The
Garland Library
of
War and Peace

The
Garland Library
of
War and Peace

Under the General Editorship of

Blanche Wiesen Cook, *John Jay College, C.U.N.Y.*

Sandi E. Cooper, *Richmond College, C.U.N.Y.*

Charles Chatfield, *Wittenberg University*

Digest of
International Law

by

Green Haywood Hackworth

(in eight volumes)

Vol. I
Chapters I-V

with a new introduction
for the Garland Edition by

Martin Bagish

Garland Publishing, Inc., New York & London
1973

Library of Congress Cataloging in Publication Data

Hackworth, Green Haywood, 1883-
   Digest of international law.

   (The Garland library of war and peace)
   Reprint of the 1940-44 ed., which was issued
as Dept. of State publication 1506, 1521, 1708, 1756,
1927, 1961, 1998, 2100.
   Covers the documents and files accumulated in the
Dept. of State since 1906.
   1. International law. 2. United States--Foreign
relations. I. Title. II. Series. III. Series:
United States. Dept. of State. Publication 1506
[etc.]
JX237.H32   341   70-147741

ISBN 0-8240-0489-2

Introduction

Green Haywood Hackworth was born on 23
January 1883 and received his law degree in 1912.
Three years later he was admitted to practice before
the Supreme Court of the United States, and in 1916
he was appointed law clerk in the Department of
State. In 1918, Hackworth was promoted to Assistant
Solicitor of the Department of State. By 1925, when
he became Solicitor, he was responsible for drafting
numerous treaties and international agreements. In
1930, Hackworth represented the United States as a
delegate to a conference for the codification of
international law held at The Hague. He became legal
adviser to the Department of State in 1931 and, upon
the death of Elihu Root in 1937, President Roosevelt
appointed him to the Permanent Court of Arbitration
at The Hague.

Throughout the 1940s, Judge Hackworth represented the United States at numerous meetings of
advisers and ministers of foreign affairs and accompanied Secretary of State Cordell Hull to the Moscow
Conference in 1943. He was a member of the
American delegation at the Dumbarton Oaks conference on International Organizations in 1944, and in
1945, was adviser to Secretary of State Edward R.
Stettinius at the Mexico City conference where the

5

INTRODUCTION

Act of Chapultapec was signed. Hackworth served as chairman of the United Nations committee of jurists which framed the tentative statutes for the International Court of Justice under the United Nations Charter, and was an adviser to the United States delegation at the San Francisco conference when the Charter was adopted. In 1946, he was elected to the International Court of Justice and served on the Court for six years.

With this experience Judge Hackworth was well qualified to compile the massive Digest of International Law. *As early as 1877 the Department of State published a general digest of international law comprising the latest definitions and examples found in foreign relations between countries. Other digests were printed by the State Department in 1886, 1887, and 1906, but they were all abbreviated and limited in scope and depth.*

The first attempt at a more inclusive digest came in 1940 with the following volumes. Valuable not only for the examples of material which explain and define the role of international law, the Digest *also demonstrates the degree of acceptance among nations of mutually respected international practices. Covering the period from 1906 to 1939, the volumes emphasize those occasions when the world's powers, great and small, attempted to improve their communication and regulate more precisely the methods and forms to be used in relation with each other.*

The period between the wars was one of great

optimism, when, for a time, it seemed as if nations were willing to submit to some form other than force in their dealings. World War I had shattered a similar period of optimism which developed after the horror of modern warfare was revealed during the Crimean War, 1854-1856. Then, various conferences on subjects of international interest were held, some concerned with devising rules for the conduct of warfare, in the hopes of limiting the bloodshed and reducing the number of innocent victims. The 1899 and 1907 meetings at The Hague were the most important of these conferences. Meetings and organizations to develop the mechanisms and methods for a peaceful arbitration of disputes among nations, including the League of Nations and the International Court of Justice, built upon the earlier examples of the Hague Conferences.

The Digest *presents the accepted forms in international relations used by the community of nations until 1939. They are illustrated by multiple examples of disputes and their solutions under international law. They range from elaborate definitions of sovereignty to the rules for waging war under a multitude of conditions, to the pacific settlement of disputes regarding fisheries, water rights, trading arrangements, and all manner of possible disputation. The origins of crises, the contending positions of the disputants, and the alternative theories of international jurists concerning the issues are also included, as are numerous and important cases. All of this material,*

7

INTRODUCTION

the thematic discussions and the specific cases which relate to them, are cross-indexed in the last volume. Consequently, the Digest *not only provides basic definitions of international law, but also serves as an important guide to further research into specific cases. For example, anyone interested in the Lansing-Ishii agreement can find procedures under international law used to draw up the agreement, a discussion of its public as well as secret provisions, and a list of pertinent documents relating to it in cited government files.*

The Digest *is primarily a presentation of ideas concerning international relations that have been codified through the years by trial and error into international law. One receives the impression that Judge Hackworth compiled the* Digest *not only for its encyclopedic value, but to signify the proud record of man's attempt to bring equity and justice through international law to all countries. The problem is that national sovereignty and the claims of the nation-state have not diminished or been adapted to an international system. There has, in fact, been little progress towards the achievement of world order. One must, therefore, be very careful when attempting to apply examples given in these volumes as evidence of the workings and nature of international law.*

Martin Bagish
with Hilary Conroy

Colloquium in Diplomacy
and Peacekeeping
University of Pennsylvania

DIGEST

OF

INTERNATIONAL LAW

BY

GREEN HAYWOOD HACKWORTH

Legal Adviser of the Department of State

VOLUME I

CHAPTERS I–V

UNITED STATES
GOVERNMENT PRINTING OFFICE
WASHINGTON : 1940

DEPARTMENT OF STATE

PUBLICATION 1506

_____

For sale by the
Superintendent of Documents
Government Printing Office
Washington, D. C.
Price $2.00

PREFACE

As early as 1877 the Department of State felt the need for a digest of international law in the conduct of its daily work. In that year "A Digest of the Published Opinions of the Attorneys-General, and of the Leading Decisions of the Federal Courts, with reference to International Law, Treaties, and Kindred Subjects", prepared by the Honorable John L. Cadwalader, Assistant Secretary of State, was published by the Government Printing Office. Mr. Cadwalader explained in the preface to the publication that "In considering questions relating to international law, or arising under treaty provisions, the want of some ready means of reference to conclusions which have formerly been reached on the same or kindred questions has constantly been experienced." The topics in that small volume of less than 300 pages were arranged alphabetically, the volume concluding, for example, with the subject-headings "War" and "Warrants". It was the forerunner of other more recent and more comprehensive digests prepared under the auspices of and published by the Government.

In 1886 there was published, pursuant to a resolution of Congress approved by the President on July 28 of that year, 24 Stat. 345, a second digest of international law prepared by Dr. Francis Wharton, who was then Chief Examiner of Claims of the Department of State. Less than a year later, in 1887, a second edition of that digest consisting of 4,000 copies was printed. The second edition contained certain new material in the Appendix to the third volume. Wharton stated in the "Preliminary Remarks" to his work that if the records of the Department of State covered by his three volumes should be printed as a whole "they would cover four hundred volumes of the ordinary law-book size" and that it "would be difficult for one seeking in haste to find rulings on some pending question of international law, to come to an accurate result from the study, in the short time assigned to him, of so vast a mass of authorities".

By an act of Congress, approved February 20, 1897, provision was made for "revising, reindexing, and otherwise completing and perfecting by the aid of such documents as may be useful, the second edition of the Digest of International Law of the United States". 29 Stat. 579, 584. This resulted in the publication by the Government in 1906—twenty years after the first publication of Wharton's Digest— of "A Digest of International Law" in seven volumes, together with an index volume, prepared by the Honorable John Bassett Moore, who had previously been Assistant Secretary of State.

Approximately thirty-five years have elapsed since the publication of that invaluable work. During this time many changes in the international structure have taken place and many new situations, unique in character, have arisen—some as a result of a World War (1914–18) and others flowing from the more normal processes of evolution. (A considerable portion of the manuscript of this work was prepared before the outbreak of the European war in 1939.) The documents and files accumulated in the Department of State since 1906, which it is the purpose of the present digest to cover, are more voluminous than those for the entire period prior to that year.

The material contained in Moore's Digest is not duplicated in the present publication. In general the outline of that Digest, and of the earlier publication by Wharton, has been followed for the convenience of those who may desire to use the Digests together. Certain departures in arrangement, however, will be noted. For example, the chapters on "Domicil", "Conventional and Diplomatic Relations", and "Intervention", have been omitted; but material on those subjects is incorporated at appropriate places in other chapters.

No effort has been made to include all available material on any given topic. On the contrary, difficulty has been experienced in eliminating material and selecting that thought to be most representative. For the most part the Digest represents the position of the Government of the United States on the subjects discussed as revealed by the voluminous records of the Department of State and to a lesser degree by decisions of the Federal courts, opinions of the attorneys general, etc. The importance of a proper understanding of the facts of a situation in an evaluation of opinions and pronouncements relating to it, has been recognized by the attention given to the historical and factual settings of the material presented.

Because of their large number and importance the prime quotations have been placed in the same type as the text. They are, however, readily distinguishable from the text by differences in leading and marginal indention. An index to the entire Digest will be found in the final volume.

A work of such wide scope as this cannot be accomplished by the labors of a single worker. I have been fortunate in having associated with me a small group of energetic and resourceful people engaged in research, and I gratefully acknowledge their invaluable help. I express my indebtedness to Miss Marjorie Whiteman, Mr. Durward V. Sandifer, Miss Katherine B. Fite, Mr. Sidney D. Spear, Mr. John W. Halderman, Mr. William W. Bishop, Jr., Mr. John Maktos, Mr. Frederick M. Diven, Mr. E. Barbour Hutchison, and Miss Alberta

Colclaser for their assistance, during varied periods of time, in collecting and analyzing vast quantities of material.

For their cooperation in the initiation of the work, I am indebted to the Secretary of State, the Honorable Cordell Hull, and former Under Secretary of State, the Honorable William Phillips, who saw the need for a new digest of international law covering the period since 1906 and desired that I should undertake the work. I am indebted to the Honorable Wilbur J. Carr, the Honorable George S. Messersmith, and the Honorable Breckenridge Long, who, successively, as Assistant Secretaries of State, gave their valued cooperation. I also express my gratitude for the cooperation of Mr. Charles B. Hosmer, Executive Assistant to Assistant Secretary Long, Mr. Edward Yardley, Director of Personnel, Dr. E. Wilder Spaulding, Chief of the Division of Research and Publication, and his predecessor, the late Dr. Cyril Wynne, and for the faithful work of Miss Alice M. Ball, Chief of the Special Documents Section, who, with her assistants, so carefully edited the manuscript for printing. I express my appreciation of the helpfulness of Miss Martha L. Gericke, Librarian, and of Mr. David A. Salmon, Chief of the Division of Communications and Records, who, together with their staffs, have been extremely obliging in making available the books and manuscript records of the Department. To each of these officials, as well as to others of my colleagues who have been helpful in reading portions of the manuscript, I am deeply indebted.

G. H. H.

WASHINGTON, D.C., 1940.

CONTENTS

CHAPTER I

CHAPTER II

Chapter III

Chapter IV

CHAPTER I

INTERNATIONAL LAW

GENERAL NATURE

§1

International law consists of a body of rules governing the relations between states. It is a system of jurisprudence which, for the most part, has evolved out of the experiences and the necessities of situations that have arisen from time to time. It has developed with the progress of civilization and with the increasing realization by nations that their relations *inter se*, if not their existence, must be governed by and depend upon rules of law fairly certain and generally reasonable. Customary, as distinguished from conventional, international law is based upon the common consent of nations extending over a period of time of sufficient duration to cause it to become crystallized into a rule of conduct. When doubt arises as to the existence or non-existence of a rule of international law, or as to the application of a rule to a given situation, resort is usually had to such sources as pertinent treaties, pronouncements of foreign offices, statements by writers, and decisions of international tribunals and those of prize courts and other domestic courts purporting to be expressive of the law of nations.

Whether international law is law in a strictly *legal* or Austinian [1] sense, depends upon the meaning attributed to the word *law*. Although international law is readily distinguishable in many respects from domestic law, it is nonetheless a system of law possessing certain characteristics peculiar to itself as well as certain others common to municipal law. An infinite number of factors have contributed to its growth. Thus, phases of the so-called "law of nature", doctrines of equity and morality, as well as certain principles common to local law, etc., have become infused in and made a part of international law.

In the case of the *S.S. Lotus*, decided by the Permanent Court of Definition International Justice on September 7, 1927, pursuant to the terms of

---

[1] Austin was of the view that "To the aggregate of the rules . . . established [by political superiors], or to some aggregate forming a portion of that aggregate, the term *law*, as used simply and strictly, is exclusively applied", that "The so called law of nations consists of opinions or sentiments current amongst nations generally", and that "It therefore is not law properly so called." I Austin, *The Province of Jurisprudence Determined* (2d ed. 1861) 2, 128.

a special agreement between France and Turkey signed on October 12, 1926, the Court stated:

> . . . Now the Court considers that the words "principles of international law", as ordinarily used, can only mean international law as it is applied between all nations belonging to the community of States.

.   .   .   .

Binding upon states

International law governs relations between independent States. The rules of law binding upon States therefore emanate from their own free will as expressed in conventions or by usages generally accepted as expressing principles of law and established in order to regulate the relations between these co-existing independent communities or with a view to the achievement of common aims. Restrictions upon the independence of States cannot therefore be presumed.

> The *S. S. Lotus* (France *v.* Turkey), Per. Ct. Int. Jus., Judgment 9, Sept. 7, 1927, Ser. A, No. 10, pp. 16, 18; II Hudson, *World Court Reports* (1935) 20, 33, 35.

In the course of its judgment of September 13, 1928, with reference to the indemnity to be allowed in the *Chorzów Factory* case (Germany *v.* Poland), the Permanent Court of International Justice stated:

> . . . The rules of law governing the reparation are the rules of international law in force between the two States concerned, and not the law governing relations between the State which has committed a wrongful act and the individual who has suffered damage. Rights or interests of an individual(the violation of which rights) causes damage are always in a different plane to [*from*] rights belonging to a State, which rights may also be infringed by the same act. The damage suffered by an individual is never therefore identical in kind with that which will be suffered by a State; it can only afford a convenient scale for the calculation of the reparation due to the State.

> Per. Ct. Int. Jus., Judgment 13, Sept. 13, 1928, Ser. A, No. 17, pp. 4, 28; I Hudson, *World Court Reports* (1934) 646, 663.

The United States Court of Claims, in the case of *Galban and Company, a Corporation,* v. *The United States,* stated:

> International law is a system of rules founded upon long-established customs and acts of states and international agreements, not inconsistent with the principles of natural justice, which Christian and civilized states recognize as obligatory in their relations and dealings with each other, as well as with the citizens and subjects of each.

> 40 Ct. Cls. (1905) 495, 504.

International law has been defined "as consisting of those rules of conduct which reason deduces, as consonant to justice, from the nature of the society existing among independent nations:

with such definitions and modifications as may be established by general consent"; . . . also, as "a complex system, composed of various ingredients. It consists of general principles of right and justice, equally suitable to the government or individuals in a state of natural equality and to the relations and conduct of nations; of a collection of usages, customs, and opinion, the growth of civilization and commerce, and of a code of conventional or positive law." . . .

H. Rept. 1916, 69th Cong., 2d sess., p. 2.

It is a trite observation that there is no such thing as a standard of international law extraneous to the domestic law of a kingdom, to which appeal may be made. International law, so far as this Court is concerned, is the body of doctrine regarding the international rights and duties of states which has been adopted and made part of the law of Scotland.

Mortensen v. *Peters*, VIII *Session Cases*, Court of Justiciary (1906) 93, 101 (Lord Dunedin, Lord President of the Court of Session in Scotland, speaking); XLIII Scot. L. R. (1906) 872, 876.

William Howard Taft, Chief Justice of the United States, as sole arbitrator in the cases of *Central Costa Rica Petroleum Company* (Great Britain v. Costa Rica) and the *Royal Bank of Canada* (Great Britain v. Costa Rica), in the course of his opinion, October 18, 1923, stated:

The merits of the policy of the United States in this non-recognition [of the government of Tinoco in Costa Rica between 1917 and 1919] it is not for the arbitrator to discuss, for the reason that in his consideration of this case, he is necessarily controlled by principles of international law, and however justified as a national policy non-recognition on such a ground may be, it certainly has not been acquiesced in by all the nations of the world, which is a condition precedent to considering it as a postulate of international law.

. . . .

These are, so far as I am advised, the only authorities to be found either in decided cases or in text writers applying the principles of estoppel to bar a nation seeking to protect its nationals in their rights against the successor of a *de facto* government.

. . . .

. . . Arguments for and against such a rule occur to me; but it suffices to say that I have not been cited to text writers of authority or to decisions of significance indicating a general acquiescence of nations in such a rule. Without this, it cannot be applied here as a principle of international law.

General acquiescence of nations

18 A.J.I.L. (1924) 147, 153, 156, 157. The arbitration between Costa Rica and Great Britain was held pursuant to the terms of a convention signed at San José on Jan. 12, 1922. 116 Br. & For. St. Paps. (1922) 438.

Now, it is a recognized prerequisite of the adoption in our municipal law of a doctrine of public international law that it

shall have attained the position of general acceptance by civilized
nations as a rule of international conduct, evidenced by international treaties and conventions, authoritative textbooks,
practice and judicial decisions. It is manifestly of the highest
importance that the Courts of this country before they give the
force of law within this realm to any doctrine of international
law should be satisfied that it has the hall-marks of general assent
and reciprocity.

Lord Macmillan, speaking in *Compania Naviera Vascongado* v. *Steamship
"Cristina" and Persons Claiming an Interest Therein*, [1938] A.C. 485, 497.

A recognition of the principles of international law is regarded
as fundamental to the existence of a state in the modern sense.

Wilson, *Handbook of International Law* (2d ed. 1927) 2.

. . . It is . . . not necessary to prove for every single rule
of International Law that every single member of the Family of
Nations consented to it. No single State can say on its admit-
tance into the Family of Nations that it desires to be subjected to
such and such a rule of International Law, and not to
others. . . .

On the other hand, no State which is a member of the Family
of Nations can at some time or another declare that it will in
future no longer submit to a certain recognised rule of the Law
of Nations. The body of the rules of this law can be altered by
common consent only, not by a unilateral declaration on the
part of one State.

I Oppenheim's *International Law* (5th ed., by Lauterpacht, 1937) 18.

From the papers in the Record Office it has been decided to
select two opinions of the Law Officers, separated by an interval
of nearly a century, which in some measure serve to illustrate
a general point of view. A study of these documents, which may
be taken as fairly representative of responsible official opinion,
makes it clear that it is impossible to associate the British Law
Officers with the formal doctrines either of the *a priori* or of the
positivist schools. On the one hand, it is clearly assumed that
there is an objective law of nations, binding as such upon civilised
states, irrespective of their assent to specific rules. On the other
hand, it is equally clear that the content of this law in relation
to particular matters can only be ascertained by reference to
custom and practice.

.   .   .   .

**"General
obligation"
differs from
"origin"**
Neither of these two opinions is in form a statement of doctrine
formally propounded as such by the government of this country,
but a study of the practice analysed in the present work makes
it clear that they fairly represent the general theory of international law which is implicit in British diplomatic action.
This theory avoids the errors in which the more extreme theoretical writers of the two opposing schools have been involved.
For the most part these errors arise from confusing the question
of the general obligation of international law with the question

of the historical origin of its particular rules. In the opinions quoted this confusion is avoided. It is clearly emphasised that international law as a whole is binding upon all civilised states irrespective of their individual consent, and that no state can by its own act release itself from the obligation either of the general law or of any well-established rule. At the same time it is equally clear that the existence of any particular rule of law which may be in dispute is a question of fact to be proved by the evidence of practice. In other words, consent is the legislative process of international law, though it is not the source of legal obligation. A rule once established by consent (which need not be universal) is binding because it has become a part of the general law, and it can then no longer be repudiated by the action of individual states.

I Herbert Arthur Smith, *Great Britain and the Law of Nations* (1932) 1, 12–13.

In Hall's treatise on International Law, in connection with his   "True law" discussion of the question whether international law constitutes a branch of "true law", it is stated:

. . . During the continuance of this state of uncertainty as to the proper limits of law, it is impossible, in dealing with international law, to ignore the two broad facts, that it is habitually treated as law, and that a certain part of what is at present acknowledged to be law is indistinguishable in character from it.
. . . The doctrines of international law have been elaborated by a course of legal reasoning; in international controversies precedents are used in a strictly legal manner; the opinions of writers are quoted and relied upon for the same purposes as those for which the opinions of writers are invoked under a system of municipal law; the conduct of states is attacked, defended, and judged within the range of international law by reference to legal considerations alone; and finally, it is recognised that there is an international morality distinct from law, violation of which gives no formal ground of complaint, however odious the action of the ill-doer may be. It may fairly be doubted whether a description of law is adequate which fails to admit a body of rules as being substantially legal, when they have received legal shape, and are regarded as having the force of law by the persons whose conduct they are intended to guide.

.   .   .   .

. . . If the rules known under the name of international law are linked to the higher examples of typical positive law by specimens of the laws of organised communities, imperfectly developed as regards their sanction, the weakness and indeterminateness of the sanction of international law cannot be an absolute bar to its admission as law; and if there is no such bar, the facts that international rules are cast in a legal mould, and are invariably treated in practice as being legal in character, necessarily become the considerations of most importance in determining their true place. That they lie on the extreme frontier of law is not to be denied; but on the whole it would seem to be more correct, as

it certainly is more convenient, to treat them as being a branch
of law, than to include them within the sphere of morals.

Hall's *International Law* (8th ed., by Higgins, 1924) 14–16.

With reference to the subject of the decadence of the law of nature
in its relation to international law, the General Claims Commission,
established by the United States and Mexico pursuant to the convention concluded on September 8, 1923, in a decision by Presiding Commissioner van Vollenhoven and Commissioner MacGregor, in the case
of the *North American Dredging Company of Texas* (United States v.
Mexico), stated:

Law of
nature

 12. It being impossible to prove the illegality of the said provision [a Calvo clause], under the limitations indicated, by adducing
generally recognized rules of positive international law, it apparently can only be contested by invoking its incongruity to the
law of nature (natural rights) and its inconsistency with inalienable, indestructible, unprescriptible, uncurtailable rights of nations. The law of nature may have been helpful, some three
centuries ago, to build up a new law of nations, and the conception
of inalienable rights of men and nations may have exercised a
salutary influence, some one hundred and fifty years ago, on the
development of modern democracy on both sides of the ocean;
but they have failed as a durable foundation of either municipal or
international law and can not be used in the present day as
substitutes for positive municipal law, on the one hand, and for
positive international law, as recognized by nations and governments through their acts and statements, on the other hand.
Inalienable rights have been the cornerstones of policies like those
of the Holy Alliance and of Lord Palmerston; instead of bringing
to the world the benefit of mutual understanding, they are to
weak or less fortunate nations an unrestrained menace.

Opinions of the Commissioners (1927) 21, 26, docket 1223.

After discussing the law of nature in the introduction to *De jure belli ac
pacis*, published in 1625, and in chapter I thereof, Grotius stated that there
was in his time "hardly any law common to all nations" outside "the sphere
of the law of nature". Grotius, *De jure belli ac pacis* (Classics of International
Law, translation, 1925) 15, 44. Vattel, writing in 1758, differentiated between "the *voluntary* Law of Nations" in contradistinction "to the *necessary*
Law of Nations, which is the inner law of conscience". Vattel, *Le droit des
gens, ou principes de la loi naturelle, appliqués à la conduite et aux affaires des
nations et des souverains* (Classics of International Law, translation, 1916) 3,
10a, 11a.

In discussing the influence of the doctrine of the law of nature upon
international law, Professor Brierly states:

 . . . Modern legal writers, especially in England, have sometimes ridiculed the conception of a law of nature, or they have
recognized its great historical influence but treated it as a super-

stition which the modern world has rightly discarded. Such an attitude, however, proceeds from a misunderstanding of the medieval idea; for under a terminology which has ceased to be familiar to us the phrase stands for something which no progressive system of law either does or can discard. Some knowledge of what a medieval writer meant by the term is necessary if we would understand either how international law arose, or how it develops to-day.

A long and continuous history, extending at least as far back as the political thought of the Greeks, lies behind the conception; but its influence on international law is so closely interwoven with that of Roman law that the two may here be discussed together. The early law of the primitive Roman city-state was able to develop into a law adequate to the needs of a highly civilized world empire, because it showed a peculiar capacity of expansion and adaptation which broke through the archaic formalism which originally characterized it, as it characterizes all primitive law. In brief, the process of expansion and adaptation took the form of admitting side by side with the *jus civile*, or original law peculiar to Rome, a more liberal and progressive element, the *jus gentium*, so called because it was believed or feigned to be of universal application, its principles being regarded as so simple and reasonable that it was assumed they must be recognized everywhere and by every one. This practical development was reinforced towards the end of the Republican era by the philosophical conception of a *jus naturale* which, as developed by the Stoics in Greece and borrowed from them by the Romans, meant, in effect, the sum of those principles which ought to control human conduct, because founded in the very nature of man as a rational and social being. In course of time *jus gentium*, the new progressive element which the practical genius of the Romans had imported into their actual law, and *jus naturale* the ideal law conforming to reason, came to be regarded as generally synonymous. . . .

The effect of such a conception as this, when applied to the theory of the relations of the new national states to one another is obvious; for it meant that it was not in the nature of things that those relations should be merely anarchical; on the contrary they must be controlled by a higher law, not the mere creation of the will of any sovereign, but part of the order of nature to which even sovereigns were subjected. Over against the theory of sovereignty, standing for the new nationalistic separation of the states of Europe, was set the theory of a law of nature denying their irresponsibility and the finality of their independence of one another.

. . . .

The medieval conception of a law of nature is open to certain criticisms. In the first place, when all allowances have been made for the aid afforded by Roman law, it has to be admitted that it implied a belief in the rationality of the universe which seems to us to be exaggerated. It is true that when medieval writers spoke of natural law as being discoverable by reason, they meant that the best human reasoning could discover it, and not, of course, that the results to which any and every individual's reasoning led him was natural law. . . .

Marginal notes:

Origin of law of nature

Criticism

Value

In the second place, when medieval writers spoke of natural law as able to overrule positive law in a case of conflict, they were introducing an anarchical principle which we must reject. . . .

These are valid criticisms, but they do not affect the permanent truths in the conception of a law of nature, and those truths are in fact recognized and acted upon as fully to-day as they ever were. For one thing it stands for the existence of *purpose* in law, reminding us that law is not a meaningless set of arbitrary principles to be mechanically applied by courts, but that it exists for certain ends, though those ends have to be differently formulated in different times and places. Thus where we might say that we attempt to embody social justice in law, giving to that term whatever interpretation is current in the thought of our time, a medieval thinker might have said that positive law ought to conform to the higher law of nature. . . . Even a slight acquaintance with the working of the English Common law shows it perpetually appealing to reason as the justification of its decisions, asking what is a reasonable time, or what is a reasonable price, or what a reasonable man would do in given circumstances. . . .

'The grandest function of the law of nature', Sir Henry Maine has written, 'was discharged in giving birth to modern international law.' But in the seventeenth and eighteenth centuries the medieval tradition began to be distorted by later writers, whose use of the old terminology in senses of their own went far to justify the obloquy which has been poured on the whole conception in modern times.

Brierly, *The Law of Nations* (1928) 9–18.

The tribunal (A. Nerincx, president) established by the United States and Great Britain pursuant to the provisions of the special agreement of August 18, 1910, discussed at length the question whether it was authorized under the terms of the agreement to invoke principles of equity in deciding the *Cayuga Indians* case. Although the conclusion was reached that the decision in the case might rest upon a strictly legal basis, the tribunal spoke as follows regarding its authority to invoke equity as a basis for the decision:

Equity

But there are special circumstances making the equitable claim of the Canadian Cayugas especially strong.

.   .   .   .

In the second place, we must bear in mind the dependent legal position of the individual Cayugas. Legally they could do nothing except under the guardianship of some sovereign. They could not determine what should be the nation, nor even whether there should be a nation legally. . . . American Courts have agreed from the beginning in pronouncing the position of the Indians an anomalous one. Miller J., in United States *v.* Kagama, 118 U.S. 375, 381. When a situation legally so anomalous is presented, recourse must be had to generally recognized principles of justice and fair dealing in order to determine the rights of the individuals involved. The same considerations of equity that have repeatedly been invoked by the courts where strict regard to the legal personality of a corporation would lead to inequitable results or to results contrary to legal policy, may be invoked here. In such cases courts have not hesitated to look behind the legal person and consider the human individuals who were the real beneficiaries. Those considerations are even more cogent where we are dealing with Indians in a state of pupilage toward the sovereign with whom they were treating.

There is the more warrant for so doing under the terms of the treaty by virtue of which we are sitting. It provides that decision shall be made in accordance with principles of international law and of equity. Merignhac considers that an arbitral tribunal is justified in reaching a decision on universally recognized principles of justice where the terms of submission are silent as to the grounds of decision and even where the grounds of decision are expressed to be the "principles of international law." He considers, however, that the appropriate formula is that "international law is to be applied with equity." *Traité théorique et pratique de l'arbitrage international*, § 303. It is significant that the present treaty uses the phrase "principles of international law and equity." When used in a general arbitration treaty, this can only mean to provide for the possibility of anomalous cases such as the present.

"International law and equity"

An examination of the provisions of arbitration treaties shows a recognition that something more than the strict law must be used in the grounds of decision of arbitral tribunals in certain cases; that there are cases in which—like the courts of the land—these tribunals must find the grounds of decision, must find the right and the law, in general considerations of justice, equity, and right dealing guided by legal analogies and by the spirit and received principles of international law. Such an examination shows also that much discrimination has been used in including or not including "equity" among the grounds of decision provided for. In general, it is used regularly in general claims arbitration treaties. As a general proposition, it is not used where special questions are referred for arbitration

. . . .

In the treaties cited, to which the United States has been a party, it will be noted how discriminatingly the language is chosen. How can it be said that the phrase "principles of equity" is of no significance when the different phrases are shown to have been so carefully chosen to fit different occasions?

. . . .

But it is not necessary to rest the case upon this proposition. It may be rested upon the strict legal basis of Article IX of the Treaty of Ghent, and in our judgment is to be decided by the application of that covenant to the equitable claim of the Canadian Cayugas to their share in the annuity.

Nielsen's Report (1926) 203, 307, 313–315, 317, 321. For a detailed examination of the provisions of specific arbitration treaties and agreements omitted from the quotation just set forth, see *ibid.* 315–321.

"Law and equity"   The tribunal established by the United States and Norway under the special agreement of June 30, 1921 for the arbitration "in accordance with the principles of law and equity" of the claim of Norway on behalf of Norwegian nationals whose ships and ship-building material, etc., had been requisitioned by the Government of the United States in 1917, in its decision of October 13, 1922 stated:

> The words "law and equity" used in the special agreement of 1921 can not be understood here in the traditional sense in which these words are used in Anglo-Saxon jurisprudence.
> The majority of international lawyers seem to agree that these words are to be understood to mean general principles of justice as distinguished from any particular system of jurisprudence or the municipal law of any State.
>
> Award of the Tribunal of Arbitration (Per. Ct. Arb., The Hague) 27; MS. Department of State, file 411.57N83/451; Scott, *Hague Court Reports* (2d ser. 1932) 39, 65.

Umpire Plumley, in his decision in the *Aroa Mines (Limited)* case (Great Britain *v.* Venezuela), arbitrated in accordance with the protocols of February 13 and May 7, 1903, stated:

Absolute equity   The phrase, "absolute equity," used in the protocols the umpire understands and interprets to mean equity unrestrained by any artificial rules in its application to the given case.

.   .   .   .

> The guide, commonly safe and constant and usually to be followed, is international law.   But if in the given case, not easily to be assumed, it should occur that its precepts are opposed to justice, or lead away from it, or are in disregard of it, or are inadequate or inapplicable, then the determination must be made by recourse to the underlying principles of justice and equity applied as best may be to the cause in hand.   The umpire will apply the precepts of international law in all cases where such use will insure justice and equity for this reason, if for no other— that well-defined principles and precepts which have successfully endured the test of time and the crucible of experience and criticism are safe in use, and should never carelessly be departed from in order that one may step out into a way unknown to walk by a course unmarked.   But these precepts are to be used as a means to the end, which end is justice.
>
> Ralston's Report (1904) 344, 386–387; protocols of Feb. 13 and May 7, 1903, *ibid.* 292, 294.

Article I of the protocol of February 17, 1903, between the United States and Venezuela, contained the provision that "The commissioners [to be subsequently appointed] or, in case of their disagreement, the umpire, shall decide all claims upon a basis of absolute equity, without regard to objections of a technical nature, or of the provisions of local legislation". The United States, in referring to this provision of the protocol and in protesting against the decision of Umpire Barge in the case of the *Orinoco Steamship Company* (United States *v.* Venezuela), a decision which was subsequently reopened, stated:

> The equity meant is clearly not local equity, that is, not necessarily the equity of the United States or the equity of Venezuela, but the spirit of justice applied to a concrete question irrespective of local statute, ordinance or interpretation.

Secretary Root to the American Minister, W. W. Russell, Feb. 28, 1907, 1908 For. Rel. 774, 784; 2 Treaties, etc. (Malloy, 1910) 1870, 1871.

It is further urged that absolute equity should control the decisions of the Commission and that equitably sufferers from the acts of revolutionists should be recompensed. But this subject may be viewed from two standpoints. It is as inequitable to charge a government for wrongs it never committed as it would be to deny rights to a claimant for a technical reason. **Equity—two viewpoints**

In the view of the umpire, the true interpretation of the protocol requires the present tribunal, disregarding technicalities, to apply equitably to the various cases submitted the well-established principles of justice, not permitting sympathy for suffering to bring about a disregard for law.

Sambiaggio case (Italy *v.* Venezuela), Ralston's Report (1904) 666, 692; protocols of Feb. 13 and May 7, 1903, *ibid.* 643, 645.

The Statute of the Permanent Court of International Justice contains the provision (art. 38):

> The Court shall apply:
> 1. International conventions, whether general or particular, establishing rules expressly recognized by the contesting States; **Statute of the Permanent Court**
> 2. International custom, as evidence of a general practice accepted as law;
> 3. The general principles of law recognized by civilized nations;
> 4. Subject to the provisions of Article 59, judicial decisions and the teachings of the most highly qualified publicists of the various nations, as subsidiary means for the determination of rules of law.
> This provision shall not prejudice the power of the Court to decide a case *ex aequo et bono*, if the parties agree thereto.

Per. Ct. Int. Jus., Ser. D, No. 1, Statute and Rules of Court and Other Constitutional Documents, Rules or Regulations (3d ed. Mar. 1936), p. 21.

The Mixed Claims Commission, United States and Germany, established pursuant to the agreement of August 10, 1922, between the two countries, held in Administrative Decision No. II that in its adjudications the commission would be controlled by the terms of the Treaty of Berlin but that where "no applicable provision is found in **Mixed Claims Commission** that instrument, in determining the measure of damages the Commission may apply":

    (a) International conventions, whether general or particular, establishing rules expressly recognized by the United States and Germany;
    (b) International custom, as evidence of a general practice accepted as law;
    (c) Rules of law common to the United States and Germany established by either statutes or judicial decisions;
    (d) The general principles of law recognized by civilized nations;
    (e) Judicial decisions and the teachings of the most highly qualified publicists of all nations, as subsidiary means for the determination of rules of law; but
    (f) The Commission will not be bound by any particular code or rules of law but shall be guided by justice, equity, and good faith.

Decisions and Opinions, 7–8.

SANCTION

§2

Whether the answer to the question as to how international law is made effective is to be found in the will of the state, in the state's ultimate responsibility for its own action or failure to act, in its fear of war or reprisals, in the effect of world opinion, or in a combination of any two or more of these, it is certain that states, sovereigns, parliaments, and public officials usually feel either bound by the commonly accepted precepts of international law or under the necessity of explaining their departure from those precepts. Whatever be the sanction upon which the enforcement of international law rests, its effectiveness increases as the nations of the world find it not only to their benefit but also to the benefit of the community of nations to conduct their relations according to certain generally accepted standards possible of performance and at the same time fair and reasonable.

The tribunal, established by the United States and Great Britain under the convention signed on January 27, 1909, for the arbitration of the *North Atlantic Coast Fisheries* case, stated in the course of its decision that—

every State has to execute the obligations incurred by Treaty *bona fide*, and is urged thereto by the ordinary sanctions of International Law in regard to observance of Treaty obligations. Such sanctions are, for instance, appeal to public opinion, publication of correspondence, censure by Parliamentary vote, demand for arbitration with the odium attendant on a refusal to arbitrate, rupture of relations, reprisal, etc.

Decision of Sept. 7, 1910, North Atlantic Coast Fisheries Tribunal of Arbitration (Per. Ct. Arb., The Hague, 1910) 104, 123; Scott, *Hague Court Reports* (1916) 141, 167.

Secretary Root stated in 1908:

Why is it that nations are thus continually yielding to arguments with no apparent compulsion behind them, and before the force of such arguments abandoning purposes, modifying conduct, and giving redress for injuries? A careful consideration of this question seems to lead to the conclusion that the difference between municipal and international law, in respect of the existence of forces compelling obedience, is more apparent than real, and that there are sanctions for the enforcement of international law no less real and substantial than those which secure obedience to municipal law.

It is a mistake to assume that the sanction which secures obedience to the laws of the state consists exclusively or chiefly of the pains and penalties imposed by the law itself for its violation. It is only in exceptional cases that men refrain from crime through fear of fine or imprisonment. In the vast majority of cases men refrain from criminal conduct because they are unwilling to incur in the community in which they live the public condemnation and obloquy which would follow a repudiation of the standard of conduct prescribed by that community for its members. . . . Not only is the effectiveness of the punishments denounced by law against crime derived chiefly from the public opinion which accompanies them, but those punishments themselves are but one form of the expression of public opinion. Laws are capable of enforcement only so far as they are in agreement with the opinions of the community in which they are to be enforced. As opinion changes old laws become obsolete and new standards force their way into the statute books. Laws passed, as they sometimes are, in advance of public opinion ordinarily wait for their enforcement until the progress of opinion has reached recognition of their value. The force of law is in the public opinion which prescribes it. *(Public opinion)*

Root, "The Sanction of International Law", in *Proceedings of the American Society of International Law* (1908) 14, 16–17.

President Taft stated in 1911:

International law has no sanction except in the conscience of nations, and nations have not anywhere near the conscience that individuals have . . . . yet either the utilitarian spirit, or perhaps a real conscience in all nations, has ultimately brought about a sanction for what we call international law, without any power to enforce it, but simply from the general public opinion of all the peoples of the world. Begun by individuals, reasoned from their own consciences and from their own sense of justice, without any power to enforce their opinion, and finally but reluctantly adopted by nations by common consent, the history of the growth of international law may well command our admiration, our wonder, and our hope for a growth in the scope and *("Conscience of nations")* sanction of such law in the future that should make us all optimists.

President Taft, speaking at the annual banquet of the American Society of International Law, Apr. 29, 1911, *Proceedings of the Society* (1911) 340, 341.

When it was reported that the Italian merchant vessel *Ancona* had been sunk on November 7, 1915, by a submarine flying the Austro-Hungarian flag, before the passengers and crew were all able to take to the lifeboats, the Italian Minister of Foreign Affairs stated that it was his Government's duty "to denounce solemnly to all nations the circumstances" of the sinking of the vessel and to state that "Their sentiments of justice and humanity will cause them without doubt to judge, as it deserves, the conduct of an enemy which is obviously contrary to the dictates of civilization and the recognized principles of international law."

The Italian Minister of Foreign Affairs (Sonnino) to the Italian Embassy at Washington, telegram, left at the Department of State on Nov. 15, 1915, MS. Department of State, file 865.857An2/22; 1915 For. Rel. Supp. 613.

In instructing the American Embassy at Vienna to protest against the sinking of the *Ancona*, Secretary Lansing said:

As the good relations of the two countries must rest upon a common regard for law and humanity, the Government of the United States can not be expected to do otherwise than to demand that the Imperial and Royal Government denounce the sinking of the *Ancona* as an illegal and indefensible act, that the officer who perpetrated the deed be punished, and that reparation by the payment of an indemnity be made for the citizens of the United States who were killed or injured by the attack on the vessel.

Secretary Lansing to Frederic Courtland Penfield, Ambassador in Austria-Hungary, telegram, 1011, Dec. 6, 1915, MS. Department of State, file 865.857An2/76a; 1915 For. Rel. Supp. 623, 624–625.

In the course of his decision in the case of the *S.S. F. J. Lisman*, Judge Joseph C. Hutcheson, Jr., as sole arbitrator, made the following comment on international law:

One of those who has long believed that in "the glorious uncertainty of law", its ever-changing content under the steady pressure of the changing life it serves, its continuous, though slow, progression from the actual to the ideal, is to be found its greatest source of strength . . . the Arbitrator has stepped confidently over the threshold into a new wonderland of law, fascinated equally by "the glorious uncertainty" of international law, the delicacy and precision of its formal adjustments, and by the greatness of its unquestioned testimony to the fact that not force, but just opinion, is at last the source of law, at least

"Just opinion"

with lawminded nations and peoples, and particularly with the United States and Great Britain.

Report and Decision of the Arbitrator in the *Claim of Edward J. Ryan, Trustee in Bankruptcy of the Interocean Transportation Company of America, Incorporated* v. *The United States of America (S.S. F. J. Lisman)*, "Under Treaty Series No. 756, May 19, 1927, Arrangement Effected by Exchange of Notes between the United States and Great Britain for the Disposal of Certain Pecuniary Claims Arising out of the Recent War", transmitted to the Department of State on Oct. 5, 1937, MS. Department of State, file 441.11In85/146a; 32 A.J.I.L. (1938) 593, 613.

SOURCE

CUSTOM

§3

It is sometimes difficult to determine whether the practice of states in a given respect has been of sufficient duration and uniformity to result in the development of a rule of international law. On many subjects the practice is well settled; on others it is changing or developing; on still others it cannot be said that there exists an established practice.

The case of *Lübeck* v. *Mecklenburg-Schwerin* involved a dispute concerning the sovereignty (particularly fishing rights) over the Bay of Lübeck. In 1874 Mecklenburg-Schwerin issued an ordinance relating to the use of the Bay of Lübeck and requested Lübeck to promulgate a similar ordinance in her territory, which was done. Mecklenburg-Schwerin contended before the German Staatsgerichtshof that this action of Lübeck, together with certain correspondence, constituted a recognition of the rights of Mecklenburg-Schwerin in the bay. The contention was rejected. The court said:

Unity by no means prevails in the literature as to how international law originates. In general, agreements and customary law are named as the sources of international law. [Origin of customary law]

.   .   .   .

With respect further to customary law, in so far as it should arise without any agreement at all, an actual practice is presupposed, which must be continued and permanent, according to a correct view (Hatschek, work cited, § 2, page 9; Heilborn, work cited, § 7, page 38). And if, as is generally recognized, no general rules can be drawn up as to the number of customary acts and their duration, one single case of usage does not suffice as a rule (Heilborn, work cited, page 38). Triepel does not assume anything different when he says, on page 99, work cited, that under certain conditions one single act of international practice based on usage may suffice for a conclusion as to the existence of a rule of international law to be ventured. In addition the usage must, if it is to lead to the formation of customary law, be [Number of acts necessary] confirmed by the proper organs of the state and can generate law only between those countries in the intercourse between which it has become customary. (Hatschek, work cited, § 2, page 9; Heilborn, work cited, § 7, page 38 ff.) Statements of other members of a state and with respect to other states may be of importance in the recognition of the genesis of a right, but cannot in themselves alone establish international customary law. If we look into the case before us from these legal standpoints, the events in connection with the publication of the Mecklenburg Ordinance of October 10, 1874, in Travemünde form the only case of usage between the parties in litigation. Everything else has occurred either between other states, such as the correspondence between Lübeck and Prussian authorities regarding the carrying on of fishing in Travemünde Bay by Dahme fishermen, or it did not involve the confirmation of usage in intercourse of states with each other but only intra-state events. . . . The single confirmation of usage, such as may perhaps be found in the publication of the Mecklenburg Ordinance of October 10, 1874, in Travemünde, can however not be regarded as sufficient for the establishment of a customary international law because of the absence of further circumstances, even if we might wish to deduce from the rest of the case that at that time a conviction of the necessity for that usage existed among the leading Lübeck officials. That does not mean that the publication of the Mecklenburg Ordinance by Lübeck is without any significance for the litigation before us; that matter will be gone into below.

⁝

It follows from what has been said that Mecklenburg-Schwerin can not base its claim to the territorial sovereignty claimed by it on a generally recognized principle of international law. How far the rest of the evidence adduced justifies this claim is to be considered.

I(2) *Zeitschrift für Ausländisches Öffentliches Recht und Völkerrecht* (1929) 180, 183–186, translation.

In 1926 the French steamship *Lotus* and the Turkish steamship *Boz-Kourt* collided on the high seas, causing the death of eight Turkish nationals; and upon the arrival of the *Lotus* at Istanbul, Turkey, criminal proceedings were instituted, pursuant to Turkish law, against Lieutenant Demons, a French citizen, the officer of the watch on board the *Lotus* at the time of the collision. When the differences that arose between France and Turkey as a result of this action on the part of Turkey were submitted to the Permanent Court of International Justice, France sought to establish that the Turkish Government had acted in conflict with international law and that there had grown up a rule of customary international law establishing the exclusive jurisdiction of the state whose flag a merchant vessel flies, over everything occurring on board such vessel on the high seas, particularly in collision cases. In support of this thesis the agent of the French Government drew the attention of the Court to the fact that questions of jurisdiction in collision cases, which frequently arise before civil courts, are but rarely encountered in the criminal courts; and he deduced from this that, in practice, prosecutions occur only before the courts of the state whose flag is flown and that that circumstance was proof of a tacit consent on the part of states and showed what "positive international law is in collision cases". The Court rejected this contention and said:

> In the Court's opinion, this conclusion is not warranted. Even if the rarity of the judicial decisions to be found among the reported cases were sufficient to prove in point of fact the circumstance alleged by the Agent for the French Government, it would merely show that States had often, in practice, abstained from instituting criminal proceedings, and not that they recognized themselves as being obliged to do so; for only if such abstention were based on their being conscious of having a duty to abstain would it be possible to speak of an international custom. The alleged fact does not allow one to infer that States have been conscious of having such a duty; on the other hand, as will presently be seen, there are other circumstances calculated to show that the contrary is true.

Failure to act

The *S. S. Lotus* (France *v.* Turkey), Per. Ct. Int. Jus., Judgment 9, Sept. 7, 1927, Ser. A, No. 10, pp. 25, 28; II Hudson, *World Court Reports* (1935) 20, 40, 42.

INTERNATIONAL AGREEMENTS

§4

Conventional international law, so-called, is not to be confused with customary international law. While a convention—such as certain of the Hague conventions—may, and often does, embody well-established international law, it may at the same time include provisions which are not established international law but which the contracting parties agree should govern the relations between them. The convention as such is binding only on the contracting parties and ceases to be binding upon them when they cease to be parties to it. Those provisions of a convention that are declaratory of international law do not lose their binding effect by reason of the abrogation of or withdrawal from the convention by parties thereto, because they did not acquire their binding force from the terms of the convention but exist as a part of the body of the common law of nations. Provisions of conventions that are not international law when incorporated therein may develop into international law by general acceptance by the nations.

In the case of the *S. S. Lotus* (France *v.* Turkey), discussed *ante*, § 3, France invoked especially the authority of conventions which, "whilst creating exceptions to the principle of the freedom of the seas by permitting the war and police vessels of a State to exercise a more or less extensive control over the merchant vessels of another State, reserve jurisdiction to the courts of the country whose flag is flown by the vessel proceeded against" in support of the proposition that there had grown up a rule of customary international law establishing the exclusive jurisdiction of the state whose flag is flown, over everything which occurs on board a merchant vessel on the high seas, even when the act committed produces effects on a vessel flying another flag, in particular in cases of collisions. In rejecting the French contention with respect to the authority of the conventions relied upon as precedents, the Court said:

Not necessarily international law

Finally, as regards conventions expressly reserving jurisdiction exclusively to the State whose flag is flown, it is not absolutely certain that this stipulation is to be regarded as expressing a general principle of law rather than as corresponding to the extraordinary jurisdiction which these conventions confer on the state-owned ships of a particular country in respect of ships of another country on the high seas. Apart from that, it should be observed that these conventions relate to matters of a particular kind, closely connected with the policing of the seas, such as the slave trade, damage to submarine cables, fisheries, etc., and not to common-law offences. Above all it should be pointed out that the offences contemplated by the conventions in question only concern a single ship; it is impossible therefore to make any deduction from them in regard to matters which concern two ships and consequently the jurisdiction of two different States.

Per. Ct. Int. Jus., Judgment 9, Sept. 7, 1927, Ser. A, No. 10, pp. 25, 27; II Hudson, *World Court Reports* (1935) 20, 40, 41–42.

In a memorandum transmitted by the Secretary of State to the American Ambassador at London, Walter Hines Page, with an instruction of December 1, 1916, reply was made to a memorandum of July 15, 1916 from the British Government, relating generally to the removal by the British authorities of alien enemies of Great Britain—reservists—from American vessels while navigating on the high seas. The United States referred to the fact that there had been certain treaties on the general subject. After listing such treaties, the memorandum continued:

It can hardly be said that these treaties demonstrate a practice of nations to remove "enemy subjects employed in the service of an enemy state" from neutral ships without bringing them before the Prize Court. If these treaties can be regarded as representing a practice of nations, as the British Government suggest, it was a practice recognized as permissible only under treaty agreement. The Government of the United States is not aware of any proof that these treaty provisions were declaratory of international law, or that they were so considered at the time of their signature or subsequently. The more reasonable view to take of them is that they represent an exception to the general practice of nations, just as the rule of "free ships, free goods," provided for in many of the same treaties, was an exception to the practice of nations and was not generally adopted until about the middle of the last century. This view is borne out by the consistent practice of Great Britain and the United States during the very period when these treaties were in force.

Secretary Lansing to Mr. Page, instruction 4520, Dec. 1, 1916, MS. Department of State, file 341.662a/270a, enclosure; 1916 For. Rel. Supp. 667, 669.

Sir Frederick Pollock has stated:

. . . Treaties and conventions between particular states may define any portion of those rules, or add to or vary the existing rules, but any conventional rule so laid down is binding only on the parties to it. Acts of this kind may go to show, according to the nature of the case and the particular circumstances, the existence of general usage which the parties wished to record for convenience in apt words and an authentic form (though this is not common), or the dissatisfaction of the parties with existing usage and their desire to improve on it, or the absence of any settled usage at all antecedent to the particular agreement. It is, therefore, impracticable, with one exception to be mentioned, to make any general statement as to the value of treaties and similar instruments as evidence of the law of nations. The exceptional case, which is of increasing frequency and importance, is where an agreement or declaration is made not by two or three states as a matter of private business between themselves, but by a considerable proportion, in number and power, of civilized states at large, for the regulation of matters of general and permanent interest. Such acts have of late been the result of congresses or conferences held for that purpose, and they have been so framed as to admit of and invite the subsequent adhesion of Powers not originally parties to the proceedings. There is no doubt that, when all or most of the great Powers have deliberately agreed to certain rules of general application, the rules approved by them have very great weight in practice even among states which have never expressly consented to them. It is hardly too much to say that declarations of this kind may be expected, in the absence of prompt and effective dissent by some Power of the first rank, to become part of the universally received law of nations within a moderate time. As among men, so among nations, the opinions and usage of the leading members in a community tend to form an authoritative example for the whole. . . .

Relation to customary law

On the whole, then, the law of nations rests on a general consent which, though it may be supplemented, influenced, and to some extent defined, by express convention, can never be completely formulated under existing conditions. This is as much as to say that the law of nations must be classed with customary law.

Pollock, "The Sources of International Law", in 2 Col. L. Rev. (1902) 511–512.

On August 6, 1914 Secretary Bryan sent telegraphic instructions to the missions of the United States at London, Paris, Berlin, Vienna, St. Petersburg (Leningrad), and Brussels to inquire whether the Governments at those capitals were willing to agree that the laws of

Unratified convention

naval warfare included in the Declaration of London in 1909 should
be applicable to the European War, provided that all the countries at
war would agree to such application. The United States expressed
the belief that the acceptance of the declaration by the belligerents
would prevent grave misunderstandings between belligerents and
neutrals. To this inquiry the Governments at Berlin and Vienna
replied that "the Declaration of London would be observed by them
upon condition of a like observance on the part of their adversaries".
The British Government informed the United States that it had
adopted the Declaration of London "with certain modifications and
additions". France and Russia "adhered to the position of the British
Government". Mr. Lansing, Acting Secretary of State stated, in this
connection, in an instruction to the Ambassador at London, Walter
Hines Page, on September 26, 1914:

> This Government in seeking general acceptance of the Declara-
> tion as a code of naval warfare for the present war had in mind
> the adoption of the Declaration as a whole and not such part of
> it as might be acceptable to certain belligerents and not to other
> belligerents. It considered that the Declaration was to be ap-
> plied as a complete code of which no rule could be ignored or
> supplemented, and in so doing it followed Article 65 of the Dec-
> laration, which stipulates: "The provisions of the present Declara-
> tion must be treated as a whole and cannot be separated."
>
> The only reasonable explanation for the inclusion in the Dec-
> laration of this requirement is that the instrument is composed
> largely of compromises on the part of the Governments repre-
> sented at the Conference. Although the Declaration is intro-
> duced with a general statement that "the signatory powers are
> agreed" that the rules contained in the Declaration "correspond
> in substance with the generally recognized principles of interna-
> tional law," the proceedings of the Conference as well as the
> documents relating to it prove that an agreement on many of the
> articles was reached through reciprocal concessions. Being con-
> ceived in compromise and concession the Declaration was ac-
> cepted by the Government of the United States at the Conference
> in London in the earnest hope that it might finally compose the
> differences which existed as to neutral rights and neutral duties,
> although in so accepting this Government was compelled to
> abandon certain rules of conduct which it had heretofore always
> maintained.

MS. Department of State, file 763.72112/126; 1914 For. Rel. Supp. 216,
225, 227–228. Subsequently, on Oct. 22, 1914, the United States withdrew
its suggestion that the Declaration of London be adopted "as a temporary
code of naval warfare to be observed by belligerents and neutrals during
the present war". Mr. Lansing, Acting Secretary of State, to Mr. Page,
telegram of Oct. 22, 1914, and Mr. Page to the Secretary of State, telegram
of Oct. 23, 1914, MS. Department of State, files 763.72112/189 and 763.72112/
213; 1914 For. Rel. Supp. 257–258.

In 1924, when the Rumanian Government, without a special agreement on the subject, declined to give assurances that if property of American citizens in Bessarabia should be expropriated adequate compensation would be paid, the United States took the position that—

> should property in Bessarabia belonging to American citizens be expropriated they would under the generally accepted principles of international law, be entitled to adequate compensation and that it is not necessary for this Government to resort to any special agreement in order to obtain for its nationals the treatment to which they are justly entitled under the law of nations.
>
> Secretary Hughes to the American Chargé d'Affaires ad interim at Bucharest, no. 265, Feb. 21, 1924, MS. Department of State, file 371.1151-Sa5/5.

In the decision of Henri Fromageot (president of the tribunal established by the United States and Great Britain pursuant to the terms of the special agreement of August 18, 1910) in the case of *The Wanderer* (Great Britain *v.* United States), it was held that, since under international law "no nation can exercise a right of visitation and search over foreign vessels pursuing a lawful avocation on the high seas, except in time of war or by special agreement", it was necessary for the United States to show that the seizure on the high seas of the British sealing schooner *Wanderer* in 1894 by the United States revenue cutter *Concord* was done pursuant to the provisions of a special agreement and that "Any such agreement being an exception to the general principle [of international law], must be construed *stricto jure.*"

> Nielsen's Report (1926) 459, 462.

WORKS OF WRITERS

§5

In the case of *West Rand Central Gold Mining Company, Limited* v. *The King*, wherein it was contended on behalf of the company that by international law the sovereign of a conquering state is liable for the obligations of the conquered state, passages from various writers on international law were cited in support of the contention. With respect to the value to be attached to the works of writers on international law the court said:

> . . . In regard to this class of authority it is important to remember certain necessary limitations to its value. There is an essential difference, as to certainty and definiteness, between municipal law and a system or body of rules in regard to inter-

national conduct, which, so far as it exists at all (and its existence is assumed by the phrase "international law"), rests upon a consensus of civilized States, not expressed in any code or pact, nor possessing, in case of dispute, any authorized or authoritative interpreter; and capable, indeed, of proof, in the absence of some express international agreement, only by evidence of usage to be obtained from the action of nations in similar cases in the course of their history.   It is obvious that, in respect of many questions that may arise, there will be room for difference of opinion as to whether such a consensus could be shewn to exist.   Perhaps it is in regard to the extra-territorial privileges of ambassadors, and in regard to the system of limits as to territorial waters, that it is least open to doubt or question.   The views expressed by learned writers on international law have done in the past, and will do in the future, valuable service in helping to create the opinion by which the range of the consensus of civilized nations is enlarged.   But in many instances their pronouncements must be regarded rather as the embodiments of their views as to what ought to be, from an ethical standpoint, the conduct of nations inter se, than the enunciation of a rule or practice so universally approved or assented to as to be fairly termed, even in the qualified sense in which that word can be understood in reference to the relations between independent political communities, "law." The reference which these writers not infrequently make to stipulations in particular treaties as acceptable evidence of international law is as little convincing as the attempt, not unknown to our Courts, to establish a trade custom which is binding without being stated, by adducing evidence of express stipulations to be found in a number of particular contracts.

[1905] 2 K. B. 391, 401–402.

DECISIONS OF TRIBUNALS

§6

In discussing the "law behind the cases" decided by the Permanent Court of International Justice, Professor Lauterpacht says that—

it is convenient to consider here shortly the part played by the pronouncements of the Permanent Court, and of other international tribunals, as a source of international law.   The authority, in this respect, of decisions of international tribunals is in a different category from that of municipal tribunals.   The part played by the latter as a source of international law in the international sphere . . .   results from the fact that municipal courts are organs of the State.   Their decisions within any single State, when endowed with sufficient uniformity and authority, may be regarded as expressing the *opinio juris* of that State. When, further, a point of international law is covered by a series of concordant and authoritative decisions of municipal courts of various States, then such decisions may be regarded as evidence of international custom.   So conceived, such decisions are not

Difference of
opinion

Personal
views

Municipal
decisions—
evidence of
custom

a subsidiary means for determining rules of international law in
the meaning of Article 38 (4) [of the Statute of the Permanent
Court of International Justice], but 'evidence of a general practice accepted as law' in the meaning of Article 38 (2).[2] ([2]This
view, it must be observed, does not command general agreement.
See on this subject *British Year Book of International Law*, 1929,
pp. 75–92.) Decisions of international courts are not a source of
international law in this sense. They are not evidence of the
practice of States or of what States conceive to be the law. International tribunals, when giving a decision on a point of international law, do not necessarily express the view of either of the
disputants. They do not choose between two conflicting views
advanced by the disputants. They state what the law is, inde- International
pendently of the views of the parties to the dispute. . . .   decisions—
Their decisions are the product of the administration of existing evidence of
law; they are, in theory, evidence of the existing rules of law. rules of law
But that does not mean that they do not in fact constitute a
source of international law. For the distinction between the
evidence and the source of many a rule of law is more speculative
and less rigid than is commonly supposed. . . .
    The position is the same with regard to other courts, including International
international tribunals. It is not of the slightest importance law—a pre-
whether the pronouncements of the Permanent Court are evi- diction
dence or source of international law so long as it is clear that
their substance by showing what are rules of international law
is identical with rules of international law. What are rules of
international law? They are rules which, in the opinion of a
sound and learned international lawyer, the Court will apply.
This is what Mr. Justice Holmes once called the bad man's
interpretation of the law. The test is, what will the Court say?
It is particularly in this practical aspect, namely, in its ability to
predict the nature of the decision, that law is a science. This
is, of course, not the assertion of the rigid positivist view. For
while it must be assumed that the judge will apply existing law,
the latter—contrary to the positivist view—is not the soulless
product of an inanimate automaton. Now, for the reasons
stated, the decisions of the Court are, as a matter both of legal
principle and of actual experience, one of the weighty factors
which will influence its future decisions. They are evidence of
what the Court considers to be the law; they show what the
Court will do in fact; for most practical purposes they show,
therefore, what international law is. In fact they are identical
with the sources of law enumerated in the first three paragraphs
of Article 38; in form they may be a subsidiary means for determining what these sources are. The effect is the same. The
Court was therefore technically fully justified in declaring in
the Judgment concerning *Certain German Interests in Polish
Upper Silesia* that the object of Article 59 is 'to prevent legal
principles accepted by the Court in a particular case from being
binding upon other States or in other disputes.' . . . They
are not binding *upon States*. Neither are they *binding* upon the
Court. But no written provision can prevent them from showing authoritatively what international law is, and no written
provision can prevent the Court from regarding them as such.

The fact that they have been established by the Court itself will not tend to diminish their authority in its eyes. It is in their inherent power, and not in the fourth paragraph of Article 38 of the Statute . . .—which by referring to 'decisions' might seem to exclude, inadvertently, Advisory Opinions—that the source of the authority of the Court's pronouncements . . . and the explanation of their actual influence will be found. The Statute cannot give life to a source of law which circumstances do not permit to become effective. On no occasion has the Court found it necessary to refer to an individual writer as representing the 'teachings of the most highly qualified publicists of the various nations.'

Lauterpacht, *The Development of International Law by the Permanent Court of International Justice* (1934) 9–12. For the text of article 38 of the Statute of the Permanent Court of International Justice, referred to in the above quotation, see *ante* §1.

In the course of its decision of September 7, 1927, in the case of the *S.S. Lotus* (France *v.* Turkey), the Permanent Court of International Justice stated:

Diversity of local decisions

So far as the Court is aware there are no decisions of international tribunals in this matter; but some decisions of municipal courts have been cited. Without pausing to consider the value to be attributed to the judgments of municipal courts in connection with the establishment of the existence of a rule of international law, it will suffice to observe that the decisions quoted sometimes support one view and sometimes the other. . . . It will suffice to observe that, as municipal jurisprudence is thus divided, it is hardly possible to see in it an indication of the existence of the restrictive rule of international law which alone could serve as a basis for the contention of the French Government.

Per. Ct. Int. Jus., Judgment 9, Sept. 7, 1927, Ser. A, No. 10, pp. 28–29; II Hudson, *World Court Reports* (1935) 20, 42–43. See also *ante* §§ 3 and 4.

RELATION TO MUNICIPAL LAW

§7

Nations are required by international law to maintain a certain standard of conduct in their relations with one another, and, accordingly, the laws of well-regulated states and their administration are probably, for the most part, consistent with international law. But if a statute (constitution or decree) contains provisions contrary to international law, and if the authorities of the state find themselves under the necessity of enforcing it, international law still subsists. In such a circumstance the defense that the law is domestic and must be administered is unavailing so far as the international relations of the state are concerned.

The Constitution of the United States expressly recognizes the exist- Constitution of U. S.
ence of international law in the provision that "The Congress shall
have Power . . . To define and punish Piracies and Felonies committed on the high Seas, and Offences against the Law of Nations."

Art. I, sec. 8.

The Constitution also contains the provision that: "The judicial Power
shall extend to all Cases, in Law and Equity, arising under this Constitution,
the Laws of the United States, and Treaties made, or which shall be made,
under their Authority;—to all Cases affecting Ambassadors, other public
Ministers and Consuls;—to all Cases of admiralty and maritime Jurisdiction;—to Controversies to which the United States shall be a Party;—to
Controversies between two or more States;—between a State and Citizens
of another State;—between Citizens of different States;—between Citizens
of the same State claiming Lands under Grants of different States, and
between a State, or the Citizens thereof, and foreign States, Citizens or
Subjects." Art. III, sec. 2.

Provision is also contained in the same instrument that: "In all Cases
affecting Ambassadors, other public Ministers and Consuls, and those in
which a State shall be Party, the Supreme Court shall have original Jurisdiction." Art. III, sec. 2.

It is further provided that: "This Constitution, and the Laws of the
United States which shall be made in Pursuance thereof; and all Treaties
made, or which shall be made, under the Authority of the United States,
shall be the supreme Law of the Land; and the Judges in every State shall
be bound thereby, any Thing in the Constitution or Laws of any State to
the Contrary notwithstanding." Art. VI, clause 2.

Finally, the eleventh amendment of the Constitution contains the provision that: "The Judicial power of the United States shall not be construed
to extend to any suit in law or equity, commenced or prosecuted against one
of the United States by Citizens of another State, or by Citizens or Subjects
of any Foreign State."

In overruling the demurrer in the case of *Kansas* v. *Colorado*, Chief American decisions
Justice Fuller, in delivering the opinion of the Supreme Court, stated:

Sitting, as it were, as an international, as well as a domestic
tribunal, we apply Federal law, state law, and international law,
as the exigencies of the particular case may demand . . .

185 U.S. (1902) 125, 146–147.

Justice Brewer, in the course of the decision on the amended bill in
the case of *Kansas* v. *Colorado*, said:

. . . Nor is our jurisdiction ousted, even if, because Kansas and
Colorado are States sovereign and independent in local matters,
the relations between them depend in any respect upon principles
of international law. International law is no alien in this tribunal. In *The Paquete Habana*, 175 U.S. 677, 700, Mr. Justice
Gray declared:

"International law is part of our law, and must be ascertained and administered by the courts of justice of appropriate jurisdiction, as often as questions of right depending upon it are duly presented for their determination."

206 U.S. (1907) 46, 97.   See also the case of *The Lusitania*, in which it was held that "The United States courts recognize the binding force of international law."   251 Fed., 715, 732 (S.D.N.Y., 1918).

"International Law is a part of our law" and must be administered whenever involved in causes presented for determination, even in a State court.

Elizabeth Riddell, executrix v. *Sophie V. Fuhrman & others*, 233 Mass. (1919) 69, 73, 123 N.E. 237, 239.

In *MacLeod* v. *United States*, it appeared that military officials of the United States in possession of Manila had required the plaintiff to pay duties on goods imported into a certain locality claimed by the United States but actually in possession of the *de facto* government of the insurgents.   The Supreme Court of the United States ordered the duties refunded, as having been exacted contrary to international law. In construing the statute ratifying the Executive order under which the duties were collected—which did not require the payment of duties under the circumstances—the Court said:

The statute should be construed in the light of the purpose of the Government to act within the limitation of the principles of international law, the observance of which is so essential to the peace and harmony of nations, and it should not be assumed that Congress proposed to violate the obligations of this country to other nations, which it was the manifest purpose of the President to scrupulously observe and which were founded upon the principles of international law.

229 U.S. (1913) 416, 434.

In the case of *The Over The Top*, where a British vessel and her cargo had been seized by officers of the United States Coast Guard in October 1924, because of alleged illegal entry of liquors at a point nineteen miles distant from the coast of the United States (claimed to be within one hour's sailing distance), the contention was advanced that, regardless of the municipal legislation of the United States (section 447 of the Tariff Act of 1922, making it unlawful for a vessel to unload any part of its cargo at any other place than a port of entry), the acts complained of by the United States—in instituting libels against the vessel and cargo—could not constitute offenses against the United States when committed by foreign nationals, on foreign vessels, on the high seas at a point beyond the territorial jurisdiction of the United States.   In dismissing the libels on the ground that the acts complained of had not been made a crime either by the laws of the United States or by the convention of January 23, 1924 between the United States and Great Britain, Judge Thomas of the District Court of the United States for the District of Connecticut said:

> If we assume for the present that the national legislation has, by its terms, made the acts complained of a crime against the United States even when committed on the high seas by foreign nationals upon a ship of foreign registry, then there is no discretion vested in the federal court, once it obtains jurisdiction, to decline enforcement. International practice is law only in so far as we adopt it, and like all common or statute law it bends to the will of the Congress. It is not the function of courts to annul legislation; it is their duty to interpret and by their judicial decrees to enforce it—and even when an act of Congress is declared invalid, it is only because the basic law is being enforced in that declaration. There is one ground only upon which a federal court may refuse to enforce an act of Congress and that is when the act is held to be unconstitutional. The act may contravene recognized principles of international comity, but that affords no more basis for judicial disregard of it than it does for executive disregard of it. These libels, therefore, cannot be attacked upon the ground that the territorial jurisdiction of the United States cannot be extended beyond the three-mile sea zone under international law.
> [2] If, however, the court has no option to refuse the enforcement of legislation in contravention of principles of international law, it does not follow that in construing the terms and provisions of a statute it may not assume that such principles were on the national conscience and that the congressional act did not deliberately intend to infringe them. In other words, unless it unmistakably appears that a congressional act was intended to be in disregard of a principle of international comity, the presumption is that it was intended to be in conformity with it.

Conflicting statute

Presumption of conformity

Schroeder v. *Bissell, Collector (The Over The Top)*, 5 F. (2d) (1925) 838, 842; Treaty Series 685; 4 Treaties, etc. (Trenwith, 1938) 4225.

The selective draft law of the United States, approved on May 18, 1917 (40 Stat. 76, 77–78), subjected to draft for military service all resident aliens of a prescribed age who had declared their intention to become citizens of the United States. With reference to this law, Circuit Judge Gilbert stated in the case of *United States* v. *Siem* that "We make no question of the power of Congress to enact that law, for neither existing treaties nor international law could divest Congress of the power, if it chose to exercise it, of requiring military service of such resident aliens, as international law is not in itself binding upon Congress, and treaties stand upon no higher plane than statutes of the United States."

International law and Congress

299 Fed. 582, 583 (C.C.A. 9th, 1924).

In another case, decided by the District Court of the United States for the Eastern District of New York, the court stated that "the rules of international law, like those of existing treaties or conventions, are subject to the express acts of Congress, and the courts of the United States have not the power to declare a law unconstitutional, if it be within the authority given to Congress as to legislation, even though the law itself be in contravention of the so-called law of nations. The Nereide, supra; Respublica v. De Longchamps, 1 Dall. (1 U.S.) 111, 1 L. Ed. 59; The Scotia, 14 Wall. (81 U.S.) 170, 20 L. Ed. 822; Opinions of the Attorney General, vol. 10, at page 521, and also the cases hereinbefore cited."

United States ex rel. Pfefer v. *Bell*, 248 Fed. 992, 995 (E.D.N.Y., 1918).

When the French, German, and British Governments submitted claims to Cuba on account of losses alleged to have been sustained by their nationals because of acts of Cuban revolutionary forces in 1895–98, the Cuban Government advanced the following reasons for objecting to the arbitration of the claims:

(f) That the Constitution provides in one of its transitory provisions, that the Republic of Cuba did not recognize any debt or liability except that legitimately incurred for the benefit of the revolution by the Chiefs of Corps of the Liberating Army, after the 24th of February, 1895, and prior to the 19th of September of the same year, on which date the Constitution of Jimaguayú was promulgated, and the debts and liabilities subsequently incurred by the revolutionary Government or its legitimate representatives abroad. Congress will determine said debts and liabilities, and resolve accordingly for the payment of those that are legitimate.

. . . .

(j) The present Government of the Republic of Cuba is legally unable to assent to arbitration of the above mentioned claims, because it would infringe the constitutional provision whereby the liabilities of Cuba are limited to the debts expressly mentioned in the Constitution.

The views of the Cuban Government having been transmitted to the Government of the United States, the latter expressed the following opinion:

Constitutional or statutory provisions

. . . It is doubtful, however, whether either in the preliminary examination of the claims by the Cuban Government or in their subsequent arbitration, if one should be agreed upon, the First Transient Provision of the Constitution of Cuba would play an important part. For so thinking there are two reasons. The first of these is that a government is not permitted to set up, as a final answer to demands for the performance of international obligations, provisions of its municipal law, either constitutional or statutory. This principle has been clearly established on many occasions, and very notably in the settlement of the so-called Alabama claims by means of the award of the Geneva Tribunal. In the second place, it is by no means clear that the First Transient Provision forbids the Cuban Government to recognize claims not therein mentioned. The language of the provision is that the Republic of Cuba "does not recognize" any other debts or obligations than those therein mentioned, and that the Cuban Congress "shall examine said debts and obligations and decide upon the payment of those which are found legitimate." The debts and obligations thus referred to are those "legitimately contracted in favor of the revolution" by commanders of the liberating army before September 19, 1895, and by the revolutionary government after that date. These words indicate that the object of the first transient provision was primarily to recognize and provide for the payment of a certain class of claims. It gave no recognition to other claims; but, in view of the principle above mentioned, it can scarcely be construed as having been intended to forbid the Cuban Government to recognize claims for which it might be liable under international law.

Undated memorandum from the Legation of Cuba to the Department of State, MS. Department of State, file 437.00/60; 1913 For. Rel. 344, 345; the Department of State to the Legation of Cuba, undated memorandum handed to the Cuban Minister, Dr. Pablo Desvernine, on July 12, 1913, MS. Department of State, file 437.00/60; 1913 For. Rel. 347–348.

In 1912 the Mexican Government requested the prevention by the Government of the United States of the introduction of arms and war material through the port of El Paso, Texas, for the use of the rebels in Mexico, on the ground that the introduction of these articles involved violation of the neutrality laws of the United States. In reply, the Acting Secretary of State pointed out that—

the duties of neutrality under the law of nations cannot be either expanded or contracted by national legislation. The United States for instance has here in excessive caution required from its citizens duties more stringent than those imposed by the law of nations; but those statutes, while they may make offenders penally liable in this country, do not themselves put either these persons or this Government under any extraterritorial obligation. Our own statutes bind only our own government and citizens, and those within our jurisdiction. If they impose on us a larger duty than is imposed upon us by international law, they do not correspondingly enlarge our duties to foreign nations. Since, therefore, these statutes only qualify as offenses certain specified transactions which would not otherwise have such character, and, therefore, since under these circumstances only those acts are bad which are really prohibited, it is evidently necessary that the act complained of should clearly fall within the statutes, in order that it may be regarded as illegal.

Not changed by local law

Mr. Huntington Wilson, Acting Secretary of State, to the Mexican Ambassador (Crespo y Martínez), Mar. 8, 1912, MS. Department of State, file

812.113/221; 1912 For. Rel. 740, 741–742. See also the telegram from the Mexican Ambassador to Mr. Wilson, Mar. 5, 1912, MS. Department of State, file 812.00/3059; 1912 For. Rel. 737–738. Subsequently (Mar. 14, 1912) a joint resolution of Congress was approved authorizing the President, whenever he should find that in any American country "conditions of domestic violence exist which are promoted by the use of arms or munitions of war procured from the United States", to make proclamation thereof, and providing that it should thereafter be unlawful to export arms or munitions of war from the United States to any such country (37 Stat. 630). President Taft issued a proclamation on the same day, making the terms of the joint resolution applicable to Mexico. On Mar. 16 following, Mr. Wilson, Acting Secretary of State, explained in a note to the Mexican Ambassador that "This action was taken not because of any obligation so to do resting upon this Government by reason of the rules and principles of international law, which obligations were already far more than met by the existing so-called neutrality statutes of the United States, but solely from a sincere desire to promote the return of peace to Mexico and the welfare of a neighboring nation." No. 134; see MS. Department of State, file 812.-113/216, enclosure; 1912 For. Rel. 747–748.

Laws "in advance" of international requirements

In connection with the controversy that arose between the United States and Germany, during the period of American neutrality in the World War, concerning the alleged shipment from American ports of motorboats, speed boats, and component parts of submarines which were said to be consigned to the enemies of Germany, Secretary Lansing pointed out that "If the municipal statutes of the country should be in advance of the requirements of international law, I understand that it is not for a foreign government to protest against their infraction so long as the infraction does not extend to the Law of Nations and so long as the municipal laws are impartially administered."

Secretary Lansing to the German Ambassador, Count von Bernstorff, Jan. 7, 1916, MS. Department of State, file 763.72111El 1/57; 1915 For. Rel. Supp. 818.

See the views of the following writers on the relation between international law and the municipal law of the United States: Scott, "The Legal Nature of International Law", in 1 A.J.I.L. (1907), pt. II, pp. 831, 851; Willoughby, "The Legal Nature of International Law", in 2 A.J.I.L. (1908) 357–358; Picciotto, *The Relation of International Law to the Law of England and of the United States of America* (1915) 126; Foulke, "Definition and Nature of International Law", in 19 Col. L. Rev. (1919) 429, 465–466; Moore, "The Relation of International Law to National Law in the American Republics", in the *Proceedings of the American Society of International Law* (1915; pub. 1916) 11, 12–22; Moore, "Fifty Years of International Law", in 50 Harv. L. Rev. (1937) 395, 397–399.

British decisions

In the course of the judgment of the court (King's Bench Division) in the case of *West Rand Central Gold Mining Company, Limited* v.

The King, decided on June 1, 1905, Lord Alverstone (C. J.) commented at some length upon the proposition urged by Lord Robert Cecil, counsel for the claimant, that "international law forms part of the law of England". He said:

> . . . It is quite true that whatever has received the common consent of civilized nations must have received the assent of our country, and that to which we have assented along with other nations in general may properly be called international law, and as such will be acknowledged and applied by our municipal tribunals when legitimate occasion arises for those tribunals to decide questions to which doctrines of international law may be relevant. But any doctrine so invoked must be one really accepted as binding between nations, and the international law sought to be applied must, like anything else, be proved by satisfactory evidence, which must shew either that the particular proposition put forward has been recognised and acted upon by our own country, or that it is of such a nature, and has been so widely and generally accepted, that it can hardly be supposed that any civilized State would repudiate it. . . . the expressions used by Lord Mansfield when dealing with the particular and recognised rule of international law on this subject, that the law of nations forms part of the law of England, ought not to be construed so as to include as part of the law of England opinions of text-writers upon a question as to which there is no evidence that Great Britain has ever assented, and a fortiori if they are contrary to the principles of her laws as declared by her Courts. The cases of *Wolff* v. *Oxholm* . . . and *Rex* v. *Keyn* . . . are only illustrations of the same rule—namely, that questions of international law may arise, and may have to be considered in connection with the administration of municipal law.

[1905] 2 K.B. 391, 406–408. See also in this connection *Commercial and Estates Company of Egypt* v. *The Board of Trade,* [1925] 1 K.B. 271, 283–284, 294–296.

In delivering the judgment of the Judicial Committee of the Privy Council in the case of the Swedish steamship *Zamora* on April 7, 1916, Lord Parker of Waddington stated that, although a British prize court is bound by an act of the Imperial Parliament, there is no power in the Crown by Order in Council to prescribe or alter the law which the prize court has to administer. King's Orders in Council

IV *Lloyd's Reports of Prize Cases* (1918) 1, 62, 84, 89, 90–91, 95–96; [1916] 2 A.C. 77, 88, 91, 92–93, 96–97.

In this connection see also the following cases: *The Alwina,* [1918] A.C. 444, 450; *The Stigstad,* [1919] A.C. 279, 284 *et seq.; The Leonora,* [1919] A.C. 974, 983 *et seq.*

110090—40——4

In the case of the Swedish steamship *Håkan*, the British prize
court (Sir Samuel Evans, president of the court, delivering the judgment rendered on July 3 1916) held:

> There is no doubt that the law to be administered in this
> Court is the law of nations (or international law, as it is often
> called), and not our municipal law.

V *Lloyd's Reports of Prize Cases* (1919) 161, 169.

See the views of the following writers on the relation between international law and the municipal law of Great Britain: Westlake, "Is International Law a Part of the Law of England?" in 22 L.Q. Rev. (1906) 14,
26; I Pitt Cobbett, *Cases on International Law* (5th or Grey's ed. 1931)
21–22; I Oppenheim's *International Law* (5th ed., by Lauterpacht, 1937)
36–38.

Germany

Article 4 of the Constitution of the German Reich of August 11,
1919 contains the provision that "The universally recognised rules of
International Law are considered as binding constituent parts of
German Federal [or national] Law."

Giese, *Verfassung des Deutschen Reiches vom 11. August 1919* (Berlin, 1925)
56, translation.

Dr. Friedrich Giese in his comment upon article 4 of the German
Constitution states:

> 3. The effect of Art. 4 is that international law, in so far and
> to the extent that it is universally recognized, is absolutely equal
> to German national law in validity, and forms in the same way a
> direct source of law for German executive and judicial officials, as
> well as nationals, so that, for example, a civil suit can be based
> directly on a principle of international law, for example, a claim
> of the violation of extra-territoriality. But international law is
> not therefore any higher system of law than German national
> legislation. In case of a plain contradiction between a principle
> of German law and a principle of international law that is alleged
> to be universally accepted, the judge or administrative official
> has to apply, not international law but German law; in this case,
> in fact, the deviation of the German principle of law contradicts
> the "universal" recognition of the principle of international law.
> On the other hand, preference is to be given international law in
> case of conflict, if the recognition of a rule of international law
> by the Reich can be proven. Thus the defect consists in the
> Reich, despite its recognition, not having yet changed the con-
> flicting German rule of law and brought it into harmony with
> international law, to do that which is its duty under international
> law. Prot. V. A. 406. The universally recognized rules of inter-
> national law are considered as part of the law of the Reich; hence
> according to Art. 13, take unqualified precedence over State laws
> that deviate therefrom.

**Where con-
flict with
statutes**

Ibid. 57–58, translation.

By the terms of the Aufbringungsgesetz (Industrial Charges Act) of 1927, a German federal law, an extraordinary tax was imposed in order to enable Germany to pay her war indemnity in accordance with the Dawes plan. When the tax was levied upon a firm of Italian nationals ("Dr. G." and the members of his family), the company having been registered and having its seat of business in Germany, it was contended on the part of the company that Italian nationals were exempt from the payment of the tax under article 5 of the treaty of commerce of October 31, 1925, between Germany and Italy, which exempted the nationals of the contracting parties from the payment of "compulsory loans and contributions" when in the territory of the other and that the imposition of the tax was contrary to international law and hence contrary to article 4 of the German Constitution quoted *ante*.

The German Federal Court for Revenue Matters (Reichsfinanzhof), in a decision of August 8, 1928, held that these contentions must be rejected; that the company must be regarded as a German company; that the tax could not be regarded as a "compulsory loan" or "contribution"; and that—

> If the act [for raising funds] were in conflict to that extent with universally recognized principles of international law, which is not the case, its validity and its binding character for the tax courts would not be prejudiced thereby. Rather would the Industrial Charges Act [*Aufbringungsgesetz*], as a law promulgated later and containing a special system of regulations, take precedence in this respect over any general principle of international law which might be in conflict therewith, or over any other law of the Reich.

> .II(2) *Zeitschrift für Ausländisches Öffentliches Recht und Völkerrecht* (1931) 88, 91–92, translation.

The Belgian Council of Prizes took the position in the course of its decision in 1919 in the case of *The Agiena* that it was not bound by national law in cases where that law was contrary to international law. The Belgian prize court stated in this connection that— **Belgium**

> it is accordingly quite indifferent whether the question in dispute is or is not covered by Belgian law, from the moment when it has been established that its solution can be derived from other sources of an equal, or a superior degree, of international law; . . . the circumstance that the Council should necessarily render judgment in accordance with the principles of this law and is not bound by national laws rather constitutes for the interested parties a guarantee of impartial justice . . .

> 1920 *Moniteur Belge* 404, 405; quoted from the translation in 16 A.J.I.L. (1922) 117, 118.

Numerous decisions of international tribunals have dealt with the relation between international law and municipal law.

In the decision in the case of the *Aroa Mines (Limited)* (Great Britain *v.* Venezuela) disallowing the claim of a British company for losses sustained by reason of the seizure of its property by revolutionary troops in Venezuela—there being no proof of any fault or lack of due diligence on the part of the titular and respondent Government—Umpire Plumley, in construing the provisions of the protocols of 1903 between the two countries, considered not only the contemporaneous correspondence of the two Governments at the time of the drafting of the protocols but also the then-existing legislation and views of certain Latin American countries with respect to the non-liability of states under domestic law for acts which may be contrary to international law. He said:

> By a proper application of the usually accepted international law governing such commissions [as this one], controlling courts, and defining the diplomatic conduct of nations there could be no question that national laws must yield to the law of nations if there was a conflict.

> .   .   .   .

> The definition of international law, making it under one form of expression and another the rules which determine the general body of civilized states in their dealings with one another, necessarily excludes state statutes from doing the same thing.

> .   .   .   .

> The right of states to give protection to their subjects abroad, to obtain redress for them, to intervene in their behalf in a proper case, which generally accepted public law always maintains, makes these municipal statutes under discussion in direct contravention thereto and therefore inadmissible principles by those states who hold to these general rules of international law.

> Ralston's Report (1904) 344, 378, 379; protocols of Feb. 13 and May 7, 1903, *ibid.* 292, 294.

In January 1917 the Government of Costa Rica under President Alfredo González was overthrown by Federico Tinoco, who established a new constitution in June of that year. In September 1919 his government fell, and, after a provisional government under Barquero, the old constitution was restored and elections were held under it. Two claims, one the *Central Costa Rica Petroleum Company* (Great Britain *v.* Costa Rica) and the other the *Royal Bank of Canada* (Great Britain *v.* Costa Rica), which arose in connection with acts of the Tinoco government, were submitted to Chief Justice Taft as sole arbitrator pursuant to the terms of a convention signed on January 12, 1922 by Great Britain and Costa Rica. In his decision (October 18, 1923), the Chief Justice explained that the courts of Costa Rica might be under the necessity of enforcing Costa Rican law but that an international tribunal would follow international law. He said:

> However this may be, these restrictions upon each claimant would seem to be inapplicable to a case like the present where is involved the obligation of a restored government for the acts or contracts of a usurping government. The courts of the restored government are bound to administer the law of the restored government under its constitution and their decisions are necessarily affected by the limitations of that instrument. This may prevent the courts from giving full effect to international law that may be at variance with the municipal law which under the restored constitution the national courts have to administer. It is obvious that the obligations of a restored government for the acts of the usurping *de facto* government it succeeds cannot, from the international standpoint, be prejudiced by a constitution which, though restored to life, is for purposes of this discussion, exactly as if it were new legislation which was not in force when the obligations arose.

Conflict between local and international law

> Nor is it an answer to this, to suggest that in the case here under consideration, the restored constitution may be construed not to prevent the Costa Rican courts from giving effect to the principles of international law, already stated. It is enough that the restored constitution is the controlling factor in the exercise of any jurisdiction to be exercised by those courts, and that other nations may object to a tribunal which must give consideration to legislation enacted after the fact, in reaching its decision.

> This is not an exceptional instance of an essential difference between the scope and effect of a decision by the highest tribunal of a country and of an international tribunal. The Constitution of the United States makes the Constitution, laws passed in pursuance thereof, and treaties of the United States the supreme law of the land. Under that provision, a treaty may repeal a statute, and a statute may repeal a treaty. The Supreme Court cannot under the Constitution recognize and enforce rights accruing to aliens under a treaty which Congress has repealed by statute. In an international tribunal, however, the unilateral repeal of a treaty by a statute would not affect the rights arising under it and its judgment would necessarily give effect to the treaty and hold the statute repealing it of no effect.

18 A.J.I.L. (1924) 147, 159–160.

The tribunal selected by Norway and the United States from the panel of the Permanent Court of Arbitration, under the special agreement of June 30, 1921 for the arbitration of certain Norwegian claims against the United States, stated in the course of the decision in the case on October 13, 1922, allowing the Norwegian claims to a considerable extent, that—

should the public law of one of the Parties seem contrary to international public policy ("Ordre Public International"), an International Tribunal is not bound by the municipal law of the States which are Parties to the arbitration.

.   .   .   .

This Tribunal is therefore a regular legal institution, which possesses by consent of the two Parties a compulsory jurisdiction, independent of the national courts of the Parties. Both Parties come before the Tribunal on a footing of perfect equality. The Tribunal cannot ignore the municipal law of the Parties, unless that law is contrary to the principle of the equality of the Parties, or to the principles of justice which are common to all civilised nations. But the Tribunal is not bound by the special rules instituted in any of the two countries for the purpose of restricting (for instance in favour of the sovereign against its own "justiciables") the equality between parties which would otherwise be the basis of justice as applied between private litigants.

The Tribunal cannot agree, therefore, with the contention of Norway that it should be entirely free to disregard the municipal law of the United States, when this has been implicitly accepted by Norwegian citizens in their dealings with American citizens, although this law may be less favourable to their present claims than the municipal laws of certain other civilised countries.

But the Tribunal cannot agree, on the other hand, with the contention of the United States that it should be governed by American Statutes whenever the United States claim jurisdiction.

This Tribunal is at liberty to examine if these Statutes are consistent with the equality of the two Contracting Parties, with Treaties passed by the United States, or with well established principles of international law, including the customary law and the practice of judges in other international courts.

After careful examination of the Constitution of the United States, of the American Jurisprudence quoted by both parties, and of the American legislation passed by Congress from 1916 onwards (commencing with the National Defence Acts of June 1916, and with particular reference to the legislation of 1917 which mobilised the industries of the United States), the Tribunal agrees with the contention of the United States that there was nothing in this emergency legislation, under the special circumstances, that was contrary to international law.

Award of the Tribunal of Arbitration (Per. Ct. Arb., The Hague) 26, 27–28; MS. Department of State, file 411.57N83/451; Scott, *Hague Court Reports* (2d ser. 1932) 39, 64, 65–66.

In the course of the decision of the Claims Commission established by France and Mexico (convention of Sept. 25, 1924), in the case of *Georges Pinson* (France *v.* Mexico), the president of the commission, J. H. W. Verzijl, pointed out that as a general principle of interpretation municipal law must, in doubtful cases, always be read in the sense that insures its conformity with international law and that—

it is incontestable and uncontested that international law is superior to "domestic" law (Politis) and that, as the Permanent Court of International Justice has formulated it so simply in its Order No. 7 relative to certain German interests in Polish Upper Silesia (bottom of page 19): "With regard to international law and the Court which is the organ thereof, national laws are mere facts", so that every international tribunal, because of its nature, is obliged and authorized to examine them in the light of international law, a thesis which has, moreover, been maintained many times and applied by different international courts.

"Superiority" of international law

The second claim cannot be maintained, for the same reason, that of the superiority of international law to the national law of states. The thesis which the arbitrator very properly formulated in the Montijo case (Moore: Digest of International Arbitrations, page 1440), namely, that a treaty is "superior to the Constitution, which latter must give way" and that "the legislation of the republic must be adapted to the treaty, not the treaty to the laws", is of equal value with respect to the mutual relations between the Constitution and unwritten international law. Following this line of reasoning, I believe that I should make the most explicit reservations with regard to the Mexican thesis maintained on page 56 of the collection of documents cited above, § 6, on *La cuestión internacional mexicano-americana, durante el Gobierno del Gral. Don Alvaro Obregón,* which the Mexican Agent has obliged me to study carefully in order to learn that if "there should be a Constitution (with the effect of ordering the confiscation of foreign property rights), as it would be the supreme law of the country it would have to be placed above treaties for the latter cannot have greater force than the Constitution itself." This thesis, absolutely contrary to the very axioms of international law, can be explained only by regrettable confusion between two very different hypotheses, namely: that of the pre-existence of a constitutional provision prohibiting the Government from approving or ratifying treaties of a given scope in the future or prohibiting the Parliament from approving them, and that of the promulgation of a constitutional provision which comes into contradiction with an already existing treaty or rule of customary international law. If, in the first case, it is extremely doubtful that such a treaty concluded despite the prohibitive provision of the Constitution may be considered as legally valid, since the constitutional organs would have exceeded the limits which the Constitution sets to their power to represent the State in the act of contracting the international engagement in question, the situation is essentially different in the latter case, for under the hypothesis of the preexistence of treaties or rules of customary law, that very fact would absolutely prevent the state from validly promulgating constitutional provisions contrary to the said treaties or rules: the existence of these latter in itself involves a corresponding restriction of the sovereignty of the State. Further, we must never lose sight of the fact that this question of fundamental importance does not come up in the same way before an international tribunal as before a national court. In fact, the latter, an expression of the sovereignty of the State, may find itself obliged by its national legislation to apply the Constitution, without examining its conformity with international law, even if it should have to admit its non-conformity with the said law. That point of view is, however, entirely foreign to international tribunals.

Decision of Oct. 19, 1928, sentence 1, *La réparation des dommages causés aux étrangers par des mouvements révolutionnaires, jurisprudence de la Commission Franco-Mexicaine des Réclamations*, 1924–1932 (Paris, 1933) 1, 72–73, translation.

Although Guatemala contended in the case of *P. W. Shufeldt* (United States *v.* Guatemala), arbitrated by the two Governments under a protocol signed on November 2, 1929, that a decree of May 22, 1928 abrogating Shufeldt's concession was the constitutional act of a sovereign state exercised by the National Assembly of Guatemala and that it could not be questioned by an international tribunal, the arbitrator—Sir Herbert Sisnett, Chief Justice of British Honduras—in his decision of July 24, 1930, with reference to this contention, held:

Municipal
law not a bar

. . . This may be quite true from a national point of view but not from an international point of view for "it is a settled principle of international law that a sovereign can not be permitted to set up one of his own municipal laws as a bar to a claim by a foreign sovereign for a wrong done to the latter's subject"

Decision of July 24, 1930, *Shufeldt Claim*, Department of State Arbitration Ser. 3 (1932) 851, 876–877.

Crimes

With regard to crimes as defined by international law, that law has no means of trying or punishing them. The recognition of them as constituting crimes, and the trial and punishment of the criminals, are left to the municipal law of each country.

In re Piracy Jure Gentium, [1934] A.C. 586, 589.

The Permanent Court of International Justice, in its judgment of May 25, 1926, in the case of *German Interests in Polish Upper Silesia and the Factory at Chorzów*, held:

Interpretation of
municipal
law

It might be asked whether a difficulty does not arise from the fact that the Court would have to deal with the Polish law of July 14th, 1920 [which was invoked by Poland in taking over the Chorzów factory]. This, however, does not appear to be the case. From the standpoint of International Law and of the Court which is its organ, municipal laws are merely facts which express the will and constitute the activities of States, in the same manner as do legal decisions or administrative measures. The Court is certainly not called upon to interpret the Polish law as such; but there is nothing to prevent the Court's giving judgment on the question whether or not, in applying that law, Poland is acting in conformity with its obligations towards Germany under the Geneva Convention.

Per. Ct. Int. Jus., Judgment 7 (Merits), May 25, 1926, Ser. A, No. 7, pp. 4, 19; I Hudson, *World Court Reports* (1934) 510, 521.

In its decision in the case between Brazil and France concerning the *Payment in Gold of Brazilian Federal Loans issued in France,* the Permanent Court of International Justice said:

Though bound to apply municipal law when circumstances so require, the Court, which is a tribunal of international law, and which, in this capacity, is deemed itself to know what this law is, is not obliged also to know the municipal law of the various countries. All that can be said in this respect is that the Court may possibly be obliged to obtain knowledge regarding the municipal law which has to be applied. And this it must do, either by means of evidence furnished it by the Parties or by means of any researches which the Court may think fit to undertake or to cause to be undertaken. — *Decisions of municipal courts*

Once the Court has arrived at the conclusion that it is necessary to apply the municipal law of a particular country, there seems no doubt that it must seek to apply it as it would be applied in that country.

.   .   .   .

Of course, the Court will endeavour to make a just appreciation of the jurisprudence of municipal courts. If this is uncertain or divided, it will rest with the Court to select the interpretation which it considers most in conformity with the law.

Per. Ct. Int. Jus., Judgment 15, July 12, 1929, Ser. A, Nos. 20/21, pp. 93, 124–125; II Hudson, *World Court Reports* (1935) 402, 428.

DEVELOPMENT

§8

In delivering the opinion of the Supreme Court in the case of *New Jersey* v. *Delaware,* Justice Cardozo commented upon the development of international law with respect to boundaries. He said:

In 1783, when the Revolutionary War was over, Delaware and New Jersey began with a clean slate. There was no treaty or convention fixing the boundary between them. There was no possessory act nor other act of dominion to give to the boundary in bay and river below the circle a practical location, or to establish a prescriptive right. In these circumstances, the capacity of the law to develop and apply a formula consonant with justice — *Growth by adjudication*

and with the political and social needs of the international legal
system is not lessened by the fact that at the creation of the
boundary the formula of the *Thalweg* had only a germinal existence. The gap is not so great that adjudication may not fill it.
Lauterpacht, The Function of Law in the International Community, pp. 52, 60, 70, 85, 100, 110, 111, 255, 404, 432. Treaties
almost contemporaneous, which were to be followed by a host of
others, were declaratory of a principle that was making its way
into the legal order. Hall, International Law, 8th ed., p. 7.
International law, or the law that governs between states, has at
times, like the common law within states, a twilight existence
during which it is hardly distinguishable from morality or justice,
till at length the *imprimatur* of a court attests its jural quality.
Lauterpacht, *supra*, pp. 110, 255; Hall, *supra*, pp. 7, 12, 15, 16;
Jenks, The New Jurisprudence, pp. 11, 12. "The gradual consolidation of opinions and habits" (Vinogradoff, Custom and
Right, p. 21) has been doing its quiet work.

> 291 U.S. (1934) 361, 383–384.

Although Sir Samuel Evans held in the case of *The Berlin*, decided
on October 29, 1914, that the vessel was not within the category of
coast fishing vessels entitled to freedom from capture under the laws
of war (the vessel being, on account of her size, equipment, and
voyage, a deep-sea fishing vessel engaged in a commercial enterprise
forming a part of the trade of the enemy country), he stated in the
course of the decision:

> In this country I do not think any decided and reported case
> has treated the immunity of such vessels as a part or rule of the
> law of nations . . .

**Rule devel-
oped**

> But after the lapse of a century I am of opinion that it has
> become a sufficiently settled doctrine and practice of the law of
> nations that fishing vessels plying their industry near or about the
> coast (not necessarily in territorial waters), in and by which the
> hardy people who man them gain their livelihood, are not properly
> subjects of capture in war so long as they confine themselves to
> the peaceful work which the industry properly involves.

> [1914] P. 265, 272.
> A discussion of the evolution of international law is contained in the
> arbitral award in *The Island of Palmas Case* (United States and Nether-
> lands), published by the International Bureau of the Permanent Court of
> Arbitration (The Hague, 1928), pp. 26–28, and in Scott, *Hague Court Re-
> ports* (2d ser. 1932) 83, 100–101.

Professor Roscoe Pound describes the change occurring in the field of
international law in the nineteenth and twentieth centuries in the
following words:

**Growth of
international
law**

> . . . the facts of international life call for creative juristic
> activity. The facts of an international law that must govern
> peoples, not personal sovereigns, that must deal with large in-

determinate groups, swayed in varying proportion by all the conflicting elements that enter into public opinion for the time being, not with individual men or with small, continuous cohesive groups of individuals, demand a theory that shall grow out of these facts and interpret them for us in terms of effective effort toward perceived ends, . . .

. . . Much of the strength of Grotius' international law, which enabled it to become a real body of living law so quickly, was in this: that it grew out of and grew up with the political facts of the time and its fundamental conception was an accurate reflection of an existing political system which was developing as the law was doing and at the same time.

Grotius' law reflected the period

.   .   .   .

When sovereignty passed from the sovereign king to the sovereign people, when kings began to reign but not rule, when wars came to be waged not by one king against another with relatively small highly trained standing armies but between whole peoples with all their powers, economic and even spiritual as well as military and naval, a profound change took place in the facts to which international law was to be applied, the effects whereof have been manifest increasingly in the present century.

Change in international scene

.   .   .   .

Recently there has been a conspicuous revival of philosophy of law throughout the world. The nineteenth-century historical school has lost its uncontested headship of the science of law and has begun visibly to break up. A new social philosophical and a new sociological jurisprudence have been making great strides. Moreover this development of new methods in legal science and breaking up of the old historical school goes along with a general abandonment of the nineteenth-century historico-metaphysical thinking in every field and revival of faith in the efficacy of effort. (. . . For the war showed visibly the role which human initiative may play in the building of institutions and the shaping of events. It palpably overturned the pyschological presuppositions of nineteenth-century thought. The conception of a slow and internally ordered succession of events and of institutions, whereby things perfect themselves by evolving to the limit of their idea, has ceased to reign.

New processes of thought developing

Among the new philosophies of action or those which succeed to them the jurist of the immediate future, thinking of a great task of social engineering, as it were, whereby the conflicting or overlapping interests and claims and demands of the peoples of this crowded world may be secured or satisfied so far as may be with a minimum of friction and a minimum of waste, must find the basis of a new philosophical theory of international law. We shall not ask him for a juristic romance built upon the cosmological romance of some closed metaphysical system. But we may demand of him a legal philosophy that shall take account of the social psychology, the economics, the sociology as well as the law and politics of today, that shall enable international law to take in what it requires from without, that shall give us a functional critique of international law in terms of social ends, not an analytical critique in terms of itself, and above all that shall conceive of the legal order as a process and not as a condition.

Pound, "Philosophical Theory and International Law", in *Bibliotheca Visseriana* (1923) 71, 75–76, 78, 89.

On July 26, 1934 the Judicial Committee of the Privy Council concluded that actual robbery was not an essential element in the crime of piracy *jure gentium* and that a frustrated attempt to commit a piratical robbery was equally piracy *jure gentium*. In the course of its consideration of the question, the Judicial Committee had occasion to consider various definitions of piracy *jure gentium*. After considering numerous early views with respect to the law of piracy and in particular the case of *R.* v. *Joseph Dawson* (13 St. Tr., col. 451) which arose in 1696, Viscount Sankey, L. C., stated:

A "living and expanding code"

But over and above that we are not now in the year 1696, we are now in the year 1934. International law was not crystallized in the 17th century, but is a living and expanding code. In his treatise on international law, the English text-book writer Hall (1835–94) says at p. 25 of his preface to the third edition (1889) (1): "Looking back over the last couple of centuries we see international law at the close of each fifty years in a more solid position than that which it occupied at the beginning of the period. Progressively it has taken firmer hold, it has extended its sphere of operation, it has ceased to trouble itself about trivial formalities, it has more and more dared to grapple in detail with the fundamental facts in the relations of States. The area within which it reigns beyond dispute has in that time been infinitely enlarged, and it has been greatly enlarged within the memory of living man." Again another example may be given. A body of international law is growing up with regard to aerial warfare and aerial transport, of which Sir Charles Hedges in 1696 could have had no possible idea.

In re Piracy Jure Gentium, [1934] A.C. 586, 592–593.

Function of jurisprudence

Henri Fromageot, president of the tribunal established by the United States and Great Britain pursuant to the terms of the special agreement of August 18, 1910, explained the function of jurisprudence in the development of international law in his decision in the case of *Eastern Extension, Australasia and China Telegraph Company, Limited* (Great Britain v. United States), as follows:

Where no express rule

. . . In our opinion, however, even assuming that there was in 1898 no treaty and no specific rule of international law formulated as the expression of a universally recognised rule governing the the case of the cutting of cables by belligerents, it can not be said that there is no principle of international law applicable. International law, as well as domestic law, may not contain, and generally does not contain, express rules decisive of particular cases; but the function of jurisprudence is to resolve the conflict of opposing rights and interests by applying, in default of any specific provision of law, the corollaries of general principles, and so to find—exactly as in the mathematical sciences—the solution of the problem. This is the method of jurisprudence; it is the method by which the law has been gradually evolved in every country resulting in the definition and settlement of legal relations as well between States as between private individuals.

Nielsen's Report (1926) 73, 75–76.

The World War made people profoundly sceptical as to the value, the efficacy, and even the existence of international law. After seeing so many treaties broken, so many rules ignored, so much that is arbitrary ruling in the relations between nations, doubt and pessimism were beginning to get the upper hand. People spoke of the ruin, the bankruptcy of international law, of the impossibility of permanently subjecting the activity of States to hard and fast rules of law. *Effect of World War*

But this first impression did not last. Little by little it was recognized that international law has no more disappeared as a result of the excesses of the late war than criminal law has ceased to remain in force in spite of the crimes that are committed. This was remarked, even during the course of hostilities, by Sir Frederick Pollock: "Law does not cease to exist because it is broken, or even because for a time it may be broken on a large scale; neither does the escape of some criminals abolish penal justice."

A calmer, more dispassionate scrutiny of the situation brought the conviction that, far from having been fatal to it, the trial it has undergone has been, in the end, a very good thing for international law; it has brought sharply into light certain changes which had already taken place in the life of the nations, but which had not as yet been fully realized; it gave an opportunity of testing the value of a great many rules, and revealed the existence of many problems for which international law offers no solution. It was thus possible to take stock of the rules of international law and to reach the conclusion that some of those rules are outworn, hence no longer sound, that others, while still sound theoretically, are no longer entirely suited to modern conditions, and lastly, that there are cases where the law presents loopholes which ought to be filled.

.   .   .   .

As a matter of fact, everybody does not view the question from the same angle. Some recommend that international law be readapted to the new circumstances. Others urge that it must be changed, by substituting new principles for the old. The general conviction is, however, that international law has already entered, or is about to enter, on a new phase of its evolution.

Politis, *The New Aspects of International Law* (Washington, 1928) 1, 2.

CODIFICATION

§9

Two views

In general there are two views of codification, namely (1) that it should consist of restating existing international law, and (2) that it should consist of stating what it is conceived that international law should be. At times both criteria are adopted in the formulation of a single code. Efforts toward codification have dealt especially with the subjects of the laws of war and neutrality in the field of public international law and also with subjects included within the scope of administrative law and private international law. The codification of international law was undertaken as early as the seventeenth century, but little was accomplished in that direction until near the middle of the nineteenth century.

Hague conventions, 1907

The Second Hague Peace Conference (which met from June 15 to October 18, 1907) made considerable progress in codifying international law, although much that it accomplished was the result of compromise. The work of this Conference—at which forty-four states were represented—nevertheless had a marked effect in clarifying important phases of international law. The Conference adopted thirteen conventions on the following subjects: (I) Pacific Settlement of International Disputes; (II) Recovery of Contract Debts; (III) Commencement of Hostilities; (IV) Laws and Customs of War on Land; (V) Neutral Powers and Persons in Land Warfare; (VI) Enemy Merchantships at the Outbreak of Hostilities; (VII) Conversion of Merchantships into Warships; (VIII) Automatic Submarine Contact Mines; (IX) Bombardment by Naval Forces in Time of War; (X) The Geneva Convention and Maritime Warfare; (XI) Restrictions on Capture in Maritime War; (XII) Establishment of an International Prize Court; and (XIII) Neutral Rights and Duties in Maritime War.

> *Deuxième Conférence Internationale de la Paix, La Haye 15 Juin–18 Octobre 1907* (The Hague, 1907) 689, *Acte Final;* I Scott, *Proceedings of the Hague Peace Conferences* (1920) 599–677.

Declaration of London, 1909

On February 26, 1909 the Declaration of London was signed by the powers represented at the International Naval Conference. It contains provisions (many of which represent compromises) on (I) Blockade in Time of War; (II) Contraband of War; (III) Unneutral Service; (IV) Destruction of Neutral Prizes; (V) Transfer to Neutral Flag; (VI) Enemy Character; (VII) Convoy; (VIII) Resistance to Search; and (IX) Compensation. Its ratification was advised and consented to by the Senate of the United States on April 24, 1912, but it was not ratified by any power.

> See note from Ambassador Bryce to Secretary Root, Mar. 27, 1908, 1909 For. Rel. 294, 295; report of the American delegates to Secretary Root, Mar 2, 1909, *ibid.* 304; *Correspondence and Documents Respecting the Internationa*

Naval Conference, Held in London, December 1908–February 1909, Miscellaneous, No. 4 (1909), Cd. 4554; *Proceedings of the International Naval Conference, Held in London, December 1908–February 1909*, Miscellaneous, No. 5 (1909), Cd. 4555. For a copy of the Declaration of London, see *ibid.* p. 381; 1909 For. Rel. 316, 318.

At the Sixth International Conference of American States held at Habana, Cuba, in 1928, conventions relating to (1) Rights and Duties of States in the Event of Civil Strife, (2) Status of Aliens, (3) Commercial Aviation, (4) Consular Agents, (5) Maritime Neutrality, (6) Diplomatic Officers, (7) Asylum, (8) Treaties, and (9) Private International Law, were signed. The first five of these conventions have been ratified by the United States. American Republics

Report of the Delegates of the United States of America to the Sixth International Conference of American States (1928) 228, 194, 177, 210, 216, 203, 225, 197, 96. The conventions ratified by the United States are to be found, in the order named above, in: 46 Stat. 2749, 2753; 47 Stat. 1901, 1976, 1989; 4 Treaties, etc. (Trenwith, 1938) 4725, 4722, 4729, 4738, and 4743.

In connection with the general subject of the codification of international law by the American republics, see the thirty projects of conventions for the preparation of a code on public international law, submitted by the American Institute of International Law to the Commission of Jurists at its meeting in Rio de Janeiro in 1927 (20 A.J.I.L., Spec. Supp. 1926, 300–384); and the twelve projects of public international law and project of a general convention of private international law, revised by the Commission of Jurists at its meeting in 1927 and submitted to the Sixth International Conference of American States (Report of the representatives of the United States of America on the International Commission of Jurists, June 10, 1927, MS. Department of State, file 710.C2/240; 22 A.J.I.L., Spec. Supp. 1928, 234–272, 273–327, texts of projects).

The Seventh International Conference of American States held at Montevideo, Uruguay, in 1933, concluded conventions on the following subjects, among others: Political Asylum, Extradition, and the Rights and Duties of States.

Report of the Delegates of the United States of America to the Seventh International Conference of American States (1934) 141, 151, 165. The United States has ratified (with reservations) the convention on Extradition and that on the Rights and Duties of States. 49 Stat. 3111, 3097; 4 Treaties, etc. (Trenwith, 1938) 4800, 4807.

A Commission of Jurists composed of two representatives from Great Britain, Italy, France, Japan, Netherlands, and United States, respectively, met at The Hague from December 11, 1922 to February 17, 1923, pursuant to a resolution adopted on February 4, 1922 at the Washington Conference on the Limitation of Armament. It considered the revision of the rules of warfare with reference to radio and aircraft and drew up twelve draft Rules for the Control of Radio in Time of War and sixty-two draft articles on the Rules of Aerial Warfare, which have not been adopted. Revision of the rules of warfare— 1923

3 Treaties, etc. (Redmond, 1923) 3139, 3140; *Commission of Jurists to Consider and Report Upon the Revision of the Rules of Warfare* (The Hague 1923) 230, 231, 240; General Report of the Commission of Jurists, *Algemeer Verslag der Commissie van Rechtsgeleerden, Belast Met de Studie Van-En he Uitbrengen van Bericht over de Herziening van het Oorlogsrecht* (The Hague 1923) 6, 14; MS. Department of State, files 700.00116/181, /185, /193, /215 /227; despatch from the first British delegate . . . Miscellaneous, No. 1᾽ (1924), Cmd. 2201.

The Hague, 1930

The Conference for the Codification of International Law held at The Hague from March 13 to April 12, 1930 under the auspices of the League of Nations, at which 48 states were represented, considered three subjects, namely—(a) Nationality, (b) Territorial Waters, and (c) Responsibility of States for Damage Caused in their Territory to the Person or Property of Foreigners. It succeeded in concluding a convention on Certain Questions Relating to the Conflict of Nationality Laws and also three protocols.

Convention on Certain Questions Relating to the Conflict of Nationality Laws League of Nations Publication C.24.M.13.1931.V; *Protocol Relating to Military Obligations in Certain Cases of Double Nationality, ibid.* C.25.M.14. 1931.V; *Protocol Relating to a Certain Case of Statelessness, ibid.* C.26.M.15 1931.V; *Special Protocol Concerning Statelessness, ibid.* C.27.M.16.1931.V. The convention just referred to came into force on July 1, 1937. The Protocol on Military Obligations entered into effect as to the Government of the United States and other governments parties to it on May 25, 1937. 50 Stat. 1317; 4 Treaties, etc. (Trenwith, 1938) 5261.

"Harvard Research"

The Research in International Law, organized by the Harvard Law School in 1927, has prepared drafts representing the collective views of a group of Americans especially interested in international law, on the following subjects: (1) Nationality, (2) Responsibility of States for Damage Done in Their Territory to the Person or Property of Foreigners, (3) Territorial Waters, (4) Diplomatic Privileges and Immunities, (5) Legal Position and Functions of Consuls, (6) Competence of Courts in Regard to Foreign States, (7) Piracy, (8) Law of Extradition, (9) Jurisdiction With Respect to Crime, (10) Law of Treaties, and (11) Rights and Duties of Neutral States in Naval and Aerial War.

23 A.J.I.L., Spec. Supp. (Apr. 1929); Research in International Law (Harvard Law School, 1932) 10, 15 *et seq.;* 29 A.J.I.L. Supp. (1935); 33 *idem* (1939) 167.

Institut de Droit International; International Law Association

In addition, the Institut de Droit International, organized at Ghent in 1873, and the International Law Association, known from 1873 to 1895 as the Association for the Reform and Codification of the Law of Nations, have formulated and adopted drafts on numerous subjects.

The texts of the drafts of the Institut de Droit International are contained in the *Annuaire de l'Institut de Droit International* for the respective years. The texts of the drafts of the International Law Association are similarly contained in the reports of the respective conferences of the International Law Association.

CHAPTER II

STATES, TERRITORIES, AND GOVERNMENTS

STATES

GENERAL NATURE

§10

The terms *state* and *nation* are frequently used interchangeably. The term *nation*, strictly speaking, as evidenced by its etymology (*nasci*, to be born), indicates relation of birth or origin and implies a common race, usually characterized by community of language and customs. The term *state*—a more specific term—connotes, in the international sense, a people permanently occupying a fixed territory, bound together by common laws and customs into a body politic, possessing an organized government, and capable of conducting relations with other states. The term thus refers to an organization or institution—a relation between people. States, generally speaking, may be broadly classified as sovereign or independent states and as dependent or semi-sovereign states.

Charles Cheney Hyde has expressed the following views:

A State or person of international law must, according to enlightened practice, possess the following qualifications:

First, there must be a people. According to Rivier, it must be sufficient in numbers to maintain and perpetuate itself. This requirement could not, he declares, be met by a casual gathering of individuals or by a chance group of bandits or by a society of pirates.

Secondly, there must be a fixed territory which the inhabitants occupy. Nomadic tribes or peoples are thus excluded from consideration.

Thirdly, there must be an organized government expressive of the sovereign will within the territory, and exercising in fact supremacy therein.

Fourthly, there must be an assertion of right through governmental agencies to enter into relations with the outside world. The exercise of this right need not be free from external restraint. Independence is not essential. It is the possession and use of the right to enter into foreign relations, whether with or without restriction, which distinguishes States of international law from the larger number of political entities given that name and which are wholly lacking in such a privilege. ⁚ illustrates the difference between Ecuador and Alaska, and between Cuba and South Carolina.

Fifthly, the inhabitants of the territory must have attained a degree of civilization such as to enable them to observe with respect to the outside world those principles of law which by common assent govern the members of the international society in their relations with each other.

I Hyde, *International Law*, etc. (1922) 16–17.

Section 3 of the act of Congress approved June 5, 1794 prohibited the fitting out or arming of vessels with intent to "be employed in the service of any foreign prince or state to cruise or commit hostilities upon the subjects, citizens or property of another foreign prince or state with whom the United States are at peace". In interpreting the meaning of the phrase "foreign prince or state", the District Court of the United States for the Northern District of Florida on May 16, 1916 said:

. . . By reference to standard dictionaries, as well as authorities on international law, it will be found very well settled that a "state or nation" denotes a political community organized under a distinct government recognized and conformed to by its citizens and subjects as the supreme power. A "prince," in the general acceptation of the term according to authorities when applied in the law of nations, signifies a sovereign, a king, emperor, or ruler; one to whom power is delegated or vested. Necessarily, when the statute of 1794 described the contending factions, parties, or belligerents as "any foreign prince or state . . . against . . . another foreign prince or state," it described a sovereign or a political community entitled to admission into the family of nations; and, as such, political recognition was essential to the operation of the statute as it read.

1 Stat. 381, 383; *The Lucy H.*, 235 Fed. 610, 614 (N. D. Fla., 1916). For a definition of the term *foreign country*, see *Burnet* v. *Chicago Portrait Co.*, 285 U. S. (1932) 1.

The state as a person of international law should possess the following qualifications: *a*) a permanent population; *b*) a defined territory; *c*) government; and *d*) capacity to enter into relations with other states.

The federal state shall constitute a sole person in the eyes of international law.

Arts. 1 and 2, convention on rights and duties of states, signed at Montevideo on Dec. 26, 1933, 49 Stat. 3097, 3100; 4 Treaties, etc. (Trenwith, 1938) 4807, 4808.

The report made to the First Assembly of the League of Nations by the Fifth Committee (on Admission to the League), December 6, **Liechtenstein** 1920, said with reference to the Principality of Liechtenstein:

The Government of the Principality of Liechtenstein has been recognised *de jure* by many States. She has concluded a number of Treaties with various States.

The Principality of Liechtenstein possesses a stable Government and fixed frontiers.

. . . .

There can be no doubt that juridically the Principality of Liechtenstein is a sovereign State, but by reason of her limited area, small population, and her geographical position, she has chosen to depute to others some of the attributes of sovereignty. For instance, she has contracted with other Powers for the control of her Customs, the administration of her Posts, Telegraphs and Telephone Services, for the diplomatic representation of her subjects in foreign countries, other than Switzerland and Austria, and for final decisions in certain judicial cases.

Liechtenstein has no army.

For the above reasons, we are of opinion that the Principality of Liechtenstein could not discharge all the international obligations which would be imposed on her by the Covenant.

Liechtenstein was denied admission to the League by vote of the Assembly on December 17, 1920.

League of Nations, *Records of the First Assembly: Plenary Meetings* (1920) 667, 652.

The Principality of Liechtenstein uses Swiss currency and is included in the Swiss customs union. With reference to the latter, see Swiss Minister in London (Paravicini) to the British Foreign Office, Mar. 28, 1924; the British Secretary of State for Foreign Affairs (MacDonald) to Minister Paravicini, Apr. 26, 1924, Gr. Br. Treaty Ser. no. 20 (1924), Cmd. 2152.

Replying to an inquiry as to the status of the Principality of Liechtenstein, the Department of State, on Oct. 16, 1925, said that "While the Principality of Lichtenstein is recognized as an independent State, this Government has no diplomatic representative to the Government of that Principality." The Under Secretary of State (Grew) to Henry W. Carlisle, Oct. 16, 1925, MS. Department of State, file 800.01/36.

On May 6, 1931 the Department of State made the following reply to another inquiry with reference to the status of the Principality of Liechtenstein:

"This Government has regarded Lichtenstein as being an independent Principality and so regarded it when under date of March 24, 1910, the President issued a Proclamation making the minimum tariff rates prescribed in Section 1 of the Tariff Act approved August 5, 1909, applicable to the Principality of Lichtenstein. This Proclamation is published in the United States Statutes at Large, Volume 36, Part 2, pages 2637 and 2638.

"For your information it may be added that this Government has assigned a separate immigration quota to the Principality of Lichtenstein."

The Assistant Secretary of State (Rogers) to Messrs. Otterbourg, Steindler & Houston, May 6, 1931, MS. Department of State, file 860B.01/7.

Lord Curzon, the delegate of the British Empire, speaking at the first meeting of the Council of the League of Nations on January 16, 1920, said:

It has sometimes been said that the League of Nations implies the establishment of a Super-State, or a Super-Sovereignty. League of
The very title "League of Nations" should be sufficient to dispel Nations

this misconception. The League does not interfere with nationality. It is upon the fact of nationhood that it rests . . .
The League is an association of sovereign States.

League of Nations, *Official Journal* (1920) 21.

. . . Whatever the League of Nations may be it is not a State. It has none of the attributes of a sovereign power. It does not govern and it makes no laws. The council of the League of Nations is not the parliament or executive power of the League of Nations. By the Treaty of Versailles, the council merely acts as an intermediary between the associated powers and any particular power as for instance a mandatory power. As it exercises no sovereign power it has no *majestas* and therefore the *crimen laesae majestatis* cannot be committed against the League of Nations or its Council. It is unnecessary to determine the exact docket in Constitutional or International law in which the League of Nations must be placed, it is sufficient to say that as a political institution it is *sui generis;* but whatever it may be it certainly is not a State and according to our law the *crimen laesae majestatis* can only be committed against a State.

Rex v. *Christian*, South African Law Reports, [1924] Appellate Division, 101, 136.

In its instruction of June 17, 1929 to the chairman of the American Delegation to the Conference for the Revision of the Geneva Convention of 1906 and for Framing a Code for Prisoners of War, the Department of State said:

International Red Cross; Sovereign Order of Malta

This Government has no objection to the presence of representatives of the International Red Cross and the Sovereign Order of Malta at the meetings held for a revision of the Geneva Convention of July 6, 1906 and for the formulation of a code for prisoners of war.

This Government, however, is strongly opposed to granting the International Red Cross or the Sovereign Order of Malta plenipotentiary status at the Conference in question, and since these organizations are not sovereign states it would oppose any proposal destined to allow either of them to vote in the Conference or to sign any instrument emanating from the Conference. Moreover it feels that since these organizations are not sovereign states they should not be given any function in the administration of the code after its adoption by the powers. In its note of February 18, 1929, this Government so informed the Swiss Government.

The Acting Secretary of State (Clark) to Eliot Wadsworth, June 17, 1929, MS. Department of State, file 514.2a12/71a.

SOVEREIGNTY

§11

The Supreme Court of Montana, in holding invalid an act of the State legislature providing for compensation to former soldiers and sailors in the World War, said:

> The sovereign power of the United States in the family of nations is vested exclusively in the United States government. Sovereignty in its full sense imports the supreme, absolute, and uncontrollable power by which any independent state is governed; and, although the states of the Union were called sovereign and independent states under the Declaration of Independence, they were never in their individual capacity strictly so, because they were always, in respect to some of the higher powers of sovereignty, subject to the control of a common authority, and were never separately recognized or known as members of the family of nations.

State ex rel. Mills v. *Dixon*, 66 Mont. (1923) 76, 86, 213 Pac. 227, 230.

In the case of *Duff Development Company, Limited* v. *Government of Kelantan and Another* in which the House of Lords affirmed an order staying proceedings against the Government of Kelantan on the ground that the Sultan of Kelantan was an independent sovereign ruler and the state was an independent sovereign state over which the court had no jurisdiction, Viscount Finlay made the following remarks regarding the relation between sovereignty and independence:

Sovereignty and independence

> The question put was as to the status of the ruler of Kelantan. It is obvious that for sovereignty there must be a certain amount of independence, but it is not in the least necessary that for sovereignty there should be complete independence. It is quite consistent with sovereignty that the sovereign may in certain respects be dependent upon another Power; the control, for instance, of foreign affairs may be completely in the hands of a protecting Power, and there may be agreements or treaties which limit the powers of the sovereign even in internal affairs without entailing a loss of the position of a sovereign Power.

[1924] A. C. 797, 814. See also the concurring opinions of Viscount Cave, Lord Dunedin, and Lord Carson, *ibid.* 808–809, 820, 830.

In his award in the *Island of Palmas* case, April 4, 1928, Max Huber, the arbitrator, made the following general observations with respect to sovereignty:

> Sovereignty in the relation between States signifies independence. Independence in regard to a portion of the globe is the right to exercise therein, to the exclusion of any other State, the functions of a State. The development of the national organisation of States during the last few centuries and, as a corollary,

Territorial
sovereignty

the development of international law, have established this principle of the exclusive competence of the State in regard to its own territory in such a way as to make it the point of departure in settling most questions that concern international relations. The special cases of the composite State, of collective sovereignty, etc. do not fall to be considered here and do not, for that matter, throw any doubt upon the principle which has just been enunciated. Under this reservation it may be stated that territorial sovereignty belongs always to one, or in exceptional circumstances to several States, to the exclusion of all others. The fact that the functions of a State can be performed by any State within a given zone is, on the other hand, precisely the characteristic feature of the legal situation pertaining in those parts of the globe which, like the high seas or lands without a master, cannot or do not yet form the territory of a State.

.   .   .   .

Territorial sovereignty, as has already been said, involves the exclusive right to display the activities of a State. This right has as corollary a duty: the obligation to protect within the territory the rights of other States, in particular their right to integrity and inviolability in peace and in war, together with the rights which each State may claim for its nationals in foreign territory. Without manifesting its territorial sovereignty in a manner corresponding to circumstances, the State cannot fulfill this duty. Territorial sovereignty cannot limit itself to its negative side, i. e. to excluding the activities of other States; for it serves to divide between nations the space upon which human activities are employed, in order to assure them at all points the minimum of protection of which international law is the guardian.

Per. Ct. Arb., official report (The Hague, 1928) 16–17; Scott, *Hague Court Reports* (2d ser. 1932) 83, 92, 93.

In its judgment rendered on August 17, 1923 in the case of the *S.S. Wimbledon,* involving the refusal of the German authorities to permit the above-mentioned British steamship (chartered to a French company) laden with munitions, to pass through the Kiel Canal, the Permanent Court of International Justice said with respect to the relation of state sovereignty to international engagements:

Sovereignty
and inter-
national
agreements

The argument has also been advanced that the general grant of a right of passage to vessels of all nationalities through the Kiel Canal cannot deprive Germany of the exercise of her rights as a neutral power in time of war, and place her under an obligation to allow the passage through the canal of contraband destined for one of the belligerents; for, in this wide sense, this grant would imply the abandonment by Germany of a personal and imprescriptible right, which forms an essential part of her sovereignty and which she neither could nor intended to renounce by anticipation. This contention has not convinced the Court; it conflicts with general considerations of the highest order. It is also gainsaid by consistent international practice and is at the same time contrary to the wording of Article 380 which clearly contemplates time of war as well as time of peace. The Court declines to see in the conclusion of any Treaty by which a State undertakes to perform or refrain from performing a particular act an abandonment of its sovereignty. No doubt any convention creating an obligation of this kind places a restriction upon the exercise of the sovereign rights of the State, in the sense that it requires them to be exercised in a certain way. But the right of entering into international engagements is an attribute of State sovereignty.

Per. Ct. Int. Jus., Ser. A, No. 1, p. 25; I Hudson, *World Court Reports* (1934) 168, 175.

In the course of the opinion in the case of *United States* v. *Curtiss-Wright Export Corp. et al.*, upholding the constitutionality of the joint resolution of Congress approved on May 28, 1934 to prohibit the sale of arms or munitions of war in the United States under certain conditions, the Supreme Court speaking through Mr. Justice Sutherland said:

As a result of the separation from Great Britain by the colonies acting as a unit, the powers of external sovereignty passed from the Crown not to the colonies severally, but to the colonies in their collective and corporate capacity as the United States of America. Even before the Declaration, the colonies were a unit in foreign affairs, acting through a common agency—namely the Continental Congress, composed of delegates from the thirteen colonies. That agency exercised the powers of war and peace, raised an army, created a navy, and finally adopted the Declaration of Independence. Rulers come and go; governments end and forms of government change; but sovereignty survives. A political society cannot endure without a supreme will somewhere. Sovereignty is never held in suspense. When, therefore, the external sovereignty of Great Britain in respect of the colonies ceased, it immediately passed to the Union. *See Penhallow* v. *Doane*, 3 Dall. 54, 80–81.

Sovereignty never held in suspense

.   .   .   .

It results that the investment of the federal government with the powers of external sovereignty did not depend upon the affirmative grants of the Constitution. The powers to declare and wage war, to conclude peace, to make treaties, to maintain diplomatic relations with other sovereignties, if they had never been mentioned in the Constitution, would have vested in the federal government as necessary concomitants of nationality. Neither the Constitution nor the laws passed in pursuance of it have any force in foreign territory unless in respect of our own citizens (see *American Banana Co.* v. *United Fruit Co.*, 213 U. S. 347, 356); and operations of the nation in such territory must be governed by treaties, international understandings and compacts, and the principles of international law. As a member of the family of nations, the right and power of the United States in that field are equal to the right and power of the other members of the international family. Otherwise, the United States is not

Not dependent upon constitutional grant

completely sovereign. The power to acquire territory by discovery and occupation (*Jones* v. *United States*, 137 U.S. 202, 212), the power to expel undesirable aliens (*Fong Yue Ting* v. *United States*, 149 U.S. 698, 705 *et seq.*), the power to make such international agreements as do not constitute treaties in the constitutional sense (*Altman & Co.* v. *United States*, 224 U.S. 583, 600, 601; Crandall, Treaties, Their Making and Enforcement, 2d ed., p. 102 and note 1), none of which is expressly affirmed by the Constitution, nevertheless exist as inherently inseparable from the conception of nationality. This the court recognized, and in each of the cases cited found the warrant for its conclusions not in the provisions of the Constitution, but in the law of nations.

48 Stat. 811; 299 U.S. (1936) 304, 316–318.

Original theory of sovereignty

. . . In the original theory it was not the state that was the sovereign, but a person or persons *within* a state that were 'sovereign' over the rest. . . .

Unfortunately for the clearness of our thinking on political matters the hold of sovereignty on the imagination was so strong that instead of formulating a new theory political science merely tried to adapt the old theory to new conditions. Sovereignty, it was felt, must be somewhere or a state would not be a state, for philosophers and lawyers had come to speak of sovereignty almost as if it were a substance, instead of being merely an abstract idea invented by their predecessors to explain the political facts of their time; and as it was no longer possible to maintain that there was always a person or persons exercising unlimited authority over all the others, men began to attribute the sovereignty to the people as a whole. . . . Still another device for retaining the doctrine of sovereignty while adapting it to modern conditions has been to attribute sovereignty to the personified state itself; and this is the usage still current in the literature of international law. But this has only added to the confusion. We may properly speak of states as 'independent' in the sense to be explained later; but it is meaningless to say that they are 'sovereign', that is to say, superior, when we are speaking of their relations to one another . . .

The theory of sovereignty . . . is not only inconsistent with the subjection of states to any kind of law, but it is in fact an impossible theory for a world which contains more states than one.

Brierly, *The Law of Nations* (2d ed. 1936) 36, 38–39.

An act of Congress approved on February 17, 1898 (30 Stat. 248), amending section 4347 of the Revised Statutes, provided that—

no merchandise shall be transported by water under penalty of forfeiture thereof from one port of the United States to another port of the United States, either directly or via a foreign port, or for any part of the voyage, in any other vessel than a vessel of the United States.

In reply to a question raised by the Secretary of the Navy as to whether coal for the use of the Navy might be transported by sea from ports on the Atlantic coast to ports on the Pacific coast of the United States in vessels of foreign registry, the Attorney General of the United States advised the Secretary of the Navy that this section did "not apply to property owned by the Government". In expressing the opinion that a prohibition in a statute of general application does not extend to or affect the sovereign, unless its language requires that such a meaning shall be given to it, the Attorney General stated:

> . . . It is a well-settled principle of statutory construction that a prohibition of this character does not extend to, or affect, the sovereign, unless its language requires that such a meaning shall be given to it. This rule is thus stated in Bacon's Abridgment, title "Prerogative," 3–5: "Where a statute is general, and thereby any prerogative, right, title, or interest is vested or taken from the King, in such case he shall not be bound unless the statute is made by express words to extend to him." This rule has been fully adopted with respect to the United States. (*U.S.* v. *Knight,* 14 Peters, 301; *U.S.* v. *Herron,* 20 Wallace, 251, 255.) In the last-mentioned case the Supreme Court says it is "the settled rule of construction that the sovereign authority of the country is not bound by the words of a statute, unless named therein." If, therefore, there had been nothing in the language of this statute to indicate whether it was or was not intended to apply to merchandise owned by the United States, the rule of construction to which I have referred would require that it be held not to have such application.

Prohibitions against local sovereign strictly construed

26 Op. Att. Gen. (1908) 415, 417.

However, in an opinion of Jan. 2, 1908, the Attorney General informed the Secretary of the Treasury that coal imported for the use of the Navy was subject to the duties prescribed by paragraph 415 of the act of Congress approved on July 24, 1897 (30 Stat. 151, 190), although the section did not specifically mention the payment of duties by the United States. In this instance, the act specifically prescribed in two other sections that the United States was exempt from the payment of duties on articles mentioned in those sections. Attorney General Bonaparte stated in the latter opinion:

> ". . . The maxim *expressio unius est exclusio alterius* applies here with full force, as in the case of *Arredondo* v. *United States* (6 Peters, 691, 725)." *Ibid.* 466, 469.

Under the terms of article II of a contract between the Panama Railroad Company and the Republic of Colombia, entered into prior to the conclusion, on November 18, 1903, by the United States and Panama, of the convention for the construction of a ship canal, 2 Treaties, etc. (Malloy, 1910) 1349, the Republic of Colombia bound itself not to establish any other railroad on the Isthmus of Panama. After the convention of 1903 became effective, the United States licensed the United Oil Company to lay a pipe line across the

Isthmus, and this action was alleged by the Panama Railroad Company to constitute a breach of the concession contract on the part of the United States. In informing the Secretary of War, on July 24, 1908, that this did not constitute a breach of the contract, Attorney General Bonaparte stated:

Agreements in derogation of sovereignty strictly construed

. . . I do not think this action of the Government can be considered, either in letter or in spirit, a violation of the stipulation not to establish another railroad. Whether the construction of a pipe line will, in any wise, affect the business of the railroad is matter of conjecture; but, in any event, the agreement of the Colombian Government not to establish another railroad, being in derogation of its rights of sovereignty, is to be strictly construed and can not, in my opinion, be reasonably extended to a prohibition against permitting the establishment of a pipe line.

27 Op. Att. Gen. (1909) 19, 25–26.

Article 1 of the convention for the regulation of aerial navigation, signed at Paris on October 13, 1919, provides as follows:

Sovereignty over the air-space

The High Contracting Parties recognise that every Power has complete and exclusive sovereignty over the air space above its territory.

For the purpose of the present Convention the territory of a State shall be understood as including the national territory, both that of the Mother Country and of the colonies, and the territorial waters adjacent thereto.

3 Treaties, etc. (Redmond, 1923) 3768, 3772–3773. This treaty was signed but not ratified by the United States.

The convention on commercial aviation signed by the United States and other American republics at Habana on February 20, 1928 provides in article I:

The high contracting parties recognize that every state has complete and exclusive sovereignty over the air space above its territory and territorial waters.

47 Stat. 1901, 1902; 4 Treaties, etc. (Trenwith, 1938) 4729, 4730.

Section 6 of the Air Commerce Act of the United States of May 20, 1926 provides in paragraph (a):

"The Congress hereby declares that the Government of the United States has, to the exclusion of all foreign nations, complete sovereignty of the air-space over the lands and waters of the United States, including the Canal Zone. Aircraft a part of the armed forces of any foreign nation shall not be navigated in the United States, including the Canal Zone, except in accordance with an authorization granted by the Secretary of State." 44 Stat. 568, 572.

Condominium

The conjoint exercise of sovereignty over a region by two or more states is denominated "condominium". The joint action of Great

Britain and Egypt in the Sudan and that of Great Britain and France in the New Hebrides have been referred to by writers as examples of condominium.

On January 19, 1899 an agreement was signed by Great Britain and Egypt relating to the joint administration of the Sudan. The first The Sudan three articles of this agreement read as follows:

ART. I. The word "Soudan" in this Agreement means all the territories south of the 22nd parallel of latitude, which—

1. Have never been evacuated by Egyptian troops since the year 1882; or

2. Which, having before the late rebellion in the Soudan been administered by the Government of His Highness the Khedive were temporarily lost to Egypt, and have been reconquered by Her Britannic Majesty's Government and the Egyptian Government, acting in concert; or

3. Which may hereafter be reconquered by the two Governments acting in concert.

II. The British and Egyptian flags shall be used together, both on land and water, throughout the Soudan, except in the town of Suakin, in which locality the Egyptian flag alone shall be used.

III. The supreme military and civil command in the Soudan shall be vested in one officer, termed the "Governor-General of the Soudan." He shall be appointed by Khedivial Decree on the recommendation of Her Britannic Majesty's Government, and shall be removed only by Khedivial Decree, with the consent of Her Britannic Majesty's Government.

91 Br. & For. St. Paps. (1898–99) 19.

Section 1 of article 11 of the treaty of alliance between Great Britain and Egypt, signed on August 26, 1936, contains the following provision in respect to the Sudan:

1. While reserving liberty to conclude new conventions in future, modifying the agreements of the 19th January and the 10th July, 1899, the High Contracting Parties agree that the administration of the Sudan shall continue to be that resulting from the said agreements. The Governor-General shall continue to exercise on the joint behalf of the High Contracting Parties the powers conferred upon him by the said agreements.

The High Contracting Parties agree that the primary aim of their administration in the Sudan must be the welfare of the Sudanese.

Nothing in this article prejudices the question of sovereignty over the Sudan. [Italics added.]

Gr. Br. Treaty Ser. no. 6 (1937), Cmd. 5360. For the agreement of July 10, 1899, see 91 Br. & For. St. Paps. (1898–99) 21.

New
Hebrides

On August 6, 1914 Great Britain and France concluded a protocol respecting the New Hebrides which provided in article 1:

> 1. The Group of the New Hebrides, including the Banks and Torres Islands, shall form a region of joint influence, in which the subjects and citizens of the two Signatory Powers shall enjoy equal rights of residence, personal protection, and trade, each of the two Powers retaining sovereignty over its nationals and over corporations legally constituted according to its law for the purpose of carrying on agricultural, industrial, commercial or other enterprises, and neither exercising a separate authority over the Group.

The rights and obligations of French and British nationals were extended to the subjects or citizens of other powers. Provision was made for the joint administration of the islands by the two Governments under two high commissioners, one appointed by each Government.

Gr. Br. Treaty Ser. no. 7 (1922), Cmd. 1681.

CLASSIFICATION

GENERAL DISCUSSION

§12

States may be said to fall into two general classifications, i.e. independent and dependent states. They may be more specifically classified as simple, composite, neutralized, vassal or semi-sovereign, and protected states. Variations in types of these classes are numerous. International law is not especially concerned with names or classifications of states or with their internal organization, so long as they are able and willing to perform their international obligations. The nature of the legal bonds existing between political units of a state, a member of the family of nations, is regulated by domestic law. The extent to which the sovereignty of a state is centralized, decentralized, or divided, under a particular union, federation, protectorate, etc., may, however, have an important bearing upon the external relations of the state with which international law is concerned.

SIMPLE STATES

§13

Simple states are those that possess a single central political authority representing the state. France, Italy, Netherlands, and Japan are examples of simple states.

Personal
union

In a personal union of states two sovereign states have the same ruler, each state retaining its separate and distinct identity. The relation that existed between Belgium and the Independent State of the Congo from 1885 to 1908, when the Congo Free State was ceded to and annexed by Belgium, has frequently been referred to as an example of a personal union of states.

> See the treaty of cession and annexation between Belgium and the Independent Congo State, signed Nov. 28, 1907, published in 3 A.J.I.L. Supp. (1909) 73; 100 Br. & For. St. Paps. (1906–7) 705, 706; 101 Br. & For. St. Paps. (1907–8) 728. Official correspondence and documents relating to the cession and annexation of the Congo Free State by Belgium are published in 1907 For. Rel., pt. II, pp. 791–829; 101 Br. & For. St. Paps. (1907–8) 731 *et seq.*

On December 10, 1918 the Danish Minister addressed a note to the Secretary of State in which he said:

> The Danish Government has, in accordance with a federal act of November 30th 1918 passed by the parliaments of Denmark and Iceland, recognized Iceland as a sovereign State. Denmark and Iceland are united under the same sceptre and His Majesty the King has in His title adopted the names of the two States. Denmark takes care of the foreign affairs on behalf of Iceland, and Iceland declares itself perpetually neutral.

> Minister Brun to Secretary Lansing, Dec. 10, 1918, MS. Department of State, file 859a.01/4. For the text of the Danish law of Nov. 30, 1918, which came into effect on Dec. 1, 1918, providing for the union of Denmark and Iceland, see 111 Br. & For. St. Paps. (1917–18) 703.

On January 5, 1935 the Department of State wrote:

> Iceland is considered to be a completely sovereign state which bears a personal union with Denmark through a common king. Laws passed by the legislative body of Iceland must have the approval of the King in Copenhagen. At the close of each session of the Icelandic Parliament an emissary presents himself in Copenhagen bearing these laws for the King's signature. In proclaiming Icelandic laws the King states "We Christian X, King of Iceland and Denmark". It will be noticed that the order of countries is reversed in his title, depending upon the country to which the proclamation has reference.

> The Department of State to Richard J. Robertson, Jan. 5, 1935, MS. Department of State, file 859A.01/34.
> The relation between Denmark and Iceland is regarded by certain writers as a real union rather than a personal union. See I Oppenheim's *International Law* (5th ed., by Lauterpacht, 1937) 158, n. 2.

COMPOSITE STATES

§14

Composite states are those composed of two or more states. They are in turn classified as real unions, confederated states, and federal states.

Real
union

A real union exists when two sovereign states are bound together by international agreement so that they form a single international person. The union of Sweden and Norway (generally regarded as a real union), which came into existence in 1814, was dissolved in 1905. That between Austria and Hungary (which originally came into existence in 1723) ceased in 1918.

> 1905 For. Rel. 853 *et seq.*; 98 Br. & For. St. Paps. (1904–5) 794–837
> For a brief history of the dissolution of the Austro-Hungarian Dual Monarchy, and particularly the events of October and November 1918, see Malbone W. Graham, *New Governments of Central Europe* (1924) 123–137.

Confederated
states

A confederated state—or band of states—comprises an organization of states in which each retains its internal and, to a greater or lesser extent, its external sovereignty. There is at the present time no organization of states among the principal states of the world commonly denominated a confederated state.

A federal state consists of a union of states wherein the sovereignty for external purposes is exercised by a central government, although, the fundamental law permitting, the component members may, consistently with such a union, exercise certain limited external powers.

Federal
states

Examples of federal states are: United States of America, Brazil, Argentina, Switzerland, Mexico, and Venezuela.

> In 1918 a constitution was adopted by the Russian Socialist Federal Soviet Republic (R.S.F.S.R.) Batsell, *Soviet Rule in Russia* (1929) 80. On July 6, 1923 the Constitution of the Union of Soviet Socialist Republics (U.S.S.R.) was confirmed by the second session of the Central Executive Committee of the Union of Soviet Socialist Republics, which resolved that the Constitution should be put into force at once and that it should be submitted for definitive confirmation to the Second Congress of Soviets of the Union of Soviet Socialist Republics. On Jan. 31, 1924 the Constitution was definitively confirmed by the Second Congress. For an English translation of this Constitution, see *ibid.* 304; *Soviet Union Year-Book* (1930) 1. For an English translation of the Constitution of the Union of Soviet Socialist Republics adopted at Moscow on Dec. 5, 1936, by the Eighth All-Union Congress of Soviets, see *International Conciliation, No. 327* (Feb. 1937) 143.
>
> An Austrian Federal Constitution was adopted by the Austrian Constituent Assembly on Oct. 1, 1920. Dareste, *Les constitutions modernes*: Europe, vol. 1 (1928), pp. 289, 290; for an English translation of this Constitution, see 113 Br. & For. St. Paps. (1920) 883. For recent developments with respect to Austria, see *post* §66.
>
> The Republics of Costa Rica, Guatemala, Honduras, and El Salvador signed a pact of union on Jan. 19, 1921 establishing the "Federation of Central America". This pact was subsequently ratified by the Governments of Honduras, Guatemala, and El Salvador. It failed of ratification in Costa Rica. Pursuant to its provisions, a Central American Provisional Federal Council was installed in Tegucigalpa, Honduras, on June 13, 1921, and on July 20, 1921 the National Constituent Assembly of the Federation of Central America was officially inaugurated in that city. A Political Constitution

for "the new Republic" was signed on Sept. 9, 1921. The Costa Rican Minister in the United States (Beeche) to Secretary Colby, Feb. 1, 1921, MS. Department of State, file 813.00/1050; the Honduran Minister of Foreign Affairs (Uclés) to Secretary Hughes, June 16, 1921, *ibid.* 813.00/1088; the Chargé in Honduras (Spencer) to Secretary Hughes, no. 169, July 21, 1921, *ibid.* 813.00/1095. See also 1921 For. Rel., vol. I, pp. 145–157.

The Federation of Central America was short-lived. Early in the year 1922 decrees were issued in Guatemala, Honduras, and El Salvador reassuming independent sovereignty in their respective countries. MS. Department of State, files 813.00/1177, 813.00/1191, 815.01/-.

It is not always possible to state categorically that a state belongs solely in any one of the classifications discussed above. A state may in certain respects fall within one classification and in other respects within another. It may, in fact, belong in a class peculiar to itself. Such, for example, is the British Empire. Oppenheim states: **Other types**

> The attempt to state the present position of the self-governing Dominions is beset by several difficulties. It is not easy to distinguish between the political and the legal situation, nor between their constitutional and their international position. . . . Again, those relations are in a state of continual transition and do not always make uniform and parallel progress as between the mother country and all of the Dominions, so that what is true to-day of relations with one Dominion may not be true to-morrow of relations with the same Dominion, or to-day of relations with any other Dominion. **British Empire**
>
> .   .   .   .
>
> . . . It [the British Empire] is apparently *sui generis* and defies classification. It is not a Federal State because there is no organ which has power both over the member-States and their citizens. It is not a Confederation because there is no treaty which unites the member-States and no organ which in fact has power over them. It is not a Real Union because there is no treaty which unites the member-States and because each of the Dominions can enter into separate treaties, and 'full powers' to sign them are issued upon the advice of the Dominion Cabinet. It is not a Personal Union . . . because it is the essence of that relationship that two or more distinct Crowns should be accidentally (and often temporarily) united in the same holder and may even (as in the case of Great Britain and Hanover) be governed by different laws of descent, whereas "the Crown in the British Empire is one and undivided."

I Oppenheim's *International Law* (5th ed., by Lauterpacht, 1937) 175, 182–183.

Representatives of the Dominion of Canada, the Commonwealth of Australia, the Union of South Africa, the Dominion of New Zealand, and India signed the Treaty of Versailles (June 28, 1919), together with the representatives of "His Majesty the King of the United Kingdom of Great Britain and Ireland and of the British **Signatories of the Treaty of Versailles**

Dominions beyond the seas, Emperor of India". As signatories of that treaty, Canada, Australia, South Africa, New Zealand, and India were named as original members of the League of Nations in the annex to the Covenant of the League (pt. I of the Treaty of Versailles).

3 Treaties, etc. (Redmond, 1923) 3329, 3336, 3345, 3521.

Imperial Conference of 1926

The Report of the Inter-Imperial Relations Committee of the Imperial Conference of 1926, which was attended by representatives of Great Britain, Canada, Australia, New Zealand, Union of South Africa, Irish Free State, Newfoundland, and India, defined the position of the "self-governing communities composed of Great Britain and the Dominions" as follows:

> . . . *They are autonomous Communities within the British Empire, equal in status, in no way subordinate one to another in any aspect of their domestic or external affairs, though united by a common allegiance to the Crown, and freely associated as members of the British Commonwealth of Nations.*

> . . . Every self-governing member of the Empire is now the master of its destiny. In fact, if not always in form, it is subject to no compulsion whatever.

Equality of status, so far as Britain and the Dominions are concerned, is thus the root principle governing our Inter-Imperial Relations. But the principles of equality and similarity, appropriate to *status*, do not universally extend to function.

III.—SPECIAL POSITION OF INDIA

It will be noted that in the previous paragraphs we have made no mention of India. Our reason for limiting their scope to Great Britain and the Dominions is that the position of India in the Empire is already defined by the Government of India Act, 1919. We would, nevertheless, recall that by Resolution IX of the Imperial War Conference, 1917, due recognition was given to the important position held by India in the British Commonwealth. Where, in this Report, we have had occasion to consider the position of India, we have made particular reference to it.

Imperial Conference, 1926: Summary of Proceedings, Parliamentary Papers (1926), Cmd. 2768, pp. 14, 15.

The report of the conference pointed out that the existing title of His Majesty the King, proclaimed under the Royal Titles Act of 1901, namely, "George V, by the Grace of God, of the United Kingdom of Great Britain and Ireland and of the British Dominions beyond the Seas, King, Defender of the Faith, Emperor of India", "hardly accorded with the altered state of affairs arising from the establishment of the Irish Free State as a Dominion". The report recommended that "subject to His Majesty's approval, the necessary legislative action should be taken to secure that His Majesty's title should henceforth read:

" 'George V, by the Grace of God, of Great Britain, Ireland, and the British Dominions beyond the Seas, King, Defender of the Faith, Emperor of India.' " Parliamentary Papers (1926), Cmd. 2768, pp. 15, 16.

An act of Parliament of Apr. 12, 1927 provided for royal proclamation "to make such alteration in the style and titles at present appertaining to the Crown as to His Majesty may seem fit". 17 Geo. V, c. 4.

The title recommended by the Imperial Conference of 1926 was in fact proclaimed by the King on May 13, 1927. *London Gazette*, no. 33274, May 13, 1927, p. 3111.

As to the later status of India, see the Government of India Act, 1935, 25 and 26 Geo. V, c. 42.

The Statute of Westminster (Dec. 11, 1931) reads in part as follows:

1. In this Act the expression "Dominion" means any of the following Dominions, that is to say, the Dominion of Canada, the Commonwealth of Australia, the Dominion of New Zealand, the Union of South Africa, the Irish Free State and Newfoundland. **Statute of Westminster, 1931**

2.—(1) The Colonial Laws Validity Act, 1865, shall not apply to any law made after the commencement of this Act by the Parliament of a Dominion.

(2) No law and no provision of any law made after the commencement of this Act by the Parliament of a Dominion shall be void or inoperative on the ground that it is repugnant to the law of England, or to the provisions of any existing or future Act of Parliament of the United Kingdom, or to any order, rule or regulation made under any such Act, and the powers of the Parliament of a Dominion shall include the power to repeal or amend any such Act, order, rule or regulation in so far as the same is part of the law of the Dominion.

3. It is hereby declared and enacted that the Parliament of a Dominion has full power to make laws having extra-territorial operation.

4. No Act of Parliament of the United Kingdom passed after the commencement of this Act shall extend, or be deemed to extend, to a Dominion as part of the law of that Dominion, unless it is expressly declared in that Act that that Dominion has requested, and consented to, the enactment thereof.

.   .   .   .

10.—(1) None of the following sections of this Act, that is to say, sections two, three, four, five and six, shall extend to a Dominion to which this section applies as part of the law of that Dominion unless that section is adopted by the Parliament of the Dominion, and any Act of that Parliament adopting any section of this Act may provide that the adoption shall have effect either from the commencement of this Act or from such later date as is specified in the adopting Act.

(2) The Parliament of any such Dominion as aforesaid may at any time revoke the adoption of any section referred to in subsection (1) of this section.

(3) The Dominions to which this section applies are the Commonwealth of Australia, the Dominion of New Zealand and Newfoundland.

11. Notwithstanding anything in the Interpretation Act, 1889, the expression "Colony" shall not, in any Act of the Parliament of the United Kingdom passed after the commencement of this Act, include a Dominion or any Province or State forming part of a Dominion.

12. This Act may be cited as the Statute of Westminster, 1931.

22 Geo. V, c. 4.

Canada

On November 19, 1926 the British Chargé d'Affaires ad interim addressed a communication to the Secretary of State, stating that his Government desired to confide the handling of matters at Washington relating to Canada to an Envoy Extraordinary and Minister Plenipotentiary accredited to the Government of the United States. The Secretary of State replied on November 20, 1926 that it would be agreeable to the President to accord formal recognition to the Canadian Minister at the convenience of His Majesty the King and the Government of Canada.

The British Chargé d'Affaires (Chilton) to Secretary Kellogg, no. 723, Nov. 19, 1926, and Mr. Kellogg to Mr. Chilton, Nov. 20, 1926, MS. Department of State, file 701.4211/53. A Canadian Minister was received by the President on Feb. 18, 1927. *Ibid.* 701.4211/62.

In construing the provisions of the so-called "Johnson act", approved on April 13, 1934 and entitled "An Act to prohibit financial transactions with any foreign government in default on its obligations to the United States" (48 Stat. 574), Attorney General Cummings informed Secretary Hull (May 5, 1934) as follows:

It has also been asked whether or not Canada, a member of the commonwealth of nations which compose the British Empire, is to be regarded as a political subdivision of Great Britain. The question should properly be answered in the negative, and this conclusion was suggested in Congress (Cong. Rec. Vol. 78, p. 6052), but it appears to be immaterial in view of my conclusion above stated concerning the intention of Congress as applied to the obligations of political subdivisions. Canada, I believe, is not in default.

37 Op. Att. Gen. (1936) 505, 512.

The South Africa Act, enacted on September 20, 1909, provided for the proclamation of the Union of South Africa, embracing the Cape of Good Hope, Natal, the Transvaal, and Orange River Colony. The preamble to that act declared that it was desirable "for the welfare and future progress of South Africa that the several British Colonies therein should be united under one Government in a legislative union under the Crown of Great Britain and Ireland".

Union of South Africa, 1909

9 Edw. VII, c. 9.

In a note dated July 29, 1929 the British Ambassador informed the Secretary of State of the desire of "His Majesty's Government in the Union of South Africa" to accredit a Minister to the Government of the United States for the handling of matters relating to the Union of South Africa. "Such a Minister", he said, "would be accredited by His Majesty The King to the President of the United States of America and he would be furnished with credentials which would enable him to take charge of all affairs relating to the Union of South Africa. He would be the ordinary channel of communication with the United States Government on these matters. The arrangements proposed would not denote any departure from the principle of the diplomatic unity of the Empire, that is to say, the principle of consultative co-operation amongst all His Majesty's representatives as amongst His Majesty's Governments themselves, in matters of common concern. The methods of dealing with matters which may arise concerning more than one of His Majesty's Governments would therefore be settled by consultation between the representatives of His Majesty's Governments concerned." The Secretary of State replied under date of August 6, 1929 that the Government of the United States would be happy to receive a diplomatic representative of "His Majesty's Government in the Union of South Africa, . . . in the capacity of Envoy Extraordinary and Minister Plenipotentiary".

> Sir Esme Howard to Secretary Stimson, no. 424, July 29, 1929 and the Acting Secretary of State (Cotton) to Sir Esme Howard, Aug. 6 1929, MS. Department of State, file 701.48A11/19.
>
> A Minister from the Union of South Africa was received by the President on Nov. 5, 1929. *Ibid.* 701.48A11/35..

On December 6, 1921 articles of agreement for a treaty were concluded between Great Britain and Ireland, wherein it was agreed that the Irish Free State should have "the same constitutional status in the Community of Nations known as the British Empire as the Dominion of Canada, the Commonwealth of Australia, the Dominion of New Zealand, and the Union of South Africa, with a Parliament".

The Irish Free State

The Constitution of the Irish Free State of 1922 provided in article 1 that "The Irish Free State . . . is a co-equal member of the Community of Nations forming the British Commonwealth of Nations."

> 114 Br. & For. St. Paps. (1921) 161. The act of Parliament of Mar. 31, 1922 declared that the articles of agreement of Dec. 6, 1921 should have the force of law as from the passing of that act. 12 Geo. V, c. 4.
>
> For the text of the Constitution of the Irish Free State of 1922, see schedule annexed to 13 Geo. V, c. 1.

On June 24, 1924 the British Ambassador addressed a note to the Secretary of State, in which he stated that his Government had come to the conclusion that it would be desirable "that the handling of matters at Washington exclusively relating to the Irish Free State should be confided to a Minister Plenipotentiary accredited to the United States Government", and expressed the hope that the Government of the United States would concur in the appointment of an Irish Free State Minister at Washington on the footing outlined in the note. The Secretary of State replied on June 28, 1924 that the President would be pleased to receive a duly accredited Minister Plenipotentiary of the Irish Free State.

> Sir Esme Howard to Secretary Hughes, no. 564, June 24, 1924, and Mr. Hughes to Sir Esme Howard, June 28, 1924, MS. Department of State, file 701.4111/487. A Minister from the Irish Free State was received by the President on Oct. 7, 1924. *Ibid.* 701.41d11/18.
>
> For a history of the establishment of the Irish Free State and a description of its status in 1927, see the opinion of Judge Peters of the Supreme Court of New York in the case of *Irish Free State et al.* v. *Guaranty Safe Deposit Co. et al.*, 129 Misc. (N.Y., 1927) 551, 559–562, 222 N.Y. Supp. 182, 191–193.
>
> A new Constitution for the former "Irish Free State" came into effect on Dec. 29, 1937. Article 4 contains provision that "The name of the State is Éire, or, in the English language, Ireland." The First Secretary of the British Embassy (Broadmead) to the Chief of the Division of European Affairs (Moffat), Jan. 1, 1938, MS. Department of State, file 841D.011/44. The name of the Irish Free State Legation in Washington was changed on Dec. 29, 1937 to "the Irish Legation or the Legation of Ireland". Memorandum from the Irish Free State Legation, Dec. 27, 1937, *ibid.* 841D.014/8.

NEUTRALIZED STATES

§15

The term *neutralized state* means not only that the state has announced its intention to remain neutral in wars between other states within the ordinary acceptation of the term *neutrality* but also that it has accepted a special status for itself by becoming "perpetually" neutral "towards all other states" (see treaty of May 11, 1867, concerning the neutrality of Luxemburg, cited *post*, this section) and that it has the guaranty of other states in a conventional undertaking that its "perpetual" neutral status and "the inviolability of its territory" shall be "invariably maintained" (see agreements on the neutrality of Switzerland, cited *post*, this section). The conventional undertakings of the guaranteeing parties may impose conditions upon the neutralized state such as demolition of fortifications, etc. In some instances neutralization of territory has been declared by unilateral act, as, for example, that by Iceland in 1918 and that by the Holy See in 1929. Such a declaration differs from neutralization as it is usually understood, i. e. there is an absence of a multilateral conventional guaranty.

The Chargé d'Affaires in Switzerland was instructed by the Department of State on November 30, 1917 to present the following communication to the Swiss Minister of Foreign Affairs:

In view of the presence of American forces in Europe engaged in the prosecution of the war against the Imperial German Government, the Government of the United States deems it appropriate to announce for the assurance of the Swiss Confederation and in harmony with the attitude of the co-belligerents of the United States in Europe, that the United States will not fail to observe the principle of neutrality applicable to Switzerland and the inviolability of its territory, so long as the neutrality of Switzerland is maintained by the Confederation and respected by the enemy.

Secretary Lansing to Mr. Wilson (telegram), Nov. 30, 1917, MS. Department of State, file 763.72111N39/133A; 1917 For. Rel., Supp. 2, p. 758.

The declaration concerning the permanent neutrality of Switzerland signed on Mar. 20, 1815, at the Congress of Vienna, by Austria, Spain, France, Great Britain, Portugal, Prussia, Russia, and Sweden was acceded to by Switzerland on May 27 of that year. I Hertslet, *Map of Europe by Treaty* (1875) 64–69; Act of Acceptance by the Swiss Confederation of May 27, 1815, *ibid.* 170; general treaty between the powers signed June 9, 1815, *ibid.* 208, 259–260; "Act, signed by the Protecting Powers, Austria, France, Great Britain, Prussia and Russia, for the Acknowledgment and Guarantee of the Perpetual Neutrality of Switzerland, and the Inviolability of its Territory", Nov. 20, 1815, *ibid.* 370. See also the Declaration of Berne of Mar. 14, 1859, *Recueil des traités, conventions et actes diplomatiques concernant l'Autriche et l'Italie* (1859) 760.

With respect to the application of Switzerland to accede to the League of Nations, under the terms of article I of the Covenant, the Council of the League on February 13, 1920 adopted the following resolution:

The Council of the League of Nations, while affirming that the conception of neutrality of the Members of the League is incompatible with the principle that all Members will be obliged to co-operate in enforcing respect for their engagements, recognises that Switzerland is in a unique situation, based on a tradition of several centuries which has been explicitly incorporated in the Law of Nations; and that the Members of the League of Nations, signatories of the Treaty of Versailles, have rightly recognised by Article 435 that the guarantees stipulated in favour of Switzerland by the Treaties of 1815 and especially by the Act of November 20, 1815, constitute international obligations for the maintenance of peace. The Members of the League of Nations are entitled to expect that the Swiss people will not stand aside when the high principles of the League have to be defended. It is in this sense that the Council of the League has taken note of the declaration made by the Swiss Government in its message to the Federal Assembly of August 4, 1919, and in its Memorandum of January 13, 1920, which declarations have been confirmed by the Swiss delegates at the meeting of the Council and in accordance with which Switzerland recognises and proclaims the duties of solidarity which membership of the League of Nations imposes upon her, including therein the duty of co-operating in such economic and financial measures as may be demanded by the

League of Nations against a covenant-breaking State, and is prepared to make every sacrifice to defend her own territory under every circumstance, even during operations undertaken by the League of Nations, but will not be obliged to take part in any military action or to allow the passage of foreign troops or the preparation of military operations within her territory.

In accepting these declarations, the Council recognises that the perpetual neutrality of Switzerland and the guarantee of the inviolability of her territory as incorporated in the Law of Nations, particularly in the Treaties and in the Act of 1815, are justified by the interests of general peace, and as such are compatible with the Covenant.

In view of the special character of the constitution of the Swiss Confederation, the Council of the League of Nations is of opinion that the notification of the Swiss declaration of accession to the League, based on the declaration of the Federal Assembly and to be carried out within two months from January 10, 1920 (the date of the coming into force of the Covenant of the League of Nations), can be accepted by the other Members of the League as the declaration required by Article I for admission as an original Member, provided that confirmation of this declaration by the Swiss people and Cantons be effected in the shortest possible time.

League of Nations, *Official Journal* (1920) 57–58. Thereafter, Switzerland was admitted to the League of Nations on Mar. 8, 1920.

By a memorandum dated Apr. 29, 1938 (submitted to the Secretary General for communication to the Council of the League of Nations), the Swiss Federal Council stated that Switzerland "will continue to collaborate with the League in all questions in which her status as a neutral country is not involved; but she considers herself entitled to ask that her absolute neutrality be explicitly recognized within the framework of the League" and requested a declaration by the Council "that the traditional neutrality of the Confederation is consistent with the provisions of the Covenant". League of Nations pub. C.146. M.87. 1938. V; *ibid., Official Journal* (1938) 385.

"In consideration of the position of Switzerland as a perpetually neutral State, the Council of the League agreed in 1920 that Switzerland should not participate in measures of a military character. The Swiss Government now ask the Council to go further in this direction, and to recognise that Switzerland will not participate in any sanctions whatsoever.

.   .   .   .

". . . the Council of the League is to-day disposed to comply with the Swiss request." Report of the representative of Sweden, May 14, 1938, submitting a draft resolution for the approval of the report to the Council of the League of Nations, League of Nations pub. C.191.(1).M.103.(1).1938.V; *ibid., Official Journal* (1938) 369.

On May 14, 1938 the Council of the League of Nations adopted a resolution approving the report and taking note that Switzerland "invoking her perpetual neutrality, has expressed the intention not to participate any longer in any manner in the putting into operation of the provisions of the Covenant relating to sanctions and declares that she will not be invited to do so". Representatives of China and the Union of Soviet Socialist Republics abstained from voting. League of Nations, *Official Journal* (1938) 369, 375; see also *ibid.* pub. C.191(1).M.103(1).1938. V.

By the terms of article 435 of the Treaty of Versailles (signed June 28, 1919), note was taken of the agreement reached between the French Government and the Swiss Government for the abrogation of the special status of the "neutralized zone of Savoy" (France), as laid down in paragraph 1 of article 92 of the final act of the Congress of Vienna and in paragraph 2 of article 3 of the Treaty of Paris of Nov. 20, 1815, as being "no longer consistent with present conditions". 3 Treaties, etc. (Redmond, 1923) 3329, 3516–3517.

Article 31 of the Treaty of Versailles provides:

> Germany, recognizing that the Treaties of April 19, 1839, Belgium which established the status of Belgium before the war, no longer conform to the requirements of the situation, consents to the abrogation of the said Treaties and undertakes immediately to recognize and to observe whatever conventions may be entered into by the Principal Allied and Associated Powers, or by any of them, in concert with the Governments of Belgium and of the Netherlands, to replace the said Treaties of 1839. If her formal adhesion should be required to such conventions or to any of their stipulations, Germany undertakes immediately to give it.

Similar provisions were included in the Treaties of Saint-Germain-en-Laye with Austria (signed September 10, 1919) and Trianon with Hungary (signed June 4, 1920).

3 Treaties, etc. (Redmond, 1923) 3329, 3349, 3149, 3180, 3539, 3566.

The treaty signed at London on Nov. 15, 1831, by the plenipotentiaries of Austria, France, Great Britain, Prussia, and Russia, on the one hand, and of Belgium, on the other, provided in article 7 that Belgium should be independent and "perpetually neutral". In article 25, the five powers first named guaranteed "the execution of all the foregoing articles". In the treaty between Belgium and Holland, signed at London on Apr. 19, 1839, concerning the separation of their respective territories, it was provided (art. 7) that Belgium should be "perpetually neutral", and the provisions of this treaty were guaranteed by Austria, France, Great Britain, Prussia, and Russia in article 1 of a treaty signed by them with Belgium, at London, on the same date. XI Martens' *Nouveau recueil* (1837) 390, 394, 404; XVI Martens' *Nouveau recueil* (1842), pt. 2, pp. 773, 777, 788, 790.

The preamble of the treaty of mutual guarantee between the United Kingdom, Belgium, France, Germany, and Italy, initialed at Locarno on October 16, 1925, took note "of the abrogation of the treaties for the neutralisation of Belgium".

Gr. Br. Treaty Ser. no. 28 (1926), Cmd. 2764. The treaty was formally signed at London on Dec. 1, 1925.

On April 24, 1937 the Ambassadors of France and Great Britain in Belgium addressed a note to the Belgian Minister of Foreign Affairs in which it was said:

1. The Governments of the United Kingdom of Great Britain and Northern Ireland and of the French Republic have not

failed during the last few months to give their full attention to the desire of the Belgian Government to have the international rights and obligations of Belgium clarified in certain respects where this is rendered necessary by her geographical position and by the delays which may still occur before the negotiation and conclusion of the general Act intended to replace the Treaty of Locarno.

2. The Government of the United Kingdom and the Government of the Republic, being anxious to give full expression to their sympathy with this desire of the Belgian Government, have agreed to make the following declaration:—

3. The said Governments have taken note of the views which the Belgian Government has itself expressed concerning the interests of Belgium, and more particularly—

> (1) the determination expressed publicly and on more than one occasion by the Belgian Government: (*a*) to defend the frontiers of Belgium with all its forces against any aggression or invasion, and to prevent Belgian territory from being used, for purposes of aggression against another State, as a passage or as a base of operations by land, by sea or in the air; (*b*) to organise the defence of Belgium in an efficient manner for this purpose;
>
> (2) the renewed assurances of the fidelity of Belgium to the Covenant of the League of Nations and to the obligations which it involves for Members of the League.

4. In consequence, taking into account the determination and assurances mentioned above, the Government of the United Kingdom and the Government of the Republic declare that they consider Belgium to be now released from all obligations towards them resulting from either the Treaty of Locarno or the arrangements drawn up in London on the 19th March, 1936, and that they maintain in respect of Belgium the undertakings of assistance which they entered into towards her under the abovementioned instruments.

In his replies of the same date, the Belgian Minister of Foreign Affairs acknowledged the communication, with thanks.

Ambassadors Ovey and Laroche to the Belgian Minister of Foreign Affairs (Spaak), Apr. 24, 1937; Mr. Spaak to Mr. Laroche, Apr. 24, 1937; Mr. Spaak to Mr. Ovey, Apr. 24, 1937. See Parliamentary Papers (1937), Cmd. 5437. Counselor Atherton to Secretary Hull, no. 3032, Apr. 27, 1937, enclosure, MS. Department of State, file 740.0011 Mutual Guarantee (Locarno)/889.

The "arrangements" of Mar. 19, 1936, referred to in the above quotation, are published in Parliamentary Papers (1936), Cmd. 5134.

On October 13, 1937 the German Minister of Foreign Affairs addressed a note to the Belgian Minister in Berlin, reading in part as follows:

1. The German Government has taken note of the views which the Belgian Government itself saw fit to express in regard to:

a) the policy of independence which it intends in full sovereignty to pursue;

b) its determination to defend with all its force the frontiers of Belgium against any aggression or invasion and to prevent Belgian territory from being used, in view of an aggression against another state, as a passageway or as a base for operations on land, at sea, or in the air, and to organize Belgian defense effectively for this purpose.

2. The Government of the Reich recognizes as a fact that the inviolability and the integrity of Belgium are of common interest to the Western Powers. It confirms its determination not to infringe on this inviolability and this integrity under any circumstance and at all times to respect Belgian territory except, it goes without saying, in the event that Belgium should, in an armed conflict in which Germany may be engaged, cooperate in military action against Germany.

3. The Government of the Reich, like the Royal British Government and the French Government, is ready to assist Belgium in the event that Belgium should be the object of an attack or invasion.

Ambassador Gibson to Secretary Hull, no. 61, Oct. 18, 1937, MS. Department of State, file 740.0011 Mutual Guarantee (Locarno)/942. For the position of the Belgian Government referred to in the above correspondence, see the statement made by the King of the Belgians to his Council of Ministers on Oct. 14, 1936, enclosure to despatch 1020 from Ambassador Morris to Secretary Hull, Oct. 15, 1936, *ibid.* 755.00/35. A portion of the statement is quoted by Charles Cheney Hyde in 31 A.J.I.L. (1937) 82.

The Congo Free State was a neutralized state, with the King of the Belgians as its sovereign, between 1885 and 1908, on which latter date it was ceded to and annexed by Belgium (*ante* §13). For the Congo Act of 1885, see XVII Hertslet, *Complete Collection*, etc. (1890) 62, 67–68, 116. For correspondence between Germany, United States of America, France, and Great Britain in the fall of 1914 on the subject of "the neutralization of the colonies lying within the conventional free-trade zone" of the Congo, see 1914 For. Rel. Supp. 112, 117, 134.

. . . [The] attitude of the United States toward Luxembourg is characterized by the fact that we have accredited a minister to that country and that we regard Luxembourg as an independent Luxemburg
and neutral state whose territory is occupied by the armed forces of a nation with which the United States is at war.

Secretary Lansing to the American Minister in the Netherlands (Garrett), no. 632, Aug. 22, 1918, MS. Department of State, file 763.72/10584; 1918 For. Rel., Supp. 1, p. 300.

Article II of the treaty signed at London on May 11, 1867 stipulated that the Grand Duchy of Luxemburg should "henceforth form a perpetually Neutral State" under the "collective guarantee" of Great Britain, Austria, France, Prussia, and Russia and that it should "be bound to observe the same Neutrality towards all other States". III Hertslet, *Map of Europe by Treaty* (1875) 1801, 1803.

The Report of the Fifth Committee to the First Assembly of the League of Nations, dated December 6, 1920, regarding the application of the Grand Duchy of Luxemburg for admission to the League, stated that the President of the Luxemburg Government had requested that the Grand Duchy on being admitted should preserve its neutrality under the guaranty of the League (the neutrality being that recognized by the Treaty of London of May 11, 1867); that Luxemburg did not expect to be released from the obligations imposed upon the members of the League by the terms of article 16 of the Covenant; that it agreed to leave its territory open for the passage of such troops as the Council of the League might authorize; that it would participate in the retaliatory measures of an economic or financial nature which might be enacted against any state in "rebellion against the League"; that its only request was that it should not be in any way compelled to participate in military operations which the members of the League might undertake in common, or to defend its territory by arms against foreign aggression; and that later, in a letter dated November 28, 1920, addressed by the Luxemburg delegation to the chairman of the subcommittee, the reservations previously made by Luxemburg were withdrawn, the delegation stating that the Luxemburg Government would find no difficulty in undertaking all the obligations which the terms of the Covenant (article 10 in particular) imposed on members of the League.

Luxemburg was admitted to the League on December 16, 1920.

League of Nations, *Records of the First Assembly: Plenary Meetings* (1920) 586, 610–612.

On April 28, 1923 the Government of Luxemburg stated in a communication addressed to the League that "the Treaty of London of May 11th, 1867, which is still in force, imposes perpetual neutrality upon the Grand-Duchy of Luxemburg; and this neutrality is proclaimed in solemn terms in the first article of our Constitution. The Grand-Duchy of Luxemburg forms an independent, indivisible, inalienable and perpetually neutral state."

League of Nations, *Official Journal* (1923) 722.

Article III of the general treaty of peace and amity, signed in Washington on December 20, 1907 by the Central American republics, contained the following provision:

Honduras

Taking into account the central geographical position of Honduras and the facilities which owing to this circumstance have made its territory most often the theater of Central American conflicts, Honduras declares from now on its absolute neutrality in event of any conflict between the other Republics; and the latter, in their turn, provided such neutrality be observed, bind themselves to respect it and in no case to violate the Honduranean territory.

1907 For. Rel., pt. 2, pp. 692, 693.

By the general treaty of peace and amity signed by the Central American republics at Washington on Feb. 7, 1923, the provisions of the treaty of Dec. 20, 1907 were abrogated. *Conference on Central American Affairs, Washington, December 4, 1922–February 7, 1923* (1923) 287, 294.

The Organic Statute of the State of Albania, drawn up at London by the Conference of Ambassadors on July 29, 1913, contained the provision in article 3 thereof that "Albania is neutralized; its neutrality is guaranteed by the six Powers"—namely, Germany, Austria-Hungary, France, Great Britain, Italy, and Russia.

Albania

> IX Martens, *Nouveau recueil général* (3d ser., Triepel, 1919) 650. translation. In considering, on Dec. 4, 1920, Albania's application for admission to the League of Nations, doubt was expressed by the Fifth Committee for the study of requests for admission of states to the League of Nations as to whether its status as of 1913 continued to exist. Albania was admitted to membership in the League on Dec. 17, 1920, apparently without reference to her status as a neutralized state. League of Nations *Records of the First Assembly*, Meetings of the Committees, vol. II, pp. 189, 190, 212-214; *ibid.: Plenary Meetings* (1920) 643–651, 668–670. As to the declaration by the Governments of the British Empire, France, Italy, and Japan. signed at Paris on Nov. 9, 1921, in regard to the procedure to be followed by the Council of the League in the event that Albania should find it impossible to maintain intact her territorial integrity, see 12 League of Nations **Treaty Series** (1922) 382.

The treaty signed by the Holy See and Italy on February 11, 1929, containing the provision that the Vatican City shall be regarded as "neutral and inviolable territory", reads in part as follows:

2. Italy recognises the sovereignty of the Holy See in the international domain as an attribute inherent in its nature and in conformity with its traditions and the requirements of its mission in the world.

Holy See; Vatican City

3. Italy recognises the full ownership and the exclusive and absolute dominion and sovereign jurisdiction of the Holy See over the Vatican, as at present constituted, together with all its appurtenances and endowments; by this means is created the Vatican City for the special purposes and under the conditions prescribed by the present treaty. The boundaries of the said City are indicated in the plan forming annex I to the present treaty, of which it forms an integral part.

.   .   .   .

4. The sovereignty and exclusive jurisdiction over the Vatican City, which Italy recognises as appertaining to the Holy See, precludes any intervention therein on the part of the Italian Government and any authority other than that of the Holy See.

.   .   .   .

9. In accordance with the rules of international law all persons having permanent residence within the Vatican City shall be subject to the sovereignty of the Holy See.

.   .   .   .

12. Italy recognises the right of the Holy See to active and passive legation in accordance with the general rules of international law.

.   .   .   .

24. As regards the sovereignty appertaining to it in the international sphere, the Holy See declares that it desires to remain and will remain aloof from rivalries of a temporal nature between other States and from international congresses convened to deal with them, unless the contending parties make a joint appeal to its mission of peace. In any event the Holy See reserves the right to exercise its moral spiritual influence.

Consequently, the Vatican City shall always and in all circumstances be regarded as neutral and inviolable territory.

130 Br. & For. St. Paps. (1929), pt. I, pp. 791–795, 799.

Iceland

By the terms of the Danish law providing for the union of Denmark and Iceland signed November 30, 1918, it was stipulated that "Denmark shall . . . give notice [to foreign powers] that Iceland declares herself permanently neutral".

Art. 19, pt. 7, of the Danish law of Nov. 30, 1918, 111 Br. & For. St. Paps. (1917–18) 703, 706.

Philippine Islands

Section 11 of the Philippine Independence Act of 1934 contains the following provision:

The President is requested, at the earliest practicable date, to enter into negotiations with foreign powers with a view to the conclusion of a treaty for the perpetual neutralization of the Philippine Islands, if and when Philippine independence shall have been achieved.

48 Stat. 456, 463.

With respect to the neutralization of Tangier, see *post* §17, on "Protectorates".

VASSAL OR SEMI-SOVEREIGN STATES

§16

The extent of the sovereignty retained by a vassal or semi-sovereign state is not determined by general rules of international law. It is ascertained in each instance by the facts of the particular case.

Bulgaria

Under the terms of article I of the Treaty of Berlin, signed on July 13, 1878 by Great Britain, Austria-Hungary, France, Germany, Italy, Russia, and Turkey, Bulgaria was "constituted an autonomous and tributary Principality under the suzerainty of His Imperial Majesty the Sultan". On October 5, 1908 Prince Ferdinand of Bulgaria proclaimed the independence of Bulgaria as a monarchial state, and Bulgaria ceased to be a vassal state.

1878 For. Rel. 895, 896; 69 Br. & For. St. Paps. (1877–78) 749, 751; IV Hertslet, *Map of Europe by Treaty* (1891) 2759, 2766; 1908 For. Rel. 57. For the recognition of Bulgaria, see *post* §38.

Egypt was formerly a vassal state under the suzerainty of Turkey. Egypt
A state of war having come into existence in November 1914 between
Turkey and the Allied Powers, Great Britain—then in occupation of
Egypt—announced the termination of the suzerainty of Turkey and
declared a protectorate over Egypt, by unilateral declaration, on
December 18, 1914.

> 1914 For. Rel. Supp. 128–129, 152–153; 108 Br. & For. St. Paps. (1914),
> pt. II, p. 185. See the discussion of Egypt as a protectorate, *post* §17. On
> the recognition of Egypt as a new state in 1922, see *post* §40.

On December 1, 1911, at the time of the fall of the Manchu dynasty, Outer
Mongolia
the Mongol princes effected a *coup d'état* and declared their independence. On November 3, 1912 a convention and protocol were
signed at Urga by Mongolia and Russia, wherein the Russian Government undertook to assist Mongolia to maintain the autonomous regime
she had established and Mongolia undertook to admit neither Chinese
troops nor the colonization of Chinese nationals. Subsequently, on
November 5, 1913, by a declaration and exchange of notes between
Russia and China, China recognized autonomous Outer Mongolia,
and Russia recognized Outer Mongolia as part of the territory of
China under Chinese suzerainty. Still later, on June 7, 1915, Russia,
China, and Outer Mongolia signed (at Kiachta [Kyakhta]) a treaty
whereby China and Russia recognized "the autonomy of Outer Mongolia forming part of Chinese territory", and Outer Mongolia recognized the suzerainty of China. Outer Mongolia also agreed not to
enter into conventions with foreign powers regarding matters of a
political or territorial nature, and Russia gained certain extraterritorial privileges.

> The Ambassador in St. Petersburg (Leningrad), Curtis Guild, to the
> Secretary of State, no. 464, Jan. 6, 1913 (containing translations of the
> agreement and protocol of Nov. 3, 1912), MS. Department of State, file
> 761.93/95; the Chargé d'Affaires in St. Petersburg (Leningrad), Charles S.
> Wilson, to the Secretary of State, no. 655, Dec. 23, 1913 (containing transla-
> tions of notes exchanged on Nov. 5, 1913), *ibid.* 761.93/109, enclosures;
> the Minister in Peking (MacMurray) to the Secretary of State, no. 691,
> July 17, 1915 (containing translation of the treaty of June 7, 1915), *ibid.*
> 761.93/113, enclosure.
>
> The texts of the above agreements are published in II MacMurray,
> *Treaties and Agreements With and Concerning China* (1921) 992, 1066,
> 1239. See also *China Year Book* (1914) 630, 633; *ibid.* (1921–22) 571,
> 587 *et seq.; ibid.* (1923) 674.

On November 22, 1919, following the Russian Revolution, the
President of the Chinese Republic by mandate "canceled" the independence of Outer Mongolia. Russia protested that this action was
in violation of the 1913 and 1915 agreements referred to in the text,
ante. A period of considerable disorder followed, and on July 6, 1921

Outer Mongolia declared its independence. On November 5, 1921 a treaty was signed at Moscow between the Soviet Government and the Government of Outer Mongolia, providing that the two Governments "recognize each other as the only governments in the territories of Russia and Mongolia". China protested against this action (in 1922), observing that Mongolia "is a part of Chinese territory".

> 1919 For. Rel., vol. I, pp. 399–402; 1920 For. Rel., vol. I, pp. 756, 757 759; *China Year Book* (1923) 674 *et seq.; ibid.* (1924) 578, 581; *ibid.* (1928) 379; *ibid.* (1938) 27–28.

Article 5 of the agreement between China and the Union of Soviet Socialist Republics signed on May 31, 1924 stated:

> The Government of the Union of Soviet Socialist Republics recognizes that Outer Mongolia is an integral part of the Republic of China and respects China's sovereignty therein.

Under the Mongol Constitution of November 1924, an independent People's Republic with all supreme power vested in the Great Assembly of the people and in the government elected by the latter, was established.

> The Minister in China (Schurman) to the Secretary of State, no. 2297 June 5, 1924, MS. Department of State, file 761.93/487, enclosure 1; *China Year Book* (1938) 31; *ibid.* (1928) 381.

On March 12, 1936 a protocol was signed by the Union of Soviet Socialist Republics and the Mongolian People's Republic, providing for "mutual support by every means in the aversion and anticipation of the threat of military attack, and also mutual assistance and support in the event of any attack by any third party" upon either of the parties to the agreement. The Government of China protested against the protocol in a note of April 7, 1936 to the Soviet Government, on the ground that Outer Mongolia "being an integral part of the Republic of China, no foreign state has the right to conclude with it any treaty or agreement" and that the action "constitutes . . . an infringement of the sovereignty of China and a violation of the stipulations of the Sino-Soviet Agreement of 1924".

> For the protocol of 1936, see the despatch of Ambassador William C. Bullitt to the Secretary of State, no. 1521, Apr. 9, 1936, MS. Department of State, file 761.93–Outer Mongolia/17, enclosure; *China Year Book* (1938) 30–31. For the reply of the Soviet Government of Apr. 8, 1936 and the subsequent note of the Government of China, see *ibid.* 31–32.

PROTECTORATES

§17

The word *protectorate* usually describes the relation between a protecting and a protected state, although the term is sometimes used with reference to the relation between a protecting state and an area or people not possessing the status of a state. It is also sometimes used as a term descriptive of the country which is under protection.

On February 7, 1923 the Permanent Court of International Justice rendered an advisory opinion on the following question:

> Whether the dispute between France and Great Britain as to the Nationality Decrees issued in Tunis and Morocco (French zone) on November 8th, 1921, and their application to British subjects, is or is not, by international law, solely a matter of domestic jurisdiction (Article 15, paragraph 8, of the Covenant).

The Court held that the dispute referred to was not, by international law, solely a matter of domestic jurisdiction. In the course of its opinion the Court, in discussing the relation between the French Government and the French Protectorates of Tunis and of the French Zone of Morocco, said:

> A. The French Decrees relate to persons born, not upon the territory of France itself, but upon the territory of the French Protectorates of Tunis and of the French zone of Morocco. Granted that it is competent for a State to enact such legislation within its national territory, the question remains to be considered whether the same competence exists as regards protected territory.
>
> The extent of the powers of a protecting State in the territory of a protected State depends, first, upon the Treaties between the protecting State and the protected State establishing the Protectorate, and, secondly, upon the conditions under which the Protectorate has been recognised by third Powers as against whom there is an intention to rely on the provisions of these Treaties. In spite of common features possessed by Protectorates under international law, they have individual legal characteristics resulting from the special conditions under which they were created, and the stage of their development. *[margin note: Powers of protecting state]*
>
> The position in the present case is determined by the international documents enumerated below:
>
> (a) As regards Tunis: The Treaty of Casr-Said of May 12th, 1881, between France and Tunis; the Treaty between the same Powers signed at La Marsa on June 8th, 1883; the correspondence between France and Great Britain, 1881–1883 (British Case, Appendix No. 6, and French Counter-Case, pages 77 *et seq.*; Supplementary Documents submitted by the British Government). . . .
>
> (b) As regards Morocco: the Treaty of Fez of March 30th, 1912, between France and Morocco; the Anglo-French Declaration regarding Egypt and Morocco, dated April

8th, 1904; Sir Edward Grey's note to M. Daeschner, dated November 14th, 1911. (French Counter-Case, page 139 British Counter-Case, Appendix No. 9); letter from M. Kiderlen-Waechter, Secretary of State for Foreign Affairs of the German Empire to M. Jules Cambon, Ambassador of the French Republic at Berlin, dated November 4th, 1911 (read during the hearing by the French Agent).

The question whether the exclusive jurisdiction possessed by a protecting State in regard to nationality questions in its own territory extends to the territory of the protected State depends upon an examination of the whole situation as it appears from the standpoint of international law. The question therefore is no longer solely one of domestic jurisdiction as defined above. (See Part IV.)

B. The French Government contends that the public powers (*puissance publique*) exercised by the protecting State, taken in conjunction with the local sovereignty of the protected State constitute full sovereignty equivalent to that upon which international relations are based, and that therefore the protecting State and the protected State may, by virtue of an agreement between them, exercise and divide between them within the protected territory the whole extent of the powers which international law recognises as enjoyed by sovereign States within the limits of their national territory. This contention is disputed by the British Government.

The Court observes that, in any event, it will be necessary to have recourse to international law in order to decide what the value of an agreement of this kind may be as regards third States, and that the question consequently ceases to be one which, by international law, is solely within the domestic jurisdiction of a State, as that jurisdiction is defined above.

Per. Ct. Int. Jus., Advisory Opinion, Ser. B, No. 4, pp. 21, 27–28; I Hudson, *World Court Reports* (1934) 145, 154, 158–159.

By an exchange of notes on May 24, 1923, the British and French Governments agreed to proceed no further with the case submitted to the Permanent Court arising out of the nationality decrees promulgated in Tunis, Nov. 8, 1921, each Government reserving the point of view which it had maintained in the diplomatic correspondence and in the preliminary proceedings at The Hague. The two Governments also agreed that no further proceedings should take place at The Hague in respect to the corresponding nationality decrees issued in Morocco (French Zone), each Government maintaining, however, its position and reserving its rights. 18 League of Nations Treaty Series (1923) 306.

As to the international personality of a protected state and its diplomatic relations with other states, see Secretary Hughes to Ambassador Harvey, Oct. 27, 1923, MS. Department of State, file 881.00/854; 1923 For. Rel., vol. II, pp. 581–582.

Monaco

In reply to an inquiry addressed to the Department of State on November 14, 1907 regarding the status of Monaco, the Department quoted from Hall (5th ed., p. 29, n. 1) as follows:

"The legal position of Monaco is far from clear. By the treaty of Peronne in 1641 the principality placed itself under the protection of France. In 1815 it was provided as part of the settlement of Europe that the protectorate should be transferred to Sardinia, and by the treaty of Turin in 1817 the necessary arrangements were made. Monaco unquestionably continued to be a protected state until after the cession of Nice to France by Italy; but in 1861 it took upon itself, without the concurrence of Italy, to cede a portion of its territory to France, which thus became interposed between it and the Italian frontier. In the particular circumstances of the case the act was tantamount to a repudiation of the Italian protectorate, Italy neither protested at the time nor has she subsequently asserted her rights, she therefore most likely has acquiesced. France has not assumed a protectorate. It consequently would seem most probable that Monaco is legally independent."

The actual relation of Monaco to other States is in accordance with Hall's conclusion. By reference to the Almanach de Gotha, 1907, p. 970, it will be seen that consular representatives of Germany, the Argentine, Austria-Hungary, Belgium, Bolivia, Chile, Spain, France, Great Britain, Greece, Italy, Luxembourg, Mexico, Norway, the Netherlands, Peru, Portugal, Roumania, Russia and Sweden, are accredited to Monaco,—several of them being also the consular representatives of the respective powers at Nice.

Consuls representing Monaco have been recognized by the United States at San Francisco and New York. In 1874 Mr. Emile de Loth was appointed Vice-Consul at Monaco, under the United States Consulate at Nice, and received an exequatur from His Serene Highness, the Prince of Monaco. Mr. de Loth continued in that capacity until 1906, when the Consular agency was discontinued for lack of business.

In Hertslet's and Martens' collections of treaties, will be found conventions between Monaco and Austria, Belgium, France, Great-Britain, the Netherlands, Russia and Switzerland, all with one exception, being conventions for extradition of criminals. The United States has no convention [bilateral] with Monaco.

The Assistant Secretary of State (Bacon) to Dr. Eugene Murray-Aaron, Nov. 19, 1907, MS. Department of State, file 9901.

By a treaty signed by France and the Principality of Monaco on July 17, 1918, the former assured to the latter "the defence of its independence and sovereignty" and guaranteed "the integrity of its territory as though that territory formed part of France". Monaco undertook, on its part, to exercise its rights of sovereignty entirely in accord with the political, military, naval, and economic interests of France (art. I). It was provided in article II that measures concerning the international relations of Monaco and measures relating either directly or indirectly to the exercise of a regency or to the succession to the crown should always form the subject of a prior understanding between Monaco and France. It was provided further that the crown might only be transmitted "whether through a marriage, by adoption or otherwise, to a person possessing French or Mon-

Treaty of 1918 between France and Monaco

egasque nationality and agreeable to the French Government".
Under article III Monaco confirmed a previous undertaking given to
the French Government "not to alienate the Principality, either
wholly or in part in favour of any Power other than France". The
same article stated:

> In the event of the Crown falling vacant, especially in default
> of an heir, whether direct or adoptive, the territory of Monaco
> shall form, under the protectorate of France, an autonomous
> State called the State of Monaco. In such an event private
> immovable property not devoted to a public use which, on that
> account, might form the subject of a special claim on the part of
> the rightful claimants, shall be repurchased by the State of
> Monaco with the aid, if necessary, of the French State.

> 111 Br. & For. St. Paps. (1917–18) 727.
> In article 436 of the Treaty of Versailles the high contracting parties
> declared and placed on record that they had taken note of the foregoing
> treaty. 3 Treaties, etc. (Redmond, 1923) 3329, 3519.

"Crown
Colonies"
and "pro-
tectorates"

Thus the term "protectorate" gradually changed its meaning
from that of a pact with the ruler of a State, which maintained
its internal but not its external sovereignty, to a declaration of
the territorial status of a region included in the Empire, in which
not only the external, but in varying degrees the internal sovereignty also, had passed to the controlling Power, in many cases
(since unexplored regions were included) without even the
"treaty" consent of the people. Powers of administration
coequal with those of a colony have been assumed.

The inhabitants of a British protectorate are styled "British
protected persons," and do not enjoy the status of British subjects, although, as Hall points out, the term "British subject" is
defined in the African Order 1889 as "including all persons enjoying His Majesty's protection." The "natives," however, are
separately defined as "the subjects of any country within the
limits of this Order not being British subjects." The wording is
therefore ambiguous, but in practice the natives of a protectorate,
who do not already enjoy the status of British subjects, have
apparently no rights or privileges either within or beyond the
limits of the protectorate. . . .

A Crown colony is annexed territory, and an integral part of
the King's dominions, acquired either by conquest, settlement,
or cession, and since all inhabitants born in it have the status of
British subjects, herein appeared to reside the chief distinction
between it and a protectorate.

> Lugard, *Dual Mandate in British Tropical Africa* (1923) 35–36.

It is stated in Halsbury:

> . . . There is no statutory or authoritative definition of the
> term "protectorate," although it appears in two recent statutes.
> . . . Protectorates are not British territory in the strict sense;
> but it is understood that no other civilised Power will interfere
> in their affairs . . . [Footnote: See and compare the Berlin

Convention, July 1878, as to "spheres of influence," out of which protectorates seem to have been evolved.] They are administered under the provisions of Orders in Council issued by virtue of powers conferred upon His Majesty by the Foreign Jurisdiction Act, 1890 . . . "or otherwise vested in His Majesty," which latter phrase may be taken to be intended to bring in aid any exercise of the royal prerogative that may be necessary to supplement His Majesty's statutory powers. Some protectorates consist of territories adjacent to colonies, for which, not being under the control of any responsible government, it has become necessary to provide some kind of administration for the purposes of law and order. Such are the Protectorates of Sierra Leone . . . and the Gambia . . . which are administered by the Governments of the colonies of the same name respectively.

X Halsbury, *Laws of England* (1909) 521.

"Territories comprised in the [British] East African Protectorate, save such as formed part of the dominions of the Sultan of Zanzibar, were annexed to the British dominions as from July 23rd, 1920, and became the Colony of Kenya. . . .

". . . The above excepted portion is called Kenya Protectorate." *Laws of England,* Supp. 27 (1937), vol. X, p. 43; Colonial Reports—Annual, No. 1806, *Kenya Colony and Protectorate, 1936* (London, 1937) 3–4. See also 131 Parliamentary Debates, House of Commons (1920) 1980, July 12, 1920, and the *London Gazette,* no. 32162, Dec. 14, 1920, p. 12287.

As to the status of the Bechuanaland, see *The King* v. *Earl of Crewe,* [1910] 2 K.B. 576, 603–604, 611, and as to the status of Swaziland, see *Sobhuza II* v. *Miller and Others,* [1926] A.C. 518, 522–524.

The British Ambassador on December 18, 1914, transmitted to the Department of State a copy of instructions from his Government stating that it considered the suzerainty of Turkey over Egypt to be terminated and that it had advised the King to place Egypt under his protection. It was stated in the instructions that the Egyptian Government would arrange for the issue of a Khedival decree providing that the consular and other foreign courts should continue to exercise, in Egypt, their accustomed jurisdiction to the extent to which the arrangements which would have to be made by the military authorities for the maintenance of public order, were not inconsistent therewith. It was further stated that the British Government had appointed a High Commissioner for Egypt who would also be the Minister of Foreign Affairs in the Egyptian Government and that the British Government would, therefore, ask the Government of the United States to instruct its representatives in Cairo to address all his official communications in the future to the High Commissioner as Minister of Foreign Affairs.

Egypt, 1914

Ambassador Spring Rice to Secretary Bryan, no. 434, Dec. 18, 1914, MS. Department of State, file 883.00/51; see also 1914 For. Rel. Supp. 152. The note from the British Government was merely acknowledged by the Government of the United States on Dec. 21 following. See MS. Department of State, file 883.00/53.

Recognition
by U. S.,
1919
Acting under instructions from the Department of State the Diplomatic Agent and Consul General at Cairo wrote to the British Special High Commissioner in that city on April 22, 1919:

> I have the honor to state that I have been directed by my Government to acquaint you with the fact that the President recognizes the British Protectorate over Egypt, which was proclaimed by His Majesty's Government on December 18, 1914.
>
> In according this recognition the President must of necessity reserve for further discussion the details thereof, along with the question of the modification of any rights belonging to the United States which may be entailed by this decision.

The Consul General at Cairo (Gary) to the Acting Secretary of State, no. 457, Apr. 26, 1919, MS. Department of State, file 883.00/162; 1919 For. Rel., vol. II, pp. 203, 204.

Article 17 of the treaty of peace signed at Lausanne on July 24, 1923 declared that the renunciation by Turkey of all rights and titles over Egypt and over the Sudan would be regarded as effective as of Nov. 5, 1914. Gr. Br. Treaty Ser. no. 16 (1923), Cmd. 1929.

Egypt was formerly a vassal state. See *ante* §16. The British protectorate over Egypt terminated on Feb. 28, 1922. For the recognition by the United States of Egypt as an independent state in 1922, see *post* §40.

Tonga.—Replying to an instruction requesting information regarding the Constitution and Government of Tonga, the Consul at Suva, Fiji Islands, on July 16, 1930, transmitted to the Department of State a report reading in part as follows:

"In 1900 under a treaty dated May 18, 1900, ratified at Nukualofa, February 16, 1901, the British Government established a protectorate over Tonga. Under the treaty Tonga agreed to have no relations with foreign powers concerning the alienation of land or any part of the sovereignty or for any demands for monetary compensation.

"The British Government undertakes to protect the government and territory of Tonga from external hostile attacks and for this purpose is to have access to the waters and harbors of Tonga and suitable sites for naval bases and fortifications.

"The British Government has the right to appoint a suitable person as British Agent and Consul in Tonga to exercise extraterritorial judicial powers over the British and foreigners in Tonga and to advise the Tongan Government. The treaty provides that the British Agent and Consul shall not interfere in any way in the internal affairs and administration of Tonga where interests of British subjects and other foreigners are not concerned. Changes among the leading officials and new appointments are to be made in consultation with the British Agent and Consul."

Consul Roberts to Secretary Stimson, no. 186, July 16, 1930, MS. Department of State, file 846M.01/19. For the text of the treaty of May 18, 1900, see 107 Br. & For. St. Paps. (1914), pt. I, p. 521. For the text of the British proclamation of Feb. 16, 1901 relative to the exercise of British jurisdiction in Tonga, see 94 Br. & For. St. Paps. (1900–1901) 1307.

On May 29, 1915 the Department of State instructed the Ambassador in Great Britain to give notice, pursuant to the provisions of the act of Mar. 4, 1915 (the so-called "Seamen's Act"), 38 Stat. 1164), to the British Secretary of State for Foreign Affairs of the intention of the Government of the United

States to abrogate article X of the treaty of Oct. 2, 1886 between the United States and the King of Tonga. 2 Treaties, etc. (Malloy, 1910) 1781; 25 Stat. 1440; Secretary Bryan to Ambassador Page, May 29, 1915, MS. Department of State, file 711.0021/44c; 1915 For. Rel. 11.

On March 3, 1921 the Ambassador in London, under instructions from the Department of State, acknowledged the denunciation of the whole treaty (with the exception of art. VI) which had been given by the British Government on July 28, 1919, with the statement that it was understood that the provisions of article VI of the treaty remained in force. MS. Department of State, files 711.4121/26, 711.4121/27.

North Borneo.—As to the British protectorate of North Borneo, see X Halsbury, *Laws of England* (1909) 524; 79 Br. & For. St. Paps. (1887–88) 237; 1907 For. Rel., pt. 1, pp. 542–548; 47 Stat. 2198; 4 Treaties, etc. (Trenwith, 1938) 4261 (convention delimiting the boundary between the Philippine Archipelago and the state of North Borneo.)

Malay States.—"The federated Malay States constitute a protectorate of a different order, based on an agreement . . . [Footnote: Signed in July 1895, between the Governor of the Straits Settlements on behalf of the Government of Her late Majesty and the rulers of Perak, Salangor, the Negri Sembilan, itself a confederation of states, and Pahang.] with the Governments of four independent native States, by which they agreed to accept a British resident-general as agent and representative of the British Government under the Governor of the Straits Settlements, who is named High Commissioner." X Halsbury, *Laws of England* (1909) 523.

Kelantan, etc.—Article 1 of a treaty between Great Britain and Siam of Mar. 10, 1909, provided:

"The Siamese Government transfers to the British Government all rights of suzerainty, protection, administration and control whatsoever, which they possess over the States of Kelantan, Tringganu, Kedah, Perlis and adjacent islands . . ." 102 Br. & For. St. Paps. (1908–9) 126; Gr. Br. Treaty Ser. no. 19 (1909), Cd. 4703. The states referred to are discussed under the heading "Protectorates" in X Halsbury, *Laws of England* (1909) 524.

In response to an interrogation in the House of Commons on Feb. 28, 1923 as to whether the sovereignty of the state of Kelantan was subject to, and limited by, the rights conferred upon Great Britain by the Anglo-Siamese treaty of 1909, or by the agreement of 1910 between the High Commissioner for the Malay States and the Rajah of Kelantan, the Under Secretary of State for Foreign Affairs replied:

"His Majesty's Government do not regard the Treaty and Agreement referred to, which are still in force, as derogating from the sovereignty of the Sultan of Kelantan, and His Majesty's Government recognise the State of Kelantan as an independent sovereign State." 160 Parliamentary Debates, House of Commons (1923) 1937–1938, Feb. 28, 1923; Consul General Skinner to Secretary Hughes, no. 14,688, Mar. 2, 1923, MS. Department of State, file 846e.01/1.

In the case of *Duff Development Company, Limited* v. *Government of Kelantan and Another* an action had been brought on an award of an arbitrator making certain declarations in favor of the company and directing the Government of Kelantan to pay the costs of arbitration and award. An appeal was taken to the House of Lords from an order staying all further proceedings in the matter on the ground that the Sultan of Kelantan was an individual sovereign ruler and the state of Kelantan an individual sovereign state over which the court had no jurisdiction. The order was affirmed by the House of Lords on Apr. 10, 1924. [1924] A.C. 797.

Trengganu.—An agreement between Great Britain and Trengganu, signed at Singapore on Apr. 22, 1910, established a British "Protectorate" over Trengganu, "a self-governing Malayo-Mohammadan State". 103 Br. & For. St. Paps. (1909–10) 987.

Perlis.—An agreement concluded between His Britannic Majesty and the Raja of the Mohammedan state of Perlis on Apr. 28, 1930 declared in article 1 that Perlis should continue to be under the protection of Great Britain, which should exercise the rights of suzerainty. 132 Br. & For. St. Paps. (1930), pt. I, p. 216.

Korea (Chosen)

The agreement of November 17, 1905 between Japan and Korea provided that the Government of Japan should have control and direction of the external relations of Korea and that the diplomatic and consular representatives of Japan should have charge of the subjects and interests of Korea in foreign countries (art. I); that Japan should see to the execution of treaties actually existing between Korea and other powers (art. II); and that the Government of Japan should be represented in Korea by a Resident General, primarily for the purpose of taking charge of and directing matters relating to diplomatic affairs (art. III). On November 24, 1905 the American Minister in Seoul was instructed to withdraw from Korea, and the diplomatic representation of the United States concerning matters relating to Korea was transferred to Tokyo.

The Secretary of State, on March 8, 1906, instructed the Embassy in Tokyo to inquire whether the Japanese Government would acquiesce in the American representative at Seoul, Korea, being styled as Agent and Consul General, thus following the usual precedent in the case of protected countries and facilitating business relations with the Japanese Resident General. On March 23, 1906 the Japanese Minister of Foreign Affairs replied that—

> in view of the fact that all the diplomatic affairs concerning Korea are, according to the agreement between Japan and Korea, to be transacted through this department, and those matters relating to foreign countries, of which the resident-general at Seoul takes charge, are limited to such local affairs of Korea as would come within the scope of the functions exercised by the foreign consuls, it is believed that no inconvenience would be experienced by the United States official at Seoul in the way of maintaining official relations with the resident-general in the capacity of consul-general, and consequently the Imperial Government regret that they are unable to see their way to consent to the said official's adopting the special designation of agent besides that of consul-general.

1905 For. Rel. 612–614; Mr. Wilson, Chargé d'Affaires, to Secretary Root, no. 419, Mar. 28, 1906, MS. Department of State, 82 Despatches, Japan. See also 1906 For. Rel., pt. II, pp. 1033, 1035.

This protectorate ceased upon the annexation of Korea by Japan under the treaty between them of Aug. 22, 1910, which took effect on the date of its promulgation (Aug. 29, 1910). The Japanese Ambassador, Y. Uchida, to the Acting Secretary of State, Huntington Wilson, Aug. 24, 1910, and enclosures, MS. Department of State, file 895.00/483; 1910 For. Rel. 681–683.

The Empire of Morocco, while constituting a single geographic entity nominally under a sultan, consists of three areas or zones, namely, the French Zone, the Spanish Zone, and the Tangier Zone. Each Zone is administered independently of the others pursuant to international agreements, the provisions of some of which require uniformity in all three zones in respect of certain matters, such as customs; telegraph, telephone, and postal services and charges; coasting trade; and control of "contraband of arms". Morocco

From periods long antedating the establishment of these Zones, the United States and other powers exercised, pursuant to treaties between them and Morocco, certain extraterritorial jurisdiction over their nationals and "protected persons" in Morocco through their own courts presided over by their respective consular and diplomatic officers. By virtue of agreements between these powers and Morocco (and between certain of the powers themselves, as well as between some of them and Morocco), the situation in and with relation to Morocco has undergone marked changes since the beginning of the twentieth century. The extraterritorial jurisdiction has for the most part given way to other forms of administrative and judicial procedure—the United States and Great Britain (Great Britain, so far as the Spanish Zone only is concerned) being the only powers still claiming and exercising extraterritorial jurisdiction over their nationals in Morocco. France has abandoned extraterritorial rights in the Spanish Zone, and Spain has abandoned extraterritorial rights in the French Zone. The sequence and essential features of some of the more important events that have characterized this transitional process by which, on the one hand, the jurisdiction of the powers generally over their nationals in Morocco as a whole and the part played by those powers in the domestic affairs of that country have been diminished and, on the other hand, the part played by most of them in the Zone of Tangier and by certain of them in the rest of Morocco has been augmented and the political status of Morocco changed, are briefly outlined in the pages that follow in this section, dealing particularly with Morocco as a protectorate. (For a discussion of extraterritoriality in Morocco, see ch. VII, under the general subject of "Extraterritoriality".)

On April 8, 1904 Great Britain and France announced by a declaration respecting Egypt and Morocco:

> The Government of the French Republic declare that they have no intention of altering the political status of Morocco.

His Britannic Majesty's Government, for their part, recognize that it appertains to France, more particularly as a Power whose dominions are coterminous for a great distance with those of Morocco, to preserve order in that country, and to provide assistance for the purpose of all administrative, economic, financial, and military reforms which it may require.

The declaration also stated (art. VIII) that the two parties recognized the interest of Spain in Morocco.

Gr. Br. Treaty Ser. no. 6 (1905), Cmd. 2384; 1 A.J.I.L. Supp. (1907) 6. See also the secret accords of Dec. 14–16, 1900 and Nov. 1, 1902 between France and Italy, Rouard de Card, *Accords secrets entre la France et l'Italie concernant le Maroc et la Lybie* (1921) 45, 47, and the agreement of Oct. 3, 1904 between France and Spain, 102 Br. & For. St. Paps. (1908–9) 432, concerning Morocco.

In 1905 the German Kaiser while on a Mediterranean cruise disembarked at Tangier and in reply to the address of welcome in his honor declared that he considered the Sultan an absolutely independent sovereign and expressed the hope that Morocco would remain "open to the peaceful rivalry of all nations, without monopoly or annexation, on the basis of absolute equality". Upon the insistence of Germany a conference was subsequently proposed by the Sultan to discuss suitable reforms to be introduced in Morocco. The conference met at Algeciras, Spain, on January 16, 1906. With the exception of Norway, all the powers signatory to the Madrid Convention of 1880 (relating to the subject of "protection" in Morocco), as well as Russia, were represented at the conference.

Ministère des Affaires Étrangères (France), *Documents diplomatiques, Affaires du Maroc*, 1901–5 (Paris, 1905), no. 234, pp. 205–206; *Conférence Internationale d'Algeciras, Procès-verbaux des séances plénières de la conférence;* 1905 For. Rel. 668.

The General Act of the International Conference of Algeciras, signed April 7, 1906, assigned to France, Spain, and Switzerland the duty of designating military officers to assist the Sultan of Morocco in establishing and maintaining in the eight ports open to commerce an adequate police force. The Diplomatic Body at Tangier was also given certain duties in these respects (arts. 3 and 8). Other reforms provided for in the act related, generally speaking, to the suppression of traffic in arms and ammunition, the establishment of a state bank, improvements in the collection of taxes and the creation of new revenues, customs matters, the repression of fraud and smuggling, public services, and public works. The act provided (arts. 102–103) that the enforcement of the regulations concerning customs and the repression of fraud and smuggling should be the exclusive concern of France and Morocco in the region bordering on Algeria, and of Spain and Morocco in the Riff and in general in the regions bordering on the Spanish possessions. Germany, Austria-Hungary, Belgium, Spain, United States, France, Great Britain, Italy, Netherlands, Portugal, Russia, and Sweden were signatories to the act. The Sultan did not sign the act but subsequently adhered to it.

In connection with its signature the United States announced (by reservation) that it had "no political interest in Morocco and no desire or purpose . . . animated it to take part in this conference other than to secure for all peoples the widest equality of trade and privilege with Morocco and to facilitate the institution of reforms in that country" and that it signed "without assuming obligation or responsibility for the enforcement thereof". In advising and consenting to the ratification of the act, the Senate of the United States (on December 12, 1906) stated, *inter alia*, that in doing so the United States had no purpose "to depart from the traditional American foreign policy which forbids participation by the United States in the settlement of political questions which are entirely European in their scope".

For the Act of Algeciras and the additional protocol of Apr. 7, 1906, see 2 Treaties, etc. (Malloy, 1910) 2157, 2181, 2183; 34 Stat. 2905, 2944, 2946; 1906 For. Rel., pt. 2, p. 1495.

The rights of the United States in Morocco are further defined by the treaty of peace and friendship of Sept. 16, 1836 (8 Stat. 484; 1 Treaties, etc. [Malloy, 1910] 1212) and by the convention as to protection of July 3, 1880, frequently referred to as the "Madrid Convention" (*ibid.* 1220; 22 Stat. 817). For the early treaty concluded in 1787 between the United States and Morocco, see 1 Treaties, etc. (Malloy, 1910) 1206; 8 Stat. 100. See also Rev. Stat., secs. 4083–4130.

On May 16, 1907, France and Spain, and Great Britain and Spain entered into simultaneous agreements for the preservation of the territorial *status quo* "in the Mediterranean and in that part of the Atlantic Ocean which washes the shores of Europe and Africa". 100 Br. & For. St. Paps. (1906–7) 570–571; 1 A.J.I.L. Supp. (1907) 425.

In an agreement of Feb. 9, 1909 between France and Germany, Germany resolved not to interfere with the "particular political interests" of France in Morocco, while France undertook to respect German economic interests in that country (102 Br. & For. St. Paps. [1908–9] 435–436; 6 A.J.I.L. Supp. [1912] 31), and in a further convention of Nov. 4, 1911 between the same countries Germany agreed not to interfere with or object to "the action of France for the purpose of lending her assistance to the Moroccan Government", including the possible "military occupation of the Moroccan territory", the possible "representation and protection of Moroccan subjects and interests abroad" by French diplomatic and consular agents, and the possible representation of His Majesty the Sultan of Morocco "before foreign representatives" in Morocco, while France declared that she was "firmly attached to the principle of commercial liberty in Morocco" and undertook not to countenance inequality in certain matters. This convention (art. 9) also envisioned the abolition of foreign consular courts in Morocco under the extraterritorial privileges enjoyed by foreign powers upon the establishment of a judiciary system "based upon the judiciary legislative regulations of the Powers interested". *Ibid.* 62, 63; 104 Br. & For. St. Paps. (1911) 948–953.

By the treaties of peace terminating the World War, Germany, Austria, and Hungary renounced their rights under the Act of Algeciras and the Franco-German agreements of 1909 and 1911 (*ante*). They also renounced their capitulatory rights in "the French Protectorate in Morocco". This result was effected in the case of Germany by articles 141–146 of the Treaty of Versailles, in the case of Austria by articles 96–101 of the Treaty of Saint-Germain-en-Laye, and in the case of Hungary by articles 80–85 of the Treaty of Trianon. 3 Treaties, etc. (Redmond, 1923) 3329, 3395–3396, 3149, 3183–3184, 3539, 3570–3571.

For information regarding the adherences of Morocco, Italy, Sweden, Great Britain, Russia, and Austria-Hungary to the convention of Nov. 4, 1911, see *Ministère des Affaires Étrangères*, (France) *Documents diplomatiques, 1912, Affaires du Maroc,* VI, 1910–12 (Paris, 1912), nos. 656 *et seq.* pp. 642 *et seq.* Belgium, Holland, and Portugal also adhered to the 1911 convention. Maxwell Blake, the Chargé d'Affaires in Tangier, to the Secretary of State (telegram) Mar. 26, 1916, MS. Department of State, file 881.00/615. For the recognition by Spain of the French protectorate in Morocco, see the treaty between France and Spain regarding Morocco signed Nov. 27, 1912, article 1 of which refers especially to the 1911 agreement between France and Germany, cited *post*, in this section, under the "Spanish Zone".

French protectorate; treaty, 1912

A French protectorate was established over Morocco by the Franco-Moroccan protectorate treaty signed at Fez on March 30, 1912. The treaty provided that there should be established in Morocco "a new régime admitting of the administrative, juridical, educational, economic, financial and military reforms which the French Government may deem useful" (art. I). It gave the French Government the right to establish such military occupation of Morocco as it might deem necessary (art. II); to have a French resident commissioner general in Morocco to exercise therein the functions of the French Government; and to be "the sole intermediary of the Sultan near foreign representatives" (art. V). France was given the control of Moroccan foreign relations, including the protection of Moroccan subjects and interests abroad, etc., and the Sultan undertook not to conclude any act of an international nature without the previous approval of France (art. VI).

On January 8, 1913 the French Ambassador in Washington communicated the text of the treaty to the Secretary of State and inquired whether the United States would give its adherence to it, and on January 22, 1913 the Secretary replied that the treaty was "not sufficiently detailed and concrete in its provisions to permit of submission to this country's treaty making power".

106 Br. & For. St. Paps. (1913) 1023 (French text); 6 A.J.I.L. Supp. (1912) 207 (English text); the French Ambassador (Jusserand) to Secretary Knox, Jan. 8, 1913, MS. Department of State, file 881.00/531; Mr. Knox to Mr. Jusserand, Jan. 22, 1913, *ibid.*; 1914 For. Rel. 905, 906.

All the signatories to the Act of Algeciras have either adhered to the Franco-Morocco protectorate treaty of 1912 or recognized the protectorate established by the treaty: Belgium adhered in Jan. 1913; the Netherlands adhered on Apr. 22, 1913; Portugal adhered in May 1913; and Great Britain adhered on Dec. 19, 1914. MS. Department of State, files 881.00/569, 881.00/558, 881.00/565; 108 Br. & For. St. Paps.(1914), pt. II, p. 185. Russia "was among the first, if not the first power to recognize this protectorate"; Spain recognized the French protectorate by the treaty signed on Nov. 27, 1912 (cited *post*, under the "Spanish Zone"); Sweden "accorded recognition to the French Protectorate" on Jan. 31, 1913; Italy recognized the protectorate on Feb. 12, 1913; and Austria-Hungary recognized the protectorate on Mar. 5, 1913. MS. Department of State, files 881.00/559, /562, /563, /567, /571, /590. As to the recognition of the protectorate by the United States, see *infra*.

On January 2, 1917 Secretary Lansing, in an informal note to the French Ambassador, reverted to the latter's notes of July 31, August 26, and October 3, 1916 regarding the recognition of the French protectorate in Morocco and said he had reached the conclusion that, owing to the pressure of business before the United States Senate, which would have to approve any treaty between the two countries on the subject, and in view of the desire of the French Government that the United States should take prompt action regarding the Moroccan situation, the best mode of procedure would be to consider separately the "question of the recognition of the Protectorate and the question of our capitulatory and other rights in Morocco, as . . . [had] been done . . . by all the European Powers in respect to their relations to Morocco". He stated that he was prepared to recognize in a formal note the French protectorate and to recommend concurrently that the item of salary for the American Minister in Morocco in the appropriation bill then pending in the Congress be changed to an item of salary for a "Diplomatic Agent" in that country. He added that there would remain for later negotiation "the question of our capitulatory and other rights in Morocco, which could be taken up in due time".

On January 15, 1917 Secretary Lansing addressed a note to Ambassador Jusserand, stating that the Government of the United States formally recognized "the establishment of the French Protectorate over the French Zone of the Sheriffian Empire". In reply, the Ambassador in a note of January 19, 1917, while expressing his appreciation of the recognition of the French protectorate in Morocco, pointed out that the protectorate established by France and Morocco under the terms of the treaty of March 1912 covered "the whole of that country" and that every power, Spain included, had recognized that the French protectorate was "coextensive with the total area of Morocco". Subsequently, on October 20, 1917, the Secretary of State addressed another note to the French Ambassador, informing him of the decision of the United States to recognize, and of its formal recognition of, the "Protectorate of France over Morocco subject to the special rights and privileges of Spain in Morocco" and subject to his informal note to the Ambassador of January 2.

> Secretary Lansing to Ambassador Jusserand, no. 1631, Jan. 2, 1917, MS. Department of State, file 881.00/631; Mr. Lansing to Mr. Jusserand, Jan. 15, 1917, *ibid.* 881.00/634; Mr. Jusserand to Mr. Lansing, Jan. 19, 1917, and Mr. Lansing to Mr. Jusserand, no. 1977, Oct. 20, 1917, *ibid.* 881.00/633; 1916 For. Rel. 800–808; 1917 For. Rel. 1093–1096.

The Franco-Moroccan protectorate treaty of March 30, 1912 stipulated in article 1:

Spanish Zone

> The Government of the Republic will come to an understanding with the Spanish Government regarding the interests which this government has in virtue of its geographical position and territorial possessions on the Moroccan coast.

Treaty of Nov. 27, 1912

In fulfilment of this obligation France concluded a treaty with Spain on November 27, 1912 recognizing that "in the Spanish zone of influence" Spain should have the right to maintain peace and to assist the Moroccan Government in introducing reforms (art.1). The treaty delimited the boundary between the Spanish and French Zones and provided for a commission to mark the boundary (arts. 2–4). It also provided that the region should remain under the civil and religious authority of the Sultan and be governed by a Calif (Khalifa)—under the supervision of a Spanish High Commissioner—to reside ordinarily at Tetuan. By the terms of article 5 Spain bound herself "not to transfer or relinquish in any manner, even temporarily, its rights as to the whole or any part of the territory composing its zone of influence". By the terms of article 19 the contracting parties reciprocally engaged to consult with each other as to "All future modifications of customs duties", and by the terms of article 22 it was provided that "Moroccan subjects who are natives of the Spanish zone of influence will be under the protection of the Spanish diplomatic and consular agents in foreign countries". It was further provided that the Spanish High Commissioner should be the only intermediary in the intercourse which the Calif might have with foreign official agents, that Spain would "see to the observance of the treaties" (art. 1), and that international agreements concluded in the future by His Shereefian Majesty would not extend to the Spanish Zone except with the previous consent of the King of Spain (art. 26).

> 106 Br. & For. St. Paps. (1913) 1023, 1025 (French texts); 6 A.J.I.L. Supp. (1912) 207, 7 A.J.I.L. Supp. (1913) 81 (English texts). The Spanish Zone in Morocco has not been recognized by the United States.
> On Apr. 28, 1913 the Spanish Legation in Tangier notified Maxwell Blake, Chargé d'Affaires of the United States in that place, that His Shereefian Majesty had chosen His Imperial Highness, Mouley Mehdi, as Calif in the

Zone of Spanish influence in Morocco "who will immediately begin to perform the functions devolving upon him in virtue of paragraphs 3 and 4 of Art. I of the Hispano-French Convention of November 27, 1912" and that "The Government of His Majesty the King of Spain, on its part, has appointed His Excellency Lieutenant-General, Don Felipe Alfau as High Commissioner of the Zone of Spanish influence in Morocco".

Mr. Blake to the Secretary of State, no. 389, May 5, 1913, MS. Department of State, file 881.00/543, enclosure 1.

In communications in 1915, 1917, and 1923, the Spanish Government requested that the United States relinquish capitulatory rights in the Spanish Zone. The United States took the position in Mar. 1923 that capitulations could only be relinquished by treaty. It suggested the settlement of certain outstanding claims of American citizens and protégés in that Zone as a necessary preliminary to formal recognition of the Zone by the United States, the question of capitulations to be considered later as a separate matter. For material on capitulations, see "Extraterritorial Jurisdiction", chapter VII.

On July 26, 1927 the Spanish Embassy indicated that it was willing to study the claims of American citizens in Spanish Morocco and requested a statement of them. Thereafter the two Governments agreed that the claims should be considered by a commission consisting of the Spanish Consul General and the American Diplomatic Agent at Tangier.

With his despatch 311 of July 12, 1928, the American Diplomatic Agent at Tangier, Maxwell Blake, submitted the joint report signed by himself and the Spanish Consul General at Tangier, Señor Antonio Pla. The Blake–Pla agreement was subsequently modified in certain particulars by the Blake–Jordana agreement of May 13, 1929. (General Jordana had succeeded Señor Pla at Tangier.) The question of claims and the recognition of the Spanish protectorate were subsequently complicated by the action of the Spanish Government in refusing to allow certain claims, and parts of claims, that had been approved by the two representatives and in conditioning their settlement upon a surrender by the United States of capitulatory rights in the Spanish Zone, as a result of which there was failure of agreement on any of the questions.

Señor Mariano Amaedo to Secretary Kellogg, July 26, 1927, MS. Department of State, file 452.11/198; Secretary Kellogg to the Spanish Ambassador, Señor Don Alejandro Padilla, Nov. 7, 1927, *ibid.* Señor Padilla to Mr. Kellogg, Feb. 11, 1928, *ibid.* file 452.11/201; the Diplomatic Agent at Tangier to the Department of State, July 12, 1928 and May 17, 1929, nos. 311 and 392, *ibid.* files 452.11/208, 452.11/217; the Ambassador in San Sebastián, Ogden H. Hammond, to the Secretary of State, no. 1338, Aug. 20, 1929, *ibid.* file 452.11/230.

For subsequent correspondence in 1930 and 1936 bearing upon the refusal of the United States to extend recognition (because of the insistence of the Spanish Government that recognition and relinquishment of capitulations be linked together as conditions precedent to the settlement of the outstanding claims), see "Extraterritorial Jurisdiction", ch. VII, § 179.

The French Ambassador, on January 16, 1916, informed the Secretary of State that under the terms of the treaty of March 30, 1912 establishing the French protectorate over the Moroccan Empire the Resident Commissioner General of the French Government (Minister of Foreign Affairs of the Sultan) was the Sultan's only intermediary with foreign representatives; that he alone had charge of all questions affecting foreigners in the Shereefian Empire; and that, as a consequence, he alone could issue exequaturs to foreign consuls. He stated, however, that the French Government had consented to waive its treaty rights in the Spanish Zone and that the Sultan had "empowered the Khalifa of Tetuan" to issue exequaturs to foreign consuls in that Zone.

> Ambassador Jusserand to Secretary Lansing, MS. Department of State, file 702.0081/1; 1916 For. Rel. 808–809.

Under articles 141–144 of the Treaty of Versailles, Germany renounced all her rights in Morocco under treaties, agreements, etc., including the Act of Algeciras, and agreed that German public property should "pass to the Maghzen without payment", while the property of German nationals might be liquidated. Subsequently, France took the position that these clauses were applicable to the whole of Morocco, including the Spanish and Tangier Zones. In 1919 France proceeded to sell former German property in Tangier at public auction, and on January 17, 1920 the Shereefian flag was hoisted over the former German Legation in Tangier. Germany protested these actions, and exchanges of notes followed between France and Germany, in which France apparently maintained her position with respect to the Tangier Zone but receded from her position with respect to the Spanish Zone, because of the fact that article 26 of the treaty of November 27, 1912 between France and Spain contained a provision that international agreements of the Sultan should come into operation in the Spanish Zone only with the previous consent of Spain, and the Treaty of Versailles did not *ipso facto* become applicable to that Zone.

> Kurt-Fritz von Graevenitz, *Die Tanger-Frage* (Berlin, 1925) 48–52. For the provisions of the Treaty of Versailles, see 3 Treaties, etc. (Redmond, 1923) 3329, 3395–3396.

Tangier Zone

When representatives of foreign powers were first received by the Sultan of Morocco, toward the end of the eighteenth century, they were not allowed to take up official residence at Fez, the sacred seat of the Shereefian court, and Tangier became the "diplomatic capitol" and place of residence of foreign diplomatic representatives. The Sultan designated a Vizier for Foreign Affairs to reside there as an intermediary between him and the foreign representatives. In 1840 the Sultan issued a *dahir* by the terms of which the representatives of the Christian powers constituting the *Conseil Sanitaire* were authorized to issue regulations regarding sanitary affairs and public health upon the coast of this Empire. The strategic position of Tangier and the circumstance that various nations have held Tangier in the past tend to explain its peculiar position as an internationalized zone.

A convention between France and Spain, signed on October 3, 1904, contained provision (in art. IX) that the city of Tangier should retain "the special character which the presence of the diplomatic corps and its municipal and sanitary institutions have given it". Article 61 of the Act of Algeciras (signed April 7, 1906) provides that the quota of tax on city buildings in Tangier "shall be turned over to the International Sanitary Council, which shall decide as to its use until the creation of a municipal organization". The Franco-Moroccan protectorate treaty of 1912 provides in article I that "the City of Tangier shall retain the distinctive characteristic for which it has been known and which will determine its municipal organization". The treaty between France and Spain regarding Morocco, signed on November 27, 1912, stipulates in article 7 that "the city of Tangier and its outskirts will be provided with a special government, which will be determined hereafter; they will form a zone included within the following described limits". The convention relative to the institution of the international municipality at Tangier, concluded by France, Spain, and Great Britain on November 5, 1914, and a Shereefian *dahir* of the same date, contained provision for an international administration for the city, but because of the World War it did not become effective.

102 Br. & For. St. Paps. (1908–9) 432, 434 (convention of Oct. 3, 1904); 2 Treaties, etc. (Malloy, 1910) 2157, 2171 and 34 Stat. 2905, 2927 (Act of Algeciras); 106 Br. & For. St. Paps. (1913) 1023 and 6 A.J.I.L. Supp. (1912) 207, 208 (treaty of Mar. 30, 1912); 7 A.J.I.L. Supp. (1913) 81, 84 and 106 Br. & For. St. Paps. (1913) 1025 (treaty of Nov. 27, 1912); Graham Stuart, *International City of Tangier* (1931) 93, 286, 296 (convention of Nov. 5, 1914).

The Tangier Zone is administered under a "Convention Regarding the Organisation of the Statute of the Tangier Zone"—generally referred to as the Statute of Tangier—signed at Paris on December 18, 1923 by Great Britain, France, and Spain, the convention being subsequently modified by an agreement signed on July 25, 1928 between the same countries and Italy. Generally speaking, under the terms of the statute of 1923, the boundaries of the Zone are determined by paragraph 2 of article 7 of the agreement of November 27, 1912 between France and Spain regarding Morocco; the "sovereign rights of His Majesty the Sultan" are recognized by article 25; the Zone is permanently neutralized and demilitarized by article 3; the "most extensive legislative and administrative powers" are delegated to the Zone by His Shereefian Majesty by article 5, except in diplomatic matters, which are reserved to France by article V of the Franco-Moroccan protectorate treaty of 1912; the protection in foreign countries of Moroccan subjects of the Tangier Zone and their interests is entrusted to France by article 6; treaties concluded by France on be- Statute, 1923 half of Morocco extend to Tangier only with the consent of the international legislative assembly of the Zone, but treaties to which all the powers signatories of the Act of Algeciras are parties apply automatically to the Zone (art. 8). Other articles deal with freedom of worship (arts. 11 and 26), the abrogation of capitulations as a result of the establishment at Tangier of the Mixed Court (arts. 13 and 48), economic equality (art. 7), and the administration of the native population by the appointed agents of the Sultan (arts. 25 and 29). Still other articles provide for the establishment of a Committee of Control, consisting of the consuls of the powers signatories of the Act of Algeciras (art. 30), for the establishment of an international legislative assembly (art. 34), and for the appointment of an administrator to carry out the decisions of the assembly and direct the international administration of the Zone (art. 35). Article 49 provides that the diplomatic agencies at Tangier shall be replaced by consulates.

> Gr. Br. Treaty Ser. no. 23 (1924), Cmd. 2203.
>
> For the text of the final protocol of the Conference for the Amendment of the Tangier Statute with Agreements and Special Provisions, together with the exchanges of notes, July 25, 1928, see Gr. Br. Treaty Ser. no. 25 (1928), Cmd. 3216, and MS. Department of State, file 881.00/1420. Prior to the conference in 1928, the United States made reservation, as it did in 1923, of its rights in Morocco and Tangier. *Ibid.* file 881.00/1385; vol. II, § 179.
>
> In 1922 the Department of State instructed the Embassy in Paris to inform the French Government that the United States had never adhered to the Franco-Moroccan protectorate treaty of Mar. 30, 1912, although it had recognized the French protectorate over Morocco, and that consequently the rights of the United States under the Act of Algeciras with regard to concessions for public works remained unimpaired by any subsequent special agreements to which it was not a party; also that—
>
> "This Government is further firmly of the opinion that the granting of an exclusive port concession at Tangier to a company a majority of whose shares are controlled by one nation, taken in conjunction with the fact that this company is granted administrative control of the port for ninety-nine (99) years, is a violation of the principle of the 'open door' established by the Act of Algeciras.
>
> "The United States Government, as a signatory of the Act of Algeciras, is unable, under the Constitution of the United States, to view with equanimity violations of that Act and, hence, has no other course open to it than to communicate with other signatory Powers with a view to taking common counsel regarding action that may be taken for the protection of the principle of the 'open door' and of the rights of the United States."
>
> The Acting Secretary of State (Phillips) to the Chargé d'Affaires (Whitehouse), no. 432, Sept. 21, 1922, MS. Department of State, file 881.156/36.

In May 1924 the British, French, and Spanish Ambassadors in the United States invited the United States to adhere to the convention of December 18, 1923. The Department of State in its replies of July 11, 1924, while not indicating a willingness to adhere to the convention, expressed a readiness to consider the possibility of suspending its extraterritorial rights in the Tangier Zone provided certain assurances were given. However satisfactory assurances were not received, with the result that, upon being notified that the statute was to become effective, the United States made "full reservation of all rights of this Government and its nationals, whether by virtue of custom or of conventional arrangement, which may be affected by any effort to bring into force the provisions of the convention of December 18, 1923".

For references to the pertinent correspondence see "Extraterritorial Jurisdiction", ch. VII, § 179.

In response to an inquiry from the Diplomatic Agent and Consul General at Tangier for instructions as to the attitude of the Government of the United States toward the furnishing of war supplies by American nationals at that place to either side in the Spanish revolution, the Department replied on July 22, 1936:

Article 3 of the Statute of Tangier would seem to prohibit the use of the Zone as a base of military operations. The Department is not in possession of sufficient facts to enable it to determine whether the refueling of the vessels in question would be in contravention of this article. It is, however, of the opinion that any repeated refueling of the Spanish war vessels in Tangier during the present uprising would be in violation of the provisions of the article.

While this Government has not accepted the Statute of Tangier and its provisions are not, therefore, applicable to American nationals, nevertheless the Department, in the interest of international cooperation for the avoidance of complications, would not be disposed to support American nationals in Tangier in any efforts to furnish supplies to either side to the present conflict, contrary to the policy adopted by the constituted authorities of the Tangier Zone.

Mr. Blake, Diplomatic Agent and Consul General, to Secretary Hull, telegram 8, July 21, 1936, and Mr. Hull to Mr. Blake, telegram 7, July 22, 1936, MS. Department of State, file 852.00/2190.

A very comprehensive review of the origin, development, and present status of the Tangier Zone is contained in a despatch dated Dec. 6, 1938 from Maxwell Blake, Diplomatic Agent and Consul General at Tangier, to the Secretary of State, no. 1405, MS. Department of State, file 881.01/50.

Tunis.—A treaty of friendship between France and Tunis signed on May 12, 1881 provided for French control of Tunisian foreign relations and for the occupation of Tunis by such French military forces as might be deemed necessary for the maintenance of order. A convention between the same countries signed on June 8, 1883 provided for the undertaking of internal reforms and for French financial assistance to Tunis, and confirmed the treaty of May 12, 1881. Turkey recognized the French protectorate of Tunis in article 120 of the unratified Treaty of Sèvres of Aug. 10, 1920 and in article 16 of the Treaty of Lausanne of July 24, 1923, and

renounced all right and title therein.   72 Br. & For. St. Paps. (1880–81)
247; 74 Br. & For. St. Paps. (1882–83) 743; Gr. Br. Treaty Ser. no. 11
(1920), Cmd. 964; *ibid.* no. 16 (1923), Cmd. 1929.   See also the convention
signed by France and the United States on Mar. 15, 1904 concerning "relations in Tunis", 33 Stat. 2263; 1 Treaties, etc. (Malloy, 1910) 544.

Annam, Cambodia, Tongking, and Laos.—As to French protectorates
over the territories of Annam, Cambodia (Cambodge), Tongking (Tonkin),
and Laos—all in Indo-China—see *Annuaire du Ministère des Colonies*
(France), *1936–1937* (Paris, 1936) 375, 387, 405, 409, 415, 421.

Andorra.—The Republic of Andorra, a small autonomous state, is under
the divided suzerainty of France and the Spanish Bishop of Urgel.

San Marino.—San Marino, a republic entirely surrounded by Italian
territory, is under the protection of Italy.

Free City of Danzig.—Articles 100–108 of the Treaty of Versailles established the Free City of Danzig under the protection of the League of Nations
Article 103 provided that a constitution for the Free City of Danzig should
be drawn up by the duly appointed representatives of the city in agreement
with the High Commissioner to be appointed by the League of Nations and
that the constitution should be placed under the guaranty of the League
By article 104 the Principal Allied and Associated Powers undertook to
negotiate a treaty, between the Polish Government and the Free City, to
come into force at the time of the establishment of the city.   One of the
objects of the treaty was to "provide that the Polish Government shall
undertake the conduct of the foreign relations of the Free City of Danzig as
well as the diplomatic protection of citizens of that city when abroad"
3 Treaties, etc. (Redmond, 1923) 3329, 3383–3386.   For the text of the
convention signed by Poland and the Free City of Danzig on Nov. 9, 1920
see 6 League of Nations Treaty Series (1921) 191.   For a discussion of the
peculiar status of the Free City of Danzig, see the Advisory Opinion of
Aug. 26, 1930 of the Permanent Court of International Justice, expressing
the opinion that the special League status of the Free City of Danzig was
not such as to enable it to become a member of the International Labor
Organization, at least until Poland had consented to certain matters in
advance.   Per. Ct. Int. Jus., Advisory Opinion, Aug. 26, 1930, Ser. B, No
18, pp. 11, 12–13; II Hudson, *World Court Reports* (1935) 669, 674, 675–676,
678.

See also the following agreements between the United States and Poland
signed on behalf of Danzig: exchange of notes according mutual unconditional most-favored-nation treatment in customs matters, Feb. 10, 1925;
declaration by which the Free City of Danzig became a "contracting party"
to the treaty of friendship, commerce, and consular rights of June 15, 1931
between the United States and Poland, Mar. 9, 1934; declaration by which
the Free City of Danzig became a contracting party to the extradition
treaty of Nov. 22, 1927 between the United States and Poland, Aug. 22,
1935; arrangement of Dec. 4, 1937 between the United States and Poland
"effecting the adherence of the Free City of Danzig to the agreement between the United States of America and Poland" concerning the mutual
recognition of ship-measurement certificates, effected by exchanges of notes
signed Jan. 17, Mar. 14, and Apr. 22, 1930, and Oct. 5, 1934.   4 Treaties
etc. (Trenwith, 1938) 4558, 4572, 4593, 4561, 4594; 48 Stat. 1507, 1680; 49
Stat. 2282; 49 Stat. 3256; Ex. Agree. Ser. 71 and 111.   On Sept. 11, 1929
the Polish Legation at Washington deposited "the adherence of the Free
City of Danzig to the Treaty for the renunciation of war, signed on August

27, 1928". Secretary Stimson to the Polish Chargé d'Affaires (Lepkowski), Sept. 11, 1929, MS. Department of State, file 711.60K12 Anti-war/19; 46 Stat. 2343; 4 Treaties, etc. (Trenwith, 1938) 5130.

Island of Cyprus.—Prior to its annexation by Great Britain on Nov. 5, 1914 (see *post* §66), the island of Cyprus was "occupied and administered" by England under the terms of article I of the convention between Great Britain and Turkey signed on June 4, 1878. 69 Br. & For. St. Paps. (1877–78) 744, 746, 769.

Article 65 of the Treaty of Lausanne (signed on July 24, 1923) contained provision for the restoration of property in Turkish territory to persons who, on Oct. 29, 1914, were Allied nationals, and article 64 of the same treaty contained provision that the term *Allied nationals* included those in a state or territory under the protection of one of the Allied states. In 1929 the Anglo-Turkish Mixed Arbitral Tribunal held that claimants who resided in Cyprus on Aug. 29, 1914, and whose property had been seized by Turkey after the outbreak of war between Turkey and Great Britain, were entitled to the benefits of articles 64 and 65 of the Treaty of Lausanne, on the ground that Cyprus constituted a "protectorate" of Great Britain on Aug. 29, 1914, within the meaning of the Lausanne Treaty. Gr. Br. Treaty Ser. no. 16 (1923), Cmd. 1929; *Parounak et Bédros Parounakian c. Gouvernement turc,* IX *Recueil des décisions des tribunaux arbitraux mixtes* (1929–30) 748, 751–753.

RIGHTS AND DUTIES OF STATES

GENERAL RIGHTS AND DUTIES

§18

On the subject of the general rights and duties of states, Stockton says:

There are certain rights and duties of a fundamental nature inherent to sovereign states. They can be classified as follows:

1. The right of independence and legal equality among other states.
2. The right of self-preservation.
3. The right of respect for the dignity and honor of the state.
4. The right of exclusive jurisdiction over its own territory.
5. The right to hold and acquire property.

These rights, to a less degree, exist in and toward states not fully sovereign.

The duties of a state corresponding to these rights require a proper observance of them in international relations, accompanied by the recognition of the obligations of good faith, a redress for wrongs, and good-will, comity, and courtesy in their intercourse.

These may be termed the rights and obligations existing in the normal times of peace. In time of war other rights and obligations arise peculiar to that state of affairs, embracing the status of belligerents and of neutrals.

Stockton, *Outlines of International Law* (1914) 97–98.

Convention
of 1933

The convention on rights and duties of states, signed by the United States and other American republics at Montevideo on December 26, 1933, provides:

ARTICLE 3

The political existence of the state is independent of recognition by the other states. Even before recognition the state has the right to defend its integrity and independence, to provide for its conservation and prosperity, and consequently to organize itself as it sees fit, to legislate upon its interests, administer its services, and to define the jurisdiction and competence of its courts.

The exercise of these rights has no other limitation than the exercise of the rights of other states according to international law.

ARTICLE 4

States are juridically equal, enjoy the same rights, and have equal capacity in their exercise. The rights of each one do not depend upon the power which it possesses to assure its exercise, but upon the simple fact of its existence as a person under international law.

ARTICLE 5

The fundamental rights of states are not susceptible of being affected in any manner whatsoever.

   .   .   .   .

ARTICLE 8

No state has the right to intervene in the internal or external affairs of another.

49 Stat. 3097, 3100; 4 Treaties, etc. (Trenwith, 1938) 4807, 4808–4809.

Equality

Among the rules of conduct prescribed for the United States by the statesmen who formulated its foreign policy, none was conceived to be more fundamental or more distinctively American than that which forbade intervention in the political affairs of other nations. The right of the government to intervene for the protection of its citizens in foreign lands and on the high seas never was doubted; nor was such action withheld in proper cases. But, warned by the spectacle of the great European struggles that had marked the attempts of nations to control one another's political destiny, the statesmen of America, believing that they had a different mission to perform, planted themselves upon the principle of the equality of nations as expounded by Grotius and other masters of international law. This principle was expressed with peculiar felicity and force by Vattel, who declared that nations inherited from nature "the same obligations and rights," that power or weakness could not in this respect produce any difference, and that a "smal republic" was "no less a sovereign state than the most powerful kingdom." The same thought was tersely phrased by Chief-Justice Marshall, in his celebrated affirmation: "No principle is more universally acknowledged than the perfect equality of nations. Russia and Geneva have equal rights." And as the Declaration of Independence proclaimed life, liberty, and the pursuit of happiness to be "inalienable rights" of individual men, so the founders of the American republic ascribed the same rights to men in their aggregate political capacity as independent nations.

Moore, *American Diplomacy* (1905) 131–132.

. . . No principle of general law is more universally as[c]-knowledged than the perfect equality of nations. All sovereign states, without respect to their relative power, are equal. Under this equality, whatever is lawful for the one is equally lawful for another and whatever is unjustifiable in one is equally so in another.

The Penza, 277 Fed. 91, 93 (E.D.N.Y., 1921).

Until the last two decades of the nineteenth century all jurists agreed that membership of the Family of Nations bestowed so-called fundamental rights on States. . . . Such rights were chiefly enumerated as the rights of existence, of self-preservation, of equality, of independence, of territorial supremacy, of holding and acquiring territory, of intercourse, and of good name and reputation. It was maintained that these fundamental rights are a matter of course and self-evident, since the Family of Nations consists of sovereign States. But no unanimity existed with regard to the number, the appellation, and the contents of these alleged fundamental rights. Hardly two text-book writers agreed on details with regard to the fundamental rights. . . . That condition of things has led to a searching criticism of the whole matter, and several writers . . . have urged, rightly, it is believed, that the notion of fundamental rights of States should totally disappear from the treatises on the Law of Nations. Yet it must be taken into consideration that under the wrong heading of fundamental rights a good many correct statements have been made for hundred of years, and that numerous real rights and duties are customarily recognised which are derived from the very membership of the Family of Nations. They are rights and duties which do not arise from international treaties between States, but which the States customarily enjoy and are subject to simply as international persons, and which they grant and receive reciprocally as members of the Family of Nations.

I Oppenheim's *International Law* (5th ed., by Lauterpacht, 1937) 217–218.

OWNERSHIP AND TRANSFER OF PROPERTY

§19

In the course of his opinion in the case of the *State of Russia* v. *National City Bank of New York et al.*, in which the court granted a motion for the substitution of the United States of America in the place of the state of Russia as plaintiff, under an assignment effected by an exchange of notes between the President of the United States and the People's Commissar for Foreign Affairs of the Union of Soviet Socialist Republics on November 16, 1933, Circuit Judge Manton said:

Right to acquire property

> The United States is in the nature of a corporate entity, and has a common-law right to acquire property. Fay v. United States, 204 F. 559 (C.C.A. 1); United States v. Rubin (D.C.) 227 F. 938. Therefore a lawful assignment to it is effective. One government may transfer property rights to another government. Hijo v. United States, 194 U.S. 315, 24 S. Ct. 727, 48 L. Ed. 994; Herrera v. United States, 222 U.S. 558, 32 S. Ct. 179, 56 L. Ed. 316.

> 69 F. (2d) 44, 47 (C.C.A. 2d., 1934).

In 1907 some 12 or 15 Japanese vessels, having crews of about 30 men each and carrying, in some instances, cannon and, so far as known, in all cases, guns, clubs, knives, and other weapons, approached the fur-seal rookeries on the Pribilof Islands and landed parties thereon who killed, skinned, and removed a number of seals from their rookeries or breeding ground, besides killing and removing a number of seals within the limits of the maritime jurisdiction of the United States. A guard, maintained by the United States for the protection of the islands, interrupted some of the marauders and, as they refused to surrender and attempted to escape with the skins of the slaughtered seals, fired upon them, killing some and wounding others. Boats discovered approaching the shore with the evident purpose of committing like depredations were fired upon by the guard and driven away, and there was reason to believe that some casualties occurred among the crews of those vessels. A certain number of the raiders surrendered to the guard, were taken prisoners, and subsequently were tried in an Alaskan court.

Defense of property rights

In an opinion dated April 15, 1908 Attorney General Bonaparte informed the Secretary of State that the guard maintained by the United States on the Pribilof Islands was justified in taking the action that it did and that the United States had undoubted property rights in the seals on those islands and was justified, as any other property-owner would be, in protecting those rights from violent invasion.

> 26 Op. Att. Gen. (1908) 587.

In connection with the proposed leasing of lands by the United States for the purpose of locating permanent monuments thereon to mark the boundary line between the United States and Canada (under article IV of the treaty signed on April 11, 1908 by the United States and Great Britain), Attorney General Wickersham informed Secretary Knox on November 30, 1910:

> There is nothing in the Constitution which prohibits the United States purchasing land within a State without the consent of the state legislature, for "undoubtedly, the United States may purchase lands within the States and build and use public structures upon them without the consent of the legislature of the State," as "the United States, being a *legal person*, is capable as any other person is to purchase and hold lands" (10 Op. 35, 38), and "payment of the purchase money for the land may be made, though the legislature of the State has not consented to the purchase." (15 Op. 212.)

28 Op. Att. Gen. (1912) 484, 485; 1 Treaties, etc. (Malloy, 1910) 815, 821.

SUCCESSION IN CASE OF UNSUCCESSFUL REVOLT

§20

In the case of the *State of Yucatan* v. *Argumedo et al.*, an action for an accounting and for a permanent injunction was brought in the New York courts against the defendant in respect to 900,000 pesos of gold allegedly removed by him from the treasury of Yucatán during a five-week period in 1915 when he was governor thereof and the State was in a condition of revolution. His government in that State was subsequently overthrown by the Carranzista forces. General Carranza's *de facto* government in Mexico was recognized by the United States on October 19, 1915. The Supreme Court of the State of New York, in granting a motion for a temporary injuction *pendente lite*, said:

> It makes no difference that the recognition followed by a few days the institution of this action, for the recognition of the Carranza government relates back to its inception; and all acts of the plaintiff government of Yucatan, such as the bringing of this action, are ratified. The plaintiff, as the recognized state government, is vested with all state property, including title to the state funds accumulated during previous *de facto* regimes and to the cause of action which accrued to the state when its funds were misappropriated. See *United States* v. *McRae*, L.R. (8 Eq. p. 69) speaking of the right of the United States to succeed to all the property of the *de facto* government of the Confederate States after the suppression of the rebellion; *United States* v. *Prioleau*, L.J. (N.S.), 35 Ch. 7; *King of the Two Sicilies* v. *Willcox*, 1 Sim. (N.S.), 301. Practically all of the cases on the right of a

state to sue proceed upon the theory that the state is continuous
and the right of action really resides in the aggregate body of the
people who are merely represented by particular governmental
organizations which may change in character or personnel.

. . .   .

Continuity of the state

. . . In the case of *The Sapphire*, 11 Wall. 164 [20 L. Ed.
127], the United States Circuit Court not only held that a suit
could be maintained in our courts by the emperor of France to
recover damages for an injury to a vessel which was the public
property of the state, but that the right to recover was not
affected by the deposition of the emperor during the pendency
of the appeal. This was on the theory that the continuity of
the state itself and its title to the property of the state is not
affected by changes in the personnel of the government. The
English law is now to the same effect. *United States* v. *Wagner*,
L.R. (2 Ch. App. 582).

92 Misc. (Sup. Ct., N.Y. Cy., spec. term, 1915) 547, 554, 555–556, 157
N.Y. Supp. 219, 225, 226.

On the subject of the continuing obligation of the state for obligations of a
previous government, see *post* §56; on the subject of the succession of states
and its effect on public debts and obligations, etc., see *post* §§ 79–82.

In the case of the *Irish Free State et al.* v. *Guaranty Safe Deposit
Co. et al.*, the Irish Free State sought to establish that it was the owner
of and entitled to the possession of approximately $2,500,000 on
deposit in the United States with the defendant. The money represented the balance of subscriptions to two loans "of an organization
which was seeking [in 1919–21] to set up by force in Ireland a republic
of Ireland, which would be free and independent of any allegiance
whatsoever to the government of Great Britain and Ireland". It
was admitted that no such republic was established. The court held
that "the British Government never recognized the De Valera organization"; that the so-called Irish Republic never existed as a
de facto government; that, consequently, the Irish Free State was not
the successor of any such *de facto* government; and that the Irish
Free State succeeded the only government in existence in Ireland at
the time it came into being, "to wit, the de jure government of Great
Britain and Ireland". The court (in dismissing the complaint of the
Irish Free State) held that since the Irish Free State "did not succeed
the revolutionary organization, but merely the de jure government in
Ireland", it had shown "no derivative title to the funds in question"

The court further held that "as the government of Great Britain and
Ireland has made no claim to the funds, the only parties entitled to the
possession of the money are the original subscribers" and a bondholder's
committee. 129 Misc. (Sup. Ct., N.Y. Cy., spec. term, 1927) 551, 553, 559,
563, 222 N.Y. Supp. 182, 202, 203.

MANDATES

GENERAL BACKGROUND

§21

By article 119 of the Treaty of Versailles, Germany renounced "in favour of the Principal Allied and Associated Powers all her rights and titles over her oversea possessions". Provision for "mandates" over those possessions was incorporated in article 22 of the Covenant of the League of Nations (pt. I of the Treaty of Versailles), reading as follows:

Treaty of Versailles, art. 119

Covenant of the League, art. 22

> To those colonies and territories which as a consequence of the late war have ceased to be under the sovereignty of the States which formerly governed them and which are inhabited by peoples not yet able to stand by themselves under the strenuous conditions of the modern world, there should be applied the principle that the well-being and development of such peoples form a sacred trust of civilisation and that securities for the performance of this trust should be embodied in this Covenant.
>
> The best method of giving practical effect to this principle is that the tutelage of such peoples should be entrusted to advanced nations who by reason of their resources, their experience or their geographical position can best undertake this responsibility, and who are willing to accept it, and that this tutelage should be exercised by them as Mandatories on behalf of the League.
>
> The character of the mandate must differ according to the stage of the development of the people, the geographical situation of the territory, its economic conditions and other similar circumstances.
>
> Certain communities formerly belonging to the Turkish Empire have reached a stage of development where their existence as independent nations can be provisionally recognised subject to the rendering of administrative advice and assistance by a Mandatory until such time as they are able to stand alone. The wishes of these communities must be a principal consideration in the selection of the Mandatory.
>
> Other peoples, especially those of Central Africa, are at such a stage that the Mandatory must be responsible for the administration of the territory under conditions which will guarantee freedom of conscience and religion, subject only to the maintenance of public order and morals, the prohibition of abuses such as the slave trade, the arms traffic and the liquor traffic, and the prevention of the establishment of fortifications or military and naval bases and of military training of the natives for other than police purposes and the defence of territory, and will also secure equal opportunities for the trade and commerce of other Members of the League.
>
> There are territories, such as South-West Africa and certain of the South Pacific Islands, which, owing to the sparseness of their population, or their small size, or their remoteness from the centres of civilisation, or their geographical contiguity to the

"A" mandates

"B" mandates

"C" mandates

territory of the Mandatory, and other circumstances, can be best administered under the laws of the Mandatory as integral portions of its territory, subject to the safeguards above mentioned in the interests of the indigenous population.

In every case of mandate, the Mandatory shall render to the Council an annual report in reference to the territory committed to its charge.

The degree of authority, control, or administration to be exercised by the Mandatory shall, if not previously agreed upon by the Members of the League, be explicitly defined in each case by the Council.

A permanent Commission shall be constituted to receive and examine the annual reports of the Mandatories and to advise the Council on all matters relating to the observance of the mandates.

3 Treaties, etc. (Redmond, 1923) 3331, 3391, 3342–3343. The United States participated in the negotiation of the Treaty of Versailles and signed but did not ratify it.

Treaty of Sèvres, 1920

In articles 94–96 of the unratified treaty of peace signed at Sèvres on August 10, 1920 by Turkey and the Allied Powers, provision was made for a mandatory regime in Syria, Mesopotamia (Iraq), and Palestine.

Treaty of Lausanne, 1923

Articles 2 and 3 of the treaty of peace signed at Lausanne on July 24, 1923 by Turkey and the Allied Powers, recited boundaries for Turkey which excluded the territories (Syria, Iraq, and Palestine) already placed under mandates, subject to the future settlement of the boundary of Iraq. No specific mention was made in the treaty of the mandatory system. Under article 16 Turkey renounced "all rights and title whatsoever over or respecting the territories situated outside the frontiers laid down" in the treaty and "the islands other than those over which her sovereignty" was recognized therein, "the future of these territories and islands being settled or to be settled by the parties concerned". Turkey undertook in article 25 to recognize the full force of the treaties of peace and additional conventions made by the other contracting powers with the Central European Powers.

Gr. Br. Treaty Ser. no. 11 (1920), Cmd. 964; ibid. no. 16 (1923), Cmd. 1929.

The mandates were divided into three categories, dependent upon their state of development and ability to conduct their affairs as indicated in article 22 of the Covenant. The "A" mandates were allocated by the Council of Ambassadors at San Remo on April 25, 1920.

Allocation

The allocation of the "B" and "C" mandates was determined by the Supreme Council of the Allies on May 7, 1919. The terms of the mandates were drawn up by the mandatory powers and approved by

..he Council of the League of Nations. The territories placed under
mandates and the powers to which they were assigned were as follows:

Territories	Mandatory powers	
"A" Mandates—		
Syria and the Lebanon	France	In the Near
Palestine and Trans-Jordan	⎫	East
Iraq (Mesopotamia) (since termina-⎬His Britannic Majesty		
ted)	⎭	
"B" Mandates—		
Ruanda-Urundi	King of the Belgians	
Part of the Cameroons	⎫	
Part of Togoland	⎬France	In Africa
Tanganyika	⎪	
Part of the Cameroons	⎬His Britannic Majesty	
Part of Togoland	⎭	
"C" Mandates—		
Territory which formerly constituted	His Britannic Majesty to be exercised	
the German Protectorate of South-	on his behalf by the Government of	
West Africa	the Union of South Africa	
All the former German islands situated		In the
in the Pacific Ocean lying north of		Pacific
the Equator (comprising the Caro-	His Majesty the Emperor of Japan	
line Islands, including Yap and the		
Pelew [or Palau] Islands, Marianne		
or Ladrone Islands [except Guam],		
and Marshall Islands)		
Former German island of Nauru	His Britannic Majesty (administered	
(Pleasant Island)	by Australia)	
The former German Colony of New	His Britannic Majesty to be exercised	
Guinea (Kaiser Wilhelm's Land,	on his behalf by the Government of	
Bismark Archipelago, and German	the Commonwealth of Australia	
Solomon Islands [Bougainville and		
Buka]) and the former German is-		
lands situated in the Pacific Ocean		
and lying south of the Equator,		
other than the islands of the Samoan		
group and the island of Nauru		
Western Samoa, former German Col-	His Britannic Majesty to be exercised	
ony of Samoa	on his behalf by the Government of	
	the Dominion of New Zealand	

League of Nations, *Official Journal* (1922) 1013, 1007, 1505, 862, 874, 886, 865, 869, 880; *ibid.* (1921) 89, 87, 93, 85, 91. Copies of the mandates with respect to Syria and the Lebanon, Palestine (and Trans-Jordan), Iraq, Ruanda-Urundi, Tanganyika, the Cameroons, Togoland, and the former German islands situated in the Pacific lying north of the equator, may also be found in 43 Stat. 1821; 44 Stat. 2184; 47 Stat. 1817; 43 Stat. 1863, 1778, 1790; 44 Stat. 2427, 2422, 2433; 42 Stat. 2149; in 4 Treaties, etc. (Trenwith 1938) 4169, 4227, 4335, 3954, 4153, 4160, 4239, 4235, 4244; and in 3 Treaties etc. (Redmond, 1923) 2723.

See the agreement of July 2, 1919 between the United Kingdom, Australia and New Zealand, vesting the administration of the island of Nauru in an administrator to be appointed for five years by the Australian Government 113 Br. & For. St. Paps. (1920) 151. For the agreement of May 30, 192 between the same parties, see 135 Br. & For. St. Paps. (1932) 248. See also the Report to the Council of the League of Nations on the Administratio of Nauru, submitted by Australia, in the respective years, particularly fo 1928, p. 3; Charteris, "The Mandate Over Nauru Island", in *British Yea Book of International Law* (1923–24) 137 *et seq.*

Pursuant to article 22 of the Covenant of the League, a Permanent Man dates Commission consisting of nine members was established by the Counc of the League on Nov. 29, 1920. Its membership was increased to ten by resolution of Sept. 8, 1927. League of Nations, *Official Journal* (Nov.– Dec. 1920) 87; *ibid.* (1927) 1120; *ibid.* (1925) 143.

"On the 12th March, 1920, the Supreme Council of the Allied Powers aske the Council of the League of Nations if the Council would be prepared t accept, in the name of the League, a Mandate for the protection of Armeni

"On the 11th April the Council of the League of Nations answered . . that the League of Nations had not the financial or the military means fo enabling it to assume an efficient protection of Armenia. Moreover, th Covenant contemplated that a Mandate would be given to States under th general supervision of the League of Nations, but not to the League Nations itself.

.   .   .   .

"On the 26th April, the Supreme Council informed the Council of th League of Nations that on the 25th April it had written to President Wilso asking if the United States would accept a Mandate for Armenia."

League of Nations, *Official Journal* (Nov.–Dec., 1920) 89–90; *ibi* (Apr.–May, 1920) 85–86; *L'Europe nouvelle*, Apr. 24, 1920, p. 514; *ibi* May 8, 1920, pp. 607–608; the Ambassador in Italy (Johnson) to Secretar Colby (from San Remo), telegrams of Apr. 25 and 28, 1920, MS. Departme of State, files 763.72119/9726 and 763.72119/9751.

On May 24, 1920 President Woodrow Wilson sent a message to Congre in which he stated: "In response to the invitation of the council at S Remo, I urgently advise and request that the Congress grant the Executi power to accept for the United States a mandate over Armenia." 59 Con Rec., pt. 7, p. 7533, May 24, 1920. On June 1, the Senate passed the fo lowing resolution as reported from the Committee on Foreign Relations:

"*Resolved by the Senate (the House of Representatives concurring),* That t Congress hereby respectfully declines to grant to the Executive the power accept a mandate over Armenia as requested in the message of the Preside dated May 24, 1920." *Ibid.* pt. 8, pp. 8073–8074, June 1, 1920, 66th Con 2d sess.

For the discussion in the Senate on the resolution, see *ibid.* 7875–7890, 7914–7920, 7960–7962, 7964–7971, 8051–8073. See also S. Doc. 281, 66th Cong., 2d sess., serial no. 7671 (Moseley's report); H. Rept. 1101, 66th Cong., 2d sess. (2 pts.), serial no. 7656 (report of the Committee on Foreign Affairs, to which was referred S. Con. Res. 27, declining to grant to the Executive the power to accept a mandate over Armenia, recommending that the resolution pass); 59 Cong. Rec., pt. 8, pp. 8156, 8459, 8579, June 1, 1920.

In 1920 the United States addressed a series of notes to Great Britain advocating an "open-door" policy in mandated territories and protesting in principle against the establishment of exclusive or monopolistic concessions in those regions. This correspondence referred particularly to economic conditions in Mesopotamia (Iraq) and Palestine, and to the so-called "San Remo oil agreement" signed by Great Britain and France on April 24, 1920, by which Great Britain conceded certain rights to France in the output of oil in Mesopotamia. In a note addressed to the British Secretary of State for Foreign Affairs on May 12, 1920, the Ambassador in Great Britain, acting under instructions from the Department of State, said: *Attitude of U. S.*

> The Government of the United States desires to point out that during the Peace negotiations at Paris leading up to the Treaty of Versailles, it consistently took the position that the future Peace of the world required that as a general principle any alien territory which should be acquired pursuant to the Treaties of Peace with the Central Powers must be held and governed in such a way as to assure equal treatment in law and in fact to the commerce of all nations. It was on account of and subject to this understanding that the United States felt itself able and willing to agree that the acquisition of certain enemy territory by the victorious powers would be consistent with the best interests of the world. The representatives of the principal Allied Powers in the discussion of the mandate principles expressed in no indefinite manner their recognition of the justice and far-sightedness of such a principle and agreed to its application to the Mandates over Turkish territory. *Equality of treatment*

The British Secretary of State for Foreign Affairs replied on August 9, 1920 that the assignment to Great Britain of the mandate for Mesopotamia "had been made and accepted subject to no friendly arrangement whatever with any Government regarding economic rights". He stated that it was far from the intention of Great Britain to establish on its own behalf any kind of monopoly in Mesopotamia and that the San Remo oil agreement aimed at no monopoly and did not exclude other interests or give exclusive rights to the mandatory power, Mesopotamia being free to develop the oil wells in any way it might deem advisable, consistent with the interests of the country. He also stated that it was the opinion of the British Government that the terms of the mandates could properly be discussed only at the Council of the League by the signatories of the Covenant.

In a note addressed to the British Secretary of State for Foreign Affairs on November 20, 1920, Secretary Colby stated that the Government of the United States was unable to concur in the last-mentioned view of the British Government. He said:

Desire to be consulted

> . . . Such powers as the Allied and Associated nations may enjoy or wield, in the determination of the governmental status of the mandated areas, accrued to them as a direct result of the war against the Central Powers. The United States, as a participant in that conflict and as a contributor to its successful issue, cannot consider any of the associated powers, the smallest no less than itself, debarred from the discussion of any of its consequences, or from participation in the rights and privileges secured under the mandates provided for in the treaties of peace

He requested that the draft mandates be communicated to the Government of the United States, as one of the powers directly interested in the terms of the mandates, for consideration before their submission to the Council of the League.

> Ambassador Davis to Lord Curzon, British Secretary of State for Foreign Affairs, no. 317, May 12, 1920 (enclosure to despatch 3061 from the Embassy in London, June 18, 1920); Ambassador Davis to Secretary Colby (telegram), Aug. 11, 1920; Mr. Colby to Mr. Davis, no. 1040, Nov. 23, 1920 MS. Department of State, files 800.6363/143, 800.6363/163, 800.6363/196a 1920 For. Rel., vol. II, pp. 651, 652, 663, 668.

In February following, the Department of State instructed the Ambassador to France to deliver to the President of the Council of the League a copy of the note of November 20, 1920 to the British Government and to request that no final decision be taken by the Council on any point touching the question of mandates until after the views of the Government of the United States had been submitted The President of the Council replied that the Council would not reach any conclusion with regard to the "A" mandates until the United States had had an opportunity to express its views and that it would defer its consideration of the "B" mandates until its next session in May or June of that year. He invited the United States in the name of the Council, to take part in the discussions in regard to "A" and "B" mandates at the forthcoming meeting, but the invitation was not accepted by the United States.

> Secretary Colby to Ambassador Wallace (telegrams) Feb. 20 and 21, 1921 President da Cunha to Secretary Colby, Mar. 1, 1921 (enclosure to despatch 2209 from the Embassy in Paris, Mar. 3, 1921): MS. Department of State files 862i.01/34, 862i.01/68; 1921 For. Rel., vol. I, pp. 88–93.

On August 4, 1921 the Department of State instructed the Ambassador in Great Britain to communicate to the British Secretary of State or Foreign Affairs a restatement of the general principles which the United States deemed to be involved in the mandate question, pointing out, *inter alia*, that there could be "no valid or effective disposition" of the overseas possessions of Germany "without the assent of the United States as one of the participants" in the victory; that the sole purpose of the United States in raising objection to the allocation or terms of mandates was "to safeguard" its "interests" and "the fair and equal opportunities" which it was believed it should enjoy in common with the other Powers"; and that since the allocation and administration of territories formerly under Turkish rule was made possible only through the victory over Germany, the United States assumed that, although it did not declare war on Turkey, there would be no disposition to discriminate against the United States or to refuse to safeguard equality of commercial opportunity in those territories. Similar instructions were sent to the Embassies in France, Italy, Belgium, and Japan.

The British Secretary of State for Foreign Affairs replied on December 22, 1921 by stating that his Government was quite willing to meet the wishes of the United States and suggesting that the British Government give the American Government certain guaranties in respect to the mandates, possibly by an exchange of notes. The French Government, on the same day, and the Belgian Government on February 11, 1922, communicated similar views to the Government of the United States.

> Secretary Hughes to Ambassador Harvey, telegram 448, Aug. 4, 1921, MS. Department of State, file 800.01M31/60; Mr. Hughes to the Ambassadors in France and Italy and the Chargé d'Affaires in Japan (telegrams), Aug. 7, 1921, *ibid.* files 800.01M31/61a, 800.01M31/61b, 800.01M31/61c; Mr. Hughes to the Embassy in Paris, telegram 415, Sept. 7, 1921, *ibid.* file 862s.01/5; Lord Curzon, British Secretary of State for Foreign Affairs, to Mr. Harvey, Dec. 22, 1921 (enclosure to despatch 811 from the Embassy in London, Dec. 23, 1921), *ibid.* 800.01M31/87; Mr. de la Rocca, for the French Minister of Foreign Affairs, to Ambassador Herrick, Dec. 22, 1921 (enclosure to despatch 1094 from the Embassy in Paris, Dec. 29, 1921), *ibid.* 800.01M31/89; Mr. Jaspar, Belgian Minister of Foreign Affairs, to Mr. Wadsworth, the American Chargé d'Affaires in Brussels, Feb. 11, 1922 (enclosure to despatch 1442 from the Embassy in Brussels, Feb. 15, 1922), *ibid.* 862s.01/7; 1921 For. Rel., vol. I, pp. 922, 925; *ibid.* vol. II, pp. 106, 111.
>
> A suggestion concerning the giving of guaranties by an exchange of notes, in respect to "A" mandates, was made a few days later by the British Foreign Office. Mr. Crowe, Under Secretary of State for Foreign Affairs, to Mr. Harvey, Dec. 29, 1921 (enclosure to despatch 831 from the Embassy in London, Dec. 30, 1921), MS. Department of State, file 867n.01/215; 1921 For. Rel., vol. II, p. 115.

On April 3, 1922 the Department of State instructed the Ambassador in Great Britain to transmit a note to the British Secretary of State for Foreign Affairs stating with respect to the mandate for

Palestine—concerning which the British Government was anxious to remove the existing uncertainties in order that a legalized civil administration might be established as early as possible—that the capitulatory rights which the United States possessed in Turkey in common with other powers rested upon the provisions of a treaty and that these rights could not be modified or abrogated except by a treaty. It was added that for these reasons alone, and apart from general considerations previously advanced by the United States, a treaty regarding the mandate would be desirable. Such a treaty, it was stated, could recite the mandate in full and "should contain appropriate undertakings on the part of His Majesty's Government for the suitable protection of the rights and interests of the United States". An instruction to the same effect with respect to the "B" mandates and embodying certain suggestions with regard to their terms was sent to the Ambassador on April 4, 1922. Similar instructions were sent to the Embassies in France and Belgium.

> Secretary Hughes to Ambassador Harvey (London), telegrams 96 and 97, Apr. 3 and 4, 1922, MS. Department of State, files 867n.01/216a 800.01M31/105b; Secretary Hughes to Ambassador Herrick (Paris), telegram 104, Apr. 4, 1922, *ibid.* 800.01M31/105c; Secretary Hughes to Ambassador Fletcher (Brussels), Apr. 6, 1922, *ibid.* 862s.01/7; Secretary Hughes to the Embassy in Paris, telegram 106, Apr. 6, 1922, *ibid.* 800.01M31/106b

"A" MANDATES

§22

Approval

On July 24, 1922 the Council of the League of Nations approved the British mandate for Palestine and the French mandate for Syria and the Lebanon, subject to certain understandings to be entered into by the Governments of France and Italy with regard to the mandate for Syria.

> League of Nations, *Official Journal* (1922) 825. France and Italy having come to an understanding on the points indicated by the Council, the mandates entered into force on Sept. 29, 1923. *Ibid.* (1923) 1355.

Syria and the Lebanon

The mandate for Syria and the Lebanon contains provisions with reference to the framing of an organic law for the mandated territory, the maintenance of troops, the ceding or leasing of land, freedom of worship, native schools, sacred shrines, taxation, commerce, the exercise of professions, freedom of transit, the development of natural resources, etc. The mandatory was given the exclusive control of the foreign relations of Syria and the Lebanon, including the diplomatic and consular protection of Syrian and Lebanese nationals outside of the territory and the right to issue exequaturs to foreign consuls within the mandated territory. Extradition treaties between

France and foreign powers were made applicable to Syria and the Lebanon pending the conclusion of special extradition agreements. Privileges and immunities of foreigners, including the benefits of consular jurisdiction and protection formerly enjoyed by capitulation or usage in the Ottoman Empire, were made inapplicable in Syria and the Lebanon, but a provision was incorporated (art. 5) for the reestablishment, under certain conditions, of these privileges at the expiration of the mandate. The mandatory is required to render an annual report to the Council of the League, and the consent of the Council is required for the modification of the terms of the mandate.

League of Nations, *Official Journal* (1922) 1013.

By the convention of April 4, 1924 between France and the United States, in which the terms of the mandate are set forth, the United States "consents to the administration" of the mandate by France, and the United States and its nationals are assured the rights and benefits secured by the mandate to states members of the League of Nations and their nationals. It is also provided, *inter alia*, that the United States shall be furnished with a "duplicate of the annual report" to be made by France and that nothing in the convention shall be affected by a modification in the terms of the mandate unless the United States shall have assented to such modification (art. 6). Agreement: France- U. S., 1924

43 Stat. 1821; 4 Treaties, etc. (Trenwith, 1938) 4169.

Prior to signing the foregoing convention, the United States inquired of the French Government (October 24, 1923) as to any agreements with regard to Syria which the latter might have entered into with a third power. In a note addressed to the French Minister of Foreign Affairs on December 18, 1923 the American Ambassador acknowledged the Foreign Minister's note of November 2 stating that the benefits of certain assurances made to Italy by France with respect to Syria and the Lebanon would be assured to the United States; he stated his assumption that the French Government would also be prepared to accord the United States and its nationals most-favored-nation treatment with respect to any other agreements relating to Syria and the Lebanon concluded by it with other governments. On this understanding, he said, it would be possible to proceed with the signing of the convention. The French Minister of Foreign Affairs replied on April 4, 1924 that his Government willingly gave that assurance. Most-favored-nation treatment

The Chargé d'Affaires (Whitehouse) to the French Minister of Foreign Affairs (Poincaré), Oct. 24, 1923; Mr. Poincaré to Ambassador Herrick, Nov. 2, 1923; Mr. Herrick to Mr. Poincaré, Dec. 18, 1923; Mr. Poincaré to Mr. Herrick, Apr. 4, 1924 (enclosures to despatch 4084 from the Embassy in Paris, Apr. 10, 1924): MS. Department of State, file 890d.01/164,/198; 1923 For. Rel., vol. II, pp. 4, 6; 1924 For. Rel., vol. I, p. 738.

Extradition treaties

The French Minister of Foreign Affairs also informed the American Ambassador (April 4, 1924) that, under the terms of article 7 of the mandate, the extradition treaties between the United States and France were applicable in Syria and the Lebanon. The Ambassador, acting under instructions from the Department of State, replied:

> In order . . . that there may be no misunderstanding with regard to the position of nationals of Syria and the Lebanon in the United States, my Government desires me to state that . . . the Government of the United States could not assure the application to such nationals in the United States of the provisions of the Extradition Treaty of 1909 [with France] in the absence of a treaty provision so providing.

Consuls

The French Minister of Foreign Affairs further assured the American Ambassador (April 4, 1924) that his Government would see no objection to the establishment, in any part of Syria and the Lebanon, of American consuls, vice consuls, and consular agents who would enjoy the treatment accorded by international custom, the consuls and vice consuls to benefit by the existing provisions of the Franco-American consular convention of 1853, it being understood that such consuls and vice consuls would be American citizens. To this the Ambassador replied:

> In order . . . that there may be no misunderstanding with regard to the position of nationals of Syria and the Lebanon in the United States, my Government desires me to state that the provisions of the Consular Convention of 1853 would not be applicable with respect to such nationals in the absence of a treaty provision specifically providing for such application . . . At the same time I take pleasure in informing you that, upon the conclusion and ratification of the mandate convention, my Government will raise no objection to the assumption by the diplomatic and consular officers of France of the protection of the interests of the nationals of Syria and the Lebanon in the United States.

> The French Minister of Foreign Affairs (Poincaré) to Ambassador Herrick, Apr. 4, 1924; Mr. Herrick to Mr. Poincaré, Apr. 4, 1924 (enclosures to despatch 4084 from the Embassy in Paris, Apr. 10, 1924): MS. Department of State, file 890d.01/198; 1924 For. Rel., vol. I, pp. 738, 740.

Boundary agreement

On October 31, 1931 the British and French Governments concluded an agreement with regard to the frontiers of Syria and the Jebel Druse on the one hand and Trans-Jordan on the other, which was approved by the Council of the League on January 30, 1932. In August 1932 the United States called to the attention of the British and French Governments the view of the United States that the transfer of territory accomplished by this agreement was legally inapplicable to the United States and its nationals until the United States had assented to the changes. The French Government replied (January 12, 1933) that it saw no objection to asking the United States to approve the new frontier without, however, prejudging the question whether there had been a modification of the terms of the mandate within the meaning of article 6 of the Franco-American convention of 1924. The British Government had made a similar reply (January 4, 1933). On May 18 following, the United States informed the two Governments that it assented to the alterations in the frontiers as set forth in the agreement.

> Consul Gilbert to Secretary Stimson, no. 235, Feb. 17, 1932; the Acting Secretary of State (Castle) to Ambassador Edge, no. 1280, Aug. 18, 1932; Mr. Castle to the Chargé d'Affaires (Atherton), no. 165, Aug. 18, 1932; Mr. Edge to Mr. Stimson, no. 3271, Jan. 19, 1933; Mr. Atherton to Mr. Stimson, no. 607, Jan. 10, 1933; the Under Secretary of State (Phillips) to the Chargé d'Affaires (Marriner), no. 1686, May 18, 1933; Mr. Phillips to Mr. Atherton, no. 513, May 18, 1933: MS. Department of State, files 790D.90i15/1, /6, /7, /13, /14, /24, /25.

A treaty of friendship and alliance was signed by France and Syria on September 9, 1936, and by France and the Lebanon on November 13, 1936, looking to the admission of Syria and the Lebanon into the League of Nations and the termination of the mandate. On August 4, 1936 the United States informed the French Government that article 6 of the convention of 1924 with France and the well-established position of the United States gave it the right to be consulted not only with respect to the termination of the French mandate over Syria and the Lebanon but also with respect to the conditions under which the territory should be administered upon the cessation of the mandatory relationship. In reply (August 25, 1936) the French Foreign Office, in addition to describing generally the nature of the agreements in negotiation, stated that their texts when ratified would be communicated to the United States. *Agreements of termination, 1936*

> The Counselor of Embassy in Páris (Wilson) to Secretary Hull, no. 57, Oct. 27, 1936, MS. Department of State, file 751.90D/66; Consul General Marriner to Secretary Hull (telegram), Nov. 13, 1936, *ibid.* 890d.01/432; Mr. Marriner to Mr. Hull, no. 112, Nov. 19, 1936, *ibid.* 890E.01/75; *L'Europe nouvelle*, Nov. 28, 1936, Supp. 48; League of Nations, *Official Journal* (1937) 287–289, 329, 333, 573–589.
>
> The Under Secretary of State (Phillips) to Ambassador Straus, no. 1440, Aug. 4, 1936, and Mr. Wilson to Mr. Hull, no. 3021, Aug. 27, 1936, MS. Department of State, files 890d.01/420A, 890d.01/423.

On November 2, 1917 Lord Balfour sent a letter to Lord Rothschild regarding the establishment of a national home in Palestine for the *Palestine*

Jewish people (since referred to as the Balfour declaration), reading as follows:

I have much pleasure in conveying to you, on behalf of His Majesty's Government, the following declaration of sympathy with Jewish Zionist aspirations which has been submitted to and approved by the Cabinet.

Balfour declaration, 1917

"His Majesty's Government view with favour the establishment in Palestine of a national home for the Jewish people, and will use their best endeavors to facilitate the achievement of this object, it being clearly understood that nothing shall be done which may prejudice the civil and religious rights of existing non-Jewish communities in Palestine or the rights and political status enjoyed by the Jews in any other country."

London *Times*, Nov. 9, 1917; 1917 For. Rel., Supp. 2, vol. I, p. 317; Handbooks Prepared Under the Direction of the Historical Section of the Foreign Office (Great Britain), no. 162, *Zionism*, p. 44; *Report of the Commission on Palestine Disturbances of August, 1929, March, 1930* (Cmd. 3530) 11. See also the joint resolution of Congress approved on Sept. 21, 1922, concerning the establishment of a national home for the Jewish people (42 Stat. 1012); H. Rept. 1038, 67th Cong., 2d sess., serial no. 7957; H. Rept. 1172, 67th Cong., 2d sess., serial no. 7959.

Terms

The British mandate for Palestine, approved by the Council of the League of Nations on July 24, 1922, stated that the Principal Allied Powers were agreed that the mandatory should be responsible for the establishment of the national Jewish home in Palestine and gave the mandatory full powers of legislation and administration of Palestine. It contained provisions for the facilitation of Jewish immigration and the acquisition of Palestinian citizenship by Jews taking up their permanent residence in Palestine and for the recognition of an appropriate Jewish agency to advise and cooperate with the administration of Palestine; and it contained other provisions generally relating to the development of the country, the protection of holy places, the freedom of worship, the raising of volunteer troops, etc. A number of sections of the mandate were similar to those contained in the French mandate for Syria and the Lebanon.

Trans-Jordan

A memorandum presented to the Council of the League of Nations by Great Britain declaring (under article 25 of the mandate) certain provisions of the mandate inapplicable to Trans-Jordan, was approved by that body on September 16, 1922.

League of Nations, *Official Journal* (1922) 823, 825, 1007, 1188, 1390.

In 1924, after some correspondence, Great Britain agreed that the convention then in negotiation between the United States and Great Britain with regard to Palestine should be applicable to Trans-Jordan, and the United States agreed that, while she should be consulted with reference to any general changes in the administration of Trans-Jordan, it was unnecessary to consult her with reference to minor administrative changes, on the understanding—which was agreed to by Great Britain—that changes which might be made in the administration of the territory would not conflict with the terms of the convention. The British Secretary of State for Foreign Affairs (MacDonald) to Ambassador Kellogg, July 17, 1924 (enclosure to despatch 606 from the Embassy in London, July 24, 1924), and Secretary Hughes to Ambassador Kellogg, no. 325, Aug. 22, 1924, MS. Department of State, file 867n.01/400; the British Foreign Office to Mr. Kellogg, Nov. 10, 1924 (enclosure to despatch 850 from the Embassy in London, Nov. 12, 1924), *ibid.* 867n.01/407.

The convention signed by the United States and Great Britain on December 3, 1924 regarding Palestine, is similar to the convention concluded in 1924 with France regarding Syria and the Lebanon, with the exception that it contains specific provision that the agreements relating to extradition and consular rights between the United States and Great Britain shall apply to the mandated territory. In view of the assurances by the British Foreign Office that the Palestine administration had every intention of treating United States consular officers in as favorable manner as the consular representatives of other states, the United States did not insist on the insertion of a stipulation to that effect in the convention with Great Britain. On July 17 and November 10, 1924 the British Foreign Office assured the American Embassy in London that American nationals in Palestine would receive most-favored-nation treatment and that any special privileges granted to subjects of any other power would automatically be accorded to American citizens in Palestine.

Agreement: U.S.–Gr. Br., 1924

44 Stat. 2184; 4 Treaties, etc. (Trenwith, 1938) 4227; the British Secretary of State for Foreign Affairs (MacDonald) to Ambassador Kellogg, July 17, 1924 (enclosure to despatch 606 from the Embassy in London, July 24, 1924), and Secretary Hughes to Ambassador Kellogg, no. 325, Aug. 22, 1924, MS. Department of State, file 867n.01/400; the British Foreign Office to Mr. Kellogg, Nov. 10, 1924 (enclosure to despatch 850 from the Embassy in London, Nov. 12, 1924), *ibid.* 867n.01/407.

In 1932 the Government of the United States took the position that any tariff privileges accorded by Great Britain, under the Import Duties Act of 1932, to Palestine should also accrue to the United States under the most-favored-nation provisions of the convention of commerce and navigation between Great Britain and the United States (signed July 3, 1815), since it considered that Palestine "is a 'foreign country' within the meaning of the term as used in Article 2 of the Convention".

Assistant Secretary of State (Rogers) to the British Chargé d'Affaires ad interim (Osborne), Aug. 27, 1932, MS. Department of State, files 641.67N3/2, 641.67N3/11; 8 Stat. 228–229; 1 Treaties, etc. (Malloy, 1910) 624, 625.

On September 1, 1928 the Council of the League of Nations adopted a resolution acknowledging that the agreement between Great Britain and Trans-Jordan, recognizing the existence of an independent gov-

Gr. Br. and Trans-Jordan, 1925

ernment in Trans-Jordan under the rule of the Amir, etc., signed on February 20, 1928, was in conformity with the principles of the mandate for Palestine, which remained fully in force.

> League of Nations, *Official Journal* (1928) 1451–1453. For the terms of the agreement, see Gr. Br. Treaty Ser. no. 7 (1930), Cmd. 3488.

Report of Palestine Royal Commission, 1937   In 1936 the British Government appointed a Royal Commission to inquire into the cause of disturbances in Palestine and into the manner in which the mandate for Palestine was being implemented in relation to the obligations of the mandatory toward the Arabs and Jews, and to make recommendations for the removal of any well-founded grievances. The commission's report, dated June 22, 1937, recommended the partition of Palestine, the termination of the mandate, the creation of a new mandate for the holy places, and the creation of independent Arab and Jewish states which should bear a treaty relationship with the mandatory, in accordance with the precedent set in Iraq and Syria.

> Parliamentary Papers (1937), Cmd. 5479.
> For the letter dated Nov. 9, 1938 from the Government of the United Kingdom to the Secretary General of the League of Nations, transmitting the report of the Palestine Partition Commission, and the statement on Palestine issued by His Majesty's Government in the United Kingdom on Nov. 9, 1938, see League of Nations, *Official Journal* (1939) 24 (Parliamentary Papers, 1938, Cmd. 5854 and Cmd. 5893).

In connection with the question of consultation with the United States in respect to any changes that might be proposed in Palestine as a result of the report of the Royal Commission, the British Foreign Office stated that it was of the view that the rights of the United States and its nationals were recited in articles 2 and 6 of the Anglo-American convention of 1924, and according to article 7 thereof "must remain intact whatever changes may be made in the Mandate for Palestine, unless the United States assent to such a change", that the consent of the United States would not therefore be required to any change in the Palestine mandate unless the specific rights in question were thereby affected, and that should any changes suggested by the British Government affect these rights, the British Government would immediately inform the United States and seek its consent thereto. The British Government also intended, it was stated, to keep the United States fully informed of any proposals it might put forward to the Council of the League for the modification of the mandate.

In reply, the United States referred to the proposal in the report of the Royal Commission to terminate the mandate for Palestine and to replace it by a treaty system and stated that its attitude set forth in correspondence with Great Britain concerning the latter's termination of its "special relations" in Iraq (*post*, this section) was fully applicable to the proposed termination of the Palestine mandate. It was explained, at the same time, that the position of the United States was "based exclusively on its obligation and purpose to provide for the protection of American interests in Palestine on a basis of equality with those of other governments and their nationals", and it was requested that any proposals in regard to the modification of the Palestine mandate should be communicated to the United States "in ample time to enable it to determine what, if any, observations it may desire to make with a view to the preservation of American rights in Palestine".

The British Foreign Office to Ambassador Bingham, July 7, 1937 (enclosure to despatch 3183 from the Embassy in London, July 8, 1937), and Secretary Hull to Ambassador Bingham, no. 1869, July 27, 1937, MS. Department of State, file 867n.01/776.

A draft mandate for Iraq was submitted by Great Britain to the Secretary General of the League of Nations on December 6, 1920. Subsequently, that Government deemed it best to determine its relations with Iraq by a special treaty of alliance, at times referred to as Iraq a treaty of "relations". Such a treaty, containing provisions with reference generally to the status of Iraq and the rendering of assistance by Great Britain to that country, was signed by the Governments of Great Britain and Iraq on October 10, 1922, and ratifications thereof were exchanged on December 19, 1924. It was provided, *inter alia*, in the treaty that the King of Iraq should himself issue exequaturs to foreign representatives in Iraq after Great Britain had agreed to their appointment, and that the treaty should remain in force for 20 years, at the end of which time it might be terminated (art. 18).

Gr. Br. Treaty Ser. no. 17 (1925), Cmd. 2370.
On Sept. 27, 1924 the British Government presented a formal communication to the Council of the League of Nations reciting the acceptance by Great Britain of a mandate for Iraq and referring to the conclusion of the treaty of alliance. In this communication Great Britain undertook, *inter alia*, for as long as the treaty was in force, the responsibility for the fulfilment by Iraq of the provisions of the treaty, assumed the obligation to make an annual report to the Council of the League, and agreed that no modifications of the treaty would be made without the consent of the Council of the League. The Council of the League, on the same day, accepted the undertakings of the British Government. League of Nations, *Official Journal* (1924) 1346–1347; MS. Department of State, file 890g.01/116; Parliamentary Papers (1925), Cmd. 2317.
On Jan. 13, 1926 the two countries signed another treaty abrogating article 18 of the treaty of 1922 and stipulating that the treaty of 1922 should remain in force for 25 years from Dec. 16, 1925, unless before that time Iraq should have become a member of the League of Nations. This treaty was approved by the Council of the League on Mar. 11, 1926. Gr. Br. Treaty Ser. no. 10 (1926), Cmd. 2662; League of Nations, *Official Journal* (1926) 503.

In 1925 the United States informed the British Government that it was not disposed to question in principle the necessity for a modification of the mandatory arrangement with reference to Iraq but that it had noted with apprehension the omission from the modified arrangement of provisions similar to those in the mandate for Syria and the Lebanon respecting the establishment of capitulations upon the termination of the mandatory arrangements and the observance of the principle of equality of opportunity in the exploitation of the natural resources of the mandated territory; that no arrangement to which it was not a party could modify its rights in Iraq by virtue of the capitulations of the Ottoman Empire; and that "American nationals should be placed on an equal footing with the nationals of any of the Allied Powers with respect to economic and other rights in Iraq".

T ripartite convention, 1930

A tripartite convention was signed on January 9, 1930, by the United States, Great Britain, and Iraq, by the terms of which the United States consented to the regime established in Iraq, and the United States and its nationals were guaranteed all the rights and benefits secured to members of the League of Nations and their nationals. It was also agreed that no modification of the special relations existing between Great Britain and Iraq—other than the termination of such special relations under article 7—should affect the rights of the United States as defined in the convention unless such change had been assented to by the latter. Under the terms of article 7 it was agreed that the convention should cease to have effect on the termination of the special relations between Great Britain and Iraq. By a protocol to the convention it was declared that there would be a suspension of the capitulatory regime in Iraq, so far as the United States was concerned, during the period of the special relations existing between Great Britain and Iraq defined in the convention; and, by an exchange of notes of the same date, Great Britain agreed to furnish the United States with duplicates of the annual reports to be made concerning the mandate.

> The Counselor of Embassy (Sterling) to Secretary Kellogg, no. 75, May 21, 1925, MS. Department of State, file 890g.01/127; 47 Stat. 1817; 4 Treaties, etc. (Trenwith, 1938) 4335.

On November 4, 1929 Great Britain announced to the League of Nations its intention to recommend Iraq for admission to membership in the League of Nations in 1932.

Treaty of alliance, 1930

On June 30, 1930 a new treaty of alliance was signed by Great Britain and Iraq, looking to the "complete freedom, equality and independence" of Iraq, Great Britain being granted certain rights in Iraq and the treaty to become operative upon the entry of Iraq into the League of Nations.

Permanent Mandates Commission, Minutes, 16th sess., p. 183; League of Nations pub. C.538.M.192.1929.VI; Gr. Br. Treaty Ser. no. 15 (1931), Cmd. 3797.

Special military, judicial, and financial agreements and a "British officials agreement" had been concluded between Great Britain and Iraq on Mar. 25, 1924. Gr. Br. Treaty Ser. no. 17 (1925), Cmd. 2370, pp. 9, 27, 34, 37. A new judicial agreement between the two countries (initialed on June 30, 1930 but not signed until March 4, 1931) approved by the Council of the League on January 22, 1931 subject to the consent of those powers whose nationals enjoyed privileges under the 1924 judicial agreement, became effective by the exchange of ratifications thereof on May 21, 1931, such consent having been given. The United States consented (June 19, 1931) to the substitution of this agreement of 1931 for the earlier agreement of 1924. Gr. Br. Treaty Ser. no. 33 (1931), Cmd. 3933; League of Nations, *Official Journal* (1931) 183, 186, 785; the Chargé d'Affaires (Atherton) to the British Secretary of State for Foreign Affairs (Henderson), June 19, 1931 (enclosure to despatch 2037 from the Embassy in London, June 19, 1931), MS. Department of State, file 741.90G9 Judicial/17.

Pursuant to the Council's resolutions of January 13, 1930 and January 22, 1931 (relating generally to the subject of the termination of mandates), the Permanent Mandates Commission of the League rendered a report in June 1931, in which it was stated that the emancipation of mandated territory should be made dependent upon two classes of preliminary conditions, namely:

(1) The existence in the territory concerned of *de facto* conditions which justify the presumption that the country has reached the stage of development at which a people has become able, in the words of Article 22 of the Covenant, "to stand by itself under the strenuous conditions of the modern world";

Termination of mandates

(2) *Certain guarantees* to be furnished by the territory desirous of emancipation to the satisfaction of the League of Nations, in whose name the mandate was conferred and has been exercised by the Mandatory.

In addition to these preliminary considerations, the Mandates Commission listed five conditions to be fulfilled before a mandated territory could be released from the mandatory regime: (a) a settled government, (b) capability of maintaining its territorial integrity and political independence, (c) ability to maintain public peace, (d) adequate financial resources, and (e) laws and a judicial organization to afford equal and regular justice to all. It was suggested in the report that the state being released from mandate should make a declaration covering the following points: (a) protection of minorities, (b) privileges and immunities of foreigners in the Near Eastern territories, including consular jurisdiction and protection, (c) interests of foreigners in judicial, civil, and criminal cases, not guaranteed by capitulations, (d) freedom of religion and exercise of religious, educational, and medical activities, (e) financial obligations regularly assumed by the former mandatory power, (f) rights legally acquired under the mandate regime, and (g) maintenance in force of international conventions to which the mandatory power acceded on behalf of the mandated territory. The report also stated that the state being released from mandate, if theretofore subject to the economic equality clause, "should consent to secure to all States Members of the League of Nations the most-favoured-nation treatment as a transitory measure on condition of reciprocity".

> League of Nations, *Official Journal* (1930) 77; *ibid.* (1931) 183; Permanent Mandates Commission, Minutes, 20th sess., pp. 228–229; League of Nations pub. C.422.M.176.1931.VI.

Report of the Permanent Mandates Commission In accordance with the resolution of the Council of the League of Nations of September 4, 1931, accepting the principles laid down by the Permanent Mandates Commission as outlined above and requesting the commission to submit its opinion on the British proposal for the emancipation of Iraq, the Permanent Mandates Commission submitted a favorable report in the fall of 1931 with reference to the termination of the British mandate for Iraq. The Council of the League on January 28, 1932 adopted a resolution noting this report and declaring itself "prepared, in principle, to pronounce the termination of the mandatory régime in Iraq" when that state should have entered into undertakings before the Council in conformity with the suggestions contained in the report of the Permanent Mandates Commission, the declaration of the termination of the mandate to be made after the examination of such undertakings on the part of Iraq and not to become effective until the date of the admission of Iraq to the League of Nations.

> League of Nations, *Official Journal* (1931) 2055–2056, 2058; Permanent Mandates Commission, Minutes, 21st sess., pp. 221–225; League of Nations pub. C.830.M.411.1931.VI; *ibid., Official Journal* (1932) 474, 479; see also despatch 244 from the Embassy in London, July 22, 1932, MS. Department of State, file 890G.01/317.

On May 19, 1932 the Council of the League of Nations approved the declaration of guaranties by Iraq and recommended that "the Powers concerned, whose nationals enjoyed capitulation rights in the former Ottoman Empire, renounce, before the admission of Iraq to the League of Nations, the maintenance of these former jurisdictional privileges in favour of their nationals in the future". On June 12 following, the Prime Minister of Iraq addressed a letter to the Secretary General of the League requesting that Iraq be admitted as a member of the League. On September 1, 1932 Great Britain informed the Secretary General that, in conformance with the Council's resolution of May 19, 1932, all the governments concerned had consented "to renounce the maintenance in Iraq, on the termination of the mandatory régime, of the capitulatory rights which they possessed in the former Ottoman Empire". Iraq was formally admitted to the League of Nations by action of the Assembly on October 3, 1932.

League of Nations, *Official Journal* (1932) 1213, 1216; the Chargé d'Affaires at London (Atherton) to Secretary Stimson, no. 244, July 22, 1932, MS. Department of State, file 890G.01/317. For the text of the declaration by the Iraq Government, see League of Nations, *Official Journal* (1932) 1347.

On the admission of Iraq to the League, see League of Nations pub. A.17.1932.VII; enclosure to despatch 336 (Political) from the Consulate at Geneva, Sept. 3, 1932, MS. Department of State, file 890G.01/325; League of Nations, *Official Journal* (1932) 1850; *ibid.*, Spec. Supp. 104, p. 48.

Although the Government of Great Britain was of the view that articles 6 and 7 of the tripartite convention of 1930 conferred no right on the United States to be consulted as to the obligations which the League might require Iraq to undertake as conditions of the termination of the mandatory regime and of her election as a member of the League of Nations, the British Foreign Office advised the United States (on April 1, 1932 in reply to an inquiry from the United States dated March 1, 1932) that she would be happy to keep it informed of the progress of events in regard to the termination of the mandatory regime in Iraq. While the Government of the United States was of the view that the rights of the United States and its nationals in Iraq would be adequately safeguarded upon the termination of the special relations between Iraq and Great Britain—under the declaration of Iraq to the Council, to the benefits of which nationals of the United States would be entitled under the terms of article 7 of the tripartite convention of 1930—it nevertheless instructed the Ambassador in London, on June 17, 1932, to bring to the attention of the appropriate authorities the following views:

. . . while the American Government concedes that by the terms of the Tripartite Convention it waived its right to consultation with respect to the actual termination of the mandate, it considers that the right was retained to be consulted with respect to the conditions under which Iraq is to be administered upon such termination. This Government is therefore of the opinion that in addition to the most-favored-nation treatment which, by virtue of the provisions of the Tripartite Convention of January 9, 1930, it will enjoy in Iraq upon the termination of the special relations, it is also entitled to a voice in the determination of the conditions upon which that most-favored-nation treatment is to be based.

Accordingly the American Government desires to make a full reservation of its position in this matter and, with a view to avoiding any possible misconception which may arise in the future, to make clear that its action in refraining from insisting upon a fulfillment of its rights in the case of Iraq is not to be construed as an abandonment of the principle established in 1921 that the approval of the United States is essential to the validity of any determination which may be reached regarding mandated territories.

> The Second Secretary of Embassy (Cox) to Mr. Baxter, British Foreign Office, Mar. 1, 1932, and Mr. Rendel, British Foreign Office, to Mr. Cox, Apr. 1, 1932 (enclosures to despatch 2716 from the Embassy in London to the Secretary of State, Apr. 5, 1932), MS. Department of State, file 890G.-01/303; the Acting Secretary of State (Castle) to Ambassador Mellon, no. 84, June 17, 1932, *ibid.*
>
> The foregoing correspondence was brought to the notice of the Permanent Mandates Commission at the request of the British Foreign Office. League of Nations, *Official Journal* (1933) 152–154; Department of State, *Press Releases*, weekly issue 162, p. 300 (Nov. 3, 1932). See also MS. Department of State, file 890G.01/351.

"B" MANDATES

§23

Terms

The terms of the "B" mandates (listed in §21, *ante*) were finally approved by the Council of the League of Nations on July 20, 1922. In each of the "B" mandates the mandatory is charged with certain responsibilities and given full powers of legislation and administration. Provisions are contained in each prohibiting the establishment of military or naval bases, the erection of fortifications, and the organization of military forces; other provisions relate to slavery, compulsory labor, traffic in arms and liquors, the transfer of land, usury, etc. Each mandatory is required to secure to all nationals of states members of the League the same rights as are enjoyed by its own nationals with respect to entry into and residence in the territory, protection, acquisition of property, exercise of professions and trades, transit, and complete economic, commercial, and industrial equality. The mandates also contain provisions with respect to the submission of annual reports by the mandatories to the Council of the League.

> League of Nations, *Official Journal* (1922) 791–793, 810, 861, 862–892. "The Council, at its meeting on July 18th [1922], approved the texts of the [B] mandates in principle, subject to formal amendments . . . entrusted to a drafting committee." *Ibid.* 793; League of Nations, pub. A6(a)1922, *Supplementary Report to the Third Assembly on the Work of the Council and on the Measures Taken to Execute the Decisions of the Assembly (July–August 1922)*, pp. 12–13.

In June and July 1922, Great Britain transmitted to the United States copies of the draft "B" mandates for Tanganyika, the Cameroons, and Togoland; France transmitted a copy of the draft mandate for the Cameroons; and Belgium transmitted a copy of the draft mandate for Ruanda-Urundi.

> *Aide-mémoire* from the British Chargé d'Affaires (Chilton) to the Secretary of State (Hughes) received June 29, 1922, MS. Department of State, file 800.01M31/125; Ambassador Herrick to Secretary Hughes, no. 2086, June

30, 1922, *ibid.* 862q.01/8; the Belgian Chargé d'Affaires (de Selys) to Secretary Hughes, July 6, 1922, *ibid.* 862S.01/10.

The United States having objected to the provisions contained in the British, French, and Belgian mandates relating to the supervision of missionaries in the mandated territories, the "B" mandates, as approved by the Council of the League on July 20, 1922, included an article similar to article II(1) of the American-Japanese convention of 1922, a provision which was expressly referred to by the United States as satisfactory in that regard.

League of Nations, *Official Journal* (1922) 810; Secretary Hughes to Ambassador Herrick, telegram 222, July 13, 1922, MS. Department of State, file 862q.01/9; Mr. Hughes to the Embassy in Belgium, telegram 15, Feb. 2, 1923, *ibid.* 862S.01/16. For subsequent correspondence containing the acquiescence of the United States with respect to these provisions, see Mr. Hughes to the Embassy in Paris, telegram 48, Feb. 1, 1923, *ibid.* 862q.01/17; Mr. Hughes to the Embassy in London, telegram 61, Mar. 21, 1923, *ibid.* 800.01M31/152. For the 1922 convention, see *post*, §24.

Treaties were signed by the United States and France on February 13, 1923, and by the United States and Belgium on April 18, 1923, conventions between the United States and Great Britain were signed on February 10, 1925, covering the French mandates for the Cameroons and Togoland, respectively, the Belgian mandate for Ruanda-Urundi, and the British mandates for the Cameroons, Tanganyika, and Togoland, respectively. By the agreements, the United States consented (subject to the terms of the respective agreements) to the administration of the mandated territories by the mandatories, and the United States and its nationals were assured all the rights and benefits secured under the terms of specified articles of the mandates to members of the League of Nations and their nationals. Other provisions of the agreements relate to the protection of vested American property rights in the mandated territories, the furnishing of duplicates of the annual reports to be made by the mandatories, and extradition treaties. Each of the agreements contains the provision that nothing therein shall be affected by any modification of the terms of the mandate unless such modification shall have been assented to by the United States.

Treaties: U.S. and the mandatories

43 Stat. 1778, 1790, 1863; 44 Stat. 2422, 2427, 2433; 4 Treaties, etc. (Trenwith, 1938) 4153, 4160, 3954, 4235, 4239, 4244.

For correspondence between the United States and Great Britain concerning the form of the preambles of the Anglo-American conventions, in which the British Government expressed the view that Germany after the entry into force of the Treaty of Versailles retained no rights in the territories under mandate which she could subsequently transfer to the United States, see Counselor Wheeler to the Secretary of State, telegram 533, Nov. 30, 1923, MS. Department of State, file 800.01M31/184; Ambassador Kellogg to the British Secretary of State for Foreign Affairs (MacDonald) no. 54, Feb. 18, 1924 (enclosure in despatch 986 from the Embassy in London, Jan. 7, 1925), *ibid.* 800.01M31/205.

"C" MANDATES

§24

Terms

The terms of the "C" mandates (listed in §21, *ante*) were approved by the Council of the League of Nations on December 17, 1920. In addition to containing provisions with respect to the fixing of boundaries, these mandates prohibit the supply of intoxicating spirits to natives, prohibit slave trade and forced labor "except for essential public works and then only for adequate remuneration", prohibit military training of natives except for internal or local police, provide that no military or naval base shall be established or fortification erected in the mandated territory, provide for freedom of worship, permit missionaries to enter and reside, permit the mandatory full power of administration and legislation over the territory, require an annual report by the mandatory to the Council of the League, and require the consent of the Council for any modification of the terms of the mandate.

Unlike the "B" mandates, the "C" mandates contain no provision for equality of economic opportunity in the mandated territories for nationals of states members of the League of Nations, nor do they contain any provision with respect to laws relating to the holding or transfer of land.

League of Nations, *Official Journal* (1921) 12, 85–94.

Island of Yap

Prior to the approval of the "C" mandates by the Council of the League, considerable correspondence took place between the United States, on the one hand, and Japan, Great Britain, France, Italy, and the Council of the League of Nations, on the other hand, concerning the disposition of the island of Yap. Briefly, the United States stated (November 9, 1920) that it was of the opinion that "for reasons vitally affecting international communications, the Supreme Council at the previous request of President Wilson, reserved for future consideration the final disposition of the Island of Yap in the hope that some agreement might be reached by the Allied and Associated Governments to place the Island under international control and thus render it available as an international cable station" and that for this reason the island of Yap was not included in the action of the Supreme Council of May 7, 1919, assigning the mandate of the former German possessions in the Pacific north of the equator to Japan. Upon receipt of replies from the British and Japanese Foreign Offices that they considered the Supreme Council's decision as definitive, the United

States pointed out that the mandate for the island of Yap had not as yet (December 4 and 6, 1920) been approved by the Council, a circumstance which admitted of the "present determination of the conditions or terms of authority, control and administration" of the island, and that it was essential that the free and unhampered use of the island for purposes of international communications should not be limited or controlled by any one power.

The Council of the League of Nations having approved the mandate on December 17, 1920, Secretary Colby addressed a note to that body (February 21, 1921) reiterating the position of the United States, stating that it could not regard itself as bound by the terms of the mandate, protesting against the Council's decision, and requesting that the question be reopened as the Council had obviously acted under a misapprehension of the facts. The President of the Council replied (March 1, 1921) that the League was concerned not with the allocation but with the administration of the mandated territories, the former being a function of the Supreme Council, and that any misunderstanding in regard to the allocation of the mandate of the island of Yap to Japan would seem to be one between the United States and Principal Allied Powers rather than between the United States and the League.

Notes were sent by the United States in April 1921 to Japan, Great Britain, France, and Italy, similar in form, repeating the position of the United States, expressing the view that neither the Supreme Council nor the League of Nations had authority to bind the United States without its consent, pointing out that the United States sought no exclusive interest in the island of Yap and had no desire "to secure any privileges without having similar privileges accorded to other Powers", and stating that it could not recognize "the validity of the mandate to Japan".

Secretary Colby to the Chargé d'Affaires (Bell), telegram 417, Nov. 9, 1920, MS. Department of State, file 862i.01/49a and also enclosures 58a, 49b, 58b; Under Secretary Davis to Mr. Bell, telegram 442, Dec. 6, 1920, ibid. files 862i.01/46a, 862i.01/59 and 862i.01/61a; Secretary Colby to the Council and President thereof, League of Nations, Feb. 21, 1921 (quoted in telegraphic instruction 107 to the Ambassador in France, Feb. 21, 1921), ibid. file 862i.01/34; President da Cunha to Secretary Colby, Mar. 1, 1921 (enclosure to despatch 2209 from the Embassy in Paris, Mar. 3, 1921), ibid. 862i.01/68; Secretary Hughes to Mr. Bell (telegram), Apr. 2, 1921, ibid. files 862i.01/46, /84a, /84b, /84c; 1921 For. Rel., vol. I, pp. 89, 93–95; 1921 For. Rel., vol. II, pp. 263–287.

A convention was signed on February 11, 1922 by the United States and Japan, by the terms of article I of which the United States consented (subject to the provisions of the convention) to the administration by Japan of all the former German islands in the Pacific lying north of the equator, and by the terms of article II of which the United States was assured certain rights in the mandated territory, including the benefits of the engagements of Japan in certain articles of the mandate. Article III assures the United States and its nationals "free access to the Island of Yap on a footing of entire equality with Japan or any other nation and their respective nationals in all that relates to the landing and operation of the existing Yap-Guam cable or of any cable which may hereafter be laid or operated by the United States or by its nationals connecting with the Island of Yap". The same article also assures the United States certain rights with respect to radio-telegraphic communication, while the succeeding article (art. IV) grants the United States and its nationals specific rights, privileges, and exemptions in relation to electrical communications.

> 42 Stat. 2149; 3 Treaties, etc. (Redmond, 1923) 2723. See also the exchanges of notes of February 11, 1922, between the two Governments concerning the treatment to be accorded nationals and vessels of the United States visiting the harbors and waters of the islands under mandate. *Ibid.* 2727–2728; MS. Department of State, files 862i.01/185, 862i.01/185a; 1922 For. Rel., vol. II, pp. 599–600.

Agreements have not been concluded by the United States with reference to the other "C" mandates.

In reply to an inquiry from the United States concerning most-favored-nation treatment of the United States in all "C" mandate territories, the British Foreign Office stated in a note of March 14, 1925 (which was formally acknowledged by the American Embassy) that the governments of the dominions were willing that an assurance be given the United States (embodied, if desired, in the form of a binding agreement) that—

> so long as the terms of the mandates remain unaltered, United States nationals and goods will be treated in all respects on a footing equal to that enjoyed by the nationals and goods of any state member of the League of Nations, with the exception of those within the British Empire, subject only to the proviso that this shall not involve the violation of any existing treaty engagements towards third parties.

> Counselor Wheeler to Lord Balfour, British Secretary of State for Foreign Affairs, no. 318, July 26, 1922 (enclosure to despatch 2473 from the Embassy in London, June 5, 1923), MS. Department of State, file 800.01M31/171; Mr. Villiers, British Foreign Office to the American Chargé d'Affaires (Sterling) Mar. 14, 1925 (enclosure to despatch 1111 from the Embassy in London, Mar. 16, 1925), *ibid.* 800.01M31/213; Secretary Kellogg to the Embassy in London, telegram 133, Apr. 25, 1925, *ibid.*

GOVERNMENTS

DISTINCTION BETWEEN THE STATE AND ITS GOVERNMENT

§25

Once a state has come into existence it continues until it is extinguished by absorption or dissolution. A government, the instrumentality through which a state functions, may change from time to time both as to form—as from a monarchy to a republic—and as to the head of the government without affecting the continuity or identity of the state as an international person.

. . . The state is a community or assemblage of men, and the government the political agency through which it acts in international relations. State of Texas v. White, 7 Wall. 700, 19 L. Ed. 227; Cherokee Nation v. Georgia, 5 Pet. 52, 8 L. Ed. 25; Foulke, International Law, vol. 1, pp. 62, 82, 102, 192. The foreign state is the true or real owner of its property, and the agency the representative of the national sovereignty. The Sapphire, supra [78 U.S. (11 Wall.) 164; 20 L. Ed. 127]; The Rogdai (D.C.) 278 F. 294.

. . . the state is perpetual, and survives the form of its government.

Lehigh Valley R. Co. v. State of Russia, 21 F. (2d) 396, 400, 401 (C.C.A. 2d, 1927).

The Government of the United States has at present no official relations with the administration now functioning in Mexico. This fact, however, does not affect the recognition of the Mexican State itself, which for years has been recognized by the United States as an "international person", as that term is understood in international practice. The existing situation simply is that there is no official intercourse between the two States.

The Acting Secretary of State (Phillips) to Attorney General Newton of the State of New York, Oct. 31, 1922, MS. Department of State, file 702.1211/1117a; 1922 For. Rel., vol. II, p. 715.

For a discussion of the nature of a state, see §§ 10 and 12. The distinction between a state and its government is also dealt with in chapter III on the subject of " Recognition ".

CLASSIFICATION

DE JURE GOVERNMENTS

§26

Henry Wheaton quotes the following definition of a *de jure* government, as distinguished from a *de facto* government:

"A *de jure* government is one which, in the opinion of the person using the phrase, ought to possess the powers of sovereignty,

> though at the time it may be deprived of them. A *de facto* government is one which is really in possession of them, although the possession may be wrongful or precarious."

I Wheaton's *Elements of International Law* (6th Eng. ed., by Keith 1929) 43.

DE FACTO GOVERNMENTS

GENERAL CHARACTERISTICS

§27

With reference to discussions concerning the proposed recognition by Great Britain of the Soviet Union, Sir Frederick Pollock, in a letter of February 4, 1924 to the London *Times*, made the following statements:

> The *de facto* Government of a given territory is that which controls the public services and performs the usual functions of political authority. This is present matter of fact. But recognition of a Government as *de facto* by a foreign Power implies the further judgment that the Government so recognised is apparently capable of maintaining itself against any adverse claims, whatever their merits may be.
>
> A *de facto* Government is also *de jure*, or in English lawful, when (1) it derives its power by regular succession under the Constitution or custom of the land, which is the most normal case; or (2) it had not a legal origin, but has acquired the consent of the governed by express ratification, such as, in our time, a popular vote, or by general acquiescence coupled with the absence of any effective adverse claim. These are often not plain matters of fact, but the subject of conflicting opinions. There may be a considerable unsettled interval, as in France between the *Ancien Regime* and the Consulate. Modern history is full of dispossessed princes and rulers claiming to be still *de jure* the heads of their States, and recognised by some foreign States and not by others. Such were the Stuarts in the 18th century, who failed after seeming to be on the point of success, and the Bourbon dynasty in France, who, two generations later, succeeded for a time after a seemingly hopeless exile.

London *Times*, Feb. 5, 1924.

De facto authorities

With reference to a communication received from an American consular officer at Veracruz, Mexico, in January 1924, referring to acts of the *"De facto* Government" at that place, the Department of State, on January 11, instructed the officer to "refer to de la Huerta faction not as 'de facto government' but as 'de facto authorities' ".

Secretary Hughes to Consul Wood (telegram), Jan. 11, 1924, MS. Department of State, file 612.112/19.

INSURGENT AND REVOLUTIONARY GOVERNMENTS

§28

By an exchange of notes dated June 2, 1914 the Governments of the United States and Great Britain agreed that they would withhold all diplomatic support from their respective citizens or subjects who claimed, directly or indirectly, any right, title, or interest in oil properties in Mexico which they had acquired subsequent to April 20, 1914, or might acquire in the future, directly or indirectly, by reason of the cancelation of contracts, leases, or other forms of conveyance, or by reason of the confiscation or taking by *de facto* authorities of properties in which American citizens or British subjects were interested, on the ground of default in contractual obligations or noncompliance with legal requirements, provided such default or noncompliance was unavoidable because of military operations or political disturbances in Mexico. The distinct understanding was expressed, however, that the agreement would not apply to any case in which failure of the American or British owner of interest in oil properties in Mexico to perform the contractual obligations or to comply with the legal requirements was not the direct result of the political unrest prevailing in Mexico at the time of default, or to any case of *bona-fide* transfer.

A similar understanding was entered into on the same date by an exchange of notes between the United States and the Netherlands.

Acts with respect to property

Oil interests: Huerta regime

> Secretary Bryan to the British Ambassador (Spring Rice), June 2, 1914, MS. Department of State, file 812.6363/95; Mr. Spring Rice to Mr. Bryan, June 2, 1914, *ibid.* 812.6363/88; 1914 For. Rel. 707–708.

On July 1, 1914 General Aguilar, Governor of the State of Veracruz, issued a decree declaring null and without legal value all the leases, concessions, and contracts celebrated during the administration of General Huerta. The Department of State instructed the American Vice Consul at Tampico on November 3, 1914 to state to the appropriate authorities that in the opinion of the Government of the United States the provisions of the decree should not be applicable to American citizens who had acquired title or interest in lands in the State of Veracruz, or had instituted or carried on proceedings looking to such acquirement during the Huerta regime, "in strict conformity with and under regularly established and applicable previously existing proceedings or acquirements", and that American citizens having interests "so incepted or acquired" should have reasonable opportunity to show proof that in acquiring such interests they had conformed to such laws. This statement, it was said, was not to be understood as applying to persons who claimed, directly or indirectly, title or interest in oil lands which they had acquired since April 20, 1914, by reason of the cancelation of contracts, leases, or other forms of conveyance or by reason of the confiscation or the taking by *de facto* authorities of interests in oil lands in which American citizens or other foreigners were interested, on the ground of default in contractual obligations or non-compliance with legal requirements, provided such default or non-compliance was unavoidable because of military operations or political disturbances in Mexico.

> Vice Consul Bevan to Secretary Bryan, no. 1190, Aug. 27, 1914, MS. Department of State, file 812.6363/132; the Acting Secretary of State (Lansing) to Mr. Bevan (telegram), Nov. 3, 1914, *ibid.* 812.6363/143; 1914 For. Rel. 711, 716.

Mining
interests:
Huerta
regime

Agreements similar in nature to those regarding the protection of their respective nationals' rights in oil interests in Mexico were made by the United States and Great Britain (June 24, 1914) and by the United States and Spain (July 2–July 6, 1914), with reference to the protection of the rights of their citizens or subjects who acquired mines, mining interests, or mining rights in Mexico subsequent to January 1, 1913.

> Secretary Bryan to the British Chargé d'Affaires (Barclay), June 24, 1914, MS. Department of State, file 812.63/7a; Mr. Barclay to Mr. Bryan, no. 207, June 24, 1914, *ibid.* 812.63/8; 1914 For. Rel. 718, 720.

On August 29, 1914 General Carranza, as first chief of the constitutionalist army "in charge of the Executive" in Mexico, issued a decree declaring null and void all matters transacted or decisions rendered since February 19, 1913 by the Departamento de Fomento and later, during the Huerta regime, by the so-called "Departamento de Agricultura y Colonización". By a circular of the Departamento de Fomento, dated September 3, 1914, an order was issued to carry out the dispositions of this decree, and all denouncements, rectifications, reductions, titles issued, and all acts executed within the mining branch by the mining agencies of the republic of Mexico or by the Departamento de Fomento were thereby declared null and void. As a matter of equity, interested persons were allowed 60 days to make application for the revalidation of proceedings or issuance of new titles. All the payments required by the mining law in connection therewith were to be made again to the then-existing government.

The Department of State, on October 16, 1914, requested the Brazilian Minister in Mexico (at that time in charge of American interests in that country) to state to the appropriate authorities that it was the view of the Government of the United States that its citizens who had acquired title or interest in mines or mining rights in Mexico, or who had instituted or carried on proceedings looking to such acquirement during the Huerta regime, in strict conformity with and under regularly established, applicable and previously existing mining laws of Mexico, should not be bound by a decree annulling such proceedings or acquirements or requiring them to make repayment of amounts payable under Mexican laws during such period, and that American citizens holding titles so incepted or acquired should have reasonable opportunity to show proof that their titles were in conformity with such laws. It was declared that this statement should not be understood as applying to persons who claimed, directly or indirectly, title or interest in mines or mining rights which they had acquired since January 1, 1913, by reason of cancelation of contracts, leases, or other forms of conveyance or by reason of the confiscation or the taking by *de facto* authorities of mines or mining rights in which American citizens or other foreigners were interested, on ground of default in contractual obligations or non-compliance with legal requirements, provided such default or non-compliance was unavoidable because of military operations or political disturbances in Mexico.

The Mexican Foreign Office informed the Brazilian Minister on October 28, 1914 that, although it was true that titles had been issued and applications had been made in accordance with preexisting laws, all decisions had been passed at the caprice of the "dictator", and for that reason such decisions had no legal value.

The Department of State further requested the Brazilian Minister on November 4, 1914 to protest again to authorities in Mexico along the lines of its communication of October 16, 1914.

The American Consul at Chihuahua reported to the Department of State on November 21, 1914 that Mr. Louis Lane, on August 26, 1913, had filed claims to 12 *pertenencias* of mineral land before the proper office in the city of Chihuahua and that he now wished to know what steps should be taken to protect his titles, in view of the Carranza decree of August 29, 1914. The Consul said that he had addressed a note to the Acting Governor of the State of Chihuahua describing Lane's case and asking what steps he should pursue to protect his interests and that the Governor had replied that he would advise Lane to comply with the Carranza decree, paying the taxes and fees in the present case to the State government, in return for which the State government would issue a receipt which would serve to protect him against the enforcement of penalties of the Carranza decree in the future. The Consul stated that, in his opinion, since the mining interests of the Republic of Mexico were exclusively under the central government and since, further, no relations were then maintained between the State of Chihuahua and the central government, the advice of the Acting Governor, if followed, would imperfectly protect Lane's rights, and that the re-paying of taxes once paid to a superior *de facto* authority, to an inferior and not coordinate authority, might come to constitute the first in a series of re-payments to a line of succeeding governments, which would amount to an intolerable hardship upon him.   The Department of State replied on December 14, 1914:

> So far as concerns the individual cases of American citizens affected by this decree, it would seem that the Department could offer them no further advice than to inform them of the above action which it has taken, and to say to them that, if they consider it advisable to attempt to comply with the provisions of the decree, under generally accepted principles of international law, they are entitled to pay taxes to persons in de facto authority.

On December 23, 1914 the Brazilian Minister in Mexico informed the Department of State that the provisional government of General Carranza had issued a decree extending the time for revalidation of mining titles from November 3, 1914 to March 31, 1915, but had left standing the regulations and penalties in the circular of September 3, 1914 containing the decree of August 29, 1914.

> The Brazilian Minister in Mexico (de Oliveira) to Secretary Bryan, telegram of Sept. 28, 1914 and no. 43 of Sept. 29, 1914, MS. Department of State, files 812.63/15, 812.63/22; Acting Secretary Lansing to Mr. de Oliveira, telegram of Oct. 16, 1914, *ibid.* 812.63/15; Mr. de Oliveira to Mr. Bryan, no. 65, Oct. 28, 1914, and no. 68, Oct. 30, 1914, *ibid.* 812.63/33,/34; Mr. Lansing to Mr. de Oliveira, telegram 313, Nov. 4, 1914, *ibid.* 812.63 /30; Consul Letcher to Mr. Bryan, no. 557, Nov. 21, 1914, *ibid.* 812.63/36; the Director of the Consular Service (Carr) to Mr. Letcher, no. 323, Dec. 14, 1914, *ibid.* 812.63/36; Mr. de Oliveira to Mr. Bryan, telegram 251, Dec. 23, 1914, *ibid.* 812.63/38; 1914 For. Rel. 718–729.

The American Vice Consul at Ensenada, Lower California, informed the Department of State on February 8, 1915 that mining titles in that district granted during the period in which General Huerta governed Mexico had been nullified by the succeeding authorities.   In reply the Department of State instructed him to inform the appropriate authorities that the Government of the United States expected that American owners of mining titles in his district "who acquired their titles in good faith and in conformity with Mexican law" should not be deprived of such titles "except upon terms of acceptable compensation and by due processes of law".

> The Director of the Consular Service (Carr) to Consul Guyant, Mar. 3, 1915, MS. Department of State, file 812.63/42; 1915 For. Rel. 892.

Title to
personal
property

The case of *O'Neill et al.* v. *Central Leather Company et al.* involved the question of the ownership of certain hides claimed by the defendant under a title based on their seizure in Mexico by insurgent forces under General Villa in November 1913, and the sale thereof in January 1914, which was subsequently approved by the Carranza regime. The Court of Errors and Appeals of New Jersey found that the United States had not recognized this regime either as the Government of Mexico or as a belligerent but that it had recognized the existence of a condition of "actual war" in Mexico between the Huerta and Carranza forces. It stated:

> The next question is whether the commander of an army in actual possession of a large territory who observes the ordinary laws of war, has the right, according to those laws, to seize private property to meet his military necessities. We need not go so far as to consider whether in the absence of government in Mexico as the president has decided, a military government under such circumstances would be entitled to be considered a *de facto* government so as to deprive us of any right to question its acts as to the property of Mexicans within the Mexican territory controlled by it. *American Banana Co.* v. *United Fruit Co.*, 213 U. S. 347. We need only inquire into the rights of parties to a war under the laws that govern that situation. These rights do not depend on the existence of belligerency in the technical sense, but on the existence of belligerency in the sense of actually existing warfare. . . . there may be a recognition of a condition of political revolt, a situation between recognition of the existence of war in a material sense and of war in a legal sense. . . . The reason[s] for permitting an armed force to levy contributions or even to confiscate property in territory occupied by them, apply as well to insurgents conducting war in a material sense as to recognized belligerents conducting war in a legal sense. The reason is the necessity of carrying on the usual operations of government and of supporting the army. . . .

> .   .   .   .

> The right to levy contributions is distinctly a conqueror's right and rests upon paramount force; it does not depend upon the recognition of belligerency with all that accompanies it, nor is its exercise limited to recognized belligerents; existing warfare and actual occupancy of the territory are the conditions necessary. Since the right exists under the laws of war, it must be exercised in accordance with those laws. It must not be confused with mere brigandage or looting. . . . In the present case the rules of war were complied with. General Villa's forces were in actual possession of Torreon, and the Laguna district. By agreement between him and the citizens, a war contribution was assessed in the district by commissions appointed by the taxpayers. An assessment was made against Martinez who as a partisan of Huerta was then in hiding. He failed to pay and his name was included in a general order to seize the property of those who refused to pay their share of the contribution. In pursuance of that order these hides were seized, and sold by General Villa. The proceedings subsequently had the approval of Carranza. We think that sale passed a title not open to inquiry in our courts.

87 N.J.L. (1915) 552, 555–558, 559, 94 Atl. 789, 791, 792.

The judgment of the Court of Errors and Appeals of New Jersey in the foregoing case was affirmed by the Supreme Court of the United States on March 11, 1918 in the case of *Oetjen* v. *Central Leather Company*, on the ground that the government of Carranza was recognized as the *de facto* government of Mexico by the Government of the

Effect of recognition

United States on October 19, 1915 and as the *de jure* government on August 31, 1917 and that "when a government which originates in revolution or revolt is recognized by the political department of our Government as the *de jure* government of the country in which it is established, such recognition is retroactive in effect and validates all the actions and conduct of the government so recognized from the commencement of its existence".

The Court said further:

> It is not necessary to consider, as the New Jersey Court did, the validity of the levy of the contribution made by the Mexican Commanding General, under rules of international law applicable to the situation, since the subject is not open to re-examination by this or any other American court.
>
> 246 U.S. (1918) 297, 302–303, 304. See also *Ricaud et al.* v. *American Metal Company, Limited*, decided the same day, wherein the Court followed the holding in *Oetjen* v. *Central Leather Company. Ibid.* 304.

In the case of *Compania Minera Ygnacio Rodriguez Ramos, S.A.* v. *Bartlesville Zinc Co. et al.* suit was brought by a Mexican corporation against the Bartlesville Zinc Company and others for damages for the conversion of 48 cars of ore allegedly taken from the plaintiff in Mexico by unknown parties and shipped to El Paso, Texas, where it was unlawfully appropriated by the defendants. The defense was that the ore had been seized and confiscated by Francisco Villa as a military necessity and had been sold to parties in Mexico from whom one of the defendants purchased it in good faith. The Supreme Court of Texas said:

> . . . Under the well-settled principles of international law, the Villa government in Mexico, although for a considerable period of time it controlled all of northern Mexico by paramount force, did not establish its legal right to rule, its acts were unlawful and are not entitled to the dignity of acts of government that the courts of a foreign nation should or can respect.
>
> It is argued by defendant in error that the Villa government exercised governmental power and was absolute over large areas of the Republic of Mexico; that, by certain acts the government of the United States recognized it as a de facto government.
>
> Belligerent rights may have been conceded to the Villa faction, and it may be conceded that his organization exercised powers of government over a very large area of Mexico. Yet that adds little to its pretensions of legality. If it had been successful, its legality would have been established, and its acts would be entitled to the respect due to another government.
>
> The recognition of the Villa faction in Mexico, as belligerents, could not be referred to as any sort of recognition of it as a government, certainly not a de jure government, and certainly not a recognition of the legality of its acts against the de jure government of Mexico, nor of the validity of its decrees and acts respecting private property. The acts of Villa in seizing private property

or by sale attempting to divest title to it in itself being an act against the de jure government of Mexico, and one violative of rights of property, it does not appear that the courts of this country are under any duty whatever to respect and give effect to such wrongful acts.

. . . the Villa faction in Mexico was vested with no legal governmental powers, never attained to any, and its acts in seizing or confiscating property were not the acts of a government, and being wrongful could not divest title.

It does appear that the acts of the agents of Villa are attributable to the Villa government and were done under its authority. We base our decision upon the holding that the acts of Villa and his agents were not the acts of a foreign government that the courts will respect, and being wrongful, no title passed to the purchaser.
We do not subscribe to the principle as announced and applied by the Court of Errors and Appeals of New Jersey in O'Neill v. Central Leather Co., 87 N.J. Law, 552, 94 Atl. 789, L.R.A. 1917A, 276, that title can be passed to private property seized by a military commander "exercising paramount force"; that the right to confiscate property "is one of the rights of the military occupant of a country." This is entirely too broad, and makes lawlessness and banditry too easy and leaves the right of property with too little or no safeguards or protection. Undoubtedly the weight of authority, and almost all authority, is to the contrary. The great law writers and jurists do not ascribe such dignity or recognition to mere paramount force. There must be something more. Paramount force must make good its right to rule, and some legitimate governmental authority must back its acts and be responsible for them. After paramount force fails, no responsibility can be placed for its acts. Where property is destroyed or taken and used under the emergencies and necessities of a belligerent in action in legitimate warfare, personal liability may not attach against the military officer taking, using, or destroying it; but certainly afterwards, if the property exists and its identity is fixed, no title has passed, but remains in the legal owner.

115 Tex. (1925) 21, 24–25, 26, 31, 275 S.W. 388, 389, 390, 392.
This case was discussed by the Supreme Court of Texas in its decision in the case of *Terrazas* v. *Holmes et al.* in which the court said in respect thereto:

"The Villa faction or government failed to make good its right to govern, failed to establish itself as a government, did not become a government, its acts fell with it, and its seizure and sale of the property passed no title. Under the principles of international law, no recognition can be given its acts as being those of a rightful or lawful government." 115 Tex. (1925) 32, 275 S.W. 392, 395.

In June 1918 the Soviet Government issued a decree expropriating sawmills and woodworking establishments and in 1919, under that decree, agents of the Government seized a mill or factory, including a quantity of wood belonging to the plaintiff, a company incorporated

Luther v. Sagor and Co.

in 1898 in Russia. In August 1920 agents of the Soviet Government sold some of the wood in question to James Sagor and Company who imported it into England where action for possession was brought by the plaintiff.

It appears from the decision of the Court of Appeal, King's Bench Division, that in April 1921 the British Foreign Office wrote to the defendant's attorneys stating that the British Government recognized the Soviet Government as the *de facto* government of Russia and that a government known as the "Provisional Government" came into power in Russia in March 1917 and was recognized by the British Government and remained in power until December 13, 1917, when it was dispersed by the Soviet authorities. In the course of his opinion Lord Justice Bankes stated that from the last-mentioned date "I think it must be accepted that the Soviet Government assumed the position of the sovereign Government and purported to act as such."

The court held that the British Government had recognized the Soviet Government as the *de facto* government of Russia existing at a date before the decree of June 1918, that therefore the validity of that decree and the sale of the wood to the defendants could not be impugned in the courts of Great Britain, and that the defendants were consequently entitled to judgment.

In the course of his opinion Lord Justice Scrutton stated:

> . . . What the Court cannot do directly it cannot in my view do indirectly. If it could not question the title of the Government of Russia to goods brought by that Government to England, it cannot indirectly question it in the hands of a purchaser from that Government by denying that the Government could confer any good title to the property. This immunity follows from recognition as a sovereign state. Should there be any government which appropriates other people's property without compensation, the remedy appears to be to refuse to recognize it as a sovereign state.
>
> *Aksionairnoye Obschestvo Dlia Mechanicheskoyi Obrabotky Diereva A. M. Luther (Company for Mechanical Woodworking, A. M. Luther)* v. *James Sagor and Company*, [1921] 3 K. B. 532, 544, 555–556.

U. S. v. Belmont

The case of *United States* v. *Belmont et al., Executors*, decided by the Supreme Court of the United States in 1937, involved a decree of the Soviet Government assuming to dissolve a Russian corporation and expropriate all its assets, including a deposit account with a bank in New York. On November 16, 1933 the Government of the United States recognized the Soviet Government and entered into an agreement with it by which amounts due it from American nationals were assigned to the United States. The Court held that, as between the United States and the depositary, the deposit belonged to the United States and stated that the effect of the recognition by the United States of the Soviet Government was "to validate, so far as this country is concerned, all acts of the Soviet Government here involved from the commencement of its existence".

> 301 U.S. (1937) 324, 330.   With respect to the contention that the public policy of the United States forbids the taking of private property without just compensation, the Court said that "the answer is that our Constitution, laws and policies have no extraterritorial operation, unless in respect of our own citizens". *Ibid.* 332.

In *MacLeod* v. *United States* action had been brought by a merchant to recover import duties paid to the United States at Manila in 1899 at the instance of the military government in the Philippine Islands. Duties on the same goods had previously been exacted by the local government when they were imported into the island of Cebu, one of the Philippine Islands not at that time under the control of the military authorities of the United States.   In holding that the duties paid at Manila should be refunded, the Supreme Court said:

Taxation

Philippine Islands, 1899

> The statement of the facts shows that the insurgent government was in actual possession of the custom-house at Cebu, with power to enforce the collection of duties there, as it did.   Such government was of the class of *de facto* governments described in 1 Moore's International Law Digest §20.

.   .   .   .

> A state of war as to third persons continued until the exchange of treaty ratifications (*Dooley* v. *United States,* 182 U. S. 222, 230), and, although rice, not being contraband of war, might have been imported (7 Moore's International Law Dig., pp. 683, 684), the authority of the military commander, until the exchange of ratifications, may have included the right to control vessels sailing from Manila to trade in the enemy's country and to penalize violations of orders in that respect.   But whatever the authority of the commander at Manila or those acting under his direction to control shipments by persons trading at Manila and in vessels sailing from there of American registration, such authority did not extend to the second collection of duties upon a cargo from a foreign port to a port occupied by a *de facto* government which had compulsorily required the payment of like duties.

> 229 U.S. (1913) 416, 428, 431–433.

On May 31, 1910, during the Nicaraguan revolution, the Department of State informed the Consul at Bluefields that the Navy Department had telegraphed to Commander Gilmer that the capture of the former customs house at the Bluff by the Madriz faction did not affect the fact that Bluefields, with certain adjacent territory for which goods hitherto passing the customs house were intended, ap-

Nicaraguan revolution, 1910

peared to remain as theretofore under the *de facto* control of the Estrada faction. The Government of the United States, therefore it was stated, admitted the right of the Estrada faction to collect customs for Bluefields and denied the right to the other faction. In as much as the Government of the United States did not recognize either faction as a government of Nicaragua but merely as in *de facto* control of portions of the country, proclamations on the part of either of them which were inconsistent with that attitude, were without effect on the United States and its citizens, it was added.

The attitude of the United States in this respect was further elaborated by the Secretary of State in telegrams to the Consuls at Bluefields and Managua, June 19, 1910, in which it was stated that the Government of the United States simply insisted that "each faction" should "collect duties only for territory under its de facto control" and refused "to permit the collection of double duties".

> The Acting Secretary of State (Wilson) to the Consulate at Bluefields (telegram), May 31, 1910, MS. Department of State, file 6369/1005A; Secretary Knox to the Consuls at Managua and Bluefields (telegrams), June 19 1910, *ibid.* files 6369/1060–A and B; 1910 For. Rel. 750, 753.

The Consul at Chihuahua, Mexico, informed the Department of State on March 23, 1912 that the provisional government of the insurrectionary forces in that place had demanded the mine taxes due to the Federal Government at the close of the month. He was instructed by the Department on March 27 following, that such taxes should be paid under protest, that the protest should be made a matter of record in each case so far as possible, and that properly authenticated receipts should be secured for all taxes paid. Americans were entitled, it was said, to pay taxes to persons in *de facto* authority. It was further stated that the Ambassador in Mexico City was being instructed to lay the matter before the Mexican Government, calling attention to the exaction of taxes by insurrectionary forces and stating that the Government of the United States would regard payment of such taxes to persons exercising *de facto* authority as completely relieving American citizens from further obligation with reference to taxes paid in that way.

> The Acting Secretary of State (Wilson) to Consul Letcher (telegram) Mar. 27, 1912, MS. Department of State, file 812.00/3353; 1912 For. Rel. 907.

The Consul at Chihuahua was further instructed on April 27, 1912 with respect to forced loans levied on American citizens by the rebel military authorities, that, bearing in mind the instructions of March 27, 1912 above referred to, he should informally protest to the appropriate persons exercising *de facto* authority in his district against all arbitrary, illegal, or confiscatory exactions made by such persons upon

American citizens or their property. In the matter of forced loans, it was said, he should distinguish between levy in the form of war taxes equally applied according to a fixed percentage among all the inhabitants of the country, whether natives or foreigners, and exactions levied arbitrarily upon only a part of the community.

On August 24, 1912 the Consul at Chihuahua informed the Department that he had been advised by the Ambassador in Mexico City that the Mexican Government would not attempt a second collection of taxes paid to rebel authorities and that the Ambassador had instructed him to advise Americans to that effect.

Secretary Knox to Consul Letcher (telegram), Apr. 27, 1912, MS. Department of State, file 312.11/285; Consul Letcher to Secretary Knox (telegram), Aug. 24, 1912, *ibid.* 812.512/6; 1912 For. Rel. 909, 910.

The Government of the United States took a similar position in subsequent cases with respect to the collection a second time of taxes, fines, customs duties, etc.:

In Mar. 1914 the United States protested when the Constitutionalist authorities were reported to be collecting back taxes from American mining companies, which had previously been paid to the central administration in Mexico. Secretary Bryan to Consul Hostetter, telegram of Mar. 16, 1914, MS. Department of State, file 812.512/211; 1914 For. Rel. 736.

In Aug. 1914 the United States protested with reference to a report that "no payment made to [an] officer of the Huerta Government [a *de facto* authority] since March 1st, 1913 is valid". Vice Consul Silliman to Secretary Bryan, telegram of Aug. 19, 1914, MS. Department of State, file 812.512/403; Mr. Bryan to Mr. Silliman, telegram of Aug. 22, 1914, *ibid.* 812.512/403; 1914 For. Rel. 756. The Mexican Foreign Office replied on Oct. 1, 1914 that proper orders had been issued that no new payments should be made on the properties of American companies involved. Secretary Bryan to the Brazilian Minister in Mexico (de Oliveira), telegram of Aug. 27, 1914, MS. Department of State, file 812.512/412; Mr. de Oliveira to Mr. Bryan, no. 52, Oct. 6, 1914, *ibid.* 812.512/468; 1914 For. Rel. 757–758.

In September 1914 the United States declined to admit that taxes might be exacted a second time where payments were made to Huerta officials when they could have been made to the Constitutionalist authorities in the territory occupied by the Constitutionalists, since it was "well nigh impossible" for Americans to determine what authorities were in control in certain sections at given times. Vice Consul Silliman to Secretary Bryan, telegram of Aug. 29, 1914, and Mr. Bryan to Mr. Silliman, telegram of Sept. 2, 1914, MS. Department of State, file 812.512/415; Mr. Silliman to Mr. Bryan, telegram of Sept. 18, 1914, *ibid.* 812.512/437; 1914 For. Rel. 757–758.

In Mar. 1915 the Department of State instructed the Consul at Mexico City to advise American citizens that they were entitled under international law "to pay taxes upon their property in Mexico to persons in *de facto* authority . . . and that . . . they would do well to consider the matter of the local control of the territory in which their properties are situated". The Director of the Consular Service (Carr) to Consul General Shanklin, no. 710, Mar. 12, 1915, MS. Department of State, file 812.512/558; 1915 For. Rel. 964.

When a fine of a million Mexican dollars was placed by General Villa upon the chamber of commerce in Monterrey, Mexico, the Department of State instructed the Consul General that it was proper to protest if the tax was "confiscatory or discriminatory" but that the United States was not justified in inquiring into the purpose of the tax or the use to be made of it, if it was levied by a competent *de facto* authority. Secretary Bryan to Consul General Hanna, telegrams of Mar. 18 and 23, 1915, MS. Department of State, file 312.115/156; 1915 For. Rel. 994–995.

In May 1915 the Department of State advised the Sierra Consolidated Mines Company that, having paid taxes upon its property located in the State of Chihuahua to the authorities exercising control in that State, it should be relieved of further payment of such taxes and protested to the Carranza Government—with reference to its mining decree of May 1, 1915—that "the United States Government does not recognize the decree referred to as having any force in the territory outside of the control of Carranza authorities or any application to American mining property located in such territory". The Assistant Secretary of State (Lansing) to the Sierra Consolidated Mines Company, May 18, 1915, MS. Department of State, file 812.512/624; the Director of the Consular Service (Carr) to the Special Agent (Silliman), May 18, 1915, *ibid.* 812.512/634; 1915 For. Rel. 915, 916.

In June 1915 the Department protested against subjecting American property in Lower California to denouncement for non-payment of taxes, when taxes had previously been paid to the *de facto* authorities at Chihuahua, Mexico. The Acting Secretary of State (Osborne) to Consul Guyant, no. 226, June 21, 1915, MS. Department of State, file 812.512/676; 1915 For. Rel. 973.

In May 1916, with reference to a report that the local collector for the Carranza regime had declared that taxes paid to the previous *de facto* authorities must be paid again, the Consul at Nogales, Mexico, was instructed to advise the appropriate authorities that Americans were entitled to be relieved from further obligations with respect to such taxes. The Director of the Consular Service (Carr) to Consul Simpich, no. 553, May 19, 1916, MS. Department of State, file 812.512/1197; 1916 For. Rel. 720.

When the Mexican Government issued a decree in April 1920 closing Sonora ports on the border, the Department of State took the position that "American citizens are entitled to pay customs duties to persons exercising *de facto* authority in that state and having made such payment to be free from further obligations in the matter". Secretary Colby to Ambassador Fletcher, telegram 121, Apr. 22, 1920, MS. Department of State, file 612.1123/196.

Where export taxes were demanded in advance by the Peláez forces in *de facto* control of Port Lobos, the American Consul at Tampico was advised by the Department of State that Americans affected were entitled to pay customs duties and taxes to those in *de facto* authority and, having paid them, to be free from further obligations in the matter but that they must decide for themselves whether they would pay taxes in advance. Consul Dawson to Secretary Colby, telegram of May 5, 1920, and Mr. Colby to Mr. Dawson, telegram of May 8, 1920, MS. Department of State, file 812.6363/673; 1920 For. Rel., vol. III, p. 162.

Replying to the report of a consul that rebel forces in Sonora, Mexico, were exacting forced loans and payments from American citizens in his district under the guise of one kind of tax or another, the Department of State, on March 29, 1929, after stating that international law recognizes the right of *de facto* authorities actually in control of areas either by revolt or by occupation to compel obedience to their demands, instructed him to—

> protest orally to the appropriate persons now exercising *de facto* authority in your district, first, against the payment of all taxes to insurrectionary authorities by American citizens on the ground that such payment is not in accordance with local law, thus giving basis for the protest of the taxpayers themselves; second, and particularly, and on the additional ground of unfair discrimination, you will orally protest against all arbitrary or confiscatory exactions levied against American property or upon American citizens, when the levy in whatever form, whether as war or other taxes, or as "forced loans" or other similar measures or contributions, is not equally applied according to a fixed percentage amongst all the inhabitants, whether natives or foreigners, but is applied arbitrarily upon that part only of the community which includes Americans.

Forced loans

In an instruction of the same date to the Ambassador in Mexico, the Department, after quoting the above instructions to the consul, said that—

Finality of payments

> you will bring the foregoing regarding . . . taxes to the attention of the Mexican Government and will state that the Government of the United States will regard payments of taxes of all kinds, made to *de facto* authorities in control of certain disturbed areas in Mexico under the circumstances set out in the telegrams, as constituting a due and proper payment of such taxes in the amounts paid and as completely relieving American citizens so paying such taxes from any and all further obligation in regard to such payment.

In reply to a report from a consul that Mexican Federal officers were taking steps to enforce re-payment to the Federal Government of taxes already paid to the rebel leaders, the Department on May 3, 1929 stated that it was instructing the Ambassador in Mexico to protest to the Mexican Government. On May 8, 1929 the Department instructed the Ambassador as follows:

> International law and custom governing this question is so clearly recognized that it is difficult to understand the seeming insistence of local Mexican authorities in running contrary thereto. In taking the position that taxes and customs paid to *de facto* authorities in control of an area (whether they be rebel authorities or authorities of a foreign country) must be considered as if they were paid to the regular authorities of a country, this Government is not invoking a principle that has not been recognized by itself. In the celebrated Castine case which arose out of the occupation by British troops of the port of Castine in Maine, the Supreme Court of the United States itself held that

Castine, Maine

goods imported into Castine during its occupation by British troops were not subject to payment of customs duties under the laws of the United States after the British withdrew, and the United States resumed the exercise of its sovereignty which, during British occupation, had been suspended. (See *United States* v. *Rice*, 4 Wheaton, p. 246.)

Mr. Fish, Secretary of State, commenting upon the demand by the Mexican authorities for duty on goods imported into Mazatlán while that port was in the occupation of insurgents stated as to the practice of the United States that "since the close of the Civil War in this country suits have been brough' against importers for duties on merchandise paid to insurgen' authorities. Those suits, however, have been discontinued, tha' proceeding probably having been influenced by the judgment o' the Supreme Court adverted to," that is, the judgment of the Supreme Court in the Castine case noted above. (I Moore' *Digest*, p. 41 *et seq.*, particularly p. 49.)

This Government confidently expects that the Mexican authorities will recognize this principle. It is no fault of Americans in Mexico that the regular constituted Mexican Government may not have been able at certain times and in given areas to enforce its own power and collect its own taxes, nor to protect American from the imposition of taxes and other duties by rebels, and therefore Americans, who were in no wise responsible for th' conditions in such areas, must not now be punished for th' forced payment by them of taxes to rebels because of this inabilit' of the regular Mexican authorities to protect them against such payment.

Secretary Stimson to Consul Damm, telegram of Mar. 29, 1929, MS Department of State, file 812.00 Sonora/463; Secretary Stimson to Ambassador Morrow, telegram 217, Mar. 29, 1929, *ibid.* 812.00 Sonora/465 Mr. Morrow to Mr. Stimson, telegram 175, Apr. 1, 1929, *ibid.* 812.0 Sonora/477; Mr. Stimson to Mr. Damm, telegram of May 3, 1929, *ibia* 812.512/3495; Mr. Stimson to Mr. Morrow, telegram 361, May 8, 192' *ibid.* 812.512/3501a.

On October 23, 1912 the Department of State telegraphed to th' Chargé d'Affaires in Mexico saying that the Consul at Veracruz ha' been informed that the port of Veracruz had been closed by order o' the Federal Government under section 6 of the customs regulation' The Chargé was instructed to inform the Mexican Government tha' the Department understood that insurrectionary forces had take' and were then in possession of Veracruz and to communicate to th' Mexican Foreign Office the following position of the United State' with reference to the closure, by mere executive or legislative act, o' Mexican ports held by insurgents:

Closure of port held by insurgents

As a general principle a decree by a sovereign power closing t' neutral commerce ports held by its enemies, whether foreign c' domestic, can have no international validity and no extra' territorial effect in the direction of imposing any obligation upo' the governments of neutral powers to recognize it or to contribut' toward its enforcement by any domestic action on their part. If the sovereign decreeing such a closure have a naval force sufficient to maintain an effective blockade and if he duly proclaim and maintain such a blockade, then he may seize, subject to the adjudication of a prize court, vessels which may attempt to run the blockade. But his decree or acts closing ports which are held adversely to him are by themselves entitled to no international respect. The Government of the United States must therefore regard as utterly nugatory such decrees or acts closing ports which the United States of Mexico do not possess, unless such proclamations are enforced by an effective blockade.

The Acting Secretary of State (Wilson) to Mr. Schuyler, MS. Department of State, file 612.1123/5; 1912 For. Rel. 901.

On June 17, 1914 the Spanish Ambassador inquired of the Department of State as to the right of consular officers of a Mexican revolutionary party to exercise, in the United States, functions of an international character, such as the clearance of vessels. Replying on June 26, 1914, the Department said that "the Government of the United States has not recognized the belligerency of the Mexican faction above-mentioned nor, of course, has it extended any recognition to persons claiming to be Consular representatives of that faction". In a further communication of July 31, 1914, the Department said:

Consular officers

. . . I have the honor to call to your attention the fact that the constitutionalist party in Mexico, to the reputed consular agents of which in the United States you referred, is in possession of some at least of the ports of Mexico, and, therefore, has the power to prescribe the conditions upon which foreign commerce can be carried on with these ports. Presumably one of the conditions imposed is that the formal documents of vessels coming to those ports from abroad must be certified to by a consular agent of the party in control of the ports, and apparently if such certification were prohibited in the United States, it would result in the discontinuance of commerce between this country and those ports of Mexico. It is not believed that the maritime nations of the world would consider such a result as desirable.

In any event, the Department is not aware of any effective measures which it could take under the laws of the United States to prohibit the exercise of the consular acts above-mentioned.

Ambassador Riaño to the Secretary of State (Bryan), June 17, 1914, and the Assistant Secretary of State (Osborne) to Ambassador Riaño, no. 305, June 26, 1914, MS. Department of State, file 702.1211/421; Mr. Bryan to Señor Riaño, July 31, 1914, *ibid.* 702.1211/424.

In response to a request for information regarding the payment of invoice fees on shipments of merchandise destined to Mexican east-coast ports during the Provisional Government of de la Huerta, the Department of State, on May 26, 1920, wrote that—

> according to the Department's information, American exporters at Laredo, Eagle Pass, El Paso, and Nogales are paying consular and other fees to commercial agents of the *de facto* authority now actually functioning in Mexico. The Department's information also indicates that exports are moving freely through the ports above mentioned.

Commercial agents

> However, this Government has not recognized the *de facto* authority mentioned or its so-called commercial agents now stationed at various places in the United States, and for that reason, it is felt that the matter of clearing vessels destined to Mexican ports with or without consular service, as well as the question of payment of consular fees to such commercial agents, must be left to the judgment of individual exporters or to the owners of vessels, as the case may be.

Secretary Polk to the J. A. Medina Company, MS. Department of State, file 612.119/2862; 1920 For. Rel., vol. III, p. 168.

MILITARY GOVERNMENTS

§29

General nature

Mr. Justice Day, in delivering the opinion of the United States Supreme Court in the case of *MacLeod* v. *United States*, said:

Philippine Islands, 1898

> When the Spanish fleet was destroyed at Manila, May 1, 1898, it became apparent that the Government of the United States might be required to take the necessary steps to make provision for the government and control of such part of the Philippines as might come into the military occupation of the forces of the United States. The right to thus occupy an enemy's country and temporarily provide for its government has been recognized by previous action of the executive authority and sanctioned by frequent decisions of this court. The local government being destroyed, the conqueror may set up its own authority and make rules and regulations for the conduct of temporary government, and to that end may collect taxes and duties to support the military authority and carry on operations incident to the occupation. Such was the course of the Government with respect to the territory acquired by conquest and afterwards ceded by the Mexican Government to the United States. *Cross* v. *Harrison*, 16 How. 164. See also in this connection *Fleming* v. *Page*, 9 How. 603; *New Orleans* v. *Steamship Co.*, 20 Wall. 387; *Dooley* v. *United States*, 182 U.S. 222; 7 Moore's International Law Digest, §§ 1143 *et seq.*, in which the history of this Government's action following the Mexican War and during and after the Spanish-American War is fully set forth, as well as Taylor on International Public Law, chapter IX, Military Occupation and Administration, §§ 568 *et seq.*, and 2 Oppenheim on International Law, §§ 166 *et seq.*

There has been considerable discussion in the cases and in works of authoritative writers upon the subject of what constitutes an occupation which will give the right to exercise governmental authority. Such occupation is not merely invasion, but is invasion plus possession of the enemy's country for the purpose of holding it temporarily at least. 2 Oppenheim, § 167. What should constitute military occupation was one of the matters before The Hague Convention in 1899 respecting laws and customs of war on land, and the following articles were adopted by the nations giving adherence to that Convention, among which is the United States (32 Stat. II, 1821):

" Article XLII. Territory is considered occupied when it is actually placed under the authority of the hostile army.

"The occupation applies only to the territory where such authority is established, and in a position to assert itself.

"Article XLIII. The authority of the legitimate power having actually passed into the hands of the occupant, the latter shall take all steps in his power to reestablish and insure, as far as possible, public order and safety, while respecting, unless absolutely prevented, the laws in force in the country."

229 U.S. (1913) 416, 424–426.

It is unquestioned that upon the occupation by our military forces of the port of Manila it was their duty to respect and assist in enforcing the municipal laws then in force there until the same might be changed by order of the military commander, called for by the necessities of war. (Hall's International Law, 4th ed., sec. 155; Taylor's International Law, secs. 576, 578.)

The commander of our forces had the right to take possession of the machinery for the collection of the revenues within the occupied district, and to make such collections. (Hall's International Law, sec. 158; Taylor's International Law, sec. 531.) It was therefore well within the authority of General Merritt to make the order he did, continuing the Spanish tariff in force at that port until the same might be changed by higher military authority.

While our occupation of Manila became permanent by subsequent treaty, our possession at the time of the collection of these duties was temporary only, and in point of law was no different from the usual military occupation of belligerent territory. It was foreign territory in our temporary possession, and during such possession we were exercising there the restricted rights of a belligerent. . . .

For all practical purposes it was foreign territory, and our military forces there were governing under the rules of international law, and in a sense legislating under such rules until receiving notice of different legislation by a superior power. It was a government *de facto*, military in character, and subject only to higher military authority actually put in force.

Ho Tung & Co. v. *The United States*, 42 Ct. Cls. (1907) 213, 227–228.

On November 5, 1916 the Emperors of Germany and Austria-Hungary proclaimed Poland an independent state with an hereditary monarchy and constitution, the exact boundaries of the kingdom to be decided later. Subsequently, on November 18, 1916, the Allied Powers issued a declaration reading in part as follows:

Poland, 1916

> By a proclamation published on November 6, 1916, at Warsaw and at Lublin, the German Emperor and the Austrian Emperor, King of Hungary, announced that they had agreed to the creation "in the Polish regions" occupied by their troops of an autonomous state under the form of an hereditary and a constitutional monarchy and to the organization, instruction, and direction of any army belonging to that state.
>
> It is a universally admitted principle of the modern right of nations that, by reason of its precarious and *de facto* character of possession, a military occupation resulting from the operations of war may not imply a transfer of sovereignty over the territory occupied and consequently does not involve any right of disposing of this territory to the profit of any one.
>
> In disposing without right of the territory occupied by their troops, the German Emperor, and the Austrian Emperor, King of Hungary, have not only committed an action which is null and void, but have once more shown contempt for one of the fundamental principles upon which the constitution and the existence of civilized states repose.

Disposition
of territory

> The Ambassador in France (Sharp) to the Secretary of State (Lansing), no. 4006, Dec. 5, 1916, MS. Department of State, file 860c.01/9; 1916 For. Rel. Supp. 796–798.

French
occupation
of Ruhr

With reference to the French occupation of the Ruhr, the Department of State, in an instruction to the Ambassador in France, dated March 5, 1923, said:

> The entrance by France into the Ruhr regions is believed to be a matter that should be dealt with purely as a question of fact irrespective of any consideration as to the legality or the propriety of the action taken by France, and without manifesting any criticism or approval of such action. The position taken by neutral powers towards the belligerent occupation of foreign territory furnishes a counterpart to the conduct suggested. Sovereignty over foreign territory is not transferred by such occupation, which is essentially provisional, notwithstanding the fact that during the time of such occupation the lawful sovereign is deprived of the power to exercise its rights as such sovereign. The relinquishment of power to the occupant and the act of depriving the lawful sovereign of power result directly from the action of the occupying power in obtaining actual control of the occupied territory. Neutral States are permitted by international law to accept this result and irrespective of the merits of the occupant's cause to deal with it accordingly. Neutral States are not to be considered as taking sides in the conflict if they act in accordance with this principle of international law.

No transfer
of sovereignty

·   ·   ·   ·   ·   ·   ·

France must, as the power occupying the Ruhr, be considered to be able to exercise, without objection by foreign neutral States, the fullest administrative powers, and must as an incident of such occupation, be deemed to be able to fix the conditions under which foreign trade may be conducted. If neutral States and their citizens are not discriminated against and there is no abuse of power, it is difficult to find any basis upon which objection could be made to the right of the occupying power to make collection of duties or to license exports or to establish embargoes.

. . . .

Notwithstanding the broad powers exercised by the occupying power there are two forms of conduct that should be guarded against and protested against in a special manner: (*a*) where any discrimination is applied against American traders in favor of traders who are French nationals, making it possible for these nationals to take advantage, for their own benefit, of existing conditions; (*b*) any action that would have the result of duplicate export taxes being exacted. Only one authority can, in contemplation of law, exercise control over a particular place at any one time. The sole authority to exact an export license is the government, whether of France or of Germany, which actually asserts and exercises control over localities in the Ruhr from which exports are made. . . . Thus where exports are actually controlled by the French Government that Government should be required to adopt the following course: Either to prevent levying by foreign authority of any other like taxes or if payments have been exacted by a foreign authority within the Ruhr to respect such payments. If it is to be considered that France in fact controls the region of the Ruhr, any German administrative agencies that may be allowed to operate within this region must be considered, from an international standpoint, to be agencies of France. The Government of the United States is justified in taking this position and in demanding in cases where second payments have been exacted in territory which has been declared to be under the control of the French a refunding of the second payments.

Administrative powers

. . . .

Notwithstanding the fact that the region of the Ruhr is not French territory, but German, the rights of the occupying power in this region are vast. The rights of the occupying State as tested by the powers of a belligerent occupant of hostile territory enable the occupying power to be the judge in the last analysis of the existence of its own emergency and the extent to which such emergency may exist. The quasi-neutral State is not to be considered as occupying the position of spokesman of the inhabitants (inhabitants of German nationality in this case) of the region concerned; and the quasi-neutral power is not in a position to make complaint of ruthless treatment of such inhabitants except to the extent that it may generally in cases of barbarities which shock the sensibilities of civilization, raise its voice in protest against such barbarities. Thus with a view to seeing whether the exact conduct complained of is a violation of the solid rights of its own, the quasi-neutral State must ever be on the alert.

.   .   .   .

Responsibility of occupant

It is believed, in a word, that the United States should make a demand for the recognition of the principle that occupation by the Government of France carries with it responsibility of the French for any occurrences within the region of the Ruhr which the Government of the United States may fairly regard as being contrary to international law; and that the occupying power will be held to strict accountability for any abuses of power, such as above indicated, and in particular for the levying of double taxes on exports and for any discriminatory acts that are distinctly adverse to American citizens.

Secretary Hughes to Ambassador Herrick, telegram 85, Mar. 5, 1923, MS. Department of State, file 611.629 Ruhr/1; 1923 For. Rel., vol. II, p. 194.

By article III of the treaty concerning relations with Cuba signed on May 22, 1903, it was agreed that the United States might "exercise the right to intervene for the preservation of Cuban independence, the maintenance of a government adequate for the protection of life, property, and individual liberty". After referring to this provision of the treaty, to the fact that serious revolutionary disturbances existed in Cuba, and to the further fact that "life, property, and individual liberty" were no longer safe throughout the island, President Theodore Roosevelt advised the Cuban Minister in Washington (on September 14, 1906) that it was imperative that there should be "an immediate cessation of hostilities and some arrangement which will secure the permanent pacification of the island" and that he was sending the Secretary of War (Taft) and the Assistant Secretary of State (Bacon) to Habana, as the special representatives of the United States to render such aid as was possible toward these ends.

Cuba, 1906–9

On September 29, 1906 Mr. Taft, as Secretary of War of the United States and Provisional Governor of Cuba, issued a proclamation reciting:

The failure of [the Cuban] Congress to act on the irrevocable resignation of the President of the Republic of Cuba, or to elect a successor, leaves this country without a government at a time when great disorder prevails, and requires that pursuant to a request of President Palma, the necessary steps be taken in the name and by the authority of the President of the United States to restore order, protect life and property in the island of Cuba and islands and keys adjacent thereto, and for this purpose, to establish therein a provisional government.

The provisional government hereby established by direction and in the name of the President of the United States will be maintained only long enough to restore order and peace and public confidence, and then to hold such elections as may be necessary to determine those persons upon whom the permanent government of the Republic should be devolved.

In so far as is consistent with the nature of a provisional government established under authority of the United States, this will be a Cuban government conforming, as far as may be, to the constitution of Cuba. The Cuban flag will be hoisted as usual over the government buildings of the island. All the executive departments and the provincial and municipal governments, including that of the city of Habana, will continue to be administered as under the Cuban Republic. The courts will continue to administer justice, and all laws not in their nature inapplicable by reason of the temporary and emergent character of the Government will be in force.

President Roosevelt has been most anxious to bring about peace under the constitutional government of Cuba, and has made every endeavor to avoid the present step. Longer delay, however, would be dangerous.

In view of the resignation of the cabinet, until further notice the heads of all departments of the central government will report to me for instructions, including Maj. Gen. Alejandro Rodriguez, in command of the rural guard and other regular government forces, and Gen. Carlos Roloff, treasurer of Cuba.

Until further notice, the civil governors and alcaldes will also report to me for instructions.

I ask all citizens and residents of Cuba to assist in the work of restoring order, tranquillity, and public confidence.

On October 3, 1906 Mr. Taft, as Provisional Governor, issued the following decree:

In compliance with instructions received from the President of the United States and in accordance with my proclamation of the 29th of September, I have resolved:

First. The diplomatic representatives of the Republic of Cuba in foreign countries are confirmed in their respective positions and they shall continue in the discharge of their duties in representation of the Republic of Cuba under the provisional administration of the United States.

Diplomatic and consular representatives

Second. The provisional government recognizes the foreign diplomatic representatives accredited to the Government of the Republic of Cuba, without necessity of the formalities or any other steps for the change, and shall continue to maintain with the same, through the Department of State, the diplomatic relations.

Third. Cuban consuls in foreign countries shall continue in the performance of their duties, and foreign consuls residing in Cuba are also recognized by the provisional government.

Minister Morgan to Secretary Root, no. 217, Oct. 13, 1906, MS. Department of State, file 244/322–324; 1906 For. Rel., pt. 1, pp. 480–481, 489, 491, 492–494; President Roosevelt to the Cuban Embassy, Sept. 14, 1906, MS. Department of State, file 244/155–156. The treaty of May 22, 1903 (33 Stat. 2248, 2249; 1 Treaties, etc. [Malloy, 1910] 362, 364), containing the so-called "Platt amendment", was abrogated as of June 9, 1934 by the exchange of ratifications of the treaty of relations signed on May 29, 1934 (48 Stat. 1682; 4 Treaties, etc. [Trenwith, 1938] 4054.)

The earlier military occupation of Cuba by the United States, which took place as a result of the war between the United States and Spain, ceased on May 20, 1902, an independent republican government having been inaugurated at that time under President Tomás Estrada Palma.   1902 For. Rel. 6.

On November 10, 1906 the Ambassador in Japan reported to the Department of State that the Japanese Government had refused to grant an exequatur to a Cuban Consul on the grounds that in 1902 the United States had agreed with Japan for the representation of Cuban interests by United States Consuls pending the appointment of Cuban Consuls, that this consul was commissioned by a Cuban president who had resigned his office, and that Cuba had come under a provisional government established by the United States.   The Department of State (on November 12, 1906) instructed the Ambassador to inform the Japanese Government that—

> the Provisional Government of Cuba exists under the Cuban constitution and that it is so established pending the election of a President; that a commission given a Cuban Consul by Mr. Palma prior to September 29, 1906, is still valid; that authority for American Consuls to act for Cuba was asked in 1902 only subject to their being displaced by regularly appointed Cuban Consuls; and that this Government, which itself treats the independent foreign relations of the people of Cuba as unimpaired, hopes that a Consul who had been lawfully commissioned by the President of Cuba may be recognized.

The Japanese Government promptly agreed to issue the exequatur as requested.

> Ambassador Wright to Secretary Root (telegram), Nov. 10, 1906, and Mr. Root to Mr. Wright (telegram), Nov. 12, 1906, MS. Department of State, file 2209; Mr. Wright to Mr. Root, no. 101, Nov. 23, 1906, *ibid.* 2209/1–3; 1906 For. Rel., pt. II, pp. 1019–1020.

Elections

The Advisory Commission, appointed by Provisional Governor Charles E. Magoon (so designated on October 13, 1906), to draw up a series of new laws for the Government of the Republic of Cuba, drafted a new electoral law which was put into effect by a decree of the Provisional Governor of April 1, 1908.   On August 1 following, provincial and municipal elections were held in conformity with this law under the supervision of the American authorities in charge of the Government of Cuba, and, on November 14 following, a general election was held for the selection of a president and the members of the Cuban legislature.   Following the election, José Miguel Gomez was installed as President on January 28, 1909, and the Provisional Government terminated on that date.

Ambassador Morgan to Secretary Root, no. 641, Apr. 13, 1908; Provisional Governor Magoon to Secretary Root (telegrams), Aug. 1 and Nov. 14, 1908; Ambassador Morgan to Secretary Root (telegram), Jan. 28, 1909: MS. Department of State, files 1943/91, 1943/117, 1943/178, 1943/193.

On April 9, 1914 Mexican military forces arrested and marched a commissioned officer of the U.S.S. *Dolphin*, together with seven men of the crew of the whaleboat of the *Dolphin*, through the streets of Tampico, and, while apologies were given by the commander of the Huertista forces at Tampico and an expression of regret was given by General Huerta himself, Admiral Mayo's demand that the flag of the United States be saluted was refused. On April 20 following, President Woodrow Wilson asked the Congress to approve the use of the armed forces of the United States "in such ways and to such an extent as may be necessary to obtain from General Huerta and his adherents the fullest recognition of the rights and dignity of the United States". On the following day the naval forces of the United States occupied the port of Veracruz, Mexico, and on the succeeding day the Congress, by resolution, stated that the President was "justified" in the employment of the armed forces to enforce his demands. On April 30th the port of Veracruz was turned over to the United States Army, and on May 2, 1914 Brigadier General Frederick Funston issued an order establishing a military government.

Veracruz, 1914

General Funston to the Secretary of War (telegram), May 2, 1914, MS. Department of State, file 812.00/11820. The order of May 2, 1914 establishing the military government is printed in 1914 For. Rel. 495. See also *ibid*. 448 *et seq*.

The Huerta regime having been overthrown, General Carranza—after repeated requests by the United States for such assurances prior to the evacuation of Veracruz—issued a decree on November 8, 1914 stating that upon the reoccupation of Veracruz by the Mexican authorities no exaction would be made from the inhabitants of the port of taxes or any other contributions of a Federal character that might have been previously paid to the foreign authorities which temporarily occupied the port, and that, in order to be entitled to the privileges granted by that decree, it would be sufficient for the interested persons to present to the tax collector's office receipts showing that such payments were made to the authorities established during the American occupation of Veracruz. On the following day he issued a decree granting general amnesty to all persons who had served as employees in the several branches of the public administration that had exercised *de facto* control during the temporary occupation of Veracruz by the American forces.

On November 10, 1914 General Aguilar, Military Governor of the State of Veracruz, issued a decree stating that, upon the evacuation of Veracruz by American forces and its occupation by Mexican authorities, no exaction would be made from the inhabitants of the port for either municipal or State dues that had been previously paid by them to the foreign authorities who occupied the port and that in order to enjoy the benefits of that decree it would be sufficient to present receipts showing the payments made to the officers of the administration in control during the American occupation.

Evacuation   In instructing General Funston, in command at Veracruz, to evacuate the city on November 23, the War Department (on November 20, 1914) said:

> . . . You will bring with you to the United States all funds in your possession from whatever source derived, both United States funds and Mexican customs receipts and taxes. You will also bring with you all the records, accounts, and money papers necessary to establish the integrity and accuracy of your financial and other administration. You will make an inventory of all goods in the customs house keeping the original thereof and leaving a copy with Consul Canada. You may also leave with Consul Canada such copies of accounts or other data as may be required by whomsoever may continue the government of the city. Do not make any arrangements with local Mexicans or with Mexican representatives from outside the city that could make it seem that you are recognizing the right of Carranza to jurisdiction over the city. It is merely desired that you get out in the best practical fashion, leaving things in as good shape as possible and making no declaration that could be interpreted as committing this Government to the recognition of the authority of any individual or faction.

The American forces left the harbor of Veracruz on November 23, 1914.

> The Brazilian Minister in Mexico (de Oliveira) to the Secretary of State (Bryan), telegram of Nov. 10, 1914, MS. Department of State, file 812.00/13730; Mr. Bryan to Mr. de Oliveira, telegram of Nov. 13, 1914, *ibid.* 812.00/13766a; the Acting Secretary of War (Breckinridge) to General Funston, telegram of Nov. 20, 1914, *ibid.* 812.00/13975; Consul Canada to Secretary Bryan, telegram of Nov. 26, 1914, *ibid.* files 812.00/13897, 812.00/13907. See also 1914 For. Rel. 618–627.
>
> For the earlier correspondence with reference to the requests of the United States for assurances on the subject of re-payment of taxes, etc., see Secretary Bryan to Minister de Oliveira, telegram of Sept. 15, 1914, MS. Department of State, file 812.00/13630a; the Acting Secretary of State (Lansing) to Mr. de Oliveira, telegram of Sept. 22, 1914, *ibid.* 812.00/13384; Mr. Bryan to Mr. de Oliveira, telegram of Oct. 7, 1914, *ibid.* 812.00/13431a; Mr. de Oliveira to Mr. Bryan, no. 66, Oct. 28, 1914, *ibid.* 812.00/13699; the Acting Secretary of State (Lansing) to Mr. de Oliveira, telegram of Nov. 1, 1914, *ibid.* 812.00/13610; 1914 For. Rel. 598–618. See also § 28, *ante.*

Haiti, 1915   During the course of repeated revolutionary disturbances in Haiti in 1914 and 1915 negotiations were undertaken for the conclusion of an agreement between the United States and Haiti whereby Haiti would give assurances to the United States with respect to certain matters in connection with the recognition of a new regime in that country. During the period when efforts were being made looking to the negotiation of the agreement, President Théodore's government was overthrown by that of General Sam, and on July 28, 1915 General Sam was murdered by a mob. On that date the Navy Department issued orders to Rear Admiral Caperton, commander of the United States forces in Haitian waters, to land marines at Port-au-Prince.

> 1915 For. Rel. 461–476.

On August 12, 1915 Rear Admiral Caperton issued the following proclamation:

> I am directed by the United States Government to assure the Haitian people that the United States has no object in view except to insure, to establish, and to help maintain Haitian independence and the establishment of a stable and firm government by the Haitian people.
> Every assistance will be given to the Haitian people in their attempt to secure these ends. It is the intention to retain the United States forces in Haiti only so long as will be necessary for this purpose.

On September 3, 1915, he issued an additional proclamation announcing martial law in the city of Port-au-Prince and "the immediate territory now occupied by the forces now under my command".

> Consul Livingston to Secretary Bryan, no. 250, Aug. 12, 1915, MS. Department of State, files 838.00/1266, 838.00/1288. The proclamations are printed in 1915 For. Rel. 481, 484.

On September 16, 1915—the same date that the government of Dartiguenave, the newly elected president, was recognized by the United States—the treaty with respect to the finances, economic development, and tranquillity of Haiti, between the United States and Haiti, was signed. The treaty contained provisions for the appointment by Haiti of a general receiver and financial adviser upon the nomination by the President of the United States, the establishment of a customs receivership, and the settlement of pecuniary claims, as well as provisions regarding the public debt of Haiti, the alienation of territory by Haiti, and the impairment of her independence. Article X provided that the Haitian Government should create an efficient constabulary composed of native Haitians and that this constabulary should be organized and officered by Americans. Article XIV provided:

> The high contracting parties shall have authority to take such steps as may be necessary to insure the complete attainment of any of the objects comprehended in this treaty; and, should the necessity occur, the United States will lend an efficient aid for

the preservation of Haitian Independence and the maintenance of a government adequate for the protection of life, property and individual liberty.

39 Stat. 1654, 1658; 3 Treaties, etc. (Redmond, 1923) 2673, 2675–2676.

Under an agreement between the United States and Haiti of Aug. 7, 1933, the Haitian Garde, trained and partly officered by United States marines, was to be turned over to the complete command of Haitian officers on Oct. 1, 1934. However, this date was advanced by President Franklin D. Roosevelt, and the withdrawal of the American forces from Haiti was completed on Aug. 15, 1934. Pursuant to the provisions of an act of Congress approved on June 19, 1934, the United States made a gift to the Haitian Government of "(a) Equipment, supplies, materials; (b) buildings on land belonging to the Government of Haiti and land leased from private owners; and (c) three emphyteutic leases and one permanent easement covering four parcels of land used by the United States as a radio station at Port-au-Prince, Haiti", which the Haitian Government felt would be useful to it. Ex. Agree. Ser. 46; Department of State, *Press Releases*, weekly issue 255, pp. 103–104 (Aug. 15, 1934); 48 Stat. 1117.

The convention concluded on February 8, 1907 between the United States and the Dominican Republic contained provision for the assistance of the United States in the collection and application of the customs revenue to the liquidation of the Dominican debt which amounted at that time to over $30,000,000, nominal or face value. Articles II and III of the convention provided as follows:

II. The Dominican Government will provide by law for the payment of all customs duties to the General Receiver and his assistants, and will give to them all needful aid and assistance and full protection to the extent of its powers. The Government of the United States will give to the General Receiver and his assistants such protection as it may find to be requisite for the performance of their duties.

III. Until the Dominican Republic has paid the whole amount of the bonds of the debt its public debt shall not be increased except by previous agreement between the Dominican Government and the United States. A like agreement shall be necessary to modify the import duties, it being an indispensable condition for the modification of such duties that the Dominican Executive demonstrate and that the President of the United States recognize that, on the basis of exportations and importations to the like amount and the like character during the two years preceding that in which it is desired to make such modifications, the total net customs receipts would at such altered rates of duties have been for each of such two years in excess of the sum of $2,000,000 United States gold.

35 Stat. 1880, 1883–1884; 1 Treaties, etc. (Malloy, 1910) 418, 420. The convention of Feb. 8, 1907 was abrogated on Oct. 24, 1925, in accordance with the provisions of article VII of the convention between the United States and the Dominican Republic signed on Dec. 27, 1924. 44 Stat. 2162; 4 Treaties, etc. (Trenwith, 1938) 4091.

On November 29, 1916 Captain Knapp, commander of the cruiser force of the United States Atlantic Fleet, issued a proclamation in which, after quoting the provisions of article III of the convention, he stated that the Government of the Dominican Republic had violated the article "on more than one occasion" and that it had "from time to time explained such violation by the necessity of incurring expenses incident to the repression of revolution"; that the United States had urged certain necessary measures which the Dominican Government had been unwilling or unable to adopt and that "in consequence domestic tranquility has been disturbed and is not now established, nor is the future observance of the treaty by the Government of Santo Domingo assured"; and that "to insure the observance of the provisions of the aforesaid treaty" and "to maintain the domestic tranquility" of that republic, it was thereby "placed in a state of Military Occupation" by the forces under his command and was made "subject to Military Government and to the exercise of military law applicable to such occupation". He added:

This military occupation is undertaken with no immediate or ulterior object of destroying the sovereignty of the Republic of Santo Domingo, but, on the contrary, is designed to give aid to that country in returning to a condition of internal order that will enable it to observe the terms of the treaty aforesaid, and the obligations resting upon it as one of the family of nations.

Dominican statutes, therefore, will continue in effect in so far as they do not conflict with the objects of the Occupation or necessary regulations established thereunder, and their lawful administration will continue in the hands of such duly authorized Dominican officials as may be necessary, all under the oversight and control of the United States Forces exercising Military Government.

The ordinary administration of justice, both in civil and criminal matters, through the regularly constituted Dominican courts will not be interfered with by the Military Government herein established; but cases to which a member of the United States Forces in Occupation is a party, or in which are involved contempt or defiance of the authority of the Military Government, will be tried by tribunals set up by the Military Government.

John Brewer, American Legation in the Dominican Republic, to Secretary Lansing, no. 143, Dec. 6, 1916, enclosing the Proclamation of Occupation and Military Government, by Captain Knapp, MS. Department of State, file 839.00/1968; 1916 For. Rel. 220, 245–247.

Elections having been held in March 1924, the Military Governor, Brigadier General Harry Lee of the United States Marine Corps, relinquished his authority as such upon the assumption of office by Horacio Vasquez, the newly elected president, on July 12, 1924. The evacuation of the American forces, which began on July 16 following, was completed on Sept. 18, 1924. *Annual Report of the Secretary of the Navy, Fiscal Year 1924* (1925) 50, 51; Minister Russell to Secretary Hughes, telegram 55, Sept.

18, 1924, MS. Department of State, file 839.00/2861; 1924 For. Rel., vol. I, pp. 618–643.

A military occupant, especially one who has conquered and subjugated a country, has supreme power over the territory occupied, and, to all intents and purposes, is the sovereign during the period of occupation. The belligerent military occupant, for example, possesses an unquestioned right to regulate all intercourse between the territory under his control and the outside world. The situation . . . is different in some respects from that obtaining in Belgium during the World War. In that case Germany was in the position of a military invader, as distinguished from a conqueror, . . . yet, in the case of Belgium, the German Government announced in November, 1914, that exequaturs of neutral consular officers in Belgium would be regarded as having expired. Minister Whitlock, however, remained in Brussels and continued to enjoy diplomatic privileges and immunities until the severance of diplomatic relations between the United States and Germany (February 3, 1917) when the German authorities withdrew his diplomatic privileges. Nevertheless, Mr. Whitlock remained in Brussels until the end of March 1917, when he and other American officials in Belgium were ordered by this Government to withdraw.

Opinion of the Legal Adviser of the Department of State, May 7, 1936, MS. Department of State, file 765.84/4525.

During the military occupation [of the Philippine Islands], and while a state of war yet existed between the two countries, the United States expressly recognized the continuance of the municipal laws of the conquered territory. The military occupancy, though absolute and supreme, operated only upon the political conditions of the people without affecting private rights of person and property. Under these municipal laws partnerships were formed and joint-stock associations organized, and the ordinary and commercial transactions of the country proceeded, as nearly alike as the changed conditions would admit, as before. And after peace was declared the authority of the United States was directed to be exerted for the security of the persons and property of the people of the islands and for the confirmation of all their private rights and relations. The municipal laws of the territories in respect to these private rights and property were to be considered as continuing in force, to be administered by the ordinary tribunals as far as practicable.

The Philippine Sugar Estates Development Company (Limited) v. *The United States,* 39 Ct. Cls. (1904) 225, 247.

In the case of *Galban and Company, a Corporation* v. *The United States,* an American company sought to recover the amount of duties paid by it to the military government of Cuba on goods imported into Cuba during the period of the first military occupation of Cuba by the United States, on the ground that Cuba was a part of the territory of the United States. The Court of Claims held that by the terms of the treaty of December 10, 1898, between the United States and Spain, sovereignty passed from Spain to the inhabitants of Cuba and that the United States as military occupant held the island in trust for the inhabitants of Cuba. The court stated, *inter alia:*

. . . True, when, pursuant to the treaty, the United States oc- Allegiance cupied the island, the inhabitants thereof during such occupancy undoubtedly owed allegiance to the United States, i. e., fidelity and obedience for the protection they received, but that did not divest them of their inherent rights.

.   .   .   .

During the occupation the people of the island were for a Trust brief time, and while in preparation therefor, denied the right of relations self-government, but when the people had by their "voluntary action" organized a "stable government" the United States withdrew and left "the government and control of the island to its people," the rightful owners. The territory being foreign, and occupied for a specific purpose, the United States could exercise no right of ownership, jurisdiction, sovereignty, or control which would operate to make the island territory of the United States. To have done so would have been a violation of their trust and an act of bad faith toward the Cuban people. The powers and functions which were exercised by the United States were strictly in line with their duties as a trustee for the protection and security of persons and property, having in view the restoration of confidence, and the encouragement of the people to resume the pursuits of peace. In furtherance of that trust it became, among other things, necessary, and there were collected from May 30, 1900, to April 29, 1902, at Sagua La Grande, Cuba, as set forth in the findings, duties aggregating $51,104.20 on goods, and merchandise imported thereto from the United States by the claimant corporation, a citizen of the United States.

.   .   .   .

Such being the case, should the merchandise of a citizen of the United States imported into Cuba from the United States have been exempted from the payment of such duties because the United States were, for the pacification thereof, exercising the functions of government over the island?

To have done so would have been an act of bad faith toward the people of Cuba, as they were entitled not only to have the revenues honestly collected, but were entitled to have all the revenues accruing to the island, from whatever source, applied to the pacific object of the occupation.

40 Ct. Cls. (1905) 495, 507–509. The court relied upon *Neely* v. *Henkel* for the proposition that Cuba was, during the occupation thereof, foreign territory and that, as between the United States and Cuba, the island was held in trust for the inhabitants of Cuba. 180 U.S. (1901) 109.

On the subject of the application of local law by the military occupant, see also *El Emporio Del Cafe, S.A.* (Mexico *v.* United States), *Opinions of the Commissioners* (1927) 7, 8, docket 281; *David Gonzalez* (Mexico *v.* United States), *ibid.* 9, docket 290.

Status of
Legation

With reference to the status of the Legation in Santo Domingo during the military occupation, Secretary Lansing advised Minister Russell, on December 20, 1916, that the "position of Legation should be practically same as before proclamation of military government, and it should be understood that it is civil representative of American Government in Santo Domingo, and will advise on all points with military government, which is carrying on the government for the Republic".

MS. Department of State, file 839.00/1967; 1916 For. Rel. 249.

Local
administra-
tion

On August 8, 1917 the Navy Department transmitted to the Department of State the Annual Report of the Military Government of the Dominican Republic from November 29, 1916 to June 30, 1917, signed by Captain Knapp and reading in part as follows:

After the issuance of the Proclamation of Military Government, I waited for some days to see if the members of the Provisional Government would in any way cooperate with the Military Government in carrying on the ordinary administration of affairs. The hope that I had in this direction proved to be unfounded; and I was assured by persons most familiar with conditions here that I could expect no assistance of the kind. I established the offices of the Military Government in the Government Palace. Upon taking possession, it was found that the President and all of the members of the Cabinet had come to their offices after the Proclamation of Military Government, had cleaned out their desks, and had not since appeared in the Government Palace. It was an evident case of desertion. Under the circumstances, as the affairs of government had to go on under intelligent administration, I placed the several Departments of the Dominican Government in charge of officers under my command.

Navy Department to Secretary Lansing, Aug. 8, 1917, MS. Department of State, file 839.00/2043; 1917 For. Rel. 709, 711.

For a discussion of the relation between the government established under a military occupant and the local government, particularly with reference to the extent to which the occupant administers the territory for and in the name of the local government, see memorandum of the Office of the Solicitor for the Department of State of Mar. 18, 1918, wherein it was stated:

"In view of all the foregoing, it would seem that the Military Government in force in the Dominican Republic must be regarded as administering affairs for the Government of that Republic, and in any event, that the provisions of the treaty of 1907 between the United States and the Dominican Republic must be considered in present force and effect, so that if the Military Government desires to modify the tariff duties of the Republic, it should proceed as provided for in Article 3 of that treaty."

MS. Department of State, file 839.00/2099; 1918 For. Rel. 382. See also memorandum of the Solicitor of July 10, 1918, MS. Department of State, file 839.00/2099; 1918 For. Rel. 389.

The Secretary of the Navy on February 4, 1918 transmitted to the Secretary of State a despatch from the Military Governor of the Dominican Republic requesting an amendment of the Dominican tariff law to permit the importation of certain necessary articles. The Department of State in a reply, dated February 25, 1918, informed the Secretary of the Navy that it considered the question of the amendment of Dominican law one to be initiated and determined by the military government of the Dominican Republic subject to the approval of the Department of State. The Secretary of the Navy was requested to inform the Military Governor of this opinion and of the fact that the Department of State approved the desired amendment.

> The Second Assistant Secretary of State (Adee) to the Secretary of the Navy (Daniels), Feb. 25, 1918, MS. Department of State, file 639.003/44; 1918 For. Rel. 380.
>
> For the discussion that took place in 1920 between the Navy Department and the Department of State as to the nature and status of the military government in the Dominican Republic, when the Military Governor asked that certain instructions be issued to the general receiver of Dominican customs through the Department of State and the Bureau of Insular Affairs of the War Department, see 1920 For. Rel., pt. II, pp. 132–154.

Article XLVIII of the Hague convention respecting the laws and customs of war on land, concluded on October 18, 1907, states:

> If, in the territory occupied, the occupant collects the taxes, dues, and tolls imposed for the benefit of the State, he shall do so, as far as is possible, in accordance with the rules of assessment and incidence in force, and shall in consequence be bound to defray the expenses of the administration of the occupied territory to the same extent as the legitimate Government was so bound.

Taxes, customs, etc.

> 36 Stat. 2277, 2307; 2 Treaties, etc. (Malloy, 1910) 2269, 2289.

In 1921 the American High Commissioner at Constantinople (Istanbul) informed the Department of State that the Greek authorities in Smyrna had demanded the payment of consumption taxes claimed to be in arrears. The United States took the position that it could not recognize the Greek administration in Turkey in any other light than as a military occupant executing the terms of the armistice with Turkey and that it did not recognize the right of the Greek administration to levy taxes other than those provided for by the capitulations or to appropriate those to their own use.

> The American High Commissioner (Rear Admiral Bristol) to the Acting Secretary of State, telegram 28, Jan. 24, 1921, MS. Department of State, file 667.003/102; Secretary Colby to Rear Admiral Bristol, telegram 13, Feb. 19, 1921, *ibid.* 667.003/104; Consul General Horton to Secretary Colby, no. 292, Mar. 2, 1921, *ibid.* 867.512/86; Consul General Horton to Secretary Hughes (telegram), July 23, 1921, and Mr. Hughes to Mr. Horton (telegram), July 29, 1921, *ibid.* 667.003/132; 1921 For. Rel., vol. II, pp. 154–163.

CHAPTER III

RECOGNITION

IN GENERAL

§30

Recognition may be of new states, of new governments, or of belligerency. It is evidenced, in the case of a new state or government, by an act officially acknowledging the existence of such state or government and indicating a readiness on the part of the recognizing state to enter into formal relations with it. The existence in fact of a new state or a new government is not dependent upon its recognition by other states. By recognition of belligerency, as here used, is meant the recognition by a state that a revolt within another state has attained such a magnitude as to constitute in fact a state of war, entitling the revolutionists or insurgents to the benefits, and imposing upon them the obligations, of the rules of war.

Definition

BY WHOM DETERMINABLE

§31

Whether and when recognition will be accorded is a matter within the discretion of the recognizing state. It is extended by the authority in whom appropriate power is vested by the law of the recognizing state. In the United States recognition has in the past usually been accomplished by the President acting solely on his own responsibility, but, occasionally, in the case of new states, it has been accomplished by the President with the cooperation of Congress. Thus Secretary Hughes declared in a letter of August 13, 1921 to Representative Garner:

Executive prerogative

> . . . The question of the recognition of a foreign government is purely a domestic one for the United States, to be decided by the Executive. [MS. Department of State, file 812.00/25133.]

Similarly Secretary Kellogg asserted in a letter to Senator Swanson dated December 14, 1927 that—

> the President has absolute power to recognize any country and, by and with the advice and consent of the Senate, to appoint an ambassador or minister without any law authorizing it or any

treaty between the two countries. . . . Congress must make an appropriation for the salaries. [MS. Department of State, file 711.672/600A.]

In every instance in which recognition has been accorded by the United States since 1906, the act has been that of the President, taken solely on his own responsibility.

Congress has exhibited little inclination to contest the prerogative of the Executive to accord or withhold recognition at his discretion, although attempts have been made on a number of occasions through resolutions to determine the action to be taken with respect to certain governments. For example, on January 2, 1913, a joint resolution was introduced in the Senate declaring:

S. J. Res.,
Jan. 2, 1913

That the present republican Government of China is hereby recognized by the United States of America, with all the powers and privileges of their intercourse and relations with this Government properly appertaining to and in general extended to independent and sovereign governments and nations.

In a memorandum transmitted to the Chairman of the Senate Committee on Foreign Relations by Secretary Knox on February 4, 1913 the following opinion was expressed with reference to this joint resolution:

In introducing the resolution Senator Bacon spoke as follows:

"It has been a subject matter of discussion almost ever since the foundation of this Government as to whether the function of the recognition of an independent government, or, when there has been a change in government, the recognition of the stability and authority of a government is a function which belongs to the executive or to the legislative branch of the Government. When I say 'legislative' I should properly say the law-making branch of the Government, which includes both the two Houses and the President.

"By some it is contended, and has been contended with much earnestness, that it is a function which exclusively belongs to the executive branch of the Government, whereas by others it has been contended with equal earnestness that it belongs to the law-making power of the Government. I believe the more conservative view is that which is represented by the opinion of many, that the initiative can be taken by either the Executive alone or by the law-making power, embracing the joint action of both the legislative and the executive branches of the Government—the Congress and the President—acting in a legislative capacity. In my opinion, the ultimate power of decision is with the law-making power, and where the final action in such case has been taken by the Executive it has been final through the acquiescence and approval of the Congress. But without now stopping to discuss the question I simply make the statement in order that my attitude may not be misunderstood in introducing the joint resolution. I move that it be referred to the Committee on Foreign Relations."

In regard to this aspect of the question it is perhaps sufficient to point out that Mr. Moore, in his International Law Digest, sums up some 170 pages of precedent and opinions in the following words:

"In the preceding review of the recognition, respectively, of new states, new governments, and belligerency, there has been made in each case a precise statement of facts, showing how and by whom the recognition was accorded. In every case, as it appears, of a new government and of belligerency, the question of recognition was determined solely by the Executive."

It should be noted that in the case of China the question involved is the recognition of a new Government and not a new State.

In a "Memorandum upon the Power to Recognize the Independence of a New Foreign State", presented to the Senate in January, 1897, by Mr. Hale (see Senate Document No. 56, Fifty-fourth Congress, second session) the statement is made that—

"It will be shown, both by the terms of the Constitution itself and by the uniform practice thereunder, that the recognition of independence of a new foreign power is an act of the Executive (President alone, or President and Senate), and not of the legislative branch of the Government, although the executive branch may properly first consult the legislative."

Speaking on the proposition "That the power to recognize belligerency or independence of a foreign government is executive in its nature has been recognized by the weight of authority in Congress, and almost without exception by the executive branch", the report continues:

"*Acquiescence by Congress.*—It is entirely erroneous to suppose that the present question is a novel one. The boundaries between the legislative and executive powers in relation to foreign affairs have been debated since the very foundation of the Government. The right to recognize the independence of a foreign state was discussed with great ability at the time of the South American revolutions, and received some attention again at the time of the revolution in Texas. The weight of authority, legislative as well as executive, was strongly against the right of Congress to interfere. In each case the President, when the time came for recognition, acted in concert with Congress, for the obvious reason that affirmative action might involve the nation in war, and thus force Congress to make large appropriations and otherwise assist in the settlement of the controversy thus opened. The question has occasionally arisen since for discussion, as in 1864 and 1877. It has never been fully debated, however, since the time of Monroe.

"The number of instances in which the Executive has recognized a new foreign power without consulting Congress (because not anticipating consequences which made such consultation neces-

sary) has been very great. No objection has been made by
Congress in any of these instances. The legislative power has
thus for 100 years impliedly confirmed the view that the right to
recognize a new foreign government belonged to the Executive;
and if it is correct doctrine that the same power can not be exercised for the same purpose by two different branches of the Government, this implied approval is conclusive of the whole present
controversy."

MS. Department of State, file 893.00/1529a; 1913 For. Rel. 88–92.

In a joint resolution passed by the House of Representatives on Feb. 29,
1912 it was resolved:

"That the United States of America congratulates the people of China on
their assumption of the powers, duties and responsibilities of self-government, and expresses the confident hope that, in the adoption and maintenance of a republican form of government, the rights, liberties and happiness
of the Chinese people will be secure and the progress of the country insured."

In communicating the text of this resolution to the Legation at Peking, the
Department of State instructed it as follows with reference to the matter of
giving it publicity:

". . . It may be regarded as an expression of the sympathy of the
American people, through their representatives, with the new order of things
in China. Due care should be taken, however, particularly with the leaders
now assembled at Peking, that this action be not confused with recognition,
which is a prerogative of the Executive and as to which it is the present intention of the President and the Department to proceed in harmony with the
other powers by entering automatically into effective informal relations with
the *de facto* provisional government, pending the establishment of such
ultimate government as may merit formal recognition."   The Acting Secretary of State (Wilson) to Minister Calhoun, Mar. 2, 1912, MS. Department
of State, file 893.00/1146a.   See also 1912 For. Rel. 71.

In connection with the resolution introduced in the Senate on
December 3, 1919 requesting the President "to withdraw" the recognition theretofore accorded Carranza, President Wilson protested that
the proposed action of the Congress constituted an encroachment upon
the Executive jurisdiction. He said:

. . . I should be gravely concerned to see any such resolution
pass the Congress. It would constitute a reversal of our constitutional practice which might lead to very grave confusion in regard
to the guidance of our foreign affairs. I am confident that I am
supported by every competent constitutional authority in the
statement that the initiative in directing the relations of our
Government with foreign governments is assigned by the Constitution to the Executive, and to the Executive only. Only one
of the two Houses of Congress is associated with the President by
the Constitution in an advisory capacity, and the advice of the
Senate is provided for only when sought by the Executive in
regard to explicit agreements with foreign governments and the
appointment of the diplomatic representatives who are to speak
for this Government at foreign capitals. The only safe course,

am confident, is to adhere to the prescribed method of the Constitution. We might go very far afield if we departed from it.

S. Con. Res. 21, 66th Cong., 2d sess.; President Wilson to Senator Albert B. Fall, Dec. 9, 1919, S. Doc. 285, 66th Cong., 2d sess., vol. 1, pp. 843C, 843D.

The courts of the United States have uniformly adhered to the view that the recognition of foreign governments is a political matter not subject to judicial inquiry or decision. In general they have not discussed the prerogatives of the executive, as distinguished from the legislative, branch of the government in the performance of this function.

Position of courts

The conduct of the foreign relations of our Government is committed by the Constitution to the Executive and Legislative— "the political"—Departments of the Government, and the propriety of what may be done in the exercise of this political power is not subject to judicial inquiry or decision. *United States* v. *Palmer*, 3 Wheat. 610; *Foster* v. *Neilson*, 2 Pet. 253, 307, 309; *Garcia* v. *Lee*, 12 Pet. 511, 517, 520; *Williams* v. *Suffolk Ins. Co.*, 13 Pet. 415, 420; *In re Cooper*, 143 U.S. 472, 499. It has been specifically decided that "Who is the sovereign, *de jure* or *de facto*, of a territory is not a judicial, but is a political question, the determination of which by the legislative and executive departments of any government conclusively binds the judges, as well as all other officers, citizens and subjects of that government. This principle has always been upheld by this court, and has been affirmed under a great variety of circumstances." *Jones* v. *United States*, 137 U.S. 202, 212.

Oetjen v. *Central Leather Company*

246 U.S. (1918) 297, 302.

What government is to be regarded here as representative of a foreign sovereign state is a political rather than a judicial question, and is to be determined by the political department of the government. Objections to its determination as well as to the underlying policy are to be addressed to it and not to the courts. Its action in recognizing a foreign government and in receiving its diplomatic representatives is conclusive on all domestic courts, which are bound to accept that determination, although they are free to draw for themselves its legal consequences in litigations pending before them. . . .

Guaranty Trust Co. of New York v. *United States*

We accept as conclusive here the determination of our own State Department that the Russian State was represented by the Provisional Government through its duly recognized representatives from March 16, 1917 to November 16, 1933, when the Soviet Government was recognized.

304 U.S. (1938) 126, 137. For cases in accord, see *Russian Government* v. *Lehigh Valley Railroad Company*, 293 Fed. 133 (S.D.N.Y., 1919); *Russian Government* v. *Lehigh Valley Railroad Company*, 293 Fed. 135 (S.D.N.Y., 1923), application for a writ of prohibition denied, 265 U.S. (1924) 573; *Lehigh Valley R. Co.* v. *State of Russia*, 21 F. (2d) 396 (C.C.A. 2d, 1927), petition for writ of certiorari denied, 275 U.S. (1927) 571; *The Rogdai*, 278

Fed. 294 (N.D. Cal., 1920); *State of Russia* v. *Bankers' Trust Co. et al.*, 4 F. Supp. 417 (S.D.N.Y., 1933); *Agency of Canadian Car & Foundry Co., Limited, et al.* v. *American Can Co.*, 253 Fed. 152 (S.D.N.Y., 1918), 258 Fed. 363 (C.C.A. 2d, 1919); *Russian Socialist Federated Soviet Republic* v. *Cibrario*, 235 N.Y. (1923) 255, 262, 139 N.E. 259, 262; *Waldes et al.* v. *Basch et al.*, 109 Misc. 306 (Sup. Ct., N.Y. Cy., spec. term, 1919), 179 N.Y. Supp. 713, 715–716; *State of Yucatan* v. *Argumedo et al.*, 92 Misc. 547 (Sup. Ct., N.Y. Cy., spec. term, 1915), 157 N.Y. Supp. 219, 224–225.

Judicial notice

The courts take judicial notice of the action of the Executive in recognizing or refusing to recognize a foreign government. In the case of the *United States* v. *Belmont et al., Executors* the United States sued to recover a sum of money deposited by a Russian corporation with August Belmont prior to 1918, basing its claim to the money upon the assignment made by the Soviet Government on November 16, 1933, to the United States of all amounts due to the Soviet Government from American nationals. In the course of its opinion, reversing the decision of the circuit court of appeals and holding that the complaint constituted sufficient cause of action, the Supreme Court said:

> We take judicial notice of the fact that coincident with the assignment set forth in the complaint, the President recognized the Soviet Government and normal diplomatic relations were established between that Government and the Government of the United States, followed by an exchange of ambassadors.

301 U.S. (1937) 324, 330. Accord: *United States ex rel. Cardashian* v. *Snyder, United States Marshal et al.*, 44 F. (2d) 895, 896 (Ct. of App. D.C., 1930); *Russian Volunteer Fleet* v. *United States*, 68 Ct. Cls. (1929) 32, 33, reversed on other grounds, 282 U.S. (1031) 481; *The Penza*, 277 Fed. 91, 92–93 (E.D.N.Y., 1921).

MODE

§32

In general

Recognition is essentially a matter of intention. It may be express or implied. The mode by which it is accomplished is of no special significance. It is essential, however, that the act constituting recognition shall give a clear indication of an intention (1) to treat with the new state as such, or (2) to accept the new government as having authority to represent the state it purports to govern and to maintain diplomatic relations with it, or (3) to recognize in the case of insurgents that they are entitled to exercise belligerent rights. "Recognition cannot be accomplished by inference merely but by the full and formal entrance into international relations through the public action of the respective executives of the two countries." Secretary Colby to the Chargé d'Affaires in Mexico (Summerlin), May 25, 1920, MS. Department of State, file 812.00/24071; 1920 For. Rel., vol. III, p. 167. An act which would normally have the effect of recognition—

short of one involving formal diplomatic relations with a foreign state or government—may be deprived of that quality by an express declaration of the government performing it that it is not intended to constitute recognition.

Recognition of new states usually carries with it recognition of the government of the state so recognized, since states can speak and act only through their governments. In a majority of the cases referred to below, recognition of new states by the United States was accomplished through a formal note sent by the American diplomatic representative at the capital of the country in question to the Foreign Office, under instructions from the Department of State. This was true in the cases of Bulgaria in 1909; Albania, Estonia, Latvia, Lithuania, and Egypt, all in 1922; and Saudi Arabia in 1931. In certain other instances a formal note was sent by the Department of State to the diplomatic representative in the United States of the state in question. This was the method followed in the cases of Armenia in 1920, and Finland and Yugoslavia in 1919. Poland was recognized in 1919 by means of a telegram from the Secretary of State, then in Paris, to the President of the Polish Provisional Government. Formal reception by the President of an Afghan mission in 1921 was considered to constitute recognition of Afghanistan. Recognition of the Czechoslovak National Council in 1918 as a *de facto* belligerent government was made through a formal public announcement issued by Secretary Lansing, and the recognition of the Government of the Republic in 1918 was made through establishment of relations with it, including the acceptance of its agent in the United States and the negotiation of loans to it. Iraq was recognized in 1931 by accrediting a chargé d'affaires to the King. In the case of Iceland recognition resulted from the conclusion of certain bilateral agreements. *New states*

Perhaps the method of recognizing a new government recurring most frequently in the foreign relations of the United States is, as in the case of the recognition of new states, the sending of a note by the representative of the United States at the foreign capital announcing the decision of his Government to establish relations with the new government. It may however assume a variety of forms. Several of the many forms employed are enumerated in the following memorandum: *New governments*

> In the practice of the United States, there are several formulae of recognition.
> The first and most usual is, the notification, by the American representative at the foreign capital, that he is instructed to enter into relations with the new government. This is ordinarily supplemented by informing the foreign minister (if there be one) in Washington in a like sense. *Methods of recognition*

The second, and the course very generally followed in other countries, is the acknowledgment, by the President, of a letter addressed to him by the head of the new foreign government announcing his assumption of authority. (It is in this way that King George V is reported to intend to recognize General Huerta as Constitutional *interim* President of the United Mexican States—that being the style and title used by General Huerta in his formal letter of announcement.)

The third, also usual in the intercourse of states, is the reception of an envoy by the President, in audience for the purpose of presenting his letters of credence.

The fourth is the reception, by the President, of the continuing diplomatic agent of the foreign state, for the purpose of making oral announcement of the change of government. In both these two latter cases, the complimentary addresses of the envoy and the President suffice to define and accentuate the scope of the recognition so effected.

A fifth method may be available, namely, the formal delivery by the American envoy at the foreign capital, to the head of the new government, of a message of recognition from the President, or of a congratulatory resolution of the American Congress if one have been passed.

The sixth method, which was adopted in the case of Portugal and Spain (and, I think, in the case of the French Republic, 1871) is to supplement the recognition of a provisional or interim government by a formal announcement of recognition, made by the American envoy, upon the adoption of a new form of government by the national assembly of the foreign state.

Memorandum of Mar. 28, 1913 of the Second Assistant Secretary of State (Adee) to Secretary Bryan, MS. Department of State, file 893.00/1669; 1913 For. Rel. 100–102.

Greece, 1924

In view of this situation I wish to suggest for your consideration the desirability of resuming, on a formal basis, the relations between the United States and Greece. This could be done by the accrediting to the Greek Government of a Chargé d'Affaires ad interim and by the reception of the Greek Chargé d'Affaires in Washington. No change in personnel would be necessary. Mr. Atherton, who has been acting as our representative in Greece, could be instructed to take up formal relations with the Greek Minister for Foreign Affairs pending the appointment of a Minister. This action would be similar to that recently taken in the case of Mexico.

The appointment of a Minister, in my opinion, should be delayed until Greece has determined the question which is now being agitated as to whether the country shall continue as a Kingdom or become a Republic. The King of Greece has recently left the country pending the decision of this question, a Regent is functioning in his place. The ultimate decision as to the form of government is one with which I feel we should in no way interfere but this does not preclude the resumption of formal relations with the Greek Government through a Chargé d'Affaires ad interim, postponing the formal accrediting of a Minister to the head of the State until Greece has herself decided—and Mr. Venizelos has proposed a plebiscite to decide the question—whether there shall be a Kingdom or a Republic.

Secretary Hughes to President Coolidge, Jan. 25, 1924, MS. Department of State, file 868.01/196a; 1924 For. Rel., vol. II, pp. 265–266. The method suggested was followed.

Pursuant to instructions from the Department of State dated September 15, 1930, the Chargé d'Affaires at La Paz notified the head of the Military Junta that he had been instructed by the Government of the United States to enter into full diplomatic relations with the Government of Bolivia. The Chargé also requested the head of the Junta to set a date upon which the newly appointed Minister could present his credentials and, in discussing the question of credentials, informed him that these documents were addressed to the President of Bolivia and inquired whether it would be convenient to present them in that form. The head of the Junta stated that he would perfer to have the credentials addressed to His Excellency, General Carlos Blanco Galindo, President of the Military Junta of the Government of Bolivia. The Department informed the Legation in a telegram of September 19:

Bolivia, 1930

> General policy for many years has been to address credentials to the heads of nations without names, although in few cases names have been inserted through error. Unless Junta insists upon new credentials Department prefers to make no change, although new credentials will be issued immediately if Junta unwilling to accept letters Mr. Feely now holds.

Chargé Hibbard to Secretary Stimson, no. 63, Sept. 18, 1930, MS. Department of State, file 824.01/19; Mr. Stimson to the Legation at La Paz, no. 39, Sept. 19, 1930, *ibid.* 123 Feely, Edward F./25.

The Minister in Honduras inquired by telegram on January 24, 1925 whether he should participate in the inaugural ceremonies on February 1 of the newly elected President of Honduras; he also inquired as to the form in which recognition should be extended to the new constitutional government. On January 26 the Department of State replied:

Official attendance at inaugural: Honduras, 1925

> You are authorized to take part in the inaugural ceremonies on February 1 in whatever manner that may be customary in Honduras when a new constitutional government is being inaugurated, and you are authorized thereafter to make such official calls on the officials of the new government as may be customary. You are also authorized in your discretion to send a note to the new Minister for Foreign Affairs expressing the gratification of the Government of the United States that it has now been possible to resume formal diplomatic relations with the Honduran Government. [Paraphrase.]

Minister Dennis to Secretary Hughes, no. 13, Jan. 24, 1925, and Mr Hughes to Mr. Dennis, no. 11, Jan. 26, 1925, MS. Department of State file 815.00/3535.

Nicaragua,
1926

Referring to an inquiry concerning the recognition of President Díaz of Nicaragua, who took the oath of office on November 14, 1926, the Department of State said:

The American Charge d'Affaires attended this inauguration under instructions from the Department of State as a sign of the official recognition of the Diaz Government by the Government of the United States. I understand that representatives of Great Britain and Honduras attended the inauguration of President Diaz as a sign of recognition by those Governments.

Secretary Kellogg to Senator Pepper, Jan. 15, 1927, MS. Department of State, file 817.00/4423.

Exequaturs

. . . This Government cannot, in any event, grant an exequatur to a Consul from a non-recognized Government.

Secretary Colby to the Commissioner at Riga, Evan E. Young, Sept. 11 1920, MS. Department of State, file 702.60i11/orig.; 1920 For. Rel., vol III, p. 661.

Upon sending consular officers to Chile in 1924, at a time when the Chilean Government was not recognized by the United States, the Department of State instructed the Embassy at Santiago as follows

It is the opinion of the Department that the formal and unconditional acceptance of an exequatur issued by the government in power in a state may be regarded as constituting recognition of such government as the government of the country.

Consequently it is desired that you inform the authorities of the government now in control in Chile: First, that the Government of the United States would of course be happy to have the vice consuls under reference perform their functions as such in the territory of Chile; secondly, that the performance of the consular function must of course remain subject to approval by the *de facto* authorities; thirdly, that the Government of the United States is willing to make use of the exequaturs issued by the government now in control in Chile on condition that it be definitely understood that this action in no way implies or is to be considered as representing recognition of that government by the Government of the United States as the Government of Chile; fourthly, that it is your desire to determine whether that government is willing to agree to such an understanding and to allow the use of the exequatur by the vice consuls on such terms.

[Paraphrase.]

On November 11, 1924 the Embassy reported the receipt of a note from the Minister of Foreign Affairs in which it was said that no objection was seen to this plan. The Department of State accordingly on November 21, 1924, instructed the Embassy to forward the exequaturs to the consular officers, together with explanations of the conditions attached to their acceptance.

The Department of State to the Embassy at Santiago, Oct. 31, 1924, MS. Department of State, file 122.352/11a; the Embassy at Santiago to the Department of State, Nov. 11, 1924, and the Department of State to the Embassy at Santiago, Nov. 21, 1924, *ibid.* 122.352/12.

In a public statement of June 7, 1921 concerning a suggestion that the signature of a treaty of amity and commerce, proposed to the government of General Obregón in Mexico, would constitute recognition by the Government of the United States of the Mexican Government, Secretary Hughes said: {Signature of treaty: Mexico, 1921}

The question of recognition is a subordinate one, but there will be no difficulty as to this, for if General Obregon is ready to negotiate a proper treaty it is drawn so as to be negotiated with him and the making of the treaty in proper form will accomplish the recognition of the Government that makes it. In short, when it appears that there is a government in Mexico willing to bind itself to the discharge of primary international obligations, concurrently with that act its recognition will take place. This Government desires immediate and cordial relations of mutual helpfulness and simply wishes that the basis of international intercourse should be properly maintained.

Secretary Hughes to the Chargé d'Affaires in Mexico (Summerlin), June 8, 1921, MS. Department of State, file 711.1211/8a; 1921 For. Rel., vol. II, pp. 406–407.

On July 25, 1928, the Envoy Extraordinary and Minister Plenipotentiary to China, appointed by the President of the United States, and the Minister of Finance, appointed by the National Government of the Republic of China, entered into a treaty of commerce; and while this treaty has not as yet been ratified by the Senate, it contains a clear recognition by the Executive Department of this government of both the National Government of the Republic of China and of its accredited representative. This recognition by the Executive Department would seem to satisfy the requirements of the law; but, if this is not enough, we have been advised by a telegram from the Secretary of State that the Minister Plenipotentiary and Envoy Extraordinary of the National Government of China has been officially received by this government, so that the recognition of the former is now settled beyond question. {China, 1928}

Republic of China v. *Merchants' Fire Assur. Corporation of New York, Same* v. *Great American Ins. Co.;* 30 F. (2d) 278, 279 (C. C. A. 9th, 1929). For a further statement concerning the recognition of the Nationalist Government by the United States, see *post* §51.

Continuation
of relations:
Peru, 1931

The National Junta Government of Peru, headed by David Samanez Ocampo, which came into power on March 11, 1931 as a result of the overthrow of the Military Junta headed by Sanchez Cerro on March 1, 1931 (a Junta headed by Jiminez having been in power for a brief period during the interim), adopted the theory that it was but a continuation of the revolutionary movement initiated in August 1930. According to telegraphic reports of May 15, 1931 from the Ambassador in Lima to the Department of State, this theory was accepted by most of the Latin American countries, with the consequent result that they considered no special action on their part necessary in the matter of recognition. The United States had continued for some time to conduct informal relations with the Junta through the Ambassador in Lima and finally, on May 19, the Department authorized him to answer the Peruvian Government's note of March 12, informing the Embassy of the establishment of the Junta and stating that the change in government "makes no difference in the diplomatic relations between the United States and Peru". The Ambassador informed the Department on May 21 that the British, Japanese, Brazilian, and Belgian Governments were extending recognition, using a formula similar to that adopted by the Department.

> Ambassador Dearing to Secretary Stimson, no. 624, Apr. 12, 1931, MS. Department of State, file 823.01/70; Mr. Dearing to Mr. Stimson, no. 224, May 15, 1931, *ibid.* 823.01/78; Mr. Stimson to Mr. Dearing, no. 35, May 19, 1931, *ibid.* 823.01/79; Mr. Dearing to Mr. Stimson, no. 229, May 21, 1931, *ibid.* 823.01/82.

Resumption
of relations:
Chile, 1925

Upon the return of President Alessandri to Chile in March 1925, after being nominally on leave of absence from the country since September 1924, the question arose as to the manner in which relations might be resumed with his government. The Solicitor for the Department of State said in an opinion of March 18, 1925 with reference to this point:

> As to the mode of resumption of diplomatic relations, it may be observed that this Government has not recognized any régime as the Government of Chile since Alessandri's departure. As the individual who resumes office is identical with him who left it, there may be little formality required in dealing with him as the head of the Government of Chile. Perhaps the mode of recognition is unimportant. The time of according recognition is also partly a matter of policy. All the circumstances connected with the Alessandri case may combine to encourage the United States to believe that no delay should ensue.

> Opinion of the Solicitor, Mar. 18, 1925, MS. Department of State, file FW825.01/42.

During the course of negotiations between the United States and Turkey looking toward a resumption of diplomatic relations, the Minister of Foreign Affairs of Turkey expressed a doubt that it was possible under international law to accredit ambassadors through an exchange of notes. The High Commissioner having requested instructions concerning this matter, the Department of State replied:

> It is not considered by the Government of the United States that any written agreement, treaty, convention, protocol or exchange of notes of a formal character is a necessary or, as a matter of fact, even a usual condition precedent to a resumption of diplomatic relations. Ambassadors and ministers are not accredited through an exchange of notes but through the presentation of letters of credence to the Chief of State, the "agréments" as a matter of courtesy having previously been requested and received.
>
> The procedure outlined above represents the practice of the Government of the United States. For example, in 1919 diplomatic relations were established by the United States with Poland and Czechoslovakia, but as yet no treaties or conventions have been negotiated between these two countries and the Government of the United States. While of the opinion that diplomatic relations and treaty relations are not interdependent, the United States would, however, in deference to the point of view of Turkey, be prepared to accomplish the resumption of diplomatic and consular relations in a protocol or in an exchange of notes. The following may be cited as instances in which there have been exchanges of correspondence as one of the steps in the resumption of diplomatic relations: Brazil, 1827; Mexico, 1923; and Nicaragua, 1926. While making reference to the resumption of diplomatic relations, these notes have also been concerned with the settlement of certain questions outstanding between the two Governments.
> [Paraphrase.]

High Commissioner Bristol to Secretary Kellogg, no. 5, Jan. 30, 1927, and Mr. Kellogg to Mr. Bristol, no. 4, Feb. 1, 1927, MS. Department of State, file 711.672/552.

Recognition has occasionally been extended through joint action by a number of governments, but it has been the usual practice of the United States to refrain from participating in such joint action. (See especially its refusal to agree to joint action in the recognition of the government of Colonel Franco in Paraguay in 1936, *post* §47. See, however, the joint note of December 9, 1924 extending recognition to Tuan Chi-jui in China, *post* §51.) It has, however, in some instances conferred with other governments before extending recognition and in some cases acted simultaneously with them (see especially the recognition of certain Central American governments, *post* §47). The procedure followed in conferring with other Latin American governments concerning the recognition of the Cuban Government in

1934 was described in a letter from the Assistant Secretary of State
(Welles) in response to a private inquiry:

> I have received your letter of January 23, 1934, and am pleased
> to learn your approval of the course followed by the President in
> conferring with the diplomatic representatives of the various
> Latin American countries prior to recognition of the present
> Cuban Government.
> This matter was handled in an entirely informal way, and there
> were no written invitations, et cetera. In this case, once the
> President had decided upon the desirability of conferring with the
> Latin American representatives, invitations were extended by
> telephone, during the morning of January 22. At the conference
> that afternoon the President advised the diplomatic representa-
> tives of our information on the Cuban situation, which was to the
> effect that the Government of Dr. Mendieta was maintaining
> order and performing the normal functions of government, and
> that it appeared to enjoy the substantial support of the Cuban
> people and of the organized political groups; and that in view of
> this situation, we intended to extend recognition to the Govern-
> ment of Dr. Mendieta. No written record appears to have been
> kept of this meeting. At four o'clock the afternoon of January
> 23, the Chargé d'Affaires at Habana, acting under instructions,
> extended formal recognition to the Cuban Government through
> the Cuban Secretary of State, Dr. Torriente.

MS. Department of State, file 837.01/102.

PREREQUISITES

§33

It has been the practice of the Government of the United States to
require the fulfilment of certain conditions by new governments as a
prerequisite to recognition. The special policy pursued by the United
States during a part of the period since 1906, with reference to the
recognition of governments coming into power in disregard of *constitutional* procedure, has assumed a political importance which has
tended to obscure the pattern of uniformity obtaining in the practice
of recognition in other instances. Aside from this prerequisite of
"constitutionalism" adopted in the recognition of Central American
governments and inaugurated by President Woodrow Wilson with
reference particularly to certain other of the American republics, the
prerequisites during this period have conformed substantially to the
so-called *de facto* policy of recognition instituted by Jefferson.

General practice

". . . The time element as such does not enter into considerations
affecting recognition of a new government", declared the Department
of State in a letter of May 16, 1936 to Representative Tinkham, concerning the recognition of the government of Colonel Franco in Paraguay, "except that, as set forth in my previous letter to you [of April 2

1936], it is the rule of the United States 'to defer recognition of another executive in its place until it shall appear that it is in possession of the machinery of the state, administering the government with the assent of the people thereof and without substantial resistance to its authority, and that it is in a position to fulfill all the international obligations and responsibilities incumbent upon a sovereign state under treaties and international law'. You will appreciate that the length of time necessary for a new government to satisfy our government upon these points will vary to a great extent in each case."

> Secretary Hull to Representative Tinkham, May 16, 1936, MS. Department of State, file 834.01/37. In the letter of Apr. 2, 1936, mentioned in the above quotation, the Department had said:
>
> "The general policy of the American Government with respect to the recognition of foreign governments is expressed in the following extract from an instruction sent to the American Minister at Bogotá by the Acting Secretary of State on September 8, 1900:
>
> "'The policy of the United States, announced and practiced upon occasion for more than a century, has been and is to refrain from acting upon conflicting claims to the de jure control of the executive power of a foreign state; but to base the recognition of a foreign government solely on its de facto ability to hold the reins of administrative power. When, by reason of revolution or other internal change not wrought by regular constitutional methods, a conflict of authority exists in another country whereby the titular government to which our representatives are accredited is reduced from power and authority, the rule of the United States is to defer recognition of another executive in its place until it shall appear that it is in possession of the machinery of the state, administering government with the assent of the people thereof and without substantial resistance to its authority, and that it is in a position to fulfill all the international obligations and responsibilities incumbent upon a sovereign state under treaties and international law. When its establishment upon such de facto basis is ascertained, it is recognized by directing the United States representative formally to notify its proper minister of his readiness to enter into relations with it, and thereafter by the still more formal process of receiving and issuing new credentials for the respective diplomatic agents.' (Moore—International Law Digest—Volume I, pages 138–139.)" *Ibid.* 834.01/34.

The general practice followed by the Government of the United States, aside from the special cases mentioned at the beginning of this section, was described in a memorandum of March 28, 1913, prepared by the Assistant Secretary of State (Adee) for the Secretary of State, with special reference to the question of recognizing the Government of the Republic of China:

> It will, I think, simplify the matter to keep in mind the distinction between the recognition necessary to the conduct of international business between two countries and the recognition of the *form* of government professed by a foreign country.
> In the former case, ever since the American Revolution entrance upon diplomatic intercourse with foreign states has been *de facto*, dependent upon the existence of three conditions of

fact: the control of the administrative machinery of the state; the general acquiescence of its people; and the ability and willingness of their government to discharge international and conventional obligations. The form of government has not been a conditional factor in such recognition; in other words, the *de jure* element of legitimacy of title has been left aside, probably because liable to involve dynastic or constitutional questions hardly within our competency to adjudicate, especially so when the organic form of government has been changed, as by revolution, from a monarchy to a commonwealth or vice versa. The general practice in such cases has been to satisfy ourselves that the change was effective and to enter into relation with the authority in *de facto* possession.

MS. Department of State, file 893.00/1669; 1913 For. Rel. 100–102. See, to the same effect, memorandum of Mar. 7, 1910, by the Assistant Secretary of State (Adee) with reference to the question raised by the Minister in Panama as to whether President Mendoza's induction into office had been accomplished in accordance with constitutional formalities. MS. Department of State, file 819.00/225.

The exact phraseology of the formula of recognition thus concisely stated by Mr. Adee has varied from time to time, not all these prerequisites being given explicit statement on every occasion. However, the essential tests adopted in determining the question of recognition have varied but little. Attention is invited especially to the following instances of recognition set forth in the following sections of this chapter: Persia, 1909, §50; Haiti, 1911, §47; Peru, 1914, 1919, §47; China, 1913, §51; Chile, 1924, §47; Argentina, Bolivia, and Peru, 1930, §47; Spain, 1931, §48; Bolivia, 1936, §47; Ecuador, 1937, §47. In nearly all these instances the ability and willingness of the new government to discharge its international

International obligations

obligations has been stressed as a prerequisite to recognition. In those instances in which this has not been stated explicitly, it has probably been considered implicit in the requirement that the government be stable and in control of the machinery of government. In some instances this factor has been considered of paramount importance. This was especially true in the case of the long-deferred recognition of the Union of Soviet Socialist Republics (see *post* §48). In the steps which finally led to the recognition of the Mexican Government in 1923, its ability and willingness to fulfil its international obligations played a primary part. Secretary Hughes declared in an instruction of June 8, 1921 to the Embassy in Mexico:

. . . Whenever Mexico is ready to give assurances that she will perform her fundamental obligation in the protection both of persons and of rights of property validly acquired, there will be no obstacles to the most advantageous relations between the two peoples.

MS. Department of State, file 711.1211/8a; 1921 For. Rel., vol. II, pp. 406–407.

In an address prepared by President Harding, released on July 31, 1923, but not delivered on account of his death, it was said:

". . . It is not for us to suggest what laws she shall have relating to the future, for we willingly acclaim Mexico as the judge of her own domestic policy. We do, however, maintain one clear principle which lies at the foundation of all international intercourse. When a nation has invited intercourse with other nations and has enacted laws under which investments have been legally made, contracts entered into, and property rights acquired by citizens of other jurisdictions, it is an essential condition of international intercourse that lawful obligations shall be met and that there shall be no resort to confiscation and repudiation." *Address Prepared by President Warren G. Harding on our Foreign Relations,* intended to be delivered at San Francisco, California, July 31, 1923 (Washington: Government Printing Office, 1923) 7. See also Secretary Hughes to Mr. John Barton Payne, May 5, 1923, MS. Department of State, file 711.1211/86a; 1923 For. Rel., vol. II, pp. 536–548.

For an exchange of views concerning the content of the term *international obligations,* see Secretary Stimson to Ambassador Culbertson, nos. 49 and 55, July 16 and 27, 1932, MS. Department of State, files 825.00 Revolutions/158, 825.00 Revolutions/171; Mr. Culbertson to Mr. Stimson, no. 156, July 29, 1932, *ibid.* file 825.00 Revolutions/173; Mr. Stimson to Mr. Culbertson, nos. 58 and 62, July 29 and Aug. 12, 1932, *ibid.* files 825.01/100, 825.00 Revolutions/183; Mr. Culbertson to Mr. Stimson, nos. 1241 and 218, Aug. 24 and Oct. 16, 1932, *ibid.* 825.516/228, 825.00 Revolutions/226; Mr. Stimson to Mr. Culbertson, no. 85, Oct. 20, 1932, *ibid.* file 825.01/147A.

While a number of factors contributed to the refusal of the United States to recognize the Soviet Government prior to 1933, the policy of non-recognition was based principally upon the failure of that Government to observe certain international obligations to which the United States attached great importance. The features of the policy pursued by the Soviet Government, which were decisive in the refusal of the United States to recognize it, were set forth at some length in a note of August 10, 1920 from the Department of State to the Italian Ambassador. U. S. S. R.

Secretary Colby to the Italian Ambassador (Avezzana), Aug. 10, 1920, MS. Department of State, file 760c.61/300b; 1920 For. Rel., vol. III, pp. 463, 466–468.

They were also set forth at considerable length in a letter of July 19, 1923, from Secretary Hughes to Mr. Gompers, President of the American Federation of Labor, reading as follows: Hughes to Gompers, July 19, 1923

. . . We are not concerned with the question of the legitimacy of a government as judged by former European standards. We recognize the right of revolution and we do not attempt to determine the internal concerns of other States. The following words of Thomas Jefferson, in 1793, express a fundamental principle: "We surely cannot deny to any nation that right whereon our own Government is founded,—that everyone may govern itself according to whatever form it pleases, and change these forms at its own will; and that it may transact its business with foreign nations through whatever organ it thinks proper, whether king, convention, assembly, committee, president or anything else it may choose. The will of the nation is the only thing essential to be regarded." It was undoubtedly this principle which was invoked by the representative of the Department of State, in the statement which you quote as having been made in February, 1921, before the House Committee on Foreign Affairs on the consideration of House Resolution 635, 66th Congress, 3d Session. It must be borne in mind, however, that while this Government has laid stress upon the value of expressed popular approval in determining whether a new government should be recognized, it has never insisted that the will of the people of a foreign State may not be manifested by long continued acquiescence in a regime actually functioning as a government. When there is a question as to the will of the nation it has generally been regarded as a wise precaution to give sufficient time to enable a new regime to prove its stability and the apparent acquiescence of the people in the exercise of the authority it has assumed. The application of these familiar principles, in dealing with foreign States, is not in derogation of the democratic ideals cherished by our people, and constitutes no justification of tyranny in any form, but proceeds upon a consideration of the importance of international intercourse and upon the established American principle of non-intervention in the internal concerns of other peoples.

But while a foreign regime may have securely established itself through the exercise of control and the submission of the people to, or their acquiescence in, its exercise of authority, there still remain other questions to be considered. Recognition is an invitation to intercourse. It is accompanied on the part of the new government by the clearly implied or express promise to fulfill the obligations of intercourse. These obligations include, among other things, the protection of the persons and property of the citizens of one country lawfully pursuing their business in the territory of the other and abstention from hostile propaganda by one country in the territory of the other. In the case of the existing regime in Russia, there has not only been the tyrannical procedure to which you refer, and which has caused the question of the submission or acquiescence of the Russian people to remain an open one, but also a repudiation of the obligations inherent in international intercourse and a defiance of the principles upon which alone it can be conducted.

The persons of our citizens in Russia are for the moment free from harm. No assurance exists, however, against a repetition of the arbitrary detentions which some of them have suffered in the past. The situation with respect to property is even more palpable. The obligations of Russia to the taxpayers of the United States remain repudiated. The many American citizens who have suffered directly or indirectly by the confiscation of American property in Russia remain without the prospect of indemnification. We have had recent evidence, moreover, that the policy of confiscation is by no means at an end. The effective jurisdiction of Moscow was recently extended to Vladivostok and soon thereafter Moscow directed the carrying out in that city of confiscatory measures such as we saw in Western Russia during 1917 and 1918.

What is most serious is that there is conclusive evidence that those in control at Moscow have not given up their original purpose of destroying existing governments wherever they can do so throughout the world. Their efforts in this direction have recently been lessened in intensity only by the reduction of the cash resources at their disposal.

.   .   .   .

While this spirit of destruction at home and abroad remains unaltered the question of recognition by our Government of the authorities at Moscow cannot be determined by mere economic considerations or by the establishment in some degree of a more prosperous condition, which of course we should be glad to note, or simply by a consideration of the probable stability of the regime in question. There cannot be intercourse among nations any more than among individuals except upon a general assumption of good faith. We would welcome convincing evidence of a desire of the Russian authorities to observe the fundamental conditions of international intercourse and the abandonment by them of the persistent attempts to subvert the institutions of democracy as maintained in this country and in others. It may confidently be added that respect by the Moscow regime for the liberties of other peoples will most likely be accompanied by appropriate respect for the ˙essential rights and liberties of the Russian people themselves. The sentiment of our people is not deemed to be favorable to the acceptance into political fellowship of this regime so long as it denies the essential bases of intercourse and cherishes, as an ultimate and definite aim, the destruction of the free institutions which we have laboriously built up, containing as they do the necessary assurances of the freedom of labor upon which our prosperity must depend.

Mr. Gompers to Secretary Hughes, July 9, 1923, and Mr. Hughes to Mr. Gompers, July 19, 1923, MS. Department of State, file 861.01/623; 1923 For. Rel., vol. II, pp. 760–764. For a further statement of the reasons for the continued non-recognition of Russia, see *post* §48. For a letter from Secretary Hughes to Senator Borah, Chairman of the Committee on Foreign Relations, Jan. 21, 1924, transmitting information relative to propaganda carried on in the United States directed from Russia, see *Recognition of Russia, Hearings Before a Subcommittee of the Committee on Foreign Relations, United States Senate*, 68th Cong., 1st sess., pursuant to S. Res. 50, pt. 2 (Washington, 1924).

In the course of its consideration of the matter of recognizing the Socialist government of Chile, the Department of State instructed the Embassy in Chile on July 16, 1932: "Your understanding is correct that it is the policy of this Government not to associate recognition with the particular type of government or particular organization which a country may determine to adopt" [paraphrase]. Secretary Stimson to Ambassador Culbertson, no. 49, July 16, 1932, MS. Department of State, file 825.00 Revolutions/158.

Constitu-
tional
procedure

The element of "constitutionality" has on occasion entered into the prerequisites applied by the United States with reference to the recognition of governments established upon the substitution of one form of government for another. Upon the overthrow of the monarchy in Portugal in October 1911, the Department of State withheld recognition "pending the obvious reestablishment of constitutional order". This was explained to mean, however, the establishment of "conditions showing that the freely expressed wish of the Portuguese people accepts and gives national sanction to the proclaimed republic". It was essentially an application of Jefferson's formula of "the will of the nation substantially declared". Secretary Jefferson to the Minister in France (Morris), Nov. 7, 1792, I Moore's Dig. 120.

> The Acting Secretary of State (Adee) to Minister Gage, Oct. 8, 1910, MS. Department of State, file 853.00/89; Secretary Knox to Mr. Gage, Oct. 18, 1910, *ibid.* 853.00/103; 1910 For. Rel. 825–828.

A somewhat similar statement was made in the case of the Chinese Republic by President Taft who declared in his message to Congress on December 3, 1912:

China, 1912

> . . . A constituent assembly, composed of representatives duly chosen by the people of China in the elections that are now being held, has been called to meet in January next to adopt a permanent constitution and organize the Government of the nascent Republic. During the formative constitutional stage and pending definitive action by the assembly, as expressive of the popular will, and the hoped-for establishment of a stable republican form of government, capable of fulfilling its international obligations, the United States is, according to precedent, maintaining full and friendly de facto relations with the provisional Government.

> 1912 For. Rel. xxi–xxii. Special factors prompted the delay in the recognition of the Government of Greece between 1920 and 1924 (see *post* §48). Upon the establishment of a republic in Spain in 1931, recognition was not delayed pending constitutional reorganization (see *post* §48).

The test of compliance with constitutional procedure has also been applied by the Government of the United States in certain instances in Latin America involving merely the substitution of one government for another, rather than a change in the form of government. These instances fall into two groups, namely, those coming under the so-called "Wilsonian policy" and those determined by the Central American policy adopted in accord with the Central American treaties of December 20, 1907 and February 7, 1923.

Wilson's
policy

When President Wilson came into office on March 4, 1913 he was faced with the immediate necessity of deciding the question of the recognition of the Huerta government in Mexico. Huerta had been elected Provisional President on February 20, 1913, after the arrest of President Madero on February 18 and his resignation while in prison on February 19. On account of the subsequent assassination of Madero, the delay on the part of Huerta in giving specific assurances requested by the United States, and certain other considerations, the Taft administration had withheld recognition of Huerta. On March 6 Secretary Bryan approved the action of the Ambassador in Mexico, as Dean of the Diplomatic Corps, in handing to the Minister of Foreign Affairs a note stating that the Diplomatic Corps had "entered into communication with the Provisional Government without committing themselves in any way as regards formal recognition", it being "left to their respective Governments to determine when such recognition shall be accorded".

MS. Department of State, file 812.00/6489; 1913 For. Rel. 758.

Five days later President Wilson issued a formal public statement setting forth the principles which would guide his action not only with respect to the recognition of Huerta but also with respect to any such cases that might arise in the future:

Cooperation is possible only when supported at every turn by the orderly processes of just government based upon law, not upon arbitrary or irregular force. We hold, as I am sure all thoughtful leaders of republican government everywhere hold, that just government rests always upon the consent of the governed, and that there can be no freedom without order based upon law and upon the public conscience and approval. We shall look to make these principles the basis of mutual intercourse, respect, and helpfulness between our sister republics and ourselves. We shall lend our influence of every kind to the realization of these principles in fact and practice, knowing that disorder, personal intrigues, and defiance of constitutional rights weaken and discredit government and injure none so much as the people who are unfortunate enough to have their common life and their common affairs so tainted and disturbed. We can have no sympathy with those who seek to seize the power of government to advance their own personal interests or ambition. We are the friends of peace, but we know that there can be no lasting or stable peace in such circumstances. As friends, therefore, we shall prefer those who act in the interest of peace and honor, who protect private rights, and respect the restraints of constitutional provision. Mutual respect seems to us the indispensable foundation of friendship between states, as between individuals.

Statement of Mar. 11, 1913

MS. Department of State, file 710.11/102a; 1913 For. Rel. 7.

The general features of this policy were further elaborated in a circular instruction of Nov. 24, 1913 to diplomatic missions:

"The purpose of the United States is solely and singly to secure peace and order in Central America by seeing to it that the processes of self government there are not interrupted or set aside.

"Usurpations like that of General Huerta menace the peace and development of America as nothing else could. They not only render the develop-

ment of ordered self government impossible; they also tend to set law
entirely aside, to put the lives and fortunes of citizens and foreigners alike
in constant jeopardy, to invalidate contracts and concessions in any way
the usurper may devise for his own profit and to impair both the national
credit and all the foundations of business, domestic or foreign.

"It is the purpose of the United States therefore to discredit and defeat
such usurpations whenever they occur.

.   .   .   .   .   .

"Its fixed resolve is that no such interruption of civil order shall be tolerated in so far as it is concerned. Each conspicuous instance in which
usurpations of this kind are prevented will render their recurrence less and
in the end a state of affairs will be secured in Mexico and elsewhere upon
this continent which will assure the peace of America and the untrammeled
development of its economic and social relations with the rest of the world."

MS. Department of State, file 812.00/11443d; 1914 For. Rel. 443–444.

In reporting to Congress on the Mexican situation on August 27,
1913, President Wilson stated that he had given the following instructions to ex-Governor John Lind, of Minnesota, whom he had sent to
Mexico as his personal representative in an attempt to reach an
agreement with Huerta:

A satisfactory settlement seems to us to be conditioned on—

(a) An immediate cessation of fighting throughout Mexico, a
definite armistice solemnly entered into and scrupulously
observed;
(b) Security given for an early and free election in which all
will agree to take part;
(c) The consent of General Huerta to bind himself not to be a
candidate for election as President of the Republic at this
election; and
(d) The agreement of all parties to abide by the results of the
election and cooperate in the most loyal way in organizing and
supporting the new administration.

Huerta rejected these proposals.

1913 For. Rel. 820, 822, 823–827. Huerta ultimately resigned on July
15, 1914, and on Oct. 19, 1915 the government of General Carranza was
recognized as the *de facto* government of Mexico, Carranza having given
satisfactory assurances with respect to the disposition of outstanding questions. *De jure* recognition was extended to him on Aug. 31, 1917 after his
election. See *post* §47.

The policy thus formulated with immediate reference to the situation in Mexico was shortly given further application. Governor

Dominican
Republic,
1913–16

Céspedes, of the Province of Puerto Plata in the Dominican Republic,
having organized a separate government in opposition to that of
President Bordas, the Department of State instructed the Chargé
d'Affaires on September 4, 1913 to take the first opportunity to
communicate to Governor Céspedes "the profound displeasure felt
by this Government at his pernicious revolutionary activity, for which

this Government will not fail to fix the responsibility". This was supplemented by an instruction of September 9 to the Minister:

> . . . The President directs me to say for your instruction that the influence of this Government will be exerted for the support of lawful authorities in Santo Domingo, and for the discouragement of any and all insurrectionary methods. You will carry with you a copy of the President's statement of last March which sets forth fully, and in such a way as to leave no doubt, his position on two important points, namely: First, that we can have no sympathy with those who seek to seize the power of government to advance their own personal interests or ambition; and second, that the test of a republican form of government is to be found in its responsiveness to the will of the people, its just powers being derived from the consent of the governed.

In a later instruction of April 4, 1914, the Minister was informed that too much emphasis could not be placed on these two points: "(1) that the President of the United States feels strongly that the best results will be accomplished only by officers of the Government who are chosen by the people"; and "(2) that changes in laws and in personnel of the Government should be by constitutional methods and not by revolution".

> Secretary Bryan to Chargé Curtis, Sept. 4, 1913, MS. Department of State, file 839/860; Secretary Bryan to Minister Sullivan, Sept. 9, 1913 and Apr. 4, 1914, *ibid.* files 839.00/912a, 839.00/1136; 1913 For. Rel. 425–427; 1914 For. Rel. 223–224.

Upon the outbreak of a revolution in Ecuador in December 1913 Secretary Bryan sent the following instruction to the Minister on December 18: Ecuador, 1913

> Call the Government's attention to the President's statement of policy, communicated in Department's March 6 [*12*] and ascertain if there is anything we can do to discourage the revolutionists and support the constitutional Government. Ascertain the reasons given by the revolutionists for their attack. In Santo Domingo our Minister recently secured a cessation of hostilities on condition that desired reforms would be effected peacefully, and yesterday a special election was held there. We shall be pleased to resort to whatever means the United States can properly employ to cause the revolutionists to follow constitutional methods of obtaining redress. [Paraphrase.]

> MS. Department of State, file 822.00/326. No action was taken in pursuance of this instruction.

Oreste Zamor having been elected President by the National Assembly of Haiti on February 8, 1914 (subsequent to the resignation Haiti, 1914 under military pressure on January 27, 1914 of President Oreste), Secretary Bryan instructed the Minister on February 26:

> . . . You will immediately seek an interview with the Minister for Foreign Affairs of the de facto Government at Port au Prince and state to him that the Government of the United States will be probably disposed to recognize the Government of Oreste Zamor as the duly elected constitutional government of the Republic of Haiti, since it appears from the support which it received in the north and in the other parts of the Republic that the advent of this Government is based upon the consent of the governed.
>
> You will further state that the Government of the United States has always considered that there can be no freedom without order based upon law and upon public conscience and approval; that the United States will always lend its influence to the realization of these principles in practice; and that, desiring the peace and prosperity of all its sister republics, this Government desires to extend its genuine disinterested friendship and aid for the continuance of peace and prosperity in Haiti.

Upon the receipt of certain assurances from President Zamor, recognition was extended to him on March 1, "as constitutional President duly elected by the Haitian Congress, . . . fully established in power with the assent of the people".

> Secretary Bryan to Minister Smith, Feb. 26 and Mar. 1, 1914, MS. Department of State, files 838.00/855, 838.00/864; 1914 For. Rel. 334–341.
>
> Zamor was overthrown on Oct. 29, 1914 and was followed in rapid succession in the presidency by Théodore, Sam, and Bobo, none of whom was recognized by the United States. Dartiguenave, who was elected on Aug. 12, 1915, was recognized by the United States on Sept. 16 following, coincidentally with the signing of the treaty of that date with Haiti. See *post* §47.

Cuba, 1917

The Minister in Cuba reported to the Department of State on February 12, 1917 that an organized revolution against the Government existed in two and probably in three provinces, the immediate cause for the revolutionary activities apparently being dissatisfaction over the conduct of recent elections, especially in the Province of Santa Clara. The next day Secretary Lansing instructed the Minister to issue the following statement as coming from the Government of the United States:

> The Government of the United States has received with the greatest apprehension the reports which have come to it to the effect that there exists organized revolt against the Government of Cuba in several provinces and that several towns have been seized by insurrectionists.
>
> Reports such as these of insurrection against the constituted Government cannot be considered except as of the most serious nature since the Government of the United States has given its

confidence and support only to Governments established through legal and constitutional methods.

During the past four years the Government of the United States has clearly and definitely set forth its position in regard to the recognition of governments which have come into power through revolution and other illegal methods and at this time desires to emphasize its position in regard to the present situation in Cuba. Its friendship for the Cuban people, which has been shown on repeated occasions, and the duties which are incumbent upon it on account of the agreement between the two countries force the Government of the United States to make clear its future policy at this time.

MS. Department of State, file 837.00/1068; see also 1917 For. Rel. 356. The Cuban Congress met on May 7, counted the electoral vote, and proclaimed Menocal and Nuñez elected President and Vice President. The revolutionary disturbances were successfully suppressed. Minister Gonzales to Secretary Lansing, May 7, 1917, MS. Department of State, file 837.00/1336; 1917 For. Rel. 401–411.

The policy of not recognizing revolutionary governments also received application during Wilson's administration in Central America but was there based partially upon the Central American treaty of 1907 (see *post*, this section). It was not applied with respect to the recognition of any non-American government, nor was it applied with respect to the recognition of new governments in American republics other than those referred to above (see especially recognition of governments coming into power in Peru in 1914 and 1919, *post* §47). The policy was invoked in a few instances subsequent to the termination of Wilson's administration in 1921 (see especially the recognition of the Saavedra government in Bolivia in 1921, *post* §47, and the delay of three years in the recognition of the government which overthrew the existing government in Ecuador in July 1925, *post* §47). The administration of President Hoover definitely abandoned the test of "constitutionality" as a prerequisite to the recognition of new governments, except in Central America. Secretary Stimson declared in an address delivered before the Council on Foreign Relations in New York City, on February 6, 1931:

Further development

The present administration has refused to follow the policy of Mr. Wilson and has followed consistently the former practice of this Government since the days of Jefferson. As soon as it was reported to us, through our diplomatic representatives, that the new governments in Bolivia, Peru, Argentina, Brazil, and Panama were in control of the administrative machinery of the state, with the apparent general acquiescence of their people, and that they were willing and apparently able to discharge their international and conventional obligations, they were recognized by our Government. And, in view of the economic depression, with the consequent need for prompt measures of financial stabilization, we did this with as little delay as possible in order to give those sorely pressed countries the quickest possible opportunities for recovering their economic poise.

Such has been our policy in all cases where international practice was not affected or controlled by preexisting treaty.

The United States and the Other American Republics, Department of State Latin American Ser. 4 (1931) 8. For the facts concerning the recognition of the new governments in Bolivia, Peru, Argentina, Brazil, and Panama, mentioned by Mr. Stimson, see *post* §47.

Central
America;
treaty of 1907

. . . In view of the imminent danger of war in the summer of 1907 [between Nicaragua and the other Central American Governments], the Presidents of the United States and Mexico jointly offered their mediation. This was accepted by all of the Central American governments, it being agreed that a conference should be held in Washington to settle all outstanding difficulties and to establish the basis for peaceful relations between the Central American republics.

The Conference adopted eight treaties. The United States and Mexico, though their delegates were present at the Conference, did not sign the treaties. To the first treaty, the General Treaty of Peace and Amity, was added an annex upon which has subsequently been based the recognition policy of the United States toward Central America. Its principal provisions are the following:

'ARTICLE I. The Government of the High Contracting Parties shall not recognize any other Government which may come into power in any of the five Republics as a consequence of a *coup d'etat*, or of a revolution against the recognized Government, so long as the freely elected representatives of the people thereof, have not constitutionally reorganized the country.

'ARTICLE II. No Government of Central America shall in case of civil war intervene in favor of or against the Government of the country where the struggle takes place.

'ARTICLE III. The Governments of Central America, in the first place, are recommended to endeavor to bring about, by the means at their command, a constitutional reform in the sense of prohibiting the reelection of the President of a Republic, where such prohibition does not exist, secondly to adopt all measures necessary to effect a complete guarantee of the principle of alternation in power.'

The United States and Nicaragua: A Survey of the Relations from 1909 to 1932, Department of State Latin American Ser. 6 (1932) 43–44. The treaty of Dec. 20, 1907 is printed in 2 Treaties, etc. (Malloy, 1910) 2397.

Severance of
relations:
Nicaragua,
1909

In his note of December 1, 1909 to the Nicaraguan Chargé d'Affaires announcing the severance of relations with Nicaragua, Secretary Knox, after describing the situation created by the Zelaya government, said:

In view of the interests of the United States and of its relation to the Washington conventions, appeal against this situation has long since been made to this Government by a majority of the Central American Republics.

He added further:

> To insure the future protection of legitimate American interests, in consideration of the interests of the majority of the Central American Republics, and in the hope of making more effective the friendly offices exerted under the Washington conventions, the Government of the United States reserves for further consideration at the proper time the question of stipulating also that the constitutional Government of Nicaragua obligate itself by convention, for the benefit of all the Governments concerned, as a guaranty for its future loyal support of the Washington conventions and their peaceful and progressive aims.

MS. Department of State, file 6369/272; 1909 For. Rel. 455, 457.

Thomas C. Dawson, the Minister in Panama, who was designated on Oct. 11, 1910 as special agent of the United States near the Provisional Government of Nicaragua, was instructed to proceed at once to Nicaragua "and there immediately enter into relations with the executive power of the Provisional Government of Managua" and to present, in part, the following views for that purpose:

"First. The reestablishment of a constitutional government and the election of a constitutional president, which should take place at the earliest practicable date, the absolute freedom of all elections being guaranteed by the Provisional Government. The constitution to be adopted should be thoroughly liberal in character and provide suitable guaranties for foreigners. The constitutional inhibitions of commercial monopolies should be affirmed." The Acting Secretary of State (Adee) to Minister Dawson, Oct. 11, 1910, MS. Department of State, file 817.00/1432a; 1910 For. Rel. 763.

In the course of a conversation with the Minister of Costa Rica at the Department of State on Oct. 3, 1910, the Acting Secretary of State (Adee), speaking with reference to the Central American treaty of Dec. 20, 1907, said:

"I referred to Article 1 of the additional convention of Washington by which the five Central American states bound themselves not to recognize any revolutionary government until the people should have chosen national representatives. While that article was not binding upon the United States, our uniform policy was quite in accordance with its precepts." MS. Department of State, file 817.00/1431.

Following serious revolutionary disturbances against the government of President Díaz, led principally by General Mena, former Minister of War, during the course of which the United States found it necessary to land United States marines to protect American interests, the Department of State, on September 4, 1912, instructed the Minister at Managua to communicate to the Government of Nicaragua a declaration of the policy of the United States, reading in part as follows:

Nicaragua, 1912

> In discountenancing Zelaya, whose régime of barbarity and corruption was ended by the Nicaraguan nation after a bloody war, the Government of the United States opposed not only the individual but the system, and this Government could not

countenance any movement to restore the same destructive régime. The Government of the United States will, therefore, discountenance any revival of Zelayaism and will lend its strong moral support to the cause of legally constituted good government for the benefit of the people of Nicaragua, whom it has long sought to aid in their just aspiration toward peace and prosperity under constitutional and orderly government. [Paraphrase.]

The Acting Secretary of State (Wilson) to Minister Weitzel, Sept. 4, 1912, MS. Department of State, file 817.00/1940b; 1912 For. Rel. 1043.

General treaty of peace and amity, 1923

. . . In 1922, to avert impending trouble, the Presidents of Nicaragua, Honduras, and El Salvador met on board the *Tacoma*, a war vessel of the United States, and signed an agreement reaffirming and strengthening the 1907 treaties. Article V of the "Tacoma Agreement" provided for another conference to which all the Central American countries would be invited, and at the suggestion of the three signatory nations, the invitations for this conference were issued by the United States. The conference, which met in Washington, in article II of the General Treaty of Peace and Amity signed February 7, 1923, not only reiterated the provisions of the 1907 treaty regarding the nonrecognition of Governments coming into power through a *coup d'état* or revolution but also strengthened it. This article reads as follows:

"Desiring to make secure in the Republics of Central America the benefits which are derived from the maintenance of free institutions and to contribute at the same time toward strengthening their stability, and the prestige with which they should be surrounded, they declare that every act, disposition or measure which alters the constitutional organization in any of them is to be deemed a menace to the peace of said Republics, whether it proceed from any public power or from the private citizens.

"Consequently, the Governments of the Contracting Parties will not recognize any other Government which may come into power in any of the five Republics through a *coup d'etat* or a revolution against a recognized Government, so long as the freely elected representatives of the people thereof have not constitutionally reorganized the country. And even in such a case they obligate themselves not to acknowledge the recognition if any of the persons elected as President, Vice-President or Chief of State designate should fall under any of the following heads:

"(1) If he should be the leader or one of the leaders of a *coup d'etat* or revolution, or through blood relationship or marriage, be an ascendent or descendent or brother of such leader or leaders.

"(2) If he should have been a Secretary of State or should have held some high military command during the accomplishment of the *coup d'etat*, the revolution, or while the election was being carried on, or if he should have held this office or command within the six months preceding the *coup d'etat*, revolution, or the election."

The United States and Nicaragua: A Survey of the Relations from 1909 to 1932, Department of State Latin American Ser. 6 (1932) 45.

Article V of the treaty of February 7, 1923 provided further:

> The Contracting Parties obligate themselves to maintain in their respective Constitutions the principle of non-re-election to the office of President and Vice-President of the Republic; and those of the Contracting Parties whose Constitutions permit such re-election, obligate themselves to introduce a constitutional reform to this effect in their next legislative session after the ratification of the present Treaty.

For the text of the treaty, see *Conference on Central American Affairs, Washington, December 4, 1922—February 7, 1923* (1923) 287–295.

The United States promptly lent its support to the rules embodied in this treaty by instructing the Legation in Honduras to give the widest publicity to the following declaration:

> The attitude of the Government of the United States with respect to the recognition of new Governments in the five Central American Republics whose representatives signed at Washington on February 7, 1923, a general Treaty of Peace and Amity, to which the United States was not a party, but with the provisions of which it is in the most hearty accord, will be consonant with the provisions of Article II thereof which stipulates that the contracting parties— *(Policy of the United States)*
>
> . . . will not recognize any other Government which may come into power in any of the five Republics through a coup d'etat or a revolution against a recognized Government, so long as the freely elected representatives of the people thereof have not constitutionally reorganized the country. And even in such a case they obligate themselves not to acknowledge the recognition if any of the persons elected as President, Vice-President or Chief of State designate should fall under any of the following heads:
>
> 1) If he should be the leader or one of the leaders of a coup d'etat or revolution, or through blood relationship or marriage, be an ascendent or descendent or brother of such leader or leaders.
>
> 2) If he should have been a Secretary of State or should have held some high military command during the accomplishment of the coup d'etat, the revolution, or while the election was being carried on, or if he should have held this office or command within the six months preceding the coup d'etat, revolution, or the election.

This was supplemented by a further instruction to the Legation in Honduras on July 14, 1923:

> The position of the Government of the United States with reference to the recognition of new governments in Central America was set forth in the Department's No. 26, June 30, 3 p. m., and any modifications made by the congresses of any of the Central American States in the Treaty of Peace and Amity of February 7, 1923, ratifying that Treaty would, of course, have

no effect upon the policy of the United States, which is not even a signatory of the Treaty. As clearly stated in the above mentioned telegram from the Department, the policy of the Government of the United States in recognizing new governments in the five Central American Republics will be in accord with the requirements of Article II of the General Treaty of Peace and Amity as signed at Washington on February 7, 1923. [Paraphrase.]

> Secretary Hughes to Minister Morales, nos. 26 and 28, June 30 and July 14' 1923, MS. Department of State, files 815.00/2609, 815.00/2624; 1923 For· Rel., vol. II, pp. 432–435. For a similar declaration, see Secretary Stimson to the Minister in El Salvador (Curtis), no. 63, Dec. 7, 1931, MS. Department of State, file 816.00 Revolutions/31.
>
> At the date this policy was announced the treaty was not in force, having been ratified only by Nicaragua.

This policy was consistently followed in the recognition of Central American governments. In an instruction of December 9, 1925 to the Minister in Nicaragua, explaining why the Government of the United States could not recognize Chamorro if he should assume the presidency, Secretary Kellogg said:

> The policy of the Government of the United States with respect to the recognition of new governments in Central America has been publicly announced a number of times and is in accord with the policy expressly adopted by the Central American nations, in pursuance of the General Treaty of Peace and Amity of February 7, 1923.
> Furthermore the Department is convinced that a continued and positive application of this policy by all of the Republics of Central America as well as by the Government of the United States, which should endeavor to set an example to the rest, is necessary to the promotion of ordinary political development in Central America and to the discouragement of the tendency to settle political difficulties of an internal character by the use of force and of unconstitutional measures which has resulted in such deplorable conditions in the past.
> [Paraphrase.]

> MS. Department of State, file 817.00/3354. See also Secretary Stimson to the Minister in Guatemala (McCafferty), no. 76, Dec. 20, 1930, *ibid.* 814.00 Revolutions/68; statement to the press by Secretary Stimson, Sept. 17, 1930 (explaining the basis for the difference in policy with reference to the recognition of Central American governments), Department of State, *Press Releases*, weekly issue 51, pp. 192–193 (Sept. 17, 1930); statement by the Assistant Secretary of State (White) to the Honduran Minister, Nov. 16, 1932, MS. Department of State, file 815.00 Revolutions/361.

Modification of policy

The policy has undergone certain modifications since that time. Subsequent to the denunciation of the treaty of 1923 by Costa Rica and El Salvador (effective as of January 1, 1934), the other three Central American governments reached an agreement upon the initiative of President Sacasa of Nicaragua that they would recognize the treaty of 1923 as binding among themselves but not with respect to Costa Rica and El Salvador; and they thereupon extended recognition to President Martinez of El Salvador. (See *post* §47.) The United States at once extended recognition to President Martinez, explaining that—

> In view of the denunciation of El Salvador of the 1923 Central American Treaty of Peace and Amity, and the recognition of the present Government of El Salvador on January 25 by Nicaragua, Honduras, and Guatemala (Costa Rica having also denounced the Treaty and previously recognized El Salvador) the Department has today instructed the Chargé d'Affaires ad interim in San Salvador to extend formal recognition of El Salvador.

Secretary Hull to all missions in Latin America, including Mexico but excluding El Salvador, Jan. 26, 1934, MS. Department of State, file 816.01/412.

In a letter of Jan. 25, 1934 to President Roosevelt recommending the recognition of the Martinez government, the Acting Secretary of State (Welles) said:

"The Government of the United States has not recognized the Martinez government in El Salvador, as you will recall, because of the fact that so long as the provisions of the Central American Treaty of Peace and Amity of 1923 remained binding upon the Central American governments, the republics of Central America could not themselves extend recognition and it was believed that since the Central American republics had entered into that treaty for the announced purpose of discouraging revolutions in Central America, the Government of the United States should cooperate with them in that effort. Now, however, since the Government of Costa Rica is no longer bound by the provisions of that treaty in view of its denouncement thereof and in view of the announcement by the Governments of Guatemala, Nicaragua, and Honduras that the provisions of the treaty are no longer binding upon El Salvador and Costa Rica, and since all of the governments of Central America have accorded official recognition to the Martinez government in El Salvador, there would seem to be every reason why this Government without delay should resume official relations with the Government of El Salvador and accord formal recognition to President Martinez." MS. Department of State, file 816.01/412.

In response to an inquiry from the Legation in Nicaragua concerning the action of the Constituent Assembly of Guatemala in amending the constitution of 1927, extending the presidential term of General Jorge Ubico, the Department of State, on October 8, 1935 said:

> It is the desire of the Department that you should not make any further statement which might give the impression of committing the Government of the United States to any action in consonance with any of the provisions of the Central American General Treaty of Peace and Amity of February 7, 1923, or which might have the implication of intending to suggest the possibility of any such action [paraphrase].

Minister Lane to Secretary Hull, no. 77, Sept. 20, 1935; the Under Secretary of State (Phillips) to Mr. Lane, no. 337, Sept. 25, 1935; Mr. Hull to Mr. Lane, no. 58, Oct. 8, 1935. MS. Department of State, file 814.00/1255.

Action similar to that taken in Guatemala was taken in Honduras, a new constitution being promulgated on Apr. 15, 1936, containing in article 202 the provision that the term of office of President Carías should terminate on Jan. 1, 1943. Minister Keena to Secretary Hull, no. 337, Apr. 3, 1936, MS. Department of State, file 815.00/4688; Mr. Keena to Mr. Hull, no. 34, Apr. 1, 1936, and Mr. Hull to Mr. Keena, no. 16, Apr. 3, 1936, *ibid.* file 815.00/4683.

CONDITIONAL AND LIMITED RECOGNITION

§34

New states

The United States has not, strictly speaking, accorded conditional recognition to any state in the period since 1906. In two or three instances certain assurances have been required coincidently with recognition. Before extending recognition to Albania on July 28, 1922, the United States obtained from the Albanian Government through Commissioner Blake, who had been sent to Albania to report on conditions there, the following assurances contained in a note of June 25 from the Minister of Foreign Affairs:

> In connection with the two points you bring forth in your letter as needing settlement, before you could take any steps in favor of the official recognition of the Government of Albania by that of the United States, allow me to communicate to you that:

Albania, 1922

> 1. The Albanian Government will recognize the passports given by the authorities of the United States of America, to persons of Albanian origin, who are naturalized Americans in conformity with the American laws concerning nationalities.
> 2. In case a commercial treaty is concluded between the Government of the United States of America and that of Albania, the latter promises to insert in the said treaty, the most favored nation clause. Meanwhile, following the official recognition of the Government of Albania by that of the United States, and pending the conclusion of the treaty above mentioned, the American interests in Albania will receive the most favored nation treatment.

Commissioner Blake to Secretary Hughes, no. 3, Aug. 2, 1922, MS. Department of State, file 875.00/77. The note was in response to a communication from Mr. Blake dated June 23, 1922. The laws necessary to give effect to the assurances were not finally enacted until Dec. 28, 1925. Minister Hart to Secretary Kellogg, no. 46, Dec. 28, 1925, *ibid.* 711.75/10.

Egypt, 1922

The text of the note which the Diplomatic Agent and Consul General at Cairo was instructed on April 25, 1922 to communicate to the Egyptian Minister of Foreign Affairs extending recognition to Egypt, contained the proviso that this recognition was "subject to the maintenance of the rights of the United States of America as they have hitherto existed". The Department of State stated that this was intended "to leave no room for doubt of the maintenance of capitulatory and commercial rights and most-favored nation treatment of the United States".

> Secretary Hughes to the Diplomatic Agent and Consul General (Howell), Apr. 25, 1922, MS. Department of State, file 883.01/10a; 1922 For. Rel., vol. II, p. 105.

In some instances the United States has insisted upon the fulfilment of certain conditions other than those ordinarily required as a prerequisite to recognition, as a condition precedent to the extension of recognition to new governments, or it has sought to obtain adequate assurances that certain steps would be taken by the recognized government. It was the insistence by the United States upon the fulfilment of certain conditions by Mexico and the refusal of Mexico to agree to them as a condition precedent to recognition, that delayed for some time the recognition of the government of General Obregón. The government of General Obregón declined to conclude a treaty of amity and commerce (proposed by the United States on May 27, 1921) partly on the ground that it constituted conditional recognition to which Mexico could not consent.

New governments

Mexico, 1921

> For the correspondence on this subject, see memorandum of the Mexican Foreign Office to the American Embassy, June 4, 1921, enclosure 2 in despatch 3949, June 10, 1921, from the Embassy in Mexico, MS. Department of State, file 711.1211/19; 1921 For. Rel., vol. II, pp. 408, 412–413. General Obregón to President Harding, June 11, 1921, MS. Department of State, file 812.00/26059; President Harding to General Obregón, July 21, 1921, enclosure to instruction to the Embassy in Mexico, July 21, 1921, *ibid.* 812.00/25114½; 1921 For. Rel., vol. II, pp. 416–423.

The elections in Nicaragua in the fall of 1924, resulting in the election of Solorzano to the presidency, were reported by the American Legation to have been marked by sustained pressure and intimidation by the government of the Conservative and Liberal Republican parties, by the refusal of electoral privileges, by the misuse by the Government of the telegraph service and liquor supply, and by the alteration of ballots. Although the Department decided to accord recognition to Solorzano, it instructed the Legation that before making known its decision to Solorzano certain assurances should be obtained from him. Solorzano accordingly gave the following assurances in a letter of December 12, 1924 to the Legation:

Nicaragua, 1924

> . . . One. I make definite assurance that the 1928 elections will be carried out in full freedom and fairness for all parties and strictly in accordance with the provisions of the Dodds electoral law and that the latter will not be modified except in strict ac-

cordance with the advice of Dr. Dodds or another suitable electoral expert in accord with the Department of State.

Two. I give definite formal engagement that immediately upon
assuming office I will form a constabulary in order to provide a
suitable means to maintain order upon the withdrawal of the
American marines for which I will request the assistance of the
government of the United States in its training and organization
according to the convention for the limitation of armaments
signed at Washington February 7th 1923.

Three. I give formal definite engagement that I will undertake
adequate and satisfactory measures with which the government
of the United States could cooperate for the solution of the
economic problems of Nicaragua, and,

Four. I shall consider the expediency of obtaining the cooperation of as many political elements in Nicaragua as possible
in forming my government.

Walter C. Thurston to Secretary Hughes, no. 250, Nov. 28, 1924, and Mr.
Hughes to Mr. Thurston, no. 151, Dec. 10, 1924, MS. Department of State,
file 817.00/3216; Mr. Thurston to Mr. Hughes, no. 264, Dec. 13, 1924, *ibid.*
817.00/3242; 1924 For. Rel., vol. II, pp. 504–507.

U. S. S. R.,
1933

In a note of November 16, 1933 Mr. Litvinov, the People's Commissar for Foreign Affairs of the Union of Soviet Socialist Republics,
informed President Roosevelt that "coincident with the establishment of diplomatic relations" between the United States and the
Soviet Union it would "be the fixed policy" of his Government to
refrain from any subversive activities of any character against the
United States, and not to permit the prosecution of such acts from its
territory. (For the text of this assurance, see *post* §48.) Mr.
Litvinov, on behalf of his Government, gave additional assurances
with respect to the right of American citizens to enjoy liberty of conscience and of religious worship, including the right to conduct services; to lease, erect, or maintain churches or other buildings for
religious purposes; to collect offerings for religious purposes; and to
give religious instruction to their children in the Soviet Union. He
stated in a further note that his Government was prepared to include
in a consular convention to be negotiated immediately following the
establishment of diplomatic relations, provisions in which nationals
of the United States should be granted rights with reference to legal
protection not less favorable than those enjoyed in the Union of
Soviet Socialist Republics by nationals of the nations most favored in
this respect. He further stated in answer to an inquiry from President Roosevelt that the right to obtain economic information was
limited in the Union of Soviet Socialist Republics, as in other countries, only in the case of business and production secrets and in the
case of the employment of forbidden methods (bribery, theft, fraud,
etc.) to obtain such information. Finally, Mr. Litvinov, on behalf
of the Government of the Soviet Union, released and assigned to the

Government of the United States all such sums of money as might be admitted to be due or found to be due from American nationals to the Soviet Union as the successor of prior governments of Russia, and waived all claims arising out of activities of the military forces of the United States in Siberia subsequent to January 1, 1918.

> MS. Department of State, files 711.61/343⅜, /343⅝, /343⅞, /343⅝, /343⅝, /343⅞. For printed texts of this correspondence, see *Establishment of Diplomatic Relations With the Union of Soviet Socialist Republics*, Department of State Eastern European Ser. 1 (1933).
>
> For other instances in which the fulfilment of certain conditions was required, either as a prerequisite to or coincident with recognition, see *post*, the refusal of the United States to recognize the Arias government in the Dominican Republic in August 1916, §47; and the recognition of President Dartiguenave in Haiti on Sept. 16, 1915, §47.

RECOGNITION OF NEW STATES

AFGHANISTAN

§35

Great Britain having recognized the independence of Afghanistan in 1919, the Afghan Government sent a mission abroad in 1921 to visit various foreign countries. With reference to the reception of this mission by the President of the United States, the Secretary of State informed the President in a letter of July 18, 1921 that the Department of State had been notified by the Viceroy to the Secretary of State for India on August 9, 1919 that Afghanistan is "officially free and independent in its affairs, both internal and external". The President received the mission at the White House on July 26, 1921, at which time it delivered an autographed letter from the Amir Amanullah Khan of Afghanistan to the President announcing the accession of the Amir to the throne of Afghanistan. In his letter of July 29, 1921 acknowledging the receipt of the Amir's letter, the President said:

Reception of mission

> It is my wish that the relations between the United States and Afghanistan may always be of a friendly character, and I shall be happy to cooperate with Your Majesty to this end. I am constrained, however, to confirm to Your Majesty what was stated orally to G. Mohemmed Wali Khan, that with respect to the United States the question of the creation of a Diplomatic Mission and of the appropriate action to that end by the Congress of the United States must be reserved for further consideration.

In a telegram of August 25, 1921 to the Chargé in Persia, the Department stated that formal recognition of independence had been neither asked for by the mission from Afghanistan nor granted.

However, in a letter of April 26, 1933 to Senator Ashurst the Department said that "it was generally accepted that recognition had been accorded to the regime of King Amanullah" through the reception of the Afghan mission.

> Secretary Hughes to President Harding, July 18, 1921, MS. Department of State, file 033.90h11/14a; Amir Amanullah Khan of Afghanistan to President Harding, undated, and President Harding to Amir Khan, July 29, 1921, *ibid.* 890h.001Am1/1; Mr. Hughes to Chargé Engert, Aug. 25, 1921, *ibid.* 707.1190h/-; 1921 For. Rel., vol. I, pp. 258–262; Secretary Hull to Senator Ashurst, Apr. 26, 1933, MS. Department of State, file 890h.01/23.

ALBANIA

§36

Request for recognition

The Minister of Foreign Affairs of Albania informed the Department of State in a note of January 28, 1922 that the Conference of Ambassadors, consisting of the representatives of Great Britain, France, Italy, and Japan, by a decision of November 9, 1921, had recognized Albania as a sovereign and independent state. The Minister requested that the Government of the United States "follow the example of the above named powers" and "recognize the Albanian Government as the de jure government of the Albanian State".

On April 24, 1922 the Department of State requested the Ambassador in Italy to report the designation of representatives who had been sent to Albania by other powers, to which the Ambassador replied on April 27 that England and Italy had sent ministers, that France was represented only by a consul at Scutari, and that Japan had no representative. He stated that the other countries which had accorded *de jure* recognition were Finland, Switzerland, Belgium, and Yugoslavia, and that, of these, only Yugoslavia was represented, having a chargé d'affaires.

> The Minister of Foreign Affairs of Albania, Fan Noli, to Secretary Hughes, no. 263, Jan. 28, 1922, MS. Department of State, file 875.01/175; Ambassador Child to Secretary Hughes, Dec. 13, 1921, *ibid.* 875.01/158; Mr. Child to Mr. Hughes, no. 251, Apr. 3, 1922, *ibid.* 875.6363/20; Mr. Hughes to Mr. Child, Apr. 24, 1922, *ibid.* 875.01/191; Mr. Child to Mr. Hughes, Apr. 27, 1922, *ibid.* 875.01/192; 1922 For. Rel., vol. I, pp. 594–598.

Recognition

In a telegraphic instruction of April 27, 1922 the Department informed Consul General Blake, then at Tangier, that it was considering the recognition of Albania but that before taking action it desired that he proceed to Albania and report "as to conditions in that country, stability of present government and existing or prospective American interests there". This instruction was supplemented by a mail instruction of May 9, 1922 which, after stating that the letter of January 28, 1922 from the then Minister of Foreign Affairs remained unacknowledged, said:

> The Department understands that in the past two years five sweeping cabinet changes, one change of the Council of Regency and two armed outbreaks have occurred in Albania. Furthermore, until recently the outcome of the serious controversies with neighboring countries in which Albania was involved has been in doubt. In view of the uncertainty regarding the stability of the Albanian administration which arose from these domestic and foreign difficulties it has not been felt, hitherto, that an act of recognition by this Government would be opportune.
>
> The international status of Albania has, however, been so affected by the decisions regarding that country which were taken by the Conference of Ambassadors on November 9, 1921, that the Department is no longer disinclined, in principle, to recognize that country and is only awaiting your report to take definite action.
>
> You are, therefore, instructed to advise the Department by telegraph on the general political situation in Albania as soon after your arrival in that country as you feel yourself properly qualified to do so, making special reference to the Albanian administration's attitude towards the protection of American interests and its degree of willingness to accord most-favored-nation treatment to the United States, and adding your recommendations as to the most suitable course of action to follow.
>
> The principal consideration in favor of early recognition by this country is that such action might be helpful to the existing or potential economic and philanthropic interests in Albania of American citizens. You are expected, therefore, to make a careful survey of such interests which may now exist and to indicate to the Department, by written reports, or, in cases of exceptional urgency, by telegraph, such definite opportunities, economic or other, as are now open to Americans or which might be opened to them on the recognition of Albania by the United States.

Secretary Hughes to the Diplomatic Agent and Consul General at Tangier (Denning) for Blake, no. 4, Apr. 27, 1922, MS. Department of State, file 123B58/175; 1922 For. Rel., vol. I, p. 598; Mr. Hughes to Mr. Blake, May 9, 1922, MS. Department of State, file 123B58/175.

Commissioner Blake reported as follows on June 28, 1922:

> Although the Albanian State has not yet definitely emerged from the stages of hopeful experiment, it is nevertheless sufficiently established in fact to command international support. Its existence responds to political exigencies in the Adriatic and [is] equally supported by the positive nationalist will of the people. The State is founded upon the basis of popular representation, but pending the delimitation of its precise boundaries by an international commission now actively pursuing its task and the subsequent assembly of the constitutional convention, popular government is nearer a generic term than a practice. The Government as yet can be given little credit for constructive

achievement owing to financial embarrassment, inexperienced leadership and totally immigrating [*inorganic*] administration.

.   .   .   .

After careful consideration of all aspects of the situation, based upon information drawn from various parts of the country and from individuals of all views and religious complexion, the propriety and expediency of immediately according American recognition of Albania is respectfully recommended for the following reasons.

1st. As an act of spontaneous moral encouragement to the Albanian people in a critical phase of their struggle for independence who in spite of grave difficulties have given sufficient evidence of political stability to cause their admission to the League of Nations as a sovereign State and their recognition as such by some twenty European countries.

2d. Material factors are equally worthy of consideration. The country has important commercial possibilities and possesses rich natural resources awaiting development. If the American Government without due cause continues officially to hold aloof legitimate American enterprises are at a disadvantage and a policy of delay and over-caution might be detrimental to present American prestige, now a great asset. Furthermore, suspicion might arise in evil quarters that the delay was for the purpose of associating improper conditions with recognition, a phase of affairs which I am confident the Secretary of State would desire to avoid under all the circumstances. As American recognition sooner or later is an inevitable corollary to the existing state of affairs it follows that prompt action to this end should have urgent attention especially as Parliament assembles early in September when important measures for the development of the country are expected to be presented for definite ratification.

He recommended that if recognition were accorded, a Legation should be established and a Minister Plenipotentiary to Albania should be immediately designated. The Department accordingly instructed him on July 25 that on July 28 he should extend to the Minister of Foreign Affairs of Albania written notification of the *de jure* recognition of Albania by the United States. He was instructed that in extending this recognition he should state that the Government of the United States "has taken cognizance of the successful maintenance of a national Albanian Government".

The Commissioner in Albania (Blake) to Secretary Hughes, June 28, 1922, MS. Department of State, file 875.01/215; Mr. Hughes to Mr. Blake, July 25, 1922, *ibid.* 875.01/223a; 1922 For. Rel., vol. I, pp. 602–604.

BALTIC STATES: ESTONIA, LATVIA, LITHUANIA

§37

The British Chargé d'Affaires in Washington on October 31, 1918 transmitted a memorandum to the Department of State in which was set forth views regarding the advisability of the general policy of granting provisional recognition to the national councils and other representative bodies of the smaller nationalities formerly forming part of the Russian Empire, for the purpose of stimulating their passive resistance under German occupation and so encouraging them in their determination to secure self-determination. The Department replied on November 27 that, while the information in the hands of the Government of the United States tended to confirm the description of the situation as to political, social, and military conditions outlined in the memorandum, nevertheless, public and official declarations which had been made by the Government of the United States on various occasions proclaiming its friendship and loyalty to Russia and the Russian people caused it to feel in honor bound to refrain from adopting any premature action before the meeting of the Peace Conference.

Policy of non-recognition

> Mr. Barclay to Secretary Lansing, no. 1206, Oct. 31, 1918, and Mr. Lansing to Mr. Barclay, no. 322, Nov. 27, 1918, MS. Department of State, file 861.00/3117; 1918 For. Rel. (Russia), vol. II, pp. 841–842, 851–852.

In a telegram of August 23, 1919 to the Commissioner at Helsingfors, the Department stated that it understood that the Peace Conference did not recognize the independence of Estonia or any of the Baltic provinces, although it considered them as entitled to autonomy and to self-determination short of complete independence.

> Secretary Lansing to the Commissioner at Helsingfors, Aug. 23, 1919, MS. Department of State, file 861.01/109.

In a telegraphic instruction of July 16, 1920 to the Commissioner at Riga, the Department of State said that its attitude toward the recognition of the Baltic states had not altered. The basis for the Department's policy in this matter was set forth at some length in a note of August 10, 1920 to the Italian Embassy in Washington concerning the general position of the Government of the United States with reference to Russia. The Department asserted that it was confident that "restored, free and united Russia" would "again take a leading place in the world, joining with the other free nations in upholding peace and orderly justice", and added:

> Until that time shall arrive the United States feels that friendship and honor require that Russia's interests must be generously

protected, and that, as far as possible, all decisions of vital importance to it, and especially those concerning its sovereignty over
the territory of the former Russian Empire, be held in abeyance.
By this feeling of friendship and honorable obligation to the great
nation whose brave and heroic self-sacrifice contributed so much
to the successful termination of the war, the Government of the
United States was guided in its reply to the Lithuanian National
Council, on October 15, 1919, and in its persistent refusal to recognize the Baltic States as separate nations independent of Russia.

.   .   .   .

To summarize the position of this Government, I would say,
therefore, in response to your Excellency's inquiry, that it would
regard with satisfaction a declaration by the Allied and Associated Powers, that the territorial integrity and true boundaries of
Russia shall be respected.   These boundaries should properly
include the whole of the former Russian Empire, with the exception of Finland proper, ethnic Poland, and such territory as may
by agreement form a part of the Armenian State.   The aspirations of these nations for independence are legitimate.   Each was
forcibly annexed and their liberation from oppressive alien rule
involves no aggressions against Russia's territorial rights, and
has received the sanction of the public opinion of all free peoples.

The Acting Secretary of State (Colby) to Commissioner Young, July 16,
1920, MS. Department of State, file 860n.01/6; Mr. Colby to the Italian
Ambassador (Avezzana), Aug. 10, 1920, *ibid.* 760c.61/300b; 1920 For. Rel.,
vol. III, pp. 463–468.

On April 1, 1921 the Embassy in Paris transmitted by telegraph to
the Department of State a copy of the note addressed by the Inter-
Allied Conference to Estonia and Latvia extending *de jure* recognition to them.   The note stated in part that the powers desired "to
indicate thereby the sympathy that they feel for the Esthonian [and
Lithuanian] people and to render homage to the efforts which it has
made with a view to organizing its national life in order and peace".

Ambassador Wallace to Secretary Hughes, no. 221, Apr. 1, 1921, MS.
Department of State, file 860i.01/28.

De jure
recognition
recommended

In response to a telegraphic request from the Secretary of State of
May 7, 1921 that he report at once his opinion as to the probability
of any early Bolshevik effort, military or peaceful, to absorb the Baltic states and the probability of success of such effort as affecting
possible recognition of Estonia and Latvia by the United States, the
Commissioner at Riga reported on May 9 that there was no indication of a disposition on the part of the Bolsheviks to endeavor to
effect through military measures the conquest and absorption of the
Baltic states.   He added that he unhesitatingly recommended the
immediate *de jure* recognition of Estonia and Latvia with the *de jure*
recognition of Lithuania coincidentally or immediately following similar action by European powers.

Secretary Hughes to Commissioner Young, May 7, 1921, MS. Department of State, file 760n.61/6a; Mr. Young to Mr. Hughes, May 9, 1921, *ibid.* 760n.61/7; 1921 For. Rel., vol. II, p. 755.

In a letter of July 24, 1922 Secretary Hughes advised the President that in his opinion the time had come to extend recognition to the Baltic governments. He said that the Estonian, Latvian, and Lithuanian Governments had been in continuous existence since 1919 and had brought about stable economic and political conditions within their respective jurisdictions. He added that the United States had maintained informal intercourse with these Governments for two years or more, an American Commissioner having been stationed at Riga and American Consuls at Riga, Reval (Tallinn), and Kovno (Kaunas), while unofficial representatives of these Governments had been received informally in the United States. He stated that if the President approved, he proposed to make the following announcement:

Recognition

"The Government of the United States recognizes the Governments of Esthonia, Latvia and Lithuania."

To accompany this announcement was the following statement:

"The Governments of Esthonia, Latvia and Lithuania have been recognized either de jure or de facto by the principal Governments of Europe and have entered into treaty relations with their neighbors.

"In extending to them recognition on its part, the Government of the United States takes cognizance of the actual existence of these Governments during a considerable period of time and of the successful maintenance within their borders of political and economic stability.

"The United States has consistently maintained that the disturbed condition of Russian affairs may not be made the occasion for the alienation of Russian territory, and this principle is not deemed to be infringed by the recognition at this time of the Governments of Esthonia, Latvia and Lithuania which have been set up and maintained by an indigenous population."

The President having given his approval, the Commissioner at Riga was instructed on July 25 to extend recognition to the three states simultaneously on July 28.

Secretary Hughes to President Harding, July 24, 1922, MS. Department of State, file 860n.01/56A; President Harding to Mr. Hughes, *ibid.* 860n.01/60; Mr. Hughes to Commissioner Young, July 25, 1922, *ibid.* 860n.01/52a; Mr. Young to Mr. Hughes, July 28, 1922, *ibid.* 860n.01/53.

With a despatch of August 16, 1922 the Commissioner at Riga transmitted to the Department copies of an exchange of notes between the Conference of Ambassadors and the Lithuanian Government by which the former extended *de jure* recognition to Lithuania. This recognition was made conditional upon the Lithuanian Government's accepting and observing the provisions of the Treaty of Versailles (arts. 331 to 345), so far as they affected the regulation of navigation on the Niemen River. This condition was accepted by the Lithuanian Minister of Foreign Affairs in his note of August 4, 1922.

> Commissioner Young to Secretary Hughes, no. 2509, Aug. 16, 1922, MS. Department of State, file 860M.01/143.

BULGARIA

§38

Recognition   On October 5, 1908 Bulgaria declared its independence of Turkey. The Ambassador in Paris reported in a telegram of April 1, 1909 to the Department of State that the Bulgarian Minister in Paris had expressed regret to him that the United States had not acted independently of Europe and recognized the independence of Bulgaria. The Ambassador said that he had replied that it seemed undesirable for the United States to depart from its traditional policy by taking the lead in a purely European matter. The Department approved the action of the Ambassador and said in its instruction to him of April 7:

> Besides the reason as stated by you for the non-recognition of Prince Ferdinand as Czar of Bulgaria, by the United States in advance of recognition by the European powers, it may be stated that it is the rule and policy of the United States to recognize only *de facto* governments, disregarding political and *de jure* claims.
>
> The Czardom of Bulgaria cannot be *de facto* until made so by the recognition of the Powers who, by the Treaty of Berlin, regulated the status of Bulgaria and the other states of the Near East.

Having been informed by the Embassy in London that Bulgaria had been recognized by the principal European powers, the Department, on May 3, 1909, instructed the Minister at Bucharest as follows:

> The President directs that you express, by formal communication through the appropriate channels, his felicitations to His Majesty, the Czar, upon the admission of Bulgaria to the community of sovereign and independent States.

> Ambassador Leischman to Secretary Root, Oct. 5, 1908, MS. Department of State, file 5072/13; Ambassador White to Secretary Knox, Apr. 1, 1909, and Mr. Knox to Mr. White, no. 350, Apr. 7, 1909, *ibid.* 15921/75; Mr. Knox to Chargé Hutchinson, May 3, 1909, *ibid.* 5072/33; 1909 For. Rel. 45

CZECHOSLOVAKIA

§39

The Ambassador in Italy reported to the Department of State in a telegram of May 7, 1918 that the Italian Government had recognized the Czechoslovak Army as an allied army with autonomy, the supreme authority—judicial, political, and military—being vested in the Czechoslovak National Council. The Council consisted of Tomas Garrigue Masaryk, President; Milan Štefánik, Vice President; and Eduard Beneš, Secretary General. The Ambassador reported that the Council had its headquarters in Paris with bureaus in Rome, New York, Geneva, London, and Moscow. He said that the recognition of the Council by the Italian Government had been accorded because the political program and aspirations of the Council were identical with those of the Entente and in accordance with their collective aspirations.

Autonomy of Czechoslovak Army

> Ambassador Page to Secretary Lansing, May 7, 1918, MS. Department of State, file 763.72/9893½; 1918 For. Rel., Supp. I, vol. I, pp. 802-803.

A political program embodying the following articles was reported to Secretary Lansing by the French Ambassador in Washington on June 15, 1918 as having been proposed by the Czechoslovak National Council:

Recognition of Czechoslovak National Council

1. Recognition by the Government of the Republic of the existence of a Czecho-Slovak state.
2. *De facto* recognition of the Czecho-Slovak National Council as constituting the lawful Government of that state.
3. *De facto* recognition of all the prerogatives of a government as appertaining to the National Council and in particular—

> (a) In financial matters. A loan (there is no question of subsidies) should be granted to it; the first would be in the amount of 20,000,000 francs.
> (b) Every customary facility should be awarded to it in its relations with its foreign agents (passports, cipher telegrams, diplomatic pouches).

4. A bureau which would serve as a permanent channel of communication between the National Council and the French Government should be created near that Government.

The Ambassador in a later note of June 29 informed the Secretary that his Government had recognized "the National Council as the supreme organization of the Czecho-Slovak movement in the Entente countries".

Recognition was extended by the United States in the form of a public announcement of September 3, 1918, reading as follows:

> The Czecho-Slovak peoples having taken up arms against the German and Austro-Hungarian Empires, and having placed

organized armies in the field which are waging war against those
Empires under officers of their own nationality and in accordance
with the rules and practices of civilized nations; and

The Czecho-Slovaks having, in prosecution of their independent purposes in the present war, confided supreme political
authority to the Czecho-Slovak National Council,

The Government of the United States recognizes that a state
of belligerency exists between the Czecho-Slovaks thus organized
and the German and Austro-Hungarian Empires.

It also recognizes the Czecho-Slovak National Council as a
de facto belligerent government clothed with proper authority
to direct the military and political affairs of the Czecho-Slovaks.

The Government of the United States further declares that
it is prepared to enter formally into relations with the *de facto*
government thus recognized for the purpose of prosecuting the
war against the common enemy, the Empires of Germany and
Austria-Hungary.

On October 14, 1918 the British Chargé in Washington informed
the Department of State that his Government had, on September 3,
1918, entered into the following agreement with the Czechoslovak
National Council:

1. His Majesty's Government will until the organization of the
future Czecho-Slovak Government maintain relations with the
Czecho-Slovak National Council and will deal with it direct on
all questions within the competence of such Council.

2. His Majesty's Government agree to the Czecho-Slovak
armies being placed under the general control of the Czecho-
Slovak National Council in all matters other than those which
fall within the sphere of the Allied commanders in chief under
whose command the units of the Czecho-Slovak armies may be
placed.

3. The Czecho-Slovak National Council will frame a budget
for the maintenance of its administration and of its armies, but
due regard shall be paid therein to any arrangements made for
the advance of funds to Czecho-Slovak forces under existing agreements between the British and Allied Governments.

4. In the event of a loan being advanced to the Czecho-Slovak
National Council on behalf of the future Czecho-Slovak Government, His Majesty's Government agree to participate therein on
terms of equality with their allies.

5. The Czecho-Slovak National Council will on behalf of the
future Czecho-Slovak Government forthwith institute a financial
commission and will invite His Majesty's Government to appoint
a member thereof. The Czecho-Slovak budget will be placed
under the control of this commission.

6. His Majesty's Government will recognize the right of the
Czecho-Slovak National Council to be represented at any Allied
conference when questions affecting the interests of the Czecho-
Slovaks are under discussion.

7. His Majesty's Government will recognize the passports
issued by the Czecho-Slovak National Council or by its duly
authorized representatives.

8. The Czecho-Slovak National Council will appoint a representative in London through whom relations with His Majesty's Government will be maintained.

9. His Majesty's Government will recognize and will treat as alien friends and as members of an allied nation all persons who may be certified to them as Czecho-Slovak by the Czecho-Slovak representative in London or by his authorized agents or to whom passports may be issued by the Czecho-Slovak National Council or its authorized representatives.

10. His Majesty's Government will treat official communications passing between the Czecho-Slovak National Council and its representatives in London upon the same footing as communications passing between a friendly Government and its representative in London.

In consequence of the action thus taken by France, the United States, and Great Britain, the Czechoslovak National Council announced to the American Ambassador in France, on October 14, 1918, that a Czechoslovak Provisional Government had been established on September 26, 1918 with its official seat in Paris. The new Czechoslovak Government and the Czechoslovak deputies met on October 28, 1918 at Prague and passed the first Czechoslovak law formally constituting the independent Czechoslovak State.

Ambassador Jusserand to Secretary Lansing, June 15 and 29, 1918, MS. Department of State, files 763.72/10415, 763.72/10592; Mr. Lansing to the Ambassador in Japan (Morris), Sept. 3, 1918, *ibid.* file 763.72/11343c; the British Chargé d'Affaires (Barclay) to Mr. Lansing, no. 1135, Oct. 14, 1918, *ibid.* 861.00/3068; the Ambassador in France (Sharp) to Mr. Lansing, Oct. 16, 1918, *ibid.* 861.00/2967; 1918 For. Rel., Supp. 1, vol. I, pp. 813–851.

For the text of the Czechoslovak law of Oct. 28, 1918, see Reparation Commission, annex 766c, MS. Department of State, file 462.00R29/845; and for a résumé of the law, see *Exposé sommaire des travaux législatifs de l'Assemblée Nationale Tchécoslovaque* (Prague, 1920) 5.

The question of purchasing securities issued by the Czechoslovak Relations Government having arisen, the Secretary of the Treasury of the with Czecho-United States addressed a letter to the Department of State on slovakia October 4, 1918 in which he made the following inquiry:

I understand that the Department of State has recognized the Czecho Slovak Government as a *de facto* belligerent government at war with Germany. As I have under consideration making advances to said Government under the authority of the Second Liberty Bond Act and the acts amendatory thereof and supplemental thereto, I shall be obliged if you will advise me if my understanding as above stated is correct, and also whether the Department of State can affirmatively advise me that in its opinion the necessary formalities have been complied with so that the obligations of the Czecho Slovak Government, when executed in conformity with the documents furnished to you and by such person as you shall designate to the Treasury Department, would be regarded by the Department of State as valid and binding internationally, and would have its sanction.

The Department replied on November 14, 1918:

> In response to your letter of October 4, I take pleasure in advising you that the United States Government on September 3, 1918 accorded recognition to the Czecho-Slovak National Council as a de facto belligerent government clothed with proper authority to direct the military and political affairs of the Czecho-Slovaks. The Czecho-Slovak National Council is, in the opinion of this Department, a foreign government engaged in war with the enemies of the United States. I am of the opinion that obligations executed at this time by President Mazaryk in the name and on behalf of the Czecho-Slovak National Council, purchased at par by the Secretary of the Treasury under the authority of the Liberty Bond Acts, will be valid and binding internationally, and such obligations will have the sanction of this Department.

Subsequently, from November 15, 1918 to April 15, 1919, six loans were made to the Czechoslovak Government under the authority of the Second Liberty Bond Act, which authorized the Secretary of the Treasury with the approval of the President to purchase at par obligations of "foreign governments" then engaged in war with the enemies of the United States.

> The Secretary of the Treasury (McAdoo) to the Secretary of State (Lansing), Oct. 4, 1918, MS. Department of State, file 860F51/3½; Mr. Lansing to Mr. McAdoo, Nov. 14, 1918, *ibid.* See also *ibid.* 860F01/148½.

In a letter of November 5, 1918 Dr. Masaryk, President of the Czechoslovak National Council, informed the Department of State that the Czechoslovak National Council had appointed Mr. Charles Pergler its Commissioner in the United States and accredited him to "the Government of the United States as the political and diplomatic representative of the Council in the United States with plenary power" and requested that all communications and documents intended for the Czechoslovak National Council be directed to Mr. Pergler. The Department replied on November 14 that it would be pleased to "accept Mr. Pergler in the capacity mentioned".

> Dr. Masaryk to Secretary Lansing, Nov. 5, 1918, and Mr. Lansing to Dr. Masaryk, Nov. 14, 1918, MS. Department of State, file 701.60f11/2b.

In a letter of December 27, 1918 to the Secretary of the Treasury, the Acting Secretary of State (Polk) referred to the Department's letter of November 14 with respect to advances to be made to the Czechoslovak National Council and enclosed "a copy of a letter of November 21, from Mr. Charles Pergler, Czecho-Slovak Commissioner in the United States, in the absence of Mr. Masaryk, enclosing a full power issued by Mr. Masaryk, dated November 15, 1918, and a copy of a telegram from the American Ambassador at Paris, dated

December 19, 1918, communicating the text of the decision of the
Government of the Czecho-Slovak Republic, of December 11, 1918—
both empowering Mr. Pergler to act for his Government in loan matters". The Acting Secretary of State added:

> . . . In view of the enclosed documents, the authenticity of
> which I have no reason to doubt, I desire to state that obligations
> executed at this time by Mr. Charles Pergler, in the name and on
> behalf of the Czecho-Slovak Republic, will be valid and binding
> internationally, and that such obligations will have the sanction
> of this Department.
>
> Mr. Polk to Mr. McAdoo, Dec. 27, 1918, MS. Department of State, file
> 860F.51/19a.

On January 7, 1919 Secretary Lansing telegraphed the Department
from Paris that "pending a decision regarding the recognition of the
Czecho-Slovak Republic" it had been suggested that a consular officer
be sent to Prague as Consul and Diplomatic Agent or Commissioner.
The Department replied on February 7:

> Your 182, January 7th, indicates that the Czecho-Slovak
> Republic has not been formally recognized as such. On Novem-
> ber 5, 1918, President Masaryk informed the Department
> that the Czecho-Slovak National Council (Government) had
> appointed Mr. Charles Pergler, its commissioner in the United
> States. In order to authorize Pergler to sign obligations for
> advances made by the Treasury Department, full powers for this
> purpose were obtained and transmitted to the Department
> by Ambassador Sharp in his 6370 December 19th. These powers
> run in the name of the Czecho-Slovak Republic, and it is under-
> stood that obligations for advances are being signed by Pergler
> in the name of the Czecho-Slovak Republic. As the powers of the
> Czecho-Slovak representative here must flow from the govern-
> ment in existence for the time being, it would seem that no other
> course could well be followed; but in order that the Department
> may not act contrary to your views the foregoing is submitted
> to you for any suggestions which you may desire to make. It
> is understood that the recognition of the Czecho-Slovak National
> Council as a de facto belligerent government applied also to the
> succeeding so-called Provisional Government and also to the
> government of the present Czecho-Slovak Republic. In order
> to hold the government of the Czecho-Slovak Republic responsible
> for the advances made to the Council and to the Provisional
> Government, it would seem necessary that some degree of recog-
> nition for this purpose should be accorded to the government of
> the Republic and it is believed that the recognition resulting
> from entering into loan agreements with Pergler, and his execu-
> tion of obligations in the name of the Republic is sufficient for
> this purpose. If, however, it seems to you that further Act of
> recognition is necessary or desirable, it would seem advisable
> that it should be taken as soon as possible.

To this Mr. Lansing replied on February 14, 1919 that he did not "consider any further act of recognition of the Czechoslovak Republic . . . desirable at the present time, in view of the fact that the frontiers of this State have not yet been definitely determined".

> The American mission to the Acting Secretary of State (Polk), no. 182, Jan. 7, 1919, MS. Department of State, file 125.0060F; Mr. Polk to the American mission, no. 622, Feb. 7, 1919, *ibid.* 860F.01/28A; the American mission to Mr. Polk, no. 742, Feb. 14, 1919, *ibid.* 860F.01/29.

Mr. Richard Crane, who had been appointed Minister to Czechoslovakia, reported that he had presented his letter of credence on June 2 [?3], 1919 to the Acting Minister of Foreign Affairs. He was formally received by President Masaryk on June 11.

> The Acting Secretary of State (Polk) to the Commission to Negotiate Peace, Apr. 23, 1919, MS. Department of State, file 125C853/6b; the Commission to Negotiate Peace to Mr. Polk, undated, received June 4, 1919, *ibid.* 123C853/15; Minister Crane to Mr. Polk, no. 1, June 15, 1919, *ibid.* 123C853/30; 1919 For. Rel., vol. II, pp. 85–93.

EGYPT

§40

The Department of State was notified in a note of March 16, 1922 from the British Ambassador that his Government had decided "with the approval of Parliament, to terminate the Protectorate declared over Egypt on December 18th, 1914, and to recognise her as an Independent Sovereign State". The Ambassador stated the conditions under which his Government had accorded recognition to Egypt and said that the Egyptian Government would "be at liberty to reestablish a Ministry for Foreign Affairs and thus to prepare the way for the diplomatic and consular representation of Egypt abroad".

The Department instructed the Diplomatic Agent and Consul General at Cairo on March 28, 1922 that such intercourse with the Egyptian Government as was essential for the conduct of the affairs of the Agency should be informal, so as to avoid giving the impression of recognition. The Agent and Consul General was instructed to refrain from discussing the subject of recognition and to inform the Department what powers, if any, had officially recognized the Egyptian Government and what steps to that end had been taken by them. He reported in a telegram of April 17, 1922 that all the great powers had recognized the Egyptian Government, including England, Italy, France, and Germany, and that most of the smaller powers had extended recognition.

On April 25 the Department informed the British Ambassador that the Government of the United States had decided to recognize the independence of Egypt, and on the same date the Diplomatic Agent and Consul General at Cairo was instructed to communicate to the Egyptian Minister of Foreign Affairs the following note:

> I take pleasure in informing Your Excellency that the President has decided to recognize the independence of Egypt this recognition being subject to the maintenance of the rights of the United States of America as they have hitherto existed.

The Department stated that the qualification included in this note was intended "to leave no room for doubt of the maintenance of capitulatory and commercial rights and most-favored nation treatment of the United States". The Agent and Consul General reported on April 26 that he had delivered a note to the Minister of Foreign Affairs in pursuance of the Department's instructions.

The British Embassy to Secretary Hughes, no. 194, Mar. 16, 1922, MS. Department of State, file 883.00/403; Mr. Hughes to the Diplomatic Agent and Consul General (Howell), Mar. 28, 1922, *ibid.* 883.01/–; Mr. Hughes to the British Ambassador (Geddes), Apr. 25, 1922, *ibid.* 883.01/11a; Mr. Hughes to Mr. Howell, Apr. 25, 1922, *ibid.* 883.01/10a; 1922 For. Rel., vol. II, pp. 103–106.

Mr. Howell to Mr. Hughes, nos. 22 and 24, Apr. 17 and 26, 1922, MS. Department of State, files 883.01/7, 883.01/11.

The rank of the Diplomatic Agent and Consul General at Cairo was raised to the grade of Envoy Extraordinary and Minister Plenipotentiary on June 24, 1922, and the first Egyptian diplomatic representative to this country presented his letter of credence to the President on January 22, 1924.

Minister Howell to Secretary Hughes, no. 31, June 24, 1922, MS. Department of State, file 123H836/14; the Assistant Secretary of State (Adee) to the Egyptian Minister, Seifoullah Yousry Pasha, Jan. 19, 1924, *ibid.* 701.8311/13b.

FINLAND

§41

The Consul at Helsingfors reported to the Department of State on December 4, 1917 that the President of the Senate of Finland had on that day before the Diet proclaimed Finland a free and independent republic. The President had asked the Consul to ascertain whether the United States would recognize Finland as an independent state and if so whether Finland might send delegates to lay their point of view before the Department of State. The Consul advised recognition. The Ambassador in Russia, in response to the request of the Department for his views, stated that he did not see how Finland could be recognized before the Constituent Assembly acted but that he saw no objection to permitting the Finnish delegation to visit the United

Independence

States. Accordingly, the Department informed the Ambassador that it did not object to the coming to the United States of a deputation from Finland but that it was not yet prepared to assume any position regarding recognition. It added in a later telegram that it did not intend to indicate indifference to the request of Finland but that, owing to present political conditions in Russia, it was impossible at that time to give a definite answer to the inquiry regarding recognition.

> Consul Haynes to Secretary Lansing, Dec. 4, 1917, MS. Department of State, file 861.00/766; Ambassador Francis to Mr. Lansing, Dec. 14, 1917, and Mr. Lansing to Mr. Francis, Dec. 15, 1917, *ibid.* 861.00/835; 1918 For. Rel. (Russia), vol. II, pp. 733–736.

Attitude of foreign governments

The American Minister in Sweden reported on December 29, 1917, that the Swedish Government, while expressing sympathy with the new Government of Finland, was withholding recognition. The Danish Government recognized the independence of Finland on January 10. The Department of State was informed by the British Government on January 30 that it was prepared to inform the Finnish people that it was ready to give formal recognition to their Government as soon as the Finns should have expressed by some unmistakable method, such as an election, their sanction of their own independence. In the meantime the British Government proposed to treat the existing Government as the *de facto* authorities in Finland.

> Minister Morris to Secretary Lansing, Dec. 29, 1917, MS. Department of State, file 861.00/880; Mr. Grant-Smith, the Chargé in Denmark, to Mr. Lansing, Jan. 11, 1918, *ibid.* 861.00/941; memorandum of the Assistant Secretary of State (Phillips), Jan. 30, 1918, *ibid.* 860d.01/32; 1918 For. Rel. (Russia), vol. II, pp. 739–745.

Policy of U. S.

The policy of the United States with reference to recognition of the independence of Finland was explained to the Finnish delegates by the Secretary of State in a conference of February 27, 1918. In reply to the request of the delegates that the United States extend recognition to Finland, the Secretary replied that the Government of the United States "was very sympathetic with Finland's aspirations for independence and that we were disposed to recognize the Government there as *de facto* and that we sincerely hoped in a short time a stable constitutional government would be established". He said further "that the Commissioners must appreciate the fact that at present it would be unwise for this Government to take any official action in view of the disorder and confusion which prevailed in Finland; but that we looked forward hopefully to a satisfactory ending of these unfortunate conditions and that when that time came I [he] should be glad to receive them again". Finally, he added that he "was speaking unofficially and personally to them on this subject" but that he "was anticipating the time when I [he] could speak with more authority".

MS. Department of State, file 860d.00/41; 1918 For. Rel. (Russia), vol. II, pp. 755–756.

The unstable conditions referred to by the Secretary continued, and on August 23, 1918 the Department of State instructed the Consul at Helsingfors that it concurred in his opinion that any action or consultations relative to recognition of the *de facto* government of Finland should be deferred until the situation was more clearly defined than it was at that time. The country was occupied for a time by the Germans, and an effort was made to establish a monarchy with Frederick Carl of Hesse as King. This effort collapsed with the withdrawal of Germany, and the Consul at Helsingfors reported in a telegram of November 16 that the Senate and the Diet had agreed on November 15 to entrust General Mannerheim with forming a new government. The Department declared again on November 22 in an instruction to the Consul that it was not at that time prepared to recognize the independence of Finland or of any separate government.

Secretary Lansing to Consul Haynes, Aug. 23, 1918, MS. Department of State, file 860d.00/255; Mr. Haynes to Mr. Lansing, Oct. 11, 1918, *ibid.* 860d.00/301; the Acting Secretary of State (Polk) to Mr. Haynes, Nov. 22, 1918, *ibid.* 860d.00/324. For general papers relating to this period, see 1918 For. Rel. (Russia), vol II, pp. 756–814.

The American Commission to Negotiate Peace (at Paris) stated, Recognition in a telegram of March 1, 1919 to the Department of State, that it believed that the general elections expected to take place on March 1, 1919 could alone determine whether the present Government of Finland had the "people's mandate". It said that in case the election should result in a clear manifestation of the public will the Commission would be disposed to raise without delay the question of provisional recognition by the Allied and Associated Governments and requested the Department's views. The Department replied that it concurred in the views of the Commission, that it believed the impending elections should determine whether the present government had the "people's mandate", and that if this proved to be the case the United States should grant provisional recognition at once, "not only to clarify the situation but also to steady the new government". Although, according to a report of March 11, 1919 from the American Consul at Helsingfors, the election did not give a decisive majority to any one party, the Department stated in a telegram of March 20 to the Consul that it felt that recognition should be given Finland after the formation of the new government on April 1 and authorized him to let the Finnish authorities know informally that the United States felt that "recognition as a *de facto* government could be given to any properly constituted government established on democratic principles and with a policy not in conflict with the Allies, which may result from the recent Finnish elections". The Commission to Negotiate Peace reported to the Department on May 5 that at a meeting held on May 3 the so-called "Council of Ministers of Foreign Affairs", at which representatives of the United States, Great Britain, France, and Japan were present, had reached the following agreement concerning the independence of Finland:

> 1. That the Governments of the United States of America and Great Britain would forthwith severally recognize the independence of Finland and the *de facto* Government.
> 2. That after the recognition of the independence of Finland and after the appointment of official diplomatic representatives, the Governments of America, Great Britain, and France would issue instructions to their representatives to urge the Finnish Government to accept the decisions of the Peace Conference in regard to the frontiers of Finland. Furthermore, the Finnish Government would be urged to treat the Red Finns who had fought with the Allies in a liberal and generous spirit by the grant of an amnesty.
> 3. That Baron Makino (the Japanese representative) would forthwith communicate the above decisions to his Government with a view to its taking similar action.

The Secretary of State accordingly informed the Finnish Minister of Foreign Affairs, in a note dated May 7, 1919, that the United States recognized the independence of Finland, and the Government of which he was a member as the *de facto* government of Finland.

> The Commission to Negotiate Peace to the Acting Secretary of State (Polk), Mar. 1, 1919, and Mr. Polk to the Commission to Negotiate Peace, Mar. 4, 1919, MS. Department of State, file 860d.01/10; Consul Haynes to Mr. Polk, Mar. 11, 1919, and Mr. Polk to Mr. Haynes, Mar. 20, 1919, *ibid.* 860d.00/380; the Commission to Negotiate Peace to Mr. Polk, May 5, 1919, *ibid.* 860d.01/21; Secretary Lansing to the Finnish Minister of Foreign Affairs (Holsti), May 7, 1919, *ibid.* 860d.01/71; 1919 For. Rel., vol. II, pp. 210–215.

De jure recognition

Mr. A. H. Saastamoinen presented his letter of credence as Minister of Finland on May 19, 1919 and was received by the President on August 21, 1919. On December 20 he addressed a note to the Department of State pointing out that the Government of Finland was not only *de facto* but also *de jure* and expressing the hope that the United States would make appropriate recognition of that fact. In reply the Department stated that as complete diplomatic relations had been established the Government of the United States had accredited Mr. Alexander Magruder to the Minister of Foreign Affairs of the Government of Finland as Chargé d'Affaires ad interim. In a telegram of the same date to the American Commissioner at Helsingfors the Department stated that the note which it had addressed to the Finnish Minister in Washington was considered "to constitute full recognition of Finland as from May 7, 1919".

Minister Saastamoinen to the Acting Secretary of State (Polk), May 19, 1919, MS. Department of State, file 701.60d11/24; Mr. Tumulty, Secretary to President Wilson, to Secretary Lansing, Aug. 21, 1919, *ibid.* 701.60d11/29; Mr. Saastamoinen to Mr. Lansing, no. 1321, Dec. 20, 1919, and Mr. Lansing to Mr. Saastamoinen, Jan. 12, 1920, *ibid.* 860d.01/53; 1919 For. Rel., vol. II, pp. 218–223, 224–227.

ICELAND

§42

The American Legation in Copenhagen reported in a despatch of December 6, 1918 that the Danish-Icelandic treaty of union had been signed by the King on November 30, 1918 and had taken effect immediately. The Danish Legation in Washington stated in a note of December 10, 1918 that it had been directed to notify the Department of State that— *(margin note: Iceland—a sovereign state)*

> The Danish Government has, in accordance with a federal act of November 30th 1918 passed by the parliaments of Denmark and Iceland, recognized Iceland as a sovereign State.

Minister Grant-Smith to Secretary Lansing, no. 1933, Dec. 6, 1918, MS. Department of State, file 859a.01/10; Minister Brun to Mr. Lansing, Dec. 10, 1918, and Mr. Lansing to Mr. Brun, Jan. 3, 1919, *ibid.* 859a.01/4.

In response to an inquiry concerning the recognition of Iceland, the Department of State said in a letter of December 13, 1933:

> It is noted that you allude to a race for recognition between Reykjavik and Moscow, and in this connection, you are advised that there has been no question of recognition by the United States of the Icelandic Government, evidence of which is found in the conclusion of treaties with Iceland in the past few years.
>
> It is presumed that you refer to the appointment of a resident representative of the United States to Iceland. In this connection, you are informed that the matter of sending a resident representative to Iceland has been given careful consideration for a number of years, but that it has not been found feasible to do so.

Mr. Moffat, Chief of the Division of Western European Affairs, to Mr. Peterson, December 13, 1933, MS. Department of State, file 859a.01/32.

The United States has concluded the following agreements with Iceland: Arbitration treaty, May 15, 1930 (46 Stat. 2841; 4 Treaties, etc. [Trenwith, 1938] 4074); relief from double income tax on shipping profits, exchange of notes signed May 22, 1922, Aug. 9 and 18, 1922, Oct. 24, 25, and 28, 1922, and Dec. 5 and 6, 1922 (47 Stat. 2612–2616; Ex. Agree. Ser. 14); reciprocal recognition of load-line certificates, exchange of notes, Jan. 16, 1932 (47 Stat. 2693; Ex. Agree. Ser. 30).

As a result of a suggestion made by Minister Coleman in a despatch of Aug. 29, 1932, when Mrs. Ruth Bryan Owen was sent to Denmark as Minis-

ter on Apr. 13, 1933 her letter of credence was addressed to "His Majesty
Christian X, King of Denmark and Iceland". Iceland had not previously
been used by the Department in the title of the King. Minister Coleman
to Secretary Stimson, no. 133, Aug. 29, 1932, MS. Department of State,
file 124.59A/1; Secretary Hull to Minister Owen, Apr. 13, 1933, *ibid.* 123
Owen, Ruth Bryan/5.

IRAQ

§43

In the tripartite convention of January 9, 1930 between the United
States, Great Britain, and Iraq concerning the rights of the United
States of America and of its nationals in Iraq, it was declared (par.
9 of the preamble) that the United States recognized Iraq as an independent state. This convention having come into force through the
exchange of ratifications in London on February 24, 1931 and its proclamation by the President on March 11, 1931, the United States, on
May 6, 1931, accredited Mr. Alexander K. Sloan as Chargé d'Affaires
to Iraq. Mr. Sloan was accredited to "His Majesty Faisal I, King of
Iraq". As Iraq was still at this time a class-A mandate, it should be
observed that article 5 of the treaty of October 10, 1922 between
Great Britain and Iraq, defining the status of the mandate, provided
that the King of Iraq should have "the right of representation in
London and in such other capitals and places as may be agreed upon
by the High Contracting Parties". For a discussion of the status of
Iraq as a class-A mandate, see *ante* §22.

47 Stat. 1817, 1819; 4 Treaties, etc. (Trenwith, 1938) 4335, 4336; Secretary Stimson to Mr. Sloan, May 6, 1931, MS. Department of State, file
123SL52/140.

For the text of the treaty of October 10, 1922 between Great Britain and
Iraq, see Gr. Br. Treaty Ser. no. 17 (1925), Cmd. 2370.

POLAND

§44

Kingdom
proclaimed

In a manifesto published November 5, 1916 the Empires of Germany and of Austria-Hungary proclaimed Poland as an independent
state with an hereditary monarchy and a constitution. The Department of State instructed the Chargé d'Affaires in Berlin on November 14 to notify the Consul at Warsaw that when officials of the new
kingdom of Poland assumed office, he should deal with them as
de facto officials but should not attend any official ceremonies. This
action was stated to have been taken out of scrupulous regard for the
neutrality of the United States.

Mr. Grew to Secretary Lansing, Nov. 5, 1916, MS. Department of State, file 860c.01/1; Mr. Lansing to Mr. Grew, Nov. 14, 1916, *ibid.* 860c.01/3; 1916 For. Rel. Supp. 796–797.

In an instruction of October 8, 1917 to the Ambassador in France, the Department of State said that it had been advised that a Polish National Committee had been organized with headquarters in Paris under the presidency of Roman Dmowski and that there had been organized, with headquarters in Chicago, a Polish National Department, constituting a federation of all important Polish organizations in the United States. The Department requested the Ambassador to inform the members of the Polish National Committee that he would gladly transmit to his Government a formal definite request by their committee for recognition, the request to state:

Polish National Committee

(1) Purposes of committee;
(2) Factions or parties represented by the committee;
(3) Nature of recognition desired.

Such a request was accordingly transmitted to the Department by the Ambassador on October 19, and on November 10 the Department instructed him to inform President Dmowski that the Department had received his request and that the Government of the United States extended recognition to the Polish National Committee "as an official Polish organization".

In the meantime, the Ambassador in Russia had reported his attendance at formal ceremonies on October 15, at which had been read by the Russian Minister of Foreign Affairs the following formal declaration:

> I now declare that the other great powers of the Entente adhering to the principles proclaimed by the Russian Government in its manifesto to the Poles dated March 17 [March 30, new style] recognize that the creation of an independent and indivisible Poland constitutes one of the conditions of a solid and just peace and of a reign of right in Europe.

The British, Italian, American, and French Ambassadors made formal favorable responses to this declaration.

Secretary Lansing to Ambassador Sharp, Oct. 8, 1917, MS. Department of State, file 860c.01/29a; Mr. Sharp to Mr. Lansing, Oct. 19, 1917, *ibid.* 860c.01/40; Mr. Lansing to Mr. Sharp, Nov. 10, 1917, *ibid.* 860c.01/61; Ambassador Francis to Mr. Lansing, Oct. 17, 1917, *ibid.* 860c.01/39; 1917 For. Rel., Supp. 2., vol. I, pp. 765–778.

Mr. Ignace Jan Paderewski addressed a letter on behalf of the Polish National Committee to the Department of State on December 18, 1917 inquiring whether the Department would authorize the committee to establish in Washington or New York a consular bureau for the purposes of identifying Poles and issuing certificates of Polish nationality to all Poles whose loyalty and irreproachable conduct would be guaranteed by reliable and responsible citizens. The Department replied that it saw no objection to the establishment of such an agency but that the Government of the United States would not be willing that it should, at that time, assume a consular character, since to do so would require the issuance of formal commissions by a recognized government and the issuance of exequaturs by the Department of State thereunder.

> Secretary Lansing to Mr. Paderewski, Dec. 20, 1917, MS. Department of State, file 860c.01/91; 1917 For. Rel., Supp. 2, vol. I, p. 790.

Allied declaration

Mr. Dmowski, the President of the Polish National Committee, submitted to the American Ambassador in France, on November 23, 1917, the proposition that the powers at war against Germany make an agreement, which they would include in their war aims, along the following lines:

> 1. The reconstitution of an independent Polish state comprising Polish territories which before the war belonged to Russia, Germany and Austria. This Polish state to be in possession of the Polish part of Silesia and of a part of the Baltic coast with the mouths of the Vistula and the Niemen; to have proper extension and a sufficiently large population to enable it to become an efficient factor of European equilibrium.
> 2. The emancipation of nationalities in Austria-Hungary which remain actually under German and Magyar supremacy: the incorporation of the Polish, Italian, Serbo-Croatian and Roumanian territories into the national states to which they belong on account of their nationality; the creation of an independent Czechish state comprising Bohemia, Moravia, the Czechish part of Silesia and the northern part of Hungary inhabited by the Slovaks.

> Ambassador Sharp to Secretary Lansing, Nov. 23, 1917, MS. Department of State, file 860c.01/55; 1917 For. Rel., Supp. 2, vol. I, pp. 785–789.

In his address of January 8, 1918 at the joint session of the two houses of Congress in outlining a peace program of the Allied and Associated Powers, President Wilson included the following point:

> XIII. An independent Polish state should be erected which should include the territories inhabited by indisputably Polish populations, which should be assured a free and secure access to the sea, and whose political and economic independence and territorial integrity should be guaranteed by international covenant.

> 1918 For. Rel., Supp. 1, vol. I, pp. 12–16.

Recognition of autonomy and belligerency

The Polish Army was recognized as autonomous and co-belligerent under the supreme political authority of the Polish National Committee by France on October 6, by Great Britain on October 15, and by the United States on November 1, 1918.

Mr. Dmowski to Secretary Lansing, Oct. 18, 1918, MS. Department of State, file 763.72/12496; Mr. Lansing to Mr. Dmowski, Nov. 1, 1918, *ibid.* 763.72/12651a; 1918 For. Rel., Supp. 1, vol. I, pp. 878–881.

On January 22, 1919 Secretary Lansing, who was in Paris with the American Commission to Negotiate Peace, notified the Department of State that acting under direction from the President he had sent the following telegram to Mr. Paderewski according full recognition to the Polish Provisional Government:

Recognition of Provisional Government

> The President of the United States directs me to extend to you as Prime Minister and Secretary for Foreign Affairs of the Provisional Polish Government his sincere wishes for your success in the high office which you have assumed and his earnest hope that the Government of which you are a part will bring prosperity to the Republic of Poland.
>
> It is my privilege to extend to you at this time my personal greetings and officially to assure you that it will [be] a source of gratification to enter into official relatio.ıs with you at the earliest opportunity. To render to your country such aid as is possible at this time as it enters upon a new cycle of independent life, will be in full accord with that spirit of friendliness which has in the past animated the American people in their relations with your countrymen.

The American Minister in Poland presented his letters of credence to General Pilsudski, the chief of the Polish state on May 2, 1919.

The Commission to Negotiate Peace to the Acting Secretary of State (Polk), Jan. 22, 1919, MS. Department of State, file 860c.01/206; Minister Gibson to Mr. Polk, no. 1, May 2, 1919, *ibid.* 123G35/139; 1919 For. Rel., vol. II, pp. 740–744. See also *Mission of the United States to Poland*, S. Doc. 177, 66th Cong., 2d sess.

SAUDI ARABIA

§45

In a note of September 29, 1928, addressed to the Secretary of State, the Acting Director of Foreign Affairs of the Kingdom of Hejaz and Nejd and its dependencies requested that formal recognition be extended by the Government of the United States to the Kingdom of Hejaz and Nejd. A similar request was transmitted to the Department of State through the Legation at Cairo. The Department instructed the Legation, on January 7, 1929, to seek an early opportunity of conveying to the Hejazi Agent at Cairo, under appropriate informal circumstances and orally, a message to the effect that, while the friendly tone of the communication from the Acting Director of Foreign Affairs was much appreciated and accordingly reciprocated, the question of the recognition by the United States of the Kingdom

Recognition requested

of Hejaz and Nejd was one to which the Secretary of State found it impracticable to reply definitively at that time. The Legation was instructed to say further that the Department felt confident that at an appropriate time the question of recognition would receive sympathetic consideration.

In response to a despatch of January 11, 1930 from the Legation expressing the view that the time had come for favorable consideration of the formal request for recognition of the Kingdom of Hejaz and Nejd, the Department said that, as the final decision would be largely influenced by the character and extent of American commercial interest, actual as well as potential, in the Hejaz, it would be glad to receive any available information on that subject. It added that it would not be in a position to give further consideration to the question of recognition of Hejaz until the character of American representation in Iraq had been determined.

> The Acting Director of Foreign Affairs, Fuad Hamza, to Secretary Kellogg, Sept. 29, 1928, MS. Department of State, file 890f.01/8; Minister Gunther to Mr. Kellogg, no. 73, Nov. 9, 1928, and Assistant Secretary Castle to Mr. Gunther, no. 24, Jan. 7, 1929, *ibid.* 890f.01/10; Mr. Gunther to Secretary Stimson, no. 315, Jan. 11, 1930, and Assistant Secretary Shaw to Mr. Gunther, no. 100, Feb. 28, 1930, *ibid.* 890f.01/15.

Recognition

On February 10, 1931 the Department of State advised the Embassy in London in part as follows:

> Upon the receipt of the present instruction, and after a study of the accompanying documents, it is desired that a member of the Embassy staff seek an early interview with the Hejazi Minister in London. At this interview the American representative should state that he is calling under instructions from his Government to inform the Hejazi Minister that the Government of the United States is now in a position to give favorable and sympathetic consideration to the request for the recognition of the Hejaz and Nejd and its Dependencies which was contained in the note addressed on September 29, 1928, to the Secretary of State by the Acting Director for Foreign Affairs at Mecca. He should add that before taking further steps in the matter the American Government would be interested to learn whether the Government of His Majesty King Ibn Saud would be prepared to enter into a treaty of friendship, commerce and navigation providing for unconditional most-favored-nation treatment. At the same time this Government would be glad to receive information with respect to the provisions of the Hejazi and Nejdi laws governing the administration of justice in civil, commercial, criminal and personal status cases in which foreigners are involved. The American representative should express the hope that the Hejazi Minister will be good enough to communicate the foregoing to his Government at Mecca with the request that any reply which that Government may wish to make be communicated through the Minister to your Embassy.

With a despatch of April 14, 1931 the Embassy transmitted the text of a note dated April 13 from the Royal Legation of Hejaz and Nejd in London stating that the Hejazi Government was ready to enter, with the United States Government, into a treaty of friendship, commerce, and navigation, providing for most-favored-nation treatment. The note added:

> His Majesty's Government have the honour to inform the American Government that the Hedjaz and Nejd laws, governing the administration of justice in civil, commercial, and criminal cases are The Islamic Laws. In addition, a special council is provided for commercial cases. With regard to cases of Personal Status, non-Moslem foreigners are treated according to special laws in common with other non-Moslem Europeans.

The Department instructed the Embassy by telegram on May 1 to inform the Hejazi Minister that the United States extended "full recognition to the Government of His Majesty King Ibn Saud of the Hejaz and Nejd and its Dependencies" and to request him to communicate this fact to the Foreign Office at Mecca. In announcing the recognition to the press on May 2, 1931, the Department said that in extending recognition the Government of the United States had taken "cognizance of the actual existence of that Government [the Government of King Ibn Saud] during a considerable period of time and of the successful maintenance within its borders of political and economic stability".

Secretary Stimson to Ambassador Dawes, no. 666, Feb. 10, 1931, MS. Department of State, file 890f.01/29A; Mr. Dawes to Mr. Stimson, no. 1832, Apr. 14, 1931, *ibid.* 890f.01/33; Mr. Stimson to Mr. Dawes, no. 113, May 1, 1931, *ibid.* 890f.01/34A. See also Department of State, *Press Releases,* weekly issue 85, p. 395 (May 3, 1931).

The name of the former Kingdom of Hejaz and Nejd and its dependencies was changed to the Kingdom of Saudi Arabia by a decree of Sept. 18, 1932.

YUGOSLAVIA

§46

On October 14, 1918 the Serbian Chargé d'Affaires in Washington stated in a note addressed to the Secretary of State that he had been instructed by his Government to bring to the attention of the Government of the United States a statement reading in part as follows:

> After our country was attacked in this manner, and for these motives, the Royal Government declared, in the month of November, 1914, in the National Parliament, that Serbia was fighting for her existence, and at the same time for the liberation and union of her Serb, Croat, and Slovene brothers-in-race, oppressed by the Germans and the Magyars.

Our allies, resolved not to hesitate to make any sacrifice that would aid them to achieve this aim, have, in the course of the war, and especially since the intervention of the United States, declared that it was their intention to reestablish Poland in all its parts, with an exit on the Baltic Sea, and to collaborate with the Czech-Slovaks as their allies.

We believe, in consequence, that we are within our rights when we await a declaration on their part, according to which they will proclaim Serbia as their loyal ally since the beginning of the war, and will, therefore, also consider as such the brothers-in-race of the Serbs, Croats and Slovenes of Austria-Hungary, and that they are ready to favor their union with Serbia in a free and democratic state, such as was provided for in the Declaration of Corfu.

The Department of State replied on October 28 that the United States had expressed itself freely in support of the right of the Yugoslavs to be entirely freed from Austrian domination but that at that time it did not feel it could go further in declaring a policy manifestly depending upon the self-determination of the peoples involved.

Chargé Simitch to Secretary Lansing, Oct. 14, 1918, and Mr. Lansing to Mr. Simitch, Oct. 28, 1918, MS. Department of State, file 763.72119/2261; 1918 For. Rel., Supp. 1, vol. I, pp. 842–844, 857.

With an undated note received by the Department of State on January 6, 1919, the Serbian Chargé d'Affaires submitted the following communication from his Government:

In accordance with the decision of the Central Committee of the National Council of Zagreb which represents the State of all the Serbian Croatian and Slovene provinces within the boundaries of the former Austro-Hungarian Monarchy, a special Delegation has arrived at Belgrade on the 1st of December. This Delegation by one [a] solemn address, presented to His Highness the Crown Prince, has proclaimed the Union of all the Serbian Croatian and Slovene provinces of the former Dualist Monarchy into one single State with the Kingdom of Serbia under the Dynasty of His Majesty King Peter and under the regency of the Crown Prince Alexander. In the reply to this address His Royal Highness the Crown Prince has proclaimed the Union of Serbia with the above mentioned independent State of Slovenes, Croats and Serbs into one single Kingdom: "Kingdom of the Serbs, Croats and Slovenes." His Highness has accepted the regency and will form a common Government. On the 17th of December His Royal Highness the Crown Prince received in audience a delegation from Montenegro. This Delegation has submitted to His Highness on the 26th of November the decisions of the Great National Assembly of the Kingdom of Montenegro. By virtue of these decisions His Majesty King Nikolas I, and His dynasty have been declared destitute of all the rights upon [to] the throne of Montenegro and the Kingdom of Montenegro, united to Serbia under the dynasty of Karageorgevitch, is included in the Kingdom of the Serbs, Croats and Slovenes. His Royal Highness the Crown Prince has declared that He accepts with pleasure and thanks these decisions. A common Government for the new Kingdom has been organized on the 21st of December. The Legations, Consulates and other Missions of the Kingdom of Serbia will be the Legations, Consulates and other Missions of the Kingdom of the Serbs, Croats and Slovenes.

In acknowledging the receipt of this note the Department said, on February 10, 1919, that—

the Government of the United States welcomes the union of the Serbian, Croatian and Slovene provinces within the boundaries of the former Austro-Hungarian Monarchy to Serbia and recognizes the Serbian Legation as the Legation of the Kingdom of the Serbs, Croatians and Slovenes. Recognition

In taking this action, however, the United States Government recognizes that the final settlement of territorial frontiers must be left to the Peace Conference for determination according to the desires of the peoples concerned.

The Secretary of State had made public in Paris on February 7, 1919 the following statement with regard to the union of the Yugoslav peoples:

On May 29, 1918, the Government of the United States expressed its sympathy for the nationalistic aspirations of the Jugo Slav race and on June 28 declared that all branches of the Slavish race should be completely freed from German and Austrian rule. After having achieved their freedom from foreign oppression the Jugo Slav[s] formerly under Austro-Hungarian rule on various occasions expressed the desire to unite with the Kingdom of Servia. The Servian Government on its part has publicly and officially accepted the union of the Serb, Croat and Slovene peoples. The Government of the United States, therefore, welcomes the union while recognizing that the final settlement of territorial frontiers must be left to the Peace Conference for determination according to desires of the peoples concerned.

Chargé Simitch to the Acting Secretary of State (Polk), received Jan. 6, 1919, and Mr. Polk to Minister Grouitch, no. 2, Feb. 10, 1919, MS. Department of State, file 860h.01/21; the Commission to Negotiate Peace to Mr. Polk, Feb. 6, 1919, *ibid.* 860h.01/26; 1919 For. Rel., vol. II, pp. 892–900.

Armenia.—In a telegram of Oct. 25, 1918 the Ambassador in France transmitted to the Department of State a request from the President of the Armenian National Delegation that Armenia be recognized as a belligerent in the same manner that the Czechoslovaks had been recognized. Apparently this request was never granted. However, the Supreme Council of the Allied Powers made the following decision on Jan. 19, 1920, which was communicated to the Department by Ambassador Wallace in a telegram of that date:

"It is agreed: (1) That the Government of the Armenian State shall be recognized as a *de facto* government on the condition that this recognition in no way prejudges the question of the eventual frontier . . ." [Ellipses in original text.]

In a telegram of Apr. 23, 1920 addressed to the representative of the Armenian Republic in Washington, the Secretary of State informed him that by direction of the President the Government of the United States recognized "as of this date, the *de facto* Government of the Armenian Republic" but that such action in no way predetermined the territorial frontiers, which, it was understood, were matters for later determination.

Ambassador Sharp to Secretary Lansing, Oct. 25, 1918, MS. Department of State, file 763.72/11903; 1918 For. Rel., Supp. 1, vol. I., p. 894.   Ambassador Wallace to Secretary Lansing, Jan. 19, 1920, MS. Department of State, file 763.72119/8740; Secretary Colby to the representative of the Armenian Republic, Apr. 23, 1920, *ibid.* 860j.01/242a; 1920 For. Rel., vol. III, pp. 775–778.   See *The Republic of Armenia, A Memorandum on the Recognition of the Government of the Republic of Armenia, Submitted by the Special Mission of the Republic of Armenia to the United States*, S. Doc. 151, 66th Cong., 1st sess.

Replying to an inquiry as to the status of Armenia, the Department of State, in a letter of Jan. 4, 1934, said that—

"the Socialist Soviet Republic of Armenia, to which it is assumed you have reference, is a component part of the Transcaucasian Socialist Federated Soviet Republic.   The latter is one of seven constituent republics composing the Union of Soviet Socialist Republics, the Government of which was recognized by the Government of the United States on November 16, 1933.

". . .   the recognition which the United States accorded in 1920 to the 'de facto Government of the Armenian Republic' is no longer effective since the Armenian Republic has ceased to exist as an independent state."

MS. Department of State, file 860j.01/633.

RECOGNITION OF NEW GOVERNMENTS

AMERICAN REPUBLICS

§47

Argentina   President Irigoyen of Argentina was forced out of office by a *coup d'état* accomplished by General Uriburu on September 6, 1930. Formal notice of the establishment of the Provisional Government under the provisional presidency of General Uriburu was given the American Embassy in a note received on September 9, in which it was stated that it was the purpose and desire of the Provisional Government to maintain and develop so far as possible the cordial relations between the two countries.   The American Ambassador recommended to the Department of State that recognition be extended promptly to the new regime, saying that he believed that it would be able to maintain itself in power until it had realized its declared purpose of holding, at the earliest possible date, elections of national senators and deputies and of a president and vice president. The Ambassador was informed that there seemed to be no possibility of immediate recognition.

Ambassador Bliss to Secretary Stimson, nos. 124 and 126, Sept. 7 and 9, 1930, MS. Department of State, files 835.00 Revolutions/2, 835.00 Revolutions/5; the Acting Secretary of State (Cotton) to Mr. Bliss, no. 100, Sept. 11, 1930, *ibid.* 835.01/7.

The Department of State requested the Embassy, on September **Recognition** 13, 1930, to inform it promptly of any reliable information respecting the control exercised by the Provisional Government over the provinces and concerning the relations of the Government, understood to be composed largely of members of the Conservative Party, with other political elements. The Ambassador replied that the Provisional Government had full control of all the provinces, exercising that control either through civilian or military interventors, the normal government machinery functioning in only two provinces. He said that the Socialist Party, while protesting the illegality of the Provisional Government, acknowledged it and expressed faith in the integrity of its intentions and that all other parties in the capital and the provinces, except the Radical Party, approved and supported the Provisional Government. The Department instructed him (September 16) "to inform the Minister for Foreign Affairs on next Thursday that your Government has instructed you to establish full diplomatic relations with the new Argentine Government, thus according recognition to it".

The Acting Secretary of State (Cotton) to Ambassador Bliss, no. 101, Sept. 13, 1930, MS. Department of State, file 835.00 Revolutions/7; Mr. Bliss to Secretary Stimson, no. 132, Sept. 14, 1930, *ibid.* 835.00 Revolutions/8;·Mr. Stimson to Mr. Bliss, no. 104, Sept. 16, 1930, *ibid.* 835.01/18.

In pursuance of the instruction of Sept. 16 the Ambassador handed a note to the Minister of Foreign Affairs of Argentina extending recognition on September 18. Mr. Bliss to Mr. Stimson, no. 976, Sept. 20, 1930, *ibid.* 835.01/42.

In reaching the conclusion to accord recognition to these three **Grounds** Governments, the evidence has satisfied me that these provisional Governments are *de facto* in control of their respective countries, and that there is no active resistance to their rule. Each of the present Governments has also made it clear that it is its intention to fulfill its respective international obligations and to hold, in due course, elections to regularize its status.

The action of the United States in thus recognizing the present Argentine, Peruvian, and Bolivian Governments does not represent any new policy or change of policy by the United States toward the nations of South America or the rest of the world.

I have deemed it wise to act promptly in this matter in order that in the present economic situation our delay may not embarrass the people of these friendly countries in reestablishing their normal intercourse with the rest of the world.

Statement by the Secretary of State, Department of State, *Press Releases*, weekly issue 51, p. 192 (Sept. 17, 1930). For text of statement made by the Secretary in explanation of his assertion that this action did not represent any new policy or change of policy, see *ibid.* pp. 192–193 (Sept. 17, 1930).

Bolivia

A *coup d'état* accomplished by the Republican leader, Bautista Saavedra, resulted in the overthrow of the Government of Bolivia on July 12, 1920 and the resignation of the President.   The American Minister reported to the Department of State on July 19 that he was assured by Saavedra that the new Government would respect all treaties.   He reported further on July 20:

Peru yesterday recognized new Government.   Representatives here of all other countries unanimous in opinion that there should be no recognition now but unless something now unforeseen should occur in next few days provisional recognition of *de facto* Government with ample guarantees [to] foreigners and foreign interests pending holding of fair elections might be made.   I feel that we should recognize the new Government as soon as possible but make it sufficiently provisional to provide for any changes which would be mainly in the personnel if at all.

An election of the new Congress having been carried out on November 14, 1920, the Department instructed the Legation as follows on December 9:

The general elections recently held in Bolivia appear to demonstrate without question that the present Government of Bolivia is supported by the great majority of the Bolivian people.   From the information which you have conveyed to the Department the elections appear to have been conducted on the whole, in an orderly and legal manner and conditions in the Republic appear to be completely tranquil.   You have informed the Department that the Congress recently elected will meet in convention on December 20, to revise the Constitution and to elect a provisional President.

In view of these circumstances the President has determined to recognize the Government of Bolivia, as soon as a provisional President is elected, as the *de facto* Government of Bolivia. Formal relations with the Bolivian Government will be entered into when it is permanently established.

You will therefore be instructed by the Department, as soon as this Government is advised of the election by the Congress of a provisional President, to extend recognition on behalf of this Government to the Government of Bolivia as the *de facto* Government of that Republic.

Minister Maginnis to Secretary Colby, July 12, 19, and 20, 1920, MS. Department of State, files 824.00/55, 824.00/67, 824.00/66; the Acting

Secretary of State (Davis) to Mr. Maginnis, Dec. 9, 1920, *ibid.* file 824.00/154c; 1920 For. Rel., vol. I, pp. 372–386.

Saavedra was inaugurated on January 28, 1921, and on January 31 the Department sent identic telegrams to its representatives in Brazil and Argentina reading as follows:

> The Department desires you to inform the Minister of Foreign Affairs that the Government of the United States, in view of the fact that the election of Dr. Bautista Saavedra to the Presidency of Bolivia was conducted in conformity with the provisions of the Bolivian Constitution as amended by the Constitutional Convention elected in November 1920, has now determined to extend recognition to the existing Government of Bolivia, not as the *de facto* Government, but as the Constitutional Government of that Republic. This Government will delay the formal act of recognition for a few days until assured that the stability of the present Bolivian Government will not be menaced by any outbreak or disorders. The Government of Argentina will receive notification of the date on which the United States will extend recognition.
>
> You should inquire also whether the Government of Argentina finds itself in agreement with the decision of the United States, and whether it will be disposed to proceed simultaneously with the United States in extending formal recognition to the Government of Bolivia. You may say to the Minister of Foreign Affairs that it is the belief of the Department that the Governments of Argentina, Brazil, and the United States have contributed to the peaceful and orderly development of Constitutional Government in this hemisphere, and have also given significant evidence of the similarity in the ideals of the three Republics, by their action in postponing recognition of the new Bolivian Government until that Government had definitely shown that it represented the will of the great majority of the Bolivian people, and until it had been established in accordance with the provisions of the Bolivian Constitution.
> [Paraphrase.]

De jure recognition

Both Governments agreed to act simultaneously with the United States, and formal recognition was accordingly extended on February 9.

Secretary Colby to the Ambassador in Argentina (Stimson), no. 13, Jan. 31, 1921, MS. Department of State, file 824.00/153 supp.; Mr. Stimson to Mr. Colby, Feb. 2, 1921, *ibid.* 824.00/176; the Ambassador in Brazil (Morgan) to Mr. Colby, Feb. 6, 1921, *ibid.* 824.00/178; the Minister in Bolivia (Maginnis) to Mr. Colby, Feb. 9, 1921, *ibid.* 824.00/181; 1921 For. Rel., vol. I, pp. 281–287.

The Military Junta established under the presidency of Colonel Osorio by *coup d'état* of June 27, 1930 was not recognized by the

Military Junta, 1930

United States until September. On September 16 the following instruction was issued to the newly appointed Minister:

> The Department desires that you inform the Minister for Foreign Affairs, or the official in charge of that Ministry, on next Thursday, that your Government has instructed you to establish full diplomatic relations with the existing Governmental Junta. You should say that you are ready to present your letters of credence to such person as may be indicated as empowered to receive the credentials of foreign ministers. [Paraphrase.]

> Mr. Hibbard to Secretary Stimson, nos. 42, 43, and 44, June 27 and 28, 1930, MS. Department of State, files 824.00/508, 824.00/507, 824.00/509; Mr. Stimson to Mr. Hibbard, no. 38, Sept. 16, 1930, *ibid.* 824.01/15.

> Minister Feely reported on September 23 that he had on that date presented his credentials and assumed charge of the Legation. Mr. Feely to Mr. Stimson, no. 65, Sept. 23, 1930, *ibid.* 123 Feely, Edward F./26. Argentina, Bolivia, and Peru were recognized on the same day. See statement by Mr. Stimson concerning this action, *ante*, this section.

Recognition of Toro Junta, 1936

Upon the resignation of President Luis Tejada Sorzano from the presidency on May 17, 1936, the Government was taken over by a mixed Junta of army officers and civilians headed by Colonel Toro. The American Ambassador in Argentina reported in a telegram of May 18, 1936, that the chairman of the peace conference which was attempting to bring about an agreement for the termination of the war between Bolivia and Paraguay had received a telegram from the Minister of Foreign Affairs of the new Bolivian regime announcing the assumption of governmental powers by the Junta and making a formal declaration that the Buenos Aires protocols and all other existing treaties to which Bolivia was a party would be strictly respected. The Ambassador stated that it was the opinion of the executive committee that recognition probably might be accorded by the six mediating nations within a few days and should be approximately simultaneous and as nearly as possible by identic notes. Secretary Hull replied on May 19 that he concurred in the belief expressed at the meeting of the executive committee that recognition of the new Bolivian Government might well be accorded simultaneously by identic notes by the six mediating nations, thus following the desirable precedent created in the case of the recognition of the existing Government in Paraguay. He added, however, that it was believed that it would be wise to await developments for at least a few days in order to ascertain public reaction in Bolivia to the change of government and more specifically to determine the final composition and authority of the new regime.

The Chargé d'Affaires in Bolivia (Muccio) to Secretary Hull, nos. 21 and 28, May 17 and 18, 1936, MS. Department of State, files 824.00/752, 824.00/762; Ambassador Weddell to Mr. Hull, no. 109, May 18, 1936, and Mr. Hull to Mr. Weddell, no. 109, May 19, 1936, *ibid.* file 824.01/40.

The Legation on May 24 communicated to the Department of State the text of a note which it had received from the Minister of Foreign Affairs requesting it to take up with the Government of the United States the question of formal recognition. The note stated that the Junta had the "support of the people and of the Army" and was "now definitely consolidated" and that the Junta Government in international matters was "one of sincere intimacy of Bolivia to all friendly nations, of a close and harmonious cooperation, and the strictest observance of existing pacts". The Embassy in Buenos Aires reported on May 29 that the executive committee of the peace conference recommended to the respective governments that their representatives in La Paz tender notes of recognition simultaneously on May 30. Secretary Hull accordingly instructed the Legation on May 30 to deliver the following note simultaneously with the delivery of notes by the other mediatory powers:

> I have the honor to acknowledge the receipt of your Excellency's note of (insert date) by which, after stating that your Government enjoys the support of the people and that it intends to respect its international obligations, you request that the question of the continuation of normal friendly relations be taken up with my Government.
>
> In view of the affirmation set forth in your note under reference, my Government has instructed me to state that it will be pleased to maintain with the Government of Bolivia the friendly relations that are traditional between our two countries.

Support of peoples; international obligations

The note was delivered, according to instructions, on the same day at 5 p.m.

Mr. Muccio to Mr. Hull, no. 29, May 24, 1936, MS. Department of State, file 824.01/43; Mr. Weddell to Mr. Hull, no. 116, May 29, 1936, *ibid.* 824.01/47; Mr. Hull to Mr. Muccio, no. 29, May 30, 1936, *ibid.* 824.01/43; Mr. Muccio to Mr. Hull, no. 32, May 30, 1936, *ibid.* 824.01/48.

Colonel Toro resigned on July 13, 1937, and the provisional presidency was turned over to Colonel Busch. The Bolivian Minister in Washington called on the Under Secretary of State on July 19, 1937 and read to him a declaration from his Government containing the assurance that Bolivia would scrupulously maintain all its international obligations and that it desired to continue its friendly relations with the Government of the United States. Acting under instruction the Minister stated that, in the opinion of his Government, no formal act of recognition of the new regime was required as the Government headed by Colonel Toro was a Government of the Army and as the

Busch Junta, 1937

Army had merely replaced one officer with another. The Minister was informed by the Under Secretary of State that the Government of the United States would desire a little time, in accordance with the traditional policy, to ascertain whether the existing government enjoyed a substantial measure of popular support and whether it was able to carry out the ordinary functions of government.

> Chargé Muccio to Secretary Hull, nos. 38 and 39, July 14, 1937, MS. Department of State, files 824.00/801, 824.00/802; memorandum of conversation with Minister Guachalla, *ibid.* file 824.00/836.

Substantially similar telegraphic instructions were addressed by the Department to the missions in Buenos Aires, Rio de Janeiro, Montevideo, and Santiago on July 19:

Basis of recognition

> Please call on the Foreign Minister at an early moment and inform him that your Government is desirous of consulting with him and learning his views with regard to the desirability of recognizing the new Bolivian Government, in this respect following the desirable precedent created in the case of recognition of the present Government in Paraguay, as well as of the Toro Government in Bolivia.

International obligations; stability; "composition and authority"; support

> . . . you may state that it is the opinion of this Government that the statement issued by Colonel Busch at the time he assumed office, which has been reiterated by the Bolivian Minister here, fully covers the Bolivian intention to respect its international obligations, which would cover the Chaco protocols. Please make inquiry, however, as to the Minister's opinion with regard to the stability of the new Government, its composition and authority, and the measure of popular support which it would seem to possess.

The four Governments consulted were unanimous in their opinion that formal relations with the Bolivian Government should be promptly established. On July 22 Secretary Hull instructed the Legation at La Paz to deliver a note to the Acting Minister of Foreign Affairs acknowledging the receipt of the note from the Bolivian Foreign Office received by the Legation on July 17, and to say:

> In view of the statements contained in your note under reference and of the declarations made by the Chief Executive that his Government intends to respect Bolivia's international obligations and the legitimate rights of private property, my Government has instructed me to state that it will be pleased to maintain with the Government of Bolivia the cordial relations which have existed between our two countries.

The note was delivered on the same date.

> Secretary Hull to Ambassador Weddell, no. 57, July 19, 1937, MS. Department of State, file 824.01/60A; Mr. Hull to Mr. Muccio, no. 21, July 22, 1937, *ibid.* 824.01/58. Previously the Department of State had telegraphed Mr. Weddell: "Inasmuch as the change of government in Bolivia

was effected by a coup d'état without any semblance of conformity to the constitution, the Department believes that recognition is necessary. The Busch regime has already given evidence of its desire to honor its international engagements. Upon receipt of information that the Busch regime is maintaining public order and is effectively administering the Government, and after consultation with the other Governments represented upon the Chaco Committee, this Government will probably proceed at once to give consideration to according recognition." Mr. Hull to Mr. Weddell, no. 56, July 17, 1937, *ibid.* 824.01/57A.

As a result of a wide-spread revolution in Brazil, President Washing- Brazil ton Luis resigned in the latter part of October 1930. A Military Junta took over the Government, and on November 3 Getulio Vargas assumed the presidency of the Provisional Government. The American Ambassador was officially notified of the change in Government by the Foreign Office on October 26 and was given the following assurances:

> "Allow me also to inform Your Excellency that the junta recognizes and respects all national obligations contracted abroad, existing treaties with foreign powers, the public debt, foreign and domestic, existing contracts and other obligations legally entered into."

Ambassador Morgan to Secretary Stimson, nos. 124, 131, and 138, Oct. 24 and 27, and Nov. 3, 1930, MS. Department of State, files 832.00 Revolutions/146, 832.00 Revolutions/160, 832.00 Revolutions/184.

The Ambassador stated in a telegram of November 4 that all the Recognition requisites for recognition contained in the statement issued by the Secretary of State on September 17, 1930, at the time of the recognition of the Governments of Argentina, Bolivia, and Peru, seemed to have been fulfilled except in regard to the holding of elections. (For the Secretary's statement of September 17, 1930, see *ante*, this section.) He said that in announcing his program upon taking over the Government, President Vargas had stated that there would be a "reform of electoral system relating especially to the guaranteeing freedom of vote" and "reform of the electorate having been accomplished the nation will be consulted regarding the choice of representatives with full power to revise the federal statutes in order to increase public and individual liberty and guarantee the autonomy of the states against violations by the Central Government". After inquiring of the Ambassador regarding the attitude of other states toward the new administration, the likelihood of any counter-revolution or independent uprising against its authority, and its readiness and willingness to recognize its international obligations, and after receiving a satisfactory report from the Ambassador, Secretary Stimson, on November 8, 1930, instructed him to reply to the note of November 3 by stating that the Government of the United States would "be happy to continue with the new Government the same friendly relations as with its predecessors". The Ambassador reported in a telegram of the same date that, as instructed by the Department, he had handed a note personally to the Minister of Foreign Affairs acknowledging receipt of the latter's note of November 3.

> Ambassador Morgan to Secretary Stimson, no. 139, Nov. 4, 1930, MS. Department of State, file 832.01/2; Mr. Stimson to Mr. Morgan, no. 78, Nov. 5, 1930, *ibid.* 832.00 Revolutions/199; Mr. Morgan to Mr. Stimson, no. 144, Nov. 7, 1930, *ibid.* 832.00 Revolutions/200; Mr. Stimson to Mr. Morgan, no. 81, Nov. 7, 1930, *ibid.* 832.01/6B; Mr. Morgan to Mr. Stimson, Nov. 8, 1930, *ibid.* 832.01/22; Mr. Stimson to Mr. Morgan, no. 82, Nov. 8, 1930, *ibid.* 832.01/3; Mr. Morgan to Mr. Stimson, no. 145, Nov. 8, 1930, *ibid.* 832.01/7.

Chile

Recognition was not extended by the Government of the United States to the government of General Altamirano who became Acting President of Chile in September 1924, when President Alessandri left the country under pressure from a Military Junta, nominally on a six months' leave of absence. The reasons for withholding recognition were stated in telegraphic instructions of September 15 and October 9, 1924 to the Embassy in Santiago, as follows:

> Department appreciates desirability of avoiding any steps which might have an unfavorable reaction on the local situation. However, the attitude of the Government of the United States so far as the recognition of the new regime is concerned must be guided not simply by the sincerity and objectives of those in control but also with adequate respect for those general principles which must govern our policy in extending recognition to any administration which may come into power in another nation by extra-constitutional means. At the present time it does not seem clear that the Government of the United States would be justified in assuming that the new regime was sufficiently established to warrant formal relations. For the present you will maintain frank, friendly, but informal relations, and you may make it clear that the United States is only pursuing that course which it invariably takes in like cases in other parts of the world. [Paraphrase.]

> Secretary Hughes to Ambassador Collier, no. 43, Sept. 15, 1924, MS. Department of State, file 825.00/287; 1924 For. Rel., vol. I, p. 359.

International obligations; stability; acquiescence of the people

> In determining upon the recognition of a new government in a foreign state, the Government of the United States must, of course, first be guided not only by the assurance that international obligations will be carried out by the new government, but also by satisfactory evidence that it is in a position to maintain stability and retain its power through the acquiescence of the people. . . . Keeping all of these factors in view, it is the desire of the Department for the present to maintain a position of reserve while omitting no opportunity to indicate friendship for the Chilean people and courtesy towards the new regime. [Paraphrase.]

Secretary Hughes to Ambassador Collier, no. 51, Oct. 9, 1924, MS. Department of State, file 825.01/15.

The American Ambassador reported the formation of a new Junta on January 31, 1925 and said that it had declared its purpose to procure the prompt return of Alessandri. On March 23 he reported that Alessandri had returned and that his reception by the people had been an unprecedented triumph. The Department accepted the Chilean view that Alessandri's return marked merely a resumption of his official duties and that such resumption was in accord with the requirements of the Constitution. It accordingly instructed the Embassy on March 19: *(margin: Resumption of relations)*

> When Alessandri resumes office, formal relations may be maintained with his Government. It is not considered that any formal communication or any special action is necessary in this connection, nor that any comment or explanation should be made with reference to this action. [Paraphrase.]

Ambassador Collier to Secretary Hughes, no. 16, Jan. 31, 1925, MS. Department of State, file 825.00/377; Mr. Collier to Secretary Kellogg, no. 32, Mar. 23, 1925, *ibid.* 825.00/407; Mr. Kellogg to Mr. Collier, no. 11, Mar. 19, 1925, *ibid.* 825.01/41.

Upon the resignation of Ibáñez as President of Chile on July 26, 1931, the President of the Senate resigned as Vice President and, in pursuance of the Constitution, turned over the power to Montero, who thus became Vice and Acting President. The American Ambassador reported on July 27 that it was the opinion of the Chilean Under Secretary of Foreign Affairs that, since the transfer of authority had followed the Constitution, the question of recognition did not arise. The Department of State replied that it concurred "in the view that no recognition of new Chilean Government is necessary". *(margin: Montero government, 1931: recognition not necessary)*

Ambassador Culbertson to Secretary Stimson, nos. 79, 83, and 82, July 26 and 27, 1931, MS. Department of State, files 825.00 Revolutions/7, 825.001 Montero, Juan/1, 825.00 Revolutions/10; the Acting Secretary of State (Castle) to Mr. Culbertson, no. 31, July 27, 1931, *ibid.* 825.01/47.

On June 4, 1932 Montero (who had been elected to the presidency in October 1931) was overthrown and succeeded by a Military Junta. In a telegram to the Department of State dated June 6, 1932, the Ambassador recommended delaying recognition for the time being. To this the Department replied: *(margin: Military Junta, June 4, 1932)*

> We must of course delay any decision as to recognition until we are in a position to determine whether the de facto Government can satisfy the usual requirements of international practice, namely, that it is in control of the country and that there is no active resistance to it, and that it intends to fulfill its international obligations. *(margin: Consent of people; international obligations)*

Ambassador Culbertson to Secretary Stimson, no. 54, June 6, 1932, MS. Department of State, file 825.00 Revolutions/69; Mr. Stimson to Mr. Culbertson, no. 25, June 6, 1932, *ibid.* 825.00 Revolutions/73.

After several shifts in the control of the Junta, Davila assumed power on June 15; and on July 14 the Chilean Foreign Office gave the following assurances to the American Embassy:

> The new Government, in carrying out the principles contained in its program of action, will respect its international obligations, it will insure domestic order and it will endeavor to strengthen the bonds of every kind which unite us with friendly countries. With the purpose of establishing normal conditions in the public administration, it has already taken the measures which will permit it to consult the will of the people on the first Sunday of October.

The Department informed the Embassy on July 16 that, because of the impossibility of speaking with confidence concerning the stability of the existing regime, it was not disposed to accord recognition at that time but would await developments. The Embassy was accordingly instructed not to make any reply to the note from the Minister of Foreign Affairs. It was advised that the fact that the new regime had already proposed certain measures which, although they had not as yet been enforced against the property of American nationals, indicated an intention of the new Government to resort to a standard radically departing from that usually deemed to assure adequate protection of foreign property under international practice, made it necessary that unusual care should be exercised before recognizing that regime.

Ambassador Culbertson to Secretary Stimson, no. 132, July 14, 1932, MS. Department of State, file 825.00 Revolutions/157; Mr. Stimson to Mr. Culbertson, no. 49, July 16, 1932, *ibid.* 825.00 Revolutions/158.

Recognition of Oyanedel government

On September 13, 1932 Davila resigned and delivered the executive power to his Minister of the Interior, General Blanche, who assumed the provisional presidency on September 14. Blanche in turn resigned on October 2, and the executive power was assumed by Oyanedel. The Ambassador reported on October 2 that Oyanedel was supposed to succeed constitutionally to the vice-presidency under article 66 of the Constitution, on the ground that his government inherited the constitutional right to govern from Montero. In a telegram of October 6 the Ambassador said that he believed that, unless we could obtain the usual guaranties, our best policy would be to allow the present informal relations to continue and to recognize the new president when he should take office after the elections which were planned for October 30.

Ambassador Culbertson to Secretary Stimson, nos. 205, 214, and 216, Sept. 13 and Oct. 2 and 6, 1932, MS. Department of State, files 825.00 Revolutions/197, 825.00 Revolutions/210, 825.00 Revolutions/219.

The Department is of course not bargaining concerning the matter of recognition and you must be careful to avoid giving any appearance of bargaining. International obligations

.   .   .   .

The Department is of the opinion that there should be some assurance given by the new government concerning its respect for international obligations. Of course the Department has no desire to contest the government's theory of its constitutionality, but on account of practical considerations must know where it stands in the matter of the government's respect for international obligations.

Please give the Department your opinion concerning the stability of the new government. The Department desires to be informed especially as to whether it has the general acquiescence of the people, whether its orders are carried out by the administrative authorities throughout the country, and whether there are any subversive movements.

[Paraphrase.]

Secretary Stimson to Ambassador Culbertson, no. 83, Oct. 12, 1932, MS. Department of State, file 825.00 Revolutions/225.

On October 16 the Ambassador reported the receipt of a note from the Foreign Office in which the assurance was given that "the Government of Chile as a Constitutional Government" would "respect its international obligations in the interest of foreigners in conformity with the laws and the political constitution of the State". Although his report regarding the stability of the Government was not entirely reassuring in all respects, upon receipt of information on October 19 that elections for the presidency would be held on October 30 the Department authorized the Ambassador to send an official note to the Minister of Foreign Affairs on October 21, stating that the Government of the United States would be pleased to carry on with the Government of Chile cordial and friendly relations. This instruction was carried out on October 21.

Ambassador Culbertson to Secretary Stimson, nos. 218 and 220, Oct. 16 and 19, 1932, MS. Department of State, files 825.00 Revolutions/226, 825.00 Revolutions/228; Mr. Stimson to Mr. Culbertson, no. 85, Oct. 20, 1932, ibid. file 825.01/147A; Mr. Culbertson to Mr. Stimson, no. 222, Oct. 21, 1932, ibid. 825.01/148.

The government of President González of Costa Rica was overthrown by force of arms by Federico Tinoco, Minister of War, on January 27, 1917. On February 9 the Minister in Costa Rica was instructed to inform General Tinoco that he had been instructed to hand him for his information a copy of the following cablegram which had been sent to the American Legations in the other four Central Costa Rica

American capitals, for presentation to the respective governments there:

Elected by legal and constitutional means

The Government of the United States has viewed the recent overthrow of the established Government in Costa Rica with the gravest concern and considers that illegal acts of this character tend to disturb the peace of Central America and to disrupt the unity of the American Continent. ¶ In view of its policy in regard to the assumption of power through illegal methods, clearly enunciated by it on several occasions during the past four years, the Government of the United States desires to set forth in an emphatic and distinct manner its present position in regard to the actual situation in Costa Rica which is that it will not give recognition or support to any Government which may be established unless it is clearly proven that it is elected by legal and constitutional means.

The Minister was instructed to say to General Tinoco that the desire which the Government of the United States had of seeing the "will of the people prevail in governmental matters in Costa Rica" had "forced it to the conclusion that no Government except such as may [might] be elected legally and established according to the Constitution shall [should] be considered entitled to recognition".

Minister Hale to Secretary Lansing, Jan. 27, 1917, MS. Department of State, file 818.00/54; Mr. Lansing to Mr. Hale, Feb. 9, 1917, *ibid.* 818.00/79b; 1917 For. Rel. 301–307.

On December 20, 1907 the Central American states had concluded an additional convention to the general treaty of peace and amity between them, providing in article I that—

The Governments of the High Contracting Parties shall not recognize any other Government which may come into power in any of the five Republics as a consequence of a *coup d'etat*, or of a revolution against the recognized Government, so long as the freely elected representatives of the people thereof have not constitutionally reorganized the country. [1907 For. Rel., pt II, p. 696.]

Recognition withheld

The Department instructed the Minister in Costa Rica on February 17 that, by authorization of the President, he should inform General Tinoco, in response to an inquiry from him, "that even if he is elected he will not be given recognition by the United States". The following statement was transmitted to General Tinoco through the Legation on February 22 and made public in the United States and in Central America:

In order that citizens of the United States may have definite information as to the position of this Government in regard to any financial aid which they may give to, or any business transactions which they may have with those persons who overthrew the Constitutional Government of Costa Rica by an act of armed rebellion, the Government of the United States desires to advise them that it will not consider any claims which may in the future arise from such dealings, worthy of its diplomatic support.

Secretary Lansing to Minister Hale, Feb. 17 and 22, 1917, MS. Department of State, files 818.00/84, 818.00/90a; 1917 For. Rel. 308.

On July 4, 1917 Señor R. Fernández Guardia, who had been acting as Special Agent of General Tinoco in Washington, informed the Department that he had been instructed to withdraw from Washington. He stated at some length the views of the *de facto* government of General Tinoco concerning the refusal of the United States to recognize that government because it had come into power through a revolution, concluding in part as follows:

Tinoco withdraws his representative

From the text above quoted [art. I of the convention of December 20, 1907] it will be clearly seen that the principle adopted has no further reach than to prevent recognition of governments that emanate from force so long as they have not been confirmed by the popular will freely expressed; certainly it was never intended to take away the sacred right of rebellion, for that would be equivalent to condemning the peoples to be the victims of tyranny; and such will surely be the fate of the Central American peoples if the United States persists in its purpose to apply the new principle without the limitation stipulated in the Additional Treaty above cited, for the right of rebellion is the only true guaranty possessed by the peoples against bad governors and that guaranty cannot be renounced without losing at the same time the right to liberty.

. . . .

On this point I am constrained to remind your excellency, in the case of Costa Rica, that in view of the preponderating position occupied by the United States in America, and of the influence it exercises—particularly in the Republics of Central America—the fact that the Washington Government refuses to recognize the legally constituted Government of Costa Rica, and seeks to justify its refusal by invoking a principle that is no part of international law, will probably be interpreted as unjustified intervention, and it is to be feared that this procedure on the part of the United States will not tend to strengthen the confidence reposed in that great country by the Republics of Latin America; because the Governments of Guatemala, Honduras, Nicaragua and El Salvador, having recognized the legitimacy of the Costa Rican Government, the fact that your excellency's Government persists in its refusal of recognition, despite the doctrine it has itself maintained, lends itself to the supposition that what really hangs in doubt before the United States is the independence and sovereignty of the Costa Rican Republic as well as of Central America and also of all the Latin American Republics.

. . . .

. . . Because intervention is not exclusively an act committed through armed forces. When adopted towards a small and weak nation, the mere unfriendly attitude of a great and powerful government suffices to produce the effects of intervention to a greater or less degree. So true is this that your excellency cannot but be aware that in consequence of the attitude assumed by the Washington Government respecting Costa Rica, the country is living in a continuous state of concern which, doubtless in abuse of the name of the United States, is being kept alive by persons who are propagating the idea that the Government of this country is supporting, or at least looks with approval upon, their efforts to disturb the public order.

> Señor R. Fernández Guardia to Secretary Lansing, July 4, 1917, MS. Department of State, file 818.00/177; 1917 For. Rel. 332–337.

Closing of legation

The attitude of Tinoco toward the Legation at San José having become increasingly unsatisfactory, the Department on November 26, 1918 instructed the Chargé d'Affaires to close the Legation and return to the United States, leaving the archives in charge of Consul Chase.

> Mr. Lansing to Mr. Johnson, Nov. 26, 1918, MS. Department of State, file 711.18/11; 1918 For. Rel. 275.

Fall of Tinoco

On August 1, 1919 Tinoco asked permission from the Costa Rican Congress to leave the country on account of illness, and on August 9 his brother Joaquin resigned as Designado, Juan B. Quiros being selected in his place. Joaquin Tinoco was assassinated on August 10, and on August 12 Federico Tinoco sailed from San José.

> Consul Chase to Secretary Lansing, Aug. 1, 10, and 11, 1919, MS. Department of State, files 818.00/803, 818.00/816, 818.00/820; Vice Consul Montgomery to Mr. Lansing, Aug. 12, 1919, ibid. 818.00/826; 1919 For. Rel., vol. I, pp. 848–854.

Refusal of recognition to Quiros

Obtain an official interview with Quiros, informing him of the attitude assumed by the Government of the United States in telegram to San Jose dated February 9, 3 P.M., 1917. You may say that the Government of the United States continues to feel as set forth in that telegram that any person elected to the position of president of Costa Rica in free, open elections held under the constitution of Costa Rica, violated by Federico Tinoco, would appear to be [have] good claim to recognition.

> Secretary Lansing to Consul Chase, Aug. 19, 1919, MS. Department of State, file 818.00/829; 1919 For. Rel., vol. I, p. 854.

Election of Acosta

Tinoco's resignation was presented to the Costa Rican Congress on August 20, 1919, and Quiros was elected for the balance of his term. The Department of State informed the Minister in Honduras on August 27:

Department cannot recognize Government of Quiros in Costa Rica, it being a creature of Tinoco. Government must be formed in accord with old constitution and free election must occur.

On August 30 it instructed the Consul at San José:

You may make it public that the Government of the United States will not recognize Juan Bautista Quiros as present President.

The governmental power should be deposited in the hands of Francisco Barquero, successor to the executive power under the Alfredo Gonzalez régime. Barquero should hold free and open elections for president at earliest possible date. Were this done, it would appear that the necessary legal formalities had been complied with to constitute a legitimate government worthy of recognition by the Government of the United States.

Quiros turned the presidency over to Barquero and elections were held on December 7, resulting in the election of Julio Acosta to the presidency. The Consul at San José was directed on August 2, 1920 to communicate to the Minister of Foreign Affairs the fact that the President had issued instructions to recognize the existing government of Costa Rica, and the Consul announced the recognition to President Acosta at an audience on August 3, 1920.

Consul Chase to Secretary Lansing, Aug. 21, 1919, MS. Department of State, file 818.00/844; Mr. Lansing to Minister Jones, Aug. 27, 1919, *ibid.* 818.00/846; Mr. Lansing to Mr. Chase, Aug. 30, 1919, *ibid.* 818.00/866a; Mr. Chase to Mr. Lansing, Sept. 3 and Dec. 8, 1919, *ibid.* files 818.00/872, 818.00/944; 1919 For. Rel., vol. I, pp. 855–865. Mr. Chase to Mr. Lansing, no. 779, May 14, 1920, MS. Department of State, file 818.00/983; Secretary Colby to Mr. Chase, Aug. 2, 1920, *ibid.* 818.00/991a; Mr. Chase to Mr. Colby, no. 823, Aug. 6, 1920, *ibid.* 818.00/999; 1920 For. Rel., vol. I, pp. 833–836.

Negotiations were initiated on July 1, 1933 between President Machado and the opposition parties in Cuba, with the American Cuba Ambassador (Welles) acting as mediator, the purpose of negotiations being to reach an agreement under which President Machado should retire and be replaced by a man satisfactory to all parties. Prolonged negotiations failed to produce a satisfactory basis for an agreement, but it having become apparent to President Machado that the Army would no longer support him, he requested Congress for a leave of absence on August 12 and deposited the presidency in General Herrera, a ranking cabinet minister. He left Cuba immediately, Machado– arriving in Nassau on August 13. In pursuance of a prior arrange- De Cespedes ment, General Herrera at once appointed Dr. Carlos Manuel de Cespedes, former Secretary of State and former Cuban Minister in Washington, Secretary of State and deposited the presidency in him in accordance with the provisions of the Constitution. Since the succession of De Cespedes to the presidency had been in accord with constitutional procedure, the Government of the United States considered it unnecessary to accord formal recognition to the new administration.

In a telegram of August 13, the Ambassador informed the Department of State that, after the passage by the Cuban Congress on the preceding night of the necessary legislation in accordance with the Constitution, De Cespedes had formally taken the oath of office as President that day. The Ambassador requested that he be authorized at once to state that the Embassy had established official relations with the De Cespedes government, since it was unquestionably constitutional in its formation, since the cabinet was of a high-class representative character, and since the situation demanded that the government receive the official support of the United States at once. He was accordingly authorized at once to send to President de Cespedes a message of congratulations upon his assumption of the responsibilities as President of the Republic. President de Cespedes acknowledged the message in a telegram addressed to President Roosevelt on August 14.

> Ambassador Welles to Secretary Hull, nos. 134, 152, and 156, Aug. 8, 12, and 13, 1933, MS. Department of State, files 837.00/3616, 837.00/3650, 837.00/3649; President de Cespedes to President Roosevelt, Aug. 14, 1933, *ibid.* file 837.00/3663; the Assistant Secretary of State (Welles) to John Martin, Jan. 30, 1934, *ibid.* 837.01/94.

Non-recognition of Grau San Martin, 1933

As a result of a revolutionary outbreak on September 4, 1933, De Cespedes, with his cabinet, resigned on September 5. The control of the government was for a time assumed by a committee of five members of the revolutionary group. Grau San Martin, one of the members of the committee, assumed the office of Provisional President on September 10. Ambassador Welles reported to the Department of State on September 6 that it would be desirable for the President to withhold recognition, as the stability and coherence of the new government appeared uncertain and it appeared to have no support outside of the capital. The position of the United States was set forth in the following statement released to the press on September 11:

Consent of people; order; obligations

The chief concern of the Government of the United States is as it has been that Cuba solve her own political problems in accordance with the desires of the Cuban people themselves. It would seem unnecessary to repeat that the Government of the United States has no interest in behalf of or prejudice against any political group or independent organization which is today active in the political life of Cuba. In view of its deep and abiding interest in the welfare of the Cuban people and the security of the Republic of Cuba, our Government is prepared to welcome any government representing the will of the people of the Republic and capable of maintaining law and order throughout the Island. Such a Government would be competent to carry out the functions and obligations incumbent upon any stable government. This has been the exact attitude of the United States Government from the beginning.

President Roosevelt further explained the position of the United States in a statement to the press on November 24, 1933, saying in part that—

> we have not believed that it would be a policy of friendship and of justice to the Cuban people as a whole to accord recognition to any provisional government in Cuba unless such government clearly possessed the support and the approval of the people of that Republic. We feel that no official action of the United States should at any time operate as an obstacle to the free and untrammeled determination by the Cuban people of their own destinies.

> Ambassador Welles to Secretary Hull, no. 191, Sept. 5, 1933, 1 p.m., no. 195, Sept. 5, 1933, 4 p.m., no. 224, Sept. 10, 1933, no. 202, Sept. 6, 1933, MS. Department of State, files 837.00/3747, 837.00/3757, 837.00/3803, 837.00/3767; Department of State, *Press Releases*, weekly issue 207, p. 152 (Sept. 11, 1933); *ibid.*, weekly issue 217, pp. 294–295 (Nov. 24, 1933).

In response to inquiries made through the American Ambassador as to whether the Government of the United States would give assurances that it would extend recognition to the Government of Cuba if the Grau San Martin regime should be replaced by a new government headed by Colonel Carlos Mendieta, the Department of State replied on January 14, 1934:

Mendieta government, 1934

> It is not possible to give an assurance of recognition of any individual before conditions projected become an accomplished fact. Previous statements have made the position of the President quite clear. A Cuban Provisional Government will be accorded recognition by the Government of the United States if it is supported by a substantial majority of the Cuban people, and is in a position to maintain law and order and normal governmental functions. There is no objection to a reiteration of this to any leaders or parties, but this Government cannot put itself in the position of giving to any individual or group an assurance of recognition in anticipation of the consummation of the conditions which have been consistently set forth. [Paraphrase.]

Grau San Martin turned over the office of Provisional President to Carlos Hevia on January 15, 1934, and Hevia took the oath of office the next day. Hevia in turn deposited the presidency, on January 18, in the Secretary of State, Dr. Marquez Sterling, who called a meeting of the leaders of the revolutionary parties at which Carlos Mendieta was elected Provisional President. In a report of January 22 the Ambassador informed the Department of State:

Order;
normal
functions;
support

> The Government is maintaining order and is carrying out the normal functions of government.
> As the Department is aware, it is supported by all the political groups except those of the extreme left and except possibly the adherents of Machado.

The Ambassador was accordingly instructed on January 23:

> Under authorization of the President you will please extend immediately to the Government of Cuba on behalf of the United States a formal and cordial recognition.

Recognition was extended the same day.

> Ambassador Caffery to Secretary Hull, no. 16, Jan. 14, 1934, and the Acting Secretary of State (Phillips) to Mr. Caffery, no. 12, Jan. 14, 1934, MS. Department of State, file 837.00/4609; Mr. Caffery to Mr. Phillips, nos. 24, 26, 43, and 60, January 15, 16, 18, and 22, 1934, *ibid.* files 837.00/4619, 837.00/4622, 837.00/4634, 837.00/4664; Mr. Hull to Mr. Caffery, no. 15, Jan. 23, 1934, *ibid.* file 837.01/70; Mr. Caffery to Mr. Hull, no. 68, Jan. 23, 1934, *ibid.* 837.01/71.

Dominican
Republic

The Government of the United States became concerned in 1912 and 1913 over the threat, caused by revolutionary disturbances in the Dominican Republic, to the continued operation of the customs receivership established under the convention of February 8, 1907 between the Dominican Republic and the United States (see text of convention, 35 Stat. 1880; 1 Treaties, etc. [Malloy, 1910] 418–420). In November 1912 the Department of State had approved the recommendation (made by two Special Commissioners sent to the Dominican Republic by the United States) that the "rebels be formally notified that they will not be recognized if the Government is overturned by force". Upon the outbreak of a revolution in September 1913 against the government of General Bordas, headed by Governor Céspedes, of the Province of Puerto Plata, the Department at once took the position that it would not recognize the revolutionary government if it should succeed. In a long instruction of September 9 the Secretary of State informed the Minister in Santo Domingo that the President had directed him to say that the influence of the Government of the United States would "be exerted for the support of lawful authorities in Santo Domingo, and for the discouragement of any and all insurrectionary methods". The Minister was informed that the President's statement of March 12, 1913 (1913 For. Rel. 7) set forth fully, and in such a way as to leave no doubt, his position on two important points, namely:

> First, that we can have no sympathy with those who seek to seize the power of government to advance their own personal

interests or ambition; and second, that the test of a republican form of government is to be found in its responsiveness to the will of the people, its just powers being derived from the consent of the governed.

The Minister was further instructed on September 12 to hand the following statement to Céspedes:

Firm in its intention to cooperate with the legally constituted Government in order that revolutionary activity may cease, the Department of State makes known to the revolutionists and those who foment revolutions the following:

Under the Convention of 1907, the Dominican Republic cannot increase its debt without the consent of the United States of America, and this Government will not consent that the Dominican Government increase its debts for the purpose of paying revolutionary expenses and claims. Moreover, this administration would look with disfavor on any administrative act that would have for its object increase of the taxes, thereby imposing a burden upon the people, for the purpose of satisfying revolutionists. And should the revolution succeed, this Government, in view of the President's declaration of policy, would withhold recognition of the de facto government, and consequently withhold the portion of the customs collections belonging to Santo Domingo as long as an unrecognized de facto government should exist.

The policy thus expounded was firmly adhered to by the Department and reiterated in numerous instructions.

Secretary Knox to Minister Russell, Nov. 25, 1912, MS. Department of State, file 839.00/714 and 1912 For. Rel. 376; Secretary Bryan to Minister Sullivan, Sept. 9, 1913, MS. Department of State, file 839.00/912a; Mr. Bryan to the Consul at Santiago, Sept. 12, 1913, *ibid.* 839.00/872, 839.00/872c and 1913 For. Rel. 425–427; Mr. Bryan to Mr. Sullivan, Feb. 27 and Apr. 4, 1914, MS. Department of State, files 839.00/1071, 839.00/1136; 1914 For. Rel. 212–223.

Finally, in August 1914, President Wilson sent two Commissioners to the Dominican Republic for the purpose of endeavoring to bring about, by conference with the political leaders, an agreement upon a program for the holding of elections for the establishment of a regular and constitutional government. As a result of the conferences held by the Commissioners, agreement was reached by the Dominican leaders upon the selection of Dr. Ramón Báez as Provisional President, who was inaugurated on August 28, 1914 and recognized on the same date by the United States.

Recognition of Provisional President Báez, 1914

Plan of President Wilson, handed to Commissioners Fort and Smith, 1914, MS. Department of State, file 839.00/1582; Commissioner Fort to Secretary Bryan, Aug. 25, 1914, *ibid.* 839.00/1490; Chargè White to Mr. Bryan, Aug. 28, 1914, *ibid.* 839.001/17; Mr. Bryan to Mr. White, Aug. 28, 1914, *ibid.* 839.00/1498a; 1914 For. Rel. 247–251.

An agreement was reached between the Commissioners and the Provisional President for the election on October 18 and 19, 1914 of a regular president and congress, this election to be supervised by observers designated by the Commissioners. Jiménez was elected President in the elections held in pursuance of this agreement; his election was confirmed by the National Assembly on December 5; he was proclaimed President on the same day; and he was promptly recognized by the Government of the United States.

Election and recognition of Jiménez, 1914

> Agreement between the United States Peace Commission and the Provisional President, Sept. 8, 1914, MS. Department of State, file 839.00/1548; Chargè White to Secretary Bryan, Dec. 5, 1914, *ibid.* 839.00/1639; Secretary Bryan to Minister Sullivan, Dec. 5, 1914, *ibid.* 839.00/1641; 1914 For. Rel. 250–259.

In early May 1916, General Arias and his followers succeeded through their revolutionary activities in forcing the resignation of President Jiménez. After some delay, on July 25, Congress elected Dr. Francisco Henríquez Provisional President for a period of five months. The Department instructed the Minister on August 26 that the Provisional Government would not be recognized "until it shows itself to be favorable to our interpretation of convention as to control, constabulary and other reforms and proves itself free from dominion of Arias". The Provisional Government having given unsatisfactory assurances with reference to these matters, the Department again, on September 8, instructed the Minister that, "unless financial control and establishment of constabulary definitely assured and made binding in future", it felt that it could not change its attitude toward the government of Henríquez. As it proved impossible to reach an agreement with the existing government and in view of the increasing seriousness of the situation, Admiral Caperton was authorized by President Wilson under date of November 26, 1916 to issue a proclamation of occupation and military government in the Republic of Santo Domingo. The proclamation was issued on November 29.

Military government, 1916

> Minister Russell to Secretary Lansing, May 7 and July 25, 1916. MS. Department of State, files 839.00/1822, 839.00/1900; Mr. Lansing to Mr. Russell, Aug. 26 and Sept. 8, 1916, *ibid.* 839.00/1912, 839.00/1923; Mr. Brewer, in charge of the Legation archives, to Mr. Lansing, no. 143, Dec. 6, 1916, *ibid.* file 839.00/1968; 1916 For. Rel. 223–247.

Recognition of Provisional Government, 1922

Acting under the authority conferred upon it by the plan for the withdrawal of the military government, which had been signed at Santo Domingo on September 18, 1922 on behalf of the United States by Commissioner Welles and Minister Russell and on behalf of the Dominican Republic by certain Dominican leaders, the commission, named in the plan for the purpose and composed of five of the principal political leaders, on October 2, 1922 selected Señor Juan Bautista

Vicini Burgos as Provisional President. The Provisional President was duly installed on October 21, and Commissioner Welles was instructed to deliver to him a message from President Harding assuring him "of the hearty good will of the Government and people of the United States, and of their sincere hope for the successful functioning of your [his] Government".

> Commissioner Welles to Secretary Hughes, Oct. 2, 1922, MS. Department of State, file 839.00/2610; Mr. Hughes to Mr. Welles, Oct. 4 and 20, 1922, *ibid.* files 839.00/2611c, 839.00/2630; Mr. Welles to Mr. Hughes, Oct. 21, 1922, *ibid.* file 839.00/2635; 1922 For. Rel., vol. II, pp. 68–74.

Pursuant to the provisions of the plan for the withdrawal of the military government and the holding of elections, General Horacio Vasquez was elected President. His election was confirmed by the electoral college on July 3, 1924, and he was inaugurated on July 12, 1924. Congratulations on his inauguration were sent to him by President Coolidge in a telegram of July 11. *Vasquez elected President, 1924*

> Minister Russell to Secretary Hughes, nos. 30 and 38, July 3 and 12 1924, MS. Department of State, files 839.00/2844, 839.001V44/Orig.; President Coolidge to President Vasquez, July 11, 1924, *ibid.* file 839.001-V44/a.
> The military government came to an end on July 12, 1924, the evacuation of the American forces being completed on September 18 of the same year. *Annual Report of the Secretary of the Navy*, Fiscal Year 1924 (1925) 50, 51; Minister Russell to Secretary Hughes, Sept. 18, 1924, MS. Department of State, file 839.00/2861; 1924 For. Rel., vol. I, p. 643.

Following the occupation of Santo Domingo by revolutionary forces under the leadership of General Estrella Urena, on February 26, 1930, an agreement was reached under which Estrella Urena was appointed Secretary of the Interior, becoming President in accordance with the Constitution, upon the resignation of President Vasquez on March 2, 1930. On March 1 Secretary Stimson instructed the Legation in Santo Domingo that as all legal forms were to be followed in the transfer of the executive power no question of recognition would be raised. *Estrella Urena government, 1930*

> Minister Curtis to Secretary Stimson, nos. 19 and 28, Feb. 26 and 28, 1930, MS. Department of State, files 839.00 Revolutions/16, 839.00 Revolutions/32; the Acting Secretary of State (Cotton) to Minister Curtis, no. 14, Mar. 1, 1930, *ibid.* file 839.00 Revolutions/45.

In despatches of January 13 and 20, 1906 the Legation in Ecuador notified the Department of State that a successful revolution had been carried out under the leadership of General Alfaro and that the insurgent government had requested the Legation to inform the Department that General Alfaro had assumed entire charge of the Republic. Subsequently, the Minister informed the Department that after waiting one month (former President Garcia had relinquished *Ecuador* *Revolution, 1906* his position and was on his way to Europe), he had requested an audience with the Supreme Chief, General Alfaro, who had received him on February 15, thus putting an end to a situation "which was becoming intolerable". He said that the visits of the remainder of the Diplomatic Corps would follow. He added that General Alfaro was in control of the Republic and seemed likely to remain so.

> Minister Lee to Secretary Root, nos. 7, 10, and 13, Jan. 13 and 20, and Feb. 16, 1906, MS. Department of State, 19 Despatches, Ecuador; 1906 For. Rel., pt. I, pp. 623–624. The Minister acted under instruction of the Department of State.

Military Junta, 1925

On July 9, 1925 the Government of Ecuador was overthrown by a Military Junta headed by General Gomez de la Torre. The Legation reported to the Department of State (on July 15) the receipt of a note from the Minister of Foreign Affairs of the Provisional Government, formally notifying it of the change of government, stating that the new government was "firmly and permanently constituted" and that it would "take the greatest pleasure in continuing to cultivate the good relations of friendship" with the Government of the United States. The Legation added that the seizure of the government by the new regime was entirely extraconstitutional, and on July 30 it reported that General de la Torre had been made head of the Provisional Government. The Department had, on the preceding day, instructed the Legation:

> Until the present political situation shall have crystallized, the Department desires that you should carefully avoid any action which might be construed to constitute recognition of the regime at present in control in Ecuador. Any communications with the authorities of the *de facto* regime should be friendly but personal and strictly informal, omitting the use of titles such as Minister for Foreign Affairs, etc. [Paraphrase.]

> The Chargé d'Affaires in Ecuador (de Lambert) to Secretary Kellogg, no. 28, July 10, 1925, and Mr. Kellogg to Mr. de Lambert, no. 19, July 14, 1925, MS. Department of State, file 822.00/590; Mr. de Lambert to Mr. Kellogg, no. 31, July 15, 1925, *ibid.* 822.00/594.

> In reply to its inquiry of Aug. 10 the Department informed the Embassy in Lima that following its policy of "withholding recognition from regimes which come into power through extra constitutional methods" it had "not recognized as other than the *de facto* authorities, the regime . . . functioning in Ecuador" and said that it did not contemplate extending formal recognition until the regime "regularizes its position or until a legally constituted government is set up". Secretary Kellogg to Ambassador Poindexter, no. 57, Aug. 12, 1925, *ibid.* 822.01/10.

Recognition withheld

In a conversation of September 10, 1925 Secretary Kellogg told Señor Elizalde, Minister from Ecuador on special mission, that the Government of the United States had no hostility toward his Government but that it had been the policy of the United States to delay, as in the case of Chile, recognizing revolutionary governments because it wished to encourage constitutional and stable governments.

MS. Department of State, file 822.01/27.

Isidro Ayora was appointed Provisional President of the Republic in April 1926, subsequently assuming absolute control of the Government. The United States, the last state to recognize Ayora's government, instructed its Minister at Quito on August 13, 1928 to deliver the following note to the Minister of Foreign Affairs: *Recognition*

> I have the honor to inform Your Excellency that I have been given instructions to say that the progress made by the Republic of Ecuador during the past three years since the *coup d'état* of July 9, 1925, and the tranquillity prevailing in Ecuador during that period, have been observed by my Government with a great deal of satisfaction. Having full confidence that the Government of Dr. Ayora has the support of the majority of the people of Ecuador, and is both capable and desirous of maintaining an orderly internal administration, and of observing with scrupulous care all international obligations, my Government is pleased to extend to it as from this date full recognition as the *de jure* Government of Ecuador. [Paraphrase.]

Support; order; obligations

The note was delivered on August 14.

Minister Bading to Secretary Kellogg, nos. 13 and 1041, Apr. 3, 1926 and Feb. 8, 1928, MS. Department of State, files 822.002/74, 822.01/53; Mr. Kellogg to Mr. Bading, no. 24, Aug. 13, 1928, *ibid.* file 822.01/64a; Mr. Bading to Mr. Kellogg, no. 33, Aug. 14, 1928, *ibid.* 822.01/65.

The armed forces of the state took over control of the Government upon the resignation of the entire Cabinet, and of Dr. Antonio Pons, Acting President, on September 27, 1935, and delegated the executive power to Federico Paez. The American Legation was formally notified of the assumption of power by the new Government through a note from the Minister of Foreign Affairs, dated October 1, in which it was stated that the Government found itself firmly constituted and desired "to continue cultivating the good relations of friendship which until now it has maintained with the Government [of the United States]". On the same day the Department inquired of the Legation whether it could be maintained that Paez, who was understood to have been Minister of Public Works in the Cabinet of ex-President Pons, succeeded to the presidency in accordance with the provisions of article 79 of the Constitution of 1929. The Legation replied that in abolishing the 1929 Constitution the present regime had *ipso facto* dispelled any semblance of constitutionality. It stated, however, that the Paez government apparently was firmly established. *Paez government, 1935*

On October 8 Secretary Hull instructed the Legation as follows:

Stability;
obligations

> In view of the report received from you that the existing government apparently is firmly established, and in view of the note addressed to you by the Minister for Foreign Affairs, which the Department presumes may be taken as a declaration of the intention of the present regime to fulfill its international obligations, it is desired that after receiving confirmation, which may be oral, from the Minister for Foreign Affairs of the above-mentioned assumption, a note be addressed to the Minister in reply to his note, saying that the Government of the United States will be happy to continue the cordial relations which it has maintained with the Government of Ecuador. [Paraphrase.]

> Minister Gonzalez to Secretary Hull, nos. 45 and 47, Sept. 28 and Oct. 2, 1935, MS. Department of State, files 822.00 Revolutions/70, 822.00 Revolutions/73; Mr. Hull to Mr. Gonzalez, nos. 22 and 23, Oct. 1 and 8, 1935, *ibid.* 822.00 Revolutions/72, 822.01/73B.

Enriquez
government,
1937

The Minister in Quito advised the Department of State on October 23, 1937 that the Army had resolved that the Ecuadoran Assembly was not representative of the people and that General Enriquez had forced the resignation of President Paez and assumed the supreme power, pending the convocation of a new Assembly. The next day he reported that the *coup d'état* had been consummated without any apparent opposition and that as the constitutional succession had been disregarded the question of recognition of the new Government arose. On October 27 the Department instructed the Minister:

> Please cable briefly . . . stating whether in your opinion the new government has the substantial support of public opinion in Ecuador, whether it is able to discharge the normal functions of Government, whether it is capable of maintaining public order and whether it intends to comply with its international obligations. . . . Pending authorization from the Department, you should avoid any action which might be construed as constituting recognition by this Government of the new Ecuadoran Government.

The Legation replied on the following day that—

Tranquillity
and order;
respect for
law; obliga-
tions

> . . . Minister for Foreign Affairs . . . has sent a note informing me of the change of government. He states that complete tranquillity and order prevails and that the Ecuadorean Government in its foreign relations "proposes to continue its policy of respect for law and the inviolability of international treaties and conventions. It desires to offer to all nations its friendly cooperation for the normal development of cultural and commercial interchange and for the preservation of peace and progress." He concludes with the statement that his Government will be pleased to continue cultivating the good relations of friendship which it happily maintains with the United States.
> The situation is not yet sufficiently clarified to permit a categorical answer on the points raised by the Department. . . . For

the moment public opinion is apathetic and awaiting developments.

On November 2 the Legation in Quito was instructed to acknowledge the note from the Minister of Foreign Affairs of the new Government, and to say:

> In view of the assurances given in your note, that in the conduct of its relations with other States, the Government of which you are a member proposes to continue its policy of respect for law and the inviolability of international treaties and conventions and desires to offer to all foreign States its friendly cooperation for the normal development of cultural and commercial interchange and for the preservation of peace and progress, I have been instructed by my Government to say that it will be pleased to continue to maintain with your Government the cordial relations that have happily existed between the Government of Ecuador and the Government of the United States. [Paraphrase.]

> Minister Gonzalez to Secretary Hull, no. 61, Oct. 23, 1937, MS. Department of State, file 822.00 Revolutions/84; Mr. Gonzalez to Mr. Hull, no. 62, Oct. 24, 1937, and Mr. Hull to Mr. Gonzalez, no. 48, Oct. 27, 1937, *ibid.* 822.00 Revolutions/86; Mr. Gonzalez to Mr. Hull, no. 63, Oct. 28, 1937, *ibid.* 822.00 Revolutions/87; the Acting Secretary of State (Welles) to Mr. Gonzalez, no. 50, Nov. 2, 1937, *ibid.* 822.01/82.

Following the overthrow of the Herrera government by a military coup d'état on December 6, 1921, General Orellana was elected Provisional President of Guatemala on December 6 by the old Congress, which had existed at the time of Cabrera's downfall in 1920. On February 22, 1922 the Legation notified the Department of State that General Orellana, the only official candidate, had been elected to the presidency. Under instructions of April 15 from the Department the Chargé d'Affaires in Guatemala informed General Orellana that the President had determined to recognize his Government as the Government of the Republic. **Guatemala, 1922**

> Mr. McMillin to Secretary Hughes, Dec. 6 and 9, 1921, MS. Department of State, files 814.00/567, 814.00/578; 1921 For. Rel., vol. II, pp. 182–187. Mr. Curtis to Mr. Hughes, Feb. 22, 1922, MS. Department of State, file 814.00/653; Mr. Hughes to Chargé Southgate, Apr. 15, 1922, *ibid.* 814.00/666; 1922 For. Rel., vol. II, pp. 459–460.

The government of Provisional President Palma, who had been elected by Congress on December 12, 1930 to serve during the incapacity of President Chacon, was overthrown on December 16, 1930 by a revolution headed by General Orellana. The Guatemalan Congress having accepted the resignation of Provisional President Palma on December 17 and appointed General Orellana as Provisional President, the Minister advised the Department of State that this appointment was illegal because it was contrary to article 65 of the **Orellana government, 1930**

Constitution and to the Central American treaty of peace and amity of February 7, 1923 (for relevant provisions, see *ante* §33).

> Minister McCafferty to Secretary Stimson, no. 95 of Dec. 12, 1930, and nos. 106, 109, and 110 of Dec. 17, 1930, MS. Department of State, files 814.001CH34/17, 814.00 Revolutions/59, 814.001 Orellana, Manuel/1, 814.00 Revolutions/60.

In a telegram of December 20, 1930 to the Legation the Department set forth at some length its position with reference to the recognition of the revolutionary government of Orellana. It pointed out that the position of the Government of the United States with regard to the Central American governments was somewhat different from that of other countries and that the policy of the United States with reference to the recognition of new governments in those republics had been publicly stated by Secretary Hughes on June 30, 1923 (for text, see *ante* §33). The quotation of this statement was followed by a quotation from the statement made by Secretary Stimson on September 17, 1930, in announcing the recognition of the Argentine, Peruvian, and Bolivian Governments (for text, see *ante*, under Argentina, this section). The Department then concluded:

> The policy set forth in these statements still represents the policy of this Government, and it is desired that you so informally and orally advise the Provisional Government of Guatemala. Although it is not the purpose of the Department to make a public statement at the present time, you may in conversation advise leading Guatemalans of the policy thus set forth.
> . . . As previously stated the Department upholds the treaties of 1923. In order that any action taken by the present Guatemalan Government may not bring about a long period of non-recognition, it is the desire of the Department that the Minister study the situation and advise it what steps may be taken by the authorities in control of the Government to put it back on a constitutional basis, and also whether it is his opinion that there is a prospect of such steps being taken.
> [Paraphrase.]

> Secretary Stimson to Minister McCafferty, no. 76, Dec. 20, 1930, MS. Department of State, file 814.00 Revolutions/68.

Andrade government, 1931

Reina Andrade was thereupon installed constitutionally as Provisional President through his election as first Vice President, followed by the acceptance of Chacon's resignation by Congress on January 2, 1931. The Minister reported in reply to instructions from the Department that there appeared to be no objection to Andrade's government from any quarter, that it was meeting with the general support of the authorities and the people, that conditions were practically normal, and that the call for elections had been issued to take place on February 6, 7, and 8. He was accordingly instructed to extend recognition to the government of Señor Andrade on the afternoon of January 8, and this was done.

> Minister Whitehouse to Secretary Stimson, no. 2, Jan. 2, 1931, MS. Department of State, file 814.00/1041; Mr. Stimson to Mr. Whitehouse, no. 2, Jan. 3, 1931, *ibid.* 814.01/32A; Mr. Whitehouse to Mr. Stimson, nos. 6 and 7, Jan. 3 and 5, 1931, *ibid.* files 814.01/31, 814.00/1044; Mr. Stimson to Mr. Whitehouse, no. 3, Jan. 6, 1931, *ibid.* file 814.01/35A; Mr. Whitehouse to Mr. Stimson, no. 254, Jan. 8, 1931, *ibid.* 814.01/43.

> The other four Central American governments in reply to a circular inquiry from the Department of State had unanimously agreed that recognition should be extended after the issuance of the call for an election. MS. Department of State, files 814.01/29, /30, /32B, /33, /35.

Early in August 1911 the government of President Simon of Haiti was overthrown by General Leconte, and a proclamation was issued on August 5 proclaiming the latter chief of the executive power. The Department of State advised the Minister on August 13 that it was considered most important to have in writing the assurances he had received orally from General Leconte concerning the protection of American interests. President Leconte was inaugurated on August 15, and on that day Minister Furniss received the following note from the Counselor of State: **Haiti**

> Replying to your letter of yesterday I am pleased to assure you that the government of Gen. Leconte will consider it an honor faithfully to fulfill all engagements regularly and legally entered into in the name of the Republic, and that the interests of the United States as well as all others will be the objects of his protection; and that you may be certain that any claims produced will be examined with the greatest impartiality. Gen. Leconte on his part hopes to be able to count on the sincere support of the heads of missions in order to obtain from their citizens the invariable respect for the laws through which they expect to obtain protection, violation of which his Government is firmly resolved never to allow. It is my profound conviction that in this as well as in all other relations the kind assistance of the American Legation and the other legations will not be wanting. **Leconte government, 1911**

Secretary Knox instructed the Minister on August 18:

> If you are satisfied that the Government of General Leconte is in full possession of the machinery of government with the acquiescence of the people of Haiti and is in position to meet its international responsibilities, you will inform the Haitian Minister for Foreign Affairs that you are authorized to enter into full relations with it. **Control of government; consent; international responsibilities**

> Minister Furniss to Secretary Knox, Aug. 6, 1911, MS. Department of State, file 838.00/629; Mr. Knox to Mr. Furniss, Aug. 13, 1911, *ibid.* 838.00/647; Mr. Furniss to Mr. Knox, Aug. 15, 1911, *ibid.* 838.00/651; Mr. Knox to Mr. Furniss, Aug. 18, 1911, *ibid.* 838.00/660; Mr. Furniss to Mr. Knox, no. 923, Aug. 21, 1911, *ibid.* 838.00/672; 1911 For. Rel. 281–290.

President Oreste, who had been elected President in May 1913, abdicated on January 27, 1914; and after Charles and Oreste Zamor had occupied Port-au-Prince, the latter was elected President on February 8. The American Minister having been assured in writing by the Government of its stability and its ability to protect the interests of foreigners and of the natives, he was instructed on February 26:

> . . . You will immediately seek an interview with the Minister for Foreign Affairs of the de facto Government at Port au Prince and state to him that the Government of the United States will be probably disposed to recognize the Government of Oreste Zamor as the duly elected constitutional government of the Republic of Haiti, since it appears from the support which it received in the north and in the other parts of the Republic that the advent of this Government is based upon the consent of the governed.

Upon the further assurance from President Zamor that all matters in which the United States might be interested would have due consideration after recognition, the Minister was instructed on March 1:

> The Government formed by General Oreste Zamor, as constitutional President duly elected by the Haitian Congress, being now fully established in power with the assent of the people, you are instructed to recognize it.

> Minister Smith to Secretary Bryan, Jan. 27 and Feb. 8 and 10, 1914, MS. Department of State, files 838.00/779, 838.00/821, 838.00/831; Mr. Bryan to Mr. Smith, Feb. 26, 1914, *ibid.* file 838.00/855; Mr. Smith to Mr. Bryan, Feb. 28, 1914, and Mr. Bryan to Mr. Smith, Mar. 1, 1914, *ibid.* 838.00/864; 1914 For. Rel. 334–341.

In the face of a revolution headed by Davilmar Théodore, President Zamor fled the capital on October 29, 1914. Théodore was elected constitutional President by the National Assembly of Haiti on November 7, 1914 and was inaugurated on November 10. On November 12 the Legation was instructed by the Department of State that if, in its opinion, the Government headed by Théodore
was *de facto*, it should inform him that recognition by the United States would be granted him as Provisional President "when a commission to be named by the Haitian Government with full powers to act upon certain questions of interest to this Government and to the Republic of Haiti is in position to give necessary assurances". The Department stated that it desired this commission to consist of three persons who should come to Washington to negotiate a convention or conventions with the United States. President Théodore indicated his willingness to appoint the commission but insisted on recognition not as Provisional President but as President, as he had been regularly elected by the National Assembly in accordance with the

Haitian Constitution. The Department informed the Legation on November 21 that, if the election of Théodore had been in strict conformity with the Constitution, the United States would formally recognize him as President "but not until after the arrival in Washington of duly appointed commission bearing credentials of the Haitian Government for the adjustment of the matters stated in the Department's telegrams". By further instruction of November 24 the Department added that, in order that there might be no misconstruction of the conditions it had stated, it would "formally recognize Théodore as President of Haiti as soon as Haitian Commission in Washington has signed satisfactory protocols covering all matters mentioned".

As serious disturbances broke out in the Haitian Senate during the course of interpellation of the Minister of Foreign Affairs concerning the negotiations with the United States, the Department modified its conditions somewhat in an instruction of December 12:

> You may further say to the Government that the question of recognition will be considered on its merits and that recognition will be granted whenever this Government is satisfied that there is in Haiti a government capable of maintaining order and meeting the country's obligations to outside nations. Such a government is impossible however unless it rests upon the consent of the governed and gives expression to the will of the people. It will be necessary, therefore, for us to have information as to the fiscal standing and general plans of the Government and as to its attitude toward foreigners and the obligations which it owes to the citizens of other nations, including its attitude on the subjects relating to the Mole of St. Nicholas.

Consent of governed; international obligations

> Minister Bailly-Blanchard to Secretary Bryan, Nov. 7, 1914, and Mr. Bryan to Mr. Bailly-Blanchard, Nov. 12, 1914, MS. Department of State, file 838.00/1020; Mr. Bryan to Mr. Bailly-Blanchard, Nov. 16, 1914, *ibid.* 838.00/1024; Mr. Bailly-Blanchard to Mr. Bryan, Nov. 28, 1914, and the Acting Secretary of State (Lansing) to Mr. Bailly-Blanchard, Nov. 21, 1914, *ibid.* 838.00/1028; Mr. Bailly-Blanchard to Mr. Bryan, Dec. 4, 1914, *ibid.* 838.00/1044; Mr. Bryan to Mr. Bailly-Blanchard, Dec. 12, 1914, *ibid.* 838.51/379a; 1914 For. Rel. 359–367.

No agreement on a basis for recognition was reached, Théodore having been overthrown in March 1915 and his successor, Sam, murdered by a mob on July 28, 1915. General Bobo assumed the position of Chief Executive, but resigned almost at once (August 7). On August 10 the Department informed the Chargé d'Affaires at Port-au-Prince that the Navy Department had instructed Admiral Caperton (who had landed American forces) that elections might take place whenever the Haitians wished it and that he should confer with the Admiral to the end that in some way the following things should be made perfectly clear:

Dartiguenave government, 1915

Order;
customs con-
trol, etc.; con-
stitutional
government

First. Let Congress understand that the Government of the United States intends to uphold it, but that it can not recognize action which does not establish in charge of Haitian affairs those whose abilities and dispositions give assurances of putting an end to factional disorders.

Second. In order that no misunderstanding can possibly occur after election, it should be made perfectly clear to candidates as soon as possible and in advance of their election, that the United States expects to be entrusted with the practical control of the customs, and such financial control over the affairs of the Republic of Haiti as the United States may deem necessary for an efficient administration.

The Government of the United States considers it its duty to support a constitutional government. It means to assist in the establishing of such a government, and to support it as long as necessity may require. It has no design upon the political or territorial integrity of Haiti; on the contrary, what has been done, as well as what will be done, is conceived in an effort to aid the people of Haiti in establishing a stable government and in maintaining domestic peace throughout the Republic.

The government of President Dartiguenave, who was elected on August 12, was recognized on September 16, the same day on which a treaty with Haiti was signed covering the matters which the Department had insisted upon as a prerequisite to recognition.

> Admiral Caperton to the Secretary of the Navy, Aug. 7, 1915, MS. Department of State, file 838.00/1243; Secretary Lansing to Chargé Davis, Aug. 10, 1915, *ibid.* 838.00/1246a; Mr. Davis to Mr. Lansing, Aug. 12 and Sept. 17, 1915, *ibid.* files 838.00/1250, 838.00/1313; 1915 For. Rel. 478–491. For text of the treaty of Sept. 16, 1915, see 39 Stat. 1654; 3 Treaties, etc. (Redmond, 1923) 2673–2677.

President
Borno, 1922

The American High Commissioner, Brigadier General John H. Russell, who had been appointed on February 11, 1922 to represent the President in Haiti for certain purposes, advised Secretary Hughes on April 11 that Louis Borno had been elected President by the Council of State on the preceding day. Borno had been held eligible for the presidency by a unanimous vote of the Court of Cassation, and the official election decree had appeared in the previous day's *Moniteur*. Secretary Hughes instructed Commissioner Russell on April 17 that if he was "satisfied with the regularity and constitutionality of Borno's election" he was authorized to state that the Government of the United States would recognize him as having been elected President.

> Secretary Hughes to Commissioner Russell, Feb. 11, 1922, MS. Department of State, file 123R914/1a; Commissioner Russell to Mr. Hughes, Apr. 11, 1922, and Mr. Hughes to Chargé Dunn, Apr. 17, 1922, *ibid.* 838.00/1855; Commissioner Russell to Mr. Hughes, Apr. 13, 1922, *ibid.* 838.00/1856; 1922 For. Rel., vol. II, pp. 461–471.

The "President's Commission for the Study and Review of Conditions in the Republic of Haiti", named by President Hoover on February 7, 1930, found that the election of a new president by the means practiced in the previous two elections, namely, by the Council of State, would not be accepted quietly by the populace. Opposition leaders representing the so-called "patriotic groups" were consulted, and a plan was adopted whereby it was agreed that "delegates elected by the patriotic groups should select a neutral candidate who would later be elected President by the Council of State". Through this method Eugene Roy became the candidate. Although some difficulty thereafter arose regarding the election of Roy as President, the Department of State maintained the position that the Haitian Government was obligated to carry out the plan agreed upon with the President's Commission and that the United States would not recognize a temporary president elected in violation of that plan. On April 21, 1930 Roy was elected President. Under authorization from the Department he was immediately recognized by the American High Commissioner as the President-elect.

President Roy, 1930

The Acting Secretary of State (Cotton) to the Legation at Port-au-Prince, nos. 30 and 42, Mar. 22 and Apr. 10, 1930, MS. Department of State, files 838.00 Elections/13, 838.00 Elections/33; Commissioner Russell to Secretary Stimson, no. 73, Apr. 21, 1930, *ibid.* file 838.00 Elections/74. See text of the Commission's report of Mar. 26, 1930, *ibid.* 838.00 Commission of Investigation/124.

In a letter of April 23, 1907 addressed to President Theodore Roosevelt, Miguel R. Dávila stated that he had taken possession of the office of Provisional President of Honduras "with the support of the great majority of the citizens" and that the program of his government would be one of "peace and guaranties for persons and interests, both national and foreign". Señor Angel Ugarte, who had been designated by President Dávila as his Minister in the United States, addressed a note to the Acting Secretary of State, dated July 4, 1907, containing the following assurances:

Honduras

1. The provisional government over which General Don Miguel R. Dávila presides in Honduras has been recognized throughout the Republic and in the neighboring countries and is performing its functions in a normal and peaceful manner;

Provisional presidency of Dávila

2. There is no apprehension of internal disturbances, as under the amnesty granted by my Government the defeated parties to the late conflict are returning to their homes in the full enjoyment of their rights and guaranties;
3. As to foreign affairs—that is, the difficulties which may arise in Central America—my Government has adopted a policy of strict neutrality toward the probable contestants; and
4. The aims pursued by my Government in soliciting the recognition of the American Government are, substantially, to

gain the ear of the Department of State regarding Central American political matters, with the hope of being aided in its efforts toward the conservation of peace or the maintenance of its own neutrality.

International obligations; constitutionality

Having been assured in addition by Señor Ugarte that the Constitution would govern beginning September 15, the Department extended recognition to the Provisional Government of General Dávila, saying in part in its note of August 23, 1907 to Provisional Minister Ugarte:

> Being advised of the competency of the provisional government to perform international obligations, and being satisfied with the steps taken to revive the constitutional régime in Honduras and to provide for the election of the executive thereof, the President has directed the recognition of the provisional government and will, upon his return to Washington, have the pleasure to receive Mr. Angel Ugarte in personal audience for the purpose of presenting the credentials which he bears as the appointed envoy extraordinary and minister plenipotentiary of the provisional government of Honduras.

> Provisional President Dávila to President Roosevelt, Apr. 23, 1907, MS. Department of State, file 3691/485; Provisional Minister Ugarte to the Acting Secretary of State, July 4 and Aug. 8, 1907, *ibid.* files 7357/2, 7357/5; the Acting Secretary of State (Adee) to Señor Ugarte, Aug. 23, 1907, *ibid.* file 7357/1; Mr. Adee to Minister Lee, Aug. 23, 1907, *ibid.* 7357/8a; 1907 For. Rel., pt. II, pp. 601–606.

Recognition refused

In the early part of 1923 the Department of State was constantly receiving reports of impending revolution in Honduras. Accordingly, in an instruction of June 30, 1923, Secretary Hughes authorized the Minister to communicate to the President and other political leaders in Honduras a statement declaring that the attitude of the United States in the matter of recognition would be consonant with the provisions of article II of the general treaty of peace and amity of February 7, 1923, which provided in substance that the contracting parties (the Central American states) would "not recognize any other Government which may come into power in any of the five Republics through a *coup d'état* or a revolution against a recognized Government so long as the freely elected representatives of the people thereof have not constitutionally reorganized the country". (For text of the note and of article II of the treaty, see *ante* §33, p. 188). The Legation reported in a despatch of July 5, 1923 that President Gutiérrez had declared that he was in perfect accord with the general treaty of peace and amity. However, the contending candidates for the presidency failed to reach an agreement, with the result that the Honduran Congress failed to elect a president before February 1, 1924, the date for the assumption of office by the new president. In a telegraphic instruction of February 9 to the Legation the Department of State said:

> In its telegram of January 26 the Department indicated that if the Gutierrez Government took definitely agreed upon steps at once to assure the holding of free elections, the Department might be willing to continue relations with his administration after February 1. The measures promised were not carried out by Señor Lopez Gutierrez . . .
>
> The Government of Lopez Gutierrez has not been recognized by the Government of the United States since February 1 . . . However, the actions taken by him have made it impossible for this Government to accord him recognition. The Department desires, therefore, that you avoid all formal diplomatic relations and that you confine your contacts to informal and oral representations, when it is found necessary to make such representations for the protection of American interests and to carry out instructions from the Department. . . . You are authorized discreetly to make it clear to the authorities of the Gutierrez administration that no legally constituted Government is recognized at present by the Government of the United States. . . .
> [Paraphrase.]

> Secretary Hughes to Minister Morales, no. 26, June 30, 1923, MS. Department of State, file 815.00/2609; Mr. Morales to Mr. Hughes, no. 423, July 5, 1923, *ibid.* 815.00/2632; 1923 For. Rel., vol. II, pp. 432–434.
> Mr. Hughes to Mr. Morales, no. 20, Feb. 9, 1924, *ibid.* 815.00/2858. The Legation was instructed on Feb. 18 to notify all American consular officers in Honduras that the Government of the United States did not recognize any regime in Honduras. Mr. Hughes to Mr. Morales, no. 25, Feb. 18, 1924, *ibid.* 815.00/2887.

As the revolutionary condition continued Secretary Hughes (on April 8, 1924) instructed Mr. Sumner Welles, who was at that time acting as special representative of the President of the United States in the Dominican Republic, to proceed to Honduras as special representative of the President for the purpose of mediating between the revolutionary forces and the Government. In a lengthy instruction of April 10, the Department told Mr. Welles that it desired that he should bear in mind the importance of bringing about the eventual establishment of a government in Honduras which could properly be recognized by the United States, and continued:

Mediation, 1924

> . . . The Government of the United States announced in a public declaration of June 30, 1923 [text, *ante* §33], that its attitude with respect to the recognition of new governments in Central America would be in accord with the provisions set forth in Article II of the General Treaty of Peace and Amity, signed at Washington in 1923. It would appear, under the conditions existing in Honduras, that the most appropriate solution would be either (1) that a constitutional President should be elected by the

Policy in accord with 1923 treaty

existing Congress, if that can be arranged, or (2) that a provisional government be established of such a character as to assure that new elections could be held under conditions of freedom and fairness. However, the Government of the United States will not make any particular solution a prerequisite to recognition by this Government, so long as the new administration is of such a character as properly to be considered as constitutionally established and fairly representative of the will of the people. In fact, it would be ready to make known its sympathy and moral support to any provisional government which might give evidence of a satisfactory character, of an intention to reestablish constitutional order. [Paraphrase.]

The other Central American governments were invited to participate in the mediation conferences, and on April 28 Mr. Welles reported that, at a preliminary conference participated in by the principal Honduran leaders, General Vicente Tosta had been unanimously selected Provisional President and a preliminary peace convention signed. Under this convention, signed at Amapalá, General Tosta assumed the provisional presidency, with the agreement that he should convoke elections for a national constituent assembly 30 days after having taken office and that he should carry out a number of other specified steps designed to bring about a satisfactory settlement of existing difficulties.

> Secretary Hughes to Commissioner Welles, nos. 14 and 2, Apr. 8 and 10, 1924, MS. Department of State, files 815.00/3077a, 815.00/3077a supp.; Mr. Welles to Mr. Hughes, no. 14, Apr. 28, 1924, *ibid.* 815.00/3139; 1924 For. Rel., vol. II, pp. 301–315.
>
> On May 16 the Department instructed the Legation that if it was satisfied that the Provisional Government had thus far complied with the terms of the Amapalá agreement it might inform that Government orally that the Government of the United States would treat unofficially with it and would extend to it appropriate moral support to assist it in making effective the program called for by the Amapalá agreement. The Acting Secretary of State (Grew) to Minister Morales, no. 67, May 16, 1924, MS. Department of State, file 815.01/1.

Recognition of Barahona, 1925

In a telegram of January 21, 1925 the Legation reported the election of Barahona to the presidency and requested instructions as to the action which should be taken with reference to the matter of his recognition. On the next day the Department of State authorized the Minister to make the following statement:

Constitutional government

The Government of the United States is gratified that it has been possible to reach a solution of the problem of establishing in Honduras a constitutional government with which the Government of the United States and those of the other Central American republics can maintain cordial relations without inconsistency with the provisions of the General Treaty of Peace and Amity signed at the Washington conference of 1923. The Government of the United States contemplates with pleasure the resumption of formal relations with the Government of Honduras upon the inauguration on February 1st of the new constitutional authorities. [Paraphrase.]

The Minister was instructed on January 26:

> You are authorized to participate in the inaugural ceremonies to take place on the 1st of February in whatever manner is customary in Honduras when the inauguration of a new constitutional government takes place, and thereafter you may make the customary official calls on the appropriate officials of the new government. You may in addition, if it seems to you advisable, address to the Minister of Foreign Affairs a note expressing the gratification of the Government of the United States that it has now been possible for diplomatic relations to be resumed with the Government of Honduras. [Paraphrase.]

> Chargé Dennis to Secretary Hughes, no. 11, Jan. 21, 1925, and Mr. Hughes to Mr. Dennis, no. 9, Jan. 22, 1925, MS. Department of State, file 815.00/3527; Mr. Hughes to Mr. Dennis, no. 11, Jan. 26, 1925, *ibid.* 815.00/3535.

President Madero, who had been elected President of Mexico in November 1911, was placed under arrest on February 18, 1913 at the behest of General Huerta, commander in chief of the government forces. Pursuant to a written agreement deposited at the American Embassy, Madero resigned on February 19, the Minister of Foreign Affairs becoming President and then resigning, thus making possible the constitutional election of Huerta as Provisional President. *[margin: Mexico]* *[margin: Huerta government, 1913]*

> Ambassador Wilson to Secretary Knox, Feb. 18, 19, and 20, 1913, MS. Department of State, files 812.00/6245, /6244, /6246, /6264, /6277; 1913 For. Rel. 699–725.

On February 20, 1913 the Ambassador requested immediate instructions "as to the question of recognition of the Provisional Government, now installed and evidently in secure possession", calling attention to the fact that the "Provisional Government takes office in accordance with the Constitution and precedents" [paraphrase]. The Department of State replied in a telegram of February 21:

> In view of the statements and tenor of your recent telegrams, the Department is disposed to consider the new Provisional Government as being legally established and to believe that it apparently intends to reestablish peace and order throughout Mexico, and to hope that it has the support of the majority of the Mexican people. It will, however, be evident to those now in responsible control in Mexico that, especially in view of the situation which has prevailed for the past two years or more, this Government must very carefully consider the question of their ability and earnest disposition to comply with the rules of international law and comity, the obligations of treaties, and the general duties to foreigners and foreign governments incidental to international intercourse. *[margin: Conditions of recognition]*

You are instructed, therefore, to say to those seeking recognition as the new Provisional Government that the Government of the United States will be glad to receive assurances that the outstanding questions between this country and Mexico, which, among other things, have done so much to mar the relations between the two Governments, which should be so especially friendly, will be dealt with in a satisfactory manner. These questions and the grievances of this Government against Mexico are set forth in general terms in the Department's note of September 15, 1912, to which the attention of the new Provisional Government should be invited.

In the interest of definiteness, however, and for the sake of an unequivocal understanding, the Department desires you to say that the questions which it is most necessary and desirable to have dealt with and got out of the way are as follows:

This Government desires settlement of the Tlahualilo controversy at the earliest possible date, either by direct agreement between the Mexican Government and the Tlahualilo Co. or by a submittal of this question to arbitration;

It desires settlement of the question of the Chamizal tract by direct agreement between the two countries;

It desires that the immediate matters regarding the equitable distribution of the waters of the Colorado River be arranged for by convention;

That the border claims growing out of battles at Aguaprieta and Juárez in 1911 be settled on the terms and according to the arrangement suggested by this Government after full consideration and arrival at the conviction that the requests made of the Mexican Government are just and fair;

That the Alamo murders be settled by the payment of $10,000 for each of the murdered men, and the prompt punishment of the guilty parties;

That the administration of justice throughout Mexico shall be raised to such a plane that this Government will no longer be compelled, by manifestly unfair and improper action on the part of certain Mexican courts, to make diplomatic representations in favor of its unjustly treated nationals;

And, finally, but most important, that the Mexican Government agree in principle to the settlement of all claims resulting from the loss of life by American citizens and damages to American property on account of the recent political disturbances in Mexico by presentation thereof to a mixed international commission which shall award damages therefor.

You will point out that no greater assurance could be given of a disposition to cement and maintain friendly relations with this Government than to give the assurances which you are above instructed to secure.

[Paraphrase.]

Ambassador Wilson to Secretary Knox, Feb. 20, 1913, 8 p.m. and 9 p.m., MS. Department of State, files 812.00/6287, 812.00/6288; Mr. Knox to Mr. Wilson, Feb. 21, 1913, *ibid.* file 812.00/6325a; 1913 For. Rel. 725–736.

The Ambassador reported in a telegram of February 24 that he had sent a note to General Huerta in the sense of the Department's instruction of Feb. 21, marked "Personal—Unofficial", and that the President had sent him a verbal assurance that the matters referred to would have immediate action in preference to everything else. Mr. Wilson to Mr. Knox, no. 36, Feb. 24, 1913, MS. Department of State, file 312.11/1170; 1913 For. Rel. 736.

Ex-President Madero was killed as a result of an attack upon the party which was escorting him from the presidential palace to the penitentiary. Recognition of the Huerta regime was accordingly delayed until such time as the Government of the United States might "be disposed to accord formal recognition as a provisional government to those in de facto authority". The Ambassador reported on February 24 that he was disposed to accept the Government's version of the killing of Madero and to consider it a closed incident and that the cooperation of the Department in this direction would be of infinite value.

> Ambassador Wilson to Secretary Knox, Feb. 23, 1913, MS. Department of State. file 812.00/6321; Mr. Knox to Mr. Wilson, Feb. 24, 1913, *ibid.* 812.00/6324; Mr. Wilson to Mr. Knox, Feb. 24, 1913, 7 p.m., *ibid.* 812.00/6353; 1913 For. Rel. 731–737.

Acting in pursuance of his general policy with respect to Central and South American states announced in a public statement of March 11, 1913, President Wilson declined to recognize Huerta's government, principally upon the ground that it was a "usurpation" of power in violation of constitutional procedure which rendered "the development of ordered self government impossible". It would be the purpose of the United States, he declared, "to discredit and defeat such usurpations wherever they occur". (For an exposition of the principal aspects of President Wilson's policy, with special reference to Mexico, see *ante* §33.) Ex-Governor John Lind, of Minnesota, was sent to Mexico by President Wilson during the summer of 1913 as his "personal representative", but Huerta rejected the terms of settlement offered as a basis for recognition. (For the text of the terms contained in Lind's instructions, see *ante* §33, and 1913 For. Rel. 821–827.) *Refusal to recognize Huerta*

Huerta finally resigned on July 15, 1914, and his successor in the provisional presidency, the Minister of Foreign Affairs (Carbajal), dissolved the government and permitted General Carranza to take control of the capital. The policy of the United States with respect to the accession of Carranza to the presidency was stated in a telegram of July 23 to the Vice Consul at Mexico City, with directions that the statement be communicated to Carranza: *Carranza assumes authority, 1914*

> . . . We have been forced by circumstances into a position in which we must practically speak for the rest of the world. It is evident that the United States is the only first-class power that can be expected to take the initiative in recognizing the new Government. It will in effect act as the representative of the other powers of the world in this matter and will unquestion-

ably be held responsible by them for the consequences. Every step taken by the Constitutionalist leaders from this moment on and everything which indicates the spirit in which they mean to proceed and to consummate their triumph must of necessity, therefore, play a very important part in determining whether it will be possible for the United States to recognize the government now being planned for.

Secretary Bryan to Vice Consul Silliman, July 23, 1914, MS. Department of State, file 812.00/14052a; 1914 For. Rel. 568–569, 588–589.

Recognition of Carranza

General Carranza was slow in consolidating his authority, but finally, on October 11, 1915, Secretary Lansing sent a telegram to the principal American diplomatic missions in Europe stating that the Secretary of State, the Ambassadors of Argentina, Brazil, and Chile, and the Ministers of Bolivia, Uruguay, and Guatemala had met in conference on October 9, 1915 and had given to the press the following statement:

The Conferees, after careful consideration of the facts, have found that the Carrancista party is the only party possessing the essentials for recognition as the de facto government of Mexico, and they have so reported to their respective Governments.

Recognition by these powers followed shortly after this announcement. On October 19 the Department of State addressed a communication to the confidential agent of the Carranza government stating that--

the President of the United States takes this opportunity of extending recognition to the de facto Government of Mexico, of which General Venustiano Carranza is the Chief Executive.

Secretary Lansing to the principal American missions in Europe, Oct. 11, 1915, MS. Department of State, file 812.00/16509b; Secretary Lansing to the confidential agent of the *de facto* government of Mexico, Oct. 19, 1915, *ibid.* 812.00/16532b; 1915 For. Rel. 767, 771.

Ambassador Fletcher presented his letters of credence to General Carranza, First Chief of the Constitutionalist Army, charged with the executive power of the Union, on Mar. 3, 1917, and the Mexican Ambassador, Señor Bonillas, was accorded formal recognition as Ambassador of the *de facto* government of Mexico on Apr. 17, 1917. Ambassador Fletcher to Secretary Lansing, no. 14, Mar. 13, 1917, MS. Department of State, file 123F63/149; Mr. Lansing to Mr. Fletcher, Apr. 21, 1917, *ibid.* 701.1211/189; 1917 For. Rel. 910–912, 915.

Carranza was elected President on Mar. 11, 1917 and informed the President of the United States of that fact in an autographed letter of May 1, 1917, to which the President replied on Aug. 31. Mr. Fletcher to Mr. Lansing, Apr. 27, 1917, MS. Department of State, file 812.00/20846; President Carranza to President Wilson, May 1, 1917, *ibid.* 812.001C23/30; Mr. Lansing to Mr. Fletcher, no. 285, Aug. 31, 1917, *ibid.* 812.001C23/1; 1917 For. Rel. 912–913, 938, 943.

As the result of a movement organized in the State of Sonora under the leadership of Governor Calles, having for its purpose the overthrow of the Carranza government, Carranza and his Cabinet abandoned the capital, and he was killed in an attack on his party on May 21, 1920 while *en route* to Veracruz. The Mexican Congress, in extraordinary session, elected Adolfo de la Huerta Provisional President on May 24. The American Chargé d'Affaires in Mexico was instructed on May 25 that— *De la Huerta, Provisional President, 1920*

> this Government has not been advised that the succession to the Presidency upon the death of the late incumbent has been effected in orderly pursuance of the provisions of the Mexican Constitution. The change appears to have been in fact revolutionary and the Executive designation appears to be a provisional expedient resting on the so-called plan of Agua Prieta, devised and carried out by a decree of de la Huerta as "Acting Supreme Chief of the Liberal Constitutionalist Army," modifying the existing electoral law and convoking the Congress which has elected him Provisional President.
>
> You should therefore be cautious in any necessary dealings with the parties now in possession, not to permit any imputation that the present régime has been even *de facto* recognized by the Government of the United States. Recognition cannot be accomplished by inference merely but by the full and formal entrance into international relations through the public action of the respective executives of the two countries.

> Chargé Summerlin to Secretary Colby, May 7, 22, and 24, 1920, MS. Department of State, files 812.00/23943, 812.00/24053, 812.00/24071; Mr. Colby to Mr. Summerlin, May 25, 1920, *ibid.* file 812.00/24071; 1920 For. Rel., vol. III, pp. 145–154, 167.

> General Obregón was elected President on Sept. 5, 1920, and recognition of the new regime was accordingly withheld pending his accession to the presidency. Confidential agent of the Government of Mexico (Pesqueira) to Secretary Colby, Oct. 26,1920, MS. Department of State,file 812.00/24701½. See also, in general, 1920 For. Rel., vol. III, pp. 162–199.

Under instructions from the Department of State, the Chargé d'Affaires in Mexico presented to President Obregón on May 27, 1921 the text of a proposed treaty of amity and commerce. The treaty was intended to settle the outstanding difficulties between the United States and Mexico (principally the question concerning the retroactive character of article 27 of the Constitution of 1917) and to establish commercial relations on a normal basis. The Chargé d'Affaires reported in his despatch of June 3 that he had stated to President Obregón "that the signing of the proposed Treaty would constitute recognition by the United States Government", that is, "the act of recognition and the signing of the document would be concurrent". However, General Obregón declined to agree to this proposal, maintaining that this was conditional recognition which it was impossible for Mexico to accept. (See *ante* §34.) The United States refused to accord *Failure of negotiations* recognition without receiving satisfactory assurances prior to or at the time of recognition with reference to the matters covered by the proposed treaty.

> Chargé Summerlin to Secretary Hughes, no. 3929, June 3, 1921, MS. Department of State, file 711.1211/17; memorandum of the Mexican Foreign Office to the American Ambassador, June 4, 1921 (enclosure 2 to despatch 3949, June 10, 1921, from the Embassy in Mexico), *ibid.* 711.1211/19; 1921 For. Rel., vol. II, pp. 404–406, 408, 412.

Joint commission

The *impasse* thus reached continued to block recognition. Finally in April 1923, as a result of a suggestion made by General Obregón, an agreement was reached for the submission of the outstanding difficulties to four commissioners, two to be appointed by each Government. It was publicly announced that the Commissioners should meet "for the purpose of expressing impressions and of reporting them to their respective authorities". The American Commissioners, Mr. Charles Beecher Warren and Mr. John Barton Payne, were appointed on May 2, 1923, and the Commissioners held the first meeting in Mexico City on May 14 following.

> Chargé Summerlin to Secretary Hughes, no. 23, Apr. 14, 1923, and Mr. Hughes to Mr. Summerlin, no. 30, Apr. 17, 1923, MS. Department of State, file 711.1211/62; Mr. Summerlin to Mr. Hughes, no. 24, Apr. 19, 1923, and Mr. Hughes to Mr. Summerlin, no. 31, Apr. 20, 1923, *ibid.* 711.1211/63; Mr. Hughes to Mr. Payne, May 5, 1923, *ibid.* 711.1211/86a; Mr. Summerlin to Mr. Hughes, no. 42, May 14, 1923, *ibid.* 711.1211/98; 1923 For. Rel., vol. II, pp. 532–548.

The subjects to be considered by the Commissioners were summarized as follows in the instructions issued to the two American Commissioners by the Secretary of State:

Instructions to American Commissioners

First. To the obtaining of satisfactory assurances against confiscation of the subsoil interests in lands owned by American citizens prior to May 1st, 1917.

Second. To the restoration or proper reparation for the taking of lands owned by American citizens prior to May 1st, 1917.

Third. To the making of appropriate claims conventions.

It will be your task thoroughly to explore existing conditions in order to ascertain and report what practicable adjustment may be had, consistent with the principles which this Government has maintained in the interest of permanent friendly relations with Mexico. It is not my purpose to give rigid instructions, but rather to indicate the range of your inquiry, and certain points which should be considered, reserving for specific instructions the particular questions which may arise in the course of your negotiations.

The Secretary concluded his instructions by saying that—

the assurance that is desired is one that will voice not simply a personal sentiment or intention, but will show that the good faith of Mexico, through her constituted authorities, is pledged to a course of conduct which will relieve this Government of the uncertainties and apprehensions of recent years, and will enable the people of the United States to give full play to their earnest desire to cultivate the most friendly relations with the people of their sister Republic.

Secretary Hughes to Mr. Payne, May 5, 1923, and Mr. Hughes to Mr. Warren, May 5, 1923, MS. Department of State, files 711.1211/86a, 711.-1211/86b; 1923 For. Rel., vol. II, pp. 536–548.

The Commissioners concluded their conferences on August 15, 1923. They signed jointly a declaration concerning the questions which had arisen out of the Mexican agrarian legislation and a declaration relating to the legislation concerning subsoil rights. They also approved of the drafts of two conventions, a special claims convention and a general claims convention, and declared that they would be forthwith signed in the event that diplomatic relations should be resumed between the two Governments. The reports of the Commissioners were submitted to the Governments by the Commissioners, that of the Mexican Commissioners receiving the approval of President Obregón and that of the American Commissioners the approval of President Coolidge.

Secretary Hughes to Chargé Summerlin, no. 119, Aug. 22, 1923, MS. Department of State, file 711.1211/157b; the First Secretary of the Mexican Embassy (Téllez) to Mr. Hughes, Aug. 25, 1923, *ibid.* 711.1211/163; 1923 For. Rel., vol. II, pp. 550–551. For the declarations adopted by the Commissioners and the text of the claims conventions, see *Proceedings of the United States–Mexican Commission, Convened in Mexico City, May 14, 1923* (Washington, 1925) 43–62.

An agreement was accordingly reached under which statements were released to the press in Washington and in Mexico City simultaneously on August 31, announcing the renewal of diplomatic relations between the two Governments. The American Chargé d'Affaires formally presented his credentials to the Mexican Minister of Foreign Affairs on September 3 under instructions from the Department, Mr. Téllez, in like manner, presenting his credentials as Chargé d'Affaires to the Department of State at the same time.

Recognition

Secretary Hughes to Chargé Summerlin, nos. 119 and 121, Aug. 22 and 25, 1923, MS. Department of State, files 711.1211/157b, 711.1211/158a; M r. Summerlin to Mr. Hughes, no. 85, Aug. 27, 1923, and the Acting Secretary of State (Phillips) to Mr. Summerlin, no. 124, Aug. 28, 1923, *ibid.* file 711.1211/161; Mr. Summerlin to Mr. Hughes, no. 88, Aug. 31, 1923, *ibid.* 711.1211/165; Mr. Phillips to Mr. Summerlin, no. 131, Aug. 31, 1923, *ibid.* 812.01/20a; 1923 For. Rel., vol. II, pp. 550–555.

As a part of the agreement reached by the Commissioners and approved by the two Governments, the general claims convention was signed in Washington on Sept. 8 and the special claims convention was signed in Mexico City on Sept. 10, 1923. 43 Stat. 1730, 1722; 4 Treaties, etc. (Trenwith, 1938) 4441, 4445.

Nicaragua

Juan Estrada
government

Through a note of September 12, 1910 from his representative in Washington to the Department of State, Señor Juan Estrada, who had proclaimed himself Provisional President of Nicaragua, requested recognition of his government by the United States, stating that he was in peaceful and unrestricted possession of the Republic and making the following representations:

1. That a general election will be held within one year, the date to be fixed by a constitutional convention convoked for that purpose.

2. That the Provisional Government will endeavor to improve and rehabilitate the national finances, to which end the aid of the Department of State will be asked in securing a loan in the United States.

3. That such loan will be secured by a percentage of the custom revenues, to be collected in a manner agreed upon between the two Governments.

4. That those responsible for the death of Cannon and Groce will be prosecuted and punished and a suitable indemnity paid to the families of the deceased.

5. That, in order to facilitate compliance with the foregoing and in event there exist necessity for formal agreement, the Department of State is requested to send to Nicaragua a commission for that purpose.

Señor Castrillo to Secretary Knox, Sept. 12, 1910, MS. Department of State, file 817.00/1395; 1910 For. Rel. 762.

Diplomatic relations having been severed on December 1, 1909, Mr. Dawson, the American Minister in Panama, was designated special agent of the United States near the Provisional Government of Nicaragua on October 11, 1910. He reported on October 28 that the Provisional President, his Minister of Foreign Affairs (Díaz), and his Minister of Finance (Mena) were willing to agree to the following:

First. To call election to take place November twentieth of members of constitutional convention to meet December fifteenth to elect President and Vice President for a period of two years and to adopt a (democratic) constitution.

Second. To support in the convention Estrada for President and Diaz for Vice-President, Estrada not to be candidate to succeed himself.

Third. To pledge now their influence that the constitution adopted shall renew and strengthen abolition of monopolies guarantee foreigners rights, provide for free popular election for the President who is to succeed Estrada and that the convention will authorize the Executive to make arrangements with the United States as indicated in paragraphs two, three and four yours of October eleven, four p.m. The above would be gladly accepted by most Liberals. A popular presidential election is at present impracticable and dangerous to peace. Delay in Government acquiring solid and internationally recognizable status very dangerous.

Mr. Dawson was instructed in a telegram on November 2, 1910:

> You may express the Department's satisfaction with the engagement so soon as it shall have been signed by all the important factional leaders, including Mena, or earlier, if in your judgment such engagement constitutes a substantial contribution to the cause of harmony in Nicaragua. You will not fail to impress upon all concerned the Department's view that this engagement is not only binding as between the signatories but also constitutes a solemn pledge to this and other foreign governments that public order will be maintained and that any violation of the agreement cannot but be disastrous to Nicaragua.

Mr. Dawson to Secretary Knox, Oct. 28, 1910, MS. Department of State, file 817.00/1445; the Acting Secretary of State (Adee) to Mr. Dawson, Nov. 2, 1910, *ibid.* 817.00/1446; 1910 For. Rel. 763–767.

The documents referred to in the two preceding telegrams were signed on Nov. 6, 1910. The note from the Nicaraguan Foreign Office transmitting the signed documents to the American Minister set forth the program "including mixed commission for unliquidated claims one member to be named by Nicaragua another by the United States, and, if a third be necessary, to be chosen by the first two, the Department to have the right to modify this feature". It also requested a loan and the sending of a financial expert from the United States. Mr. Dawson to Mr. Knox, Nov. 6, 1910, MS. Department of State, file 817.00/1459.

American Consul Moffat, on December 31, 1910, reported the unanimous election of Estrada and Díaz as President and Vice President, respectively. On January 1, 1911 President Taft sent the following message to President Estrada: _{Formal recognition}

> I send your excellency my most cordial felicitations for the New Year, with which I hope will begin an era of progress, peace, and prosperity for the people of Nicaragua. I congratulate you upon your assumption of the presidency by popular mandate unanimously expressed through the Assembly recently elected, and I assure you, and through you the Government and people of Nicaragua, of the sincere sympathy and friendship of the Government and people of the United States in the work of regeneration which we hope will be so successful. I add my wishes for your own personal welfare.

A new American minister was thereafter accredited to Nicaragua on January 20, 1911.

President Taft to President Estrada, Jan. 1, 1911, MS. Department of State, file 817.00/1517A; Secretary Knox to Minister Northcott, Jan. 20, 1911, *ibid.* 123.N81/29B; 1911 For. Rel. 648–654.

On October 25, [1925] General Chamorro seized the fortress dominating Managua and informed the American Minister that it was his express purpose to drive the Liberals from the cabinet and restore the Conservative Party to the power which it enjoyed before the last election. He stated that he wished Solorzano to remain President and himself to be appointed Minister of War _{Chamorro regime, 1926}

and to have complete control of all arms.   The American Minister immediately informed him that any Government assuming power by force would not be recognized by the Government of the United States.   Chamorro forced Solorzano to sign a joint document agreeing (1) that the coalition pacts should be broken and be considered as of no value henceforth; (2) that the Government be entirely Conservative; (3) that full amnesty be granted to all participants in his military operations; (4) that the Government pay Chamorro 10,000 cordobas for the expenses of his uprising besides paying the troops; (5) that Chamorro be made General in Chief of the Army.   Chamorro thus gained complete control.   The middle of November he sent twelve hundred men to Leon and stated that they would be held there until Vice President Sacasa who was then in hiding should resign and he intimated that if milder means could not produce Sacasa's resignation sterner measures might be adopted toward relatives and friends of the Vice President.   Sacasa escaped and is now in the United States.

Chamorro was elected Senator on January 3, and states his intention of being elected first designado on January 11, whereupon he will cause Solorzano to resign and through intimidation will keep Sacasa from returning to the country and he will thus be President.

Coup d'état

The Legation in Managua has been instructed to inform Chamorro that the United States would not recognize any Government headed by him since such a government would be founded on a *coup d'etat* and hence is debarred of recognition under the General Treaty of Peace and Amity of 1923.   The Nicaraguan Minister in Washington has also been definitely told that Chamorro will not be recognized if he assumes the presidency and it is hoped that this categoric statement made both here and in Managua may prove effective in preventing his taking this step. The Department feels that the signatories of the 1923 Treaty should make clear to Chamorro their position in the matter and it hopes that the Government to which you are accredited will instruct its representative in Managua by telegraph to tell Chamorro immediately that he will not be recognized by it should he assume the presidency during the present presidential term of office.   This statement should be made before January 11, and should also be made public.   The Legation at Managua reports on January 5, that Chamorro maintains that he can obtain recognition from the other Central American States.

Secretary Kellogg to the Legations at Guatemala, El Salvador, Honduras and Costa Rica, Jan. 7, 1926, MS. Department of State, file 817.00/3383A.

All the Central American governments stated that they would not recognize Chamorro if he should assume the presidency.   *Ibid.* files 817.00/3384 /3385, /3387, /3390.

Chamorro assumed the presidency on January 17, 1926, after the Nicaraguan Congress had granted Solorzano a leave of absence, sentenced Vice President Sacasa to two years' banishment, and declared the vice-presidency vacant.   The United States consistently maintained its policy of refusing to recognize Chamorro's regime. On March 11 the Department of State instructed the Minister in Nicaragua:

> As it appears likely that you may be consulted and your opinions asked, you may in such event say that it has always been the feeling of the Department that the only possible and legal solution of the present situation in Nicaragua would be for Chamorro to withdraw and permit Solorzano to return to office [paraphrase].

Non-recognition of Chamorro

Finally on October 30, 1926, acting in accordance with article 106 of the Constitution, Chamorro deposited the presidency in the Second Designate, Senator Uriza, the First Designate being absent in the United States. The Department's position regarding Uriza's government was stated in an instruction of November 3:

> It is the view of the Department that the Uriza regime has no constitutional basis whatever and that it is merely a transition between the Chamorro regime and a government which can be recognized. The Department does not contemplate according any form of moral support to Uriza. [Paraphrase.]

Secretary Kellogg to Señor Don Salvador Castrillo, Jan. 22, 1926, MS. Department of State, file 817.00/3416; the Acting Secretary of State (Grew) to Minister Eberhardt, no. 20, Mar. 11, 1926, *ibid.* 817.00/3497a; Secretary Kellogg to the Chargé d'Affaires (Dennis), no. 105, Nov. 3, 1926, *ibid.* 817.00/3997.

Having been advised of the plan under which the Senators and Deputies who had been expelled by General Chamorro from the previous Congress were to be invited to return and to resume their seats, and a designate then selected who would succeed to the presidency, the Department of State on November 6 advised the Legation:

Díaz government recognized

> The Department would give very careful consideration to the prompt recognition as the Constitutional President of Nicaragua of a Designate who should be elected by a Congress which might be considered to be the duly constituted Congress of Nicaragua. . . . If a Constitutional Government should be established which the United States could recognize, customary support would be given to it. [Paraphrase.]

On November 11 the Department instructed the Chargé d'Affaires:

> The Department will consider favorably according immediate recognition to the new President if the designation should be carried out in conformity with the present plans as reported by you, which are understood to be in accordance with the provisions of the Constitution . . .
> If the proposed plans are actually carried out the Department authorizes you to attend the inaugural ceremonies. [Paraphrase.]

Adolfo Díaz was duly elected designate by the Congress on November 11 and took the oath of office as President on November 14. The American Chargé d'Affaires attended his inaugural ceremonies and delivered a note to the Minister of Foreign Affairs on November 17 formally notifying the Nicaraguan Government of the extension of recognition to the new regime by the Government of the United States.

> Secretary Kellogg to Chargé Dennis, nos. 106 and 108, November 6 and 11, 1926, MS. Department of State, files 817.00/4016, 817.00/4037; Mr. Dennis to Mr. Kellogg, nos. 196, 200, and 202, Nov. 11, 14, and 17, 1926, *ibid.* 817.00/4044, 817.00/4059, 817.00/4070.

Panama

On January 2, 1931 a successful *coup d'état* was carried out against the government of President Arosemena, of Panama, under the direction of the "Acción Comunal". The President resigned on January 3, having first accepted the resignation of the Minister of Government and appointed in his place Dr. Harmodio Arias. The members of the Arosemena Cabinet then met and elected Dr. Arias as Provisional President (nominally in pursuance of article 81 of the Constitution); the members of the Cabinet thereafter promptly resigned. In the meantime the Supreme Court met in formal session, rendered a decision holding the election of Designados of October 1, 1930 unconstitutional, and called Dr. Ricardo Alfaro (elected First Designate in 1928) to take charge of the presidency. Arias at once took the oath of office as Provisional President to serve until such time as Alfaro could return to Panama from the United States. This procedure was intended to make the succession to the presidency legal and in accordance with the Constitution, in the hope that no questions would be raised in the matter of the recognition of the new government.

> Minister Davis to Secretary Stimson, nos. 96, 98, 7, and 17, Jan. 2 and Jan. 4, 1931, MS. Department of State, files 819.00 Revolutions/1, 819.00 Revolutions/2, 819.00/1539, 819.00/1541. For a summary of the events leading up to the selection of Alfaro as President, see Mr. Davis to Mr. Stimson, no. 307, Jan. 6, 1931, *ibid.* 819.00 Revolutions/29.

The Minister reported in a telegram to the Secretary of State on January 4:

> The following statement has been made to the press by the Minister of Foreign Affairs of the *de facto* government:
>
> "In my opinion recognition of the new government of Panama is not required by foreign governments as I consider that the change has been accomplished in a constitutional manner."
> [Paraphrase.]

On the same day the Minister reported the receipt of an official note from the Minister of Foreign Affairs advising him of the change of government and "expressing the hope that the relations between the Ministry and the Legation will [would] continue to be as cordial as in the past". The Department replied on January 5:

> The Department desires that you should not at present make a reply to the note. Pressing business which it is necessary to take up in writing should be transacted through memoranda from the Legation to the Ministry for Foreign Affairs, but not addressed to any individual in his official capacity.

> .   .   .   .

> The failure of the Department to forward instructions to you up to the present time concerning the matter of recognition, has not been the result of any misgivings with regard to the constitutionality of the appointment of Señor Arias as Provisional President, but has been due rather to a desire to allow time to determine whether the new Government would have sufficient stability and control of the country to establish and continue its authority. It is not probable that the Department will take action until after the return of Dr. Alfaro to Panama, and the assumption of control of the Government by him, and its decision at that time will be determined by the developments which take place. It is desired that you keep the Department informed concerning the extent to which the new authorities have control over the country, concerning any armed opposition which may arise against the new Government, and concerning the prospect of the new Government having the power to maintain itself in office. The Department also desires to know whether it has the support of the majority of the country.
> [Paraphrase.]

The Minister telegraphed the Department on January 14:

> The following governments consider present government constitutional continuation of Arosemena government and have continued normal diplomatic relations: Italy, Spain, Ecuador, Costa Rica, Germany, Colombia, and Mexico.
> New government apparently has support of great majority of residents of capital and has been well received throughout the republic. Opposition from deposed authorities improbable in immediate future. Question of satisfying extreme element of group which carried out revolution will be Dr. Alfaro's chief problem.
> Alfaro will arrive tomorrow and is planning to take oath of office Friday January 16th. I am informed invitation will be extended diplomatic corps to attend inauguration and reception. Unless otherwise instructed immediately by cable I shall not attend.

To this the Department replied on January 15:

> The Department is inclined to consider Alfaro's coming into office as a constitutional devolution. Furthermore the ordinary standards of international law for the recognition of new Governments would appear to be met with. The Department's only preoccupation on this score in the past has been the question of

Constitutional devolution; stability

stability and your present statement that the new Government apparently has the support of the great majority of the residents of the capital and has been well received throughout the Republic, and that opposition from the deposed authorities is improbable in the immediate future, leads the Department to feel that you should attend the inauguration of Doctor Alfaro and carry on normal diplomatic relations thereafter with his Government. You are authorized to do so.

Minister Davis to Secretary Stimson, nos. 18 and 19, Jan. 4, 1931 (2 p.m. and 3 p.m.), MS. Department of State, files 819.00 Revolutions/14, 819.00 Revolutions/15; Mr. Stimson to Mr. Davis, no. 6, Jan. 5, 1931, *ibid.* file 819.00 Revolutions/21; Mr. Davis to Mr. Stimson, no. 32, Jan. 14, 1931, *ibid.* 819.00 Revolutions/33; Mr. Stimson to Mr. Davis, no. 32, Jan. 15, 1931, *ibid.* 819.00 Revolutions/35.

Paraguay

The Ayala government was overthrown by a revolutionary movement which broke out in Paraguay on February 17, 1936, Colonel Franco being selected Provisional President two days later. On February 20 the Legation reported to the Department of State:

I have just received two notes from the Ministry for Foreign Affairs. The first announces that Colonel Franco today took oath as provisional president "by decision of the plebiscitary decree of the liberating army," and that he has constituted his cabinet . . .

The second notifies this Legation that the Minister for Foreign Affairs, "has fixed tomorrow, Friday, the 21st, from nine to eleven o'clock to receive in special audience the members of the diplomatic corps accredited before the Government of Paraguay."

In a further telegram of the same date the Minister reported:

At a meeting of the diplomatic corps this evening my colleagues, with the uncertain exception of the Argentine Chargé d'Affaires, decided to call at the Foreign Office tomorrow morning in compliance with Dr. Stefanich's invitation. They do not, with the exception of the Mexican [omission ?], regard such action as implying recognition. I stated that I must await instructions.

In so far as can be judged the present de facto government appears able to maintain itself for the immediate future although in many quarters there still exists a feeling of uncertainty. If formal recognition is to be accorded upon this basis I can see no grounds for refusal and it would seem advisable not to delay. It would also be conducive to friendly relations with the new government if I could join my colleagues in their call at the Foreign Office tomorrow.

In a telegram of February 21 the Department approved the action of the Minister in refraining from attending the meeting called at the Foreign Office and said:

With reference to the last paragraph of your cable No. 24, it would seem as yet premature in any event to determine whether the new government in Paraguay meets with a substantial measure of popular support; whether it is able to maintain itself in power; whether it is able to carry out the functions of a stable government; and finally, whether it intends to comply with its international obligations previously contracted.

In a telegraphic instruction of March 3 to the Legation in Asunción, the Department said:

It is the belief of this Government that it would be wise with reference to the matter of recognition, so far as may be possible, to act in harmony with the other mediatory powers who are represented at the Chaco Peace Conference, and it is also of the opinion that it would be clearly desirable that formal assurances should be made by the new Paraguayan regime declaring its firm intention to uphold all of the peace agreements which have been previously concluded at the Chaco Peace Conference. [Paraphrase.]

Minister Howard to Secretary Hull, no. 21 of Feb. 19, 1936, no. 22 of Feb. 19, 1936, no. 23 of Feb. 20, 1936 (4 p.m.), no. 24 of Feb. 20, 1936 (7 p.m.), MS. Department of State, files 834.00/794, /795, /796, /797; Mr. Hull to Mr. Howard, nos. 2 and 4, Feb. 21 and Mar. 3, 1936, *ibid.* 834.00/796, 834.01/12.

On March 5, 1936, President Franco sent a telegram direct to President Roosevelt:

. . . This provisional government was constituted sixteen days ago with unanimous support of all the Paraguayan people, having given its attention from first moment to issuing official declarations regarding its will faithfully to carry out international obligations and pacts in force as well as with regard to democratic principles which will guide new organization of the State and the resolution proceed without delay with the repatriation of captives of war. *Assurances by Franco*

Mr. Braden, the American delegate to the peace conference, reported on March 8 that it was the opinion of the executive committee of the peace conference that the fact that the provisions of article 4 of the protocol of January 21, 1936, concerning repatriation of Bolivian and Paraguayan prisoners of war, had been complied with, together with the declaration of the Paraguayan Government contained in Franco's telegrams to the presidents of the neutral states of his intention to respect the Buenos Aires protocols, placed the conference in a position where it should recommend recognition to the participating governments.

The Department of State declined to assent to a proposal by the executive committee that recognition be extended to the Paraguayan Government by means of a joint note signed by the six chiefs of mission in Asunción and suggested in a telegram of March 11 to the Embassy at Buenos Aires the use of identic notes. On March 13 it communicated to the Legation at Asunción the text of a note to be delivered to the Foreign Office at such time as the conference should determine to extend recognition to the new government. After adverting to certain statements made by the Paraguayan Government to the peace conference, the note concluded:

International
obligations

> As a result of its deliberation and after consulting with the governments of the other mediatory nations represented at the Peace Conference, the Government of the United States has with much pleasure reached the conclusion that it is the express intention of the Government of Paraguay to respect in every way the peace protocols signed in Buenos Aires on June 12, 1935, and on the 21st of January, 1936, as well as its other international obligations.
>
> Consequently, I have the honor to inform Your Excellency that my Government will be pleased to maintain with the Government of Paraguay the friendly relations that are traditional between our two countries.

The Department adhered to its view that recognition by means of identic notes was to be preferred, saying in a telegram of March 13 to the Embassy at Buenos Aires:

> . . . From every point of view it seems better to follow the established precedent that recognition be accorded by each of the governments involved as an independent act of individual sovereignty.

Notes were delivered simultaneously on March 14.

> President Franco to President Roosevelt, Mar. 5, 1936, MS. Department of State, file 834.01/30; Ambassador Weddell to Secretary Hull, no. 55, Mar. 8, 1936, *ibid.* 834.01/20; Mr. Hull to Mr. Weddell, no. 30, Mar. 11, 1936, *ibid.* 834.01/23; the Acting Secretary of State (Phillips) to Minister Howard, no. 9, Mar. 13, 1936, *ibid.* 834.01/25; Mr. Phillips to Mr. Weddell, no. 32, Mar. 13, 1936, *ibid.* 834.01/27; Mr. Weddell to Mr. Hull, no. 63, Mar. 13, 1936, *ibid.* 834.00/28; Mr. Howard to Mr. Hull, no. 47, Mar. 14, 1936, *ibid.* 834.01/29.

Paiva
government

The Provisional Government of President Franco was overthrown on August 14, 1937, and Felix Paiva, former Vice President, was sworn in as President on August 16. The Minister in Asunción informed the Department in a telegram of August 17:

> I have just been invited by the Under Secretary for Foreign Affairs to meet this afternoon together with my colleagues Dr. Luis Argana Minister of Justice and Public Instruction, and Acting Minister for Foreign Affairs pending arrival tomorrow of Dr. Baez. The Under Secretary states that it is not the intention of this meeting to imply recognition of the new government which he states is being requested through the Paraguayan Legations. While my acceptance would undoubtedly be conducive to the creation of friendly feeling I shall make no move pending instructions.

His report having arrived too late for instructions to be issued, he informed the Department on August 18:

> Meeting not in a body, diplomats called at various times between 4:30 and 6 o'clock. Failing instructions I did not call. Minister for Foreign Affairs stated that the Government is returning to the constitution of 1870 and that international obligations will be respected.

In a telegraphic instruction of August 18, 1937 to the Embassy at Buenos Aires with reference to the matter of recognition of the Paiva government, the Department said:

> It is the opinion of the Department that a declaration by the new Paraguayan regime, similar to that made by the Government of Colonel Busch in Bolivia, to the effect that the Government will respect all international obligations, should constitute a satisfactory safeguard for the Peace Conference negotiations. The Department desires that you report the views of the delegates of the other mediatory powers concerning the content of notes of recognition. It is the desire of the Department that you should not take any position concerning recognition without prior authorization pending a further consideration of the matter. [Paraphrase. For the assurances of the Busch government, see §47.]

Mr. Spruille Braden, delegate to the Chaco Peace Conference, informed the Department on August 25:

> Paraguayan Minister for Foreign Affairs' telegram to Conference President, while not as specific as desired, was considered as warranting mediatory powers proceeding to recognize. Argentina and Chile intend to do so tomorrow; Peru tomorrow or next day. I recommend that the United States recognize tomorrow if possible. I would appreciate being advised when recognition is extended.
>
> Paraguayan Minister for Foreign Affairs' telegram of August 24 follows:
>
> "Having taken charge today of the portfolio of foreign relations I comply with the duty of sending Your Excellency and your honorable colleagues the expression of my personal salutation declaring that it is the intention of my Government to collaborate for the preservation of that entity in order to carry to a good end the purposes which created it, without detriment to the agreements adopted in its previous deliberations."

The Department accordingly instructed the Minister in Asunción on August 26:

> You will request an interview with the Minister for Foreign Affairs at the earliest opportunity today and hand to him a note containing the following statement. Compliance with agreements
>
> "I have been instructed by my Government to inform Your Excellency that, having noted with satisfaction the statement regarding foreign policy and the Chaco Peace Conference negotia-

tions made by His Excellency the President of Paraguay and published on August 22, as well as Your Excellency's telegram of August 24 to the President of the Peace Conference, the Government of the United States of America will be pleased to maintain the friendly relations that have so happily existed between our two countries."

The Minister reported the delivery of the note on August 27.

Minister Howard to Secretary Hull, no. 23, Aug. 17, 1937, and Mr. Hull to Mr. Howard, no. 12, Aug. 17, 1937, MS. Department of State, file 834.01/39; Mr. Howard to Mr. Hull, no. 25, Aug. 18, 1937, *ibid.* file 834.01/40; Mr. Hull to Ambassador Weddell, nos. 73 and 74, Aug. 18 and 20, 1937, *ibid.* files 724.34119/978, /979; Mr. Weddell to Mr. Hull, no. 156, Aug. 25, 1937, *ibid.* file /988; Mr. Hull to Mr. Howard, no. 16, Aug. 26, 1937, *ibid.* /993C; Mr. Howard to Mr. Hull, no. 29 *bis*, Aug. 27, 1937, *ibid.* /994.

Peru

On February 4, 1914 a revolution headed by Augusto Durand overthrew the existing Government of Peru, and on the same date a Junta government was formed under the presidency of Colonel Oscar Benavides, ex-Chief-of-Staff. The American Legation reported to the Department of State on February 8:

. . . The question of recognition is now being raised . . . No evidence of organized opposition to present régime, nor does any seem probable. Believe ultimate recognition inevitable. Request instructions.

The Department instructed the Legation on February 12:

Control of executive power; acquiescence

The Junta created by the Congress being in uncontested exercise of executive power and such exercise being freely acquiesced in by the people, you are instructed to recognize the Junta as a Provisional Government pending the establishment of a permanent executive.

Benavides was elected Provisional President by Congress on May 15 and was immediately sworn in. The Minister was instructed on May 26 to call on the Minister for Foreign Affairs the following day and to inform him that "the United States recognizes the Government of Colonel Benavides as the Provisional Government of Peru".

Minister McMillin to Secretary Bryan, Feb. 4 and 8, 1914, MS. Department of State, files 823.00/116, /121; Mr. Bryan to Mr. McMillin, Feb. 12 and May 26, 1914, *ibid.* /127a, /178a; 1914 For. Rel. 1061–1067.

Leguia executed a *coup d'état* on July 4, 1919, seized and imprisoned President Pardo, and assumed the provisional presidency by a proclamation on the following day. The Department of State inquired of the Minister by telegram on August 5:

In your opinion is will of majority of people of Peru expressed in support of action of Leguia in overthrowing Pardo and calling for new elections?

The Minister replied on August 9:

> Leguia unquestionably has now and had at the time of elections a strong popular following. Whether this was sufficient to elect I do not know. He had absolute control over army. I am therefore of the opinion that he will be able to overcome any and all opposition that may arise against his rule for the present and near future. The same forces that aided him in taking the Government from Pardo will enable him to hold it, at least for the present now that Pardo is out of power and out of the Republic.

He further stated:

> Allied Ministers seem to be of this opinion. I believe that a majority of the people have acquiesced in overthrow [of] Pardo Government but not in calling new congressional elections.

The election for a new Congress was held on August 26, resulting in an overwhelming victory for the Government, and on August 28 the Department instructed the Minister:

> In view of the facts reported in your August 26th, 8 p.m., you are instructed to address an informal communication to the Minister of Foreign Affairs of the Leguia government informing him that the Government of the United States extends to Mr. Leguia recognition as the head of the *de facto* Government of Peru.

Minister McMillin to the Acting Secretary of State (Phillips), July 4 and 5, 1919, MS. Department of State, files 823.00/254, 823.00/257; Secretary Lansing to Minister McMillin, Aug. 5, 1919, *ibid.* file 823.00/287; Mr. McMillin to Mr. Lansing, Aug. 9, 1919, *ibid.* 823.00/291; Mr. McMillin to Mr. Lansing, Aug. 26, 1919, and Mr. Lansing to Mr. McMillin, Aug. 28, 1919, *ibid.* 823.00/297; 1919 For. Rel., vol. II, pp. 720–728, 732–736.

Under pressure of a revolutionary outbreak President Leguia resigned on August 25, 1930, and the executive power was assumed by a Junta on August 28, headed by Colonel Sanchez Cerro. The Chargé d'Affaires reported on August 29:

Sanchez Cerro Junta

> . . . The Foreign Office has informed diplomatic representatives in Lima by note August 28 . . . that the new Council of Government would strictly comply with Peru's international agreements and maintain the good relations which unite Peru with the United States.

With an informal note of August 29, 1930 the Peruvian Ambassador transmitted the following message from the Peruvian Minister of Foreign Affairs to the Assistant Secretary of State (Castle):

> Please let it be known that the Government Junta will comply strictly with international treaties and commitments and with foreign financial undertakings, guaranteeing their fulfilment.

The Chargé d'Affaires (Mayer) to Secretary Stimson, nos. 150, 161, and 166, Aug. 25, 28, and 29, 1930, MS. Department of State, files 823.00 Revolutions/8, 823.00 Revolutions/21, 823.00 Revolutions/26; Ambassador de Freyre to Assistant Secretary Castle, Aug. 29, 1930, *ibid.* file 823.00 Revolutions/43.

Acquiescence of people; control of territory; obligations

The Ambassador in Lima recommended on September 13, 1930 that the Cerro Junta be recognized by the Government of the United States, saying that it was his belief:

> First. That the junta government is acquiesced in by practically the entire population of the country;
> Second, that it controls all Peruvian territory and is maintaining public order;
> Third, that it is willing and able and is living up to its international obligations;
> Fourth, that it intends eventually to restore the country to a constitutional regime.

He was thereupon instructed by telegram on September 16:

> The Department desires that on Thursday next you inform the Minister for Foreign Affairs that your Government has instructed you to enter into full diplomatic relations with the new Peruvian Government, thus according recognition to it. [Paraphrase.]

Ambassador Dearing to Secretary Stimson, no. 207, Sept. 13, 1930, MS. Department of State, file 823.01/20; Mr. Stimson to Mr. Dearing, no. 109, Sept. 16, 1930, *ibid.* 823.01/23. For a statement to the press on Sept. 17 by the Secretary of State setting forth the grounds upon which the Department acted in extending recognition to Peru, as well as to Bolivia and Argentina, see *ante*, this section, under Argentina.

Ocampo Junta: Relations not affected by change in government

Sanchez Cerro and his entire Junta resigned on March 1, 1931, and after a number of temporary shifts in the government a Junta headed by David Samanez Ocampo took over the government on March 11. The Embassy transmitted to the Department of State on March 13 the text of a note from the Foreign Office dated March 12 containing a formal notification of the establishment of the new Junta and saying that it was "resolved to comply strictly with the international obligations concluded by Peru". In a telegraphic instruction of May 8 the Department advised the Ambassador:

> . . . Information in the Department's possession indicates that recognition has been extended only by Spain and Norway and that particular circumstances determined their action. It has been indicated by you that the British, Japanese and Brazilian Governments are prepared to follow our lead. The Department desires to know the attitude of the Latin American countries such as Chile and Argentina.
> The Department . . . desires to be informed of your considered opinion concerning the stability of the existing regime and whether the Peruvian people are apt to give it support in the next succeeding months. It is understood by the Depart-

ment that the navy supports the regime. Does it have the support of the army, or is the army's allegiance divided, and is there likely to be a movement against the Government in the near future? Is it your opinion that recognition would tend to stabilize conditions in Peru?

[Paraphrase.]

To this the Ambassador replied on May 15:

The present Peruvian Government . . . has at present the support of the army, navy and police and the acquiescence of people in general and seems likely to continue for the immediate future.

. . . .

. . . Chile and Argentina consider that full diplomatic relations exist with the present Peruvian Government and are acting accordingly. Most other Latin American countries and the Papal State take the same position and feel that no special recognizing action on their part is necessary.

. . . .

In my opinion to accord full diplomatic relations will tend to stabilize conditions in Peru and by regularizing our intercourse will greatly facilitate our current business.

The Department accordingly instructed the Ambassador on May 19:

You may answer Peruvian Government's note of March 12 last and state that the change in Government in Peru will make no difference in the diplomatic relations between the United States and Peru.

Ambassador Dearing to Secretary Stimson, nos. 80, 112, 116, and 624 Mar. 1, 11, and 13, and Apr. 12, 1931, MS. Department of State, files 823.00 Revolutions/125, 823.002/151, 823.00 Revolutions/169, 823.01/70; Mr. Stimson to Mr. Dearing, no. 30, May 8, 1931, *ibid.* file 823.01/76; Mr. Dearing to Mr. Stimson, no. 224, May 15, 1931, *ibid.* 823.01/78; Mr. Stimson to Mr. Dearing, no. 35, May 19, 1931, *ibid.* 823.01/79.

The Ambassador informed the Department on May 20 that he had carried out its instruction, and on May 21 he reported that the British, Japanese, Brazilian, and Belgian Governments were extending recognition using a similar formula. Mr. Dearing to Mr. Stimson, nos. 225 and 229, May 20 and 21, 1931, *ibid.* files 823.01/80, /82.

Sanchez Cerro was elected to the presidency on October 11, 1931 and was assassinated on April 30, 1933. He was succeeded by General Benavides who was elected President by the Constituent Assembly. The presidential election held on October 11, 1936 was Benavides declared invalid by formal resolution (November 4, 1936) of the government National Electoral Board, and the Constituent Assembly adopted a report on November 13 continuing Benavides in office until December 8, 1939. The Ambassador stated in his telegram of November 14 to the Department of State that the Constituent Assembly would cease

to function on December 8, 1936 and that Benavides would rule with
the assisting military cabinet. In a further telegram to the Department of November 16, the Ambassador expressed the opinion that
what had happened should be regarded as a purely internal matter
and that diplomatic representatives should simply continue to conduct
relations with the Government, not signalizing the event by any
special action. He said that he would act in accord with this view
unless the Department considered some other course more desirable.
He was instructed on November 19 that in the event the Diplomatic
Corps should be invited to attend ceremonies to mark Benavides'
continuance in office, he should accept and attend.

> Ambassador Dearing to Secretary Stimson, no. 1310, Dec. 7, 1931, MS.
> Department of State, file 823.00/802; Mr. Dearing to Secretary Hull, no.
> 132 of Apr. 30, 1933 (2 p.m.), no. 134 of Apr. 30, 1933 (8 p.m.), no. 4798 of
> Nov. 5, 1936, no. 66 of Nov. 14, 1936, no. 70 of Nov. 16, 1936, *ibid.* files
> 823.00/966, /968, /1232, /1237, /1238; the Acting Secretary of State (Moore)
> to Mr. Dearing, no. 50, Nov. 19, 1936, *ibid.* file 823.001B43/19.

El Salvador

As a result of a military *coup d'état* carried out on December 4, 1931,
President Araujo was compelled to leave El Salvador, taking refuge
in Guatemala after having deposited the presidential powers in the
Third Designate, Dr. Olano. General Martinez, the Vice President,
at once assumed the presidency. On December 20 the Department of
State sent the following telegraphic instruction to the Ministers in
Guatemala, Honduras, Nicaragua, and Costa Rica:

> Having made a very careful study of the matter, the Depart-
> ment has reached the conclusion that the Government headed by
> General Martinez may not properly be recognized under the terms
> of Article two of the General Treaty of Peace and Amity of 1923.
> With regard to that article it appears (1) that General Martinez
> has acceded to the Presidency through a *coup d'état* and that the
> government has not been reorganized in a constitutional manner
> by a Congress freely elected by the people; and (2) that even if
> such a reorganization should be accomplished, General Martinez
> could not be recognized in view of the fact that he occupied the
> office of Minister of War within six months prior to the *coup d'état.*

Policy
guided by
1923 treaty

> It has been stated by the Department on a number of occasions
> that the Government of the United States is guided in its relations
> with the Republics of Central America by the principles embodied
> in the treaty of 1923. This Government, therefore, finds it
> impossible to recognize General Martinez as President of El
> Salvador.
> [Paraphrase.]

The Ministers were instructed to advise the Governments to which
they were accredited of the position of the United States and to express
the hope that they would find it possible to follow a similar course in
order that the signatories of the 1923 treaty and the United States
might act in harmony and that the principles embodied in that treaty

might thus be made effective. All the Central American governments stated that they would be guided by the principles of the treaty of 1923 in deciding upon the recognition of the Salvadoran Government.

MS. Department of State, files 816.01/28, /29, /30, /35. The Minister in Guatemala (Whitehouse) to Secretary Stimson, no. 65, Dec. 4, 1931, MS. Department of State, file 816.001 Araujo, Arturo/40; Mr. Stimson to the Chargé in Costa Rica (Werlich), no. 42, Dec. 20, 1931, *ibid.* 816.01/27A, and identic telegrams to Guatemala, Honduras, and Nicaragua.

The Minister in El Salvador was recalled to Washington on January 10, 1932, and the Legation was left in the care of a Chargé d'Affaires, *Non-recognition* who was instructed that he should be guided by the following principles with reference to the existing situation in El Salvador:

(1) On account of the provisions of the treaty of 1923 Martinez cannot be recognized under any circumstances. No animus against the Martinez faction is involved in this policy which is dictated by the clear provisions of the treaty. The other Republics of Central America are in accord with this policy. It would be of no use for Martinez or his supporters to send a representative to the United States to seek recognition. . . .

(2) The Department hopes very earnestly that at the earliest possible moment there may be established in Salvador a government of a character permitting its recognition by the United States and by the Republics of Central America . . . The Department does not desire to express any opinion concerning the eligibility of any individual for appointment as First Designate, its only concern being that the selection made shall be of a person whom it will be possible to recognize in accordance with the provisions of the treaty of 1923. . . . It is desired that you bring these considerations appropriately to the attention of the military authorities in control of the existing regime.
[Paraphrase.]

Martinez was declared constitutional President by the Legislative Assembly on February 4, 1932. The Government of the United States, nevertheless, adhered strictly to its decision not to recognize him.

The Acting Secretary of State (Phillips) to Representative Black, June 7, 1933, MS. Department of State, file 816.01/300; Secretary Stimson to Chargé McCafferty, no. 6, Jan. 13, 1932, *ibid.* 816.01/50A; Mr McCafferty to Mr. Stimson, no. 30, Feb. 5, 1932, *ibid.* 816.00/839.

Immediately after the denunciation of the treaty of 1923 by Costa Rica and El Salvador, which became effective on January 1, 1934, Costa Rica extended recognition to Martinez. Upon the initiative *Recognition* of President Sacasa of Nicaragua, the other three Central American states accorded recognition on January 25 in pursuance of an agreement that they would recognize the treaty of 1923 as binding among themselves but not with respect to Costa Rica and El Salvador.

At the same time they agreed to call a conference to consider a revision of the treaty. Under authorization from President Roosevelt, the Chargé in El Salvador was authorized on January 26 to extend recognition to the Government of El Salvador on behalf of the United States, and in a circular telegram of the same date all the other missions in Latin America were advised of this action as follows:

> In view of the denunciation by El Salvador of the 1923 Central American Treaty of Peace and Amity, and the recognition of the present Government of El Salvador on January 25 by Nicaragua, Honduras, and Guatemala (Costa Rica having also denounced the Treaty and previously recognized El Salvador) the Department has today instructed the Chargé d'Affaires ad interim in San Salvador to extend formal recognition to the Government of El Salvador.

> The Minister in Costa Rica (Sack) to Secretary Hull, no. 81, Jan. 5, 1934, MS. Department of State, file 816.01/351; the Minister in Nicaragua (Lane) to Mr. Hull, no. 26, Jan. 24, 1934, *ibid.* 816.01/399; the Chargé in Guatemala (Lawton) to Mr. Hull, no. 12, Jan. 25, 1934, *ibid.* 816.01/404; Mr. Lane to Mr. Hull, no. 28, Jan. 25, 1934, *ibid.* 816.01/405; the Minister in Honduras (Lay) to Mr. Hull, no. 7, Jan. 25, 1934, *ibid.* 816.01/409; Mr. Hull to the Chargé d'Affaires in El Salvador, (McCafferty), no. 4, Jan. 26, 1934, and Mr. Hull to all missions in Latin America, including Mexico but excluding El Salvador, Jan. 26, 1934, *ibid.* file 816.01/412.

Venezuela

Because of the persistent refusal of the government of General Castro, of Venezuela, to heed the requests of the United States for redress for serious injuries inflicted upon American interests by the Venezuelan authorities, the United States severed diplomatic relations with Venezuela on June 13, 1908. The protection of American interests in Venezuela was entrusted to the Brazilian Legation in Caracas. On December 19, 1908 the Brazilian Ambassador in Washington communicated to the Department of State the text of a telegram received from the Brazilian representative in Venezuela, reading in part:

> Reaction initiated against General Castro. Minister for Foreign Affairs saw me to day, asked [me to] make . . . known (to) American Government wish (of) President Gomez to settle satisfactorily all international questions.

Buchanan—
High Com-
missioner

The President accordingly appointed William I. Buchanan as High Commissioner to represent him in the conduct of negotiations looking to the reestablishment of diplomatic relations with Venezuela. The formal instructions to Commissioner Buchanan, dated December 21, 1908, reviewed the circumstances under which relations had been severed and, after referring to the wish indicated by President Gomez to reestablish relations, stated:

> The purpose indicated by President Gomez will naturally involve an acceptance of the proposal of the United States for the

arbitration of the pending claims and the disavowal of the discourtesies referred to in the instructions to the American Chargé.

The latter may be in the most general terms and is not deemed to be of primary importance. Indeed, courteous expressions of respect and good will from the new Administration might be deemed a sufficient reversal of the former tone to answer.

It is not deemed necessary that you should complete definitively the signing and submission to arbitration of the pending claims, but it will be sufficient if you receive from the Government of President Gomez an explicit statement committing Venezuela to the arbitration of those claims, referring to my communication to Mr. Russell of February 28, 1907, stating fully the character of the claims.

Commissioner Buchanan was then instructed to obtain a settlement of the outstanding claims and to incorporate the agreement with respect to them in the form of a protocol, as a prerequisite to the reestablishment of diplomatic relations. Such a protocol was signed on February 13, 1909, containing provisions for the settlement by reference to arbitration of three claims, that is, those of the Orinoco Steamship Company, the Orinoco Corporation, and the United States and Venezuela Company. Separate agreements were entered into for the settlement of the Jaurett and the New York and Bermudez Company claims. *Settlement of claims*

On January 18, 1909 Mr. Buchanan informed the Venezuelan Minister of Foreign Affairs that immediately upon his advising his Government of the signing of a protocol satisfactorily arranging for the settlement of existing differences he had been authorized by the Secretary of State to say that the United States would at once send its Minister to Caracas and would be glad to receive a Minister from Venezuela. *Relations resumed*

> Secretary Root to the Chargé d'Affaires in Venezuela (Sleeper), June 12, 1908, MS. Department of State, file 4832/9A; the Brazilian Ambassador in Washington (Nabuco) to Mr. Root, Dec. 19, 1908, *ibid.* 4832/68; Mr. Root to Commissioner Buchanan, Dec. 21, 1908, *ibid.* 4832/68; Mr. Buchanan to Secretary Bacon, Feb. 26, 1909, *ibid.* 4832/91; 1909 For. Rel. 609–616.

EUROPE

§48

A revolutionary outbreak instituted by the Nationalists in Albania resulted in the overthrow in June 1924 of the government headed by Ahmet Bey. The Nationalist forces occupied Tirana on June 11, the members of the Cabinet and other officials having fled to Durazzo. In a telegram of June 19 the American Minister informed the Department of State: *Albania*

The Cabinet was announced on June 17 with Fan Noli as Prime Minister . . .

Formal written announcement was made to the foreign representatives. I have not made a reply. It appears very questionable whether the one remaining regent, Peci, had legal authority to authorize the formation of a cabinet.

. . . I shall maintain friendly but informal relations with the leaders although I intend to refrain, pending the receipt of instructions, from any act which could properly be construed to constitute recognition.

[Paraphrase.]

The Department replied on June 24:

Unless there has been a change in the head of the state, it would not appear that the question of recognition arises. There would be no objection to your continuing to maintain with the present government the relations which you have had with its predecessors if the government is, in your opinion, properly constituted, is stable, and is in control of the country, and you are authorized in your discretion to do so.   [Paraphrase.]

The Minister reported on July 2:

. . . The only regent who remains and whose term ends in the fall has departed on an indefinite leave of absence allegedly on account of his health, and his functions have been assumed ostensibly by the Prime Minister by whom it is stated that elections will not be held until the first of next March. Consequently there is no head of the state. . . . No further pretension to legal status under the Constitution is made.

I propose to refrain from sending communications of a formal character to the Minister for Foreign Affairs but in case of need I shall leave with him impersonal memoranda of important conversations.

[Paraphrase.]

In an instruction of October 2 the Department said:

The Department's telegram No. 30 of June 24, 1 p.m., was sent upon the assumption that a change of cabinet had taken place and not a change in the head of the state. However, it now appears that Fan Noli is performing the function of sole Regent as well as acting as Prime Minister.

It is further understood by the Department that the relations which you have had up to the present with the Albanian Government have been informal in character and that the Department is consequently at this time free to adopt the policy best calculated to meet the needs of the existing situation; that is, either (1) to act formally by granting an exequatur to Tashko and instructing you to establish formal relations or (2) to withhold action of this character with the understanding that informal relations would be conducted by you with the Albanian Government as at present.

It is desired by the Department that you should suspend action on the request for an exequatur.
[Paraphrase.]

The Ambassador in Italy (Fletcher) to Secretary Hughes, no. 114, June 11, 1924, MS. Department of State, file 875.00/140; Minister Grant-Smith to Mr. Hughes, nos. 284, 287, and 56, June 11, 16, and 19, 1924, *ibid.* files 875.00/149, 875.00/151, 875.002/10; Mr. Hughes to Mr. Grant-Smith, no. 39, June 24, 1924, *ibid.* file 875.01/243; Mr. Grant-Smith to Mr. Hughes, no. 62, July 2, 1924, *ibid.* 875.01/245; Chargé Kodding to Mr. Hughes, no. 323, Aug. 30, 1924, *ibid.* 875.01/250; Mr. Hughes to Mr. Grant-Smith, no. 49, Oct. 2, 1924, *ibid.* 702.7511/13; 1924 For. Rel., vol. I, pp. 309–312.

On January 5, 1925 the American Minister reported further:

The Prime Minister who left the capital last June upon its occupation by the Nationalists has returned accompanied by most of his colleagues and has announced the resignation of his cabinet. A new one is being formed with Ahmet Zogu as Prime Minister . . . Ahmet Zogu is without question the dictator of Albania. As he has foreign support he will undoubtedly remain so for some time. [Paraphrase.]

Having been informed by the Minister on January 14 that the new regime appeared to be relatively stable, the Department of State replied on January 22:

It is the opinion of the Department that nothing is to be gained by withholding recognition indefinitely . . . *Assurances*
Consequently if it is possible for you to obtain definite assurances from Ahmet Zogu that the prosecution [of the murderers of Coleman and de Long, American citizens] will be pushed, the Department would consider sending instructions in the near future for you to extend recognition.
[Paraphrase.]

The Minister advised the Department on January 29:

Ahmet Bey has replied to my informal written inquiry that . . . every possible measure has been taken for the arrest and exemplary punishment of those responsible [for the murder of Coleman and de Long] and that he is confident that the result will be satisfactory.
. . . In view of the statement made by Ahmet Bey it appears that nothing would be gained by deferring recognition any longer.
[Paraphrase.]

The Department accordingly instructed the Minister on January 31:

The Department authorizes you to extend recognition to the new government in Albania and to acknowledge the receipt of the official notification to the Legation of the establishment of the Republic. [Paraphrase.]

Minister Grant-Smith to Secretary Hughes, Jan. 5, 1925, and Mr. Hughes to Mr. Grant-Smith, no. 2, Jan. 10, 1925, MS. Department of State, file 875.01/258; Mr. Grant-Smith to Mr. Hughes, no. 4, Jan. 14, 1925, and Mr. Hughes to Mr. Grant-Smith, no. 3, Jan. 22, 1925, *ibid.* 875.01/260; Mr. Grant-Smith to Mr. Hughes, no. 8, Jan. 29, 1925, and Mr. Hughes to Mr. Grant-Smith, no. 5, Jan. 31, 1925, *ibid.* 875.01/265.

Recognition of monarchy

On September 3, 1928 the Albanian Minister in Washington notified the Department of State that an Albanian constitutional convention had unanimously voted the restoration of the monarchy and on September 1, 1928 had elected President Zogu as King of the Albanians. The Department instructed the Minister on September 12 to address a note to the Minister of Foreign Affairs saying:

Note has been taken by my Government of the action of the Albanian Constitutional Assembly changing the form of the Government of Albania to that of a Constitutional Monarchy and proclaiming President Ahmed Zogu "Zog First King of the Albanians". Under instructions from my Government I take pleasure in informing Your Excellency that the Government of the United States extends recognition to the Kingdom of Albania, with the understanding that the exchange of notes of June 22 [23–25], 1922 between the United States and Albania and the provisions of Albanian law enacted in pursuance thereof will continue in force. [Paraphrase.]

The Acting Secretary of State (Clark) to Minister Hart, no. 30, Sept. 5, 1928, MS. Department of State, file 875.01/279; Mr. Hart to Secretary Kellogg, no. 58, Sept. 6, 1928, and Mr. Kellogg to Mr. Hart, no. 35, Sept. 12, 1928, *ibid.* 875.01/280. For the text of the note of June 25, 1922, see *ante* §34.

In a telegram of November 19, 1921 the Department of State instructed the Commissioner at Vienna:

Austria

By the exchange of ratifications November 9 [8], 1921, and by Executive Proclamation November 18 [17?], 1921, diplomatic relations between the United States and Austria may be resumed.

You are instructed to request your provisional recognition as Chargé d'Affaires pending arrival letters of credence.

As soon as you have been received, you will advise the Department thereof and request the Foreign Office to recognize the diplomatic secretaries of your staff and, as Military Attaché, Lieutenant Colonel Allen L. Briggs. Also request temporary recognition pending issuance of exequaturs following consular appointments: Carol H. Foster, Consul in charge at Vienna, Robert Heingartner, Consul on detail, and Joseph Burt, Vice Consul.

When you have been recognized by the Government inform consuls and direct them to function and to take over any furniture, archives and other American Government property which may still be in the hands of Spanish Consuls in charge of American interests.

He reported on November 30 that the Austrian Government had recognized him as Chargé d'Affaires and received him as such on November 26.

> Secretary Hughes to Commissioner Frazier, Nov. 19, 1921, MS. Department of State, file 123F861/132a; Chargé Frazier to Mr. Hughes, Nov. 30, 1921, *ibid.* 123F861/134; 1921 For. Rel., vol. I, p. 279.

The Secretary of State instructed the American Commission to Negotiate Peace (on November 5, 1919) to communicate the following to Ellis Loring Dresel if it approved:

> You will proceed to Berlin and assume the title of American Commissioner. It is not contemplated that you should have at present any official relations with the German Government. Germany Spanish Embassy continues to handle the diplomatic affairs of this Government and Department merely desires to have an official representative at Berlin from whom it can receive information of interest and importance. While you will do for American citizens everything compatible with your present instructions, your chief mission consists in keeping Department and Mission at Paris fully informed of political and economic conditions in Germany, the present attitude of the German Government toward American citizens and institutions as well as toward naturalized citizens of German origin, the aspirations of foreign governments in Germany, the military, economic and financial situation, etc. It is highly important that you maintain friendly and intimate relations with the representatives of Allied Governments in Germany, bearing in mind that the rupture of diplomatic relations between the German Government and the United States still continues, and that you are not a diplomatic officer accredited to Germany. You will avoid all acts which might convey the idea that your presence or that of other American officials in Germany means a resumption of diplomatic relations.

> MS. Department of State, file 124.62/66; 1919 For. Rel., vol. II, p. 244.
> On May 12, 1920 the Department of State instructed the Commissioner that American consular officials in Germany for the present "were considered part of the Commission and their offices wherever established should be considered as branches of the Commission and not as having a Consular character". It added that the consular officers should not perform any consular work aside from passport and visa work and economic observations. In an instruction of June 18, 1920, in response to an informal inquiry from the German Foreign Office, the Department declined to receive an unofficial German representative in Washington. Commissioner Dresel to Secretary Colby, June 8, 1920, and Mr. Colby to Mr. Dresel, June 18, 1920, MS. Department of State, file 701.6211/479; 1920 For. Rel., vol. II, pp. 258–259.

The American Commissioner was instructed on November 14, 1921:

> By the exchange of ratifications November 11, 1921, and by Executive Proclamation November 14, 1921, diplomatic relations between the United States and Germany may be resumed.

You are instructed to request your provisional recognition as Chargé d'Affaires *ad interim* pending arrival of letters of credence.

As soon as you have been received, you will advise the Department thereof and request the Foreign Office to recognize the diplomatic secretaries of your staff, and [here follow a list of military attachés and lists of consular appointments].

They should also proceed to their respective posts as soon as the principal officers go there.

You should at once furnish Consul General Coffin with a copy of this telegram and have him instruct those officers now in Germany but not already at posts named to proceed immediately to such posts prepared as soon as you notify them that you have been formally received, to request temporary recognition from local authorities, pending receipt of formal recognition, and to take over offices, furniture, archives and other American Government property which may now be in hands of Spanish Consuls in charge of American interests.

He reported on November 16 that he had been recognized by the German Government as of that date.

Secretary Hughes to Commissioner Dresel, Nov. 14, 1921, MS. Department of State, file 707.1162/9b; Chargé Dresel to Mr. Hughes, Nov. 16, 1921, *ibid.* 123D811/29; 1921 For. Rel., vol. II, pp. 33–34.

Greece   Former King Constantine, who had abdicated the throne of Greece on June 1, 1917 in favor of his son Alexander, was recalled to the throne of Greece following an election held in November 1920, resulting in a defeat of the Venizelos government and a plebiscite held on December 5, 1920 showing a majority in favor of his return. The Department of State decided to delay recognition and accordingly instructed the Minister on January 7 as follows:

Department feels that if information is requested of its attitude as regards recognition of King Constantine you should state that you have no instructions.

.   .   .   .

Our final decision will be made upon the usual receipt of notice from the King of his assumption of office.

The Minister was instructed further on January 15:

The Greek Chargé d'Affaires by note dated January 12 informed the Department of State that he was in receipt of orders from his Government to the effect that King Constantine had returned to Greece on the 6th of last December and had assumed the function as King. The Greek Chargé was thereupon called to the State Department and told confidentially that while the Department, after consultation with the President, is inclined to consider favorably the recognition of King Constantine it could not accept the form in which the note was sent as a formal announcement of accession. The Greek Chargé was therefore asked to advise the Greek Government that before a reply was given by the Department of State it would be necessary that a formal announcement signed by King Constantine and addressed to the President of the United States be received.

It is the opinion of the Department that as King Constantine's accession to the throne was the result of an election which brought about the overthrow of Venizelos followed by a plebiscite which returned King Constantine a favorable majority his recognition should no longer be refused. The Department has taken no definite action however in this regard.

The reason for the form in which the announcement of the accession of King Constantine had been given, was explained at some length in a telegram of January 18 from the Minister in Greece:

> . . . Greek Government explains failure formally to announce accession Constantine due to fact that he never ceased to be King; he simply resumed throne after enforced absence. . . . I respectfully suggest that Department would do great service by drawing from Greek Government explicit acknowledgment of legitimacy of former regime by admission that King Constantine succeeds to throne made vacant by death of King Alexander. On this basis early recognition by United States after proper formalities have been complied with it seems to me would be right and proper. If on the contrary we permit theory now being followed to go unchallenged all acts of Venizelos Government likely to be invalidated as hundreds have already been. . . . Of countries represented here, only Holland and Spain have entered into full relations with King; Russian Minister sees him socially, likewise Roumanian Chargé d'Affaires.

Recognition was consequently further delayed pending the determination of the actual status of King Constantine as head of the Government of Greece. In a telegram of March 16, the American Chargé d'Affaires in Greece (at the request of the Minister of Foreign Affairs) communicated to the Department the following statement:

> The present Royal Government recognizes all obligations resulting from treaties, conventions or agreements concluded with foreign powers or private persons by the Government administering the affairs of the country during the time when the Royal authority was exercised by the late lamented son of His Majesty King Constantine.

The Chargé stated that this represented a frank declaration that the Greek Government regarded the reign of Alexander as illegal, and added that the French and British Governments were withholding recognition. The Department continued to withhold its recognition.

Minister Capps to Secretary Polk, Nov. 15 and Dec. 6, 1920, MS. Department of State, files 868.00/222, 868.00/232; 1920 For. Rel., vol. II, pp. 705–710.

The Acting Secretary of State (Davis) to Mr. Capps, Jan. 7 and 15, 1921, MS. Department of State, files 868.001C76/20, 868.001C76/21; Mr. Capps to Mr. Davis, Jan. 18, 1921, *ibid.* file 868.001C76/22; Chargé Hall to Secretary Hughes, Mar. 16, 1921, *ibid.* 868.001C76/32; 1921 For. Rel., vol. II, pp. 138–150.

A new letter of credence had been issued to the Minister in Athens upon the accession of Alexander to the throne following the abdication of his father. The Acting Secretary of State (Davis) to President Wilson, Dec. 28, 1920, MS. Department of State, file 868.001C76/49; 1920 For. Rel., vol. II, pp. 709–710.

Recognition policy

King Constantine abdicated on September 27, 1922 and was succeeded by the Crown Prince, who took the oath of office as George II. The policy of the Department of State with reference to the recognition of the government of George II was summarized as follows in a letter of October 9, 1923 to Representative Rogers:

The events which attended the revolution which ousted Constantine are a matter of record. You will recall that Constantine fled the country and that his prominent supporters and Cabinet ministers were arrested and after summary trials were executed under circumstances of revolting cruelty. The British Government, which heretofore has maintained a Chargé d'Affaires in Athens, although not recognizing Constantine, withdrew this representative, while the representatives of others of the Powers, including that of the United States, took occasion to interpret to the Greek authorities the unfortunate impression which the execution of the Greek ministers had caused on public opinion generally.

The Government which succeeded that of Constantine was frankly based on military power and has not yet legalized its positions by holding elections, although it has repeatedly indicated its intention to do so, only to postpone the election from month to month for the past eight months.

Meanwhile the negotiation of a treaty of peace between the Allied Powers, Greece and Turkey was undertaken at Lausanne and it seemed undesirable, pending the conclusion of these negotiations, for the United States to take separate action in the matter of the recognition of Greece. Although the negotiations have been concluded and peace has now been ratified by Greece and Turkey, the Greek Government has not yet held the promised elections; and, while I do not desire to indicate that the Department has adopted it as a definite policy that such election will be awaited before recognition is extended, this is an important consideration.

The Chargé d'Affaires in Greece (Caffery) to Secretary Hughes, no. 129, Sept. 27, 1922, MS. Department of State, file 868.001C76/69; the Chief of the Division of Near Eastern Affairs (Dulles) to Representative Rogers, Oct. 9, 1923, *ibid.* 868.01/175.

In a letter of January 25, 1924 to President Coolidge, Secretary Hughes recommended the immediate recognition of the Greek Government, saying in part:

The treatment of American interests in Greece by the Greek authorities has been satisfactory. While there are a number of outstanding questions between the two countries, particularly the question of the 1918 Loan Agreement with Greece and the funding of Greek indebtedness to the United States, these are questions which have been held in abeyance in the absence of formal recognition and do not afford at this time adequate ground for withholding recognition. It would be desirable to negotiate a commercial treaty with Greece but this again is a matter which would naturally follow rather than precede recognition.

.   .   .   .

The appointment of a Minister, in my opinion, should be delayed until Greece has determined the question which is now being agitated as to whether the country shall continue as a Kingdom or become a Republic. The King of Greece has recently left the country pending the decision of this question, a Regent is functioning in his place. The ultimate decision as to the form of government is one with which I feel we should in no way interfere but this does not preclude the resumption of formal relations with the Greek Government through a Chargé d'Affaires ad interim, postponing the formal accrediting of a Minister to the head of the State until Greece has herself decided—and Mr. Venizelos has proposed a plebiscite to decide the question— whether there shall be a Kingdom or a Republic.

Acting with the approval of the President, the Department of State (on January 26) instructed the Chargé d'Affaires to deliver a formal communication to the Greek Minister of Foreign Affairs on January 29, quoting the following letter from the Secretary of State accrediting him as Chargé:

I have the honor to inform you that Mr. Ray Atherton, a Secretary of Legation in the Diplomatic Service of the United States, has been ordered to assume the duties of Chargé d'Affaires ad interim of the United States at Athens. I accordingly hereby accredit Mr. Atherton in the foregoing capacity and ask that you will give credence to what he shall say on the part of the Government of the United States. My knowledge of Mr. Atherton's qualifications encourages the hope that he will conduct the affairs of the Legation at Athens in a manner gratifying to the Government of Greece.

Recognition

It said further:

This act will constitute formal recognition of the Government of Greece by the United States. As it is the desire of this Government to avoid any interference in the decision of the constitutional question at present under consideration in Greece, you will be accredited to the Minister for Foreign Affairs. The Department intends to delay the accrediting of a Minister to the head of the State pending the decision by Greece of this action. [Paraphrase.]

Secretary Hughes to Chargé Atherton, no. 8, Jan. 18, 1924, MS. Department of State, file 868.01/192; Mr. Atherton to Mr. Hughes, no. 23, Jan. 23, 1924, *ibid*. 868.01/194; Mr. Hughes to President Coolidge, Jan. 25, 1924, *ibid.* 868.01/196a; Mr. Hughes to Mr. Atherton, no. 13, Jan. 26, 1924, *ibid.* 868.01/197; 1924 For. Rel., vol. II, pp. 265–268.

The letter was delivered on Jan. 29 in accordance with these instructions. Mr. Atherton to Mr. Hughes, no. 29, Jan. 29, 1924, MS. Department of State, file 868.01/199.

On being advised by the American Legation on Apr. 16 of the receipt of a formal note from the Greek Foreign Office advising it of the action of the National Assembly on Mar. 25 in dethroning the Glucksburg dynasty and establishing a republic, the Department of State replied (Apr. 17) that it did not consider that the establishment of the new regime in Greece would necessitate any change in its instructions of Jan. 26.   Mr. Atherton to Mr. Hughes, no. 63, Apr. 16, 1924, *ibid.* 123L36/159; Mr. Hughes to Mr. Atherton, no. 46, Apr. 17, 1924, *ibid.* 868.01/218; 1924 For. Rel., vol. II, pp. 272–274.

In a telegram of December 20, 1921 the Department of State informed the Commissioner at Budapest:

Hungary

By the exchange of ratifications December 17, 1921, and by Executive Proclamation December 21 [20], 1921, diplomatic relations between the United States of America and Hungary may be resumed.

You are instructed to request your provisional recognition as Chargé d'Affaires pending arrival letters of credence as Chargé d'Affaires *pro tempore.*

As soon as you have been received, you will advise the Department thereof and request the Foreign Office to recognize the diplomatic secretaries of your staff and, as Military Attaché, Major Henry W. T. Eglin, Acting General Staff.   Also request temporary recognition, pending issuance of exequaturs, following consular appointments: Edwin C. Kemp, Consul in charge at Budapest, Digby A. Willson, Vice Consul, Walter S. Reineck, Vice Consul.

When you have been recognized by the Hungarian Government inform consuls and direct them to function and to take over any furniture, archives and other American Government property which may still be in the hands of Spanish Consuls in charge of American interests.

The Commissioner notified the Department on December 30 that he had been granted provisional recognition as Chargé d'Affaires as from December 26.

Secretary Hughes to Commissioner Grant-Smith, Dec. 20, 1921, MS. Department of State, file 123Sm61/183a; Chargé Grant-Smith to Mr. Hughes, Dec. 30, 1921, *ibid.* 123Sm61/184; 1921 For. Rel., vol. II, pp. 260–261.

The American Commissioner sent to Budapest in December 1919 had been advised that—

"no formal recognition has yet been given by the government of the United States and that   . . .   [he was] not accredited as a diplomatic representative to the Hungarian Government."   Secretary Lansing to Commissioner Grant-Smith, Dec. 10, 1919, MS. Department of State, file 123Sm61/163a; 1919 For. Rel., vol. II, pp. 410–412.

In his annual message to Congress of December 6, 1910 President
Taft said that the National Skoupchtina "having expressed its will
that the Principality of Montenegro be raised to the rank of kingdom"   Montenegro
the Prince of Montenegro had "on August 15 last assumed the title
of King of Montenegro", and that it had given him pleasure "to
accord to the new kingdom the recognition of the United States".
This recognition was accomplished through a letter sent to Nicolas,
King of Montenegro, on July 12, 1910, to which the latter replied on
August 17, 1910.

> 1910 For. Rel. xi.   President Taft to King Nicolas, July 12, 1910, MS.
> Department of State, file 873.00/8a; Minister Moses to Secretary Knox, no.
> 12, Sept. 24, 1910, *ibid.* 873.00/11.
> Following the adoption of the Constitution of the Kingdom of the Serbs,
> Croats, and Slovenes and the recognition by other governments of the
> Kingdom, in which had been incorporated the former Kingdom of Monte-
> negro, the Government of the United States on Jan. 21, 1921, informed the
> Montenegrin Consul General in charge of the Montenegrin Legation that
> "in view of the present status of Montenegro, this Government no longer
> considers it necessary to accord recognition to her diplomatic and Consular
> officers".   The diplomatic and consular officers of the United States were
> informed of this action by a circular instruction of Feb. 8, 1921.   The Act-
> ing Secretary of State (Polk) to the Montenegrin Consul General (Dix), Jan.
> 21, 1921, *ibid.* 702.7311/32a; Secretary Colby to the diplomatic and con-
> sular officers, no. 16, Feb. 8, 1921, *ibid.* 702.7311/36b; 1921 For. Rel., vol.
> II, pp. 945–949.

Following the outbreak of a revolution in Portugal in October 1910,
the Provisional President of Portugal sent to the American Secretary   Portugal
of State a telegram announcing that monarchical institutions had
been abolished, a Republic proclaimed, and a Provisional Government installed.   He stated that public order was assured by the action
of the Government and the solidarity of the citizens.   The Minister
at Lisbon inquired on October 7 whether he should transact ordinary
business with the Provisional Government by unofficial action, to
which the Department of State replied:

> . . . You will keep up such intercourse with the responsible   Provisional
> de facto authorities as may be necessary for full security of any   relations
> American interests and maintain provisional relations pending the
> obvious reestablishment of constitutional order, when you will
> receive further instructions.

In reply to a further inquiry from the Minister, the Department
explained (October 18) that the phrase "obvious reestablishment of
constitutional order" had reference to "conditions showing that the
freely expressed wish of the Portuguese people accepts and gives
national sanction to the proclaimed republic".

In a despatch of February 10, 1911 the Legation informed the De-   Request for
partment of the disappointment of the Portuguese Government over   recognition
the fact that the United States had not extended formal recognition

to the new Government and gave the following statement of the views of the Portuguese authorities:

> During the course of a conversation yesterday with the minister for foreign affairs, he brought up the subject of recognition and at length expressed his regret that the United States had not followed the example of Brazil and other Latin-American countries by tendering unqualified recognition soon after the proclamation of the Republic. He said that it had been a great surprise to the members of the Provisional Government to see the United States follow the lead of the monarchical European countries in its attitude toward the Portuguese Republic.
>
> I endeavored to explain to the minister that the action of our Government with respect to the new Republic is based on the precedents of the policy which has been followed by the United States in what concerns the recognition of provisional governments in other countries and that as soon as the Portuguese people shall determine, by means of a decisive vote of the Constituent Assembly or in any other unquestionable manner, the form and character of the future government of the country, I felt sure that the United States would be among the first to establish official relations with the government which shall be constituted in accordance with the will of the people of Portugal. As examples I mentioned the attitude of the United States with respect to the proclamation of the Republic in France and Brazil. Mr. Machado replied that he understood the attitude of the United States on this question to be based on precedent, but he thinks an exception should be made in this case in view of the undisputed control of the country by the Republicans, in accordance with the unanimous, in his opinion, wishes of the Portuguese people. He went on to say that, while the Provisional Government does not wish to beg recognition from any country, he hoped that the United States, as a Republic, would see fit to encourage the infant Republic by early recognition. I agreed to transmit his statement to you, but I gave him no encouragement and avoided a prolonged discussion of the subject. It is now rumored that the Constituent Assembly will meet in May, but nothing definite has been decided and the electoral law has not yet been decreed.

The Legation was instructed on June 6, 1911 that—

Recognition

> So soon as the Constituent Assembly, which meets on the 19th instant, shall have expressed the voice of the people and settled upon the form of government to be adopted by Portugal, you are . . . to inform the minister for foreign affairs of its official recognition by the Government of the United States of America. You will be prepared to do this if possible the same day that the Constituent Assembly takes definite and final action.

This was done on June 19.

> Provisional President Braza to Secretary Knox, Oct. 5, 1910, MS. Department of State, file 853.00/82; Minister Gage to Mr. Knox, Oct. 7, 1910, and the Acting Secretary of State (Adee) to Mr. Gage, Oct. 8, 1910, *ibid.*

853.00/89; Mr. Knox to Mr. Gage, Oct. 18, 1910, *ibid.* 853.00/103; 1910 For. Rel. 825–828.

Chargé Lorillard to Mr. Knox, no. 83, Feb. 10, 1911, MS. Department of State, file 853.00/169; Mr. Knox to Mr. Lorillard, June 6, 1911, *ibid.* 853.00/190; Mr. Lorillard to Mr. Knox, no. 160, June 20, 1911, *ibid.* 853.00/206; 1911 For. Rel. xxii, 689–692.

On December 5, 1917 a revolution broke out in Portugal culminating in the issuance of a decree by the Revolutionary Junta on December 9 dissolving the Congress of the Republic. The Dean of the Diplomatic Corps (the Brazilian Ambassador) received a note from the Junta dated December 9, announcing the assumption of power by the Junta and stating that it would use its "best efforts to maintain the relations which so happily existed between the Portuguese Republic and the friendly and allied nations, duly respecting all obligations taken towards them by the Portuguese nation". By mutual agreement this note was merely acknowledged on December 11. The Portuguese Legation in Washington, in a note of December 12, notified the Department of State of the assumption of power by the Junta and of its publication of a proclamation "guaranteeing the enjoyment of all rights, faithfully maintain[ing] the English alliance and all the international obligations assumed in the name of the nation".

Recognition of Paes government

Minister Birch to Secretary Lansing, nos. 192, 194, and 335, Dec. 10, 11, and 20, 1917, MS. Department of State, files 853.00/334, /335, /359; Minister d'Alte to Mr. Lansing, Dec. 12, 1917, *ibid.* file 853.00/340.

The American Legation, on December 15, recommended that recognition be extended to the new Government and, on December 24, telegraphed:

> All the foreign representatives here, with the exception of Cuba, have established relations with the new Portuguese Government. I desire to have the instructions of the Department concerning the attitude of the United States in this matter. The new government appears to enjoy general public support and its authority is recognized throughout the country. [Paraphrase.]

The Department of State replied on the same day:

Elections

> The Department hereby authorizes you to continue the transaction of business with the new Portuguese Government, and to advise the new Minister of Foreign Affairs orally that formal recognition will be extended to the new Government of Portugal by the Government of the United States after elections shall have been held and the government established in accordance with the constitution. [Paraphrase.]

Minister Birch to Secretary Lansing, nos. 203 and 215, Dec. 15 and 24, 1917, MS. Department of State, files 853.00/338, 853.00/345; Mr. Lansing to Mr. Birch, no. 171, Dec. 24, 1917, *ibid.* file 853.00/337.   Similar action was taken by the British and French Governments.   Mr. Birch to Mr. Lansing, no. 206, Dec. 17, 1917, *ibid.* 853.00/339.

The American Minister reported on January 24, 1918:

> The diplomatic representatives of the Allied Powers accredited at Lisbon, after numerous conferences at which the political situation was discussed fully, have decided to inform their respective governments that in their opinion, under the present conditions, it is unwise to continue further the provisional character of existing diplomatic relations with the Portuguese Government.   This step is fully justified by public opinion in Portugal.
>
> .   .   .   .
>
> It is my understanding that this procedure will satisfy Mr. Sidonio Paes as it will involve his full recognition as Chief of the State and especially of his authority to issue and to receive letters of credence.
>
> [Paraphrase.]

Having been informed by the Legation that it was the intention of the Government to hold elections but that the date was uncertain, the Department of State (on February 5) instructed it as follows:

> You may textually inform Mr. Paes that this Government, animated by its historic friendship with Portugal, would be gratified if the amicable relations already established between the United States and the Provisional Government since it came into power might continue.   This Government however cannot but feel, in conformity with its traditions, that formal recognition of Mr. Paes as President of the Republic of Portugal should be deferred until the Portuguese people may voice their choice in the coming elections.

The elections were held on April 29, resulting in the election of Paes as President, and on May 13 the Legation was instructed to join with the Allied ministers in according full recognition to Paes as President of the Republic of Portugal.   The Minister reported to the Department of State on May 16 that he and the Allied ministers had together called at the Foreign Office and that they had handed to the new Minister of Foreign Affairs individual notes according full recognition to the new Government.

Minister Birch to Secretary Lansing, no. 234, Jan. 24, 1918, and the Acting Secretary of State (Polk) to Mr. Birch, no. 183, Jan. 28, 1918, MS. Department of State, file 853.00/354; Mr. Birch to Mr. Lansing, no. 244, Jan. 30, 1918, and Mr. Polk to Mr. Birch, no. 186, Feb. 5, 1918, *ibid.* 853.00/357; Mr. Birch to Mr. Lansing, nos. 346 and 357, Apr. 29 and May 9, 1918, *ibid.* files 853.00/372, 853.00/373; the Department of State to the British Embassy, May 25, 1918, *ibid.* file 853.00/374; Mr. Birch to Mr. Lansing, no. 363, May 16, 1918, *ibid.* 853.00/375.

Changes in the presidency occurred on June 1, 1926, and on June 18, in accordance with constitutional procedure but preceded by armed disturbances. They were considered not to raise the question of recognition. Minister Dearing to Secretary Kellogg, no. 1497, June 7, 1926, *ibid.* 853.00/704; Mr. Kellogg to Mr. Dearing, no. 20, June 21, 1926, *ibid.* 853.00/702; Mr. Dearing to Mr. Kellogg, no. 36, June 22, 1926, *ibid.* 853.01/7.

The American Embassy in Madrid was officially notified in a note of April 17, 1931 from the Spanish Foreign Office of the establishment of a Provisional Government with Alcala Zamora as President, the King having turned over the Government to Zamora on April 14 and having left the country the following day. The Foreign Office expressed the hope that the Embassy would "find it appropriate to recommend" to the Government of the United States "the desirability of recognizing with the greatest urgency this new form of government as applied by the Spanish nation in the exercise of its sovereignty". The Ambassador had stated in a telegram of April 16 to the Department of State that he could not advise immediate recognition of the new regime but added that some sort of *modus vivendi* would be necessary for dealing with it unless he was to be legally accredited. He was instructed on the same day to be guided in his conduct of current business by the attitude of the representatives of France, Great Britain, Germany, and Italy, and to either—

Spain

Provisional Republican Government

> (1) Seek a conference with the Provisional President and inform him orally that although you have no instructions up to the present governing the extension of recognition to his government, you hope that there may not be any interruption in the free conduct of relations between the governments of the two countries and that consequently you are prepared to continue to deal with the Foreign Office upon an informal basis, or
> (2) Merely continue to maintain with the Foreign Office relations on matters of current business.
> [Paraphrase.]

The Ambassador replied on April 17:

> With reference to the alternative instructions you gave me . . . I considered it preferable to follow the first and accordingly communicated orally with the Provisional President this afternoon at one o'clock. . . . I was received most cordially by the President and he assented at once to my suggestion which I made as if on my own initiative, without mentioning your instructions on this point. [Paraphrase.]

Ambassador Laughlin to Secretary Stimson, nos. 18, 19, 21, and 337, Apr. 14, 15, 16, and 18, 1931, MS. Department of State, files 852.00/1815, /1817, /1818, 852.01/48; Mr. Stimson to Mr. Laughlin, no. 10, Apr. 16, 1931, *ibid.* file 852.01/17; Mr. Laughlin to Mr. Stimson, nos. 22 and 24, Apr. 16 and 17, 1931, *ibid.* files 852.00/1819, 852.01/19.

On April 19 the Department of State requested information from the Ambassador as follows:

> Is the Department correct in its understanding that the Provisional Government, with the exception of Catalonia, with whom they are in agreement regarding the means of determining eventual relationship, is by popular consent in complete control of Spain? Is it your opinion that public order is now being maintained by the Provisional Government and that it is capable of continuing to maintain such order? Have Spain's financial and other obligations been recognized by the Provisional Government? Would you recommend at this time prompt recognition, and if so, at what specific time and on what terms?
>
> It is the Department's opinion that this Government should not become involved in a race to recognize the new Government, but on the other hand, it does not desire to be conspicuous in withholding recognition after action has been taken by the other great powers. It is considered however, that the Spanish situation is primarily one of European concern and the Department is of the opinion therefore that the motives of the other powers or their action in the matter of recognition may not necessarily apply to any action that may be taken by us. The Department would like to have a full expression of your opinion.
> [Paraphrase.]

The Ambassador answered the first question in the affirmative. As to the second question, he referred to his previous telegram stating that good order was being maintained in general and that there were no active elements of disturbance, but that such elements were certainly latent in Catalonia and that recognition by the great powers would unquestionably strengthen the hand of the Government. In response to the third question he stated that in repeated public statements the new Minister of Finance had asserted that the new Government would respect the financial engagements entered into by the monarchy. As to the fourth question he recommended prompt recognition. Accordingly the Department instructed him on April 21:

Financial engagements

> As soon as you have ascertained that your British colleague has taken action, you should deliver a note to the Minister for Foreign Affairs (acknowledging his communication of April 17, quoted in your telegram No. 25, April 18, noon) and stating that "the Government of the United States of America takes pleasure in according recognition to the Provisional Government of Spain."

On the following day the Ambassador reported that his British colleague had extended recognition on behalf of Great Britain at 12:30 that day and that he had been received by the Minister of State for Foreign Affairs at 4:30 that afternoon for the delivery of the note authorized in the Department's instruction.

Ambassador Laughlin to Secretary Stimson, no. 26, Apr. 18, 1931, and Mr. Stimson to Mr. Laughlin, no. 11, Apr. 19, 1931, MS. Department of

State, file 852.01/30; Mr. Laughlin to Mr. Stimson, no. 27, Apr. 20, 1931, and Mr. Stimson to Mr. Laughlin, no. 12, Apr. 21, 1931, *ibid.* 852.01/33; Mr. Laughlin to Mr. Stimson, no. 28, Apr. 22, 1931, *ibid.* 852.01/36.

The civil conflict in Spain, which began in July 1936, having terminated with the final disappearance of the previously recognized Republican (Loyalist) Government, the Secretary of State sent the following telegram on April 1, 1939 to the Minister of Foreign Affairs of the Nationalist Government, headed by General Francisco Franco:

The Government of the United States desires to establish diplomatic relations with Spain and the President is prepared to nominate as Ambassador near the Spanish Government Mr. Alexander W. Weddell, at present Ambassador of the United States to the Argentine Republic. Upon receiving a telegram from Your Excellency that the appointment of Mr. Weddell is acceptable, the Government of the United States is prepared formally to reopen its mission in Spain and to send a Chargé d'Affaires ad interim pending the arrival of the Ambassador. At the same time there will be submitted to the President for his approval the name of the representative whom the Spanish Government may desire to send as Ambassador to Washington.

Recognition of Nationalist Government

To this the Minister of Foreign Affairs replied on the following day:

I understand that the telegram which Your Excellency sent to me yesterday signifies full recognition on the part of your republic of the national government as the sole and legitimate one of Spain. As soon as Your Excellency explicitly confirms this to me the request for a placet [*agrément*] which you make for the designation of an ambassador will be considered and I shall ask Your Excellency that until the sending of an ambassador by Spain your Government regard Mr. Cardenas, who up to now has been our unofficial agent in your country, as Chargé d'Affaires of Spain.

On April 3 the Secretary of State informed the Minister of Foreign Affairs that his understanding of the telegram of April 1 was correct, saying:

. . . I may state that the expressed desire of the Government of the United States to establish diplomatic relations, as well as its request for the *agrement* of the name of a new Ambassador, carried with it de jure recognition of Your Excellency's Government as the National Government of Spain. Pending the appointment of a Spanish Ambassador here, this Government is glad as from today to accept Mr. Cardenas as Chargé d'Affaires of Spain.

Pending the receipt of the *agrement* requested for Mr. Weddell as Ambassador of the United States, I will request Your Excellency to receive Mr. H. Freeman Matthews, at present First Secretary of the Embassy of the United States in Paris, as Chargé d'Affaires ad interim. Mr. Matthews will serve as

Chargé d'Affaires ad interim until the arrival of an Ambassador of the United States.

Mr. Matthews was received at Burgos by the Minister of Foreign Affairs on April 13. Señor de Cárdenas took possession of the Spanish Embassy in Washington on April 3, and on April 19 he informed the Department of State of his appointment as Ambassador of Spain to the United States. He was advised on April 26 that the Secretary of State would be glad to receive him upon the arrival of his letters of credence and to arrange an audience with the President for the presentation of his letters.

> Secretary Hull to General Francisco Gómez Jordana, Minister of Foreign Affairs, Apr. 1, 1939, MS. Department of State, file 852.01/573A; General Jordana to Mr. Hull, Apr. 2, 1939, and Mr. Hull to General Jordana, Apr. 3, 1939, *ibid.* 852.01/576; Chargé d'Affaires (Matthews) to Mr. Hull, no. 5, Apr. 13, 1939, *ibid.* 123M431/174; the Spanish Chargé d'Affaires (de Cárdenas) to Mr. Hull, no. 145–01, Apr. 3, 1939, *ibid.* 701.5211/613; Señor de Cárdenas to Mr. Hull, no. 145–06, Apr. 19, 1939, and Mr. Hull to Señor de Cárdenas, Apr. 26, 1939, *ibid.* 701.5211/618.

Russia

Upon the abdication of the Emperor of Russia, Nicholas II, on March 17, 1917, a Provisional Government was formed consisting of a Council of Ministers appointed by a committee of twelve named by the Duma. The Ambassador reported to the Department of State in a telegram of March 18:

Provisional Government

. . . No opposition to Provisional Government . . . Absolute quiet prevails here and throughout Russia so far as known. Rodzyanko and Milyukov both assure me that the entire army accepts the authority of Provisional Government and all appearances and advices confirm same. Plan of Provisional Government is to call a constituent assembly or convention whose members will be elected by the whole people and empowered to organize a good government. Whether that will be republic or constitutional monarchy is not decided but the conclusions of the assembly will be accepted universally and enforced by the army and navy. No concerted action in diplomatic conference; no meeting held or called. It has been customary for British, French and Italian Ambassadors to call daily together at the Foreign Office and they called upon Milyukov Friday, yesterday and to-day but have not formally recognized the Provisional Government. Milyukov tells me confidentially that Buchanan has authority from his Government for recognition but is waiting till Italian and French Ambassadors are likewise authorized. I request respectfully that you promptly give me authority to recognize Provisional Government as first recognition is desirable from every viewpoint. This revolution is the practical realization of that principle of government which we have championed and advocated, I mean government by consent of the governed.

The Ambassador was authorized in a telegraphic instruction of March 20 to call on the Minister for Foreign Affairs of the new Government "and ask for an appointment with the head of the Provisional Government to acquaint him with the desire of this Government to open relations with the new Government of Russia" and was instructed to state that the Government of the United States "recognizes the new Government of Russia, and that you, as ambassador of the United States, will be pleased to continue intercourse with Russia through the medium of the new Government".

Ambassador Francis to Secretary Lansing, Mar. 17, 1917, MS. Department of State, file 861.00/281; the Russian Ambassador (Bakhméteff) to Mr. Lansing, Mar. 18, 1917, *ibid.* 861.00/287; Mr. Francis to Mr. Lansing, Mar. 18, 1917, and Mr. Lansing to Mr. Francis, Mar. 20, 1917, *ibid.* 861.00/-284; 1918 For. Rel. (Russia), vol. I, pp. 1–12.

The Ambassador was formally received by the Council of Ministers on March 22 and announced the recognition of the Provisional Government by the United States. Mr. Francis to Mr. Lansing, Mar. 22, 1917, MS. Department of State, file 861.00/296; 1918 For. Rel. (Russia), vol. I, pp. 12–13.

The Provisional Government was overthrown by the Bolshevik *coup d'état* of November 7, 1917. The Department of State instructed the Ambassador on December 6 that the President desired that all American representatives in Russia should withhold direct communication with the Bolshevik government. On December 9 the Ambassador reported the policy he had been pursuing with reference to the matter of recognition as follows:

Bolshevik coup d'état

. . . Reference to my cables will show how carefully I have avoided every appearance that could be construed as recognition or in any way strengthening government of Lenin and Trotsky, having persistently refused appeals of military attaché to permit Bolshevik government to place in Embassy guard of soldiers obeying Soviet commands and to permit him to procure from Smolny permit for my personal automobile. As recognition of Provisional Government six days after its organization was made at psychological moment and when followed by recognition of other Governments, as it was, had effect of strengthening and establishing that Government so any apparent recognition of this government would have had like result. In such policy I will [did] not [rely on] own judgment but was in thorough accord with all Allied missions here with whom you directed close relations should be established.

Ambassador Francis to Secretary Lansing, Nov. 7, 1917, MS. Department of State, file 861.00/632; the Minister in Sweden (Morris) to Mr. Lansing, Nov. 9, 1917, *ibid.* 861.00/631; Mr. Lansing to Mr. Francis, Dec. 6, 1917, *ibid.* 861.00/796a; Mr. Francis to Mr. Lansing, Dec. 9, 1917, *ibid.* 861.00/786; Mr. Lansing to American diplomatic representatives in European countries,

Japan, China, and Siam, Dec. 15, 1917, *ibid.* 861.01/9a; 1918 For. Rel. (Russia), vol. I, pp. 224–225, 287–290, 294, 317.

American diplomatic and consular representatives were finally withdrawn from Russia on Aug. 15 and Sept. 14, 1918, respectively. Ambassador Francis to Secretary Lansing, Aug. 15, 1918, MS. Department of State, file 861.00/2734; Mr. Lansing to Ambassador Sharp, Sept. 14, 1918, *ibid.* 123 P 78/48b; Consul Poole to Mr. Lansing, Sept. 25, 1918, *ibid.* 861.00/2799; 1918 For. Rel. (Russia), vol. I, pp. 632–640, 671–673.

While withholding recognition of the government, the Department of State issued the following instructions to the Ambassador in France on July 7, 1920 concerning trade relations with Soviet Russia.

Trade at own risk

Restrictions which have heretofore stood in way of trade and communication with Soviet Russia were today removed by action of State Department. Such of these restrictions however as pertain to shipment of materials susceptible of immediate use for war purposes will for present at least be maintained. Political recognition present or future of any Russian authority exercising or claiming to exercise governmental functions is neither granted nor implied by this action. It should be emphasized moreover that individuals or corporations availing themselves of present opportunity to trade with Russia will do so on their own responsibility and at their own risk. The assistance which the United States can normally extend to its citizens who engage in trade or travel in some foreign country whose government is recognized by United States cannot be looked for in present case since there is no official or representative Russian authority with which this Government can maintain those relations usually subsisting between nations.

The Acting Secretary of State (Davis) to Ambassador Wallace, July 7, 1920, MS. Department of State, file 661.1115/96a; 1920 For. Rel., vol. III, p. 717.

In a letter of October 27, 1919 to Senator Lodge, Chairman of the Committee on Foreign Relations, Secretary Lansing said:

". . . The study which has been made of the Bolshevist movement, some of the results of which are furnished herewith, show conclusively that the purpose of the Bolsheviks is to subvert the existing principles of government and society the world over, including those countries in which democratic institutions are already established. They have built up a political machine which, by the concentration of power in the hands of a few and the ruthlessness of its methods, suggests the Asiatic despotism of the early Tsars. The results of their exercise of power, as shown by the documents presented in the accompanying memorandum, have been demoralization, civil war, and economic collapse." S. Doc. 172, 66th Cong., 2d sess., p. 3.

The United States declined an invitation to participate in the Conference convened at Genoa in 1922, pursuant to a resolution adopted by the Allied Governments in conference at Cannes, to which the Soviet Government was invited. It subsequently declined to participate in a committee of experts which the Conference proposed to set up for the purpose of conducting an inquiry into economic conditions in Russia, and said in part, in explanation of its refusal, in an instruction of May 17, 1922 to the Ambassador in Italy:

> The Genoa Conference has been so conducted as to give foremost place to question of recognition of Soviet regime and Soviet representatives have been facilitated in presenting impossible demands, as, for example, for a huge loan to Soviet regime for which there is not the slightest prospect. Further, the Soviet representatives in their memorandum of May 11th have set up barriers to political relations which might as well be recognized as such first as last. This Government has no intention of continuing such fruitless discussions or of participating in conference which merely furnishes a stage for declarations illadjusted to the objects sought.

Subsequently, upon the suggestion of the Secretary of Commerce (Hoover), the Department of State tentatively considered the possibility of sending an expert commission to Russia to study the economic situation there. The matter having been informally discussed by the American Ambassador in Germany with the representative of Russia in Berlin, the latter handed the following statement to the Ambassador (on September 16):

> The Russian Government is interested in the highest degree in every step which can bring nearer the reestablishment of commercial relations between Russia and the United States of America. It is evident that such commerical relations must be based upon equality of rights and reciprocal benefits. The Russian Government is therefore ready to begin at once preliminary official exchange of opinions as to reopening of regular relations with a duly authorized American delegation. . . . The Russian Government would eagerly welcome any measure which being based upon mutual interest and equality would allow both the United States and Russia to acquire the necessary information as to the business conditions of the two countries. . . . It is from this viewpoint that Russia cannot consider as a measure promoting the desired end the nomination of an American committee of inquiry for Russia which would put Russia in a condition of inferiority.

In view of the refusal of the Soviet Government the matter was considered to be terminated.

Secretary Hughes to the Italian Ambassador (Ricci), Mar. 8, 1922, MS. Department of State, file 550.E1/78a; 1922 For. Rel., vol. I, pp. 392–394.

Secretary Hughes to the Ambassador in Italy (Child), May 17, 1922, MS. Department of State, file 550.E1 Russia/9b; Mr. Hughes to the Secretary of Commerce (Hoover), July 15, 1922, *ibid.* 861.50Am3/25; the Ambassador in Germany (Houghton) to the Acting Secretary of State (Phillips), Sept. 16, 1922, and Mr. Phillips to Mr. Houghton, Sept. 18, 1922, *ibid.* 861.50Am3/17; 1922 For. Rel., vol. II, pp. 791–834.

In the course of the ensuing years up to the time of the recognition of the Union of Soviet Socialist Republics by the United States in 1933, a number of statements were made giving the reasons for the continued refusal to recognize the Soviet Government. In his annual message to Congress of December 6, 1923 President Coolidge said:

Union of Soviet Socialist Republics

> Our diplomatic relations, lately so largely interrupted, are now being resumed, but Russia presents notable difficulties. We have every desire to see that great people, who are our traditional friends, restored to their position among the nations of the earth. We have relieved their pitiable destitution with an enormous charity. Our Government offers no objection to the carrying on of commerce by our citizens with the people of Russia. Our Government does not propose, however, to enter into relations with another régime which refuses to recognize the sanctity of international obligations. I do not propose to barter away for the privilege of trade any of the cherished rights of humanity. I do not propose to make merchandise of any American principles. These rights and principles must go wherever the sanctions of our Government go.

International obligations

On December 16, 1923 Mr. Tchitcherin, People's Commissar for Foreign Affairs, sent the following request for recognition directly to President Coolidge by telegraph:

Tchitcherin's request

> It has been the constant endeavor of Soviet government to bring about resumption of friendly relations with United States of America based upon mutual trust. With this end in view it has repeatedly announced its readiness to enter into negotiations with American government and to remove all misunderstandings and differences between the two countries. After reading your messages to Congress, Soviet Government, sincerely anxious to establish at last firm friendship with people and government United States, informs you of its complete readiness to discuss with your government all problems mentioned in your message, these negotiations being based on principle mutual non-intervention internal affairs. Soviet government will continue wholeheartedly to adhere this principle expecting same attitude from American government. As to question of claims mentioned your message Soviet government is fully prepared to negotiate with view its satisfactory settlement on assumption that principle reciprocity recognized all round. On its part Soviet government is ready to do all in its power so far as dignity and interests of its country permit to bring about the desired end of renewal of friendship with United States of America.

Non-intervention; claims

The Consul at Reval (Tallinn) was instructed on December 18 to hand the following statement to the Soviet representative there for communication to Tchitcherin:

> With respect to the telegram to President Coolidge from Tchitcherin of December 16th, the Secretary of State today made the following statement in reply

"There would seem to be at this time no reason for negotiations. The American Government, as the President said in his message to the Congress, is not proposing to barter away its principles. If the Soviet authorities are ready to restore the confiscated property of American citizens or make effective compensation, they can do so. If the Soviet authorities are ready to repeal their decree repudiating Russia's obligations to this country and appropriately recognize them, they can do so. It requires no conference or negotiations to accomplish these results which can and should be achieved at Moscow as evidence of good faith. The American Government has not incurred liabilities to Russia or repudiated obligations. Most serious is the continued propaganda to overthrow the institutions of this country. This Government can enter into no negotiations until these efforts directed from Moscow are abandoned." *Restoration of property, etc.*

The Consul reported on December 19 that he had that day handed the statement to the Soviet representative.

1923 For. Rel., vol. I, p. vii; People's Commissar for Foreign Affairs (Tchitcherin) to President Coolidge, Dec. 16, 1923, and Secretary Hughes to Consul Quarton, Dec. 18, 1923, MS. Department of State, file 711.61/71; Mr. Quarton to Mr. Hughes, Dec. 19, 1923, *ibid.* 711.61/72; 1923 For. Rel., vol. II, pp. 787–788.

On October 10, 1933 President Roosevelt addressed the following letter to the President of the All Union Central Executive Committee of the Union of Soviet Socialist Republics:

Since the beginning of my Administration, I have contemplated the desirability of an effort to end the present abnormal relations between the hundred and twenty-five million people of the United States and the hundred and sixty million people of Russia. *Letter of President Roosevelt*

It is most regrettable that these great peoples, between whom a happy tradition of friendship existed for more than a century to their mutual advantage, should now be without a practical method of communicating directly with each other.

The difficulties that have created this anomalous situation are serious but not, in my opinion, insoluble; and difficulties between great nations can be removed only by frank, friendly conversations. If you are of similar mind, I should be glad to receive any representatives you may designate to explore with me personally all questions outstanding between our countries.

Participation in such a discussion would, of course, not commit either nation to any future course of action, but would indicate a sincere desire to reach a satisfactory solution of the problems involved. It is my hope that such conversations might result in good to the people of both our countries.

To this President Kalinin replied:

I have always considered most abnormal and regrettable a situation wherein, during the past sixteen years, two great re-

publics—the United States of America and the Union of Soviet
Socialist Republics—have lacked the usual methods of communication and have been deprived of the benefits which such communication could give.   I am glad to note that you also reached the
same conclusion.

There is no doubt that difficulties, present or arising, between
two countries, can be solved only when direct relations exist
between them; and that, on the other hand, they have no chance
for solution in the absence of such relations.   I shall take the
liberty further to express the opinion that the abnormal situation,
to which you correctly refer in your message, has an unfavorable
effect not only on the interests of the two states concerned, but
also on the general international situation, increasing the element
of disquiet, complicating the process of consolidating world
peace and encouraging forces tending to disturb that peace.

In accordance with the above, I gladly accept your proposal
to send to the United States a representative of the Soviet Government to discuss with you the questions of interest to our
countries.   The Soviet Government will be represented by Mr.
M. M. Litvinov, People's Commissar for Foreign Affairs, who
will come to Washington at a time to be mutually agreed upon.

Recognition   As a result of the negotiations conducted, in pursuance of these
letters, in Washington between Mr. Litvinov and officials of the Government of the United States, a series of notes were exchanged on
November 16, 1933 between President Roosevelt and Mr. Litvinov
relating, *inter alia*, to the right of religious worship of American citizens
in Russia, to the conclusion of a consular convention according most-
favored-nation treatment to the United States, to prosecution for
economic espionage, to the assignment of certain claims and property
rights by the Union of Soviet Socialist Republics to the United States,
and to the renunciation by the Soviet Government of all claims arising out of activities of military forces of the United States in Siberia,
subsequent to January 1, 1918.   In a note of the same date Mr.
Litvinov informed the President "that coincident with the establishment of diplomatic relations" between the Government of the United
States and that of the Union of Soviet Socialist Republics it would be
the fixed policy of the Government of the Union of Soviet Socialist
Republics:

1. To respect scrupulously the indisputable right of the
United States to order its own life within its own jurisdiction in
its own way and to refrain from interfering in any manner in the
internal affairs of the United States, its territories or possessions.

2. To refrain, and to restrain all persons in government service
and all organizations of the Government or under its direct or
indirect control, including organizations in receipt of any financial
assistance from it, from any act overt or covert liable in any way
whatsoever to injure the tranquillity, prosperity, order, or security of the whole or any part of the United States, its territories
or possessions, and, in particular, from any act tending to incite

or encourage armed intervention, or any agitation or propaganda having as an aim, the violation of the territorial integrity of the United States, its territories or possessions, or the bringing about by force of a change in the political or social order of the whole or any part of the United States, its territories or possessions.

3. Not to permit the formation or residence on its territory of any organization or group—and to prevent the activity on its territory of any organization or group, or of representatives or officials of any organization or group—which makes claim to be the Government of, or makes attempt upon the territorial integrity of, the United States, its territories or possessions; not to form, subsidize, support or permit on its territory military organizations or groups having the aim of armed struggle against the United States, its territories or possessions, and to prevent any recruiting on behalf of such organizations and groups.

4. Not to permit the formation or residence on its territory of any organization or group—and to prevent the activity on its territory of any organization or group, or of representatives or officials of any organization or group—which has as an aim the overthrow or the preparation for the overthrow of, or the bringing about by force of a change in, the political or social order of the whole or any part of the United States, its territories or possessions.

Notes were thereupon exchanged, dated November 16, 1933, stating the mutual decision of the two Governments to establish normal diplomatic relations.

President Roosevelt to the President of the All Union Central Executive Committee (Mikhail Kalinin), Oct. 10, 1933, MS. Department of State, file 711.61/287A; President Kalinin to President Roosevelt, Oct. 17, 1933, *ibid.* 711.61/287½; Secretary Hull to the Embassy in Paris, Oct. 21, 1933, *ibid.* 711.61/291A; the People's Commissar for Foreign Affairs (Litvinov), to President Roosevelt, Nov. 16, 1933, *ibid.* 711.61/343⅜; President Roosevelt to Mr. Litvinov, Nov. 16, 1933, *ibid.* 711.61/343A; Mr. Litvinov to President Roosevelt, Nov. 16, 1933, *ibid.* 711.61/343⅛.

For the exchange of notes concerning the assurances given by Mr. Litvinov on behalf of the Union of Soviet Socialist Republics, see MS. Department of State, files 711.61/343 2/8, /343⅜, /343 4/8, /343⅝, /343 6/8, /343⅞. For the printed text of this correspondence, see *Establishment of Diplomatic Relations with the Union of Soviet Socialist Republics*, Department of State Eastern European Ser. 1 (1933).

For pertinent facts regarding the establishment of the Russian Socialist Federal Soviet Republic and the Union of Soviet Socialist Republics, see *ante* §14.

AFRICA

§49

On December 3, 1930 the Chargé d'Affaires at Monrovia, Liberia, reported to the Department of State that President King had informed him that he would resign that day on account of the opposition to his reform program. (President King's reform program had resulted **Liberia** from the investigation and report of an international commission consisting of three members, one American, one British, and one Liberian, appointed early in 1930. For the text of the report, see *Report of the International Commission of Inquiry into the Existence of Slavery and Forced Labor in the Republic of Liberia* (1930), Department of State pub. 147; *International Commission of Inquiry in Liberia,* League of Nations pub. C.658.M.272.1930.VI.) The Department instructed the Chargé d'Affaires on the same day that until the receipt of further instructions he should not address by their title the new officials who might assume control.

> Chargé Reber to Secretary Stimson, no. 169, Dec. 3, 1930, and Mr. Stimson to Mr. Reber, no. 109, Dec. 3, 1930, MS. Department of State, file 882.001/54.

The Minister having reported on May 28, 1931 that Edwin Barclay had been elected to the presidency by a decisive majority, he was advised on the following day that after careful consideration the conclusion had been reached that, pending the investigation by the experts appointed by the International Committee set up by the League of Nations and an examination of their findings with particular reference to the social and humanitarian reforms so urgently needed in Liberia, it would not be desirable for him to present his credentials.

> Minister Mitchell to Secretary Stimson, no. 46, May 28, 1931, MS. Department of State, file 882.001 Barclay, Edwin/8; the Acting Secretary of State (Castle) to Mr. Mitchell, no. 41, May 29, 1931, *ibid.* 123 Mitchell, Charles E./57.
>
> In response to an inquiry from President Barclay, the Department authorized the Minister to state informally to him that, since the decision of the the Government of the United States with respect to recognition would depend to a considerable extent upon the attitude of Liberia regarding the report and recommendations of the experts appointed by the League Committee no useful purpose would be served by the suggested visit of a Liberian envoy to the United States in advance of the next meeting of the International Committee. Mr. Mitchell to Mr. Stimson, no. 79, Oct. 3, 1931, and Mr. Stimson to Mr. Mitchell, no. 52, Oct. 6, 1931, *ibid.* 882.01/27.
>
> Barclay was formally inaugurated as President on Jan. 4, 1932. Mr. Mitchell to Mr. Stimson, no. 3, Jan. 4, 1932, *ibid.* 882.001 Barclay, Edwin/10.

The International Committee, on which the United States was officially represented, continued for a period of over three years during which time it presented to Liberia two plans of reform, both of which Liberia refused to accept. On May 18, 1934 the Council of the League formally withdrew its offer of assistance.

> Commissioner Winship to Secretary Hull, no. 2, Sept. 3, 1933, MS. Department of State, file 882.01 Foreign Control/661. For the report of the American member of the International Committee setting forth in full the record of the activities of the Committee, see Chargé Reber to Mr. Hull, May 26, 1934, *ibid.* 882.01 Foreign Control/842, enclosure. For the

text of the report of Harry A. McBride, Special Assistant to the Secretary of State, dated Oct. 3, 1934, see the note from the Secretary of State to the British Ambassador, Oct. 17, 1934, *ibid.* 882.01 Foreign Control/841, enclosure.

On May 14, 1935 the Department of State inquired of the Chargé Recognition d'Affaires in Liberia whether he saw any cause for delaying recognition and stated that, if not, it was its purpose to request authority from the President to recognize the Barclay regime shortly after the Liberian Congress had withdrawn its repudiationist legislation. The Chargé d'Affaires replied that he saw no reason whatever to delay recognition after the Liberian Congress repealed the Moratorium Act and ratified the Firestone agreements, that conditions were not perfect but that they were improving, and that he felt very strongly that recognition would place the Government of the United States in a better position to assist in the formation and operation of Barclay's reform plan. Upon assurances from the Secretary of State that President Barclay and the Liberian Government were "faithfully endeavoring to carry out their plan for Liberia's rehabilitation", the President approved the proposed recognition, and, upon being advised that the Liberian legislature had taken final action on the legislation, the Department of State sent instructions for the recognition (by appropriate ceremony and the transmittal of a note) of the Government of President Barclay.

Secretary Hull to Chargé Hibbard, no. 5, May 14, 1935, MS. Department of State, file 882.01 Foreign Control/945; Mr. Hibbard to Mr. Hull, no. 14, May 17, 1935, *ibid.* 882.01 Foreign Control/948; Mr. Hull to President Roosevelt, May 28, 1935, *ibid.* 882.01/48; Mr. Hibbard to Mr. Hull, no. 17, June 6, 1935, *ibid.* 882.01 Foreign Control/951; Mr. Hull to Mr. Hibbard, no. 9, June 8, 1935, *ibid.* 882.01/48A; Mr. Hibbard to Mr. Hull, no. 20, June 14, 1935, *ibid.* 882.01/52.

On December 16, 1936 the British Chargé d'Affaires at Monrovia presented his letter of credence to the Secretary of State of Liberia. Department of State, XV *Press Releases*, weekly issue 377, pp. 529–531 (Dec. 17, 1936).

The Sultan of Morocco, Abd el Aziz, having been overthrown by Morocco Mulai Hafid, the latter, in a note of September 7, 1908 addressed to the Dean of the Diplomatic Corps, formally requested recognition by the powers signatory to the Act of Algeciras. In response to separate memoranda concerning the question of recognition left at the Department of State on September 14 by the French Embassy and the Spanish Legation, the Department of State replied on October 9:

The Government of the United States having carefully considered the observations submitted by the French memorandum, as well as by a similar memorandum from the Spanish Government received through its legation at Washington, is now prepared to announce its readiness to assent to the recognition of Mulai Hafid in general terms, without undertaking to express views as to minor points of difference concerning which the directly interested powers may not have reached an accord, but provided that substantial guaranties shall be given by Mulai Hafid of his purpose and ability to accept and discharge all conventional obligations incurred by former sovereigns of Morocco, as well as those of the Algeciras act as those growing out of treaty rights and international law, so that the interests of the United States and its citizens in Morocco shall rest on equal footing with those of other nations.

A joint note prepared upon the initiative of the French and Spanish Governments was delivered to Mulai Hafid by the Dean of the Diplomatic Corps at Tangier on November 18. (For the text of the note, see 1908 For. Rel. 648–649.) Mulai Hafid replied on November 29, 1908, accepting all the terms of the collective note with only a slight reservation as to the verification of certain debts, which was not regarded as important by the powers. The United States indicated in a telegram of December 17, 1908 to Minister Gummeré that it found the reply satisfactory, and on January 6, 1909 the Minister reported that all the powers having found the note satisfactory the Dean of the Diplomatic Corps had, on January 5, delivered a note to Mulai Hafid informing him of his recognition by the powers signatory to the Act of Algeciras.

> Memorandum from the French Embassy to the Department of State, Sept. 14, 1908, MS. Department of State, file 2151/215; the Secretary of Legation (Philip) to Secretary Root, no. 381, Sept. 15, 1908, *ibid.* 2151/223; Mr. Root to the French Ambassador, Oct. 9, 1908, *ibid.* 2151/217–218; note sent to Mulai Hafid by the powers, Nov. 18, 1908, *ibid.* 2151/234; Minister Gummeré to Mr. Root, Dec. 7, 1908, *ibid.* 2151/299–300; Mr. Root to Mr. Gummeré, Dec. 17, 1908, *ibid.* 2151/293; Mr. Gummeré to Mr. Root, Jan. 6, 1909, *ibid.* 2151/313; 1908 For. Rel. 646–655; 1909 For. Rel. 433.

NEAR EAST

§50

Afghanistan Following the revolution in 1928 resulting in the overthrow of King Amanullah, Nadir Kahn, who eventually succeeded to the throne, neither notified the Government of the United States officially of his accession, which was done in the case of certain of the European powers, nor requested American recognition through any official channel. Under the circumstances the Department considered that the recognition accorded to Afghanistan in 1921 did not extend to the new regime of Nadir Kahn.

Subsequent to the assassination of King Nadir Kahn in the latter part of 1933 and the accession to the throne of Mohammed Zahir, the

Government of the latter transmitted to the Department of State (through the Embassy in Paris in July 1934) a letter addressed by the King to President Roosevelt announcing the death of his father and his accession to the throne. The King expressed the desire of his Government "to strengthen the political and economic relations, which it had and has still now with the High Government of the United States". In recommending to the President that recognition be extended to the Afghanistan Government, the Department of State pointed out that all the great powers had recognized it and that the present regime appeared to be a stable one.

The President stated in a letter to King Mohammed Zahir (transmitted through the Embassy in Paris with an instruction of August 28, 1934):

> I cordially reciprocate the sentiment which you express and, in extending recognition to Your Majesty's Government, take this opportunity of assuring you of my hope that friendly relations will always exist between the United States and Afghanistan.

> The Chargé d'Affaires in France (Marriner) to Secretary Hull, nos. 493 and 1019, June 30 and July 3, 1934, MS. Department of State, files 890h.001 Zahir/4, 890h.001 Zahir/7; the Acting Secretary of State (Phillips) to President Roosevelt, Aug. 21, 1934, ibid. file 890h.01 Zahir/12; Mr. Phillips to the Ambassador in France (Straus), no. 549, Aug. 28, 1934, ibid. 890h.001 Zahir/13.

In a despatch of July 18, 1909 the Legation at Teheran reported to the Department of State that the city had been occupied by revolutionary forces, that the Shah had fled, and that the Crown Prince had been proclaimed Shah. The ex-Shah had taken asylum in the Russian Legation and had formally abdicated on July 17 in favor of the Crown Prince. On July 22 the Department instructed the Legation: *Persia*

> You will notify the Minister for Foreign Affairs of the readiness of the Legation to enter into full relations with the Government of the new Shah, and express the wishes of your Government for the prosperity and tranquillity of Persia under his rule.

> The Chargé d'Affaires in Persia (De Billier) to Secretary Knox, no. 205, July 18, 1909, MS. Department of State, file 5931/472; Mr. De Billier to Mr. Knox, July 22, 1909, and Mr. Knox to Mr. De Billier, July 22, 1909, ibid. 5931/462; 1909 For. Rel. 495–496.

The Minister at Teheran advised the Department of State on October 31, 1925 that the Mejliss had passed a law that day abolishing the Kajar sovereignty. On November 1 he reported the receipt of an official communication from the Minister of Foreign Affairs informing him of this action and stating that the Provisional Government of the country had been entrusted to His Highness, Pahlevi, *Recognition of Reza Shah Pahlevi* until a constituent assembly should be formed to make a permanent arrangement. The Minister was instructed on November 3:

> The Department approves your acknowledging the receipt of the circular quoted in your 78, November 1, 7 p.m. in the form suggested in your 79, November 2, 11 p.m. [strictly personal and unofficial in form]. You are further authorized, in the exercise of your discretion to carry on the affairs of the Legation with the Provisional Government, conforming as far as possible to the general procedure followed in this matter by the other diplomatic representatives in Teheran.
>
> In view of the fact that the Government of Reza Khan is described in this circular note as a Provisional Government and as the note makes reference to a permanent arrangement pursuant to action by the Constituent Assembly, it is assumed by the Department that the question of formal recognition does not arise at the present time and that the Department will have further opportunity before extending recognition to consider the legality of the new regime and its attitude toward the fulfilment of the international undertakings of the former Government. [Paraphrase.]

On November 5 he was further instructed:

> The Department authorizes you to deliver to the Persian Government a note in which you may state that the Government of the United States extends recognition to the Provisional Government inaugurated in Persia in pursuance of the recent decision by the National Assembly of Persia, pending the final decision which is to be made by the Constituent Assembly. It is desired that you add that this recognition is extended with the understanding that the new regime will scrupulously observe the international agreements between the United States and Persia. [Paraphrase.]

International agreements

Having been advised by the Legation that Pahlevi had taken the oath of office before Parliament on December 15, the Department of State authorized the Legation (in an instruction of December 16) to address the following note to the Minister of Foreign Affairs:

> My Government has taken note of the action of the Constituent Assembly of Persia in investing the Constitutional Monarchy of Persia in his Imperial Majesty, Reza Shah Pahlevi and has been advised that His Majesty has taken the oath. I now take pleasure in informing Your Excellency, under instructions from my Government, that the Government of the United States extends recognition to the Government of Persia, it being understood, as set forth in my communication of November 7, 1925 (See Department's 56, November 5, 6 p.m.) that all international treaties and agreements between the United States and Persia will be scrupulously observed.

Chargé Amory to Secretary Kellogg, nos. 77 and 78, Oct. 31 and Nov. 1, 1925, MS. Department of State, files 891.01/23, 891.01/24; Mr. Kellogg to

Mr. Amory, no. 53, Nov. 3, 1925, *ibid.* file 891.01/25; Mr. Amory to Mr. Kellogg, no. 81, Nov. 5, 1925, and Mr. Kellogg to Mr. Amory, no. 56, Nov. 5, 1925, *ibid.* 891.01/27; Mr. Amory to Mr. Kellogg, no. 88, Dec. 15, 1925, and Mr. Kellogg to Mr. Amory, no. 62, Dec. 16, 1925, *ibid.* 891.01/40.

The Department of State was notified on April 27, 1909 by the Ambassador in Constantinople (Istanbul) that Sultan Abdul Mohamid Turkey had been dethroned and that his brother Rechad had been placed on the throne and would reign under the name of Mohamid V. Similar notification was received on the same date from the Turkish Ambassador in Washington. On April 28 President Taft sent a telegram of congratulations to the new Sultan, and the Turkish Ambassador was informed of this act.

Ambassador Leishman to Secretary Knox, Apr. 27, 1909, MS. Department of State, file 10044/167; President Taft to Sultan Mohamid V, Apr. 28, 1909, *ibid.* 10044/168A; 1909 For. Rel. 581–584.

In instructing you to return to Constantinople in capacity of Commissioner, Department merely desired to have official representative stationed at Constantinople from whom it could receive Informal information of interest and importance. Inasmuch as Swedish relations, Legation continues to handle diplomatic affairs of this Govern- 1919 ment, it is not necessary that you should have at present any official relations with Turkish Government. It is highly important that you maintain friendly and intimate relations with the representatives of the Allied countries in Constantinople and cooperate with them generally. While you will do for American citizens everything compatible with present instructions your chief mission consists in keeping Department and Embassy at Paris fully informed of conditions in Turkey; political conditions in general, present attitude of Turkish Government towards Americans and American institutions and towards naturalized citizens of Ottoman origin; the relations of the several Allied representatives, the aspirations of foreign governments in Turkey, military, economic and financial situations, conditions of travel, etc. You should bear in mind that your mission is not identical with the Allied High Commissioners sent to Constantinople by the Governments at war with Turkey.

The Acting Secretary of State (Polk) to Commissioner Heck, Jan. 21, 1919, MS. Department of State, file 123H35/60a; 1919 For. Rel., vol. II, pp. 810–811.

Consul General Ravndal, who was designated on May 3, 1919 to succeed Commissioner Heck, was instructed to bear in mind that the rupture of diplomatic relations between Turkey and the United States still continued and that he was not a diplomatic officer accredited to Turkey. He was accordingly cautioned to avoid all acts which might convey the idea that his presence or that of other American officials in Turkey meant a resumption of diplomatic relations. Mr. Polk to Commissioner Ravndal, May 3, 1919, MS. Department of State, file 123R19/138; 1919 For. Rel., vol. II, p. 812.

In August 1919, Admiral Bristol, the senior United States naval officer stationed at Constantinople, was appointed High Commissioner by the

President with instructions, dated Aug. 28, 1919, to be guided by the instructions previously given to Commissioners Heck and Ravndal. Secretary Lansing to President Wilson, Aug. 5, 1919, MS. Department of State, file 123B773/1; Secretary Lansing to High Commissioner Bristol, no. 192, Aug. 28, 1918, *ibid.* 123B773/1c.

Recognition

The signing of the treaty of peace and of a treaty of extradition on August 6, 1923 at Lausanne by the representatives of the United States and the representatives of "The Government of the Grand National Assembly of Turkey" constituted recognition of that Government by the United States. The nature of the relations of the Government of the United States with Turkey subsequent to the World War, and as a result of the signing of these treaties, was described by the Department of State in a letter of July 9, 1932:

> The Government of the United States has not expressly recognized any Government in Turkey since the severance of diplomatic relations between the United States and Turkey on April 20, 1917.
>
> No recognition was accorded by the Government of the United States to any Government in Turkey during the period April 20, 1917, to August 6, 1923.

Intention to reestablish relations

> On August 6, 1923, two treaties were signed at Lausanne by duly authorized representatives of the Government of the United States and "The Government of the Grand National Assembly of Turkey". While these treaties have not been ratified by either country, this Department considers that the signing of the treaties in behalf of the United States without reservation, together with the intention of this Government at that time to reestablish relations with Turkey, constitute formal recognition by this Government of "The Government of the Grand National Assembly of Turkey" as from August 6, 1923.
>
> The Department considers that the present Government of the Republic of Turkey is a continuation of the Government of the Grand National Assembly of Turkey.

The Assistant Secretary of State (Rogers) to Messrs. Davis, Wagner, and Heater, July 9, 1932, MS. Department of State, file 311.6754 Ottoman Bank/4.

By an exchange of notes of Feb. 17, 1927 the United States and Turkey agreed to establish diplomatic and consular relations "based upon the principles of international law" and to proceed to the appointment of ambassadors as soon as possible. Mr. Grew was accordingly duly accredited as Ambassador to Turkey on May 27, 1927. High Commissioner Bristol to Secretary Kellogg, no. 2186, Feb. 27, 1927, MS. Department of State, file 711.672/580; Secretary Kellogg to Ambassador Grew, May 27, 1927, *ibid.* 123G861/300A.

For the text of the treaties with Turkey, see Senate confidential print, 68th Cong., 1st sess., Ex. D; 67 Cong. Rec., pt. 6, pp. 6250 *et seq.*

FAR EAST

§51

As a result of revolutionary disturbances in China in 1911 the China Emperor formally abdicated the throne on February 12, 1912 in favor of a republican form of government, at the same time conferring upon Yuan Shih Kai full power to organize such a government. Three days later Yuan was unanimously elected Provisional President by the Nanking assembly which had been set up by the revolutionists, to which position he had previously been elected by the Peking assembly. He was inaugurated at Peking on March 10, 1912.

> Minister Calhoun to Secretary Knox, Feb. 16, 1912, MS. Department of State, file 893.00/1073; 1912 For. Rel. 62–66.

On March 2, 1912 the Department of State communicated to the J. Res. of Minister at Peking the text of a joint resolution passed by the House Feb. 29, 1912 of Representatives on February 29 relative to the recognition of the Chinese Republic, instructing him to use due care in giving it publicity in order that this action should not be confused with recognition (for the text of the resolution, see *ante* §31).

> The Acting Secretary of State (Wilson) to Minister Calhoun, Mar. 2, 1912, MS. Department of State, file 893.00/1146a.

On May 6 the Department of State inquired of the Legation at Department's Peking how far the situation in China was in its judgment "responsive inquiry to the conditions of recognition of governments under international law" and in what respects the Provisional Government still fell short of the requirements. The Legation replied the next day that:

> The present coalition Government is nominally in possession of 20 Provinces, under military governors the extent of whose submission to the central Government is problematical. The north and south are not yet well fused, but the only organized resistance is in Mongolia, Kanush, Turkestan and Thibet. There is acquiescence but not hearty support on the part of the wealthy and educated, and the real will of the mass of the people is not known. The National Council cannot therefore be considered representative. The Government was established by the political manoeuvers of a few, not by general demand of the people. But it is the only government in sight, and recognition would strengthen its hold on the country, particularly if given by concerted action of the powers. [Paraphrase.]

Accordingly, on July 20, the Department instructed the Ambassadors to France, Germany, Great Britain, Italy, Japan, Russia, and Austria to communicate the following confidential memorandum to the Governments to which they were accredited:

> The powers are in full accord, the American Government believes, in the view that a stable central government is the first desideratum in China and that formal recognition by the powers, when granted, would go far to confirm the stability of the established government.
>
> The Provisional Government appears now to be generally in possession of the administrative machinery, to be maintaining order, and to be exercising its functions with the acquiescence of the people. The situation accordingly seems to resolve itself to the question whether there are any substantial reasons why recognition should longer be withheld.
>
> Would the Government of (insert name of country) now be disposed to consider whether the present Chinese Government may not be regarded as so far substantially conforming to the accepted standards of international law as to merit formal recognition?
> [Paraphrase.]

The replies to this inquiry were not favorable to recognition.

> The Acting Secretary of State (Wilson) to Minister Calhoun, May 6, 1912, MS. Department of State, file 893.51/873a; Minister Calhoun to Secretary Knox, May 7, 1912, *ibid.* 893.00/1304; Mr. Knox to the Ambassadors in France, Germany, Great Britain, Italy, Japan, Russia, and Austria, July 20, 1912, *ibid.* 893.00/1383b; 1912 For. Rel. 78–82.
>
> For the replies of the various governments, see *ibid.* files 893.00/1391, /1399, /1403, /1406, /1413, /1414, /1420; 1912 For. Rel. 82–86.

President's message, Dec. 3, 1912   In his message to Congress on December 3, 1912 President Taft made the following reference to the matter of the recognition of the Chinese Republic:

> The political disturbances in China in the autumn and winter of 1911–12 resulted in the abdication of the Manchu rulers on February 12, followed by the formation of a provisional republican government empowered to conduct the affairs of the nation until a permanent government might be regularly established. The natural sympathy of the American people with the assumption of republican principles by the Chinese people was appropriately expressed in a concurrent resolution of Congress on April 17, 1912. A constituent assembly, composed of representatives duly chosen by the people of China in the elections that are now being held, has been called to meet in January next to adopt a permanent constitution and organize the Government of the nascent Republic. During the formative constitutional stage and pending definitive action by the assembly, as expressive of the popular will, and the hoped-for establishment of a stable republican form of government, capable of fulfilling its international obligations, the United States is, according to precedent, maintaining full and friendly de facto relations with the provisional Government.

1912 For. Rel. xxi–xxii. See also the joint resolution introduced in the Senate by Senator Bacon on Jan. 2, 1913. S. J. Res. 146, 49 Cong. Rec., p. 914.

On Feb. 4, 1913 Secretary Knox sent to the Chairman of the Senate Committee on Foreign Relations a long memorandum entitled *Memorandum on the Recognition of the "Republican Government of China"*. For the text of the memorandum, see 1913 For. Rel. 88–92.

In a despatch of March 18, 1913 the Legation at Peking gave an extended account of conditions existing in China and stated its reasons for believing that recognition should be extended at once. The Legation concluded:

> Taking all these facts into consideration, it seems to me that even the most discouraging features of the situation in China are not of a sort to recommend delay in recognizing the new Government.
>
> There is no rival government contending with it for the possession of the country. The Manchus are not offering any resistance to it. It was established, in fact, by the cooperation of the Manchu Government, which abdicated with the object of preventing further civil strife. It has complete possession of all the provinces of China proper and of Manchuria. Outer Mongolia declared its independence before the Republic was formed. Tibet is engaged in strife with the Republic, but Tibet has always been autonomous, as indeed is true also of Mongolia. The elections just held throughout the 22 provinces, in spite of the delays and deadlocks occurring in some, show that the people who really take any interest in the political situation mean to stand by the Republic. But even if it should prove true that a dictatorship or an empire is to succeed the present Government it would be no more than has happened in the case of other republics recognized by the United States, and there is nothing in the anticipation of such an event to encourage us to withhold from this struggling Republic a sympathetic recognition by the Mother of Republics.

Chargé Williams to Secretary Bryan, no. 782, Mar. 18, 1913, MS. Department of State, file 893.00/1607; 1913 For. Rel. 96–98.

The Secretary of State on April 2, 1913 handed the following *aide-mémoire* to the representatives in Washington of countries having treaty relations with China, namely, Austria-Hungary, Belgium, Brazil, Cuba, Denmark, France, Germany, Great Britain, Italy, Japan, Mexico, Netherlands, Norway, Peru, Portugal, Russia, Spain, and Sweden:

> The President wishes me to announce to you, and through you to your Government, that it is his purpose to recognize the Government of China on the 8th of April upon the meeting of its Constituent Assembly. He wishes me to say that he very earnestly desires and invites the cooperation of your Government and its action to the same effect at the same time.

MS. Department of State, file 893.00/1596a; 1913 For. Rel. 108–109.

The Governments of Brazil, Mexico, Peru, and Cuba promptly assented to the President's proposal, announcing the issuance of instructions to their diplomatic representatives to recognize the Republic of China in cooperation with the American Minister.   1913 For. Rel. 109.

On Apr. 11 the Netherland Government informed the Department of its intention to recognize the Chinese Government "as soon as the Chinese President is definitely elected" (MS. Department of State, file 893.00/1615), and on the same day the Spanish Minister orally informed the Department that in as much as Spain had "no political interests in China, the recognition by the Spanish Government of the new Republic of China will follow the recognition of that Government by the majority of the other Powers" (*ibid.* 893.00/1663½).

The other governments to whom the *aide mémoire* was sent declined to recognize the Chinese Government at that time. *Ibid.* files 893.00/1687½ (Japan), 893.00/1667 (Great Britain), 893.00/1613 (France), 893.00/1603 (Denmark), 893.00/1606 (Austria-Hungary), 893.00/1605 (Italy); 1913 For. Rel. 109–115.

Recognition by U. S., May 2, 1913

The Department on April 6, 1913 instructed the Legation at Peking to communicate a message to the President of China as coming from the President of the United States when the National Assembly should have convened with a quorum and organized for business by the election of its officers.   The message was delivered to President Yuan on May 2, 1913.

Secretary Bryan to the Chargé d'Affaires (Williams), Apr. 6, 1913, MS. Department of State, file 893.00/1598a; Mr. Williams to Mr. Bryan, no. 841, May 6, 1913, *ibid.* 893.00/1681; 1913 For. Rel. 109–119.

Li Yuan-hung becomes President

President Hsü, who had been elected in 1918, resigned on June 2, 1922, and Li Yuan-hung temporarily assumed the duties of President. Upon the American Minister's suggestion that the question of recognition did not arise, as the change was not in the form of government but only in its head, he was instructed on June 16 to deal with "the situation as a new administration and not as a new government".

Minister Schurman to Secretary Hughes, June 2 and 12, 1922, MS. Department of State, files 893.00/4412, 893.00/4450; Mr. Schurman to Mr. Hughes, June 13, 1922, and Mr. Hughes to Mr. Schurman, June 15, 1922, 5 p.m., *ibid.* file 893.00/4465; Mr. Schurman to Mr. Hughes, June 15, 1922, and Mr. Hughes to Mr. Schurman, June 16, 1922, 8 p.m., *ibid.* 893.001L-76/3; 1922 For. Rel., vol. I, pp. 711–720.

Tuan Chi-jui recognized

On November 25, 1924 the American Legation notified the Department of State that it had received a formal note from the Minister of Foreign Affairs dated November 24, announcing the assumption of the office of Chief Executive of the Republic of China on that day by Tuan Chi-jui.   His government was designated as the Provisional Government of the Republic of China.   The Legation said that it was the unanimous opinion of the chiefs of mission that Tuan Chi-jui "was the *de facto* government", and for this reason the senior minister had been authorized to reply to the Minister of Foreign Affairs that the heads of legations would call individually on Tuan Chi-jui in a day or two, to pay to him personal respects as the head of the Provisional *de facto* Government, the senior minister to make it entirely clear that such action would in no way imply formal *de jure* recognition. The Department instructed the Legation on November 26 that the Minister should associate himself with the action thus proposed to be taken, making it entirely clear that his action was in no sense to be interpreted as implying formal recognition.

The following joint note signed by the diplomatic representatives in Peking of Great Britain, Japan, France, Italy, Belgium, Netherlands, and United States, was sent to the Chinese Foreign Office on December 9, 1924:

> The representatives at Peking of the United States of America, Belgium, Great Britain, France, Italy, Japan, and The Netherlands declare in the names of their governments that taking note of the communication addressed to them on November 24th by the Wai Chiao Pu announcing the assumption of office by the provisional chief executive and of the mandates issued by the new chief executive on the same date they will lend their full support to the provisional government in Peking under the present provisional chief executive and that they have entered into de facto relations with the same on the understanding that this provisional government has been constituted with the concurrence of the nation for the purpose of taking charge of the affairs of the Chinese Republic pending the establishment of a formal government representing all the provinces and parties in the Republic and on the understanding that it is the intention of the provisional government and of any formal government that may hereafter be established to respect and duly fulfill all treaties conventions and other engagements entered into by the former Manchu and Republican governments and all rights privileges and immunities enjoyed by foreigners in China by virtue of such international engagements which according to international usage can only be modified by mutual consent of the contracting parties. They further declare that on the above understanding their governments are willing and anxious to proceed as soon as practicable with the carrying out of the measures contemplated in the Washington treaties and resolutions.

The Portuguese representative at Peking subsequently signed the note. The Chinese Government replied on December 24 assuring the powers that it would continue to respect all treaties, conventions, and other engagements entered into by China.

The Chargé d'Affaires (Mayer) to Secretary Hughes, no. 456, Nov. 25, 1924, and Mr. Hughes to Mr. Mayer, no. 295, Nov. 26, 1924, MS. Department of State, file 893.00/5796; Mr. Mayer to Mr. Hughes, no. 472, Dec. 4, 1924, *ibid.* 893.01/144; Mr. Mayer to Mr. Hughes, no. 478, Dec. 9, 1924, and Mr. Hughes to Mr. Mayer, no. 449, Dec. 10, 1924, *ibid.* 893.01/149; the

Minister in Portugal (Dearing) to Mr. Hughes, no. 60, Dec. 16, 1924, *ibid.* 893.01/157; the Minister in China (Schurman) to Mr. Hughes, no. 501 Dec. 24, 1924, *ibid.* 893.01/162; 1924 For. Rel., vol. I, pp. 399–409.

Recognition of Nationalist Government

Tuan Chi-jui fled from Peking on April 9, 1926, and for a considerable time no government was able to maintain its authority for any substantial period. In the meantime, the Nationalist Government, with its capital at Canton, extended and consolidated its authority. By an instruction of June 23, 1928 the Minister at Peking was authorized, at an appropriate early date, to commence conversations with the Nationalist authorities for revision of the tariff provisions of the treaties between the United States and China. A treaty was signed on July 25, 1928. On August 10, 1928 the Legation at Peking was informed by the Department:

> Department considers that the signing of the treaty on July 25 with representative of the Nationalist Government constitutes technically recognition of that Government and that ratification by the Senate is not necessary to give effect to the recognition.

On September 11 the Legation was instructed further:

> In reply to inquiries you should invite attention to the fact that the Governments of the United States of America and the Republic of China, through their duly accredited representatives, on July 25 signed a formal treaty modifying certain provisions in the treaties in force between the two nations and establishing a new arrangement in substitution therefor. You may also state that the Legation has been authorized to conduct its relations with the Nationalist Government of China on a basis of full recognition.

> Minister MacMurray to Secretary Kellogg, no. 208, May 14, 1926, MS. Department of State, file 893.00/7397; Mr. Kellogg to Mr. MacMurray, nos. 12 and 202, Jan. 15, 1927 and June 23, 1928, *ibid.* files 893.01/253, 893.01/289; Mr. MacMurray to Mr. Kellogg, no. 529, July 12, 1928, *ibid.* file 893.01/302; Mr. Kellogg to Mr. MacMurray, nos. 265 and 310, Aug. 10 and Sept. 11, 1928, *ibid.* files 893.01/317, 893.01/339a. For the treaty signed July 25, 1928, see 45 Stat. 2742; 4 Treaties, etc. (Trenwith, 1938) 4020.

RECOGNITION OF BELLIGERENCY

§52

The term *belligerency* presupposes the existence of a state of war between two or more states, or actual hostilities amounting to civil war within a single state. It is in the latter sense that the term *belligerency* is here used. The existence of war between two states does not require recognition on the part of neutral states in order to entitle the contending parties to the rights and to subject them to the obligations of belligerents.

The question whether recognition of belligerency shall be extended to an insurgent force is a matter for determination by the recognizing state. There is no obligation to recognize that such a status exists; in fact there may be strong reasons why recognition should not be extended. Recognition of a state of belligerency before the conflict has assumed the proportions of civil war, as distinguished from an uprising which the recognized government may be able readily to suppress, may be regarded by the established government as premature and as a gratuitous interference by the foreign state in a matter entirely domestic in character. On the other hand situations may develop during the course of a civil conflict wherein the interests of the foreign state on land or sea are so affected as to make it imperative, as a matter of policy, to recognize the existence of a state of belligerency. *No obligation to recognize* *Premature recognition*

Although the United States has been called upon in numerous instances during the past 30 years to define its policy toward civil conflicts of varying degrees of intensity in other states, it has—with two possible exceptions—in no instance recognized a state of belligerency in such a civil conflict. These two possible exceptions, namely, the recognition in 1918 of Czechoslovakia and of Poland as co-belligerents in the World War were not, strictly speaking, acts of recognition of belligerency in civil strife but were measures taken by the United States and certain other powers in the prosecution of the war.

On September 3, 1918 the Government of the United States announced its recognition of the existence of "a state of belligerency . . . between the Czecho-Slovaks thus organized [the Czechoslovak National Council] and the German and Austro-Hungarian Empires". It also recognized "the Czecho-Slovak National Council as a *de facto* belligerent government clothed with proper authority to direct the military and political affairs of the Czechoslovaks". This action was declared to have been taken "for the purpose of prosecuting the war against the common enemy, the Empires of Germany and Austria-Hungary". *Czechoslovakia*

> Secretary Lansing to the Ambassador in Japan (Morris), Sept. 3, 1918, MS. Department of State, file 763.72/11343c; 1918 For. Rel., Supp. 1, vol. I, pp. 824–825. For further material concerning this matter, see *ante* §39.

On June 4, 1917 the President of the French Republic issued a decree providing for the creation of an autonomous Polish Army, fighting under its own national colors. Shortly thereafter a Polish National Committee was established in Paris, with the approval of the French Government, which was recognized as the Polish official organization by the Governments of France, Great Britain, Italy, and the United States. Finally, on October 6, 1918, the Polish National Committee was recognized by France as the supreme political authority of the Polish Army, and the Army was recognized as autonomous, *Poland* allied, and co-belligerent. Similar recognition was extended by Great Britain on October 15. Secretary Lansing on November 1 sent the following communication to the President of the Polish National Committee:

> This Government's position with respect to the Polish cause and the Polish people could hardly be more clearly defined than was outlined by the President in his address before the Congress of January 8, 1918. Therefore, feeling as it does a deep sympathy for the Polish people and viewing with gratification the progress of the Polish cause, this Government experiences a feeling of genuine satisfaction in being able to comply with your request by recognizing the Polish Army, under the supreme political authority of the Polish National Committee, as autonomous and co-belligerent.

> The President of the Polish National Committee (Dmowski) to Secretary Lansing, Oct. 18, 1918, MS. Department of State, file 763.72/12496; Mr. Lansing to Mr. Dmowski, Nov. 1, 1918, *ibid.* 763.72/12651a; 1918 For. Rel., Supp. 1, vol. I, pp. 878–881.

> The relevant passage in the address by President Wilson on Jan. 8, 1918, to which reference was made by Secretary Lansing, was point XIII of his peace program. It read:

> "XIII. An independent Polish state should be erected which should include the territories inhabited by indisputably Polish populations, which should be assured a free and secure access to the sea, and whose political and economic independence and territorial integrity should be guaranteed by international covenant." *Ibid.* 16.

Method

Recognition of belligerency by a state not a party to the contest is frequently announced in a formal proclamation of neutrality between the contending parties, but, as in the case of new states and new governments, such recognition is not necessarily express. It may be implied from any act indicating a clear intention to accord regular belligerent rights to the insurgents. Accordingly, in dealing with insurgent groups or entities whom it is not desired to recognize as having a belligerent status, care is usually exercised to make it clear that it is not thereby intended to extend recognition. Recognition by the parent state may likewise be either explicit or implicit, as, for example, through the proclamation of a blockade of ports held by insurgent forces. Questions have occasionally arisen whether formal acquiescence by a foreign state in such a blockade might not constitute a recognition by it of a status of belligerency between the contending forces.

> See Minister Smith to Secretary Bryan, Feb. 12, 1914, and Mr. Bryan to Mr. Smith, Feb. 13, 1914, MS. Department of State, file 838.00/834; Mr. Smith to Mr. Bryan, Feb. 17, 1914, and no. 57 of Feb. 20, 1914, *ibid.* files 838.00/847, 838.00/871; the Assistant Secretary of State (Osborne) to Mr. Smith, no. 23, Mar. 12, 1914, *ibid.* 838.00/871; 1914 For. Rel. 382–384.

If . . . the contest be between two sections of a country, a long or short period may exist between the beginning of hostilities and the prosecution of hostilities upon such a large and organized scale as to constitute war. As the established government naturally seeks to minimize the gravity of the contest, and as a voluntary concession of belligerent rights to the insurgents would be in itself a confession of their success, the parent government is not inclined to recognize the contest as war and extend to revolutionists the rights of belligerents. As, however, the mere existence of hostilities affects neutrals, and as a neutral is responsible for the propriety of his conduct, it finds itself necessarily forced to decide whether the hostilities as prosecuted are of such a nature and extent as to amount to war. Belligerency is a fact and must be recognized as any other fact. The recognition of belligerency is at one and the same time a matter of policy, but the policy depends upon the existence of the fact, and the propriety of recognition not only depends upon the mere fact but upon the influence of war upon the interests of the neutral acting in behalf of its subjects or citizens. A recognition of belligerency before actual war exists can, therefore, be considered as the recognition of a non-existent fact, and as such goes far to create the status which it professes to recognize, since premature recognition of belligerency is regarded as an unfriendly act likely to entail unpleasant controversies.

Admitting, however, actual fact as the test of belligerency, it is evident that the fact may appear in different light to different neutrals, for a neutral in the neighborhood of any insurrection is likely to be more intimately affected by war than a neutral at a distance. The industry and commerce of a neutral within the sphere of hostilities are affected more intimately than the industry and commerce of a remote nation, and a neutral within the range of hostilities might, therefore, be more inclined to recognize belligerency by reason of geographical location and commercial interests and, indeed, would be justified in so doing, whereas a nation remote from the war would not feel the same necessity and would not have the same justification. Again, war may exist in the interior of a country and its effects may not extend beyond the boundaries of the country, or war may exist either on the coast or in proximity to it in such a way as to influence shipping and commerce. In the latter case a neutral with commercial interests may find it necessary to recognize war, whereas it would be indisposed to recognize the status if the war were actually confined to the interior. If hostilities are extended to the sea and the war becomes at one and the same time a maritime contest, the neutral may find itself obliged in the interest of its commerce to take action at an earlier stage than would otherwise be the case.

.   .   .   .

. . . In any case it is for the foreign state to determine for itself whether the advantages to it and its legitimate interests will counterbalance the disadvantages which may result from recognition. [On this point the language of Hall's Int. Law, 5th ed., p. 34, is here quoted.] Decision by foreign state

.   .   .   .   .   ;   ;

**Recognition
justified**

Admitting that a state has the right to determine for itself, so far as its interests are concerned, whether hostilities amount to war and, therefore, permit a recognition of belligerency, and that the right so to do is not merely a legal right and, as such, admitted by writers of international law and, indeed, a duty incumbent upon it to protect the interests of its subjects and citizens when jeopardized or influenced by the existence of war, it is necessary for the state to determine,—and for the state alone, when recognition should be granted and each case must be determined by its special circumstance, although certain general and well recognized principles may serve as a guide. The mere declaration of independence by a section of a community is not of itself sufficient. A contest within the interior of a state not affecting foreign countries would seem not to justify recognition. But even in this case if hostilities were actually conducted on a large scale, with a government organized, capable of and actually maintaining law and order within the sphere of its operations with chances of ultimate success, it is believed that recognition in such a case would not be premature. If, however, hostilities are extended to the seaboard, involving the coast which is in possession of the insurgents and if the maritime contest is waged and in existence, it would seem both in theory and in fact that in recognizing belligerency a foreign state would be acting in its own interests if it recognized a state of war, provided that the coast was in the possession of the belligerents; that the contest was waged on a large scale; that military forces were organized and under the command of responsible forces; and that the operations were extended to the territorial waters, as in the case of a blockade. The language of Hall is clear and unmistakable, to the effect that the presumption would be in such a case in favor of the recognition of belligerency.

Tests

If it is a fact that the Nicaraguan insurgents actually possess the Atlantic seaboard and exercise authority in that quarter; if they have established a provisional government for the maintenance of law and order; if they have organized armed forces actually in the field under competent, duly commissioned or responsible officers; if they have invested a port and actually can or do prevent the ingress or egress of foreign vessels, and if they have at their disposal vessels sufficient to maintain the blockade from sea and land forces sufficient to invest the port by land, it would seem that the United States may in its discretion and for the protection of its own interests recognize the status of belligerency as created by the insurgents and as an existent fact. If the facts are such as stated, it would appear that the United States may properly recognize the belligerency of the insurgents. The principle of law would seem to be clear but its application depends upon the existence or non-existence of the facts, and the facts should be such, it would seem, as to create a presumption that the state of affairs either is likely to be permanent and result in the formation of a state, or that the status is likely to continue for such a period of time or indefinitely as to make the recognition necessary or advisable in the interests of citizens of the United States.

Opinion of the Solicitor for the Department of State, Nov. 18, 1909, MS.
Department of State, file 6369/698.

The recent political events in Mexico received attention from
this Government because of the exceedingly delicate and difficult
situation created along our southern border and the necessity
for taking measures properly to safeguard American interests.
The Government of the United States, in its desire to secure a
proper observance and enforcement of the so-called neutrality
statutes of the Federal Government, issued directions to the
appropriate officers to exercise a diligent and vigilant regard for
the requirements of such rules and laws. Although a condition
of actual armed conflict existed, there was no official recognition
of belligerency involving the technical neutrality obligations of
international law.

Annual message of President Taft, 1911 For. Rel. xi.
As to the status of the insurgent forces under General Villa in Nov. 1913
and Jan. 1914 and of the then-unrecognized Carranza regime, see *O'Neill
et al.* v. *Central Leather Company et al.*, 87 N.J.L. (1915) 552, 553, 554, 556–557,
94 Atl. 789, 790, 792; and *Compania Minera Ygnacio Rodriguez Ramos, S.A.*
v. *Bartlesville Zinc Co. et al.*, 115 Tex. (1925) 21, 24–25, 26, 27, 31, 275 S.W.
388, 389, 390, 392 (both discussed *ante*, under "Insurgent and Revolutionary
Governments", §28).

On March 3, 1929 revolutionary disturbances broke out simul- Mexico, 1929
taneously in the States of Veracruz, Sonora, and Coahuila, Mexico.
The Mexican Government immediately put on foot a vigorous military
campaign which resulted in the suppression of the insurrection in May
1929. The belligerency of the insurrectionary forces was not recognized by the Government of the United States. It recognized only
that there was an armed uprising against the regularly constituted
Government of Mexico which had adopted measures of suppression.
A number of instructions were issued concerning the attitude to be
maintained by American diplomatic and consular representatives
toward the Government and the insurrectionary forces.

While Department desires that you report facts regarding
conditions in your district regardless [of] whether such facts
redound to credit of Federals or rebels, your attention is invited
to the fact that this Government maintains diplomatic relations
with the present constituted Government of Mexico, that it has
authorized the sale of arms and munitions to that Government,
that it is permitting the exportation of arms and munitions to
Mexico in favor of that Government but does not permit rebel
forces to acquire arms and munitions in the United States and Non-
that it has not recognized belligerency of the insurrectionists. recognition
Your attitude will be guided accordingly and you will exercise
caution so that no action on your part may be construed as
recognizing the belligerency of rebel forces.

Secretary Stimson to Consul Jones (Douglas, Arizona), Apr. 3, 1929, MS.
Department of State, file 812.00 Sonora/521.

The American Consul at Ciudad Juarez advised the Department yesterday that he had been informed by the rebel authorities that American aviators were being accepted for service in the rebel army. You are instructed at your early convenience and in the exercise of your discretion . . . to point out to the Mexican Government that . . . the Government of the United States will expect that such Americans when taken prisoners will not be regarded by the Government of Mexico as guilty of treason but, on the contrary, that any American fighting in the rebel army will, if taken prisoner, be treated by the regular Government forces in accordance with the laws of war as recognized between nations, and not in accordance with domestic law when the latter differs from such laws of war. You are instructed further to say that this is not intended to involve, even by implication, a recognition of the belligerency of the rebel forces, the sole purpose and desire of the Government of the United States being to avoid a distressing and unfortunate accident or incident which might prove most embarrassing to both Governments. [Paraphrase.]

Treatment of prisoners

Secretary Stimson to Ambassador Morrow, no. 233, Apr. 4, 1929, MS. Department of State, file 812.00 Sonora/513.

. . . Inasmuch as this Government does not recognize the belligerency of the insurrectionists the question of neutrality does not arise and consequently this Government can only recognize the duly constituted authorities of Mexico with which it maintains official relations. You may so inform those parties who have expressed their wish that this Government adopt "a strictly neutral stand".

You will immediately, orally and unofficially inform those rebel leaders who have threatened or may threaten retaliatory measures against Americans and American interests in your district that the Government of the United States must insist upon the observance of the principles of international law in so far as the lives, property and interests of American citizens are concerned, and it will seek infliction of due and proper punishment upon all persons responsible for the violation of those principles.

Americans and their interests

As instructed in the Department's telegram of March 29, 4 p.m., in case any *de facto* authority in your district violates any of the foregoing principles, you will immediately report the facts thereof to the nearest American consular officer on the border with the request that he immediately notify the nearest immigration officer to the end that such *de facto* authorities may not, after maltreating American citizens or their property or interests in Mexico, find immunity for their acts in a safe refuge in the United States. You will notify the Department of all such action taken.

Your despatch No. 65, March 30, indicates that you informed Mexican Federal authorities that you "could take only a purely neutral stand" and that it was your "duty to maintain friendly relations with both factions." As already explained to you there can be no question of neutrality in the present situation and this Government does not recognize two warring factions

No question of neutrality

in Mexico, but only the regular Government which it has formally recognized and with which it is on terms of peace and amity.

Secretary Stimson to Consul Jones (Douglas, Arizona), Apr. 10, 1929, MS. Department of State, file 812.00 Sonora/638.

. . . While the United States has recognized the existence of a condition of hostilities in certain areas in Mexico, this does not imply recognition of a legal state of war, the parties to which have been treated as belligerents. The belligerency of the rebels has not been recognized nor has this Government recognized in this conflict even a semi-belligerency in the form of a recognition that the military operations in Mexico are between two rival warring factions. This Government has recognized only that there is an armed uprising against the regularly constituted Government of Mexico which has adopted measures of suppression which seem now about to be successful. The rebels, therefore, have no international legal status and it would seem that nationally they stand as illegal groups of armed men attempting to overthrow their own government, and therefore probably having the status of traitors. They are from the standpoint of legal principle, both international and national, in no better position than ordinary outlaws and bandits. Representations of the strongest character may therefore be made to them against injuries by them to American life and American property.

It is of the utmost importance that you keep these legal distinctions in mind as otherwise this Government may find itself in a position where it is not properly fulfilling its international obligations.

Secretary Stimson to Consul Damm (Nogales, Arizona), Apr. 25, 1929, MS. Department of State, file 812.00 Sonora/837.

A revolution broke out in Brazil in the early part of October 1930, Brazil, 1930 resulting in the overthrow of the existing Government on the 24th of that month. On October 15 the Secretary of State made public the following statement:

Nothing has come to the notice of the Department in the news from Brazil which changes the attitude of this Government from exercising the same friendly offices toward the Government of Brazil which we would exercise toward any government with which we are in friendly relations. Under those circumstances, the Government of Brazil has a perfect right to buy munitions in this country.

In a note of October 22, 1930 the Brazilian Ambassador requested Embargo that the Government of the United States impose an embargo on the shipment of arms and munitions to Brazil, "with the exception of such limitations and exceptions as the President might prescribe as being approved as lawful with regard to exportation of arms or munitions of war for shipment from the United States to the Federal Government of Brazil". On October 22 President Hoover issued a proclamation imposing an embargo upon the shipment of arms and munitions to Brazil, invoking as authority for such action the joint resolution of January 31, 1922. In a statement released to the press on October 23 the Secretary of State gave the following explanation of the reasons for the issuance of this proclamation:

> Some accounts in the press this morning reported that our action in placing an embargo upon the sale of arms and munitions to revolutionists in Brazil was unprecedented. While it is true that this is the first occasion where the United States has placed an embargo on the shipment of arms and munitions to a South American country, it is misleading to call it an unprecedented action, as it is our regular action under similar circumstances. We have placed embargoes on the shipment of arms and munitions on various occasions when there were conditions of domestic violence in Central America, Mexico, Cuba, and the Orient. It just happens that a situation requiring the application of this principle has not hitherto come up in South America, and there has therefore hitherto been no occasion for applying the general principle. There is nothing unprecedented in the principle which we have applied many times before. It is very important that people should not misunderstand it as a new principle. It is important for the reason that the revolutionists who may be hurt by our action in placing an embargo may assert that we are taking sides for some ulterior reason with one or the other of the combatants. Instead of that, we are acting according to general principles of international law. Those principles declare that where we are in friendly relations through diplomatic channels with a government which has been recognized as the legitimate government of a country, that government is entitled to the ordinary rights of any government to buy arms in this country; while the people who are opposing and trying to overthrow that government and are not yet recognized as belligerents are not entitled to that right. It is not a matter of choice on our part, but is a practice of mankind known as international law. We have no personal bias and are doing nothing but attempting to carry out the law of mankind.

> Department of State, *Press Releases*, weekly issues 55, and 56, pp. 250–251, 264–267 (Oct. 15 and 22, 1930).

The American Consul at São Paulo reported on August 1, 1932 that the members of the civil and military households of the Governor of the State of São Paulo had handed him a request for "the recognition of belligerency between the State of São Paulo and the dictatorship". The Consul said that he had replied verbally that he could not receive the communication officially but that he would be glad to examine it and request instructions from the Embassy. On August 2 the Department of State approved the action of the Consul and said:

São Paulo's request

> . . . Neither the extent of the hostilities which have thus far taken place nor the effects of these hostilities on the rights and

interests of the United States appear to require any definition of our relation to the two parties to the conflict. It is moreover of course evident that a declaration according belligerent rights under present conditions would be a gratuitous and unfriendly act to the Government of Brazil.

Consul Cameron to Secretary Stimson, Aug. 1, 1932, MS. Department of State, file 832.00 Revolutions/286; the Acting Secretary of State (Castle) to Mr. Cameron, Aug. 2, 1932, *ibid.* 832.00 Revolutions/295.

For a discussion of acts falling short of recognition of belligerency, see *post* §53.

For a discussion of the effect of recognition of belligerency, see *post* §55.

ACTS FALLING SHORT OF RECOGNITION

§53

The conduct of informal relations with the officials or agents of a new state or government does not in itself imply recognition. In order that recognition may be implied from any act short of explicit recognition, the act must be of such unequivocal character as to leave no doubt of the intention of the state performing or participating in it to deal with the new state or government officially as such. It frequently happens that the establishment or the maintenance of informal relations is most desirable, if not imperative, prior to the establishment of formal relations. Such necessary intercourse may be maintained in a number of ways with unrecognized states or governments. Thus unaccredited diplomatic or other agents, including commissioners, may be sent to a state, either to obtain information or to conduct informal negotiations or relations, as in the case of Albania in 1922 (see *ante* §48) and in the case of the Baltic states for two or three years prior to their recognition by the United States in 1922 (see *post*, this section). Consular officers of different countries have been stationed in "Manchukuo" without an implication of recognition (see *post*, this section). So also representatives of a state (diplomatic and consular) stationed in a foreign state at the time a change of government therein takes place may continue at their posts and conduct affairs informally with the new government without attendant recognition by their government. In the same manner agents from an unrecognized state or government may be permitted to act or continue to act, as the case may be, in another state, informally without recognition of the sending state or government (see Finland, *ante* §41).

Upon the overthrow of an existing government in a foreign state with which the United States maintains diplomatic relations, it has been the practice of the United States to carry on informal relations New states and new governments with the new government, pending recognition, both through the diplomatic representative of the foreign state in this country (when such representative is authorized by the new government to act for it) and through the American diplomatic representative in the foreign country. Most acts normally necessary to the maintenance of relations can be performed so long as there is no indication that they are intended to constitute recognition. The Acting Secretary of State (Wilson) in a letter of February 25, 1913 to the Secretary to President Taft, stated with reference to the situation in China:

> In the recognition of the changes of form of administration in foreign governments, the policy of this country for nearly a century and a half has been to apply the de facto test and be satisfied that the new authority in power exists with the acquiescence of the governed and is in a position to discharge all international obligations pertaining to the state. It has also been the policy to enter into practical relations with the temporary government of such a state, pending final organization. On February 13, 1912, the Foreign Office at Peking notified the American Legation that China had entered upon a formative period and that the Provisional United Government had decided to continue the foreign minister accredited to the United States under the temporary designation of "Provisional Diplomatic Agent". On February 14, 1912, the Chinese Minister officially informed this Government that the Emperor in abdicating had vested Yuan Shih-Kai with power to adopt and establish a Republican form of government and that pending the establishment of such a government, the diplomatic and consular officers of China abroad are and [to] continue in the discharge of their functions. Pursuant to established policy, the Chinese Minister was promptly admitted to full relations with this Department and the American Minister at Peking was permitted to continue in the exercise of his office. The two countries are therefore practically in full relations during the formative or provisional period.

MS. Department of State, file 893.00/1548a; 1913 For. Rel. 92–93.

During the course of the Portuguese revolution of 1910 the Acting Secretary of State (Adee) instructed the American Minister in Portugal on October 8:

> You will keep up such intercourse with the responsible de facto authorities as may be necessary for full security of any American interests and maintain provisional relations pending the obvious reestablishment of constitutional order, when you will receive further instructions.

MS. Department of State, file 853.00/89; 1910 For. Rel. 827.

In response to a telegram of July 13, 1923 from the Legation in Peking, the Department said in its reply of July 24:

. . . The Department is not of the opinion that the withdrawal of recognition from the Government at Peking would necessitate withdrawing from Peking the Legations, which would continue to operate there for the maintenance of de facto relations with the authorities of the Chinese Government, for the transaction of mutual business, for the supervision of their respective Consular offices, and for the exercise with respect to their national interests, of such protection as might be possible under the circumstances. [Paraphrase.]

Minister Schurman to Secretary Hughes, no. 261, July 16, 1923, and Mr. Hughes to Mr. Schurman, no. 147, July 24, 1923, MS. Department of State, file 393.1123-Lincheng/203.

In an instruction of April 20, 1923 to the Embassy in Mexico City, the Department of State expressed its agreement with the text of a statement to be made public with reference to the appointment of two commissioners by the United States and two by Mexico for the purpose of examining the questions outstanding between the two countries, with a view to reaching a mutual understanding on the reestablishment of diplomatic relations. This agreement was made, subject to the following explanatory statement:

Commissioners or agents, etc.

The Department does not desire to raise any question concerning the mere use of words, since the purpose of the present negotiations is to reach an appropriate and sound understanding for the resumption of diplomatic relations. On the other hand, the effort to reach such an understanding should not be considered as changing the existing situation in the event of a failure to reach an understanding that is mutually satisfactory. Therefore the United States requires that it be understood that in the arrangements for the meeting of the Commissioners, in the use of the words "the Governments of the United States and Mexico" in the proposed identic public statement and in the proceedings, which are intended to be of the most friendly character, on the part of the American Commissioners, the United States does not intend thereby to change its position or to give recognition. The Government of the United States intends to approach the consideration of all the pending questions in the liberal spirit of friendship but it insists on maintaining its position intact until a common understanding is reached. For this reason the appointment of Commissioners and their negotiations with Mexican Commissioners and exchange of courtesies in Mexico must not be considered as having the effect of extending recognition to the government at present functioning in Mexico. [Paraphrase.]

Secretary Hughes to the Chargé d'Affaires in Mexico (Summerlin), no. 31, Apr. 20, 1923, MS. Department of State, file 711.1211/63; 1923 For. Rel., vol. II, p. 534.

The Provisional President of Mexico, Señor de la Huerta, in June 1920 selected Señor Fernando Iglesias Calderón to come to Washington as the confidential agent of his regime. On June 22, 1920 the Department of State telegraphed to the American Consul at Nuevo Laredo that it desired

that the courtesies due to distinguished private citizens be extended to
Señor Calderón and his party.   The Acting Secretary of State (Davis) to
Consul Robertson (telegram), June 22, 1920, MS. Department of State, file
701.1211/253; 1920 For. Rel., vol. III, p. 173.

On December 7, 1921 a special trade delegation of the so-called
"Far Eastern Republic" to the United States called at the Department of State.   In the course of the conversation, the Acting Chief
of the Division of Russian Affairs pointed out to the delegation that
no delegations from countries not recognized by the United States
would be received officially by the Government of the United States
or by the Secretary of State but that the Division of Russian Affairs
of the Department of State would be pleased to discuss matters
informally with the representatives of the Far Eastern Republic.

MS. Department of State, file 861a.01/216; 1921 For. Rel., vol. II, pp.
750–751.

The Commissioner at Riga advised the Department of State in a
telegram of August 27, 1920 that he had received a note from the
Estonian authorities adverting to the appointment of a new American
consul at Reval (Tallinn) and expressing a desire to appoint an Estonian Consul to the United States who would "be charged with
representing our [that] Government in political affairs".   The Department instructed the Commissioner on September 11—

> to assure the Esthonian *de facto* authorities that this Government
> in stationing a consul at Reval was acting on the assumption that
> such a move would be agreeable and helpful to the Esthonian
> people in their effort to reestablish their commerce and industry.
> You will tactfully convey the idea that if this Consular officer
> is not welcome, he can very easily be withdrawn.   This Govern-
> ment cannot, in any event, grant an exequatur to a Consul from
> a non-recognized Government.   You will explain, in a friendly
> spirit, that embarrassment will be the only result of an attempt
> to force this particular issue at the present time.

The Department stated later that it would have no objection to the
sending to this country of an unofficial Estonian agent with a status
similar to that enjoyed by those of Lithuania and Latvia, and subsequently the Estonian Government appointed such an unofficial
representative.

Commissioner Young to Secretary Colby, Aug. 27, 1920, and Mr. Colby
to Mr. Young, Sept. 11, 1920, MS. Department of State, file 702.60i11/orig.;
Mr. Colby to Mr. Young, Sept. 23, 1920, *ibid.* 702.60i11/1; Consul Albrecht
to Mr. Colby, Oct. 6, 1920, *ibid.* 702.60i11/3; 1920 For. Rel., vol. III, pp.
659–664.

Dr. C. C. Wu, who had been sent to the United States as a representative
of the Nationalist Government of Nanking, was received informally by the
Secretary of State on May 28, 1928, having been introduced by letter by

the Chinese Minister of the non-recognized regime in Peking. MS. Department of State, file 701.9311/342.

On March 5, 1919 the Department of State instructed the Consul General at Nantes, France:

Proceed Constantinople early as practicable for purpose reestablishing Consulate General. . . . You and other consular officers are sent in a purely consular capacity without exequatur subject to permission to act being granted by the *de facto* authorities in control and with the express understanding that your resumption of duties with regard to American commerce should have no political significance or be regarded as a recognition of the rightfulness of control of such local authorities. You will confine your work strictly to consular duties.

Consular officers

The Acting Secretary of State (Polk) to Consul General Ravndal (telegram), Mar. 5, 1919, MS. Department of State, file 123R19/130a; 1919 For. Rel., vol. II, p. 811.

Prior to the change in the Government of Chile in 1924 requests had been made for exequaturs for two American Vice Consuls, but the exequaturs were received subsequent to the change and were issued by the new regime. The Embassy was informed by the Department of State that the act of formally and unconditionally accepting an exequatur issued by the regime functioning in a state might be deemed to involve recognition of that regime as the government of the country. It was accordingly instructed to inform the authorities that the Government of the United States would be willing to make use of the exequaturs issued by the existing government but upon condition that it be understood definitely that this action did not in any sense constitute recognition of the new Chilean Government.

Exequaturs

The Embassy in Santiago to Secretary Hughes, no. 82, Oct. 27, 1924, MS· Department of State, file 123M226/16; the Acting Secretary of State (Grew) to the Embassy in Santiago, no. 58, Oct. 31, 1924, *ibid.* 122.352/11a. For the text of the instruction of Oct. 31, 1924, see *ante* §32.

A somewhat similar question arose when the Chilean Embassy in Washington inquired whether the Department of State would be willing to receive the commissions of certain Chilean consular officers in the United States signed by President Alessandri and countersigned by the Minister of Foreign Affairs, before the regime then functioning in Chile had overthrown the Alessandri Government. The conclusion was reached that the Department could not properly grant exequaturs upon the basis of consular commissions granted by the Alessandri regime which had ceased to exist and that if it should grant exequaturs to Chilean consuls upon commissions presented by the existing regime, it would thereby recognize it as the *de jure* government of Chile. The Embassy was accordingly informally notified that the Department would not be able to receive the commissions of the Chilean consular officers in question or to grant them exequaturs but that if the Embassy should request that these officers be permitted to perform their functions in the United States without formal exequaturs, the Department would be disposed to grant it.

> Memorandum of the Solicitor's Office, Nov. 4, 1924, and memorandum by the Division of Latin American Affairs, Nov. 5, 1924, MS. Department of State, file 702.2511/161.

The Legation at Quito informed the Department of State on July 21, 1925 that the Ecuadoran Consul General at New York had resigned and that it was the desire of the existing regime (which the United States had not recognized) to appoint his successor and perhaps other consular officers in the United States without delay, and stated that it had been requested to ascertain whether the Government of the United States would grant exequaturs to new Ecuadoran consular officers or what measures it was willing to take to enable such officers to carry out their functions. The Department replied on July 28:

> Although it is not possible for the Department to issue exequaturs to consular officers possessing commissions from a regime which has not been recognized, upon the request of the Ecuadoran Legation it would be disposed to permit consular officers appointed by the Government at present functioning in Ecuador to perform their duties provisionally without exequaturs. [Paraphrase.]

> Minister de Lambert to Secretary Kellogg, no. 33, July 21, 1925, MS. Department of State, file 822.00/596; Mr. Kellogg to Mr. de Lambert, no. 25, July 28, 1925, *ibid.* 702.2211/57.

Continuation of functions

Department has advised Secretary of Treasury and Governor of New York that it is informed that Muñoz will perform the functions of the Consulate General of Guatemala in New York, and that it considers it desirable as a practical matter that agents of this Government should raise no question as to lack of formal recognition of Muñoz and to deal with him in the transaction of business as with his predecessor. You may informally advise authorities to this effect, making it clear that such action does not constitute recognition but is taken simply to avoid inconvenience and loss to commercial interests.

> Secretary Hughes to the Chargé d'Affaires in Guatemala (Curtis) Jan. 28, 1922, MS. Department of State, file 702.1411/80a; 1922 For. Rel., vol. II, pp. 458–459.

Transfer of consuls

A question having arisen during the deliberations of the Advisory Committee of the League of Nations concerning the status of consuls in "Manchukuo" (unrecognized), the Department of State, in response to a request for instructions from the American Minister to Switzerland, said:

Upon the assignment of consular officers of the United States to posts in China and upon the transfer of such officers from post to post in that State, the usual procedure is for the Government of the United States to notify the Government of China through the medium of the Legation of the United States in Peiping. In pursuance of long established practice the Government of the United States does not make a request for exequaturs for consuls of the United States in China. It is understood by the Department that a similar practice is followed by other powers enjoying extraterritorial jurisdiction in China. An American Vice Consul at Canton was transferred in February, 1933 to Mukden and an American Vice Consul at Tsinan was transferred to Harbin.

According to the Department's information the customary procedure indicated above was adopted.

[Paraphrase.]

The Minister in Switzerland (Wilson) to Secretary Hull, no. 177, May 10, 1933, and Mr. Hull to Mr. Wilson, no. 101, May 12, 1933, MS. Department of State, file 793.94 Advisory Committee/41; Mr. Wilson to Mr. Hull, no. 181, May 13, 1933, and Mr. Hull to Mr. Wilson, no. 103, May 18, 1933, *ibid.* 793.94 Advisory Committee/42.

"Manchukuo".—In a telegram of Mar. 2, 1932 the Legation at Peiping advised the Department of State of the official announcement on Mar. 1 of the establishment of the "new State of Manchukuo". The Department instructed the Legation on Mar. 3 that if any notification were received with regard to the establishment of the new regime in Manchuria, it should inform the Department but should take no additional action in the absence of further instructions.

The Minister of Foreign Affairs of the newly formed regime informed the Department in a telegram of March 12 of the establishment of the "State" of "Manchukuo" and said that its diplomatic intercourse would conform to several principles, including:

"First, That Government shall conduct affairs of State according primary principle of faith and confidence and spirit of harmony and friendship and pledges maintain and promote international peace.

"Second. That Government shall respect international justice in accordance with international laws and conventions.

"Third. That Government shall succeed those liable obligations due Republic of China by virtue of treaty stipulations with foreign countries in light of international laws and conventions and that these obligations shall be faithfully discharged."

The Minister of Foreign Affairs stated that it was earnestly desired that the Government of the United States "will fully understand purport of establishment of State Manchuria hereinbefore stated and formal diplomatic relations be established between your Government and State of Manchuria". This telegram was filed without acknowledgment.

Pu Yi was installed as Chief Executive or "Regent" of the new regime in Manchuria on Mar. 9, 1932.

Minister Johnson to Secretary Stimson, no. 294, Mar. 2, 1932, and Mr. Stimson to Mr. Johnson, no. 76, Mar. 3, 1932, MS. Department of State, file 893.01 Manchuria/17; the Minister of Foreign Affairs of "Manchukuo", Hsieh Chieh Shih, to Mr. Stimson, Mar. 12, 1932, *ibid.* 893.01 Manchuria/38; Consul General Myers to Mr. Stimson, Mar. 17, 1932, *ibid.* 893.01 Manchuria/111. For correspondence concerning events preceding establishment of "Manchukuo", see *Conditions in Manchuria, Message from the President of the United States Transmitting in Response to Senate Resolution No. 87 a Report by the Secretary of State Relative to Conditions in Manchuria*, S. Doc. 55, 72d Cong., 1st sess.

The policy of the United States with reference to the recognition of any change that might be brought about impairing the treaty rights of the United States in connection with the question of the sovereignty, the independence, or the territorial and administrative integrity of the Republic of China, had been previously set forth in the following identic note addressed to the Chinese and Japanese Governments on Jan. 7, 1932:

"With the recent military operations about Chinchow, the last remaining administrative authority of the Government of the Chinese Republic in South Manchuria, as it existed prior to September 18, 1931, has been destroyed. The American Government continues confident that the work of the neutral commission recently authorized by the Council of the League of Nations will facilitate an ultimate solution of the difficulties now existing between China and Japan. But in view of the present situation and of its own rights and obligations therein, the American Government deems it to be its duty to notify both the Imperial Japanese Government and the Government of the Chinese Republic that it can not admit the legality of any situation *de facto* nor does it intend to recognize any treaty or agreement entered into between those Governments, or agents thereof, which may impair the treaty rights of the United States or its citizens in China, including those which relate to the sovereignty, the independence, or the territorial and administrative integrity of the Republic of China, or to the international policy relative to China, commonly known as the open-door policy; and that it does not intend to recognize any situation, treaty, or agreement which may be brought about by means contrary to the covenants and obligations of the Pact of Paris of August 27, 1928, to which treaty both China and Japan, as well as the United States, are parties." Department of State, *Press Releases*, weekly issue 119, pp. 41–42 (Jan. 7, 1932).

The policy of the Government of the United States was further set forth in a letter of Feb. 23, 1932 from Secretary Stimson to Senator Borah, Chairman of the Senate Committee on Foreign Relations, reading in part as follows:

". . . We see no reason for abandoning the enlightened principles which are embodied in these treaties [the nine-power treaty and the Kellogg-Briand pact]. We believe that this situation would have been avoided had these covenants been faithfully observed, and no evidence has come to us to indicate that a due compliance with them would have interfered with the adequate protection of the legitimate rights in China of the signatories of those treaties and their nationals.

"On January 7th last, upon the instruction of the President, this Government formally notified Japan and China that it would not recognize any situation, treaty, or agreement entered into by those Governments in violation of the covenants of these treaties, which affected the rights of our Government or its citizens in China. If a similar decision should be reached and a similar position taken by the other governments of the world, a caveat will be placed upon such action which, we believe, will effectively bar the legality hereafter of any title or right sought to be obtained by pressure or treaty violation, and which, as has been shown by history in the past, will eventually lead to the restoration to China of rights and titles of which she may have been deprived."

Ibid., weekly issue 126, p. 205 (Feb. 24, 1932).

In its resolution of Mar. 11, 1932 the Assembly of the League of Nations adopted a principle of non-recognition similar to that thus announced by the United States. The Assembly declared that it was "incumbent upon the Members of the League of Nations not to recognise any situation, treaty or agreement which may be brought about by means contrary to the Covenant of the League of Nations or to the Pact of Paris". League of Nations, *Official Journal*, Spec. Supp. 101 (1932), pp. 87, 88; Department of State, *Press Releases*, weekly issue 128, pp. 256–257 (Mar. 11, 1932).

Japan recognized "Manchukuo" through a protocol signed on Sept. 15, 1932. Ambassador Grew to Secretary Stimson, no. 232, Sept. 15, 1932, MS. Department of State, file 893.01 Manchuria/467.

The United States accepted membership on the Commission of Enquiry—the so-called "Lytton Commission"—selected by the Council of the League of Nations on Jan. 14, 1932, pursuant to a resolution of the Council dated Dec. 10, 1931, which stated that the purpose of the Commission was "to study on the spot and to report to the Council on any circumstance which, affecting international relations, threatens to disturb peace between China and Japan, or the good understanding between them upon which peace depends". For the report of the Lytton Commission, signed at Peiping on Sept. 4, 1932, see League of Nations pub. C. 663.M.320.1932.VII; *Manchuria, Report of the Commission of Enquiry Appointed by the League of Nations* (1932), Department of State pub. 378.

The Assembly of the League of Nations adopted a report with regard to the Sino-Japanese dispute on Feb. 24, 1933, containing the following declarations with reference to the matter of recognition:

"In view of the special circumstances of the case, the recommendations made do not provide for a mere return to the *status quo* existing before September, 1931. They likewise exclude the maintenance and recognition of the existing regime in Manchuria, such maintenance and recognition being incompatible with the fundamental principles of existing international obligations and with the good understanding between the two countries on which peace in the Far East depends.

"It follows that, in adopting the present report, the Members of the League intend to abstain, particularly as regards the existing regime in Manchuria, from any act which might prejudice or delay the carrying out of the recommendations of the said report. They will continue not to recognise this regime either *de jure* or *de facto*. They intend to abstain from taking any isolated action with regard to the situation in Manchuria and to continue to concert their action among themselves as well as with the interested States not members of the League."

League of Nations, Information Section, *Assembly Report on the Sino-Japanese Dispute* 22.

Acting under authority of the resolution of Feb. 24, 1933 of the Assembly, the Advisory Committee appointed to follow the situation in Manchuria invited the United States, on Feb. 25, 1933, "to cooperate" in the work of the Committee, the purpose of which was "to aid the members of the League in concerting their action and their attitude among themselves and with the non-member states". On Mar. 11, 1933 the Government of the United States, in accepting the invitation, specified that it would cooperate in such a manner as might "be found appropriate and feasible" and that it would exercise "independence of judgment with regard to proposals" which might be made or action which might be recommended by the Advisory Committee. The American representative on the Advisory Committee was instructed to participate in the deliberations of the Committee without voting therein. League of Nations, *Official Journal*, Spec. Supp. 112 (1933), pp. 24, 99.

A circular note drawn up by the Advisory Committee of the League of Nations on June 7, 1933, with reference to the matter of non-recognition of the existing regime in Manchuria, was communicated by the Secretary General to the members of the League of Nations on June 14 and to the United States on June 12, 1933. The note stated that the Committee had so far investigated the following subjects—

". . . question of the participation of the present Government of Manchuria in international Conventions; postal services and stamps; question of the international non-recognition of the currency of 'Manchukuo'; problems that may be raised by the acceptance by foreigners of concessions or appointments in Manchuria; question of passports; position of consuls; application of the import and export certificate system under the Geneva Opium Convention (1925) and the Limitation Convention (1931)."

The Committee recommended the action which should be taken by the interested governments with regard to these matters. With reference to the first point the Committee said that it was clear that, in deciding to continue not to recognize either *de jure* or *de facto* the existing regime in Manchuria, the members of the League of Nations had in view that, should "Manchukuo" manifest its intention of acceding to certain general international conventions, they would take all steps in their power to prevent such accession. With regard to "Closed Conventions", under which the parties have to be consulted as to the admission of new members, the Committee stated that the members of the League should act in conformity with the Assembly's recommendation by refusing to agree to the admission of "Manchukuo".

With regard to "Open Conventions", that is, conventions providing that states might accede by unilateral act, the Advisory Committee proposed that the states with which acts of accession were deposited should previously consult the contracting parties to the convention in question, should the "Manchukuo Government" express a desire to accede thereto. The members of the League parties to such a convention would then have an opportunity, in conformity with the Assembly's recommendation, to oppose the adherence of "Manchukuo" to the convention. As to conventions concluded under the auspices of the League of Nations, it was stated that the Secretary General could not receive any accession from "Manchukuo". With regard to postal services, the Committee stated that the Chinese Government had announced on July 24, 1932 that, in virtue of article 27 of the universal postal convention, it had requested the Universal Postal Union to notify all member states as follows:

"1. That all postal service in Manchuria has been temporarily suspended;
"2. That all mails destined for Europe and America will henceforth be forwarded respectively via the Suez Canal and the Pacific Ocean. The Chinese Government requests that all post offices of the Member States will do the same with their mails destined for China;

"3. That all stamps issued by the puppet government will be invalid. All mail matter or parcels bearing these illegal stamps will be charged postage due."

The Committee said that, apart from this communication, it was of the opinion that it would suffice to remind the members of the League that "Manchukuo" was not a member of the Universal Postal Union.

With reference to the currency question, the Committee said that it had concluded that, since domestic currency was created by domestic law and was actually utilized in the same way as any other object of value bought or sold in the international market, it considered it inexpedient to propose that governments should pass legislation prohibiting transactions in "Manchukuo" currency. However, it called the attention of the interested countries having an official foreign exchange market to the desirability of taking any available useful measures in order not to admit official quotations in "Manchukuo" currency.

With regard to the matter of concessions, the Committee stated that it considered that it rested with each member of the League to decide for itself whether it was desirable to call the attention of its nationals to the special risks attendant upon the acceptance of concessions or appointments in Manchuria.

As to passports, the Committee stated that it did not consider that a government which did not recognize the existing regime in "Manchukuo", either *de jure* or *de facto*, could regard as a passport the document issued by authorities dependent on the "Manchukuo Government", and could not, therefore, allow any of its agents to visa such a document. It added, however, that an identity document or a *laissez-passer* from the consul of the country which an inhabitant of "Manchukuo" wished to visit, might be accepted. It stated that these considerations applied with even greater force to diplomatic passports or diplomatic visas.

The Committee said that it considered that interested states could, without infringing the report adopted by the Assembly, make provision, if necessary, for replacing their consuls in Manchuria. It added:

". . . The despatch of consuls under the circumstances does not imply recognition of 'Manchukuo', as those agents are appointed for the purpose of keeping their Governments informed and protecting their nationals."

With reference to the Geneva opium convention of 1925, chapter V, the Committee recommended to the members of the League, and to interested states non-members, that applications for the export to "Manchukuo" territory of opium or other dangerous drugs should not be granted unless the applicant produced an import certificate in accordance with the convention of such a nature as to satisfy the government to which application was made that the goods in question were not to be imported into "Manchukuo" territory for a purpose contrary to the convention. It added that a copy of the export authorization should accompany the consignment, but governments should refrain from forwarding a second copy of the export authorization to "Manchukuo", since such action might be interpreted as a *de facto* recognition of "Manchukuo".

Sir Eric Drummond, Secretary General of the League of Nations, to Secretary Hull, June 12, 1933, MS. Department of State, file 793.94 Advisory Committee/46. For the text of the circular of June 7, 1933, see also League of Nations, *Official Journal*, Spec. Supp. 113 (1933) pp. 10–13.

The practice followed by the United States with regard to these recommendations was set forth in the following statement published by the League of Nations on Nov. 8, 1933:

"The United States Minister, Mr. Hugh Wilson, advised the Secretary-General that the views of *the American Government* in regard to the principle of non-recognition remained unchanged, that the American Government concurred, except in a few particulars, in the conclusions arrived at by the Advisory Committee, and that the procedure followed by the American Government was in substance in accordance, except in a few particulars, with the procedure recommended by the Advisory Committee." "Measures Consequent upon the Non-Recognition of Manchukuo", note by the Secretary General of the League, Nov. 8, 1933, League of Nations, *Official Journal* (1934) 17–18.

The Minister of Foreign Affairs of the regime in "Manchukuo" informed the Department of State in a telegram of Mar. 1, 1934 that "His Excellency Mr. Pu Yi, Chief Executive" had on that date acceded to the throne as "Emperor of Manchoutikou, Manchou Empire". He stated that "this Government earnestly desires relations between Your Excellency's nation and this nation to develop most favorably in the future". The telegram was filed without acknowledgment. The Minister of Foreign Affairs, Hsieh Chieh Shih, to Secretary Hull, Mar. 1, 1934, MS. Department of State, file 893.01 Manchuria/1017. On Jan. 18, 1938 the Department informed an inquirer that Japan, El Salvador, and Italy were the only states that had extended recognition to "Manchukuo". The Chief of the Division of Far Eastern Affairs (Hamilton) to Miss Trechtenberg, Jan. 18, 1938, *ibid.* 893.01 Manchuria/1491. Germany announced its intention to recognize "Manchukuo" on Feb. 20, 1938, and a treaty between Germany and "Manchukuo" was signed at Berlin on May 12, 1938. Hungary extended recognition on Jan. 10, 1939. 33 A.J.I.L. (1939) 366.

Visaing of travel documents

On April 4, 1912 the Minister at Peking informed the Department of State that he had been requested by the Minister of Foreign Affairs of the Provisional Government of the Republic of China to instruct certain consuls to visa section-6 certificates (travel documents for teachers, students, merchants, and certain others) issued by local provisional governments. He inquired whether compliance with this request would involve recognition of the Provisional Government and was instructed on April 5, 1912 that:

Compliance with the request of Chinese Foreign Minister referred to in your April 4 does not involve formal recognition; it would be in harmony with our *de facto* relations with the present administration. You may instruct consuls to comply with this understanding. [Paraphrase.]

Minister Calhoun to Secretary Knox, Apr. 4, 1912, and the Acting Secretary of State (Wilson) to Mr. Calhoun, Apr. 5, 1912, MS. Department of State, file 151.096/28; 1912 For. Rel. 76–77.

"NOTE 12. Travel document issued by unrecognized government. When the travel document presented by an applicant is one issued by a government not recognized by the United States, the applicant will execute his application on Form 257, in duplicate. A signed photograph will be affixed to each copy of the form with mucilage or glue and impressed with the legend machine. Offices not having a legend machine will use the impression seal. The passport-visa stamp will be placed on the duplicate form to be given to the applicant. In no case should the visaed form be attached to the travel document. (See note 194.)

"NOTE 194. Passports issued by governments not recognized by the United States. An alien may present a passport issued by a government not recognized by the United States. However, no notations or stamps of any sort will be placed on the passport nor will the seal of the consulate be placed thereon, in the absence of special instructions. In the case of an applicant holding such a passport, who is applying for a passport visa, the procedure indicated in note 12 will be followed."

Supplement A of the Consular Regulations, Notes to section 361: Admission of aliens into the United States (revised to Jan. 1, 1936).

The rule contained in note 12 was originally embodied in paragraph 31 of General Instruction Consular No. 926 of June 12, 1924 (Diplomatic Serial No. 273), which comprised regulations governing the entry of aliens into the United States.

The Solicitor's Office of the Department of State held in an opinion of May 21, 1931 that the visaing of passports issued by the Peruvian Junta Government, headed by David Samanez Ocampo, would not constitute recognition. MS. Department of State, file 823.01/84.

In an instruction of Dec. 30, 1932 to the Chargé d'Affaires at London, the Department of State said:

"Since official recognition has not been extended by the United States to the Government of Afghanistan, it would not be proper to issue Shah Mahmood Khan a diplomatic visa or a non-immigrant visa under Section 3(1) of the Immigration Act of 1924, as these classifications indicate the recipient's official position. He may, however, be courteously referred to the Consulate General for consideration of an application for a visa under Section 3(2) of the Act of 1924, as a temporary visitor. If a visa under this category is issued at the Consulate General, it should not be placed upon the Minister's Afghan passport but upon a Form 257 Consular, in conformity with the procedure set forth in Note 18 [note 12 in the regulations as revised to Jan. 1, 1936], Section 361, Consular Regulations.

"Although, as indicated, it would not be proper to issue a visa in this case under a classification recognizing an official status of the recipient, there would appear to be no objection to considering that he comes within the provisions of Section 2 of the Act of June 4, 1920, . . . which exempts an official of a foreign government from the payment of non-immigrant passport application and visa fees."

The Assistant Secretary of State (Carr) to the Chargé d'Affaires (Atherton), no. 338, Dec. 30, 1932, MS. Department of State, file 033.90H11 Mahmood Kahn, Shah/2.

In 1933 the Secretary of State authorized the Embassy in Paris to:

Issue diplomatic visas to Litvinov and members of his party placing visas on Soviet passports without requiring personal appearance of applicants. . . . the Government of the United States does not consider that the issue of diplomatic visas in

Diplomatic visa

these cases constitutes a precedent nor does it regard such acts as constituting recognition of the existing regime in Russia. [Paraphrase.]

> Secretary Hull to the Chargé d'Affaires (Marriner), no. 312, Oct. 24, 1933, MS. Department of State, file 711.61/292.

Authentication of signatures

When the question arose whether the Consul at Chihuahua should recognize the signature of the Governor of the State of Chihuahua on a legal document, he was instructed that, assuming the Governor to be an appointee of the de la Huerta regime then in control at Mexico City, the Department must decline to authorize him to recognize the Governor's official signature.

> Secretary Colby to Consul Stewart, June 19, 1920, MS. Department of State, file 812.00/24217; 1920 For. Rel., vol. III, p. 173.

In response to a request of September 28, 1924 from the Consul General at Valparaiso asking whether he was authorized to legalize documents issued by officials appointed by the military government in Chile and to authenticate their signatures (although the new government had not been recognized by the United States), the Department of State replied that such legalization and authentication might be performed "indicating that the officials in question are the *de facto* authorities now functioning in Chile".

> Consul General Deichman to Secretary Hughes, Sept. 28, 1924, and Mr. Hughes to Mr. Deichman, Oct. 3, 1924, MS. Department of State, file 193.55/383. A similar instruction was sent to the Embassy in Chile on Oct. 9, with the additional statement that "Such legalization with such indication does not constitute recognition of a new government." Secretary Hughes to Ambassador Collier, no. 52, Oct. 9, 1924, *ibid.* 825.01/13; 1924 For. Rel., vol. I, p. 360.

In a letter of December 7, 1925 the Director of the Veterans Bureau inquired whether acceptance by the Veterans Bureau of documents certified by Soviet notaries whose official character had in turn been attested by representatives of friendly governments, would entail recognition by the United States of the Soviet Government and be objectionable to the Department of State. In an opinion of December 14, 1925 the Solicitor's Office of the Department concluded that—

> the authority to accord recognition on the part of the Government of the United States to a foreign Government is conferred by the Constitution on the President; that recognition is a matter of intention and is not to be implied except from action on the part of the Executive, or from action taken by his authority which clearly indicates an intention to accord recognition; that neither of the two other branches of the Government, the Legislative or Judicial, can effectively accord political recognition to a foreign Government; and that action taken by the Veterans Bureau in the exercise of authority conferred upon it by Congress

could not properly be regarded as recognition of the Soviet régime.

The Veterans Bureau was accordingly advised that the Department perceived no objection to the acceptance of such certificates.

Director of the Veterans Bureau (Hines) to the Secretary of State (Kellogg), Dec. 7, 1925, and the Under Secretary of State (Grew) to General Hines, Dec. 23, 1925, MS. Department of State, file 103.9992/2974; General Hines to Mr. Kellogg, Feb. 17, 1926, and the Assistant Secretary of State (Harrison) to General Hines, Mar. 18, 1928, *ibid.* 103.9992/3001; opinion of the Solicitor's Office, Dec. 14, 1925, *ibid.* F.W. 103.9992/2974.

In reply to an inquiry from the Legation in Peking as to whether it should, in compliance with a request from the Chinese Foreign Office, certify to the official character of the Foreign Office seal, reading "Ministry of Foreign Affairs, Peking, China", the Department of State instructed the Legation to say that it was unable to comply with the request in view of the fact that the United States had not recognized the existing regime in China but that the Consul General at Shanghai might authenticate a certification of the seal by the local Chinese authorities. The certificate was desired for use in the United States Court for China. Minister MacMurray to Secretary Kellogg, no. 562, Nov. 18, 1926, and Mr. Kellogg to Mr. MacMurrary, no. 275, Nov. 20, 1926, MS. Department of State, file 193.51/11.

On the question as to the attitude that the American Legation and the Panama Canal authorities should assume toward the new government which had been installed in Panama as a result of the *coup d'état* carried out on January 2, 1931, it was stated:

The Department has no objection to the Canal authorities recognizing the signatures of the present authorities in the transaction of urgent and necessary business, provided it is made clear that this does not imply recognition of the authorities as the *de facto* Government. Any business with the present authorities should be postponed that can be postponed. [Paraphrase.]

Minister Davis to Secretary Stimson, no. 15, Jan. 3, 1931, 3 p.m., MS. Department of State, file 819.00 Revolutions/12; Mr. Stimson to Mr. Davis, no. 4, Jan. 3, 1931, 7 p.m., *ibid.* 819.00 Revolutions/16.

This Department perceives no objection to the proposal for exchanging the official publications in question [patent publications] but considers that in view of the fact that this Government has not recognized "Manchukuo" the exchange of publications should be handled informally through the American Consulate General, Mukden, Manchuria. The publications of the United States Patent Office should be addressed to The American Consul, American Consulate General, Mukden, Manchuria, via Japan. [*Exchange of publications*]

The Assistant Secretary of State (Moore) to the Secretary of Commerce (Roper), Feb. 25, 1937, MS. Department of State, file 021/1896.

In an instruction of February 28, 1913 to the Ambassador in Mexico City, Secretary Knox said, with special reference to the manner in [*Form of intercourse*] which relations should be conducted with the Provisional Government of President Huerta, that—

> the exact forms of correspondence and modes of address, whether they be maintained as usual or whether the de facto officials be addressed by name with et ceteras added, are not in themselves very material so long as the exact attitude of the United States and the theory upon which it is dealing with the Mexican authorities is made quite clear to them.

MS. Department of State, file 812.00/6431a; 1913 For. Rel. 747–748. This instruction was supplemented by one of July 10, 1913:

> ". . . Since this Government is maintaining diplomatic relations with the central administration at Mexico City on the basis of the actual fact of its existence, the Department desires you, when you become cognizant of the fact that some one other than Mr. de la Barra is in charge of the business of the Mexican foreign office, to continue to make such representations as you are from time to time instructed to make to the central administration at Mexico City in the same manner as in the recent past, this indication applying equally to whoever may succeed Mr. de la Barra as Acting Secretary of State and whoever is subsequently appointed in his stead as Minister for Foreign Affairs. This of course does not raise any question of recognition."

MS. Department of State, file 812.002/29.

Secretary Kellogg instructed the Minister in Nicaragua on Jan. 12, 1926, concerning the manner in which relations should be maintained with General Chamorro in the event that he should assume the presidency, as follows:

> ". . . It is desired that you should in such case address personal letters only, refraining from all official communications with the Minister for Foreign Affairs. Such letters should be addressed to the Minister personally, all titles of office being omitted. Any representations that you make should be confined strictly to the protection of the interests of American citizens. You should not visa passports issued by the new authorities. The Department will not request exequaturs for American Consular officers in Nicaragua under the new regime nor will exequaturs be accorded to the Consuls of that regime in the United States nor will a new Minister accredited by that regime be received." [Paraphrase.] MS. Department of State, file 817.00/3389.

In some instances relations with the officials of non-recognized governments have been restricted to oral intercourse. Thus, in an instruction of Apr. 6, 1932 to the Legation in El Salvador, the Acting Secretary of State (Castle) said:

> ". . . It is the Department's understanding that the discussions you have had with Martinez and various officials of his regime have been on the basis of entirely informal and personal talks in an effort to be helpful in the present difficulties in which Salvador finds itself due to the fact that the present regime cannot be recognized by the other Central American countries and the United States, in view of the 1923 Treaty.
>
> "We are of course anxious that the present situation in Salvador may be regularized as soon as possible, so that we can extend recognition to a government there. Please maintain the conversations you have on the subject on the informal and personal basis mentioned hereinabove."

MS. Department of State, file 816.01/141. See also Secretary Stimson to Ambassador Culbertson, no. 25, June 6, 1932, *ibid.* 825.00 Revolutions/73.

On September 14, 1924 the Ambassador in Chile requested instructions concerning the manner in which he might reply to a formal communication from the Foreign Office advising him of various resolutions dictated by the Junta of Government which had assumed the executive power of the Republic. He stated that there had been much discussion at a meeting of the Diplomatic Corps as to whether this note could be answered without implying recognition, and, if so, whether it should be answered verbally in an informal manner or in writing; and if in writing, in what terms; also whether Señor Solar, who signed the communication as Minister of Foreign Affairs, could be so addressed. The Department of State authorized him—

> to acknowledge the note from Señor Aldunate by means of an informal communication addressed to Señor Aldunate personally without describing his office, expressing appreciation for the information and saying that it has been received in an informal and unofficial manner and communicated to your Government for its information. [Paraphrase.]

Ambassador Collier to Secretary Hughes, no. 62, Sept. 14, 1924, and Mr. Hughes to Mr. Collier, no. 44, Sept. 16, 1924, MS. Department of State, file 825.00/288.

Speaking with reference to a statement made by the American Minister in Helsingfors to the Minister of Foreign Affairs of Finland that under no circumstances could he meet the Soviet representative, Secretary Hughes said in an instruction of August 28, 1924:

> With respect to the representative at the capital to which you are accredited, of a régime not recognized by the Government of the United States, there should be no difficulty in informal and courteous relations, as between two gentlemen. I did not have any difficulty when I attended the celebration of the Centenary of Brazilian Independence at Rio de Janeiro in 1922, in meeting the representative of Mexico and having cordial relations with him, although the Mexican Government had not been recognized by the Government of the United States. Of course such personal and private relations must depend largely on the character and bearing of others, but the usual courtesies of a personal character need never embarrass this Government in maintaining its policy of non-recognition. [Paraphrase.]

Secretary Hughes to the Chargé d'Affaires (Hall), no. 19, Aug. 28, 1924, MS. Department of State, file 707.1161/13.

To avoid the possibility that recognition might be inferred from official attendance at diplomatic or formal social functions given by high officials of a non-recognized government or by the entertainment at such functions of such officials by American diplomatic representa- *Diplomatic or social functions*

tives, the Department of State has on occasion advised American diplomatic representatives to act in their personal capacity under such circumstances. For example:

> . . . it should be said for your information that the Department does not consider that such non-recognition [by the United States of a foreign government] is in itself a valid reason why you or the members of your staff should feel obliged to abstain from participating in a function at which such a representative is a guest of honor. Attendance at a gathering of this kind would not imply recognition and hence would be entirely permissible in the course of the friendly and courteous if necessarily informal relations which should ordinarily prevail between your mission and that of a Government not recognized by the United States.

The Acting Secretary of State (Castle) to the Ambassador in France (Herrick), no. 2882, Aug. 30, 1928, MS. Department of State, file 701.1651/9.

Since this Government does not recognize the present regime in Russia, you will not have any relations with the present representative of that regime in Turkey in his representative capacity. Such relations as may develop between you and him will consequently fall into two categories: (1) relations arising out of the fact that he is Dean of the Diplomatic Corps, and (2) relations of a personal nature arising out of the fact that during the course of your official and social life in Turkey you will inevitably be thrown into more or less frequent contact with him upon occasions when he will not be acting in his capacity as Dean of the Diplomatic Corps.

In dealing with the Soviet representative in his capacity of Dean of the Diplomatic Corps, you should, in general, treat him in the same manner as you would treat him were he the representative of a government recognized by the Government of the United States, except that you should exercise care not to take any step which might carry with it the implication that this Government has recognized the Soviet regime or that you are in a position to establish relations with him as the representative of that regime. There is, of course, no need for you to refrain from such purely social and unofficial relationships with him as may tend to arise out of your association in the Diplomatic Corps and his special position in that body.

If you should ascertain that it is the custom in Turkey for newly arrived Ambassadors or Ministers to call on the Dean of the Diplomatic Corps, the Department perceives no objection to your calling in due course upon the present Dean, despite the fact that he does not represent a government which is recognized by the Government of the United States. In making such a call you should leave your official card, writing on it "The Dean of the Diplomatic Corps", in order to avoid any possibility of its being made to appear that you are entering into relations with him in his representative capacity. In the course of any subsequent relations with him, you should make use of your personal card.

Secretary Hull to the Ambassador in Turkey (Skinner), Sept. 5, 1933, MS. Department of State, file 707.1161/49A.

Although recognition of the newly established Government in Paraguay will be solely dependent upon this Government's intent to extend such recognition, the attendance by you at a meeting of the foreign representatives accredited to Paraguay which the new Foreign Minister called would undoubtedly be regarded in Paraguay as admitting . . . recognition and would make it necessary for this Government officially to declare that such recognition was not thereby intended. [Paraphrase.]

Secretary Hull to Minister Howard, no. 2, Feb. 21, 1936, MS. Department of State, file 834.00/796.

Similar instances are:

Attendance by American Minister at Independence Day reception at Chilean Legation in Costa Rica. Minister Eberhardt to Secretary Stimson, no. 68, Sept. 13, 1932, and Mr. Stimson to Mr. Eberhardt, no. 36, Sept. 15, 1932, ibid. 825.01/124.

Entertainment of Soviet delegates by the American delegation to Telecommunication Conference, 1932. Commissioner Sykes to Secretary Stimson, no. 49, Nov. 2, 1932, ibid. 574.G1P43/461; Mr. Stimson to Mr. Sykes, no. 49, Nov. 4, 1932, ibid. 574.G1P43/467.

Attendance by American Minister in Costa Rica at official dinner given in honor of the Salvadoran special mission. Minister Sack to Secretary Hull, no. 4, Jan. 22, 1934, and Mr. Hull to Mr. Sack, no. 3, Jan. 22, 1934, ibid. 816.01/390.

Attendance by American Minister in Asunción at banquet in honor of Papal Legate by Provisional President Paiva. Minister Howard to Secretary Hull, no. 28, Aug. 19, 1937, and Mr. Hull to Mr. Howard, no. 14, Aug. 21, 1937, ibid. 834.01/42.

On November 27, 1920 the Chargé d'Affaires in Mexico advised the Department of State:

The Foreign Office has informed the chiefs of foreign missions in writing that General Obregón will take the oath of office as constitutionally elected President of the Republic at midnight November 30th in the Chamber of Deputies. The communication states further that there will be a box reserved for the diplomatic corps.

The French Chargé d'Affaires states he has received instructions to attend and I understand that the Belgian and Italian Ministers have decided to attend but not in uniform, the Spanish Minister is awaiting instructions, the Japanese Chargé d'Affaires says he will act in accord with the Embassy.

He was instructed that—

Foreign Office be informed in writing that although you are not authorized to be present officially at Obregón inauguration, you will be pleased to attend in private capacity.

The Chargé d'Affaires (Summerlin) to Secretary Colby, Nov. 27 and 29 (4 p.m.), 1920, Mr. Colby to Mr. Summerlin, Nov. 29 and 30, 1920, MS. Department of State, files 812.00/24782, /24788; 1920 For. Rel., vol. III, pp. 196–197.

In response to a request from the Governor of California for advice as to whether several United States governors should attend the inaugural ceremonies of President-elect Obregón of Mexico to which they had been invited, the Department of State replied:

"The State Department has no advice to give on the question but I call your attention to the obvious fact that the governors are undoubtedly invited because they are governors. In view of the fact that recognition has not yet been accorded to Mexico their attendance would undoubtedly receive the significance in the minds of the Mexicans which their high official station in this country must of necessity suggest. It is a matter for you to consider in these aspects, and one upon which naturally the Department is reluctant to advise, although we clearly perceive the possibility of misconstruction and other regrettable results as the sequel of such a visit." Secretary Colby to Governor Stephens, Nov. 20, 1920, MS. Department of State, file 812.00/24776; 1920 For. Rel., vol. III, p. 195.

In accordance with the desire expressed in your letter of today, there is sent to you enclosed a translation of the telegram from the King of Greece announcing the death of his father, the late King.

Communication between heads of states

As we have of late had no official intercourse with the Greek Government, neither with the present King nor with his father, it would be consistent with our past action to acknowledge the receipt of this communication through the American Chargé d'Affaires at Athens rather than for the President to telegraph an answer in his own name.

Secretary Hughes to George B. Christian, Jr., Secretary to President Harding, Jan. 13, 1923, MS. Department of State, file 868.001C76/83; 1922 For. Rel., vol. II, p. 413.

At a time when the United States had not extended recognition to the Government of Liberia, the Secretary of State at the direction of the President acknowledged a telegram of congratulations from President Barclay to President Roosevelt, addressing President Barclay as "His Excellency the President of Liberia". The reply was communicated through the Liberian Consul General in Baltimore. The Chargé d'Affaires in Liberia (MacVeagh) to Secretary Hull, no. 18, Apr. 20, 1934, and the Acting Secretary of State (Phillips) to Mr. MacVeagh, no. 6, Apr. 21, 1934, MS. Department of State, file 811.001 Roosevelt, F.D./1518.

"President Mikhail Kalinin, All Union Central Executive Committee" of the Union of Soviet Socialist Republics, although unrecognized, was included among the heads of states to whom was cabled President Roosevelt's message of May 16, 1933, to the nations participating in the Disarmament Conference and the International Monetary and Economic Conference. Department of State, Treaty Information Bulletin 44 (May 1933) 2–7.

International conferences

The American delegates to the Child Welfare Congress are not accredited to the Chilean regime and neither are they given the power to bind the Government of the United States in any way, but they are merely designated as delegates "on the part of the United States to the Fourth Pan American Congress on Child Welfare to be held at Santiago, Chile, October 12 to 19, 1924." It is not considered therefore that their participation in such a Congress could be construed to constitute recognition of the regime functioning at the present time in Chile as the Chilean Government. It is nevertheless the desire of the Department that if you should feel that an attempt will be made so to construe it you should address an informal note to the Foreign Office saying that participation of the delegates from the United States in the Congress in question is not to be considered as a recognition of the regime now functioning in Chile as the Government. [Paraphrase.]

Secretary Hughes to the Ambassador in Chile (Collier), no. 49, Oct. 8, 1924, MS. Department of State, file 540.55G4/37a.

At the Bolívar Congress in 1926 certain delegates raised the question of the advisability of making a joint statement to the effect that, since the commission was purely fraternal and commemorative, nothing occurring there could have the effect of recognition of unrecognized governments—the statement having reference to the participation of the Nicaraguan and Ecuadoran Governments in the congress. The chairman of the American delegation was instructed as follows:

The Department concurs in your view that the mere participation of Nicaraguan and Ecuadorean delegates could not be considered to constitute recognition of the existing regimes in those countries and it prefers that you should not raise the question or be a party to any statement. However, you should not sign any document bearing the signatures of, or to be signed by the delegates of Nicaragua and Ecuador in their representative capacity. [Paraphrase.]

Commissioner South to Secretary Kellogg, no. 46, June 15, 1926, and Mr. Kellogg to Mr. South, no. 48, June 16, 1926, MS. Department of State, file 819.415C/64.

In 1929 the Acting Postmaster General informed the Secretary of State that there was a movement on the part of the representatives of the Government of the United States to invite the Universal Postal Union to hold its next congress in Washington and inquired whether there would be any difficulty with regard to the admission of the Soviet delegates to this congress. The Secretary stated in his reply:

It should be added, however, inasmuch as it appears to be customary for the Government of the country in which the Congress is to take place to issue the invitations for the Congress, that this Government would not be in a position to extend an invitation to attend the Congress to a régime not recognized by this Government.

Office of the Postmaster General to the Secretary of State (Stimson), June 6, 1929, MS. Department of State, file 571.A11/34; Secretary Stimson to Postmaster General Brown, June 10, 1929, ibid. 571.A11/36.

The question of the effect, with reference to the matter of recognition, of becoming a party to a multilateral treaty along with an unrecognized government, was examined at the time of the sending of the American delegation to the conference at Geneva in 1925 on

Multilateral treaties

the supervision of the international trade in arms and ammunition and in implements of war. The delegation was instructed as follows:

It is assumed that no action by the American Delegation or by this Government should be construed or open to a fair construction as constituting recognition of the régime now functioning in Russia.

The bare participation of the United States through an American Delegation in a conference to deal with traffic in arms called by the League of Nations in which delegates representing the Soviet régime are also participants would signify nothing.

Again, the bare signature of a multi-lateral Convention by American delegates which was signed also by Soviet delegates would not in itself constitute recognition of the Soviet Government as the Government of Russia, although possibly the formal ratification of the Convention without explanation might be subject to divergent constructions. It may be observed in this connection that the Allied Powers in permitting Russia to sign with them the so-called Straits Convention at Rome on August 14, 1923, did not regard their action as constituting recognition of the Soviet régime. No reservations were made by them.

.   .   .   .

. . . it would be highly unwise for a country, such as our own, not recognizing the Soviet régime, to undertake any contractual obligation with respect to Russia so long as it was represented by a régime not recognized by us.

Reservations

Accordingly, it is desired that, as a safeguard against any possible misconstruction of the attitude of the United States in signing a Convention at Geneva, or in accepting a Convention signed in its behalf, appropriate reservation be made covering the three following points: First, the effect of signing; secondly, the effect of failure on the part of the United States to object to the operation of Article 32 of the Convention; and, thirdly, the suspension of the operation of the Convention as between the United States and a signatory or adhering Power represented by a régime not recognized by the United States until such Power or signatory is represented by a Government recognized as such by the United States. . . .

It may be observed that this Government has consented in correspondence with other interested Powers to permit Russia to adhere to the treaty concerning Spitzbergen under terms which could in no wise be regarded as implying recognition of its Soviet Government.

Secretary Kellogg to the Honorable Theodore E. Burton, Chairman of the American Delegation, et al., no. 2, Apr. 16, 1925, MS. Department of State, file 500A14/167c. The necessity for making these reservations did not arise, however, as the Soviet Government did not participate in the conference. For the text of the convention signed at the conference on June 17, 1925, see Department of State, Treaty Information Bulletin 18 (Mar. 1931) 21–50.

The treaty relating to Spitzbergen, signed at Paris on Feb. 9, 1920, to which reference was made in the instruction of Apr. 16, 1925, contained the following provision in article 10:

"Until the recognition by the High Contracting Parties of a Russian Government shall permit Russia to adhere to the present Treaty, Russian nationals and companies shall enjoy the same rights as nationals of the High Contracting Parties." 43 Stat. 1892; 4 Treaties, etc. (Trenwith, 1938) 4861. See also Secretary Kellogg to the Norwegian Minister (Bryn), Feb. 2, 1926, MS. Department of State, file 857H.01/64; and Secretary Stimson to the French Ambassador (Claudel), Dec. 21, 1931, *ibid.* 857H.01/95. The Union of Soviet Socialist Republics did not adhere to the treaty until May 7, 1935.

In signing the international sanitary convention of June 21, 1926, revising the convention of June 17, 1912, the American delegation made the following reservation:

"The Plenipotentiaries of the United States of America formally declare that their signing the International Sanitary Convention of this date is not to be construed to mean that the United States of America recognizes a régime or entity acting as Government of a signatory or adhering Power when that régime or entity is not recognized by the United States as the Government of that Power. They further declare that the participation of the United States of America in the International Sanitary Convention of this date does not involve any contractual obligation on the part of the United States to a signatory or adhering Power represented by a régime or entity which the United States does not recognize as representing the Government of that Power, until it is represented by a Government recognized by the United States.

"The Plenipotentiaries of the United States of America declare, furthermore, that their Government reserves to itself the right to decide whether from the standpoint of the measures to be applied a foreign district is to be considered as infected and to decide what measures shall be applied to arrival in its own ports under special circumstances."

4 Treaties, etc. (Trenwith, 1938) 4962, 5014.

Similar reservations were made by the United States in signing the following agreements: convention for the safety of life at sea at London on May 31, 1929 (International Conference on Safety of Life at Sea, London, Apr. 16 to May 31, 1929, *Report of the Delegation of the United States of America and Appended Documents*, Department of State Conference Ser. 1 (1929) 246; 50 Stat. 1121, 1122; 4 Treaties, etc. [Trenwith, 1938] 5134); international load-line convention at London on July 5, 1930 (*ibid.* 5287, 5332; 47 Stat. 2228, 2388); and the narcotic drugs convention at Geneva on July 13, 1931 (48 Stat. 1543, 1584; 4 Treaties, etc. [Trenwith, 1938] 5351, 5369). Apparently through inadvertence such a reservation was not made at the time of the signing of the convention for the suppression of counterfeiting currency at Geneva on Apr. 20, 1929 (MS. Department of State, file 511.4A6/424). Reservations were not made by the American delegation in signing the universal postal conventions at Stockholm on Aug. 28, 1924 (44 Stat. 2221) and at London on June 28, 1929 (46 Stat. 2523).

The grounds upon which the Department's action in the matter of reservations was based were set forth at some length in an instruction of July 26, 1931 to the Legation at Bern in response to a telegram from the Legation suggesting that the reservation which had been made in signing the narcotic drugs convention should be expunged:

> While the Department entertains no doubt that this Government's refusal to recognize the régime in any country can not be affected by its mere signature of or adherence to a multilateral treaty to which the unrecognized régime is a party, the Department considers it desirable in order to avoid any possible misconstruction of its position to make the reservations incorporated in the narcotics convention.
>
> . . . Any possible technical implication of recognition which might be alleged to be involved in the adherence by an unrecognized régime to a treaty to which the United States is a party but which the unrecognized régime did not sign would appear to be too tenuous to warrant even any explanatory declaration or reservation. But when the United States and the unrecognized régime both sign a convention or when the United States signs a convention which is left open for subsequent signature as is the case in the Narcotics Convention under consideration, the Department considers it desirable to accompany its signature by a reservation of the kind incorporated in the Narcotics Convention.

The Acting Secretary of State (Castle) to Minister Wilson, no. 85, July 26, 1931, MS. Department of State, file 511.4A6/424.

In response to an inquiry from the American delegation to the Telecommunication Conference at Madrid on October 4, 1932, whether at the time of signature of the convention the delegation should make a statement relative to unrecognized regimes similar to that made in signing the convention for safety of life at sea in London, the delegation was instructed:

> No statement should be made by the delegation with reference to unrecognized governments. . . . it is considered by the Government of the United States that the adherence to or signature of a multilateral treaty by a government which has not been recognized by this Government, and which has been signed by the United States or to which the United States is a party does not constitute recognition of such government by the United States. It is considered evident that a view contrary to this would make it possible for a non-recognized nation or government to make compulsory recognition by other states, parties to a multilateral treaty, whether they had become parties by adherence or by signature, and without their consent. It is the opinion of the United States that such a result is legally impossible. Recognition is primarily a matter of intent. An intention to recognize another government cannot properly be imputed to the United States on account of a unilateral act performed by the other government. Signature or accession by another government to a multilateral treaty is believed to be a unilateral act upon the part of such government. In view of the foregoing considerations it is not considered necessary that

the delegation should make any statement on the subject at the time that the convention is signed.   [Paraphrase.]

Commissioner Sykes to Secretary Stimson, no. 21, Oct. 4, 1932, MS. Department of State, file 574G1/873; Mr. Stimson to Mr. Sykes, no. 29, Oct. 13, 1932, *ibid.* 574G1/883.

In connection with the signature of the international sanitary convention for air navigation, the following views were expressed regarding the subject of the making of reservations and the question of recognition:

Recognition, as has repeatedly been stated, is primarily a matter of intent.   Intent to recognize cannot validly be imputed from the mere failure to raise objection or make reservation where no direct contractual obligation is undertaken.

If the treaty carries with it mutual and reciprocal obligations requiring the governments to have dealings with each other or to recognize official acts of each other, the signing of the treaty without reservation would carry with it an implication that the signatories are prepared to treat with each other on an equal footing.   For example, the Fur Seals Convention of 1911, between the United States, Great Britain, Russia and Japan, provides in Article 1 that the High Contracting Parties

"mutually and reciprocally agree that their citizens and subjects respectively, and all persons subject to their laws and treaties, and their vessels, shall be prohibited, while this Convention remains in force, from engaging in pelagic sealing in the waters of the North Pacific Ocean, ... and that every such person and vessel offending against such prohibition may be seized, except within the territorial jurisdiction of one of the other Powers, and detained by the naval or other duly commissioned officers of any of the Parties to this Convention, to be delivered as soon as practicable to an authorized official of their own nation at the nearest point to the place of seizure, or elsewhere as may be mutually agreed upon; and that the authorities of the nation to which such person or vessel belongs alone shall have jurisdiction to try the offense and impose the penalties for the same."

The Article further provides that witnesses and proofs necessary to establish the offense, so far as they are under the control of any of the parties to the Convention, shall be furnished with all reasonable promptitude to the proper authorities having jurisdiction to try the offense.   Obviously, the signing with a non-recognized government of a multilateral treaty containing provisions in the nature of those recited, requiring as they do affirmative inter-governmental cooperation or dealings with an unrecognized government, would constitute recognition of the non-recognized government.   On the other hand, where a treaty or convention is of such a character as would permit of its being carried into operation without such inter-governmental coopera- tion or exchange of communications, *i.e.,* where there do not exist reciprocal affirmative duties and obligations on the part of the signatories, the signing of such a treaty or convention with a non-recognized government would not constitute recognition. It is not necessary that a government, in order to avoid the implication of recognition of a government with which it does not desire to have diplomatic relations, should object, except in cases of the character indicated above, to the signing of a multilateral agreement to which a non-recognized government is or may become a party, or that it should make reservation as to such government. There is all the greater reason why this should not be necessary if some of the parties to the agreement have recognized such government.

Opinion of the Legal Adviser of the Department of State, Mar. 15, 1932, MS. Department of State, file 512.4A1A1/22½. No provision for such a reservation was included in the instruction to the Minister at The Hague concerning the signing of this convention. Department of State to Minister Swenson, no. 268, Oct. 20, 1933, *ibid.* 512.4A1A1/86.

Adherence

I have the honor to acknowledge the receipt of your note of January 27, 1926, by which you inform me that the Soviet regime in Russia has given the Italian Government notice of its adhesion to the International Office of Public Hygiene; that this adhesion seems to be in accordance with the provisions of the Convention of December 9, 1907, and that your Government does not see how it could be disputed. In view of the fact that the Government of the United States has not recognized the Soviet regime, you add that your Government would attach value to knowing the view of this Government on the question.

In reply I have the honor to state that as Russia was one of the original signatories of the Arrangement of December 9, 1907, and duly deposited its ratification with the Italian Ministry for Foreign Affairs, and as there has been at no time notification given to the Government of the United States of the withdrawal of Russia from the said Arrangement, it is the view of the Government of the United States that Russia is still a party to the Arrangement by reason of its ratification above mentioned.

Inasmuch as this Government does not recognize the Union of Socialist Soviet Republics, it attaches no significance to the action reported in your note. This Government desires moreover that it shall be understood that its failure to object to the action reported in your note implies no recognition of the Soviet Regime.

Secretary Kellogg to the French Ambassador (Berenger), Mar. 24, 1926, MS. Department of State, file 512.4A1a/285.

In a letter of August 18, 1928 from the Assistant Secretary of State (Castle) to President Coolidge, informing him of the sending of a circular telegram to various American diplomatic missions instructing them to invite the governments to which they were accredited to adhere to the treaty for the renunciation of war and of the fact that the French Foreign Office was sending a similar note to the Soviet Government, it was stated that:

Inasmuch as this is a question of adherence and not of original signature, it can not possibly involve any recognition by this

Government of the Soviet regime. In fact, we are already parties to more than one treaty to which the Soviet Government has adhered.

MS. Department of State, file 711.0012 Anti-War/266.

In a note of July 24, 1929 the Department of State informed the French Foreign Office that the treaty had come into force through the ratification of Japan, all the other signatories having previously ratified the treaty. It transmitted therewith the instruments of adherence which had been deposited with the Government of the United States and requested the French Government to forward to the existing Soviet regime an enclosed set of the instruments of ratification of all the signatory governments and of the instruments evidencing the adherence of other governments. Secretary Stimson to the French Minister of Foreign Affairs, July 24, 1929, *ibid.* 711.0012 Anti-War/869.

The conclusion reached by the Department of State concerning the effect of adherence by a non-recognized power to a multilateral treaty was further elaborated in a memorandum prepared by the Under Secretary of State on Oct. 23, 1928, after a conference with certain other officials of the Department:

"1. Adherence to a multilateral treaty by a government recognized by other governments adherent or signatory to such treaty, would not constitute a recognition of such adhering power by the other powers who had not theretofore recognized and did not wish to recognize such adherent.

"A contrary view would place it within the power of the non-recognized nation to force recognition upon other powers parties to a multilateral treaty (by signature or adherence) against their will, which is legally impossible.

"In this connection it was agreed that in this case France and other powers that had recognized Russia had the right to enter into treaty relations with Russia as provided in the Peace Pact, notwithstanding the United States . . . had not recognized Russia . . . ; and further that this treaty relation between France and other powers and Russia with reference to the Peace Pact might be created through the adherence of Russia to the multilateral Peace Pact . . . without involving the United States in the matter of recognition.

"2. It was also agreed that if the United States wished to indicate in connection with this adherence of Russia to the Peace Pact that such adherence did not constitute recognition by the United States of Russia, an appropriate time to make such an announcement would be when the treaty, having been ratified by all the powers signatory to it, came into force, and notification of that fact was communicated to those powers which had adhered.

"In this connection it was further agreed that while a strict reading of the Peace Pact might require that the United States telegraphically notify the other Governments immediately upon the deposit of the adherence of Russia, and furnish them with a certified copy of it (Article 3), yet the treaty had been drawn apparently with the thought that adherence to the treaty should be made after the treaty itself came into force and effect; that in practice it had worked out as to the Peace Pact that nations were depositing both actual instruments of adherence and notices of intention to adhere before the treaty became operative; that in these circumstances it would be entirely proper for the United States to hold the instrument of adherence unacknowledged until the treaty should come into effect; and at that time an acknowledgment could be made and notification to other powers could be given in such terms as should be then deemed expedient.

"3. It was further agreed that the mere fact that the United States Government was the depositary of the Peace Pact, and of the ratifications thereof and adherences thereto, did not give to the United States any special rights or position or impose upon it any special obligations with reference to this treaty; that the United States was merely the custodian of the documents concerned, which were international documents rather than national documents, and as custodian or depositary was charged with the administrative duties required by Article III; and that as a depositary, we possessed no discretionary rights with reference to the receipt or the refusal of a proffered adherence or ratification."

MS. Department of State, file 711.6112 Anti-War/75.

In 1928 Secretary Kellogg said:

It is considered by the Government of the United States that the signing of a bilateral treaty by it with another State, such as that which was signed with the Nationalist Government, constitutes recognition. It is not considered, however, that adherence to a multilateral treaty of which the United States is a signatory or to which it is a party, by an unrecognized government, involves recognition of the latter by the United States. It is erroneous to attribute to the Government of the United States the doctrine that adherence to a multilateral treaty by governments to which previous recognition had not been accorded, constitutes recognition of such governments. Adherence by another government is its own unilateral act. Intention is a matter of primary importance in recognition, and intention on the part of the United States to recognize such a government could not be imputed to it from an act of the other government. [Paraphrase.]

Secretary Kellogg to Chargé Neville, no. 123, Nov. 19, 1928, MS. Department of State, file 711.9412 Anti-War/75.

Business transactions

The Ecuadoran Legation in Washington having addressed a note on April 11, 1927 to the Department of State requesting that the War Department be asked to release to the Surplus Property Division 4,000 haversacks needed to complete an order from Ecuador, the question arose whether such a sale would constitute a recognition of the Government of Ecuador. The Department concluded that:

. . . While there are certain acts which cannot fail to have the effect of recognizing a government, such as accrediting diplomatic representatives, negotiation of treaties and conventions, etc., recognition is for the most part a matter of intention. Intention to recognize could not be imputed from a sale of the character here contemplated, and even though intention to recognize should be imputed to this Government by Ecuador, this Government would not be estopped to deny that the transaction had that effect.

The Ecuadoran Legation was accordingly notified (in a note of June 7, 1927) that when it should desire to take delivery of the haversacks, shipping instructions would be furnished to the War Department.

> The Assistant Secretary of War (MacNider) to the Secretary of State (Kellogg), May 16, 1927; Opinion of the Solicitor of the Department of State, June 6, 1927; the Department of State to the Ecuadoran Legation, June 7, 1927. See MS. Department of State, file 822.24/25. The sale was to be made subject to the act approved June 5, 1920 (41 Stat. 949).

In reply to an inquiry from the Legation in China as to whether there would be any objection to the signing by it of a lease with certain officials of the Soviet Government covering property belonging to that Government, the Department of State advised against the signing of such a lease.

> Minister MacMurray to Secretary Kellogg, no. 1, Jan. 3, 1929, and Mr. Kellogg to Mr. MacMurray, no. 11, Jan. 8, 1929, MS. Department of State, file 124.9318/131.
>
> In 1923 the Department of State advised the Department of the Interior that no objection was perceived to the placing by the Patent Office of the Soviet Board of Inventions on the mailing list "provided the matter be not arranged formally or in writing with the authorities of the so-called Soviet Government". The Assistant Secretary of the Interior (Goodwin) to the Secretary of State (Hughes), Sept. 14, 1923, and Secretary Hughes to the Secretary of the Interior, Oct. 5, 1923, *ibid.* 021/1075.
>
> A similar position was taken by the United States in a number of other instances in the years prior to the recognition of the Soviet Government by the United States in 1933: admission of trained zoologist from Russia (the Secretary of Agriculture (Jardine) to the Secretary of State (Kellogg), Nov. 29, 1926, and Mr. Kellogg to Mr. Jardine, Dec. 16, 1926, *ibid.* 102.7502/3); exchange of educational publications (the Secretary of the Interior (Wilbur) to the Secretary of State (Stimson), May 9, 1929, and the Assistant Secretary of State (Castle) to Secretary Wilbur, June 14, 1929, *ibid.* 102.65/232); collaboration with public-health service (the Assistant Secretary of the Treasury (Heath) to the Secretary of State (Stimson), Feb. 7, 1930, and the Acting Secretary of State (Cotton) to the Secretary of the Treasury (Mellon), Mar. 6, 1930, *ibid.* 811.42761/23); establishment of a Soviet agricultural agency (the Acting Secretary of Agriculture (Dunlap) to the Secretary of State (Stimson), May 23, 1930, and the Assistant Secretary of State (Carr) to the Secretary of Agriculture, June 11, 1930, *ibid.* 861.01B11/50).
>
> The Secretary of State (Kellogg) advised the Secretary of Commerce (Hoover) on July 28, 1926:
>
> "If the Commissioner of Patents should determine that the provisions in the decrees mentioned [of the Soviet Government] meet the condition prescribed by the Act of Congress of February 20, 1905, on which the benefits of that Act may be extended to citizens of foreign countries, the Department perceives no objection to the registration by the Patent Office of Russian trade-marks. The Department would regard such registration merely as the determination of a fact not involving the political recognition of the Soviet régime." *Ibid.* 811.54361/18.

Belligerency

Any act involving relations with an insurgent or a revolutionary regime must fall short of recognition of belligerency unless it indicates a clear intention on the part of the recognizing state to treat the insurgents or revolutionists as belligerents, enjoying all the rights and subject to all the obligations normally attaching to the status of belligerency. (For the general discussion of recognition of belligerency, see *ante* §52.)

Arms
embargoes

Acting under the authority of certain joint resolutions of Congress various Presidents of the United States have issued proclamations placing restrictions on the exportation of arms and munitions of war to countries in which revolutionary disturbances existed. In no case has such action been considered as constituting recognition of the insurgents as belligerents. Nor was the joint resolution of Congress, approved January 8, 1937 (50·Stat. 3), prohibiting the exportation of arms, ammunition, and implements of war to Spain regarded as constituting recognition by the United States of the belligerency of the insurgents under General Franco, although the resolution applied equally to the recognized Government of Spain and to the insurgents.

The joint resolution of Apr. 22, 1898 authorized the President "to prohibit the export of coal or other material used in war from any seaport of the United States until otherwise ordered by the President or by Congress." 30 Stat. 739. This resolution was amended on Mar. 14, 1912 to read:

"That whenever the President shall find that in any American country conditions of domestic violence exist which are promoted by the use of arms or munitions of war procured from the United States, and shall make proclamation thereof, it shall be unlawful to export except under such limitations and exceptions as the President shall prescribe any arms or munitions of war from any place in the United States to such country until otherwise ordered by the President or by Congress." 37 Stat. 630.

This latter resolution was in turn superseded by that approved Jan. 31, 1922, which contains practically the same phraseology as the earlier resolution except that it is also applicable to "any country in which the United States exercises extraterritorial jurisdiction". 42 Stat. 361.

A number of proclamations have been issued under authority of these resolutions: no. 604, Oct. 14, 1905, exportation of arms to the Dominican Republic (34 Stat. 3183–3184); no. 1185, Mar. 14, 1912, exportation of arms or munitions of war to Mexico (37 Stat. 1733); no. 1263, Feb. 3, 1914, revoking proclamation of Mar. 14, 1912 concerning exportation of arms or munitions of war to Mexico (38 Stat. 1992); no. 1315, Oct. 19, 1915, exportation of arms or munitions of war to Mexico (39 Stat. 1756); no. 1530, July 12, 1919, exportation of arms or munitions of war to Mexico (41 Stat. 1762–1763); no. 1621, Mar. 4, 1922, exportation of arms or munitions of war to China (42 Stat. 2264–2265); no. 1683, Jan. 7, 1924, exportation of arms or munitions of war to Mexico (43 Stat. 1934–1935); no. 1689, Mar. 22, 1924, exportation of arms or munitions of war to Honduras (43 Stat. 1942–1943); no. 1693, May 2, 1924, exportation of arms or munitions of war to Cuba (43 Stat. 1946–1947); no. 1697, May 15, 1924, exportation of arms or munitions of war to Honduras (43 Stat. 1950–1951); no. 1709, Aug. 29, 1924, revoking proclamation of May 15, 1924 concerning exportation of arms or munitions of war to Cuba (43 Stat. 1965–1966); no. 1783, Sept. 15, 1926, exportation of arms or munitions of war to Nicaragua (44 Stat. 2625–2626); no. 1885, July 18, 1929, revoking proclamation of Jan. 7, 1924 concerning exportation of arms or munitions of war to Mexico (46 Stat. 3001); no. 1923, Oct. 22, 1930, exportation of arms or munitions of war to Brazil (46 Stat. 3036–3037); no. 1939, Mar. 2, 1931, revoking proclamation of Oct. 22, 1930 concerning exportation of arms or munitions of war to Brazil (46 Stat. 3050); no. 2089, June 29, 1934, exportation of arms or munitions of war to Cuba (49 Stat. 3399–4400).

The joint resolution of Jan. 8, 1937 prohibiting the shipment of arms to Spain provided in part:

"That during the existence of the state of civil strife now obtaining in Spain it shall, from and after the approval of this Resolution be unlawful to export arms, ammunition, or implements of war from any place in the United States, or possessions of the United States, to Spain or to any other foreign country for transshipment to Spain or for use of either of the opposing forces in Spain." 50 Stat. 3.

The joint resolution of May 1, 1937 amending the joint resolution of Aug. 31, 1935 (49 Stat. 1081), as amended and extended on Feb. 29, 1936 (49 Stat. 1152), provided in section 1(c):

"Whenever the President shall find that a state of civil strife exists in a foreign state and that such civil strife is of a magnitude or is being conducted under such conditions that the export of arms, ammunition, or implements of war from the United States to such foreign state would threaten or endanger the peace of the United States, the President shall proclaim such fact, and it shall thereafter be unlawful to export, or attempt to export, or cause to be exported, arms, ammunition, or implements of war from any place in the United States to such foreign state, or to any neutral state for transshipment to, or for the use of such foreign state." 50 Stat. 121–122.

Article 1 of the convention on duties and rights of states in the event of civil strife signed at Habana on Feb. 20, 1928 to which the United States is a party provides:

"The contracting states bind themselves to observe the following rules with regard to civil strife in another one of them:

.   .   .   .

"3. To forbid the traffic in arms and war material, except when intended for the government, while the belligerency of the rebels has not been recognized, in which latter case the rules of neutrality shall be applied." 46 Stat. 2749, 2750; 4 Treaties, etc. (Trenwith, 1938) 4725.

On Mar. 14, 1921 Secretary Hughes informed Senator Henry Cabot Lodge, Chairman of the Foreign Relations Committee:

"In view of the long continued civil strife in China, the powers allied and associated in the war, and also certain of the neutral powers, mutually agreed, through their diplomatic representatives in Peking, in May, 1919, to restrict shipments from their respective countries to China of arms and munitions of war, and material destined exclusively for their manufacture, until the establishment of a government whose authority should be recognized throughout the whole country. The powers thus cooperating were the United States, Great Britain, France, Japan, Spain, Portugal, Russia,

Brazil, the Netherlands, Denmark, Belgium, and Italy. . . . This Government was enabled to exercise the control over the export of arms and munitions to China, in pursuance of the policy thus adopted, on the basis of the provisions of the espionage act of June 15, 1917, as enforced by the War Trade Board." MS. Department of State, file 693.119/444a; 1921 For. Rel., vol. I, p. 551.

The American schooner *Lucy H.* was seized by the United States on a libel of information charging the violation of the Neutrality Act as finally amended April 20, 1818 and embodied in the Penal Code of 1910 (35 Stat. 1090; 18 U.S.C. §23), the pertinent provisions of which read:

> Whoever, within the territory . . . of the United States fits out and arms . . . any vessel, with intent that such vessel shall be employed in the service of any foreign prince or state, or of any colony, district, or people, to cruise or commit hostilities against the subjects, citizens, or property of any foreign prince or state, or of any colony, district, or people, with whom the United States are at peace . . . and every such vessel . . . her tackle . . . materials . . . stores . . . shall be forfeited.

Application of neutrality act

The sufficiency of the libel was challenged on the ground that the regime against whom the vessel was designed to be used was not a "foreign prince or state, or . . . any colony, district, or people, with whom the United States are at peace" within the meaning of the statute, it being alleged that the regime was in fact only an insurrectionary force. The court pointed out that the Supreme Court in the case of *The Three Friends* (166 U.S. 54) had specifically held that "the word 'people,' taken in connection with the words 'colony' and 'district,' covered any insurgent or insurrectionary body of people acting together, undertaking, and conducting hostilities, although its belligerency had not been recognized". In holding that the same rule applied to the provision with reference to "hostilities against" such foreign insurrectionary bodies or peoples, the district court said:

> It may be true that for a political community to be entitled to political recognition under the law of nations, it should have the attributes of sovereignty. In that event the provisions of the statute "any foreign prince or state" would necessarily embrace such a community. If recognition followed, that recognition would take place in the orderly way prescribed by rules governing such matters in national intercourse. There would be the necessary representative, the formal demand, and the formal action of the political department of the recognizing power.
>
> Interpreting one section of the Neutrality Act after the amendments of 1818, the Supreme Court, in the case of Wiborg v. United States, 163 U. S. 647, 16 Sup. Ct. 1127, 1197, 41 L. Ed. 289, text, observed:
>
> "It [the Neutrality Act] was undoubtedly designed in general to secure neutrality in wars between two other nations, or between

contending parties recognized as belligerents, but its operation is not necessarily dependent on the existence of such state of belligerency."

Congress undertook to preserve the neutrality of the United States, not only in wars between states and nations recognized, but also in insurrections and political revolts in foreign countries where such contests produce a situation in which both factions are striving for exclusive dominion. If the United States is to preserve neutrality toward other nations and peoples as Congress designed, its ports cannot be used as a base of operations for military expeditions or enterprises which may not only go in furtherance of or in assisting an insurrectionary force, but which in its very nature, in the absence of strife, might incite revolt. Manifestly, therefore, Congress, in the addition of the words "Colony, district or people," to the second branch of this section sought to provide for a situation which, and to describe a body of persons whom, it was impracticable to recognize politically.

There is no apparent reason for restricting the interpretation of the amendment to the first branch of the section, as stated in The Three Friends, supra, and there certainly is nothing in the opinion to warrant the view that the words "foreign prince or state, or of any colony, district or people," as used in the second branch of the section, against whose "subjects, citizens or property" hostilities were intended, should receive a more strict application. Indeed, such a construction would fail utterly to compass what President Madison moved Congress to do by his earnest appeal for "more efficient laws to prevent violations of the neutrality of the United States as a nation at peace," by permitting belligerent parties to arm and equip vessels within the waters of the United States for military purposes.

From what is said it follows that the construction placed on the first branch of the particular section of the Neutrality Act is equally applicable to the second branch of the section, and consequently political recognition of the objects of the hostilities is not required as a condition precedent to a violation of the act, and the exceptions numbered 6 and 7 will be overruled.

235 Fed. 610, 615 (N.D. Fla., 1916).

Blockades of ports in the control of insurgent forces have not infrequently been proclaimed by the established government, and in some instances the insurgents themselves have proclaimed blockades. In such cases it has been the practice of the United States to recognize such blockades only "if the sovereign decreeing such a closure have a naval force sufficient to maintain an effective blockade and if he duly proclaim and maintain such a blockade". *Blockades*

The Acting Secretary of State (Wilson) to the Chargé d'Affaires in Mexico (Schuyler), Oct. 23, 1912, MS. Department of State, file 612.1123/5.

For similar declarations, see (1) the Acting Secretary of State (Bacon) to the Minister in Haiti (Furniss), Nov. 27, 1908, *ibid.* 2126/322 and 1908 For. Rel. 439–440; (2) Secretary Knox to the Minister in Costa Rica (Merry), Nov. 21, 1909, MS. Department of State, file 6369/272 and 1909 For. Rel.

454–455; (3) Secretary Knox to the Consul at Managua (De Olivares), May 19, 1910, MS. Department of State, file 6369/951a and 1910 For. Rel. 746–747; (4) Secretary Knox to Consul Moffat at Bluefields, June 19, 1910, MS. Department of State, file 6369/1060c and 1910 For. Rel. 753; (5) Secretary Hughes to the Chargé d'Affaires in Mexico (Summerlin), no. 45, Jan. 19, 1924, MS. Department of State, file 812.00/26772; (6) Secretary Stimson to the Chargé d'Affaires in Brazil (Thurston), July 16, 1932, *ibid.* 832.00 Revolutions/260; (7) Secretary Stimson to the Consul at São Paulo, Brazil (Cameron), Sept. 27, 1932, *ibid.* 832.00 Revolutions/389.

In reply to a *note verbale* of Aug. 20, 1936 from the Spanish Foreign Office to the American Embassy advising the Embassy that certain ports in the possession of the insurgents and certain others in possession of the Government had "been declared a war zone" and that consequently entry into them by merchant ships would not be permitted, the Department of State instructed the Embassy on Aug. 25 to reply as follows:

"My Government directs me to inform you in reply that, with the friendliest feelings toward the Spanish Government, it cannot admit the legality of any action on the part of the Spanish Government in declaring such ports closed unless that Government declares and maintains an effective blockade of such ports. In taking this position my Government is guided by a long line of precedents in international law with which the Spanish Government is doubtless familiar." Department of State, XV *Press Releases*, weekly issue 361, pp. 192–193 (Aug. 27, 1936).

As of possible interest, see the *Oriental Navigation Company* case before the United States–Mexican General Claims Commission under the convention of Sept. 8, 1923, *Opinions of the Commissioners* (1929) 23–47, docket 411.

Reservation of rights

In the light of recent occurrences, particularly in regard to cases affecting American interests and property, it is appropriate that the revolutionary party should understand that the United States reserve all claims and rights growing out of acts or omissions of the revolutionary party to which this Government or its citizens may be entitled under international law. Such timely reservation is not to be deemed to imply admission of a full state of revolutionary belligerency with the rights and obligations attaching thereto under the doctrines of international law.

Secretary Knox to the Consul at Bluefields, Nicaragua (Moffat), Nov. 21, 1909, MS. Department of State, file 6369/272; 1909 For. Rel. 454.

Orozco revolutionary government

The Department of State on April 14, 1912 instructed the Consul at Chihuahua to deliver to General Orozco, who had established a revolutionary government purporting to be the Provisional Government of Mexico, a copy of the following statement of the attitude of the United States:

Life and property

The enormous destruction, constantly increasing, of valuable American properties in the course of the present unfortunate disturbances, the taking of American life contrary to the principles governing such matters among all civilized nations, the increasing dangers to which all American citizens in Mexico are subjected, and the seemingly possible indefinite continuance of this unfortunate situation compel the Government of the United

States to give notice that it expects and must demand that American life and property within the Republic of Mexico be justly and adequately protected, and that this Government must hold Mexico and the Mexican people responsible for all wanton or illegal acts sacrificing or endangering American life or damaging American property or interests there situated.

Meanwhile, it should be apparent to all sections of the Mexican people that those who spread baseless rumors or provoke just resentment by attacks upon Americans or other foreign persons or property are working against the best interests and the honor of their country, for which the United States is known to hold, and in the present grave situation is manifesting, the greatest and most sincere friendship, and are seeking for their own selfish ends to burden the future of their countrymen with heavy obligations of enormous damages for their wrongful acts.

How strongly the Government of the United States deprecates even the very few cases of participation by its citizens in the present insurrectionary disturbances is well known to the people of Mexico, and was shown by the President's proclamation of March 2 and the various other acts of this Government looking to the same end. The Government of the United States must insist and demand that American citizens who may be taken prisoners, whether by one party or the other, as participants Prisoners in the present insurrectionary disturbances, shall be dealt with in accordance with broad principles of equitable justice and humanity, as well as in accordance with the principles of international law which may be involved, and to which the people of Mexico have given their assent and adherence in numerous international engagements. This Government must hold the Mexican people strictly responsible for any departure from such principles.

Notwithstanding press reports that certain Mexican officers have announced a contrary policy, the Government of the United States has every confidence in the disposition of the Government of Mexico in the premises, and must request that appropriate instructions be immediately issued to the proper military officers and officials in the sense indicated.

In a telegram of April 20, 1912, addressed to the Acting Secretary of State, General Orozco requested recognition by the Government of the United States, giving a number of reasons as to why such recognition should be extended. On May 30, 1912 the Department instructed the Consul at Chihuahua:

. . . Make unofficial but firm demand of Orozco for an explanation of his proclamation in so far as it affects Americans. Informally, but vigorously protest against any effort on his part, direct or indirect, to evade the obligation to protect noncombatants imposed by the rules of civilized warfare and by civilization. Remark upon the disastrous consequences of departure from proper procedure in such cases. Demand ample protection to all American citizens and their interests and safe conduct and transportation facilities to the Texas border for any who may wish to leave Mexico. Suggest safe conduct for other foreigners.

Discreetly inform Americans of any danger you believe to exist; also suggest to them the desirability of their withdrawal as soon as possible from rebel territory, whenever you think it requisite. [Paraphrase.]

Again, on July 29, 1912, the Department instructed the Consul at Ciudad Juráez to say to General Orozco that he must at once inform his subordinate insurrectionary leaders that there must be no maltreatment of Americans or of their property. In reply to representations made to him, General Orozco informed the Consul that he would listen to him "personally but not officially". He made no promise of compliance with the request made by the Department.

Recognition of belligerency was never extended by the United States Government in favor of Orozco.

> Consul Letcher to Secretary Knox, Apr. 11, 1912, MS. Department of State, file 812.00/3576; the Acting Secretary of State (Wilson) to Ambassador Wilson, Apr. 14, 1912, *ibid.* 812.00/3593a; General Orozco to Acting Secretary Wilson, Apr. 20, 1912, *ibid.* 812.00/3670; Secretary Knox to Consul Letcher, May 30, 1912, *ibid.* 812.00/4070; Secretary Knox to Consul Edwards, July 29, 1912, *ibid.* 812.00/4500; Mr. Edwards to Mr. Knox, July 31, 1912, *ibid.* 812.00/4531; 1912 For. Rel. 781–825.

Protests to insurgents

The United States destroyer *Kane* having been bombed near Gibraltar on August 30, 1936, the Department of State instructed the Consul at Seville on August 30 in part as follows:

> Since the plane making the attack was unidentified, the President has directed that this incident be brought to the attention of the Spanish Government through our Embassy at Madrid and informally to the attention of General Franco through you, with the request that both sides issue instructions in the strongest terms, as the American Government feels confident they will desire to do, to prevent another incident of this character.
>
> Take up this matter immediately informally with General Franco or in his absence with the officer in command at Seville in the sense of the foregoing, endeavor to obtain a categorical statement as to whether the plane making this attack was an insurgent plane, and urge and insist upon definite assurance that appropriate instructions will immediately be issued to the insurgent armed forces. Telegraph immediately and fully the result of your representations.
>
> You will, of course, understand that it is not intended that the action which we are instructing you to take shall have any bearing on the subject of recognition of any kind.

> Secretary Hull to the Consul at Seville, Aug. 30, 1936, MS. Department of State, file 852.00/2889.

The following message has been received from our Legation at Lisbon:

> "Note just received from Amoedo, insurgent representative in Lisbon, contains warning that, beginning today and until the 15th

of December, in the zone between Cape San Antonio, Province of Alicante, and the town Marbella, Province of Malaga, frequent aerial attacks against presumed enemy vessels will take place, and that offensive mines will be placed at the entrance of the ports of this zone."

Please request General Queipo de Llano to inform General Franco, as Commander-in-Chief of the insurgent land and sea forces, as well as the insurgent naval headquarters at Cadiz that during the period mentioned in Amoedo's note it is highly probable that American merchant and naval vessels will be passing through waters adjacent to and possibly within the zone declared liable to "frequent aerial attacks against presumed enemy vessels", and that we cannot admit the right of insurgent airplanes to attack American vessels within or outside the zone.

The Acting Secretary of State (Moore) to the Consul at Seville, Dec. 3, 1936, MS. Department of State, file 852.00/3949.

Speaking with reference to reports that the Consul who had returned to Bilbao in territory controlled by the insurgent forces in Spain was returning in a diplomatic capacity, the Department of State said in a telegram of November 15 to the Ambassador in Spain that it had made it clear that the Consul would return to his post in his capacity as Consul only and that, as in the case of the consulate at Málaga, the Consul at Bilbao would resume his duties because it was felt that conditions made it safe for him to do so. The Department declared that the maintenance of consulates in insurgent territory involved no question of recognition.

Return of consul to insurgent territory

Ambassador Bowers to Secretary Hull, no. 394, Nov. 14, 1937, and Mr. Hull to Mr. Bowers, Nov. 15, 1937, MS. Department of State, file 125.199/52.

On November 24, 1937 the Department of State instructed the Ambassador in Spain to address an informal and personal letter to General Franco concerning sentences imposed upon certain American citizens by the judicial authorities of the insurgents. The Department said that it had given careful consideration to this step and was "convinced that the sending of such a personal letter would have no bearing whatever upon, and raise no question in connection with, the subject of recognition". Upon the suggestion of the Ambassador, he was authorized to address General Franco as "His Excellency, General Francisco Franco".

Form of address of General Franco

Secretary Hull to Ambassador Bowers, no. B–385, Nov. 24, 1937, MS. Department of State, file 352.1121 Fernandez, Antonio/117; Mr. Hull to Mr. Bowers, no. B–386, Nov. 26, 1937, *ibid.* 352.1121 Fernandez, Antonio/119½.

EFFECT OF NON-RECOGNITION

§54

Legislative
decrees: ter-
ritorial effect

In the cases of *M. Salimoff & Co. et al.* v. *Standard Oil Co. of New York* and *Same* v. *Vacuum Oil Co.*, the former owners of petroleum property in Russia, nationalized by a decree of the Soviet Government dated June 20, 1918, joined in an equitable action for an accounting with respect to oil taken from lands formerly belonging to the plaintiffs and sold to the defendants by the Soviet Government. (*Izvestia*, June 22, 1918, no. 127 (391), p. 4, cols. 3 and 4.) The Court of Appeals of New York, in affirming the orders of the Appellate Division dismissing the plaintiffs' complaint, adverted to the following statement made by the Secretary of State concerning the status of the Soviet Government:

> 2. The Department of State is cognizant of the fact that the Soviet régime is exercising control and power in territory of the former Russian Empire and the Department of State has no disposition to ignore that fact.
> 3. The refusal of the Government of the United States to accord recognition to the Soviet régime is not based on the ground that that régime does not exercise control and authority in territory of the former Russian Empire, but on other facts.

It then continued:

> It follows that the question as to the validity of acts and decrees of a régime, not the subject of diplomatic recognition, becomes a matter to be decided by the courts in an appropriate case.

> .   .   .   .

> . . . The question with us is whether, within Russia, the Soviet decrees have actually attained such effect as to alter the rights and obligations of parties in a manner we may not in justice disregard, even though they do not emanate from a lawfully established authority, recognized politically by the government of the United States.

> .   .   .   .

> The legitimate conclusion is that the existing government cannot be ignored by the courts of this state, so far as the validity of its acts in Russia is concerned, although the attempt is here made to nullify such acts and create a cause of action in tort in favor of Russian nationals against American corporations, purchasers for value from the Soviet government of property in Russia in accordance with Soviet law.

> .   .   .   .

> Nonrecognition is no answer to defendant's contention, no reason for regarding as of no legal effect the laws of an unrecognized government ruling by force, as the Soviet government in Russia concededly was. "Within its own territory the Soviet was a sovereign power."   W. S. Andrews, J., in 12 Cornell Law Quarterly, 441.

262 N.Y. (1933) 220, 224, 225, 228, 186 N.E. 679, 681, 682–683. See the dictum of the court of appeals in its earlier opinion in the case of *Sokoloff* v. *The National City Bank of New York*, 239 N.Y. (1924) 158, 163, 165–166, 145 N.E. 917, 918, 919. Cf. the case of *Bourne* v. *Bourne*, 204 N.Y. Supp. 866, 873 (Sup. Ct., App. Div., 1st Dept., 1924).

The fall of one governmental establishment and the substitution of another governmental establishment which actually governs, which is able to enforce its claims by military force and is obeyed by the people over whom it rules, must profoundly affect all the acts and duties, all the relations of those who live within the territory over which the new establishment exercises rule. Its rule may be without lawful foundation; but, lawful or unlawful, its existence is a fact, and that fact cannot be destroyed by juridical concepts. The State Department determines whether it will recognize its existence as lawful, and, until the State Department has recognized the new establishment, the court may not pass upon its legitimacy or ascribe to its decrees all the effect which inheres in the laws or orders of a sovereign.

Russian Reinsurance Company et al. v. *Stoddard*, 240 N.Y. (1925) 149, 158, 147 N.E. 703, 705.

The cases of the *Banque de France* v. *Equitable Trust Co. of New York*, and *Same* v. *Chase National Bank of the City of New York* involved an action by the Bank of France to recover gold purchased by it in 1917 in Russia and entrusted for safekeeping to the State Bank of the Russian Empire at Petrograd (Leningrad) to be held for account of the Bank of France. The defendants alleged that the gold in their possession was not the property of the plaintiff but the property of the State Bank of the Union of Soviet Socialist Republics and that the gold delivered to the State Bank of the Russian Empire had been confiscated under decrees of the Russian Socialist Federal Soviet Republic. In denying the plaintiff's motions to strike out these defenses in the defendants' answer, Judge Goddard of the District Court of the United States for the Southern District of New York said:

That there is an existing government in Russia Sovereign within its own territory cannot be and is not entirely ignored even by our own country, although it has not recognized such government. For instance, in proceedings to naturalize Russian citizens, the executive and judicial branches of our own government acknowledge the existence of "the present Government of Russia" to the extent of requiring such applicants for citizenship to forswear allegiance to "the present Government of Russia." Russian Government v. Lehigh Valley R. Co. (D.C.) 293 F. 133, 135.

. . . .

. . . there has now developed what I think will be generally regarded as the rule here. It holds to the principle that the refusal of the political department to recognize a government should not be allowed to affect private rights which may depend upon proving the existing conditions in such state.

Justice requires that effect should be given by our courts, even though we do not recognize the Russian Government, to those acts in Russia upon which the rights of our citizens depend, provided that in so doing our judicial department does not encroach upon or interfere with the political branch of our government.

33 F. (2d) 202, 205, 206 (S.D.N.Y., 1929). In the case of *Gurdus* v. *Philadelphia National Bank* the Supreme Court of Pennsylvania rejected the defendant's contention that the court below should have taken judicial notice of the fact that the Kerensky government, in power at the time certain leather was sold, was overthrown on Nov. 7, 1918 by the Soviet Republic, which was not recognized by the United States, so paralyzing the judiciary of Russia as to prevent the defendant from forcing his correspondent in Moscow to account for the money paid. It affirmed the judgment below in favor of the plaintiff for damages resulting from refusal to deliver certain merchandise purchased in Russia and said that the evidence showed that up to the time the money was paid the Soviet Republic had not interfered with the operations of the defendant's agent. It declared that "under such circumstances no court could judicially notice this alleged situation" and added that, even assuming that the court could take judicial notice of the fall of the Kerensky government and of the control attained by the Soviet Government, the defendant would be likewise bound to take notice of these facts and to act accordingly. 273 Pa. (1922) 110, 116 Atl. 672, 674.

Extraterritorial effect

Action was brought in the case of *Petrogradsky Mejdunarodny Kommerchesky Bank* v. *The National City Bank of New York* by a Russian bank chartered in 1869 by the Russian Imperial Government to recover the balance of money deposited by it with the defendant in 1911 and 1915. By decrees of the Soviet Government in 1917 the bank was declared to be merged in the People's or State Bank. Its assets were confiscated, its liabilities canceled, and its shares extinguished. By a later decree in 1920 the People's or State Bank was itself abolished. The defendant alleged, *inter alia*, that the plaintiff corporation had been dissolved and was no longer a juristic person and that its former directors had no authority to speak for it. In directing judgment for the plaintiff and in holding that the directors (of which the court remarked that a quorum was still alive) had authority to act for the corporation, the New York Court of Appeals said, speaking through Chief Justice Cardozo:

We think the plaintiff is not dissolved, but is still a juristic person with capacity to sue.

The decrees of the Soviet Republic nationalizing the Russian banks are not law in the United States, nor recognized as law. . . . We do not recognize the decrees of Soviet Russia as competent to divest the plaintiff of the title to any assets that would otherwise have the protection of our law. At least this must be so where the title thus divested is transferred to the very government not recognized as existent. For the same reason we do not admit their competence in aid of a like purpose to pass sentence of death on the expropriated owner. Death, if it has followed, is not death by act of law. Hervey, The Legal Effects of Recognition in International Law, passim, 38 Harv. L. Rev. 818, 822; cf. Noel-Henry, Les Gouvernements de Fait devant le Juge, pp. 98, 107, 108.

In saying this we assume, though we are not required to decide, that the decrees were intended to extinguish the life of the nationalized banks, and not merely to strip them of ownership or usufruct (cf., however, *Russian C. & I. Bank* v. *Comptoir d'Escompte de Mulhouse*, [1925] App. Cas. 112; *Banque* etc., v. *Goukassow*, [1925] App. Cas. 150; *Employers' Liability Assur. Corp., Ltd.*, v. *Sedgwick & Co.*, [1927] App. Cas. 95; Wohl, Nationalization of Joint Stock Banking Corporations in Soviet Russia, 75 U. of Penn. L. Rev. 385, 386, 392, 395, with references to decisions in France and Germany).

. . . .

. . . The corporation survives in such a sense and to such a degree that it may still be dealt with as a *persona* in lands where the decrees of the Soviet Republic are not recognized as law.

253 N.Y. (1930) 23, 28, 29, 36, 170 N.E. 479, 481, 484.

In the case of *The People of the State of New York, by Beha* v. *Russian Reinsurance Company of Petrograd, Russia* involving a similar action, in which it appeared that, after the domestic creditors and policyholders had been paid, a surplus remained, the court ordered the return of the surplus to the companies for the satisfaction of the claims of foreign creditors and policyholders through the usual remedies at law. With reference to the decision in the *Petrogradsky* case, Chief Justice Cardozo, in his opinion for the court, said:

"The present state of the law in respect of these Russian corporations driven from their domicile and there subjected to decrees of confiscation and extinction has been expounded with a full review of the decisions in a recent judgment of this court. *Petrogradsky Mejdunarodny Kommerchesky Bank* v. *National City Bank*, 253 N.Y. 23, 170 N.E. 479; cf. *Severnoe Securities Corporation* v. *London & Lancashire Ins. Co.*, 255 N.Y. 120, 174 N.E. 299. The ruling was that they were still juristic persons, and that their boards of directors, represented by a quorum, were still competent to act. The doctrine of that decision controls the case at hand. True, of course, it is that a court of equity will not decree the payment of a fund to the corporations or their officers if the situation gives notice that waste or spoliation of the assets is threatened or intended. Nothing of the kind appears. The fund will not be paid to the corporations until opportunity has been given to the creditors to enforce their demands against the surplus by execution or attachment if they have failed to protect themselves already by filing proofs of claim. . . ." 255 N.Y. (1931) 415, 425–426, 175 N.E. 114, 117.

See also *In re People, by Beha, Superintendent of Insurance, In re First Russian Insurance Company*, 255 N.Y. (1931) 428, 175 N.E. 118–120; *In re People, by Beha, Superintendent of Insurance, In re Moscow Fire Insurance Company of Moscow, Russia, In re Northern Insurance Company of Moscow, Russia*, 255 N.Y. (1931) 433, 175 N.E. 120–121; *In re People, by Beha, Superintendent of Insurance, In re Second Russian Insurance Company*, 255

N.Y. (1931) 436, 175 N.E. 121–122; *In re People, by Beha, Superintendent of Insurance, In re First Russian Insurance Company*, 255 N.Y. (1931) 440, 175 N.E. 122–123.

In granting a motion by the plaintiff in the case of *Hennenlotter* v. *Norwich Union Fire Ins. Soc., Limited, et al.*, for an order to bring in as additional parties defendant to the action a Russian corporation and a Norwegian corporation, the Supreme Court of Kings County, New York, said:

> "It is urged that the Russian corporation is now an arm or part of the Soviet government of Russia, and that, since our government has refused to recognize the Soviet government of Russia, it is impossible to make it a party. In my opinion, the Russian corporation is to be regarded, not as an agent or instrumentality of the Soviet government, but as still being the pre-Soviet corporation, unaffected by the acts or decrees of the present government of Russia, and qualified to act, be sued, or appear as it existed prior to the revolution. James & Co. v. Second Russian Ins. Co., 208 App. Div. 141, 203 N.Y.S. 232; Gumoens v. Equitable Trust Co. of New York (Sup.) 201 N.Y.S. 96." 207 N.Y. Supp. 588 (Sup. Ct., Kings Cy., spec. term, 1924).

> In the case of *Wulfsohn et al.* v. *Russo-Asiatic Bank* the Russo-Asiatic Bank, a Russian corporation doing business in China, brought an action to recover the sum of $160,000 alleged to be due on an exchange transaction. The defendant contended among other things that the Russo-Asiatic Bank had been nationalized by certain decrees of the Soviet Government and that consequently it had no legal capacity to sue. The Circuit Court of Appeals for the Ninth Circuit (in affirming the judgment of the United States Court for China in favor of the plaintiff) declared that since the plaintiff had continued to do business with the defendant after the decrees in question it was estopped from questioning the corporate existence of the plaintiff or its right to maintain this action. 11 F. (2d) 715, 718 (C. C. A. 9th, 1926).

In an action on contracts of reinsurance in the case of *Fred S. James & Company* v. *Second Russian Insurance Company*, the defendant urged that although it was engaged in insurance business in New York its corporate life had been ended by a decree of the Soviet Government nationalizing the business of insurance companies in Russia. At the time the case was decided (1925) the Soviet Government was not recognized by the United States. The New York Court of Appeals, in holding that the liability of the defendant, which had assets available for seizure in New York, was not extinguished by the Soviet decree of nationalization, said:

> . . . Our concern is not so much with the consequences intended by the authors of the decree as with those that will be permitted in other jurisdictions where the intentions of its authors are without effect as law. . . . Far from suspending its activities since the promulgation of the decree which is said to have ended its existence, it has since then written policies of insurance covering millions of dollars of risks, has collected premiums in large amounts and by the admissions of its answer, is doing business to-day. If the Russian government had been recognized by the United States as a government de jure, there might be need, even then, to consider whether a defendant so circumstanced,

continuing to exercise its corporate powers under the license of our laws, would be heard to assert its extinction in avoidance of a suit. Cf. Thompson on Corporations, §6569; 2 Morawetz, Private Corporations (2d Ed.) §1003; 37 Harvard Law Review, 610.

In the existing situation, the refinements of learning that envelop and to some extent obscure the definition of de facto corporations are foreign to our inquiry. So long, at least, as the decree of the Russian government is denied recognition as an utterance of sovereignty, the problem before us is governed, not by any technical rules, but by the largest considerations of public policy and justice. *MacLeod* v. *U.S.*, 229 U.S. 416, 428, 429, 33 S. Ct. 955, 57 L. Ed. 1260. When regard is had to these, the answer is not doubtful. The defendant asks us to declare its death as a means to the nullification of its debts and the confiscation of its assets by the government of its domicile. Neither the public policy of the nation, as established by President and Congress, nor any consideration of equity or justice, exacts an exception in such conditions to the need of recognition. We do not say that a government unrecognized by ours will always be viewed as nonexistent by our courts, though the sole question at issue has to do with a transaction between the unrecognized government and a citizen or subject of a government by which recognition has [*?not*] been given. . . . We deal now with the single question whether the defendant has an existence sufficient to subject it to suit in the domestic forum. That is a question which the law of the forum will determine for itself. Liability to be sued is quite distinct from liability to be held in judgment upon the facts developed in the suit. We keep our ruling within these limits, and hold that the defendant is amenable to the process of our courts.

. . . As to the Soviet decree, we think its attempted extinguishment of liabilities is *brutum fulmen*, in England as well as here, and this whether the government attempting it has been recognized or not. Russia might terminate the liability of Russian corporations in Russian courts or under Russian law. Its fiat to that effect could not constrain the courts of other sovereignties, if assets of the debtor were available for seizure in the jurisdiction of the forum (*Barth* v. *Backus*, 140 N.Y. 230 [35 N.E. 425, 23 L.R.A. 47, 37 Am. St. Rep. 545]; *Matter of People* [*City Equitable Fire Ins. Co.*], 238 N.Y. 147, 152 [144 N.E. 484]; cf. *Matter of Barnetts' Trusts*, 1902, 1 Ch. 847).

239 N.Y. (1925) 248, 255, 256, 257, 146 N.E. 369, 370, 371.

The Court of Appeals of New York held in the case of *Joint-Stock Co. of Volgakama Oil & Chemical Factory* v. *National City Bank of New York*, an action by a Russian corporation for the recovery of a sum of money deposited with the defendant some seven months after the establishment of the Soviet regime in Russia, that the decrees of the Soviet Government, as set forth in the pleadings, did not have the effect of terminating the existence of the corporation and accordingly affirmed a judgment below granting the plaintiff's motion for summary judgment. 240 N.Y. (1925) 368, 375, 148 N.E. 552, 555. Accord: *Moscow Machine Tool and Engine Company* v. *Richard et al.*, 240 N.Y. (1925) 707, 148 N.E. 768.

In the case of *Russian Reinsurance Company et al.* v. *Stoddard*, the plaintiff, incorporated in Russia in 1899 and authorized to transact business in the State of New York in 1906, brought an action to compel the return of certain securities deposited by it under a trust agreement for the protection of policyholders and creditors in the United States. The trustee resisted the claim on the ground, *inter alia*, that the plaintiff corporation was no longer in existence or if in existence had no capacity to sue on account of a decree of the Soviet Government, which was not then recognized by the United States, nationalizing the business of insurance. The New York Court of Appeals reversed the judgment of the appellate division reversing the judgment of dismissal in a lower court and affirmed that judgment. With reference to the effect upon the rights of the parties of the fact that the United States had not recognized the Soviet Government, the court of appeals said in part:

". . . The State Department determines only that question [of political recognition]. It cannot determine how far the private rights and obligations of individuals are affected by acts of a body not sovereign, or with which our government will have no dealings. That question does not concern our foreign relations. It is not a political question, but a judicial question. The courts in considering that question assume as a premise that until recognition these acts are not in full sense law. Their conclusion must depend upon whether these have nevertheless had such an actual effect that they may not be disregarded. In such case we deal with result rather than cause. We do not pass upon what such an unrecognized governmental authority may do, or upon the right or wrong of what it has done; we consider the effect upon others of that which has been done, primarily from the point of view of fact rather than of theory.

.   .   .   .

"We grant admission to the courts of this state to foreign corporations because of comity. We have not admitted to our comity the Soviet Republic, and the plaintiff denies allegiance to it. The claim based upon comity with a government of the Czar which may exist as a juridical concept, but is in fact not functioning and is without representative here, is tenuous. It should not prevail where injustice follows to one of our own nationals.

"Our inability to protect by our judgment this defendant against a second recovery upon the same cause of action presents a strong consideration against assuming jurisdiction of this action. *Mahr* v. *Norwich Union Fire Insurance Co.*, 127 N.Y. 452, 28 N.E. 391. The corporation is deprived of no substantial right or benefit, if our courts refuse to entertain jurisdiction of an action brought by it until the time comes when a government which we recognize rules the country of plaintiff's corporate domicile, or at least until the plaintiff corporation is able to re-establish its existence in that domicile, and the machinery provided by its charter for the management of its affairs is again functioning. If it is urged that by so doing we may enable the Soviet government in case of recognition by the State Department to assert here an unjust claim based upon confiscation, the answer is that the responsibility rests upon that branch of our government to determine in the first instance whether and upon what terms the Soviet government should hereafter be recognized, and the courts will then determine, subject to any rights granted by treaty, whether they will enforce any claim asserted by that government.

"To the extent that until that time the courts should not take jurisdiction of this equitable cause of action, both justice and common sense require us to give effect to the conditions existing in Russia, though those conditions are created by a force which we are not ready to acknowledge as entitled to recognition as a state or government." 240 N.Y. (1925) 149, 158, 168–169, 147 N.E. 703, 705, 707, 709.

In a *per-curiam* opinion rendered the same day in the case of the *First Russian Insurance Co. et al.* v. *Beha* the court said that the considerations which led to a reversal in the case of *Russian Reinsurance Company* v. *Bankers' Trust Company* [?*Stoddard*] were not presented by the record in this case and added:

". . . The continued existence of the corporation and the authority of the directors are conclusively established by the findings which have been unanimously affirmed. The defendant holds the property and is sued as an officer of the state, and there is no danger of recovery against him in another jurisdiction." 240 N.Y. (1925) 601, 148 N.E. 722.

Twenty-two actions were combined in the case of *Dougherty* v. *Equitable Life Assur. Soc. of United States* involving suits brought against the defendant on certain policies of insurance by its branch organized in Russia under the laws of the Imperial Government. The court of appeals reversed the decision of the appellate division in favor of the plaintiffs and dismissed the complaints, holding in effect that the insurance contracts written in Russia between the defendant's branch there and the insured who were Russian citizens residing in Russia were to be governed by Russian law and that, since by Russian law the contractual obligation itself had been destroyed, no cause of action in favor of the plaintiffs remained. With reference to the effect of the decrees issued by the Soviet Government at a time when it had not been recognized by the United States and of the subsequent recognition of the Soviet Government by the United States, Judge Crane said in his opinion speaking for the court:

"The question now for us to determine is, What effect these laws and decrees of an established government, binding upon the citizens of Russia in Russia, have upon this defendant's contracts, made in Russia with Russian citizens, to be determined and interpreted and given effect, if any, according to Russian law. Of course, we start with the premise that the United States has now recognized the Soviet Republic, and that the government of Russia is in all respects to be treated as any other power in Europe.

.   .   .   .

"The plaintiffs, respondents, have referred to certain of our cases as indicating that the recognition of the Soviet Republic by this country gives no validity to previous decrees. All of these, with one exception, had to do with contracts made out of Russia, most of them with contracts made in New York, to be governed by New York law.

.   .   .   .

"Recognition does not compel our courts to give effect to foreign laws if they are contrary to our public policy. Some writers have suggested that non-recognition was an insufficient reason for the refusal of our courts to enforce the laws of another country; rather, it should have been that those laws were contrary to our public policy. ('The Unrecognized Government in American Courts,' by Professor Borchard, 26 American Journal of International Law [1932] 261, 268; 'Judicial Aspects of Foreign Relations,' Louis L. Jaffe; 'Comparative and International Aspects of American Gold Clause Abrogation,' by Arthur Nussbaum, vol. XLIV, Yale Law Journal, p. 53 [Nov. 1934].)

"However, it cannot be against the public policy of this state to hold nationals to the contracts which they have made in their own country to be performed there according to the laws of that country. When they have specifically stipulated that the laws of their native land shall govern their acts, we give effect to those laws after recognition by this country the same as we would give effect to the laws of any nation which had not developed out of revolution.

"Our conclusion, therefore, is that, since recognition, the Soviet decrees became the laws of Russia, governing the policies here in question, and that obligations thereunder were at an end." 266 N.Y. (1934) 71, 83–84, 88, 90, 193 N.E. 897, 900, 902, 903.

Guaranty Trust Co. of New York v. *United States*, decided by the Supreme Court of the United States, involved an action by the United States under an assignment from the Soviet Government of November 16, 1933 to recover the sum of $5,000,000 deposited with the Guaranty Trust Company of New York by the Provisional Government of Russia in July 1917. The Court held that the statute of limitations runs against a foreign government and that the United States as assignee could claim no greater rights than the assignor. Although ruling that notice of repudiation given by the Guaranty Trust Company to the diplomatic representatives of the Provisional Government of Russia must "so far as our own [American] courts are concerned, be taken as notice to the state whom they represented" (the Government of the United States having continued to recognize the representative of the Provisional Government), the Court said with reference to the right of the Soviet Government to maintain a suit in the courts of the United States:

Non-recognized state in local courts: as plaintiff

It is not denied that, in conformity to generally accepted principles, the Soviet Government could not maintain a suit in our courts before its recognition by the political department of the Government. For this reason access to the federal and state courts was denied to the Soviet Government before recognition. *The Penza*, 277 Fed. 91; *The Rogdai*, 278 Fed. 294; *R.S.F.S.R.* v. *Cibrario*, 235 N.Y. 255; *Preobazhenski* v. *Cibrario*, 192 N.Y. Supp. 275.

304 U.S. (1938) 126, 137.

In the case of *Russian Socialist Federated Soviet Republic* v. *Cibrario*, cited by the Supreme Court, the New York Court of Appeals in affirming a judgment dismissing a complaint brought by the existing *de facto* Soviet Government, said with reference to the "right" of such a non-recognized government to become a plaintiff:

"We reach the conclusion, therefore, that a foreign power brings an action in our courts not as a matter of right. Its power to do so is the creature of comity. Until such government is recognized by the United States, no such comity exists. The plaintiff concededly has not been so recognized. There is, therefore, no proper party before us. . . .

"We are the more ready to reach this conclusion because to hold otherwise might tend to nullify the rule that public policy must always prevail over comity. More than once during the last 70 years our relations with one or another existing but unrecognized government have been of so critical a character that to permit it to recover in our courts funds which might strengthen it or which might even be used against our interests would be unwise. We should do nothing to thwart the policy which the United States has adopted." 235 N.Y. (1923) 255, 262, 263, 139 N.E. 259, 261, 262.

In *The Penza* and *The Tobolsk* the Russian Socialist Federal Soviet Republic and Mr. Ludwig C. A. K. Martens, as agent and representative thereof, filed a libel seeking possession of two steamers. In dismissing the libel the court said, "The Soviet Republic never having been recognized as a soverign state by this government, it may not maintain this libel in the federal courts. Its alleged agent would have no better or greater rights than his principal." 277 Fed. 91, 94 (E.D.N.Y., 1921).

However, non-recognition does not in general abridge the rights of citizens of a state the government of which has not been recognized to sue in our courts. For example, in the case of the *Russian Volunteer Fleet* v. *United States* the petitioner sued to recover just compensation for the requisitioning by the United States Shipping Board Emergency Fleet Corporation, under authority delegated to it by the President, of contracts for the construction of two vessels. The Court of Claims held itself to be without jurisdiction to entertain the action on the ground that, since the United States had not recognized the Government of the Union of Soviet Socialist Republics, there could be no reciprocity as required by section 155 of the Judicial Code. That section limited the rights of aliens to prosecute claims against the Government of the United States in the Court of Claims to those cases in which the government of which the alien was a citizen or a subject accorded a similar privilege to the citizens of the United States. The Supreme Court granted a writ of certiorari and reversed the judgment on the ground that the act of June 15, 1917, under which the action had been brought, made no reference to section 155 of the Judicial Code and that to deny a right of action to the plaintiff under such circumstance, in the absence of any other remedy, would be contrary to the fifth amendment to the Federal Constitution. The Court said that it did not "regard it as an admissible construction of the act of June 15, 1917 to hold that the Congress intended that the right of an alien friend to recover just compensation should be defeated or postponed because of the lack of recognition by the Government of the United States of the régime in his country". It added that the question as presented was "not one of a claim advanced by or on behalf of a foreign government or régime, but . . . simply one of compensating an owner of property taken by the United States".

68 Ct. Cls. (1929) 32, 33, 35–36; 282 U.S. (1931) 481, 492.

In a telegram of June 27, 1928 the Minister in China stated that in response to an inquiry whether the United States Government was prepared to recognize the Nationalist Government as having capacity to sue in the United

States Court for China as a *de facto* government, for the purpose only of filing a suit in that court, he intended to say:

> "In reply to your letter of June 20th I beg leave to inform you that the American Government has been for sometime and now is in de facto relationship with the Nationalist regime established at Nanking. With reference to your specific enquiry whether the Nationalist Government have the capacity to sue in the United States Court for China for and on behalf of the Republic of China, I must advise you that this question appears to be one for judicial determination."

The Department of State approved this reply. Minister MacMurray to Secretary Kellogg, no. 499, June 27, 1928, and Mr. Kellogg to Mr. MacMurray, no. 208, June 28, 1928, MS. Department of State, file 893.01/292.

As
defendant

In the case of *Wulfsohn* v. *Russian Socialist Federated Soviet Republic*, an action brought against the existing *de facto* Soviet Government on account of furs owned by the plaintiff which had been stored in Russia and confiscated by the Soviet Government, the New York Court of Appeals reversed an order of the lower courts denying the motion to vacate a writ of attachment. At the time when the case was decided (1923) the existing Soviet Government was not recognized by the United States. In reversing the order of the lower courts, the court of appeals said:

> . . . We have an existing government sovereign within its own territories. There necessarily its jurisdiction is exclusive and absolute. It is susceptible of no limitation not imposed by itself. This is the result of its independence. It may be conceded that its actions should accord with natural justice and equity. If they do not, however, our courts are not competent to review them. They may not bring a foreign sovereign before our bar, not because of comity, but because he has not submitted himself to our laws. Without his consent he is not subject to them. Concededly that is so as to a foreign government that has received recognition. [Here follows the citation of cases.] But whether recognized or not the evil of such an attempt would be the same. "To cite a foreign potentate into a municipal court for any complaint against him in his public capacity is contrary to the law of nations and an insult which he is entitled to resent." (*De Haber* v. *Queen of Portugal*, 17 Q.B. 171.) In either case to do so would "vex the peace of nations." In either case the hands of the state department would be tied. Unwillingly it would find itself involved in disputes it might think unwise. Such is not the proper method of redress if a citizen of the United States is wronged. The question is a political one, not confided to the courts but to another department of government. Whenever an act done by a sovereign in his sovereign character is questioned it becomes a matter of negotiation, or of reprisals or of war.

234 N.Y. (1923) 372, 375–376, 138 N.E. 24, 25–26.

In holding in the case of *Nankivel et al.* v. *Omsk All-Russian Government et al.* that an action could not be maintained against the defendant government on the ground that it had ceased to exist at the time that the suit was begun, the Court of Appeals of New York said in the course of its opinion with reference to the position of a non-recognized government as a defendant:

> So long as it maintained an independent existence it was immune from suit for its governmental acts in our courts without its consent. Lack of recognition by the United States government, we have recently held, does not permit an individual suitor to bring a de facto government before the bar. *Wulfsohn* v. *Russian Socialist Federated Soviet Republic*, 234 N.Y. 372. To sue a sovereign state is to insult it in a manner which it may treat with silent contempt. It is not bound to come into our courts and plead its immunity. It is liable to suit only when its consent is duly given. *People of Porto Rico* v. *Rosaly*, 227 U.S. 270. When defendant was extinguished by conquest, it became, so far as its continued corporate existence is concerned, as if it had never existed. *Williams* v. *Bruffy*, 96 U.S. 176, 185.

237 N.Y. (1923) 150, 156, 142 N.E. 569, 570–571. Accord: *Voevodine* v. *Government of the Commander-in-Chief of the Armed Forces in the South of Russia et al.*, 232 App. Div. (1931) 204, 249 N.Y. Supp. 644; 257 N.Y. (1931) 557, 178 N.E. 793.

. . . It is to be noted that the answer sets up that the shipments of gold in question were shipped by the State Bank of the Union of Soviet Socialist Republics, and that it appears from the pleadings of the plaintiff that its gold was seized by the Government of Russia and that the State Bank of the Union of Soviet Socialist Republics was a part of said government, so that the plaintiff is here asserting that the gold in question is claimed by the Union of Soviet Socialist Republics in opposition to the plaintiff's rights, and the result is a suit brought in this jurisdiction which involves the title to property claimed by the Russian Government, and that leads to the consideration of the question: Who is the sovereign de facto or de jure in Russia? And this is not a judicial but is a political question, and it is immaterial whether the foreign sovereign has been recognized or not. Wulfsohn v. Russian Republic, supra; Jones v. United States, 137 U.S. 202, 11 S. Ct. 80, 34 L. Ed. 691.

Furthermore, it is alleged by the plaintiff itself that the Union of Soviet Socialist Republics is a foreign government, so that as in the Wulfsohn Case, it is unnecessary for that fact to be made known to the court by a formal "suggestion" through the State Department. Thus, it appears that this court is not in a position to pass upon the issue, not because of nonrecognition but simply for the reason, as stated by Judge Andrews in Wulfsohn v. Russian, etc., Republic, supra, at page 376 of 234 N.Y. (138 N.E. 26): "They may not bring a foreign sovereign before our bar, not because of comity, but because he has not submitted himself to our laws. Without his consent he is not subject to them."

110090—40——25

Banque de France v. *Equitable Trust Co. of New York*, 33 F. (2d) 202, 207 (S.D.N.Y., 1929).

The claimants are entitled to compensation, unless there has been a failure of competent proof that they are the surviving children of the deceased employee, or that their respective ages are as found by the State Industrial Board, or that they were still in existence at the time of the award. The claimants are said to reside in Russia. Appellants contend that the birth certificates were insufficient to comply with section 121–a of the Workmen's Compensation Law because they depend upon the authentication of officials of Soviet Russia, which is not recognized by the United States of America. The non-recognition of the present government in Russia does not require the rejection of this proof. It has been judicially determined that there does in fact exist a government, sovereign within its own territory, in Russia. . . . In the present case the private rights under our law of the surviving children of a workman, killed in a New York employment, are involved. The act of an official of the Soviet Government in authenticating proof of relationship and age is required to bring about equity and justice. There is no practical way to reach the result contemplated by our humane statute otherwise. In support of the action of the State Industrial Board in accepting this proof, we have also a certificate of the general consul of the Republic of Poland for the city of Minsk in Russia that the signature of the Russian official having charge of foreign affairs is genuine. We are also informed by what is not denied to be authentic record proof, although not a part of the record, that the War and Navy Departments and United States Veteran's Bureau are accepting proofs of relationship executed in similar manner.

Werenjchik et al. v. *Ulen Contracting Corporation et al.*, 229 App. Div. (1930) 36, 240 N.Y. Supp. 619, 620–621.

The widow of an American citizen, who died intestate in Mexico City, having been appointed administratrix by one of the Mexican civil courts, instituted an action in the Supreme Court of New York to obtain payment upon a number of notes made by the defendant in favor of the deceased. The court granted the defendant's motion for judgment on the pleadings, the contention being that an administratrix appointed by a Mexican court could maintain no action in the courts of the United States so long as the executive department of the United States Government declined to recognize the government functioning in Mexico. Judge McAvoy in granting the motion said:

". . . The foreign court is erected in Mexico, whose present government is not yet admitted to recognition as a sovereign by our federal authority. It seems obvious that judicial power cannot be contemplated as in an existence apart from the sovereignty under the sway of which it operates. It is but a branch of government, coeval and coexistent therewith, without distinct entity or being. The Mexican government is not *de facto* here, since recognition alone can make it so. It may have all the attributes of a ruling faction, a colony, a district of people, or maintain any other form of suzerainty in its established domain, but its power as a government remains nil without our patent of recognition. As the parent of the court it cannot have notice, either judicial or administrative, and surely the creature cannot be possessed of a power not given its creator. The duty to declare the legal incapacity to sue is paramount to a consideration of the evils attendant upon the failure of justice resultant upon this policy of international relations." For the text of this opinion, in the case of *Pelzer* v. *United Dredging Company*, which was apparently unreported, see Edwin D. Dickinson, "The Unrecognized Government or State in English and American Law", in 22 Mich. L. Rev. (1923–24) 30.

Having procured letters of administration in New York, the widow then moved to amend her pleadings by dropping her status as administratrix appointed in Mexico and asserting the status acquired under New York law. This motion was granted by the Supreme Court but reversed on appeal to the appellate division, the latter remarking in its opinion that the action of the Supreme Court had apparently been based upon the theory that New York letters were ancillary to the Mexican letters. Holding this procedure to be improper, the court said:

". . . But the letters granted by the Surrogate's Court are not ancillary to any original letters elsewhere issued. Indeed, if they were ancillary to those granted in Mexico, the Surrogate's Court would have had no authority to issue them, for the same reasons which prompted the dismissal of the complaint in this action. A substitution of parties is only permissible where one has lawfully succeeded to the rights and interests formerly held by another party. But the New York administratrix has not derived any rights from the original Mexican administratrix, and hence must be regarded as an independent official, despite the fact that May S. Pelzer happens to be the same individual who was appointed as administratrix in the unrecognized jurisdiction." *Pelzer* v. *United Dredging Company*, 193 N.Y. Supp. 676, 678 (Sup. Ct., App. Div., 1st Dept., 1922). For the opinion of the Supreme Court on the plaintiff's motion to amend, see 193 N.Y. Supp. 675.

. . . as this Government does not recognize the belligerency of the Mexican insurrectionists, such rebels as may enter the United States either singly or in groups may be subject to detention by United States Federal authorities along the border, pursuant to the provisions and procedure of the so-called neutrality statutes.

Secretary Stimson to Senator Ashurst, Apr. 12, 1929, MS. Department of State, file 812.00 Sonora/662.

EFFECT OF RECOGNITION

§55

In the case of *Garvin* v. *Diamond Coal & Coke Co. et al.* the father of the plaintiffs, a subject of Austria-Hungary, had been accidentally killed in the course of his employment with the defendant company. On appeal from a decision of the court of common pleas in favor of the plaintiffs, the company contended that the claim submitted was barred by the statute of limitations, alleging that the statute began to run on the date of the recognition of the Czechoslovak Republic by the United States. In refusing to accept this contention, the court said:

Status of
territory

> We have examined the documents, etc., called to our attention, to ascertain, inter alia, the action taken by our government, and find it did in September, 1918, recognize the existence of such republic, and later sent a representative thereto. At the time of such recognition, however, the republic had an army in the field but no territory, and, so far as appears, the United States never recognized the territory here in question as that of the Czechoslovak Republic. The mere fact that such a republic was recognized proves nothing as to territory, especially as to that claimed to have been thereafter acquired. Furthermore, no treaty between any nations touching the territory here in question, made in time to affect this litigation, has been called to our attention. In the absence of adequate political action recognizing a change of boundaries, we cannot assume the place in question ceased to be enemy territory until the war ended. An opposite conclusion is reached in two cases, cited by appellant, viz. *Kolundjija* v. *Hanna Ore Mining Co.* (Minn.) 193 N.W. 163, and *Waldes et al.* v. *Basch*, 109 Misc. Rep. 306, 179 N.Y. Supp. 713. The former, however, was by a divided court and in the latter such conclusion was not necessary to a decision of the case, for as some of the plaintiffs were alien enemies, being subjects of Germany, the suit failed without reference to the status of the other plaintiffs. Notwithstanding these authorities, for which we have great respect, there is, in our opinion, a distinction between the recognition of a revolutionary people and the territory which they may acquire.

278 Pa. (1924) 469, 472–473, 123 Atl. 468, 469. *Contra: Kolundjija et al.* v. *Hanna Ore Mining Company*, 155 Minn. (1923) 176, 193 N.W. 163–165; *Waldes et al.* v. *Basch et al.*, 109 Misc. (1919) 306, 179 N.Y. Supp. 713 (Sup. Ct., N.Y. Cy., spec. term).

The case of *Inland Steel Co.* v. *Jelenovic et al.* involved an appeal from an award of the industrial board of Indiana granting compensation to the dependent heirs of Ivan Jelenovic who lost his life as a result of an accident which arose out of and in the course of his employment with the company. The company contended that the claim was barred by the statute of limitations, alleging that the statute began to run at the time that the United States recognized the Kingdom of the Serbs, Croats, and Slovenes on February 5, 1919 rather than on July 2, 1921, the date of the approval of the joint resolution of Congress declaring the war with Austria-Hungary at an end (42 Stat. 105). The Appellate Court of Indiana held that the recognition by the United States of the Serb-Croat-Slovene state did not change the alien enemy status of the plaintiffs but that they continued to be alien enemies until July 2, 1921, saying in the course of its opinion:

It is, of course, a well-settled principle, conceded by appellant, that war suspends the operation of the statute of limitations against alien enemies residing in enemy territory. However, it is argued by appellant that whereas appellees were residents of that portion of Austria-Hungary which, after the war began, was incorporated in, and became a part of, the kingdom of the Serbs, Croats, and Slovenes, and whereas the latter kingdom was duly recognized by the United States, February 5, 1919, it must necessarily follow that from the date of such recognition appellees ceased to be alien enemies. Not so. Appellant misconceives the effect of recognition by the executive, and particularly of the Serbian state by the executive department of the United States. The United States by this executive act of recognition did not intend to, nor did it, change the status of any persons whom Congress by prior declaration of war had made alien enemies. It was intended merely as a recognition by appropriate diplomatic act of the existence of the new kingdom, and as an expression of readiness to enter into relationship such as the United States usually establishes with friendly powers. Recognition was extended before peace treaties had settled territorial and other rights, in part, because of our relations with Serbia during the war, and in part, perhaps, because of a desire to stabilize certain conditions in anticipation of the conclusion of definitive peace treaties.

An act of recognition, within the powers delegated to the national executive, is conclusive in all courts in respect to everything which it actually decides, but no further. Certain it is that neither Congress nor the President regarded the act of recognition as terminating the war.

Status of alien enemies

84 Ind. App. (1926) 373, 375–376, 150 N.E. 391, 392–393.

In the opinion of the Supreme Court of the United States in the case of *Guaranty Trust Co. of New York* v. *United States* there appears the following note:

Recognition of Provisional Government of Russia

The United States accorded recognition to the Provisional Government March 16, 1917 and continued to recognize it until November 16, 1933, when the Soviet Government was recognized. During that period the United States declined to recognize the Soviet Government or to receive its accredited representative, and so certified in litigations pending in the federal courts. The Penza, *supra;* The Rogdai, *supra.* It recognized Mr. Bakhmeteff as Russian Ambassador from July 5, 1917 until June 30, 1922, when he retired, having designated Mr. Ughet as custodian of Russian property in the United States. Mr. Ughet, after his appointment as Financial Attache April 7, 1917, continued to be recognized as such by the United States until November 16, 1933. He was recognized by the United States as Charge d'Affaires ad interim, during the absence of the Ambassador from December 3, 1918 to July 31, 1919. Their diplomatic status as stated was certified in the present suit by the Secretary of State, who stated that he considered Mr. Ughet's status unaffected by the termination of the Ambassador's duties.

Their status was certified to by the Department on October 31, 1918 and July 2, 1919, respectively, in Lehigh Valley Railroad Co. *v.* State of Russia, 293 Fed. 133. Mr. Bakhmeteff's status as Ambassador was certified May 18, 1919 in Agency of Canadian Car & Foundry Co. *v.* American Can Co., 258 Fed. 363, 368; on April 6, 1920 in The Rogdai, 278 Fed. 294, 295; on June 24, 1919 in The Penza, 277 Fed. 91, 93. Certificate with respect to both Mr. Bakhmeteff and Mr. Ughet was given February 19, 1923 and with respect to Mr. Ughet December 22, 1927. On the faith of the two last mentioned certificates the Court, in the Lehigh Valley Railroad case, *supra*, as stated by the Government's brief in the present case, ordered to be paid to Mr. Ughet approximately $1,000,000, of which more than $700,000 was paid to the United States Treasurer "on account of interest due on obligations of the Provisional Government of Russia by the Treasurer."

304 U.S. (1938) 126, 138–139.

Termination of relations with Provisional Government

On November 16, 1933, the date of the exchange of notes between the President of the United States and Mr. Litvinov, People's Commissar for Foreign Affairs, providing for the establishment of diplomatic relations between the United States and the Union of Soviet Socialist Republics, the Department of State replied to a letter of October 21, 1933 from Mr. S. Ughet, Russian financial attaché, requesting that his present status be discontinued at the earliest convenience of the Department of State. It said that in view of the recognition of the Union of Soviet Socialist Republics by the Government of the United States it ceased to recognize him as Russian financial attaché as of that date.

The Russian Financial Attaché (Ughet) to the Chief of the Division of Eastern European Affairs (Kelley), Oct. 21, 1933, and the Acting Secretary of State (Phillips) to Mr. Ughet, Nov. 16, 1933, MS. Department of State, files 701.6111/767 and 701.6111/729A.

The two cases disposed of in the decision in *Oetjen* v. *Central Leather Company* involved suits in replevin to establish title to two large consignments of hides which the plaintiff claimed he owned as assignee of a Mexican company, and to which the defendants claimed title by purchase from a Texas corporation which had purchased the hides from General Francisco Villa on January 3, 1914. At the time of the seizure of the hides by Villa, in satisfaction of an assessment imposed upon the owner, and their subsequent sale to the Texas corporation, Villa was an agent of Carranza who was in revolt against the Government of Mexico. In holding that the subsequent recognition by the United States of the government of Carranza as the *de facto* and *de jure* government of Mexico gave validity to the acts of the Carranza government from its inception, the Supreme Court said:

It is also the result of the interpretation by this court of the Retroactive
effect principles of international law that when a government which originates in revolution or revolt is recognized by the political department of our government as the *de jure* government of the country in which it is established, such recognition is retroactive in effect and validates all the actions and conduct of the government so recognized from the commencement of its existence. *Williams* v. *Bruffy*, 96 U.S. 176, 186; *Underhill* v. *Hernandez*, 168 U.S. 250, 253. See the same case 65 Fed. Rep. 577.

246 U.S. (1918) 297, 301, 302–303.

The Court of Errors and Appeals of New Jersey, from whose decision appeal was made to the Supreme Court, arrived at the same result, prior to the recognition of Carranza by the United States, but upon a different ground, namely, that Carranza's government, exercising paramount authority in the territory under his control, had power to pass a valid title to property appropriated as a legitimate act of war. *O'Neill et al.* v. *Central Leather Company et al.*, 87 N.J.L. (1915) 552, 94 Atl. 789. In accord with the *Oetjen* case and involving a similar set of facts, see *Ricaud et al.* v. *American Metal Company, Limited*, 246 U.S. (1918) 304–310.

For a decision held to have been controlled by the *Ricaud* case, involving a question of ownership of a quantity of coffee seized by an agent of the Carranza government in 1914, see *Monteblanco Real Estate Corp.* v. *Wolvin Line et al.*, 147 La. (1920) 563, 85 So. 242. The Supreme Court of New Jersey, in the case of *Molina* v. *Comision Reguladora del Mercado de Henequen*, cited the *Oetjen* and *Ricaud* cases as controlling so far as the retroactive effect of recognition and the validity of the acts of the Carranza government were concerned but held that the act of sequestration involved in the case gave custody only to the property in question and did not transfer title. 92 N.J.L. (1918) 38, 104 Atl. 450.

For opinions citing with approval the decision in the *Oetjen* case, see *Banque de France* v. *Equitable Trust Co. of New York, same* v. *Chase National Bank of the City of New York*, 33 F. (2d) 202, 206 (S.D.N.Y., 1929); *Day-Gormley Leather Co.* v. *National City Bank of New York*, 8 F. Supp. 503, 505–506 (S.D.N.Y., 1934); *M. Salimoff & Co. et al.* v. *Standard Oil Co. of New York, same* v. *Vacuum Oil Co.*, 262 N.Y. (1933) 220, 226, 186 N.E. 679, 681.

In the case of *Terrazas* v. *Holmes et al.*, the plaintiff, a former governor of the State of Chihuahua in Mexico, brought action to recover certain cattle which had belonged to him and which had been seized by the forces of General Carranza, and later by those of General Villa. Citing the *Oetjen* and the *Ricaud* cases, the Supreme Court of Texas held that the action of Carranza had the effect of divesting the plaintiff of title to the property in question since his government had been subsequently recognized by the United States, despite the fact that the defendant's agent had purchased the cattle from the insurgent government of Villa which failed to established its authority. 115 Tex. (1925) 32, 43–44, 275 S.W. 392, 395. Accord: *Terrazas* v. *Donohue, et al.*, 115 Tex. (1925) 46, 275 S.W. 396.

We take judicial notice of the fact that coincident with the assignment [made by the Soviet Government to the United States on November 16, 1933] set forth in the complaint, the President recognized the Soviet government, and normal diplomatic relations were established between that government and the government of the United States, followed by an exchange of ambassadors. The effect of this was to validate, so far as this country is concerned, all acts of the Soviet government here involved from the commencement of its existence. The recognition, establishment of diplomatic relations, the assignment, and agreements with respect thereto, were all parts of one transaction, resulting in an international compact between the two governments. That the negotiations, acceptance of the assignment and agreements and understandings in respect thereof were within the competence of the President may not be doubted.

> *United States* v. *Belmont et al., Executors*, 301 U.S. (1937) 324, 330. For the facts in the case, see *ante* pp. 136–137.

The case of *United States* v. *Bank of New York & Trust Company* involved an action in equity brought by the United States for an accounting by the defendant company with respect to certain funds deposited with the defendant by the Moscow Fire Insurance Company after New York creditors and shareholders had been paid, the claim of the United States being based upon the assignment made by the Soviet Government at the time of its recognition on November 16, 1933. The motion of the defendant to dismiss the complaint for insufficiency was granted by the District Court of the United States for the Southern District of New York on the ground that the action being one *in rem*, the jurisdiction of the State courts of New York should not be disturbed, the fund in question having been paid into the bank under a decree of the Court of Appeals of New York. This decree was affirmed by the Circuit Court of Appeals for the Second Circuit on the same grounds, but, with respect to the contention of the defendant that the assignor had no title or interest not based upon confiscation, a concept so repugnant to public policy in this country that it would not be recognized and endorsed, the court said:

> We take judicial notice of the recognition of the Soviet Government by the United States on November 16, 1933, which was the day on which the assignment here relied upon was made. Underhill v. Hernandez, 168 U.S. 250, 18 S. Ct. 83, 42 L. Ed. 456. By that act of recognition the decrees under which this Russian corporation was dissolved and its property confiscated by the Soviet Government became as valid as they would have been had they been passed at a time when we had already recognized the Soviet Government. The effect of recognition was to that extent retroactive. Ricaud v. American Metal Co., 246 U.S. 304, 38 S. Ct. 312, 62 L. Ed. 733; Oetjen v. Central Leather Co., 246 U.S. 297, 38 S. Ct. 309, 62 L. Ed. 726. When our government recognized that government, the public policy of this country to recognize the validity of Soviet decrees within Soviet territory was established. No one will question the power of the government of the domicile of a corporation to destroy what it has created. . . . When the now recognized Soviet Government issued its decrees to that effect this corporation was dead. . . . There can be no serious dispute that its property and all its corporate rights in

Russia were subject to such disposition as actually took place in accordance with Russian law. The Russian State obviously could, and this record shows that it did, confiscate everything belonging to this corporation within the confines of Russia. It could, and did, acquire for itself every right the corporation in Russia possessed. It became the corporation there so far as we are now concerned. It had all its property and rights as fully as though the corporation had lawfully assigned them to it before dissolution. To that extent our public policy as to confiscatory decrees, so far as it may be expressed by our courts, is of no moment. When the executive branch recognized the Soviet Government, the judicial branch became bound to recognize the validity of Soviet decrees in Soviet territory from the beginning of the Soviet régime. Oetjen v. Central Leather Co., supra. See, also, Lazard Bros. & Co. v. Midland Bank, Ltd., [1933] A.C. 289, H. of L., for the rule in England. Consequently we must for present purposes take the Soviet Government to have become to all intents and purposes the Russian insurance corporation in Russia which owned the deposit in New York subject to the fulfillment of the conditions upon which the deposit was made with the New York Superintendent of Insurance.

This decree was affirmed by the Supreme Court which said in the course of its opinion:

The government also insists that the courts of the state had lost jurisdiction of the funds, prior to the time when the present suits were begun, by reason of the fact that the funds were the property of the Russian government which our government had recognized. But, whatever the effect of recognition, it is manifest that it did not terminate the state proceedings. The state court still had control of the property and questions as to the rights of the parties who were before it, or of those who might come before it, were legal questions which the court had jurisdiction to decide.

10 F. Supp. 269 (S.D.N.Y., 1934); 77 F. (2d) 866, 868 (C.C.A. 2d, 1935); 296 U.S. (1936) 463, 478–479.

. . . It is enough that it is now the recognized sovereign; the action by the chief executive of the United States government conclusively binding this court and all courts in this country. This deprives of any weight whatsoever defendant's contention that his accounting, which he admits he is obligated to make "to the proper authorities," should be postponed until "a stable form of government is established." In view of the action of our government, it is merely incumbent upon this court to find that the authorities who directed the bringing of this suit are "the proper authorities" and that they in fact constitute "a stable form of government." Recognition is never accorded until, in the opinion of the executive, the government recognized is stable, and on this political question the opinion of the executive, whether right or wrong, is the only opinion that can be considered.

State of Yucatan v. *Argumedo et al.*, 92 Misc. (Sup. Ct., N.Y. Cy., spec. term, 1915) 547, 157 N.Y. Supp. 219, 224–225.

Government as litigant

The courts have also held that recognition operates retroactively to accord to the government recognized legal capacity to act as plaintiff or defendant in suits instituted prior to the date of their recognition. The decision in the case of the *State of Yucatan* v. *Argumedo et al.* was on a motion to continue *pendente lite* a temporary injunction against the defendant, who had been in control of the government of the State of Yucatán for a short time in 1915 and had taken with him when he fled the country 900,000 pesos of gold from the treasury of the State, to restrain him from unlawfully appropriating the money to his own use. The government of General Carranza having been recognized as the *de facto* government of Mexico shortly after this action was instituted, the court said, in granting the motion, with reference to the retroactive effect of this recognition:

> It makes no difference that the recognition followed by a few days the institution of this action, for the recognition of the Carranza government relates back to its inception, and all acts of the plaintiff government of Yucatan, such as the bringing of this action, are ratified. . . . When a de facto government is recognized and becomes the de jure government, the recognition relates back to the inception of the government, and it thereupon becomes lawful from the beginning.

> 92 Misc. (Sup. Ct., N.Y. Cy., spec. term, 1915) 547, 157 N.Y. Supp. 219, 225. In the case of *Republic of China* v. *Merchants' Fire Assur. Corporation of New York,* wherein it appeared that recognition of the National Government of the Republic of China was accorded by the United States after the United States Court for China had dismissed the action brought by the National Government on the ground that not having been recognized it had no legal capacity to sue, the Circuit Court of Appeals for the Ninth Circuit took judicial notice of the intervening recognition and reversed the decision. 30 F. (2d) 278, 279 (C. C. A. 9th, 1929).

Territorial limitation

The argument that the plaintiff in error may at some future time, if the Soviet régime is recognized by our government, be compelled to pay again what it is obliged to pay now, is fallacious. It is only the acts performed in its own territory that can be validated by the retroactive effect of recognition. Acts theretofore performed outside its own territory cannot be validated by recognition. The former are illustrated in Underhill v. Hernandez, 168 U.S. 250, 18 S. Ct. 83, 42 L. Ed. 456, where the acts in question were performed in Venezuela; Oetjen v. Central Leather Co., supra, and Ricaud v. American Metal Co., 246 U.S. 304, 38 S. Ct. 312, 62 L. Ed. 733, where there were acts of confiscation in Mexico; and the English case of Luther v. Sagor [1921] 3 K.B. 532, acts performed in Russia. The latter are illustrated by Kennett v. Chambers, supra; U.S. v. Trumbull (D.C.) 48 F. 99; Agency of Canadian Car Co. v. American Can Co., supra.

Following these principles, we agree with the contention of the defendant in error that the state of Russia, as a plaintiff, may continue the prosecution through the agency vested in Mr. Ughet, and the plaintiff in error will be protected as against any possible future claims of a subsequent recognized government of Russia, if payment be made as directed in this judgment.

Lehigh Valley R. Co. v. *State of Russia*, 21 F. (2d) 396, 401 (C.C.A.2d, 1927).

The general statement contained in the opinion in *Salimoff & Co.* v. *Standard Oil Co.*, 262 N.Y. 220, 186 N.E. 679, to the effect that recognition of a de facto government as a de jure government is retroactive in effect and validates all the acts of the government so recognized from the commencement of its existence, must be read in connection with its context, and, as so read, it did not refer to acts sought to be given effect extraterritorially.

Vladikavkazsky Ry. Co. v. *New York Trust Co.*, 263 N.Y. (1934) 369, 379, 189 N.E. 456, 460.

The following quotation bearing on consequences of recognition of belligerency is set forth in the case of *The Three Friends* [166 U.S. (1896) 1, 63]:

". . . the recognition of belligerency involves the rights of blockade, visitation, search and seizure of contraband articles on the high seas, and abandonment of claims for reparation on account of damages suffered by our citizens from the prevalence of warfare." *Belligerency*

And

"Recognition of belligerency does not confer upon the community recognized all the rights of an independent state, but it grants to its government and subjects the rights and imposes upon them the obligations of an independent state in all matters relating to the war." (Lawrence, Principles of International Law, Section 162.)

Recognition presupposes the existence of what is equivalent to war between the parties in opposition and serves to clothe each with such rights with respect to the recognizing state as might be claimed in a conflict being waged between two independent states. The consequences are such as to confer a distinct benefit upon the insurgents to whom recognition is accorded and to increase proportionally the burdens of the Government opposing them. A foreign state, therefore, is not free thus to aid an insurgent cause except under special conditions which relieve the former from the normal duty of restraint. The according of recognition to insurgents who have not achieved such degree of success as gives them an organization purporting to have the characteristics of a state, constitutes the giving of aid to a cause or movement which at the time is incapable of assuming those responsibilities of a belligerent. Such premature recognition may give grounds for a complaint by the established government that recognition is designed primarily to aid the insurrection.

Within a month after the beginning of the Civil War in the United States Great Britain, on April 30, 1861, recognized the confederate states as belligerents and on May 13, 1861 issued a neutrality proclamation.   Other European states followed Great Britain in recognizing the confederate states as belligerents.

The action of Great Britain was regarded by the United States as premature and was later declared by a British statesman to have been accomplished "with unfriendly haste".

Having recognized a state of belligerency Great Britain was held to have failed to perform her neutral obligations by allowing the construction, fitting out and departure from British ports of confederate cruisers for which that country was required to pay damages to the United States.

Opinion of the Solicitor for the Department of State, Oct. 13, 1930, MS. Department of State, file 832.01/23.

In an opinion of Nov. 18, 1909 the Solicitor said:

"The consequences of belligerency naturally enter into a question of the propriety of its recognition and may often in themselves be determinative." MS. Department of State, file 6369/698.

On November 1, 1918 the Polish Army was recognized by the United States as autonomous and co-belligerent under the supreme political authority of the Polish National Committee.   On February 21, 1918 the representative of the Polish National Committee in the United States, Ignace Jan Paderewski, informed the Department of State that the Polish National Committee had selected Michael Kwaspiszewski to act as its representative in the United States in charge of the issuance of certificates of Polish nationality to Poles born in Germany and Austria, as well as Russian Poland.   He requested permission to open subagencies in certain centers of Polish immigration in the United States at which applications for certificates could be received and transmitted for consideration to the main agency.   In response to a request from the Department for advice in the matter, the Attorney General replied that he saw no objection to the establishment of such subagencies or to the issuance of the certificates but that the classification of alien enemies (defined by Rev. Stat., sec. 4067) could not be altered without the consent of Congress and that the status of such Poles as alien enemies could not be altered by the issuance of passports.

In a letter of August 20, 1920 the Department of State accordingly authorized the issuance of such certificates saying:

It is to be understood that the terms "consideration of the public authorities which the Government of the United States has agreed to extend to Poles to whom these certificates are issued," implies that whenever the holder of a certificate of this character applies to any official of the Department of Justice for a permit to enter forbidden areas or for a permit to do any other act forbidden by the restrictions contained in the President's proclamations relating to alien enemies, special and liberal consideration will be given to his application.

Polish National Committee: passports

It is understood that these certificates will not be issued by your Committee to persons of Polish nationality whose loyalty to the United States has not previously been satisfactorily established.

Secretary Lansing to Mr. Paderewski, Mar. 26, 1918, MS. Department of State, file 860c.01/79; Mr. Lansing to Mr. Paderewski, Aug. 20, 1918, *ibid.* 800c.01/94; 1918 For. Rel., Supp. 2, pp. 210–213.

For the general discussion of recognition of belligerency and for acts falling short of recognition of belligerency, see *ante* §§52, 53.

CONTINUITY OF STATES

§56

It follows from the fact of continuity of state life that all rights and title to property belonging to a state continue to vest in it regardless of changes in its government. The extension or failure to extend recognition to the government does not affect such continuity. This is the view taken by the courts. The courts do, however, consider themselves bound by the decision of the executive as to the government authorized to represent the foreign state.

Title to state property

. . . the rights of a sovereign state are vested in the state rather than in any particular government which may purport to represent it, *The Sapphire, supra,* [11 Wall. (1870) 164] 168, and suit in its behalf may be maintained in our courts only by that government which has been recognized by the political department of our own government as the authorized government of the foreign state.

.   .   .   .   .   .

We accept as conclusive here the determination of our own State Department that the Russian State was represented by the Provisional Government through its duly recognized representatives from March 16, 1917 to November 16, 1933, when the Soviet Government was recognized. There was at all times during that period a recognized diplomatic representative of the Russian State to whom notice concerning its interests within the United States could be communicated, and to whom our courts were open for the purpose of prosecuting suits in behalf of the Russian State. In fact, during that period suits were brought in its behalf in both the federal and state courts, which consistently ruled that the recognized Ambassador and Financial Attache were authorized to maintain them.

Guaranty Trust Co. of New York v. *United States,* 304 U.S. (1938) 126, 137–138.

In an action for damages resulting from the destruction of certain property belonging to the Imperial Russian Government while in the custody of the defendant (brought by the attorneys for the Russian Government upon the authority of Boris Bakhméteff, who

Russian Government v. Lehigh Valley R. Co., and other cases

had been accredited to the United States as Ambassador by the
Provisional Government, successor to the Imperial Russian Government, on July 5, 1917), the District Court of the United States for
the Southern District of New York denied a motion to dismiss the
action on the ground that there was in existence no "Russian government" and therefore no plaintiff. The court, declaring itself to be
bound by the action of the political department of the Government in
continuing to recognize Bakhméteff as the Ambassador of the Russian
Government in the United States, said:

> It may, however, be observed that the importance of recogniz-
> ing governmental continuity, quite irrespective of considerations
> as to the existing form of a foreign government, or as to the human
> beings in control at any particular time, is well illustrated in this
> case, where it is sought to deprive a foreign state forever of the
> opportunity to be heard in an effort to recover for the loss of
> property which belonged to the foreign state; i.e., the "Russian
> government," by whatever name called. It may also be noted,
> in passing, that the executive and judicial branches of the govern-
> ment have recognized "the present government of Russia" in
> proceedings to naturalize Russian subjects. Since the fall of
> the Imperial Russian government, such applicants for citizenship
> forswear allegiance to "the present government of Russia."

In further proceedings in the same case, the district court (in its
opinion of October 2, 1923) said with reference to this point:

> Does the fact that the government to [by] which Mr. Bakhme-
> tieff was accredited has fallen, and that no other government in
> Russia has been recognized by the United States, cause these
> actions to be abated? Or does the fact that the custody of the
> property for which Mr. Bakhmetieff has been responsible was
> considered by our government to vest in Mr. Ughet, whose diplo-
> matic status was not considered to be altered save them? That
> the real party in interest is the state of Russia, and that Russia,
> the state, still lives and is a continuing entity in the contempla-
> tion of the law, is true.

The view taken by the district court in these two decisions was sustained on appeal by the Circuit Court of Appeals for the Second Circuit, which declared in its decision of August 8, 1927:

> . . . We must judicially recognize that the state of Russia
> survives.
>
>   .   .   .   .
>
> The granting or refusal of recognition has nothing to do with
> the recognition of the state itself. . . . The suit did not abate
> by the change in the form of government in Russia; the state is
> perpetual, and survives the form of its government. The Sap-
> phire, supra. The recognized government may carry on the suit,
> at least until the new government becomes accredited here by
> recognition.

293 Fed. 133, 134 (S.D.N.Y., 1919); *Russian Government* v. *Lehigh Valley R. Co.*, 293 Fed. 135, 137–138 (S.D.N.Y., 1923); *Lehigh Valley R. Co.* v. *State of Russia*, 21 F. (2d) 396, 400, 401 (C.C.A. 2d, 1927).

At another point in the same opinion, speaking with reference to the capacity of Mr. Bakhméteff to authorize the prosecution of the action, and to the status of Mr. Ughet, the financial attaché of the Russian Embassy, subsequent to the termination of Bakhméteff's duties in the United States on June 30, 1922, the circuit court of appeals said:

". . . Mr. Ughet, by the State Department's determination, is entitled to the custody in the United States of the property of Russia, and as part of that duty he was authorized to continue the suits for the state of Russia. This duty becomes obvious. It became important to avoid efforts to destroy the right of action as a basis of keeping its property, when motions to dismiss were made and delays occurred which would give rise to the bar of limitation to sue. The question of Mr. Ughet's power under his agency is generally important, because of the change in name of the plaintiff in the action to the state of Russia in substitution of the Imperial Russian Government. We must judicially recognize that the state of Russia survives." 21 F. (2d) 396, 400 (C.C.A. 2d, 1927). Petition for a writ of certiorari was denied, 275 U.S. (1927) 571.

An application to the Supreme Court, subsequent to the second decision, for a writ of prohibition was denied. *Ex parte: In the matter of the Lehigh Valley Railway Company*, 265 U.S. (1924) 573.

It will be noted that fundamentally there is no controversy touching the real ownership of the transport; she belongs to Russia; no adverse claim, either public or private, is involved. By Russia, of course, I do not refer to any particular political group or organization, but to the national entity or sovereignty. . . . the Russian sovereignty may speak through different representatives, and it may have business agents as well as diplomatic agents; but all must derive their authority from a single source. The national will must be expressed through a single political organization; two conflicting "governments" cannot function at the same time. *The Rogdai*

278 Fed. 294, 296 (N.D. Cal., 1920).

. . . The plaintiff, as the recognized state government, is vested with all state property, including title to the state funds accumulated during previous de facto régimes and to the cause of action which accrued to the state when its funds were misappropriated. See United States v. McRae, L. R. 8 Eq. 69, speaking of the right of the United States to succeed to all the property of the de facto government of the Confederate States after the suppression of the rebellion; United States v. Prioleau, L.J. (N.S.) 35 Ch. 7; King of the Two Sicilies v. Willcox, 1 Sim. (N.S.) 301. Practically all of the cases on the right of a state to sue proceed upon the theory that the state is continuous and the right of action really resides in the aggregate body of the people who are merely represented by particular governmental organizations which may change in character or personnel. *State of Yucatan* v. *Argumedo et al.*

92 Misc. (Sup. Ct., N.Y. Cy., spec. term, 1915) 547, 157 N.Y. Supp. 219, 225–226.

*Voevodine v.
Government of
the Command-
er-in-Chief of
the Armed
Forces in the
South of Rus-
sia et al.*

The property of such a government belongs to the state, as sovereign, and, upon the overthrow of the de facto government, another government replacing it would succeed to the representative right of such de facto government in all of its property. Here, if plaintiff had dealt with Morosoff as the agent of the government in a purely commercial transaction, or had acquired a lien upon the property in his possession, a different question would be presented. The right of succession may be made subject to all charges or liens arising. *United States of America* v. *Prioleau*, [1865] 2 H. & M. 559, 71 Eng. Reprint Vice Chancellor's Court, page 580.

.   .   .   .

In conclusion, we hold that, so long as the Denikin government lasted, plaintiff could not have enforced any claim as against its property held by Morosoff, and, when that government fell, its property did not become a trust fund for creditors to be distributed by the courts of this state, but remained rather to be taken over by a successor government whenever claims thereto may be presented through actions in our courts by such government after it shall have been previously recognized by the government of the United States. *Russian Socialist Federated Soviet Republic* v. *Cibrario*, 235 N.Y. 255.

232 App. Div. (1931) 204, 208, 209, 249 N.Y. Supp. 644; 257 N.Y. (1931) 557, 178 N.E. 793. In a *per curiam* decision the New York Court of Appeals affirmed the decision of the appellate division in this case, in favor of the defendant. 257 N.Y. (1931) 557, 178 N.E. 793.

In the case of the *Agency of Canadian Car & Foundry Co. Limited, et al.* v. *American Can Co.*, a suit by two American corporations for the recovery of certain sums of money from the defendant company (also an American corporation), which had come into the possession of the defendant through certain transactions with the Russian Government during the World War, the District Court of the United States for the Southern District of New York held that an agreement entered into on December 18, 1917 between the plaintiff companies and the Russian supply committee in America, representing the Russian Government, constituted a complete defense to any action by or on behalf of the Russian Government with respect to this money. With reference to the effect of the change in form of the Russian Government, the court said:

Since the notable precedent of The Sapphire, 78 U.S. (11 Wall.) 164, 20 L. Ed. 127, the principle is firmly established in our courts that the rights and liabilities of a state are unaffected by a change either in the form or personnel of its government, however accomplished, whether by revolution or otherwise. No other doctrine is thinkable, at least among nations which have any conception of international honor.

253 Fed. 152, 155–156 (S.D.N.Y., 1918); affirmed, 258 Fed. 363, 368–369 (C.C.A. 2d, 1919).

Suit was instituted in the case of the *State of Russia* v. *Bankers' Trust Co. et al.* by Serge Ughet, recognized by the United States as the financial attaché of the Russian Embassy, in the name of the state of Russia for the recovery of a deposit which had been transferred by agreement from the Bankers' Trust Co. and segregated in a special fund in the National City Bank of New York. The District Court of the United States for the Southern District of New York, in allowing a set-off and counter claim interposed by the National City Bank based upon a separate indebtedness incurred by the Imperial Russian Government, said:

State of Russia v. *Bankers' Trust Co. et al.*

> . . . Unquestionably the money when deposited in the Bankers' Trust Company was owned by the Russian state, whatever may have been the prevailing government, and the joint depositors in whose names it was placed were merely acting as agents for their country under an authority recognized by the American executive.

In an opinion rendered February 6, 1934 the Circuit Court of Appeals, Second Circuit, granted a motion for the substitution of the United States in the place of the state of Russia as plaintiff, the motion being based upon the assignment by the Soviet Government to the United States, at the time of the recognition of the latter by the United States on November 16, 1933, of all amounts due it or that might be found to be due it, as the successor of prior governments of Russia, or otherwise, from American nationals.

In its decision on the merits on April 6, 1936 the court held that the set-off was properly allowable.

4 F. Supp. 417–418 (S.D.N.Y., 1933); 69 F. (2d) 44, 46 (C.C.A. 2d, 1934); 83 F. (2d) 236 (C.C.A. 2d, 1936).

In advising Secretary Hull (on May 5, 1934) concerning the interpretation of the so-called "Johnson act" (approved April 13, 1934, 48 Stat. 574), particularly as to whether the Soviet Government, as the successor to prior governments of Russia, was to be regarded as in default in the payment of its obligations or any part thereof to the Government of the United States—within the meaning of the Johnson act—"in view of the fact that no payment has been made on the bonds issued to the Government of the United States by the Provisional Government, on account of loans made to that Government by the United States" during the period of the World War, "the Provisional Government having been the immediate predecessor of the Soviet Government", Attorney General Cummings stated:

Soviet Government

> The proceedings in the House of Representatives indicate acceptance of the view that our Government regards the Soviet Government as responsible for the obligations incurred by prior Russian governments. (Cong. Rec. Vol. 78, p. 6049.) The posi-

tion of our Government in this respect accords with accepted principles of international law, as illustrated by the following authorities:

Moore, Int. Law Digest, v. 1, sec. 96, quoting Secretary of State Adams (August 10, 1818):

"No principle of international law can be more clearly established than this: That the *rights* and the *obligations* of a nation in regard to other States are independent of its internal revolutions of government. It extends even to the case of conquest. The conqueror who reduces a nation to his subjection receives it subject to all its engagements and duties toward others, the fulfillment of which then becomes his own duty."

Halleck, Int. Law (3d ed.) v. 1, p. 90:

"Public debts, whether due to or from the revolutionized State, are neither cancelled nor affected by any change in the constitution or internal government of a State."

The same rule is stated, in substance, in Kent's Commentaries (12th ed.) v. 1, p. 26, and in an opinion of Attorney General Griggs, 22 Op. 583, 584. In connection with, and in support of, these statements the authors cite 1 Whart. Int. Law Dig., sec. 5; Hall, Int. Law (4th ed.), pp. 104, 105; Rivier, Principes due Droit des Gens, I, pp. 70–72; *United States* v. *MacRae*, L. R. 8 Eq. 69; Vattel, Droit des Gens, liv. II, ch. XII, §§183–197; Grotius, De Jur. Bel., lib. II, cap. IX §8.

This view, in fact, was stated in Congress (Cong. Rec. Vol. 78, p. 6048) to have suggested the insertion of the provision in Section 2 of the statute excluding from its operation public corporations controlled by the United States, which are permitted to engage in the transactions prohibited to individuals and private corporations, if administratively determined to be desirable. I, therefore, regard the Soviet Government as in default, within the contemplation of the statute.

37 Op. Att. Gen. (1936) 505, 513–514

CHAPTER IV

TERRITORY AND SOVEREIGNTY OF STATES

ACQUISITION AND LOSS

GENERAL OBSERVATIONS

§57

In the award in the *Island of Palmas* case, the arbitrator, Dr. Max Huber, stated:

It is admitted by both sides that international law underwent profound modifications between the end of the Middle-Ages and the end of the 19th century, as regards the rights of discovery and acquisition of uninhabited regions or regions inhabited by savages or semi-civilised peoples. Both Parties are also agreed that a juridical fact must be appreciated in the light of the law contemporary with it, and not of the law in force at the time when a dispute in regard to it arises or falls to be settled. The effect of discovery by Spain is therefore to be determined by the rules of international law in force in the first half of the 16th century—or (to take the earliest date) in the first quarter of it, i.e. at the time when the Portuguese or Spaniards made their appearance in the Sea of Celebes.

Changes in law of discovery

. . . . .

As regards the question which of different legal systems prevailing at successive periods is to be applied in a particular case (the so-called intertemporal law), a distinction must be made between the creation of rights and the existence of rights. The same principle which subjects the act creative of a right to the law in force at the time the right arises, demands that the existence of the right, in other words its continued manifestation, shall follow the conditions required by the evolution of law. . . . It seems therefore incompatible with this rule of positive law [effective occupation] that there should be regions which are neither under the effective sovereignty of a State, nor without a master, but which are reserved for the exclusive influence of one State, in virtue solely of a title of acquisition which is no longer recognized by existing law, even if such a title ever conferred territorial sovereignty. For these reasons, discovery alone, without any subsequent act, cannot at the present time suffice to prove sovereignty over the Island of Palmas (or Miangas); and in so far as there is no sovereignty, the question of an abandonment properly speaking of sovereignty by one State in order that the sovereignty of another may take its place does not arise.

Successive rules.

Arbitral Award in the Island of Palmas Case, United States and the Netherlands, Apr. 4, 1928 (Per. Ct. Arb.) 26–27; Scott, *Hague Court Reports* (2d ser. 1932) 83, 100–101.

On the subject of the maintenance of sovereignty the arbitrator said:

". . . If a dispute arises as to the sovereignty over a portion of territory, it is customary to examine which of the States claiming sovereignty possesses a title—cession, conquest, occupation, etc.—superior to that which the other State might possibly bring forward against it. However, if the contestation is based on the fact that the other Party has actually displayed sovereignty, it cannot be sufficient to establish the title by which territorial sovereignty was validly acquired at a certain moment; it must also be shown that the territorial sovereignty has continued to exist and did exist at the moment which for the decision of the dispute must be considered as critical. This demonstration consists in the actual display of State activities, such as belongs only to the territorial sovereignty.

.   .   .   .

"Manifestations of territorial sovereignty assume, it is true, different forms, according to conditions of time and place. Although continuous in principle, sovereignty cannot be exercised in fact at every moment on every point of a territory. The intermittence and discontinuity compatible with the maintenance of the right necessarily differ according as inhabited or uninhabited regions are involved, or regions enclosed within territories in which sovereignty is uncontestably displayed, or again, regions accessible from, for instance, the high seas. It is true that neighbouring States may by convention fix limits to their own sovereignty, even in regions such as the interior of scarcely explored continents where such sovereignty is scarcely manifested, and in this way each may prevent the other from any penetration of its territory. The delimitation of Hinterland may also be mentioned in this connection.

"If, however, no conventional line of sufficient topographical precision exists or if there are gaps in the frontiers otherwise established, or if a conventional line leaves room for doubt, or if, as e.g. in the case of an island situated in the high seas, the question arises whether a title is valid *erga omnes*, the actual continuous and peaceful display of state functions is in case of dispute the sound and natural criterium of territorial sovereignty."

Award, *ibid.*, 16, 18–19; Scott, *ibid.*, 92, 94.

In the arbitral award in the *Clipperton Island* case the King of Italy pointed out that—

the proof of an historic right of Mexico's is not supported by any manifestation of her sovereignty over the island, a sovereignty never exercised until the expedition of 1897; and the mere conviction that this was territory belonging to Mexico, although general and of long standing, cannot be retained.

Arbitral Award of His Majesty the King of Italy on the Subject of the Difference Relative to the Sovereignty over Clipperton Island (France-Mexico), Jan. 28, 1931, 26 A.J.I.L. (1932) 390, 393.

By a convention of March 14, 1908 Norway and Sweden agreed to submit to the final decision of a tribunal of arbitration the question of the maritime boundary between the two countries so far as this boundary had not been determined by the Royal resolution of March 15, 1904. In its decision of October 23, 1909, fixing the boundary by points on an official map, the tribunal, accepting the premise that the maritime territory in question was divided automatically between Norway and Sweden by the peace of Roskilde in 1658, stated in part that— *(Application of former rules)*

> in order to ascertain which may have been the automatic dividing line of 1658 we must have recourse to the principles of law in force at that time.
>
> .   .   .   .
>
> . . . we shall be acting much more in accord with the ideas of the seventeenth century and with the notions of law prevailing at that time if we admit that the automatic division of the territory in question must have taken place according to the general direction of the land territory of which the maritime territory constituted an appurtenance, and if we consequently apply this same rule at the present time in order to arrive at a just and lawful determination of the boundary.

Decision of the Permanent Court of Arbitration in the Matter of the Maritime Boundary Dispute Between Norway and Sweden, Oct. 23, 1909, The Hague (translation), 4 A.J.I.L. (1910) 226, 231, 232.

No unanimity exists among writers on the Law of Nations with regard to the modes of acquiring territory on the part of the members of the Family of Nations. The topic owes its controversial character to the fact that the conception of State territory has undergone a great change since the appearance of the science of the Law of Nations. When Grotius created that science, State territory used to be still, as in the Middle Ages, more or less identified with the private property of the monarch of the State. Grotius and his followers applied, therefore, the rules of Roman Law concerning the acquisition of private property to the acquisition of territory by States. Nowadays, however, the acquisition of territory by a State can mean nothing else than the acquisition of *sovereignty* over such territory. Under these circumstances the rules of Roman Law concerning the acquisition of private property can no longer be applied. Yet the fact that they have been applied in the past has left traces which can hardly be obliterated; and they need not be obliterated, since they contain a good deal of truth in agreement with the actual facts. But the different modes of acquiring territory must be taken from the real practice of the States, and not from Roman Law, although the latter's terminology and common-sense basis may be made use of. *(Roman law)*

I Oppenheim's *International Law* (5th ed., by Lauterpacht, 1937) 428–429.

Recent
trends

The problems which arise to-day are not in all respects the same as those which had to be solved in the earlier periods of colonial expansion. New methods of acquisition have been introduced to meet the altered conditions. Some rules, such as those connected with Discovery, have sunk into the background; others, for instance those concerned with the acquisition of a part only of the sovereignty, have been brought from an obscure position into the foreground. New rules have been framed. Yet old rules have been retained, developed, and adapted to new situations; and for a proper understanding of the law of to-day a knowledge of its growth since the end of the Middle Ages is essential.

Older
rules

But it is not necessary to deal with the past merely in order to show how the present rules have grown up. The contention, which has been put forward in Arbitration Proceedings, that titles which had their beginnings in past ages must be judged to-day according to the law as it existed at those times, is probably not universally sound—it is sufficient in this connection to refer here to the extended scope which has been given to the doctrine of Effective Occupation in modern times. But such a principle is frequently the right one to apply. . . . and in disputes as to territorial titles it is sometimes necessary to know which State was pointed out by the law of a particular time as having the best claim to certain territory at that time.

.   .   .   .

International law places no veto on the acquisition of territory merely on account of its relative backwardness or advancement. It does, however, prescribe the mode or modes of acquisition which must be employed, according to the condition of the territory, if a valid title to it is to be obtained.

.   .   .   .

I.—Areas which are *territoria nullius* and open to acquisition by Occupation may consist of:

Acquirable
territory

(1) Uninhabited lands; unless they are unsuitable for permanent habitation and are being used for the purposes for which they are suitable, or are islands which are situated within territorial waters, or have been formed by alluvium from occupied territory.

(2) Lands inhabited by individuals who are not permanently united for political action.

(3) Lands which have been abandoned by their former occupants.

(4) Lands which have been forfeited because they have not been occupied effectively.

(5) Seas that are almost or entirely surrounded by land which fulfils one of the above conditions.

(6) The belt of the ocean bordering on land which fulfils one of the above conditions to a distance of at least three marine miles from the shore occupied, with possible extensions in the cases of bays and straits.

(7) The soil beneath the bed of the open sea—by starting from beneath territorial waters.

(8) Portions of the open sea adjoining the territorial belt—by accretions to the neighbouring land.

II.—Lands inhabited by any permanent political society can be acquired only by Conquest, Cession or Prescription.

III.—The open sea, though *territorium nullius*, is not now susceptible of sovereignty, save in certain cases where prescriptive rights are claimed to sedentary fisheries on the sea-bed.

IV.—States may, by agreement, bind themselves not to make particular acquisitions. Apart from such agreements, the above conditions apply, from the legal point of view, to territory situated in any part of the world, although, so far as the American continent is concerned, they are dominated by political considerations arising out of the Monroe Doctrine.

Lindley, *Acquisition and Government of Backward Territory in International Law* (London, 1926) v–vi, 1, 80–81. As to whether polar ice areas may be subjected to sovereignty, see *post* §67.

From time to time various states have made declarations of policy or have entered into conventional undertakings which purport to eliminate certain areas from the realm of acquirable territories, either absolutely or conditionally. Such undertakings were contained in Limitations the treaty signed at Christiania (Oslo) on November 2, 1907 by Great Britain, France, Germany, Norway, and Russia concerning the independence and territorial integrity of Norway; in the assurances given to Great Britain by Siam in 1909 that the latter would not cede or lease to any foreign government any territory in certain portions of the Malay Peninsula; in the Lansing-Ishii agreement of November 2, 1917; and in the nine-power treaty signed at Washington on February 6, 1922, regarding the sovereignty, independence, and territorial integrity of China, etc.

Minister Peirce to Secretary Root, no. 98, Feb. 12, 1908, MS. Department of State, file 6924/7–9, and 1907 For. Rel., pt. II, pp. 926–928; Minister King to Secretary Knox, no. 484, May 13, 1909, MS. Department of State, file 10883/32–38, enclosures, and 1909 For. Rel. 539; 3 Treaties, etc. (Redmond, 1923) 2720–2722; 44 Stat. 2113; 4 Treaties, etc. (Trenwith, 1938) 4872. Attention is also called to the Monroe Doctrine.

In connection with the subject of the assertion of territorial jurisdiction by the Executive, William Howard Taft stated that "Of course the decision of Congress or the treaty making power upon such an issue would be binding upon the Courts, but in the absence of the decision of either the action of the President is conclusive with the Courts."

Taft, *Our Chief Magistrate and His Powers* (1916) 118.

The President is competent to recognize the acquisition of territory by discovery and occupation. Thus shall [*small*] uninhabited islands in the Pacific [Midway and Wake Islands] have been taken possession of by naval commanders.

Wright, *Control of American Foreign Relations* (1922) 274.

DISCOVERY

§58

The statement has frequently been made that at the time of the European explorations in the Western Hemisphere discovery was a sufficient basis for a claim to sovereignty over the newly discovered lands. It is not always clear whether writers use the term *discovery* to mean discovery alone or whether they mean to include within that term the formal taking of possession in the name of the sovereign which has usually accompanied the discovery. In the *Island of Palmas* award the arbitrator, Max Huber, laid down a strong caveat as to the soundness of "the view most favourable to the American arguments . . . that discovery as such, i.e., the mere fact of seeing land, without any act, even symbolical, of taking possession, involved *ipso jure* territorial sovereignty and not merely an 'inchoate title', a *jus ad rem*, to be completed eventually by an actual and durable taking of possession within a reasonable time".

> Arbitral Award in the Island of Palmas Case, United States and the Netherlands, Apr. 4, 1928 (Per. Ct. Arb.) 26–27; Scott, *Hague Court Reports* (2d ser. 1932) 83, 100. Dr. Huber was speaking of the first quarter of the sixteenth century.

Modern researches have clarified to a considerable extent the actual practices of the principal powers engaged in explorations in the earlier age of discoveries. The authors of a recent study of this problem conclude, *inter alia*, that—

> it may be stated first of all that, throughout this lengthy period [a period of several centuries], no state appeared to regard mere discovery, in the sense of "physical" discovery or simple "visual apprehension," as being in any way sufficient *per se* to establish a right of sovereignty over, or a valid title to, *terra nullius*. Furthermore, mere disembarkation upon any portion of such regions—or even extended penetration and exploration therein—was not regarded as sufficient itself to establish such right or title. Nor did merely giving names to regions, capes, headlands, islands, valleys, peninsulas, rivers, streams, gulfs, harbors or bays have any such results. It should be added, however, that the term "discovery" was often rather loosely applied, and, in some instances, according to the attendant circumstances, may have been intended to include the performance of a formal ceremony of taking possession. It is, of course, obvious that, in such in-

stances, more had occurred than a discovery in the sense of a mere visual apprehension.

Next, it may be asserted on the basis of the facts that the formal ceremony of taking of possession, the symbolic act, was generally regarded as being wholly sufficient *per se* to establish immediately a right of sovereignty over, or a valid title to, areas so claimed and did not require to be supplemented by the performance of other acts, such as, for example, "effective occupation." A right or title so acquired and established was deemed good against all subsequent claims set up in opposition thereto unless, perhaps, transferred by conquest or treaty, relinquished, abandoned, or successfully opposed by continued occupation on the part of some other state. Naturally enough, the details of these formal ceremonies of taking of possession did vary, often quite markedly, among the various nations concerned, but still, and most important of all, what may be termed the ultimate legal effect thereof was the same. Thus, the Portuguese and the French . . . were usually content with the performance of ceremonies very simple in nature, such as the mere erection of a cross or other monument bearing the royal arms. The Dutch also adhered to the simplicities and usually erected no religious symbols whatever. On the other hand, the Spanish and the English usually employed a considerably greater degree of formality in their ceremonies, the former particularly being accustomed to observe an elaborate ritual.

Keller, Lissitzyn, and Mann, *Creation of Rights of Sovereignty Through Symbolic Acts, 1400–1800* (1938) 148–149. See also Simsarian, "The Acquisition of Legal Title to *Terra Nullius*", in 53 Pol. Sci. Q. (1938) 111–128.

It is the opinion of the Department that the discovery of lands unknown to civilization, even when coupled with a formal taking of possession, does not support a valid claim of sovereignty unless the discovery is followed by an actual settlement of the discovered country. In the absence of an act of Congress assertative in a domestic sense of dominion over Wilkes Land this Department would be reluctant to declare that the United States possessed a right of sovereignty over that territory.

Discoveries in Antarctic

Secretary Hughes to A. W. Prescott, May 13, 1924, MS. Department of State, file 811.014/101.

In the penultimate paragraph of your letter you state that, in order to avoid any misunderstanding, you would add that possession of all the land which Mr. Amundsen may discover will, of course, be taken in the name of His Majesty, the King of Norway. In my opinion rights similar to those which in earlier centuries were based upon the acts of a discoverer, followed by occupation or settlement consummated at long and uncertain periods thereafter, are not capable of being acquired at the present time. Today, if an explorer is able to ascertain the existence of lands still unknown to civilization, his act of so-called discovery, coupled with a formal taking of possession, would have no significance, save as he might herald the advent of the settler; and where for climatic or other reasons actual settlement would be an impossi-

Amundsen trans-polar flight

bility, as in the case of the Polar regions, such conduct on his part would afford frail support for a reasonable claim of sovereignty. I am therefore compelled to state, without now adverting to other considerations, that this Government cannot admit that such taking of possession as a discoverer by Mr. Amundsen of areas explored by him could establish the basis of rights of sovereignty in the Polar regions, to which, it is understoood, he is about to depart.

Secretary Hughes to the Norwegian Minister, H. H. Bryn, Apr. 2, 1924, MS. Department of State, file 857.014/6.

. . . I have the honor, acting under instructions from my Government which has been made acquainted with Your Excellency's note of April 2, 1924, to say that the Norweigian Government wishes to emphasize, in order that its position in regard to this question may not be misunderstood, that when in the Legation's note of February 25, 1924, the statement was made that possession of all the land, which might be discovered by Captain Amundsen, would be taken in the name of His Majesty the King of Norway, this did not involve that the Norwegian Government had the intention to invoke a possible discovery of new land as a basis for a claim to sovereignty. It only meant that the Norwegian Government claimed the right to priority in acquiring subsequently the sovereignty by settlement or by other procedure sanctioned by International Law. My Government will at a later date, if occasion should arise, take up for further discussion the considerations and principles set forth in Your Excellency's above mentioned note.

Mr. Bryn to Mr. Hughes, Nov. 12, 1924, *ibid.* 857.014/16.

. . . However, according to the view that has prevailed at any rate since the 19th century an inchoate title of discovery must be completed within a reasonable period by the effective occupation of the region claimed to be discovered. This principle must be applied in the present case, for the reasons given above in regard to the rules determining which of successive legal systems is to be applied (the so-called intertemporal law).

. . . .

The title of discovery . . . would, under the most favourable and most extensive interpretation, exist only as an inchoate title, as a claim to establish sovereignty by effective occupation. An inchoate title however cannot prevail over a definite title founded on continuous and peaceful display of sovereignty.

Arbitral Award in the Island of Palmas Case, United States and the Netherlands, Apr. 4, 1928 (Per. Ct. Arb.) 27–28, 60; Scott, *Hague Court Reports* (2d ser. 1932) 83, 101, 128.

. . . the discovery of new channels of trade in regions not belonging to any State cannot by itself be held to confer an effective right to the acquisition of the sovereignty of the said regions by the State, whose subjects the persons who in their private capacity make the discovery may happen to be.

Award of His Majesty the King of Italy with Regard to the Boundary Between the Colony of British Guiana and the United States of Brazil, June 6, 1904, Cd. 2166 (1904) 4; 99 Br. & For. St. Paps. (1905–6) 930.

In the Clipperton Island arbitration under the agreement of March 2, 1909 between France and Mexico, the latter claimed sovereignty as the successor of Spain, whose title, it was argued, was founded upon discovery. In the course of the decision rendered on January 28, 1931 the arbitrator stated:

. . . However, even admitting that the discovery had been made by Spanish subjects, it would be necessary, to establish the contention of Mexico, to prove that Spain not only had the right, as a state, to incorporate the island in her possessions, but also had effectively exercised the right. But that has not been demonstrated at all.

Arbitral Award of His Majesty the King of Italy on the Subject of the Difference Relative to the Sovereignty over Clipperton Island (France-Mexico) Jan. 28, 1931, 26 A.J.I.L. (1932) 390, 393.

OCCUPATION

§59

Occupation is an *original*, as distinguished from a *derivative*, mode of acquisition of territory. It involves the intentional appropriation by a state of territory not under the sovereignty of any other state. It does not involve the transfer of sovereignty from one state to another. Occupation is usually—though not necessarily—associated with the discovery of the territory in question by the occupying state.

The power to acquire territory by discovery and occupation (*Jones* v. *United States*, 137 U.S. 202, 212), . . . exist[s] as inherently inseparable from the conception of nationality. This the court recognized, and in each of the cases cited found the warrant for its conclusions not in the provisions of the Constitution, but in the law of nations.

United States v. Curtiss-Wright Export Corp. et al., 299 U. S. (1936) 304, 318.

In his decision of June 6, 1904, as arbitrator between Great Britain and Brazil under the treaty concluded at London on November 6, 1901, the King of Italy stated that—

to acquire the sovereignty of regions which are not in the dominion of any State, it is indispensable that the occupation be effected In name of in the name of the State which intends to acquire the sovereignty state of those regions.

Award of His Majesty the King of Italy with Regard to the Boundary Between the Colony of British Guiana and the United States of Brazil, Cd. 2166 (1904) 4; 99 Br. & For. St. Paps. (1905–6) 930.

Settlement

Secretary Hughes stated in 1924 that "actual settlement" was required for a valid claim of sovereignty over a discovered country.

Quoted *ante* §58.

To the same effect, see I Oppenheim's *International Law* (5th ed., by Lauterpacht, 1937) 439–440, where settlement is considered to be one element of possession, the other being a formal act or announcement indicating the intention of the occupying state to assert its sovereignty. In addition to possession, this authority requires the establishment of an administration over the territory in order to meet the tests of effective occupation.

For a contrary view, see Lindley, *Acquisition and Government of Backward Territory in International Law* (London, 1926) 6–7, where the author points out that certain uninhabited islands are under the undoubted sovereignty of various states. See also Smedal, *Acquisition of Sovereignty over Polar Areas* (Oslo, 1931; translation by Chr. Meyer) 38–39, and Von der Heydte, "Discovery, Symbolic Annexation and Virtual Effectiveness in International Law", in 29 A.J.I.L. (1935) 462–465, where the author develops the thesis that "Without prejudice to the general principle which requires effective occupation, sovereignty over a region completely uninhabited and seldom frequented is acquired merely by symbolic annexation."

Governmental control

. . . International law in the 19th century, having regard to the fact that most parts of the globe were under the sovereignty of States members of the community of nations, and that territories without a master had become relatively few, took account of a tendency already existing and especially developed since the middle of the 18th century, and laid down the principle that occupation, to constitute a claim to territorial sovereignty, must be effective, that is, offer certain guarantees to other States and their nationals.

Arbitral Award in the Island of Palmas Case, United States and the Netherlands, Apr. 4, 1928 (Per. Ct. Arb.) 27; Scott, *Hague Court Reports* (2d ser. 1932) 83, 101.

. . . There is no reason to invoke the obligation contained in Art. 35 of the Act of Berlin of 1885 . . . Since this Act of Berlin was subsequent to the French occupation here under consideration, concerns only territories on the coasts of Africa, and binds only the signatory states, of which Mexico is not one, in their mutual relations, it can have no weight in the present case. Besides, Art. 35, strictly speaking, has nothing to do with the taking of possession, but imposes an obligation which presupposes an occupation which has already taken place and is already valid.

Arbitral Award of His Majesty the King of Italy on the Subject of the Difference Relative to the Sovereignty over Clipperton Island (France-Mexico), Jan. 28, 1931, 26 A.J.I.L. (1932) 390, 394.

Chapter VI of the general act of the Conference of Berlin of Feb. 26, 1885 consisted of a declaration concerning the essential conditions to be fulfilled in order that new occupations on the coasts of the African Continent might be considered effective. Article 35 (the second of the two articles under this chapter) recognized the obligation on the part of the signatory powers to maintain, in the territories occupied by them on the coasts of Africa, an authority sufficient to protect acquired rights and, should the case arise, freedom of commerce and transit under the conditions agreed upon. 76 Br. & For. St. Paps. (1884–85) 19.

The convention for the revision of the general act of Berlin, etc., signed at St. Germain-en-Laye on September 10, 1919, replaced the Berlin act as between the signatory powers which have ratified it. Article 10 of this convention reads as follows: *Revision of Berlin declaration*

> The Signatory Powers acknowledge their obligation to maintain in the regions under their control actual authority and police forces sufficient to insure protection for persons and property and, if the case should arise, freedom for commerce and transit.

4 Treaties, etc. (Trenwith, 1938) 4849, 4853; 49 Stat. 3027, 3039.

The convention was signed and ratified by the United States, Belgium, British Empire, France, Italy, Japan, and Portugal. Ethiopia adhered. It will be noted that article 10 of the 1919 convention is not limited to any particular regions in Africa, as was article 35 of the Berlin act referred to, *ante.*

In view of the adoption by Great Britain, Germany, France, and the United States, both before and after the Berlin Conference, of the principle of effective occupation, and of the fact that, during recent years, no colonial Power appears to have taken exception to the applicability of the rule to new occupations, it seems to be justifiable to say that all recent acquisitions of territory, whether on the coasts of Africa or not, are subject to it.

.   .   .   .

An erroneous notion as to what is required for effective occupation appears to have been entertained by the Peruvian Government in 1912. That Government, according to the Peruvian Consul-General, had not protested earlier against the crimes known to exist in the Putumayo for the reason that "it could be proved that they were committed almost exclusively by Colombians, and that this very fact would support a claim of effective occupation by Colombia, which would go far to sustain that country's pretensions to possession." It would seem, on the contrary, that the very fact of the absence from the Putumayo of an authority sufficient to protect the natives from violence, and particularly from such crimes as were revealed by the report of the British Consul-General and by the winding-up proceedings in the English Court in connection with the Peruvian Amazon Company, Limited, was in itself sufficient to show that no effective occupation had taken place. [Cd. 6678 (1913) 7, 8.]

Lindley, *Acquisition and Government of Backward Territory in International Law* (London, 1926) 157–158.

. . . occupation cannot be held to be carried out except by effective, uninterrupted, and permanent possession being taken in the name of the State, and . . . a simple affirmation of rights of sovereignty or a manifest intention to render the occupation effective cannot suffice;

. . . the effective possession of a part of a region, although it may be held to confer a right to the acquisition of the whole of a region which constitutes a single organic whole, cannot confer a right to the acquisition of the whole of a region which, either owing to its size or to its physical configuration, cannot be deemed to be a single organic whole *de facto* . . .

Award of His Majesty the King of Italy with Regard to the Boundary Between the Colony of British Guiana and the United States of Brazil, June 6, 1904, Cd. 2166 (1904) 4; 99 Br. & For. St. Paps. (1905–6) 930.

The question remains whether France proceeded to an effective occupation, satisfying the conditions required by international law for the validity of this kind of territorial acquisition. In effect Mexico maintains, secondarily to her principal contention which has just been examined, that the French occupation was not valid, and consequently her own right to occupy the island which must still be considered as *nullius* in 1897.

In whatever concerns this question, there is, first of all, ground to hold as incontestable, the regularity of the act by which France in 1858 made known in a clear and precise manner, her intention to consider the island as her territory.

On the other hand, it is disputed that France took effective possession of the island, and it is maintained that without such a taking of possession of an effective character, the occupation must be considered as null and void.

It is beyond doubt that by immemorial usage having the force of law, besides the *animus occupandi*, the actual, and not the nominal, taking of possession is a necessary condition of occupation. This taking of possession consists in the act, or series of acts, by which the occupying state reduces to its possession the territory in question and takes steps to exercise exclusive authority there. Strictly speaking, and in ordinary cases, that only takes place when the state establishes in the territory itself an organization capable of making its laws respected. But this step is, properly speaking, but a means of procedure to the taking of possession, and, therefore, is not identical with the latter. There may also be cases where it is unnecessary to have recourse to this method. Thus, if a territory, by virtue of the fact that it was completely uninhabited, is, from the first moment when the occupying state makes its appearance there, at the absolute and undisputed disposition of that state, from that moment the taking of possession must be considered as accomplished, and the occupation is thereby completed.

Arbitral Award of His Majesty the King of Italy on the Subject of the Difference Relative to the Sovereignty over Clipperton Island (France-Mexico), Jan. 28, 1931, 26 A.J.I.L. (1932) 390, 393–394.

In its judgment of April 5, 1933 (see *post* §§64, 70) the Permanent Court of International Justice concluded that Danish sovereignty extended over the entire island of Greenland and was not limited to the colonized portions. It pointed out, however, that this conclusion was based to a large extent upon two considerations, namely, "the absence of any claim to sovereignty by another Power, and the Arctic and inaccessible character of the uncolonized parts of the country". The Court, moreover, was dealing with extremely ancient claims, the history of the exploration and settlement involved in the case going back as far as the tenth century.

Eastern Greenland case

> Per. Ct. Int. Jus., Ser. A/B, No. 53 (Apr. 5, 1933), pp. 22, 50–51; III Hudson, *World Court Reports* (1938) 175. See Hyde, "The Case Concerning the Legal Status of Eastern Greenland" (editorial comment), in 27 A.J.I.L. (1933) 732.

Effective occupation as generally required does not imply its extension to every nook and corner. It is sufficient to dispose at some places within the territory of such a strong force that its power can be extended if necessary over the whole region in order to guarantee a certain minimum of legal order and legal protection within the boundaries, and to exclude any interference from a third State (virtual effectiveness).

Effectiveness

> Von der Heydte, "Discovery, Symbolic Annexation and Virtual Effectiveness in International Law", in 29 A.J.I.L. (1935) 463.

In its decision of October 23, 1909 in the maritime boundary dispute between Norway and Sweden (*ante* §57), the tribunal called attention to the following factual considerations as supporting its decision to assign Grisbådarne to Sweden:

Exploitation

a. The circumstances that lobster fishing in the shoals of Grisbadarna has been carried on for a much longer time, to a much larger extent, and by much larger numbers of fishers by the subjects of Sweden than by the subjects of Norway.

b. The circumstance that Sweden has performed various acts in the Grisbadarna region, especially of late, owing to her conviction that these regions were Swedish, as, for instance, the placing of beacons, the measurement of the sea, and the installation of a lightboat, being acts which involved considerable expense and in doing which she not only thought that she was exercising her right but even more that she was performing her duty; whereas Norway, according to her own admission, showed much less solicitude in this region in these various regards.

> Decision of the Permanent Court of Arbitration in the Matter of the Maritime Boundary Dispute between Norway and Sweden, Oct, 23, 1909, The Hague (translation), 4 A.J.I.L. (1910) 226, 233.

A State does not gain sovereignty over a No-man's-land by sending scientific expeditions to the land; nor by establishing wireless stations or scientific posts in the land. Such acts on the part of the State are, however, of importance if it wishes to acquire sovereignty. A wireless station is, for instance, an excellent point of support to a colonization. If its staff is given police authority, it will be able, on behalf of the State, to control the area around the station and in that way to bring the latter under the authority of the State. Scientific expeditions may yield a knowledge of the country which will stimulate and facilitate a colonization. Also acts which do not form an expression of sovereignty over the territory may become of importance in a dispute on sovereignty, because the court may be of opinion that weight should be attached to them for the sake of equity. This specially applies when the court is not bound in its decision to existing law, but is free to seek the most reasonable solution. In a sovereignty dispute it will therefore be in the interest of the State to be able to demonstrate the highest degree of activity in the disputed territory.

Smedal, *Acquisition of Sovereignty over Polar Areas* (Oslo, 1931; translation by Chr. Meyer) 39.

In discussing the arguments of the United States in the Island of Palmas arbitration, Max Huber, the arbitrator, said:

In the last place there remains to be considered *title arising out of contiguity*. Although States have in certain circumstances maintained that islands relatively close to their shores belonged to them in virtue of their geographical situation, it is impossible to show the existence of a rule of positive international law to the effect that islands situated outside territorial waters should belong to a State from the mere fact that its territory forms the *terra firma* (nearest continent or island of considerable size). Not only would it seem that there are no precedents sufficiently frequent and sufficiently precise in their bearing to establish such a rule of international law, but the alleged principle itself is by its very nature so uncertain and contested that even Governments of the same State have on different occasions maintained contradictory opinions as to its soundness. The principle of contiguity, in regard to islands, may not be out of place when it is a question of allotting them to one State rather than another, either by agreement between the Parties, or by a decision not necessarily based on law; but as a rule establishing *ipso jure* the presumption of sovereignty in favour of a particular State, this principle would be in conflict with what has been said as to territorial sovereignty and as to the necessary relation between the right to exclude other States from a region and the duty to display therein the activities of a State. Nor is this principle of contiguity admissible as a legal method of deciding questions of territorial sovereignty; for it is wholly lacking in precision and would in its application lead to arbitrary results. This would be especially true in a case such as that of the island in question, which is not relatively close to one single continent, but forms part of a large archipelago in which strict delimitations between the different parts are not naturally obvious.

There lies, however, at the root of the idea of contiguity one point which must be considered also in regard to the Island of Palmas (or Miangas). It has been explained above that in the exercise of territorial sovereignty there are necessarily gaps, intermittence in time and discontinuity in space. This phenomenon will be particularly noticeable in the case of colonial territories, partly uninhabited or as yet partly unsubdued. The fact that a State cannot prove display of sovereignty as regards such a portion of territory cannot forthwith be interpreted as showing that sovereignty is inexistent. Each case must be appreciated in accordance with the particular circumstances.

It is however, to be observed that international arbitral jurisprudence in disputes on territorial sovereignty (e.g. the award in the arbitration between Italy and Switzerland concerning the Alpe Craivarola; Lafontaine, Pasicrisie internationale, p. 201–209) would seem to attribute greater weight to—even isolated—acts of display of sovereignty than to continuity of territory, even if such continuity is combined with the existence of natural boundaries.

As regards groups of islands, it is possible that a group may under certain circumstances be regarded as in law a unit, and that the fate of the principal part may involve the rest. Here, however, we must distinguish between, on the one hand, the act of first taking possession, which can hardly extend to every portion of territory, and, on the other hand, the display of sovereignty as a continuous and prolonged manifestation which must make itself felt through the whole territory.

In the conclusion the arbitrator stated:

> The title of contiguity, understood as a basis of territorial sovereignty, has no foundation in international law.

Arbitral Award in the Island of Palmas Case, United States and the Netherlands, Apr. 4, 1928 (Per. Ct. Arb.) 39–40, 60; Scott, *Hague Court Reports* (2d ser. 1932) 83, 111–112, 128.

The claim to unoccupied territory on the ground of proximity is familiar in international law, though it has not always passed without protest. The principle is described as contiguity or continuity, according as the territory in question is or is not separated by water. . . .

The right of a state to islands within its maritime belt has been universally recognized, and Lord Stowell's well-known decision in the case of the *Anna*, . . . besides asserting that islands formed of alluvium beyond the three-mile limit belong to the mainland, suggests that the same is true of those occupying a strategic position.

The German Prize Code . . . recognizes "islands situated not more than six sea miles from the coast" as belonging to a neutral state on the mainland for the purpose of measuring the maritime belt, free from belligerent operations, and Dana . . . asserts that "islands adjacent to the coast, though not

formed by alluvium or increment, are considered as appurtenant, unless some other Power has obtained title to them by some
of the recognized modes of acquisition."

Peru, following a suggestion of Lord Palmerston in 1834,
asserted that the proximity of the Lobos Islands to Peru would
give her a *prima facie* claim to them, although they were over
twenty miles distant. . . . A similar basis was offered by
Venezuela as a claim to the Aves Islands, . . . by Hayti to
Navassa, . . . and among others, by Spain and later Argentine to the Falklands, . . . although the latter are almost two
hundred and fifty miles from the mainland. All of these claims
gave rise to considerable controversy, the result of which seems
to support Mr. Fish's contention in the Navassa case that the
utmost to which the argument amounts "is a claim to a *constructive* possession, or rather to a right of possession; but in
contemplation of international law such claim of a right to possession is not enough to establish the right of a nation to exclusive territorial sovereignty (Vattel, Bk. 1, Chap. xviii, sec. 208),"
. . . which, according to Mr. Webster in the Lobos Island case,
must be supported by "unequivocal acts of absolute sovereignty
and ownership." . . .

The continuity of unoccupied or savage territory with that
occupied by a civilized state has been stated as grounds for territorial claims, especially in the modern "hinterland" and "sphere
of influence" theories. The colonial charters in America commonly granted jurisdiction "from sea to sea" and Calhoun in
1844 felt able to assert: "That continuity furnishes a just foundation for a claim of territory, in connection with those of discovery
and occupation, would seem unquestionable."

The present law, in view of the generally accepted Declaration
of the West African Conference of 1885, would seem to justify no
claims to territory beyond that effectively controlled, although the
adjacent state may justly claim the right of notification, with an
option to make good the *constructive* claim by actual occupation.

Wright, "Territorial Propinquity", in 12 A.J.I.L. (1918) 520–522.
For material on the "sector principle", see *post* §67.

Notification

. . . An obligation for the Netherlands to notify to other
Powers the establishment of suzerainty over the Sangi States or
of the display of sovereignty in these territories did not exist.

Such notification, like any other formal act, can only be the
condition of legality as a consequence of an explicit rule of law.
A rule of this kind adopted by the Powers in 1885 for the African
continent does not apply *de plano* to other regions, and thus the
contract with Taruna of 1885, or with Kandahar-Taruna of 1889,
even if they were to be considered as the first assertions of
sovereignty over Palmas (or Miangas) would not be subject to
the rule of notification.

Arbitral Award in the Island of Palmas Case, United States and the
Netherlands, Apr. 4, 1928 (Per. Ct. Arb.) 59; Scott, *Hague Court Reports*
2d ser. 1932) 83, 128.

The regularity of the French occupation has also been questioned because the other Powers were not notified of it. But it must be observed that the precise obligation to make such notification is contained in Art. 34 of the Act of Berlin cited above, which, as before mentioned, is not applicable to the present case. There is good reason to think that the notoriety given to the act, by whatever means, sufficed at the time, and that France provoked that notoriety by publishing the said act in the manner above indicated.

Arbitral Award of His Majesty the King of Italy on the Subject of the Difference Relative to the Sovereignty over Clipperton Island (France-Mexico) Jan. 28, 1931, 26 A.J.I.L. (1932) 390, 394.

ACCRETION, EROSION, AND AVULSION

§60

A state's territory may be increased or decreased by processes of accretion or erosion, respectively. Accretion may result not only in additions to the mainland but also in the formation of deltas, islands, and bars within the maritime belt of the littoral state. Such accretions can generally be brought about only by erosion from other lands. The process, therefore, by which territory is gained by one state may, though not necessarily, involve the loss of territory by another state. This is often true with respect to changes in boundary streams. When changes in the bed and channel of a boundary stream are brought about by natural and gradual processes of erosion and accretion, the boundary follows the varying course of the stream, but when sudden and violent changes in the channel of the stream occur, whether from natural or artificial causes, and the stream suddenly leaves its old bed and forms a new one, the process is known as avulsion, and the resulting change in the channel does not bring about a change in the boundary. In the latter case, in the absence of an agreement to the contrary, the middle of the old channel, if it previously marked the boundary, continues to do so even though the old bed may have been entirely abandoned by the stream.

Article V of the Treaty of Guadalupe Hidalgo of 1848 between the United States and Mexico provided, *inter alia*, that the boundary line between the two countries should begin in the Gulf of Mexico, three leagues from land, opposite the mouth of the Rio Grande, and should run thence up the middle of the river, "following the deepest channel, where it has more than one, to the point where it strikes the southern boundary of New Mexico; thence, westwardly, along the whole southern boundary of New Mexico", etc. 9 Stat. 922, 926–928; 1 Treaties, etc. (Malloy, 1910) 1107, 1109–1110.

U.S. and Mexico, 1848

This definition of the boundary line was amended in part, particularly as regards the Colorado River, by article I of the Gadsden treaty of 1853, by providing among other things that from a point on that river 20 English miles below its junction with the Gila the boundary should follow "the middle of the said river Colorado until it intersects the present line between the United States and Mexico". 10 Stat. 1031, 1032; 1 Treaties, etc. (Malloy, 1910) 1121, 1122.

1853

The boundary convention concluded between the two countries on November 12, 1884 stipulated (in art. I) that the dividing line should continue to be that described in the treaties and should "follow the center of the normal channel" of the Rio Grande and the Colorado River, "notwithstanding any alterations in the banks or in the course of those rivers, provided that such alterations be effected by natural causes through the slow and gradual erosion and deposit of alluvium and not by the abandonment of an existing river bed and the opening of a new one." Article II of this convention provided that any other change wrought by the force of the current, whether by the cutting of a new bed or, when there was more than one channel, by the deepening of another channel than that which marked the boundary at the time of the "survey made under the aforesaid Treaty", should produce no change in the dividing line as "fixed by the surveys of the International Boundary Commissions in 1852" and that the line then fixed should continue to follow the middle of the original channel bed, even though this should become wholly dry or be obstructed by deposits. *Ibid.* 1159, 1160; 24 Stat. 1011, 1012.

1884

Provision was contained in article II of the boundary convention of March 1, 1889 between the two countries for the establishment of an International Boundary Commission, which, by article I of that convention was given exclusive jurisdiction to pass upon differences or questions arising from alterations or changes taking place in the Rio Grande or the Colorado River where they form the boundary. The Commission was to decide whether these changes had occurred "through avulsion or erosion, for the effects of articles I and II of the convention of November 12, 1884" (art. IV). 26 Stat. 1512, 1513–1514; 1 Treaties, etc. (Malloy, 1910) 1167–1168. The convention was to run for a period of five years from the date of the exchange of ratifications thereof; it was renewed several times and finally by the water boundary convention of 1900 was continued in effect indefinitely, subject to the right of either party to dissolve the Commission upon six months' notice to the other party (*ibid.* 1192, 1193; 31 Stat. 1936, 1937).

1889

1900

Practical difficulties arose with reference to the application of the provisions of the convention of 1884 because of changes effected in the bed of the river by slow and gradual erosion coupled with avulsion, as a result of which the river frequently abandoned its old channel and left separated from it land known as *bancos*. These *bancos* were left at distances from the new river bed, and, by reason of the successive deposits of alluvium, the old channel became effaced and the *bancos* became confused with the land contiguous thereto, although by the terms of the convention of 1884 they remained subject to the jurisdiction of the country from which they had been separated. To remedy the situation a new convention was entered into in 1905 providing for the elimination of the *bancos* from the effects of the convention of 1884 and making them a part of the country on whose side they were thus formed, unless the *banco* should have an area of over 250 hectares or a population of more than 200 souls. In either of these latter events the land was to be considered as still belonging to the country from which it had become detached, the old bed of the river remaining the boundary in such cases. Private property rights on *bancos* eliminated from the effects of the convention of 1884 were to remain unaffected by such changes in sovereignty. 35 Stat. 1863, 1867; 1 Treaties, etc. (Malloy, 1910) 1199, 1200–1201.

1905

In 1895 the Mexican Commissioner on the International Boundary Commission submitted to the Commission a case known as the "El Chamizal", relating to the complaint of one Pedro I. Garcia. Garcia alleged that the tract of land known as "El Chamizal" had been acquired by his grandfather in 1827 and that it was in the public and peaceable possession of his grandfather and those claiming under him up to the year 1873, "in which year in consequence of the abrupt and sudden change of the current of the Rio Grande, the land in question was by that fact left on the other side of said river, or on the side of what is called today El Paso, Texas" (Report of William Cullen Dennis, agent for the United States in the Chamizal Arbitration, Sept. 8, 1911, MS. Department of State, file 711.1215/381, p. 9).

El Chamizal case

The Boundary Commission having been unable to agree upon the allocation of the *banco*, a convention was signed by the two Governments on June 24, 1910 submitting to arbitration the question "whether the international title to the Chamizal tract is in the United States of America or Mexico" (36 Stat. 2481, 2483; 3 Treaties, etc. (Redmond, 1923) 2729, 2730).

Arbitration

The Government of the United States maintained that the Chamizal tract, consisting of some 600 acres, had been formed by processes of slow and gradual erosion and accretion and therefore became territory of the United States under the treaties of 1848 and 1853 and the convention of 1884. The Government of Mexico contended that it had been formed by avulsion, that the old river bed as it existed

Contentions

at the time of the survey of the boundary in 1852 still marked the boundary between the two countries, and that consequently the tract was Mexican territory. Specifically, the contentions of the parties as set forth in the decision of the Commission were as follows:

By the Treaties of 1848 and 1853 the Rio Grande, from a point a little higher than the present City of El Paso to its mouth in the Gulf of Mexico, was constituted the boundary line between the United States and Mexico.

The contention on behalf of the United States of Mexico is that this dividing line was fixed, under those treaties, in a permanent and invariable manner, and consequently that the changes which have taken place in the river have not affected the boundary line which was established and marked in 1852.

On behalf of the United States of America it is contended that according to the true intent and meaning of the Treaties of 1848 and 1853, if the channel of the river changes by gradual accretion the boundary follows the channel, and that it is only in case of a sudden change of bed that the river ceases to be the boundary, which then remains in the abandoned bed of the river.

It is further contended on behalf of the United States of America that by the terms of a subsequent boundary Convention in 1884, rules of interpretation were adopted which became applicable to all changes in the Rio Grande, which have occurred since the river became the international boundary, and that the changes which determined the formation of the Chamizal tract are changes resulting from slow and gradual erosion and deposit of alluvion within the meaning of that Convention, and consequently changes which left the channel of the river as the international boundary line.

The Mexican Government, on the other hand, contends that the Chamizal tract having been formed before the coming in force of the Convention of 1884, that convention was not retroactive and could not affect the title to the tract, and further contends that even assuming the case to be governed by the Convention of 1884 the changes in the channel have not been the result of slow and gradual erosion and deposit of alluvion.

Finally the United States of America have set up a claim to the Chamizal tract by prescription, alleged to result from the undisturbed, uninterrupted, and unchallenged possession of the territory since the Treaty of 1848.

Award of June 15, 1911, Chamizal Arbitration, United States and Mexico (Washington, 1911) 7, 12–13.

The Commission, with the Mexican Commissioner dissenting, rejected the fixed-line theory of the Mexican Government, principally upon the ground that the whole course of action of the parties since **Decision** the conclusion of the treaty of 1848 indicated that it was the intention of the parties that the boundary should follow the river, the boundary to shift with the river, except in cases in which it abandoned its old channel and cut a new channel, in which case the boundary would remain in the old bed of the river. The claim of the United States to the territory by right of prescription was rejected, by unanimous vote, principally on the ground that the political control exercised by the local and Federal Governments had been constantly challenged and questioned by the Republic of Mexico.

The decision of the Commission on the principal question, with the American Commissioner dissenting, was based essentially upon the conclusion that it was the intent of the treaties of 1848 and 1853 and of article I of the convention of November 12, 1884 that titles to newly formed land should be transferred to the other country only when it was formed through "slow and gradual erosion and deposit of alluvium" and that the erosion as well as the deposit must be by a slow and gradual process. The Commission held that a much discussed change occurring in 1864 had not been caused by such slow erosion and that consequently the title to that part of the *banco* formed in 1864 should remain in Mexico. The Commission declared that it was not called upon to define the boundary line in exact terms and that consequently the fact that no evidence had been offered which would enable it to fix the line did not affect its right to reach the conclusion stated.

The Presiding Commissioner, E. Lafleur, of Canada (the Mexican Commissioner, F. B. Puga, concurring in part), said:

> Upon the application of the Convention of 1884 to the facts of this case the commissioners are unable to agree.
>
> The Presiding Commissioner and the Mexican Commissioner are of the opinion that the evidence establishes that from 1852 to 1864 the changes in the river, which during that interval formed a portion of the Chamizal tract, were caused by slow and gradual erosion and deposit of alluvium within the meaning of Article I of the Convention of 1884.
>
> . . . .
>
> With respect to the nature of the changes which occurred in 1864, and during the four succeeding years, the Presiding Commissioner and the Mexican Commissioner are of opinion that the phenomena described by the witnesses as having occurred during that period can not properly be described as alterations in the river effected through the slow and gradual erosion and deposit of alluvium.
>
> . . . .
>
> The Presiding Commissioner and the Mexican Commissioner consider that the changes referred to in this testimony can not by any stretch of the imagination, or elasticity of language, be characterized as slow and gradual erosion.
>
> The case of *Nebraska* v. *Iowa* (143 U.S. 359), decided by the Supreme Court of the United States in 1892, is clearly distinguishable from the present case. In *Nebraska* v. *Iowa* the court, applying the ordinary rules of international law to a

fluvial boundary between two States, hold [*sic*] that while there might be an instantaneous and obvious dropping into the Missouri River of quite a portion of its banks, and while the disappearance, by reason of this process, of a mass of bank might be sudden and obvious, the accretion to the other side was always gradual and by the imperceptible deposit of floating particles of earth. The conclusion was, therefore, that notwithstanding the rapidity of the changes in the course of the channel, and the washing from the one side onto the other, the law of accretion controlled on the Missouri River, as elsewhere.

In the present case, however, while the accretion may have been slow and gradual, the parties have expressly contracted that not only the accretion, but the erosion, must be slow and gradual. . . . If it had been called upon, in the case just cited, to decide whether the degradation of the bank of the Missouri River had occurred through a slow and gradual process the answer would undoubtedly have been in the negative.

In the case of *St. Louis* v. *Rutz* (138 U.S., 226) the Supreme Court of the United States, dealing with facts very similar to those established by the evidence in the present case, found that the washing away of the bank of the Mississippi River did not take place slowly and imperceptibly, but, on the contrary, the caving in and washing away of the same was rapid and perceptible in its progress; that such washing away of said river bank occurred principally at the rises or floods of high water in the Mississippi River, which usually occurred in the spring of the year; that such rises or floods varied in their duration, lasting from four to eight weeks before the waters of the river would subside to their ordinary stage or level; that during each flood there was usually carried away a strip of land from off said river bank from 240 to 300 feet in width, which loss of land could be seen and perceived in its progress; that as much as a city block would be cut off and washed away in a day or two, and that blocks or masses of earth from ten to fifteen feet in width frequently caved in and were carried away at one time.

If the degradation of the bank of the Mississippi River, above described, was found by the Supreme Court not to be slow and imperceptible progress, it is difficult to understand how the destruction of land, houses and forests, described by the witnesses in the present case, can be regarded as examples of slow and/ gradual erosion.

. . . .

. . . Applying this principle [that laid down in *Nebraska* v. *Iowa*], *mutatis mutandis*, to the present case, the Presiding Commissioner and the Mexican Commissioner are of opinion that the accretions which occurred in the Chamizal tract up to the time of the great flood in 1864 should be awarded to the United States of America, and that inasmuch as the changes which occurred in that year did not constitute slow and gradual erosion within the meaning of the Convention of 1884, the balance of the tract should be awarded to Mexico.

Award of June 15, 1911, Chamizal Arbitration, United States and Mexico (Washington, 1911) 7, 30–33, 35.

The American Commissioner, Anson Mills, concurred in part—as indicated above—in the findings of the Presiding Commissioner "to the effect that the Treaties of 1848 and 1853 did not establish a fixed and invariable line; that the Treaty of 1884 was retroactive, and in the finding of the Presiding Commissioner and the Mexican Commissioner to the effect that the United States has not established a title to the Chamizal tract by prescription". He dissented "*in toto* from so much of the opinion and award as assumes to segregate the Chamizal tract and to divide the parts so segregated between the two nations, and from that part of the opinion and award which holds that a portion of the Chamizal tract was not formed through 'slow and gradual erosion and deposit of alluvium' within the terms of the Treaty of 1884". He explained that "The reasons for the dissent are threefold: First, because in his opinion, the Commission is wholly without jurisdiction to segregate the tract or to make other findings concerning the change at El Chamizal than 'to decide whether it has occurred through avulsion or erosion, for the effects of articles 1 and 2 of the Convention of November 12, 1884,' (and article 4, Convention of 1889). Secondly, because in his opinion, the Convention of 1884 is not susceptible to any other construction than that the change of the river at El Chamizal was embraced within the first alternative of the Treaty of 1884. And, thirdly, because, in his opinion, the finding and award is vague, indeterminate and uncertain in its terms and impossible of execution." *Ibid.* 36. He declared that articles I and III of the arbitration convention of 1910 taken together meant that the two Governments had "asked this Commission a specific and definite question and that the Commission is 'solely and exclusively' empowered and required to give a specific and definite answer—either that the international title to the Chamizal tract as defined in the Convention is in the United States, or that it is in Mexico". He pointed out that neither the Mexican Government nor the Government of the United States had, from the time that the question of the Chamizal tract first arose in 1867 down to and through the close of the proceedings on June 2, 1911, advanced the slightest suggestion that there could be any question regarding a division of the tract. *Ibid.* 37. He was of the opinion that the case of *Nebraska* v. *Iowa*, relied upon in the decision, was not a "precedent" for "dividing the tract in question between the parties" for the reason that the Supreme Court of the United States was not confined to such narrow limits as those prescribed by the conventions of 1884 and 1910 (*ibid.* 1938). He was further of the opinion that the case of *St. Louis* v. *Rutz*, also relied upon in the decision, was not in point, stating:

An analogous case would have been presented here if after the river had invaded Mexican territory by rapid erosion, making for itself a bed five hundred yards wide, as one witness testified it did (U.S. Case, App., p. 118), an island had subsequently arisen to the south of the thread of the stream. That island would have belonged to Mexico whether it subsequently became joined to the south bank or not, or even though it might have become joined by accretion after its formation to the north bank, but there is not a suggestion in the evidence that such a fact ever occurred. On the contrary, the evidence indisputably shows that the north bank did not even move south simultaneously with the destruction of the south bank but that it grew up in a long course of years by the slow and gradual deposit of alluvium.

The American Commissioner is constrained to hold, therefore, that the majority of the Commission have failed to apply to the case the express rules laid down by the Convention of 1884; and by this failure have departed from the terms of the submission and invalidated the award.

Ibid. 44–45.

The Mexican Commissioner pointed out in his "Individual opinion" that he differed "from the opinion of his learned colleagues in definitely judging the subject of the Chamizal in the matter of the fixedness and invariability of the boundary line of 1852, and also in regard to the retrospective application of the convention of 1884" (*ibid.* 49–50).

Mexican Commissioner

At the session of the Commission on June 15, 1911 in which the award was read, the agent for the United States protested against the decision and award on the following grounds:

Protest of U.S. agent

1. Because it departs from the terms of submission in the following particulars:

> *a.* Because in dividing the Chamizal tract it assumes to decide a question not submitted to the Commission by the Convention of 1910 and a question the Commission was not asked to decide by either party at any stage of the proceedings;
> *b.* Because it fails to apply the standard prescribed by the Treaty of 1884;
> *c.* Because it applied to the determination of the issue of erosion or avulsion a ruling or principle not authorized by the terms of the submission or by the principles of international law or embraced in any of the treaties or conventions existing between the United States and Mexico;
> *d.* Because it departs from the jurisdictional provision of the Treaty of 1889 creating the International Boundary Commission.

2. Because the award is uncertain and indefinite in its terms, incapable of being made certain, and impossible of application.

3. Because the award fails to "state the reasons upon which it is based" in this that it fails to state specifically whether the alleged rapid and violent erosion by which it finds a portion of the Chamizal tract was formed comes within the terms of the Treaty of 1884 or is governed by the principles of international law, and fails to

state reasons for the inferential finding that it comes within the provisions of the Treaty of 1884, in spite of the fact that these questions were repeatedly argued by agent and counsel for the United States.

4. Because of essential error of law and fact.

Report of William Cullen Dennis, agent for the United States, Sept. 8, 1911, MS. Department of State, file 711.1215/381, pp. 78–79; *Minutes of the Meetings of the International Boundary Commission, June 10 and 15, 1911, Containing the Award in the Chamizal Case* (Washington, 1911) 56–57. The award is also printed in 1911 For. Rel. 573 *et seq.*

For the proceedings of the International Boundary Commission in the *El Chamizal* case, see *Proceedings of the International (Water) Boundary Commission, United States and Mexico* (Washington, 1903), vol. I, pp. 42–95.

By a communication of Aug. 24, 1911, the Government of the United States notified the Government of Mexico that—

"For the reasons set forth by the American Commissioner in his dissenting opinion, and by the American Agent in his suggestion of protest, the United States does not accept this award as valid or binding." MS. Department of State, file 711.1215/350a ; 1911 For. Rel. 598.

The next and perhaps the most important question is as to the effect of the sudden and violent change in the channel of the river that occurred in the year 1876, and which both parties properly treat as a true and typical avulsion. It is settled beyond the possibility of dispute that where running streams are the boundaries between States, the same rule applies as between private proprietors, namely, that when the bed and channel are changed by the natural and gradual processes known as erosion and accretion, the boundary follows the varying course of the stream; while if the stream from any cause, natural or artificial, suddenly leaves its old bed and forms a new one, by the process known as an avulsion, the resulting change of channel works no change of boundary, which remains in the middle of the old channel, although no water may be flowing in it, and irrespective of subsequent changes in the new channel. *New Orleans* v. *United States*, 10 Pet. 662, 717; *Jefferis* v. *East Omaha Land Co.*, 134 U.S. 178, 189; *Nebraska* v. *Iowa*, 143 U.S. 359, 361, 367, 370; *Missouri* v. *Nebraska*, 196 U.S. 23, 34–36. **State boundaries**

State of Arkansas v. State of Tennessee, 246 U.S. (1918) 158, 173.

See also *State of Oklahoma* v. *State of Texas*, 260 U.S. (1923) 606, 636–637; *New Mexico* v. *Texas*, 275 U.S. (1927) 279, 301–302.

During a period of nearly a century from 1823 to 1912–13, gradual erosion occurred on the Mississippi side and gradual accretion took place on the Louisiana bank of the Mississippi River. As a result of this alluvial action the river gradually and imperceptibly moved eastward and northward a distance of five or six miles. In 1912–13 the river, by a sudden avulsion, cut a new channel across the bar thus formed by accretion on the Louisiana side and separated a large portion of it from the Louisiana shore. A bill was brought in the Supreme

Court of the United States in 1928 to establish the proper interstate boundary at this point. The case was decided in February 1931, after the report of a special master. The Court held that the changes between the years 1823 and 1912–13 were due to gradual erosions and accretions and therefore adhered to the State of Louisiana, the boundary changing with the shifts of the river. The change in 1912–13, however, was due to an avulsion, and therefore the boundary was not changed, territorial sovereignty remaining unaffected.

The Court pointed out that there was no disagreement between the parties as to the applicable legal principles but only as to the correctness of the master's fact-findings and conclusions.

Louisiana v. *Mississippi*, 282 U.S. (1931) 458.

The former treaties with Mexico followed the usual rule that where gradual changes occur in the course of the bounding river the boundary will follow the river, but not in cases of avulsion. The treaty proclaimed June 5, 1907 (35 Stat. 1863), made the river the boundary also as to "Bancos" theretofore or thereafter created by avulsion unless they were of an area of over 250 hectares or were populated by over two hundred souls, and the Boundary Commission was to determine the status of each Banco and mark it out on the ground. Article 4 gave the option to an inhabitant of a Banco thus transferred to remain on it or to remove, to keep his property or dispose of it, and to retain his old citizenship or to acquire that of the country to which he was transferred.

Shapleigh et al. v. *Mier*, 83 F. (2d) 673, 675 (C.C.A. 5th, 1936). Affirmed, 299 U.S. (1937) 468.

For a discussion of the subject of *Bancos*, see ch. V, *post*.

Title to accreted land

A point of land projecting into Manila Bay on the island of Luzon had been gradually formed by the action of the sea since 1811, "about three-quarters since 1856, and a part since 1871", in which latter year the Spanish Law of Waters of 1866 became effective in the Philippines. The property was formerly used by the Spanish Navy and at the time of the suit here in question was occupied by the United States as a naval station. Plaintiffs sued to recover possession of the land, claiming title under conveyances from the owner of the upland. The Supreme Court of the United States, in 1912, affirmed the decision of the Philippine courts that, under III Partidas, tit. 28, laws 3, 4, 6, 24, and 26, and the Law of Waters of 1866, the title to the accretions remained in the Government.

In its opinion, written by Mr. Justice Holmes, the Supreme Court pointed out that the problem of ownership of accession to the shore by alluvial action had been a confused and vexed one under the Spanish law. It appeared clear, he said, that the civil law gave the alluvial increase of river banks to the riparian owner and that under that law the right of alluvion was not recognized for lakes and ponds.

Continuing, the Court stated:

> The seashore flowed by the tides, unlike the banks of rivers, was public property; in Spain belonging to the sovereign power. . . . The Spanish commentators do not help us, as they go little beyond a naked statement one way or the other. It seems to us that the best evidence of the view prevailing in Spain is to be found in the codification which presumably embodies it. . . . [Article 4 of the Law of Waters of 1866 provides:] "The lands added to the shores by the accessions and accretions caused by the sea belong to the public domain. When they are not (longer) washed by the waters of the sea, and are not necessary for objects of public utility, nor for the establishment of special industries, nor for the coast guard service, the Government shall [will?] declare them property of the adjacent estates, in increase of the same."
>
> . . . .
>
> . . . Of course we are dealing with the law of the Philippines, not with that which prevails in this country, whether of mixed antecedents or the common law.

Ker and Company v. *Couden*, 223 U.S. (1912) 268, 275, 277–279.

In a later case arising in New Jersey, the Court, again speaking through Mr. Justice Holmes, stated:

> The first ground of the defendant's claim is a grant from the State to the defendant's predecessors in title of land flowed by tidewater at the date of the deed, June 28, 1900, which included the strip in controversy. There seems to be no doubt from the decision of the Court of Errors and Appeals that this grant put an end to the right of the complainants to build wharves or otherwise to encroach upon the granted land, that being regarded as merely a license, revoked by the grant. The defendant contends that the effect was greater still, and relies upon a statement in the decision referred to, that "if the land was formerly fast land, [as this was said to have been] and the title was lost by erosion, it became the property of the State, not merely as long as it remained under water, but, if the State made a riparian grant, absolutely." This form of statement remained unchanged notwithstanding the criticism in a concurring opinion by White, J., 83 N.J. Eq. 656. But we agree with the District Court that it means no more than we have stated, and is shown to mean no more not only by the authority cited but by the following words in the opinion: "The title lost by erosion was then lost forever, unless it was regained by accretion, and the right of accretion was the compensation of the former owner for his loss." We presume from this language that in New Jersey as elsewhere by the common law the right of accretion is not like the permissive right to use land still under water, but is a right as against the State as well as its grantees, when as here the grantees have not filled in the land. In some countries that inherit the Roman law the rule may be different. *Ker & Co.* v. *Couden*, 223

Common-law rule

U.S. 268. We conclude that the conveyance by the State did not give the defendant a title to land added by accretion to the complainants' premises, and that it does not matter that this conveyance was by metes and bounds. The boundaries however indicated were good until changed by the gradual work of the ocean and then were modified in accordance with what we believe to be the common law. *Banks* v. *Ogden,* 2 Wall. 57.

Stevens v. *Arnold,* 262 U.S. (1923) 266, 269–270.

Loss by alluvial action

The owner of an island in the Ohio River brought suit to set aside harbor lines established in Pittsburgh by the Secretary of War under section 12 of the act of Congress of September 19, 1890 (26 Stat. 426, 455) and section 11 of the act of March 3, 1899 (30 Stat. 1121, 1151) and to restrain any prosecution for having reclaimed and occupied partially submerged land outside of the prescribed limits. The complainant argued, *inter alia,* that in 1865 the high- and low-water lines along the shore of the island had been definitely fixed by commissioners acting under a Pennsylvania statute of 1858 and that "by virtue of the statute, and the action of the Commissioners under it in fixing the high-water line as a permanent boundary, the right of the owners of the island to accretions beyond that line was taken away, while at the same time they were no longer subject to loss or diminution of their land by reason of its submergence 'through the avulsion of floods or freshets or through gradual erosion'". The complainant also argued that, regardless of the statute, the submergence of portions of the island during subsequent years had not affected its title, which remained absolute, including the reclamation and improvement of the submerged land inside the former line of high water.

In upholding the power of the Federal Government to fix the harbor lines for the protection of the harbor of Pittsburgh and in affirming the dismissal of complainant's bill, the Supreme Court, speaking through Mr. Justice Hughes, said:

> It is the established rule that a riparian proprietor of land bounded by a stream, the banks of which are changed by the gradual and imperceptible process of accretion or erosion, continues to hold to the stream as his boundary; if his land is increased he is not accountable for the gain, and if it is diminished he has no recourse for the loss. But where a stream suddenly and perceptibly abandons its old channel, the title is not affected and the boundary remains at the former line. . . . The doctrine that the owner takes the risk of the increase or diminution of his land by the action of the water applies as well to rivers that are strong and swift, to those that overflow their banks, and whether or not dykes and other defenses are necessary to keep the water within its proper limits. It is when the change in the stream is sudden, or violent, and visible, that the title remains the

same. It is not enough that the change may be discerned by comparison at two distinct points of time. It must be perceptible when it takes place. "The test as to what is gradual and imperceptible in the sense of the rule is, that though the witnesses may see from time to time that progress has been made, they could not perceive it while the process was going on." *County of St. Clair v. Lovingston, supra* (p. 68).

. . . It is alleged "that subsequent to the establishment in 1865 by said Commissioners of the line of high water mark, as aforesaid, a considerable amount of the soil of the shore of said Brunot's Island on the so-called back channel, within the said high water mark was washed away from time to time by heavy floods and freshets, so that a large part of the upland of the island, that is the land above high water mark, became and was overflowed and slightly submerged by water, but said land was not submerged to an extent sufficient to permit of navigation of any kind thereover." There is no other statement on the point save that the bill asserts that the complainant was entitled to reclaim "keeping at all times within the lines of the part that had been torn away by the violence of the waters."

It is manifest that these allegations are inadequate to support the complainant's contention. The determining words are that the land was "washed away from time to time by heavy floods and freshets," and the reference is to what occurred in many years. This is far from a statement that at any particular time there was such a sudden, violent, and visible change as to justify a departure from the ordinary rule which governs accretion and diminution albeit the stream suffer wide fluctuations in volume, the current be swift, and the banks afford slight resistance to encroachment.

For example, the general principle of accretion, which has that of diminution as its correlative, applies to such rivers as the Mississippi and the Missouri, notwithstanding the extent and rapidity of the changes constantly effected. . . .

The present case falls within the category first mentioned, and according to general principles of law the owner would bear the losses caused by the washings of the river.

Philadelphia Company v. *Stimson, Secretary of War*, 223 U.S. (1912) 605, 614, 624–625, 627.

CESSION

§61

Cession of territory involves the transfer of sovereignty by means of an agreement between the ceding and the acquiring states. It is a *derivative* mode of acquisition. The cession may comprise a portion only of the territory of the ceding state or it may comprise the totality of its territory. In the latter situation, as for example in the treaty of August 22, 1910 between Japan and Korea, the ceding state disappears and becomes merged into the acquiring state.

The consent of the population of ceded territory is not essential to the validity of the cession, although Grotius (bk. II, ch. vi, sec. 4) apparently held the opposite view. It is worthy of note, however, that in recent years cessions of territory have frequently been conditioned upon the will of the people as expressed in a plebiscite.

> In its scant century and a half of history the plebiscite, as a means of determination of questions of sovereignty, has suffered great fluctuations of fortune.
>
> .   .   .   .
>
> Abandoned by diplomats, condemned by the majority of writers on international law, and forgotten by the world at large, the plebiscite nevertheless stood as a goal for many a national group and, with the World War, came to the fore, together with the principle of self-determination, as the hoped-for means of regeneration for many a subject nationality, and found its place in the platform of numerous liberal and radical movements for permanent peace.
>
> I Sarah Wambaugh, *Plebiscites Since the World War* (1933) 3–4. See this work for detailed discussion of the several plebiscites held or attempted to be held in the years 1920–26 and the preparations for the plebiscite in the Saar Basin Territory.

During the course of the negotiations for the cession of the Danish West Indies to the United States, the American Minister in Denmark informed the Department of State by telegram on April 27, 1916 of the text of the Danish *contre-projet* reading in part as follows:

> The United States Government will be aware from previous negotiations respecting the questions now at issue that a cession of these islands which from olden times have belonged to the Danish Crown will only seem justifiable to Danish public opinion if the Danish public feel convinced that both the islands and their inhabitants will gain by the union with the United States, a great power in their vicinity, this position being preferable to a continued union with Denmark. This point of view manifested itself during the previous negotiations in the wish that the inhabitants of the islands might, through voting, be given an opportunity of expressing themselves respecting the contemplated cession. It is not impossible that this point of view will again be brought forward by the Danish Rigsdag.

On June 9, 1916 Secretary Lansing informed the American Minister that:

> This Government regrets that it cannot favor submitting the question of transfer of the islands to a vote of the inhabitants.

In a new Danish counter project of June 28, 1916 it was stated:

> The Danish Government waive the claim that the convention should be made dependent on the vote of the inhabitants on the islands ceded . . .

Minister Egan to Secretary Lansing, no. 240, Apr. 27, 1916, MS. Department of State, file 711.5914/56; Mr. Lansing to Mr. Egan, no. 110, June 9, 1916, *ibid.* 711.5914/59; Mr. Egan to Mr. Lansing, no. 268, June 30, 1916, *ibid.* 711.5914/63; 1917 For. Rel. 617, 622, 625.

After the signing of the treaty there was considerable pressure in Denmark for a plebiscite in the islands before parliamentary approval should be given to the treaty. This movement rested to a large extent upon the doubts entertained as to the manner in which an American administration would deal with the negroes in the islands. On October 5, 1916 the American Minister in Denmark telegraphed the Department of State that it had been agreed instead to arrange for thorough consideration by a parliamentary commission of the views of the inhabitants of the islands. His message stated:

> Parliamentary committee has reached a series of conclusions relative to its course of procedure. It insists that the whole of the diplomatic correspondence pertaining to the sale be submitted to it. When the material has been considered by the committee the latter will decide upon what persons shall be called upon to furnish information. At the meeting yesterday telegrams were despatched to the West Indian colonial boards to the effect that the committee was desirous of conferring with members of the boards. They must be selected in such a manner that the prevailing views are represented. They are to arrive in Copenhagen within the time limit set for the work of the committee. Governor Helweg Larsen who has resigned is now in New York City. He is due here October 26th, also he will be requested to furnish information. This procedure does away with the demand of Socialist party for a referendum in the islands.

Minister Egan to Secretary Lansing, no. 364, Oct. 5, 1916, MS. Department of State, file 711.5914/154; 1917 For. Rel. 682.

As regards the treaties of peace terminating the World War, it has been stated:

> The conclusion is inevitable that the Peace Treaties ending the World War have so far not established a universal or even general practice of a settlement of territorial questions on the basis of the principle of self-determination by the plebiscite. Nor have they eliminated acquisitions of territory on the implied principle if not the expressed term of conquest.
>
> Assuming that the ratification of the treaties by the constitutional agencies of the countries involved does establish an [? in] international law the norms on which the treaty provisions are built, we come to the inevitable conclusion that these treaties have given international legal validity to a practice which by the will of the one of two contending parties, enforced upon the other, establishes the use of the plebiscite in some territorial cessions and

prohibits the expression of popular consent or disapproval in others.

> Mattern, "The Employment of the Plebiscite in the Determination of Sovereignty", in 38 *Johns Hopkins University Studies in Historical and Political Science* (1920) no. 3, p. 194 [492].
>
> See also the discussion in connection with the acquisition of territorial sovereignty by conquest, *post* §62.

Self-determination

The principle of self-determination, as enunciated by President Wilson in a series of addresses, played an important role in the process of territorial readjustments following the World War. In his address of May 27, 1916 before the League to Enforce Peace President Wilson said:

> We believe these fundamental things: First, that every people has a right to choose the sovereignty under which they shall live.

In his address to the Senate of January 22, 1917 he stated:

> And there is a deeper thing involved than even equality of right among organized nations. No peace can last, or ought to last, which does not recognize and accept the principle that governments derive all their just powers from the consent of the governed, and that no right anywhere exists to hand peoples about from sovereignty to sovereignty as if they were property.

> 53 Cong. Rec., pt. 9, p. 8854; 54 Cong. Rec., pt. 2, p. 1742.

In his address of February 11, 1918, delivered before a joint session of the two houses of Congress, President Wilson declared:

> . . . National aspirations must be respected; peoples may now be dominated and governed only by their own consent. "Self-determination" is not a mere phrase. It is an imperative principle of action . . .

In this address he laid down four fundamental principles, among them:

> Second, that peoples and provinces are not to be bartered about from sovereignty to sovereignty as if they were mere chattels and pawns in a game, even the great game, now forever discredited, of the balance of power;

> .   .   .   .

> Fourth, that all well defined national aspirations shall be accorded the utmost satisfaction that can be accorded them without introducing new or perpetuating old elements of discord and antagonism that would be likely in time to break the peace of Europe and consequently of the world.

Finally, in his Mount Vernon address of July 4, 1918, President Wilson advanced as one of the fundamental ends to be achieved:

The settlement of every question, whether of territory, of sovereignty, of economic arrangement, or of political relationship, upon the basis of the free acceptance of that settlement by the people immediately concerned ...

.   .   .   .

These great objects can be put into a single sentence. What we seek is the reign of law, based upon the consent of the governed and sustained by the organized opinion of mankind.

56 Cong. Rec., pt. 2, pp. 1952–1953; *ibid.*, pt. 9, p. 8671.

In the present case, as the United States expressly disclaimed any intention to exercise sovereignty, jurisdiction, or control over the island, "except for the pacification thereof," the ownership of the island, upon the relinquishment by Spain of her sovereignty over it, immediately passed to the inhabitants of Cuba, who, in the resolutions referred to, were declared to be free and independent, and in whom, therefore, abstractly considered, sovereignty resided.

Art. I, Treaty of Paris, 1898

Had the language been "Spain cedes to the United States the island of Cuba," as by Article II she did Porto Rico, that would have divested her of all title to and, by consequence, all sovereignty over Cuba, both of which would then immediately have passed to the United States, as they did in the case of Porto Rico; subject, however, to the rights of the people. True, when, pursuant to the treaty, the United States occupied the island, the inhabitants thereof during such occupancy undoubtedly owed allegiance to the United States, i.e., fidelity and obedience for the protection they received, but that did not divest them of their inherent rights.

Galban and Company, A Corporation, v. *The United States,* 40 Ct. Cls. (1905) 495, 506–507.

On July 15, 1904 Attorney General Moody advised the Secretary of the Treasury that Miraflores Island "did not belong to Porto Rico before the cession, and by the treaty of peace title to it was transferred from Spain to the United States. (24 Opin., 8.)" and that he was "accordingly of opinion that the United States now possesses a valid and complete title to the whole of the island in question".

Miraflores

25 Op. Att. Gen. (1906) 193, 194.

Article 1 of the convention between the United States and Denmark for the cession of the Danish West Indies, signed August 4, 1916, provided:

Danish West Indies

His Majesty the King of Denmark by this convention cedes to the United States all territory, dominion and sovereignty, possessed, asserted or claimed by Denmark in the West Indies including the Islands of Saint Thomas, Saint John and Saint Croix together with the adjacent islands and rocks.

This cession includes the right of property in all public, government, or crown lands, public buildings, wharves, ports, harbors, fortifications, barracks, public funds, rights, franchises, and privileges, and all other public property of every kind or description now belonging to Denmark together with all appurtenances thereto.

In this cession shall also be included any government archives, records, papers or documents which relate to the cession or the rights and property of the inhabitants of the Islands ceded, and which may now be existing either in the Islands ceded or in Denmark. Such archives and records shall be carefully preserved, and authenticated copies thereof, as may be required shall be at all times given to the United States Government or the Danish Government, as the case may be, or to such properly authorized persons as may apply for them.

Article 3 provided:

It is especially agreed, however, that:

1) The arms and military stores existing in the Islands at the time of the cession and belonging to the Danish Government shall remain the property of that Government and shall, as soon as circumstances will permit, be removed by it, unless they, or parts thereof, may have been bought by the Government of the United States; it being however understood that flags and colors, uniforms and such arms or military articles as are marked as being the property of the Danish Government shall not be included in such purchase.

2) The movables, especially silver plate and pictures which may be found in the government buildings in the islands ceded and belonging to the Danish Government shall remain the property of that Government and shall, as soon as circumstances will permit, be removed by it.

.   .   .   .

5) Whatever sum shall be due to the Danish Treasury by private individuals on the date of the exchange of ratifications are reserved and do not pass by this cession; and where the Danish Government at that date holds property taken over by the Danish Treasury for sums due by private individuals, such property shall not pass by this cession, but the Danish Government shall sell or dispose of such property and remove its proceeds within two years from the date of the exchange of ratifications of this convention; the United States Government being entitled to sell by public auction, to the credit of the Danish Government, any portion of such property remaining unsold at the expiration of the said term of two years.

39 Stat. 1706–1710; 3 Treaties, etc. (Redmond, 1923) 2558–2560.

CONQUEST

§62

Conquest is the taking of possession of territory of an enemy state by force; it becomes a mode of acquisition of territory—and hence of transfer of sovereignty—only if the conquered territory is effectively reduced to possession and annexed by the conquering state.

It has been argued on behalf of Norway that after the disappearance of the two Nordic settlements, Norwegian sovereignty was lost and Greenland became a *terra nullius*. Conquest and voluntary abandonment are the grounds on which this view is put forward.

Eastern Greenland Case

The word "conquest" is not an appropriate phrase, even if it is assumed that it was fighting with the Eskimos which led to the downfall of the settlements. Conquest only operates as a cause of loss of sovereignty when there is war between two States and by reason of the defeat of one of them sovereignty over territory passes from the loser to the victorious State. The principle does not apply in a case where a settlement has been established in a distant country and its inhabitants are massacred by the aboriginal population. Nor is the fact of "conquest" established. It is known now that the settlements must have disappeared at an early date, but at the time there seems to have been a belief that despite the loss of contact and the loss of knowledge of the whereabouts of the settlements one or both of them would again be discovered and found to contain the descendants of the early settlers.

Per. Ct. Int. Jus., Ser. A/B, No. 53 (Apr. 5, 1933), pp. 22, 46–47; III Hudson, *World Court Reports* (1938) 171–172.

. . . On May 24, 1900, Lord Roberts, the Commander-in-Chief of the British forces operating against the Boer States, issued the following proclamation:—

.   .   .   .   .   .

" . . . the territories known as the Orange Free State are annexed to, and form part of, Her Majesty's dominions, and that provisionally, and until Her Majesty's pleasure is fully declared, the said territories will be administered by me with such powers as aforesaid.

Orange Free State

"Her Majesty is pleased to direct that the new territories shall henceforth be known as the Orange River Colony."

.   .   .   .   .   .

A similar proclamation, published September 1, 1900, purported to annex the South African Republic. . . .

Now at this date the Boer forces had by no means been subjugated; their organized resistance still remained, and was, indeed, very vigorous and effective. Both in the Transvaal and in the Orange Free State the British subsequently met with con-

South African Republic

siderable reverses; and these reverses were inflicted by burghers who could not be considered other than the legitimate combatants of States whose independence was still in existence, and whose Governments still issued orders which were obeyed. Indeed, from September 1, 1900, to September 1, 1901, the British losses amounted to 1,857 officers and 34,531 men; so that it was manifestly impossible to claim that the armed contention was at an end. The position, then, assumed by the British authorities was juridically invalid, because it was unsupported by conditions *de facto*. As General Den Beer Poortugael, a leading European authority, writing in 1901, observed on the subject: "L'annexion est un fait juridique parfait, et peut donc être reconnu, lorsque la conquête a eu lieu dans des conditions qui répondent aux exigences du droit des gens. Mais, la guerre étant une action entre deux parties, il ne suffit pas pour établir la légalité du fait, que l'une de ces parties déclare que la contestation avec l'autre a pris fin. Il y faut le consentement libre de l'autre partie, ou du moins une supériorité de force devant laquelle, en fait, la seconde partie soit obligée de s'incliner, qu'elle ne puisse nier, à laquelle elle doive se soumettre." . . .

British statesmen, too—e.g. Sir William Harcourt and Mr. Bryce (now Lord Bryce)—condemned the proclamations. The latter speaking in the House of Commons of that of May 24, 1900, described it as "a monstrous proclamation, a proclamation absolutely opposed to the first principles of international law, a proclamation based upon a paper annexation made seven days before, which purported to treat the inhabitants of the two Republics[1] ([1] This was said by inadvertence; for, as we have seen, the proclamation of May 24 referred only to the Orange Free State.) as rebels—rebels, forsooth, on the basis of this paper annexation." . . .

As soon as these proclamations were made, the President of the Orange Free State and the President of the South African Republic protested against them (June 11 and September 3, respectively), which they declared to be null and void, and contrary to the law of nations. They added that their nations remained free and independent, and refused to submit to British authority.

"Reasons"

Certain reasons have been suggested for the issue of the proclamations. In the first place, it was said that the British military authorities interpreted the departure of President Kruger for Europe as implying the disappearance of the Government of the South African Republic. But the departure, or expulsion, or death of the head of a Government does not necessarily put an end to that Government or to the juridical personality of the State. The Germans in 1870, despite their licentious conduct in many respects, advanced no such pretension. The Imperial Government had fallen, but they acknowledged its temporary substitute—the Government of National Defence—as the legitimate Government. . . . Secondly, judging from a proclamation of September 9, 1900, it appears that the object of the annexation was to prevent the "late South African Republic" from granting concessions, and so on the one hand raising money for the prosecution of hostilities, and on the other compromising the future of the country by burdening it with obligations imposed through military exigencies.

Notwithstanding the formal proclamations, it is fair to add that the British authorities did not on that account consider *in fact* that the countries had thereby been annexed; at all events, they made no attempt to apply in practice the various principles underlying annexation and change of sovereignty.

The Turco-Italian War, 1911, furnished another example of premature annexation on the part of Italy. The first Italian act of occupation took place on October 5, 1911, when Italian vessels transported landing parties to take possession of Tripoli. Already in the middle of October public opinion in Italy declared in favour of annexation; and towards the end of the same month an announcement was made that the Italian Government had notified the Powers "of the cessation of Ottoman rule in North Africa," and that the newly acquired Italian possessions there extended from the Egyptian frontier on the east to Tunis on the west, and southward to the British and French zones of influence in Central Africa. These boundaries, however, were mentioned neither in the decree of annexation nor in the circular addressed by the Marquis di San Giuliano to the Powers. On November 5, exactly a month after the first act of occupation, the King of Italy issued a decree to the effect that Tripolitana and Cyrenaica were placed under the full and complete sovereignty of the Kingdom of Italy, that an Act of Parliament would establish the final regulations for the administration of the said regions, and that until this Act was promulgated provision would be made by royal decrees; it added that the decree would be laid before Parliament for the purpose of converting it into law. At the same time, the Italian Foreign Office sent a note to the Powers as follows:

Tripolitania and Cyrenaica

" . . . by a royal decree dated to-day, Tripolitana and Cyrenaica have been definitely and irrevocably submitted to the full and complete sovereignty of the Kingdom of Italy.

" . . . Tripolitana and Cyrenaica have ceased to be a part of the Ottoman Empire, but we are at present prepared to examine in a liberal and conciliatory spirit the means of settling in the most suitable and honourable manner for Turkey the consequences of irrevocably accomplished facts.

"Certainly we could not maintain these conciliatory intentions if Turkey persisted in uselessly prolonging the war. We, however, trust that the Great Powers' work of concord will bring her to take without delay wise decisions, and resolutions responding to her true interests and those of the whole civilized world. In any case, Italy will co-operate in obtaining such results by showing herself as ready to agree upon equitable terms of peace as she is resolute in her determination to adopt the most efficacious means of imposing it with the shortest possible delay." . . .

Two days later (November 7), General Caneva, accompanied by his staff and a guard of honour, read the royal decree before the Arab notables in Tripoli.

It appears that the annexation had not been notified to the Turkish Government. None the less, the Porte hastened to protest against the proceeding. . . . This protest is expressed so precisely and pointedly that it is desirable to give it *verbatim:*

"The Imperial Ottoman Government learns that the Italian Government, having *motu proprio* promulgated a decree proclaiming the annexation of the Ottoman provinces of Tripoli and Bengazi, communicates the same to the Powers. The Sublime Porte protests in the most energetic manner against this proclamation, which it considers as null and valueless, both in law and in fact. Such an act is effectively null because it is contrary to the most elementary principles of international law, and equally so because Turkey and Italy are still in a state of war and because the Turkish Government intends to preserve and to defend by force of arms its sovereign rights, which are imprescriptible and inalienable, over these two provinces. On the other hand, this proclamation and its communication to the Powers constitute a double and formal violation of the engagements solemnly contracted under treaties, especially those of Paris and Berlin, as well by Italy towards the Great Powers as by the latter towards the Ottoman Government, with reference to the territorial integrity of the Empire. Under these conditions the annexation proclaimed by the Italian Government remains juridically null, just as it is inexistent in fact." . . .

In point of fact, at the date of the alleged annexation there had been no subjugation whatever. . . . The Italian army had entered into occupation of little more than the main points on the coast of the provinces. It had taken possession of only five towns at considerable distances from each other. The interior remained in the hands of the Turks and Arabs, who from time to time made assaults on the Italian forces near the ports occupied. There was not even effective occupation, according to the provisions laid down in the Hague Regulations and Article 34 of the General Act of Berlin (February 26, 1885), which forbids fictitious annexation of territory.

Like the British premature proclamations in South Africa, the Italian decree was generally condemned. According to a statement made by Sir Edward Grey in the House of Commons, November 8, 1911—that is, three days after the decree was published—the British Government then regarded the annexation as inoperative. Even in Italy objections to it were raised on the ground of international law, whatever grounds policy might furnish. Thus, Professor Diena held . . . that juridically the acts in question possessed no international validity—his phrase is "internazionalmente irrilevanti"; and that Tripolitana and Cyrenaica really ceased in law to form part of the Ottoman Empire only as a result of the Sultan's firman annexed to the treaty of peace, which Italy promptly communicated to the other Powers. . . .

On the other hand, Professor Anzilotti of Rome maintained that there were two kinds of occupation: firstly, occupation pure and simple, secondly, occupation with the object of conquest and annexation; and he held that the latter kind would entitle the occupant to transfer to himself the sovereignty over the country occupied. . . . It is, however, untenable. If adopted, it would inevitably involve the suppression of the entire doctrine of military occupation as embodied in modern international law. It would, more than ever, put a weaker State at the mercy of a more powerful. The purely temporary provisional character of occupation would vanish; and the first act of invasion might well signalize one of two arbitrary and terrible alternatives— the total destruction of all on the invaded territory who offered resistance, or the immediate appropriation of the invaded territory and the bringing of all under the yoke of the invader's sovereignty. That is, the moment the invaders arrived, with a view to taking possession of the country and permanently retaining it, they would consider the people their subjects, and would thus be in a position to regard resistance as high treason, and to compel all, non-combatants and armed forces alike, to take part in military operations against their own country. Their refusal, due to their patriotism and devotion to their country, would be looked upon by the invader as a crime punishable with death; their unswerving and self-sacrificing fidelity would be treated as the vilest offence that man is capable of; their martyrdom would be regarded as the condign punishment of a traitor.

Phillipson, *Termination of War and Treaties of Peace* (1916) 22–28.

By a note of October 18, 1912 the Italian Chargé d'Affaires in Washington informed the Secretary of State that "the state of war between Italy and Turkey has terminated by the conclusion of a treaty of peace signed at Lausanne on October 18th instant between plenipotentiaries of the two nations". The Italian Chargé d'Affaires concluded his note by requesting the United States to "recognize the sovereignty of Italy over Tripoli and Cyrenaica". In reply the Acting Secretary of State merely stated that the United States was "much gratified" to learn that the state of war had been terminated between Italy and Turkey.

1912 For. Rel. 632.

There have been certain tendencies, particularly since the World War, to denounce conquest as a means of acquiring territorial sovereignty. Recent trends

Article 10 of the Covenant of the League of Nations provides:

The Members of the League undertake to respect and preserve as against external aggression the territorial integrity and existing political independence of all Members of the League.

The declaration of the American republics, transmitted on August 3, 1932 to the Governments of Paraguay and Bolivia by representatives of the United States, Colombia, Uruguay, Cuba, Mexico, Peru, Brazil, Argentina, Chile, Guatemala, Venezuela, Haiti, Dominican

Republic, Honduras, Ecuador, Panama, Nicaragua, Costa Rica, and San Salvador, stated in conclusion:

> The American nations further declare that they will not recognize any territorial arrangement of this controversy which has not been obtained by peaceful means nor the validity of territorial acquisitions which may be obtained through occupation or conquest by force of arms.

The anti-war treaty of non-aggression and conciliation, signed at Rio de Janeiro on October 10, 1933 by the representatives of Argentina, Brazil, Chile, Mexico, Paraguay, and Uruguay, to which treaty the United States adhered on August 10, 1934, contains the following provisions:

> The states designated below . . .
> To the end of condemning wars of aggression and territorial acquisitions that may be obtained by armed conquest, making them impossible and establishing their invalidity through the positive provisions of this treaty.
>
> .   .   .   .
>
> . . . have agreed upon the following:
>
> .   .   .   .
>
> They declare that as between the high contracting parties territorial questions must not be settled by violence, and that they will not recognize any territorial arrangement which is not obtained by pacific means, nor the validity of the occupation or acquisition of territories that may be brought about by force of arms.

3 Treaties, etc. (Redmond, 1923) 3336, 3339. Telegrams to Paraguay and Bolivia, Aug. 3, 1932, MS. Department of State, file 724.3415/19586 (translation). 49 Stat. 3363, 3375; 4 Treaties, etc. (Trenwith, 1938) 4793–4794.

See also Secretary Stimson's note of Jan. 7, 1932 (*ante* §53); the resolution of the League of Nations of Mar. 11, 1932, League of Nations *Official Journal*, Spec. Supp. 101, pp. 87–88 (*ante* §53); and article 11 of the convention on rights and duties of states signed at Montevideo, Dec. 26, 1933, 49 Stat. 3097, 3101; 4 Treaties, etc. (Trenwith, 1938) 4807, 4809. For a recent discussion of the subject of the acquisition of territory by force, see Hyde, "Conquest Today", in 30 A.J.I.L. (1936) 471–476.

PRESCRIPTION

§63

In the case of *Louisiana* v. *Mississippi*, the Supreme Court of the United States, speaking through Chief Justice Fuller, said:

> The question is one of boundary, and this court has many times held that, as between the States of the Union, long acquiescence in the assertion of a particular boundary and the exercise of dominion and sovereignty over the territory within it, should be accepted as conclusive, whatever the international rule might be

in respect of the acquisition by prescription of large tracts of country claimed by both.

202 U.S. (1906) 1, 53–54.

The case of *State of Maryland* v. *State of West Virginia* involved an original bill in equity filed in the Supreme Court by the State of Maryland on October 12, 1891, pursuant to an act of the Maryland General Assembly of January 1890 directing the Attorney General to take such steps as were necessary to secure an adjudication of the boundary dispute between the two States. The controversy related to the true location of that portion of the boundary line between the two States lying between Garrett County, Maryland, and Preston County, West Virginia, from the headwaters of the Potomac to the Pennsylvania line. In brief, Maryland contended that the line should be run from the "Potomac Stone" while West Virginia contended that the "Deakins" line, run from the Fairfax stone, was the proper boundary (see plate 1, 217 U.S. (1910) 1, 27). Maryland rested its case upon the construction of the charter granted by King Charles I, on June 20, 1632, to Lord Baltimore. West Virginia relied upon the fact that, for a long period of time, the so-called "Deakins" line had been recognized and acted upon as the established true boundary line.

The Court conceded, in its opinion, that in the light of present knowledge, it was quite possible, as Maryland argued, that a meridian line from the Potomac stone more fully conformed with the terms of the charter than did one drawn from the Fairfax stone. The Court then pointed out, however, that the Potomac stone had not even been located until six years after the filing of the suit before the Court, whereas the Fairfax stone had a long and important history, which is set out in some detail in the opinion.

The Court reached the following conclusion:

> the fact remains that after the Deakins survey in 1788 the people living along the line generally regarded that line as the boundary line between the States at bar. . . .
> A perusal of the record satisfies us that for many years occupation and conveyance of the lands on the Virginia side has been with reference to the Deakins line as the boundary line. The people have generally accepted it, and the facts in this connection cannot be ignored.

The Court then quoted with approval from *Virginia* v. *Tennessee*, 148 U.S. (1893) 503, 522, 523, and *Louisiana* v. *Mississippi*, 202 U.S. (1906) 1, 53, and concluded:

> The effect to be given to such facts as long continued possession "gradually ripening into that condition which is in conformity with international order," depends upon the merit of

individual cases as they arise. I Oppenheim, International Law, §243. In this case we think a right, in its nature prescriptive, has arisen, practically undisturbed for many years, not to be overthrown without doing violence to principles of established right and justice equally binding upon States and individuals. *Rhode Island* v. *Massachusetts*, 12 Pet. 657.

.   .   .   .

We think, for the reasons which we have undertaken to state, that the decree in this case should provide for the appointment of commissioners whose duty it shall be to run and permanently mark the old Deakins line, beginning at a point where the north and south line from the Fairfax Stone crosses the Potomac River and running thence northerly along said line to the Pennsylvania border.

217 U.S. (1910) 1, 41, 44–45. For the final decree, see *ibid.* 577.

In denying the contention of the State of Tennessee that the boundary should be a line equidistant between the opposite banks of the river instead of the "thalweg" because such was the boundary acquiesced in for many years by the States of Arkansas and Tennessee and their predecessors in sovereignty, the Supreme Court of the United States said:

It is said that Arkansas has interpreted the line to be at a point equidistant from the well-defined and permanent banks of the river, that Tennessee likewise has recognized this boundary, and that by long acquiescence on the part of both States in this construction, and the exercise of jurisdiction by both in accordance therewith, the question should be treated as settled. The reference is to certain judicial decisions, and two acts of legislation. In *Cessill* v. *State* (1883), 40 Arkansas, 501, which was a prosecution for unlicensed sale of liquors upon a boat anchored off the Arkansas shore, it was held that the boundary line, as established by the original treaties and since observed in federal legislation, state constitutions, and judicial decisions was the "line along the river bed equidistant from the permanent and defined banks of the ascertained channel on either side." This was followed in subsequent decisions by the same court. *Wolfe* v. *State* (1912), 104 Arkansas, 140, 143; *Kinnanne* v. *State* (1913), 106 Arkansas, 286, 290. The first pertinent decision by the Supreme Court of Tennessee is *State* v. *Muncie Pulp Co.* (1907), 119 Tennessee, 47, in which a similar conclusion was reached, partly upon the ground that it had been adopted by the courts of Arkansas. The legislative action referred to consists of two acts of the General Assembly of the State of Tennessee (Acts 1903, p. 1215, c. 420; Acts 1907, p. 1723, c. 516), each of which authorized the appointment of a commission to confer and act with a like commission representing the State of Arkansas to locate the line between the States in the old and abandoned channel at the place that we now have under consideration; and the Act of 1907 further provided that if Arkansas should fail to appoint a commission, the Attorney General of Tennessee should

Effect of particular statutes and decisions

be authorized to institute a suit against that State in this court to establish and locate the boundary line. These acts, far from treating the boundary as a line settled and acquiesced in, treat it as a matter requiring to be definitely settled, with the cooperation of representatives of the sister State if practicable, otherwise by appropriate litigation.

The Arkansas decisions had for their object the establishment of a proper rule for the administration of the criminal laws of the State, and were entirely independent of any action taken or proposed by the authorities of the State of Tennessee. They had no particular reference to that part of the river bed that was abandoned as the result of the avulsion of 1876; on the contrary, they dealt with parts of the river where the water still flowed in its ancient channel. The decision of the Supreme Court of Tennessee in *State* v. *Muncie Pulp Co.*, 119 Tennessee, 47, sustained the claim of the State to a part of the abandoned river bed which, by the rule of the *thalweg*, would be without that State. The combined effect of these decisions and of the legislation referred to, all of which were subsequent to the year 1876, falls far short of that long acquiescence in the practical location of a common boundary, and possession in accordance therewith, which in some of the cases has been treated as an aid in setting the question at rest. *Rhode Island* v. *Massachusetts*, 4 How. 591, 638, 639; *Indiana* v. *Kentucky*, 136 U.S. 479, 510, 514, 518; *Virginia* v. *Tennessee*, 148 U.S. 503, 522; *Louisiana* v. *Mississippi*, 202 U.S. 1, 53; *Maryland* v. *West Virginia*, 217 U.S. 1, 41.

State of Arkansas v. *State of Tennessee*, 246 U.S. (1918) 158, 171–172.

. . . it is insisted that Arkansas and Mississippi by their respective constitutions have fixed the boundary line, as it is now claimed to be by the State of Mississippi, and that such boundary line has become the true boundary of the States irrespective of the decision of this court in *Iowa* v. *Illinois, supra,* followed in *Arkansas* v. *Tennessee, supra.* We have examined the constitutions and decisions of the respective States, and find nothing in them to change the conclusions reached by this court in determining the question of boundary between States.

.   .   .   .

We are unable to find occasion to depart from this rule [of the *thalweg*] because of long acquiescence in enactments and decisions, and the practices of the inhabitants of the disputed territory in recognition of a boundary, which have been given weight in a number of our cases where the true boundary line was difficult to ascertain.

State of Arkansas v. *State of Mississippi*, 250 U.S. (1919) 39, 44, 45.

In 1923 the State of Michigan instituted an original suit in equity in the Supreme Court of the United States to determine the boundary between Michigan and Wisconsin from the mouth of the Montreal River at Lake Superior to the ship-channel entrance from Lake Mich- *Michigan* v. *Wisconsin* igan into Green Bay. The decision of the Court, rendered in 1926, was based upon the "rule, long-settled and never doubted by this court, . . . that long acquiescence by one state in the possession of territory by another and in the exercise of sovereignty and dominion over it is conclusive of the latter's title and rightful authority".

For purposes of convenience, the Court dealt separately with the three different sections of the disputed boundary. With regard to the Montreal River section, after a review of the historical background, the Court concluded "that the description in the Michigan Enabling Act [June 15, 1836, 5 Stat. 49] of the line from the mouth of the Montreal to the Lake of the Desert was inserted under the mistaken belief that the river connected with the lake; that this mistake was discovered as early as 1841, of which discovery Michigan, long prior to the admission of Wisconsin, had knowledge; that the line as now claimed by Wisconsin was surveyed and marked by Cram and Burt at the dates already stated [1840–1841, 1847]; that Michigan not only assented to the result of these surveys, but actively participated in securing the insertion of the description of that line in the Wisconsin Enabling Act [Aug. 6, 1846, 9 Stat. 56–57] and herself substantially adopted it by the [Michigan] Constitution of 1850; and that for a period of more than 60 years she stood by without objection with full knowledge of the possession, acts of dominion, and claim and exercise of jurisdiction on the part of the State of Wisconsin over the area in question".

The Court stated:

In addition to this, the line as claimed by Wisconsin has been, from the time of the Burt survey, accepted as the true boundary by the United States and, in its surveys, plats and maps, sales and other acts in respect of the public lands, continuously and consistently recognized, with the knowledge of Michigan and without protest on her part. Indeed, nothing appears to indicate dissatisfaction with the boundary thus established until the adoption of the Constitution of 1908, and, even then, except to the extent that this may be regarded as a continuing assertion of a claim to the boundary as there set forth or as originally described in the Michigan Enabling Act, the matter was allowed to rest until 1919.

To meet this situation, it is contended that the State of Michigan through all these years labored under a mistake in respect of the real facts and that this was the result of excusable ignorance on her part. The contention is devoid of merit. The material facts, since at least the date of the Wisconsin Enabling Act, have been so obvious that knowledge of them on the part of the Michigan authorities, if it were not shown, as it is shown, by the evidence, must necessarily be assumed.

Notwithstanding, the State of Michigan at this late day insists that the boundary now be established by a decree of this court in accordance with the description contained in her Constitution of 1908. Plainly, this cannot be done. That rights of the character here claimed may be acquired on the one hand and lost on the other by open, long-continued and uninterrupted possession of territory, is a doctrine not confined to individuals but applicable to sovereign nations as well, *Direct United States Cable Co.* v. *Anglo-American Telegraph Co.*, [1877] L.R. 2 A.C. 394, 421; Wheaton, International Law, 5th Eng. Ed. 268–269; 1 Moore, International Law Digest, 294 *et seq.*, and, *a fortiori*, to the quasi-sovereign states of the Union. . . . That rule [*supra*] is applicable here and is decisive of the question in respect of the Montreal River section of the boundary in favor of Wisconsin.

In considering the Menominee River section of the boundary the Court stated:

Some of these islands, comparatively small in area and of little consequence, have never been surveyed or any definite acts of dominion exercised over them by either state. But to this we attach no importance. The assertion and exercise of dominion by Wisconsin over the islands on the Michigan side of the channel was begun and has continued in virtue of, and in reliance upon, the readjustment of the boundary set forth in the Wisconsin Enabling Act. The rule is well-settled in respect of individual claimants that actual possession of a part of a tract by one who claims the larger tract, under color of title describing it, extends his possession to the entire tract in the absence of actual adverse possession of some part of it by another. *Clarke's Lessee* v. *Courtney*, 5 Pet. 319, 354; *Hunnicutt* v. *Peyton*, 102 U.S. 333, 368; *Ellicott* v. *Pearl*, 10 Pet. 412, 442; *Smith* v. *Gale*, 144 U.S. 509, 525–526; *Montoya* v. *Gonzales*, 232 U.S. 375, 377; *Houston Oil Co. of Texas* v. *Goodrich*, 213 Fed. 136, 142. Upon like grounds and with equal reason, under circumstances such as are here disclosed, the principle of the rule applies where states are the rival claimants. It results that the Wisconsin Enabling Act, together with the Act of Admission, gave color of title in that state to all of the islands within the limits there described; and that her original and continued possession, assertion and exercise of dominion and jurisdiction over a part of these islands, pursuant to such legislation and with the acquiescence of Michigan, extended Wisconsin's possession, dominion and jurisdiction to all of them, in the absence of actual possession of, or exercise of dominion over, any territory within the boundary by Michigan. The fact that the islands constitute separated tracts of land is of no consequence here, whatever its effect might be under other conditions. In applying the rule, the area within the described boundary, both land and water, must be considered as together constituting a single tract of territory.

Constructive possession

In discussing the Green Bay section of the boundary the Court said:

In determining the boundary through this section, the question is not embarrassed by differences of description. The calls of the Michigan Enabling Act are down the channel of the

Menominee to "the centre of the most usual ship channel of the Green Bay of Lake Michigan; thence through the centre of the most usual ship channel of the said Bay to the middle of Lake Michigan." The Wisconsin Enabling Act calls for the same boundary.

The evidence shows that there are two distinct ship channels, to either of which this description might apply. . . . The evidence as to which of the two ship channels was the usual one at the time of the adoption of the Michigan Enabling Act is not only conflicting, but of such inconclusive character that, standing alone, we could base no decree upon it with any feeling of certainty. . . . If it were necessary, we should, of course, undertake the task—as we should be bound to do—of reaching a conclusion from these dubious premises. But, it is not necessary, for, as in the case of the two sections of the boundary just discussed, the title of Wisconsin to the disputed area now in question, is established by long possession and acquiscence; and this conclusion is justified by evidence and concessions of the most substantial character.

. . . The explanation relied upon is that the State of Michigan, as a result of her excusable ignorance, has not been aware of the real facts and, therefore, should not be held to have lost rights by long acquiescence which she otherwise might have had. This view cannot be accepted and may be dismissed with a reference to what we have already said as to the same defense in respect of the Montreal River section.

Michigan v. *Wisconsin*, 270 U.S. (1926) 295, 307–308, 313–318.

In the case of *Louisiana* v. *Mississippi*, the State of Mississippi asserted, as a separate and alternative defense, that its title to the disputed territory could not then be assailed because of long-continued possession and exercise of sovereignty and dominion, with the acquiescence of Louisiana. The master appointed by the Court found:

5. That Mississippi did not by possession or exercise of sovereignty or dominion acquire right or title to the disputed territory . . .

In sustaining the master's finding, the Supreme Court said:

The first knowledge that complainant's witnesses had of any claim on behalf of Mississippi or its citizens was shortly before this action was brought. It appears that in or about 1923 Mississippi sold some of the land in question for delinquent taxes. On the assessment rolls of Issaquena County, Mississippi, the purchasers at these tax sales first appeared as owners in 1925-1926. The respondent put in evidence assessment rolls for certain years between 1848 and 1926. They show that after 1883 certain of the lands within the original boundary of Tullos Island are marked "in river," or "in Mississippi River," and from time to time these lands so designated were assessed for taxation, sometimes for nominal amounts and sometimes for substantial sums. At times "Island No. 98" appears as a separate item on the rolls, although the surveys show that at those times the island had disappeared. It is described as of greatly varying sizes in different years. The evidence to be drawn from this source is quite contradictory and fails to show any dominion by Mississippi over the disputed territory.

The record sustains the master's finding that there is no proof that Louisiana or its citizens knew of or acquiesced in any purported dominion of Mississippi over the disputed territory. The respondent has failed to meet the test laid down in *Michigan* v. *Wisconsin*, 270 U.S. 295, with respect to exercise of sovereignty and dominion over the disputed territory, and acquiescence by complainant in such alleged possession. The master's fifth finding is sustained.

282 U.S. (1931) 458, 462, 466–467. See also *ante* §60.

It is a settled principle of the law of nations that a state of things which actually exists and has existed for a long time should be changed as little as possible . . .

Decision of the Permanent Court of Arbitration in the Matter of the Maritime Boundary Dispute Between Norway and Sweden, Oct. 23, 1909, The Hague (translation), 4 A.J.I.L. (1910) 226, 233.

In 1906 a dispute arose between the United States (claiming under the Treaty of Paris of December 10, 1898) and the Netherlands concerning the ownership of the Island of Palmas (or Miangas), each nation claiming the island as a territory attached for a long period of time to its possessions lying relatively close to the island. Following a lengthy diplomatic correspondence, a special agreement was signed on January 23, 1925 to refer the controversy to arbitration. Article I of the special agreement provided: "The sole duty of the arbitrator shall be to determine whether the Island of Palmas (or Miangas) in its entirety forms a part of territory belonging to the United States of America or of Netherlands territory." 44 Stat. 2007, 2008; 4 Treaties, etc. (Trenwith, 1938) 4512, 4513.

Island of Palmas Arbitration

The decision of the arbitrator, Max Huber, announced on April 4, 1928, was that "The Island of Palmas (or Miangas) forms in its entirety a part of Netherlands territory." It was stated in the course of his decision:

In the opinion of the Arbitrator the Netherlands have succeeded in establishing the following facts:

. . . .

c. Acts characteristic of State authority exercised either by the vassal state or by the suzerain Power in regard precisely to the Island of Palmas (or Miangas) have been established as occurring at different epochs between 1700 and 1898, as well as in the period between 1898 and 1906.

The acts of indirect or direct display of Netherlands sovereignty at Palmas (or Miangas), especially in the 18th and early 19th centuries are not numerous, and there are considerable gaps in the evidence of continuous display. But apart from the consideration that the manifestations of sovereignty over a small and distant island, inhabited only by natives, cannot be expected to be frequent, it is not necessary that the display of sovereignty should go back to a very far distant period. It may suffice that such display existed in 1898, and had already existed as continuous and peaceful before that date long enough to enable any Power who might have considered herself as possessing sovereignty over the island, or having a claim to sovereignty to have, according to local conditions, a reasonable possibility for ascertaining the existence of a state of things contrary to her real or alleged rights.

It is not necessary that the display of sovereignty should be established as having begun at a precise epoch; it suffices that it had existed at the critical period preceding the year 1898. It is quite natural that the establishment of sovereignty may be the outcome of a slow evolution, of a progressive intensification of state control. This is particularly the case, if sovereignty is acquired by the establishment of the suzerainty of a colonial power over a native State, and in regard to outlying possessions of such a vassal state.

Now the evidence relating to the period after the middle of the 19th century makes it clear that the Netherlands Indian Government considered the island distinctly as a part of its possessions and that, in the years immediately preceding 1898, an intensification of display of sovereignty took place.

Since the moment when the Spaniards, in withdrawing from the Moluccas in 1666, made express reservations as to the maintainance [*sic*] of their sovereign rights, up to the contestation made by the United States in 1906, no contestation or other action whatever or protest against the exercise of territorial rights by the Netherlands over the Talautse (Sangi) Isles and their dependencies (Miangas included) has been recorded. The peaceful character of the display of Netherlands sovereignty for the entire period to which the evidence concerning acts of display relates (1700–1906) must be admitted.

There is moreover no evidence which would establish any act of display of sovereignty over the island by Spain or another Power, such as might counter-balance or annihilate the manifestations of Netherlands sovereignty. As to third Powers, the evidence submitted to the Tribunal does not disclose any trace of such action, at least from the middle of the 17th century onwards. These circumstances, together with the absence of any evidence of a conflict between Spanish and Netherlands authorities during more than two centuries as regards Palmas (or Miangas), are an indirect proof of the exclusive display of Netherlands soverignty.

This being so, it remains to be considered first whether the display of state authority might not be legally defective and therefore unable to create a valid title of sovereignty, and secondly whether the United States may not put forward a better title to that of the Netherlands.

As to the conditions of acquisition of sovereignty by way of continuous and peaceful display of state authority (so-called prescription), some of which have been discussed in the United States Counter Memorandum, the following must be said:

The display has been open and public, that is to say that it was in conformity with usages as to exercise of sovereignty over colonial states. A clandestine exercise of state authority over an inhabited territory during a considerable length of time would seem to be impossible.

.   .   .   .

There can further be no doubt that the Netherlands exercised the state authority over the Sangi States as sovereign in their own right, not under a derived or precarious title.

Finally it is to be observed that the question whether the establishment of the Dutch on the Talautse Isles (Sangi) in 1677 was a violation of the Treaty of Münster and whether this circumstance might have prevented the acquisition of sovereignty even by means of prolonged exercise of state authority, need not be examined, since the Treaty of Utrecht recognized the state of things existing in 1714 and therefore the suzerain right of the Netherlands over Tabukan and Miangas.

.   .   .   .

The Netherlands title of sovereignty, acquired by continuous and peaceful display of state authority during a long period of time going probably back beyond the year 1700, therefore holds good.

Arbitral Award in the Island of Palmas Case, United States and the Netherlands, Apr. 4, 1928 (Per. Ct. Arb.) 57–60, 63; Scott, *Hague Court Reports* (2d ser. 1932) 83, 126–129, 131.

Without thinking it necessary to discuss the very controversial question as to whether the right of prescription invoked by the United States is an accepted principle of the law of nations, in the absence of any convention establishing a term of prescription, the commissioners are unanimous in coming to the conclusion that the possession of the United States in the present case was not of such a character as to found a prescriptive title. Upon the evidence adduced it is impossible to hold that the possession of El Chamizal by the United States was undisturbed, uninterrupted and unchallenged from the date of the Treaty of Guadalupe Hidalgo in 1848 until the year 1895, when, in consequence of the creation of a competent tribunal to decide the question, the Chamizal case was first presented. On the contrary it may be said that the physical possession taken by citizens of the United States and the political control exercised by the local and federal governments, have been constantly challenged and questioned by the Republic of Mexico, through its accredited diplomatic agents. *Chamizal arbitration*

Possession challenged

As early as 1856, the river changes threatening the valley of El Paso had caused anxious inquiries, which resulted in a reference of the matter to the Hon. Caleb Cushing for his opinion.

In January, 1867, Don Matias Romero forwarded to Mr. Seward, Secretary of State, a communication from the perfecture [sic] of Brazos relating to the controversy between the people of El Paso del Norte (now Juarez) and the people of Franklin (now El Paso, Texas) over the Chamizal tract, then in process of formation. From that time until the negotiation of the Convention of 1884, a considerable amount of diplomatic correspondence is devoted to this very question, and the Convention of 1884 was an endeavor to fix the rights of the two nations with respect to the changes brought about by the action of the waters of the Rio Grande.

The very existence of that convention precludes the United States from acquiring by prescription against the terms of their title and, as has been pointed out above, the two republics have ever since the signing of that convention treated it as a source of all their rights in respect of accretion to the territory on one side or the other of the river.

Another characteristic of possession serving as a foundation for prescription is that it should be peaceable.

.   .   .   .

It is quite clear from the circumstances related in this affidavit that however much the Mexicans may have desired to take physical possession of the district, the result of any attempt to do so would have provoked scenes of violence and the Republic of Mexico can not be blamed for resorting to the milder forms of protest contained in its diplomatic correspondence.

In private law, the interruption of prescription is effected by a suit, but in dealings between nations this is of course impossible, unless and until an international tribunal is established for such purpose. In the present case, the Mexican claim was asserted before the International Boundary Commission within a reasonable time after it commenced to exercise its functions, and prior to that date the Mexican Government had done all that could be reasonably required of it by way of protest against the alleged encroachment.

Under these circumstances the Commissioners have no difficulty in coming to the conclusion that the plea of prescription should be dismissed.

Award of June 15, 1911, Chamizal Arbitration, United States and Mexico, (Washington, 1911) 7, 29–30. For a further discussion of this case, see *ante* §60.

ABANDONMENT

§64

Abandonment, as a means of losing sovereignty over territory, involves the voluntary relinquishment of possession of and authority over the territory. Cases of abandonment in recent times are extremely rare. Jurists seem to be in agreement that an intention to abandon must clearly appear but that this intention need not be expressed and may be gathered from the circumstances surrounding the supposed withdrawal of state authority.

It follows from these premises that Clipperton Island was legitimately acquired by France on November 17, 1858. There is no reason to suppose that France has subsequently lost her right by *derelictio*, since she never had the *animus* of abandoning the island, and the fact that she has not exercised her authority there in a positive manner does not imply the forfeiture of an acquisition already definitely perfected.

Arbitral Award of His Majesty the King of Italy on the Subject of the Difference Relative to the Sovereignty over Clipperton Island (France-Mexico), Jan. 8, 1931, 26 A.J.I.L. (1932) 390, 394.

As regards voluntary abandonment, there is nothing to show any definite renunciation on the part of the kings of Norway or Denmark.

During the first two centuries or so after the settlements perished, there seems to have been no intercourse with Greenland, and knowledge of it diminished; but the tradition of the King's rights lived on, and in the early part of the XVIIth century a revival of interest in Greenland on the part both of the King and of his people took place. **Eastern Greenland Case**

That period was an era of adventure and exploration. The example set by the navigators of foreign countries was inspiring, and a desire arose in Norway and Denmark to recover the territory which had been subject to the sovereignty of the King's ancestors in the past. The expeditions sent out in 1605 and 1606 under Lindenow to "Our Country of Greenland", the efforts to assure respect on the part of foreign Powers for the King's rights there and the claim to exclude foreigners from the Greenland trade all show that the King considered that in his dealings with Greenland he was dealing with a country with respect to which he had a special position superior to that of any other Power. This special position can only have been derived from the sovereign rights which accrued to the King of Norway from the submission made to him by the early Nordic settlers and which descended to the Danish-Norwegian kings. It must have covered the territory which is known as Greenland to-day, because the country was inhabited. The expedition in 1605 brought back some of the inhabitants, whereas Spitzbergen was admittedly uninhabited. Lastly, as there were at this date no colonies or settlements in Greenland, the King's claims cannot have been limited to any particular places in the country.

That the King's claims amounted merely to pretensions is clear, for he had no permanent contact with the country, he was exercising no authority there. The claims, however, were not disputed. No other Power was putting forward any claim to territorial sovereignty in Greenland, and in the absence of any competing claim the King's pretensions to be the sovereign of Greenland subsisted.

Per. Ct. Int. Jus., Ser. A/B, No. 53 (Apr. 5, 1933), pp. 22, 47–48; III Hudson, *World Court Reports* (1938) 172.

REVOLUTION AND SECESSION

§65

Revolution and secession constitute a historically familiar method of effecting changes in territorial sovereignty. They usually involve a declaration of independence from former political ties, withdrawal from the jurisdiction of the former sovereign, and the maintenance of the new independent status as the result either of military operations or of the acceptance of the situation by states in a position to challenge it.

Bulgaria proclaimed her independence on October 5, 1908. Finland was declared a free Republic before the Diet by the President of the Senate on December 4, 1917, and the independence of Finland was formally proclaimed on December 7, 1917. Lithuania formally declared her independence on December 11, 1917, and the claims of the Taryba (Council of State of Lithuania), with a request for recognition, were communicated to the United States on February 7, 1918. The Declaration of Independence of the Czechoslovak nation was adopted in Paris on October 18, 1918 by the Czechoslovak National Council, which had been recognized by the United States and the Allies as the Provisional Government of the Czechoslovak state and nation. Latvia's independence was proclaimed on November 18, 1918.

> Minister Knowles to Secretary Root, no. 33, Bulgarian ser., Oct. 6, 1908, MS. Department of State, file 5072/19–20; 1908 For. Rel. 57. Consul Haynes to Secretary Lansing, Dec. 4, 1917, MS. Department of State, file 861.00/766; 1918 For. Rel., Russia, vol. II, p. 733; 1918 U.S. Naval War College, Int. Law Docs., p. 47, n. 1. 2 *Official U.S. Bulletin*, no. 303, May 7, 1918, p. 8; Chargé Wilson to Secretary Lansing, no. 2355, Feb. 9, 1918, MS. Department of State, file 861.00/1261, enclosure; 1918 For. Rel., Russia, vol. II, pp. 817–819. President Masaryk to Secretary Lansing, Oct. 18, 1918, MS. Department of State, file 861.00/3124; 1918 For. Rel., Supp. 1, vol. I, pp. 847–851; 2 *Official U.S. Bulletin*, no. 441, Oct. 19, 1918, p. 3. Minister Coleman to Secretary Hughes, no. 1517, Nov. 24, 1923 (calling attention to the fifth anniversary of Latvia's independence), MS. Department of State, file 860p.00/46.

. . . By the Declaration of Independence, "the Representatives of the United States of America" declared the United [not the several] Colonies to be free and independent states, and as such to have "full Power to levy War, conclude Peace, contract Alliances, establish Commerce and to do all other Acts and Things which Independent States may of right do."

As a result of the separation from Great Britain by the colonies, acting as a unit, the powers of external sovereignty passed from the Crown not to the colonies severally, but to the colonies in their collective and corporate capacity as the United States of America. Even before the Declaration, the colonies were a unit in foreign affairs, acting through a common agency—namely, the Continental Congress, composed of delegates from the thirteen colonies. That agency exercised the powers of war and peace, raised an army, created a navy, and finally adopted the Declaration of Independence. Rulers come and go; governments end and forms of government change; but sovereignty survives. A political society cannot endure without a supreme will somewhere. Sovereignty is never held in suspense. When, therefore, the external sovereignty of Great Britain in respect of the colonies ceased, it immediately passed to the Union. *See Penhallow* v. *Doane*, 3 Dall. 54, 80–81. That fact was given practical application almost at once. The treaty of peace, made on September 23, 1783, was concluded between his Britannic Majesty and the "United States of America." 8 Stat.— European Treaties—80.

United States v. Curtiss-Wright Export Corp. et al., 299 U.S. (1936) 304, 316–317.

Article III of the treaty between the United States and the Republic of Colombia, signed at Bogotá on April 6, 1914, for the settlement of differences arising out of the events which took place on the Isthmus of Panama in November 1903, provides:

Panama

The Republic of Colombia recognizes Panama as an independent nation . . .
In consideration of this recognition, the Government of the United States will, immediately after the exchange of the ratifications of the present Treaty, take the necessary steps in order to obtain from the Government of Panama the despatch of a duly accredited agent to negotiate and conclude with the Government of Colombia a Treaty of Peace and Friendship, with a view to bring about both the establishment of regular diplomatic relations between Colombia and Panama and the adjustment of pecuniary liability as between the two countries, in accordance with recognized principles of law and precedents.

42 Stat. 2122, 2125; 3 Treaties, etc. (Redmond, 1923) 2538, 2539–2540. Ratifications were exchanged at Bogotá on Mar. 1, 1922, and the treaty was proclaimed by the President on Mar. 20, 1922.

See *ante*, Recognition of New States, §§35–46.

In the confusion of post-war Europe revolutionary movements led to the establishment of several independent regimes, among them Azerbaijan, Armenia, Fiume, Georgia, and Ukraine, each of which enjoyed only brief existence.

ANNEXATION

§66

On May 16, 1913 the Embassy in Vienna transmitted to the Department of State the following despatch concerning the announced annexation of the island of Ada-Kaleh by Hungary:

Ada-Kaleh

> on the 15th instant the annexation by Hungary of the island of Ada-Kaleh was officially announced by the Austro-Hungarian Government. Ada-Kaleh is a small island in the Danube of about a square mile in area; it is situated near Orsova close to the point where the three frontiers of Hungary, Servia and Rumania meet; a short distance below the island the Danube flows through the gorge of the Iron Gate.
>
> In the readjustment of Balkan frontiers which took place after the Congress of Berlin the island was forgotten. By an exchange of Notes, however, in 1878 between the Ottoman Empire and the Kingdom of Hungary it was agreed that Turkey should exercise jurisdiction over the island and maintain a Governor there. . . .
>
> At the time of writing it is not clear whether the Turkish Governor remonstrated against the annexation but he is supposed to have disappeared.
>
> Ambassador Kerens to Secretary Bryan, no. 491, May 16, 1913, MS. Department of State, file 864.014. "By a decision of the Supreme Council, dated July 28, 1919, Ada Kaleh was allocated to Rumania (see London Daily Telegraph' May 1, 1923). The Turkish title to this island was finally extinguished by Article 132 of the Treaty of Sèvres and Article 16 of the Treaty of Lausanne." I *Treaties of Peace 1919–1923* (Carnegie Endowment for International Peace, 1924), introduction by Martin, xxxvii; II *idem* 825, 966.

Island of Cyprus

By virtue of a convention, annex, and agreement between Great Britain and Turkey, dated respectively June 4, July 1, and August 14, 1878, the island of Cyprus was placed under British administration. Following the outbreak of war between the two countries in 1914, the Cyprus (Annexation) Order in Council was issued on November 5, 1914. This Order pointed out that the former conventional arrangements were annulled by the outbreak of war and decreed the annexation of Cyprus to "form part of His Majesty's Dominions".

In article 20 of the treaty of peace signed at Lausanne on July 24, 1923, Turkey recognized the annexation of Cyprus by Great Britain. Letters patent issued on March 10, 1925 declared that the island of Cyprus should thereafter be known as "the Colony of Cyprus". Provision was made for the government thereof under a governor and commander in chief. The letters patent were proclaimed and published on May 1, 1925.

London Gazette, no. 28963, Nov. 3, 1914, 2d Supp., p. 8998; *ibid.*, no. 28965, Nov. 6, 1914, p. 9012; Gr. Br. Treaty Ser. no. 16 (1923), Cmd. 1929. 121 Br. & For. St. Paps. (1925), pt. I, p. 99.

In answer to the inquiry of the American High Commissioner in Constantinople (Istanbul) as to whether the United States considered capitulations still in force in Rhodes (Rodi), the Department of State, on September 23, 1922, said that, pending final determination of the status of territories detached from Turkey, it considered that Rhodes had not yet ceased to be a part of Ottoman territory to which capitulatory rights of the United States still extended. {Island of Rhodes}

On September 12 the High Commissioner made further inquiry with particular reference to the statement of an official of the Italian High Commission in Constantinople to the effect that Rhodes was annexed to Italy by proclamation in 1915 and that foreigners residing there were subject not to the Ottoman capitulations but to the jurisdiction of the Italian courts. In its reply of October 28, 1922 the Department referred to its communication of September 23, 1922 and in amplification thereof said that—

> the Department would be unable to regard the alleged proclamation, even if authentic, as constituting in itself a legal transfer of territory which has as yet received no sanction in ratified treaties. You will recall that by Article 122 of the unratified Treaty of Sèvres, Turkey ceded the islands of the Dodecanese and Cástellorizzo to Italy. In accordance, however, with the terms of a Convention between Italy and Greece, signed on the same day as the Treaty of Sèvres, Italy relinquished in favor of Greece her rights over all of these island[s] save Cástellorizzo and Rhodes. But a clause of this Convention provided that if and when, within a period of fifteen years, Great Britain should cede Cyprus to Greece, Italy would consent to hold a plebiscite in Rhodes, with a view to determining the final status of the island. It would thus appear that while Rhodes has been under Italian occupation since the Turco-Italian war of 1911–12, the question of the ultimate disposition of this island is still in abeyance.
>
> In these circumstances, and pending the ratification of an international instrument or of the international instruments which will dispose of the question of Rhodes, the Department considers that, as in other territories detached from the Ottoman Empire whose status remains undetermined, the capitulations are still in force.

Acting Secretary Phillips to High Commissioner Bristol, telegram 149, Sept. 23, 1922, MS. Department of State, file 711.673/163; Secretary Hughes to Rear Admiral Bristol, no. 256, Oct. 28, 1922, *ibid.* 867.014/8.

Turkey renounced all rights and title over the island of Rhodes in article 15 of the Treaty of Lausanne (July 24, 1923). Gr. Br. Treaty Ser. no. 16 (1923), Cmd. 1929.

Austria

On March 14, 1938 the German Ambassador in the United States transmitted the following note to the Department of State:

I have the honor, at the request of the German Government, to notify Your Excellency of the following law of March 13, 1938, concerning the reunion of Austria with the German Reich:

The Reich Government has decided the following law which is promulgated herewith:

ARTICLE I

The Federal Constitutional Law of March 13, 1938 decided by the Austrian Federal Government concerning the reunion of Austria with the German Reich herewith becomes a law of the German Reich. The text thereof is as follows:

"On the basis of Article 3, paragraph 2 of the Federal Constitutional Law governing extraordinary measures within the realm of the Constitution, Federal Law Journal I, number 255/1934, the Federal Government has resolved:

Article 1. Austria is a state (land) of the German Reich.

Article 2. On Sunday, April 10, 1938, there will take place a free and secret plebiscite of German men and women of Austria over 20 years of age on the reunion with the German Reich.

Article 3. In the plebiscite the majority vote cast will be decisive.

Article 4. The necessary prescriptions for the carrying out and supplementation of Article 2 of this Federal Constitutional Law will be made by means of Decrees.

Article 5. This Federal Constitutional Law enters into force the day of its promulgation.

The Federal Government is charged with the execution of this Federal Constitutional Law.

Vienna, March 13, 1938."

ARTICLE II

The law now prevailing in Austria remains in force until further notice. The introduction of Reich law into Austria will be effected by the Leader and Reich Chancelor or by the Reich Minister empowered by him to do so.

ARTICLE III

The Reich Minister of the Interior is empowered, in agreement with the Reich Minister concerned, to issue the necessary legal and administrative prescriptions for the carrying out and supplementation of this Law. The Law enters into force the day of its promulgation.

Linz, *March 13, 1938.*

The Leader and Reich Chancelor

The Reich Minister of the Interior

The Reich Minister for Foreign Affairs

The Deputy of the Leader

The former Austrian diplomatic representatives in foreign countries have received the order to place themselves, along with their personnel, under the German representatives.

Ambassador Dieckhoff to Secretary Hull, Department of State, XVIII *Press Releases*, weekly issue 442, pp. 374–375 (Mar. 15, 1938).

On March 19, 1938 the Department of State released the following statement to the press:

On March 17, 1938, the Minister of the Republic of Austria, Mr. Edgar Prochnik, informed the Department of State that, as a result of the developments which have occurred in Austria, that country has ceased to exist as an independent nation and has been incorporated in the German Reich; that therefore the Austrian mission to this country, of which he has been the head, has been abolished; and that the affairs of the mission have been taken over by the Embassy of Germany. The German Ambassador has informed the Department of State that he has assumed the functions hitherto performed by the Minister of Austria.

The Department further stated that appropriate consideration was being given to the "technical steps" on the part of the Government of the United States necessitated by the changed status of the Austrian Republic.

Department of State, Mimeographed Press Release, Mar. 19, 1938.

On Apr. 6, 1938 the Ambassador in Berlin, upon instruction of the Secretary of State, delivered a note to the German Minister of Foreign Affairs, in which he stated that the Government of the United States found itself "under the necessity as a practical measure of closing its Legation at Vienna and of establishing a Consulate General" and requested provisional consular status for certain American consular officers. Department of State, XVIII *Press Releases*, weekly issue 445, pp. 465–467 (Apr. 6, 1938).

For a summary of the attitude of the United States Government toward territorial changes in Europe in 1938 and 1939, see circular instruction of Jan. 4, 1940 (diplomatic serial 3176), MS. Department of State, file 840.0144/1.

POLAR AND SUBPOLAR REGIONS

PROBLEMS

§67

The progress that has been made toward the discovery and exploration of the polar regions has given rise to many new problems in international law.

The announcement of the discovery of the North Pole raised in several quarters, among others the British and Canadian Parliaments, the question whether the act of discovery gave to the United States any right of possession over the North Pole.

Polar ice areas

In searching for the answer to this question, it is necessary to ascertain the rules of the Law of Nations that govern analogous cases.

What was previously presumed, proved to be correct, that at the North Pole there is no land, but only ice resting on the deep sea, and in order to reach the Pole, it must be approached for a long distance over the ice resting on the deep sea.

What is the law applicable to the sea? Originally formulated by Queen Elizabeth, and more fully expounded by the Hollander, Hugo Grotius, the freedom of the high seas was controverted in the reign of Charles the First by the publication of the treatise *Mare Clausum* written some years before by England's ablest jurist of that time, John Selden.

At various times all or almost all the nations of the world have taken a hand in the controversy of the freedom of the high seas. And each state has argued on the side that at the time seemed best for its own individual interests. But in the long run the family of nations has pronounced without equivocation in favor of the freedom of the seas. Naturally if the North Polar Sea were open there would be no question of its being as free as any part of the broad Atlantic and Pacific Oceans.

The North Polar Sea, however, is covered with ice. Ice, unlike the water of the high seas, is a solid substance upon which mankind can build habitations and live for an indefinite period of time. Thus during the Russo-Japanese War, the Russians built during the winter seasons a railroad on the ice over Lake Baikal and established a station mid-way across the frozen lake. And over that piece of railroad they forwarded many thousands of men and great quantities of stores and implements of war. *In that sense* it might be urged that men might permanently occupy the ice cover of the Polar Sea. But the ice at the North Pole is never at rest. It is in continual motion. It moves slowly in a direction from Bering's Strait towards the Atlantic Ocean. Consequently any habitation fixed upon it would be continually moving. And such possible occupation would be too precarious and shifting to and fro to give any one a good title. And so the rules of the Law of Nations that recognize the freedom of the high seas, would seem to apply naturally to a moving and shifting substance like the North Polar Sea ice at all points beyond the customary three-mile limit from the shore. [Italics added.]

Balch, "The Arctic and Antarctic Regions and the Law of Nations", in 4 A.J.I.L. (1910) 265–266.

The view that the ice covering the Arctic Ocean cannot be occupied, has been expressed by States having interest in these regions. When Peary, in 1909, returned from his last expedition and telegraphed to President Taft: "I have the honour to place the North Pole at your disposal", the United States advanced no claim of sovereignty over the Pole. The reason for this was that they were of opinion that the Pole, being situated in the sea, could not be the subject of sovereignty . . .

Before Roald Amundsen made his polar flights in 1925 and 1926, he was authorized to take into possession on behalf of Norway any land he might discover, but not areas of ice in the Polar Sea.

.   .   .   .

The reasons why sovereignty over the ice in the Arctic Sea cannot be admitted, are making themselves felt in the same degree with regard to corresponding formations of ice in the Antarctic regions. Moreover, floating ice is here sometimes met with so far north, and under such conditions, that the question of sovereignty can hardly be raised.

Along the coasts of the Antarctic Continent, there is a special formation of ice generally called shelf-ice, or, the Barrier. It stretches from the land towards the sea. Its height varies from Antarctic some few feet to over a hundred feet above the level of the sea, but it is usually of about the latter dimension. Its surface is approximately horizontal, but it terminates on the sea side in vertical cliff faces . . . It is a question whether the Barrier is afloat or resting on solid ground. The question can not be answered generally, as there are a series of barriers, most of which are not yet sufficiently explored.

.   .   .   .

If we now raise the question whether the Ross Barrier can be subjected to sovereignty, then the question is least difficult to answer with regard to that part of the Barrier which rests on solid ground. It must be put on a par with a land territory, and it can be occupied. Doubts arise when the question affects that part of the Barrier which is afloat. We are of opinion that since there is no natural border line between the two parts of the Barrier, and as the latter appears externally as a whole, the same principle should apply to the whole extent of the Barrier.

In appearance it resembles a land territory rather more than a sea territory. At the Barrier edge all navigation obviously ceases. In this instance it is difficult to plead the considerations that have formed the rule that the sea cannot be made subject to the sovereignty of a State. We are, therefore, of opinion that good reasons favour the view that the Ross Barrier should be regarded as land and can be the object of sovereignty.

The question thus raised is not without practical importance. If a State takes effective possession of Ross Barrier, it will be able to reserve for its subjects the right of whaling within a reasonable territorial limit. At present the Ross Barrier is not submitted to sovereignty, and all nations must therefore have the right to carry on whaling up to the very edge of the Barrier.

What has been said above of the question of sovereignty in respect of Ross Barrier, applies also to other barriers resembling the Ross Barrier.

The question whether ice areas covering the sea can be occupied Opinions of has often been dealt with in the literature of international law. publicists

Rolland maintains, for instance, that a permanent surface of ice extending from the coast out towards the sea should be considered a continuation of the land and can be submitted to sovereignty . . . Waultrin and Balch are of the opinion that sovereignty can be acquired over immobile ice . . . Scott holds that a floating field of ice is not capable of being submitted to sovereignty, but he does not seem to have thought of the barriers . . . Lindley does not find any reason for excepting from occupation the regions around the two Poles . . . Clute is of opinion that even if large areas of the Arctic Sea are frozen up, it must still be regarded as an open sea and cannot be submitted to sovereignty. . . . Oppenheim mentions the question whether the North Pole can be occupied. In his opinion it must be answered in the negative "as there is no land on the North Pole " . . . Breitfuss suggests the division of the Arctic Ocean between five polar States, and recommends that their sovereignty shall not only include the land and islands lying there, but also, to a certain extent—to be decided by international agreement—"the areas of the sea which are covered with ice fields["] . . . Lakhtine, who also gives an opinion especially on the Arctic Sea, says that the sea areas covered with more or less immobile ice fall within the sovereignty of the polar States . . .

Pearce Higgins who has published the latest edition of Hall's book: "A Treatise on International Law", and also Fauchille, hold the view that, as it is impossible to settle permanently in the polar regions proper, sovereignty cannot be acquired over them. The opinion that and [*any ?*] areas in the polar regions cannot be submitted to sovereignty is, however, without any foundation. The fictitious occupations made by several States in Antarctica is a proof hereof. That it may be difficult to settle permanently in the immediate vicinity of the South Pole, is a case apart. It may also be difficult to settle permanently in the Sahara or in the upper parts of the high chains of mountains in Asia or South America, but it is not denied for that reason that a State may possess sovereignty over this desert and these mountain tracts.

Smedal, *Acquisition of Sovereignty over Polar Areas* (Oslo, 1931; translation by Chr. Meyer) 29–32.

Another problem that has arisen in connection with recent polar explorations is whether the peculiar geographic and climatic characteristics of these regions require a modification of the usual tests of effective occupation.

Settlement

The statement by Secretary Hughes to the effect that actual settlement is required as the basis of a claim of sovereignty over newly discovered polar lands is set out in part *ante* §58. In that same statement he also said:

Antarctic

So far as this Department is informed the exploration of parts of the Antarctic Continent by American, Belgian, British, French, German, Norwegian, Russian, Swedish, and other travelers has not been followed by permanent settlement upon any part of the continent.

It is the understanding of this Department that the so-called Ross Dependency of New Zealand has no permanent population. This part of the Antarctic Continent lies immediately east of Wilkes Land.

It is likewise the understanding of this Department that the portion of the so-called Dependency of the Falkland Islands upon the mainland of the Antarctic Continent which is referred to as "Graham's Land" in the British Letters Patent of July 21, 1908, and of March 28, 1917, and which was discovered by Captain N. B. Palmer in 1820–21 and named Palmer Land by the United States Geographic Board on November 6, 1912, has no permanent population, although it is understood that British and other whalers use the shoal waters near shore in summer for anchorage.

Secretary Hughes to A. W. Prescott, May 13, 1924, MS. Department of State, file 811.014/101.

The diverse and lively interests of opposing states banish a judicial spirit in appraising the value of conflicting claims. . . . If, on account of the rigour of climatic conditions in the polar regions, there is to be a relaxation of the requirements of the law demanding occupation as the mode of acquiring a right of sovereignty over newly found lands, it should be kept within rigid bounds, and never regarded as applicable to kindred efforts in the temperate zones. The relaxation should be confined to the waiving of settlement as a necessary condition for the perfecting of a right of sovereignty, provided a claimant state may establish that by some other process it is in a position to exercise control over what it claims as its own. This requirement should be applied in all polar regions. In those of the Arctic, it might, however, be recognized that the sovereign of contiguous territory projecting itself into the Arctic Circle was, by reason of that fact, in a position to exercise requisite control over an extensive area, or at least in a position to make proof of the fact. Yet in such case, the doctrine of contiguity should not be permitted to supplant the need of proof, as by acknowledging the possession of a power of control when none was found to exist. In the Antarctic regions no assumption of the requisite power should be derived from the mere assignment of a claimed area to a particular dependency of the claimant. No bare notification of a claim should be deemed to suffice to beget a right of sovereignty, or be accepted as a substitute of proof of the requisite power to control.

Hyde, "Acquisition of Sovereignty over Polar Areas", in 19 *Iowa L. Rev.* (1934) 293–294.

In 1929 the Norwegian Minister communicated a note to the Secretary of State, reading in part as follows:

The Norwegian Government has taken it for granted that the Government of the United States of America, whichever [*whatever*] intentions it may have to claim sovereignty to certain parts of the Antarctic regions, . . . does not intend to base such possible claims to sovereignty or claims of priority to sovereignty in the South Polar Regions upon the flights of Commander Byrd. In any case, the Norwegian Government assumes that possible claims of this nature do not comprise any part of the territory immediately circumjacent to the South Pole, which, as will be known, was taken possession of in the name of the King of Norway by Captain Roald Amundsen in December 1911, under the name of Haakon VII's Plateau, nor to comprise the territories on both sides of Captain Amundsen's route to the South Pole south of Edward VII's Land and including i.a. Queen Maud's Range.

My Government has instructed me to add that while it is not its intention at the present time to claim sovereignty to the territories referred to above, it considers that the said discovery and annexation constitute a valid basis for a claim of priority to acquire such territories whenever the requirements of interna· tional law as to effective occupation of a new territory shall have been fulfilled.

In reply Secretary Stimson said:

My attention has been called to your note of April 15, 1929, regarding Commander Byrd's scientific expedition into the Antarctic regions, which apparently has not been acknowledged. I therefore hasten to express to you the Department's regret at this apparent oversight.

The reference to your Government's statement regarding the basis for a claim of priority to sovereignty over certain enumerated territories, as indicated on page two of your note, has been noted, but since it is assumed that this was merely brought to the Department's attention for its information, no comment by the Department would seem to be called for at this time.

Minister Bachke to Secretary Stimson, Apr. 15, 1929, and Mr. Stimson to Mr. Bachke, Dec. 7, 1929, MS. Department of State, file 857.014/63.

Claims made by Admiral Byrd

. . . despatches and publications of Admiral Byrd indicate that he has claimed for the United States all territory which he has discovered or explored to the east of 150° west longitude during his two Antarctic expeditions and that the name "Marie Byrd Land" has been applied to all such territory.

Secretary Hull to Representative Dunn, Mar. 28, 1936, MS. Department of State, file 800.014 Antarctic/94.

A detailed geographic and geological report on the newly discovered Marie Byrd Land was transmitted by Commander Byrd to the Secretary of the Navy by radio and was issued as a press release by the Navy Department on June 28, 1929. This report concluded:

"A very conservative estimate shows that we have seen at least 20,000 square miles statute of hitherto unknown Antarctic areas."

The Acting Secretary of the Navy (Standley) to the Secretary of State (Hull), Aug. 11, 1934, *ibid.* 800.014 Antarctic/64, enclosure.

On December 1, 1929 the Department of State released the following statement to the press:

On November 17, 1928, the British Ambassador at Washington addressed a note to the Department of State in which he said that His Majesty's Governments in different countries of the Empire had learnt that an American expedition under Commander Byrd had started on a voyage of scientific research in the Antarctic regions. Those Governments had watched with especial interest the progress of the expedition on account of the interest which they themselves take in the regions where they understood Commander Byrd would conduct the bulk of his research. The Department would recall that certain regions of the Antarctic formed the subject of discussions at the Imperial Conference in London in 1926, a copy of the summary of the proceedings of which was transmitted to the Department. His Majesty's Governments wished the expedition every success, and, if desired, would issue instructions to appropriate authorities to afford Commander Byrd every assistance while the expedition was in the Ross Dependency and the Falkland Islands Dependencies.

.   .   .   .   .   .

The Undersecretary of State on November 15, 1929, wrote the Chargé d'Affaires at the British Embassy in Washington that his attention had been called to the British note of November 17, 1928, which apparently had not been acknowledged. He, therefore, hastened to express the Department's regret at this apparent oversight, and at the same time expressed its appreciation of the interest of His Majesty's Governments in Commander Byrd's expedition.

The Ambassador's reference to the summary of the proceedings of the Imperial Conference of 1926 had been noted, but since it was assumed that this was merely brought to the Department's attention for its information, no comment by the Department seemed to be called for at this time.

Department of State, *Press Releases*, weekly issue 10, pp. 81–82 (Dec. 1, 1929) ; MS. Department of State, file 800.014 Antarctic/15½ (copy).

The official summary of the proceedings of the British Imperial Conference of 1926 contains the following list of areas in the Antarctic "to which", it was stated, "a British title already exists by virtue of discovery":

> "(i.) The outlying part of Coats Land, viz., the portion not comprised within the Falkland Islands Dependencies.
> (ii.) Enderby Land.
> (iii.) Kemp Land.
> (iv.) Queen Mary Land.
> (v.) The area which lies to the west of Adélie Land and which on its discovery by the Australian Antarctic Expedition in 1912 was denominated Wilkes Land.
> (vi.) King George V Land.
> (vii.) Oates Land."

Imperial Conference, 1926: Summary of Proceedings, Parliamentary Papers (1926), Cmd. 2768, pp. 33–34; the British Ambassador, Sir Esme Howard, to Secretary Kellogg, no. 526, Nov. 17, 1928, MS. Department of State, file 031 Byrd South Polar Expedition/38, enclosure; excerpt printed in Department of State *Press Releases*, weekly issue 10, pp. 81–82 (Dec. 1, 1929).

In response to inquiries concerning sovereignty over "Little America", the Department of State pointed out that Admiral Byrd had claimed for the United States all the territory explored by him *east* of longitude 150° W. ("Marie Byrd Land") but that "Little America" is situated to the *west* of longitude 150° W. and therefore would not be included in the territory which he had claimed for the United States.

> Assistant Secretary Moore to Miss Florence Helland, June 8, 1936, MS. Department of State, file 800.014 Antarctic/101. Similar letters were sent to Silver, Burdett and Company, July 6, 1936, and L. A. Chase, Mar. 22, 1937, *ibid.* files 800.014 Antarctic/103, /111.

On January 29, 1934 the British Ambassador in Washington addressed a note to the Secretary of State, reading in part as follows:

Ross Dependency

> The United States Government will doubtless be aware that an expedition to the Antarctic led by Admiral Byrd left New Zealand on December 12th for a base in Ross dependency which was established on his previous expedition in 1928–1929. . . .
>
> His Majesty's Government in New Zealand understand that the expedition has the official backing of the United States Government and in these circumstances they feel it necessary to state that their attention has been drawn to articles in certain newspapers reporting that it is intended to establish a post office at Admiral Byrd's base in Ross dependency and that certain members of the expedition were before leaving the United States formally sworn in before the Postmaster General of the United States with the object of acting as postmasters at this post office. It is also understood that special stamps in connection with the expedition have been issued by the United States Government, and it has been reported that these will be used to frank letters posted at the expedition's base. While His Majesty's Government in New Zealand recognise that some allowance must be made for the absence of ordinary postal facilities in Ross dependency, they would point out that if a United States post office were to be officially established in the dependency, or if the United States Government were to sanction the use of United States postage stamps there without permission from the sovereign Power, such acts could not be regarded otherwise than as infringing the British sovereignty and New Zealand administrative rights in the dependency as well as the laws there in force.
>
> Although it is understood that the expedition is operating a wireless station in Ross dependency, no licence for such a station was applied for, and similarly although it is understood that United States aircraft are being imported into the dependency for the purpose of making flights in or over its territory, the competent authorities received no application for permission for such flights. Since on his previous expedition Admiral Byrd established a wireless station at his base and carried aircraft to the dependency, and was not then required to obtain a licence

or formal permission he may have thought it unnecessary to do so on this occasion. His Majesty's Government in New Zealand are indeed willing to regard their offer of facilities as covering now, as on the previous expedition, permission both for the wireless station and for the flights over the dependency, but they would nevertheless point out that they would have preferred prior application to have been made to the competent authority by or on behalf of the expedition in accordance with the relevant legislation applicable.

His Majesty's Government in New Zealand are not aware whether the expedition to the Ross dependency led by Mr. Lincoln Ellsworth is proceeding under the auspices of the United States Government, but should this be the case they would wish to draw the attention of the United States Government to the same points in connection with the operation of a wireless station and aeroplane flights.

His Majesty's Government in New Zealand trust that the United States Government will bear the above mentioned points in mind in the case of any United States expeditions under official auspices which may proceed in the future to territory under New Zealand administration.

On February 24, 1934 the Department sent the following reply:

I desire to assure you that any facilities given to the expedition by the New Zealand authorities are greatly appreciated. It does not seem necessary at this time to enter into a discussion of the interesting questions which are set forth in your note. However, I reserve all rights which the United States or its citizens may have with respect to this matter.

Reservations

Sir Ronald Lindsay to Secretary Hull, no. 33, Jan. 29, 1934, MS. Department of State, file 031 Byrd South Polar Expedition/142; Assistant Secretary Moore to Sir Ronald Lindsay, Feb. 24, 1934, *ibid.*

On November 14, 1934 the following informal note was sent to the British Ambassador:

Referring to your recent inquiry, I beg to inform you that so far as I am advised the only action taken by my Government relative to the Byrd Expedition to the Antarctic since your note of January 29, 1934, and my reply thereto of February 24, 1934, consists in the Postmaster General of my Government having instructed a representative of his Department to proceed to Little America, Admiral Byrd's base, "for the purpose of assuming charge of the handling of the mail at that place".

It is understood that His Majesty's Government in New Zealand bases its claim of sovereignty on the discovery of a portion of the region in question. While it is unnecessary to enter into any detailed discussion of the subject at this time, nevertheless, in order to avoid misapprehension, it is proper for me to say, in the light of long established principles of international law, that I can not admit that sovereignty accrues from mere discovery unaccompanied by occupancy and use.

In reply, the following note, dated December 27, was handed to the Secretary of State by the British Ambassador on December 29:

With reference to the letter which you were so good as to address to me on November 14th last, I have the honour, under instructions from His Majesty's Principal Secretary of State for Foreign Affairs, at the instance of His Majesty's Government in New Zealand to inform you that the supposition that the British claim to sovereignty over the Ross Dependency is based on discovery alone, and, moreover, on the discovery of only a portion of the region, is based on a misapprehension of the facts of the situation.

2. The Dependency was established and placed under New Zealand Administration by an Order in Council of 1923 in which the Dependency's geographical limits were precisely defined. Regulations have been made by the Governor General of New Zealand in respect of the Dependency and the British title has been kept up by the exercise in respect of the Dependency of administrative and governmental powers, e.g. as regards the issue of whaling licences and the appointment of a special officer to act as magistrate for the Dependency.

3. As I had the honour to state in my Note No. 33 of January 29th last, His Majesty's Government in New Zealand recognize the absence of ordinary postal facilities in the Dependency and desire therefore to facilitate as far as possible the carriage of mail by United States authorities to and from the Byrd Expedition. As regards Mr. Anderson's present mission, they understand that he is carrying letters to which are, or will be, affixed special stamps printed in the United States and that these stamps are to be cancelled and date-stamped on board the Expedition's vessel. They also understand that these stamps are intended to be commemorative of the Byrd Expedition and have been issued as a matter of philatelic interest.

4. In the above circumstances His Majesty's Government in New Zealand have no objection to the proposed visit of Mr. Anderson. They must, however, place it on record that, had his mission appeared to them to be designed as an assertion of United States sovereignty over any part of the Ross Dependency or as a challenge to British sovereignty therein, they would have been compelled to make a protest.

On February 7, 1935 the following note was addressed to the British Ambassador by the Secretary of State:

I have received your note No. 402 dated December 27, 1934, concerning the British claim to sovereignty over the Ross Dependency. It is noted that His Majesty's Government in New Zealand have no objection to the proposed visit of Mr. Anderson.

The Government of the United States considers that no useful purpose would be served by a discussion at this time of the questions raised in your note. In the circumstances, I consider it desirable merely to reaffirm the statement contained in my note of February 24, 1934, to the effect that the United States reserves all rights which this country or its citizens may have with respect to the matter.

Secretary Hull to Sir Ronald Lindsay, Nov. 14, 1934, MS. Department of State, file 031 Byrd South Polar Expedition/161; Sir Ronald Lindsay to Mr. Hull, no. 402, Dec. 27, 1934, *ibid.* 031 Byrd South Polar Expedition/166; Mr. Hull to Sir Ronald Lindsay, Feb. 7, 1935, *ibid.*

On January 6, 1939 the Department of State, referring to notes exchanged between the British and French Governments regarding aerial navigation in the Antarctic region, instructed the American Embassies in London and Paris to inform the British and French Governments that the Government of the United States reserved all rights which it or its citizens might have with respect both to the question of aerial navigation in the Antarctic and to those underlying questions of territorial sovereignty involved.

Aerial navigation

U.S. reservations

The Acting Secretary of State (Welles) to the American Embassies in London and Paris, Jan. 6, 1939 (telegrams), MS. Department of State, file 741.5127/3.

The notes referred to, which were exchanged at Paris on Oct. 25, 1938, stated in part that—

". . . the Ministry for Foreign Affairs were so good as to inform His Majesty's Embassy that the Government of the Republic were prepared to recognise the free right of passage of British Commonwealth aircraft over Adélie Land on the understanding that reciprocal rights would be accorded to French aircraft over British Commonwealth territories in the Antarctic.

". . . His Majesty's Governments in the United Kingdom, the Commonwealth of Australia, and New Zealand accept an arrangement on the above-mentioned basis." Gr. Br. Treaty Ser. no. 73 (1938), Cmd. 5900.

French claims to Adélie Land are based on discovery of the land by Dumont d'Urville in 1840, who named the land in honor of his wife, Adélie. A French decree of April 1, 1938 established the limits of the French Antarctic possessions designated as Adélie Land, which by decree of November 21, 1924 had been placed under the jurisdiction of the colonial government of Madagascar, along with St. Paul, Amsterdam, and Kerguelen Islands, and Crozet Archipelago. Article 1 of the decree of April 1, 1938, in translation, reads:

French Antarctic claim

The islands and territories situated to the South of the 60th parallel of South Latitude and between the 136th and 142nd meridians of Longitude East of Greenwich are under French sovereignty.

Vice Consul Gannett to Secretary Hull, Apr. 6 and May 14, 1938, MS. Department of State, files 851.014/83, /86; *Journal officiel*, Apr. 6, 1938, no. 82, pp. 4098–4099.

In a despatch of February 24, 1939 the Embassy of the United States in Paris transmitted to the Department of State copies of a note from the French Foreign Office setting forth the claim of the French Government to Adélie Land. On May 16, 1939 the Department instructed the Ambassador to France to transmit a note to the French Minister of Foreign Affairs in the following terms:

> My Government understands that France bases its claims to the territory in question on the discovery of the coast of that region by the distinguished French explorer, Admiral Dumont d'Urville, in 1840; on the subsequent publication of the facts of his discovery and the action taken by him in connection therewith; and on the decrees of March 27, 1924, November 21, 1924, and April 1, 1938. So far as my Government is aware, Admiral Dumont d'Urville did not even land on the coast claimed for France by him, nor has any French citizen visited the area south of the 60th parallel south latitude and between the 136th and 142nd meridian east longitude since then.
>
> While my Government believes that it is unnecessary at this time to enter into any detailed discussion of the subject, nevertheless, in order to avoid misapprehension, I am instructed to inform Your Excellency that in the light of established principles of international law the United States Government cannot admit that sovereignty accrues from mere discovery.
>
> The Counselor of Embassy (Wilson) to Secretary Hull, no. 3896, Feb. 24, 1939, and the Counselor of the Department of State (Moore) to Ambassador Bullitt, no. 1487, May 16, 1939, MS. Department of State, file 741.5127/7.

Norwegian
Antarctic
claim

The Norwegian Legation informed the Department of State on January 14, 1939 that by a Royal decree of that day there was placed under the sovereignty of Norway that part of the coast of the Antarctic Continent which stretches from the boundary of the "Falkland Islands Dependencies" on the west (boundary of "Coats Land") to the boundary of "Australian Antarctic Dependency" on the east (longitude 45° East) with the territory situated within the said coast and with the adjacent waters, and that the Ministry of Justice had been authorized to take the necessary steps concerning the exercise of police authority in that region. In acknowledging receipt of the note the Department stated:

U.S.
reservation

> Without at this time desiring to enter into a discussion of the various territorial and other questions suggested by the contents of the Royal Decree to which you have drawn my attention, I wish to inform you that the United States reserves all rights which it or its citizens may have in the area mentioned.

On February 16, 1939 the Norwegian Minister transmitted to the Department of State two copies of the Royal decree of January 14,

1939, and the Department in acknowledging the receipt of this note stated:

> In the foregoing connection Mr. Hull refers to the Department's note of January 16, 1939, by which were reserved all rights appertaining to the United States in the area mentioned.

The Norwegian Minister (Morgenstierne) to Secretary Hull, Jan. 14, 1939 (translation), and the Counselor of the Department of State (Moore) to Mr. Morgenstierne, Jan. 16, 1939, MS. Department of State, file 800.014 Antarctic/132; the Norwegian Minister to the Secretary of State, Feb. 16, 1939 (enclosures), and the Secretary of State to Mr. Morgenstierne, Mar. 6, 1939, *ibid.* 800.014 Antarctic/145.

Sector principle.—Certain states have advanced in recent years in connection with claims to jurisdiction in polar regions the suggestion of the so-called "sector principle", a brief account of which follows.

Russia.—On Nov. 13, 1916 the Russian Ambassador in Washington sent a note to the Department of State calling attention to the annexation of certain newly discovered lands in the Arctic. The Russian Government claimed as "part and parcel of the Empire" several Arctic islands lying near the Asiatic coast as constituting "an extension Northward of the Continental tableland of Siberia." On Nov. 12, 1924 the People's Commissar for Foreign Affairs sent a telegram to the Department confirming the claim to these islands and contending that they were situated west of the line "which under Article 1 of the Washington Convention between Russia and the United States, dated March 18/30, 1867, defines the boundary west of which the United States of America undertook not to prefer any claim".

The Soviet decree of Apr. 15, 1926 claimed sovereignty over all territory, discovered or undiscovered, lying in the Arctic Ocean north of the coast of the Soviet Union to the North Pole, between meridian 32°4'35'' east of Greenwich and meridian 168°49'30'' west of Greenwich. The decree by its terms did not apply to lands in this area which had been recognized by the Soviet Government "as property of another State" and set out the boundaries of the area in greater detail than is here given. Ambassador Bakhméteff to Secretary Lansing, no. 767, Nov. 13, 1916, MS. Department of State, file 861.014/2 (translation); People's Commissar for Foreign Affairs (Tchitcherin) to Secretary Hughes, Nov. 12, 1924 (telegram, translation), *ibid.* 861.0144/75; Under Secretary Grew, memoranda of conversations with the Norwegian Minister (Bryn), June 4 and June 12, 1926, *ibid.* 861.014/74.

Great Britain.—In the Antarctic regions three sector claims have been advanced on behalf of Great Britain. In as much as there are no "contiguous" territories extending into this area, as Canada and Russia extend into the Arctic, these Antarctic-sector claims must rest upon a different theory from the Arctic claims. Moreover, the sectors claimed by Great Britain in the South Polar regions far exceed the areas which would be embraced by the projection southward to the pole of the meridians bounding the respective mainland territories to which these sectors are assigned for administrative purposes.

In a letter written in 1924 Secretary Hughes called attention to the following official notices of the British Government:

"(a) 'British Letters Patent appointing the Governor of the colony of the Falkland Islands to be Governor of South Georgia, the South Orkneys, the South Shetlands, the Sandwich Islands, and Graham's Land, and providing for the Government thereof as Dependencies of the Colony.— Westminster, July 21, 1908' (British and Foreign State Papers, Volume CI, 1907–8, pages 76–7);

"(b) 'British Letters Patent, passed under the Great Seal of the United Kingdom, providing for the further Definition and Administration of certain Islands and Territories as Dependencies of the Colony of the Falkland Islands.—Westminster, March 28, 1917' (British and Foreign State Papers, Volume CXI, 1917–18, pages 16–17), contains the following statement:

> " 'Now we do hereby declare that from and after the publication of these our Letters Patent in the Government "Gazette" of our Colony of the Falkland Islands, the Dependencies of our said Colony shall be deemed to include and to have included all islands and territories whatsoever between the 20th degree of west longitude and the 50th degree of west longitude which are situated south of the 50th parallel of south latitude; and all islands and territories whatsoever between the 50th degree of west longitude and the 80th degree of west longitude which are situated south of the 58th parallel of south latitude.'

"(c) Orders in Council, July 30, 1923, (The London Gazette, July 31, 1923, page 5211), including the following:

> " 'And whereas the coasts of the Ross Sea, with the islands and territories adjacent thereto, . . . are a British settlement . . .

> " 'From and after the publications of this Order in the Government Gazette of the Dominion of New Zealand that part of His Majesty's Dominions in the Antarctic Seas, which comprises all the islands and territories between the 160th degree of East Longitude and 150th degree of West Longitude which are situated south of the 60th degree of South Latitude shall be named the Ross Dependency.' "

He stated that:

"So far as this Department is informed the exploration of parts of the Antarctic Continent by American, Belgian, British, French, German, Norwegian, Russian, Swedish, and other travelers has not been followed by permanent settlement upon any part of the continent."

The British Order in Council of Feb. 7, 1933 placing a large Antarctic sector under the authority of the Commonwealth of Australia stated that—

"that part of the territory in the Antarctic Seas which comprises all the islands and territories other than Adélie Land situated south of the 60th degree of South Latitude and lying between the 160th degree of East Longitude and the 45th degree of East Longitude is territory over which His Majesty has sovereign rights."

Secretary Hughes to A. W. Prescott, May 13, 1924, MS. Department of State, file 811.014/101. *London Gazette*, No. 33911, Feb. 14, 1933, p. 1011.

Canada.—On Feb. 20, 1907 Senator Poirier presented the following motion in the Canadian Senate:

"That it be resolved that the Senate is of opinion that the time has come for Canada to make a formal declaration of possession of the lands and islands situated in the north of the Dominion, and extending to the north pole."

Debates of the Senate of the Dominion of Canada, 1906–7, 10th Parliament, 3d sess. (1907) 266–271. In the course of his argument, Senator Poirier allocated so-called "polar sectors" to Norway and Sweden, Russia, United States (Alaska), and Canada.

The motion was not adopted, but on June 27, 1925 an amendment to the Northwest Territories Act was assented to, providing that scientists and explorers should obtain permits to enter the Canadian Arctic (Statutes of Canada, 1925, 15–16 Geo. V., ch. 48). In discussing this measure in the Canadian House of Commons on June 1, 1925 Mr. Stewart, Minister of the Interior, stated in response to a question that Canada claimed all the territory "right up to the North Pole".

Debates of the House of Commons of the Dominion of Canada, 14th Parliament, 4th sess. (1925), vol. LX, p. 3925. See also *ibid.*, pp. 3926, 4238, for further statements by the Minister of the Interior. In 1926 Canada issued an Order in Council providing that all persons entering the territories of the Canadian Arctic should secure permits. This requirement has been fulfilled by the scientists and explorers of many nations since that time. Minister Phillips to Secretary Stimson, no. 1219, Nov. 21, 1929, MS. Department of State, file 842.014/42.

Norway.—In 1930 the Norwegian Government had occasion to express its disapproval of the sector theory. In a despatch of Mar. 1, 1930 the Minister to Norway informed the Department of State, in connection with a current Norwegian exploring expedition in the Antarctic:

"The Minister for Foreign Affairs told me the other day that Norway has no intention of annexing territory charted by the *Norvegia* but that it would object to applying the sector principle to the south polar regions and that freedom of the seas would be claimed."

In a Norwegian note of Aug. 8, 1930, formally recognizing Canada's sovereignty over the Sverdrup Islands, the following stipulation appears:

". . . my Government is anxious to emphasize that their recognizance of the sovereignty of His Britannic Majesty over these islands is in no way based on any sanction whatever of what is named 'the sector principle.' "

Minister Swenson to Secretary Stimson, no. 1594, Mar. 1, 1930, MS. Department of State, file 857.014/80; Gr. Br. Treaty Ser. no. 25 (1931), Cmd. 3875 (reprint of Canadian Treaty Ser. no. 17 (1930), exchange of notes between His Majesty's Government in Canada and the Norwegian Government respecting sovereignty over the Otto Sverdrup Islands). See, however, Norwegian decree of Jan. 14, 1939, claiming a portion of the coast of Antarctica for Norway, *ante*, this section.

United States.—When a private citizen suggested to President Hoover that the United States should take the initiative in bringing about an international arrangement for the partitioning of the Arctic region into national sectors of five contiguous countries (United States, Canada, Denmark, Norway, and Russia), the proposal was called to the attention of the Navy Department, which stated that the course of action proposed—

"(a) Is an effort arbitrarily to divide up a large part of the world's area amongst several countries;

"(b) Contains no justification for claiming sovereignty over large areas of the world's surface;

"(c) Violates the long recognized custom of establishing sovereignty over territory by right of discovery;

"(d) Is in effect a claim of sovereignty over high seas, which are universally recognized as free to all nations, and is a novel attempt to create artificially a closed sea and thereby infringe the rights of all nations to the free use of this area.

"I, therefore, consider that this government should not enter into any such agreement as proposed."

The Secretary of the Navy (Adams) to the Secretary of State (Stimson), Sept. 23, 1929, MS. Department of State, file 800.014 Arctic/26.

Nansen Land.—Fridtjof Nansen Land (formerly Franz Josef Land) is situated north of the Russian mainland Novaya Zemlya between 42° and 65° E. in about the same latitude as northern Spitsbergen. It thus lies within the so-called "sector" claimed by Russia. Norway has not recognized the sector principle nor admitted the validity of the Russian claim to Fridtjof Nansen Land. On its own behalf, Norway has advanced claims based upon discovery as well as upon numerous sealing, hunting, relief, and other expeditions, dating from 1865. MS. Department of State, file 800.014 Arctic/31; Minister Swenson to Secretary Stimson, no. 1436, June 15, 1929, *ibid.* 861.014/97; Smedal, *Acquisition of Sovereignty over Polar Areas* (Oslo, 1931; translation by Chr. Meyer) 69–73.

Wrangel Island.—Wrangel Island is situated approximately 80 nautical miles to the north of the coast of Siberia and about 160 nautical miles west of the longitude of the boundary meridian in Bering Strait between Alaskan and Russian territory. Wrangel Island likewise lies within the so-called "sector" claimed by Russia and was specifically mentioned in the Russian declarations of 1916 and 1924 (*ante*). Since 1924 a Soviet colony has been maintained in exclusive possession of the island. Although previously seen by other explorers, the first recorded landings on Wrangel Island were made in 1881 by parties from American Government vessels who claimed the island for the United States. In 1921 occupation was begun by a group organized under Canadian leadership for the purpose of exploiting the resources of the island and establishing British sovereignty. In 1923 an American company purchased the holdings of the Canadian group and took over the operation of their enterprises on the island. The employees of this firm were removed from Wrangel Island by a Soviet ship which reached the island in the latter part of Aug. 1924, confiscated a stock of furs, removed the British flag and hoisted the Soviet flag. At about the same time the British and Canadian Governments disclaimed any interest in establishing sovereignty over the island. The United States has not relinquished its claim to Wrangel Island. Assistant Secretary Johnson to Ginn and Company, Dec. 20, 1928, MS. Department of State, file 811.014/150; the British Colonial Minister (Amery) to Vilhjalmur Stefansson, Mar. 14, 1925 (copy left with Department of State on May 12, 1925), *ibid.* 861.0144/125; Mr. Stefansson to the Chief of the Division of Eastern European Affairs

(Young), May 27, 1925, and Mr. Young to Mr. Stefansson, June 10, 1925, *ibid.* 861.0144/135. See also 1923 For. Rel., vol. I, pp. 278–286.

Herald Island.—Herald Island, situated about 38 nautical miles in an easterly direction from Wrangel Island, also lies within the Russian-claimed "sector" and was likewise specifically claimed in the Russian declarations of 1916 and 1924. It was discovered in 1849 by a British naval captain who took possession in the name of Great Britain. An American naval commander landed on the island in 1855, and two parties from American naval vessels landed in 1881. In September 1924 a group of Americans visited the island, found it unoccupied, and raised the American flag, claiming the island on behalf of the United States. In acknowledging the receipt of this information in 1926, the Department of State pointed out that there was no information then available to show that any Russian had ever landed on Herald Island. Representative Albert E. Carter to Secretary Kellogg, Apr. 6, 1926, and Mr. Kellogg to Mr. Carter, May 4, 1926, MS. Department of State, file 861.014/70; Mr. Carter to Mr. Kellogg, Apr. 16, 1926, *ibid.* 861.014/71.

Sverdrup Islands.—On Nov. 21, 1930 the American Legation at Oslo reported to the Department of State that, by a note of Nov. 5, 1930, the Norwegian Government had recognized the sovereignty of Canada over the Arctic islands known as "Sverdrup's Islands". The Minister further stated that Norway did not thereby acknowledge the so-called sector principle "which means the direct extension of Canada's borders converging to the North Pole" and that Canada had agreed to give favorable consideration to Norwegian requests for fishing, trapping, hunting, and other industrial rights on these islands, in the event that existing regulations for the protection of aboriginal tribes should be relaxed. It was also reported that Captain Otto Sverdrup, the Norwegian explorer and discoverer of the islands, received from the Canadian Government the sum of $67,000 in recognition of his services. Minister Philip to Secretary Stimson, no. 4, Nov. 21, 1930, MS. Department of State, file 841.014/35. Gr. Br. Treaty Ser. no. 25 (1931), Cmd. 3875 (reprint of Canadian Treaty Ser. no. 17 (1930), exchange of notes between His Majesty's Government in Canada and the Norwegian Government respecting sovereignty over the Otto Sverdrup Islands). The texts of the notes exchanged are set out in this publication.

RECENT CHANGES

SPITSBERGEN

§68

In his message to Congress on December 3, 1912 President Taft said:

The great preponderance of American material interests in the subarctic island of Spitzbergen, which has always been regarded politically as "no man's land," impels this Government to a continued and lively interest in the international dispositions to be made for the political governance and administration of that region.

1912 For. Rel. xx.

International conference, 1914

On June 16, 1914 an international conference convened in Christiania (Oslo), Norway, to consider the government of the archipelago of Spitsbergen which had theretofore been generally recognized as *terra nullius*. Represented at the Conference were United States, Germany, Denmark, France, Great Britain, Norway, Netherlands, Russia, and Sweden. The United States had tentatively prepared a plan of government for the archipelago, a copy of which was furnished to its delegates, but, in view of the fact that a number of the delegates to the Conference deemed it undesirable to consider that plan as a whole, the American delegation refrained from submitting the plan to the Conference and joined with the other delegations in considering the plan submitted by the delegations of Norway, Russia, and Sweden for the international administration of the archipelago.

On July 9, 1914 the Secretary of State instructed the American delegates to make it clear to the representatives at the Conference that the United States did not desire any part in the control of the government to be organized in Spitsbergen or to assume any responsibility therefor. It simply desired, he said, that the rights of its nationals in the islands be recognized and properly secured and that the rights and property interests of its citizens be given the same protection and recognition by the government to be organized as was accorded to citizens of other countries.

The Conference adjourned on July 30, 1914 to meet again in February 1915, without having signed any acts. Owing to the outbreak of the World War, the Conference never reconvened.

Secretary Bryan to the American Legation at Christiania, July 9, 1914 (telegram), MS. Department of State, file 850d.00/320a. For the instructions of the Department of State to the delegation of the United States, see Secretary Bryan to Mr. Collier and Minister Schmedeman, May 23, 1914, MS. Department of State, file 850d.00/271a. For the minutes of the Spitsbergen Conference, see *ibid.* 850d.00/335; 1914 For. Rel. 974–981.

"Terra nullius"

The unique feature of the situation is this: Although the islands of Spitzbergen were discovered over two centuries ago and have been frequently visited since their discovery, no nation has ever considered it worth its while to occupy them or to assert sovereignty over them. The intense cold and the long period of the year when they are ice-bound necessarily made an attempt to develop their resources extremely difficult, so that they seemed to be an undesirable possession, a probable source of expense rather than a source of profit. This was the prevailing opinion of those governments whose vessels visited occasionally those barren shores in search of furs and whales. Thus the archipelago remained unoccupied, and it became generally recognized that Spitzbergen was *terra nullius*, a "no-man's land." Doubtless in recent years more than one government would have been willing to have annexed the territory in view of its possible mineral wealth, but having so long acquiesced in the declaration that it was *terra nullius* none has had the hardihood to claim sovereignty over the archipelago.

This extraordinary political state of the islands, to which a parallel will be hard to find in modern times, would have excited little interest but for the recent discovery of the richness of the coal deposits and the presence of a mining population, which gave promise of being permanent. If this population increased and persons of different nationalities settled in the islands laying claim to lands already claimed by others, how would these people be governed and to what authority could they appeal to settle their conflicting claims and to protect them in the enjoyment of their rights? That was the problem in 1914 and is the problem still which the Powers interested will have to solve. And in view of the fact that the principle of *terra nullius* must be considered as a factor it is by no means easy of solution.

Admitting that it is necessary to establish some form of government in the archipelago, the question presented is, Upon what theory can a government be established over a territory owned by no nation? What basis is there for the exercise of sovereign rights?

. . . .

Since a similar state of affairs has never before arisen to perplex the statesmen of the world, there is no use in seeking a solution in past examples. Indeed, so unusual is the situation, that comparisons and conclusions drawn from historical experience are entirely wanting, and the problem must be solved by a consideration of the fundamental principles underlying governmental institutions. It must be determined whether the nature of sovereignty admits of the possibility of the exercise of sovereign power on land without the existence of territorial sovereignty. Such a question leads into the field of political philosophy, into an analysis of the abstract idea of sovereignty, and into a consideration of its origin, extent, and exercise.

Lansing, "A Unique International Problem", in 11 A.J.I.L. (1917) 764-765.

A treaty relating to Spitsbergen, signed at Paris on February 9, Treaty, 1920 1920 by the plenipotentiaries of the United States, Great Britain, Denmark, France, Italy, Japan, Norway, Netherlands, and Sweden, recognized, subject to the stipulations contained therein, "the full and absolute sovereignty of Norway over the Archipelago of Spitsbergen, comprising, with Bear Island or Beeren-Eiland, all the islands situated between 10° and 35° longitude East of Greenwich and between 74° and 81° latitude North, especially West Spitsbergen, North-East Land, Barents Island, Edge Island, Wiche Islands, Hope Island or Hopen-Eiland, and Prince Charles Foreland, together with all islands great or small and rocks appertaining thereto". By the terms of the treaty the islands were demilitarized and equality among the parties thereto was provided with reference to freedom of access, commerce, mining, hunting, fishing, and communications. Provision was also contained in the treaty for the recognition by Norway of the rights of "Occupiers of land" and of other "acquired rights" (arts. 2, 6, and 7) in Spitsbergen, and with respect to the procedure by which private claims to land were to be investigated and validated (annex).

> 43 Stat. 1892, 1894, 1895–1898, 1901; 4 Treaties, etc. (Trenwith, 1938) 4861–4864, 4865; Gr. Br. Treaty Ser. no. 18 (1924), Cmd. 2092. For a brief discussion of the treaty, see Nielsen, "The Solution of the Spitsbergen Question", in 14 A.J.I.L. (1920) 232–235.

Annexation by Norway

In despatches addressed to the Department of State on July 18 and August 16, 1925, the Legation at Oslo reported that the Storting had enacted a law concerning the Spitsbergen Archipelago and Bear Island, jointly designated as Svalbard, providing that this region was to be considered as an integral part of the Kingdom of Norway, effective August 14, 1925.

> Minister Swenson to Secretary Kellogg, nos. 638 and 656, July 18 and Aug. 16, 1925, MS. Department of State, files 857.014/24, /25.
> A translation of this Norwegian law appears in 122 Br. & For. St. Paps. (1925) 986–990.

BOUVET ISLAND

§69

Norwegian occupation

In connection with the occupation of Bouvet Island, situated at 54°26′ S. latitude and 3°24′ E. longitude in the South Atlantic Ocean, by a Norwegian expedition on December 1, 1927, the Legation at Oslo reported to the Department of State on January 30, 1928 that Consul Lars Christensen, of Sandefjord, had notified the Norwegian Foreign Office on August 1, 1927 that he intended to send the vessel *Norvegia* on a scientific expedition into the Antarctic waters west of Bouvet Island and had requested authority to instruct the captain of the vessel to take possession on behalf of Norway of unoccupied territories and of fishing rights pertaining thereto; that the Minister of Foreign Affairs had issued the requested full powers, the authorization being restricted to territories which had not previously been occupied by any other government in accordance with the rules of international law; and that on December 2, 1927 Consul Christensen had notified the Foreign Office of the receipt of a telegram from the captain of the *Norvegia* stating that he had occupied Bouvet Island on December 1, 1927, had placed a depot there, and had hoisted the Norwegian flag.

The island was placed under Norwegian sovereignty by Royal decree of January 23, 1928, and by this decree the Minister of Justice was authorized to make preparations regarding the exercise of police authority in the island.

An article appeared in the press on January 18, 1928 to the effect that a Norwegian sealing company had been granted exclusive rights by the British Colonial Department to use the Bouvet and Thompson Islands as sealing bases. The Norwegian Government thereupon (in a note of January 19, 1928) advised the British Foreign Office of the authority granted Consul Christensen and of the occupation effected by the *Norvegia* expedition. The Norwegian note discussed the history of the island, stated that it had never previously been visited by any-one, although British explorers had been in the neighborhood, and pointed out that the island did not lie in either the Falkland or Ross sectors claimed by Great Britain.

The British Government sent two different replies to the Norwegian note. The first, dated February 13, 1928, referred to the published summary of the proceedings of the British Imperial Conference of 1926 (*ante* §§14 and 67) and stated that the purpose of the communication was merely to avoid complications that might arise from activities of the expedition in the areas referred to in that report. The second note, dated February 15, 1928, took the position that a valid British title to Bouvet Island existed as the result of the landing and taking possession in 1825 by the captain of the British sealer *Sprightly*. By a note of April 24, 1928 to the British Government, the Norwegian Government reaffirmed the validity of its occupation and maintained that its title was securely founded in international law. Norway denied that Bouvet Island had actually been visited by the British expedition in 1825 and took the position that, in any event, a formal act at the time of the alleged landing without the effective taking of possession was an insufficient basis for a claim to sovereignty and that even if an inchoate title had been acquired in 1825, that title would have become invalidated by British inactivity for about one hundred years. *British claim*

On November 19, 1928 the Department of State was notified by the Legation at Oslo that on November 13, 1928 the British Under Secretary of State for Foreign Affairs had informed the Norwegian Minister in London that Great Britain had withdrawn its claim to Bouvet Island and had no objection to its becoming a Norwegian possession. This report was confirmed in a despatch of November 21, 1928 from the Embassy in London which stated that— *Recognition of Norwegian claim*

> in an official reply to a question in the House of Commons on November 19, 1928, the Under Secretary of State for Foreign Affairs stated that after a careful review of all the issues involved, and having regard to the friendly relations existing be-

tween the two countries, His Majesty's Government have decided to waive the British claim to Bouvet Island in favor of Norway.

Minister Swenson to Secretary Kellogg, no. 1119, Jan. 30, 1928, MS. Department of State, file 857.014/49; the Norwegian Minister, H. H. Bachke, to Mr. Kellogg, Dec. 12, 1928, *ibid.* 857.014/58; Mr. Swenson to Mr. Kellogg, nos. 1136, 1179, and 1309, Feb. 27, May 3, and Nov. 19, 1928, *ibid.* files 857.014/50, /52, /56; the Counselor of Embassy (Atherton) to Mr. Kellogg, no. 3189, Nov. 21, 1928, *ibid.* file 857.014/57.

In a despatch dated Mar. 29, 1930, the Legation at Oslo informed the Department of State that the Norwegian Storting had enacted a law defining the status of Bouvet Island and providing for such legislation as was then considered necessary regarding private property rights, the administration of justice, etc. Mr. Swenson to Secretary Stimson, no. 1615, Mar. 29, 1930, *ibid.* 857.014/82.

GREENLAND

§70

Declaration of the U.S.

There was appended to the convention between the United States and Denmark for the cession of the Danish West Indies, a declaration made on August 4, 1916 by the Secretary of State that "the Government of the United States of America will not object to the Danish Government extending their political and economic interests to the whole of Greenland".

39 Stat. 1706, 1715; 3 Treaties, etc. (Redmond, 1923) 2558, 2564; 1917 For. Rel. 694, 700.

Danish-British negotiations

The American Ambassador in Great Britain telegraphed to the Secretary of State on May 20, 1920 that he had received a note from the British Foreign Office stating that the Danish Minister had requested the British Government to recognize Danish sovereignty over Greenland and that the British Secretary of State for Foreign Affairs had informed the Danish Minister that his Government was prepared to do so, subject to the condition that, in the event of Denmark's wishing to dispose of the territory, she would grant the British Empire the right of preemption, since the geographic position of Greenland made the question of ownership a matter of great importance to the British Empire as a whole and to Canada in particular. (The British Government subsequently modified its position regarding Danish sovereignty over Greenland in a note to the Danish Minister to Great Britain, dated September 6, 1920, in which it was said that the British Government recognized Danish sovereignty over Greenland but that, in view of its geographic proximity to the Dominion of Canada, it reserved the right to be consulted should the Danish Government at any time contemplate the alienation of that territory.)

The Department of State instructed the Ambassador on June 5, 1920 to inform the British Foreign Office of the declaration by the United States at the time of the signature of the treaty of cession of the Danish West Indies (*ante*). He was further instructed that, "owing to the importance of its geographical position", the United States was not disposed, however, to recognize the existence in a third government of a right of preemption to acquire the territory in question if the Danish Government should desire to dispose of it and that it accordingly reserved for future consideration the position it might take in the event of a specific proposal of such a transfer.

> Ambassador Davis to Secretary Colby, May 20, 1920 (telegram), and Mr. Colby to Mr. Davis, June 5, 1920 (telegram), MS. Department of State, file 859b.01/; Per. Ct. Int. Jus., Ser. C, No. 62, Legal Status of Eastern Greenland (Application Instituting Proceedings: Danish Case and Norwegian Counter Case) (1933) 48.

On August 3, 1921 the Secretary of State addressed a note to the Danish Minister in which he set forth the position of the Government of the United States in regard to the possible transfer of Greenland, as explained in the above-mentioned instruction of June 5, 1920 to the Ambassador in Great Britain. In reply the Danish Minister, on September 29, 1921, informed the Secretary that the Danish Government had no desire to transfer its interests in Greenland and had not given to any government any right of preemption in Greenland or any part thereof.

> Secretary Hughes to Minister Brun, Aug. 3, 1921, MS. Department of State, file 859b.01/7; Mr. Brun to Mr. Hughes, Sept. 29, 1921, *ibid.* 859b.01/9.

Norwegian claim

On February 21, 1931 the Norwegian Premier and Minister of Foreign Affairs delivered a speech before the Storting on the subject of East Greenland, a summary of which was reported to be as follows:

> Mr. Mowinckel stated that Norway's viewpoint, based on the East Greenland Agreement of 1924 is that this territory is terra nullius, while Denmark maintains its right of sovereignty. Since the signing of this Agreement, however, certain questions of principle have arisen. Norwegian activities have increased all along the coast of East Greenland, and especially north of Scoresby Sound; and many Norwegian trappers and fishermen have "occupied land for use" in accordance with the terms of Article 4 of the Greenland Agreement.
>
> The Premier went on to say that in view of the fact that a Danish expedition is being sent to this region this summer and in order to avoid any collision between Norwegian and Danish interests there, the Norwegian Government has advised the Danish Government of the extent of Norwegian activities and settlements there which have taken place in conformity with the terms of the Agreement.

. . . Norway contends just as it did during the negotiations that, with regard to the question of sovereignty, Greenland rightfully should belong to Norway, the nation whose people have the greatest practical interests there. Denmark asserts that it has sovereignty over Greenland. So long as activities there continue along purely practical lines without touching questions of principle, these questions of principle can rest. However, there have arisen, especially this year, certain things which have aggravated the situation and which may make the question such an acute one that both nations, out of consideration for their mutual friendly relations, may deem it best to seek an amicable solution of the question of sovereignty over this territory.

Mr. Mowinckel concluded by saying that in accordance with the Greenland Agreement itself its provisions may be submitted to the Hague Court. Should it prove impossible to carry on scientific and practical activities on Greenland without raising questions of principle, then the sovereignty over this territory ought to be definitely settled.

Chargé Andrews to Secretary Stimson, no. 59, Mar. 7, 1931, MS. Department of State, file 857.00P.R./5.

Decree, 1931

In a note of July 11, 1931 the Norwegian Legation informed the Department of State that by Royal decree of July 10, 1931 the territory of East Greenland between 71°30′ and 75°40′ N. latitude had been placed under the sovereignty of Norway. The Legation recalled that the Department had been informed by the Norwegian Minister on November 16, 1925 that Norway had not recognized Danish sovereignty over the whole of Greenland.

On July 13, 1931 the Danish Legation delivered a note to the Department setting forth the views of the Danish Government on the controversy and the bases of Denmark's claim to sovereignty over all of Greenland, and concluding:

Denmark has on July 11th 1931 referred the case to the Permanent Court of International Justice at the Hague and claimed that the declaration of occupation and the measures taken in connection therewith be declared illegal and void.

Decree, 1932

While the *Eastern Greenland* case was pending before the Permanent Court of International Justice, Norway, by Royal decree, dated July 12, 1932, announced that the area of southeast Greenland lying between 63°40′ and 60°30′ latitude N. was under Norwegian sovereignty.

The Norwegian Chargé d'Affaires (Offerdahl) to Secretary Stimson, July 11, 1931, MS. Department of State, file 859b.01/59; the Danish Minister (Wadsted) to the Acting Secretary of State (Castle), no. 130, July 13, 1931, *ibid.* 859b.01/60; Minister Philip to Secretary Stimson, July 13, 1932, *ibid.* 859b.01/96.

On July 18, 1932 the Danish Minister at The Hague instituted proceedings before the Permanent Court of International Justice on behalf of his Government against the Norwegian Government concerning the legal status of southeastern Greenland. Counter proceedings were instituted on the same day by the Norwegian Chargé d'Affaires at The Hague against the Danish Government.

In a judgment dated April 5, 1933 the Permanent Court of International Justice held, by twelve votes to two, that Denmark possessed "a valid title to the sovereignty over all Greenland", that Norway had recognized Danish sovereignty over the whole of Greenland and consequently could not proceed with the occupation of any part thereof, and that the declaration of occupation of East Greenland promulgated by the Norwegian Government on July 10, 1931, and any steps taken in that respect by that Government, constituted a violation of the existing legal situation and were accordingly unlawful and invalid. One of the principal grounds for its judgment in the *Eastern Greenland* case was stated by the Court as follows: Danish sovereignty established

> The first Danish argument is that the Norwegian occupation of part of the East Coast of Greenland is invalid because Denmark has claimed and exercised sovereign rights over Greenland as a whole for a long time and has obtained thereby a valid title to sovereignty. The date at which such Danish sovereignty must have existed in order to render the Norwegian occupation invalid is the date at which the occupation took place, viz., July 10th, 1931. Exercise of state authority
>
> The Danish claim is not founded upon any particular act of occupation but alleges—to use the phrase employed in the Palmas Island decision of the Permanent Court of Arbitration, April 4th, 1928—a title "founded on the peaceful and continuous display of State authority over the island". It is based upon the view that Denmark now enjoys all the rights which the King of Denmark and Norway enjoyed over Greenland up till 1814. Both the existence and the extent of these rights must therefore be considered, as well as the Danish claim to sovereignty since that date.
>
> It must be borne in mind, however, that as the critical date is July 10th, 1931, it is not necessary that sovereignty over Greenland should have existed throughout the period during which the Danish Government maintains that it was in being. Even if the material submitted to the Court might be thought insufficient to establish the existence of that sovereignty during the earlier periods, this would not exclude a finding that it is sufficient to establish a valid title in the period immediately preceding the occupation.
>
> Before proceeding to consider in detail the evidence submitted to the Court, it may be well to state that a claim to sovereignty based not upon some particular act or title such as a treaty of cession but merely upon continued display of authority, involves two elements each of which must be shown

to exist: the intention and will to act as sovereign, and some actual exercise or display of such authority.

Another circumstance which must be taken into account by any tribunal which has to adjudicate upon a claim to sovereignty over a particular territory, is the extent to which the sovereignty is also claimed by some other Power. In most of the cases involving claims to territorial sovereignty which have come before an international tribunal, there have been two competing claims to the sovereignty, and the tribunal has had to decide which of the two is the stronger. One of the peculiar features of the present case is that up to 1931 there was no claim by any Power other than Denmark to the sovereignty over Greenland. Indeed, up till 1921, no Power disputed the Danish claim to sovereignty.

It is impossible to read the records of the decisions in cases as to territorial sovereignty without observing that in many cases the tribunal has been satisfied with very little in the way of the actual exercise of sovereign rights, provided that the other State could not make out a superior claim. This is particularly true in the case of claims to sovereignty over areas in thinly populated or unsettled countries.

Per. Ct. Int. Jus., Ser. A/B, No. 53, (Apr. 5, 1933) pp. 22, 45–46; III Hudson, *World Court Reports* (1938), pp. 170–171.

On Apr. 18, 1933 the agent of the Norwegian Government informed the Court that, by Royal decree dated Apr. 7, 1933, his Government had revoked the proclamation of July 12, 1932 (*ante*) and that in these circumstances it withdrew its application to institute proceedings against the Danish Government. The agent of the Danish Government by letter of the same date informed the Court that his Government, having been notified by the Norwegian Government of the withdrawal of its declaration of occupation in respect to the territories in question in southeastern Greenland, withdrew its application instituting proceedings against the latter Government. The Court therefore, on May 11, 1933, declared the proceedings terminated. Per. Ct. Int. Jus., Ser. A/B, No. 55, (May 11, 1933) p. 157; III Hudson *World Court Reports* (1938) 97.

ISLAND OF JAN MAYEN

§71

On February 9, 1920 the Norwegian Legation in Washington informed the Department of State that the island of Jan Mayen, situated in the Arctic Ocean between Norway and Greenland, had been occupied by Christoffer Evensen Ruud, a Norwegian national, in August 1917 and that he intended to prospect for ore and minerals, to establish a station for the catching of animals, and to begin seal-oil manufacturing and ore washing. Two years later, on April 21, 1922, the Legation advised the Department that Hagbard Ekerold, a civil engineer, had sent the Norwegian Foreign Office a telegram from the island, on January 16, 1922, that he had "annexed" the island in the name of the Norwegian Meteorological Institute with a view to its permanent occupation. The Legation added that part of the territory had been occupied since August 8, 1921 by the Geophysical Expedition conducted by Mr. Ekerold; that the whole of the territory had been occupied since November 12, 1921; and that during the summer and fall of 1921 a wireless station had been erected thereon.

In reply to an instruction sent by the Department to the Minister in Norway on November 9, 1922, directing him to make discreet inquiries as to whether the Norwegian Government in fact claimed the ownership of the island, the Minister, with a despatch dated July 5, 1923, transmitted a note from the Norwegian Foreign Office stating in part that the island should be considered as *terra nullius* but that, on the other hand, the Norwegian Government assumed that no question could arise regarding the annexation of the island by any other power in view of the fact that no other country had even approximately as great interests to safeguard there as Norway. In this connection it was pointed out that the Meteorological Institute had established a wireless station on the island which had already proved of extraordinary value to fisheries along the Norwegian coast, to Norwegian agriculture, and to northern Europe as a whole, in giving timely warnings of the "violent north-west storms which sweep through the open space between Spitsbergen and Iceland".

In a note dated May 17, 1926 the Norwegian Minister advised the Department of State that the Meteorological Institute had extended "its annexation" to the entire island. The Legation in Oslo was instructed by the Department to ascertain whether it was the view of the Norwegian Government that the activities of the Meteorological Institute had changed the political status of the island. On October 1, 1926 the Legation transmitted to the Department a note from the Foreign Office stating that the above-mentioned activities had greatly increased Norwegian interests on the island but that no occupation on the part of the Norwegian state had taken place.

On May 9, 1929 the Norwegian Minister in Washington informed the Department of State that by Royal decree of May 8, 1929 the island of Jan Mayen had been placed under the sovereignty of Norway and that police authority on the island was exercised by the chief of the Norwegian Meteorological Station.

On June 28, 1929 the Department of State said in a note addressed to the Norwegian Minister:

> . . . As you are doubtless aware a question has arisen in the past with regard to the rights of an American citizen, Mr. Hagbard D. I. Ekerold, and of an American company organized

by him, the Polarfront Company, to the land occupied by the Company for the establishment of two fox farms. This matter, in so far as the Department is aware, has not yet been settled.

In the circumstances I have the honor to state in acknowledging your note informing me of the placing of the Island of Jan Mayen under Norwegian sovereignty that this Government is confident that the Norwegian Government will not fail to respect the rights of Mr. Hagbard D. I. Ekerold and the Polarfront Company.

Subsequently, on August 7, 1929, the Norwegian Legation informed the Department that it was instructed to say that the occupation of Jan Mayen by Norway was in no way intended to cause changes in the rights which, according to civil law, "exist on the island".

The Norwegian Chargé d'Affaires (Arentz) to Secretary Lansing, Feb. 9, 1920, MS. Department of State, file 857.014/–; Minister Bryn to Secretary Hughes, Apr. 21, 1922, and Mr. Adee to Minister Swenson, no. 66, Nov. 9, 1922, *ibid.* 857.014/2; Mr. Swenson to Mr. Hughes, no. 244, July 5, 1923, *ibid.* 857.014/4; Minister Bryn to Secretary Kellogg, May 17, 1926, and the Acting Secretary of State (Grew) to the Chargé d'Affaires in Norway (Gade), no. 297, Aug. 25, 1926, *ibid.* 857.014/28; Mr. Swenson to Mr. Kellogg, no. 870, Oct. 1, 1926, *ibid.* 857.014/36; Minister Bachke to Secretary Stimson, May 9, 1929, *ibid.* 857.014/66; Mr. Stimson to Mr. Bachke, June 28, 1929, *ibid.* 857.014/68; the Norwegian Chargé d'Affaires (Lundh) to Mr. Stimson, Aug. 7, 1929, *ibid.* 857.014/73. See also Mr. Swenson to Mr. Stimson, no. 1614, Mar. 28, 1930, *ibid.* 857.014/81; Mr. Bachke to Mr. Stimson, Apr. 28, 1930, Department of State, *Press Releases,* weekly issue 33, p. 251 (May 13, 1930); Assistant Secretary White to Mr. Bachke, May 23, 1930, MS. Department of State, file 857.014/83.

In 1926 the Polarfront Company, a New York corporation of which Hagbard Ekerold was president, had chartered a ship and sent four men with provisions and equipment to the island of Jan Mayen and had established two fox farms on the island. In the course of the correspondence that took place between Mr. Ekerold and the Department of State regarding the company's claim to rights on the island, the Department pointed out, on Feb. 16, 1927, that the general recognition of the status of the island as *terra nullius* rendered it impossible to acquire title to property there, as ordinarily understood, because "Ownership, in its essential features, constitutes the use and enjoyment of the property owned, to the exclusion of all others in its use and enjoyment, and is secured to the owner under the authority of the Government exercising the right of sovereignty with relation both to the island and its inhabitants." *Ibid.* 857.014/34–43.

By a note of Nov. 18, 1930 the British Government recognized the sovereignty of Norway over the island of Jan Mayen. Gr. Br. Treaty Ser. no. 14 (1931), Cmd. 3792 (Exchange of notes between His Majesty's Government in the United Kingdom and the Norwegian Government respecting the recognition of Norwegian sovereignty over Jan Mayen Island).

TERRITORIAL POSSESSIONS OF THE UNITED STATES [1]

DANISH WEST INDIES (VIRGIN ISLANDS)

§72

An account of the negotiations of the proposed treaty of January 24, 1902 for the purchase of the Danish West Indies by the United States, is contained in volume I of Moore's *International Law Digest*, pages 601–610, and the diplomatic correspondence is set out in detail in 1917 *Foreign Relations*, pages 457–544. That treaty failed of ratification by one vote in the Danish Landsting on October 22, 1902.

Treaty of 1902

During 1911–13 the Minister at Copenhagen transmitted a number of despatches to the Department of State relating to reports and articles of Danish origin concerning economic conditions in the islands, the general state of Danish public opinion, the increasing efforts of German shipping interests to entrench themselves firmly in the West Indies, the effect of the completion of the Panama Canal on the future of the islands, and the possibility that Denmark might exchange them for Schleswig. The possible price of $15,000,000 for the islands was also mentioned. Informed Danes seemed to hold the view that eventually the United States would acquire the Danish West Indies but that the time was not then propitious for raising the question. As late, however, as November 1911 the Danish Minister of Foreign Affairs indicated that he was opposed to the sale of the islands.

> Minister Egan to Secretary Knox, nos. 444, 448, 464, 476, and 478, July 21, Aug. 23, and Nov. 2, 14, and 15, 1911, MS. Department of State, files 711.5914/13, /15, /16, /17, /18; Mr. Egan to Secretary Bryan, no. 694, May 27, 1913, *ibid.* file 711.5914/23 ; 1917 For. Rel. 565–588.

On March 8, 1915 the Minister in Copenhagen sent a despatch to the Department of State, reading in part as follows:

> It may seem out of place for me, especially when the most terrible events are making a crisis in the world, to return to a subject on which in the past I have written many despatches, the purchase of the Danish Antilles. For seven years I have hoped that the Department might instruct me to make such suggestions to the Danish Government as would lead to an offer of these islands to the United States at a reasonable price. . . .
>
> Once during the administration of President Taft there seemed to be some hope that the matter of the purchase of these islands might be considered as probable in the near future; the President went so far as to ask me whether they could be put

Renewed discussion.

---

[1] The discussion under this heading does not purport to cover all the territorial possessions of the United States. It relates only to certain changes occurring or inaugurated since 1906.

under the same jurisdiction as Porto Rico and what price might be asked for them. This was sometime after a number of distinguished Danes had sent to me a memorial (September 23, 1910) proposing that our Government should accept Greenland in exchange for Mindanao, the Danish Government having the right to surrender Mindanao to Germany in exchange for Northern Schleswig. The hope that Danish Schleswig may one day again become part of Denmark is still cherished by a great number of the Danes, whose very delicate position, between two great Powers, does not depress their national ardor. The knowledge that this memorial had been presented to me produced a discussion in certain groups here as to whether the Danish Government would be willing to part with St. Thomas and the other Danish Antilles.

.   .   .   .

I have been impressed by the fact that the Department, notwithstanding its present arduous and grievous occupations, has kept its eyes fastened on probable contingencies which may result from the present war and I take the liberty of calling attention to one of these possible contingencies.

In a despatch of May 24, 1915 the Minister informed the Department that in a recent interview between him and the Danish Minister of Foreign Affairs both had agreed that economic conditions in the islands were bad, that the Danish capitalists who had opposed the sale of the islands to the United States in 1902 had evidently changed their opinion as to the value of the islands to them, and that many of the most enterprising residents of the islands were emigrating to the United States to take advantage of the greater opportunities there. The two Ministers agreed, unofficially and personally, that it would be to the mutual advantage of Denmark and the United States to arrange for the transfer of the islands should the opportunity occur.

> Minister Egan to Secretary Bryan, nos. 833 and 850, Mar. 8 and May 24, 1915, MS. Department of State, files 711.5914/26, /27; 1917 For. Rel. 588–591.

Official inquiries

On June 16, 1915 the Department authorized the Minister to approach the proper officials with a view to determining whether a proposal for the purchase of the islands "would be received not unfavorably". Subsequently the Minister informed the Department that the Governor of the Danish West Indies had expressed himself as opposed to the sale, but on August 18, 1915 (following a second instruction from the Secretary of State dated August 10) he informed the Department concerning an interview with the Minister of Foreign Affairs in which the latter stated that he had always believed that it would be well for Denmark to cede the islands to the United States but that he did not know the views of his colleagues.

The Minister stated in his despatch of August 18:

> . . . Mr. de Scavenius [Minister of Foreign Affairs] . . . added that if any proposition worthy of the reputation of the United States for largeness of views and for generosity were made, it would probably be seriously considered. I asked him what he meant by largeness of views and generosity as applied to the purchase of the islands. He said that the previous experience of Denmark in her relations with the United States in regard to the sale of the islands had been so unfortunate, owing, he thought to a misunderstanding on both sides, that the prestige of both countries demanded that the United States should not propose pecuniary terms which would lead to haggling or fail to give guarantees which would effect the kind treatment of the present inhabitants, principally negroes. I answered that as to the first, the United States was not in the habit of buying anything because it was cheap, but because it felt the need of possessing it, that he was right in presuming that if my Government made any proposition it would be both generous and just, and as to the treatment of the negroes, it seemed to me we understood the character of the colored people and the way of making them content better than the Europeans. . . . He reiterated the statement that in view of past negotiations for the islands, which had not reflected credit on either country, Denmark could not make an offer of the islands to us, but that he was reasonably certain, though he spoke only personally, that if a suitable offer was made it would be seriously considered.

Secretary Lansing to Minister Egan, telegram 27, June 16, 1915, MS. Department of State, file 711.5914/26; Mr. Egan to Mr. Lansing, no. 867, July 17, 1915, and Mr. Lansing to Mr. Egan, telegram 37, Aug. 10, 1915, *ibid.* 711.5914/29; Mr. Egan to Mr. Lansing, no. 870, Aug. 18, 1915, *ibid.* 711.5914/32; 1917 For. Rel. 591–595.

During the next few months, according to reports from the Legation at Copenhagen, sentiment in Denmark in favor of selling the islands to the United States grew very rapidly. *(Favorable Danish sentiment)*

Minister Egan to Secretary Lansing, telegrams 168, 173, and 185, and despatch 889, Aug. 19, Sept. 16, and Nov. 8 and 19, 1915, MS. Department of State, files 711.5914/30, 711.5914/33, 859d.00/4, 711.5914/39; 1917 For. Rel. 595–597. As of possible interest, see also Tansill, *Purchase of the Danish West Indies* (1932) 476–481, concerning the possibility of German expansionist tendencies.

Following certain exchanges of communications in which varying amounts were discussed, the Secretary of State on January 10, 1916 sent the following telegram to the American Minister: *(Formal negotiations)*

> Please inform Foreign Office that, in view of Denmark's willingness to part with her ancient possessions in the West Indies, and, with a desire for an early and friendly conclusion of the negotia-

tions, this Government would consider an offer of the sale of the Danish West Indies for the sum of twenty-five million dollars, although not agreeing to pay that amount, which seems excessive.

Secretary Lansing to Minister Egan, telegram 67, Jan. 10, 1916, MS. Department of State, file 711.5914/44; 1917 For. Rel. 598.

Although the Department, on March 14, had telegraphed to the American Legation at Copenhagen a draft treaty of cession for submission to the Danish Minister of Foreign Affairs and had requested the original documents of certain concessions regarding which the United States proposed to assume the obligations incumbent upon Denmark, on March 27, 1916 it wired the Legation that this Government would agree to assume all legal liabilities under Article III of the proposed convention without seeing the original documents which were *en route* to it by mail on the condition that the agreement could be signed immediately. A Danish *contre-projet* was transmitted by the American Minister to the Department on April 27, 1916 and on May 23, 1916 the Minister informed the Department:

> The Minister for Foreign Affairs thinks that the time is propitious for presenting the question of the islands here.   He believes that the Government of the United States will not object to the Danish Government's extending their political and economic interests to the whole of Greenland.

The Acting Secretary of State (Polk) to Minister Egan, telegram 88, Mar. 14, 1916, MS. Department of State, file 711.5914/49a ; Secretary Lansing to Mr. Egan, telegram 92, Mar. 27, 1916, *ibid.* 711.5914/51b; Mr. Egan to Mr. Lansing, telegrams 240 and 107, Apr. 27 and May 23, 1916, *ibid.* files 711.5914/56, /59; 1917 For. Rel. 604–608, 617–622.

Early in June 1916 the Department replied to the Danish counter project, and on June 30 the American Minister transmitted to the Department a new counter project embodying most of the suggestions of the United States and concluding as follows:

> . . . The Danish Government agree with the United States Government that the present moment would be opportune for the conclusion of this convention, and should the United States Government be able to accept the draft now submitted, it will be possible to give the Danish Minister at Washington telegraphic powers in the course of eight days to sign the convention in the name of the Danish Government together with the American plenipotentiary.

The Danish Minister to the United States transmitted to the Department, July 18, 1916, a draft convention sent to him by the Danish Foreign Office and expressed the hope that the text would be satisfactory and that the convention could be promptly signed. He also enclosed a copy of a declaration regarding Greenland which it was desired that the Government of the United States should make. The Department accepted the text of the convention (July 27), explaining that some verbal changes not affecting the sense of the text had been made. On July 31 the Acting Secretary of State sent the following telegram to the Danish Minister (then at Bar Harbor, Maine):

> . . . My telegram July 27 intended to include assurance that declaration enclosed in your letter of July 18 will be given to you when treaty is signed. This will be done simultaneously with signature of treaty, it being understood that declaration stands or falls with treaty. Desire to submit treaty to Senate immediately after signature. Will consult you as to date if it is desired to submit it simultaneously to Senate and Danish Parliament.

The convention was signed in New York by Secretary Lansing and Minister Brun on August 4, 1916. By its terms the King of Denmark ceded to the United States "all territory, dominion and sovereignty, possessed, asserted or claimed by Denmark in the West Indies including the Islands of Saint Thomas, Saint John and Saint Croix together with the adjacent islands and rocks", and the United States agreed to pay therefor "twenty-five million dollars in gold coin of the United States". (As to the provisions in the convention relating to concessions, private rights, property, etc., see *post* §82.) At the same time Secretary Lansing signed a declaration that the United States would not object to the extension by Denmark of her "political and economic interests to the whole of Greenland". _{Convention signed Aug. 4, 1916}

On September 7 following, the convention was approved by the United States Senate without modification of the text but with a proviso that the convention should not be construed as imposing any trust upon the United States with respect to funds and property of the Danish National Church in the islands, such proviso to be made the subject of an exchange of notes between the two Governments so as to make it plain that the condition was understood and accepted by the two Governments, the purpose being to bring the convention clearly within the constitutional powers of the United States with respect to church establishment and freedom of religion.

The convention was ratified by Denmark on December 22, 1916 (after a favorable vote in a national plebiscite) and by the President of the United States on January 16, 1917; ratifications were exchanged at Washington on the following day (39 Stat. 1706, 1711, 1715; 3 Treaties, etc. (Redmond, 1923) 2558, 2561, 2563–2564).

In a circular instruction of April 19, 1917 consular officers of the United States were informed that the islands would be known in the future as the Virgin Islands. _{Name: Virgin Islands}

Secretary Lansing to Minister Egan, telegram 110, June 9, 1916, MS. Department of State, file 711.5914/59; Mr. Egan to Mr. Lansing, telegram 268, June 30, 1916, *ibid.* 711.5914/63; Minister Brun to the Acting Secretary of State (Polk), July 18, 1916, *ibid.* 711.5914/276; Mr. Polk to Mr. Brun, telegrams of July 27 and July 31, 1916, *ibid.* files 711.5914/236½, 711.5914/72; Mr. Polk to Mr. Egan, telegram 142, Aug. 5, 1916, *ibid.* file 711.5914/77a; Mr. Polk to President Wilson, Aug. 7, 1916, *ibid.* 711.5914/83a; the Director of the Consular Service (Carr) to the American consular officers, Apr. 19, 1917, *ibid.* 711.5914/544a. See also 1917 For. Rel. 622–627, 634–646, 706.

By section 7 of the act approved Mar. 3, 1917 Congress appropriated the sum of $25,000,000 to be paid to Denmark "in full consideration of the cession of the Danish West Indian Islands to the United States made by the convention between the United States of America and His Majesty the King of Denmark entered into August fourth, nineteen hundred and sixteen, and ratified by the Senate of the United States on the seventh day of September, nineteen hundred and sixteen" (39 Stat. 1132, 1133). Payment was made at Washington on Mar. 31, 1917.

SWAINS ISLAND

§73

On May 22, 1924 Secretary Hughes sent a letter to President Coolidge recommending Congressional action to extend the sovereignty of the United States over Swains Island. This letter, as printed in a report of the House Committee on Foreign Affairs, reads as follows:

I have the honor to invite attention to the anomalous status of Swains Island (otherwise known as Quiros, Gente Hermosa, Olosega, or Jennings Island), an isolated atoll in the Pacific Ocean, lying in latitude 11°3′ south, longitude 170°55′ west, approximately 200 miles north-by-east from Apia, Samoa, and to suggest that, if you approve, the case be brought to the attention of Congress with the recommendation that the sovereignty of the United States be extended over the island and that it be placed under the jurisdiction of the government established in American Samoa.

The following statement will indicate this Government's relation to the island for more than half a century:

It appears that in 1856, Captain Turnbull, a British subject, the alleged discoverer of Swains Island, gave the island to Eli Jennings, who is reported to have always held himself out as an American citizen. Jennings married a native woman of Upolou, Samoa, and resided on the island until his death in 1878, at which time, under his will, the island became the property of his wife, Maria Jennings. The marriage certificate and will of Eli Jennings were recorded in the American consulate at Apia. By the will of the widow, Maria Jennings, the island became, at her death in 1891, the property of her son, Eli Hutchinson Jennings.

In September, 1909, the resident commissioner in the Gilbert Islands visited Swains Island and collected approximately $85 in taxes from Eli Hutchinson Jennings for the British Government. In response to an inquiry from the American consul at Apia, this department, on November 9, 1910, instructed the consul that Mr. Jennings should file a diplomatic claim against the British Government for recovery of the amount paid as taxes, but added, "From the facts before the department, it is not clear whether Swains Island was ever in fact discovered and occupied with the sanction of the United States and whether the United States has ever actually exercised jurisdiction over the island. In the absence of further evidence on these points, it is an unsettled question whether this Government could well maintain a claim to sovereignty over this island, based on the mere occupation thereof by a private citizen." However, before the department's instruction was received by the consul the assistant high commissioner of the British Government for the western Pacific informed the consul that the British Government considered Swains Island to be American territory and that the taxes collected from Mr. Jennings would be returned to him.

During the summer of 1917 certain natives, former residents of Swains Island, appeared before the native court of Western Samoa and filed charges of cruelty against Mr. Jennings. The British Embassy at Washington, under date of January 30, 1918, informed the department that His Majesty's Government understood that Swains Island was American territory and, accordingly, transmitted to the department for consideration a copy of the evidence presented in support of the charges. The evidence was referred to the Secretary of the Navy, who caused an investigation to be made respecting the conditions obtaining on the island. Such investigation disclosed that the complaints were not justified and the department so advised the British Embassy under date of January 20, 1919.

Eli Hutchinson Jennings died at Swains Island in October, 1920. By his last will and testament all his property, including Swains Island, was left to his daughter, Anne Eliza Carruthers, wife of Irving Hetherington Carruthers, a British subject, and to his son, Alexander Jennings, as tenants in common. Irving Hetherington Carruthers, who was named sole executor and trustee, in 1921, endeavored to probate the will of his father-in-law, but no court could be found which would exercise jurisdiction. Two prior wills of members of the Jennings family purporting to devise Swains Island, were probated in the American consular court at Apia, Samoa. However, the exterritorial jurisdiction formerly exercised by the American consular court at Apia came to an end upon the conclusion on December 2, 1899, of the convention to adjust the question between the United States, Germany, and Great Britain in respect to the Samoan Islands, and the American consul at Apia, since he now exercises no judicial powers, is without authority to probate the will or to grant letters testamentary.

Mrs. Carruthers died intestate in August, 1921, and letters of administration were granted by the British high court of Western Samoa to Mr. Carruthers, who was appointed guardian of the five minor children and administrator of the estate of his deceased wife. It is understood, however, that the letters of administration granted by the British court affect only such property of the estate as is situated in Western Samoa and do not cover Swains Island, over which that court has declined to exercise jurisdiction. Both Mr. Carruthers and Mr. Jennings, who apparently is not satisfied with Mr. Carruthers's management of the property, are desirous of having the jurisdiction of the administrative and judicial authorities of the Government established in American Samoa by the Navy Department extended to Swains Island. The matter was brought to the attention of the Navy Department and that department, under date of March 30, 1921, expressed doubt whether the judicial authorities of the Government established in American Samoa were vested with requisite jurisdiction under existing circumstances of undeclared American sovereignty over Swains Island to probate the will of Eli Hutchinson Jennings.

The status of Swains Island, so far as the jurisdiction of the United States is concerned, can not accurately be defined. The island, under the name of Quiros, appears on the list of guano islands appertaining to the United States, which have been bonded under the act of Congress approved August 18, 1856. That act, the provisions of which are embodied in sections 5570–5578 of the Revised Statutes, authorizes the President, in his discretion, upon the fulfillment of the conditions enumerated therein, to declare that islands or keys not within the jurisdiction of any other government, and upon which guano deposits have been discovered by American citizens, shall appertain to the United States. It is questionable, in view of the interpretation given the act of August 18, 1856, by the courts, whether an island declared to appertain to the United States becomes thereby a part of the territorial domain thereof.

.   .   .   .

I may also mention that a further complication with regard to the status of Swains Island arises from the fact that no guano has, at least for some years, been removed from the island, and the question whether the limited jurisdiction conferred by the guano islands act continues over an island after the removal of guano has ceased does not appear to have been passed upon by the courts. While it is questionable whether the United States has acquired sovereignty over Swains Island by reason of the provisions of the act of August 18, 1856, it appears to be clear that no other country is in a position to assert claim to the island. The fact that the island is included in the list of guano islands appertaining to the United States and has since 1856 been continuously in the possession of the Jennings family, who have always regarded themselves as American citizens, and that American jurisdiction over the island has been recognized by Great Britain, the only other country which might be in a position to dispute an American claim thereto, would seem to place upon this Government the responsibility either of extending its sovereignty over Swains Island and assuming the obligations which such a course would necessarily entail, or of disclaiming the exercise of any control or jurisdiction over the island and the inhabitants thereof.

.   .   .   .

Under the circumstances, I am of the opinion that it would be desirable to have Congress indicate its desire or willingness to extend the sovereignty of the United States over Swains Island and to place it under the jurisdiction of the administrative and judicial authorities of American Samoa.

It is believed that the purpose might appropriately be accomplished by a joint resolution of Congress along the lines of the attached draft. This draft has received the approval of the Secretary of the Navy.

In a message to Congress of May 23, 1924 the President transmitted Mr. Hughes' report and recommended that Congress take the necessary action to regularize the status of Swains Island (S. Doc. 117, 68th Cong., 1st sess.) A joint resolution was introduced in the House of Representatives on June 7, 1924 (H. J. Res. 294, 68th Cong.) and its adoption recommended in the report of the Committee on Foreign Affairs (H. Rept. 1549, 68th Cong., 2d sess.) The joint resolution was duly adopted and was approved by the President on March 4, 1925. It reads as follows:

Whereas Swains Island (otherwise known as Quiros, Gente Hermosa, Olosega, and Jennings Island) is included in the list of guano islands appertaining to the United States, which have been bonded under the Act of Congress approved August 18, 1856; and

Whereas the island has been in the continuous possession of American citizens for over fifty years and no form of government therefor or for the inhabitants thereof has been provided by the United States: Therefore be it

Resolved by the Senate and House of Representatives of the United States of America in Congress assembled, That the sovereignty of the United States over American Samoa is hereby extended over Swains Island, which is made a part of American Samoa and placed under the jurisdiction of the administrative and judicial authorities of the government established therein by the United States. [43 Stat. 1357; 48 U.S.C. §1431.]

On July 3, 1925 the Acting Secretary of the Navy informed the Department of State that a report had been received from the Governor of American Samoa to the effect that the U.S.S. *Ontario* visited Swains Island on May 13 of that year and that, in obedience to the written orders of the Governor, Lt. Comdr. C. D. Edgar, U.S.N., landed, hoisted the flag, and proclaimed United States sovereignty over the island, in accordance with Public Resolution 75, 68th Congress. On July 9, 1925 the American Consulate at Apia, Western

Samoa, transmitted to the Department copies of an article concerning Swains Island and the proclamation of American sovereignty which appeared in the May number of *Ole Faatonu* (no. 5, vol. XXIII, May 1925) published by the Government of American Samoa at Pago Pago. The article reads as follows:

At 1:00 p.m., 12 May 1925, the U.S.S. "Ontario" got underway and proceed [*proceeded*] to Swains Island for the purpose of extending the sovereignty of the United States over said Island in accordance with the provisions of a Joint Resolution of the Congress of the United States. The "Ontario" arrived at Swains Island the morning of 13 May 1925 and the official party immediately went ashore.

At 3:00 p. m. the official ceremonies began. Lieutenant Commander Edgar, U.S. Navy, representing the Government of American Samoa read his orders from the Governor of American Samoa together with the Joint Resolution of Congress and proclaimed sovereignty of the United States over the Island. The American Flag was then hoisted and the "Ontario" fired the National Salute of twenty-one guns.

After the hoisting of the Flag a Samoan Pastor led the assemblage in the Samoan Hymn, after which he made an appropriate speech telling the people of the Island that heretofore they had had no father and no mother and never knew where they stood, but that now the great American Government would take care of them, and they would have a father and mother.

The Island itself is a coral formation, round in shape, from a mile and a half to two miles in diameter. There is a passage through the reef for small boats but no anchorage, as the reef drops off into deep water. In the interior is a lake or lagoon about a half mile in diameter and no outlet to the sea. The Island is low and flat and has a sandy soil. Very little is grown with the exception of coconuts.

There are about seventy people on the Island; all contented and happy.

The distance between Tutuila and Swains Island and return is about four hundred miles.

The "Ontario" left Swains Island the evening of 13 May 1925 and on the return trip made several stops in and around Manu'a [*sic*] collecting copra, returning to the Naval Station on 15 May 1925.

Secretary Hughes to President Coolidge, May 22, 1924, H. Rept. 1549, 68th Cong., 2d sess., pp. 2–4 and MS. Department of State, file 811.0141Q/26; the Acting Secretary of the Navy (Eberle) to the Secretary of State (Kellogg), July 3, 1925, *ibid.* 811.0141Q/33; the Vice Consul in Charge at Apia (Roberts) to Mr. Kellogg, no. 590, July 9, 1925, *ibid.* 811.0141Q/35, enclosure.

PALMYRA ISLAND

§74

The question of the political status of Palmyra Island (Palmyros or Samarang Island) was brought to the attention of the Government of the United States by a letter from the Governor of Hawaii, dated January 10, 1912, reading in part as follows:

> Palmyra Island is one of a chain of several islands, the others being Washington, Fanning and Christmas, in general parallel with the Hawaiian chain and lying about a thousand miles further south.
>
> .   .   .   .
>
> . . . An effort has been made to purchase Palmyra Island also and there appears to be some reason to suppose that an effort will be made to obtain it as an alleged British crown land and/or perhaps to have action taken to establish British sovereignty over it, now that the offer to purchase has been declined by its present owner.
>
> This Island, Palmyra, was discovered by the Captain of the American ship Palmyra in 1802 and was surveyed by an American war ship in 1874.
>
> It was formally taken possession of by the Hawaiian Government in 1862 and by it supposed to have [been] ceded with the other islands of the Hawaiian Government to the United States at the time of annexation. No islands, however, were mentioned by name in the cession.
>
> The private title to this island has been from a date several years before 1862 to the present time in citizens of Hawaii and one Hawaiian corporation, successively, the records of the successive transfers being in the record and probate offices in this City [Honolulu]. The present owner is Hon. H. E. Cooper, a Circuit Judge of the First Circuit of this Territory and formerly Secretary of the Territory.
>
> Thus the title to the island both as to sovereignty and as to private ownership would seem to be American without question. Apparently, however, a British war vessel attempted to take possession of the island in 1897 or earlier and it is said to be registered in the office of the British Lord High Commissioner of the Pacific at Suva, Fiji, and, as stated above, it may be that an effort will be made soon to reassert the British claim to the island. Several other islands in the Pacific seem to have been claimed successfully on behalf of different governments. . . .
>
> I therefore submit the question whether it would not be advisable for the United States Government to have a national vessel proceed to Palmyra Island and confirm the claim of American sovereignty over it in order to avoid possible difficulties in the future.

On February 3, 1912 the Department of State transmitted a copy of the Governor's letter to the Navy Department and asked to be informed of that Department's views as to the feasibility of sending a naval vessel to visit Palmyra Island in order that the claim of American sovereignty might be confirmed and also to discover whether there was any evidence on the island tending to indicate an effort on the part of Great Britain to establish sovereignty over the island. It was later arranged to send a vessel as suggested.

> Governor Frear to the Secretary of the Interior, Jan. 10, 1912, and the Secretary of State (Knox) to the Secretary of the Navy, Feb. 3, 1912, MS. Department of State, file 711.4114P18.

Naval report

On February 26, 1912 the Acting Secretary of the Navy transmitted to the Department of State a copy of a cablegram received from the commander of the Second Division, U.S. Pacific Fleet, who had just returned to Honolulu from a visit on the U.S.S. *West Virginia* to Palmyra Island. The cablegram, paraphrased, read as follows:

> The most thorough examination of every part of Palmyra Island revealed absolutely no evidence of British endeavor to claim sovereignty of Palmyra Island. It is entirely devoid of inhabitants and without habitation other than three vacated huts, very evidently belonging to Japanese bird hunters.

> The Acting Secretary of the Navy (Winthrop) to the Secretary of State (Knox), Feb. 26, 1912, MS. Department of State, file 711.4114P18/4.

American sovereignty

On April 3, 1912 the Department recommended to the Governor of Hawaii that the government of the Territory of Hawaii should "in its official acts continue to recognize Palmyra Island as a part of that Territory, and should take occasion from time to time to have that fact appear in its public documents and on the official maps of the Territory".

> The Acting Secretary of State (Wilson) to the Governor of Hawaii (through the Secretary of the Interior), Apr. 3, 1912, MS. Department of State, file 711.4114P18/4.

Early American claim; Guano Act

In a letter of April 3, 1912 the Governor of Hawaii transmitted to the Department of State a copy of an article in the Honolulu newspaper, the *Advertiser*, of June 26, 1862. The article showed that possession of Palmyra Island had been taken in the name of the United States, under the Guano Act, several years before it was taken possession of in the name of the government of Hawaii, as set forth in the Governor's letter of January 10, 1912 quoted above.

The enclosure read in part as follows:

> By the following notice, which was in the last issue of the Government gazette, it appears that Palmyra Island, located nearly a thousand miles distant from this group, has been taken possession of and formally annexed to this Kingdom

(Here follows the Notice of the Minister of the Interior June 18, 1862.)

The above may be perfectly legal and strictly in accordance with the law of nations, but our authorities, before they proceed any further, and appoint a governor, with tax collectors, judges and other officers for their newly acquired territory, should investigate the title to the claim which is now set up.

It appears that formal possession [was taken] of Palmyra Island in October 1859, for the United States Government, by Dr. G. P. Judd the Agent of the American Guano Company, who visited the island in the brig Josephine. A notice to that effect and the American flag were left on the island. The following is a copy of the notice left there:

> BE IT KNOWN TO ALL PEOPLE, that, on the 19th day of October, A. D. 1859, the undersigned, Agent of the American Guano Company, landed from the brig Josephine, and having discovered a deposit of guano thereon, doth, on this 20th day of October aforesaid, take formal possession of this Island, called, "Palmyra", on behalf of the United States, and claim the same for said Company.
>
> (Signed)   G. P. Judd,
>   Agent, A. G. Co.
>
> Witnesses:
>   C. H. Judd
>   R. Drysdale, M.D.
>   W. C. Stone.

Governor Frear to Secretary Knox, Apr. 3, 1912, MS. Department of State, file 711.4114P18/8, enclosure. See also I Moore's Dig. 568.

Since 1912 the Department of State has had occasion at various times to comment upon the political status of Palmyra Island. On September 9, 1913 it said:

Present political status

> . . . American sovereignty over Palmyra Island, so far as this Department is informed, appears to be well founded, the Island being regarded as belonging to Hawaii at the time when the Hawaiian Islands and their dependencies were annexed as a part of the territory of the United States. For the Hawaiian Proclamation of June 18, 1862, annexing the island, you are referred to William T. Brigham's Index to the Islands of the Pacific.

In 1923, in reply to a request for information from a publishing firm, the Department stated:

> . . . Palmyra Island legally passed under the full sovereignty of the United States upon the annexation of the Hawaiian Islands by this country which took place on August 12, 1898. Palmyra Island now forms a part of the territory of Hawaii.

In 1925 the Department made the following reply to a request for information from a publishing firm which had called attention to conflicting statements as to the sovereignty of the island:

In reply, you are informed that the United States Geological Survey Bulletin No. 689, page 39, contains the following paragraph:

"Palmyra Island, latitude 5°52′ N., longitude 162°06′ W., known also as Samarang Island, was annexed to Hawaii in 1862. It is an atoll occupying an area about 6 miles long and 1½ miles wide and consists of more than 50 small coral islets varying from less than half an acre to 46 acres in size, covered with brush and coconut trees." . . .

. . . "Palmyros Island", approximately in the same latitude and longitude, is listed as a Guano Island appertaining to the United States in 1860, (Moore's International Law Digest, Volume I, page 568). According to the Department's information, Palmyra was formally annexed by the Kingdom of Hawaii on June 18, 1862; in 1889, it is understood that Great Britain made a claim to annex Palmyra. In 1893, however, Palmyra was specifically included in a list of "The Hawaiian Islands and Dependencies" accompanying a communication from one of the Commissioners of the Hawaiian Provisional Government to the Secretary of State (Sen. Ex. Doc. No. 76, 52nd Cong., 2nd Sess., p. 43). In the report of the Hawaiian Commission, appointed by the President in pursuance of the "Joint resolution to provide for annexing the Hawaiian Islands to the United States," approved July 7, 1898, Palmyra Island is specifically included in the list of islands of the Hawaiian group annexed to the United States (Sen. Doc. No. 16, 55th Cong., 3rd Session, p. 4).

You are further informed that although the Statesman's Year Book includes Palmyra among the British possessions, recent British publications are not agreed as to the status of the Island. Thus the British Colonial Office List, which continued to list Palmyra as a British possession until 1917, in subsequent issues has omitted the Island from the list of British possessions. "Stewart's Handbook of the Pacific Islands of 1922", page 510 (published in Sydney, Australia), states that Palmyra is the property of Judge Cooper of Honolulu and has been leased by him to the Palmyra Copra Company.

A similar reply to a third publishing firm was made at about the same time.

The Second Assistant Secretary (Adee) to Mr. Frank L. Long, Sept. 9, 1913, MS. Department of State, file 711.4114P18/10; Assistant Secretary Harrison to the Frontier Press Company, May 10, 1923, ibid. 811.014/88; Mr. Harrison to Mr. Charles E. Funk, July 21, 1925, ibid. 711.4114P18/11; Mr. Harrison to Mr. George S. Lee, Jr., July 21, 1925, ibid. 711.4114P18/12

On January 7, 1932 the Norwegian Legation inquired as to whether there had been any exchange of correspondence between the Governments of the United States and of Great Britain as a result of the establishment of American sovereignty over Palmyra Island. The Department stated in reply that there was no record in the files of the Department of any exchange of views between the United States and Great Britain with respect to the question of sovereignty over Palmyra Island and continued:

It may be stated for the information of the Norwegian Legation that acting under the direction and authority of Kamehameha IV, King of the Hawaiian Islands, the Minister of the Interior issued on June 18, 1862, the following proclamation:

"Whereas, On the 15th day of April, 1862, Palmyra Island, in latitude 5°50′ North, and longitude 161°53′ West, was taken possession of, with the usual formalities, by Captain Zenas Bent, he being duly authorized to do so, in the name of Kamehameha IV., King of the Hawaiian Islands. *Therefore*, This is to give notice, that the said island, so taken possession of, is henceforth to be considered and respected as part of the Domain of the King of the Hawaiian Islands."

In view of the proclamation quoted, it has been considered that upon the annexation on August 12, 1898, of the Hawaiian Islands and their dependencies, Palmyra Island legally passed under the full sovereignty of the United States and that it now is a portion of the Territory of Hawaii.

Memorandum of the Norwegian Legation to the Department of State, Jan. 7, 1932, and memorandum of the Department of State to the Norwegian Legation, Jan. 19, 1932, MS. Department of State, file 811.014/232.

ISLE OF PINES
(Isla de Pinos)
§75

By article I of the Treaty of Paris of December 10, 1898, Spain relinquished all claim of sovereignty over and title to Cuba, and the United States agreed that upon occupation of the island following its evacuation by Spain it would—so long as the occupation should last—assume such obligations as might result therefrom under international law. By article II Spain ceded to the United States the island of Puerto Rico "and other islands now under Spanish sovereignty in the West Indies" (30 Stat. 1754, 1755; 2 Treaties, etc. (Malloy, 1910) 1690, 1691).

The sixth clause of the "Platt Amendment", incorporated in the convention signed by the United States and Cuba on May 22, 1903, provided that the Isle of Pines should be omitted from the proposed constitutional boundaries of Cuba and that the title thereto should be the subject of future adjustment by treaty (act of March 2, 1901,

31 Stat. 895, 898; 1 Treaties, etc. (Malloy, 1910) 362, 364). On March 2, 1904 a treaty between the United States and Cuba for the adjustment of title to the ownership of the Isle of Pines was signed at Washington. By article I the United States relinquished in favor of Cuba all claim of title to the Isle of Pines under articles I and II of the treaty of 1898. Article II recited that the considerations for relinquishment by the United States of claim of title to the island were the grants to the United States of coaling and naval stations in the island of Cuba, which had previously been made. By article III American citizens residing or holding property in the Isle of Pines were assured protection against any diminution of rights and privileges acquired prior to the date of exchange of ratifications of the treaty. This treaty remained unratified until 1925 (*post*).

In 1907 in the case of *Pearcy* v. *Stranahan* (205 U.S. 257), the Supreme Court of the United States passed upon the political status of the Isle of Pines and concluded that it was a "foreign country" within the meaning of the Dingley tariff act of 1897 (30 Stat. 151). Reviewing the official acts of the Spanish Government from 1774 to 1898, the Court concluded that "all the world knew that it was an integral part of Cuba, and in view of the language of the joint resolution of April 20, 1898 [30 Stat. 738], it seems clear that the Isle of Pines was not supposed to be one of the 'other islands' ceded by Article II. Those were islands not constituting an integral part of Cuba, such as Vieques, Culebra and Mona Islands adjacent to Porto Rico." 205 U.S. 257, 266.

In considering whether the treaty had been otherwise interpreted by the political departments of the Government of the United States, the Court alluded, *inter alia*, to a letter written to an American resident of the Isle of Pines on November 27, 1905 by Secretary Root in which he said:

> The treaty now pending before the Senate, if approved by that body, will relinquish all claim of the United States to the Isle of Pines. In my judgment the United States has no substantial claim to the Isle of Pines. The treaty merely accords to Cuba what is hers in accordance with international law and justice.
>
> At the time of the treaty of peace which ended the war between the United States and Spain, the Isle of Pines was and had been for several centuries a part of Cuba. I have no doubt whatever that it continues to be a part of Cuba and that it is not and never has been territory of the United States. This is the view with which President Roosevelt authorized the pending treaty, and Mr. Hay signed it, and I expect to urge its confirmation. [*Ibid.* 270–271.]

On March 13, 1925 the Senate of the United States advised the ratification of the treaty of March 2, 1904, with the following reservations:

1. That all the provisions of existing and future treaties, including the Permanent Treaty proclaimed July 2, 1904, between the United States of America and the Republic of Cuba shall apply to the territory and the inhabitants of the Isle of Pines.

2. The term "other foreigners" appearing at the end of Article III shall be construed to mean foreigners who receive the most favorable treatment under the Government of Cuba.

These reservations were incorporated in an exchange of notes between the two Governments dated March 17 and March 18, 1925. Ratifications of the treaty were exchanged at Washington on March 23, 1925, and it was proclaimed on the following day.

44 Stat. 1997, 1999–2001; 4 Treaties, etc. (Trenwith, 1938) 4036, 4038–4039.

PHILIPPINE ISLANDS

§76

A declaration of the policy of the Government of the United States as to the future political status of the Philippine Islands was made in the preamble to the "Jones Act" of August 29, 1916, which read as follows:

... it was never the intention of the people of the United States in the incipiency of the War with Spain to make it a war of conquest or for territorial aggrandizement; and

... it is, as it has always been, the purpose of the people of the United States to withdraw their sovereignty over the Philippine Islands and to recognize their independence as soon as a stable government can be established therein; and

... for the speedy accomplishment of such purpose it is desirable to place in the hands of the people of the Philippines as large a control of their domestic affairs as can be given them without, in the meantime, impairing the exercise of the rights of sovereignty by the people of the United States, in order that, by the use and exercise of popular franchise and governmental powers, they may be the better prepared to fully assume the responsibilities and enjoy all the privileges of complete independence:

[39 Stat. 545.]

Organic Act of 1916

On March 25, 1924 the Chairman of the Committee on Insular Affairs of the House of Representatives inquired of the Department of State as to whether the granting of independence to the Philippine Islands would be contrary to any provisions of the four-power pact (treaty of December 13, 1921 between the United States of America,

Independence a domestic matter

the British Empire, France, and Japan relating to their insular possessions and insular dominions in the region of the Pacific Ocean, 43 Stat. 1646; 4 Treaties, etc. (Trenwith, 1938) 4883). Replying on April 3, 1924 the Department of State said:

> The controversies referred to in [the treaty] . . . do not, as indicated in the declaration accompanying the Treaty, embrace questions which, under the principles of international law, lie exclusively within the domestic jurisdiction of the respective powers. The question whether independence shall be granted to the Philippine Islands is one which lies exclusively within the domestic jurisdiction of the United States. I, therefore, do not consider that the Treaty mentioned, the declaration accompanying the Treaty, or the Treaty supplementary thereto, concluded February 6, 1922, in any manner affect the exclusive right of this Government to withhold or to grant independence to the Islands in question.
>
> Representative Fairfield to Secretary Hughes, Mar. 25, 1924, and Mr. Hughes to Mr Fairfield, Apr. 3, 1924, MS. Department of State, file 811b.01/63.

In a communication of October 3, 1930, addressed to the Department of State, it was asked whether there was any obligation under any treaty entered into at any time on the part of the United States, either with Spain or directly with the Philippine people, wherein the United States was in any manner bound to a promise of independence of the Islands. Replying on October 10, 1930 the Department said that—

No treaty obligation

> there is no treaty provision by which the United States promises the independence of the Philippine Islands. Such independence lies wholly in the discretion of the United States to be exercised through the appropriate Constitutional method. The United States has made no agreement on the subject nor has there been any authoritative or official promise on the subject by either the executive or Congress. The Sixty-fourth Congress in a preamble to the present Organic Act (Statutes at Large, Vol. 39, Par. 1, p. 545) on this subject and various Presidents have made statements as to the ultimate purpose of the United States in certain circumstances or conditions. No such statements, of course, constitute an official commitment of the Government.
>
> Representative McCormick to the Department of State, Oct. 3, 1930, and Assistant Secretary Castle to Mrs. McCormick, Oct. 10, 1930, MS. Department of State, file 811b.01/139.

Act of 1933

On January 17, 1933 the so-called "Hare-Hawes-Cutting act", to enable the people of the Philippine Islands to adopt a constitution and form a government, to provide for the independence of the islands, and for other purposes, was passed by Congress over a presidential veto (47 Stat. 761–770). The act provided that it should not take effect until it should be accepted by the Philippine Legislature or by a convention called for that purpose. The first section of the act was not accepted.

H. Rept. 968, 73d Cong., 2d sess., pp. 2, 3.

Congress passed another act, the so-called "Tydings-McDuffie act", approved by the President on March 24, 1934, providing for the complete independence of the Philippine Islands upon the expiration of a period of ten years from a specified date and upon compliance with certain conditions. This act, like that of 1933, was not to take effect until accepted by the Philippine Legislature or by a convention called for that purpose by the Legislature. It authorizes the Philippine Legislature to provide for the election of delegates to a constitutional convention to formulate and draft a Constitution "for the government of the Commonwealth of the Philippine Islands". Section 2 provides that the Constitution shall be republican in form, shall contain a bill of rights, and shall provide that, "pending the final and complete withdrawal of the sovereignty of the United States" over the Islands, all citizens and officers of the Philippine Islands shall owe allegiance to the United States. Pending the attainment by the Islands of complete independence, all acts of the Legislature of the Commonwealth are to be reported to the Congress of the United States and certain acts, namely, those relating to currency, coinage, imports, and immigration, are not to become effective until approved by the President of the United States. Section 2 further provides that meanwhile the foreign affairs of the Islands "shall be under the direct supervision and control of the United States"; that the decisions of the courts of the Commonwealth shall be subject to review by the Supreme Court of the United States (as now provided by law); and that the United States shall have the right to intervene for the preservation of the government of the Commonwealth, for the protection of life, property, and individual liberty, and for the discharge of government obligations under and in accordance with the provisions of the Constitution.

Independence Act of 1934

Constitution of the Commonwealth

The act provides (sec. 3) that the Constitution to be drafted and approved by the constitutional convention should be submitted to the President of the United States and, if certified by him to conform to the act, to the people of the Philippine Islands for their ratification (sec. 4); that such ratification should be deemed an expression of the will of the people of the Philippine Islands in favor of independence; and that when obtained, and proclaimed by the President of the United States, "the existing Philippine Government shall terminate and the new government shall enter upon its rights", etc.

High
Commis-
sioner

The act authorizes the President to appoint, by and with the advice and consent of the Senate, a United States High Commissioner to the government of the Commonwealth of the Philippine Islands, to be the representative of the President in the Islands, to have access to the records of the government of the Commonwealth, and to be furnished by the Chief Executive of the Commonwealth with such information as he shall request. The government of the Commonwealth is authorized to be represented in the United States by a Resident Commissioner with a non-voting seat in the House of Representatives. (Sec. 7.)

Independ-
ence in
ten years

Section 10 of the act stipulates that on the fourth day of July immediately following the expiration of a period of ten years from the date of the inauguration of the government of the Commonwealth, the President of the United States "shall by proclamation withdraw and surrender all right of possession, supervision, jurisdiction, control, or sovereignty then existing and exercised by the United States in and over the territory and people of the Philippine Islands . . . and, on behalf of the United States, shall recognize the independence of the Philippine Islands as a separate and self-governing nation and acknowledge the authority and control over the same of the government instituted by the people thereof, under the constitution then in force".

Neutraliza-
tion

Section 11 requests the President of the United States, at the earliest practicable date, to enter into negotiations with foreign powers with a view to the conclusion of a treaty for the perpetual neutralization of the Philippine Islands, if and when Philippine independence shall have been achieved. Section 12 provides that upon the proclamation and recognition of the independence of the Philippine Islands, the President shall notify foreign governments thereof and invite their recognition of such independence.

Statutes

Section 15 repeals certain laws and parts of laws and provides for the continuance in force of others until they shall be altered, amended, or repealed by the Legislature of the Commonwealth of the Philippine Islands or by the Congress of the United States.

Act accepted

A concurrent resolution accepting the act was adopted by the Senate and House of Representatives of the Philippine Legislature in joint session on May 1, 1934.

Constitution
approved

A Constitution of the Philippines was adopted by a Philippine constitutional convention on February 8, 1935. On March 23, 1935 the President of the United States notified the Governor General of the Philippine Islands that the proposed Constitution had been submitted to him and that he certified that "the same conforms substantially with the provisions of the Act of Congress approved March 24, 1934".

48 Stat. 456–465; MS. Department of State, file 811b.01/215; H. Doc. 355, 73d Cong., 2d sess.; S. Doc. 43, 74th Cong., 1st sess.

On November 5, 1935 the Minister of the Union of South Africa presented to the Secretary of State an inquiry from the South African Department of Customs and Excise relative to the classification of the Philippine Islands for customs and statistical purposes. The Secretary of State replied that until the President of the United States shall by proclamation withdraw and surrender all right of possession, supervision, jurisdiction, control, or sovereignty in the Philippines as provided in section 10 (*a*) of the Independence Act "sovereignty over the Philippine Islands rests with the United States."

Sovereignty

Secretary Hull to the Minister of the Union of South Africa, Nov. 15, 1935, MS. Department of State, file 811b.01/261. See, to the same effect, the Legal Adviser of the Department of State to Comptroller Pearlove of the Department of Administration and Finance of Minnesota, Nov. 25, 1936, *ibid.* 811b.01/304.

In the case of *Cincinnati Soap Co.* v. *United States*, decided by the Supreme Court of the United States on May 3, 1937, involving the constitutionality of an appropriation to the Philippine treasury of certain processing taxes provided for in section 602½ of the Revenue Act of 1934 (48 Stat. 680, 763), the Court said:

> The Philippine Islands and their inhabitants, from the beginning of our occupation, have borne a peculiar relation to the United States. The Islands constitute a dependency over which the United States for more than a generation, has had and exercised supreme power of legislation and administration, *Posadas* v. *National City Bank*, 296, U.S. 497, 502, a power limited only by the terms of the treaty of cession and those principles of the Constitution which by their nature are inherently inviolable.

With reference to the effect of the Philippine Independence Act of 1934, the Court said:

> But it is contended that the passage of the Philippine Independence Act of March 24, 1934, c. 84, 48 Stat. 456, and the adoption and approval of a constitution for the Commonwealth of the Philippine Islands have created a different situation; and that since then, whatever may have been the case before, the United States has been under no duty to make any financial contribution to the islands. Undoubtedly, these acts have brought about a profound change in the status of the islands and in their relations to the United States; but the sovereignty of the United States has not been and, for a long time may not be, finally withdrawn. So far as the United States is concerned, the Philippine Islands are not yet foreign territory. By express provision of the Independence Act, we still retain powers with respect to our trade relations with the islands, with certain exceptions set forth particularly in the act. We retain powers

with respect to their financial operations and their currency; and we continue to control their foreign relations. The power of review by this court over Philippine cases, as now provided by law, is not only continued, but is extended to all cases involving the Constitution of the Commonwealth of the Philippine Islands.

Thus, while the power of the United States has been modified, it has not been abolished. Moral responsibilities well may accompany the process of separation from this country; and, indeed, they may have been intensified by the new and perplexing problems which the Philippine people now will be called upon to meet as one of its results. The existence and character of the consequent obligations and the extent of the relief, if any, which should be afforded by the United States in respect of them, are matters, not for judicial but for Congressional consideration and determination.

301 U.S. (1937) 308, 313–314, 319–320.

Diplomatic formalities

As to the honors which should be accorded the President of the Philippine Commonwealth during a visit to a foreign state, the Department of State on January 29, 1937 said that—

the Philippine Commonwealth is not an independent state and its President is not entitled to the honors usually accorded to a chief of state. Sovereignty of the Philippine Islands remains with the United States and the only official of the United States entitled to such honors is the President of the United States. When the Commonwealth Government was inaugurated, it was decided that the High Commissioner to the Philippine Islands, representing the President of the United States, should have precedence over the President of the Commonwealth and that both of those officials should be entitled in the Philippines to salutes of 19 guns.

Until such time as the Philippine Commonwealth becomes entirely free and independent of the United States, it is expected that when honors are rendered any official of the Philippine Commonwealth, the flag of the United States be displayed.

Secretary Hull to Ambassador Johnson, Jan. 29, 1937 (telegram), MS. Department of State, file 811b.001 Quezon, Manuel L./55.

In circular instructions to certain diplomatic and consular officers on Apr. 28, 1937 Assistant Secretary Carr said:

"A ruling was made at the time of the inauguration of the Commonwealth Government establishing the rank of the President of the Philippine Commonwealth as analogous to that of a Governor of a State and providing that the President of the Commonwealth would rank with, but after, the United States High Commissioner to the Philippines.

"This same ruling also prescribed that both the United States High Commissioner and the President of the Philippine Commonwealth would be entitled to a salute of nineteen guns in Philippine territory or Philippine waters, on which occasion only the flag of the United States should be flown. In consequence, the President of the Philippine Commonwealth has not recognized international status and should not be accorded the honors usually given a chief of state. Moreover, he is not entitled to any salutes or honors outside of Philippine territory or Philippine waters.

"If in connection with any ceremony or celebration outside of the Philippines involving the Philippine Islands or one of its officials, the flag of the Philippine Commonwealth is displayed, the flag of the United States should also be flown and given the honor position to the right of (observer's left), or above the Philippine flag.

"The heads of diplomatic missions, as representatives of the President of the United States, take precedence in the countries to which they are accredited over the President of the Philippine Commonwealth.

"It is requested that, when an occasion arises which in your opinion requires such action, the substance of this instruction be brought to the attention of the appropriate authorities."

MS. Department of State, file 811b.01/341a.

In a letter to the Secretary of State on April 30, 1936, with reference to the subject of extradition between the Philippine Islands and foreign countries, the Acting Attorney General said: **Extradition**

This involves, inter alia, interpretation of the provision in the Philippine Independence Act that "foreign affairs shall be under the direct supervision and control of the United States." [Sec. 2(a) (10), Act of March 24, 1934, 48 Stat. 457.] As a matter of first impression this provision appears to be somewhat indefinite and suggests the question whether the Congress contemplated that the Government of the Commonwealth of the Philippine Islands should deal with foreign nations subject to supervision and control or in just what manner, and by whom, foreign affairs affecting the Philippine Islands should be handled.

The Acting Attorney General having requested the views of the Department of State, the Secretary of State, with a letter dated May 26, 1936, submitted a memorandum reading in part as follows:

The provision of the 10th subdivision of Section 2(a) of the Act of March 24, 1934, is one of a number of provisions which the bill required should be contained in the Constitution of the Philippines and which should be in effect "pending the final and complete withdrawal of the sovereignty of the United States over the Philippine Islands". The object of these temporary provisions was to maintain the responsibility of the United States for the general conduct of the government of the Philippines during the ten-year transition period, at the end of which the islands were to become completely independent.

. . . It will be observed that the principal part of the Constitution [of the Philippine Islands adopted by the constitutional convention in pursuance of the act of Congress of March 24, 1934], which contains sixteen articles, is drawn in such form that it will become completely effective, without change, when the islands become independent. However, there is appended to the Constitution an ordinance setting forth the special relationship between the Philippine Islands and the United States during the transition period, while the United States remains sovereign in the islands. These provisions accord with the provisions contained in Section 2(a) of the Act of March 24, 1934. Thus the language of the 10th subsection of Section 1 of the ordinance is the same in phraseology as that of Section 2(a) (10) of the Act of March 24, 1934.

.   .   .   .

Both the Acts of Congress and the ordinance appended to the Constitution of the Philippines show clearly that it was intended that full sovereignty over the Philippines was to be retained by the United States during the transition period of ten years provided for in the Act. They show that, while the government of the Philippine Islands was to have a large measure of self-government, they were not to constitute a separate sovereign state under the rules of international law. In other words, it was clearly intended that the United States and the Philippine Islands should continue to constitute a single state. This is made clear, not only by the provision that the foreign affairs of the Philippines "shall be under the direct supervision and control of the United States", but also by the various other provisions contained in the Act, and repeated in the ordinance appended to the Constitution setting forth in detail the continued authority and responsibility of the United States in the Philippines during the transition period. Among them is the provision, to which special attention has already been called, under which the President of the United States may intervene for the preservation of the government of the Commonwealth of the Philippines, for the protection of life, property and liberty and "for the discharge of government obligations under and in accordance with the provisions of the constitution". . . .

. . . it is believed that it is the intent of the statutory provision in question that foreign affairs pertaining to the Philippine Islands are to be conducted and not merely supervised by the United States. The use of the adjective "direct" before the word "supervision" and the addition of the words "and control" seem to emphasize this point. Needless to say, the Government of the United States, acting through the High Commissioner to the Commonwealth of the Philippine Islands, may call upon the government of the latter for cooperation and assistance in matters pertaining to foreign affairs, including the extradition of criminals, as well as the protection of aliens in the islands, but it is believed that communications between the government of the islands and foreign governments must be carried on through the High Commissioner.

It may be well to make mention of the following provision of Section 12(9) of Article VIII of the Constitution of the Philippines:

"The President shall have power, with the concurrence of a majority of all the Members of the National Assembly, to make treaties, and with the consent of the Commission on appointments, he shall appoint ambassadors, other public ministers and

Philippines not a sovereign state

consuls, and he shall receive ambassadors and other ministers duly accredited to the Government of the Philippines."

It cannot be maintained that the provision just quoted overcomes or in any way limits the provision in the statute and ordinance that during the transition period "foreign affairs shall be under the direct supervision and control of the United States". On the contrary, it is quite clear that the provision of Section 12(9) of Article VIII of the Constitution is subject to and limited by the provision of Section 1(10) of the ordinance, just as other provisions in the principal part of the Constitution are, during the said period, subject to and limited by provisions in the ordinance. The whole object of the ordinance is to maintain the authority and responsibility of the United States in the islands during the period in question, and it necessarily follows that they place limitations upon the authority of the government of the Philippines during the same period. . . . It seems clear that, in view of the statutory provision under discussion, the President of the Philippines could not perform these functions unless expressly authorized by the Government of the United States. It has been suggested that Philippine citizens might be sent as commercial agents to foreign countries, but, for the reasons mentioned, the sending of such persons would also be subject to the authorization of the United States. The provision of the Act of March 24, 1934, under consideration evidently covers all matters concerning foreign affairs which pertain to the Philippines.

Diplomatic officers

. . . .

Unfortunately, the report of the Committee on Territories and Insular Affairs of the Senate of March 15, 1934, concerning the bill, S. 3055, which became the Act of March 24, 1934, contains no special discussion of the particular provision of the Statute in question. It may be observed, however, that the report calls attention to the fact that the bill was a "proposal to reenact the Hare-Hawes-Cutting bill" with certain exceptions having no application to the provision now under consideration. In this connection it may further be observed that in the report of the Committee, of February 24, 1932, concerning the Hare-Hawes-Cutting bill, there appears the following passage:

"It is also provided that foreign relations of the Islands shall be *exclusively* under the control and supervision of the United States, and that our Government at any time may intervene to prevent a violation of international obligations." [Italics added.]

The statutory provision in question, as construed in the Committee's report just quoted, is believed to be eminently wise. With regard to the delicate and important functions pertaining to the conduct of foreign affairs, it is impossible to have a divided authority.

For the reasons mentioned, it seems clear that it was not the intent of Congress that the Government of the Philippines should, during the period in which the United States retains sovereignty over the Philippines, deal directly with foreign governments in matters relating to the extradition of criminals.

The Acting Attorney General (Keenan) to the Secretary of State (Hull), Apr. 30, 1936, MS. Department of State, file 200.11B/13; Mr. Hull to Attorney General Cummings, May 26, 1936, *ibid.* 200.11B/16, enclosing a memorandum prepared in the Office of the Legal Adviser (200.11B/15).

With reference to the question of granting a visa to a member of the household of President Quezon of the Philippine Commonwealth, the Department of State on June 3, 1937 said:

"Philippine Government officials are considered to be foreign government officials for visa purposes in view of [the] language of [the] Philippine Independence Act."

Secretary Hull to Consul General Southard, June 3, 1937 (telegram), MS. Department of State, file 811.111 Diplomatic/10231.

GUANO ISLANDS

§77

The Department of State expressed the following opinion in 1907 regarding the legal status of guano islands appertaining to the United States:

. . . the United States possess no sovereign or territorial rights over guano islands. United States citizens who discover guano, or their assigns, are protected by this Government in the prosecution of their enterprise which extends only to appropriation and disposal of the guano thereon. This protection is extended under the Acts of Congress on the subject, compiled in Title 72 of the Revised Statutes of the United States.

The Assistant Secretary of State (Bacon) to Messrs. Dudley and Michener, Jan. 3, 1907, MS. Department of State, file 3126.

To the same effect, see: the Acting Secretary of State (Adee) to Mr. Miles Carpenter, July 22, 1907, *ibid.* Minor File, vol. 12; the Third Assistant Secretary of State (Phillips) to Mr. H. M. Walker, July 13, 1914, *ibid.* file 811.0141/13; the Acting Secretary of State (Phillips) to Representative John Jacob Rogers, Apr. 28, 1922, *ibid.* 811.0141SW2/77; the Acting Secretary of State (Castle) to Mr. R. F. Nichols, Sept. 1, 1932, *ibid.* 811.0141/54.

The act of August 18, 1856 (Sections 5570–78 R.S.; sections 1411–19, Title 48 U.S.C.) does not vest title to any of the Guano Islands to which it applies in the discoverer but merely authorizes the President, in his discretion, to protect the discoverer or his assigns in the exclusive right of occupying such island, rocks or keys for the purpose of obtaining guano and of selling and delivering the same to the United States to be used therein. In Duncan v. Navassa Phosphate Company (137 U.S. 647), the Supreme Court of the United States said, "The whole right conferred upon the discoverer and his assigns is a license to occupy the island for the purpose of removing [the] guano."

The Acting Secretary of State (Phillips) to Representative Harold Knutson, July 18, 1935, MS. Department of State, file 811.0141SE6/11.

. . . the Department has no authority to grant permission, or a concession, for the exploitation of guano in the Caribbean Sea or elsewhere.

.   .   .   .

The Department has from time to time, upon application being made by Americans who have submitted satisfactory evidence, among other things, of their discovery of guano deposits and that the island, rock, or key upon which the guano is situated is not within the lawful jurisdiction, or occupied by the citizens, of any other government, issued on behalf of the President a guano certificate. Such a certificate has been referred to by the Supreme Court of the United States as having the effect of determining that the island appertains to the United States. (See *Jones* v. *United States*, 137 U.S. (1890) 202; 34 Op. Att. Gen. (1923–25) 507, 514.

The Legal Adviser of the Department of State to Messrs. Eccleston and Knife, Sept. 2, 1936, MS. Department of State, file 811.0141SW2/144.

. . . Under the limited jurisdiction which the United States asserts over guano islands, as set forth in the statute, it would not appear that land on such islands could "belong to the United States" within the meaning of section 4660; neither does it appear that the United States exercises jurisdiction over such islands within the meaning of R.S. 4661, . . .

But looking on these islands in the broader view of territory acquired by discovery and occupation, not abandoned, nor claimed by another power, it is not perceived that there could be any reasonable objection on the part of any other Government to a change in the manner of our occupation of a guano island like Navassa, and the assertion on our part of full sovereignty thereover. Any such change, however, would appear to require the cooperation of the legislative branch of the Government.

Under present conditions, however, the Island of Navassa, while not territory of the United States within the sense of the statutes above quoted, would seem to be, internationally speaking, within the jurisdiction of the United States, and no other power would appear to have any right to object to any action which the United States might take in regard to erecting a light-house thereon.

Opinion of the Solicitor for the Department of State, Sept. 25, 1907, MS. Department of State, file 10640/3, enclosure. See also *post*, this section, the letter of July 20, 1908 from the Acting Secretary of State to the General Counsel of the Isthmian Canal Commission accompanying the memorandum from which the above excerpt is taken.

For action taken by the Executive with respect to guano and other islands, see the proclamation of Jan. 17, 1916 regarding Navassa Island; the proclamation of June 5, 1919 regarding Roncador Cay; the proclamation of Feb. 25, 1919 regarding Serrana and Quita Sueño Banks; the Executive order of June 29, 1926 regarding Johnston and Sand Islands and the Executive order of Dec. 29, 1934 regarding these two islands and others; the Executive order of May 13, 1936 regarding Jarvis, Baker, and Howland Islands; and the Executive order of Mar. 3, 1938 with respect to Canton and Enderbury Islands—all discussed *post*, this section.

In August 1909 the Department of Commerce and Labor informed the Department of State of a request for the clearance of an American schooner coastwise to Swan Island, Caribbean Sea, stating that "Swan Island is supposed to be one of the islands bonded as a guano island to which American vessels may proceed as in the coasting

Coastwise clearance

trade". The Department of State replied that it appeared that Swan Island was no longer exploited for guano but was used for raising fruit; that the law (Rev. Stat. 5578) contemplated the abandonment of guano islands by the United States after the guano had been removed; and that consequently the Department was unable to authorize the clearance of an American schooner coastwise to the island.

The Acting Secretary of Commerce and Labor (McHarg) to the Secretary of State (Knox), Aug. 3, 1909, and the Acting Secretary of State (Adee) to the Secretary of Commerce and Labor, Aug. 4, 1909 (telegram), MS. Department of State, file 20850/2. See "Swan Islands", *post*.

The Act of August 18, 1856, . . . provides the method by which jurisdiction may be acquired and the sovereignty of the United States extended over unoccupied and unclaimed islands containing guano deposits. It provides certain conditions which must be complied with by the discoverer, or those claiming through him, and when such conditions have been complied with the President may, *in his discretion*, consider the same "as appertaining to the United States."

.   .   .   .

The facts required by the statute to be established by the discoverer, or those claiming through him, before such person or persons may claim the protection of the United States, as set forth by Attorney General Black, in 9 Op. 30, are:

1. That a deposit of guano has been discovered upon the island by an American citizen.
2. That such island is not within the lawful jurisdiction of any other government.
3. That the island is not occupied by the citizens of any other government.
4. That the discoverer has taken and occupied peaceable possession [*sic*] thereof in the name of the United States.
5. That the discoverer has given notice of these facts as soon as practicable to the State Department, on his oath.
6. That the notice has been accompanied with a description of the island and its location.
7. That satisfactory evidence has been furnished to the State Department showing that the island was not taken out of the possession of any other government or people.

8. That the discoverer, his heirs, or assigns, shall give bond in such penalty as may be required by the President to deliver guano to citizens of the United States for the purpose of being used therein, and to none others, and at prices not to exceed the maximum fixed by statute.

.   .   .   .

There is no provision in the Guano Islands Act requiring the President to proclaim that the conditions of the Act have been complied with, and that a certain island or islands may be "considered as appertaining to the United States". The extension of the protection of the United States Government to any particular island rests within the discretion of the President, after determining that the statutory conditions have been complied with, but evidence of the exercise of this discretion may be manifested by the announcement or certificate of the Secretary of State.

.   .   .   .

. . . it [the certificate] is conclusive, not only upon the executive officers of the Government, but upon the courts as well.

Attorney General Sargent to Secretary Hughes, June 24, 1925, MS. Department of State, file 811.0141SW2/85; 34 Op. Att. Gen. (1923–25) 507, 512–514.

In response to an inquiry as to the person recognized by the Department of State as the owner of the Alacran Reef, the Department stated in 1926:

With respect to Alacrans Islands, the Government of Mexico produced satisfactory evidence showing that at the time of and prior to the alleged discovery of the islands by an American citizen, the islands were in the lawful jurisdiction and possession of Mexico and accordingly they were stricken from the list of guano islands "appertaining to the United States", and official notice to this effect was given by the Acting Secretary of the Treasury to the Collectors of Customs under date of November 21, 1894.

Alacran Reef (Chica, Perez, Pajaros)

The Assistant Secretary of State (Harrison) to McDonough and McDonough, Feb. 5, 1926, MS. Department of State, file 811.0141C19/18. The statement was repeated by the Department in 1928 in replying to a similar inquiry by Senator Edge. Secretary Kellogg to Senator Walter E. Edge, Jan. 31, 1928, ibid. 811.0141C19/28.

. . . Arcas Keys, which are claimed by Mexico, were never included in the Treasury list of bonded Guano Islands.

Arcas Keys

The Acting Secretary of State (Phillips) to Representative Harold Knutson, July 18, 1935, MS. Department of State, file 811.0141SE6/11.

Replying in 1913 and 1914 to inquiries as to the status of Baker Island, the Department of State merely observed that the island

Baker Island
(New Nan-
tucket,
Phoebe)

appeared on the list of guano islands appertaining to the United States bonded in the Treasury Department under the guano acts. In 1920, in reply to an inquiry concerning Baker and other guano islands, the Department stated that "These islands . . . are not dependencies of the United States but appertain to the United States, since they were first discovered by Americans." In 1927 it stated that, although Baker Island was included among British possessions in certain British publications, the Department was not aware that the British Government had made any claim of sovereignty and that the island was still regarded as appertaining to the United States under the provisions of the Guano Act of 1856. Similar statements were made by the Department to the National Geographic Society in 1932 and to a private citizen in 1933.

> The Acting Secretary of State (Osborne) to Rand McNally and Company, Sept. 6, 1913, MS. Department of State, file 811.014/9; Counselor Lansing to the Secretary of the Interior, Dec. 10, 1914, ibid. 811.014/16; the Second Assistant Secretary of State (Adee) to the Secretary of War (Bureau of Insular Affairs), Mar. 12, 1920, ibid. 811.014/50; the Assistant Secretary of State (Castle) to P. L. King, July 1, 1927, ibid. 811.0141/35; the Historical Adviser (Miller) to Ralph Graves of the National Geographic Magazine, May 2, 1932, ibid. 811.014/236; S. W. Boggs, Geographer of the Department of State, to R. G. Gifford, Aug. 7, 1933, ibid. 800.014/179.

Howland
Island
(Howland's)

Replying to an inquiry from the Department of the Interior as to the political status of Howland Island, the Department of State in 1914 stated that the island appeared on the list of guano islands appertaining to the United States bonded in the Treasury Department. Later, in 1927, it informed a publishing firm that, although Howland Island was included among British possessions in certain British publications, it was not aware that the British Government had advanced any claim of sovereignty thereto and that the island was still regarded as appertaining to the United States. Still later, in 1933, the Department said:

> . . . Howland Island appears to have been discovered in 1842 by an American citizen, who returned and took possession in 1857. Both islands [Baker and Howland] were bonded as guano islands under the provisions of the Guano Act of 1856. Although both of these islands are included among the list of British possessions in certain British publications, the Department is not aware that any formal claim of sovereignty over them has been made by the British Government.

> Counselor Lansing to the Secretary of the Interior, Dec. 10, 1914, MS. Department of State, file 811.014/16; the Assistant Secretary of State (Harrison) to Ginn and Company, Mar. 14, 1927, ibid. 811.014/130; S. W. Boggs, Geographer of the Department of State, to R. G. Gifford, Aug. 7, 1933, ibid. 800.014/179.

With respect to Jarvis Island the Department of State wrote in 1930 that "the United States has not acquiesced in any claim which may have been made to Jarvis Island by foreign governments and reserves all right with respect to the island which the United States may have". Later, in 1933, it stated: Jarvis Island

> Jarvis Island was discovered in 1835 by Michael Baker, an American. In 1858 it was visited by Captain Davis of the U. S. S. St. Mary's, who took formal possession in the name of the United States. In 1889 Great Britain took possession of the island and it has been named as British in official publications of Great Britain. However, the United States has not acquiesced in the British claim and reserves all rights with respect to the island.

> The Historical Adviser (Dennett) to C. A. Burkhart, Mar. 29, 1930, MS. Department of State, file 811.014/172 ; S. W. Boggs, Geographer of the Department of State, to R. G. Gifford, Aug. 7, 1933, *ibid.* 800.014/179.

Baker, Howland, and Jarvis Islands were formally reserved, set aside, and placed under the control and jurisdiction of the Secretary of Interior by Executive Order 7368, issued by President Roosevelt on May 13, 1936, reading as follows: Executive order, May 13, 1936

> By virtue of and pursuant to the authority vested in me by the Act of June 25, 1910, ch. 421, 36 Stat. 847, as amended by the Act of August 24, 1912, ch. 369, 37 Stat. 497, and as President of the United States, it is ordered that Jarvis Island located in the Pacific Ocean approximately in latitude 0°22'30'' S. and longitude 160°01' W. from Greenwich; Baker Island located in the Pacific Ocean approximately in latitude 0°13'30'' N. and longitude 176°33' W. from Greenwich; and Howland Island located in the Pacific Ocean approximately in latitude 0°49' N. and longitude 176°43' W. from Greenwich, as indicated upon the diagram hereto attached and made a part of this order, be, and they are hereby, reserved, set aside, and placed under the control and jurisdiction of the Secretary of the Interior for administrative purposes.
> This order shall continue in full force and effect unless and until revoked by the President or by act of Congress.

> 1 Fed. Reg. (1936), pt. I, p. 405.

On July 30, 1925 a geographic publishing firm was informed by the Department that—

> the title to Christmas Island, as between Great Britain and the United States, may be regarded as somewhat uncertain. Christmas Island was bonded as an American Guano Island December 29, 1859. . . . Christmas Island
> According to information available to the Department, Christmas Island has been occupied at one time or another by American citizens and by British subjects. By a British Order in Council,

made public on November 28, 1919, it was set forth that from and after the proclamation of the Order by publication in the Western Pacific Gazette, the boundaries of the Gilbert and Ellice Islands Colony shall be extended to include Christmas Island. The Department has not made any formal protest or claim in respect of the British Order in Council of November 28, 1919. On the other hand, this Government has never relinquished such claims as it may have by virtue of the former occupancy of Christmas Island by American citizens.

.   .   .   .

You are further informed that on a map which was compiled for the Department in 1921, Christmas Island was indicated as "Status undetermined—U.S., Br."

The Assistant Secretary of State (Harrison) to A. J. Nystrom and Company, July 30, 1925, MS. Department of State, file 841.014/27.

Later on October 12, 1929 the Department said:

. . . Christmas Island, however, has formally been incorporated in the Gilbert and Ellice Islands Colony by an Order-in-Council issued in 1919 and the Department understands that the Island was leased to the Central Pacific Cocoanut Plantations, Limited, for a term of eighty-seven years beginning in January, 1914. The United States has neither admitted nor questioned this latest claim of British sovereignty of Christmas Island, although as stated in the account of the Island, contained in Moore's International Law Digest, Volume I, page 573, the United States by formal communications addressed to the British Government in 1879 and 1888 reserved all questions which might grow out of the occupation of the Island by Great Britain.

The Assistant Secretary of State (Johnson) to William Hard, Oct. 12, 1929, MS. Department of State, file 811.014/167.

Canton and Enderbury Islands

On March 3, 1938 President Roosevelt issued Executive Order 7828 placing Canton Island and Enderbury Island under the control and jurisdiction of the Secretary of the Interior. The order stated:

By virtue of and pursuant to the authority vested in me as President of the United States, it is ordered that Canton Island, an atoll of coral formation, 50 to 600 yards wide and surrounding a lagoon about 9 miles long, which is located in the Pacific Ocean approximately in latitude 2°49′ S. and longitude 171°43′ W. from Greenwich; also Enderbury Island, 2.5 miles long and 1 mile wide, located in the Pacific Ocean approximately in latitude 3°07′ S. and longitude 171°03′ W. from Greenwich, be, and they are hereby reserved, set aside, and placed under the control and jurisdiction of the Secretary of the Interior for administrative purposes.

III Fed. Reg. (1938) 525.

On August 11, 1938 following discussions between the British and American Governments as to the status of Canton and Enderbury Islands, the following joint *communiqué* was issued simultaneously in London and Washington:

The Governments of the United States and of the United Kingdom have agreed to set up a regime for the use in common of the Islands of Canton and Enderbury in the Phoenix Group and for the employment of these islands for purposes connected with international aviation and communication, with equal facilities for each party. The details of the regime will be determined in notes to be exchanged between the two Governments.

Department of State, XIX *Press Releases*, weekly issue 463, p. 114 (Aug. 11, 1938).

By an exchange of notes dated April 6, 1939 an agreement was entered into between the United States and Great Britain regarding the joint administration of Canton and Enderbury Islands. The terms of the agreement follow:

I

The Government of the United States and the Government of the United Kingdom, without prejudice to their respective claims to Canton and Enderbury Islands, agree to a joint control over these islands.

II

The islands shall, during the period of joint control, be administered by a United States and a British official appointed by their respective Governments. The manner in which these two officials shall exercise the powers of administration reserved to them under this paragraph shall be determined by the two Governments in consultation as occasion may require.

III

The islands shall, during the period of joint control, be subject to a special joint *ad hoc* régime the details of which shall be determined by the two Governments in consultation from time to time.

IV

The islands shall be available for communications and for use as airports for international aviation, but only civil aviation companies incorporated in the United States of America or in any part of the British Commonwealth of Nations shall be permitted to use them for the purpose of scheduled air services.

V

The use of any part of either of the islands or their territorial waters for aviation purposes, except as herein agreed upon, or for any other purpose, shall be the subject of agreement between the two Governments.

VI

An airport may be constructed and operated on Canton Island by an American company or companies, satisfactory to the United States Government, which, in return for an agreed fee, shall provide facilities for British aircraft and British civil aviation companies equal to those enjoyed by United States aircraft and by such American company or companies. In case of dispute as to fees, or the conditions of use by British aircraft or by British civil aviation companies, the matter shall be settled by arbitration.

VII

The joint control hereby set up shall have a duration of fifty years from this day's date. If no agreement to the contrary is reached before the expiration of that period the joint control shall continue thereafter until such time as it may be modified or terminated by the mutual consent of the two Governments.

Ex. Agree. Ser. 145.

Johnston Island (Johnson's, Cornwallis)

Replying to an inquiry in 1914 the Department of State said that "Johnson's Island" appeared on the list of guano islands appertaining to the United States and referred the inquirer to the opinion of the Attorney General rendered on July 12, 1859 (9 Op. Att. Gen. [1869] 364) for an account of the discovery and taking possession of the island. In the 1917 *Colonial Office List*, an unofficial British publication compiled from official records, it is stated that the British "protectorate" declared over Johnston Island was "afterwards withdrawn", and the island was "acknowledged to belong to Hawaii, on condition that the right to land a cable is conceded if desired." In 1924 the Department of State informed the Secretary of Commerce that, from the information at its disposal, Johnston Island was "under sovereignty of the United States, a portion of the Territory of Hawaii." Later, in 1929, the Department stated that "Johnston Island belongs to the Hawaiian group".

The Third Assistant Secretary of State (Phillips) to H. M. Walker, July 13, 1914, MS. Department of State, file 811.0141/13; *Colonial Office List*, 1917 (London) 438 n.; the Acting Secretary of State (Grew) to the Secretary of Commerce (Hoover), July 18, 1924, MS. Department of State, file 811.014/110; the Assistant Secretary of State (Johnson) to H. H. Laughlin, Aug. 16, 1929, *ibid.* 811.014/162.

Executive Order, June 29, 1926

Executive Order 4467, issued by President Coolidge on June 29, 1926, reads as follows:

It is hereby ordered that two small islands known as Johnston Island and Sand Island, located in the Pacific Ocean, approximately in latitude 16°44′45″ North and longitude 169°30′30″ West from Greenwich, . . . be and the same are hereby reserved and set apart for the use of the Department of Agriculture as a refuge and breeding ground for native birds.

It is unlawful for any person to hunt, trap, capture, wilfully disturb or kill any bird of any kind whatever, or take the eggs of such bird within the limits of this reserve, except under such rules and regulations as may be prescribed by the Secretary of Agriculture.

Warning is expressly given to all persons not to commit any of the acts herein enumerated, under the penalties prescribed by Section 84 of the U.S. Penal Code, approved March 4, 1909 (35 Stat., 1088), as amended by the Act approved April 15, 1924 (43 Stat., 98).

This reservation to be known as Johnston Island Reservation.

In a letter of July 15, 1922 the Island of Palmyra Copra Company, Ltd., an Hawaiian corporation, notified the Department of State that it had "annexed" Kingman Reef "in the name of the United States of America, and for its own use" on May 10, 1922. The reef was described as "an atoll island charted . . . but never before claimed". The company stated that it believed that this official notification was all that was necessary "in addition to listing the same in our local tax returns". The company enclosed a certified copy of a notice of possession which, together with an American flag and copies of Honolulu newspapers, had been left in a glass jar on the island by its agent. Two clippings from the Honolulu *Advertiser*, with photographs of the island and the landing party, were also enclosed. It appeared that the company's interest was in securing Kingman Reef, dry at high tide, for a fishing base. *(margin: Kingman Reef (Kingman, Maria Shoal, Caldau, "Dangers Rock"))*

The Island of Palmyra Copra Company, Ltd., to Secretary Hughes, July 15, 1922, MS. Department of State, file 811.014K59; Second Assistant Secretary Adee to the Island of Palmyra Copra Company, Ltd., Sept. 28, 1922, *ibid.* 811.014K59/1.

On December 29, 1934 Executive Order 6935, reading as follows, was signed by President Roosevelt:

PLACING CERTAIN ISLANDS IN THE PACIFIC OCEAN UNDER THE CONTROL AND JURISDICTION OF THE SECRETARY OF THE NAVY.

WAKE ISLAND, KINGMAN REEF, AND JOHNSTON AND SAND ISLANDS.

By virtue of and pursuant to the authority vested in me by the act of June 25, 1910, ch. 421, 36 Stat. 847, as amended by the act of August 24, 1912, ch. 369, 37 Stat. 497, and as President of the United States, it is ordered that Wake Island located in the Pacific Ocean approximately in latitude 19°17′28″ N. and longitude 166°34′42″ E. from Greenwich, Kingman Reef located in the Pacific Ocean approximately in latitude 6°24′37″ N. and longitude 162°22′ W. from Greenwich, and Johnston and Sand Islands located in the Pacific Ocean approximately in latitude 16°44′32″ N. and longitude 169°30′59″ W. from Greenwich, together with the reefs surrounding all the aforesaid islands, as indicated upon the diagram hereto attached and made a part of this *(margin: Executive Order, Dec. 29, 1934)* order, be, and they are hereby, reserved, set aside, and placed under the control and jurisdiction of the Secretary of the Navy for administrative purposes, subject, however, to the use of the said Johnston and Sand Islands by the Department of Agriculture as a refuge and breeding ground for native birds as provided by Executive Order No. 4467 of June 29, 1926.

This order shall continue in full force and effect unless and until revoked by the President or by act of Congress.

Navassa
Island

In reply to a letter of December 12, 1906 inquiring whether Navassa Island in the Caribbean Sea was still under the jurisdiction and control of the United States or whether it had been abandoned or surrendered in any way, the Department of State said:

> Navassa Island has not been stricken from the list of guano islands appertaining to the United States under these Acts. The law is silent upon the subject whether the non-use of the privilege of working the guano causes a forfeiture of the privilege. (See Mr. Gresham to Mr. Gordon, October 19, 1893, Moore's International Law Digest, volume 1, page 65). Neither does the law prescribe any method by which the Government of the United States can ascertain when the guano has all been removed.

> Assistant Secretary Bacon to Messrs. Dudley and Michener, Jan. 3, 1907, MS. Department of State, file 3126.

On December 21, 1907 the Isthmian Canal Commission inquired of the Department of State regarding the political status of Navassa Island, having in mind the possible erection of a lighthouse upon the island. The Department replied, in part, that—

> it does not appear that the United States has surrendered its jurisdiction over Navassa Island under the guano acts, and . . . so far as is known to the Department, neither Haiti nor any other power has attempted to assert sovereignty over the island because of any supposed abandonment thereof by the United States.

> However, assuming that this Government still has jurisdiction over Navassa Island under the guano acts, it would seem that the Government itself has interpreted such jurisdiction to be so limited that it cannot be claimed that this or other guano islands "belong" to the United States, within the meaning of section 4660 R.S., or that the United States exercises "jurisdiction" over them within the meaning of R.S. 4661; so that there is no present authority to erect a light-house thereon by virtue of R.S. 4653–4680 defining the authority of the Light-House Board and providing for the erection of light-houses under its direction.

> Nevertheless, it would appear that internationally speaking this Government is in a position to assert full sovereignty over Navassa Island should such action be deemed desirable, and that no other government could reasonably object to such assertion. It would seem, however, that any assertion of this character

should have the cooperation of the legislative branch of the Government.

Even as the Island is at present situated it may well be that there is authority in the War Department to secure a site on the island from those at present entitled under the guano statutes, and to proceed at once to the erection of a light-house thereon with funds which are entirely under the control of the War Department or of the Isthmian Canal Commission and not subject to the restrictions governing the action of the Light-House Board.

The Acting Secretary of State (Adee) to Richard R. Rogers, General Counsel of the Isthmian Canal Commission, July 20, 1908, MS. Department of State, file 10640/3. Pertinent excerpts from the memorandum of the Solicitor for the Department of State which accompanied the Acting Secretary's letter are set forth *ante*, p. 503.

A similar letter was sent by the Department in 1911 to the Secretary of Commerce and Labor regarding the erection of a lighthouse on the island. The Acting Secretary of State (Wilson) to the Secretary of Commerce and Labor (Nagel), Apr. 22, 1911, *ibid.* 811.822/4.

By the Deficiency Appropriation Act of October 22, 1913 Congress appropriated the sum of $125,000 for the erection of a light station on Navassa Island (38 Stat. 208, 224). The Minister of Haiti, on July 5, 1915, entered a formal protest with the Department of State against the proposed erection of the light, terming "that initiative" an "invasion of the sovereign rights of the Republic of Haiti on the island". In reply the Department pointed out that exhaustive consideration had been given to the claim of Haiti to the island by Secretary Fish, as set out in his notes of December 31, 1872 and June 10, 1873 to the diplomatic representative of Haiti in Washington. The claim of Haiti was denied, the Department quoting from the note of June 10, 1873 from Mr. Fish, as follows:

Appropriation for erection of light

Haitian protest

"The Government of the United States has given patient attention to the statements and arguments ably put forward on the part of Haiti, and has carefully considered all the facts bearing upon the question, and feels confident in the justice of the position it [the United States] has assumed. I cannot doubt that this position is fully sustained by facts, by history and by the well settled principles of public law, and it is hoped that it may be regarded by Haiti as fully answering the claims advanced on her part, and thus avoid further discussion on the subject."

Minister Ménos to Secretary Lansing, July 5, 1915, and Mr. Lansing to Mr. Ménos, no. 5, July 14, 1915, MS. Department of State, file 811.822/8.

Before the erection of the light was begun President Wilson issued a proclamation dated January 17, 1916, which, after stating the pro-

Proclamation of Jan. 17, 1916

visions of the Guano Act of August 18, 1856 (11 Stat. 119; Rev. Stat., secs. 5570–5578), continued:

> AND WHEREAS, pursuant to the foregoin[g] Act of Congress, the Island of Navassa is now under the sole and exclusive jurisdiction of the United States and out of the jurisdiction of any other Government.
> AND WHEREAS, the Congress of the United States by the Act of October 22, 1913 . . . has made an appropriation for the construction of a light station on the Island of Navassa.
> Now, THEREFORE I, WOODROW WILSON, President of the United States, by virtue of the power in me vested, do hereby declare, proclaim, and make known that the said Island of Navassa in the West Indies be and the same is hereby reserved for lighthouse purposes, such reservation being deemed necessary in the public interests, subject to such legislative action as the Congress of the United States may take with respect thereto.

> 39 Stat. 1763.

On August 22, 1916 the Department of Commerce informed the Department of State that the radio station owned by the United States Government, but temporarily operated by the contractors engaged in building the light on Navassa Island, had not yet been recognized by Great Britain and that such recognition was necessary in order that communication might be established with Jamaica, the contractors' base of supplies. Upon the request of the United States, Great Britain authorized the Government of Jamaica to issue the necessary license.

> The Acting Secretary of Commerce (Sweet) to the Secretary of State (Lansing), Aug. 22, 1916, and the Assistant Secretary of State Osborne to Chargé Laughlin, no. 4210, Sept. 20, 1916, MS. Department of State, file 811.822/23; Ambassador Page to Secretary Lansing, no. 5219, Nov. 13, 1916, *ibid.* 811.822/29.

Since the date of the proclamation by President Wilson the Department of State has uniformly declared that Navassa Island forms a part of the territory of the United States. An opinion of the Solicitor, dated October 25, 1917, concluded:

> It would, therefore, appear that this Government is committed to the view that it has the right to control and use Navassa Island, and such control and use would naturally extend to purposes of war as well as those of peace.

Various letters have been written to private citizens giving a brief history of the island, citing the presidential proclamation of January 17, 1916 and observing that this action was based upon the Guano Act and also the act of October 22, 1913. In a letter written in 1927 the Department included Navassa Island as one of the "possessions of the United States, outside the territorial boundaries of the United States".

MS. Department of State, file 811.345/42; the Solicitor for the Department of State (Hackworth) to H. W. Leese, Mar. 13, 1928, *ibid.* 811.0141/37; the Acting Secretary of State (Castle) to R. F. Nichols, Sept. 1, 1932, *ibid.* 811.0141/54; the Assistant Secretary of State (Castle) to P. L. King, July 1, 1927, *ibid.* 811.0141/35. Navassa Island is similarly listed as a possession of the United States in a letter sent by the Assistant Secretary of State (Harrison) to Ginn and Company, Mar. 14, 1927, *ibid.* 811.014/130.

In connection with the preparation of a new Constitution of Haiti in 1917, the Department of State instructed the Legation by telegraph on Nov. 8, 1917 that the reference to Navassa Island as Haitian territory in article I of the proposed draft should be stricken out, because the island belonged to the United States. In a supplementary instruction of Nov. 27, 1917 the Department, after an exhaustive review of the history of the island, stated:

"From the foregoing you will observe that it is the view of this Government that it has the exclusive right to the control and use of Navassa Island on which there is at the present time a light station constructed by the authorities of this Government . . . as well as a wireless station which is under governmental supervision."

Secretary Lansing to the American Legation at Port-au-Prince, Nov. 8, 1917 (telegram), MS. Department of State, file 838.011/28a; Counselor Polk to Chargé Mayer, no. 159, Nov. 27, 1917, *ibid.* 838.011/28a (supplement).

In 1932 the American Chargé d'Affaires in Haiti reported that, in a proposed amendment to article I of the Constitution of Haiti, Navassa Island was claimed as Haitian territory. The Chargé d'Affaires stated that he had informed the Haitian Foreign Office that the island belonged to the United States but that the Minister of Foreign Affairs had replied that Haiti had always considered the island as Haitian territory and that he thought it was time some settlement was made of the question. The Department's reply to the Legation gave a summary of the history of the island, referred to the Department's answers to Haiti in 1873 and 1915, and, after stating that there had been no change in the Department's position since the latter date, instructed the Legation to inform the Haitian Government that the United States did not believe that Haiti would include any statement regarding Navassa Island in its Constitution "which is not borne out by the facts and the law". The instruction was not received until after the Assembly had taken final action on the text of the article in question, and the American Minister did not think it advisable to make representations at that time. In a subsequent despatch he asked to be instructed "to make a formal reservation of our rights, setting forth the facts outlined in the Department's instruction . . . and stating that the Island is now actually occupied by the United States for the purpose of maintaining a lighthouse there". The Department authorized the Minister to take this action, which was done.

Chargé McGurk to Secretary Stimson, no. 422, June 15, 1932, and Assistant Secretary White to Mr. McGurk, no. 207, July 5, 1932, MS. Department of State, file 838.011/125; Minister Munro to Secretary Stimson, no. 455, July 25, 1932, and Mr. White to Mr. Munro, no. 218, Aug. 13, 1932, *ibid.* 838.011/129; Mr. Munro to Mr. Stimson, no. 489, Sept. 12, 1932, *ibid.* 838.011/131, enclosure.

On Apr. 11, 1934 the Haitian Chamber of Deputies voted a resolution demanding the return of Navassa Island to Haiti. In a conversation with the Haitian Minister of Foreign Affairs on Apr. 13, 1934, the American Chargé d'Affaires informed him that the American Government's position on the subject of the ownership of the island had been clearly set forth in the Legation's note to the Foreign Office, dated Sept. 12, 1932. The Haitian Minister of Foreign Affairs volunteered the opinion that it was a mistake for the National Assembly to raise the question of sovereignty at that time. Chargé Woodward to Secretary Hull, no. 298, Apr. 18, 1934, *ibid.* 838.011/135.

In Article I of title I of the new Constitution submitted to a national plebiscite on June 2, 1935, Navassa was included as one of the "dependent Islands", which, along with Haiti's territory, "are inviolable and may not be alienated by any treaty or by any convention". Chargé Chapin to Secretary Hull, nos. 636, 658, and 664, May 29 and June 17 and 19, 1935, *ibid.* files 838.011/149, /154, /155.

Great Swan and Little Swan Islands are situated in the Caribbean Sea about 97 miles north of Patuca Point, Honduras, in latitude 17°25′ N., longitude 83°55′ W. The western island, Great Swan, is about two miles long. The eastern island, Little Swan, is about one and one-half miles long. Each is about one-half mile in breadth.

From the time of the discovery in 1857 by Americans of guano on the Swan Islands, the islands have been occupied by American citizens and exploited by American interests. The guano operations continued until 1904. Since that time an American corporation has developed and exploited the agricultural resources of the islands and has been in continuous possession. As early as 1911 a wireless station was maintained on the islands by the United Fruit Company. From June 1914 to August 31, 1927 the Weather Bureau of the United States maintained an observation station on the islands.

The Secretary of the Navy (Meyer) to the Secretary of State (Knox), Nov. 13, 1911, MS. Department of State, file 811.0141SW2/29, enclosures; memorandum, Office of the Solicitor, Aug. 14, 1924, ibid. 811.0141SW2/82½; Attorney General Sargent to Secretary Hughes, June 24, 1925, *ibid.* file 811.0141SW2/85; 34 Op. Att. Gen. (1923-25) 507, 509-513; the Acting Secretary of Agriculture (Dunlap) to the Secretary of State (Kellogg), Dec. 10, 1927, MS. Department of State, file 811.0141SW2/93.

On February 8, 1918, at the request of the Secretary of the Navy, the Acting Attorney General of the United States gave an opinion as to the status of the Swan Islands. His first conclusion, that the United States had never acquired sovereignty by virtue of the Guano Act of 1856, was based upon inadequate information and was subsequently reversed in 1925; his second conclusion was "that no other country has any proper claim to these islands, and that the United States may at any time assert its sovereignty over them by appropriate action". The factual basis for this conclusion was "that since the period of the original discovery, with the exception of the very slight lapse of time (apparently not 48 hours) between the abandonment of these islands by the Albion Chemical Co. and their so-called rediscovery and settlement by Alonzo Adams in 1904, these islands have always been claimed as occupied by citizens of the United States, and that no other Government has attempted to assert any dominion over them or right and title to any property in them".

On August 21, 1924 Secretary Hughes addressed a letter to the Attorney General pointing out that, in view of certain information in the files of the Department of State, a reconsideration of portions of the former opinion of the Attorney General would seem to be warranted. A copy of a departmental memorandum incorporating these facts was enclosed. The Attorney General replied in a letter dated June 24, 1925 in which, with reference to the opinion of February 8, 1918, he stated:

> The principal questions submitted to the Attorney General by the Secretary of the Navy were:
> (1) "Has the United States Government acquired sovereignty over the said islands by virtue of the Guano Islands Act of August 18, 1856?"
>
> .   .   .   .
>
> At the time of the rendition of the opinion of February 8, 1918, a copy of the certificate of the Secretary of State, dated February 11, 1863 [issued to the New York Guano Company, the assignees of the original discoverers], above set forth, was not before the Acting Attorney General, as shown by the statement in the opinion that "It nowhere appears, however, that any executive action was taken by the President or on his behalf . . . ." This assertion is confirmed by an examination of the statement of facts supplied by the Secretary of the Navy. Had a copy of that certificate been supplied to the Attorney General I have no doubt but that he would have answered the first question in the affirmative.

The Attorney General then referred to other facts brought out in the Department's memorandum: In a letter of March 23, 1863 addressed to Mr. U. P. Parish, Secretary Seward had said, *inter alia*, that the proofs filed by the New York Guano Company "were considered sufficient to authorize the Government to extend the protection asked for, under the Act of August 18, 1856 . . ." and that the Secretary of the Treasury, under date of February 12, 1869, had issued instructions to collectors of customs directing them to enforce the provisions of the coastwise shipping laws to guano islands appertaining to the United States, and had enclosed a list of such islands among which were the Swan Islands. As to these matters, the Attorney General said:

> . . . It appears, therefore, that the certificate set forth above was considered by both the Secretary of State and the Secretary of the Treasury as a sufficient proclamation of the extension of sovereignty over the Swan Islands, and that the conditions precedent prescribed by the Guano Islands Act had, in the opinion of the Secretary of State, at that time been complied with.

After a discussion of the meaning of the provisions of the Guano Act, with particular reference to the case of *Jones* v. *United States*, 137 U.S. (1890) 202, the Attorney General concluded:

> The fact that the Albion Chemical and Export Company, successor to the New York Guano Company, abandoned Swan Islands on February 5, 1904, and that Mr. Alonzo Adams reoccupied and took possession of the islands on February 6, 1904, does not affect the sovereignty of the United States over said islands.
>
> Sovereignty of the United States having once been extended, no act of the tenant or licensee could deprive the United States of its dominion over said islands. . . .
>
> It is my opinion, therefore, that the dominion of the United States Government was extended over the Swan Islands by the President, as evidenced by the certificate of Secretary Seward, dated February 11, 1863, and that the sovereignty of the United States attached to said islands as of that date.
>
> 31 Op. Att. Gen. (1916–19) 216, 222–223; 34 Op. Att. Gen. (1923–25) 507, 508, 511–512, 514–515; Secretary Hughes to Attorney General Sargent, Aug. 21, 1924, MS. Department of State, file 811.0141SW2/82a; Memorandum, Office of the Solicitor for the Department of State, Aug. 14, 1924, *ibid.* 811.0141SW2/82½; Mr. Sargent to Mr. Hughes, June 24, 1925, *ibid.* 811.0141SW2/85.

Honduran claim

Upon receipt of a report in 1921 that a Honduran official was *en route* to the Swan Islands to take possession of them in the name of his Government, the Department of State instructed the Legation in Honduras that, if the report were accurate, it should inquire upon what basis the Honduran Government was acting. In a note to the Legation of May 28, 1921 the Honduran Minister of Foreign Affairs stated that his Government had decided to send a commission to the islands "which form a part of the territory included under the sovereignty of this Republic", as an administrative measure but that the commission had not yet been sent. On August 11, 1921 the Legation, acting on instructions from the Department, stated that the Swan Islands appertained to the United States whose citizens had discovered them and had since remained in full possession of them and that, in the opinion of the Government of the United States, it would be easier to effect a satisfactory settlement of the contentions of the two Governments if Honduras refrained from any attempt to take possession of the islands, thus maintaining the *status quo*.

Secretary Hughes to the American Legation at Tegucigalpa, Honduras, May 23, 1921, MS. Department of State, file 811.0141SW2/66; Chargé Spencer to Mr. Hughes, May 30, 1921 (telegram), *ibid.* 811.0141SW2/67; Mr. Spencer to Mr. Hughes, no. 137, May 30, 1921 (enclosure, translation), and Mr. Hughes to Mr. Spencer, no. 425, July 12, 1921, *ibid.* 811.0141SW2/68; Minister Morales to Mr. Hughes, no. 101, May 31, 1922, *ibid.* 811.0141SW2/73.

The basis of the Honduran claim was set forth in a note to the American Legation of November 15, 1923, in which were enclosed copies of the report of a commission that had investigated the status of the Swan Islands for the Honduran Government and other material upon which Honduras relied. Discovery of the islands was asserted to have been made by the Spaniards in the early years of the sixteenth century. The title of Spain, it was said, passed to Central America by virtue of its political emancipation, and, upon the dissolution of the United Provinces of Central America in 1839, the islands remained under the exclusive jurisdiction of Honduras.

Minister Morales to Secretary Hughes, no. 538, Nov. 21, 1923, MS. Department of State, file 811.0141SW2/82. The Honduran Legation in Washington expressed similar views in a note to the Department of State in 1935. Chargé Cáceres to Secretary Hull, Dec. 12, 1935, *ibid.* 811.0141SW2/140.

In 1929 the Department of State instructed the Legation in Honduras that, if reports concerning Honduran moves to establish a guard on the islands proved to be correct, it should inform the Honduran Minister of Foreign Affairs of the extension of American "dominion" over the islands on February 11, 1863, "and that the sovereignty of the United States attached to those islands as of that date"; of the subsequent establishment by American interests of a radio and meteorological station, etc.; and of the utilization of that equipment by the United States Weather Bureau during the 1928 hurricane season and of its intended use for the same purpose in 1929. The instruction concluded:

> You will add that in view of these facts this Government hopes that the Government of Honduras will refrain from the performance of any act of assumption of jurisdiction over the Islands in question.

The Legation transmitted a note to the Honduran Foreign Office from which a reply was received on April 4, 1929, asking to be furnished with copies of the Guano Act of August 18, 1856 and the certificate of the Secretary of State, dated February 11, 1863. Copies of the documents were sent to the Legation on April 23 for delivery to the Honduran Minister of Foreign Affairs.

Minister Summerlin to Secretary Kellogg, no. 20, Feb. 24, 1929, and Mr. Kellogg to Mr. Summerlin, Mar. 1, 1929 (telegrams), MS. Department of State, file 811.0141SW2/117; Mr. Summerlin to Secretary Stimson, no. 849, Apr. 6, 1929 (enclosure), and Assistant Secretary White to Mr. Summerlin, no. 352, Apr. 23, 1929, *ibid.* 811.0141SW2/123.

The islands remain in the exclusive possession of American interests and under the jurisdiction of the United States, which has not admitted the validity of the Honduran claim. The meteorological station on the islands was maintained by the United States Weather Bureau during the cyclone seasons of 1928 and 1932.

The Secretary of State (Hughes) to the Secretary of War (Weeks), July 31, 1922, MS. Department of State, file 811.0141SW2/76; the Acting Secretary of State (Phillips) to Representative J. J. Rogers, Aug. 22, 1922, *ibid.* 811.0141SW2/77; the Assistant Secretary of State (White) to the Chargé d'Affaires in Berlin (Gordon) no. 207, Oct. 31, 1930, *ibid.* 811.0141-SW2/132; the Assistant Secretary of State (Castle) to the Cuban Chargé d'Affaires (Altunaga), Aug. 1, 1928, *ibid.* 811.0141SW2/112; the Acting Secretary of Agriculture (Marvin) to the Secretary of State (Stimson), July 13, 1932, *ibid.* 811.0141SW2/135.

Serranilla Bank

With respect to Serranilla Bank it appears from the Department's records that James W. Jennett, an American citizen on May 24, 1869 filed with the Department a declaration of discovery of guano deposits on the Island and that on September 8, 1879 and September 13, 1880 bonds were given pursuant to the provisions of Sections 5570 and 5574 of the Revised Statutes of the United States, . . .

.   .   .   .

The Serranilla Bank as well as the Islands referred to in the Proclamations appears in the list of Guano Islands considered as appertaining to the United States.

Second Assistant Secretary Adee to Mr. Edward H. Mason, May 5, 1920, MS. Department of State, file 811.822/83.

Serranilla Keys are still included in the list of bonded Guano Islands. There is, however, no record of the Department of State having issued a certificate or proclamation with regard to these Keys.

There are a number of documents in the Department's files purporting to be deeds, assignments and affidavits relating to the . . . Keys in question. The Department is not in a position either to vouch for the validity of such documents or to express an opinion regarding their legal effect, nor has it any means of assurance that the documents filed with it comprise all of the purported assignments of interest in the Keys or the guano deposits thereon. Upon receipt of documents relating to Guano Islands it has been the practice merely to place them in the Department's files, where they are open to inspection by properly authorized persons.

The Acting Secretary of State (Phillips) to Representative Knutson, July 18, 1935, MS. Department of State, file 811.0141SE6/11.

It appears from the Department's records that, in the year 1869, James W. Jennett, an American citizen, filed with the Department, as discoverer of deposits of guano in the Islands of Pedro Keys, Quita Sueño, Petrel and Roncador, a memorial claiming the benefits of the above mentioned statute [act of 1856]. *(margin: Serrana and Quita Sueño Banks, and Roncador Cay)*

On November 22, 1869, he, together with certain other persons, filed with the Department a bond, as required by the . . . provision of law, for the proper working and disposition of the deposits, which bond was approved by the Department on November 26, 1869. These islands were subsequently included in a list of Guano Islands appertaining to the United States which was published by the Treasury Department on October 12, 1871. (Moore's International Law Digest, Vol. I, p. 566.)

. . . .

It further appears that, in December, 1890, the Government of Colombia, in a communication to the Secretary of State, declared that . . . Roncador and Quita Sueño belonged to that country and inquired as to whether the removal of guano by Mr. Jennett had been authorized by the Government of the United States. This Government replied that such authorization had been given and refused to acquiesce in Colombia's claim of title to the islands.

Assistant Secretary Phillips to Mr. E. A. Alexander, Apr. 21, 1917, MS. Department of State, file 811.0141/20.

On February 25, 1919 President Wilson issued the following proclamation reserving Serrana and Quita Sueño Banks for lighthouse purposes: *(margin: Proclamation, Feb. 25, 1919)*

WHEREAS, the Congress of the United States has provided by act of August 18, 1856 (11 U. S. Statutes at Large, page 119; Secs. 5570 to 5578 U.S. Revised Statutes), that whenever any citizen of the United States, after the passage of the act, discovers a deposit of guano on any island, rock, or key, not within the lawful jurisdiction of any other Government and shall take peaceable possession thereof and occupy the same, the island, rock, or key may, at the discretion of the President of the United States, be considered as appertaining to the United States.

AND WHEREAS, pursuant to the foregoing act of Congress, Serrana and Quita Sueño Banks in the western part of the Caribbean Sea are now under the sole and exclusive jurisdiction of the United States and out of the jurisdiction of any other government.

Now, THEREFORE, I, WOODROW WILSON, President of the United States, by virtue of the power in me vested, do hereby declare, proclaim, and make known that the southwest cay of Serrana Banks and the north, or other suitable portion of Quita Sueño Banks, including any small detached cays surrounding either of these banks which the Department of Commerce may desire, be and the same are reserved for lighthouse purposes, such reservations being deemed necessary in the public interests, subject to such legislative action as the Congress of the United States may take with respect thereto.

40 Stat. 1933; 1919 For. Rel. vol. I, p. 796.

On June 5, 1919 a similar proclamation was issued by President Wilson with respect to Roncador Cay.

41 Stat. 1751, 1752; 1919 For. Rel., vol. I, pp. 797–798.

In a despatch of September 17, 1919 the American Legation at Bogotá, Colombia, transmitted to the Department of State a copy of a note from the Colombian Minister of Foreign Affairs, dated September 13, expressing surprise at the erection of light towers in "the Cays of Roncador, Quitasueno y Serranilla [sic], which belong to the territorial domain of Colombia". The note referred to the notification of Colombian title to these keys in a note to the Department of State of January 18, 1893. Prior to that note, it was said, the Government of the United States had explicitly recognized the sovereignty of Colombia over these keys by supporting the request of Sweden that the Colombian Government erect a light tower on the keys. The Department instructed the Legation on October 16, 1919 that the lighthouses, which were in operation as early as June 1919, were erected in the belief that those islands appertained to the United States.

Minister Philip to Secretary Lansing, no. 144, Sept. 17, 1919, MS. Department of State, file 811.822/64 (enclosure, translation); 1919 For. Rel., vol. I, pp. 798–801.

It will be noted from the enclosures hereto [correspondence between the Departments of Commerce and Agriculture] that to grant Mr. Eden authority to collect eggs on Serrana Cays for the purpose of sale would be an evasion of the Act of Congress of July 3, 1918, carrying into effect the treaty with Great Britain providing for the protection of birds which migrate between the United States and Canada, and that, for that reason, it is considered inadvisable to comply with Mr. Eden's request. You are instructed to inform him accordingly.

The Director of the Consular Service (Carr) to Consul Latham, Jan. 16, 1923, MS. Department of State, file 811.014/85.

On June 4, 1926 the British Ambassador in Washington addressed a note to the Secretary of State informing him that the British Government was, at that time, engaged in correspondence with the Colombian Government regarding an incident arising out of the arrest of certain British fishermen by the Colombian authorities on a charge of illegal fishing in Colombian waters. The note stated:

. . . At the time of their arrest, the fishermen were pursuing their calling on Quitafueno [*sic*] Bank, an almost totally submerged and totally uninhabited rock forty miles from Old Providence Island.

His Majesty's Government are disposed to hold that a formation of this nature cannot be regarded as subject to the sovereignty of Colombia, but they have been assured by the Colombian Minister in London that the United States Government before creating an untended light there, requested permission from the Government of Colombia to do so.

The Ambassador requested to be informed whether the United States in fact recognized the sovereignty of Colombia over Quita Sueño Bank. The Department replied in part:

This Government has never requested the permission of the Colombian Government to erect a lighthouse on Quita Sueño Banks. However, on February 12, 1919, the American Minister at Bogota, Colombia, was instructed to request the Government of Colombia to permit the erection of two lights . . . one on . . . Old Providence Island and the other on one of the Courtown Cays. In making this request the American Minister informed the Government of Colombia that the request did not signify the taking of any attitude on the part of the United States Government toward the various claims concerning the sovereignty of the islands in question. Although a light was also placed at this time on the Quita Sueño Banks the Colombian Government was not consulted with reference thereto.

Sir Esme Howard to Secretary Kellogg, no. 389, June 4, 1926, and Mr. Kellogg to Sir Esme Howard, June 12, 1926, MS. Department of State, file 811.822/106.

On April 10, 1928 the following arrangement between the United States and Colombia respecting the status of Serrana and Quita Sueño Banks and Roncador Cay was effected by an exchange of notes:

. . . whereas both Governments have claimed the right of sovereignty over these Islands; and whereas the interest of the United States lies primarily in the maintenance of aids to navigation; and whereas Colombia shares the desire that such aids shall be maintained without interruption and furthermore is especially interested that her nationals shall uninterruptedly possess the opportunity of fishing in the waters adjacent to those Islands, the *status quo* in respect to the matter shall be maintained and the Government of Colombia will refrain from objecting to the maintenance by the United States of the services which it has established or may establish for aids to navigation, and the Government of the United States will refrain from objecting to the utilization, by Colombian nationals, of the waters appurtenant to the Islands for the purpose of fishing. [4 Treaties, etc. (Trenwith, 1938) 4023–4024.]

On December 4, 1928 the Honduran Legation in Washington sent to the Department of State a note enclosing copies of notes which the Honduran Government had transmitted to the Governments of Colombia and Nicaragua, protesting against certain provisions of the treaty of boundaries and jurisdictions then recently concluded between those Governments. It was stated in the treaty that "The Roncador, Quitasueño and Serrana Keys, the possession of which is in dispute between Colombia and the United States of America, are not considered to be included in this Treaty." The Honduran Government protested that since it claimed sovereignty over Quita Sueño Bank and Roncador Cay it could not admit that these lands were subject to controversy between other countries.

The Department replied, after alluding to the Department's approval in November 1869 of the occupation of Roncador Cay and Quita Sueño by the American discoverer of guano deposits thereon:

> By a proclamation of June 5, 1919, the President of the United States declared Roncador Cay to be under the sole and exclusive jurisdiction of the United States and out of the jurisdiction of any other government.

> . . . .

> By a proclamation of February 25, 1919, the President of the United States made known that Quita Sueño Banks are under the sole and exclusive jurisdiction of the United States and out of the jurisdiction of any other Government.

> From the foregoing it will be evident that this Government has always regarded Quita Sueño Banks and Roncador Cay since their discovery by Jennett as being under the sovereignty and jurisdiction of the United States and it cannot, therefore, admit any claim of a foreign nation to sovereignty over these islands.

> Minister Olaya to Secretary Kellogg, no. 352, Apr. 10, 1928, MS. Department of State, file 811.0141C19/35; Mr. Kellogg to Dr. Olaya, Apr. 10, 1928, *ibid.* 811.0141C19/36; the Honduran Chargé d'Affaires (Izaguirre V.) to Mr. Kellogg, Dec. 4, 1928, *ibid.* 811.0141C19/44; Mr. Kellogg to Minister Bográn, Dec. 26, 1928, *ibid.* 811.0141C19/46.

EFFECTS OF CHANGE OF SOVEREIGNTY

TRANSITIONAL PERIOD

§78

Pending transfer

In a decision given November 19, 1925 the American and British claims tribunal, established under the special agreement of August 18, 1910, rejected claims advanced on behalf of British subjects on account of property destroyed by Filipino insurgents on the occasion of the occupation of Iloilo on the island of Panay by the forces of the United States. One of the grounds upon which liability of the United

States was asserted was that there had been a delay of a week in replying to a request from General Otis to Washington for permission
to occupy the place to preserve order and protect property, after the
general had been requested by the businessmen of Iloilo to do so and
had been notified by the Spanish commander that he desired to evacuate. As a consequence, it was asserted, the Spanish had evacuated
and the insurgents had taken control before the American expedition
arrived. In rejecting the claims, the tribunal stated on this phase of
the case that—

> we are of opinion that there was no duty upon the United States
> under the terms of the Protocol, or of the then unratified treaty,
> or otherwise, to assume control at Iloilo. *De jure* there was no
> sovereignty over the islands until the treaty was ratified. Nor
> was any *de facto* control over Iloilo assumed until the taking up
> of hostilities against the United States on the part of the so-called
> Filipino Republic required it on February 11, 1899. The sending
> of General Miller's force, at the request of the business men of the
> place, was an intervention to preserve peace and property. As
> between the United States and the claimants or their government,
> it was a matter of discretion whether or not to do this, and no
> fault can be imputed because of delay in undertaking such an
> intervention.

> Iloilo Claims (Great Britain *v.* United States), Nielsen's report (1926)
> 403, 404.

After the conclusion of a treaty of cession, and pending the
actual transfer of possession to the grantee, the grantor is doubtless permitted to exercise authority necessary to maintain order
and safeguard economic conditions within the territory concerned. During that interval (at least in the case of a treaty
which is to take effect from the date of signature, and is ultimately confirmed by both parties) it may be regarded as bur-
dened with the duty of impairing in no manner the value to its
successor of its new domain. The Supreme Court of the United
States has declared that while in such case "full sovereignty" does
not pass to the State to which it is transferred until actual delivery "it is also true, that the exercise of sovereignty by the ceding
country ceases, except for strictly municipal purposes, especially
for granting lands."

I Hyde, *International Law*, etc. (1922) 201.

The abandonment by Germany of her rights and titles under
Article 88 of the Treaty of Versailles merely contemplates the
possible renunciation of sovereignty over the territories in question and cannot involve the immobilization of all movable and
immovable property belonging to the State during the period
from the day of the coming into force of the Peace Treaty until
the transfer of sovereignty over Upper Silesia.

Germany undoubtedly retained until the actual transfer of sovereignty the right to dispose of her property, and only a misuse

of this right could endow an act of alienation with the character of a breach of the Treaty; such misuse cannot be presumed, and it rests with the party who states that there has been such misuse to prove his statement.

Nor would it be legitimate to construe the Treaty of Versailles in such a way as to incorporate therein certain clauses of the Armistice Convention and of the instruments following it, so as to carry back to November 11th, 1918, the decisive date as from which rights acquired by individuals, under contracts concluded by them with the Reich and German States, should be regarded as void or liable to annulment. The special provisions of Article 75 which relate to Alsace-Lorraine, a territory restored to French sovereignty as from November 11th, 1918, and according to which the decisive date is that of the French Decree of November 30th, 1918, make it clear that a date previous to the latter could not have been contemplated by the Treaty in the case of territories which only change hands by cession. The decisive date therefore, for these territories, cannot be other than that of the transfer of sovereignty.

Per. Ct. Int. Jus., Ser. A, No. 7, Case Concerning Certain German Interests in Polish Upper Silesia (The Merits), May 25, 1926, p. 30; I Hudson, *World Court Reports* (1934) 510, 530.

Sixaola territory

Representation having been made to the Department of State that the American Banana Company was suffering through eviction and seizure of its property in the so-called "Sixaola territory" in dispute between Panama and Costa Rica, the Department of State instructed the Ministers to those two countries to say that, while the United States did not controvert the power of Costa Rica and Colombia or Panama to make a provisional agreement respecting the administration of that territory pending the definite settlement of its ownership, it did not concede the power of the provisional administrator to execute judgment in the capacity of sovereign until the sovereignty of the territory was adjudicated and the courts of the sovereign had passed upon the matters involved. They were further instructed to say that the Government of the United States did not concede the right of either to prejudice the ultimate rights of American citizens therein by adverse action in advance of such definite adjudication and that it did not undertake to determine the conflicting claims of title made by that company and by other American citizens but that it would reserve in behalf of any injured American citizen, as against either Costa Rica or Panama, all rights which pertained to territory and for the infringement of which the rightful sovereign might be found responsible.

Secretary Root to Minister Merry, Jan. 27, 1906 (telegram), MS. Department of State, 22 Instructions, Central America, 637; 1906 For. Rel., pt. II, p. 1184.

In further regard to the rights of American citizens in the disputed territory the Department of State instructed the Minister to Panama on Apr. 16, 1906 as follows:

"The department is not unmindful of the contention of Costa Rica that an understanding has existed between that state and Panama whereby the former has retained temporary possession and administrative control over the district, and pending the ratification of the treaty of March 7, 1905, exercises police powers and other general attributes of *de facto* sovereignty within the territory. At the same time it is undeniable that the *de jure* sovereignty has been in Colombia and Panama since the Loubet award, accepted as it is by Panama and Costa Rica, so that either by virtue of that award or of the pending boundary treaty the territory will ultimately come under the jurisdiction of Panama. Meanwhile, certain American citizens, acting upon the assurances of the authorities of Colombia and Panama, and in accordance with the laws of those States, have gone into this territory, expended large sums in developing it, and by virtue of such acts have acquired certain possessory rights thereunder and are entitled to protection therein. In the adjustment of any conflicting claims of title which may arise or have arisen it would be improper for this department to interfere. But, on the other hand, after rights, possessory or otherwise, in this property have been acquired in good faith by American citizens and have become vested in them, the department is of opinion that they should not be divested except by due process of law by ejectment or other appropriate legal action.

"In the department's conception of this matter Costa Rica exercises at present a temporary de facto sovereignty over the territory included in the McConnell concession, subject of right to be divested at any time at the will of Panama, but actually continuing until such time as the pending boundary treaty is ratified. She exercises the powers of government that are necessary for the orderly administration of the district, but should not use this sovereignty in such a way as to impair the rights of the de jure sovereign of the territory. Her functions of government are limited by her tenure, which is of a temporary and precarious character. Her duty is to preserve the property, not to destroy it, and hand it over to her successor without the commission of any acts tending to impair the ultimate rights of the de jure owner."

Secretary Root to Minister Magoon, no. 37, Apr. 16, 1906, MS. Department of State, 1 Instructions, Panama, 142; 1906 For. Rel., pt. II, pp. 1201–1202.

LAW AND GOVERNMENT

§79

One of the most important problems arising out of the transfer of territory from one sovereign to another concerns the effect of such transfer upon political relations and private rights. Various aspects of the problem have been before the courts in recent years. In two cases, one decided in 1906 and the other in 1911, the Supreme Court of the United States discussed the underlying general principles in the following terms:

> By the general rule of public law, recognized by the United States, whenever political jurisdiction and legislative power over territory are transferred from one nation to another, the laws of the country transferred, intended for the protection of private rights, continue in force until abrogated or changed by the new government. Of course, in case of cession to the United States, laws of the ceded country inconsistent with the Constitution and laws of the United States, so far as applicable, would cease to be of obligatory force; but otherwise the municipal laws of the acquired country continue.

> *Ortega* v. *Lara*, 202 U.S. (1906) 339, 342.

> That there is a total abrogation of the former political relations of the inhabitants of the ceded region is obvious. That all laws theretofore in force which are in conflict with the political character, constitution or institutions of the substituted sovereign lose their force, is also plain. *Alvarez* v. *United States*, 216 U.S. 167. But it is equally settled in the same public law that that great body of municipal law which regulates private and domestic rights continues in force until abrogated or changed by the new ruler.

> *Vilas* v. *City of Manila*, 220 U.S. (1911) 345, 357.

On January 30, 1907 Attorney General Charles J. Bonaparte advised the Secretary of War that laws governing a territory (the Canal Zone) which has passed from one power to another continue in force thereafter only by the consent of the succeeding authority, implied from its failure to modify or repeal them.

> 26 Op. Att. Gen. (1906–8) 113, 118–119.

> . . . In the present case, in particular, the transfer of the left half of the Rhine, embracing mainly plaintiff's water right, from the canton of Zurich to the canton of Schaffhausen, by virtue of the decision by the Federal Court of November 9, 1897, . . . is to be looked upon as if the transfer has been effected by virtue of some constitutive act particularly by virtue of a voluntary cession . . . *i.e.*, as a transfer from the legal sovereignty of Zurich to that of Schaffhausen. Consequently, the transfer is governed by the ordinary principles applicable to the international succession of states . . . According to these principles the law of the state assuming sovereignty simply takes the place of that of its predecessor with respect to the territory affected by such change of sovereignty, and in such a way that the public law of the former is applicable immediately to all relations, while existing private rights, on the other hand, so far as they are not inconsistent with the new public law, are not affected by the new private law in their nature and substance but are

subject only to its rules concerning the alteration and loss of private rights . . .

Decision of the Swiss Federal Court, *In re: Pottery Works of Ziegler Bros., Canton of Schaffhausen,* Oct. 5, 1905 (translation), 1 A.J.I.L. (1907) 237, 242.

. . . The law in force at the time of the death of the testator Williams, in 1879, which, on the marriage of the parents, legitimated children born out of lawful wedlock was passed on May 24, 1866 by the legislative assembly of the Hawaiian Islands, . . . and reads as follows:

"All children born out of wedlock are hereby declared legitimate on the marriage of the parents with each other, and are entitled to the same rights as those born in wedlock."

In the year 1880, in *Kekula* v. *Pioeiwa,* 4 Hawaii, 292, the proper interpretation of the act of 1866 was directly involved. . . . The right of the plaintiff to recover depended upon the fact of his constructive legitimacy. It was held, however, that the act of 1866 did not apply to the case of an adulterous intercourse, and that the offspring of such intercourse could not inherit from the father. While it was observed in the opinion that to enforce a contrary doctrine would be opposed to good morals, it is plain that the conclusion reached was that the statute was adopted by the legislative department of the Hawaiian government with the intention that it should have the restrictive effect given to it by the court. In other words, it was decided that the statute should not be broadly construed, as was claimed on behalf of the plaintiff. The statute was not afterwards modified, the decision in the *Kekula case* has never been disapproved or doubted by the court which rendered it, it has undoubtedly become a rule of property, and was followed in the instant case. On the coming of the Hawaiian Islands under the sovereignty of the United States this statute was in force, with the construction given to it by the highest court of the country, and its continued enforcement was in effect ordained by the organic act, which, in §6, provided, "That the laws of Hawaii, not inconsistent with the Constitution or laws of the United States or the provisions of this act, shall continue in force, subject to repeal or amendment by the legislature of Hawaii or the Congress of the United States".

. . . The case at bar, however, more cogently calls upon us not to disregard the construction given to the statute by the highest court of Hawaii. Here the law in question was passed while Hawaii was an independent government, and its meaning was declared by the court of last resort of that government, and, as we have said, that law as thus construed was given recognition by the organic act. The subject with which the law deals, the rights which may have come into existence during the more than forty years in which the statute has been in force, admonish us that we may not overthrow the meaning given by the court of last resort of Hawaii, and which has prevailed for so many years.

Indeed, as the construction affixed to the statute many years before the islands were acquired was final, in effect that construction had entered into the statute at the time of acquisition and must by us be considered as if written in the law.

Kealoha v. *Castle*, 210 U.S. (1908) 149, 152–154.

Obligations of municipal corporation

The fundamental question is whether, notwithstanding the cession of the Philippine Islands to the United States, followed by a reincorporation of the city, the present municipality of Manila is liable for the obligations of the city incurred prior to the cession to the United States.

. . . . They [municipal corporations] exercise powers which are governmental and powers which are of a private or business character. In the one character a municipal corporation is a governmental sub-division, and for that purpose exercises by delegation a part of the sovereignty of the State. In the other character it is a mere legal entity or juristic person. In the latter character it stands for the community in the administration of local affairs wholly beyond the sphere of the public purposes for which its governmental powers are conferred.

In view of the dual character of municipal corporations there is no public reason for presuming their total dissolution as a mere consequence of military occupation or territorial cession. The suspension of such governmental functions as are obviously incompatible with the new political relations thus brought about may be presumed. But no such implication may be reasonably indulged beyond that result.

Such a conclusion is in harmony with the settled principles of public law as declared by this and other courts and expounded by the text books upon the laws of war and international law. Taylor[,] International Public Law, §578.

That the United States might, by virtue of its situation under a treaty ceding full title, have utterly extinguished every municipality which it found in existence in the Philippine Islands may be conceded. That it did so in view of the practice of nations to the contrary is not to be presumed and can only be established by cogent evidence.

The conclusion we reach that the legal entity survived both the military occupation and the cession which followed finds support in the cases which hold that the Pueblos of San Francisco and Los Angeles, which existed as municipal organizations prior to the cession of California by Mexico, continued to exist with their community and property rights intact. *Cohas* v. *Raisin*, 3 California, 443; *Hart* v. *Burnett*, 15 California, 530; *Townsend* v. *Greeley*, 5 Wall. 326; *Merryman* v. *Bourne*, 9 Wall. 592, 602; *More* v. *Steinbach*, 127 U.S. 70; *Los Angeles Milling Co.* v. *Los Angeles*, 217 U.S. 217.

Vilas v. *City of Manila*, 220 U.S. (1911) 345, 352, 356–358, 360. The Court held that, even if there was no adequate remedy for the collection of a claim against the municipality of Manila when reduced to judgment, a plaintiff having a valid claim against the municipality was entitled to maintain an action thereon to reduce it to a judgment.

We have now to inquire whether that part of the Sixth Amendment to the Constitution, which requires that, in all criminal prosecutions, the accused shall enjoy the right to a speedy and public trial, by an impartial jury of the State and district wherein the crime shall have been committed, which district shall have been previously ascertained by law, applies to Porto Rico. . . . It is well settled that these provisions for jury trial in criminal and civil cases apply to the Territories of the United States. . . . But it is just as clearly settled that they do not apply to territory belonging to the United States which has not been incorporated into the Union. . . . It was further settled in *Downes* v. *Bidwell*, 182 U.S. 244, and confirmed by *Dorr* v. *United States*, 195 U.S. 138, that neither the Philippines nor Porto Rico was territory which had been incorporated in the Union or become a part of the United States, as distinguished from merely belonging to it; and that the acts giving temporary governments to the Philippines, 32 Stat. 691, and to Porto Rico, 31 Stat. 77, had no such effect. The *Insular Cases* revealed much diversity of opinion in this court as to the constitutional status of the territory acquired by the Treaty of Paris ending the Spanish War, but the *Dorr Case* shows that the opinion of Mr. Justice White of the majority, in *Downes* v. *Bidwell*, has become the settled law of the court. The conclusion of this court in the *Dorr Case*, p. 149, was as follows:

> "We conclude that the power to govern territory, implied in the right to acquire it, and given to Congress in the Constitution in Article IV, §3, to whatever other limitations it may be subject, the extent of which must be decided as questions arise, does not require that body to enact for ceded territory, not made a part of the United States by Congressional action, a system of laws which shall include the right of trial by jury, and that the Constitution does not, without legislation and of its own force, carry such right to territory so situated."

The Court further held that Congress had not, subsequent to the Foraker act of April 12, 1900 (31 Stat. 77), enacted legislation which had the effect of incorporating Puerto Rico into the Union. After considering the Organic Act for Puerto Rico of March 2, 1917 (39 Stat. 951), popularly known as the Jones act, the Court stated in part:

> In Porto Rico, however, the Porto Rican can not insist upon the right of trial by jury, except as his own representatives in his legislature shall confer it on him. The citizen of the United States living in Porto Rico can not there enjoy a right of trial by jury under the Federal Constitution, any more than the Porto Rican. It is locality that is determinative of the application of the Constitution, in such matters as judicial procedure, and not the status of the people who live in it.

[margin note:] Unincorporated territory: constitutional guaranties, trial by jury

It is true that, in the absence of other and countervailing evidence, a law of Congress or a provision in a treaty acquiring territory, declaring an intention to confer political and civil rights on the inhabitants of the new lands as American citizens, may be properly interpreted to mean an incorporation of it into the Union, as in the case of Louisiana and Alaska. This was one of the chief grounds upon which this court placed its conclusion that Alaska had been incorporated in the Union, in *Rassmussen* v. *United States*, 197 U.S. 516. But Alaska was a very different case from that of Porto Rico. It was an enormous territory, very sparsely settled and offering opportunity for immigration and settlement by American citizens. It was on the American Continent and within easy reach of the then United States. It involved none of the difficulties which incorporation of the Philippines and Porto Rico presents, and one of them is in the very matter of trial by jury.

Balzac v. *People of Porto Rico*, 258 U.S. (1922) 298, 304–305, 309.

"Due process of law"

The main question in the case is whether constitutional guarantees (especially those contained in the Fifth and Sixth Amendments) extend to inhabitants of the Virgin Islands.

.   .   .   .

The law governing judicial proceedings in the Virgin Islands is declared by the Act of Congress of March 3, 1917 (39 Stat. c. 171), locally known as "the Organic Act." By this Act it is provided:

"That until Congress shall otherwise provide, *in so far as compatible with the changed sovereignty* . . . the . . . local laws, in force and effect in said Islands on the Seventeenth day of January, Nineteen Hundred and Seventeen, shall remain in force and effect in said Islands, and the same shall be administered . . . through the local judicial tribunals established in said Islands, respectively . . ." (section 3924 1/4b).

.   .   .   .

As the treaty of cession between Denmark and the United States did not bring the Virgin Islands into the United States as incorporated territory and as Congress has since the treaty done nothing to incorporate them into the United States, they must be regarded as unincorporated territory, entitled only to the protection of such laws of the United States as are applicable to possessions of that status.

The only laws of the United States applicable to the Virgin Islands are the Act of Congress of March 3, 1917, and the fundamental law of the Constitution guaranteeing certain rights to all within its protection. . . . But in the Insular Cases . . . where the Supreme Court reviewed nearly the whole range of sovereignty of the United States over its possessions, defining what laws, statutory and constitutional, are not applicable to unincorporated territories until Congress shall extend them, it is made very certain that there are constitutional rights of a natural or personal nature of which Congress can not, in legislating for such outlying territories, deprive their inhabitants. In these cases the Supreme Court clearly expressed the opinion, not on the point of the decisions, to be sure, but as a logical corrollary, that even if the people of such territories—not being possessed of the political rights of citizens—are regarded as aliens, they are entitled in the spirit of the Constitution to be protected in life, liberty and property and not to be deprived thereof without due process of law.

It was, we think, these natural or personal rights, vouchsafed by the Constitution to everyone within its operation, that Congress had in mind when by the Act of March 3, 1917, it provided for retention in the Virgin Islands of local laws and local procedure "in so far as compatible with the changed sovereignty." The Congress evidently intended that a man in the Virgin Islands might be, and, indeed, should be tried for his life under local laws of Danish origin, yet only when those laws are not incompatible with principles brought to the Islands by the change of sovereignty, the cardinal one being that of due process of law.

.   .   .   .

The proceedings below, if they had been conducted solely under Danish law, might have conformed to due process of law in that they followed, in due course, legal procedure established under Danish rule. But, while it was declared by The Organic Act that proceedings in the local courts of the Virgin Islands shall be as provided by local Danish laws, Congress wrought a change in those laws by also providing that they remain in force only so far as they are compatible with the changed sovereignty. What the change in sovereignty brought to the Islands was, we think, the right, guaranteed by the new sovereign, of "an accused to be confronted with the witnesses against him" and the right not to be "deprived of life, liberty, or property, without due process of law." The essential element of the latter is the right to be heard.

These are principles which Congress, by the Organic Act, engrafted upon the Danish laws of the Virgin Islands. Without these principles the local laws would not be compatible with the changed sovereignty. Texas & Pacific Ry. Co. v. I.C.C., 162 U.S. 197, 218, 16 Sup. Ct. 666, 40 L. Ed. 940.

Due, perhaps, to the very real difficulty of administering together two different systems of jurisprudence, it appears that these rights were not extended to the defendants in their trial before the District Court of St. Thomas and St. John, Virgin Islands of the United States. At the trial the defendants were not confronted with the witnesses against them and they were not heard in their defense in that they were not given an opportunity to speak through the cross-examination of witnesses.

Soto et al v. *United States*, 273 Fed. 628, 629, 632–635 (C.C.A. 3d., 1921).

In 1899 the United States Congress passed an act setting aside certain lands in the State of Washington as a national park (16 U.S.C. §91). In 1901 the legislature of the State of Washington passed an act ceding exclusive jurisdiction over this territory to the United States, the jurisdiction not to vest until the United States

Workmen's compensation law

should have notified the Governor of the assumption of jurisdiction over the park. In 1911 the Workmen's Compensation Act of the State of Washington was enacted and went into effect. Five years thereafter, in 1916, Congress passed an act assuming exclusive jurisdiction over Mount Rainier National Park (16 U.S.C. §95). On July 16, 1916 the Secretary of the Interior notified the Governor that the Federal Government had accepted jurisdiction over the park. In 1931 a construction firm entered into a contract with the United States to perform certain highway work in the park, and the Department of Labor and Industries of the State of Washington levied and assessed industrial insurance and medical-aid premiums against the contractor under the state Workmen's Compensation Act. The contractor applied for a writ of prohibition to prevent the collection of these premiums. In denying the writ, the Supreme Court of Washington, after discussing the case of *Rock Island & Pacific Railway Co.* v. *McGlinn* (114 U.S. (1885) 542), stated that—

> the workmen's compensation act having been in force within the territorial boundaries of Rainier National Park at the time jurisdiction thereof was ceded to the United States, the act remained in force until Congress passed an act which superseded it. Up to the present time no act of Congress has been passed which is in any respect inconsistent with the operation of the workmen's compensation act over the park.
>
> *State ex rel. Grays Harbor Construction Co.* v. *Department of Labor and industries,* 167 Wash. (1932) 507, 514, 10 Pac. (2d) 213, 215–216.

The United States Court of Claims made the following statement regarding the effect of the cession of the Philippine Islands upon the laws concerning incorporation in a case decided in 1904:

Law of incorporation

> A more serious question is presented in considering the competency of the local authorities to create the plaintiff a corporation. If that authority did not exist, then plaintiff acquired no legal existence and has none now.
>
> The company was organized under the Spanish law claimed by plaintiff to be in force in the Philippine Islands after the treaty of Paris. Articles incorporating plaintiff were executed in January, 1900, and were duly recorded in the Mercantile Registry of Manila soon thereafter. The treaty which ceded the islands to the United States was signed December 10, 1898, and ratified the following April. During this time Manila was under the military control of the United States, and the municipal law of the place was administered and enforced by the military government, except as modified by the military authorities. When the treaty ceding the islands was ratified the sovereignty of the United States became absolute. Translations of the laws then in force in the ceded territory were published and issued by authority of the Secretary of War. This included the civil code and the code of commerce, which regulated rights of property and prescribed

rules for commercial transactions and embraced the rules under which commercial associations are formed and regulated. The translation recited that the code of commerce was in force. (Division of Customs and Insular Affairs, October, 1899.) Some changes were subsequently made (laws of Philippine Commission, 1901), as, for example, the repeal of a chapter of the code (p. 132), but no changes affecting the methods of incorporating companies had been made at the time of the incorporation of this association.

The general rule of international law in regard to all conquered or ceded territory is that the old laws continue until repealed by the proper authorities. (Woolsey's Int. Law, sec. 161.)

Special privileges, grants, or franchises flowing from the grace and pleasure of the sovereign in favor of some one particular person or body distinguished from the general body of the inhabitants are the things forbidden. It needs no reference to international law to say that any exercise of authority by the ceding sovereignty, after cession, could not have force with reference to such things as grants of land, or the bestowal of special franchises, such as the construction of roads, the keeping of ferries, and the erection of bridges with the right to collect toll upon them. These are grants by the authority of the State as particular privileges which look to the promotion and protection of the public good. But the municipal laws promulgated during the time the ceding authority existed and which are generally recognized as necessary to the peace and good order of the community remained in full force and effect. Any other rule would hold in abeyance civil functions with respect to the use, enjoyment, and transfer of private property that would lead to results harmful to the inhabitants of the ceded territory and injurious to the best interests and authority of the new sovereign as well. This is something that has not been tolerated in modern times.

Even if a state of insurrection had existed at the place of incorporation the validity of certain judicial acts (which would include the incorporation of this association under the municipal law) would be valid. The force of acts not hostile in their purpose or method of enforcement to the authority of the National Government and not impairing the rights of citizens appears in *Horn* v. *Lockhart* (17 Wall., 580). The line between valid acts such as those governing the course of descents and regulating the conveyance and transfer of property, and invalid acts proceeding from an unlawful government against the authority of the rightful sovereign, was clearly drawn in *Home Ins. Co.* v. *United States* (8 C. Cls. R., 449), which was affirmed by the Supreme Court in an opinion by Mr. Justice Strong, published in 10 C. Cls. R., 145. The analogy of these cases to that at bar is close enough to establish with greater reason the rule that the internal concerns of the new inhabitants were not paralyzed by the transition from one government to another, nor suspended until the authority taking over the ceded territory ordained something to take the place of the established local law. This accords with the enlightened practice of civilized nations to recognize existing laws to the extent that the military and civil authority of the conquering nation shall not operate to disorganize society or discontinue civil government with respect to the purely domestic affairs of the people of new acquisitions.

The Philippine Sugar Estates Development Company (Limited) v. *The United States,* 39 Ct. Cls. (1904) 225, 244–247, 249.

Libel of public authorities in Philippines

The important question is here squarely presented of whether article 256 of the Spanish Penal Code, punishing "Any person who, by . . . writing, shall defame, abuse, or insult any Minister of the Crown or other person in authority . . . ," is still in force.

.   .   .   .

Appellant's main proposition in the lower court and again energetically pressed in the appellate court was that article 256 of the Spanish Penal Code is not now in force because abrogated by the change from Spanish to American sovereignty over the Philippines and because inconsistent with democratic principles of government. This view was indirectly favored by the trial judge, and, as before stated, is the opinion of three members of this court.

.   .   .   .

It cannot admit of doubt that all those provisions of the Spanish Penal Code having to do with such subjects as treason, *lése majesté*, religion and worship, rebellion, sedition, and contempts of ministers of the crown, are no longer in force. Our present task, therefore, is a determination of whether article 256 has met the same fate, or, more specifically stated, whether it is in the nature of a municipal law or a political law, and is consistent with the Constitution and laws of the United States and the characteristics and institutions of the American Government.

It is a general principle of the public law that on acquisition of territory the previous political relations of the ceded region are totally abrogated. "Political" is here used to denominate the laws regulating the relations sustained by the inhabitants to the sovereign. (American Insurance Co. *vs.* Canter [1828], 1 Pet., 511; Chicago, Rock Island and Pacific Railway Co. *vs.* McGlinn [1885], 114 U.S., 542; Roa *vs.* Collector of Customs [1912], 23 Phil., 315.)

.   .   .   .

Therefore, it has come with somewhat of a shock to hear the statement made that the happiness, peace, and prosperity of the people of the Philippine Islands and their customs, habits, and prejudices, to follow the language of President McKinley, demand obeisance to authority, and royal protection for that authority.

According to our view, article 256 of the Spanish Penal Code was enacted by the Government of Spain to protect Spanish officials who were the representatives of the King. With the change of sovereignty, a new government, and a new theory of government, was set up in the Philippines. . . .

. . . In the early days of the American Republic, a sedition law was enacted, making it an offense to libel the Government, the Congress, or the President of the United States, but the law met with so much popular disapproval, that it was soon repealed. "*In this country no distinction as to persons is recognized*, and in practice a person holding a high office is regarded as a target at whom any person may let fly his poisonous words. High official position, instead of affording immunity from slanderous and libelous charges, seems rather to be regarded as making his character free plunder for any one who desires to create a sensation by attacking it." (Newell, Slander and Libel, 3d ed., p. 245; Sillars *vs.* Collier [1890], 151 Mass., 50; 6 L.R.A., 680.)

Article 256 of the Penal Code is contrary to the genius and fundamental principles of the American character and system of government.

. . . .

The crime of *lése majesté* disappeared in the Philippines with the ratification of the Treaty of Paris. Ministers of the Crown have no place under the American flag.

To summarize, the result is, that all the members of the court are of the opinion, although for different reasons, that the judgment should be reversed and the defendant and appellant acquitted, with costs *de officio*. So ordered.

People v. *Perfecto,* 43 Phil. (1922) 887, 889, 895–902.

This brings up the interesting question whether the common law as to franchises applies in Porto Rico. There is no question that Porto Rico is a civil-law community, having not only inherited the civil law of Spain, but in so many words re-adopted it in the revision of March 1, 1902, and the Organic Acts both of 1900 and 1917 provide, the latter in §57: "That the laws and ordinances of Porto Rico now in force shall continue in force and effect." There is a well-marked distinction in all systems between public and private law, but the Spanish Civil Code, in force in Porto Rico, has not limited itself to private law.

Law of franchises

. . . .

The question at issue in the case at bar is not as to the ownership of the land of the Carretera or public highway, but as to the right of user of that Carretera by individual citizens. . . . There can be no doubt that, although private rights and civil law were retained in Porto Rico by the will of the American government when it succeeded to the sovereignty formerly held by Spain, political rights of all kinds were thenceforward to be the same in Porto Rico as on the mainland of the United States. That is to say, that all political principals [*sic*] for the future were changed from Spanish or civil law and became American or common law. It is only this class of rights which is at issue in the case at bar, and as to them whatever is law on the mainland is to be held law in Porto Rico except as changed by statute. Whatever rights exist as to the use of public places in Porto Rico are to be decided according to the principles of the freer common law prevailing in the United States. The Civil Code of Porto Rico and all rights derived therefrom are fully in force, but they are not affected by the issue now presented.

Porto Rico Railway, Light & Power Company v. *Felipe Amador et al.*, 11 P.R. Fed. 170, 174–176 (D.C. Porto Rico, 1919).

Doctrine of respondeat superior

In holding that the rule of liability of master for servant, familiar to the common law, could be followed in the case of a personal-injury claim arising in the Canal Zone in 1916, where the Supreme Court of the Zone had looked to the common law in the construction of Colombian statutes prior to the act of Congress of 1912 ratifying the order of the President of the United States continuing in force the Civil Code of the Republic of Panama in the Canal Zone, Justice Holmes, speaking for the Supreme Court, said:

By the Act of Congress of April 28, 1904, c. 1758, §2, 33 Stat. 429, temporary powers of government over the Canal Zone were vested in such persons and were to be exercised in such manner as the President should direct. An executive order of the President addressed to the Secretary of War on May 9, 1904, directed that the power of the Isthmian Commission should be exercised under the Secretary's direction. The order contained this passage, "The laws of the land, with which the inhabitants are familiar, and which were in force on February 26, 1904, will continue in force in the canal zone . . . until altered or annulled by the said commission;" with power to the Commission to legislate, subject to approval by the Secretary. This was construed to keep in force the Civil Code of the Republic of Panama, which was translated into English and published by the Isthmian Canal Commission in 1905. By the Act of Congress of August 24, 1912, c. 390, §2, 37 Stat. 560, 561, "All laws, orders, regulations, and ordinances adopted and promulgated in the Canal Zone by order of the President for the government and sanitation of the Canal Zone and the construction of the Panama Canal are hereby ratified and confirmed as valid and binding until Congress shall otherwise provide." On these facts it is argued that the defendant's liability is governed by the Civil Code alone as it would be construed in countries where the civil law prevails and that so construed the code does not sanction the application of the rule *respondeat superior* to the present case.

. . . If it be true that the Civil Code would have been construed to exclude the defendant's liability in the present case if the Zone had remained within the jurisdiction of Colombia it does not follow that the liability is no greater as things stand now. The President's order continuing the law then in force was merely the embodiment of the rule that a change of sovereignty does not put an end to existing private law, and the

ratification of that order by the Act of August 24, 1912, no more
fastened upon the Zone a specific interpretation of the former
Civil Code than does a statute adopting the common law fasten
upon a territory a specific doctrine of the English Courts.

Panama Railroad Company v. *Bosse*, 249 U.S. (1919) 41, 43–45.

. . . Guayuco Banco was cut from Mexico into the United
States during the year 1926 by a change in the course of the *Bancos*
boundary river, Rio Grande, under the provisions of the Treaty
signed March 20, 1905, and proclaimed June 5, 1907, between
Mexico and the United States, 35 Stat. 1863 [1 Treaties, etc.
(Malloy, 1910) 1199].

.   .   .   .

. . . It is true that where a large territory with its inhabitants
is transferred by conquest or by treaty to a new sovereignty that
the municipal law of the old sovereignty remains with it until
altered by the new, as "the law of the land." The courts afterwards sitting in such territory continue judicially to recognize
and apply that law as a part of the law of the forum. Fremont
v. United States, 17 How. 542, at page 556, 15 L. Ed. 241; United
States v. Perot, 98 U.S. 428, 25 L. Ed. 251; United States v.
Chaves, 159 U.S. 452, 16 S. Ct. 57, 40 L. Ed. 215. But we think
the principle has no application to the transfer by the movement
of a river of a few acres of land from one sovereignty to another.
The law of Mexico up to the date of such transfer does not
thereby become a part of the lex fori. It remains foreign law
to be proven as a fact when written by production of copies of
the Constitution and statutes, and in other respects by the testimony of experts.

The Court held that the expropriation of the land by the State of
Chihuahua under the Mexican Constitution and laws before the
transfer to the United States must be treated as valid by the courts,
redress, if any, being a matter for diplomatic settlement.

Shapleigh et al. v. *Mier*, 83 F. (2d) 673, 674, 676 (C.C.A. 5th, 1936).
Affirmed, 299 U.S. (1937) 468.

PUBLIC DEBTS AND OBLIGATIONS

§80

The matters connected with the distribution of public obligations in the case of the division of a state into distinct states, or
the cession of a portion of one state to another have engaged the
attention of numerous writers without having led to any definite
conclusion except that no universal rule of international law on
the subject can be said to exist. As a general rule, however, it
may be said that the state, through all changing forms of government, is responsible for the debts of its titular government
and even of general *de facto* governments. Public debts are not

extinguished by the division of a state into distinct states, whether by war or by mutual consent. According to the weight of authority among international law writers, however, there appears to be no legal obligation on the part of a seceding province or on the part of a country taking over a certain portion of territory from another country to assume some share of the national debt *when the identity of the parent state is maintained.* They recognize, however, a moral obligation to assume a proportionate share of the general debt of the parent government which has been incurred for the benefit of the entire country. Many of the continental writers supported by the evidence of numerous treaties, erect the moral obligation into a legal one, whereas the Anglo-American publicists—possibly influenced by the fact that their countries have been annexing and conquering countries— and in turn supported by various treaties, such as the treaties following the Franco-Prussian War of 1871 and the Spanish-American War of 1898, and the treaties of cession of Louisiana, Florida, New Mexico and California, assert vigorously the merely moral character of the obligation. Moreover, no uniform rule for the apportionment of the debt has ever been agreed upon, a further evidence of the non-legal character of the obligation. In the case of a debt raised for the purposes of the ceded territory or charged upon its local revenues, it is held by the majority of writers, who cite numerous treaties in support, that the obligation passes with the land to its new owners. While reason and authority favor this rule, it is not altogether certain that the annexing state contracts a legal obligation to pay the debts secured upon local revenues, and it is fair to conclude that it is not bound to pay war debts contracted by the conquered state or province for the very purpose of resisting conquest and annexation. Nor is a new independent state split off from a parent state legally obliged to assume any share of the debts of the parent state, although some of them may have been incurred in its special behalf. Thus, the American colonies in 1783 assumed no part of the general debt of Great Britain; on the other hand, the Spanish-American colonies practically all undertook to pay a portion of the debt of Spain.

According to strict principles of international law, the parent state which has lost a province by conquest or cession, remains liable for all but local debts of the transferred province contracted for local purposes. On equitable grounds, a reduction of the debt has, at times, been allowed by creditor governments, especially when the debt was incurred through the separated province. Where the identity of the parent state is destroyed, the conquering or annexing power or the new state becomes heir to the debts of the destroyed country. The ceded or seceding territory, however, is liable for local debts, although, as observed, there is much difficulty in establishing what is a local debt. It has been noted that a general debt, even when made a lien upon local revenues, is not a local debt and an obligation *in rem.* A local debt is one incurred only for strictly local purposes, and is the only one which carries to the annexing state or new state created, a legal obligation to pay. It is important in all cases to establish whether the debt has been contracted for local or for national purposes.

Borchard, *Diplomatic Protection of Citizens Abroad* (1915) 202–205.

The Commonwealth of Virginia brought a suit in the Supreme Court of the United States to have the share of the State of West Virginia in the public debt of Virginia, as it stood in 1861, ascertained and satisfied. The Court held that the ordinance of Wheeling, the constitution of West Virginia, and the act of Congress admitting West Virginia into the Union (12 Stat. 633) established a contractual obligation on the part of West Virginia to pay her share of the debt existing at the time of separation. Secession; *Virginia* v. *West Virginia*

The bill alleged the existence of a debt contracted between 1820 and 1861 in connection with internal improvements intended to develop the whole State. For West Virginia, it was argued that the debt had been incurred for local improvements and therefore should be divided according to the territory in which the money was expended. In dealing with this latter argument, the Court stated:

> . . . We see no sufficient reason for the application of such a principle to this case. In form the aid was an investment. It generally took the shape of a subscription for stock in a corporation. To make the investment a safe one the precaution was taken to require as a condition precedent that two or three-fifths of the stock should have been subscribed for by solvent persons fully able to pay, and that one-fourth of the subscriptions should have been paid up into the hands of the treasurer. From this point of view the venture was on behalf of the whole State. The parties interested in the investment were the same, wherever the sphere of corporate action might be. The whole State would have got the gain and the whole State must bear the loss, as it does not appear that there are any stocks of value on hand. If we should attempt to look farther, many of the corporations concerned were engaged in improvements that had West Virginia for their objective point, and we should be lost in futile detail if we should try to unravel in each instance the ultimate scope of the scheme. It would be unjust, however, to stop with the place where the first steps were taken and not to consider the purpose with which the enterprise was begun. All the expenditures had the ultimate good of the whole State in view. Therefore we adhere to our conclusion that West Virginia's share of the debt must be ascertained in a different way.

The Court decided that the "nearest approach to justice" that it could make was to adopt, as the basis of apportionment of the debt, a ratio determined by the estimated valuation of the real and personal property of the two States on the date of the separation, June 20, 1863. It rejected a ratio determined by population or land area, pointing out that "the relative resources of the debtor populations

are generally recognized . . . as affording a proper measure".
Slaves were excluded from the valuation.

Virginia v. *West Virginia*, 220 U.S. (1911) 1, 29–30, 34–35.

Conquest
of South
Africa

In the case of *West Rand Central Gold Mining Company, Limited*
v. *The King* the suppliants, by a petition of right, sought to recover
the value of two parcels of gold seized by officials of the South
African Republic before the commencement of hostilities with the
British in October 1899. It was alleged that, under the laws of the
Republic, the Government thereof had been under a liability to
return the gold or its value and that, not having done so, this obligation devolved upon the British Government as a result of the
conquest, annexation (in 1900), and succession to the sovereignty of
the Transvaal Republic. The Attorney General, on behalf of the
Crown, demurred to the petition. The demurrer was allowed, and
judgment was given for the Crown. Judgment was read by Lord
Alverstone, C. J., who first pointed out that the petition appeared
to be demurrable because it failed to show a contractual obligation
on the part of the Transvaal Government. The court then answered in the negative the question whether "all the contractual
obligations of a State annexed by Great Britain upon conquest are
imposed as a matter of course, and in default of express reservations, upon Great Britain, and can be enforced by British Municipal
law against the Crown".

> [1905] 2 K.B. 391, 400. For the discussion by the court of the writings
> of jurists whose views had been advanced to support the suppliants' con-
> tention, see *ibid.* 403–406.

> . . . A British Proclamation of June 6, 1900 [Cd. 426, p. 9],
> in which the British Government refused to recognize the validity
> of certain war debts of the South African Republic, appears to
> have been the first official document to indicate the negative policy
> which Great Britain was about to pursue with regard to the
> financial liabilities of the conquered state [the South African
> Republic]. . . .
> . . . On September 8, the British Government announced that
> all concessions would be considered on their merits. . . .
> During the years 1900–03, the German government repeatedly
> took diplomatic steps for the protection of German share- and
> bond-holders of the Netherlands South African Railway Com-
> pany. Protracted negotiations with the British Foreign and
> Colonial Offices finally resulted in a settlement. As to the legal
> views of the British Government, acknowledging no obligation
> to compensate the German holders of shares and bonds, but com-
> pensating them only *ex gratia*, the German government did not
> subscribe to them, but resorted neither to protest nor to the invoca-
> tion of an arbitration court to emphasize its dissent.

Negotiations between the Dutch and British governments first took place shortly after the outbreak of the war, and continued until 1908. Holland suggested arbitration, but Great Britain apparently did not accept it. In 1908, the Dutch Parliament was informed that the British Government was willing to settle the question amicably. Although the British Government did not change its official attitude on the legal questions involved, it finally agreed to satisfy practically all claims of the share and debenture holders.

(4) With regard to loans which had been floated by the annexed state, Great Britain, while also declining legal responsibility, actually agreed to satisfy the creditors as a matter of grace [citing Keith, *Theory of State Succession, with Special Reference to English and Colonial Law* (1907) 64–65] and when in 1909 the Union of South Africa was formed, the new Union assumed the debts of the Colonies.

Feilchenfeld, *Public Debts and State Succession* (1931) 380–381, 383–384.

Phillipson states that "In 1902 all the debts of the late South African Republic and Orange Free State were taken over, including a deficit amounting to about £1,500,000." *Termination of War and Treaties of Peace* (1916) 42.

. . . The national debt of Korea [annexed by Japan in 1910] (taken over by the Treasury of the Imperial Government) at the **Korea** end of May, 1910, was estimated to amount to 36,146,543 yen (3,702,401*l*.)

Statesman's Year-Book (1911) 996.

The declaration of the independence of the Czechoslovak nation, adopted by the Provisional Government at Paris on October 18, 1918, **Czecho-** stated: **slovakia**

Our nation will assume its part of the Austro-Hungarian pre-war public debt; the debts for this war we leave to those who incurred them.

2 *Official U.S. Bulletin*, no. 441, Oct. 19, 1918, p. 3.

On April 6, 1938, upon instruction of the Secretary of State, the Ambassador in Germany delivered a note to the German Minister of Foreign Affairs in which, alluding to the announcement made to the **Austrian** Government of the United States by the Austrian Minister on March **public debt** 17, 1938, he stated that the Government of the United States was "under the necessity for all practical purposes of accepting what he says as a fact" and that, accordingly, consideration was being given to various adjustments necessitated by the change of status of Austria. The note continued:

. . . I have to notify the German Government that the Government of the United States will look to it for the discharge of the relief indebtedness of the Government of Austria to the Government of the United States under the Debt Agreement

110090—40——36

signed May 8, 1930, and the Moratorium Agreement signed September 14, 1932, between the Government of the United States and the Government of Austria.

.   .   .   .   .   .

In addition to the sums owed this Government from the Austrian Government, consideration is required for the various dollar obligations of Austrian borrowers which are in private hands. The Austrian Government itself borrowed in the American market in 1930, the issue being part of the Austrian Government International Loan of 1930 and being secured by a first charge upon the gross receipts of the Austrian Customs and Tobacco Monopoly. . . . Furthermore, substantial amounts of bonds publicly issued in the American market by several Austrian political subdivisions and corporations, payable in dollars, are owned by citizens and residents of the United States.

On these dollar bonds in private hands, the Austrian Government and the other Austrian debtors have been making regular payments pursuant to the terms of the obligations. This Government will expect that these obligations will continue to be fully recognized and that service will be continued by the German authorities which have succeeded in control of the means and machinery of payment in Austria.

Secretary Hull to Ambassador Wilson Apr. 5, 1938 (telegram), MS. Department of State, file 863.51 Relief Credits/362a; Department of State, XVIII *Press Releases*, weekly issue 445, pp. 465–467 (Apr. 6, 1938).

For a further discussion of the Austro-German events of Mar. 1938, see *ante* §66.

On June 9, 1938 the American Ambassador in Berlin delivered the following note also to the German Foreign Office:

In pursuance to instructions received from my Government, I have the honor to bring to your Excellency's attention that according to advices received from the Foreign Bondholders Protective Council, the June 1, 1938, monthly service installment on the Austrian Government international loan of 1930 has not been paid. In this connection I have the honor to refer to my note of April 6 notifying your Excellency that the Government of the United States will look to the German Government for the discharge of the relief indebtedness of the Government of Austria to the Government of the United States and pointing out that the lien of this relief indebtedness upon the assets and revenues of Austria has been subordinated by the United States to the lien of the Austrian international loan of 1930 upon the same assets and revenues.

While no reply to this note has been received, indications were given on the occasion of the presentation of the Embassy's *aide memoire* of May 16 that your Excellency's Government was taking the position that having regard to former precedents of international law and to the principles applied therein it was not under a legal obligation to take over the external debts of the Austrian Federal Government.

The Government of the United States does not wish to omit, on the occasion of the failure of the German Government to make the contractual monthly payment due June 1 on the Austrian Loan of 1930, in spite of the express charge which it enjoys on the assets and revenues of Austria taken over by the German Government, to state its dissent from the indicated position of the German Government as to its legal responsibilities in the premises, and to express the hope that Germany may yet undertake the payments incumbent on it both under international law and under equity.

It is believed that the weight of authority clearly supports the general doctrine of international law founded upon obvious principles of justice that in case of absorption of a state, the substituted sovereignty assumes the debts and obligations of the absorbed state, and takes the burdens with the benefits. A few exceptions to this general proposition have sometimes been asserted, but these exceptions appear to find no application to the circumstances of the instant case. Both the 1930 loan and the relief loans were made in time of peace, for constructive works and the relief of human suffering. There appears no reason why American creditors of Austria should be placed in any worse position by reason of the absorption of Austria by Germany than they would have been in had such absorption not taken place. The United States Government therefore, while recognizing that the German Government is at present engaged in negotiations with numerous governments covering this and related questions, regrets that the service of the loan, affecting many American holders, should have been interrupted, reasserts its own position, and requests that as early reply as possible may be made to the note of April 6, 1938.

Department of State, *XVIII Press Releases*, weekly issue 455, pp. 694–695 (June 17, 1938).

In a note of October 19, 1938 the Ambassador of the United States in Germany reminded the German Foreign Office of its failure to answer his notes of April 6 and June 9 regarding the cessation of service upon Austrian dollar bonds. He pointed out that the German Government was currently making payments on the service of similar Austrian obligations in the hands of British, French, and other nationalities.

The German Foreign Office replied on November 17, 1938, stating that the Embassy had been orally informed (May 16, 1938) that the German Government "was not of the opinion that it was under any legal obligation to assume the foreign debts of the former Austrian Federal Government". On another occasion (July 15, 1938) the view had been expressed in conversation that Germany "supported by historical procedures, took a generally negative stand with regard to the debts of the Austrian Government, since they were brought about in order to support the incompetent Austrian state artificially created by the Paris Treaties". Subsequently (on August 5 following), the Embassy was orally informed that the German Government was awaiting the outcome of negotiations with other creditor countries before replying to the American notes. Negotiations with England and France had at that time been concluded; thereafter a conclusion had been reached with Holland, and negotiations with Switzerland were continuing. In view of these circumstances Germany protested in its note of November 17 that it had not disregarded American rights and interests and stated that it had been seeking a way by which, in spite of its "fundamental rejection of any legal obligation", it could give consideration to the American creditors of certain Austrian Government debts in a manner similar to that arranged for various other creditors. It was explained that Germany had an export surplus from its trade with the other creditor countries involved, from which foreign exchange for the payments could be drawn, and that special provisions could be agreed upon which guaranteed that the trade surplus would always permit the withdrawal of such foreign exchange, whereas this situation did not obtain with respect to German-American trade relations. The German Government further stated that it was continuing investigations to determine if it might not be possible to make some other adjustment in favor of the American creditors.

In replying to this note on November 25, 1938 the American Embassy, with particular reference to the relief indebtedness of the Government of Austria, reaffirmed the position of the United States Government as to the responsibility of the German Government for the payment of the indebtedness of the Government of Austria, and its intention to look to the German Government for payment thereof, and stated:

> . . . This inter-governmental indebtedness, incurred to obtain food for the Austrian people at a time of distress and lack of means or ordinary credit for the most necessary payments, and specifically secured on assets and revenues of Austria, has not disappeared or been annulled by the fact of the taking over of these assets and revenues by the German Government.

Referring to other funded indebtedness of the Austrian Government, the Embassy's note alluded to the offer of the German Minister of Finance, published on October 25, 1938, to indemnify the holders of a list of bonds of the Austrian Government, on which the capital and interest service was suspended after October 2, 1938, by exchanging 4½-percent bonds of the German Government, payable in Reichsmarks, for the Austrian Government bonds at the rate of 262 Reichsmarks par value of the German Government issue for each $100 par value of the bonds of the American *tranche* of the Austrian Government loan of 1930, and stated:

It appears therefore that with respect to bonds of the Austrian Government which are held by citizens or residents of the United States, the German Government while disclaiming legal responsibility is prepared to make *de facto* provision for payment as a charge on the German Government, and that it has caused the suspension of capital and interest payments by the agencies charged therewith prior to October 2, 1938. This confirmation of the position that holders of the bonds of the Austrian Federal Government must look to the German Government for the discharge of these obligations might reduce the question of legal responsibility to an academic question were adequate provision, acceptable to the bondholders, made for the payment of the obligations. Unfortunately, under the foreign exchange laws and practices of the Reich, the Reichsmark securities of the German Government tendered by the offer of October 24, 1938, as the terms of the offer are interpreted by my Government from the published text, could be accepted by residents of the United States only at the cost of a prohibitive sacrifice of the market value and income yield of securities they hold, while the German Government states in its note under acknowledgment that it has not been able to find an adjustment providing for payments in the United States comparable to the provisions made for other foreign holders of Austrian bonds.

Attention was also called to the fact that no specific mention was made in the note under acknowledgment regarding dollar bonds of Austrian political subdivisions and corporations, holders of which, as well as holders of the Austrian Government loan of 1930, had been receiving full interest service in dollars up to the time of the absorption of Austria into the German Reich.

Finally, the hope was expressed that the studies being made by the German Government would produce positive results in the near future so that the American holders of Austrian securities would not remain the only important group of holders of Austrian bonds for which no provision for payment was made.

Department of State, XIX *Press Releases*, weekly issue 479, pp. 375–379 (Nov. 27, 1938).

In a note of January 3, 1939 the German Government stated that, although it felt under no legal obligation to assume the foreign debts of the former Austrian Federal Government, agreements had already been concluded with most of the interested governments for an indemnification of creditors of Austrian loans; that in the agreements "because of their specific nature" Austrian relief debts had not been considered; that there was no intention to discriminate against American creditors; that, however, the "prevailing passivity" of the German trade balance with the United States would have to be taken into consideration and the cooperation of the United States would be necessary in order to provide adjustment of rates of loan service to altered conditions; that, on this basis, the German Government was willing to enter into negotiations with the Government of the United States; and that the offer of indemnity on the part of the German Government, referred to in the previous American note, applied equally to non-foreign and foreign holders of Austrian bonds, and American holders could avail themselves of it.

Replying to the German note on January 20, 1939, the American Chargé d'Affaires in Berlin stated that the Government of the United States could not accept the legal interpretation that the German Government was under no obligation to assume the foreign debts of the Austrian Federal Government, that it perceived no reason why the intergovernmental relief debt should be left out of present consideration, and that the United States was willing to discuss any proposals regarding payment of this debt which the German Government might desire to put forward. With regard to the privately held Austrian foreign bonds, it was pointed out, in the same communication, that the other governments with whom arrangements had been made had been guarantors of some issues of those bonds and therefore under obligations to the holders in case of default; that moreover, these governments had bilateral clearing and payments arrangements with Germany since shortly after the declaration of Germany in 1934 that the payment of German obligations to residents of foreign countries must be related to the balance of trade between Germany and the particular creditor country; and that the United States had continually protested against the principle that the responsibility of a debtor government for its debts can be made to depend on the balance of trade. The American note reiterated certain basic considerations bearing upon the right of American bondholders to receive treatment no less favorable than that extended to other holders of Austrian bonds and stated that, while the Government of the United States would be willing to facilitate any proper adjustment of the service on the bonds in question, it did not perceive in the circumstances of the Austrian bond situation any reason to depart from its established position that such adjustment of indebtedness toward private citizens was a matter for negotiation between debtors and creditors rather than between the government of the debtor country and the Government of the United States.

Department of State, XX *Press Releases*, weekly issue 487, pp. 53–55 (Jan. 25, 1939).

See Garner, "Questions of State Succession Raised by the German Annexation of Austria", in 32 A.J.I.L. (1938) 421–438, and "Germany's Responsibility for Austria's Debts", *ibid.*, 766–775.

The contention that the liability of the city [Manila] upon obligations was destroyed by a mere change of sovereignty is obviously one which is without a shadow of moral force, and, if true, must result from settled principles of rigid law. While the contracts from which the claims in suit resulted were in progress, war between the United States and Spain ensued. On August 13, 1898, the city was occupied by the forces of this Government and its affairs conducted by military authority. On July 31, 1901, the present incorporating act was passed, and the city since that time has been an autonomous municipality.

Property and obligations of municipality

·   ·   ·   ·   ·   ·   ·

Was corporate identity and corporate liability extinguished as a necessary legal result of the new charter granted in 1901 by the Philippine Commission? The inhabitants of the old city are the incorporators of the new. There is substantially identity of area. There are some changes in the form of government and some changes in corporate powers and methods of administration. The new corporation is endowed with all of the property and property rights of the old. It has the same power to sue and be sued which the former corporation had. There is not the slightest suggestion that the new corporation shall not succeed to the contracts and obligations of the old corporation. Laying out of view any question of the constitutional guarantee against impairment of the obligation of contracts, there is, in the absence of express legislative declaration of a contrary purpose, no reason for supposing that the reincorporation of an old municipality is intended to permit an escape from the obligations of the old, to whose property and rights it has succeeded. The juristic identity of the corporation has been in no wise affected, and, in law, the present city is in every legal sense the successor of the old. As such it is entitled to the property and property rights of the predecessor corporation, and is, in law, subject to all of its liabilities.

Vilas v. *City of Manila*, 220 U.S. (1911) 345, 353–354, 360–361.

It is not infrequently provided in treaties regarding the separation of territory from a parent state, either to become a new state or to form a part of or be administered by another state, that the new state or the state acquiring, administering, or controlling the territory shall assume a portion of the public debt of the state from which the territory has been separated.

See, for example, article 10 of the treaty of peace between Italy and Turkey signed on Oct. 18, 1912, VII *Martens', Nouveau recueil général* (3d ser., Triepel, 1913) 10, and 7 A.J.I.L. Supp. (1913) 61–62; articles 254–257 of the Treaty of Versailles signed by the Allied and Associated Powers and Germany, June 28, 1919, 3 Treaties, etc. (Redmond, 1923) 3441–3442; article 21 of the treaty signed by the United States, France, Great Britain, Italy, Japan, and Poland on June 28, 1919, *ibid.* 3723; articles 203–205 of the Treaty of Saint-Germain-en-Laye signed by the Allied and Associated Powers and Austria, Sept. 10, 1919, *ibid.* 3218–3222; articles 186–188 of the Treaty of Trianon signed by the Allied and Associated Powers and Hungary, June 4, 1920, *ibid.* 3608–3613; articles 134 and 135 of the Treaty of Neuilly signed by the Allied and Associated Powers and Bulgaria, Nov. 27, 1919, 112 Br. & For. St. Paps. (1919) 819; articles 18, 46–57 of the Treaty of Lausanne signed by Great Britain, France, Italy, Japan, Greece, Rumania, the Serb-Croat-Slovene State, and Turkey, July 24, 1923, 28 League of Nations Treaty Series (1924)

25, 36–47; article V of the treaty between Great Britain and Ireland, Dec. 6, 1921, 26 League of Nations Treaty Series (1924) 10, and Parliamentary Debates (186 H. C. Deb. 5s.), col. 2656 (Irish Free State released from obligation under art. V of the treaty); article 6 of the convention concerning the territory of Memel (Klaipéda) signed at Paris on May 8, 1924, 29 League of Nations Treaty Series (1924) 89.

PRIVATE RIGHTS

§81

In the transfer of sovereignty from Spain, where the church and state were closely united, to the United States, pursuant to the Treaty of Paris (December 10, 1898), where such union was incompatible with the institutions and laws of the country, many questions arose regarding the ownership of properties held by the Roman Catholic Church as well as regarding other properties held by the government but claimed by the church. Articles II and VIII of the Treaty of Paris provided for the cession of the island of Puerto Rico to the United States, together with all buildings, wharves, barracks, forts, structures, public highways, and other public property which, in conformity with law, belonged to the public domain, and as such belonged to the crown of Spain, it being understood, however, that such cession could not in any respect impair the property or the rights belonging to ecclesiastical or civic bodies. 30 Stat. 1754, 1755–1759; 2 Treaties, etc. (Malloy, 1910) 1690–1693.

Questions as to title to the churches and temples in the peaceful possession of the church at the time of the withdrawal of Spain from the island of Puerto Rico were passed upon in the decision of the Supreme Court of the United States in the case of *Municipality of Ponce* v. *Roman Catholic Apostolic Church in Porto Rico*, wherein it was held, on June 1, 1908, that the ownership of the property remained in the church notwithstanding the fact that municipalities may have furnished some of the funds for building or repairing churches. The Court said:

> . . . The Roman Catholic Church has been recognized as possessing legal personality by the treaty of Paris and its property rights solemnly safeguarded. In so doing the treaty has merely followed the recognized rule of international law which would have protected the property of the church in Porto Rico subsequent to the cession.

210 U.S. (1908) 296, 323–324.

By an act approved Mar. 4, 1909 Congress appropriated $120,000 for payment to the Catholic Church in Puerto Rico in full settlement of all claims of the church to properties then in the hands of the United States, i.e., "the building known as the Santo Domingo Barracks and the land pertaining thereto, and the site of the building formerly known as the

Ballaja Barracks, now known as the Infantry Barracks, both properties in the City of San Juan, Porto Rico", and concerning which a memorandum agreement had been signed on Aug. 12, 1908 by representatives of the church, Puerto Rico, and the United States.

S. Rept. 800, accompanying S. 8601, 60th Cong., 2d sess., serial no. 5380; 35 Stat. 945, 1018.

. . . It is therein [article VIII of the Treaty of Paris of December 10, 1898, 30 Stat. 1754, 1758] expressly provided that the relinquishment or cession "can not in any respect impair the property or rights which by law belong to the peaceful possession of property of all kind[s,] of Provinces, municipalities, public or private establishments, ecclesiastical or civic bodies, or any other associations having legal capacity to acquire and possess property in the aforesaid territories renounced or ceded, or of private individuals, of whatsoever nationality such individuals may be." This is the usual stipulation in treaties and is in effect a declaration of the rights of the inhabitants under international law. (*United States* v. *de la Arredondo*, 6 Pet., 691, 712.)

The Eastern Extension, Australasia and China Telegraph Company v. *The United States*, 46 Ct. Cls. (1911) 646, 648–649.

3. Being a valid judgment [the judgment of a Mexican *alcalde*, dated March 24, 1834, in the case of *Phillips* v. *Tenille*], rendered by a court of competent jurisdiction under the Mexican government, we think it was not affected as a valid obligation by the Revolution and change of government. For in the event of conquest or revolution "the people change their allegiance; their relation to the ancient sovereign is dissolved, but their relations to each other, and their rights of property, remain undisturbed." U.S. v. Percheman, 7 Pet. 51, 8 L. Ed. 604, opinion by Chief Justice Marshall; 15 R.C.L. 115; section 1, Schedule of Constitution of Republic; McMullen v. Hodge, 5 Tex. 34. — *Judgment of former sovereign*

4. It is also true, however, that, while the judgment rendered under the Mexican rule remained a civil obligation under the Texas Republic, it was not of itself enforceable as a judgment under the rule of the succeeding sovereignty and in its courts. It had to be recognized by the new sovereignty. The early lawmakers met this need.

Clements et al. v. *Texas Co. et al.*, 273 S.W. 993, 999 (Tex. Civ. App., 1925).

On February 3, 1923 the Council of the League of Nations adopted a resolution asking the Permanent Court of International Justice for an advisory opinion as to whether the position adopted by the Polish Government in the following respects was in conformity with its international obligations: — *Interests in realty*

(*a*) a number of colonists who were formerly German nationals, and who are now domiciled in Polish territory previously belonging to Germany, have acquired Polish nationality, particularly in virtue of Article 91 of the Treaty of Versailles. They are occupying their holdings under contracts (Rentenguts-verträge) which although concluded with the German Colonization Commission prior to the Armistice of November 11th, 1918, did not receive an "Auflassung" before that date. The Polish Government regards itself as the legitimate owner of these holdings under Article 256 of the Treaty of Versailles, and considers itself entitled to cancel the above contracts. In consequence, the Polish authorities have taken certain measures in regard to these colonists by which the latter will be expelled from the holdings which they occupy;

(*b*) the Polish authorities will not recognize leases conceded before November 11th, 1918, by the German Government to German nationals who have now become Polish subjects. These are leases over German State properties which have subsequently been transferred to the Polish State in virtue of the Treaty of Versailles, in particular of Article 256 . . .

In its advisory opinion, dated September 10, 1923, the Court concluded that Poland's action was not in conformity with law and treaty obligations. In the course of the opinion the Court stated:

It has been shown that under the *Rentengutsverträge* the purchaser has, even before Auflassung, vested rights enforceable as against the vendor. The principal question with which the Court is now confronted is the following: The sovereignty and the ownership of State property having changed, is the settler who had concluded a *Rentengutsvertrag* with the Prussian State entitled to claim from the Polish Government as the new owner the execution of the contract, including the completion of the transfer by *Auflassung?*

Three views have been suggested.

The first is that the contracts are of a "personal" nature and exist only as between the original parties, i.e. the Prussian State and the holder of the lands, so that the obligations of the former cannot be considered as having passed to Poland. The reasons why this hypothesis is not acceptable may be found both in what has been said as to the legal nature of the rights of the holder under the *Rentengutsverträge* and in what is now to be said concerning the effect of a change of sovereignty on private rights.

Equally unacceptable is the second view, that the *Rentenguts-verträge* have automatically fallen to the ground in consequence of the cession of territory. Private rights acquired under existing law do not cease on a change of sovereignty. No one denies that the German Civil Law, both substantive and adjective, has continued without interruption to operate in the territory in question. It can hardly be maintained that, although the law survives, private rights acquired under it have perished. Such a contention is based on no principle and would be contrary to an almost universal opinion and practice.

There remains the third view that private rights are to be respected by the new territorial sovereign.

The general question whether and under what circumstances a State may modify or cancel private rights by its sovereign legislative power, requires no consideration here.

The Court is here dealing with private rights under specific provisions of law and treaty, and it suffices for the purposes of the present opinion to say that even those who contest the existence in international law of a general principle of State succession do not go so far as to maintain that private rights including those acquired from the State as the owner of the property are invalid as against a successor in sovereignty.

By the Minorities Treaty Poland has agreed that all Polish nationals shall enjoy the same civil and political rights and the same treatment and security in law as well as in fact. The action taken by the Polish authorities under the Law of July 14th, 1920, and particularly under Article 5 is undoubtedly a virtual annulment of the rights which the settlers acquired under their contracts and therefore an infraction of the obligation concerning their civil rights. It is contrary to the principle of equality in that it subjects the settlers to a discriminating and injurious treatment to which other citizens holding contracts of sale or lease are not subject.

. . . .

Furthermore, Poland claims that she acquired the property of the German States unburdened, because the Peace Treaty does not in terms require her to fulfil the obligations which those States had contracted with regard to such property. The Court, as has already been seen, is of opinion that no treaty provision is required for the preservation of the rights and obligations now in question. In the opinion of the Court, therefore, no conclusion can be drawn from the silence of the Treaty of Peace contrary to that resulting from the preceding statements. On the other hand, however, the position of the Court as regards the protection of the private rights now in question appears to be supported by the provisions of that Treaty.

. . . .

If as between enemies such contracts are maintained, it seems impossible that the Treaty should have countenanced the annulment of contracts between a State and its newly acquired nationals.

Per. Ct. Int. Jus., Advisory Opinion, Ser. B, No. 6, pp. 6–7, 35–39; I Hudson, *World Court Reports* (1934) 208–209, 226–228.

In the case of *George Rodney Burt*, American-British claims arbitration under the special agreement of August 18, 1910, the United States claimed damages for the deprivation by British authorities of titles to land acquired in the Fiji Islands from native chiefs prior to the annexation of the islands by Great Britain on October 10, 1874. Burt purchased a 3,750-acre tract in 1868, evidenced by three deeds and a certificate executed by the ruling chief of the territory concerned and certain subordinate chiefs or heads of tribes supposed to have an interest in the land. He occupied and developed his tract but was driven out by wild tribesmen. In 1879 he filed a claim to the tract before the Board of Land Commissioners. The claim was disallowed, but he was given a Crown grant *ex gratia* in 1880 of 100 acres of which he took possession. After a rehearing, his claim was entirely disallowed in April 1884, and he was excluded from the 100-acre tract that he had been occupying. In its decision of October 26, 1923 the tribunal awarded the United States £10,000 on account of the Burt claim. In the award the tribunal stated:

> On these facts the precise question before this Tribunal is whether Great Britain, as the succeeding Power in the islands under the Deed of Cession of 1874, failed in any respect to observe and carry out any obligation toward Burt which it may be properly said, from the point of view of international law, to have assumed. If Burt had at the time a valid title to the lands, it is plain that under all the circumstances the Government was bound to recognize and respect it. In this connection we do not concern ourselves with the methods and the procedure adopted and employed in dealing with land titles. We have no criticism to make in this regard; on the contrary we feel that good faith is rightly attributable to the authorities at every stage and that the procedure was the customary and appropriate one for handling a situation of this nature. We look only to the general result which was reached and note that this result was the ultimate denial of Burt's right.
>
> We therefore come to the particular question involved: whether Burt had at the time of the cession such an interest as to entitle him to invoke the obligation of the succeeding Power? His title to Emuri, resting as it did upon a conveyance from the ruling Chiefs of the territory in which the land was situated, naturally depended upon the power of such chiefs to convey. . . . It stands without dispute that the most solemn and consequential act affecting land and sovereignty in the islands was performed on the theory that the Chiefs had the power to act. . . . We can not help feeling that, on the whole case, the Chiefs had the power, and that the distinction between want of power and possible abuse of power goes far towards reconciling the conflicting views.
>
> .   .   .   .   .   .
>
> 8. Passing now to the question of the subsistence of Burt's right up to the date of the cession to Great Britain, we have only to enquire whether a reasonable construction of the evidence shows any abandonment by him of his claim. The inference to our minds is irresistible that if he had not been dispossessed of Emuri by the wrongful, violent act of an uncontrolled and uncontrollable mountain tribe—an event which the Land Commissioners found to have no bearing upon his title—he would have continued in occupation, and it is not an unwarranted assumption to say that if the cession to Great Britain had taken

place in 1869, Burt would have almost automatically received a Crown grant. We fail to find anything in the subsequent events which indicates any intention on his part to abandon; on the contrary he diligently prosecuted his claim so far as the circumstances and his limited resources permitted, and was at no stage of the proceedings in default. He stood upon his rights under the conveyances from the Chiefs, and, on the view which we take, the Crown authorities by refusing to recognize his title, failed to carry out the obligation which Great Britain, as the succeeding Power in the islands, must be held to have assumed.

Nielsen's Report (1926) 588, 595–598.

In the case of *William Webster*, also decided by the American-British claims tribunal established under the special agreement of Aug. 18, 1910, the United States claimed damages on behalf of Webster for the denial of title and loss of possession of lands in New Zealand after the annexation of that country by Great Britain on Feb. 6, 1840. Webster had purchased large tracts of land (allegedly some 500,000 acres) from the native chieftains and tribes between 1836 and 1839. He had been allowed some 42,000 acres by the Lands Commission, appointed to examine the titles derived from the aborigines and to recommend grants in lieu thereof, to which he had submitted his claims in 1841. In its decision of Dec. 12, 1925 the arbitral tribunal rejected the claim, differentiating the facts in this case from those in the *Burt* case. *Ibid.* 540, 542–546.

. . . In determining appellees' rights based upon their purchase from the Mexican government, and as affected by the treaty of Guadalupe Hidalgo, it should be borne in mind that a mere change of sovereignty, even in the absence of treaty stipulations for the protection of private rights, does not divest the vested property rights of individuals.

. . . .

If it be conceded that when one nation has, by force, wrested territory from another, it has the power to destroy private rights in such territory by the confiscation of lands which had been acquired from the former government, still such course of conduct would be so contrary to every sense of justice as that no court should hold that such was the intention of the conquering nation, unless it was clearly and distinctly so declared by the political department of that nation.

State v. *Gallardo et al.*, 135 S.W. 664, 669–670 (Tex. Civ. App., 1911). Affirmed 106 Tex. (1914) 274, 166 S.W. 369.

Two grants of land were made by the Mexican authorities in 1823 and 1825 within territory which subsequently became a part of New Mexico. These grants were overlapping or conflicting to the extent of some 5,000 acres. The act of Congress of July 22, 1854 (§8, 10 Stat. 308, 309) made it the duty of the surveyor general of New Mexico "to ascertain the origin, nature, character, and extent of all claims to lands under the laws, usages, and customs of Spain

Overlapping grants

and Mexico". That officer was required to report to Congress as to the validity or invalidity of the various titles "for such action thereon as may be deemed just and proper, with a view to confirm *bona fide* grants, and give full effect to the treaty of eighteen hundred and forty-eight between the United States and Mexico" (9 Stat. 922; 1 Treaties, etc. [Malloy 1910] 1107). The so-called "Beck grant"—the one prior in point of time—was presented for confirmation to the surveyor general in May 1855, declared valid by him, and so reported to the Secretary of the Interior on September 30, 1856 for confirmation by Congress. The other grant was presented to the surveyor general for confirmation in 1857, decided to be valid, and reported to the Secretary of the Interior for confirmation by Congress on September 15, 1857. Both grants were confirmed by Congress in the act of June 21, 1860. 12 Stat. 71.

The Supreme Court of the Territory of New Mexico decided that both grants were invalid under the Mexican law and took their efficacy solely from the act of Congress and that, therefore, so far as the grants overlapped, each party had an equal undivided interest in the lands within the conflict.

The Supreme Court of the United States reversed the decision of the New Mexico court, holding that the land in question was part of the Beck grant which was prior in time in all of its steps. In the course of its opinion the Court stated:

> . . . The act of Congress was not a gratuity, it was intended to be a discharge of the obligations of the treaty between the United States and Mexico. It was a confirmation of rights which existed, and as they existed.
>
> .   .   .   .
>
> The confirmation . . . cannot be dissociated from what preceded it, and it may be said of such direct confirmation by act of Congress . . . that it constitutes a declaration of the validity of the claim under the Mexican laws and that the claim is entitled to recognition and protection by the stipulations of the treaty. . . . And if there be claims under two patents, each of which reserves the rights of the other parties, the inquiry must extend to the character of the original concession. The controversy can only be settled by determining which of these two gives the better right to the demanded premises.
>
> *Jones, Receiver* v. *St. Louis Land and Cattle Co.*, 232 U.S. (1914) 355, 360, 361.

Article 2 of the convention between the United States and Denmark for the cession of the Danish West Indies reads in part as follows:

> . . . But it is understood that this cession does not in any respect impair private rights which by law belong to the peaceful possession of property of all kinds by private individuals of whatsoever nationality, by municipalities, public or private establish-

ments, ecclesiastical or civic bodies, or any other associations having legal capacity to acquire and possess property in the Islands ceded.

39 Stat. 1706, 1707; 3 Treaties, etc. (Redmond, 1923) 2558, 2559; 1917 For. Rel. 695.

. . . whatever title, rights, and privileges the inhabitants of Texas received by virtue of land grants from the Spanish and Mexican governments, which were a part of the realty itself or were easements or servitudes in connection therewith, remained intact, notwithstanding the change in sovereignty and the subsequent adoption of the common law as a rule of decision.

Ike Miller et al. v. *Henry Letzerich et al.*, 121 Tex. (1932) 248, 254, 49 S.W. (2d) 404, 408.

The land in controversy was once part of the Mexican state *Bancos* of Chihuahua. In 1926 it was cut by avulsion from the south or right bank of the Rio Grande to the north or left bank, and became part of the United States. By the ordinary rule a change of location resulting from avulsion would have left Mexico still sovereign over the territory thus moved, the centre of the old channel remaining as the boundary. *Missouri* v. *Nebraska*, 196 U.S. 23, 35; *Nebraska* v. *Iowa*, 143 U.S. 359, 361, 367, 370. Here a different rule applied by force of a convention, proclaimed June 5, 1907 (35 Stat. 1863), whereby the boundaries were to shift in the event of future changes, with exceptions not now material as to population and area. A Boundary Commission, previously established but confirmed by the Convention, marked the change upon the ground. Sovereignty was thus transferred, but private ownership remained the same. *United States* v. *Chaves*, 159 U.S. 452, 457; *United States* v. *Percheman*, 7 Pet. 51, 86. To find the title to the land today we must know where title stood while the land was yet in Mexico.

Shapleigh et al. v. *Mier*, 299 U.S. (1937) 468, 469–470.

We conclude, therefore, that at the time the territory of Arizona was acquired from Mexico the government of the United States, and its agent, the government of Arizona, had the right to dispose of and regulate the use of all waters of *Water rights* every nature, both surface and subterranean, in the dual capacity as sovereign and as proprietor of the public domain, unhampered by any rules of either the civil or the common law, or by any previous general custom which had theretofore existed, subject only to such vested rights to the use of *specific* waters as had been acquired, either formally from the Mexican government or impliedly as a result of local custom, and to the right of use of all percolating, subterranean waters underlying lands then in private hands by the owners of such lands.

Maricopa County Municipal Water Conservation District Number One et al. v. *Southwest Cotton Company et al.*, 39 Ariz. (1931) 65, 75–76, 4 Pac. (2d) 369, 373.

Abolition of quasi-public office

In refusing to allow recovery of compensation for the abolition of the office of *procurador* which the plaintiff, a subject of Spain, had purchased in Puerto Rico prior to 1898, the Supreme Court of the United States said:

> . . . If, originally, the claimant lawfully purchased, in perpetuity, the office of Solicitor (Procurador) and held it when Porto Rico was acquired by the United States, he acquired and held it subject, necessarily, to the power of the United States to abolish it whenever it conceived that the public interest demanded that to be done. The intention of Congress in relation to the office of Solicitor or Procurador by the Foraker Act cannot be doubted—indeed, its abolition by Congress is made the ground of the present action and claim. Upon the acquisition of Porto Rico that Island was placed under military government, subject, until Congress acted in the premises, to the authority of the President as Commander-in-Chief acting under the Constitution and laws of the United States. Porto Rico was made a Department by order of the President on the eighteenth of October, 1898. By his sanction, it must be presumed, General Order No. 134 was made, abolishing the office of Solicitor or Procurador. That order was recognized by Congress, if such recognition was essential to its validity, when Congress, by the Foraker Act of 1900, provided that the laws and ordinances of Porto Rico, then in force, should continue in full force and effect, *except* "as altered or modified by military orders in force" when that act was passed. It is clear that claimant is not entitled to be compensated for his office by the United States because of its exercise of an authority unquestionably possessed by it as the lawful sovereign of the Island and its inhabitants. The abolition of the office was not, we think, in violation of any provision of the Constitution, nor did it infringe any right of property which the claimant could assert as against the United States. See *O'Reilly de Camara* v. *Brooke*, 209 U.S. 45, 49. The judgment of the Court of Claims must be affirmed.

Alvarez y Sanchez v. *United States*, 216 U.S. (1910) 167, 176.

Profession

Article VIII of the Treaty of Paris of December 10, 1898 provided that the cession of sovereignty by Spain to the United States "cannot in any respect impair the property rights which by law belong to the peaceful possession of property of all kinds" (30 Stat. 1754, 1758; 2 Treaties, etc. (Malloy, 1910) 1690, 1693).

In the case of *Bosque* v. *United States* the Supreme Court held that the right to practice law is not "property" within the protection of this article of the treaty. The Court stated that the provisions of article IX of the treaty that "Spanish subjects . . . shall also have the right to carry on their . . . professions, being subject in respect thereof to such laws as are applicable to other foreigners" (30 Stat. 1754, 1759; 2 Treaties, etc. (Malloy, 1910) 1690, 1693) referred not to the Spanish law but to the laws enacted by the new sovereignty, i.e. the laws and regulations put in force in the Philippines by the military and civil authorities of the United States.

209 U.S. (1908) 91.

Under the terms of a mortgage executed in Puerto Rico in 1894, a Puerto Rican contracted to pay some 18,000 pesos at stated times, in money current in the commerce, whatever may be the coinage in circulation, at the rate of 100 centavos (cents) of the money in circulation for each peso (paraphrase). After the cession of Puerto Rico to the United States, Congress passed an act, April 12, 1900 (31 Stat. 77, 80), providing for the retiring of Puerto Rican coins and the substitution therefor of the coins of the United States, and further that— *(Change in monetary unit)*

> all debts owing on the date when this Act shall take effect shall be payable in the coins of Porto Rico now in circulation, or in the coins of the United States at the rate of [60 cents per peso].

In 1901 the mortgagee instituted an action in a district court of Puerto Rico to collect instalments due at the rate of one dollar a peso and to obtain a declaration that future payments were to be made in the same manner. Judgment was had for the plaintiff and affirmed by the Supreme Court of Puerto Rico on the ground that the contract clearly called for payment on the basis of 100 cents of the coinage in circulation, whatever it might be, for each peso and that the mortgagee was therefore entitled to receive one dollar for each peso owed. The decision was reversed by the Supreme Court of the United States which held that the mortgagor was entitled to pay the remaining portion of the debt in American money at the rate of exchange prescribed by the statute, namely, 60 cents for each peso. The Court pointed out that, even if it were to be conceded that the strict and literal interpretation of the contract was as decided by the lower courts, such construction did not express the real intention of the parties when the contract was made. It said:

> On looking at this contract we are of opinion that it evidently contemplates only such change in coins as might occur while Porto Rico was under the same political power. It speaks of the payment of the debt in the money current in commerce, whatever may be the coinage of the money that, as such, is in circulation "in this province." The words "in this province" evidently did not contemplate any change of government, but only a possible change of coinage under the same government.
>
> .   .   .   .
>
> There was . . . no contract to pay in American money at the rate contended for by appellee. In providing for the withdrawal of all coins in circulation in Porto Rico, Congress pro-

vided at the same time for fixing the equivalent between those coins and American coins for the payment of all existing debts. This was simply fixing the value of those coins relatively to their value in American coin and with reference to the payment of debts then existing. All money then unpaid on this mortgage obligation was an existing debt within the act, and hence might be paid in American money at the rate therein specified.

Succession of Serralles v. *Esbri,* 200 U.S. (1906) 103, 113, 117–118.

In 1902, following the annexation of the South African Republic by Great Britain, the United States submitted a claim to the British Government on behalf of Robert E. Brown, an American mining engineer, based upon the failure of the South African Republic to grant Brown licenses to stake off mining claims and upon the illegal action of the South African courts in denying him redress. The views of the British Government with respect to the claim were set forth by Lord Lansdowne in a note to the American Ambassador in London, dated November 14, 1903, in which it was stated:

> As regards the first ground, His Majesty's Government are unable to find that it has ever been admitted that a conquering State takes over liabilities of this nature, which are not for debts, but for unliquidated damages, and it appears very doubtful to them whether Mr. Brown's claim could be substantiated at all or in any case for any substantial amount.
> As regards the second ground, it has never so far as His Majesty's Government are aware been laid down that the conquering State takes over liabilities for wrongs which have been committed by the Government of the conquered country and any such contention appears to them to be unsound in principle.
> In these circumstances His Majesty's Government are unable to admit that the late Mr. Brown has any claim under international law against that Government of the Transvaal as successor to the Government of the South African Republic.

A claim on Brown's behalf for £330,000, with interest, was submitted by the Government of the United States to the tribunal established under the special agreement of August 18, 1910 between the United States and Great Britain. In its decision of November 23, 1923 the tribunal held that Brown had sustained "a real denial of justice" at the hands of the former government but that liability therefor "never passed to or was assumed by the British Government". In so deciding, the tribunal, speaking through its president, Henri Fromageot, stated:

Denial of justice

> . . . It should be borne in mind that this was simply a pending claim for damages against certain officials and had never become a liquidated debt of the former State. Nor is there, properly speaking, any question of State succession here involved.

. . . We have searched the record for any indication that the British authorities did more than leave this matter exactly where it stood when annexation took place. They did not redress the wrong which had been committed, nor did they place any obstacles in Brown's path; they took no action one way or the other. No British official nor any British court undertook to deny Brown justice or to perpetuate the wrong. The Attorney General of the Colony, in his opinion, declared that the courts were still open to the claimant. The contention of the American Agent amounts to an assertion that a succeeding State acquiring a territory by conquest without any undertaking to assume such liabilities is bound to take the affirmatice [sic] steps to right the wrongs done by the former State. We cannot indorse this doctrine.

Nielsen's Report (1926) 162, 187, 197, 199, 200–201.

Subsequently, the same tribunal considered a group of claims submitted on behalf of British subjects for indemnity for wrongful imprisonment, expulsion from the country, and other indignities claimed to have been inflicted upon them by the authorities of the Hawaiian Republic prior to its annexation by the United States. It was contended on behalf of Great Britain that the *Brown* case, *ante*, was to be distinguished from these cases, in that the South African Republic had come to an end by conquest while the Hawaiian Republic came to an end by voluntary cession. In rejecting this contention and in disallowing the claims, the tribunal, speaking through its president, A. Nerincx, said:

. . . We are unable to accept the distinction contended for. In the first place, it assumes a general principle of succession to liability for delict, to which the case of succession of one state to another through conquest would be an exception. We think there is no such principle. It was denied in the Brown Case and has never been contended for to any such extent. The general statements of writers, with respect to succession to obligations, have reference to changes of form of government, where the identity of the legal unit remains, to liability to observe treaties of the extinct state, to contractual liabilities, or at most to quasi-contractual liabilities. Even here, there is much controversy. The analogy of universal succession in private law, which is much relied on by those who argue for a large measure of succession to liability for obligations of the extinct state, even if admitted (and the aptness of the analogy is disputed), would make against succession to liability for delicts. Nor do we see any valid reason for distinguishing termination of a legal unit of International Law through conquest from termination by any other mode of merging in, or swallowing up by, some other legal unit. In either case the legal unit which did the wrong no longer exists, and legal liability for the wrong has been extinguished with it.

Delicts

Hawaiian Claims, Nielsen's Report (1926) 85, 160–161.

CONTRACTS AND CONCESSIONS

§82

In an instruction of June 9, 1916 to the Minister in Denmark regarding the Danish *contre-projet* for the cession of the Danish West Indies, the Department stated:

> As to concessions and grants, this Government can undertake to assume obligations only in regard to such as may be mentioned in the treaty under negotiation. If the Danish Government believes that other concessions have been granted in the islands, it should satisfy itself as to what concessions they are and promptly notify this Government. I look to the Danish Government to inform this Government as to the particulars of any further concessions which may be in existence, for I cannot assure the maintenance of concessions or grants that have not been brought to my attention prior to the signature of the treaty and I cannot present to the Senate, with hope of obtaining its approval, a treaty that is indefinite in the obligations which it imposes on the United States.

> Secretary Lansing to Minister Egan, telegram 110, June 9, 1916, MS. Department of State, file 711.5914/59; 1917 For. Rel. 622.
>
> Subsection 4 of article 3 of the convention signed on Aug. 4, 1916 between the United States and Denmark for the cession to the United States of the Danish West Indies, listed nine concessions and licenses previously issued in the islands by the Danish Government which the United States agreed to maintain in accordance with the terms on which they had been given. 39 Stat. 1706, 1709–1710; 3 Treaties, etc. (Redmond, 1923) 2558, 2560; 1917 For. Rel. 694, 696–697.

> . . . since the powers and rights under consideration [various powers of supervision and audit, the right to receive ten percent of the profits of the bank, etc., which were reserved to the Danish Government in its concession to the National Bank of the Danish West Indies] appear to be associated with the exercise of sovereignty over the Islands, this Department is of the opinion that these powers and rights duly passed from Denmark to the United States by virtue of the transference of the sovereignty of the Islands and in accordance with the terms of the Treaty of Cession.

> The Under Secretary of State (Polk) to the Secretary of the Treasury, Apr. 6, 1920, MS. Department of State, file 811.515/249.

On April 25, 1908 the Secretary of War requested the opinion of the Attorney General as to "whether the $250,000 per annum which the Panama Railroad Company agreed to pay the Republic of Colombia as the price of its concession, in view of the fact that the railroad company's original concession has neither been formally reaffirmed since the United States succeeded to the sovereignty of the territory to which that concession related, nor adhered to in substance upon the part of the United States, is an enforceable claim payable to the United States; and whether the railroad company may not, in view of that fact, insist upon a modification of the terms of the original contract of concession". The entire capital stock of the Panama Railroad Company was, at the time of the request for an opinion, owned by the Government of the United States.

After advising the Secretary of War, on July 24, 1908, that the contract between Colombia and the Panama Railroad Company had been recognized and affirmed by officials of the United States, the Attorney General stated:

Adoption and ratification presumed

> Independently, however, of these considerations, I think it is clear that, when a new sovereign succeeds to the rights of one dispossessed of a territory in which concessions of this character have been granted, it must be presumed, in the absence of express action on its part indicating unmistakably a contrary intention to adopt and ratify such acts of its precedessor, and I can not assent to the proposition that the other party to the concession or contract has a right to repudiate its terms and thus release itself from the obligations imposed on it by its existing contracts, merely because the sovereign with whom it contracted has been, through the vicissitudes of war or revolution, or as the result of a treaty of cession, succeeded by a different sovereign in the territory to which these particular contracts relate. In my opinion any individual or corporation dealing with a sovereign power does so with notice of all the necessary incidents of its sovereignty, and among these is the possibility that its sovereign power over the territory to which the contract relates may be transferred to another.
>
> I hold, therefore, that the substitution of the United States in the several powers and rights held successively by New Granada, Colombia, and Panama by reason of contractual relations with this corporation, or its predecessors in title, does not of itself affect the rights of the sovereign power under such contract, or make a formal reaffirmation of such rights on the part of the United States necessary; and I further hold that the action of the United States with regard to the railroad company amounts to a recognition of the previously existing contractual relations, which of itself would supply the place of such formal reaffirmation, if the same were necessary.

27 Op. Att. Gen. (1908–9) 19, 21, 23–24.

At the time of the declaration of independence by Panama on November 3, 1903, the Central and South American Telegraph Company—an American firm—was operating a system of cables starting at the port of Panamá, touching at Buenaventura, and terminating at the port of Callao, under a concession contract concluded with Colombia in 1879. The contract was extended on November 30, 1903, to be

effective as from November 1. Although at first the Government of
Panama insisted on the payment of duties on supplies shipped to the
company's manager in Panama (contrary to the terms of the 1879
contract and the extension contract with Colombia), it at length
allowed the free entry into Panama of goods introduced for the cable
service but not of goods shipped to persons employed by the company,
and the company on its part allowed the Government of Panama a
rebate on its cable tariffs. However, the Government of Panama
declined officially to recognize the 1903 extension concession by Colombia. When the company moved certain of its cables into the Canal
Zone and subsequently requested official recognition by the United
States of its rights under the 1903 contract with Colombia, the Department of State replied that in the circumstances it would not be
warranted in recognizing the rights claimed by the company.

> Memorial of the Central and South American Telegraph Company to
> Secretary Root, Oct. 5, 1905, MS. Department of State, file 312/20; Mr. Root
> to the American Minister in Panama, Oct. 6, 1906 (telegram), *ibid.* 312/10a;
> the Acting Secretary of State (Adee) to the President of the Central and
> South American Telegraph Company (Scrymser), Jan. 7, 1907, *ibid.* 312/22;
> the Panaman Minister of Foreign Affairs (Arias) to the American Minister
> (Squiers), Apr. 5 and 11, 1907, *ibid.* 312/31; Mr. Root to Mr. Squiers, no.
> 47, June 8, 1907, *ibid.* 312/30–32; Mr. Squiers to Mr. Root, no. 124, June 29,
> 1907, *ibid.* 312/52–53; Señor Arias to Mr. Squiers, Jan. 20, 1908, *ibid.* 312/80;
> the Chargé d'Affaires in Panama (Weitzel) to Secretary Knox, no. 654,
> Mar. 11, 1910, *ibid.* 319.115C33/103.
>
> President Scrymser to Secretary Bryan, Sept. 15, 1913, *ibid.* 811f.73/1;
> Counselor Moore to Mr. Scrymser, Dec. 19, 1913, *ibid.* 811f.73/5.

. . . When the United States succeeded to the sovereignty
over the islands [Philippines] they were under no more obligation to continue the contracts for public or private service of
individuals or corporations than they were to continue in office
officials appointed by the Spanish Government. (*Sanchez* v.
United States, 42 C. Cls., 458; affirmed, 216 U.S., 167.)

> *The Eastern Extension, Australasia and China Telegraph Company* v.
> *The United States*, 46 Ct. Cls. (1911) 646, 653. In this case it appeared
> that in 1879, and subsequent years prior to the Spanish-American War, the
> claimant, a British company, had procured from the Spanish Government
> grants and concessions for the establishment and working of submarine
> cables in the Philippine Archipelago, the company to be paid an annual
> subsidy of £4,500.

A debt owing by Bolivia to one Pedro López Gama, a Brazilian,
having been assigned (because of the advancement of large sums of
money to him) to Alsop & Co., a firm registered in Chile but composed of American citizens, was liquidated in 1876 by means of arrangements set out in the form of a contract between the Bolivian
Government and one John Wheelwright, the liquidator of the firm

of Alsop & Co. Under the terms of the contract Bolivia admitted Alsop & Co. that she was indebted to the firm in a specified amount, and the debt was to be settled by giving the liquidator the right to a share in Bolivia's portion of the customs receipts collected at Arica (Peru), and also by giving him the right to work government silver mines along the Bolivian littoral.

In 1879 war broke out between Chile and Bolivia, and the coast province of Bolivia in which the mines were situated was occupied by Chile; shortly thereafter Peru became engaged in the war, and in 1880 Arica also passed into the possession of Chile. As a result of the war both of the sources from which the debt was to be paid passed into the hands of Chile.

The Governments of the United States and Chile having been unable to agree as to the liability of the latter to Alsop & Co., the matter was submitted to His Majesty King George V as *amiable compositeur* pursuant to a protocol of December 1, 1909 (3 Treaties, etc. [Redmond, 1923] 2508).

Although it was not alleged by the United States that the conquest of Arica and of the coast province would of itself affect the indebtedness of Bolivia or transfer the liability to Chile, it was contended (1) that Chile appropriated to her own use the proceeds of the customhouse at Arica, thereby preventing Alsop & Co. from realizing anything under the Wheelwright contract in liquidation of the debt; (2) that Chile prevented Alsop & Co. from working the government silver mines in the coast province in the way they were entitled to work them by applying Chilean law in the province from the date of the military occupation, thereby subjecting Alsop & Co. to more onerous terms than would have been the case under Bolivian law; and (3) that from time to time Chile undertook to pay the claim.

Chile, on the other hand, repudiated liability altogether, so far as the claim was based on her appropriation of the Arica customs and so far as concerned the application of Chilean law to the province she had conquered. As regards her undertakings to pay, she maintained that she was only liable to the extent of the provision made in the treaty of 1904 between her and Bolivia and that she was willing to pay that amount but that it had been refused.

By the award dated July 5, 1911 it was held that "The effect of the Chilean occupation of Arica was to put it out of the power of Peru to carry out the agreement of 1878 [between Peru and Bolivia as to the customs at Arica]; consequently Bolivia's right to any share in the customs collected at Arica determined from that moment and continued in suspense until such time as that or some new agreement was again in operation between herself and the power in possession of Arica"; that "the Wheelwright contract effected no assignment or hypothecation of the Arica customs, that the arrangement embodied in article 2 of that contract was not binding on Chile, that Chile in appropriating the proceeds of the Arica customs . . . did not receive the money to the use of Alsop & Co., and that the claim under this head for $2,337,384.28 payable in gold is not sustainable". In connection with the claim presented on account of the loss of the silver mines as a source of payment of the debt, it was pointed out that Wheelwright had been left by Chile in possession of all the mines of which he had been able to obtain control. It was held that the rights of the firm with respect to the mines were in the nature of options and that—

> . . . The right which Alsop & Co. possessed under the Wheelwright contract to work a particular "estaca" was merely a contractual right against Bolivia; until they had secured possession of the "estaca" they had nothing which could fairly be described as "property".

It was further held:

> . . . Where no possession of a particular "estaca" had been obtained, the firm had merely a contractual right, which the war put an end to so far as regards Bolivia, and which was not valid against Chile.

The *amiable compositeur* however awarded 2,275,375 bolivianos on the ground that under the treaty of peace of 1904 (and the supplementary notes and protocol) between Chile and Bolivia, the former had assumed certain obligations of Bolivia, including the obligation to pay that amount.

> Ambassador Reid to Secretary Knox, no. 1738, July 11, 1911, MS. Department of State, file 425.11A78/582 (enclosure, award); 1911 For. Rel. 38, 44, 45, 47, 53; see also 1910 For. Rel. 138–189.

Payment
of subsidy
to conces-
sionaire

The Eastern Extension, Australasia and China Telegraph Company, a British corporation, secured cable concessions in the Philippine Islands from the Spanish Government in 1879, 1897, and 1898. Under the terms of these concessions the concessionaire was to enjoy an annual subsidy of £4,500, was to pay a 10-percent tax to the State, and agreed to transmit official despatches, giving them precedence, at half the rates charged for those of a private character and free of charge on the Hongkong-Manila cable. After the cession of the islands to the United States use was made of the cables for the sending of official despatches. The company brought suit in the court of claims to recover the subsidy assured to it by Spain as its compensation for such service. The court, in sustaining a demurrer and dismissing the petition, stated:

The obligation of Spain to the claimant was not the obligation of the Philippine Archipelago, though the Spanish Government saw fit to pay the subsidy out of the revenues of the islands; but if we were to assume that it was, the United States, in the absence of treaty stipulation, such as is referred to in *Hall's International Law*, sec. 28, p. 104, would not be liable therefor. If we were to assume that the obligations of Spain to the claimant was a general debt of the Spanish Government, it would be a personal one, as laid down in *Hall's International Law*, p. 99, *note;* and being a personal obligation would not, in the absence of a treaty stipulation, attach to the United States.

. . . the court is without jurisdiction to determine the question.

48 Ct. Cls. (1912) 33, 49, 50; 46 Ct. Cls. (1911) 646. See also 231 U.S. (1913) 326, remanding the case to the Court of Claims.

Upon hearing the case on the claimant's amended petition, the Court of Claims held that no contract with the United States was shown, and the petition was accordingly dismissed. On appeal, the judgment of the Court of Claims was affirmed by the Supreme Court, which held that there was no proof of a contract, express or implied, by the United States to adopt and be bound by the concession. 251 U.S. (1920) 355, 366.

For the effects of changes of sovereignty upon treaty rights and obligations, see the chapter on "Treaties".

For the effects of changes of sovereignty upon nationality, see the chapter on "Nationality".

CHAPTER V

NATIONAL JURISDICTION AND TERRITORIAL LIMITS

THE NATIONAL DOMAIN

§83

The Supreme Court of the United States in the case of *Cunard Steamship Company, Ltd., et al.* v. *Mellon, Secretary of the Treasury, et al.*, in construing the term "territory" in the phrase "the United States and all territory subject to the jurisdiction thereof" contained in the eighteenth amendment to the Constitution of the United States, stated:

> Various meanings are sought to be attributed to the term "territory" in the phrase "the United States and all territory subject to the jurisdiction thereof." We are of opinion that it means the regional areas—of land and adjacent waters—over which the United States claims and exercises dominion and control as a sovereign power. The immediate context and the purport of the entire section show that the term is used in a physical and not a metaphorical sense—that it refers to areas or districts having fixity of location and recognized boundaries. See *United States* v. *Bevans*, 3 Wheat. 336, 390.
>
> It now is settled in the United States and recognized elsewhere that the territory subject to its jurisdiction includes the land areas under its dominion and control, the ports, harbors, bays and other enclosed arms of the sea along its coast and a marginal belt of the sea extending from the coast line outward a marine league, or three geographic miles. *Church* v. *Hubbart*, 2 Cranch, 187, 234; *The Ann*, 1 Fed. Cas., p. 926; *United States* v. *Smiley*, 27 Fed. Cas., p. 1132; *Manchester* v. *Massachusetts*, 139 U.S. 240, 257–258; *Louisiana* v. *Mississippi*, 202 U.S. 1, 52; 1 Kent's Com., 12th ed., *29; 1 Moore International Law Digest, §145; 1 Hyde International Law, §§141, 142, 154; Wilson International Law, 8th ed., §54; Westlake International Law, 2d ed., p. 187, *et seq.;* Wheaton International Law, 5th Eng. ed. (Phillipson), p. 282; 1 Oppenheim International Law, 3d ed., §§185–189, 252.

262 U.S. (1923) 100, 122.

. . . By the terms of the treaty of Guadalupe Hidalgo, which was finally ratified at the city of Queretaro on May 30, 1848, Mexico ceded to the United States all territory lying to the northward of a line drawn from the mouth of the Rio Grande westerly to the Pacific Ocean. By virtue of this treaty the United States assumed that jurisdiction over the region thus ceded, both territorial and maritime, which Mexico had theretofore asserted, and which embraced all of the ports, harbors, bays, and inlets along the coast of California and for a considerable though perhaps indefinite distance into the ocean, including dominion over the numerous islands lying therein adjacent to said coast.

> *Ocean Industries, Inc. (a Corporation)* v. *The Superior Court of California, in and for Santa Cruz County, et al.,* 200 Calif. (1927) 235, 242, 252 Pac. 722, 724.

TERRITORIAL LIMITS

RIVERS

DIVISIONAL LINES

§84

Navigable rivers

In the case of *Louisiana* v. *Mississippi*, involving a boundary controversy between the two States, Chief Justice Fuller, in delivering the opinion of the Supreme Court of the United States, adopted the rule of the thalweg and said:

> Now to repeat, the boundary of Louisiana separating her from the State of Mississippi to the east is the thread of the channel of the Mississippi river, . . .

The thalweg

> If the doctrine of the thalweg is applicable, the correct boundary line separating Louisiana from Mississippi in these waters is the deep water channel.
>
> The term "thalweg" is commonly used by writers on international law in definition of water boundaries between States, meaning the middle or deepest or most navigable channel.

> 202 U.S. (1906) 1, 48.

Where the proper authorities have named or described the center of one channel of a river as the boundary between states bordering thereon, the boundary, as thus prescribed, remains the boundary, "subject to the changes in it which come by accretion", and is not moved to any other channel of the river, although another channel may in the course of years become the most important or main channel of the river.

> *Washington* v. *Oregon,* 211 U.S. (1908) 127, 136. Petition for rehearing denied, *Washington* v. *Oregon,* 214 U.S. (1909) 205, 218.
>
> "The territorial limits of Kentucky extend across the [Ohio] river to low-water mark on the northerly shore. *Indiana* v. *Kentucky,* 136 U.S. 479, 519." *Nicoulin* v. *O'Brien,* 248 U.S. (1918) 113, 114.

"It is settled beyond the possibility of dispute that where running streams are the boundaries between States, the same rule applies as between private proprietors, namely, that when the bed and channel are changed by the natural and gradual processes known as erosion and accretion, the boundary follows the varying course of the stream; while if the stream from any cause, natural or artificial, suddenly leaves its old bed and forms a new one, by the processes known as an avulsion, the resulting change of channel works no change of boundary, which remains in the middle of the old channel, although no water may be flowing in it, and irrespective of subsequent changes in the new channel." Although the rule of the thalweg may derive its origin from the equal rights of boundary states in the navigation of a river, the rule does not cease to be applicable when navigation has been rendered impossible by the abandonment of a portion of the river bed as a result of an avulsion.

State of Arkansas v. State of Tennessee, 246 U.S. (1918) 158, 173. To the same effect, see Arkansas v. Mississippi, holding that the boundary was "the middle of the channel of navigation as it existed just previous to the avulsion". 250 U.S. (1919) 39, 45.

In holding that the boundary line between Texas and Oklahoma is along the south bank of the Red River, and not along its medial line, under a proper interpretation of the provisions of article 3 of the treaty of February 22, 1819, between the United States and Spain, the Supreme Court stated that "the bank intended by the treaty provision is the water-washed and relatively permanent elevation or acclivity at the outer line of the river bed which separates the bed from the adjacent upland, whether valley or hill, and serves to confine the waters within the bed and to preserve the course of the river" and that "the boundary intended is on and along the bank at the average or mean level attained by the waters in the periods when they reach and wash the bank without overflowing it", while the "bed" of the river includes "all of the area which is kept practically bare of vegetation by the wash of the waters of the river from year to year in their onward course, although parts of it are left dry for months at a time", and excludes "the lateral valleys which have the characteristics of relatively fast land and usually are covered by upland grasses and vegetation, although temporarily overflowed in exceptional instances when the river is at flood".

State of Oklahoma v. State of Texas, 260 U.S. (1923) 606, 631. See, in this connection, State of Oklahoma v. State of Texas, 252 U.S. (1920) 372; 256 U.S. (1921) 70, 602; 258 U.S. (1922) 574.

Where a river, "navigable or non-navigable, is the boundary between two States, and the navigable channel is not involved, in the absence of convention or controlling circumstances to the contrary, each takes to the middle of the stream", and the middle line of the stream is to be determined when the water is at its ordinary stage, "neither swollen by freshets nor shrunk by drought".

> *State of Georgia* v. *State of South Carolina*, 257 U.S. (1922) 516, 521.
>
> In the case of *New Mexico* v. *Texas*, 275 U.S. (1927) 279, the Supreme Court of the United States held that the boundary line was the middle of the main channel of the Rio Grande as it flowed in 1850 and that subsequent accretions did not affect the boundary. For the final decree, see 276 U.S. (1928) 558.

In an original suit brought in the Supreme Court of the United States in 1915, Vermont contended that the boundary between that State and New Hampshire was "the thread of the channel" of the Connecticut River for its entire course, except for a small part, but that if the Court should decide that the boundary was not the thread but "the west bank of the Connecticut River", then "such line is the westerly edge of the waters of the Connecticut River at its average and mean stage during the entire year without reference to the extraordinary freshets or extreme droughts". New Hampshire contended that the boundary was "at the top or westerly margin of the westerly bank of the Connecticut River and the east branch thereof". The Court held that a British order of the King in Council of July 20, 1764, fixing the boundary between the adjoining royal provinces of New York and New Hampshire at the "western banks of the River Connecticut", and thus including the territory which later became Vermont in the province of New York, was not intended to shift the boundary line from low-water mark to the top of the bank of the Connecticut River and pointed out that a different rule had been applied in the case of grants bounded by tidal waters, which carry only to high-water mark.

> *Vermont* v. *New Hampshire*, 289 U.S. (1933) 593, 595, 596. For decrees, see 290 U.S. (1934) 579, 589, 602.

In holding that the true boundary between New Jersey and Delaware in the Delaware River below a circle of 12 miles about the town of New Castle and in Delaware Bay below the river, is "the middle of the main ship channel in Delaware River and Bay", the Supreme Court stated:

> International law today divides the river boundaries between states by the middle of the main channel, when there is one, and not by the geographical centre, half way between the banks. . . . It applies the same doctrine, now known as the doctrine of the *Thalweg*, to estuaries and bays in which the dominant sailing channel can be followed to the sea. *Louisiana* v. *Mississippi, supra;* and compare 1 Halleck International Law, 4th ed., p. 182; Moore, Digest International Law, vol. 1, p. 617;

Matter of Devoe Manufacturing Co., 108 **U.S.** 401; *The Fame*, 8 Fed. Cas. 984, Story, J.; *The Open Boat*, 18 Fed. Cas. 751, Ware, J. The *Thalweg*, or downway, is the track taken by boats in their course down the stream, which is that of the strongest current. 1 Westlake, International Law, p. 144; Orban, Etude de Droit Fluvial International, p. 343; Kaeckenbeck, International Rivers, p. 176; Hyde, Int. Law, p. 244; Fiore, Int. Law Codified, §1051; Calvo, Dictionnaire de Droit International.

. . . .

The commentators tell us of times when the doctrine of the *Thalweg* was still unknown or undeveloped. Anciently, we are informed, there was a principle of co-dominion by which boundary streams to their entire width were held in common ownership by the proprietors on either side. 1 Hyde, International Law, p. 243, §137. Then, with Grotius and Vattel, came the notion of equality of division (Nys, Droit International, vol. 1, pp. 425, 426; Hyde, *supra*, p. 244, citing Grotius, De Jure Belli ac Pacis, and Vattel, Law of Nations), though how this was to be attained was still indefinite and uncertain, as the citations from Grotius and Vattel show. Finally, about the end of the eighteenth century, the formula acquired precision, the middle of the "stream" becoming the middle of the "channel." There are statements by the commentators that the term *Thalweg* is to be traced to the Congress of Rastadt in 1797 (Engelhardt, Du Régime Conventionnel des Fleuves Internationaux, p. 72; Koch, Histoire des Traités de Paix, vol. 5, p. 156), and the Treaty of Lunéville in 1801. Hyde, *supra*, pp. 245, 246; Kaeckenbeck, International Rivers, p. 176; Adami, National Frontiers, translated by Behrens, p. 17. . . .

In 1783, when the Revolutionary War was over, Delaware and New Jersey began with a clean slate. There was no treaty or convention fixing the boundary between them. There was no possessory act nor other act of dominion to give to the boundary in bay and river below the circle a practical location, or to establish a prescriptive right. In these circumstances, the capacity of the law to develop and apply a formula consonant with justice and with the political and social needs of the international legal system is not lessened by the fact that at the creation of the boundary the formula of the *Thalweg* had only a germinal existence. The gap is not so great that adjudication may not fill it. Lauterpacht, The Function of Law in the International Community, pp. 52, 60, 70, 85, 100, 110, 111, 255, 404, 432. . . .

It is thus with the formula of the *Thalweg* in its application to the division between Delaware and New Jersey. We apply it to that boundary, which goes back to the Peace of Paris, just as we applied it to the boundary between Illinois and Iowa, which derives from a treaty of 1763 (*Iowa* v. *Illinois; Keokuk & Hamilton Bridge Co.* v. *Illinois; Arkansas* v. *Tennessee; Arkansas* v. *Mississippi, supra*), or to that between Louisiana and Mississippi (202 U.S. 1, 16), which goes back to 1812, or between Minnesota and Wisconsin (252 U.S. 273), going back to 1846.

New Jersey v. *Delaware*, 291 U.S. (1934) **361**, 379, 381.

History

In the case of *Re Village of Fort Erie and Buffalo and Fort Erie Public Bridge Co.*, decided by the Appellate Division of the Supreme Court of Ontario on December 29, 1927, a Canadian village had assessed an international bridge built by a company over the Niagara River to a point in the State of New York. The bridge had been taxed to the international line, and the village appealed from a decision holding that it was not entitled to tax the bridge up to that line but only up to the shore of the river. The court, in dismissing the appeal, stated:

> Mr. Manning's contention is that the Village of Fort Erie is not confined in its territory to the dry land west of the river's bank, but that it extends to the international line, i.e., as far as Canadian territory extends under the river.
>
> This contention is based on the old Common Law doctrine of *ad medium filum aquae*, which is perfectly valid yet in certain cases. But it has never been applied to international waters, the English cases dealing with land and waters wholly in England, and the case of *Maclaren* v. *Attorney-General for Quebec*, [1914] A.C. 258, with the Gatineau, a river wholly in Quebec.
>
> If it could ever apply to any international waters, it could not apply to the river Niagara. By the Treaty of Peace concluded on the 3rd September, 1783, the boundary of that part was to be "the middle of the communication into Lake Erie" from Lake Ontario; the real boundary-line was not established "on the ground" till after the Treaty of Ghent, 1814, under the provisions of which a commission was appointed to fix the international boundary from the present Cornwall to Lake Superior. It is known that there was much "give and take" by and between the commissioners [boundary commissioners]—it was strongly asserted at the time, and official documents seem to bear out the contention, that most of the "give" was on one side and most of the "take" on the other. However that may be, the commissioners did not take the middle of the stream as the international line—in many cases the middle of the navigable channel was taken, and in a few what was considered an utterly inadmissable and unfounded claim was allowed for the sake of peace. It cannot be said that at any point the international line, as declared in the Utica Award of 1822, is the middle thread. But, even assuming that this principle can ever be applied to the Niagara river, it is wholly inapplicable to this case.

> 61 Ont. L.R. (1927) 502, 504; [1928] 1 D.L.R. 723, 724–725.

> As of possible interest, see the Argentine case *Don Leonardo Pereyra Iraola* v. *the Province of Buenos Aires*, 133 *Fallos de la Corte Suprema de Justicia de la Nacion* (1920) 372, 378.

In the *Grisbadarna* case (Norway and Sweden), involving a question of the delimitation of a certain part of the maritime boundary between Norway and Sweden, the tribunal refused to apply the rule of the thalweg because the documents invoked did not demonstrate that this rule was followed in the seventeenth century, the period considered material in determining the boundary.

Scott, *Hague Court Reports* (1916) 121.

In the case of *Ker and Company* v. *Couden* the Supreme Court of the United States affirmed a decision of the Philippine courts that under III Partidas, tit. 28, laws 3, 4, 6, 24, and 26, and the Law of Waters of 1866, the title to accretions along the sea was vested in the Government rather than in the owners of the private land adjacent thereto. 223 U.S. (1912) 268.

NAVIGATION

§85

Westlake states:

That the principle on which the freedom of trade and navigation is . . . claimed on international rivers does not include the rivers which are entirely comprised within the territory of a single state, as asserted by Bluntschli, appears from the condition that those who use the right of passage must have need of it for just causes. It is common for states to reserve their coasting trade for their own nationals and to prohibit the importation of foreign merchandise in ships of third countries, and no question is ever raised as to the international lawfulness of such restrictions. But a state can no more be bound to open its river ports than its seaports to foreigners. It is only when a state on an international river and an oversea state, or two states on the same international river not contiguous to one another, are desirous of such intercourse, that the vessels of either have a just cause for needing passage through the coriparian territories lower on the river in the one case or separating them in the other case, and that the doctrine of Grotius applies. The test for its application is that the navigation in question has a lawful territorial origin, and a lawful ulterior destination beyond the part of the river through which the passage is claimed. The principle asserts the free use of rivers as the vehicle of intercourse not in itself affecting the country of passage, and nothing more.

1 Westlake, *International Law* (2d ed., 1910) 147.

The "common law test of navigability, to wit, the ebb and flow of the tide", has had "no place in American jurisprudence since the decision in the case of *The Propeller Genesee Chief* v. *Fitzhugh*, 12 How. [1851] 443, and is therefore no test of riparian ownership". The term "navigable waters" means waters that are "navigable in fact".

Tests of navigability

McGilvra and Bressler v. *Ross, State Land Commissioner of the State of Washington*, 215 U.S. (1909) 70, 77–78 (involving claims to lands below high-water mark on two non-tidal lakes).

In deciding that the extension of the Hoopa Valley Reservation included the bed of the Klamath (Link) River in California, the Supreme Court pointed out that "what are navigable waters of the United States", in contradistinction to "the navigable waters of the

States", depends upon "whether the stream in its ordinary condition affords a channel for useful commerce", and that "what shall be deemed a navigable water within the meaning of the local rules of property is for the determination of the several States". It held that California, by an act of 1850 adopting the common law and thereby transferring to all riparian proprietors (or confirming in them) the ownership of the non-navigable streams and their beds, and by acts of February 24 and March 11, 1891 declaring in effect

Ownership of river bed

that the Klamath River was a non-navigable stream, had vested in the United States, as riparian owner, the title to the bed of the Klamath "if in fact it be a navigable river", and that if "in fact it be non-navigable" the same result flowed from the mere adoption of the common law.

Donnelly v. *United States*, 228 U. S. (1913) 243, 259, 262.

Poole Island in Snake River, a navigable stream forming in part the boundary line between Oregon and Idaho, is located on the Idaho side of the thread of the stream. A question regarding the title to the island having been brought before the Supreme Court of the United States in 1913, the Court pointed out that land under navigable waters passes from the United States to a State by virtue of the State's admission to the Union and that the ownership of such land by riparian proprietors who have purchased from the State depends on the law of that State. In connection with these two points the Court stated:

Coming to the effect to be given to the admission of Idaho as a State and to the disposal of the fractional subdivisions on the east bank, it is well to repeat that Snake river is a navigable stream, for there is an important difference between navigable and non-navigable waters in such a connection. Thus,

Distinction: navigable and non-navigable waters

Rev. Stat., §2476, which is but a continuation of early statutes on the subject (Acts May 18, 1796, 1 Stat. 468, c. 29, §9; March 3, 1803, 2 Stat. 229, c. 27, §17), declares: "All navigable rivers, within the territory occupied by the public lands, shall remain and be deemed public highways; and, in all cases where the opposite banks of any streams not navigable belong to different persons, the stream and the bed thereof shall become common to both:" and of this provision it was said in *Railroad Company* v. *Schurmeir*, 7 Wall. 272, 288, "the court does not hesitate to decide, that Congress, in making a distinction between streams navigable and those not navigable, intended to provide that the common law rules of riparian ownership should apply to lands bordering on the latter, but that the title to lands bordering on navigable streams should stop at the stream, and that all such streams should be deemed to be, and remain public highways." Besides, it was settled long ago by this court, upon a consideration of the relative rights and powers of the Federal and state governments under the Constitution, that lands under-lying navigable waters within the several States belong to the respective States in virtue of their sovereignty and may be used and disposed of as they may direct, subject always to the rights of the public in such waters and to the paramount power of Congress to control their navigation so far as may be necessary for the regulation of commerce among the States and with foreign nations, and that each new State, upon its admission to the Union, becomes endowed with the same rights and powers in this regard as the older ones. *County of St. Clair* v. *Lovingston*, 23 Wall. 46, 68; *Barney* v. *Keokuk*, 94 U.S. 324, 338; *Illinois Central Railroad Co.* v. *Illinois*, 146 U.S. 387, 434–437; *Shively* v. *Bowlby*, 152 U.S. 1, 48–50; *McGilvra* v. *Ross*, 215 U.S. 70.

Bearing in mind, then, that Snake river is a navigable stream, it is apparent, first, that on the admission of Idaho to statehood the ownership of the bed of the river on the Idaho side of the thread of the stream—the thread being the true boundary of the State—passed from the United States to the State, subject to the limitations just indicated, and, second, that the subsequent disposal by the former of the fractional subdivisions on the east bank carried with it no right to the bed of the river, save as the law of Idaho may have attached such a right to private riparian ownership.

However, the Court held that the island was not part of the bed of the stream or land under the water and therefore its ownership did not pass to the State but remained in the United States and subject to disposal under its laws.

Scott v. *Lattig*, 227 U.S. (1913) 229, 242.

In *Oklahoma* v. *Texas* the Supreme Court, after stating that the question of the ownership of the Red River bed depended on the navigability of the river, referred to article III of the treaty of 1819 between the United States and Spain, declaring that the navigation of the Sabine, Red, and Arkansas Rivers should be common to the inhabitants of both countries, and held that these words of the treaty did not impress the river with the legal character of a navigable stream where it was not navigable in fact, as the entire article "shows . . . that what really was intended . . . was to provide . . . that the right to navigate these rivers, wherever along the boundary they were navigable in fact, should be common to the respective inhabitants of both nations"; that there was no infer-ence of navigability from the fact that surveyors had run a meander line along the northerly bank and did not extend the township and section lines across the river; that there was no inference of navi-gability from the fact that Congress in permitting the construction of certain bridges across the river within Oklahoma had provided that there should be no interference with navigation; that any inference of navigability from appropriations by Congress and use of money in an attempt to improve the river was overcome "by the actual conditions disclosed in the course of the work"; and that, while the evidence relating to that part of the river in the eastern half of the State was not so conclusive against navigability as that relating to the western section, it established that "trade and travel neither do nor can move over that part of the river, in its natural and ordinary condition, according to the modes of trade and travel customary on water;—in other words, that it is neither used, nor susceptible of being used, in its natural and ordinary condition as a highway for commerce", its characteristics being such "that its use for transportation has been and must be exceptional, and confined to the irregular and short periods of temporary high water". The Court concluded that no part of the Red River within Oklahoma was navigable and that therefore the title to the bed did not pass to the State upon its admission to the Union.

> 258 U.S. (1922) 574, 585, 590, 591.

In the case of *Brewer-Elliott Oil & Gas Company et al.* v. *United States et al.*, an action brought by the United States to cancel leases granted the appellants by the State of Oklahoma covering part of the Arkansas River within the Osage Indian Reservation, Mr. Chief Justice Taft, delivering the opinion of the Court, stated:

> A navigable river in this country is one which is used, or is susceptible of being used in its ordinary condition, as a highway for commerce over which trade and travel are or may be conducted in the customary modes of trade and travel on water. It does not depend upon the mode by which commerce is conducted upon it, whether by steamers, sailing vessels or flat boats, nor upon the difficulties attending navigation, but upon the fact whether the river in its natural state is such that it affords a channel for useful commerce.

The Court held further that "what title, if any, the Osages took in the river bed in 1872" when their grant was made, which was 35 years before Oklahoma was admitted into the Union, was under the circumstances a federal question and that it was not for a State to adopt a retroactive rule for determining navigability which would destroy a title already accrued under federal law and grant.

> 260 U.S. (1922) 77, 86, 87. The Court found that the Arkansas River along the reservation was not navigable.

The United States brought suit (argued in 1931) to quiet title to land constituting the beds of part of the Colorado River and its tributaries, the San Juan, Green, and Grand Rivers in Utah. In deciding that the rivers were in fact navigable, at least in part, the Supreme Court of the United States said:

> . . . In accordance with the constitutional principle of the equality of States, the title to the beds of rivers within Utah passed to that State when it was admitted to the Union, if the rivers were then navigable; and, if they were not then navigable, the title to the river beds remained in the United States. The question of navigability is thus determinative of the controversy, and that is a federal question. This is so, although it is undisputed that none of the portions of the rivers under consideration constitute navigable waters of the United States, that is, they are not navigable in interstate or foreign commerce, and the question is whether they are navigable waters of the State of Utah. State laws cannot affect titles vested in the United States.
>
> The test of navigability has frequently been stated by this Court.
>
> .   .   .   .
>
> The question of that susceptibility in the ordinary condition of the rivers, rather than of the mere manner or extent of actual use, is the crucial question. The Government insists that the uses of the rivers have been more of a private nature than of a public, commercial sort. But, assuming this to be the fact, it cannot be regarded as controlling when the rivers are shown to be capable of commercial use. The extent of existing commerce is not the test. The evidence of the actual use of streams, and especially of extensive and continued use for commercial purposes, may be most persuasive, but where conditions of exploration and settlement explain the infrequency or limited nature of such use, the susceptibility to use as a highway of commerce may still be satisfactorily proved.

United States v. *Utah*, 283 U.S. (1931) 64, 75, 82.

On the subject of the ownership of river beds, see: 26 Op. Att. Gen. (1908) 441, 442, holding that there can be private property rights in the soil under the navigable waters of the United States if they have been granted by the United States or the particular State having jurisdiction in the premises; *Archer* v. *Greenville Sand and Gravel Company*, 233 U.S. (1914) 60, 68, holding that "it is a question of local law whether the title to the beds of the navigable rivers of the United States is in the State in which the rivers are situated or in the owners of the land bordering upon such rivers"; *State of Oklahoma* v. *State of Texas*, 258 U.S. (1922) 574, 582, 583, 594, holding that where the United States owns the bed of a non-navigable stream and the upland on one or both sides "it, of course, is free when disposing of the upland to retain all or any part of the river bed"; and 35 Op. Att. Gen. (1929) 251, 256, 257–258, to the effect that when "a grantor who owns the upland on both sides of the stream . . . conveys land on one side only, in the absence of language showing a different intention a conveyance carries to the middle of the stream", but when the grantor "owns the entire bed of the stream [in this instance, the Red River bed] but no part of the upland on the opposite side, . . . his grant naming the stream as the boundary line will carry as far as he owns".

On the subject of riparian rights, see: *Producers Oil Company* v. *Hanzen*, 238 U.S. (1915) 325, 339, holding that "when the United States conveys a tract of land by patent referring to an official plat which shows the same bordering on a navigable river the purchaser takes title up to the water line"; and *State of Arkansas* v. *State of Tennessee*, 246 U.S. (1918) 158, 175, 176, holding that it is for the States "to establish such rules of property as they deem expedient with respect to the navigable waters within their borders and the riparian lands adjacent to them".

See *ante*, §60, "Accretion, Erosion, and Avulsion".

See also *Philadelphia Company* v. *Stimson, Secretary of War*, a case involving the right of Congress to regulate navigation on the Ohio River, where it was held that when "the State of Pennsylvania established harbor lines [at Brunot Island in the Ohio River, in Allegheny County, Pennsylvania] and thus undertook to regulate the rights of navigation, its action, however effective as between the State and the riparian proprietors, was necessarily subject to the paramount power of Congress". 223 U.S. (1912) 605, 635.

DIVERSION

§86

Arkansas River

In 1901 the State of Kansas brought an original suit in the Supreme Court of the United States to restrict the State of Colorado and certain corporations from diverting the water in the Arkansas River for irrigation purposes in Colorado. The Court, after pointing out that the question presented was one "between two States, one [Kansas] recognizing generally the common law rule of riparian rights and the other [Colorado] prescribing the doctrine of the public ownership of flowing water", and that a State could determine for itself which rule should control, held that although the diminution of the flow of water in the river by the irrigation of Colorado had worked some detriment to the southwestern part of Kansas, yet, when the amount of the detriment was compared with the great benefit which had resulted in Colorado, "it would seem that equality of right and equity between the two States forbids any interference with the present withdrawal of water in Colorado for purposes of irrigation".

The Court dismissed the bill, without prejudice to the right of Kansas to institute new proceedings whenever it should appear that, through a material increase in the depletion of the waters of the Arkansas by Colorado, the substantial interests of Kansas were being injured "to the extent of destroying the equitable apportionment of benefits between the two States resulting from the flow of the river".

Kansas v. *Colorado et al.*, 206 U. S. (1907) 46, 95, 114, 118.

There was no claim that the navigability of the river was diminished by the division of waters. The United States filed an intervening petition claiming a right to the use of the water for the reclamation of arid lands. The Court dismissed the intervening petition of the United States on the ground that while the Federal Government had the right to preserve the navigability of a river, the control of the flow of waters within the limits of a State is, subject to the exception just mentioned, fixed by the State.

In 1911 suit was brought by Wyoming to prevent a proposed diversion in Colorado of part of the waters of the Laramie River, a nonnavigable interstate stream rising in the latter State. When the suit was brought the two corporate defendants, acting under the authority and permission of Colorado, were proceeding to divert in that State a considerable portion of the water of the river and to conduct the same into another watershed, lying wholly in Colorado, for use in irrigating lands more than 50 miles distant from the point of diversion. The topography and natural drainage were such that none of the water could return to the stream or ever reach Wyoming. The Supreme Court of the United States entered a decree enjoining the defendants from diverting more than a certain amount of water each year. Mr. Justice Van Devanter, delivering the opinion of the Court, stated that the doctrine of prior appropriation had been adopted in both States and that in both States— *Laramie River*

Doctrine of prior "appropriation" adopted in both States

> . . . The earliest settlers gave effect to a . . . rule whereby the waters of the streams were regarded as open to appropriation for irrigation, mining and other beneficial purposes. The diversion from the stream and the application of the water to a beneficial purpose constituted an appropriation, and the appropriator was treated as acquiring a continuing right to divert and use the water to the extent of his appropriation, but not beyond what was reasonably required and actually used. This was deemed a property right and dealt with and respected accordingly. As between different appropriations from the same stream, the one first in time was deemed superior in right, and a completed appropriation was regarded as effective from the time the purpose to make it was definitely formed and actual work thereon was begun, provided the work was carried to completion with reasonable diligence.

After rejecting the contention of Colorado that she as a State might rightfully divert and use the waters flowing within her boundaries in this interstate stream regardless of any prejudice that this might work to others having rights in the stream below her boundary and dismissing the objection of Wyoming to the proposed diversion on the ground that it was to another watershed from which she could receive no benefit, the Court found that the senior appropriation in Wyoming was 272,500 acre-feet out of an available supply of 288,000 acre-feet and held that there remained only 15,500 acre-feet which were subject to the junior appropriation in Colorado. The

Court enjoined Colorado from diverting more than the last-named amount of acre-feet a year from the Laramie River.

> *Wyoming* v. *Colorado et al.,* 259 U.S. (1922) 419, 459.
>
> On June 1, 1936 the Supreme Court of the United States enjoined Colorado, at the instance of Wyoming, from further diversions under meadowland appropriations of more than 4,250 acre-feet a year (the amount to which she was entitled for this purpose under the 1921 decree) measured at the headgates through which the water was diverted. Colorado claimed that the greater part of the water so diverted would return to the stream through surface drainage and percolation and that the amount actually consumed would not exceed the amount fixed in the 1921 decree. *Wyoming* v. *Colorado,* 298 U.S. (1936) 573, 586.
>
> On the doctrine of "prior appropriation", see *Bean* v. *Morris,* 221 U.S. (1911) 485; *Morris* v. *Bean et al.,* 146 Fed. 423 (C.C.D. Mont., 1906); *Bean et al.* v. *Morris et al.,* 159 Fed. 651 (C.C.A. 9th, 1908).
>
> For a case holding that in the State of Arizona the doctrine of prior appropriation is not applicable to percolating subterranean waters and stating that they are governed by the common law, see *Maricopa County Municipal Water Conservation District Number One et al.* v. *Southwest Cotton Company et al.,* 4 P. (2d) (1931) 369, 39 Ariz. 65.

Delaware River: tributaries   In 1930 New Jersey brought a suit to enjoin a proposed diversion of waters in New York from tributaries of the Delaware River to the watershed of the Hudson River in order to increase the water supply of the city of New York. The Supreme Court of the United States enjoined diversion in excess of 440 million gallons of water daily. New Jersey insisted on a strict application of the rules of the common law governing private riparian proprietors subject to the same sovereign power. The Court, Mr. Justice Holmes speaking, rejected this contention and adopted instead "the principle of equitable division", pointing out that the "removal of water to a different watershed obviously must be allowed at times unless States are to be deprived of the most beneficial use on formal grounds" and that—

> . . . It is established that a more liberal answer may be given than in a controversy between neighbors members of a single State. *Connecticut* v. *Massachusetts,* 282 U.S. 660. Different considerations come in when we are dealing with independent sovereigns having to regard the welfare of the whole population and when the alternative to settlement is war. In a less degree, perhaps, the same is true of the quasi-sovereignties bound together in the Union. A river is more than an amenity, it is a treasure. It offers a necessity of life that must be rationed among those who have power over it.
>
> *New Jersey* v. *New York et al.,* 283 U.S. (1931) 336, 341, 342.

In the case of *Connecticut* v. *Massachusetts,* decided in 1931, the Supreme Court of the United States was called upon to decide an original suit brought by Connecticut against Massachusetts to enjoin her from diverting waters from streams within her territory, the Ware and Swift Rivers, tributaries of the Connecticut, a navigable river flowing through Massachusetts and thence into Connecticut. The Special Master, to whom the case had been referred by the Court, found that the district to be served by the diversion would be faced by a water shortage in the near future and that the tributaries referred to were selected rather than other sources of water in the eastern part of Massachusetts which were polluted or liable to become so. The Court found that Connecticut had not established that she had sustained injury as a result of the diversions complained of and dismissed the bill of complaint without prejudice to her right to maintain a suit against Massachusetts whenever it should appear that substantial interests of Connecticut were being injured. The Court pointed out that, while under the common law in force in both States "each riparian owner has a vested right in the use of the flowing waters and is entitled to have them flow as they were wont, unimpaired as to quantity and uncontaminated as to quality", the municipal law of the States did not necessarily constitute a dependable guide or a just basis for the decision and that— Ware and Swift Rivers

> . . . As was shown in *Kansas* v. *Colorado*, 206 U.S. 46, 100, such disputes are to be settled on the basis of equality of right. But this is not to say that there must be an equal division of the waters of an interstate stream among the States through which it flows. It means that the principles of right and equity shall be applied having regard to the "equal level or plane on which all the States stand, in point of power and right, under our constitutional system" and that, upon a consideration of the pertinent laws of the contending States and all other relevant facts, this Court will determine what is an equitable apportionment of the use of such waters. *Wyoming* v. *Colorado*, 259 U.S. 419, 465, 470. "Right and equity"

282 U.S. (1931) 660, 669, 670.

In the case of *Washington* v. *Oregon*, a suit to obtain, *inter alia*, an apportionment between the two States of the waters of the Walla Walla River and tributaries, the complainant State alleged that Oregon was wrongfully diverting the waters and prayed for an injunction. In dismissing the complaint the Court, relying upon the rule of "priority of appropriation" as the basis of the division of the waters, said: Walla Walla River

> A priority once acquired or put in course of acquisition by the posting of a notice may be lost to the claimant by abandonment or laches. There must be no waste in arid lands of the "treasure" of a river. *New Jersey* v. *New York*, 283 U.S. 336, 342. The essence of the doctrine of prior appropriation is beneficial use, Abandonment

not a stale or barren claim. Only diligence and good faith will keep the privilege alive.

297 U.S. (1936) 517, 527.

Rio Grande   During the course of judicial proceedings relating to the proposed construction of the Elephant Butte Dam in New Mexico, entered into upon complaint of the Mexican authorities and resulting ultimately in a decision by the Supreme Court of the United States in 1909 perpetually enjoining the company which had been formed for the purpose of constructing the dam from constructing it, the United States undertook the construction of a dam near Engle, New Mexico, about one mile from the site of the then-proposed Elephant Butte Dam, and concluded a convention with the Mexican Government on May 21, 1906 providing for the equitable distribution of the waters of the Rio Grande for irrigation purposes, with special reference to the distribution of waters to be stored as a result of the construction of Eagle Dam. Article I of the convention provides that the United States shall deliver to Mexico from the waters stored by the dam a total of 60,000 acre-feet of water annually; article III provides that such delivery shall be without cost to Mexico; while article IV provides that the delivery of the water shall not be construed as "a recognition by the United States of any claim on the part of Mexico to the said waters". Article V further stipulates:

> The United States, in entering into this treaty, does not thereby concede, expressly or by implication, any legal basis for any claims heretofore asserted or which may be hereafter asserted by reason of any losses incurred by the owners of land in Mexico due or alleged to be due to the diversion of the waters of the Rio Grande within the United States; nor does the United States in any way concede the establishment of any general principle or precedent by the concluding of this treaty. The understanding of both parties is that the arrangement contemplated by this treaty extends only to the portion of the Rio Grande which forms the international boundary, from the head of the Mexican Canal down to Fort Quitman, Texas, and in no other case.

1 Treaties, etc. (Malloy, 1910) 1202, 1203. *United States* v. *Rio Grande Dam and Irrigation Company*, 174 U.S. (1899) 690, 702, 703; 184 U.S. (1902) 416. *Rio Grande Dam and Irrigation Company* v. *United States*, 215 U.S. (1909) 266; Secretary Root to the British Ambassador, Sir H. M. Durand, Nov. 2, 1905, MS. Department of State, 27 Notes, Great Britain, 420–425. For the opinion of the American-British arbitral tribunal established under the special agreement between the United States and Great Britain of Aug. 18, 1910, disallowing the claim against the United States of the *Rio Grande Irrigation and Land Company, Ltd.*, an English company formed for the actual task of constructing the Elephant Butte Dam, see Nielsen's Report (1926) 336. For correspondence relating to the

proposed construction of Engle Dam, see MS. Department of State, file 17053.

In 1907 and 1908 Mexico called the attention of the United States to two proposed diversions of water on the American side of the Rio Grande and contended that the convention of 1906 forbade any further depletion of the water supply enjoyed by Mexican land-owners around Ciudad Juárez, Mexico, pending the construction of the storage dam near Engle, New Mexico, and the delivery of the quantity of water to Mexico for which the convention provided. The Department of State, relying upon the advice of the Attorney General (May 2, 1907), replied that the proposed diversions were outside of the particular stretch of the river included within the scope of the convention. At the same time it suggested that an International Commission be appointed for the study of the equitable distribution of the waters of the Rio Grande, with a view to arriving at an international agreement acceptable to both countries. The proposal was accepted in December 1908, and a commissioner was appointed by each Government, but in 1913 the President of Mexico discontinued the negotiations until formal recognition of his admin-istration by the United States. No further negotiations took place until 1925.

Joint Commission: Rio Grande

The Mexican Ambassador (Creel) to Secretary Root, no. 5, Feb. 20, 1907, MS. Department of State, file 3487/6; Attorney General Bonaparte to Mr. Root, May 2, 1907, *ibid.* 3487/13–20.

The Mexican Chargé d'Affaires (Godoy) to Mr. Root, Feb. 6, 1908, *ibid.* 3487/21; Señor Godoy to the Acting Secretary of State (Bacon), Oct. 1, 1908, and Mr. Bacon to Señor Godoy, no. 381, Nov. 24, 1908, *ibid.* 3487/32; Señor Godoy to Mr. Root, Dec. 21, 1908, *ibid.* 17420/3; Secretary Bacon to Señor Godoy, Feb. 1, 1909, *ibid.* 17420/4; Commissioner Keblinger to Secre-tary Knox, May 21, 1912, *ibid.* 711.1216M/342.

Meanwhile the United States and Mexico, at the suggestion of the former, also appointed a Joint Commission, consisting of a commis-sioner appointed by each Government, to make recommendations with respect to the amount of water which the two Governments were respectively entitled to take from the Colorado River for irrigation purposes. It appears that the plan contemplated by the commis-sioners involved a large expenditure of money for storage reservoirs on the headwaters of the river.

Joint Com-mission: Colorado River

Secretary Root to Ambassador Thompson, no. 397, Jan. 29, 1908, MS. Department of State, file 3172/71a; the Mexican Minister of Foreign Af-fairs (Mariscal) to Mr. Thompson, Mar. 31, 1908, *ibid.* 3172/85–86. Com-missioner Keblinger to Secretary Knox, May 21, 1912, and the Acting Secretary of State (Wilson) to Senator John D. Works, May 27, 1912, *ibid.* 711.1216M/342.

Between September 1912 and May 1913 negotiations took place with reference to a draft convention providing for a preliminary commission to study and report upon a basis of distribution of the waters of the Colorado. They were broken off by the President of Mexico pending the formal recognition of his administration by the United States, and were not resumed until in January 1925.

The Acting Secretary of State (Wilson) to Ambassador Wilson, no. 775, Mar. 21, 1912, MS. Department of State, file 711.1216M/326; Ambassador Wilson to Secretary Knox, no. 1379, Apr. 27, 1912, *ibid.* 711.1216M/334; the Acting Secretary of State (Wilson) to Ambassador Wilson, no. 974, Sept. 10, 1912, *ibid.* 711.1216M/384; Mr. Adee to Ambassador Wilson, no. 1215, Feb. 8, 1913, *ibid.* 711.1216M/399; Ambassador Wilson to Mr. Knox, May 8, 1913, *ibid.* 812.00/7431; Chargé Benitez to Secretary Hughes, Jan. 6, 1925, and Mr. Hughes to Señor Benitez, Feb. 5, 1925, *ibid.* 711.1216M/534.

By an act of Congress approved August 19, 1921 (42 Stat. 171), the States of Arizona, California, Colorado, Nevada, New Mexico, Utah, and Wyoming were authorized to enter into a compact or agreement respecting the disposition and apportionment of the waters of the Colorado River. These States entered into a compact on November 24, 1922 containing provisions in article III apportioning in perpetuity to the upper and lower basins on the Colorado River system 7,500,000 acre-feet of water *per annum* (the lower basin being also permitted to increase its beneficial consumptive use of such waters by 1,000,000 acre-feet *per annum*), and agreeing that if, "as a matter of international comity", the United States should thereafter recognize any right in Mexico to the use of any waters of the Colorado River system, such waters should be supplied first from the waters which are surplus over and above the amounts so apportioned and in the event of an insufficiency of such surplus then the deficiency should be borne equally by the upper and lower basins. Article IV of the compact, after stating that the Colorado River had ceased to be navigable for commerce, provided that its use for navigation should be subservient to domestic, agricultural, and power purposes.

Colorado River compact

The approval by Congress of the compact was contained in section 13(a) of the Boulder Canyon Project Act, December 21, 1928 (45 Stat. 1057), section 20 of which provided:

Nothing in this Act shall be construed as a denial or recognition of any rights, if any, in Mexico to the use of the waters of the Colorado River system.

Conformably to exchanges of communications in 1925 and 1926 between the United States and Mexico, the Congress of the United States on March 3, 1927 passed a joint resolution (44 Stat., pt. 2, p. 1403, amending an act of May 13, 1924, 43 Stat. 118) authorizing the President to designate three commissioners to cooperate with representatives of Mexico in a study regarding the equitable use of the waters of the lower Rio Grande, the lower Colorado, and, with the concurrence of Mexico, of the Tia Juana River, for the purpose of securing information on which to base a treaty with Mexico. On June 15, 1927 the Secretary of State directed that the title of the new commission should be the International Water Commission, United States and Mexico. Report of the American Section of the International Water Commission, United States and Mexico, H. Doc. 359, 71st Cong., 2d sess., p. 2.

International Water Commission

On March 22, 1930 the American section of the Commission submitted a report to the Congress, pointing out, *inter alia*, that the Mexican section took the position that it could not suggest to its Government a modification of the existing agreements "which proclaim the navigability of the Rio Grande and Colorado unless modifications could be established which would permit a use of the waters more advantageous for the inhabitants of the two countries"; that the Colorado was an international stream and must be considered as a single geographical unit; that Mexico could not accept a smaller volume than 3,600,000 acre-feet of water *per annum* (the original claim was 4,500,000 acre-feet annually) from the Colorado River; that it had taken into consideration in arriving at its figure only lands susceptible of irrigation by ditches, irrigable lands requiring a pumping-lift under 80 feet, and those that could be cultivated at small cost, while in the United States "there were taken into consideration domestic uses of cities far away from the stream, lands to be irrigated with a pump lift of between 80 and 400 feet, and also lands that would be very costly to put under cultivation"; and that it was not the main purpose of the convention of 1906 to settle the problem of "the equitable distribution of the waters between the two countries, notwithstanding that it so states". On the other hand, it was stated that the American section took the position that, owing to the importance of conserving and using for irrigation and other beneficial purposes all the waters of the Rio Grande and the Colorado River, the theory of navigability of these streams should be abandoned; that the only instance of the international determination of waters for irrigation and other consumptive purposes between the United States and Mexico was the convention of 1906 for the equitable distribution of the waters of the Rio Grande, under which as an act of comity the United States undertook to provide Mexico with a regulated flow of water from a reservoir built by and within the United States near El Paso; that similarly it proposed to recommend as an act of comity and "as an equitable division of the waters of the

Report of American section

Colorado", to deliver to Mexico 750,000 acre-feet annually, representing the greatest amount that had been received by irrigators in that country from the stream in any one year, namely 1928, the certainty of such delivery to be conditioned on the construction by the United States of Boulder Dam; and that to approve the proposal of Mexico would mean that development of land in the United States would be restricted by the reservation of water for lands in Mexico "that are not now irrigated and which may not be irrigated for an indefinite period in the future", a surrender not required "by either international law or comity".

The report to Congress pointed out that the differences in the views of the two sections made it impossible to submit unanimous recommendations. In regard to the Tia Juana River, it stated that the Commission considered any international action on the stream unnecessary at that time although the two Governments might later find it advantageous to confirm formally an agreement reached by local authorities.

With respect to the Rio Grande the American section suggested that—

> a treaty should be entered into between the United States and Mexico whereby existing uses that have grown up in either country for the waters of the Rio Grande would be recognized and perpetuated, and under which the two countries jointly may construct reservoirs on the main river to fully regulate the flow and make available for beneficial use in the two countries the water now being wasted into the Gulf and the power that may be generated along the river below Fort Quitman, the cost of these reservoirs to be borne by the two countries in proportion to the water to be stored therein for each country, and the cost of the works for the development of power and the power therefrom to be similarly shared. [Report of the American Section of the Commission, *ante*, pp. 28–29.]

In transmitting the report of the Commission to the President the Department of State said:

> The American section of the Commission in its report expresses views on certain legal and political matters which have not been passed on or approved by this department. [*Ibid.* vii.]

Consolidation: International Boundary Commission

By an act of Congress approved June 30, 1932 (47 Stat. 382, 417), the American section of the International Water Commission, United States and Mexico, was abolished, and its powers, duties, and functions were transferred to the American section of the International Boundary Commission, United States and Mexico, established under the boundary convention of March 1, 1889. 1 Treaties, etc. (Malloy, 1910) 1167.

On August 19, 1935 Congress passed another act authorizing the President to appoint representatives to cooperate with representatives of Mexico in a study of the equitable use of the water of the lower Rio Grande, the lower Colorado River, and the Tia Juana River, for the purpose of obtaining information which might be used as a basis for the negotiation of a treaty (49 Stat. 660). The American Commissioner on the International Boundary Commission, United States and Mexico, was authorized to perform these functions. Negotiations looking to the conclusion of a treaty have been suspended until all available data shall have been assembled and compiled.

In as much as Elephant Butte Dam, constructed by the United States in compliance with its obligation under article I of the convention of 1906 between the United States and Mexico, whereby the United States agreed to deliver "60,000 acre-feet of water annually, in the bed of the Rio Grande at the point where the head works of the Acequia Madre, known as the Old Mexican Canal, now exist above the city of Juarez", is located about 130 miles from the point of the delivery of the water and as the United States has no control over the Rio Grande between these two points, the water to be delivered is beyond the control of the United States to measure. By an act of Congress approved June 4, 1936 the Secretary of State was authorized, in order to remedy this situation, to construct, operate, and maintain works for the canalization of the Rio Grande from the proposed Caballo Dam in New Mexico to the proposed international dam near El Paso, Texas, and to acquire such property as may be necessary therefor. Preliminary Report of the American Section of the International Water Commission, United States and Mexico, Aug. 1, 1935, MS. Department of State, file 711.1216A/688; Final Report, Dec. 14, 1935, ibid. 711.1216A/741; 32 Stat. 388; 49 Stat. 24, 660, 961, 1463.

Secretary Kellogg to the American Embassy in Mexico City, Aug. 12, 1926, MS. Department of State, file 711.1216B/195a; Mr. Schoenfeld to Mr. Kellogg, Nov. 23, 1926, ibid. 711.1216B/200; Report of the American Section of the International Water Commission, United States and Mexico, H. Doc. 359, 71st Cong., 2d sess., serial no. 9233; Secretary Hull to the President, Aug. 24, 1935, MS. Department of State, file 711.1216A/703.

Colorado River compact, H. Doc. 605, 67th Cong., 4th sess., serial no. 8215; for copies of the documents constituting the basic exchanges between the United States and Mexico, 1924–28, respecting the proposed study of the equitable use of the waters of the lower Colorado River and the Rio Grande, see S. Doc. 163, 70th Cong., 1st sess., serial no. 8871; for a report of the House Committee on Irrigation and Reclamation regarding the Boulder Canyon project, see H. Rept. 918, 70th Cong., 1st sess., serial no. 8836.

See also: Hearings before the House Committee on Foreign Affairs on H.R. 8371, regarding the "Equitable Use of the Waters of the Rio Grande below Fort Quitman, Texas", Apr. 17, 1924, 68th Cong., 1st sess.; H.R. 6453, providing for study regarding equitable use of waters of Rio Grande, etc., in cooperation with Mexico, S. Rept. 633, 74th Cong., 1st sess., serial no. 9879; H.R. 6453, H. Rept. 422, 74th Cong., 1st sess., serial no. 9886; report regarding extension of terms and provisions of present Rio Grande compact, H.R. 7873, S. Rept. 712, 74th Cong., 1st sess., serial no. 9879; hearings before the House Committee on Foreign Affairs on H.R. 9998 and H.R.

11768, for the purpose of authorizing construction, operation, and maintenance of Rio Grande canalization project and authorizing appropriation for that purpose, Mar. 10 and 13, 1936, 74th Cong., 2d sess.

In the case of *Arizona* v. *California et al.* the Supreme Court of the United States dismissed a suit brought by Arizona against the Secretary of the Interior and the States of California, Nevada, Utah, New Mexico, Colorado, and Wyoming in 1930 to enjoin the construction at Black Canyon on the Colorado River of a dam pursuant to the Boulder Canyon Project Act of Dec. 21, 1928 (45 Stat. 1057), and the Colorado River compact. Half of the dam was to be in Arizona. Arizona and the six defendant States signed the Colorado River compact, but Arizona did not ratify it. The Court held, *inter alia*, that the Federal Government had the power to create this obstruction in the Colorado River for the purpose of improving its navigability. It found that the contention by Arizona that the river was not navigable could not be maintained and that the fact that purposes other than navigation would be served by the construction of the dam could not invalidate the exercising of the lawful authority regarding improvement of navigation. 283 U.S. (1931) 423; see also *Arizona* v. *California et al.*, 292 U.S. (1934) 341.

On Nov. 25, 1935 Arizona requested the Supreme Court of the United States to allow it to file a bill against California and the five other States of the Colorado River basin praying in effect for a judicial apportionment of the unappropriated waters of the Colorado River. On May 25, 1936 the Court denied the petition on the ground that the United States had undertaken, in the asserted exercise of its authority to control navigation, to impound, and control the disposition of, the surplus water in the river not already appropriated, and that the United States would be an indispensable party in such a proceeding. The Court pointed out that the natural dependable flow of the river was already over-appropriated and that the prayer was for a decree of equitable division of the privilege of future appropriation. *Arizona* v. *California et al.*, 298 U.S. (1936) 558, 570–571.

On May 3, 1906, following a joint resolution of Congress of March 15, 1906, the International Waterways Commission (United States and Canada) reported (1) that "it would be a sacrilege to destroy the scenic effect of Niagara Falls"; (2) that while the Commission was not fully agreed as to the effect of diversions of water from Niagara Falls, all were of the opinion that more than 36,000 cubic feet a second on the Canadian side of the Niagara River or on the Niagara peninsula and 18,500 cubic feet a second on the American side of the Niagara River, including diversions for power purposes on the Erie Canal, "can not be diverted without injury to Niagara Falls as a whole"; and (3) that it recommended that "a treaty or legislation be had limiting these diversions to the quantities mentioned".

Niagara River

34 Stat. 824. Report of the American Members of the International Waterways Commission, United States and Canada, relating to the preservation of Niagara Falls, submitted to Congress on Mar. 19, 1906, printed in Hearings before the House Committee on Rivers and Harbors, H.R.

18024, 59th Cong., 1st sess., p. 262. For the report of the Commission, dated May 3, 1906, see *ibid.* pp. 283, 284.

The act of Congress of June 29, 1906 contained a general prohibition with respect to diversion of water from the Niagara River above Niagara Falls but authorized the Secretary of War, under certain express limitations, to issue permits for the use of water for power purposes. The act provided further that the permits so issued were not to interfere with the navigable capacity of the river, with its integrity and proper volume as a boundary stream, or with the scenic grandeur of the Falls. The permits so issued were to be revocable at will by the Secretary of War and were to terminate by statutory limitation on June 29, 1909, the date of the expiration of the act. The act requested the President to open negotiations with Great Britain "for the purpose of effectually providing, by suitable treaty with said Government, for such regulation and control of the waters of Niagara River and its tributaries as will preserve the scenic grandeur of Niagara Falls and of the rapids in said river". 34 Stat. 626. By joint resolution of Mar. 3, 1909, the act of June 29, 1906 was continued in force for two years. 35 Stat. 1169.

On January 11, 1909 a convention relating to the boundary waters between the United States and Canada was signed by the United States and Great Britain and was proclaimed by the President on May 13, 1910. Article V of the convention, after reciting the desirability of limiting the diversion of waters from the Niagara River so that the level of Lake Erie and the flow of the stream shall not be appreciably affected and of accomplishing this with the least possible injury to investments already made in the construction of power plants on each side of the river, states: *Convention of 1909, art. V*

The United States may authorize and permit the diversion within the State of New York of the waters of said river above the Falls of Niagara, for power purposes, not exceeding in the aggregate a daily diversion at the rate of twenty thousand cubic feet of water per second.

The United Kingdom, by the Dominion of Canada, or the Province of Ontario, may authorize and permit the diversion within the Province of Ontario of the waters of said river above the Falls of Niagara, for power purposes, not exceeding in the aggregate a daily diversion at the rate of thirty-six thousand cubic feet of water per second.

The prohibitions of this article shall not apply to the diversion of water for sanitary or domestic purposes, or for the service of canals for the purposes of navigation.

3 Treaties, etc. (Redmond, 1923) 2607, 2609.

On Jan. 2, 1929 the United States and Canada concluded a new treaty providing for additional diversion of waters from the Niagara River. This treaty is pending in the United States Senate. For the text of the 1929 treaty, see MS. Department of State, file 711.4216Ni/260, and 70 Cong. Rec., pt. 2, p. 1955.

In advising the Secretary of War on December 14, 1908 that the sanction of Congress was necessary for the construction of a proposed bridge across the Niagara River connecting Niagara Falls, New York, with Niagara Falls, Ontario, Canada, Attorney General Bonaparte stated:

Navigability

> Niagara River would seem to come fairly within these definitions of a navigable water of the United States. It forms a continued highway from Lake Erie to a point above the Falls over which commerce is carried on between the State of New York and a foreign country. The fact that commerce is interrupted for a few miles between the Falls and Lewiston, where it is again resumed, can not be said to affect the character of the river so as to take it out of the class of navigable waters of the United States. It seems to me an error to contend that because it can not be navigated throughout its entire course from Lake Erie to Lake Ontario, it is therefore not a navigable river of the United States, when for nearly 28 miles in all it forms a highway of commerce between this country and Canada, and I may add, when, as such, it constitutes an international boundary between this country and Canada.

27 Op. Att. Gen. (1909) 120, 123.

In an opinion of Aug. 14, 1913 Attorney General McReynolds advised President Wilson that "any diversion of water from the Niagara River in such quantity as substantially to interfere with the navigable capacity of that river or the connected lakes, or which in any substantial degree alters or modifies the course, location, or channel of either of those waterways", was prohibited by the terms of section 10 of the act of Congress approved on Mar. 3, 1899 (30 Stat. 1121, 1151) prohibiting obstructions to navigation, unless it was recommended in advance by the Chief of Engineers and authorized by the Secretary of War. 30 Op. Att. Gen. (1913–16) 217, 218.

The Congress of the United States adopted a joint resolution approved Jan. 19, 1917 (39 Stat. 867) authorizing the Secretary of War to issue permits, revocable at will, for additional diversion of water in the United States from the Niagara River. See Hearings of the Committee on Foreign Relations relating to this legislation, Feb. 10, 1917, S. 7803, H.R. 20047, 64th Cong., 2d sess.

See also Hearings before the Committee on Foreign Relations with regard to the preservation of Niagara Falls, S. Doc. 393, 59th Cong., 1st sess., serial no. 4915; Hearings of Jan. 16, 1912 on H.R. 6746, 7694, 62d Cong., 2d sess.; H. Rept. 158, to accompany S.J.Res. 3, 62d Cong., 1st sess., serial no. 6078.

St. Marys and Milk Rivers

In 1907 and 1908 negotiations occurred between the United States and Great Britain, wherein the United States proposed that an agreement be entered into apportioning the waters of the St. Marys and Milk Rivers which flow across the 49th-parallel boundary between the United States and Canada. The negotiations were later combined with the general negotiations resulting in the conclusion of the convention of January 11, 1909, article VI of which relates to the apportionment of the waters of the two rivers in question:

The High Contracting Parties agree that the St. Mary and Milk Rivers and their tributaries (in the State of Montana and the Provinces of Alberta and Saskatchewan) are to be treated as one stream for the purposes of irrigation and power, and the waters thereof shall be apportioned equally between the two countries, but in making such equal apportionment more than half may be taken from one river and less than half from the other by either country so as to afford a more beneficial use to each. It is further agreed that in the division of such waters during the irrigation season, between the 1st of April and 31st of October, inclusive, annually, the United States is entitled to a prior appropriation of 500 cubic feet per second of the waters of the Milk River, or so much of such amount as constitutes three-fourths of its natural flow, and that Canada is entitled to a prior appropriation of 500 cubic feet per second of the flow of St. Mary River, or so much of such amount as constitutes three-fourths of its natural flow.

The channel of the Milk River in Canada may be used at the convenience of the United States for the conveyance, while passing through Canadian territory, of waters diverted from the St. Mary River. . . .

The measurement and apportionment of the water to be used by each country shall from time to time be made jointly by the properly constituted reclamation officers of the United States and the properly constituted irrigation officers of His Majesty under the direction of the International Joint Commission.

Secretary Root to Ambassador Bryce, no. 88, June 15, 1907, MS. Department of State, file 5150/2; Mr. Bryce to Mr. Root, Mar. 10, 1908, *ibid.* 5150/8-9; 3 Treaties, etc. (Redmond, 1923) 2607, 2610.

The International Joint Commission between the United States and Canada was established pursuant to articles VII to XII of the convention of Jan. 11, 1909, *ibid.* 2611-2614. See *post*, pp. 616-617. The following cases decided by it arose out of applications seeking the Commission's approval for various projects:

Application of Rainy River Improvement Company, filed Apr. 4, 1912, for the erection of a dam at Kettle Falls, at the outlet of Lake Namakan, St. Louis County, Minnesota, denied on Apr. 8, 1913 for lack of jurisdiction.

Application of Clarence M. Brown, receiver of the Michigan Lake Superior Company, filed June 30, 1913, for approval of proposed lease with the United States for diversion of water from, and construction of compensating works in, the St. Marys River at Sault Ste. Marie, Michigan. The Michigan Northern Power Company was later substituted as applicant in the case. A conditional approval was granted on May 25, 1914.

Approval of diversion of waters of the St. Marys River and construction of compensating works at Sault Ste. Marie, Ontario, was sought in an application filed on Jan. 21, 1914 by the Algoma Steel Corporation. An approval conditional as to construction and operation of the proposed works was granted on May 27, 1914.

On Jan. 29, 1915 two separate applications were filed for approval of the obstruction, diversion, and use of the waters of St. Croix River at Grand Falls, in the State of Maine and the Province of New Brunswick. The two applicant companies, St. Croix Water Power Company and Sprague's Falls

Manufacturing Company (Limited), respectively, were controlled by the same interests, and the Commission, after considering the applications jointly, issued conditional approval in both cases on Nov. 9, 1915.

Approval of a submerged weir in the South Sault Channel of the St. Lawrence River at the mouth of the power canal of the St. Lawrence River Power Company at Massena, New York, was sought by the company in an application filed on Aug. 9, 1918. An interim order of approval was issued on Sept. 14, 1918 providing for the removal of the weir, unless the application, being again submitted to the Commission, should then be approved. Another application was filed on Sept. 5, 1920, and a second interim order of approval was issued on Dec. 6, 1922. A further continuance of the weir was granted for a period of two years from Sept. 14, 1923. On Jan. 25, 1928 the company submitted to the Commission an application to raise the crest of its submerged weir. The Commission adjourned *sine die* the hearing of the last-mentioned application in order to afford time for the collection of data desired by Canada and made an application by the company for a hearing a prerequisite to the holding of a further hearing. No such application has yet been filed.

Approval of an application for power development in the St. John River, at Grand Falls in New Brunswick, was sought by the New Brunswick Electric Power Commission in an application filed on Feb. 20, 1925. An order of approval was issued on June 22, 1925.

The Saint John River Power Company, which had acquired the rights of the New Brunswick Electric Power Commission, applied on June 16, 1926 for permission to construct and operate certain works in and adjacent to the St. John River, at Grand Falls, Saint John. The application was approved on June 28, 1926.

An official list of documents of the Commission relating to the cases referred to above is contained in the publication entitled *Papers Relating to the Work of the International Joint Commission* (Ottawa, 1929) 149.

In an application filed with the Commission on Sept. 6, 1929 and amended on Feb. 8, 1932, the West Kootenay Power and Light Company, Limited, sought the Commission's approval for the construction of a storage dam and compensatory works and plans therefor in Kootenay (Kootenai) River at or near Granite, British Columbia, and for the right to store water in Kootenay Lake. On Nov. 11, 1938 the Commission granted the application subject to certain supervisory control and to payment of a maximum sum of $3,000 annually to those who might be injured. The Secretary of the American section of the Commission (Smith) to the Secretary of State (Stimson), Sept. 19, 1929, MS. Department of State, file 711.42157K83/53; Mr. Smith to Mr. Stimson, Feb. 16, 1932, *ibid.* 711.42157K83/99; Secretary of the American section of the Commission (Ellis) to the Secretary of State (Hull), Nov. 14, 1938, 711.42157K83/186.

Leitha River   The Imperial Royal Administrative Court of Austria held a hearing on January 11, 1913 at which arguments were submitted against a decision of the Ministry of Agriculture authorizing diversion of water from the Leitha River. The diversion was to take place in Austrian territory. The Leitha flows into Hungary, and interested Hungarian parties complained against the diversion on the ground that they had "suffered in their ostensible usufructuary rights in the

Leitha in so far as the latter passes through Hungarian territory"
and had sustained injuries resulting from the fact that "the level
of the water-course running in the direction of Hungary has fallen
in consequence of measures put into operation on Austrian territory".
In rejecting the contention of the Hungarian parties to the litigation that "section 19 of the Lower Austrian law governing water
rights, which guarantees the municipalities against injury to their
water supply, extends also to the municipalities of a foreign state,
which might suffer prejudice, as the result of regulations enacted by
the Austrian authorities with reference to a body of water flowing
beyond the Austrian frontier, even in case the regulations applied
only to a body of water within Austrian territory", and in rejecting the claim of certain of the Hungarian parties that according to
international customary law all states are bound "in enacting
measures applying to water-courses running beyond their respective
frontiers, to respect the existing rights and juridically protected
interests in these water-courses beyond their frontiers", the Administrative Court, a national Austrian court, said:

> It must, furthermore, be borne in mind that, on the one hand,
> up to the present time, in so far as concerns the juridical condi-
> tions of water-courses flowing beyond the frontiers, we have not
> passed beyond the postulate of the mutual and fair consideration
> of the contiguous states through which the river takes its course;
> and, on the other hand, as is shown, among other writers, by
> Christian Meurer, in Vol. IV of *Zeitschrift für Politik* (1911),
> page 370 and following, opinions still widely differ regarding
> the extent to and the form in which this consideration should be
> applied. The thorough treatment which Dr. Max Huber, profes-
> sor in the University of Zürich, gave to these matters at the
> First International Aqui-Economic Conference, held at Berne
> in 1912 (*cf.* the protocol, p. 27 and following), shows that even
> the conventional settlement of questions arising in connection
> with rivers passing beyond the frontiers presents extraordinary
> difficulties in justly protecting the interests of the contracting
> states. If then, the question of adjusting these interests, in so
> far as they involve international law, is far from having been
> finally settled, we must dismiss as erroneous the assertion that the
> Austrian water law, as incorporated in the Imperial water law
> of 1869 and in the state water laws of 1870, has automatically
> introduced an international water law similar to the principle
> of international private law, according to which usufructuaries
> and other interested parties may claim rights in existing usu-
> fructuary conditions in that part of a body of water passing
> beyond the Austrian frontier and outside of Austria, when the
> possibility of damage to the usufruct in that part of the body of
> water outside of Austria is feared in consequence of measures
> enacted within Austrian territory.

7 A.J.I.L. (1913) 653, 657, 658 (translation).

With a view to regulating diversion of water from rivers for the development of hydraulic power, 16 states signed a convention at Geneva on December 9, 1923. This convention, which came into force on June 30, 1935, stipulates, *inter alia*, that it in no way affects the right of each state "within the limits of international law" to carry out on its own territory any operation for the development of hydraulic power which it may deem desirable; that should a reasonable development of power involve international investigation, such investigation shall be carried out conjointly by the states concerned with a view to arriving at the solution most favorable to their interests; and that no state shall be obliged to carry out a program of development unless it has formally accepted the obligation to do so.

> 36 League of Nations Treaty Series (1925) 75. A protocol signed on the same day provides that the convention does not modify state responsibility under international law for injury done by the construction of works for development of hydraulic power. *Ibid.* 89.

INTERNATIONAL STREAMS

EUROPEAN RIVERS

§87

On July 17 and 18, 1927 the German Constitutional Law Court (Staatsgerichtshof) rendered a provisional decision in the case of the States of *Württemberg and Prussia* v. *Baden*, involving rights of the three States in the flow of the waters of the Danube. In the upper regions of that river there is considerable seepage of water because of the character of the river's banks and bed. The waters flow underground through part of Baden, rising as a spring in its territory to form the river Aach which empties into the Lake of Constance. At the Immendingen Machine Works on the boundary of Baden a dam was constructed in 1914, causing part of the water of the Danube in the storage basin to run out underground. There were other sink areas a little below Immendingen, in Baden, at the Brühl bend, and at Fridingen in Württemberg. As a result of the seepage of water in Baden a part of the river in Württemberg, from 10 to 12 kilometers, dried up for a certain period each year, varying from 309 days in 1921 to 148 days in 1923.

Württemberg brought a suit to compel Baden to take measures to counteract the increase in the natural seepage of water. It alleged that the Immendingen Dam pressed the water into the sink holes situated within the storage basin; that that pressure was a cause of the increase in the natural sinking of the water in the Danube; and that the Baden Government had refused permission to the owner of a water-power plant, whose interests were also injured by the pressure of the water, to have the crevices in the rock in the storage basin behind the dam walled up and that this refusal was for the purpose of providing as much water as possible from the Danube for the persons interested in the Aach.

With respect to the sink holes at the Brühl, below Möhringen, it alleged that gravel banks and sand banks in the bed of the Danube were damming up the water of the river and forcing it to the right bank, where most of the sink holes were and that, during low water, owners of mills along the Danube at that point had taken measures to counteract the losses of water by filling the most important sink holes with brush, reeds, gravel, sand, and mud, and by cutting channels through the gravel banks which dammed up the water, but that the Baden Government had prohibited this work of maintenance, again in the interest of the persons concerned with the Aach. Württemberg maintained that this behavior of Baden was illegal, since it violated "the industrial regulations, the water laws of Baden itself, and, lastly, the principles of international law". Württemberg asked that the court order Baden (1) to make the walls of the dam at Immendingen watertight or to remove the dam, (2) to clear the bed of the Danube at Möhringen from the sand and gravel banks, and (3) to improve the river bed by a uniform river bottom.

Baden made a counter motion that Württemberg restore the conditions in the sink area of the Fridingen loop as they were before the construction of the Fridingen power plant and before the man-made closing of the sink holes in that district on the Krämer lot.

Prussia, alleging that it was affected by the seepage of the waters of the Danube which flows through Prussian territory after leaving Baden and Württemberg, joined Württemberg as a party plaintiff.

In deciding the case, the court stated that, so far as the German States can act as independent states, their legal relations to one another were regulated according to international law under article 4 of the Constitution of the German Reich but that in the relationship of the German States toward each other there was "a greater limitation of the basic principle of territorial sovereignty than if two entirely foreign states were opposing each other" and that, accordingly, there were obligations of the various German States toward each other "which cannot, at least to the same extent, be derived from international law applicable to all States". It pointed out that the case of the seeping of water from one river to another river occurs in nature so seldom that "rules of international law have not been formed for it". In holding that Baden must desist from injuring her neighbor at the Immendingen Dam where by damming up the water its sinking into the sole and side walls was facilitated, it relied on the "generally recognized principles of water law . . . [that] no useless consumption of water, injurious to other interested parties, may be connected with a dam", it stated that water would seep away at this point even if the dam were not there, and it held that Baden did "not need to eliminate the natural loss of water that would occur in the storage area even if the dam were not there, but only the augmented seepage caused by the dam".

As to the prohibitions of the authorities of Baden at Brühl against the making of simple channels in the sand and gravel banks, rendering it possible for the river to flow onward rather than to run off from the Danube to the Aach, it was held that Baden could not justify the prohibitions on the ground that "in this way she is only maintaining the natural conditions with respect to the water"; that, while a state "is not obliged to interfere, in the interests of another state, with the natural processes affecting an international river", the action of Baden in this particular amounted to "the neglect of any orderly work of maintenance" along this stretch of the river; and that Baden was "therefore required to eliminate the increased seepage caused by her inactivity" but that she was not under an obligation to improve the bed of the Danube in the Möhringen region "by the creation of a uniform sole of the river", as demanded by Württemburg, as this would involve "a considerable change in the natural condition", going beyond the "generally customary work of river maintenance . . . and approaches an improvement in the river".

As to the counter claim of Baden concerning measures which Württemberg had taken in the loop in the Danube lying in her territory near Fridingen, which could have resulted in only small damage to Baden, the court stated that "only considerable interference with the natural flow of international rivers can form the basis for claims under international law". It held that Württemberg was "justified in counteracting in her territory an increase of the seepage due entirely to natural causes" and that the "natural condition forms the limit for her action", since Württemberg must put up with the condition as to distribution of water which had been brought about in the past by natural means, i.e. that she was justified in closing certain artificial sink holes at the so-called "Krämer Ford", as they were not created by nature, but that she was not justified in establishing a power plant at Fridingen the water for the use of which did not return to the Danube until much farther down the river, thus depriving the Fridingen points of any possibility of seepage for a large portion of the year, a diminution in the seepage of water which Baden was not bound to bear. The court adopted the view that the "legal principles which have been developed for the common utilization of international watercourses flowing above ground require . . . application to water flowing underground" and that Württemberg was obliged "to refrain from such interference with the natural distribution of water as damages the interests of Baden to any considerable extent".

116 *Entscheidungen des Reichsgerichts in Zivilsachen* (1927) 1, 22, 30, 31–42 (second paging; translation).

A question having arisen as to the jurisdiction of the European Commission of the Danube established under the Treaty of Paris of 1856 in the region between Galatz (Galati) and Brăila, the Permanent Court of International Justice, in an Advisory Opinion rendered December 8, 1927, held that the European Commission had the same powers from Galatz to Brăila as it had on the part of the Danube below Galatz. In the course of its opinion the Court stated:

> Prior to 1815, the right to navigate rivers which separated or traversed two or more States was not regulated by any general principle or general act, and formed a subject of constant dispute. For the most part, each State sought to monopolize the navigation of streams flowing through its own territory, and even the right of an upper riparian State to access to the sea was denied. As the existence of such conditions not only hampered the development of commerce but also tended to prevent the growth of international relations appropriate to a state of peace, the Parties to the great international conflict which covered the concluding years of the XVIIIth century and the earlier part of the XIXth, introduced into the arrangements by which this long period of warfare was ended, provisions for the freedom of navigation of international streams.

After discussing the Act of Vienna of 1815, the Treaty of Paris of 1856, the Public Act concluded at Galatz in 1865, the Protocol of Paris of 1866, the Treaty of Berlin of 1878, the Additional Act signed at Galatz in 1881, the Treaty signed at London in 1883, and the pertinent provisions of the Treaty of Versailles of 1919, the Court denied the contention of the Rumanian Government that a distinction should be drawn "between so-called technical and so-called juridical powers" of the Commission, as well as the contention that the powers of the Commission were to be considered as being limited in the ports of Galatz and Brăila to a zone corresponding generally to the navigable channel to the exclusion of the harbor zones. The Court said:

> . . . The criterion for the delimitation of the powers of the European Commission and of the territorial authorities in the ports of Galatz and Braila with regard to vessels moored or otherwise at rest in these ports, and with regard to the use by vessels of the installations and services of these ports, is therefore the following: the powers of regulation and jurisdiction belong to the territorial authorities; the right of supervision,

with a view to ensuring freedom of navigation and equal treatment of all flags, belongs to the European Commission.

Per. Ct. Int. Jus., Advisory Opinion, Ser. B, No. 14, pp. 38, 46, 67; II Hudson, *World Court Reports* (1935) 140, 164, 170, 185.

Following the rendition of the Advisory Opinion negotiations were renewed by the interested governments and a draft convention was prepared to confirm the jurisdiction of the European Commission up to Brăila, but this convention was not brought into force. On May 17, 1933 representatives of France, Great Britain, Italy, and Rumania signed a *modus vivendi* and declaration which were signed by the Commission on June 25, 1933, containing provision that the European Commission's jurisdiction should extend from the sea to Brăila under certain conditions. For the text of the *modus vivendi* and the declaration of June 25, 1933, see Per. Ct. Int. Jus., Ser. E, No. 9, pp. 106, 107; *ibid.* No. 10, p. 79.

Article 32 of the convention instituting the definitive statute of the Danube, signed at Paris on July 23, 1921 (26 League of Nations Treaty Series [1924] 173, 191) provided that, in order to maintain and improve navigable conditions at the Iron Gates section of the Danube, the two riparian states concerned, that is, Rumania and Yugoslavia, and the International Commission should conclude an agreement setting up special technical and administrative services. The agreement referred to was signed at Semmering on June 28, 1932. 140 *idem* (1934) 191.

For the early history of the European Commission of the Danube, see Joseph P. Chamberlain, *The Danube* (Washington: Government Printing Office, 1918).

By articles 341 and 343 of the Treaty of Versailles the Oder River was placed under the administration of an International Commission composed of representatives of Poland, Prussia, Czechoslovakia, Great Britain, France, Denmark, and Sweden, charged with the duty of preparing a project for the revision of existing international agreements and regulations. Difficulties arose with respect to the definition of the sections of the river to which the international regime was to apply. The Warthe (Warta) and the Netze (Noteć) rise in Poland and, after flowing through Polish territory, form the German-Polish frontier for a certain distance, and then pass into German territory, where the Netze flows into the Warthe before that river joins the Oder. By the terms of article 331 of the Treaty of Versailles the Oder "and all navigable parts" thereof "which naturally provide more than one State with access to the sea" were declared "international". All parties admitted the navigability of the Warthe and the Netze in Polish territory. The Polish Government, however, contended that the parts of the streams which were in Polish territory provided only Poland with access to the sea and that therefore they did not fall within the terms of article 331. On the other hand, the six other powers on the International Commission maintained that "the fact of providing more than one State with access to the sea concerns the waterway as such and not a particular

The Oder

part of its course" and that therefore the condition prescribed by article 331 was fulfilled.

The Permanent Court of International Justice rendered a judgment on September 10, 1929, holding that the jurisdiction of the Commission extended to the section of the Warthe and the Netze situated in Polish territory. It stated that a solution "has been sought not in the idea of a right of passage in favour of upstream States, but in that of a community of interest of riparian States"; that this community of interest in a navigable river "becomes the basis of a common legal right, the essential features of which are the perfect equality of all riparian States in the user of the whole course of the river and the exclusion of any preferential privilege of any one riparian State in relation to the other"; that article 332 of the Treaty of Versailles granted freedom of navigation on waterways declared international in article 331 "to all Powers on a footing of perfect equality", a provision that would be "inappropriate, if not arbitrary, if the freedom stopped short at the last political frontier"; that the introduction of representatives of non-riparian powers on the river commissions was "not exclusively or mainly due to the desire to afford a greater measure of protection to the interests of landlocked States" but was "rather to be explained by the interest that non-riparian States may have in navigation on the waterways in question"; and that it would be difficult to understand why that interest should not be recognized "where the question of reaching the ports of the last upstream State is involved", as the interest of all states is in liberty of navigation in both directions.

3 Treaties, etc. (Redmond, 1923) 3487–3492; Per. Ct. Int. Jus., Ser. A, No. 23, pp. 25, 27, 28; *ibid.* Ser. C., No. 17–II, p. 244; II Hudson, *World Court Reports* (1935) 611, 626, 627, 628.

At the Barcelona Conference held in Mar. and Apr. 1921, forty states participated in the conclusion of a convention on the regime of navigable waterways of international concern. Attached to the convention was a statute on the regime of navigable waterways of international concern. These instruments constituted the general convention contemplated by the provisions of the peace treaties (*ante*). Articles 1 and 2 of the statute define "navigable waterways of international concern". The statute also contains provisions with reference to freedom of navigation (art. 3), equality of treatment (art. 4), interstate transportation (art. 5), and the authority of the respective states to take necessary measures for policing the territory and for applying laws and regulations relating to customs, public health, *etc.* (art. 6).

7 League of Nations Treaty Series (1921–22) 36; League of Nations, Barcelona Conference, Verbatim Records and Texts Relating to the Convention on the Regime of Navigable Waterways of International Concern and to the Declaration Recognising the Right to a Flag of States Having no Sea-Coast, Geneva 1921, pp. 430, 451.

Article 327 of the Treaty of Versailles, signed June 28, 1919, provides for freedom of navigation of Germany's inland navigating routes for the nationals of the Allied and Associated Powers. By article 331 of the treaty "the Elbe (*Labe*) from its confluence with the Vltava (*Moldau*), and the Vltava (*Moldau*) from Prague; the Oder (*Odra*) from its confluence with the Oppa; the Niemen (*Russstrom-Memel-Niemen*) from Grodno; the Danube from Ulm" are "declared international . . . and all navigable parts of these river systems which naturally provide more than one State with access to the sea, with or without transhipment from one vessel to another; together with lateral canals and channels constructed either to duplicate or to improve naturally navigable sections of the specified river systems, or to connect two naturally navigable sections of the same river" are also "declared international". Article 332 provides for equality of treatment of persons and vessels of all powers. Articles 333–337 relate to charges and maintenance of the navigability of the river by riparian states. Article 338 provides that the regime set out in articles 332–337 above shall be superseded by one to be laid down in a general convention drawn up by the Allied and Associated Powers and approved by the League of Nations. 3 Treaties, etc. (Redmond, 1923) 3487–3491. Similar provisions are contained in articles 290–310 of the Treaty of St.-Germain-en-Laye signed Sept. 10, 1919, and in articles 274–293 of the Treaty of Trianon signed June 4, 1920. *Ibid.* 3266–3272, 3665–3671.

By articles 340 and 343 of the Treaty of Versailles the Elbe River was placed under the administration of an international commission comprised of representatives of German riparian States, Czechoslovakia, Great Britain, France, Italy, and Belgium and empowered to prepare a project for the revision of existing international agreements and regulations in conformity with provisions of the treaty. A convention instituting the statute of navigation of the Elbe was signed at Dresden on Feb. 22, 1922 by Germany, Belgium, Great Britain, France, Italy, and Czechoslovakia. Article 2 thereof provides that the international commission, in addition to pronouncing upon complaints arising out of the application of the convention and claims appealed to it and deciding whether tariffs are in accordance with the convention, shall "supervise the conservation of the freedom of navigation, the maintenance in good order of the navigable channel and the improvement of that channel".

3 Treaties, etc. (Redmond, 1923) 3487–3492; 26 League of Nations Treaty Series (1924) 219, 223.

Article 362 of the Treaty of Versailles provides that Germany shall offer no objection to any proposals of the Central Rhine Commission for extending its jurisdiction—

"(1) to the Moselle below the Franco-Luxemburg frontier down to the Rhine, subject to the consent of Luxemburg;

"(2) to the Rhine above Basle up to the Lake of Constance, subject to the consent of Switzerland;

"(3) to the lateral canals and channels which may be established either to duplicate or to improve naturally navigable sections of the Rhine or the Moselle, or to connect two naturally navigable sections of these rivers, and also any other parts of the Rhine river system which may be covered by the General Convention provided for in Article 338 above."

3 Treaties, etc. (Redmond, 1923) 3497.

The Treaty of Versailles continued in force the Convention of Mannheim of Oct. 17, 1868, which superseded the definitive regulation regarding the navigation of the Rhine put into effect by the convention signed at Mayence (Mainz) on Mar. 31, 1831, by Baden, Bavaria, France, Hesse, Nassau, Netherlands, and Prussia.

For the early history of the Rhine Commission, see Per. Ct. Int. Jus., Ser. B, No. 14, pp. 38 and 39. For the convention of 1831, see IX Martens' *Nouveau recueil* (1833) 252. For the convention of 1868, see XX Martens' *idem* (1875) 355; and for an "Additional Article", dated Sept. 18, 1895, see 87 Br. & For. St. Paps. 788. For the text of the agreement of June 4, 1898 modifying the convention of Mannheim, see XXIX Martens' *Nouveau recueil général* (2d ser, 1903) 113. For the text of the pertinent provisions (arts. 354–362) of the Treaty of Versailles, see 3 Treaties, etc. (Redmond, 1923) 3493.

Article 359 of the Treaty of Versailles provides that no works shall be carried out on the Rhine where it forms the boundary between France and Germany without the previous approval of the Central Commission for Rhine Navigation. A preliminary agreement with reference to works to be undertaken was concluded by France, Germany, and Switzerland on May 10, 1922. On Dec. 18, 1929 France, Germany, and Switzerland signed at Geneva a protocol concerning technical and administrative cooperation in the work for the regulation of the Rhine between Strasburg-Kehl and Istein. Article I of this protocol provided that Germany and Switzerland should carry out the regulation of the Rhine between Strasburg-Kehl and Istein, in accordance with the scheme approved by the Central Commission for Rhine Navigation on Apr. 29, 1925.

3 Treaties, etc. (Redmond, 1923) 3496; 26 League of Nations Treaty Series (1924) 265; 104 *idem* (1930) 27.

On Sept. 28, 1927 the First Senate of the Department for the Insurance of the Sick and Invalid in Germany rendered an opinion in a case involving the question whether German law subjecting to insurance foreign ships employed in navigating German waters for a considerable length of time could be applied to such ships in view of the internationalization of the Rhine. It was held that such law was applicable to the crews of the Swiss Tug Navigation Company. 43 *Amtliche Nachrichten des Reichsversicherungsamts* (1927) 586.

It has been held that a judgment rendered by the Court for Navigation Rights on the Rhine at Rüdesheim, Germany, must be executed in France, a signatory to the Treaty of Versailles. *Badische A. G. für Reinschiffahrt und Seetransport* v. *Compagnie centrale d'assurances maritimes, Compagnie Mélusine et Union Maritime,* 55 *Clunet, Journal du droit international* (1928) 1043.

AMERICAN RIVERS

§88

Pigeon River, a small international boundary stream between the State of Minnesota and the Province of Ontario, has it source in lakes on the international boundary, whence it flows in a southeasterly direction along that boundary for about 40 miles and discharges at Pigeon Bay into Lake Superior. The boundary is approximately midstream. In 1928, 1929, and 1930, Charles W. Cox, Limited, a

Pigeon River

Canadian corporation and dealer in timber, drove quantities of pulp-wood and railway ties down the river toward Lake Superior, making use of improvements in the river, consisting of sluiceways, booms, and dams, belonging to the Pigeon River Improvement, Slide & Boom Co. (a Minnesota corporation) and refusing to pay tolls thereon. The latter company brought suit against the Canadian corporation to recover the tolls. The case was removed to a Federal court, a demurrer to the amended complaint was sustained without leave further to amend, and the judgment of dismissal was affirmed by the circuit court of appeals.

Upon appeal the Supreme Court of the United States reversed the judgment dismissing the complaint and held that the provision in article II of the Webster-Ashburton treaty of 1842 that "all the water communications and all the usual portages along the line from Lake Superior to the Lake of the Woods, and also Grand Portage, from the shore of Lake Superior to the Pigeon River, as now actually used, shall be free and open to the use of the citizens and subjects of both countries", did not preclude improvements of the stream by sluiceways, booms, and dams nor did it prevent the exaction of a non-discriminatory charge for the use of such improvements. In the course of the decision (Mr. Chief Justice Hughes rendering the opinion), it was pointed out that under the decision of the Canadian Supreme Court in the case of the *Arrow River & Tributaries, Slide & Boom Co.*, decided in 1932, it had been held that the Ontario company might impose charges upon citizens of the United States for the use of its works on the Canadian side of the line.

> *Pigeon River Improvement, Slide & Boom Co.* v. *Charles W. Cox, Limited*, 63 F. (2d) 567 (C.C.A. 8th, 1933) ; 291 U.S. (1934) 138, 148. *Arrow River & Tributaries Slide & Boom Company, Ltd.* v. *Pigeon Timber Company, Limited*, 1932 Can. Sup. Ct. 495.

Concurrent regulations, St. Clair River

At the suggestion of the War Department of the United States, the Governments of the United States and Canada in 1907 agreed on concurrent regulations requiring all up-bound vessels passing through the St. Clair River in the vicinity of Stag Island to pass through the eastern channel (in Canada) and all down-bound vessels to pass through the western channel (in the United States). These regulations were extended by concurrent action in 1909 to the St. Clair River in the vicinity of St. Clair, Michigan.

> For the regulations of the War Department in this regard, dated Jan. 8, 1907 and Apr. 24, 1909, see MS. Department of State, files 3722, 3722/4–5. For the Canadian Orders in Council of Feb. 19, 1907 and June 5, 1909, see *ibid.* 3722/1–3, 3722/7–8.
>
> The Canadian Government proposed, through the British Ambassador on July 2, 1909, that the speed of vessels in the St. Clair River be limited

to nine miles an hour. Concurrent regulations to this effect were thereupon adopted by both Governments.

For the Canadian Order in Council of Oct. 9, 1909, see *ibid*. 3722/14–15. For the regulations promulgated by the War Department, see Acting Secretary of State (Adee) to Ambassador Bryce, no. 720, Sept. 14, 1909, *ibid*. 3722/11.

On July 18, 1932 Canada and the United States signed a treaty for the construction of a deep waterway from the Great Lakes to the sea. On the same day the President of the United States issued a statement in which he explained that the treaty provided for the construction of a 27-foot waterway from the sea to all Canadian and American points on the Great Lakes; that such a depth would admit practically 90 percent of the ocean shipping of the world to the lake cities in the States of New York, Ohio, Michigan, Indiana, Illinois, Wisconsin, and Minnesota; that its influence in cheapening transportation of overseas goods would stretch widely into the interior; that the large by-product of power would benefit the Northeast; and that these benefits would be mutual with the great Dominion to the north. He also explained that the waterway would probably require 10 years for completion, during which time normal growth of traffic in the Nation would far more than compensate for any diversions from American railways and other American port facilities, and that "economic gains from improved transportation have always benefited the whole people". He stated that, under the engineers' estimates, the total cost would be about $543,000,000, of which approximately $272,000,000 would have to be expended by the United States, and that some portion of these expenditures had already been made by both countries. He quoted General Douglas MacArthur, Acting Secretary of War, to the effect that "the provisions in respect to the diversion of water from Lake Michigan . . . are sufficient to provide for the maintenance of the 9 foot waterway from Chicago to the Mississippi", and he explained that the Canadian project of a two-stage development in the International Section had been adopted instead of the original American project of a single-stage development.

Proposed Great Lakes–St. Lawrence waterway treaty

President's statement

The treaty was submitted to the Senate of the United States for advice and consent to ratification. A resolution authorizing ratification with reservations failed of passage on March 14, 1934, but no order of return to the President was made and the treaty is pending in the Senate.

Great Lakes–St. Lawrence Deep Waterway Treaty (Department of State, 1932) 10, 11, 12 containing an outline of the negotiations and a detailed summary of the provisions of the treaty) ; 78 Cong. Rec., pt. 4, p. 4474.

See also: Report on S. 10558, to provide for the improvement of navigation in the St. Lawrence River and for the construction of dams, locks, canals, and other appurtenant structures therein at and near Long Sault,

Barnhart, and Sheek Islands, S. Rept. 1203, 61st Cong., 3d sess., serial no. 5840;

Report of the Government Engineers, United States and Canada, on the improvement of the St. Lawrence River from Montreal to Ontario, made to the International Joint Commission, S. Doc. 179, 67th Cong., 2d sess., serial no. 7972;

Report from the Chief of Engineers, United States Army, on preliminary examination and survey of the St. Lawrence River between Ogdensburg, New York, and Lake Ontario, authorized by the River and Harbor Act approved Mar. 3, 1925 (43 Stat. 1186, 1191), H. Doc. 316, 70th Cong., 1st sess., serial no. 8900;

Message from the President transmitting a report of the Chairman of the United States – St. Lawrence Commission on the St. Lawrence Waterway Project, S. Doc. 183, 69th Cong., 2d sess., serial no. 8697;

Message from the President requesting the consideration of approval by the Senate of the so-called "St. Lawrence treaty with Canada", and transmitting a summary of the data prepared by the Interdepartmental Board on the Great Lakes – St. Lawrence Project, S. Doc. 110, 73d Cong., 2d sess., serial no. 9800;

Survey of the Great Lakes–St. Lawrence seaway and power project containing reports prepared by the United States Departments of War and Commerce and by the Interdepartmental Board and the Federal Power Commission, S. Doc. 116, 73d Cong., 2d sess., serial no. 9785–6;

Hearing before the House Committee on Interstate and Foreign Commerce on H. J. Res. 157, 73d Cong., 1st sess., relating to the use of the water of the St. Lawrence River in accordance with the Great Lakes–St. Lawrence deep waterway treaty, Apr. 20, 1933.

Rio Grande

In December 1895 James H. McMahan, accompanied by his son and two other young men, organized a trapping expedition along the Rio Grande, and thereafter (in January 1896) while in their boats and following the main channel of the river down stream, Mexican officers engaged in preventing smuggling appeared on the Mexican side of the river, ordered them to stop, and fired at them. Subsequently McMahan submitted a claim to the General Claims Commission organized by the United States and Mexico under the terms of the convention of September 8, 1923, alleging that, pursuant to the boundary treaties concluded between the two countries, the navigation of the Rio Grande was free to the citizens of both countries and that the party was exercising a "right" when the Mexican soldiers, for no reason whatsoever, ordered them to halt and then attacked them. After referring to article VII of the treaty of February 2, 1848, article IV of the treaty of December 30, 1853, and articles I and II of the treaty signed November 12, 1884, the majority of the Commission concluded that there was "no doubt" but that the party was "exercising a perfectly recognized right in navigating on a part of the Rio Grande which serves as boundary between the two nations" and that Mexico was entitled to exercise police powers as a territorial right "within its established limits", as provided in article VII of the treaty of 1848. After pointing out that "the boundary or dividing line between both nations in reference to the Rio Grande, is the middle of this river, following the deepest channel, which signifies that up to this point, the two nations may exercise their full territorial rights", the majority of the Commission stated that "by studying the subject of navigation on international rivers, whether they be boundary lines between two or more territories, and empty into the sea, it is found that the tendency is to establish the principle of free navigation, provided that it be always limited by the right of the riparian States to exercise police rights in that portion of the course which corresponds to them". It was held that the action taken by Mexico in this instance did not appear "excessive or contrary to the right of free navigation".

Opinions of the Commissioners (1929) 235, 239, 240, 241.

In a statement made by the Brazilian Minister of Foreign Affairs to the President of Brazil on September 30, 1907, the position was taken that freedom of navigation by foreign vessels in rivers traversing Brazilian territory rests upon concession from Brazil. The Minister stated: The Amazon

> At the same time, as far as the River Iça or Putumayo is concerned, which, as it is the natural exit of the territory to the southeast of Colombia, crosses the territories adjacent to our boundary from the Amazon to the Apaporis, we have agreed on a modus vivendi, by which Brazil permits as a concession, made of its own will and for that reason as a proof of its sovereignty, the passage of Colombian vessels and to export and import commerce by Colombia by the Brazilian district of Baizo Iça.

A treaty of April 24, 1907 between Brazil and Colombia recognized freedom of navigation on affluents of the Amazon navigable within Colombian dominion, while a treaty of August 21, 1908, concluded between them, recognized freedom of navigation for Brazilian and Colombian vessels on rivers admitted to be common property by the treaty of 1907 in perpetuity.

A treaty between Brazil and Peru concluded on September 8, 1909 provided for complete freedom of navigation on all affluents of the Amazon navigable within Peru.

Vessels of all nations were granted freedom of navigation between Bolivia and the sea under a treaty concluded on August 12, 1910 by Bolivia and Brazil.

1907 For. Rel., pt. 1, pp. 110, 111, 113 (statement of Brazilian Minister, 1907, and text of *modus vivendi* between Brazil and Colombia of 1907); *ibid.* 108 (treaty of 1907 between Brazil and Colombia); 5 A.J.I.L. Supp. (1911) 79, 82 (treaty of 1908 between Brazil and Colombia); VI Martens' *Nouveau recueil général* (3d ser., Triepel, 1913) 849, 851 (treaty of 1909 between Brazil and Peru); VII *idem* (1913) 632 (treaty of 1910 between Brazil and Bolivia).

Paraguay
River

By article 4 of the treaty of July 22, 1908, concluded at La Paz between Bolivia and Germany, the former gave to merchant vessels of the latter the right of free navigation on the Paraguay River. Such freedom for vessels of all nations was accorded by a treaty of August 12, 1910 signed at Rio de Janeiro by Bolivia and Brazil.

> IV *idem* (1911) 284; VII *idem* (1913) 632.
>
> For the decision of the Central American Court of Justice as to the "perpetual rights of free navigation" enjoyed by Costa Rica in the San Juan River and certain other waters, under the treaty of Apr. 15, 1858 between Costa Rica and Nicaragua and under the award of President Cleveland of Mar. 22, 1888, and as to the Nicaraguan right of exclusive ownership and "highest sovereignty" over the San Juan River, which right "is not absolute", see *Costa Rica* v. *Nicaragua*, 11 A.J.I.L. (1917) 181.

AFRICAN RIVERS

§89

Congo

Under a convention of April 18, 1908 signed at Berlin, France and Germany agreed to mutual freedom of navigation and commerce on the Congo River according to regulations contained in article 2 of the convention. Reciprocal freedom of navigation was also provided for in another convention between the two countries signed at Berlin on November 4, 1911.

> I Martens' *Nouveau recueil général* (3d ser., Triepel, 1909) 612; V *idem* (1912) 643, 657.

The "Convention Revising the General Act of Berlin, February 26, 1885, and the General Act and Declaration of Brussels, July 2, 1890", signed at St.-Germain-en-Laye on September 10, 1919, contains provision that "The trade of all nations shall enjoy complete freedom . . . in all the regions forming the basin of the Congo and its outlets" (art. 1 and annex) and that the navigation of the Niger shall "be entirely free for merchant vessels and for the transport of goods and passengers" (art. 5). In 1931 the Belgian Government concluded with the Union Nationale des Transports Fluviaux, known as "Unatra" an arrangement under which that company (more than half of the shares of which were owned by the Belgian Government), in consideration of the refund of the amounts involved, made reductions in its normal rates for the shipment of produce, without admitting others, including one *Oscar Chinn*, a British subject, to the benefits of the arrangement. Chinn and five others similarly affected by the arrangement had recourse to the court of first instance and the court of appeals at Leopoldville, claiming that the effect of the arrangement was virtually to establish a monopoly in favor of Unatra and asking damages for losses sustained in consequence thereof. The claims were rejected.

On April 13, 1934 the Belgian Government and the British Government agreed to submit the dispute regarding Chinn's losses in consequence of the arrangement to the Permanent Court of International Justice, which, by a judgment of December 12, 1934, held that the measures taken by the Belgian Government were not "in conflict with the international obligations" of that Government. The Court, in the course of its decision, defined the freedom of navigation referred to in the convention of St.-Germain, stating:

> According to the conception universally accepted, the freedom of navigation referred to by the Convention comprises freedom of movement for vessels, freedom to enter ports, and to make use of plant and docks, to load and unload goods and to transport goods and passengers. **"Freedom of navigation"**
>
> From this point of view, freedom of navigation implies, as far as the business side of maritime or fluvial transport is concerned, freedom of commerce also. But it does not follow that in all other respects freedom of navigation entails and presupposes freedom of commerce.
>
> What the Government of the United Kingdom is concerned with in this case is the principle of freedom of navigation regarded from the special aspect of the commercial operations inherent in the conduct of the transport business; for that Government has never contended that the impugned measures constituted an obstacle to the movement of vessels.

> . . . .

> "Whilst therefore it is certain that the Convention of Saint-Germain is also based on the idea of commercial freedom, it is however to be observed that this idea has not the same import in the Convention as in the Act of Berlin. This Act really meant by free trade the régime of the open door. By abolishing—as has already been stated—the prohibition to levy customs duties found in Article IV of the Act, the Convention has abandoned this régime; in this connection it should also be observed that Article V of the Act, the second paragraph of which corresponds to Article 3 of the Convention, contained a first paragraph which does not reappear in the Convention and which prohibited the granting of a monopoly or privilege in matters of trade.
>
> It cannot be supposed that the contracting Parties adopted new provisions with the idea that they might lend themselves to a broad interpretation going beyond what was expressly laid down.
>
> Freedom of trade, as established by the Convention, consists in the right—in principle unrestricted—to engage in any commercial activity, whether it be concerned with trading properly so-called, that is the purchase and sale of goods, or whether it be concerned with industry, and in particular the transport business; or, finally, whether it is carried on inside the country or, by the exchange of imports and exports, with other countries. Freedom of trade does not mean the abolition of commercial competition; it presupposes the existence of such competition.

Every undertaking freely carrying on its commercial activities may find itself confronted with obstacles placed in its way by rival concerns which are perhaps its superiors in capital or organization. It may also find itself in competition with concerns in which States participate, and which have occupied a special position ever since their formation, as is the case of Unatra. Mr. Chinn, a British subject, when, in 1929, he entered the river transport business, could not have been ignorant of the existence of the competition which he would encounter on the part of Unatra, which had been established since 1925, of the magnitude of the capital invested in that Company, of the connection it had with the Colonial and Belgian Governments, and of the predominant rôle reserved to the latter with regard to the fixing and application of transport rates.

The Government of the United Kingdom maintains that the reduction in transport rates together with the Belgian Government's promise temporarily to make good losses enabled Unatra to exercise a *de facto* monopoly inconsistent with freedom of trade.

The Court must therefore consider whether the alleged concentration of transport business in the hands of Unatra, of which the Government of the United Kingdom complains, and the fact that, because of this concentration, it was commercially impossible for Mr. Chinn to carry on his business, are inconsistent with the conception of freedom of trade propounded above.

"Freedom of commerce"

A concentration of business of this kind will only infringe freedom of commerce if commerce is prohibited by the concession of a right precluding the exercise of the same right by others; in other words, if a "monopoly" is established which others are bound to respect.

The Court sees nothing in the measure taken by the Belgian Government indicative of such a prohibition.

Gr. Br. Treaty Ser. no. 18 (1919), Cmd. 477; Per. Ct. Int. Jus., Ser. A/B No. 63 (Dec. 12, 1934), pp. 83, 84.

Ubangi

On April 18, 1908 France and Germany signed a treaty at Berlin, article II of which provided for mutual freedom of navigation and commerce on the Ubangi River. Mutual enjoyment of navigation was also provided for in another treaty between the two countries signed at Berlin on November 4, 1911. On September 28, 1912 the two countries signed at Paris a convention containing regulations for the navigation of the Ubangi.

I Martens' *Nouveau recueil général* (3d ser., Triepel, 1909) 612 (treaty of 1908); V *idem* (1912) 651, 657 (treaty of 1911); VII *idem* (1913) 135 (treaty of 1913).

STRAITS

§90

The Committee on Territorial Waters (the second committee) of the Divisional lines Conference on the Codification of International Law, which met at The Hague in March and April 1930, referred the general subject of "straits" to its second subcommittee. The question was so closely related to the breadth of the territorial sea, on which the second committee failed to agree, that the latter was unable to arrive at even a provisional decision on the articles drawn up by the second subcommittee on this subject. The second committee, however, considered that the articles so drafted "constitute valuable material for the continuation of the study of the question" and attached them to its report to the Conference. That part of the report (Appendix II) reads as follows:

> In straits which form a passage between two parts of the high sea, the limits of the territorial sea shall be ascertained in the same manner as on other parts of the coast, even if the same State is the Coastal State of both shores.
> When the width of the straits exceeds the breadth of the two belts of territorial sea, the waters between those two belts form part of the high sea. If the result of this delimitation is to leave an area of high sea not exceeding two miles in breadth surrounded by territorial sea, this area may be assimilated to territorial sea.
>
> .   .   .   .
>
> Under no pretext whatever may the passage even of warships through straits used for international navigation between two parts of the high sea be interfered with.
>
> League of Nations publication C.351.M.145.1930.V, pp. 125, 133, 134; *ibid.* C.230.M.117.1930.V, pp. 4, 13, 14; see also *ibid.* C.74.M.39.1929.V, pp. 55–60 (containing the replies of the governments together with the observations of the Preparatory Committee on the Bases of Discussion).

During the World War, the *Bangor*, a vessel flying the Norwegian Navigation flag and commanded by a Norwegian master but fitted and manned from New York for the purpose of rendering services to German warships, was captured by the British in the Strait of Magellan while, according to the entry in the log, the vessel was in the middle of the strait opposite Port Tamar anchorage, the strait being seven miles wide at that place, i.e. more than three miles from either shore. Counsel for the ship-owners admitted that the vessel must suffer judgment of condemnation in the British prize court unless she was immune from capture on the technical ground that she was at the time in waters alleged to be territorial waters of a neutral state. The Probate, Divorce, and Admiralty Division of the British High

Court of Justice, sitting as a prize court, held that, even on the basis of the contention of the ship-owners that the capture took place in neutral waters, the vessel and her cargo must be condemned as good and lawful prize on the ground that "a capture within the territorial waters of a neutral is, as between enemy belligerents, for all purposes rightful; and that it is only by the neutral State concerned that the legal validity of the capture can be questioned". In the course of its decision the court made the following statements:

> The limits of territorial waters, in relation to national and international rights and privileges, have of recent years been subject to much discussion. It may well be that the old marine league, which for long determined the boundaries of territorial waters, ought to be extended by reason of the enlarged range of guns used for shore protection.
>
> This case does not, in my view, call for any pronouncement upon that question. I am content to decide the question of law raised by the claimants upon the assumption that the capture took place within the territorial waters of the Republic of Chile. This assumption, of course, does not imply any expression of opinion as to the character of the Strait of Magellan as between Chile and other nations. This strait connects the two vast free oceans of the Atlantic and the Pacific. As such, the strait must be considered free for the commerce of all nations passing between the two oceans.

Free passage

> In 1879 the Government of the United States of America declared that it would not tolerate exclusive claims by any nation whatsoever to the Strait of Magellan, and would hold responsible any Government that undertook, no matter on what pretext, to lay any impost on its commerce through the strait. Later, in 1881, the Republic of Chile entered into a treaty with the Argentine Republic by which the strait was declared to be neutralized for ever, and free navigation was guaranteed to the flags of all nations.
>
> I have referred to these matters in order to show that there is a right of free passage through the strait for commercial purposes. It is not inconsistent with this that, during war between any nations entitled to use them for commerce, the strait should be regarded in whole or in part as the territorial waters of Chile, whose lands bound it on both sides.

[1916] P. 181, 184, 185.

"Considering that the Strait of Magellan as well as the canals of the southern region lie within the international limits of Chile, and consequently form part of the territory of the Republic,

"*It is decreed:*

"In reference to the neutrality established in the decree No. 1857 of November 5 last of the ministry of foreign affairs, the interior waters of the Strait of Magellan and the canals of the southern region, even in the parts which are distant more than 3 miles from either bank, should be considered as forming part of the jurisdictional or neutral sea."

Chilean decree of Dec. 15, 1914, 1916 U.S. Naval War College, *International Law Topics* 21.

By convention regarding the regime of the straits, signed at Montreux on July 20, 1936, the signatory powers agreed to "recognize and affirm the principle of freedom of transit and navigation" in the straits, a term which the convention defines as comprising the "Straits of the Dardanelles, the Sea of Marmora, and the Bosphorus". Commercial vessels have freedom of transit therein subject only to sanitary inspection and certain charges specified in the convention. Turkey may prohibit the passage of vessels of states at war with her. With respect to warships, a distinction is made between their passage in time of peace and in time of war, and certain restrictions are imposed. The Dardanelles

173 League of Nations Treaty Series (1936–37) 213, 219. While Turkey conceded free navigation to foreign merchant ships prior to the convention of 1936, it excluded war vessels. This principle had a formal recognition in a convention signed at London on July 13, 1841 (29 Br. & For. St. Paps. 703), although it had been accepted as far back as 1809 when, on Jan. 5, Great Britain and Turkey concluded a treaty of peace and commerce (1 *idem,* pt. I, pp. 768, 772). Exclusion of warships was also provided for in article X of the treaty of Paris on Mar. 30, 1856 (46 *idem* 8, 12) and in article I of the convention signed at Paris on the same date (*ibid.* 18, 21) revising the convention of 1841. The pertinent provisions of the agreements of 1856 were abrogated by the Treaty of London of March 13, 1871 (61 *idem* 7, 9), which, however, maintained the principle of freedom for merchant vessels but not for warships (with a limited exception in time of peace). Pursuant to article 23 of the treaty of peace signed at Lausanne on July 24, 1923 (28 League of Nations Treaty Series (1924) 11, 27), by which the parties agreed to recognize the freedom of transit and navigation in the straits, a convention regarding the regime of the straits was signed at Lausanne on the same date (*ibid.* 115), which also recognized such freedom.

LAKES

§91

The Supreme Court of Oregon stated in the case of *Alsos* v. *Kendall et al.:*

No rule of international law is more firmly established than that the territory of a sovereign state includes the lakes, seas, and rivers entirely inclosed within its limits.

227 Pac. (1924) 286, 289.

It is settled law in this country that lands underlying navigable waters within a State belong to the State in its sovereign capacity and may be used and disposed of as it may elect, subject to the paramount power of Congress to control such waters for the purposes of navigation in commerce among the States and with foreign nations, and subject to the qualification that where the United States, after acquiring the territory and before the creation of the State, has granted rights in such lands by way of performing international obligations, or effecting the use or improvement of the lands for the purposes of commerce among the States and with foreign nations, or carrying out other public purposes appropriate to the objects for which the territory was held, such rights are not cut off by the subsequent creation of the State, but remain unimpaired, and the rights which otherwise would pass to the State in virtue of its admission into the Union are restricted or qualified accordingly. . . . the United States early adopted and constantly has adhered to the policy of regarding lands under navigable waters in acquired territory, while under its sole dominion, as held for the ultimate benefit of future States, and so has refrained from making any disposal thereof, save in exceptional instances when impelled to particular disposals by some international duty or public exigency. It follows from this that disposals by the United States during the territorial period are not lightly to be inferred, and should not be regarded as intended unless the intention was definitely declared or otherwise made very plain.

United States v. *Holt State Bank et al.*, 270 U.S. (1926) 49, 54. See also the opinion of the Attorney General of June 19, 1912, 29 Op. Att. Gen. (1913) 455.

On the right of the United States to control the navigable waters within the several States for purposes of navigation, see *Port of Seattle* v. *Oregon & Washington Railroad Company et al.*, 255 U.S. (1921) 56, 63.

In an action involving property rights on a navigable body of water in or near the upper end of Lake Superior, the Supreme Court of the United States held that riparian rights attaching to property patented by the United States are determined by the law of the State in which they are situated and that the fact that both parties owning property bordering on a navigable stream opposite to each other acquired the property from the United States did not change the rule. *Norton, Executor* v. *Whiteside*, 239 U.S. (1915) 144.

See also the case of *Massachusetts* v. *New York et al.* holding, with reference to the Treaty of Hartford concluded by the two States on Dec. 16, 1786, wherein New York granted to Massachusetts certain land extending from Pennsylvania "to the Shore" of Lake Ontario to be held in private ownership as well as rights of navigation and fishery on the lake, that the treaty conveyed to Massachusetts no title to the bed of the lake and that "The dominion over navigable waters, and property in the soil under them, are so identified with the exercise of the sovereign powers of government that a presumption against their separation from sovereignty must be indulged, in construing all grants by the sovereign, of lands to be held in private ownership." 271 U.S. (1926) 65, 89.

In *United States* v. *Oregon* the Supreme Court held that Malheur, Mud, and Harney Lakes and connecting waters in the State of Oregon were non-navigable in 1859, the date of the admission of Oregon into the Union; that title to land within the meander line of a non-navigable lake did not pass to the State as an incident to ownership of abutting uplands granted by the United States where, prior to the approval of the survey of the uplands, the lake had been set aside by Executive order as a Federal reservation; and, with reference to an Oregon statute of 1921, that—

> in no case has this Court held that a state could deprive the United States of its title to land under non-navigable waters without its consent, or that a grant of uplands to private individuals, which does not in terms or by implication include the adjacent land under water, nevertheless operates to pass it to the State.

295 U.S. (1935) 1, 27.

On September 25, 1923 the German Criminal Court of Appeals (Division I) rendered a decision regarding the customs frontier of the Lake of Constance, a lake forming the international boundary between Württemberg and Baden, on the one hand, and Switzerland, on the other. After pointing out that in the lower lake or Zeller See the middle of the lake marked the boundary under the terms of article I of the treaty of October 1854 between the Duchy of Baden and the Canton of Thurgau and that the Überlinger See, enclosed on all three landward sides by territory of Baden, was exclusively under German sovereignty, the court considered the question of the upper lake, the status of which under constitutional and international law was disputed, one view being that this part of the lake should come under the condominium of the riparian states and another being that the median line of the lake should form the boundary. In upholding the latter view, the court said: *(margin: Lake of Constance)*

> The general rules of international law do not argue in favor of, but against the assumption of a condominium. According to these rules, the principles applying to streams also find corresponding application to inland lakes (see v. Liszt, loc. cit., page 76 and v. Martitz, loc. cit. pages 286–287). We can not see why a rule of law which has met with general recognition with regard to Lake Geneva should not also be recognized for the Lake of Constance.
> The historical development of legal relations along the Lake of Constance also contradicts the assumption of a condominium. Even Rettich, the chief supporter of the condominium theory, admits that up to the end of the eighteenth century Switzerland included the lake in her territory, up to the median line (pages 82 and 83); he maintains, however, that Switzerland later, by conclusive acts, renounced her special claims in favor of "the condominium" of the lake (page 80). This assertion has already been refuted by v. Martitz in a convincing way (p. 288); among other things, he points out that Articles 3 and 24 of the International Navigation and Port Executive Order for the Lake of Constance, of September 22, 1867 (bad. Reg. Bl. 1868, page 215) *(margin: Median line v. condominium)*

provide for separate "water territories" of the different riparian states (page 293). By a Baden-Swiss international treaty of April 25, 1878, the so-called *"Konstanzer Tritter"* was divided between Baden and the Canton of Thurgau. Single portions could not have been taken away from a condominium without the joint action of all riparian states. Even if a renunciation by Switzerland of her special rights could be assumed, the origin of a condominium could not be concluded even therefrom (v. Martitz, page 288). A condominium in which Switzerland shared, would have had to be considered neutral during a war (Rettich, page 122). But in the judgment appealed from it is actually stated that in the recent World War the riparian states exercised their rights of sovereignty as far as the middle line of the Lake of Constance by means of patrol boats with military equipment.

According to this, that opinion is to be given preference which places the Reich boundary and the customs boundary on the middle line of the Lake of Constance.

57 *Entscheidungen des Reichsgerichts in Strafsachen* (1924) 368, 369, translation.

The Great Lakes

"Boundary waters"

On January 11, 1909 there was signed at Washington a convention concerning the boundary waters between the United States and Canada. The convention defines the "boundary waters" as the waters from main shore to main shore of the lakes, rivers, and connecting waterways, or the portions thereof, along which the international boundary between the United States and the Dominion of Canada passes, including all bays, arms, and inlets thereof but not including tributary waters which in their natural channels would flow into such lakes, rivers, and waterways, or waters flowing from such lakes, rivers, and waterways, or the waters of rivers flowing across the boundary (preliminary art.)

Navigation

It is agreed therein that the navigation of all navigable boundary waters shall forever continue free and open for the purposes of commerce to the inhabitants and to the vessels of both countries equally, subject, however, to any laws and regulations of either country not inconsistent with such privilege of free navigation and equality of treatment (art. I). It is also agreed that the same right of navigation shall extend to the waters of Lake Michigan and to all canals connecting boundary waters (*ibid.*) Each high contracting party reserves to itself the "exclusive jurisdiction and control over the use and diversion . . . of all waters on its own side of the line" flowing across or into boundary waters (art. II). In addition to the uses, obstructions, and diversions provided for by special agreement between the parties, they agree that "no further or other uses or obstructions or diversions, whether temporary or permanent, of boundary waters on either side of the line, affecting the natural level or flow of boundary waters on the other side of the line, shall be made" except by authority of the respective high contracting parties and

Use, diversion, obstruction

with the approval of the International Joint Commission (art. III), to be composed of six commissioners, three to be appointed by each Government (art. VII). It is stipulated that the following order of precedence shall be observed among the various uses of the waters: (1) Domestic and sanitary purposes; (2) navigation; and (3) power and irrigation. However, the then-existing uses of boundary waters were not to be disturbed.

The high contracting parties have, under the terms of the convention, "equal and similar rights in the use of the [boundary] waters". But the requirement for an equal division may, in the discretion of the Commission, be suspended in certain cases of temporary diversions. The Commission may make its approval in any case conditional upon the construction of remedial or protective works to compensate so far as possible for the particular use or diversion proposed, and it may condition its approval upon suitable and adequate provision being made for the protection and indemnity of all interests on the other side of the line which may be injured. (Art. VIII.)

As indicated *ante* (§86), special provisions are contained in the convention with reference to the Niagara, St. Marys, and Milk Rivers (arts. V and VI).

Other questions or matters of difference arising between the high contracting parties involving the rights, obligations, or interests of either in relation to the other along the common frontier shall, upon request of either the Government of the United States or the Government of Canada, be referred to the International Joint Commission "for examination and report", such reports not to be regarded as decisions of the questions submitted and not to have the character of arbitral awards (art. IX). The Commission may, upon agreement of the parties, also act as an arbitral tribunal in certain classes of cases referred to in article X.

3 Treaties, etc. (Redmond, 1923) 2607–2614. The Senate of the United States conditioned its advice and consent to the convention on the understanding that nothing therein should affect existing rights "at the rapids of the St. Mary's River at Sault Ste. Marie". *Ibid.* 2615. See the opinion of Attorney General Wickersham of Apr. 8, 1909 construing the scope of the reservation. 27 Op. Att. Gen. (1908–9) 295, 298–300.

In 1910 the Canadian Minister of Public Works, speaking before the Canadian House of Commons in support of the convention signed on January 11, 1909, stated:

I may say that that is simply an affirmance of what has always been contended by the United States to be international law, and of what I do not think has been disputed by the jurists of this country, that is to say that so far as the waters which are wholly situate within the country are concerned, that country may make a diversion of these waters and prevent them from flowing into the boundary waters.

The United States have contended that it is a principle of international law that any country has the right to divert waters in its own country subject always, I may say, to the question of navigation.

. . . .

The question might arise between the inhabitants of Montana, Alberta and Saskatchewan, because a person or company in Montana might divert certain waters which flow to the northward and use these waters for the purposes of irrigation. The result might be to deprive a Canadian living lower down the stream upon the Canadian side of the boundary of water which would be very necessary for the purpose of irrigation. Before this treaty that could be done and he could not say a word, but under this treaty he can complain through this government, I take it, to the authorities of the United States, and it would be their duty, in carrying out the spirit of this treaty, to see that compensation is provided for the injury, and, vice versa, the same obligation that is imposed upon the people of the United States is also imposed upon the people of Canada.

Still later he said:

I think my hon. friend will find that the recognition of the international right to complain of the diversion of waters before they pass into its territory depends entirely upon the question of navigation. I am satisfied that if my hon. friend looks up the authorities he will find that that is the only case in which the sovereign right of a country is disputed. It is recognized that it pertains to the sovereign right of a country to deal with waters in its own territory, just as it would deal with any other species of property, and that right, under international law, is subject to this one consideration, that if diversion interferes with the waters in that country, if it interferes or materially affects navigation in the territory further down, the government of the country whose navigation has been affected has a right to complain under the principles of international law against such diversion. I am satisfied my hon. friend will find that the right is limited wholly to cases where it is alleged that navigation has been seriously interfered with.

Debates of the House of Commons of the Dominion of Canada, 11th Parliament, 3d sess. (1910–11), vol. I, pp. 870, 879, 893.

Diversion: the Chicago Drainage Canal

The Chicago Drainage Canal, built by the Sanitary District of Chicago created under an act of May 29, 1889 (Laws of Illinois [1889] 125), was opened in January 1900. It diverts waters of Lake Michigan through the Chicago and the Illinois Rivers to the Mississippi River in the disposal of sewage. On January 17, 1903 the Secretary of War ordered that after March 31 of that year the daily diversion of water from Lake Michigan should not exceed 250,000 cubic feet a minute. In March 1907 and in January 1913 he denied an application for the flow of more water through the Calumet Sag Channel.

In 1913 a bill in equity was filed by the United States to enjoin the Sanitary District of Chicago from diverting water from Lake Michigan in excess of the amount authorized by the Secretary of War. The suit was consolidated with an earlier suit brought by the United States in 1908 to prevent the construction of a second channel from Lake Michigan through the Calumet River, permit for which had been refused by the Secretary of War, and to prevent an increase in the flow of water in excess of the limit fixed by the Secretary of War. Repeated delays occurred in the course of litigation, and it was not until January 1925 that a decree enjoining the Sanitary District from diverting water from Lake Michigan in excess of 250,000 cubic feet a minute (4,167 cubic feet a second)—the amount authorized by the Secretary of War—was affirmed by the Supreme Court of the United States. The Court held that the withdrawal of water in excess of the amount authorized by the Secretary of War was prohibited by the act approved March 3, 1899 (30 Stat. 1151), as involving a change in the condition of the Lakes and the Chicago River and "an obstruction to their navigable · capacity". While the suit was pending, however, the Sanitary District violated the restriction in the Secretary of War's permit and increased the diversion to 8,500 cubic feet a second. Under date of March 3, 1925 a permit was issued by the Secretary of War to the district authorizing the temporary and conditional withdrawal from the lake of 8,500 cubic feet a second until December 31, 1929.

> *Sanitary District of Chicago* v. *United States*, 266 U.S. (1925) 405, 425, 429, 431–432.
>
> As to the authority of the Secretary of War in the premises, see the opinion of the Attorney General of Feb. 13, 1925, 34 Op. Att. Gen. (1923–25) 410, 419.
>
> For the historical background relating to the building of the Chicago Drainage Canal, see the opinion in *State of Wisconsin et al.* v. *State of Illinois and Sanitary District of Chicago et al.*, 278 U.S. (1929) 367, 401, 405–406.

Meanwhile, in 1922, the State of Wisconsin filed a bill in equity— amended in 1925 and 1926, when the States of Minnesota, Michigan, Ohio, Pennsylvania, and New York became co-plaintiffs—to enjoin the State of Illinois and the Sanitary District of Chicago from continuing to withdraw 8,500 cubic feet of water a second from Lake Michigan at Chicago, which had, it was alleged, resulted in lowering the levels of Lakes Michigan, Huron, Erie, and Ontario, and the St. Lawrence River not less than six inches, to the serious injury of the complainant States. The States of Missouri, Kentucky, Tennessee, and Louisiana, by leave of court, became intervening co-defendants.

The Court referred the cause to the Honorable Charles Evans Hughes as a Special Master, with authority to take the evidence and to report it to the Court with his findings of fact, conclusions of law, and recommendations for a decree, all to be subject to approval or other disposal by the Court. The Master gave full hearings, and submitted his report on November 23, 1927. The case was thereafter elaborately argued, and on January 14, 1929 the Supreme Court (Mr. Chief Justice Taft delivering the opinion) held that, with the exception of the amount of water needed for the Chicago River, the plaintiffs were entitled to have the diversions stopped by injunction but that the decree should be so framed "as to accord to the Sanitary District a reasonably practicable time within which to provide some other means of disposing of the sewage, reducing the diversion as the artificial disposition of the sewage increases from time to time, until it is entirely disposed of thereby, when there shall be a final, permanent operative and effective injunction". The cause was again referred to the Special Master to take testimony on the practical measures needed and the time required for their completion and to report his conclusions for the formulation of such a decree.

> *State of Wisconsin et al.* v. *State of Illinois and Sanitary District of Chicago et al.*, 278 U.S. (1929) 367, 419, 421.

Decree

On April 14, 1930 the Supreme Court (the Special Master having reported) issued a decree to the effect (1) that on and after July 1, 1930 the State of Illinois and the Sanitary District of Chicago should not divert any of the waters of the Great Lakes–St. Lawrence system or watershed through the Chicago Drainage Canal and its auxiliary channels or otherwise in excess of an annual average of 6,500 cubic second-feet in addition to domestic pumpage; (2) that on and after December 31, 1935 unless good cause be shown the defendants should not divert in excess of an annual average of 5,000 cubic second-feet in addition to domestic pumpage; and (3) that on and after December 31, 1938 unless good cause be shown they should not divert in excess of an annual average of 1,500 cubic second-feet in addition to domestic pumpage. These amounts, as indicated, were exclusive of the amounts drawn by the city of Chicago for domestic water-supply purposes. It was further ordered that the Sanitary District file with the clerk of the Supreme Court of the United States, semi-annually, a report setting forth the progress made in the construction of the sewage-treatment plants and their effectiveness, and also setting forth the average diversion of water from Lake Michigan during the period from the entry of the decree to the date of the report.

"The net diversion of water from Lake Michigan, the domestic pumpage of the Chicago Metropolitan area, the in-flow from the Des Plaines River, and the total flow from the main channel at Lockport for the years 1930 to 1938" were stated in the report of 1939 to be as follows:

January–June, 1930	6,820	cubic second feet
July–December, 1930	6,497	" " "
1931	6,500	" " "
1932	6,450	" " "
1933	6,270	" " "
1934	6,433	" " "
1935	6,484	" " "
1936	4,862	" " "
1937	4,989	" " "
1938	4,480	" " "

Semi-Annual Report of the Sanitary District of Chicago, filed with the Supreme Court on Jan. 9, 1939; *Wisconsin et al.* v. *Illinois et al.*, 281 U.S. (1930) 179, 201–202; *ibid.* 696–698 (decree, Apr. 21, 1930).

The decree of Apr. 21, 1930 was enlarged on May 22, 1933, at the instance of the States of Wisconsin, Minnesota, Ohio, and Michigan, by a requirement that the State of Illinois take all necessary steps, including whatever authorizations, requirements, or provisions for the raising, appropriation, and application of moneys, that might be needed in order to cause and secure the completion of adequate sewage treatment or sewage disposal plants and sewers, etc., and file a report in the office of the Clerk of the Supreme Court of the United States, on or before Oct. 2, 1933, of the action taken in compliance with the Court's order. *Wisconsin et al.* v. *Illinois et al.*, 289 U.S. (1933) 395, 710.

In notes exchanged between the Department of State and the British Embassy in Washington in 1912 and 1913, the Embassy stated that the Government of Canada considered that the building of the Calumet and Sag Channel (which had been commenced) was highly undesirable; that any diversion of water from Lake Michigan prejudicially affecting the navigation of the Great Lakes infringed the rights secured to Canada by the Webster-Ashburton treaty of 1842 (art. 7), as well as the rights of navigation in boundary waters and in Lake Michigan "to which the Dominion is entitled under the Boundary Waters Treaty of 1909"; and that the authorities of the United States "have not under the recognized principles of International Law any right to divert from Lake Michigan by any means, or for any purpose, such an amount of water as will prejudicially affect the navigation of boundary waters".

When bills were introduced in Congress in 1923 with respect to the establishment of a waterway from the Great Lakes to the Gulf of Mexico (which subsequently failed of passage), the British Embassy informed the Department that the Government of Canada was unalterably opposed to the proposed diversion from the Great Lakes watershed to that of the Mississippi, because of the great detriment to navigation from Sault Ste. Marie to tidewater, and that the diversion which had theretofore taken place at Chicago had affected harbors, the lock-sills of the Sault Ste. Marie canals, the Welland Canal and the St. Lawrence Canal, and had had a most injurious effect upon ocean shipping between Montreal and the sea.

In relation to the permit issued by the Secretary of War in 1925 (*ante*), the Canadian Government stated that, while it did "not wish to oppose any interim measure which may be necessary to protect the health of the inhabitants of the city of Chicago", the works dependent upon the levels and flow of the Great Lakes system could not be confidently carried out if diversions from the watershed were permitted without mutual assent thereto and inquired as to the measures taken to insure future curtailment in the amount of water being diverted. To this, the United States replied that the "sewage treatment program of the Sanitary District has been arranged, so as to make it possible to effect a reduction to a gross flow of 4,167 cubic feet per second by the year 1935 or before".

> For the early correspondence see: Ambassador Bryce to Secretary Knox, Nov. 29, 1912, MS. Department of State, file 711.4216M58; the Acting Secretary of State (Wilson) to Mr. Bryce, Dec. 24, 1912, *ibid.* 711.4216M58/1; Mr. Knox to Mr. Bryce, Jan. 23, 1913, decision of the Secretary of War of Jan. 8, 1913, *ibid.* 711.4216M58/2; Mr. Bryce to Secretary Bryan, Mar. 17, 1913, *ibid.* 711.4216M58/3; Mr. Robert Lansing to Chargé Barclay, July 29, 1914, *ibid.* 711.4216M58/8.
>
> For the correspondence regarding the proposed establishment of a waterway from the Great Lakes to the Gulf of Mexico, particularly with reference to the Hull bill (H.R. 5475), see: Chargé Chilton to Secretary Hughes, Feb. 13, 1924, *ibid.* 711.4216M58/22; Sir Esme Howard to Mr. Hughes, Mar. 21, 1924, and Mr. Hughes to Sir Esme Howard, Apr. 2, 1924, *ibid.* 711.4216M58/25.
>
> For correspondence regarding the permit of Mar. 3, 1925, see: the Acting Secretary of State (Grew) to Sir Esme Howard, Feb. 13, 1925, *ibid.* 711.4216M58/53; Sir Esme Howard to Mr. Hughes, Feb. 24, 1925, *ibid.* 711.4216M58/55; Secretary Kellogg to Sir Esme Howard, Mar. 21, 1925, *ibid.* 711.4216M58/58; Mr. Chilton to Mr. Kellogg, Sept. 15, 1925, *ibid.* 711.4216M58/68; Mr. Kellogg to Sir Esme Howard, Nov. 24, 1925, *ibid.* 711.4216M58/72; Sir Esme Howard to Mr. Kellogg, Feb. 5, 1926, *ibid.* 711.4216M58/80; Mr. Chilton to Mr. Kellogg, no. 299, undated (received by the Department of State on May 1, 1926), and Mr. Kellogg to Sir Esme Howard, July 26, 1926, *ibid.* 711.4216M58/97.
>
> As of possible interest see: Hearings before the Senate Committee on Foreign Relations concerning the Chicago Drainage Canal, S. Doc. 393, 59th Cong., 1st sess., serial no. 4915; hearings before the House Committee on Interstate and Foreign Commerce on H.R. 24271, concerning the Chicago Drainage Canal, Feb. 20, 1907, 59th Cong., 2d sess.; report regarding information sought by the House of Representatives from the

Secretary of War as to the effect of the diversion of water from Lake Michigan at Chicago, H. Rept. 1027, 67th Cong., 2d sess., serial no. 7959; hearings before the House Committee on Rivers and Harbors on H. Res. 305, diversion of waters of Lake Michigan, May 9, 1922, 67th Cong., 2d sess.; hearings on H.R. 12620, Illinois and Mississippi Rivers and diversion of water from Lake Michigan, Sept. 14, 1922, 67th Cong., 2d sess.; hearings on H.R. 5475, relating to the Illinois and Mississippi Rivers and diversion of waters from Lake Michigan, Mar. 17–20, 1924, Apr. 15 to May 27, 1924, 68th Cong., 1st sess.; hearings on the Illinois River and water from Lake Michigan, Feb. 11, Mar. 30, 31, and Apr. 1, 2, 3, 1926, 69th Cong., 1st sess.; hearings on improvement of the Illinois waterway, Apr. 4, 1930, 71st Cong., 2d sess.; hearings on the improvement of the Illinois waterway (locks and dams in the Illinois River), Feb. 8, 1934, 73d Cong., 2d sess.

For the report of Special Master Charles Evans Hughes to the Supreme Court of the United States (Oct. term, 1927) relating to "Lake Levels", see H. Doc. 178, 70th Cong., 1st sess., serial no. 8898.

MARGINAL SEA

CHARACTER AND EXTENT

§92

Beginning in 1916 the United States sought to prevent and to enjoin the Alaska Pacific Fisheries from maintaining a fishtrap in navigable waters at the Annette Islands off southeastern Alaska, contending that the trap was within a reservation established for the use of Indians and that it was also an obstruction to navigation. The Supreme Court, in affirming a decree granting an injunction, stated that the question before it was whether the act of Congress approved March 3, 1891 (26 Stat. 1101) embraced only the upland of the islands or included as well the adjacent waters and submerged land. In the course of the opinion the Court stated:

> That Congress had power to make the reservation inclusive of the adjacent waters and submerged land as well as the upland needs little more than statement. All were the property of the United States and within a district where the entire dominion and sovereignty rested in the United States and over which Congress had complete legislative authority. *National Bank* v. *County of Yankton*, 101 U.S. 129, 133; *Shively* v. *Bowlby*, 152 U.S. 1, 47–48, 58; *United States* v. *Winans*, 198 U.S. 371, 383.

The Court found that the term "Annette Islands" embraced the surrounding waters as well as the upland.

Alaska Pacific Fisheries v. *United States*, 248 U.S. (1918) 78, 87; *Alaska Pacific Fisheries et al.* v. *United States*, 240 Fed. 274 (C.C.A. 9th, 1917), affirmed.

Sovereignty

The Preparatory Committee for the Conference for the Codification of International Law held at The Hague in 1930, after submitting *questionnaires* to the various governments on the subject of territorial waters and receiving their replies, stated that "The replies show that the Governments agree in considering that a State has sovereignty over a belt of sea round its coast." Subsequently, the second committee, appointed by the Conference to study the subject of territorial waters, was unable to agree upon the terms of a convention, but, speaking generally, it said that—

> it was recognised that international law attributes to each Coastal State sovereignty over a belt of sea round its coasts. This must be regarded as essential for the protection of the legitimate interests of the State. The belt of territorial sea forms part of the territory of the State; the sovereignty which the State exercises over this belt does not differ in kind from the authority exercised over its land domain.
>
> This sovereignty is however limited by conditions established by international law; indeed it is precisely because the freedom of navigation is of such great importance to all States that the right of innocent passage through the territorial sea has been generally recognised.

> League of Nations pub. C.74.M.39.1929.V(Bases of Discussion), pp. 12, 17; *ibid.* C.230.M.117.1930.V, pp. 3, 6. See also *ibid.* C.351(b).M.145(b).-1930.V (Minutes of the Second Committee).

Arrest in territorial waters

In March 1920 Charles Vincenti, a citizen of the United States, was arrested while on an American motorboat in British territorial waters off Bimini, Bahama Islands, British West Indies, by a special officer of the Department of Justice and by two internal-revenue agents holding a warrant against him for unlawful sale of liquor in Maryland and was taken back to the United States, although the motorboat was fired upon and pursued by British officials. Subsequently, the Department of State informed the British Ambassador that—

> you will observe that the persons who arrested Vincenti and forcibly removed him from the Biminis Islands, acted on their own initiative and without the knowledge or approval of this Government in any way, and have been reprimanded and indefinitely suspended for their participation in the affair. Furthermore, it appears that Vincenti's bail has been exonerated and all proceedings subsequent to his unlawful arrest have been revoked. The incident is greatly regretted by this Government and I trust that the steps taken to make amends for it are entirely satisfactory to your Government.

The Ambassador replied that the action taken by the Government was satisfactory.

> Secretary Colby to Ambassador Geddes, June 10, 1920, MS. Department of State, file 611.44e244/10; Mr. Peterson to Mr. Colby, Aug. 9, 1920, *ibid.* 611.44e244/12.

In September 1927 a Coast Guard vessel of the United States, under the command of Boatswain Larry Christiansen, seized two liquor vessels near Cat Cay in the Bahamas, took them into the harbor of Cat Cay, and subsequently removed them to Florida, delivering them to officials of the United States Government. A warrant of arrest having been issued in the Bahamas against Christiansen, the British Vice Consul at Miami, Florida, demanded his extradition. After correspondence between the Government of the United States and the Government of Great Britain regarding the case, the British Embassy presented to the Department of State a communication which read in part:

> After consultation with the Governor of the Bahamas, His Majesty's Government are prepared to waive their demand for the extradition of Christiansen for trial in the Bahamas if the United States Government will make an apology for the violation of British territorial waters by Christiansen and will also give an undertaking (1) to restore the boats and cargoes seized by Christiansen with compensation for wrongful seizure, (2) bring Christiansen to trial (3) pay all·expenses incurred by the Government of the Bahamas in dealing with this incident and (4) protect all witnesses that may be required to attend Christiansen's trial.

The Department replied:

> The appropriate authorities of the Government of the United States have made an investigation of the Christiansen case and, in the light of the information before them, have reached the following conclusions:
>
> 1. That the seizures took place on the high seas, where, of course, American public vessels have the right to seize American ships;
>
> .   .   .   .
>
> 4. That in landing the seized vessels, cargo and prisoners in the Bahamas and removing them therefrom, there was a technical violation by the Coast Guard of British territorial waters.
>
> . . . the Government of the United States will, on account of this technical violation of British territorial waters by a public vessel of the United States, give an undertaking:
>
> 1. To express regret to the British Government . . . ;
> 2. To return the boats and their cargoes;
> 3. To remit the bail and drop the prosecution of the six men who were arrested in the two seizures;
> 4. To transfer Christiansen to another area;
> 5. To endeavor to prevent a recurrence of such incidents;

The Department added that charges submitted against Christiansen would be investigated; that, should a prosecution become necessary in the United States, witnesses from foreign countries would be granted immunity and expenses and the fees of any witnesses subpenaed would be paid; and that—

> Since both of the vessels seized by Christiansen were of American registry, and the owners thereof American citizens, the Government of the United States considers that any question concerning compensation to such owners is naturally one for the determination of the appropriate authorities of the United States Government.

The request for reimbursement of the expenses was later withdrawn, and the British Embassy refrained from pressing the demand for extradition.

> The Assistant Secretary of State (Castle) to the Secretary of the Treasury, Dec. 15, 1927, MS. Department of State, file 211.44eC46/12; the Secretary of the Treasury (Mellon) to the Secretary of State (Kellogg), Dec. 9, 1927, *ibid.* 211.44eC46/13; *aide-mémoire* from the British Embassy to the Department of State, Dec. 29, 1927, *ibid.* 211.44eC46/17; the Department of State to the British Embassy, Jan. 13, 1928, *ibid.* 211.44eC46/19; Sir Esme Howard to Mr. Kellogg, June 1, 1928, *ibid.* 211.44eC46/24.

A Canadian court found that the *Verna*, a boat belonging to a Canadian national, while sailing in Canadian waters with a cargo of liquor but violating no law, was seized by persons acting as officials of the United States Government who took it to the United States and sold it at auction to the Palmer Fish Company. After the sale, and while the boat was storm-bound in Canadian waters, it was taken possession of by its former owner with the aid of a Canadian customs official. Charges having been brought by the Palmer Fish Company against the former owner and the customs official before a Canadian magistrate, the latter ordered the boat restored to the former owner. In so doing, the magistrate said:

> . . . Even judicial officers are not permitted to violate the territorial jurisdiction of other countries.

> Consul Johnson to Secretary Kellogg, Oct. 27, 1927, MS. Department of State, file 811.114 Verna/—.

On December 19, 1929 the Canadian Legation submitted to the Department of State an *aide-mémoire* concerning the seizure by a United States Coast Guard vessel of the launch *Ana* in Canadian territorial waters. Upon investigation by authorities of the United States, it was found that the liquor-laden launch *Ana* was seized by American officials in American waters; that as a result of a hole in the hull the patrol boat sank shortly after the boarding of the *Ana;* that, while the *Ana* was drifting in American waters with two customs officers and two rumrunners on board, a tug with two men apparently looking for the latter was requested by the officers to tow them into shore at Wyandotte, Michigan; that an offer of $500 by the men on the tug for the release of the cargo and men was refused by the officers; that the former then started for the American Customs Patrol Base but, stating that the ice was too thick, worked toward the international boundary line and, upon reaching it, continued into Canadian waters over the protest of the officers; and that patrolmen on shore noticing the incident communicated with the United States Coast Guard Cutter 142, but by the time the patrol boat reached the rum-laden craft "it was well within Canadian waters". The cutter towed the *Ana* to the American shore, permitting the tugboat with the four men to escape. These facts, in the form of a report, having been communicated to the Canadian Legation in Washington, the latter stated:

> It appears from this report that the final seizure of the "*Ana*" was admittedly made within Canadian territorial waters, since it is stated that when Coast Guard Cutter 142 reached the "*Ana*" this vessel was "well within Canadian waters". The Canadian Legation is not aware of any reason which would justify, in these circumstances, the operation in Canadian waters of a vessel of the United States Coast Guard, and therefore requests that the action of the United States officers concerned, in entering Canadian jurisdiction, should be disavowed.

The Department of State replied:

> . . . A vessel apprehended within the waters of the United States while engaged in violation of the revenue laws of the United States, the penalty for which is forfeiture of the vessel, is by the very act forfeited to the United States at the time the wrongful act is committed, though the forfeiture must subsequently be enforced by legal process.
>
> A similar rule would appear to prevail under Canadian law, as shown by a letter dated January 20, 1921, addressed by the Canadian Commissioner of Customs to the American Consul General at Ottawa.

The letter to which reference was made requested the return of an automobile seized by authorities of the United States for having been brought from Canada without report at a customs house. The automobile had previously been seized by the Canadian authorities for unlawful entry into Canada from the United States. The Canadian Government had explained that "under our law . . . the automobile at the date of its importation became forfeited to the Crown". The Department pointed out that the automobile was returned to the Canadian Government and added:

> The interested authorities of this Government state that the action of the Coast Guard patrol boat in entering Canadian

waters was in conformity with the provisions of Article II of the treaty concluded May 18, 1908, in reference to reciprocal rights for the United States and Canada in the matters of conveyance of prisoners and wrecking and salvage. They are of the opinion that since the *Ana* was seized in American territorial waters and was never out of the custody of the United States, the action of the Coast Guard officers in going to the aid of the Customs officers was a matter of rendering assistance and not a matter of making a seizure, the seizure having previously been completed.

.   .   .   .

It is hoped that, in view of the additional details of the incident related herein, the Canadian Government will raise no further objection to the action of the Coast Guard officers in this case.

Aide-mémoire from the Canadian Legation, Dec. 19, 1929, MS. Department of State, file 811.114 Ana/1; memoranda of the Department of State to the Canadian Legation, Dec. 28, 1929 and Feb. 6, 1930, *ibid.* files 811.114 Ana/3, 811.114 Ana/6; *aide-mémoire* from the Canadian Legation to the Department of State, Dec. 23, 1930, *ibid.* file 811.114 Ana/9; memorandum of the Department of State to the Canadian Legation, Aug. 20, 1931, *ibid.* 811.114 Ana/17. While the Canadian Government persisted in the view that despite the extenuating circumstances in the case there was a technical violation of Canadian territorial waters by the Coast Guard vessel in bringing the *Ana* out of Canadian jurisdiction, discussion of the case was dropped. *Ibid.* 811.114 Ana/20.

Various points of view with reference to the breadth of the territorial waters were expressed provisionally or in principle in the second committee of the Conference for the Codification of International Law held at The Hague in 1930, at its thirteenth meeting held on April 3. The delegates of certain states were in favor of the acceptance of the principle of a zone on the high sea contiguous to the territorial sea in which the coastal state would be able to exercise certain control. The views as expressed in the meeting of April 3 on these subjects were summarized as follows:

Country	Breadth favored (miles)	Adjacent zone desired
Union of South Africa	3	—
Germany	3	Yes
United States	3	—
Belgium	3	Yes
Great Britain	3	No
Canada	3	—
Chile	6 or 3	"Without an adjacent zone" "With an adjacent zone"
China	3	—

Country	Breadth favored (miles)	Adjacent zone desired
Colombia	6	—
Cuba	6	Yes
Denmark	3	—
Egypt	3	Yes
Spain	6	Yes
Estonia	3	Yes
Finland	4	Yes
France	3	Yes
Greece	3 Would accept "two miles"	—
India	3	—
Irish Free State	3	—
Iceland	4	—
Italy	6	—
Japan	3	No
Latvia	6	Yes
Norway	4	Must be limited by "needs regarding customs and security"
Netherlands	3	—
Persia	6	Yes
Poland	3	Yes
Portugal	12 or 6	"Provided there is an adjacent zone" of 6 miles.
Rumania	6	Reserves attitude
Sweden	4	—
Czechoslovakia	No coastline	—
Turkey	6	Yes
Uruguay	6	Reserves attitude
Yugoslavia	6	Reserves attitude
Brazil	6	—
U. S. S. R.	"Use of international maritime waterways must under no conditions be interfered with"	—

In its report to the Conference, the second committee made the following statement:

The Committee refrained from taking a decision on the question whether existing international law recognises any fixed breadth of the belt of territorial sea. Faced with differences of opinion on this subject, the Committee preferred, in conformity with the instructions it received from the Conference, not to express an opinion on what ought to be regarded as the existing law, but to concentrate its efforts on reaching an agreement which would fix the breadth of the territorial sea for the future. It regrets to confess that its efforts in this direction met with no success.

League of Nations pub. C.351(b).M.145(b).1930.V, pp. 123 *et seq.; ibid.* C.230.M.117.1930.V, pp. 3, 15–17. For the earlier replies of the governments with respect to point III (the breadth of territorial waters) and the bases of discussion drafted by the Preparatory Committee of the League of Nations on the basis thereof, together with its observations thereon, see *ibid.* C.74.M.39.1929.V, pp. 22–34, 128–142.

Canada

It is a well-recognized principle, both in this country [Canada] and in the United States, that the jurisdiction of a nation is exclusive and absolute within its own territory, of which its territorial waters within three marine miles from the shore are as clearly a part as the land.

S. S. May v. *The King*, [1931] 3 D.L.R. 15, 20.

Chile

The contiguous sea, up to a distance of 3 marine miles counted from the low-water line is considered as the jurisdictional or neutral sea on the coasts of the Republic for the safeguarding of the rights and the accomplishment of the duties relative to the neutrality declared by the Government in case of international conflicts.

Chilean decree of Nov. 5, 1914, 1916 U.S. Naval War College, *International Law Topics* 19.

France

Article 2. The limit of the territorial waters is fixed by an imaginary line running out three marine miles from the great outer reefs and, where there are no such reefs, three marine miles from the shore line at low tide.

French decree of Sept. 23, 1911 making applicable to New Caledonia and its dependencies the provisions of the law of Mar. 1, 1888 forbidding fishing by foreigners in territorial waters. *Journal officiel de la République française*, Sept. 29, 1911, p. 7856, translation.

A French decree of May 21, 1913 permits foreign warships, in time of peace, to anchor in territorial waters "at a distance less than 6 miles from the shore line at low tide" under certain conditions. *Ibid.* June 13, 1913, p. 5066, translation; *ibid.* June 14, 1913, p. 5099.

Cuba

On July 31, 1908 the American Ambassador in London reported that Sir Edward Grey had called his attention to the seizure of the British schooner *Georgie*, of Nassau, Bahamas, by the Cuban revenue cutter *Baire* on May 23, thirty miles west of Santiago, the master of the schooner having declared that he was five miles from the coast at the time of seizure. Cuba had asserted that, under her customs regulations, the territorial waters of the country extend four leagues from the coast of the island and cays, and a fine of $340 had been levied against the schooner for having turtles on board in violation of

Cuban fishing regulations. Sir Edward Grey had stated that assertion of jurisdiction by the Cuban Government beyond the three-mile Great Britain limit could not be accepted; that Great Britain would resent any interference with British vessels beyond the three-mile limit and would hold the Cuban Government responsible for any acts prejudicially affecting the interests of British subjects "outside trade waters as recognized by international law"; that Great Britain had always maintained this principle; and that when a claim had formerly been put forward by Spain to maritime jurisdiction extending to six miles Great Britain had protested. He had expressed the hope that the United States would use its influence with the Cuban Government to obtain the withdrawal of the claim of jurisdiction.

In an informal note of August 18, 1908 from the Acting Secretary of State (Adee) to Governor Magoon, then Military Governor of Cuba, Mr. Adee stated that "the rule which is reported to have been announced by the Cuban Government in this case—namely, that the territorial waters of Cuba extend four leagues from the coast of the Island and of the cays belonging to it—not only fails to accord with the views now expressed by the British Government, but is out of harmony with the principles held by this Government as declared by Secretaries Seward and Olney, as well as with the generally accepted rules of international law". He expressed the hope that the Cuban Government would, "after due consideration and in view of the very disputable legality from the point of view of international law of any attempt to enforce municipal regulations beyond the three-mile limit", see fit to remit the fine which had been imposed upon the British schooner *Georgie* and to give instructions to its revenue officers to prevent the occurrence of similar seizures. On September 8, 1908 Governor Magoon informed Mr. Adee that the fine had been remitted on the ground that the vessel at the time of Remittance of fine seizure was returning to Nassau from a fishing voyage and that it had not during its voyage touched at any Cuban port nor was it bound for any port in Cuba. No comment was made upon the question of the legality of the assertion by Cuba of jurisdiction beyond the three-mile limit.

Ambassador Reid to the the Secretary of State, July 31, 1908, MS. Department of State, file 14875; the Acting Secretary of State (Adee) to Governor Magoon, Aug. 18, 1908, *ibid.* 14875/2; Governor Magoon to Mr. Adee, Sept. 8, 1908, *ibid*, 14875/4.

The discussion in the House of Commons [on April 30, 1923] had to do with the claim of the Russian Government to jurisdiction within 12 miles of the coast.

The . . . text of the discussion in Parliament to which I have referred, as officially reported, is as follows:—

.   .   .   .

Soviet claim of 12-mile limit

"Mr. McNeil [Under Secretary of State for Foreign Affairs]: The Norwegian Government, equally with His Majesty's Government, have disputed the claim of the Russian Government to a 12-mile limit of territorial waters, and the dispute is, so far as I am aware, not yet settled. On the publication of the Russian decree of May, 1921, making this claim, His Majesty's Government informed the Soviet Government of their inability to concur in any extension of territorial limits beyond three nautical miles. While not admitting that the principle of a three-mile limit can be called in question, they have nevertheless expressed their readiness to discuss with the Soviet Government a special convention for the protection of seal fisheries in these waters. In September, 1921, the Soviet Government accepted this offer, but it has not up to the present transmitted the draft convention requested by His Majesty's Government as a first step in the negotiations.

.   .   .   .

" . . . The doctrine of territorial waters is not laid down in any international instrument, but the jurisdiction of nations over their coastal waters has been accepted by usage and is now a recognized rule of international law; His Majesty's Government have always maintained that by international law and practice the general limit of territorial jurisdiction is three miles, but from time to time claims to extend the three-mile limit have been advanced by different States. Such claims, which amount to annexation of the high seas, could only be made effective by international agreement. The Imperial Russian Government put forward a claim in 1909 to extend to 12 miles the Limit of Russian territorial waters. His Majesty's Government refused to admit this claim, but consented to refer the question for discussion to The Hague Conference. The Imperial Russian Government immediately on receipt of representations from His Majesty's Government released a British vessel which had been seized outside the three-mile limit, and refrained from attempting to enforce their claim pending its discussion at an international conference. In this respect the present Russian Government, so far from adopting the policy followed by the Imperial Russian Government, has insisted on enforcing a decree made in May, 1921, which has no international sanction, and, in spite of repeated representations of His Majesty's Government in connection with the seizure of British vessels, has refused to give any satisfaction whatever."

Consul General Skinner to Secretary Hughes, May 3, 1923, MS. Department of State, file 811.114/1445.

On September 2, 1937 the American Consulate at Belize reported that on the night of August 30 the British motor vessel *Caoba* was stopped by bullets fired across its bow by the *Zambrano*, a Honduran

Coast Guard cutter, and was searched "some twelve miles outside of Puerto Cortes, Honduras". The Honduran officials suspected that an individual wanted in Honduras was hiding on the *Caoba*, but, not finding him on the vessel, they permitted it to continue its journey. The American Legation at Tegucigalpa reported on October 1, 1937:

The British Government has made formal representations to the Honduran Government relative to this stoppage of a British vessel on the high seas, reserving all rights and stating it had viewed with great surprise this unwarranted incident. The Honduran Government has orally indicated its regret and stated that a full investigation was being initiated. *British protest*

In this connection, the Department's attention is drawn to Article 153 of the new Honduran Constitution of 1936, which states in part:— *Honduran Constitution, 1936*

"Article 153.—To the State appertains the full dominion, inalienable and imprescriptible, over the waters of the territorial seas to a distance of twelve kilometers from the lowest tide mark . . ."

It has been learned that at the time of the adoption of the Constitution of 1936 the British Government presented a Note to the Honduran Government indicating its non-acceptance of this designation of territorial waters of twelve kilometers (seven and one-half miles), as in contradiction to international usage in the conception of territorial waters as being approximately three miles from the lowest tide mark.

Vice Consul Gidden to Secretary Hull, Sept. 2, 1937, MS. Department of State, file 615.44a28/1; Minister Erwin to Mr. Hull, Oct. 1, 1937, *ibid.* 615.44a28/2.

On Oct. 19, 1937 the Department of State transmitted the following instruction to the American Legation at Tegucigalpa, with reference to article 153 of the Honduran Constitution quoted in the excerpt above set forth:

"It is desired that you advise the Honduran Foreign Office in writing that your Government reserves all rights of whatever nature with regard to any effects upon American interests from an enforcement of this Constitutional provision so far as it asserts that the territorial waters of Honduras extend beyond the three-mile limit." The Acting Secretary of State (Welles) to Mr. Erwin, Oct. 19, 1937, *ibid.* 615.44a28/3.

On March 22, 1922 the Norwegian Supreme Court rendered a decision in the *Penal Case Against Jens Hansen Lund*, involving the question whether the Norwegian law of September 30, 1921, extending the customs legislation to a limit of 10 nautical miles seaward, was applicable to an alien who had sold liquor unlawfully at a place about three and one-half miles from shore. The defendant had appealed from a conviction by the mixed court (*meddomsret*) for Fredrikstad on December 20, 1921. The Supreme Court, although upholding the conviction, stated that the lower court was wrong in assuming that the extent of the Norwegian territorial waters was one league and that—

Norway

. . . By "Royal Resolution" of February 22, 1812, it is provided that the limit for territorial waters shall be calculated as up to one nautical mile from land, corresponding approximately to 1⅓ leagues. This provision is still valid. It was alleged during the proceedings before the Supreme Court that during the last war Norway limited herself to seeking enforcement of the three mile limit, *inter alia* with respect to the question of neutrality. No accurate information in regard thereto is before the Supreme Court, but in any event there can be no permanent deviation from or abandonment of the said provision as to a nautical mile as a limit for territorial waters.

Norsk retstidende (1922) 499, translation.

On June 30, 1927 the Norwegian Supreme Court rendered an opinion in the case of *Advocate Leif Rode, Public Prosecutor* v. *Paul Frantz Weber and Others,* reversing a lower court's conviction of certain persons accused of unlawful importation of liquor. The lower court had found the defendants guilty of selling liquor within four miles from a line drawn between two small rocks off the Norwegian coast. In reversing the judgment the Supreme Court held that, as the Norwegian authorities had not determined the limits of the territorial waters in the section of the coast in question, it would be unreasonable to do so in a criminal case on the basis of a line which was subject to so much dispute as the line adopted by the lower court. *Ibid.* (1927) 513.

United States

. . . There is no general statute defining the limits of the territorial waters of the United States. Reference is, however, made to sections 2760, 2867 and 3067 of the Revised Statutes dealing with the proper enforcement of the revenue laws of the United States; also to Article V of the Treaty of Guadalupe-Hidalgo, February 2, 1848, between the United States and Mexico, defining the boundary line between the two countries, and the Convention of June 15, 1846, between the United States and Great Britain, fixing the northwestern boundary.

The Assistant Secretary of State (Bacon) to the Russian Ambassador (Rosen), Oct. 3, 1907, MS. Department of State, file 8488.

. . . this Government has always adhered to the principle that its maritime jurisdiction extends for a distance of one marine league (or nearly three and one-half English miles) from its coast. This, of course, does not include any waters or bays which are so landlocked as to be, without question, only in the jurisdiction of the United States.

The Assistant Secretary of State (Wilson) to F. M. Wilmot, June 16, 1909, *ibid.* 20008.

The Government of Russia having promulgated a law in 1910 subjecting to customs regulations vessels within "twelve marine miles from extreme low-water mark from the seacoasts of the Russian Empire, whether mainland or islands", the Department of State, on January 21, 1911, instructed the American Ambassador in St. Petersburg (Leningrad) to state to the Minister for Foreign Affairs that—

> with reference to the general operation of the law over the marginal seas beyond the generally recognized three mile limit and particularly as affecting American commerce, the United States is constrained to reserve all rights of whatever nature.

In reply the Embassy stated in part:

> In discussing with me this matter and the correlated question raised by the proposal to exclude foreigners from fishing within twelve miles from the shores of Archangel Government (reported in my No. 452 of January 16th), Mr. Sazonoff [Russian Minister for Foreign Affairs] took the view that territorial jurisdiction over marginal seas is based on the theory of control from the land, and that the delimitation of this area of control at twelve miles now corresponds more nearly with actual conditions than does the three-mile limit which represented the effective range of cannon at the time when this limitation of control over the seas was recognized as a principle of international law.

In a despatch of February 3, 1912 the Embassy, after referring to the law extending jurisdiction for customs purposes and to another law that had just been passed (May 29/June 11, 1911) extending jurisdiction over fishing within 12 miles of the Pacific coast, stated that England and Japan had protested against the extension of jurisdiction and added:

> Russia contends that the three mile limit is obsolete. The distance of three miles having been set as the conventional range of a cannon, it is claimed that with the extension of the range of modern ordnance the limit of jurisdiction should be increased to correspond.

With a further despatch of July 19, 1912 the Embassy transmitted to the Department a copy of the following note which had been sent by the Russian Ministry for Foreign Affairs in the early part of 1911 in reply to a protest by Japan against the extension of Russian jurisdiction—

> in modern international law there exists no *generally accepted* rule concerning the limits of territorial waters within which sovereign state authority may be exercised.
> The question has been given widely different solutions either by international treaties or the municipal laws of a state, and very often in an unequal manner for the various protected interests (customs regulations, fisheries, criminal or civil jurisdiction, sanitary observations, etc.)

Thus an examination of the laws dealing with the question shows that a great many States in Europe and America exercise undisputed jurisdiction within limits that exceed the so-called ordinary zone of three nautical miles.

Sections 2760, 2867, and 3067 of the Revised Statutes of the United States of America, for instance, fix the limit of the jurisdiction of American customs officers at 4 marine leagues (12 nautical miles), exactly the distance set by the new Russian law of 1909.

The jurisdiction of British officers in all customs and quarantine cases also covers (under Article XXIII of chapter 35 of the British Act 9 Geo. II; Article XII of chapter 80 of Acts 39 and 40 Geo. III; and Article I of chapter 47 of Act 24 Geo. III) a 4 marine-league zone.

Finally, under the law of March 27, 1817, the customs marine zone of France reaches out 2 myriameters from the coast.

Taking into consideration the above-cited provisions of laws against which no State appears to have protested, together with the fact that Russia is not bound by any international treaty fixing the 3-marine-mile zone for the territorial waters and that therefore its area cannot be measured from the viewpoint of international law except by the range of the cannons on the coast (which now even exceed the 12-nautical-mile limit) the Imperial Government is unable to admit that the Russian law of December 10, 1909, conflicts with international law.

Lastly, the Imperial Ministry deems it its duty to recall to the Japanese Embassy's memory that the Institute of International Law (whose authority on such questions is unquestionable) did not hesitate to declare (as far back as 17 years ago, when it met at Paris, in 1894) that the "usually adopted" distance of three miles was absolutely insufficient.

Memorandum of Apr. 12, 1910 from the Russian Embassy to the Department of State, and memorandum of the Department of State to the Russian Embassy, Apr. 18, 1910, MS. Department of State, file 861.0145; Ambassador Rockhill to Secretary Knox, Sept. 30, 1910, and Mr. Knox to Mr. Rockhill, Jan. 21, 1911, *ibid.* 861.0145/2; Mr. Rockhill to Mr. Knox, Feb. 13, 1911, *ibid.* 861.0145/4; Ambassador Guild to Mr. Knox, Feb. 3, 1912, *ibid.* 861.0145/10; Chargé Wilson to Mr. Knox, July 19, 1912, *ibid.* 861.0145/14; 1912 For. Rel. 1287–1309.

The British fishing trawler *St. Hubert* was seized in 1922 at a place ten and one-half miles from the Russian shore by Soviet authorities, who alleged that the vessel was fishing illegally within the limits of Russian waters. The captain of the vessel stated that he knew only the law of the three-mile limit. However, the Soviet court held that he had violated the Soviet decree of June 1, 1921 stipulating a marginal belt of 12 miles in fishing in those waters.

Consul Grout to Secretary Hughes, Mar. 23, 1922, MS. Department of State, file 361.4154Sa2/–, containing a translation of the decision of the Soviet court, Mar. 1922.

In 1915 it was alleged by the master of the Danish steamship *Vinland* that a British cruiser, which had been hovering outside of the territorial waters of the United States, had followed her within the three-mile limit of the United States. In a note of December 16, 1915 to the British Ambassador, Secretary Lansing stated that the Government of the United States had "always regarded the practice of belligerent cruisers patrolling American coasts in close proximity to the territorial waters of the United States and making the neighborhood a station for their observations as inconsistent with the treatment to be expected from the naval vessels of a friendly power in time of war" and had "maintained that the consequent menace of such proceedings to the freedom of American commerce" was "vexatious and uncourteous to the United States". In the correspondence that ensued the United States advanced "no claim that British vessels which have been and are cruising off American ports beyond the three-mile limit have not in so doing been within their strict legal rights under international law" but, rather, based its objection to the continued presence of belligerent vessels of war cruising in close proximity to American ports upon "the irritation which it naturally causes to a neutral country".

Secretary Lansing to Ambassador Spring Rice, Dec. 16, 1915 and Apr. 26, 1916, MS. Department of State, files 763.72111V76/7, 763.72111V76/10; 1915 For. Rel. Supp. 877–881; 1916 For. Rel. Supp. 759, 763.

I have the honor to acknowledge receipt of Your Excellency's note of November 6, 1914, having reference to your previous notes of August 13th and September 8th last, the first of which notes contained announcement that by a Royal Decree of the Italian Government, dated August 6, 1914, the limits of its territorial waters were set at six nautical miles from the shore, . . .

Italian decree, 1914

In your note of November 6th, Your Excellency says [after stating that "the limits of the marginal sea are not regulated by international conventions or general rules of international law thus leaving every State at liberty to fix them within the sphere of its own sovereignty without subjecting its decision to the recognition of the other States"] that, in order to remove any possible uncertainty respecting the position of this Government, you will appreciate an explicit declaration on behalf of the United States accepting the decision of the Italian Government as embodied in the Royal Decree referred to.

I am compelled to inform Your Excellency of my inability to accept the principle of the Royal Decree, in so far as it may undertake to extend the limits of the territorial waters beyond three nautical miles from the main shore line and to extend thereover the jurisdiction of the Italian Government.

An examination into the question involved leads to the conclusion that the territorial jurisdiction of a nation over the waters of the sea which wash its shore is now generally recognized by the principal nations to extend to the distance of one marine league or three nautical miles, that the Government of the United States appears to have uniformly supported this rule, and that the right of a nation to extend, by domestic ordinance, its jurisdiction beyond this limit has not been acquiesced in by the Government of the United States.

There are certain reasons, brought forward from time to time in the discussion of this question and advanced by writers on international law, why the maritime nations might deem the way clear to extend this determined limit of three miles, in view of the great improvement in gunnery and of the extended distance to which, from the shore, the rights of nations could be defended; but it seems manifestly important that such a construction or change of the rule should be reduced to a precise proposition and should then receive in some manner reciprocal acknowledgment from the principal maritime powers; in fine, that the extent of the open or high seas should better be the result of some concerted understanding by the nations whose vessels sail them than be left to the determination of each particular nation, influenced by the interests which may be peculiar to it.

> The Acting Secretary of State (Lansing) to Ambassador di Cellere, Nov. 28, 1914, MS. Department of State, file 763.72111/628; 1914 For. Rel. Supp. 665.

On December 12, 1914 the Department of State adverted to the note from the Acting Secretary of State to the Italian Ambassador, just quoted, and stated that it had taken steps to furnish the Department of the Navy with a copy of the diplomatic correspondence on this matter, with the request that orders be issued to the public ships of the United States notifying them of the Royal decree of August 6 and giving such further instructions as might be appropriate with a view to avoiding "so far as is possible any incident which may raise a question between the governments of Italy and the United States as to the extent of the territorial waters of the former country".

> Mr. Lansing to Mr. di Cellere, Dec. 12, 1914, MS. Department of State, file 763.72111/628; 1914 For. Rel. Supp. 666, 667.

In the case of *Ex Parte Marincovich*, the District Court of Appeal of California (2d dist.) stated:

> . . . If the extent of California's jurisdiction is to be determined according to the general rule, based upon usage uniformly recognized by the law of nations, there can be no doubt that it includes a zone of water, 3 miles wide, around Catalina Island. All the writers upon public law agree that every nation has exclusive jurisdiction over the waters adjacent to its shores to a distance of 3 miles from shore, or, as it is frequently expressed, "the distance of a cannon shot from shore." The distance of 3 geographical miles was fixed at a time when no gun could force a ball farther. This rule of international usage is applicable to California just as though it were an independent, sovereign nation, save only that its right of exclusive control over such waters is limited in so far as control may have been granted to

the United States. Manchester v. Massachusetts, 139 U.S. 234, 11 Sup. Ct. 559, 35 L. Ed. 159; Humboldt L. M. Ass'n v. Christopherson, 73 Fed. 239, 19 C.C.A. 481, 46 L.R.A. 264. . . . Wheaton, International Law (8th Ed.) §177.

192 Pac. (1920) 156, 157, 48 Calif. App. 474.

In 1925 the American Embassy at Madrid transmitted to the Department of State a *note verbale* from the Spanish Foreign Office relative to the Spanish-French maritime patrol of the Moroccan coast. It was stated that the vigilance was confined to six miles and that the territorial waters within those six miles were closed to navigation between certain points. Reference was made in the note to the stipulations of article 4 of an agreement of December 18, 1923, between Great Britain, Spain, and France, as giving the right of vigilance of the territorial waters of the Zone of Tangier to Spanish, British, and French naval forces. It was added that vessels and boats found to be engaged in traffic in arms, war material, and merchandise suspected of being bound for ports not open to commerce would be delivered to the appropriate jurisdiction. The Department of State replied: {Moroccan coast}

. . . You may inform the Spanish Government that this Government does not recognize the right of either the Spanish or French Governments to interfere with American vessels outside the three mile limit, as recognized by international law, nor does it recognize the right to interfere with such vessels within the three mile limit except in the manner provided for under the Act of Algeciras.

Spanish Foreign Office to the American Embassy at Madrid, July 2, 1925; Ambassador Moore to Secretary Kellogg, July 3, 1925; and Mr. Kellogg to the American Embassy, July 31, 1925; MS. Department of State, file 881.00/1110; Gr. Br. Treaty Ser. no. 23 (1924), Cmd. 2203.

A Mexican decree dated August 30, 1935, containing provision for the extension of Mexican territorial waters from three miles to nine miles, reads in translation: {Mexican claim, 1935}

SOLE ARTICLE: Section I of article 4 of the Law of Immovable Properties of the Nation, of December 18, 1902, is amended to read as follows:

"I.—The Territorial Waters, for a distance of nine nautical miles (16,668 kilometers), counted from the mark of the lowest tide on the coasts of the mainland or on the shores of the islands forming part of the national territory."

On January 11, 1936 the Department of State instructed the Embassy in Mexico as follows:

It is desired that you advise the Mexican Foreign Office in writing that your Government reserves all rights of whatever nature so far as concerns any effects upon American commerce from enforcement of this legislation purporting to amend existing law so as to extend the territorial waters of Mexico from three miles in breadth to nine miles.

A note in the sense of the Department's instruction was delivered by the Embassy to the Mexican Foreign Office under date of March 7, 1936. The latter replied on May 6, 1936, in part, that—

the following conclusions are deduced:

1.—The territorial waters of Mexico as well as those of the United States have been fixed by the Treaty of Peace, Amity and Boundaries concluded between the two countries on February 2, 1848, at nine nautical miles or 16 kilometers 668 meters.

2.—Any doubts as to whether Article V of the said Treaty refers to territorial waters have been definitely settled by the exchange of notes between Mexico, the United States, and Great Britain. In his note of August 19, 1848, Mr. James Buchanan, Secretary of State of the United States, recognizes that the territorial waters extend for three nautical leagues as determined by the United States and Mexico in the Treaty of Peace, Amity and Boundaries signed on February 2, 1848.

3.—The Decree of August 29, 1935, published in the *Diario oficial* of August 31, 1935, conforms strictly to the provisions of Article V of the above-mentioned Treaty, since it fixes the breadth of territorial waters at nine nautical miles, that is, 16 kilometers, 668 meters.

The Government of Mexico believes that an appraisal of the foregoing facts will cause the Government of Your Excellency to consider as just and proper the decision taken by the Government of Mexico in regard to territorial waters, and therefore as unwarranted the reservation of rights made by the Government of the United States.

To this the Department of State replied on May 23, 1936:

The treaty provisions [art. V of the treaty of 1848] in question read as follows:

"The dividing line between the two Republics shall begin in the Gulf of Mexico, three leagues from land at the mouth of the Rio Grande ..."

The Foreign Office has not taken into account the remaining words of the paragraph from which the quotation is taken, which words delimit the boundary line between its eastern end in the Gulf of Mexico and its western end which is said to be "the Pacific Ocean". It will be observed that the western limit of the boundary line is *not* stated to be "three leagues from land". Moreover, the second paragraph of Article V of the Treaty of

1848 contains the following provision as to the western limit of the boundary line between the two countries:

"and, in order to preclude all difficulty in tracing upon the ground the limit separating Upper from Lower California, it is agreed that the said limit shall consist of a straight line drawn from the middle of the Rio Gila, where it unites with the Colorado, to a point on the coast of the Pacific Ocean, distant one marine league due south of the southernmost point of the port of San Diego."

It will be further observed that in the last quoted provisions of the Article upon which the Mexican Foreign Office relies, the westernmost point of the boundary line between the two countries is stated as being on the *coast* of the Pacific Ocean.

That portion of Article V of the Treaty of 1848 which the Mexican Foreign Office quotes relates only to the boundary line at a given point and furnishes no authority for Mexico to claim generally that its territorial waters extend nine miles from the coast. The British note of June 9, 1848 which is quoted by the Mexican Foreign Office recognizes the merely local applicability of the agreement between the United States and Mexico as to the easternmost part of the boundary line, when it states in giving notice that the British Government could not "acquiesce in the extent of maritime jurisdiction assumed by the United States and Mexico", that the giving of such notice is "the more necessary because the Gulf of Mexico is a great thoroughfare of maritime commerce".

Furthermore, this view of the restricted nature of the agreement is strengthened by the statements in this Department's note to the British Minister of August 19, 1848, which is also quoted by the Mexican Foreign Office, and wherein it was said that if for the "mutual convenience" of the United States and Mexico it had been proper to enter into such an arrangement, third parties had no just cause of complaint and that the Government of the United States never intended by this stipulation to question the rights which Great Britain or any other power may possess under the law of nations.

Presumably it is true as indicated by a note sent by this Department to the British Minister on January 22, 1875, that the arrangement thus made between the United States and Mexico with respect to the *Gulf of Mexico* was designed to prevent smuggling in the particular area covered by the arrangement.

Wholly aside from the question of the boundary line between the two countries, there remains to be considered the total great extent of the Mexican coast and the bordering territorial waters. To say that because the United States agreed that in one area, so far as the United States was concerned, Mexican territorial waters extended three leagues from land, therefore Mexico was entitled to claim such an extent of territorial waters adjacent to her entire coast line is an unwarranted deduction from the terms of Article V of the Treaty of 1848.

Ambassador Daniels to Secretary Hull, Nov. 27, 1935, and the Assistant Secretary of State (Moore) to the Chargé d'Affaires in Mexico (Norweb), Jan. 11, 1936, MS. Department of State, file 812.0145/12; Second Secretary MacVeagh to Mr. Hull, Mar. 9, 1936, *ibid.* 812.0145/15; the Mexican Minister of Foreign Affairs (Hay) to Mr. Daniels, May 6, 1936, and Mr. Moore to Mr. Daniels, May 23, 1936, *ibid.* 812.0145/16.

In holding that Florida had a right to regulate sponge fisheries beyond the three-mile belt of territorial waters but within the three-league territorial limits of Florida, as defined in the State Constitutions of 1868 and 1885, the District Court of the United States for the Northern District of Florida overruled contentions to the effect that the boundaries as fixed in the Constitution were void as being in conflict with the treaty of February 22, 1819 between the United States and Spain, 2 Treaties, etc. (Malloy, 1910) 1651, ceding the Floridas to the United States, and with the act of Congress of March 3, 1845 (5 Stat. 742, 743), admitting Florida into the Union.

The court (Judge Long speaking) held that the act of 1845 fixed the boundaries as set out in the treaty; that in effect it described the Gulf of Mexico as one of the boundaries; that "Under international law this means that the jurisdiction of the state extends one league into the Gulf, or 3 miles"; that the boundary could be changed by agreement "between the state and the Congress, so long as the change does not affect the territory of another state"; and that Congress had, by an act of June 25, 1868 (15 Stat. 73) and by subsequent acquiescence, approved the change of the boundary from one to three leagues from mainland into the Gulf of Mexico. The court referred also to acquiescence of foreign nations for more than 50 years in the establishment of the boundary, as an element to be taken into account.

> *Pope et al.* v. *Blanton, County Judge, et al.,* 10 F. Supp. 18 (N. D. Fla., 1935).
>
> For a discussion of the breadth of the belt of territorial waters, prepared for the use of a committee of the Norwegian Parliament, see Christopher B. V. Meyer, *Extent of Jurisdiction in Coastal Waters* (1937) 512–518, 520.

MEASUREMENT

§93

Baseline The German steamship *Düsseldorf* and her cargo of iron ore were captured by a British cruiser on February 22, 1918 within three miles of two parcels of land which, at high water, are divided from the mainland of Norway by narrow passages but are not separated in any way from the mainland at low water. The Norwegian Government claimed the release of the steamship and cargo on the ground that the seizure took place in Norwegian territorial waters. Lord Sterndale, in delivering the opinion of the British prize court, upheld the Norwegian contention, stating:

The question is from what place are the 3 miles from the coast to be reckoned. One contention on the part of the claimant was the extreme one, that wherever you get a piece of rock, however small, however uninhabited, and however uninhabitable, within the 3-mile radius from the mainland, that must also be taken as being part of the territory of the country, and the 3 miles of territorial waters must be taken from that rock. So that if it happens to be 2-3/4 miles out you will really get a distance of 5-3/4 miles from what is ordinarily called the mainland. All I say is—I give no opinion about that in this case, because it is not necessary—that I do not wish to be taken as accepting it as accurate. There was then a smaller contention—if I may call it so—and that was that at any rate an island such as the one I have mentioned of Buholmen, which is, I think, about 300 metres long, is large enough to be part of the mainland. That, again, I prefer to leave for decision when it becomes necessary to decide it, but I cannot see my way to say that two pieces of land which are not disconnected from the mainland at low water, and not separated in any way, are not part of the mainland. If that be so, taking the position given by the Crown, this capture, or part of the operation of capture, at any rate, took place within 3 miles of the Norwegian coast so defined. As I have indicated, it is a very near thing indeed whether it was not within 3 miles of what is indisputably the mainland; it is a very near thing indeed of some 100 or 200 yards. But, accepting the Crown's case to the full extent, in my opinion part of the operations of this capture took place in Norwegian territorial waters, and therefore there must be an order for the release of ship and cargo.

The Düsseldorf, [1919] P. 245, 246–247; IX *Lloyd's Reports of Prize Cases* (1923) 1, 6. An appeal was taken from so much of the judgment as disallowed the claim for costs and damages. The judicial committee of the Privy Council, in passing on the question of damages, approved the decision of the prize court with respect to the method of determining the extent of the marginal sea in this case. *Ibid.* 12; [1920] A.C. 1034.

No general statute defines the territorial waters of the United States. This Government considers, however, as asserted in Article 1 of the Convention concluded on May 19, 1924, between the United States and Germany for the Prevention of Smuggling of Intoxicating Liquors, that "three marine miles, extending from the coast-line outwards and measured from low-tide mark, constitute the proper limits of territorial waters."

W. R. Castle, Jr. to the German Chargé d'Affaires (Kiep), Oct. 6, 1927, MS. Department of State, file 811.0145/211.

For a definition of the term "shore" as used in a boundary description, see 25 Op. Att. Gen. (1906) 172, 174–176.

Prior to the Hague Conference on the Codification of International Law, held in 1930, the Preparatory Committee of the League of Nations pointed out that a question was presented "whether the breadth of territorial waters is to be measured from low-water mark following all the sinuosities of the coast, or whether an imaginary line connecting particular salient points of the coast is to be taken as the base line". After consulting the various governments, the Preparatory Committee stated:

> The majority of the States which have supplied information pronounce for the first formula, which has already been adopted in various international conventions. The second formula would necessitate detailed information as regards the choice of the salient points and the distance determining the base line between these points. The replies received do not furnish such details. In these circumstances, the first formula is the only one which can be adopted.

The subcommittee appointed by the second committee of the Conference to consider the question tentatively adopted the view that "the breadth of the territorial sea is measured from the line of low-water mark along the entire coast"; that, for the purposes of the proposed convention, "the line of low-water mark is that indicated on the charts officially used by the Coastal State, provided the latter line does not appreciably depart from the line of mean low-water spring tides"; and that elevations of the sea bed situated within the territorial sea, though only above water at low tide, "are taken into consideration" for the determination of the baseline of the territorial sea.

> League of Nations pub. C.74.M.39.1929.V, pp. 35, 38 (also contains replies of the governments) ; *ibid.* C.230.M.117.1930.V, p. 11.
>
> The same subcommittee also tentatively reported:
>
> "When a river flows directly into the sea, the waters of the river constitute inland water up to a line following the general direction of the coast drawn across the mouth of the river whatever its width. If the river flows into an estuary, the rules applicable to bays apply to the estuary."
>
> *Ibid.* 14. See also *ibid.* C.74.M.39.1929.V, pp. 61, 63, containing the replies of the governments on the same general subject.
>
> In the *Grisbadarna* case (Norway and Sweden) a tribunal composed of three jurists indicated the boundary line between Norway and Sweden in the area within the marginal seas "by tracing a line perpendicularly to the general direction of the coast". Scott, *Hague Court Reports* (1916) 122, 129.

Line between inland waters and marginal sea   On March 9, 1928 the Norwegian Legation at Washington requested of the Department of State copies of any regulations which might exist regarding the delineation of the political coastline or the drawing up of the limit between internal and territorial waters. On July 13, 1929 the Department replied:

> The geographic points for drawing up the basic lines for the territorial waters and the fishery boundary, with the exception of certain limited areas covered by special treaty or agreement, have not been determined by the United States. Agencies of the Fed-

eral Government have made their own determinations for administrative purposes; for example, the Steamboat Inspection Service has made certain decisions regarding lines separating inland waters from the high seas. However, no final determination has been made which would be binding alike upon all agencies of the Federal Government.

No general statute defines the territorial waters of the United States.

.   .   .   .

As having a possible bearing on the inquiry of the Norwegian Sea Territory Commission, I have the honor to enclose a copy each of the following publications:

1. "Pilot Rules for Certain Inland Waters of the Atlantic and Pacific Coasts, and of the Coast of the Gulf of Mexico."
    On page 11 of this publication under the heading "Boundary Lines of the High Seas", will be found the designation of the lines dividing the high seas from rivers, harbors, and inland waters. Within these lines are inland waters upon which inland rules and pilot rules apply. Outside of these lines are the high seas upon which the international rules apply.
2. "Pilot Rules for the Rivers whose waters flow into the Gulf of Mexico and their Tributaries and the Red River of the North."
    On page 21, of this publication under the heading "Boundary Lines of Inland Waters", will be found the designation of the boundary lines of the high seas and lines of demarcation of inland waters of the United States bordering on the Gulf of Mexico where the pilot rules for rivers emptying into the Gulf of Mexico apply.

It should be understood that the foregoing lines do not represent territorial boundaries, but are for navigational purposes, to indicate where inland rules begin and international rules cease to apply.

The Norwegian Minister (Bachke) to the Secretary of State (Kellogg), Mar. 9, 1928, MS. Department of State, file 811.0145/215; the Acting Secretary of Commerce (Morgan) to Mr. Kellogg, Apr. 24, 1928, *ibid.* 811.0145/217; the Secretary of the Navy (Adams) to the Secretary of State (Stimson), May 8, 1929, and W. R. Castle, Jr. to Chargé Lundh, July 13, 1929, *ibid.* 811.0145/224; the Acting Secretary of the Navy (Hughes) to Mr. Stimson, July 24, 1929, *ibid.* 811.0145/226.

INNOCENT PASSAGE

§94

Charles Cheney Hyde discusses the subject of innocent passage through territorial waters as follows:

Over its territorial waters along the marginal sea the control of the territorial sovereign is limited. While it may regulate at will matters pertaining to fisheries, the enjoyment of the underlying land, coastal trade, police and pilotage, the use of particular channels, as well as maritime ceremonial, it is not permitted to debar foreign merchant vessels from the enjoyment of what is known as the right of "innocent passage." . . .

Vessels of war, although serving no commercial purpose, are not necessarily deprived of the right of passage under normal conditions, and still less, other public ships devoted to scientific purposes.

So long as the conduct of a vessel of any kind is not essentially injurious to the safety and welfare of the littoral State, there would appear to be no reason to exclude it from the use of the marginal sea. . . . In a word, the right of so-called innocent passage vanishes whenever the conduct of a ship is harmful to the territorial sovereign. To the latter, whether a belligerent or a neutral, must be accorded the right to determine when acts of a passing ship lose their innocent character.

·　　·　　·　　·　　·　　·　　·

The territorial sovereign must itself be the judge of what violates its own rights or interests. It is not, however, likely to find occasion or be disposed to charge a violation thereof, unless apprised of the commission of a grave offense arousing in fact the interest of persons on shore or elsewhere outside of the vessel and within its territory. If a passing ship or an occupant thereof violates the local law and with respect to a stranger to the vessel, the territorial sovereign may fairly assert jurisdiction.

Whether the statutes of the littoral State are applicable to occurrences taking place within the marginal sea, and especially to acts committed on foreign passing ships, and whether also the local tribunals are clothed with requisite jurisdiction for purposes of adjudication, present questions of municipal rather than international law.

I Hyde, *International Law*, etc. (1922) 277–278, 404–405.

. . . War-ships may not pass without consent into this zone [of marginal seas], because they threaten. Merchant-ships may pass and repass, because they do not threaten.

Statement of Elihu Root, *North Atlantic Coast Fisheries Arbitration*, Oral Argument, part II (1910) 1214; XI *North Atlantic Coast Fisheries Arbitration* (S. Doc. 870, 61st Cong., 3rd sess.), p. 2007.

Article 2 of the statute on freedom of transit, signed at Barcelona on April 20, 1921 by 32 states, provides that in order to insure the application of the provisions of that article, relating to free transit, the "Contracting States will allow transit in accordance with the customary conditions and reserves across their territorial waters."

7 League of Nations Treaty Series (1921–22) 13, 27.

In 1884 the Chilean Court of Serena held that in a case of theft it had jurisdiction over a ship which was merely in passage, although it was not definitely established whether or not the vessel was in territorial waters.

Tobar y Borgoño, *Du conflit international au sujet des compétences pénales et des causes concomitantes au délit qui les influencent* (1910) 691. Article 5 of the Chilean Penal Code provides:

"The Chilean penal law is obligatory for all the inhabitants of the republic including foreigners. The crimes committed within territorial or adjacent waters are subject to the provisions of this code." *Códigos de la República de Chile* (1937) 997, translation.

In the case of *The Ship "D. C. Whitney"* v. *The St. Clair Navigation Company and The Southern Coal and Transportation Company,* a proceeding *in rem* against an American vessel arising out of a collision between two American ships in the port of Sandusky, Ohio, the Supreme Court of Canada, reversing a judgment of the Exchequer Court, Toronto Admiralty District, held that a foreign vessel bound from one port of the United States to another and passing through waters dividing Canada from the United States, which waters are made free and open to ships of both nations under the Webster-Ashburton treaty of 1842 between Great Britain and the United States, is not, even when on the Canadian side, within Canadian control so as to be subject to arrest on warrant from an admiralty court. Judge Davies, delivering the opinion of the court, stated:

. . . Jurisdiction only attaches over the *res* when it comes or is brought within the control or submits to the jurisdiction of the court and not till then. Such jurisdiction does not exist against a ship passing along the coast in the exercise of innocent passage or through channels or arms of the sea which, by international law or special convention, are declared free and open to the ships of her nationality, unless expressly given by statute.

38 Can. Sup. Ct. (1907) 303, 311; 1 Treaties, etc. (Malloy, 1910) 650.

In the case of *Government of the Netherlands* v. *Neptune Steamship Company,* the court of first instance of Middleburg, Netherlands, in holding, on September 20, 1914, that a seizure of a German vessel that was descending the River Scheldt and that had collided with a government vessel was legal, stated that if it were otherwise "the absurd consequence would necessarily follow that vessels coming from abroad and passing through Dutch territory to get to a foreign country would be relieved of the execution of the right of security to which every creditor has a right . . ."

43 *Journal du droit international privé* (1916) 657, 658, translation.

Immense quantities of shipping, bound from one foreign port to another, daily pass, on their regular course, through the territorial waters of third States; and yet international law permits such third States to enforce their municipal law upon such shipping.

Arrest of vessel

In the case of *Compañía de Navegación Nacional* (Panama *v.* United States) the United States–Panamanian Claims Commission, on June 29, 1933, disallowed a claim made by Panama based on the arrest of the company's steamer, the *David*, within a few hundred yards of Flamenco Island and probably between that island and San José Rock off the Pacific entrance of the Panama Canal. The majority of the Commission, having found that the arrest took place within the territorial waters of the Canal Zone, said:

> We now turn to the question raised by the assertion that the *David* should have been exempted from arrest under the rule of innocent passage. An exhaustive research was made into the authorities upon this question by the Agents, and the point was argued with great thoroughness. The general rule of the extension of sovereignty over the 3-mile zone is clearly established. Exceptions to the completeness of this sovereignty should be supported by clear authority. There is a clear preponderance of authority to the effect that this sovereignty is qualified by what is known as the right of innocent passage, and that this qualification forbids the sovereign actually to prohibit the innocent passage of alien merchant vessels through its territorial waters.
> There is no clear preponderance of authority to the effect that such vessels when passing through territorial waters are exempt from civil arrest. In the absence of such authority, the Commission cannot say that a country may not, under the rules of international law, assert the right to arrest on civil process merchant ships passing through its territorial waters.

Mr. Alfaro, the Panamanian Commissioner, dissenting, said:

> I am not in accord with this conclusion of the majority which is contrary to the very nature of the right of innocent passage and which considerably abridges it and does not seem to be based upon creditable authorities in international law. . . .
> It is proper to point out also that the claimant does not maintain that absolute immunity exists from the jurisdiction of the littoral authorities; that it does not allege, for example, lack of jurisdiction in the case of an offense committed within territorial waters in the course of innocent passage, although some writers deny jurisdiction even in such cases; the claimant also accepts that the ship is obliged to comply with orders and maritime regulations which contribute to the safety of navigation, or that are of a sanitary or police character. The claimant maintains only that in case of a civil action growing out of a collision occurring previously beyond the jurisdiction of the littoral authorities, the latter were without jurisdiction later to interfere with the passage of the same ship by means of a civil suit not affecting in any way territorial sovereign interests.

Hunt's Report (1934) 765, 815, 817. The Commission was established in accordance with the conventions of July 28, 1926 and Dec. 17, 1932 between the United States and Panama. Treaty Series 842 and 860; 4 Treaties, etc. (Trenwith, 1938) 4546, 4552.

The second committee appointed by the Hague Conference for the Codification of International Law in 1930 to study the subject of territorial waters, provisionally approved the following articles with reference to innocent passage:

ARTICLE 3.

"Passage" means navigation through the territorial sea for the purpose either of traversing that sea without entering inland waters, or of proceeding to inland waters, or of making for the high sea from inland waters.

Passage is not *innocent* when a vessel makes use of the territorial sea of a Coastal State for the purpose of doing any act prejudicial to the security, to the public policy or to the fiscal interests of that State.

Right of passage

Passage includes stopping and anchoring, but in so far only as the same are incidental to ordinary navigation or are rendered necessary by *force majeure* or by distress.

.   .   .   .

ARTICLE 4.

A Coastal State may put no obstacles in the way of the innocent passage of foreign vessels in the territorial sea.

Submarine vessels shall navigate on the surface.

.   .   .   .

ARTICLE 5.

The right of passage does not prevent the Coastal State from taking all necessary steps to protect itself in the territorial sea against any act prejudicial to the security, public policy or fiscal interests of the State, and, in the case of vessels proceeding to inland waters, against any breach of the conditions to which the admission of those vessels to those waters is subject.

Jurisdiction

.   .   .   .

ARTICLE 6.

Foreign vessels exercising the right of passage shall comply with the laws and regulations enacted in conformity with international usage by the Coastal State, and, in particular, as regards:

(a) the safety of traffic and the protection of channels and buoys;

(b) the protection of the waters of the Coastal State against pollution of any kind caused by vessels;

(c) the protection of the products of the territorial sea;

(d) the rights of fishing, shooting and analogous rights belonging to the Coastal State.

The Coastal State may not, however, apply these rules or regulations in such a manner as to discriminate between foreign vessels of different nationalities, nor, save in matters relating to fishing and shooting, between national vessels and foreign vessels.

.   .   .   .

ARTICLE 7.

No charge may be levied upon foreign vessels by reason only of their passage through the territorial sea.

Charges may only be levied upon a foreign vessel passing through the territorial sea as payment for specific services rendered to the vessel. These charges shall be levied without discrimination.

.   .   .   .

ARTICLE 8.

A Coastal State may not take any steps on board a foreign vessel passing through the territorial sea to arrest any person or to conduct any investigation by reason of any crime committed on board the vessel during its passage, save only in the following cases:

(1) if the consequences of the crime extend beyond the vessel; or

(2) if the crime is of a kind to disturb the peace of the country or the good order of the territorial sea; or

(3) if the assistance of the local authorities has been requested by the captain of the vessel or by the consul of the country whose flag the vessel flies.

The above provisions do not affect the right of the Coastal State to take any steps authorised by its laws for the purpose of an arrest or investigation on board a foreign vessel in the inland waters of that State or lying in its territorial sea, or passing through the territorial sea after leaving the inland waters.

The local authorities shall in all cases pay due regard to the interests of navigation when making an arrest on board a vessel.

.   .   .   .

ARTICLE 9.

A Coastal State may not arrest nor divert a foreign vessel passing through the territorial sea, for the purpose of exercising civil jurisdiction in relation to a person on board the vessel. A Coastal State may not levy execution against or arrest the vessel for the purpose of any civil proceedings save only in respect of obligations or liabilities incurred by the vessel itself in the course of or for the purpose of its voyage through the waters of the Coastal State.

The above provisions are without prejudice to the right of the Coastal State in accordance with its laws to levy execution against, or to arrest, a foreign vessel in the inland waters of the State or lying in the territorial sea, or passing through the territorial sea after leaving the inland waters of the State, for the purpose of any civil proceedings.

League of Nations pub. C.230.M.117.1930.V, Report of the Second Commission, pp. 4, 6–9. For replies of the governments to the Questionnaire of the Preparatory Committee of the League of Nations and the Bases of Discussion prepared by the latter, see *ibid.* C.74.M.39.1929.V, pp. 65–86, 145–151.

ISLANDS

§95

In the case of *Ex Parte Marincovich*, decided by the District Court of Appeal of California (2d dist., div. 2), involving a question as to the jurisdiction of the court to try a case arising within three miles of Catalina Island, Presiding Justice Finlayson said:

There is just as much reason for the extension of state sovereignty over a 3-mile belt around Catalina Island as there is for the extension of sovereignty over a 3-mile zone along and off the shore of the mainland. In the one case, as in the other, such jurisdiction is necessary to an adequate exercise of the state's police powers and to protect the coast from the effects of hostilities by other nations at war.

. . . .

We conclude, therefore, that, unless the people of the state, in their definition of the state's boundary as set forth in article 21 of the Constitution, have deliberately excluded such waters from the territory over which the State's sovereignty extends, the state has jurisdiction over a belt of water, three miles wide, around each of the islands that lie along and adjacent to our shores.

192 Pac. (1920) 156, 158, 48 Calif. App. 474.

The convention regarding the Aaland Islands signed at Geneva on October 20, 1921 provides that the territorial waters of the islands "are considered to extend for a distance of three marine miles from the low-water mark on the islands, islets and reefs not permanently submerged, . . . ".

9 *League of Nations Treaty Series* (1922), art. 2, pp. 212, 217.

In the case of *Middleton* v. *United States* the defendant was convicted of bringing aliens into the United States in violation of section 8 of the Immigration Act of 1917 (39 Stat. 874), making it a misdemeanor to "bring into or land in the United States, by vessel or otherwise", any alien unlawfully. With respect to a contention that the evidence did not show that he actually had landed aliens in the United States, the Court stated in part:

> . . . It is beyond dispute that he [Middleton] brought the aliens into the territorial waters of the United States when he came within half a mile of the Keys [of Florida], and also when he passed by the bell buoy of the Northwest Channel within three miles of an island. It does not make any difference that these islands were uninhabited; it is sufficient that they were islands of the United States.

> 32 F. (2d) 239, 240 (C.C.A. 5th, 1929).

The Preparatory Committee for the Conference for the Codification of International Law, held at the Hague in 1930, requested information from the several governments with reference to the problem of measuring territorial waters around islands. On March 16, 1929 the Government of the United States replied:

> Alluvial islands off the mouth of the Mississippi River of insufficient consistency to support life, uninhabited and resorted to only for shooting and taking birds' nests were called a kind of portico to the mainland by Sir William Scott in the *Anne* (1805) 5 C. Rob. 373, 165 English Rep. 815, and held to be part of the territory of the United States from which the protection of the territory was to be reckoned. It was stated in the opinion that whether the islands were composed of earth or solid rock did not vary the right of dominion, for right of dominion did not depend upon the texture of the soil.

> A shallow submerged reef off the coast of Florida on which a beacon was built could not be considered territory of the United States. U. S. *v.* Henning (1925) 7 Fed. (2d) 488, revised on other grounds (1926) 15 Fed. (2d) 74.

> A submerged shoal could not be considered an island. *Soult* v. *L'Africaine* (1804) 22 Fed. Cas. 13179.

> It would seem that any naturally formed part of the earth's surface, projecting above the level of the sea at low tide and surrounded by water at low tide, should be considered an island.

> League of Nations pub. C.74.M.39.1929.V, p. 145. The same document contains the replies of the other governments at pp. 48–54, and for the observations of the Preparatory Committee on the replies, see p. 50.

> At the same Conference the Committee on Territorial Waters submitted the following report of its subcommittee II as of possible interest for the continuation of the study:

> "Every island has its own territorial sea. An island is an area of land, surrounded by water, which is permanently above high-water mark.

> "Observations.

> "The definition of the term 'island' does not exclude artificial islands, provided these are true portions of the territory and not merely floating works, anchored buoys, etc. The case of an artificial island erected near

to the line of demarcation between the territorial waters of two countries is reserved.

"An elevation of the sea bed, which is only exposed at low tide, is not deemed to be an island for the purpose of this Convention. (See however the above proposal concerning the Base Line.)

"GROUPS OF ISLANDS.

"Observations.

"With regard to a group of islands (archipelago) and islands situated along the coast, the majority of the Sub-Committee was of opinion that a distance of 10 miles should be adopted as a basis for measuring the territorial sea outward in the direction of the high sea. Owing to the lack of technical details, however, the idea of drafting a definite text on this subject had to be abandoned. The Sub-Committee did not express any opinion with regard to the nature of the waters included within the group."

Ibid. C.230.M.117.1930.V, p. 13.

SEA BED AND SUBSOIL

§96

In the case of *Attorney-General for the Province of British Columbia* v. *Attorney-General for the Dominion of Canada,* involving the power of the Province to grant fishing rights in certain waters, the Privy Council held that "the right of fishing in the sea is a right of the public in general which does not depend on any proprietary title, and that the Dominion has the exclusive right of legislating with regard to it", stating at the same time that—

they are of opinion that the right of the public to fish in the sea has been well established in English law for many centuries and does not depend on the assertion or maintenance of any title in the Crown to the subjacent land.

They desire, however, to point out that the three-mile limit is something very different from the "narrow seas" limit discussed by the older authorities, such as Selden and Hale, a principle which may safely be said to be now obsolete. The doctrine of the zone comprised in the former limit owes its origin to comparatively modern authorities on public international law. Its meaning is still in controversy. The questions raised thereby affect not only the Empire generally but also the rights of foreign nations as against the Crown, and of the subjects of the Crown as against other nations in foreign territorial waters. Until the Powers have adequately discussed and agreed on the meaning of the doctrine at a Conference, it is not desirable that any municipal tribunal should pronounce on it. . . . Until then the conflict of judicial opinion which arose in *Reg.* v. *Keyn*[2] ([2] 2 Ex. D. 63) is not likely to be satisfactorily settled, nor is a conclusion likely to be reached on the question whether the shore below low water mark to within three miles of the coast forms part of the territory of the Crown or is merely subject to special powers necessary for protective and police purposes. . . . But apart from these difficulties, there is the decisive consideration that the question is not one which belongs to the domain of municipal law alone.

[1914] A.C. 153, 173, 174.

Rights above and under territorial waters

The Preparatory Committee for the Hague Conference for the Codification of International Law requested information from the respective governments with regard to the "Application of the rights of the coastal State to the air above and the sea bottom and subsoil covered by its territorial waters". On March 16, 1929 the United States replied:

Reply of U.S.

By Section 6 of the Air Commerce Act of March 20th, 1926, Congress declared that the Government of the United States possessed to the exclusion of all other nations complete sovereignty of the air space over the lands and waters of the United States, including the Canal Zone (44 Stat., 568, 572).

The Section of the Act cited finds support in the Convention relating to International Air Navigation signed by certain Powers on October 13th, 1919, in which it was recognised that every State has complete and exclusive sovereignty above its territory and territorial waters (II L.N.T.S., 173).

Court Decisions.

The sea-bottom and subsoil covered by the territorial waters, including fish and minerals, are the property of the United States or of the individual States where they border (Smith *v.* Maryland, 18 Howard 71, 74; McCready *v.* Virginia, 94 U.S. 391; Manchester *v.* Massachusetts, 139 U.S. 240, 259; Louisiana *v.* Mississippi, 202 U.S. 1, 52; Messenger *v.* Kingsbury, 158 California 611, 112 Pac. 65, 66).

After considering the replies of the governments, the Preparatory Committee observed that unanimity existed and drew up the following basis of discussion (no. 2):

The sovereignty of the coastal State extends to the air above its territorial waters, to the bed of the sea covered by those waters and to the subsoil.

The second committee appointed by the Conference provisionally approved an article to the same general effect, stating at the same time that "as regards the bed of the sea and the subsoil, there are but few rules of international law".

League of Nations pub. C.74.M.39.1929.V, pp. 18–21 (also contains replies of other governments) ; *ibid.* C.230.M.117.1930.V, p. 6.

In the case of *Alaska Gold Recovery Co. et al.* v. *Northern Mining & Trading Co.* the District Court of the United States for the District of Alaska, held that the owner of a seabeach mining claim at Nome had a right to mine certain areas between high and low tide

and the land under the waters of the shore of Bering Sea belonging
to the Government, since this right was expressly granted by section
129, *Compiled Laws of the Territory of Alaska*, 1913, which provided
that "subject only to such general limitations as may be necessary to
exempt navigation from artificial obstructions all land and shoal
water between low and mean high tide on the shores, bays, and inlets
of Bering Sea, within the jurisdiction of the United States, shall be
subject to exploration and mining".

> 7 Alaska (D. C., 2d. Div., 1926) 386, 395.

In 1933 the city of Los Angeles brought suit to quiet title to land
claimed to be tideland in Los Angeles harbor. It based its title on a
legislative grant by the State of California. The defendant company
claimed title under a patent granted by the United States after the
admission of California as a State of the Union in 1850. A decree
of the lower court dismissing the suit was reversed by the circuit
court of appeals. In 1935 the Supreme Court granted certiorari to
review the reversal and affirmed the decree of the appellate court.
The Supreme Court held that, upon the acquisition from Mexico of
the territory embracing California, "the United States acquired the
title to tidelands equally with the title to upland, but held the
former only in trust for the future States that might be erected"
out of the territory and subject to any prior grants or trusts imposed thereon by Mexico; that "if the land in question was tideland, the title passed to California at the time of her admission to
the Union"; and that in a suit to quiet title brought by a party
claiming tideland under a grant from a State, against a party claiming title under a patent from the United States purporting to convey
land bordering on the ocean, the question whether a part of the
tideland was erroneously included by the survey and patent is a
federal question. The Court, speaking through Chief Justice
Hughes, stated:

> The tideland extends to the high water mark. *Hardin* v.   **Extent of**
> *Jordan, supra; Shively* v. *Bowlby, supra; McGilvra* v. *Ross,* **tideland**
> 215 U.S. 70, 79. This does not mean, as petitioners contend, a
> physical mark made upon the ground by the waters; it means
> the line of high water as determined by the course of the tides.

After referring particularly to the case of *Attorney-General* v.
Chambers (4 De G. M. & G. (1854) 206, 214, 217), the Court concluded:

> In California, the Acts of 1911 and 1917, upon which the City
> of Los Angeles bases its claim, grant the "tidelands and sub-
> merged lands" situated "below the line of mean high tide of the
> Pacific Ocean." Petitioners urge that "ordinary high water

mark" has been defined by the state court as referring to the line of the neap tides. . . .

In determining the limit of the federal grant, we perceive no justification for taking neap high tides, or the mean of those tides, as the boundary between upland and tideland, and for thus excluding from the shore the land which is actually covered by the tides most of the time. In order to include the land that is thus covered, it is necessary to take the mean high tide line which, as the Court of Appeals said, is neither the spring tide nor the neap tide, but a mean of all the high tides.

In view of the definition of the mean high tide, as given by the United States Coast and Geodetic Survey, that "Mean high water at any place is the average height of all the high waters at that place over a considerable period of time," and the further observation that "from theoretical considerations of an astronomical character" there should be "a periodic variation in the rise of water above sea level having a period of 18.6 years," . . . the Court of Appeals directed that in order to ascertain the mean high tide line with requisite certainty in fixing the boundary of valuable tidelands, such as those here in question appear to be, "an average of 18.6 years should be determined as near as possible." We find no error in that instruction.

City of Los Angeles v. Borax Consolidated Limited et al., 5 F. Supp. (S.D. Cal., 1933) 281; 74 F. (2d) 901 (C.C.A. 9th, 1935), Borax Consolidated Ltd. et al. v. Los Angeles, 296 U.S. (1935) 10, 16, 22, 25–27. A petition for re-hearing was subsequently denied by the Supreme Court, 296 U.S. (1935) 664.

An act of the State of Washington, dated Mar. 16, 1901 (Laws of Washington, 1901, ch. 105, p. 217), set apart certain tidelands along the Pacific coast as a public highway and prohibited their lease. In the case of State ex rel. Ernst v. Savidge, the Supreme Court of Washington recognized the validity of the act by refusing to issue a mandamus to compel the execution of a lease for the mining and extraction of petroleum and natural gas. 187 Pac. (1920) 1089, 110 Wash. 81.

In Boone v. Kingsbury the Supreme Court of California held that a State has absolute power to alienate tidal and submerged lands unfit for navigation, commerce, or fisheries. 273 Pac. (1928) 797, 814, 206 Calif. 148.

FISHERIES

§97

In the case of Louisiana v. Mississippi, Chief Justice Fuller said:

The maritime belt is that part of the sea which, in contradistinction to the open sea, is under the sway of the riparian States, which can exclusively reserve the fishery within their respective maritime belts for their own citizens, whether fish, or pearls, or amber, or other products of the sea. See Manchester v. Massachusetts, 139 U.S. 240; McCready v. Virginia, 94 U.S. 391.

In Manchester v. Massachusetts, the court said: "We think it must be regarded as established that, as between nations, the minimum limit of the territorial jurisdiction of a nation over tide waters is a marine league from its coast; that bays wholly within its territory not exceeding two marine leagues in width at the mouth are within this limit; and that included in this territorial jurisdiction is the right of control over fisheries, whether the fish be migratory, free swimming fish, or free moving fish, or fish attached to or embedded in the soil. The open sea within this limit is, of course, subject to the common right of navigation; and all governments, for the purpose of self protection in time of war or for the prevention of frauds on its revenue, exercise an authority beyond this limit."

Questions as to the breadth of the maritime belt or the extent of the sway of the riparian States require no special consideration here. The facts render such discussion unnecessary.

202 U.S. (1906) 1, 52.

As to "the exclusive right of the Dominion Parliament to make or authorize the making of regulations and restrictions respecting the fisheries of Canada", see The Ship "North", et al. and His Majesty the King, et al., 37 Can. Sup. Ct. (1906) 385, 393.

The dominion of the state or nation over the seas adjoining its shores is for the purpose of protecting its coast from the effects of hostilities between other nations which may be at war, the protection of its revenue, and the preservation of order by its police. Included in this territorial jurisdiction is the right of control over fisheries, whether the fish be migratory, free-swimming fish, or fish attached to or embedded in the soil. Massachusetts v. Manchester, 152 Mass. 230, 25 N.E. 113, 9 L.R.A. 236, 23 Am. St. Rep. 820; Manchester v. Massachusetts, supra; Dunham v. Lamphere, 3 Gray (Mass.) 268; Humboldt L. M. Ass'n v. Christopherson, supra; notes to State v. Shaw, 67 Ohio St. 157, 65 N.E. 875, 60 L.R.A. 481 et seq.; 16 Am. & Eng. Enc. of L. (2d Ed.) 1132; 33 Cyc. 830.

Ex Parte Marincovich, 192 Pac. (1920) 156, 158, 48 Calif. App. 474.

In the fall of 1906 a number of protests were received by the Department of State alleging that the Government of Mexico was seizing American fishing vessels both within and beyond the three-mile limit and that proceedings were being instituted for the confiscation of such vessels. The Department, on October 6, 1906, forwarded an opinion of its Solicitor, dated October 2, 1906, to the American Embassy at Mexico City, reading in part as follows:

The right of the Mexican authorities to subject merchant vessels within the territorial waters of Mexico to the operation of local ordinances is beyond question, and whether it be convenient or inconvenient, it must be submitted to. If, however, the vessel is merely entering territorial waters driven by stress of weather, it would seem that such vessel, unless destined to a Mexican port, should not ordinarily be examined. Still, the right exists and it is too late in the day to question it as applied to merchant vessels. Comity, however, would limit its exercise to cases in which inspection is reasonably necessary or advisable.

The case is different with vessels found beyond the three mile limit. International law limits the sovereignty of a country to three miles from lowwater mark, and although Mexican sovereignty follows Mexican vessels upon the high seas until they put into a foreign port, international law does not recognize Mexican sovereignty over a foreign vessel, or any right on the part of Mexico to assume the incidents of sovereignty upon a foreign vessel, beyond the three-mile limit.

.   .   .   .

The claim to exercise the right of visit and search beyond the three-mile limit is based upon paragraph 2, article 5, of a Mexican law issued December 18, 1902, which reads as follows:

"The inspection and jurisdiction of the Federal authority may extend into the sea for fiscal purposes up to a distance of twenty kilometers measured from the line marked by low tide on the coasts of the Republic."

Expressed in English terms, it appears that Mexico claims the right to extend its laws for fiscal purposes to a distance of 12½ statute miles . . . ["A little over 10 nautical miles"] from lowwater mark. In the light of the previous statement it is at once evident that this law can only bind Mexican subjects to submit to visit and search and such foreign vessels as consent to the exercise of the right. In the absence of such consent, resistance to the exercise of the alleged right is clearly justifiable.

While it is clearly settled that territorial jurisdiction does not extend beyond the three-mile limit, still there is a tendency to permit the regulated exercise of the right of inspection beyond this limit. A distinction is taken between the general application of municipal laws beyond the limit and the extension of the revenue or customs laws for the purpose of facilitating importation. For example an unrepealed statute of the United States permits officers of revenue cutters "to board all vessels which arrive within four leagues of the coast thereof, if bound for the United States, and search and examine the same, and every part thereof, and shall demand, receive, and certify the manifest required to be on board certain vessels, shall affix and put proper fastenings on the hatches and other communications with the hold of any vessel, and shall remain on board such vessels until they arrive at the port or place of their destination." (R.S. 2760).

It cannot be claimed that the jurisdiction of the United States rightfully extends beyond the three-mile limit, except to its citizens. It would seem, however, that where foreign vessels are bound to the United States, the visitation and examination of cargo as provided for in this article may be convenient. Convenience, therefore, to both parties—to the incoming vessel as well as to the customs officers,—would seem to dictate the act and justify the policy. Such seems to be the general view, for in the statement to the British Minister Mr. Secretary Fish was able to say: "It is believed, however, that in carrying into effect the authority conferred by the Act of Congress referred to, no vessel is boarded, if boarded at all, except such a one as, upon being hailed, may have answered that she was bound to a port of the

United States." (Moore's International Law Digest, Vol. I, p. 731.)

It is to be noted, however, that only those vessels are inspected which are bound or destined to the United States; that a foreign merchant vessel outside of the three-mile limit would not be inspected even although such vessel should proceed along the entire extent of the Atlantic coast.

To this extent, therefore, the United States has extended its revenue laws. It cannot object that Mexico should claim and exercise the same right under similar circumstances. It is, however, recognized by Mexico and the United States that revenue laws can solely be applied to the purpose for which they are passed and that they cannot be extended as a cover to other and different circumstances. . . .

It would appear, therefore, in the light of authority that local jurisdiction without the consent of the party to be affected does not extend beyond the three-mile limit; that this Government has, as previously stated, extended its jurisdiction four marine leagues solely for the purpose of examining foreign vessels bound to an American port; that this extension of local law is for the purpose of convenience; that it has always been consented to and that when convenience and consent should cease the law itself would be inoperative as regards foreign vessels. The attempt to use a customs or revenue law to confer jurisdiction for other purposes and for all purposes is not and cannot be justified.

It would appear, therefore, that the statute of Mexico extending its jurisdiction beyond the three-mile limit should not affect American vessels unless such vessels are bound for a Mexican port, and that inasmuch as the statute is general in its nature and subjects all foreign vessels to examination whether such vessels be bound for a Mexican port or merely be temporarily within the limits covered by the statute, this Government should refuse to recognize the effect of the statute so far as American interests are concerned.

Secretary Root to Ambassador Thompson, no. 125, Oct. 6, 1906, and Mr. Thompson to Mr. Root, no. 268, Oct. 22, 1906, MS. Department of State, files 779/25, 779/35.

On October 22, 1906 Ambassador Thompson replied that each of the captures of American fishing vessels which had taken place during the course of the year left little room to doubt that the vessels were within the three-mile limit for a deliberate purpose foreign to stress of weather; that the Embassy had no information from any source that any captures of American vessels had taken place beyond the three-mile limit; and that the cases of the vessels seized were being handled in a regular way before the Federal courts of the country.

Ambassador Thompson to Secretary Root, Oct. 22, 1906, *ibid.* 779/36–37. The United States refrained from protesting against the seizures of the vessels, limiting its action to procuring the release of the vessels on bond during the course of the litigation. On May 3, 1909 the Department declined to submit a claim for damages on behalf of the owners of the *Silas Stearns,* one of the vessels seized. Secretary Knox to Senator Fletcher, *ibid.* 779/103.

In the case of the *Argonaut and Jonas H. French* (United States *v.* Great Britain), the Government of the United States claimed damages before the tribunal established under the terms of the special agreement of August 18, 1910, on account of the seizure on July 24, 1887 and subsequent confiscation by Canadian authorities of boats and seines belonging to the American vessels *Argonaut* and *Jonas H. French,* which had drifted within Canadian waters off Prince Edward Island, "less than three miles from the shore". In disallowing the claim the tribunal stated:

> It is a universally recognized principle of international law that a State has jurisdiction over sea-fishing within its territorial waters, and to apply thereto its municipal law, and to impose in respect thereof such prohibitions as it may think fit.
>
> .   .   .   .

Unintentional but avoidable entrance

> It must be observed that though the intention was to fish quite near the three-mile limit and though with the exercise of a very small amount of prudence it could have been foreseen that there would be a strong tide setting shore-wards, there was on board the boat no anchor or any other means of preventing it drifting within the prohibited zone.
> Nielsen's Report (1926) 509, 512, 513.

> The state of Florida may exercise its powers of sovereignty over the waters of the Gulf of Mexico within the boundary lines of the state of Florida and may regulate industries [in this case sponge fishing] having as their basis the products of such waters, or the bottoms thereof, . . .
>
> *Lipscomb, Sheriff* v. *Gialourakis,* 133 So. 104, 107 (Fla., 1931), 101 Fla. 1130.
>
> As of interest in connection with this section, see Bingham, *Report on the International Law of Pacific Coastal Fisheries* (1938). See also *post,* "Fisheries", pp. 783 *et seq.*

NATIONAL DEFENSE

§98

Italy

Paragraph 14 of the rules of maritime warfare promulgated by the Italian Ministry of the Navy in 1908, provided that the territorial waters "for the purposes of the law of war ['for rights of fishery and customs territorial waters have a greater extent'] have the extent to cannon range from shore" and that this extent "by customary law must be held to be fixed at three marine miles".

An Italian Royal decree of August 20, 1909 provided that, whenever a maritime stronghold must be placed upon a war basis, the commandant thereof can ask vessels at anchor to put to sea and such vessels are bound to go beyond "cannon range".

The Italian law of June 16, 1912 stated in article 1 that, "when it is recognized as necessary in the interest of national defense", the transit and sojourn of national or foreign merchant vessels may be prohibited "within or without the seas of the State" and that for the purposes of this law the seas of the state include the sea "within ten marine miles of the shore".

Norme di diritto internazionale marittimo in tempo di guerra (1908) 7, translation; 6 *Raccolta delle leggi e decreti del regno d'Italia* (1909) 5226, 5227; *Gazzetta ufficiale*, June 27, 1912, no. 151, p. 3788, translation.

France

A French decree of October 18, 1912 specified that French territorial waters extend out to a limit of six marine miles (11,111 meters) into the offing from the shore-line at low tide, for the purpose of the application of the rules of neutrality contained in the Thirteenth Hague Convention of October 18, 1907. The French instructions to naval commanders, dated December 19, 1912, stated (art. V) that the states that "have fixed an extent of their territorial waters in excess of three miles as regards the law of war" were Russia (cannon-range), Sweden (four miles, and the cannon-range from a fortress), Norway (four miles), Denmark (four miles), France (six miles), Spain (six miles), Portugal (six miles), and Italy (the cannon-range) and that "You will respect any limit of this nature which is found to be regularly fixed in this way before the opening of hostilities."

On May 26, 1913 the President of the French Republic issued a decree extending the limit of three miles, which was the width of the forbidden zone for the protection of the French coasts in time of war under a decree of July 19, 1909, to six miles "from the coast in the offing where the bases of fleet operations are located", except with respect to certain specified areas where the zone was indicated.

Journal officiel de la République française, Oct. 20 and 21, 1912, pp. 8976, 8996, *erratum;* XX *Revue général de droit international public, Documents* (1913) 6, 7; 1913 U.S. Naval War College, *International Law Topics and Discussions* 23, translation; *Journal officiel*, June 14, 1913, p. 5097; *ibid.* June 18, 1913, p. 5234, *erratum;* XX *Revue générale de droit international public, Documents* (1913) 56, 57.

On Sept. 29, 1915, in the case of the *Heina*, the French Prize Council (in accordance with the instructions of 1912) upheld the validity of the capture of a Norwegian vessel by the French cruiser *Condé* on Sept. 13, 1914, at a point four and five-sixths miles off the then-Danish Island of Savana, one of the Virgin Islands group, Denmark having adopted four miles as the breadth of territorial waters "as regards captures", although the Prize Council apparently would have respected the Danish rule had the capture been made within four miles of the coast. Fauchille, *Jurisprudence française en matière de prises maritimes* (1916) 119.

Netherlands

Article 17 of the Netherlands declaration of neutrality of August 5, 1914 specified three nautical miles from low-water mark as the width of the coastal waters.

II The Times (London), *Documentary History of the War* (1917), pt. 2, p. 52.

Uruguay

Article 2 of the neutrality rules, proclaimed by the Government of Uruguay on August 7, 1914, specified five miles as the width of the territorial waters.

1914 *Registro nacional* (1915) 393.

Germany

The German naval prize regulations of September 30, 1909 (as in force July 1, 1915), read in part as follows:

3. The right of capture is not to be exercised—

(a) Within neutral territorial waters, i.e., within the sea area 3 nautical miles in breadth from the coastline at low water, extending along the coast and the islands and bays belonging thereto.

107 Br. & For. St. Paps. 832, 833; Huberich and King, *Prize Code of the German Empire* (1915) 3.

On May 18, 1915 the Imperial Supreme Prize Court in Berlin, in denying the legality of the seizure of the Swedish steamship *Elida*, on October 13, 1914, by a German torpedo boat near Trelleborg off the coast of Sweden, took occasion to point out that the seizure took place outside of the three-mile limit but allegedly within four miles of the Swedish coast, the zone of territorial waters claimed by Sweden, a claim which the court stated had up to that time been recognized only by Norway, and that—

in reality the permissibility of an extension of the territorial waters is founded not so much upon the independent regulation by the single state, as upon the supposition of a tacit acknowledgement of such an extension by the other states. A mere failure to object, however, is not identical with a positive concurrence of the nations. Furthermore it must be remembered that even if the exercise by a maritime nation of certain official functions, such as those of the health and customs authorities, is tolerated beyond the three mile zone, this by no means represents a concession to the effect that in all other respects the waters in question are included within the territorial jurisdiction.

The Elida, 10 A.J.I.L (1916) 916, 918, translation.

See also article I of the declaration of neutrality of Belgium, Sept. 3, 1939 (no act of hostility permitted within three marine miles from low-water mark), XLI *Bulletin de l'Institut Juridique International* (1939) 301; article 1(2) of the proclamation of neutrality of the Netherlands, Sept. 3, 1939 (territorial sea is three marine miles wide), *ibid.* 349–350;

articles 1–4 of the decree of Sept. 15, 1939 of the President of Venezuela (for purposes of neutrality a three-mile territorial water zone understood, with an additional contiguous zone of nine nautical miles for "necessary safety, customs and sanitary police measures"), XLII *idem* 188–189.

SMUGGLING

§99

The Canadian Customs Act of 1906 (sec. 154) prohibits hovering of vessels in British waters "within one league of the coasts or shores of Canada".

Rev. Stat. of Canada, 1906, vol. I, ch. 48.

The Egyptian customs regulation of February 16, 1909 contains provision for a zone of customs supervision extending to a distance of 10 kilometers from the coastline. Laws

100 Br. & For. St. Paps. 884, 885.

For the purpose of "preventing contraband", a customs zone of 12 nautical miles in breadth has been established by Estonia by a decree of 1918.

League of Nations pub. C.74.M.39.1929.V, p. 26.

By paragraph 1 of the law of July 14, 1922, Norway established a special zone for customs inspection having a breadth of 10 nautical miles.

Ibid. 30.

On March 22, 1922 the Norwegian Supreme Court rendered an opinion in the *Penal Case Against Jens Hansen Lund* involving the question whether law 6 of September 30, 1921 was applicable to aliens. Section 1 of that law provides:

> The provisions of customs legislation concerning customs service inspection on vessels in Norwegian waters, and discharge or loading of goods from or for foreign countries and shipment of goods within the kingdom, are applicable within a seaward limit of $3\frac{1}{3}$ leagues beyond the outermost islands and islets, which are regularly overflowed by the sea.

It appeared that the defendant had sold brandy to various persons from the vessel *Kattegat* at a place about three and a half miles from shore. He contended that according to section 12 of the Norwegian penal law, an act such as the one committed by him was not an offense against Norwegian law when committed outside of the three-mile limit. The Supreme Court held that the provisions of the law of 1921 were properly applicable and that they were applicable to aliens as well as Norwegians.

> *Norsk restidende* (1922) 499, 500.

A Danish law of May 31, 1922 (no. 208) authorizes customs surveillance against smuggling of liquor and other heavily taxed articles within a zone of 16 marine miles.

> III Gidel, *Le droit international public de la mer* (1934) 442, n.

The French Customs Code of December 28, 1926 provides (arts. 477 and 478) for customs supervision within 20 kilometers of the coast.

> 26 *Lois, décrets d'intérèt général,* etc. (Sirey, 1926) 1064.

By a decree of May 30, 1927 (art. 60) Finland fixed the outer limit of her customs zone at six nautical miles.

> League of Nations pub. C.74.M.39.1929.V, p. 27.
> For a case construing the German Importation Control Order of 1920, wherein it was found that in the application of that order the coastal waters were not to be counted as territory of the Reich, see the decision of the German Criminal Court of Appeals of July 11, 1921. 56 *Entscheidungen des Reichsgerichts in Strafsachen* (1921) 135.

United States

An Anti-Smuggling Act, to provide for the more effective enforcement of the revenue laws of the United States to prevent smuggling, and for other purposes, was approved by the President on August 5, 1935. Section 1 authorizes the establishment of customs-enforcement areas. It provides:

Customs-enforcement areas

Geographical limitations

> (a) Whenever the President finds and declares that at any place or within any area on the high seas adjacent to but outside customs waters any vessel or vessels hover or are being kept off the coast of the United States and that, by virtue of the presence of any such vessel or vessels at such place or within such area, the unlawful introduction or removal into or from the United States of any merchandise or person is being or may be occasioned, promoted, or threatened, the place or area so found and declared shall constitute a customs-enforcement area for the purposes of this Act. . . . No customs-enforcement area shall include any waters more than one hundred nautical miles from the place or immediate area where the President declares such vessel or vessels are hovering or are being kept and, notwithstanding the foregoing provision, shall not include any waters more than fifty nautical miles outwards from the outer limit of customs waters.

The term "customs waters", just quoted, is defined by sections 201 and 401 of the act to include, in the case of a foreign vessel subject to a treaty between the United States and a foreign government, the waters specified by the treaty and, in the case of "every other vessel, the waters within four leagues of the coast of the United States". A customs-enforcement area shall cease to exist when the President shall "declare" that the circumstances which gave rise to its establishment have ceased to exist. Once such an area is declared any vessel in the area is subject to the law applicable in that area. The act defines the powers of customs officers and provides as to treaty obligations that—

> nothing contained in this section or in any other provision of law respecting the revenue shall be construed to authorize or to require any officer of the United States to enforce any law thereof upon the high seas upon a foreign vessel in contravention of any treaty with a foreign government enabling or permitting the authorities of the United States to board, examine, search, seize, or otherwise to enforce upon such vessel upon the high seas the laws of the United States except as such authorities are or may otherwise be enabled or permitted under special arrangement with such foreign government: . . .

Treaty vessels

Section 2 of the act provides penalties against the owner of a United States vessel violating foreign smuggling laws if, under the laws of the foreign country, a penalty is imposed for violations of the customs revenue laws of the United States. Under section 3(a) seizure and forfeiture of a vessel employed to defraud the revenue laws of the United States or to smuggle merchandise into the United States may take place whenever such vessel is found at any place at which it may be examined by a customs officer.

Seizure and forfeiture of vessel

Section 201 of title II amends section 401 of the Tariff Act of 1930. It defines a hovering vessel as follows:

> (n) . . . any vessel which is found or kept off the coast of the United States within or without the customs waters, if, from the history, conduct, character, or location of the vessel, it is reasonable to believe that such vessel is being used or may be used to introduce or promote or facilitate the introduction or attempted introduction of merchandise into the United States in violation of the laws respecting the revenue.

"Hovering vessel"

Section 203 (a) of title II (amending section 581 of the Tariff Act of 1930) makes the following provision with respect to the right of hot pursuit:

> (d) Any vessel or vehicle which, at any authorized place, is required to come to a stop by any officer of the customs, or is required to come to a stop by signal made by any vessel employed in the service of the customs displaying the ensign and pennant prescribed for such vessel by the President, shall come to a stop, and upon failure to comply, a vessel so required to come to a stop shall become subject to pursuit and the master thereof shall be liable to a fine of not more than $5,000 nor less than $1,000. It

shall be the duty of the several officers of the customs to pursue any vessel which may become subject to pursuit, and to board and examine the same, and to examine any person or merchandise on board, without as well as within their respective districts and at any place upon the high seas or, if permitted by the appropriate foreign authority, elsewhere where the vessel may be pursued as well as at any other authorized place.

Under section 205 (amending section 586 of the Tariff Act of 1930) unlawful unlading or transhipment upon the high seas adjacent to customs waters is prohibited. Section 206 of the act (amending section 587 of the Tariff Act of 1930) contains provision for the examination of hovering vessels and for the imposition of certain penalties.

49 Stat. 517. Hearings before the House Committee on Ways and Means on H.R. 5496, Anti-Smuggling Act, Mar. 8, 13 and May 1, 2, 1935, 74th Cong., 1st sess. For the Tariff Act of 1930, see 46 Stat. 590.

The Norwegian steamship *Reidun*, carrying a large quantity of alcohol with clearance for Canadian ports, when more than 500 and less than 600 miles from the nearest point of the United States, or any of its customs-enforcement areas or customs waters, transhipped liquor on several speed boats, one of which brought 765 cases into the harbor of Charleston, South Carolina. The District Court of the United States for the Eastern District of New York held that the vessel could not be seized by the United States at the port of New York for alleged violation of the provisions of the Anti-Smuggling Act of 1935, title II, section 205 (49 Stat. 517, 524), which prohibit unlading merchandise "upon the high seas adjacent to the customs waters" for the purpose of violating the law. The court stated that "It is, of course, now well settled that the customs waters of the United States include a strip of coastal waters extending outward 12 miles from low-water marks" and held that the phrase "upon the high seas adjacent to the customs waters" must mean, as to nations with which the United States has no applicable treaties, "the waters adjacent to 4 leagues of the coast" and as to "treaty nations", a distance "equivalent to one hour's steaming distance" from the coast. The court pointed out that the limitation upon the power delegated to the President in the establishment of a customs-enforcement area under the act "is that such area shall not include any waters more than 50 nautical miles outwards from the outer limit of customs waters" and expressed the opinion that "It is thus unreasonable to believe that Congress intended that the term 'adjacent' . . . meant more than 50 miles from the outer customs limit." The court held that so far as treaty nations are concerned the Anti-Smuggling Act "was not intended to extend the jurisdictional rights of the United States" beyond those agreed to with such treaty

nations. Exceptions to the libel were sustained on the ground that
the vessel at the place of transhipment was not in waters "adjacent
to customs waters of the United States" nor within the limit defined
in the treaty between the United States and Norway of May 24,
1924 (43 Stat. 1772, 1773).

The libel was then amended so as to present an additional cause
of forfeiture based on section 3 of the Anti-Smuggling Act (49 Stat.
517, 518). It was alleged by the Government that the steamship,
while at Antwerp, "was fitted out in part for the purpose of being
employed to defraud the revenue of the United States, by the unlading and transshipment of said Belgian alcohol on the high seas".
The court overruled the exceptions to the additional cause of forfeiture, holding that if the vessel was fitted out as alleged and "did
cause merchandise to be smuggled into the United States . . . it
ran the hazard of punishment by coming within the customs enforcement areas". Galston, district judge, speaking for the court, stated:

> There is no invasion here of treaty rights. There is no search   Enforcement
> and seizure on the high seas beyond customs enforcement areas   of liquor
> nor beyond one hour's sailing distance from the coast . . .   laws
> Congress may very well have intended to mete out punishment
> to those who conspire outside of the territorial jurisdiction to
> violate laws of the nation by subjecting them to apprehension
> or punishment when found within the jurisdiction.

14 F. Supp. 771, 774 (E.D.N.Y., 1936) ; 15 F. Supp. 112, 113 (E.D.N.Y.,
1936).

The eighteenth amendment to the Constitution of the United   18th amend-
States provided in section 1 that one year after its ratification—   ment

> the manufacture, sale, or transportation of intoxicating liquors
> within, the importation thereof into, or the exportation thereof
> from the United States and all territory subject to the jurisdic-
> tion thereof for beverage purposes is hereby prohibited.

Section 2 provided:

> The Congress and the several States shall have concurrent
> power to enforce this article by appropriate legislation.

The amendment was declared, in a proclamation by the Acting
Secretary of State, dated January 29, 1919, to have been ratified by
three fourths of the States. In accordance with its provisions, it took
effect on January 16, 1920. It was repealed by the twenty-first
amendment to the Constitution, which took effect on December 5,
1933 and which provides, *inter alia:*

> The transportation or importation into any State, Territory,
> or possession of the United States for delivery or use therein

of intoxicating liquors, in violation of the laws thereof, is hereby prohibited.

40 Stat. 1941; 48 Stat. 1720. *Regal Drug Corporation* v. *Wardell*, 273 Fed. 182 (C.C.A. 9th, 1921); *Dillon* v. *Gloss*, etc., 256 U.S. 368 (1921); *Druggan* v. *Anderson, U.S. Marshal, et al.*, 269 U.S. 36 (1925).

The Volstead act

The National Prohibition Act—also popularly known as the Volstead act—approved on October 28, 1919, provided (sec. 3):

No person shall on or after the date when the eighteenth amendment to the Constitution of the United States goes into effect, manufacture, sell, barter, transport, import, export, deliver, furnish or possess any intoxicating liquor except as authorized in this Act . . .

The provisions just quoted and all laws amendatory of or supplementary to them were repealed by the Liquor Law Repeal and Enforcement Act approved by the President on August 27, 1935.

41 Stat. 305, 308; 49 Stat. 872; *United States* v. *Chambers et al.*, 291 U.S. 217 (1934).

Application

6. The first section of the [18th] Amendment—the one embodying the prohibition—is operative throughout the entire territorial limits of the United States, binds all legislative bodies, courts, public officers and individuals within those limits, and of its own force invalidates every legislative act—whether by Congress, by a state legislature, or by a territorial assembly—which authorizes or sanctions what the section prohibits.

Mr. Justice Van Devanter in the *National Prohibition Cases*, 253 U.S. (1920) 350, 386.

In 1920 the Department of State received a complaint from the Italian Embassy concerning the action of the collector of customs at New York in keeping under seal liquors on board foreign vessels in the port of New York, thereby preventing distribution of daily rations to which members of Italian crews were entitled under contract and causing strikes. A similar complaint was received from the French Embassy. The former Embassy requested that, if possible, the instructions of the Treasury Department be at least temporarily suspended. On January 17, 1920 the Department of State addressed the following letter to the Secretary of the Treasury:

In view of the practice (See Moore's International Law Digest, Vol. II, p. 286, et seq.), observed by states generally, not to interfere, through their authorities, in the internal administration, order or discipline of foreign vessels in their ports, unless it becomes necessary to do so in a case involving, or threatening to involve, a breach of the peace of the port or the commission of a crime, the Department trusts that, if consistent with existing laws applicable to the matter, it will be possible to comply with the Italian Embassy's request. . . .

. . . It is requested that any regulations adopted, or any steps taken in the matter, be made applicable to all foreign vessels in United States ports.

The Treasury Department replied on January 27, 1920 that, as a result of an amendment of Treasury Decision 38218, pursuant to an opinion rendered by the Attorney General—

liquors on foreign vessels will be placed under seal while the vessels are in port and such portions thereof released from seal from time to time as may be required for use by the officers and crews . . .

and that appropriate instructions had been issued to collectors of customs at the various ports.

The Second Assistant Secretary of State (Adee) to the Secretary of the Treasury (Mellon), Jan. 17, 1920, MS. Department of State, file 811.114/204; the Assistant Secretary of the Treasury (Shouse) to the Secretary of State (Lansing), Jan. 27, 1920, *ibid.* 811.114/212.

On Jan. 23, 1920 Attorney General Palmer advised the Secretary of the Treasury that—

". . . the bringing of such liquors on shore, even by the members of the crew to whom they are issued, will be unlawful and subject the offender to prosecution; but so long as the liquors on board are properly listed as sea stores, and are not excessive in quantity, I do not think their daily distribution on board the ship can properly be interfered with by this Government." 32 Op. Att. Gen. (1919–21) 96, 97–98.

On October 6, 1922 the Attorney General of the United States informed the Secretary of the Treasury:

It is a long-established principle of municipal and international law that a nation has the right to make and enforce laws covering its territorial waters as well as its land.

.   .   .   .   .   .

If then the bringing in of liquors by foreign vessels as ship stores or otherwise constitutes a transportation or possession contrary to the Eighteenth Amendment and the National Prohibition Act, it is clearly a violation of the law that no executive or administrative officer of the Government has the power to permit.

.   .   .   .   .   .

Are we then to argue that such inflexible provisions of law, declared by our Supreme Court as the constitutional policy of our country, shall apply to our own citizens, but be abandoned when we deal with ships of a foreign nation? To do so would be a grievous surrender of our sovereignty.

.   .   .   .   .   .

I am, therefore, of the opinion that the Eighteenth Amendment and the National Prohibition Act prohibit as unlawful the possession and transportation of beverage liquors on board foreign vessels while in our territorial waters, whether such liquors are sealed or open.

Following this ruling of the Attorney General, the President of the United States requested the Secretary of the Treasury on October 6, 1922 to formulate regulations for the enforcement of the law, and on October 7, 1922 he informed the Secretary of the Treasury that—

> pending the formulation of regulations, the enforcement of the prohibition of transportation of cargoes or ship stores will not be practicable in the case of foreign vessels leaving their home ports or American vessels leaving foreign ports on or before October 14, 1922. Any earlier attempt at enforcement, in the absence of due notice and ample regulations, would be inconsistent with just dealing and have a tendency to disrupt needlessly the ways of commerce.

At the request of the Secretary of the Treasury the Department of State sent, on October 14, 1922, a circular telegram to American diplomatic and consular officers instructing them to notify shipowners within their respective districts as follows:

> The provisions of the National Prohibition Act are applicable to United States vessels leaving foreign ports after October twenty-first, and to foreign vessels leaving foreign ports after that date on coming within the territorial waters of the United States. All sales of beverage liquors on United States vessels anywhere, and on foreign vessels within the territorial waters of the United States, are unlawful after October seventh. This notice does not apply to foreign vessels passing through the Panama Canal and not touching any other port under the jurisdiction of the United States.

Protests
On October 17, 1922 the Mexican Embassy protested the shortness of notice. The Spanish Ambassador sent a note on October 20, 1922 reading in part:

> . . . Your Excellency is aware that in the majority of European countries wine is considered as forming part of food and if the Spanish sailors are denied it at their meals they will not ship.
> I merely make this remark for Your Excellency's information and that of the proper Department, but not in any way implying the assent of His Majesty's Government to the new law, and much less to the principle which inspired it.
> [Translation.]

The British Embassy transmitted the following memorandum on October 23, 1922:

> The British Merchant Marine Act and the regulations issued thereunder provide that all British ships must carry on board, as part of their medical stores, specified quantities of wines and spirits.
> It will, of course, be understood that British ships must continue to comply with British law in the same way as United States ships must comply with the law of this country.

In reply the Department of State transmitted to the British Embassy a statement, dated October 25, 1922, given to the press by the Treasury Department, and invited its attention to the fact that until the new regulations were available, enforcement of the law would continue as theretofore and that sea stores on foreign ships entering American territorial waters "can, when such stores are required for the use of the officers and crew of the vessel, be opened only from time to time for withdrawal for such purpose, but must be immediately resealed". Similar replies were made to the communications from the Mexican and Spanish Embassies.

> 33 Op. Att. Gen. (1921–23) 335, 346, 348, 349, 351. The Secretary of the Treasury (Mellon) to the Secretary of State (Hughes), Oct. 7, 1922, MS. Department of State, file 811.114/1015; the Acting Secretary of State (Harrison) to the diplomatic and consular officers, Oct. 14, 1922, *ibid.* 811.114/1032; the Secretary of the Mexican Embassy (Téllez) to the Chief of the Division of Mexican Affairs (Hanna), Oct. 17, 1922, and Mr. Hanna to Señor Téllez, Nov. 24, 1922, *ibid.* 811.114/1053, /1089; Ambassador Riaño to Mr. Hughes, Oct. 20, 1922, and Mr. Hughes to Señor Riaño, Oct. 28, 1922, *ibid.* 811.114/1063, /1069; memorandum of the British Embassy, Oct. 23, 1922, *ibid.* 811.114/1060; the Acting Secretary of State (Phillips) to Ambassador Geddes, Nov. 2, 1922, *ibid.* 811.114/1078.

A circular telegram sent to American diplomatic representatives by the Department of State under date of October 28, 1922 requested them to inform the respective Foreign Offices that, under regulations of the Treasury Department—

> both cargo and sea-stores liquors may be brought into American territorial waters, cargo liquors to be sealed and remain sealed while therein, sea-stores to be sealed on entering and remain sealed, except when opened for the withdrawal therefrom of liquors for the use of the officers and crew only, all sales and service whatever to passengers being prohibited.

> Secretary Hughes to diplomatic representatives, Oct. 28, 1922, *ibid.* 811.114/1074.

Transit through U.S.

In reply to a request by the American Consul at Guaymas, Mexico, for instructions as to whether liquors in transit from Mexico through the United States to Mexico were subject to the Volstead act (41 Stat. 305), the Department of State refered to an opinion by the Acting Attorney General, reading in part as follows:

> The National Prohibition Act applies to all the territory of the United States that is not otherwise excepted from its operation, and extends to all waters within its territorial limits, including a marine league from the shore; within those waters the manufacture, sale, transportation, possession, etc., is prohibited.
> My conclusion therefore is that the provisions of section 3005, Revised Statutes, do not apply to intoxicating liquors for bever-

age purposes, and that the National Prohibition Act prohibits "in transit" shipments of such liquors touching at the ports of or moving through the United States, though same originate in and are destined to foreign countries.

Consul Yost to Secretary Colby, Feb. 17, 1921; Mr. Colby to Mr. Yost, Feb. 19, 1921; and Attorney General Daugherty to the Secretary of the Treasury (Mellon), June 30, 1921: MS. Department of State, file 811.114/424. 32 Op. Att. Gen. (1919–21) 419, 421.

Repeal of prior law

In the cases of *Grogan* v. *Walker and Sons* and *Anchor Line, Ltd.* v. *Aldridge,* decided together by the Supreme Court of the United States, the Court held that the eighteenth amendment to the Constitution of the United States and the Volstead act (41 Stat. 305) prohibited the transportation of whiskey from a foreign port through a port of the United States to another foreign port and transhipment of intoxicating liquors from one foreign vessel to another in a port of the United States. It held that both acts were forbidden by the eighteenth amendment and the Volstead act, which, in this respect, superseded the provisions of section 3005 of the Revised Statutes of the United States, as amended, and article XXIX of the treaty between the United States and Great Britain of May 8, 1871 (17 Stat. 863)—each relating to the transportation in bond, without the payment of duty, of goods destined to British provinces. It was added that the Volstead act did not provide "for transshipment or carriage across the country from without" and that "When Congress was ready to permit such a transit for special reasons, in the Canal Zone, it permitted it in express words. Title III, §20, 41 Stat. 322."

259 U.S. (1922) 80, 89.

On August 16, 1922 Secretary Hughes made the following observations in a letter to Senator Sterling:

Proposed jurisdiction

I beg to acknowledge the receipt of your letter of July 28, 1922, in which you call attention to a bill (H.R. 7456), to be proposed as an amendment to the Tariff Act, relating to the extension of statutory provisions with regard to intoxicating liquors to a distance of six marine leagues from the coast.

.   .   .   .

. . . I am constrained to say, however, that I consider that any attempt on the part of this Government to extend its domestic legislation to the high seas, as that term is understood in international law, in the manner contemplated by the bill under consideration would be in contravention of an established rule of international law and practice.

Foreign vessels outside of the 3-mile limit

Although a nation may give effect to its laws with regard to its own vessels wherever they may be navigated, in my opinion the long observed rule with regard to the three mile limit of territorial waters stands in the way of the application of domestic legislation over vessels of other nations beyond that limit. Irrespective of what the origin of that rule may be, I consider the rule so well established that the United States cannot properly depart from it, until a general agreement respecting its alteration shall have been reached among the nations of the world in the manner indicated in the extract which you quote from the work on international law by the noted publicist Dr. Oppenheim. Of course, an exception might be made by agreement with a particular nation as to its vessels. I beg to point out to you in particular that this Government has consistently adhered to the three mile rule. Without entering into any detailed discussion of statements of authorities that might seem to some extent at variance with this general rule, I may invite attention to diplomatic discussions, decisions of international arbitral tribunals, and statements of writers on international law, from which I think it clearly appears that the rule with respect to the three mile limit is generally observed by nations as a rule of international law, and that this Government could not legally nor in a manner consistent with its attitude in the past disregard that rule.

.   .   .   .

In a decision rendered under date of December 2, 1921, by the arbitral tribunal established under the special arbitration agreement concluded August 18, 1910, between the United States and Great Britain, damages were awarded in favor of the British Government because of the action of an officer of the United States Revenue Cutter Service in boarding in 1909 British schooners engaged in hunting sea otters in the North Pacific Ocean. The tribunal in its opinion said:

"It is a fundamental principle of international maritime law that, except by special convention or in time of war, interference by a cruiser with a foreign vessel pursuing a lawful avocation on the high seas is unwarranted and illegal, and constitutes a violation of the sovereignty of the country whose flag the vessel flies.

"It is not contested that at the date and place of interference by the United States naval authorities there was no agreement authorizing those authorities to interfere as they did with the British schooners, and, therefore, a legal liability on the United States Government was created by the acts of its officers now complained of."

After quoting from Wheaton's *Elements of International Law* (8th ed., by Dana, 1866), page 258, Secretary Hughes continued:

It has been suggested that the seizure of vessels on the high **Self-preser-** seas for the purpose of preventing smuggling might be justified **vation** under the so-called right of self-preservation. This right on the part of a nation, says Mr. Hershey, in his work on international law includes "the right to preserve the integrity and inviolability of its territory with the corresponding duty of respecting that of other states". (p. 144). In order to maintain that right a nation may, say the authorities, in extreme cases commit what would ordinarily be an infraction of the law of nations and violate the territorial sovereignty or the international right of another state. (Westlake I, 299; Taylor, 405; Hall 5th ed., 269; Moore II, 402). Operations of this kind are described by Halleck as "imperfect war". (I, p. 113). From an examination of the instances in which this principle of self-preservation has been invoked, it would appear that they are limited to efforts to thwart acts of a military character. A serious question is involved in any attempt to extend the application of this so-called right of self-preservation, which has given rise to much controversy in the past, to interference with foreign vessels on the high seas with a view to the prevention of smuggling.

Hovering-acts

You refer to the statutory provisions enacted in 1799 which have been called "hovering-laws". Similar laws were enacted by Great Britain in 1736 [*1739*], but it appears they have long since been repealed. I shall not discuss the application of the provisions of these laws further than to say that municipal legislation undoubtedly supplies the rule for municipal officers, but the rule of international law will remain the criterion of international obligation by reference to which our duties toward other nations are determined except as they may be modified by special agreements.

Secretary Hughes to Senator Sterling, Aug. 16, 1922, MS. Department of State, file 811.114/900.

Negotiations with Great Britain

Meanwhile, in a note to the British Embassy in Washington, dated June 26, 1922, the Department of State, after pointing out particularly that it had been found that many of the ships engaged in the illegal smuggling of liquor into the United States were registered under the British flag and that a large quantity of liquor was being carried by such vessels from the Bahama Islands and from Bermuda to points off the coast of the United States for the purpose of being smuggled into the United States, and suggesting cooperation between the British and United States authorities with the object of restricting such smuggling, stated, *inter alia*, that the Government of the United States was prompted to inquire whether the British Government "would be disposed to enter into a treaty for the purpose of checking the illegal practices in question". It was suggested that such a treaty "might contain reciprocal provisions authorizing the authorities of each Government to exercise a right of search of vessels of the other beyond the three-mile limit of territorial waters to the extent of twelve miles from the shore".

The British Government replied on October 13, 1922 that "His Majesty's Government have consistently opposed any extension of the limit of territorial waters such as that now suggested" and that "they do not feel that they can properly acquiesce, in order to meet a temporary emergency, in the abandonment of a principle to which they attach great importance".

Subsequently, on November 30 of the same year, the British Ambassador, in a note to the Secretary of State, said that "No one . . . questions the right of any state to determine that alcoholic beverages shall not be consumed within the area of its territorial waters" and called attention to the difference between enforcing "sumptuary regulations" and declaring illegal "the passive existence, under seal within the holds or lockers of a foreign ship, of articles legally on board that ship according to the laws of its own state". He objected to forming a precedent in this latter respect.

Secretary Hughes to Ambassador Geddes, June 26, 1922, MS. Department of State, file 811.114 Gt. Brit./22 ; Mr. Geddes to Mr. Hughes, Oct. 13 and Nov. 30, 1922, *ibid.* files 811.114 Gt. Brit./39, 811.114/1142.

On December 30, 1922 the British Ambassador at Washington addressed a note to the Department of State, reading in part as follows:

In order to avoid the possibility of any misunderstanding, I am desired by my Government to make it clear that His Majesty's Government are unable to acquiesce in what they understand to be the ruling of the United States Government, namely, that foreign vessels may be seized outside the three-mile limit if it can be shown that they have established contact with the shore for illegal purposes by means of their own small boats. My Government must reserve their right to lodge a protest in any individual case in which action may be taken by the United States Government under this ruling.

The Department replied that the position of the United States was supported—

by the position taken by the British Government in the case of the British Columbian schooner *Araunah*, which was seized off Copper Island, by the Russian authorities in 1888, because it appeared that members of the crew of the schooner were illegally taking seals in Bering Sea by means of canoes operated between the schooner and the land, and it was affirmed that two of the canoes were within half a mile of the shore. Lord Salisbury stated that Her Majesty's Government were "of opinion that, even if the *Araunah* at the time of the seizure was herself outside the three-mile territorial limit, the fact that she was, by means of her boats, carrying on fishing within Russian waters without the prescribed license warranted her seizure and confiscation according to the provisions of the municipal law regulating the use of those waters". (Volume 82, British and Foreign State Papers, page 1058.)
I may add that it is not understood on what grounds the decision of His Majesty's Government in this matter was reached, in view of the position taken by Lord Salisbury in the *Araunah* case and the statement in your note No. 781 of October 13, 1922, that His Majesty's Government "are desirous of assisting the United States Government to the best of their ability in the suppression of the traffic and in the prevention of the abuse of the British flag by those engaged in it".

Ambassador Geddes to Secretary Hughes, Dec. 30, 1922, and Mr. Hughes to Mr. Geddes, Jan. 18, 1923, MS. Department of State, file 811.114/1182.

On June 2, 1923 the Treasury Department issued regulations in order to give effect to the decision in the case of *Cunard Steamship Company, Ltd., et al.* v. *Mellon, Secretary of the Treasury, et al.*, 262 U.S. (1923) 100, which involved several suits to enjoin the application of the National Prohibition Act. The regulations embraced such subjects as the extent of territorial waters, involuntary entrance of vessels, war vessels, diplomatic exemptions, cargo liquor, sea stores, and liquor for non-beverage purposes. T.D. 3484, *Internal Revenue Bulletin* (Washington, Jan.–June, 1923) 327; Second Assistant Secretary Adee to diplomatic and consular officers, June 4, 1923, MS. Department of State, file 811.114/1489.

On May 28, 1923 the Department of State instructed the Minister at Peiping that the National Prohibition Act, 41 Stat. 305, did not apply to undocumented American steamers operating on the upper Yangtze River under the American flag.

Minister Schurman to Secretary Hughes, Mar. 26, 1923, MS. Department of State, file 811.114/1323; Assistant Attorney General Willebrandt to Mr. Hughes, May 1, 1923, and Under Secretary Phillips to Mr. Schurman, May 28, 1923, *ibid.* 811.114/1408.

On July 14, 1923 the British Chargé d'Affaires ad interim stated, in a memorandum of that date, that His Majesty's Secretary of State for Foreign Affairs had pointed out that, while "the theory of the international validity of the three-mile limit would be strengthened by the conclusion of a treaty making an exception for a special purpose", "Practically however such a treaty would weaken the principle because it would form a precedent for the conclusion of further similar treaties until finally the principle would become a dead letter" and that for this latter reason Lord Curzon had felt bound to state, when questioned in Parliament, that His Majesty's Government could not accept the proposal of the Secretary of State of the United States.

Five days later Secretary Hughes replied by a *note verbale* that, by the draft treaty relative to visit and search of vessels within 12 miles of the coasts of the parties, respectively, for the purpose of preventing the illegal introduction of articles into their territories, and also relating to the carriage, within territorial waters, of certain sealed stores and cargo destined for foreign ports (which had been handed previously to the British Chargé d'Affaires on June 11, 1923), it was not intended "to propose an extension of the limits of territorial waters, and the draft proposal specifically negatived such an intention." It was further pointed out in the same communication that the proposed agreement would not interfere with legitimate commerce bound for American or foreign ports but would bear only upon "those vessels which come within twelve miles but hover off the three-mile limit for the purpose of aiding in the smuggling of intoxicating liquor, or other prohibited articles, into the territory of the United States". Finally, the British Government was invited to cooperate in molding the form of an arrangement that would be satisfactory.

The reply of the British Government, dated September 17, 1923, was to the effect that, in view of the fact that the amount of the illegal traffic in spirituous liquors sold just outside the three-mile limit appeared to have been "exaggerated", the British Government was reluctant "to weaken the authority of the general rule of international law, whereby three miles is regarded as the limit of territorial jurisdiction" and that His Majesty's Government could not agree to an extension of the three-mile limit, even for a limited purpose, until the matter had been submitted to the Imperial Conference, which would meet within a few weeks in London.

> The British Chargé d'Affaires to the Department of State, July 14, 1923, and Secretary Hughes to the British Chargé d'Affaires, July 19, 1923, MS. Department of State, file 711.419/16; the British Chargé d'Affaires (Chilton) to the Acting Secretary of State (Phillips), Sept. 17, 1923, *ibid.* 711.419/32.
>
> In discussing the subject of the American law with respect to the seizure of liquor on foreign ships, on June 28, 1923, in the House of Lords, the British Secretary of State for Foreign Affairs (Curzon) stated:
>
> "What is the legal position as interpreted by His Majesty's Government, acting upon the advice of their legal authorities? It is as follows. There are two recognised principles of International Law which prevent us from contending that the United States have committed any violation of International Law in forbidding foreign vessels to bring alcoholic liquor within their waters. The first is that foreigners and foreign ships trading with a country must comply with its laws. The second is that every sovereign independent State is supreme over all persons and property within its dominions, including ships within its territorial waters. . . .
>
> "The net result of this complex of considerations has, therefore, been that on many matters the practice has grown up that a State should not exact compliance with its own law even though a ship is within its waters, but should leave such matters to be regulated by the law of the flag State. This, however, is international practice rather than International Law and, accordingly a departure from it involves a breach, not of International Law, but of the comity of nations. The sanction for it, such as there is, is that if a State acted unreasonably towards the ships of other nations when they came within its jurisdiction, it would find that its own ships were unreasonably treated when they were within foreign jurisdiction."
>
> *Parliamentary Debates*, H.L., 5th ser., vol. 54, col. 724.
>
> In an instruction of Aug. 25, 1923 to the Chargé d'Affaires in London the Department of State stated that a precedent for concluding a special treaty arrangement with the British Government authorizing it to visit and search British vessels to a limit of 12 miles was to be found in the treaty of Dec. 27, 1774 concluded between France and Spain, whereby French and Spanish customs authorities were permitted (art. 8) to seize, up to

a distance of two leagues from the coasts, French and Spanish ships carrying forbidden goods.

Secretary Hughes to Chargé Wheeler, Aug. 25, 1923, MS. Department of State, file 711.419/31a.

Convention of 1924: U.S. and Gt. Br.

Following the exchange of the communications referred to above and others, the United States and Great Britain concluded a convention on January 23, 1924 for the prevention of the smuggling of intoxicating liquors, article I of which reads:

The High Contracting Parties declare that it is their firm intention to uphold the principle that 3 marine miles extending from the coast-line outwards and measured from low-water mark constitute the proper limits of territorial waters.

Treaty Series 685, 43 Stat. 1761.

Similar provisions are found in the following conventions between the United States and other countries: May 19, 1924, with Germany (Treaty Series 694, 43 Stat. 1815) ; June 6, 1924, with Panama (Treaty Series 707, 43 Stat. 1875) ; Aug. 21, 1924, with the Netherlands (Treaty Series 712, 44 Stat. 2013) ; Mar. 4, 1926, with Cuba (Treaty Series 738, 44 Stat. 2395) ; May 31, 1928, with Japan (Treaty Series 807, 46 Stat. 2446).

Article I of the convention of May 22, 1924 with Sweden (Treaty Series 698, 43 Stat. 1830) reads:

"The High Contracting Parties respectively retain their rights and claims, without prejudice by reason of this agreement, with respect to the extent of their territorial jurisdiction."

Similar provisions are found in the following conventions between the United States and other powers for the prevention of smuggling of intoxicating liquors: May 24, 1924, with Norway (Treaty Series 689, 43 Stat. 1772) ; May 29, 1924, with Denmark (Treaty Series 693, 43 Stat. 1809) ; June 3, 1924, with Italy (Treaty Series 702, 43 Stat. 1844) ; June 30, 1924, with France (Treaty Series 755, 45 Stat. 2403) ; Dec. 9, 1925, with Belgium (Treaty Series 759, 45 Stat. 2456) ; Feb. 10, 1926, with Spain (Treaty Series 749, 44 Stat. 2465) ; Apr. 25, 1928, with Greece (Treaty Series 772, 45 Stat. 2736) ; May 27, 1930, with Chile (Treaty Series 829, 46 Stat. 2852) ; and June 19, 1930, with Poland (Treaty Series 821, 46 Stat. 2773).

In addition to the provisions contained in article I, *supra*, the convention with Great Britain provides that the authorities of the United States may board private vessels under the British flag for the purpose of ascertaining whether the vessels, or those on board thereof, are endeavoring to import alcoholic beverages into the United States; that when there is shown a reasonable ground for suspicion a search of the vessel may be made; and that, if there is reasonable cause for belief that the vessel has committed or is attempting to commit an offense against the laws of the United States with respect to the importation of alcoholic beverages, the vessel may be seized and taken into port for adjudication. It provides that these rights shall not be exercised at a greater distance from the coast than can be "traversed in one hour by the vessel suspected of endeavoring to commit the offense" but that, in cases where the liquor is intended to be conveyed to the United States "by a vessel other than the one boarded and searched, it shall be the speed of such other vessel and not the speed of the vessel boarded, which shall determine the distance from the coast at which the right under this article can be exercised". (Art. II.)

In return for this concession by the British Government, it is provided that no penalty of forfeiture under the laws of the United States shall be applicable "to alcoholic liquors or to vessels or persons by reason of the carriage of such liquors, when such liquors are listed as sea stores or cargo destined for a port foreign to the United States, . . . on board British vessels voyaging to or from ports of the United States, . . . or passing through the territorial waters thereof, . . . provided that such liquors shall be kept under seal continuously while the vessel on which they are carried remains within said territorial waters and that no part of such liquors shall at any time or place be unladen within the United States, its territories or possessions". (Art. III.)

> 4 Treaties, etc. (Trenwith, 1938) 4225, 4226.
>
> Similar provisions are contained in the following conventions to which the United States is a party, all relating to smuggling: May 19, 1924, with Germany; May 22, 1924, with Sweden; May 24, 1924, with Norway; May 29, 1924, with Denmark; June 3, 1924, with Italy; June 6, 1924, with Panama; June 30, 1924, with France; Aug. 21, 1924, with the Netherlands; Dec. 9, 1925, with Belgium; Feb. 10, 1926, with Spain; Mar. 4, 1926, with Cuba; Apr. 25, 1928, with Greece; May 31, 1928, with Japan; May 27, 1930, with Chile; June 19, 1930, with Poland, all of which are cited *ante*.
>
> As of possible interest, see hearings before the House Committee on Foreign Affairs *in re* the treaty between Great Britain and the United States having for its purpose the abolition of smuggling of intoxicating liquors from Great Britain into the United States, Feb. 20 and Mar. 7, 1924, H. Res. 174, 68th Cong., 1st sess.
>
> On Aug. 19, 1925 Germany, Denmark, Estonia, Finland, Latvia, Lithuania, Norway, Poland and the Free City of Danzig, Sweden, and the Union of Soviet Socialist Republics signed a convention at Helsingfors (Helsinki) for the prevention of smuggling of intoxicating liquors. By article 9 thereof the contracting parties agreed not to object to the application of municipal law within a zone of 12 marine miles from the shore or from the external limits of archipelagoes. The same article provides that vessels met within that zone and escaping outside of it may be pursued and subjected to the same treatment as if they had been within the 12-mile limit. 42 League of Nations Treaty Series (1925-26) 75.

Section 2811 of the Revised Statutes of the United States provided:

Every master of any vessel laden with merchandise, and bound to any port of the United States, shall, on his arrival within four leagues of the coast thereof, . . . upon demand, produce the manifests in writing which such master is required to have

Seizure: not under treaty

on board his vessel, to such officer of the customs as first comes on board his vessel, for inspection . . .

On May 15, 1920 the *Reemplazo*, a Cuban schooner, was boarded by American customs officials while at anchor some six or seven miles from the United States coast, and demand for the manifest was made. After the officers discovered that the vessel was loaded with intoxicating liquors, little or no attention was paid to the question of the manifest. The day following the seizure of the vessel a clearance certificate from the authorities in Habana was produced showing that the schooner had cleared for a fishing trip. After the vessel had left the harbor the liquor was put on board and she sailed, intending to have the liquor transported in boats to Tarpon Springs, Florida, or in that vicinity. In order to accomplish this object she was anchored at the point where she was seized. The Circuit Court of Appeals for the Fifth Circuit reversed a decree of the lower court dismissing a libel of forfeiture against the vessel. Circuit Judge Walker, who delivered the opinion of the court holding that the seizure was not to be declared invalid because it was more than three miles from the coast, stated:

> In view of the great length of time the above-quoted provision of section 2811 has been in existence and acted on, without complaint, so far as appears, by foreign nations whose vessels are affected by the exercise of the right which the provision asserts, and of the long-continued recognition by the courts of the validity of the provision, for reasons disclosed, though not in cases calling for a decision on the question, we are of opinion that there is an absence of justification for the contention that the United States went beyond any power or jurisdiction with which it is vested in authorizing, for the protection of its revenue and the enforcement of its commercial regulations, such action as the statute in question provides for within four leagues of our coast.

> *United States* v. *Bengochea et al.*, 279 Fed. 537, 541 (C.C.A. 5th, 1922). For the corresponding section with reference to the production of manifests, contained in the act of June 17, 1930, see 19 U.S.C. §1583.

In 1922 the *Grace and Ruby*, a British schooner, sailed from the Bahama Islands, British West Indies, with a clearance for St. John, N.B., having a cargo of liquor, part of which was owned by one Sullivan, of Salem, Massachusetts, who was on board. From the Bahamas the vessel proceeded directly to a point six miles off the coast of Gloucester, Massachusetts, where Sullivan went ashore, later returning with a motorboat with which he carried liquor and three members of the crew of the *Grace and Ruby*, and transported a dory belonging to the schooner, to the shore at night. The attempt to land the liquor was discovered by the revenue officers of the United States, and the motorboat and her cargo were seized. The following day the *Grace and Ruby*, with the balance of her cargo, was seized at a point about four miles from the nearest land. The vessel was libeled for smuggling liquor into the United States in violation of sections 2872 and 2874 of the Revised Statutes of the United States (containing provision that no merchandise brought in any vessel from a foreign port should be unladen or delivered within the United States except in open day, unless by special license, nor at any time without a permit from the collector of the port, and providing for the forfeiture of the merchandise and vessel) and of the National Prohibition Act (41 Stat. 305). Exceptions were entered against the two libels on the ground of lack of jurisdiction. In overruling these exceptions, the District Court of the United States for the District of Massachusetts stated, *inter alia:*

> [2] While the question is not free from doubt, and no decision upon the point has come to my notice, it seems to me that this action on her part constituted an unlawful unlading by the Grace and Ruby at night within the territorial limits of the United States, in violation of Rev. St. §§2872, 2874. See 1 Wheaton, Criminal Law (11th Ed.) §§324, 330, 341, for a discussion of the principles involved and a collection of cases. The act of unlading, although beginning beyond the three-mile limit, continued until the liquor was landed, and the schooner was actively assisting in it by means of her small boat and three of her crew, who were on the motorboat for that purpose. It was none the less an unlawful unlading, within the section referred to, because by the transfer to the motorboat an offense was committed under section 2867, which rendered the motorboat and liquor liable to seizure and forfeiture, and the persons who aided and assisted liable to a penalty for so doing.
>
> . . . .
>
> The high seas are the territory of no nation; no nation can extend its laws over them; they are free to the vessels of all countries. But this has been thought not to mean that a nation is powerless against vessels offending against its laws which remain just outside the three-mile limit.
>
> . . . .
>
> The line between territorial waters and the high seas is not like the boundary between us and a foreign power. There must be, it seems to me, a certain width of debatable waters adjacent to our coasts. How far our authority shall be extended into them for the seizure of foreign vessels which have broken our laws is a matter for the political departments of the government rather than for the courts to determine.

283 Fed. 475, 476, 477 (D. Mass., 1922).

The *Louise F.*, a British schooner, with a cargo of liquors allegedly bound from Nassau, Bahamas, for Halifax, N.S., was forcibly seized on the high seas by a member of her crew and two others not connected with the vessel, who overpowered the officers and crew, brought her into waters of the United States, and unloaded a part of the cargo. The District Court of the United States for the Southern District of Florida held that under the circumstances neither the vessel nor her officers incurred any penalty under the Tariff Act of 1922 or any forfeiture under the Volstead act, and dismissed the libel. 293 Fed. 933 (S.D. Fla., 1923).

At a point approximately 19 miles from the coast of the United States, 25 cases of whisky were sold in 1924, from the *Over the Top*, a British vessel, to a special agent of the Internal Revenue Department. The crew of the vessel under the direction of the captain unloaded these cases to a sea-sled employed in the government service. The point where the sale took place was within one hour's sailing distance as computed by the possible speed of the sea-sled. On the day following the sale, the vessel was seized. The District Court of the United States for the District of Connecticut, in dismissing libels of forfeiture, found that the vessel had been hovering for some time off the coast of the United States at the point where she was seized and that those in command were engaged during that period in selling liquor and delivering it to boats proceeding from the coast of the United States and returning thereto. The court stated:

> My conclusion, then, is that as no statute embracing the subject-matter of sections 447, 448, 450, 453, 585, 586, 593, and 594 of the Tariff Act of 1922 has extended our territorial jurisdiction to a point on the high seas distant 19 miles from our coast, conduct which would have been in violation of these sections if performed within our territory cannot constitute an offense against the United States when performed at such a distance by foreign nationals on ships of foreign registry. If, for the purpose of our treasury, we can extend our sea jurisdiction to a point four leagues from the coast, I see no reason why we cannot extend it four leagues more. I merely observe that we have not done so yet.

. . . .

Convention not self-executing

> It must be noted that the treaty [of 1924] does not define the acts constituting an offense against the laws of the United States prohibiting the importation of alcoholic beverages. These acts are defined in the statute. . . . If, before this treaty was contracted, the unlading of merchandise by a ship of British registry at a point more than four leagues removed from the coast of the United States did not constitute a crime against the United States (and there appears to be no contention that it did), then the treaty could not and did not make it a crime.

The court held that a sale of liquor 19 miles from the coast to a government agent, so that title passed, did not constitute smuggling within section 593 of the Tariff Act of 1922 and dismissed the action.

5 F. (2d) 838, 843, 844 (D. Conn., 1925).

In the case of the *Frances Louise* the District Court of the United States for the District of Massachusetts dismissed a libel asking the forfeiture of a Canadian schooner, which had been seized outside of the limits set—one hour's sailing—by the convention of 1924 between the United States and Great Britain, stating that "both nations intended the treaty to deal with the matter in a complete way". 1 F. (2d) 1004, 1006 (D. Mass., 1924).

In the case of *The Panama* the court issued a decree of forfeiture against a British schooner and its cargo of intoxicating liquors, the seizure having been made 12.1 miles from the nearest point of shore off Galveston, Texas, and at a greater distance from shore than she could cover in one hour. Judge Hutcheson, speaking for the court, said: "I have, in The Island Home and The Rosalie M., both decided without reference to the treaty, declared my view that the right of the executive to seize and search for violations of our laws is not limited by any particular distance from the shore. Nor do I think the treaty changes this right. It merely expresses a diplomatic agreement in advance to the doing of those things which the United States already had authority to do, subject only to political accountability to foreign nations whose bottoms were searched, and I therefore overrule the contention of the defendant that the terms of the treaty have made search and seizure unlawful." 6 F. (2d) 326, 327 (S.D. Tex., 1925).

After referring to *The Grace and Ruby* and *The Henry L. Marshall* (where contact was made with "shore boats" for the purpose of delivering the cargo to the shore, as a matter of continuous carriage), the District Court of the United States for the Southern District of Texas held in the case of *The Muriel E. Winters, ibid.* 466, where the captain of the vessel admitted that she was engaged in bringing liquor from the Bahama Islands to the United States and selling it to small boats outside of the 12-mile limit, without prearrangement or further connection with the buyers that "no sort of sound legal reasoning could stretch the principle applied in those cases to cause a forfeiture of the vessel upon the theory of its introduction of liquor by constructive presence in the United States, where the transaction was finished at sea", and where the vessel "thereafter had no connection of any kind with the liquor", and that the vessel was not forfeitable upon that ground, although she was subject to forfeiture, under an amended allegation, for having unladen liquor at a point within 12 miles from shore under section 586 of the Tariff Act of 1922 (42 Stat. 858, 980).

In the case of the *Frances E.* the master and crew of a British vessel, which had been seized some 16 miles off the coast of Florida, were convicted of possessing and transporting liquor in violation of the Volstead act, although the proof showed that the vessel could not traverse the distance from shore in one hour, the jury being instructed that it might look to the speed of such vessels as were ordinarily used to transport liquor from vessels to the shore. *United States* v. *Henning et al.*, 7 F. (2d) 488, 490 (S.D. Ala., 1925).

In the case of *Ford et al.* v. *United States* the Supreme Court of the United States affirmed a conviction of conspiracy (under sec. 37 of the Criminal Code) to import liquor into the United States in violation of the prohibition law (42 Stat. 305) and section 593(*b*) of the Tariff Act of 1922 (42 Stat. 858, 982), by persons on board the British vessel *Quadra*, seized while hovering at a distance of 5.7 miles from the Farallon Islands (near San Francisco), the vessel having a speed of 6.6 miles an hour. 273 U.S. (1927) 593, 610, 618.

In the case of the *Sagatind* and the *Diamantina* the Circuit Court of Appeals for the Second Circuit affirmed decrees of a lower court dismissing libels of forfeiture against the *Sagatind*, a Norwegian steamer, and the *Diamantina*, a British vessel, and their cargoes, for violation of the prohibition and revenue statutes of the United States. The *Sagatind* was loaded with liquor in Belgium and was instructed to discharge its cargo at a point off the coast of the United States. She transhipped a quantity of liquor to the *Diamantina* at a point twenty·some miles off the New Jersey coast. There was no proof that either vessel came voluntarily within 12 miles of the coast of the United States nor was there any evidence that either vessel had made contact with the shore, although it was found that the liquor was to be sold along the coast. The vessels were seized more than 20 miles from the shore. The court agreed with the decision in the case of the *Frances Louise* that the treaties "exclusively determine the status of vessels" but that "nowhere in the treaties can any words be found indicating an intent on the part of the contracting parties to change or extend the limits of the territory of the United States" and that "in that sense the treaty is not self-executing". 11 F. (2d) 673, 675 (C.C.A. 2d, 1926). For the act of Congress, approved May 13, 1938, authorizing payment of the sum of $5,000 as a matter of grace, as an indemnity to the Norwegian Government because of the detention and treatment of the crew of the *Sagatind*, see 52 Stat. 350, 1147.

In the case of *Arch* v. *United States* the Circuit Court of Appeals for the Fifth Circuit considered an appeal from a judgment forfeiting the British vessel *Island Home* for violations of the customs laws and of the Volstead act (41 Stat. 305), particularly for unlawfully unloading liquor by means of small boats without a permit, after arrival at a point within four leagues of the United States coast, and for failure to have a manifest of the cargo. The vessel had come within the three-mile limit but subsequently had anchored outside of it, although well within 12 miles of the coast. It was contended that the seizure was illegal because made beyond the three-mile limit. In affirming the decree of forfeiture the court stated:

> . . . When she reached a point within four leagues of the shore she was as much within the jurisdiction of the United States as if actually in port, and was required to observe all the customs laws and regulations. When the Coast Guard observed her at anchor they had the authority to board her for the purpose of making inquiry as to her cargo and destination, and, finding no manifest, had the right to search without the necessity of procuring a search warrant. Tariff Act of Sept. 21, 1922, §581 (Comp. St. Ann. Supp. 1923, §5841h); Carroll v. U.S., 267 U.S. 132, 45 S. Ct. 280, 69 L. Ed. 543, 39 A.L.R. 790. Finding probable cause therefor, the seizure was justified.

Probable
cause

If the Island Home had merely sailed through the customs zone without it being shown she had the intention of anchoring within it, and clandestinely introducing her cargo into the country, or if her intention had been only to anchor without the jurisdictional limits and there sell to chance customers, the case presented would have been different. Burns v. U.S. (C.C.A.) 296 F. 468; Romano v. U.S. (C.C.A.) 9 F. (2d) 522.

13 F. (2d) 382, 384 (C.C.A. 5th, 1926).

In the case of *The J. Duffy*, a suit brought for the forfeiture of a liquor-laden British vessel and for penalties for unlawful importation of liquor into the United States, the Circuit Court of Appeals for the Second Circuit held that the offense, punishable under section 593(*b*) of the Tariff Act of 1922 (42 Stat. 858, 982), was complete when a person fraudulently or knowingly imported into the United States merchandise contrary to law or brought such merchandise into the territorial waters, and further held that it was not necessary that the merchandise should have been unloaded. The court reversed a decree of the lower court dismissing the suit. However it agreed with the lower court that "when arrested in Long Island Sound she [the vessel] was within the territorial waters of the United States".

18 F. (2d) 754 (C.C.A. 2d, 1927); 14 F. (2d) 426 (D. Conn., 1926). The forfeiture of the vessel was not decreed but penalties were imposed.

In the case of *The Mistinguette*, a French vessel bound from St. Pierre, Miquelon, to Nassau, was discovered by a United States Coast Guard vessel less than three miles from shore and headed (without lights) toward Montauk Point. She was overhauled and boarded when four and a half miles from shore. The Circuit Court of Appeals for the Second Circuit held that the vessel was "bound to the United States" within the meaning of section 584 of the Tariff Act of 1922, that that phrase "does not require that she reach a port of entry", and that officers of the customs or Coast Guard were authorized to board a vessel within four leagues of the coast, under section 581 of the Tariff Act of 1922. A lien on the vessel for penalties incurred for failure to exhibit her manifest on demand of an officer of the Coast Guard within the 12-mile limit as prescribed by sections 581, 584, and 594 of the Tariff Act of 1922 was sustained, and the decree of the lower court dismissing the libel seeking forfeiture of the cargo for violation of section 584 of the same act was reversed by the circuit court of appeals. *United States* v. *416 Cases G. T. Whiskey, etc.*, 27 F. (2d) 738, 739 (C.C.A. 2d, 1928).

In the case of *The Pictonian*, a British schooner was arrested 14 miles from the coast of the United States for violating section 3450 of the Revised Statutes of the United States, sections 584, 586, 587, and 593 of the Tariff Act of 1922 (42 Stat. 858, 980, 981, 982), providing for the seizure within 12 miles of the coast of vessels violating the customs laws of the United States, and article 2 of the convention of 1924 between the United States and Great Britain for the prevention of smuggling of intoxicating liquors into the United States (43 Stat. 1761). The defendant contended that the United States had no authority to seize a vessel at that distance; that the convention between the United States and Great Britain giving the right to seize, within an hour's sailing distance from the shore under certain circumstances, did not and could not extend the right to search and seize beyond the 12-mile limit prescribed by the statute; and that the acts alleged against the vessel were not crimes because Congress had not by law declared and could not declare them to be such when committed beyond the 12-mile limit.

A decree of forfeiture having been entered by the District Court of the United States for the Eastern District of New York, the case was appealed to the Circuit Court of Appeals for the Second Circuit, which, on June 6, 1927, reversed the decree of forfeiture. Justice Manton, speaking for the court, after stating that it was "lawful for the Pictonian to carry a cargo of liquor outside of the territorial jurisdiction of the United States" and citing *Cunard Steamship Company, Ltd., et al.* v. *Mellon, Secretary of the Treasury, et al.*, 262 U.S. (1923) 100, pointed out that section 584 of the Tariff Act of 1922 provided a penalty for failure to produce a manifest within four leagues of the coast and that since the vessel was 14 miles from the coast when boarded there was no violation of this section. The court, relying upon the decision in the case of *The Sagatind*, 11 F. (2d) 673 (C.C.A. 2d, 1926), stated that "We held there that there was no extension of the territorial jurisdiction created by the treaty of May 22, 1924."

　　3 F. (2d) 145 (E.D.N.Y., 1924) ; 20 F. (2d) 353, 354 (C.C.A. 2d, 1927).

On March 14, 1927 the Coast Guard cutter *Mascoutin* sighted the *Vinces*, a Canadian liquor-laden vessel, steaming in the direction of the South Carolina coast. She was then within seven and a half miles of the shore and within one hour's sailing distance. The *Mascoutin* pursued and overtook her when she was about twelve and three-quarters miles from the shore. She was brought into the port of Charleston where she was libeled for violation of the Tariff Act of 1922 (42 Stat. 858). The District Court of the United States for the Eastern District of South Carolina assessed penalties against the vessel and ordered forfeiture of her cargo under sections 584 and 594 of the Tariff Act of 1922 (19 U.S.C.A. §§486 and 498.) This decree was affirmed on appeal. With respect to the validity of seizure the appellate court said:

> While it is true, as contended, that the vessel never came within the 3-mile limit of the territorial waters of the United States, we think that, as she was bound for the United States with an unmanifested cargo and came within 12 miles, or 4 marine leagues, of the coast, her seizure was justified under the revenue statutes of the United States, and that these statutes constitute a valid exercise of the sovereign power of the government.

After referring to sections 431, 581, 583, 584, and 594 of the Tariff Act of 1922, *ante*, the court said:

> We think it equally clear that these statutes are valid, notwithstanding the fact that the territorial boundaries of the United States extend only to the 3-mile limit. Such provisions have been a part of every tariff act passed by Congress beginning with the statute of 1790 (1 Stat. 145) which introduced the 4-league limit (section 31) of the British hovering statutes. While in effect an assertion of extraterritorial jurisdiction, they are justified on the ground that they are necessary to territorial security and the proper enforcement of the laws of the country. Church v. Hubbart, 2 Cranch, 187, 235, 236, 2 L. Ed. 249; The Apollon, 9 Wheat. 362, 371, 6 L. Ed. 111; Manchester v. Mass., 139 U.S. 240, 268, 11 S. Ct. 559, 35 L. Ed. 159; The Cherie (C.C.A. 1st) 13 F. (2d) 992; Arch v. U.S., supra; Dickinson on Jurisdiction at the Maritime Frontier, supra.

> . . . . . .

> And we do not think that the right within the 12-mile limit to seize and proceed against vessels bound for the United States, for violation of the provisions of its revenue laws, has been limited in any way by the provisions of the Treaty with Great Britain of 1924 (43 Stat. 1761).

Territorial security and enforcement of laws

It was held that the vessel, when signaled, was within an hour's sailing distance of the shore of the United States and that the seizure was therefore expressly authorized by the convention.

27 F. (2d) 296, 299, 300 (C.C.A. 4th, 1928).

In the case of *The Marion Phillis* the Circuit Court of Appeals for the Second Circuit reversed the judgment of the lower court dismissing a libel seeking the forfeiture of the British schooner *Marion Phillis* and her cargo for failure of the master to exhibit a manifest as required of vessels "bound to the United States" by section 584 of the Tariff Act of 1922 (42 Stat. 858). The vessel had sailed from St. Pierre, Miquelon, on October 12, 1927 for Nassau, British West Indies, with a cargo of liquor. She was sighted by the Coast Guard patrol boat *Travis* about 30 miles off the New Jersey coast. On October 27 the schooner was about six and a half miles off shore and heading for the Long Island coast. She was ordered to stop and was boarded. The captain denied that he had a manifest and intimated that he had gotten within the 12-mile limit by mistake. Circuit Judge Swan, delivering the opinion of the court, said:

> It is perfectly clear that the schooner was not bound for Nassau. For three days she had sailed in the opposite direction, without stress of weather or other excuse. What, then, was her purpose? The plain and reasonable inference is that she was seeking an opportunity to discharge her cargo on or near the Long Island coast, either by proceeding herself into territorial

waters, or by meeting contact boats outside the three-mile but within the 12-mile limit, or by transshipment to smugglers beyond the 12-mile limit. Whichever method of discharge she might employ it seems to us beyond reasonable doubt that her contraband cargo was intended to be smuggled to our shores. . . .

. . . The purpose of a manifest is not merely to collect duties, but is also to inform government officials whether forbidden things are being imported. United States v. Sischo, 262 U.S. 165, 167, 43 S. Ct. 511, 67 L. Ed. 925. This purpose will be promoted by interpreting the phrase "bound to the United States" to include a vessel which hovers outside the 12-mile limit with contraband for smugglers, even though no manifest may legally be demanded unless she crosses the line. We cannot agree with the lower court's finding that the Marion Phillis was not bound to the United States.

<blockquote>36 F. (2d) 688, 689, 690 (C.C.A. 2d, 1929). See also the case of The Metmuzel, 49 F. (2d) 365 (E.D.Va., 1930), affirmed in The Metmuzel, Miller v. United States, 49 F. (2d) 368 (C.C.A. 4th, 1931); certiorari denied, 283 U.S. (1931) 866.</blockquote>

On November 1, 1930 the British motor-screw Mazel Tov, a vessel of speed not exceeding ten miles an hour, was seized by the United States Coast Guard at a point eleven and a half miles off the coast of Massachusetts. The master of the vessel took exception to the jurisdiction of the lower court on the ground that the "vessel was not seized within the territorial limits of any jurisdiction of the United States, but, on the contrary, was captured and boarded at a point more than four (4) leagues from the coast" and that "it was not the intention at any time to enter any of the territorial limits of the United States". The district court having found the facts just stated, dismissed the libels. The circuit court of appeals, to which the Government appealed, held that the convention of 1924 did not "effect a change in the customs-revenue laws of the United States wherein Congress had fixed a four league protective zone", and reversed the judgment. On certiorari the Supreme Court reversed the decision of the appellate court on the ground that "the Government itself lacked power to seize, since by the Treaty it had imposed a territorial limitation upon its own authority".

Justice Brandeis, delivering the opinion of the Court, said:

<blockquote>The Treaty, being later in date than the Act of 1922, superseded, so far as inconsistent with the terms of the Act, the authority which had been conferred by §581 upon officers of the Coast Guard to board, search and seize beyond our territorial waters [within 4 leagues (12 miles) of the coast of the United States]. Whitney v. Robertson, 124 U.S. 190, 194. For in a strict sense the Treaty was self-executing, in that no legislation was necessary to authorize executive action pursuant to its provisions.</blockquote>

The Treaty was not abrogated by re-enacting §581 in the Tariff Act of 1930 in the identical terms of the Act of 1922. A treaty will not be deemed to have been abrogated or modified by a later statute unless such purpose on the part of Congress has been clearly expressed.

Cook v. *United States,* 288 U.S. (1933) 102, 108, 118, 119, 121.

On April 1, 1930 the British vessel *Ada M.* was seized by the Coast Guard of the United States, and libels of forfeiture were filed against the cargo and the vessel as a rum-runner on the ground that she had violated sections 581, 584–586, and 594 of the Tariff Act of 1922 (42 Stat. 858). The libels alleged that the vessel was seized within 12 miles of the coast of New Jersey but did not state whether the vessel was within one hour's sailing distance from the coast. The District Court of the United States for the Southern District of New York found that the vessel was within the 12-mile limit and rendered a decree of forfeiture as to the vessel and cargo. The circuit court, to which the case was appealed, reversed this decision on the ground that the convention between the United States and Great Britain of 1924 (43 Stat. 1761) permitted seizure and forfeiture of a vessel only when the vessel was seized within one hour's sailing distance of the coast, stating that the "libel failed to allege the vessel was seized at a place from which it could reach the shore in one hour, and is therefore demurrable".

The circuit court remanded the case to the lower court for an application for leave to amend the libel and prove the speed of the vessel. The libels having been amended, the claimant argued that the amended libels did not state facts sufficient to constitute a cause of action for forfeiture or to show that the court had jurisdiction of the case. In overruling the claimant's exceptions to the amended libels the court stated:

> . . . The contention is made that, though the amended libels adequately allege a seizure within one hour's sailing distance of the seized vessel from the shore, they are still insufficient in that they do not allege a violation of the Prohibition Act (27 U.S.C.A. §1 et seq.), but rather violations of the Tariff Act of 1922 (42 Stat. 858). In effect, claimant argues that this court's jurisdiction is wholly dependent upon the Treaty of 1924.
>
> .   .   .   .
>
> Clearly, it is sufficient that the causes of forfeiture in this proceeding are based upon the provisions of the Tariff Act of 1922 which were in effect at the time of the seizure of the vessel and cargo. The Treaty with Great Britain merely modified the right of seizure and, except for that limitation, had no effect upon the right of forfeiture given by the Tariff Act.
>
> .   .   .   .

If the seizure was lawful, having in mind the modification by the Treaty of 1924, then the vessel and cargo may be libeled for either a violation of the Tariff Act or the Prohibition Act.

60 F. (2d) 449 (S.D.N.Y., 1932) ; 67 F. (2d) 333, 335 (C.C.A. 2d, 1933) ; 20 F. Supp 331, 333, 335, (S.D.N.Y., 1937).

Effect of repeal of 18th amendment on treaties

In the case of *The Ada M.* the Department of Justice requested the opinion of the Department of State regarding a contention raised by counsel for the claimants that the convention of 1924 between the United States and Great Britain for the prevention of smuggling of liquors into the United States (43 Stat. 1761) was abrogated by the repeal of the eighteenth amendment to the Constitution of the United States on December 5, 1933 (48 Stat. 1720). The Secretary of State replied that the convention "has not been terminated by reason of the repeal of the Eighteenth Amendment to the Constitution of the United States". The reasons for this conclusion were stated to be:

(1) The convention was still necessary to avoid "difficulties" since laws similar to the National Prohibition Act were in force in some states.

(2) The case of *Ford et al.* v. *United States*, 273 U.S. (1927) 593, had held that "the laws in force in the United States on the subject of alcoholic beverages", which formed the basis for the convention, included the provisions of the tariff act and the Federal conspiracy statute.

(3) In the case of *The Golmaccam*, a British vessel, 8 F. Supp. 338 (D.Maine, N.D. 1934), the view was expressed that the repeal of the eighteenth amendment did not terminate the convention.

(4) The Department had not been notified by any government with which a liquor convention was in force that it considered such convention terminated by the repeal of the amendment.

The District Court of the United States for the Southern District of New York, in granting a motion for leave to amend the libels in the case of *The Ada M.*, stated:

. . . Suppose the Treaty did drop out of the picture in 1933. The abrogation would have no effect on the right or wrong in a seizure made three years earlier. . . . The claimants' contention that the Treaty is no longer in existence is the minor premise in a syllogism the major premise of which is that the right of forfeiture is founded on the Treaty. The major premise being false, The Isabel H., supra, there is no need of discussing whether the Treaty is still in effect.

United States v. *5,870 Bags and 100 Kegs, et al.*, 20 F. Supp. 331, 333 (S.D.N.Y., 1937) ; 60 F. (2d) 449 (S.D.N.Y., 1932) ; 67 F. (2d) 333 (C.C.A. 2d, 1933). Secretary Hull to Attorney General Cummings, May 4, 1937, MS. Department of State, file 811.114 Ada M/55.

BAYS AND GULFS

MEASUREMENT

§100

The question "From where must be measured the 'three marine miles of any . . . bays' ", referred to in article I of the convention of 1818 between the United States and Great Britain, wherein the United States renounced the liberty to take, dry, or cure fish "within three marine miles of any of the . . . Bays . . . of His Brittanic Majesty's Dominions in America", with certain exceptions, was submitted, as the fifth of seven questions, to a tribunal selected from the panel of the Permanent Court of Arbitration, under the terms of a special agreement signed at Washington on January 27, 1909 by the United States and Great Britain. In its decision of September 7, 1910 the tribunal held that the term "bays" applied to "every bay on the coast in question" that might be reasonably supposed to have been considered as a bay by the negotiators; that the renunciatory clause included bays other than those under the territorial sovereignty of Great Britain, the term "bays" having been used in a "geographical" sense and not with reference "to political control"; and that, contrary to the contention of the United States, the clause applied to bays other than bays six miles or less in width *inter fauces terrae*, the tribunal stating, *inter alia*, in this last regard that— *North Atlantic Coast Fisheries arbitration*

> admittedly the geographical character of a bay contains conditions which concern the interests of the territorial sovereign to a more intimate and important extent than do those connected with the open coast. Thus conditions of national and territorial integrity, of defense, of commerce and of industry are all vitally concerned with the control of the bays penetrating the national coast line. This interest varies, speaking generally in proportion to the penetration inland of the bay; but as no principle of international law recognizes any specified relation between the concavity of the bay and the requirements for control by the territorial sovereignty, this tribunal is unable to qualify by the application of any new principle its interpretation of the Treaty of 1818 as excluding bays in general from the strict and systematic application of the three mile rule . . .

> . . . .

> from the information before this tribunal it is evident that the three mile rule is not applied to bays strictly or systematically either by the United States or by any other Power;
> . . . It has been recognized by the United States that bays stand apart, and that in respect of them territorial jurisdiction may be exercised farther than the marginal belt in the case of Delaware Bay by the report of the United States Attorney General of May 19th, 1793; and the letter of Mr. Jefferson to Mr. Genet of Nov. 8th, 1793, declares the bays of the United States

generally to be, "as being landlocked, within the body of the United States".

Historic bays   The tribunal rejected the contention of the United States "that such exceptions only should be made from the application of the three mile rule to bays as are sanctioned by conventions and established usage", stating at the same time that, while it recognized "that conventions and established usage might be considered as the basis for claiming as territorial those bays which on this ground might be called historic bays, and that such claim should be held valid in the absence of any principle of international law on the subject", the principle could not be applied to the bays in question, as desired by the United States, because not only had certain of the claims of Great Britain been recognized in the past by the United States but also (*a*) because Great Britain had, during the instant controversy, asserted a claim to these bays generally and had enforced such claims specifically in statutes and otherwise with reference to the more important bays, and—

> (*b*) Because neither should such relaxations of this claim, as are in evidence, be construed as renunciations of it; nor should omissions to enforce the claim in regard to bays as to which no controversy arose, be so construed. Such a construction by this Tribunal would not only be intrinsically inequitable, but internationally injurious; in that it would discourage conciliatory diplomatic transactions and encourage the assertion of extreme claims in their fullest extent.

The tribunal was of the further opinion that the negotiators of the convention of 1818 probably thought that everyone would know what was a bay; that in this popular sense the term must be interpreted; and that the "interpretation must take into account all the individual circumstances which for any one of the different bays are to be appreciated, the relation of its width to the length of penetration inland, the possibility and the necessity of its being defended by the State in whose territory it is indented; the special value which it has for the industry of the inhabitants of its shores; the distance which it is secluded from the highways of nations on the open sea and other circumstances not possible to enumerate in general".

Finally, it held:

Measurement of bays   In case of bays the three marine miles are to be measured from a straight line drawn across the body of water at the place where it ceases to have the configuration and characteristics of a bay. At all other places the three marine miles are to be measured following the sinuosities of the coast.

It also held that, although this rule was "correct in principle", it was not entirely satisfactory "as to its practical applicability", leaving room for doubt and differences, and in view of the fact that, in a number of treaties as well as in her instructions to naval officers stationed on the coasts in controversy, Great Britain had adopted "the rule that only bays of ten miles width should be considered as those wherein the fishing is reserved to nationals", and, although "these circumstances are not sufficient to constitute this a principle of international law", it seemed reasonable to propose this rule with certain exceptions for the consideration and acceptance of the high contracting parties; and that:

> In every bay not hereinafter specifically provided for [Baie des Chaleurs, Bay of Miramichi, Egmont Bay, St. Ann's Bay, Fortune Bay, Barrington Bay, Chedabucto and St. Peter's Bays, Mira Bay, Placentia Bay, and St. Mary's Bay] the limits of exclusion shall be drawn three miles seaward from a straight line across the bay in the part nearest the entrance at the first point where the width does not exceed ten miles.

Per. Ct. Arb., *North Atlantic Coast Fisheries Tribunal of Arbitration* (The Hague, 1910) 104, 105, 107, 134–140; MS. Department of State, file 711.438A/363; Scott, *Hague Court Reports* (1916) 146, 181–190. Dr. Drago dissented from the decision of the majority as regards question 5. He favored the 10-mile rule for the measurement of bays, at least for purposes of fishing, and otherwise objected to the decision of the majority because it was indefinite and because it recommended a procedure "without the scope of the award". *Ibid.* 195–207.

In his report (dated Nov. 14, 1910) to the Secretary of State, Chandler P. Anderson, agent of the United States before the tribunal, stated with respect to the holding of the tribunal on question 5:

"Great Britain's contention did not rest upon the assertion of territorial jurisdiction over such bays, and the award does not go to the extent of holding that Great Britain has territorial jurisdiction over the large bays, although the United States has renounced for its fishermen the right to fish therein.

"The award, therefore, still leaves American fishermen in such bays subject to American and not British law, and confers upon Great Britain or the British colonies no right to seize or interfere with American fishing vessels beyond the 3-mile limit from shore in such bays, such vessels being in a similar situation to British vessels violating their obligation under the fur-seal award, which excludes them from fishing in certain portions of the high seas.

"The award of the tribunal on this question does not define what is a bay, holding merely that the 3-mile limit of exclusion must be measured from a 'line drawn across the body of water at the place where it ceases to have the configuration and characteristics of a bay.' This answer leaves open the question of where such line is to be drawn in each particular case and also the question of whether any particular body of water has the 'configuration and characteristics of a bay.'

.   .   .   .

"The strength of the position of the United States on this question is shown by the very able argument presented in the dissenting opinion by Dr. Drago and by the fact that the British contention was not fully sustained, and that this was the only question of the seven submitted upon which the decision of the tribunal was not unanimous." S. Doc. 806, 61st Cong., 3d sess., serial no. 5943, p. 10.

An agreement was signed in Washington by Great Britain and the United States on July 20, 1912 adopting with certain modifications, the rules and method of procedure prescribed in the award in *The North Atlantic Coast Fisheries* case. 3 Treaties, etc. (Redmond, 1923) 2632.

On Nov. 14, 1910 the British Embassy addressed a note to the Secretary of State suggesting a discussion of the legislative and executive acts of Newfoundland and Canada claimed by the United States to be inconsistent with the true interpretation of the convention of 1818, preliminary to any recourse to the services of a commission of experts, conformably to the award of 1910. The suggestion was adopted.

Chargé Innes to Secretary Knox, no. 230, Nov. 14, 1910, MS. Department of State, file 711.438A/365; Mr. Knox to Mr. Innes, Nov. 26, 1910, *ibid.* 711.438A/367.

For the minutes of the conferences held in Washington, Jan. 9–14, 1911, pursuant to this agreement, see 3 Treaties, etc. (Redmond, 1923) 2627, 2628; Treaty Series 553 and 554; 1911 For. Rel. 271, 272.

Three-mile limit

From a very early date nations have generally acquiesced in the proposition that a nation's territory over which its sovereignty extends ends 3 miles from and into the bordering ocean. Ocean Industries, Inc., v. Superior Court, 200 Cal. 235, 252 P. 722. Such three miles was not a line following the exact contour of the coast, which would seem impracticable, but was three miles from the line joining headlands or points between which lie indentations or bays. But a moment's thought upon the subject is sufficient to cause appreciation of the fact that the rule of reason must be read into this formula. As, for instance, if the whole of the land bordering the Gulf of Mexico were under one sovereignty the whole of such vast sea could not well be considered as within such country's sovereignty. The practice of governments, explorers, geographers, etc., has generally confined such formula to bays which are not in fact open sea, and so the coasts of the continents have been mapped, the points between which the sea curves inward have been designated, and the waters between such points have been designated as bays. A consultation of the old discovery and navigation maps of the Spaniards, and as well the English, will show this to have been the practice on the Pacific Coast of North America, and it does not appear to have been disturbed by the Mexican sovereignty. . . . The Constitution of California (Const. Cal. 1849, art. 12) in its boundary description provides that the 3-mile limit shall be followed, and that the bays and harbors along the coast are included. It would seem to follow logically that United States national and California state sovereignty have always been in accord with this rule. . . .

Gulf of Mexico

Bay of San Pedro

It seems, therefore, and I so decide, that the Bay of San Pedro is that body of water lying landward from a line drawn from Point Lasuen to Point Firmin, and that the sovereignty of the United States and the territory of the state of California extends three miles to seaward from such line. The same conclusion was reached by the Appellate Department of the Los Angeles County California Superior Court in Criminal Appeals No. 734, People v. Haskel.

United States v. *Carrillo et al.*, 13 F. Supp. 121, 122 (S.D. Cal., 1935). In this case the defendants were under indictment for piracy, robbing and plundering a gambling vessel, the *Monte Carlo*, anchored off the shore of California.

In 1918 the Probate, Divorce, and Admiralty Division of the British High Court of Justice condemned the Norwegian steamship *Loekken* and her cargo, on the application of the Crown, on the ground that the full cargo of sulphur pyrites, which she was carrying at the time of seizure in 1916, was absolute contraband destined to Germany. The Norwegian Consul General having intervened, the question was raised as to whether the capture took place within and in violation of the territorial waters of Norway. By an arrangement between the Norwegian Government and the British Government it was agreed that for the purposes of the case the limit of territorial waters was three marine miles from the coast. It was therefore necessary for the court to determine only the baseline and whether the vessel was inside or outside "three nautical miles of it" at the time of capture. It held that the baseline should be taken, at this point, off the coast of Norway to be from Naze (or Lindesnes) on the east, to the head of the mainland off which Rauna Island lay, on the west ("a distance of about 13 miles"), that the vessel was outside the territorial waters of Norway at the time of capture, and that therefore the capture was regular. 34 T.L.R. (1918) 594. The Judicial Committee of the Privy Council agreed with the conclusion of the lower court that the vessel was outside of the territorial waters of Norway—other important questions of fact having been agreed to for purposes of the appeal—and the appeal was dismissed on Nov. 30, 1920. V *Lloyd's List Law Reports* (1920) 95, 244; IX *Lloyd's Reports of Prize Cases* (1923) 17n.

Subcommittee II of the second committee of the Conference for the Codification of International Law, held at The Hague in 1930, made the following report to the second committee on the subject of "Bays":

> In the case of bays the coasts of which belong to a single State, the belt of territorial waters shall be measured from a straight line drawn across the opening of the bay. If the opening of the bay is more than ten miles wide, the line shall be drawn at the nearest point to the entrance at which the opening does not exceed ten miles.

Observations.

> . . . This is the system adopted i.a. in the North Sea Fisheries Convention of May 6th, 1882. Other Delegations were only prepared to regard the waters of a bay as inland waters if the two zones of territorial sea met at the opening of the bay, in other words, if the opening did not exceed twice the breadth of the territorial sea. States which were in favour of a territorial belt of three miles held that the opening should therefore not exceed six miles. . . .

Most Delegations agreed to a width of ten miles, provided a system were simultaneously adopted under which slight indentations would not be treated as bays.

The absence of agreement in the second committee as to the breadth of the territorial sea, prevented that Committee from reaching even a provisional decision on the report of subcommittee II, which was merely attached as an annex to the second committee's report to the Conference.

League of Nations pub. C.230.M.117.1930. V, pp. 4, 11. For the proposals of the delegations of the United States and of France with reference to the determination of the status of the waters of a bay or estuary, and the delimitation of territorial waters in connection therewith, see *ibid.* 12. For the replies of the governments to the *questionnaire* submitted to them by the League of Nations Preparatory Committee prior to the Conference, together with the observations and bases of discussion drawn up by that Committee, see *ibid.* C.74.M.39.1929.V, pp. 39–45.

In discussing the measurement of baselines in the delimitation of bays, Meyer concludes:

6-mile
baseline

In recent times it has been assumed in several quarters that "the ordinary drawing" of the territorial limit is now based on six-mile base lines as a maximum across bays, fjords and other indentations. The preceding report shows that the British Government and its counsel, as late as 1910, have demonstrated that this mode of drawing the limit represents an entirely new principle, not used by any State, and, as we have seen, the Court of Arbitration upheld this view.

10-mile
baseline

Many have also in recent years assumed that a drawing of the limit by using base lines with a maximum length of ten miles was "a universally recognized rule in international law with regard to fishery questions". The correctness of this view was likewise emphatically denied by the British Government in 1910, not only as regards fisheries, but in all respects. It has also been definitely rejected by British and American Courts of Law. The result of the preceding investigations with regard to bays has been to show: that where no restricting stipulations, or lost rights of usage exist, the contention of Great Britain in 1910 is perfectly correct, namely that the political coast line follows the main direction of the coasts, or, as stated by the British Crown lawyers in 1841: it shall be

"Headland
to headland"
rule

drawn from headland to headland. "Sinuosities" and "envelopes" are conceptions which the United States advocated in vain before the Court of Arbitration at The Hague 1910.

Territorial
bays

As regards recognition by other States of bays as territorial when their width exceeds a certain measure, it must be noted that the British Government in 1910 contended that bays are territorial without regard to their width. The bays which were concerned in that special case, are most of them curvatures in the coast line having in some cases a breadth three times as great as their penetration into the land. According to Canadian law the Hudson Bay is territorial. Moray Firth is in fact territorial. Likewise the Firth of Clyde and Bristol Channel. No one seems to have thought that it was necessary to obtain the assent of other Powers in these cases in order to make the matter legal, except perhaps in the case of the Moray Firth out of regard for the North Sea Convention. The British Government has reserved its claim to regard the Bay of Fundy as territorial. The practice of other States furnishes also examples of bays being declared territorial regardless of their width. . . .

The drawing of the limit between enclosed waters and the territorial sea is possibly still more a matter of national legislation in sovereign States than the breadth of the territorial sea. It is also a problem which has still less been elucidated in international law. As this dividing line—"the political coast line"—forms the starting point of the territorial sea itself, it follows that up to 1927 the exact course of the latter had not in fact been authoritatively established in any country with the exception of some small coastal tracts.[1] ([1] It has afterwards been done by Iceland and Sweden.) In the case of Great Britain, such an official indication of the limits of enclosed waters has not, as far as is known, taken place since the establishment of the King's Chambers in 1604. Our investigations seem to show that no State has devoted such attention to this problem as Norway. The reason for this is possibly that States feel a marked unwillingness to indicate exact boundaries until actual events make it absolutely necessary.

Meyer, *Extent of Jurisdiction in Coastal Waters* (1937) 518–520.

DIVISIONAL LINES

§101

A question regarding the boundary line between Minnesota and Wisconsin in upper and lower St. Louis Bay was involved in the case of *Minnesota* v. *Wisconsin.* In holding that the boundary followed the "principal navigable channel", the Court pointed out that it adopted "the doctrine of *Thalweg* as opposed to the physical middle line" and stated:

The doctrine of *Thalweg*, a modification of the more ancient principle which required equal division of territory, was adopted in order to preserve to each State equality of right in the beneficial use of the stream as a means of communication. Accordingly, the middle of the principal channel of navigation is commonly accepted as the boundary. Equality in the beneficial use often would be defeated, rather than promoted, by fixing the boundary on a given line merely because it connects points of greatest depth. Deepest water and the principal navigable channel are not necessarily the same. The rule has direct reference to actual or probable use in the ordinary course, and common experience shows that vessels do not follow a narrow

[margin note:] Thalweg: principal navigable channel

crooked channel close to shore, however deep, when they can proceed on a safer and more direct one with sufficient water.

252 U.S. (1920) 273, 281, 282.

In connection with its determination of the boundary line in the Green Bay section of the Wisconsin and Michigan boundary, the Supreme Court of the United States held that Congress must have intended that the two States "should have equality of right and opportunity in respect of these waters, including navigation, fishing and other uses", and, in adopting the rule of the *Thalweg*, the Court said:

> The parties rightly assume that there is no difference between the description of the boundary through Green Bay given in the Act creating Wisconsin Territory and that specified in the Michigan Enabling Act. 270 U.S. 314. The evidence shows, and the master found: When these Acts were passed, there was no "main" or "most usual ship" channel. . . .

As it is impossible to identify any channel in the bay as that indicated by the Acts referred to, the intention of Congress must be otherwise ascertained. By principles of international law, that apply also to boundaries between States constituting this country, it is well established that when a navigable stream is a boundary between States the middle of the main channel, as distinguished from the geographical middle, limits the jurisdiction of each unless otherwise fixed by agreement or understanding between the parties. That rule rests upon equitable considerations and is intended to safeguard to each State equality of access and right of navigation in the stream. *Iowa* v. *Illinois*, 147 U.S. 1, 7. This court has held that, on occasion, the principle of the *Thalweg* is also applicable to bays, estuaries and other arms of the sea. *Louisiana* v. *Mississippi*, 202 U.S. 1, 50. *New Jersey* v. *Delaware*, 291 U.S. 361, 379.

International law

> *Wisconsin* v. *Michigan*, 295 U.S. (1935) 455, 460, 461; *Michigan* v. *Wisconsin*, 270 U.S. (1926) 295, 315, 316.

VARIOUS BAYS AND GULFS

§102

In the case of *Mortensen* v. *Peters* the High Court of Justiciary of Scotland was called upon to decide an appeal from a conviction of a Danish master of a Norwegian vessel for fishing in a prohibited manner at a point in the Moray Firth, outside of the three-mile limit but within an area closed against trawlers by the Herring Fishery Act of Scotland, 1889 (52 & 53 Vict. 23) and bylaws made pursuant thereto. The firth is a bay "about seventy-three miles wide at its mouth and over twenty miles deep". The appellate court, in upholding the jurisdiction of the lower court, said (the Lord Justice General speaking):

Moray Firth

I do not think I need say anything about what is known as the three-mile limit. It may be assumed that within the three miles the territorial sovereignty would be sufficient to cover any such legislation as the present. It is enough to say that that is not a proof of the counter proposition that outside the three miles no such result could be looked for. The locus, although outside the three-mile limit, is within the bay known as the Moray Firth, and the Moray Firth, say the respondents, is *intra fauces terrae*. Now, I cannot say that there is any definition of what *fauces terrae* exactly are. But there are at least three points which go far to show that this spot might be considered as lying therein.

1st. The dicta of the Scottish institutional writers seem to show that it would be no usurpation, according to the law of Scotland, so to consider it.

. . . .

2nd. The same statute puts forward claims to what are at least analogous places. If attention is paid to the schedule appended to section 6, many places will be found far beyond the three-mile limit—*e.g.*, the Firth of Clyde near its mouth. I am not ignoring that it may be said that this in one sense is proving *idem per idem*, but none the less I do not think the fact can be ignored.

3rd. There are many instances to be found in decided cases where the right of a nation to legislate for waters more or less landlocked or landembraced although beyond the three-mile limit has been admitted. They will be found collected in the case of the *Direct United States Cable Company* v. *Anglo-American Telegraph Company*, L.R. 2 App. Cas. 394, the bay there in question being Conception Bay, which has a width at the mouth of rather more than 20 miles.

It seems to me, therefore, without laying down the proposition that the Moray Firth is for every purpose within the territorial sovereignty, it can at least be clearly said that the appellant cannot make out his proposition that it is inconceivable that the British legislature should attempt for fishery regulation to legislate against all and sundry in such a place.

Lord Kyllachy concurring said:

It, however, seems to me vain to suggest that according to international law there is *any part* of the Moray Firth which is simply an area of open sea, and thus in the same position as if it were situated, say, in the middle of the German Ocean. For *prima facie*, at least, the whole Firth, is, as its name bears, a "bay" or "estuary", formed by two well-marked headlands, and stretching inwards for many miles into the heart of the country. All that can be said *contra* is only this—that at its outer end the Firth is very wide, and is of a size, if not also of a configuration, somewhat beyond what is usually characteristic of bays and estuaries. That may or may not be so. The cases of the Bristol Channel, the Firth of Clyde, and the Firth of Forth, would have to be considered before that proposition could be affirmed. But, be that as it may, the real question I apprehend is—whether, by international law, there is any recognised and established rule on the subject, particularly a rule so arbitrary and artificial as that of the ten-mile limit measure, for which the appellant contends.

Now as to that, it is, I think, enough to say that no such rule exists, or (which is the same thing), that we have not had presented to us any evidence of its existence. But I may add that, if negative authority may be invoked, there seems to me to be no better authority as to the existing position than the passage quoted at the discussion from Lord Blackburn's, or rather the Privy Council's, judgment in the *Conception Bay* case [*Direct United States Cable Co.* v. *Anglo-American Telegraph Co.*, L.R., 2 App. Cas. 420], in which, after reviewing existing authorities, their Lordships sum up the result thus—"It does not appear to their Lordships that jurists and text-writers are agreed what are the rules as to dimensions and configuration, which, apart from other considerations, would lead to the conclusion that a bay is or is not part of the territory of the State possessing the adjoining coasts, and it has never, that they can find, been made the ground of any judicial determination." It seems difficult in the face of this (the, I think, latest deliverance on the subject) to affirm that the statute and bye-law here in question are (if construed in the natural sense), in breach of plain and established rules of international law.

XLIII *Scottish Law Reporter* (1906) 872, 876, 878; VIII *Session Cases,* Court of Justiciary (1906) 93, 101, 102, 105; 1 A.J.I.L. (1907) 526, 534, 538. See also *post,* p. 712.

On July 13, 1906 the Canadian Parliament amended "The Fisheries Act" of 1904 (4 Edw. VII, c. 13) by adding thereto an additional subsection providing that the license fee payable for any Hudson Bay vessel or boat engaged in the whale fishery or hunting whales within the waters of Hudson Bay should be $50 a year and that, "inasmuch as Hudson Bay is wholly territorial water of Canada", the requirements as to licensing and fees "shall apply to every vessel . . . in any part of the waters of Hudson Bay, whether such vessel or boat belong to Canada, or is registered and outfitted in, or commences her voyage from, any other British or foreign country". (6 Edw. VII, c. 13.)

In October 1906, in response to an inquiry "whether any treaty exists with Canada under which United States vessels are permitted to fish in the waters of Hudson Bay, or whether the waters of Hudson Bay proper, as well as Ungava Bay and James Bay are international waters outside the three mile limit", the Department of State explained that the "rights of American citizens to fish in Hudson Bay are limited by the provisions of the treaty of 1818 between the United States and Great Britain" by article I of which it was agreed "that the inhabitants of the United States shall have liberty to take fish on certain clearly defined parts of the coast of Newfoundland and Labrador, and on the southern shores of the Magdalen Islands, and the United States renounced forever any liberty theretofore enjoyed or claimed by its inhabitants to take, dry or cure fish on or within three marine miles of His Britannic Majesty's dominions in America not so defined", and that under this treaty stipulation "citizens of the United States have no right to whale or fish in the waters of Hudson Bay within three marine miles of the shore". It added:

> Except insofar as this limitation operates, our vessels have, under the law of nations, the right to fish whale anywhere in the high seas off any British coast. As to the scope of the limitation in the treaty, the two governments have differently construed the phrase—"within three marine miles of any of the coasts, bays, creeks or harbors", the British Government contending in the case of bays, that the prescribed distance of three miles is to be measured from the headlands or extreme points of land next the entrance to the bays, and the United States claiming that the phrase indicates an imaginary line three miles distant and following the sinuosities of the shore. In the case of the American schooner *Washington*, which came before the United States and British Claims Commission under the Convention of 1853, the declaration was adverse to the British contention, and it is understood that the British Government has abandoned the "headland" theory as applied to large bodies of water.
>
> In any event, with respect to Hudson Bay, which is a body of water 900 miles long by 600 miles wide, and connected with the Atlantic Ocean by a strait about 400 miles in length and varying from 60 to 100 miles in width, the United States will take the position that citizens of the United States have the right to whale and fish within its waters outside the three mile limit.

The Second Assistant Secretary (Adee) to Mr. Ludwig Wurzburg, Oct. 8, 1906, MS. Department of State, minor file, vol. 62.

Article 3 of the peace treaty between Finland and the Russian Socialist Federal Soviet Republic, signed at Dorpat (Tartu) on October 14, 1920, provided, with certain exceptions: **Gulf of Finland**

> The breadth of the territorial waters of the contracting Powers in the Gulf of Finland shall be four nautical miles from the coast, and, in an archipelago, from the last islet or rock above sea level.

3 League of Nations Treaty Series (1921) 6, 66. Finland and the U.S.S.R. concluded an agreement on July 28, 1923 concerning the maintenance of order in the parts of the Gulf of Finland situated outside of territorial waters, the upkeep of maritime installations, and the pilotage service in the gulf. 32 *idem* (1925) 102, 112. For views of textwriters as to the status of the waters of the Gulf of Finland, which is over 40 miles wide at the

> mouth, see Jessup, *Law of Territorial Waters and Maritime Jurisdiction* (1927) 397.

On August 5, 1914 the United States concluded a convention with Nicaragua—known as the Bryan-Chamorro convention—by the terms of which Nicaragua granted in perpetuity to the United States the—

> exclusive proprietary rights necessary and convenient for the construction, operation and maintenance of an inter-oceanic canal by way of the San Juan River and the great Lake of Nicaragua or by way of any route over Nicaraguan territory, the details of the terms upon which such canal shall be constructed, operated and maintained to be agreed to by the two governments whenever the Government of the United States shall notify the Government of Nicaragua of its desire or intention to construct such canal. [Art. 1.]

The convention further provided that to enable the Government of the United States to protect—

> the Panama Canal and the proprietary rights granted to the Government of the United States by the foregoing article [meaning art. 1], and also to enable the Government of the United States to take any measure necessary to the ends contemplated herein, the Government of Nicaragua hereby leases for a term of ninety-nine years to the Government of the United States the islands in the Caribbean Sea known as Great Corn Island and Little Corn Island; and the Government of Nicaragua further grants to the Government of the United States for a like period of ninety-nine years the right to establish, operate and maintain a naval base at such place on the territory of Nicaragua bordering upon the Gulf of Fonseca as the Government of the United States may select. [Art. 2.]

Gulf of
Fonseca

In consideration of the foregoing the Government of the United States paid to Nicaragua the sum of $3,000,000 (art 3).

The Senate of the United States gave its consent to the ratification of the convention with the proviso that—

> whereas, Costa Rica, Salvador and Honduras have protested against the ratification of said Convention in the fear or belief that said Convention might in some respect impair existing rights of said States; therefore, it is declared by the Senate that in advising and consenting to the ratification of the said Convention as amended such advice and consent are given with the understanding, to be expressed as a part of the instrument of ratification, that nothing in said Convention is intended to affect any existing right of any of the said named States.

Nicaragua having accepted the understanding expressed by the Senate, the ratifications of the convention were exchanged on June 22, 1916.

3 Treaties, etc. (Redmond, 1923) 2740, 2741, 2742.

Subsequently, El Salvador protested against the 1914 convention to the Governments of Nicaragua and the United States and in 1916 instituted an action against Nicaragua in the Central American Court of Justice (established by the Central American states under an agreement entered into on December 20, 1907), alleging (1) that the establishment of a naval base by a powerful state in the immediate vicinity of El Salvador constituted "a serious menace to its free and independent life"; (2) that the Bryan-Chamorro convention "ignores and violates the rights of dominion [co-ownership] which Salvador has in the Gulf of Fonseca"; (3) that the convention "injures the primary interests of Salvador as a Central American State"; (4) that the convention was contrary to the treaty of peace and friendship signed by the Central American republics in 1907; (5) that "the treaty cannot be legally consummated" under article 2 of the Nicaraguan Constitution; and (6) that the Government of El Salvador had endeavored to discuss with Nicaragua its opposition to the Bryan-Chamorro convention "without success". In support of the argument that El Salvador, Honduras, and Nicaragua had co-ownership of the Gulf of Fonseca, El Salvador urged:

> (a) That because, for a long period of years, those waters belonged to a single political entity, to wit, the Spanish Colonial Government in Central America, and later, to the Federal Republic of the Center of America, the fact conclusively results that, on the dissolution of the federation without having effected a delimitation among the three riparian States of their sovereignty therein, the ownership of those waters continued in common in those three States.
> (b) That it matters not that in the year 1900, . . . the Governments of Honduras and Nicaragua fixed a divisionary line between the two countries in the waters of the Gulf; because that act was brought about without the intervention of El Salvador.

El Salvador petitioned the court to "fix the situation in which the Government of Nicaragua must remain . . . pending a final decision" and "in the final judgment" compel Nicaragua "to abstain from fulfilling the Bryan-Chamorro treaty."

The Government of Nicaragua took the position that it did "not dispute, or cast doubt upon, the perfectly evident fact that the Bay of Fonseca is a closed or territorial bay", but it denied that "that characteristic attaches to it by reason of the fact that the three States adjacent to the Gulf . . . formerly belonged to a single international political entity, for, besides the fact that the said States preserved their autonomy, independence and even sovereignty whilst in the federation, the true reason underlying that characteristic is

that the Gulf of Fonseca is *small in extent*, and, therefore, belongs to
the nations that own its coasts".

1916 For. Rel. 853–862; 11 A.J.I.L. (1917) 674, 677; 1907 For. Rel. 697.

In its judgment of March 9, 1917 the Central American court held,
inter alia: (1) that the Gulf of Fonseca is an "historical bay and
with the character of a closed sea", that the Government of Nicaragua
in agreeing to a concession for the establishment of a naval base
"violated the right of joint ownership which El Salvador holds in
the Gulf of Fonseca", and that the establishment of a naval base by
its nature and transcendency compromises the safety of El Salvador;
(2) that the Bryan-Chamorro convention "violates Articles 2 and 9
of the Treaty of Peace and Amity" of December 20, 1907; and (3)
that the Government of Nicaragua was obliged "to reestablish and
maintain the legal status which existed before the Bryan-Chamorro
Treaty".

> 1917 For. Rel. 1101–1104.
>
> Article 2 of the 1907 treaty between the Central American states dealt
> with the altering of the "constitutional organization" in any of the
> Central American republics, while article 9 dealt with national treat-
> ment of merchant vessels of the respective countries engaged in trade
> in territories of the other. 1907 For. Rel. 692, 693, 694. This treaty
> was superseded by the 1923 general treaty of peace and amity, articles
> 2 and 8 of which contain provisions similar to those in articles 2 and 9
> of the 1907 treaty. *Conference on Central American Affairs, Washington,
> December 4, 1922–February 7, 1923* (1923) 287, 288, 291, 294. The treaty
> has since been denounced by Costa Rica and El Salvador, effective as of
> Jan. 1, 1934. Department of State, Treaty Information Bulletin 39 (Dec.
> 1932) 4–5. The treaty remained effective as to Guatemala, Honduras,
> and Nicaragua. *Ibid.*

The Minister of Foreign Affairs of Honduras addressed a communication to the Government of El Salvador on September 30,
1916, while the Salvadoran case against Nicaragua was pending in
the court, protesting against "the pretended right of codomination
[joint ownership] which is alleged by the Government" of El Salvador in its demand against the Government of Nicaragua, and
stating that his purpose was "to declare, as my Government has
already formally declared, that she does not recognize and has not
recognized, any state of codomination with Salvador, nor with any
other Republic, in the waters of Fonseca Bay which correspond to
Honduras". In the same communication, the Honduran Minister
of Foreign Affairs pointed out that in 1900 Honduras and Nicaragua had determined by a commission the boundary line between
them in the Gulf of Fonseca, that this boundary still subsisted, and
that at no time had El Salvador "given any objection to the valid-

ity of the same". He further pointed out that "Article 13 of the Law of Salvador on navigation and waters" states:

> The territorial waters of the Republic are divided into five maritime departments, in the following manner:
> 1. Maritime Department of La Union, composing the Bay of Conchagua, that part of the Gulf of Fonseca in which are situated the Salvadorian Islands, and the territorial waters as far as the parallel of the eastern mouth of the San Miguel.

During the course of the arbitration Nicaraguan counsel referred to the attempt made by El Salvador in 1884 to negotiate a boundary convention fixing the maritime boundary between El Salvador and Honduras and to the fact that that convention was not carried into effect, because of the failure of the Honduran Congress to approve it.

1916 For. Rel. 890, 891; 11 A.J.I.L. (1917) 674, 688.

In a circular note, dated November 24, 1917, sent by Nicaragua to the Central American governments for the purpose of explaining the reasons for its rejection of this and another decision of the Central American Court, the Nicaraguan Government quoted the Honduran note to the Government of El Salvador, just referred to, and stated that "The points embraced in the protest of the Honduran Government against the joint dominion . . . coincide with the answer given by my Government to the Salvadorean suit in regard to this point." The answer of the Nicaraguan Government stated:

> While my Government realizes the dominion and possession of the three countries in the Gulf of Fonseca, which date back to the beginnings of the conquest of the American Continent, it absolutely denies that this dominion and possession have been exercised in COMMON or have constituted A COMMUNITY (of possession) BETWEEN THE SAID REPUBLICS. No legal technicality warrants considering as a community (of possession) the coexistence of contiguous sovereign countries between which the boundary line has not yet been marked, nor is the use of such terms warranted by the circumstance of concurrence or adjacency of the territories of Nicaragua, Honduras, and El Salvador to the waters of said Gulf, for what really occurred for a long time on account of this situation was that the territorial part belonging to each of the three Republics had not been separated by a formal demarkation of boundaries.

MS. Department of State, file 817.812/322.

On January 19, 1925 the German trawler *Heinrich Augustin* was seized by the Swedish gunboat *Svensksund*, 1.4 distance-minutes from an imaginary line drawn from the Tylö Lighthouse to Halland's Väderö Lighthouse, a distance of some twelve miles, at the en- Laholm Bay trance to Laholm Bay. The court of first instance at Halmstad, in deciding as to the right of aliens to fish at a place which the complainant maintained was Swedish territorial waters and which the defendant contended was high seas, said:

> The exposition of both sides has not given any definite guidance for deciding how the limit of Swedish territorial waters at Laholm Bay was determined in former days according to the Swedish law.
>
> However, in the convention between Sweden and Denmark, July 14, 1899, regarding fishing rights in the waters of these countries, the contracting parties proceeded on the basis that unless agreement was made to the contrary the fishing privileges in the whole Bay of Laholm should be reserved for Swedish citizens to a distance of one geographical mile outside of a straight line drawn from Halland's Väderö lighthouse to Tylö lighthouse. By the convention a special concession was made to Danish fishermen who were to be permitted to fish ¼ geographical mile within the outer limit. The fact that Denmark, who is Sweden's closest neighbor in regard to the fishing waters in question and at the time of the convention was undoubtedly more than any other foreign Power interested in keeping Laholm Bay open for fishing, accepted the above stipulations, without doubt gives strong support to the assumption that the Swedish Crown even before the convention maintained the conception in regard to the extension of Swedish territorial waters which was embodied in the convention.
>
> Furthermore, inasmuch as it has not been proven that the Crown at any later date has failed to uphold the same view, it may be considered as clearly demonstrated that the Crown for a considerable period has treated as Swedish fishing waters the whole Bay of Laholm within a line drawn between Halland's Väderö lighthouse and Tylö lighthouse and in addition a region situated within one geographical mile outside of this boundary.
>
> Under such circumstances and inasmuch as the Crown must be considered as having the power to determine as it has the extent of Swedish fishing waters, the region in question must be considered as Swedish waters, and as it is indisputable that the defendant on the 19th of January, 1925, with his ship was trawling within said region, and that the ship was apprehended within the same region,
>
> The Magistrate's Court finds the defendant guilty.

The decision of the court of first instance was appealed to the Göta Court of Appeal at Jönköping, which remitted the fine for illegal fishing but, for the rest, confirmed the decision of the court of first instance. A further appeal was taken to the Swedish Supreme Court which, in affirming the decision of the lower court, stated:

On the grounds established at the magistrate's court, the place where the apprehension of the trawler took place must be considered as being within Swedish territorial waters.

Minister Bliss to Secretary Kellogg, Mar. 10 and 21, 1925, MS. Department of State, files 858.0145/3, 858.0145/4; Minister Harrison to Mr. Kellogg, Dec. 7, 1927, ibid. file 858.0145/7; Till frågan om gränsen för sveriges territorialvatten (1928) 35, 120–121, translation; 24 A.J.I.L. (1930) 776, 779, 783.

In the case of *The J. Duffy*, a suit instituted for the forfeiture of a British schooner and her cargo of intoxicating liquors, Judge Thomas stated that the exact place where the arrest of the vessel occurred was doubtful but that, in view of the conclusions reached, it was immaterial. He said: *Long Island Sound*

. . . I hold that the waters of Long Island Sound proper are territorial waters and that our municipal law reaches over them.

The decision of the court was reversed on appeal so far as it held that there was no violation of section 593(*b*) of the Tariff Act of 1922 (42 Stat. 858, 982), but the Circuit Court of Appeals agreed that the waters of Long Island Sound were "territorial waters of the United States".

The J. Duffy, United States v. 2802 Cases Scotch Whisky, etc., 14 F. (2d) 426 (D. Conn. 1926); 18 F. (2d) 754, 755 (C.C.A. 2d, 1927). In Annual Digest, 1925–26, p. 126, the report of the case is followed by this note:

"NOTE.—Although the expression 'territorial waters' was used by the Court, it is submitted that 'national', that is 'internal, waters' is intended. The waters of Long Island Sound include the waters between the mainland and Long Island off New York City and are from 100 to 125 miles long and from 10 to 25 miles wide. They are not 'territorial' in the sense that the three-mile belt is."

In the case of *The Fagernes*, decided by the English Court of Appeal in 1927, Lord Justice Lawrence stated in the course of his separate opinion: *Bristol Channel*

It is common ground that there is no international treaty or convention expressly sanctioning or recognizing any territorial rights of the Crown over the Bristol Channel. Further, no evidence has been adduced that the Crown has possessed itself of, or has effectively asserted any territorial rights over, that part of the Bristol Channel where the collision occurred. In the absence of any express treaty or controlling executive act of the Government, the question arises whether there is any established general rule of international law for determining the territorial character of bays. . . .
. . . in my judgment the Attorney-General has established the proposition that, although the principle of claiming territorial rights over bays is well established as a rule of interna-

tional law, and although there is no question as to the applicability of that principle in the case of bays, the entire land boundaries of which form part of the territory of the same State and the entrances of which do not exceed six sea miles in width, yet there is no recognized general rule of international law by which it can be determined whether any given bay, with an entrance wider than six sea miles, does or does not form part of the territory of the State whose shores form its land boundary. Each such case must depend upon its own special circumstances.

[1927] P. 311, 327.

In 1927 the chairman of the International Fisheries Commission, United States and Mexico, requested, on behalf of certain fishermen, the opinion of the Department of State as to what would be considered the high seas in the Gulf of California. The Department replied:

Gulf of California

> . . . You add that these fishermen feel that they might find it necessary to go into the Gulf for protection in case of storm and still want to remain technically on the high seas.
>
> The approximate dimensions of the Gulf of California, the Department understands, measured on a large scale hydrographic chart are:
>
> > Width at southern end (Arena Point to Altata) approximately 103 nautical miles.
> > Length of the Gulf, approximately 565 nautical miles.
> > Width at narrowest part, mainland to mainland; (San Gabriel Point to San Miguel Point) approximately 47 nautical miles.
>
> In the absence of any accepted standard as to their size and conformation, it is difficult to determine in any given case whether a bay, gulf or recess in a coast line can be regarded as territorial waters. Under the applicable general principles of international law, however, as evidenced by writers on the subject, it may be stated that gulfs and bays surrounded by land of one and the same littoral State whose entrance is of such a width that it cannot be commanded by coast batteries are regarded as non-territorial. The Gulf of California has apparently not been discussed by such authorities, but the width of the Gulf leaves little doubt that it should be regarded as a part of the open sea, with the exception, of course, of the inside, marginal belts of territorial water.

Chairman O'Malley to Secretary Kellogg, Feb. 15, 1927, and Under Secretary Grew to Mr. O'Malley, Mar. 16, 1927, MS. Department of State, file 711.128/71.

Bay of Monterey

The question whether a ship engaged in fishing within the headlands of the Bay of Monterey more than three nautical miles from low-water mark along the shore line thereof was within the territorial boundaries of the State of California and subject to its laws, was passed upon by the Supreme Court of California in the case of *Ocean Industries, Inc.* v. *The Superior Court of Santa Cruz County et al.*, decided in 1927. After stating that it would take judicial notice of the political history of the world, and after relating the early history of the Spanish conquest of that part of North America and the discovery of the Bay of Monterey, the court said:

> . . . The bay of Monterey, thus designated from its first discovery as a "bay", is a body of water having headlands approximately eighteen miles apart, with receding shores, giving a total width of twenty-two miles inside the headlands, with a total depth of approximately nine miles. It thus satisfies the definition of a "bay" given by the lexicographers as a body of water around which the land forms a curve; or a recess or inlet between capes or headlands. (Webster, Title "Bay.")

It was held that "the entire bay of Monterey within its headlands and thence into the ocean for a distance of three nautical miles" is within the jurisdiction of the State of California, the court stating:

> The petitioner, however, insists that by the rules of international law the territorial jurisdiction of a maritime state does not extend beyond 3 miles from the shore line, and follows the indentations of the coast into all bays or gulfs, the headlands of which are more than 6 miles apart, and cites certain text-writers upon international law in support of that contention. These text-writers give as the reason for this rule the somewhat fantastic one that, while our modern international law was in the process of forming, the range of coast planted cannon did not exceed 3 miles. These text-writers, however, while suggesting such a rule based upon such a long-lost reason, admit that as to the stronger maritime powers of modern Europe the rule was more honored in the breach than in the observance. Britain, which has depended more upon its "Wooden Walls" than upon its coast ordnance, has always asserted its sovereignty, not only over the entire area of the bays, ports, harbors, firths, and other inlets along its much indented coast line, but also over the bays, gulfs, and inlets of its dependencies; such, for example, as the Bay of Conception in Newfoundland, which has a breadth of 15 miles. These text-writers also point out that France has always asserted sovereignty over the Bay of Cancale, which is 17 miles wide at its headlands, and that the United States asserts and has maintained its jurisdiction over the Bays of Delaware and Chesapeake, although the former has a headland width of 15, and the latter of 12 miles. . . . While it is true that by treaties and conventions between the powers chiefly in arbitration cases the fixation of a 6-mile distance between headlands of certain bays and inlets have at times been agreed upon in the settlement of international disputes, it cannot be said that there is any rule of international law upon the subject; the whole matter resting in the undisputed assertion of jurisdiction by the power of

Conception Bay

Delaware and Chesapeake Bays

possessing the inclosing shore line of the bay or inlet in question. This being so, we arrived at the conclusion that the Bay of Monterey between its headlands and the ocean adjacent to a line drawn between these headlands for a distance of 3 nautical miles is within the boundaries of the state of California and of the counties respectively of Santa Cruz and Monterey.

200 Cal. (1927) 235, 241, 245; 252 Pac. 722, 724, 725–726.

The Constitutional Law Court for the German Reich (Staats-gerichtshof) in rendering a decision in the case of *Lübeck* v. *Mecklenburg-Schwerin*, involving a boundary dispute as to Lübeck Bay, said:

Lübeck Bay

> In the first place, as far as the legal bases for the decision to be made are concerned, the view defended by Mecklenburg-Schwerin in conjunction with its experts, Langfeld, v. Gierke and Wenzel is to be rejected: it is that in the case of inlets of the sea with several riparian states, the middle lines drawn from the shore boundaries form the boundaries of the states on the water, according to generally recognized principles of international law. To be sure, it is also defended by several other teachers of international law, but frequently not without mention of the fact that it is objected to (thus for example B. Hatschek, *Völkerrecht*, page 199; the same, *Völkerrecht im Grundriss*, page 94; Strupp, *Theorie und Praxis des Völkerrechts*, section 8, No. 6b, page 43) . . . No general rules are recognized in international law, neither can they be drawn up, because the relations and the needs of the riparian states may be of many and different kinds. Historical development, which in this very case assumes special significance, may have led to a very different result. It may be possible under this that each riparian state possesses territorial sovereignty over a portion of the bay; but it is also possible that the states may exercise undivided territorial sovereignty jointly over the whole bay; it is also conceivable that no full territorial sovereignty has arisen at all and that the bay maintains rather the nature of coastal waters. And lastly, it is not precluded that one of the riparian states may have territorial sovereignty over the whole bay (see also Stoerk in Holtzendorff's *Handbuch*, volume II, page 468, and Niemeyer in his *Völkerrecht*, Sammlung Göschen, page 111). This view, that historical development and actual conditions are to be given decisive significance with regard to sovereignty in the case of bays with several riparian states, has also been defended constantly by the German Reich in negotiations with the Netherlands regarding the Wattenmeer on the lower Ems. The standpoint of Lübeck with regard to the principle is therefore the right one. This view leads also to the opinion that in one and the same part of an inlet of the sea territorial sovereignty may belong to one riparian state in one direction and to another riparian state in another direction, as in international law the boundaries for territorial sovereignty over coastal waters are not infrequently determined in different ways according to

their different emanations (sovereignty over fishing, sovereignty over customs).

With respect to rights in relation to navigation the court stated that—

Navigation

the Constitutional Law Court also considers that proof has been furnished with respect to sovereignty over navigation, that since time immemorial Lübeck has been in possession thereof, and in fact over all the disputed portion of Lübeck Bay as far as the mouth of the Harkenbeck, so that to this extent also the first motion of Lübeck is to be granted. Accordingly, Lübeck retains the possibility of regulating her maritime navigation in future also as may suit the needs at any time, without having to fear an objection by Mecklenburg-Schwerin.

To be sure, doubts may exist as to the delimitation on the seaward side, for as has already been mentioned, how far Lübeck's ownership extends cannot be determined exactly either with respect to sovereignty over navigation or sovereignty over fishing. In this case considerations of expedience must form the deciding factor, and stress is to be laid on the idea that, to avoid a clash of interest, the boundary for sovereignty over fishing and over navigation must be the same. Further, it is found to be necessary to draw the boundary correctly with regard to the needs of shipping. Therefore the line from the mouth of the Harkenbeck to Haffkrugerfeld, which otherwise might be considered, must be eliminated as not distinguishable in that location. Consequently the Constitutional Law Court decides in favor of the boundary line from the mouth of the Harkenbeck to the tower of Gömnitz and the perpendicular dropped on this line from the Brodten boundary stake, corresponding to the proposal of Lübeck.

The court also stated:

But aside from sovereignty over fishing and that over navigation, Lübeck's first motion cannot be granted in its full extent, for it has not been proved that Lübeck possessed from time immemorial all rights arising out of territorial sovereignty. . . .

In paragraph I of its Order for the protection of the shores and dunes of the coast of the Baltic Sea at Rosenhagen, Berendorf, et cetera, of October 10, 1874, Mecklenburg-Schwerin has laid claim plainly to territorial sovereignty along its coast and extending into the sea, by prohibiting the digging of sand, gravel, clay, or loam, the cutting of ordinary grass, sand grass or other growth, and the removal of seaweed or stones, without permission of the authorities, in the dune region or along the high banks along the sea coast, and also for a distance of 400 meters out into the Baltic Sea, and Lübeck publicly proclaimed this ordinance in Travemünde, upon request. It must be concluded from this that at that time Lübeck neither believed that it had full territorial sovereignty as far as the Mecklenburg-Schwerin coast nor did it actually have such sovereignty. On the other hand, at that time and in that place Mecklenburg-Schwerin was in possession of limited territorial sovereignty.

The data submitted are not sufficient for further determinations. Under such circumstances the Constitutional Law Court considers it advisable and necessary for the protection of the interests of both parties to divide the waters of the Bay disputed between them, aside from sovereignty over fishing and navigation, in such a way that the western part is placed under the territorial sovereignty of Lübeck and the eastern part under the territorial sovereignty of Mecklenburg-Schwerin.

122 *Entscheidungen des Reichsgerichts in Zivilsachen* (1929), App., pp. 1, 6, 11, translation. The dispute in this case arose as a result of a police order of Mecklenburg-Schwerin of Feb. 23, 1925 for the protection of fishery in the coastal waters of Travemünde Bay, the innermost portion of Lübeck Bay, which permitted fishing in that part of the bay only to independent Mecklenburg fishermen. *Regierungsblatt für Mecklenburg-Schwerin* (1925) 57.

With reference to events subsequent to the rendering of the opinion in the case of *Mortensen* v. *Peters*, discussed *ante*, pp. 698–700, the following statement is made by Jessup:

"Apparently the Norwegian Government made no protest in this case, and for a time foreign trawlers steered clear of the Firth.[65]   ([65] Fulton *op. cit.* [*The Sovereignty of the Sea* (1911)] p. 727.)   But they soon returned in larger numbers. Six masters were convicted of contravening the by-laws (more than three miles from shore); five were imprisoned for failure to pay the fine of one hundred pounds. At the trial, the Norwegian Vice-Consul read a protest under instructions from the Foreign Minister of Norway against the conviction of the masters of three of these vessels provided it appeared that they were charged with trawling outside territorial limits. Dr. Nansen, the Norwegian Minister in London, also made representations to the British Foreign Office, and ten days after the trial, the men were released and the fines remitted.

"The case is robbed of some of its international significance because most of the trawlers had been registered under the Norwegian flag by British subjects who sought by this fraudulent means to obtain protection for fishing in the Moray Firth. With these fishermen the Norwegian Government had no sympathy and accordingly after making a formal protest, it warned all owners of Norwegian trawlers not to fish in the Firth and not to expect Government support if they did so and were punished in Scotland. Nevertheless, the British Government decided not to continue to enforce the regulations against foreigners.

"The question of the fishery control in the Moray Firth was extensively debated in the British Parliament.

.   .   .   .   .

"It seems clear that the policy of the British Government was largely dictated by the realization that any extensive pretensions in their own waters would meet with reciprocal claims off foreign shores. The resulting injury to British fishing interests in general would have been greater than that occasioned by foreign trawling in the Moray Firth.

"In conclusion it must be stated that Great Britain does not claim the Moray Firth as part of British territorial waters."

Jessup, *Law of Territorial Waters and Maritime Jurisdiction* (1927) 430, 434, 436.

BOUNDARIES

GENERAL PRINCIPLES

§103

A decision was rendered on October 23, 1909, by an arbitral tribunal selected pursuant to the terms of a *compromis* of March 14, 1908 between Norway and Sweden, providing for submission to arbitration of a difference with reference to part of the maritime boundary between the two states so far as it had not been determined by a Royal resolution of March 15, 1904 issued before the dissolution of their union in 1905. Article 3 of the *compromis* provided that the tribunal should decide whether or not "the boundary-line shall be considered to be, either wholly or in part, determined by the boundary treaty of 1661, together with the chart appertaining to the same" and, if not, "to determine the same, taking into account the circumstances of fact and the principles of international law". ^{The *Grisbadarna* case}

Having found that beyond a certain point the boundary had not been fixed by the treaty of 1661, the tribunal proceeded to determine the uncertain part of the boundary and said:

> Whereas, in this connection, the parties have adopted, at least in practice, the rule of making the division along the median line drawn between the islands, islets, and reefs situated on both sides and not constantly submerged, as having been in their opinion the rule which was applied on this side of point A by the treaty of 1661; ^{Median line}
>
> The adoption of a rule on such grounds should, without regard to the question whether the rule invoked was really applied by said treaty, have as a logical consequence, in applying it at the present time, that one should take into account at the same time the circumstances of fact which existed at the time of the treaty; ^{Contemporaneous circumstances}

The tribunal fixed the boundary according to the principles of law in force at the time when the original boundary treaty was made. It stated that "it is a settled principle of the law of nations that a state of things which actually exists and has existed for a long time should be changed as little as possible"; pointed out that this rule is particularly applicable in a case involving private interests; and called attention to the fact that lobster fishing was the most important fishing on the Grisbadarna (Grisbådarne) banks, that this fishing was the very thing that gave the banks their value as fisheries, and that the Swedes were first to fish for lobster by means of the tackle and craft necessary to engage in fishing as far out at sea as the banks in question. It awarded the Grisbadarna banks to Sweden. In considering the state of things which it found had actually existed for a long time, the tribunal referred to acts of ownership and possession ^{*Status quo*}

exercised by the two Governments and, in this connection, took into account the maintenance of lifeboats and beacons and expense of measurements of regions.

> The *Grisbadarna* case (Norway and Sweden), Scott, *Hague Court Reports* (1916) 122, 126, 130, 134, 487; *ibid.* 133, 496 (convention of 1908); *ibid.* 136, 500 (Royal resolution of Mar. 15, 1904). The tribunal awarded the Skjöttegrunde to Norway. *Ibid.* 132–133.

The *Island of Timor* case

Under the terms of a treaty of April 20, 1859, providing for the division of the island of Timor between the Netherlands and Portugal, certain parts of territory belonging to the Netherlands within the boundaries were assigned to Portugal and *vice versa*, in order to avoid the division of native tribes. These so-called "enclaves" were abolished by a treaty signed on June 10, 1893, creating a commission for the establishment of the boundary. In order to settle the part of the boundary regarding which the commission had not arrived at an agreement, the two countries concluded a convention on October 1, 1904. However, determination of part of the boundary relating to a Portuguese enclave formerly within Dutch territory was left to a mixed commission. The commissioners were unable to agree and thereafter the two Governments concluded a convention, dated April 3, 1913, referring the dispute to a sole arbitrator chosen from the membership of the Permanent Court of Arbitration. On June 25, 1914 the arbitrator (Charles Édouard Lardy, of Switzerland) rendered an award in accordance with the contentions of the Netherlands. After quoting Heffter and Rivier to the effect that in case of doubt treaties ought to be interpreted "conformably with the real mutual intention", the arbitrator said:

> It now remains only to apply these rules to the circumstances of the case.
>
> .   .   .   .
>
> 10. The summit line proposed by the Government of the Netherlands between the source of the river Kabun (Lèos) to the south, and the source of the Noèl Meto to the north is sufficiently natural to be surveyed on land without great practical difficulties. It offers the advantage that the watercourses uniformly descend from that summit line toward the territories placed wholly under Dutch sovereignty. The survey suggested by the Portuguese Government, on the contrary, would attribute the upper and the lower part of these several streams to different sovereignties.
>
> .   .   .   .

Equity

> 12. Finally, if we take the point of view of equity, which it is important not to lose sight of in international relations, the summit line proposed by the Netherlands is not contrary to equity, in the sense that Portugal will receive more territory than it had reason to hope for. . . . If, or

the contrary, the eastern survey suggested by the Portuguese Government were adopted, the Netherlands could rightfully allege that they were being deprived of almost all the territory which theoretically was granted to them.

The arbitrator also stated that "Conventions between States . . . ought to be interpreted 'rather in the sense in which they can have some effect than in the sense in which they can produce none'."

> Scott, *Hague Court Reports* (1916) 355, 366, 383, 384; *ibid.* 390, 599 (treaty of 1859); *ibid.* 393, 601 (treaty of 1893); *ibid.* 396, 604 (convention of 1904); *ibid.* 387, 596 (convention of Apr. 3, 1913).

On January 19, 1920 the Supreme Council of the Principal Allied and Associated Powers agreed to recognize the government of the Armenian State as a *de facto* government on the condition that the recognition should not prejudge the question of the eventual frontier. The United States recognized the *de facto* government of the Armenian Republic on April 23, 1920, on the condition that the territorial frontiers should be left for later determination. The Supreme Council proposed that the President of the United States should arbitrate the question of the boundary between Turkey and Armenia. *[margin: Turkish-Armenian boundary]*

On May 17, 1920 the Secretary of State informed the American Ambassador in France that the President had agreed to act as arbitrator and, on November 22, 1920, President Wilson sent to the President of the Supreme Council of the Allied Powers a letter accompanied by his decision regarding the boundary. In explaining in his letter the broad principles which he took into account in his determination of the frontier, the President said:

> . . . According to the terms of the arbitral reference set forth in Part III, Section 6, Article 89, of the Treaty of Sèvres, the scope of the arbitral competence assigned to me is clearly limited to the determination of the frontiers of Turkey and Armenia in the Vilayets of Erzerum, Trebizond, Van and Bitlis. . . .
>
> In approaching this problem it was obvious that the existing ethnic and religious distribution of the populations in the four vilayets could not, as in other parts of the world, be regarded as the guiding element of the decision . . . The limitation of the arbitral assignment to the four vilayets named in Article 89 of the treaty made it seem a duty and an obligation that as large an area within these vilayets be granted to the Armenian state as could be done, while meeting the basic requirements of an adequate natural frontier and of geographic and economic unity for the new state. . . . The conflicting territorial desires of Armenians, Turks, Kurds and Greeks along the boundaries assigned to my arbitral decision could not always be harmonized. In such cases it was my belief that consideration of a healthy economic life for the future state of Armenia should be decisive. *[margin: Ethnic and religious grounds]* *[margin: Adequate frontier; geographic and economic unity]*

Where, however, the requirements of a correct geographic boundary permitted, all mountain and valley districts along the border which were predominantly Kurdish or Turkish have been left to Turkey rather than assigned to Armenia, unless trade relations with definite market towns threw them necessarily into the Armenian state. Wherever information upon tribal relations and seasonal migrations was obtainable, the attempt was made to respect the integrity of tribal groupings and nomad pastoral movements.

Natural barriers; ethnographic considerations

From the Persian border southwest of the town of Kotur the boundary line of Armenia is determined by a rugged natural barrier of great height. . . . The sound physiographic reasons which seemed to justify this decision was further strengthened by the ethnographic consideration. . . . The control of these headwaters should be kept, wherever possible, within the domain of the two interested states, Turkey and Mesopotamia. For these reasons the Armenian claim upon the upper valley of the Great Zab could not be satisfied.

Security

The boundary upon the west from Bitlis and Mush northward to the vicinity of Erzingan lies well within Bitlis and Erzerum vilayets. It follows a natural geographic barrier, which furnishes Armenia with perfect security. . . .

Access to sea

From the northern border of the Dersim the nature and direction of the frontier decision was primarily dependent upon the vital question of supplying an adequate access to the sea for the state of Armenia.

.   .   .   .

the arrangements providing for Armenia's access to the sea must be such as to offer every possibility for the development of this state as one capable of reassuming and maintaining that useful role in the commerce of the world which its geographical position, athwart a great historic trade route, assigned to it in the past.

Ambassador Wallace to Secretary Lansing, Jan. 19, 1920, MS. Department of State, file 763.72119/8740; Secretary Colby to the Representative of the Armenian Republic (Pasdermadjian), Apr. 23, 1920, *ibid.* 860j01/242a; Ambassador Johnson to Mr. Colby, Apr. 27, 1920, *ibid.* 763.72119/9749; Mr. Colby to Mr. Wallace, Nov. 24, 1920, *ibid.* 760j6715/61. For the President's letter of Nov. 22, 1920, see 1920 For. Rel., vol. III, p. 790; for his decision fixing in detail the boundary line, see *ibid.* 795.

Teschen agreement

The dispute between Poland and Czechoslovakia regarding the limits of their sovereignty over the Duchy of Teschen (Cieszyn) and the territory of Orava and Spisz was settled by an agreement, signed on July 28, 1920 by representatives of Czechoslovakia and the Principal Allied Powers, which, after fixing the boundary line in detail, created a boundary commission composed of a representative of each of the Principal Allied Powers as well as of Poland and Czechoslovakia "to trace on the spot the frontier line", and provided:

The Commission shall have full power to propose to the Conference of Ambassadors such modifications as may seem to it to be justified by the interests of individuals or of communities in the neighborhood of the frontier line taking into account special local circumstances.

The Polish representative (Mr. Paderewski) signed the agreement on July 30, 1920.

On March 15, 1923 the Council of Ambassadors rendered a decision with regard to the Polish frontiers in harmony with the assertions of territorial sovereignty by Poland.

> Ambassador Wallace to Secretary Colby, July 21 and 28, 1920, MS. Department of State, files 760c60F/33, 760c60F/40; Chargé Harrison to Mr. Colby, June 29 and Aug. 13, 1920, *ibid.* 760c60F/42, 760c60F/53, 760c60F/54; 1919 For. Rel., vol. I, pp. 22, 24, 27; 1920 For. Rel., vol. I, pp. 36 *et seq.*
>
> Mr. Whitehouse, Counselor of the Embassy at Paris, to the Secretary of State, No. 2988, Mar. 26, 1923, MS. Department of State, file 763.-72119/11954, enclosure F; diplomatic serial 189, Apr. 10, 1923, *ibid.* 760C6115/8.

At the termination of the second Balkan war in 1912, the Principal Allied Powers agreed that an independent state of Albania should be created. Pursuant to the Treaty of London of May 17/30, 1913, which reserved to them "the task of settling the frontiers of Albania and any other questions regarding Albania", a Conference of Ambassadors sitting at London in 1913 adopted certain decisions as to the boundaries of Albania, known as the "Protocol of London". A delimitation commission, created under one of these decisions, concluded a final protocol, signed on December 17, 1913, but the World War prevented the complete determination of the boundaries of the new state. A resolution of the League of Nations, regarding the admission of Albania as a member of the League, reserved the question of the settlement of the frontiers. On October 2, 1921 the Assembly of the League of Nations left the settlement of the Albanian boundaries to the Principal Powers. A delimitation commission appointed by the Conference of Ambassadors, which sat at Paris and which was authorized to act as the agent of the Principal Powers for the purpose of determining the boundaries, differed as to the country to which the Monastery of Saint-Naoum should be given under the protocol of London of 1913. The Conference of Ambassadors, after considering the data submitted to it, decided, on December 6, 1922— *The Monastery of Saint-Naoum*

> to inform the Serbo-Albanian Boundary Commission and the Albanian and Yugo-Slav Governments that the Conference has agreed to allocate the Saint-Naoum Monastery to Albania.

The Serb-Croat-Slovene state protested against this decision on the ground that the mission of the Conference of Ambassadors was not merely to settle the frontiers of Albania but to settle them in conformity with the decisions of the Protocol of London of 1913 according to which, it was contended, the monastery was allocated to Serbia. On June 5, 1924 the boundary question was referred to the Council of the League of Nations by the Conference of Ambassadors, acting on behalf of the Principal Powers. The Council requested the Permanent Court of International Justice to give an advisory opinion on the following question:

> Have the Principal Allied Powers, by the decision of the Conference of Ambassadors of December 6th, 1922, exhausted, in regard to the frontier between Albania and the Kingdom of the Serbs, Croats and Slovenes at the Monastery of Saint-Naoum, the mission, such as it has been recognized by the interested Parties, which is contemplated by a unanimous Resolution of the Assembly of the League of Nations of October 2nd, 1921?

On September 4, 1924 the Court gave an advisory opinion that the Principal Powers had exhausted, by the decision of the Conference of Ambassadors of December 6, 1922, their mission regarding the frontier at the Monastery of Saint-Naoum. It called attention to the fact that the Serb-Croat-Slovene state had recognized the competence of the Principal Powers to settle the boundary question and that it had voted in favor of the resolution of the League of Nations of October 2, 1921. With respect to the contention of the Serb-Croat-Slovene state that the Conference of Ambassadors was not merely to settle the Albanian boundary but to settle it in conformity with the Protocol of London of 1913, the Court stated that this raised the question whether the Albanian frontier at the Monastery of Saint-Naoum had been actually fixed in 1913 or not. The Court was of the opinion that the documents placed before it did not suffice to prove that the Conference of Ambassadors was mistaken in holding that the frontier at Saint-Naoum had not been definitely fixed in 1913.

After stating that the Paris Conference of Ambassadors had "a certain amount of latitude" in settling the frontiers of Albania, the Court quoted the decision of August 11, 1913 of the London Conference, part of which provided that "the western and southern shore of Lake Ochrida from the village of Lin as far as [jusqu'au] the Monastery of Sveti-Naoum shall form part of Albania". With respect to this decision the Court, in order to ascertain the meaning of a word in a doubtful phrase, referred to another phrase of the decision the meaning of which was clear and in which the word was used. It stated:

> . . . The Court does not think it possible to affirm that the meaning of this word in connection with a place like the Monastery of Saint-Naoum necessarily implies either its inclusion or

exclusion. It should, however, be observed that in the same paragraph, side by side with the expression *jusqu'à Saint-Naoum*, is to be found the expression: *jusqu'à Phtelia* which is shown by the facts of the case to mean: Phthelia inclusive.

And further on:

A map which has been submitted to the Court and which is described as that sent by Yougoslavia to the Conference of Ambassadors . . . contains a frontier line leaving Saint-Naoum outside Albania. . . . Moreover the map in question is unsigned and its authentic character is not established. **Maps**

. . . .

This decision [of August 11, 1913] has also been criticised on the ground that it was based on erroneous information or adopted without regard to certain essential facts. The Court refers to what it has already said regarding the definitive character of the decisions in question, and does not feel called upon to give an opinion on the question whether such decisions can—except when an express reservation to that effect has been made—be revised in the event of the existence of an essential error being proved, or of new facts being relied on. But even if revision under such conditions were admissible, these conditions are not present in the case before the Court.

These arguments make it necessary for the Court to ascertain whether, over and above the group of circumstances which led to that decision, there exist new facts or facts unknown at the time when the decision was taken; . . . **New evidence**

As concerns new facts, there are none in the present case. It is true that, according to a communication received by the Court from the Conference of Ambassadors, the Conference was unacquainted with the documents sent by the Serb-Croat-Slovene State in support of its claim for revision until June 1923. But in the opinion of the Court fresh documents do not in themselves amount to fresh facts. No new fact—properly so-called—has been alleged.

Per. Ct. Int. Jus., Advisory Opinion, Ser. B, No. 9, pp. 9, 15, 16, 18, 20, 21; 107 Br. & For. St. Paps. 656 (treaty of May 17/30, 1913).

On November 21, 1925 the Permanent Court of International Justice rendered an advisory opinion to the effect that the "decision to be taken" by the Council of the League of Nations by virtue of the authority of paragraph 2, article 3, of the Peace Treaty of Lausanne, of July 24, 1923, would be binding and would constitute a definitive determination of the frontier between Turkey and Iraq. In arriving at that conclusion the Court looked at the "intention of the Parties" to the treaty and held that the parties intended "to insure a definitive and binding solution of the dispute".

Per. Ct. Int. Jus., Advisory Opinion, Ser. B, No. 12, pp. 6, 19; I Hudson, *World Court Reports* (1934) 722. For the Treaty of Lausanne, see 28 League of Nations Treaty Series (1924) 13.

On March 1, 1927 the Judicial Committee of the Privy Council rendered an opinion in the case *Re Labrador Boundary*, which had been referred to it by the Dominion of Canada and the Colony of Newfoundland in the form of the following question: "What is the location and definition of the boundary as between Canada and Newfoundland in the Labrador Peninsula under the Statutes, Orders in Council and Proclamations?" Canada contended that the boundary should follow the coast at a distance of one mile from high-water mark, while Newfoundland maintained that the inland boundary of the territory on the shore of Labrador must be determined by the watershed of the rivers flowing into the sea on that coast. Viscount Cave, L.C., who delivered the opinion of the Committee, which was generally in favor of the contentions of Newfoundland, stated:

> When the material documents are considered from this point of view, it is evident that they contain much which supports the contention that the word "coast" is to be construed as including a considerable area of land . . .
> With regard to the limit in depth of the country which may be described as "coast", where that term is used in the wider sense, it is argued that the natural limit is to be found (in the absence of special circumstances) in the watershed which is the source of the rivers falling into the sea at that place; and there is much to be said in favour of that view. It is consistent with the doctrine of international law by which the occupation of a seacoast carries with it a right to the whole territory drained by the rivers which empty their water into its line (see Hall's International Law, 7th ed., pp. 107–8; Westlake's International Law, 1904, Part 1, pp. 112–3; and Lawrence's Principles of International Law, 7th ed. p. 153); and it is certainly difficult, in the absence of any specified boundary or of any special feature (such as a political frontier), which could be taken as a boundary, to suggest any point between the seashore and the watershed at which a line could be drawn.
> Further, the use of the watershed or "height of land" as a boundary was undoubtedly familiar in British North America at the period in question, and it is shown as a boundary in many of the maps of that time.

The opinion concluded:

> The maps here referred to, even when issued or accepted by departments of the Canadian Government, cannot be treated as admissions binding on that Government; for even if such an admission could be effectively made, the departments concerned are not shown to have had any authority to make it. But the fact that throughout a long series of years, and until the present dispute arose, all the maps issued in Canada either supported or were consistent with the claim now put forward by Newfoundland, is of some value as showing the construction put

upon the Orders in Council and statutes by persons of authority and by the general public in the Dominion.

[1927] 2 D.L.R. 401, 402, 415, 427.

In the arbitral award rendered on April 4, 1928 in the *Island of Palmas* case between the United States and the Netherlands, Max Huber, as sole arbitrator, stated:

> Among the methods of indirect proof, not of the exercise of sovereignty, but of its existence in law, submitted by the United States, there is the *evidence from maps*. . . . A comparison of the information supplied by the two Parties shows that only with the greatest caution can account be taken of maps in deciding a question of sovereignty, at any rate in the case of an island such as Palmas (or Miangas). Any maps which do not precisely indicate the political distribution of territories, and in particular the Island of Palmas (or Miangas) clearly marked as such, must be rejected forthwith, unless they contribute— supposing that they are accurate—to the location of geographical names. Moreover, indications of such a nature are only of value when there is reason to think that the cartographer has not merely referred to already existing maps—as seems very often to be the case—but that he has based his decision on information carefully collected for the purpose. Above all, then, official or semi-official maps seem capable of fulfilling these conditions, and they would be of special interest in cases where they do not assert the sovereignty of the country of which the Government has caused them to be issued.
>
> If the Arbitrator is satisfied as to the existence of legally relevant facts which contradict the statements of cartographers whose sources of information are not known, he can attach no weight to the maps, however numerous and generally appreciated they may be.
>
> The first condition required of maps that are to serve as evidence on points of law is their geographical accuracy.

MS. Department of State, file 711.5614/278; Per. Ct. Arb., Arbitral Award in the *Island of Palmas* case (1928) 36; Scott, *Hague Court Reports* (1932) 84, 108.

In the case of *Wisconsin* v. *Michigan* Mr. Justice Butler, speaking for the Supreme Court of the United States, said that "principles of International law . . . apply also to boundaries between States constituting" the United States. **International law applicable between States**

295 U.S. (1935) 455, 461.

The question is one of boundary, and this court has many times held that, as between the States of the Union, long acquiescence in the assertion of a particular boundary and the exercise of dominion and sovereignty over the territory within it, should be accepted as conclusive, whatever the international rule might **Acquiescence** be in respect of the acquisition by prescription of large tracts of country claimed by both.

Louisiana v. Mississippi, 202 U.S. (1906) 1, 53. The issue with reference to the boundary was raised when the two States enacted dissimilar legislation in regard to oyster fishing in the waters in dispute.

In the case of State of Maryland v. State of West Virginia, involving a dispute between the two States regarding their boundary from the headwaters of the Potomac to the Pennsylvania line, West Virginia claimed that the boundary line, long-recognized and established, was the one known as "Deakins" line. Mr. Justice Day, in delivering the opinion of the Supreme Court of the United States upholding this contention, stated:

Long recognition

This record leaves no doubt . . . that the Deakins line . . . had long been recognized as a boundary and served as such.

Occupation and conveyance

A perusal of the record satisfies us that for many years occupation and conveyance of the lands on the Virginia side has been with reference to the Deakins line as the boundary line. The people have generally accepted it and have adopted it, and the facts in this connection cannot be ignored.

Long-continued possession

The effect to be given to such facts as long continued possession "gradually ripening into that condition which is in conformity with international order," depends upon the merit of individual cases as they arise. 1 Oppenheim International Law §243.

Law and equity

Upon the whole case, the conclusions at which we have arrived, we believe, best meet the facts disclosed in this record, are warranted by the applicable principles of law and equity, and will least disturb the rights and titles long regarded as settled and fixed by the people most to be affected.

217 U.S. (1910) 1, 40, 41, 44, 46. See also Smoot Sand & Gravel Corporation v. Washington Airport, Inc., 283 U.S. (1931) 348, 350.

In 1910–12 the United States, by dredging from the bottom of the Potomac River and depositing the material, filled in a strip of land on the river-front of the city of Alexandria, which formerly lay below low-water mark. The United States enclosed the made land by a fence at high-water mark, but the Marine Railway Co. & Coal Company, Inc., claiming title to the adjoining land inshore, destroyed the fence and took possession, whereupon the United States brought a suit in the Supreme Court of the District of Columbia to recover possession. The defendant pleaded to the jurisdiction of the court alleging that the land was not in the District of Columbia and was a part of Virginia. The ruling of the court in favor of the United States was affirmed both by the court of appeals and by the Supreme

Court of the United States. In the course of its decision, the Supreme Court, Mr. Justice Holmes speaking, said:

> . . . If the taking possession of land were under a deed purporting to convey more than the portion actually occupied, no doubt, within reasonable limits, the sovereign power might give to it the effect of adverse possession of the whole, as against other subjects of the same power. *Montoya* v. *Gonzales*, 232 U.S. 375, 377, 378. But the effect of filling in upon the edge of a stream as against a different power is another matter. Such acts in themselves import no claim beyond the land thus occupied. . . .

> Finally, on the other hand, the Revised Statutes relating to the District of Columbia, June 22, 1874, §1, describe the District as "including the river Potomac in its course through the District," which imports an assertion by Congress that the title of the United States embraces the whole river bed; and the jurisdiction of the District over the river seems to have been exercised without dispute. For cases that have reached the reports see *Alexandria Canal Railroad & Bridge Co.* v. *District of Columbia*, 1 Mackey, 217, 225, 226. *Smoot* v. *District of Columbia*, 23 App. D.C. 266. *Evans* v. *United States*, 31 App. D.C. 544.

> It may happen that such filling as is done in this case will interrupt previously existing access to the water front. But that does not affect the right of the United States to possession of the land. What other rights, if any, the plaintiff in error may have does not concern us now.

Marine Railway Co. & Coal Company, Inc. v. *United States*, 257 U.S. (1921) 47, 65.

In the case of *Michigan* v. *Wisconsin*, a suit involving part of the boundary line from Lake Superior via the Montreal River, Lake of the Desert, and Menominee River to Green Bay, and thence through the center of the usual channel to the center of Lake Michigan, the Supreme Court of the United States held, in 1926, that long acquiescence by one State in the possession of territory and in the exercise of sovereignty over it, by another State, is conclusive of the latter's title. It called attention to the fact that the Enabling Act of June 15, 1836 (5 Stat. 49), under which Michigan became a State in 1837, described a boundary line from the mouth of the Montreal River to the Lake of the Desert; that this description was made under the mistaken belief that the river connected with the lake; that the mistake was discovered as early as 1841; that Michigan had acquiesced in the possession and claim of jurisdiction on the part of Wisconsin over the area in question; and that the territory between the two boundary lines claimed by the respective States belonged to Wisconsin.

Long acquiescence

270 U.S. (1926) 295, 308. See also *Wisconsin* v. *Michigan*, 295 U.S. (1935) 455; 297 U.S. (1936) 547.

In the case of *New Jersey* v. *Delaware* the original jurisdiction of the Supreme Court of the United States was invoked for the determination of the boundary in the Delaware Bay and River. Delaware claimed title to the bed of the river within a circle of 12 miles about the town of New Castle, while New Jersey bounded her title by the thalweg. A Special Master appointed by the Court, as well as the Court, upheld Delaware's contention. Mr. Justice Cordozo, speaking for the Court, said:

> Delaware traces her title to the river bed within the circle through deeds going back two and a half centuries and more.
>
> .   .   .   .
>
> Delaware's chain of title has now been followed from the feoffment of 1682 to the early days of statehood, and has been found to be unbroken. The question remains whether some other and better chain can be brought forward by New Jersey. Unless this can be done, Delaware must prevail.

The Court also said:

Acts of
dominion

> Apart from these acts of dominion by riparian proprietors, there are other acts of dominion by New Jersey and its agents which are relied upon now as indicative of ownership. They include the service of process, civil and criminal; the assessment of improvements for the purpose of taxation; and the execution of deeds of conveyance to the United States and others. Of all it is enough to say that they are matched by many other acts, equally indicative of ownership and dominion, by the Government of Delaware. The Master summarizes the situation with the statement that "at no time has the State of Delaware ever abandoned its claim, dominion or jurisdiction over the Delaware River within said twelve-mile circle, nor has it at any time acquiesced in the claim of the State of New Jersey, thereto, except as modified by the . . . Compact of 1905".

No acquies-
cence

> The truth indeed is that almost from the beginning of statehood Delaware and New Jersey have been engaged in a dispute as to the boundary between them. There is no room in such circumstances for the application of the principle that long acquiescence may establish a boundary otherwise uncertain. *Vermont* v. *New Hampshire*, 289 U.S. 593, 613; *Indiana* v. *Kentucky*, 136 U.S. 479, 509, 511; *Massachusetts* v. *New York*, *supra*, p. 95. Acquiescence is not compatible with a century of conflict.

291 U.S. (1934) 361, 364, 374, 376.

For material on accretion, erosion, and avulsion, see *ante* § § 60 and 84.

EFFECT OF ABSENCE OF DELIMITATION

§104

In the case of *Alberto Brown* the Panamanian Supreme Court   Jurisdiction
held, on February 5, 1929, that the Panamanian courts were without
jurisdiction over a crime committed in territory under Costa Rican
jurisdiction, even though such territory was in dispute between the
two countries.

> 27 *Registro judicial* (1929) bk. I, p. 103.

The Belgian Court of Compensation for War Damages at Verviers
denied, on September 16, 1924, claims against Belgium for damages
inflicted during the World War on property situated in the Commune
of La Calamine (formerly known as "Moresnet") on the ground
that the damages had not been caused on Belgian territory. The
territory had been claimed both by Prussia, which had been succeeded by Germany, and by the Netherlands, which had been succeeded by Belgium. The dispute went back to the time when the
commission appointed under the Treaty of Vienna of May 31, 1815
had failed to determine the limits of the territory. Under article
32 of the Treaty of Versailles of June 28, 1919, Germany recognized
"the full sovereignty of Belgium over the whole of the disputed
territory of Moresnet". During the period of the dispute sovereignty
was exercised by Belgium under a *modus vivendi*.

On May 22, 1925 the Belgian Court of Cassation, in reversing the
decision of the lower court, decided that the territory in question
was Belgian when the damages were inflicted; that the sovereignty
of Belgium over this territory should not be sought in the Treaty
of Versailles under which Germany merely recognized this sovereignty; that it must be found in the Treaty of Vienna of 1815,
which was interpreted by the Treaty of Versailles; that the latter
treaty did not result in the transfer of sovereignty to Belgium over
new territory but merely resulted in the removal of the obstacle to
Belgian sovereignty created by German contentions; and that Moresnet must be considered as having been a part of the Netherlands
since 1815 and of Belgium since 1830.

> Case of *Kepp et Consorts, Pasicrisie Belge* (1925), pt. I, pp. 253–255;
> 2 Br. & For. St. Paps. 136 (treaty of 1815) ; 3 Treaties, etc. (Redmond,
> 1923) 3329 (Treaty of Versailles).

In the case of the *German Continental Gas Company* v. *Polish
State* involving a liquidation, pursuant to Polish legislation, of property owned by the plaintiff company in Warsaw, the company contended that when the property was liquidated the territory belonged
in law to Russia, that the territory had not then been ceded to Poland,

and that, even if there had been a cession, the boundaries of the ceded territory had not yet been determined. The claimant also maintained that as long as the boundaries were undetermined Poland could not be considered as possessing the territory *de jure*. The German-Polish mixed arbitral tribunal to which the claim was submitted stated with respect to this point:

> But, whatever may be the importance of delimitation of frontiers, one cannot go so far as to contend that as long as this delimitation has not been juridically decided, the state in question cannot be considered as having any territory whatever. Here, also, the practice of international law and historical precedents indicate the contrary. In order that a state should exist and could be recognized as such with a territory without which it could not either exist or be recognized, it is sufficient that this territory should have a sufficiently certain consistency (even though its frontiers should not have been accurately delimited) and that, on this territory, the state should actually exercise national public authority in an independent manner. There are numerous examples of cases in which states have existed unquestionably, have been recognized and have been recognized mutually at a time when their frontier between them had not yet been accurately fixed. In this connection, it is unnecessary to recall the international arbitrations which have fixed the boundary between the Argentine Republic and Chile and the more recent one between Colombia and Venezuela, and one could not draw therefrom the conclusion that before these delimitations the states in question had no territory.

The tribunal pointed out that, had the measure of which complaint was made taken place in disputed territory, the fact that the boundary had not yet been fixed might have had some relevancy. It held that the measure in question was taken in territory the national Polish character of which could not be doubted since the end of 1918.

> IX *Recueil des décisions des tribunaux arbitraux mixtes* (1929–30) 336, 346, translation.

ARBITRATIONS

§105

Bolivia-Peru; treaty of 1902   On December 30, 1902 an arbitration treaty was signed between Bolivia and Peru submitting a long-standing boundary dispute existing between them to the "Government" of Argentina, in order to obtain a final decision according to which "all the territory which in 1810 belonged to the jurisdiction or district of the ancient *Audiencia* of Charcas, within the boundaries of the Viceroyalty of Buenos Aires, in virtue of the enactments of the former Sovereign, shall fall to the Republic of Bolivia; and all the territory which at that same date in virtue of enactments of like origin belonged to the Viceroyalty of Lima, shall fall to the Republic of Peru". Article 2 of the treaty provided that the boundary between the Peruvian provinces of Tacna and Arica and the Bolivian province of Carangas, having been fixed by a treaty for the demarcation of the frontier of September 23, 1902, was excepted from the present treaty. Article 4 provided that, when Royal acts and orders did not afford sufficient basis for the determination of the extent of the territory, the question should be decided in an "equitable" way approximating as much as possible the solution suggested by those acts and orders. It was provided in article 5 that possession exercised over territory by one of the parties could not prevail over titles or Royal dispositions to the contrary. The exchange of ratifications took place on March 9, 1904. On July 13 the President of Argentina accepted the office of arbitrator, which in the meantime had been offered to him under the treaty of 1902.

The President of Argentina appointed an advisory commission to assist in determining the boundaries, and the commission, after examining the pleadings, submitted its recommendations in a communication dated July 1, 1909, addressed to the Minister of Foreign Affairs of Argentina, in which it stated that the documents submitted neither established the positions taken by the respective Governments nor defined in a clear and precise manner the territories in dispute. The commission indicated the boundary line which, in its opinion, should be "equitably" established; the line described approached the line which in 1810 separated the jurisdiction and district of the ancient *Audiencia* of Charcas from the Viceroyalty of Lima. *Consultative commission*

The President of Argentina (José Figueroa Alcorta), on July 9, 1909, adopted the line suggested by the commission. In interpreting article 1 of the treaty of 1902, he found that he was not to determine the boundary of the whole *Audiencia* of Charcas and of the whole Vice Royalty of Lima in 1810—which determination would have involved countries other than Bolivia and Peru—but was merely to fix the boundaries of those two districts only so far as they related to Bolivia and Peru. He explained that he did not find that the line claimed by either of the parties had been established by the evidence and that, in reality, the disputed territory was in 1810 and practically up to the time of the rendition of the award unexplored. He held that Royal acts in effect in 1810 did not define clearly whether the disputed territory was part of the Vice Royalty of Lima or of the *Audiencia* of Charcas and that, in the circumstances, it was necessary to decide the question "equitably" as provided by article 4, which he did. *Award*

Equitable determination

The award was received very unfavorably in Bolivia. The disapprobation by the Bolivian people was so great that a mob attacked the Argentine Legation, and the Argentine Minister was forced to flee. When a circular letter of the President of Bolivia reflecting upon the President of Argentina became known, diplomatic relations were severed between the two countries. However, shortly thereafter negotiations between Bolivia and Peru resulted in the signing of a protocol on September 15, 1909 formally assenting to the decision of the arbitrator, and of another protocol on September 17, 1909 designating the boundaries of the disputed territory as agreed upon finally by the representatives of Bolivia and Peru. The latter protocol provided:

Protocols of 1909

> In order that the boundaries established by the Arbitrator may conform as nearly as possible with the natural conditions of the land, and with the convenience of both interested parties, the Governments of Bolivia and Peru have resolved, by means of the present pact, to effect the exchanges and concessions [*cessions*] of lands which by mutual agreement are considered necessary for the object sought, namely, that the frontiers of each country may remain fixed in accordance with the requirements of its security and any misunderstanding in the future be avoided.

In accordance with the provisions just quoted the line of the frontier as determined by the arbitrator was modified to conform to the wishes of both parties. It was also provided in the latter protocol that within six months from the date of the protocol both countries would name boundary commissioners to demarcate the frontier line in accordance with its stipulations.

Armed conflict occurred in 1910 in the Manuripi region, and thereafter protocols dated March 30 and April 15, 1911, respectively, were signed by the two Governments, expressing regret for the occurrences, expressing the hope that the work of demarcation under the 1909 protocol should proceed as rapidly as possible, and instructing and reorganizing the mixed commission for the demarcation of the boundary. The demarcation commission thus organized proceeded to mark the boundary during the years 1911–13. By further protocols dated May 6, 1912 and December 19, 1916 the jurisdiction of the demarcation commission was extended and the work directed. On June 2, 1925 a further protocol was signed containing provision for the appointment of another mixed commission to mark the boundary from the point where it was begun by the former demarcation commission, at the confluence of the Pachasili stream with the Suches, to the boundary of the province of Tacna.

Minister Stutesman to Secretary Knox, Nov. 26, 1909, MS. Department of State, file 534/143; Minister Pezet to the Acting Secretary of State, May 8, 1912, and the Acting Secretary of State (Wilson) to Señor Pezet, May 13, 1912, *ibid.* 723.2415/172; *Arbitraje argentino en la cuestión de límites entres las repúblicas del Perú y de Bolivia* (1909) 9 (treaty of 1902); 1909 For. Rel. 504 (treaty of 1902); 100 Br. & For. St. Paps. 803

(treaty of 1902) ; *Arbitraje Argentino*, 22, 27, 85 (recommendations of the consultative commission) ; *ibid.* 96 (award) ; 1909 For. Rel. 502, 505, 506 (protocols of Sept. 15 and 17, 1909) ; 105 Br. & For. St. Paps. 572, 581, 583 (award and protocols of 1911) ; *Peru–Bolivia Boundary Commission 1911–1913; Report, Royal Geographical Society of London* (Cambridge, 1918) ; Ireland, *Boundaries, Possessions, and Conflicts in South America* (1938) 95–108 (containing a résumé of the early history of the dispute).

By the terms of a convention of November 4, 1896 a long-standing boundary dispute between Costa Rica and Colombia was submitted to the arbitration of the President of France. Both countries accepted the award of President Loubet, dated September 11, 1900, so far as the boundary laid down by him from the central Cordilleras to the Pacific was concerned, whereby certain territory of Colombia— the Coto district—was awarded to Costa Rica; but Costa Rica protested against the boundary as laid down in the award from the Cordilleras to the Atlantic, whereby a strip of Costa Rican territory along the Sixaola River was awarded to Colombia, on the ground that the arbitrator exceeded his authority in adjudicating territory not in dispute. **Panama and Costa Rica**

Subsequently the matter was referred to Chief Justice White of the United States, as arbitrator, under a convention of March 17, 1910 between Costa Rica and Panama (successor to Colombia). Briefly speaking he held, in his award of September 12, 1914, that the thalweg of the Sixaola River was the boundary. Panama refused to accept this award on the ground that the Chief Justice had exceeded his powers under the convention and that it was inequitable that Costa Rica should gain territory both to the west and to the east of the Cordilleras.

Relations between the two countries became more and more strained, and in 1921 Costa Rican troops attempted to take possession of territory under the 1914 award and Panamanian troops attempted to re-occupy the Coto district. On March 3, 1921 the United States offered its good offices for the purpose of finding a peaceful means of settling the controversy, which offer was accepted, as was also the suggestion of the United States that, pending conclusion of an amicable settlement, the troops of both nations be brought back to the *status-quo* line with instructions not to renew hostilities. **Good offices**

The Panamanian Government having requested a declaration of the manner in which the United States Government understood its obligation in relation to the invasion of Panama by Costa Rica and its efforts to evict Panamanians from Coto, Secretary Hughes set forth at some length the position of the United States in an instruction to the American Legation of March 15, 1921. He stated that under article 1 of the Hay – Bunau Varilla treaty the United States guaranteed the "independence" of Panama and that it must "advise itself as to the extent of the sovereignty" of Panama "and hence of the territorial limits" of that state; that to do so it was necessary to examine the merits of the boundary dispute; that Panama had not taken steps to fulfil its obligation as to territory (on the Pacific side) awarded to Costa Rica by the arbitral award of the President of the French Republic and unequivocally accepted by the Porras-Anderson treaty of March 17, 1910, between Panama and Costa Rica, which territory included Coto, and also had not accepted the arbitral award (relating to the Atlantic side) of the Chief Justice of the United States; and that the guaranty of the United States was obviously conditioned upon the performance by Panama of her international obligations. As to Panama's refusal to abide by the latter award on the ground that the Chief Justice exceeded his jurisdiction as arbitrator, Secretary Hughes stated that the United States had "been unable to find any ground upon which this contention can be advanced".

Proposed plebiscites   In a lengthy note of March 18, 1921 the Panamanian Minister of Foreign Affairs expressed disagreement with the declaration and proposed that the matter be settled by holding plebiscites in the two areas. Secretary Hughes was opposed to this procedure and, in an instruction of April 27 to the Legation in Panama, said:

> . . . Unless such steps [transfer of territory under the Loubet award] are taken within a reasonable time, the Government of the United States will find itself compelled to proceed in the manner which may be requisite in order that it may assure itself that the exercise of jurisdiction is appropriately transferred and that the boundary line on the Pacific side, as defined in the Loubet award, and on the Atlantic side, as determined by the award of the Chief Justice of the United States, is physically laid down in the manner provided in Articles II and VII of the Porras-Anderson Treaty.

Mediation   On August 1 of the same year, he wrote the Minister in Panama that, "In view of the fact that the friendly mediation" of the United States had been accepted by both Costa Rica and Panama, he should transmit to the Minister of Foreign Affairs the following formal request from the Government of Costa Rica:

Boundary commission
> 1. That, in fulfillment of Article 1, of the Anderson-Porras Treaty [of 1910], the transfer be made of the jurisdiction over the territory now occupied by the civil authorities of Panama that lies indisputably to the north of the Punta Burica-Cerro Pando line, which, according to that Article, was held by both parties to be clear and indubitable; and,
> 2. That, in accordance with the stipulations of Articles 1 and 7, of the same Treaty, the President of Panama appoint an engineer

of his own choice to physically lay down the divisionary line and mark it by appropriate monuments.

The Legation was further informed that Costa Rica had appointed its engineer on the commission for the demarcation of the boundary under the provisions of article 7 of the treaty of 1910 and that Costa Rica was requesting the Chief Justice of the United States to appoint two members of the commission, as provided in the treaty. Panama declined to appoint a commissioner on the ground that the provisions of the treaty of 1910 were no longer binding upon her and that "the award pronounced in the agreed arbitration being null the arbitration convention fell into disuse *ipso facto* and *ipso jure*".

On August 18 Secretary Hughes instructed the Minister in Panama to inform the Panamanian Government that the Government of the United States was "advised by the Government of Costa Rica that since it considers that the Porras-Anderson Convention is in force, and since it believes that there is no valid reason for delaying its complete execution any longer, it is ready to assume immediately the jurisdiction over the territory" and that— _{Transfer of jurisdiction}

> . . . In view of the fact that the Government of Panama appears unwilling to carry out this delimitation in the manner provided in the Porras-Anderson Convention, and inasmuch as a reasonable time, mentioned in the note of this Government dated May 2, 1921, for the reaching of an agreement as to the manner of carrying out this delimitation, has already been afforded, there would seem to be no reason why the Government of the United States should, as the friendly mediator between the two Governments, or by virtue of its special relations to the Government of Panama, feel compelled to suggest to the Government of Costa Rica that it delay longer taking jurisdiction over the territory which is now occupied by Panama and which was adjudged to belong to Costa Rica by the terms of the Loubet Award.

Panama withdrew from the Coto district, and Costa Rica took peaceable possession of the region on September 5, 1921.

On November 18, 1921 Secretary Hughes notified the Costa Rican Minister that Professor John Hayford, Dean of the College of Engineering, Northwestern University, and Professor Ora Minor Leland, of the University of Minnesota, had been appointed by Chief Justice Taft as commissioners to delimit the boundary in accordance with article 7 of the Porras-Anderson treaty of 1910.

Active negotiations for the delimitation of the boundary were not resumed until in 1925. In a telegram of February 6, 1925 the Department reiterated the views set forth in the instructions referred to above with respect to the validity of the White award and the grounds for the interest of the United States in a settlement of the matter, and stated that, in the event of a failure of Panama and Costa Rica to reach an agreement within a reasonable time satisfactory to both, the United States would "have no other alternative than to afford facilities for the engineers appointed by the Chief Justice of the Supreme Court of the United States and by the Government of Costa Rica in demarcating the boundary line, should Panama refuse to cooperate therein".

Panama declined, however, to appoint a commissioner, and the negotiations for a settlement were continued at intervals during the ensuing years. Regular diplomatic relations were restored between Costa Rica and Panama on October 1, 1928, through the good offices of the Chilean Government, such relations having been broken off at the time of the conflict of 1921. The dispute as to the Atlantic slope boundary has appeared to be on the verge of a settlement a number of times but up to this time a mutually satisfactory agreement has not been reached.

92 Br. & For. St. Paps. 1036 (convention of 1896); *ibid.* 1038 (award of 1900); 103 *idem* (1909–10) 404 (convention of 1910); MS. Department of State, file 718.1915/221½, 8 A.J.I.L. (1914) 913 (award of 1914).

Secretary Hughes to the American Legation at Panama, Mar. 15, 1921, MS. Department of State, file 718.1915/368a. Minister Price to Secretary Hughes, no. 2940, Apr. 12, 1921, *ibid.* 718.1915/438, enclosing note from the Panamanian Minister of Foreign Affairs of Mar. 18, 1921; Mr. Hughes to the American Legation at Panama, Apr. 27 and Aug. 1, 1921, *ibid.* files 718.1915/438, 718.1915/525; Mr. Price to Mr. Hughes, Aug. 6, 1921, *ibid.* file 718.1915/539; Mr. Hughes to the American Legation at Panama, Aug. 18 and 22, 1921, and Feb. 6, 1925, *ibid.* files 718.1915/549a, /550, /701; 1921 For. Rel. 175–228.

Colombia and Venezuela

After prolonged negotiations, an arbitral convention was signed on November 3, 1916 by Colombia and Venezuela for the purpose of settling a long-standing boundary dispute. The agreement provided that the purpose of the two Governments was to settle the boundary according to an arbitral decision rendered in 1891 by the Queen Regent Maria-Cristina of Spain in the name of her minor son, Alfonso XIII. Differences of opinion between them with respect to the means to be employed in order to attain this purpose were to be settled by the arbitrator, the President of the Swiss Confederation (interpreted by a subsequent agreement of July 20, 1917, to mean "the Swiss Federal Council"). The parties entrusted to the arbitrator the tracing and marking of the frontier fixed by the award, by means of experts. The agreement recited (in article I) that Colombia considered that she had a right to take possession of the territories which the award recognized as belonging to her and which were clearly bounded by nature or by the work of the demarcation commission in 1900 and 1901, and that Venezuela considered that this could not be done until the entire frontier line had been wholly marked, and submitted the question whether the award could be partially executed. This point was to be decided within one year.

The Swiss Federal Council announced its opinion and award on March 24, 1922. It decided that the award of 1891 could be executed partially and that each Government might occupy the territory indicated in that award which was bounded by natural frontiers or which had been marked by the demarcation commission. It also decided that the work of demarcation within the jurisdiction of the Swiss Federal Council should be done by a technical commission with an arbitral character, which should complete its work by December 31, 1924, unless in case of exceptional difficulty. The decision of the Swiss Federal Council read in part as follows:

When the Spanish colonies of Central and South America proclaimed their independence, in the second decade of the nineteenth century, they adopted a principle of constitutional and international law to which they gave the name of *uti possidetis juris* of 1810, with the effect of establishing that the boundaries of the newly constituted republics would be the boundaries of the Spanish provinces which they replaced. This general principle offered the advantage of laying down an absolute rule that there is not, in law, any territory in the formerly Spanish America without a master; although there were numerous regions which had not been occupied by the Spaniards and numerous unexplored regions, or regions inhabited by uncivilized aborigines, such regions were considered to belong rightfully to each of the republics which had succeeded to the Spanish Province to which the said territories were attached in view of old royal ordinances of the mother country, Spain. Those territories, although not in fact occupied, were by common accord considered as occupied, legally, from the first moment, by the new Republic. Encroachments and inopportune attempts at colonization from the other side of the frontier, as well as *de facto* occupations, became meaningless or without legal consequences. This principle had also the advantage of eliminating, it was hoped, boundary disputes among the new States. Finally, this principle excluded the attempts of European colonizing States on territories which they might have tried to proclaim *res nullius*. The international situation of Spanish America was from the beginning entirely different from that of Africa, for example. This principle later received a general confirmation under the name of the Monroe Doctrine, but had long been the basis of South American public law.

Uti possidetis juris of 1810

Uninhabited regions

De facto occupation

. . . .

The Swiss Federal Council, on the basis of the foregoing observations of fact and of law, has reached the following conclusions:

1.

The question posed in the first article of the *Compromis* signed at Bogotá November 3, 1916, is that of knowing whether one of the contesting states "has the right to enter into possession of the territories which were recognized to it by the Spanish Arbitral Decision and which are clearly delimited by nature itself or by the work of the delimitation Commissions" or whether on the contrary, as is maintained by Venezuela, "that can not be done before the common boundary line has been integrally delimited on the ground".

By application of the principle of *uti possidetis juris* of 1810 . . . the two States are considered to have had, since 1810, the sovereignty and the legal possession of the territories forming a part of the Spanish provinces which they replaced.

.   .   .   .

Neither the *Compromis* of 1881, nor the decision itself carries prescriptions on the subject of formalities of handing over or the formalities concerning occupation and the return of the territories.

. . . This convention . . . of 1898 likewise does not contain any indications of formalities of handing over nor an indication of the set times for taking possession or for execution . . .

Formalities in transfer

If international law knows of innumerable examples of boundary treaties in which there figures an indication of formalities of handing over and of delivery of territories, it does not know of any absolute and obligatory prescriptions relative to such formalities; there is even a certain number of examples of cessions and transfers of territories in which there was no formal handing over. . . . The examples invoked in treaties in which there figure formalities of handing over and the taking of possession all concern, furthermore, real cessions of territories transferred by a state which renounces sovereignty over them to another state which acquires such sovereignty. If, therefore, there were—as is not the case—an absolute principle of international law requiring a handing over and formalities of taking possession in case of transfer of sovereignty from one state to another, that principle would not be applicable to the boundary relations between Colombia and Venezuela, because by virtue of the principle of the *uti possidetis juris* of 1810, proclaimed by the two High Contesting Parties and confirmed by the Spanish arbitral Decision, there is neither a grantor nor a grantee; each one of the States is held to have had ever since 1810 sovereignty over territories which the Spanish arbitrator has recognized to it. The state which was in occupation of the territory, the sovereignty of which has been recognized to the other state, has no title for operating the delivery of the territory which it holds without right; its possession has ceased to be legitimate from and after the day of the coming into force of the decision. The state whose occupation is contrary to the decision has no other duty than that of evacuating the territory in question and the other state may effect occupation while exercising the courtesy required for the purpose of avoiding conflicts and notifying the inhabitants.

.   .   .   .

The two Parties themselves have therefore practiced the system of partial or successive occupations.

At present, if one wished to require that the Parties should restore territories which the Spanish Decision attributed to them and which they had been occupying for about twenty years and if it were desired to require that they should wait for the final delimitation of the last of their immense common boundaries, that would have the practical result of imposing on each one of the States not only the obligation to abstain from occupying what has been recognized to it but also the obligation to await from an irregular possessor the return of its own property during an indefinite period. Finally as those territories must pertain to the State the sovereignty of which has been recognized by the Spanish Arbitrator, the administrative organization given for twenty years past to those territories would be suppressed, a necessarily ephemeral administration would have to be created, all that for the purpose of respecting an alleged principle; now that principle does not even exist obligatorily for cessions, properly so-called, of territories, and especially is contrary to the South American principle of *uti possidetis juris* of 1810, a principle consecrated by the constitutions of the two contesting countries and confirmed by the Arbitral Decision of Spain. That would also be contrary to the two Colombian-Venezuelan Agreements of 1894 and 1896 which have stipulated or confirmed the right of occupation. The Spanish Decision is now thirty years old; it cannot indefinitely remain in the condition of a juridical abstraction. In the thought of the arbitrator the authority of arbitral decisions in general requires execution of this decision everywhere where it can be executed and *pari passu* with the elimination of the obstructions which are in the way of this execution.

Administration in territory

2.

Once the right of each one of the Parties is admitted to proceed to partial and successive occupation of the territories, the sovereignty of which was recognized to it by the Spanish Decision of 1891, and which are clearly delimited by nature herself or by the work of the delimitation commissions, the question is posed of knowing which territories can be occupied.

As regards the territory delimited by natural boundaries the Spanish Decision has passed on the question so that the Swiss Arbitrator must consider those natural boundaries as definitive; there is therefore no reason to have them explored as Venezuela asks nor to decide again as regards them.

As regards the delimitations fixed by the Mixed Commission of 1900 and 1901, delimitations as to which Venezuela generally considers that they should be revised, the Colombian-Venezuelan practice is to consider the Commissioners as having arbitral powers and not as being simply technical experts; the successive treaties concluded between the Parties since 1833 have contained the principle that the *procès-verbaux* and the plans drawn up by the Commissions of the two countries must, if they are in agreement with each other, be considered as forming part of the treaty and as "having the same force and value as if they were inserted therein".

.   .   .   .

Decisions of boundary commissions definitive

The decisions of mixed commissions therefore are definitive and are not subject to revision except on the points where the Commissioners have not been able to agree and have submitted the case to the two Governments, such disagreements keeping a purely local character and not suspending the continuation of the work of marking in the other sections of the boundary line.

The Mixed Commissions themselves have always considered their decisions rendered by common agreement as definitive and have so designated them in their *procès-verbaux*.

The Swiss Federal Council decreed the organization of the technical commission of Swiss experts (organized in two sections) in May 1922, and on July 30, 1924 it notified the two Governments of the final decisions of the experts on the demarcation of the boundary line.

> *Arbitrage entre la Colombie et la Vénézuéla, Sentence arbitrale* (Neuchatel, 1922) 5–6, 101, 102, 103, 105, 108, 112, translation. The demarcation of the boundary line is not as yet completed but is slowly progressing toward completion.
>
> The early background of the case was generally as follows:
>
> On September 14, 1881 Colombia and Venezuela signed a treaty for the adjustment of the territorial difficulties which had arisen soon after the two countries separated in 1830. *Ibid.* 127. It recited that the two countries, desiring to settle their boundaries such as they existed "by the ordinances of their former common sovereign" and having considered for a period of 50 years "all the titles, documents, proofs and authorities of their archives in repeated negotiations, without being able to arrive at an agreement regarding the respective rights or the *uti possidetis juris* of 1810", submitted the question to the King of Spain as arbitrator in order to obtain a final decision according to which "all the territory which belonged to the jurisdiction of the former captaincy-general of Caracas, by royal acts of the former sovereign up to 1810, will remain jurisdictional territory of the Republic of Venezuela and all territory which, by similar acts of that date, belonged to the jurisdiction of the Vice Royalty of Santa Fé, will remain territory of the Republic now called United States of Colombia".
>
> A decision not having been rendered at the time of the death of King Alfonso XII, the two countries agreed that the question should be arbitrated by the Government of the Spanish monarchy and added, in the supplementary agreement signed at Paris on February 15, 1886 (*ibid.* 129), that the arbitrator would have the right to fix the boundary in a manner which would be most justified by existing documents "when the said documents did not present the desired clarity".

On March 16, 1891 an arbitral decision was rendered by the Queen Regent Maria-Cristina in the name of her minor son, Alfonso XIII (*ibid*. 131). The Venezuelan Government took the position that certain matters relating to the execution of the award required parliamentary action, while Colombia maintained that legislative intervention by one of the parties to an arbitration was not in accordance with international law and insisted that there should be strict and punctual compliance with the decision. After adopting the federal form of government Venezuela also contended that consent of the various states of the Federation was necessary. In order to settle the difficulties, the two countries signed, on April 4, 1894, a declaration that it was their desire to fulfil the arbitral decision of 1891, and on April 24, 1894 and, again, on November 21, 1896 treaties were signed by them further defining the boundary. (*Ibid*. 15–17.) Each failed of approval.

On December 30, 1898 a convention was signed at Caracas creating a mixed commission for the demarcation of the boundary in accordance with the arbitral decision (*ibid*. 137). Difficulties between the commissioners were to be submitted to the two Governments. However, when such difficulties were submitted, the two Governments failed to agree and the commission suspended its work in 1901 after having fixed the limits of part of the boundary.

For the text of the arbitral agreement of 1916, see *ibid*. 141. See also Ireland, *Boundaries, Possessions, and Conflicts in South America* (1938) 206–218.

Boundary difficulties between Honduras and Guatemala arose about the middle of the nineteenth century. On September 15, 1821 the peoples of the districts of Honduras and Guatemala which then, with Costa Rica, Nicaragua, and El Salvador, constituted the captaincy-general of Guatemala, declared their independence of Spain. Uncertainty with respect to the boundary gave rise to conflicts of jurisdiction in border towns. The first agreement between the two countries relating to boundaries was a general treaty of peace and friendship signed at Guatemala city on July 19, 1845. Article XIII provided that the ecclesiastical limits of the dioceses of Honduras and Guatemala, as laid down in the Royal Ordinance of *Intendentes* of 1786, was to be the boundary. Commissioners met in 1847 but found no ecclesiastical or similar document determining the episcopal jurisdiction of the dioceses during the Spanish occupation. Honduras withdrew her commissioners after submitting the proposition that article XIII referred only to uninhabited places not occupied by either state prior to independence.

The boundary question was again made the subject of a convention on March 1, 1895, article I of which contained provision for the establishment of a commission composed of an equal number of members for each of the two countries "to study the antecedents, documents, and data existing as to the limits of both Republics". The commission was to submit to the two Governments "the bases, which, in their opinion, should be adopted to celebrate a treaty to fix defin-

Guatemala and Honduras

Treaty, 1845

Convention, 1895

itively the boundary line of both Republics". It was provided in article IX that in case of disagreement between the two Governments the question should be decided by an arbitrator. The commission did not begin its work until 1908, and in 1910, as a result of a dispute over the right of Honduran engineers to make surveys on the left bank of the Motagua River, its labors came to an end.

Convention, 1914

A new convention was concluded on August 1, 1914. It was almost identical with that of 1895. Again the work of the commission appointed thereunder resulted in an *impasse* because of the insistence of Honduran engineers on the right to make surveys on the left bank of the Motagua. Although the agreement contained provision that the President of the United States should act as sole arbitrator, resort was not had at the time to the services of an arbitrator.

Mediation

During the fall and winter of 1917 events in the disputed territory threatened to result in armed conflict. In order to avert this and to adjust the differences, the Government of the United States offered its services as mediator. The offer was accepted, and in May 1918 the Honduran-Guatemalan Conference was formally opened in Washington. Briefs were submitted, together with a mass of documentary evidence, but a definitive boundary line was not evolved. At this time Guatemala was in *de facto* control of a considerable portion of the disputed territory.

Further armed conflict having taken place in 1927, the United States again tendered its good offices, but the commissioners appointed by the two Governments in dispute failed to agree upon even a provisional line, pending a definitive settlement of the boundary. In June of 1928 the United States suggested that the disputants have recourse to the International Central American Tribunal (established at the Washington Conference of 1923), but Honduras insisted that the 1914 agreement, by the terms of which recourse was to be had to the President of the United States as arbitrator, remained in force.

Convention, 1930

On July 16, 1930, following further armed clashes between the disputants and following the mediation of the United States, and a boundary conference held in Washington, a convention was signed by Guatemala and Honduras, containing provision for arbitration by a special boundary tribunal. On the same day a supplementary convention was signed containing provision for the creation of a commission of Guatemalan and Honduran engineers and a chief engineer to be appointed by the president of the tribunal, to mark the boundary line. The special boundary tribunal, appointed pursuant to the terms of the convention, was composed of Chief Justice Hughes, president, Dr. Luis Castro-Ureña, designated by Guatemala, and Dr. Emilio Bello-Codesido, designated by Honduras.

Under the terms of the agreement this special tribunal was to decide, as a preliminary matter, the question whether "the International Central American Tribunal [is] . . . competent to take cognizance of the boundary question pending between Guatemala and Honduras". It further provided that if the special tribunal should deny the competence of the International Central American Tribunal in the matter, the special tribunal should proceed to take cognizance of the frontier dispute; and that if, on the other hand, the special tribunal should recognize the competence of the International Central American Tribunal "the said Special Tribunal shall take cognizance, as [the] International Central American Tribunal, of the boundary question" (art. I). By a unanimous decision, dated January 8, 1932, the special tribunal held that the International Central American Tribunal had not the competence to decide the question and requested the parties to submit their pleas, proofs, and documents.

Article V of the convention of 1930 stipulated that "the only juridical line which can be established between their respective countries is that of the *Uti Possidetis* of 1821" and that "the Tribunal shall determine this line" but that "If the Tribunal finds that one or both parties, in their subsequent development, have established, beyond that line, interests which should be taken into account in establishing the definitive boundary, the Tribunal shall modify, as it may see fit, the line of the *Uti Possidetis* of 1821 and shall fix the territorial or other compensation which it may deem just that either party should pay to the other."

In its opinion and award on the merits, dated January 23, 1933, the tribunal stated: Opinion and award

> The Tribunal finds itself confronted at the outset with a difference between the Parties as to the significance of the phrase "*uti possidetis* of 1821" as used in Article V. Both Parties agree that the principle adopted had reference to the demarcations *Uti possidetis* which existed under the colonial regime, that is, to the administrative limits of the colonial entities of Guatemala and Honduras which became independent States. But the Parties differ as to the test to be applied in determining these limits. Guatemala contends that by reference to the "*uti possidetis* of 1821" the Parties meant to have the line drawn "in conformity with the fact rather than a theory, the fact being what the Spanish monarch had himself laid down, or permitted, or acquiesced in, or tolerated, as between Province and Province, in 1821," and that the test of that line should be "the sheer factual situation" as it was at that time. Honduras insists that the phrase "*uti possidetis*" in Article V signifies "*uti possidetis juris*," and that a line could not be considered "as being juridically based on a *uti possidetis de facto*."

Both Parties invite attention to the historic utilization of the phrase *"uti possidetis"* in Latin American settlements. But an examination of these, and of the views of eminent jurists bearing upon that use of the phrase, fails to disclose such a concensus of opinion as would establish a definite criterion for the interpretation of the expression in Article V of the present Treaty.

The Parties also seek to support their respective interpretations by reference to former Treaties between them relating to the same boundary controversy. None of these Treaties used the expression *"uti possidetis."*

.   .   .   .

In determining this initial question of interpretation, we cannot regard these former proceedings as having a controlling effect. . . .

The Treaty of 1930 is a new agreement which makes no mention of the earlier and unsuccessful efforts at settlement and must stand on its own footing. The expression *"uti possidetis"* undoubtedly refers to *possession*. It makes possession the test. In determining in what sense the Parties referred to possession,

Administrative control

we must have regard to their situation at the moment the colonial regime was terminated. . . . The concept of *"uti possidetis* of 1821"* thus necessarily refers to an administrative control which rested on the will of the Spanish Crown. For the purpose of drawing the line of *"uti possidetis* of 1821"* we must look to the existence of that administrative control. . . .

Evidence

. . . We are to seek the evidence of administrative control at that time [1821]. In ascertaining the necessary support for that administrative control in the will of the Spanish King, we are at liberty to resort to all manifestations of that will—to royal *cedulas*, or rescripts, to royal orders, laws and decrees, and also, in the absence of precise laws or rescripts, to conduct indicating royal acquiescence in colonial assertions of administrative authority. The Crown was at liberty at all times to change its royal commands or to interpret them by allowing what it did not forbid. In this situation the continued and unopposed assertion of administrative authority by either of the colonial entities, under claim of right, which is not shown to be an act of usurpation because of conflict with a clear and definite expression of the royal will, is entitled to weight and is not to be overborne by reference to antecedent provisions or recitals of an equivocal character. Statements by historians and others, of repute, and authenticated maps, are also to be considered, although such descriptive material is of slight value when it relates to territory of which little or nothing was known and in which it does not appear that any administrative control was actually exercised.

First area

The tribunal considered the significance of events with respect to establishing the boundaries of the territory in dispute, and for this purpose it divided the territory into four parts.

It first considered the Honduran claim to the territory between the Motagua River and British Honduras and stated:

> The controversy as to this claim has taken a wide range. As already stated, the attitude of the Parties upon achieving independence places in a strong light their conceptions at that time of the territorial extent of the administrative authority of the preceding colonial entities.

After reviewing early assertions of jurisdiction by Guatemala, it stated:

> While no State can acquire jurisdiction over territory in another State by mere declarations on its own behalf, it is equally true that these assertions of authority by Guatemala (and other acts on her part disclosed by the evidence), shortly after independence, . . . were public, formal acts and show clearly the understanding of Guatemala that this was her territory. These assertions invited opposition on the part of Honduras if they were believed to be unwarranted. It is therefore pertinent to inquire as to what action, if any, was taken by Honduras at or near the time of independence in relation to the territory now under consideration and in answer to the above-mentioned proceedings of Guatemala.

Assertions of authority

The tribunal pointed to the lack of Honduran opposition or attempt to exercise authority during the period following independence, as well as to the fact that Guatemala had maintained authority over that part of the territory, and stated that the Honduran assertion that Guatemala did not enjoy authority over the territory prior to independence but that such authority was "an encroachment upon territory previously held under the administration of Honduras", required "clear proof" which was lacking. The tribunal held that there was no ground for the conclusion that the assertion of administrative authority by Guatemala upon achieving independence was unfounded and that—

Clear proof

> The necessary conclusion is that there is warrant for drawing the line of *uti possidetis* of 1821 so as to assign to Honduras the territory north and west of the Motagua river.

The tribunal next considered the Guatemalan claim to the Omoa and the Cuyamel area. After reviewing the history of Omoa, it stated:

Second area

> The conclusion, then, is that at the moment of independence Omoa was in the possession of the Kingdom of Guatemala for the purposes of the Kingdom as a whole, and was not in the possession of the Province of Guatemala, as distinguished from the Kingdom, or in the possession of the Province of Honduras. Hence, the evidence affords no sufficient basis for drawing the

Possession

line of *uti possidetis* of 1821 so as to include Omoa in either Guatemala or Honduras.

A similar conclusion was reached as to the Cuyamel area.

Third area

Administrative control

With respect to the third part of the territory, situated in the Motagua Valley from a point near the confluence of the Managua and Motagua Rivers to the mouth of the Motagua, the Guatemalan Government claimed that the boundary line should run along the Merendon Range, while Honduras claimed the whole region. The tribunal found that there was no evidence of provisional administrative control by either Guatemala or Honduras in this area prior to independence and that no Royal *cédula* or official order of any kind had been produced delimiting the boundary through this territory during the Spanish occupation, and stated:

Recognition of boundary

> The question remains whether there was a recognized boundary. For the concept of possession cannot be deemed to require a *pedis possessio* of every tract of land, and it is manifestly possible to have a recognition of a boundary, up to which it is assumed that administrative authority will be exercised as the opening up and the development of territory within the boundary may require. The chief points in the evidence bearing upon this question may be noted.

Historians

Attention was called to Father Juarros' history of the kingdom of Guatemala, published in 1808, and to the fact that, while each of the two governments cited Juarros, neither accepted him as authority with respect to its own claim. The tribunal said finally, with respect to this part of the territory:

> Giving full weight to this evidence, it must be deemed to support the view that the territory of the Province of Guatemala did extend to the Motagua river. But the evidence cannot be said to furnish an adequate basis for the conclusion that both States recognized the Motagua as the boundary between them. Such a decision could not rest upon the statement of Juarros alone, unsupported by official data, and official documents lack the requisite definiteness and certainty. . . .
>
> . . . The claim of Guatemala, with respect to the territory in question, that is, that the line of *uti possidetis* of 1821 should follow the *cordillera* of Merendon, rests, not upon a factual possession or upon a right to that territory shown to have been conferred by the Spanish monarch, but upon the theory of a constructive possession of the watershed of the Motagua river. But as Guatemala states,—"The watershed was at that time [during the colonial period] for the most part a tangle of impenetrable forests that defied the explorer, and even more the surveyor. From the heights of the westerly side, and following the course of the streams that flowed into the Motagua river, the region was largely uninhabited by the Spaniard, even as late as 1821." And it is manifest that the mere physical fact of the

Constructive possession

existence of a watershed cannot be regarded as fixing the line of *uti possidetis*.

In the absence of royal delimitation, or of evidence of the exercise of administrative control, or of satisfactory proof of a recognized boundary, the Tribunal is not at liberty to allocate the territory in question, . . . to either party on the basis of a line of *uti possidetis* of 1821. Subsequent developments in this region and the corresponding equities of the respective Parties demand, however, proper recognition in determining the definitive boundary which should be established between them in this territory according to equity and justice.

The tribunal next considered the status of the territory from the confluence of the Managua and Motagua Rivers to the boundary of El Salvador, embracing the Copán region. With respect to grants of public lands during the colonial period and also following it, which were produced in evidence by both parties, it said: *Fourth area*

Deliberate and formal assertion of civil authority is shown in the making of grants of the public domain. . . . Through these land grants it is possible to trace the area in which each of the colonial entities, and the States which succeeded them, asserted administrative control. *Land grants*

In connection with the question whether the lack of adequate evidence to establish the line of *uti possidetis* of 1821 in certain parts of the territory prevented it from determining the definitive boundary to its full extent, the tribunal said:

The Treaty of 1930 contemplates the establishment of a definitive boundary between Guatemala and Honduras. . . .

In the light of the declared purpose of the Treaty, the Tribunal is not at liberty to conclude that the lack of adequate evidence to establish the line of *uti possidetis* of 1821, throughout the entire territory in dispute, relieves the Tribunal of the duty to determine the definitive boundary to its full extent. The Tribunal, by the provision of the Treaty as to the line of *uti possidetis* of 1821, is not required to perform the impossible, and manifestly is bound to establish that line only to the extent that the evidence permits it to be established. And as the Tribunal is expressly authorized in the interests of justice, as disclosed by subsequent developments, to depart from the line of *uti possidetis* of 1821, even where that line is found to exist, the Treaty must be construed as empowering the Tribunal to determine the definitive boundary as justice may require throughout the entire area in controversy, to the end that the question of territorial boundaries may be finally and amicably settled.

The criteria to be applied by the Tribunal in the exercise of this authority are plainly indicated. It is not the function of the Tribunal to fix territorial limits in its view of what might be an appropriate division of the territory merely with reference to geographical features or potential advantages of a military or economic character, apart from the historical facts of develop- *Criteria*

Equities

ment. The Treaty cannot be construed as authorizing the Tribunal to establish a definitive boundary according to an idealistic conception, without regard to the settlement of the territory and existing equities created by the enterprise of the respective Parties. So far as may be found to be consistent with these equities, the geographical features of the territory indicating natural boundaries may be considered.

In fixing the boundary, the Tribunal must have regard (1) to the facts of actual possession; (2) to the question whether possession by one Party has been acquired in good faith, and without invading the right of the other Party; and (3) to the relation of territory actually occupied to that which is as yet unoccupied. In the light of the facts as thus ascertained, questions of compensation may be determined.

In determining the definitive boundary of the area from Cerro Oscuro to Angostura on the Managua River, the tribunal said:

Possession

It thus appears that according to the line of present possession, each one of the Parties is in possession of certain portions of territory which by the line of *uti possidetis* of 1821 pertained to the territory of the other Party. But the evidence furnishes no means of measuring the respective equities of either Party with respect to these apparent encroachments of the other or to determine the balance of advantage which either Party may thereby have derived. It is also evident that the Tribunal has no sufficient basis for an attempt to rectify the line of present possession so as to secure a more equitable division of the territory in dispute.

With respect to the territory lying east and south of the Motagua River, it said:

Unsettled regions; priority of settlement

In this region in dispute . . . where it has been found impossible to establish the line of *uti possidetis* of 1821, it is manifest that neither Party can be regarded as infringing the rights of the other Party in making developments according to the demands of economic progress, so long as territory already occupied has not been invaded. In view of the nature of the territory, long uninhabited and unknown, and of the lack of authoritative delimitation, it was natural that there should have been conflicting conceptions of the extent of jurisdiction and that each Party should believe that it was entitled to advance into the unoccupied zone as its interests seemed to require. Such advances in good faith, followed by occupation and development, unquestionably created equities which enterprises subsequently undertaken would be bound to consider. When it appears that the two Parties, seeking to extend their area of possession have come into conflict, the question of priority of occupation necessarily arises. Priority in settlement in good faith would appropriately establish priority of right.

In regard to the area from Cerro Escarpado to the Tinto River flowing out of the Lagua Tinta, it said:

As to the territorial equities of the two Republics, with which the Tribunal is concerned in this region, it is apparent that Honduras could not create an equity, entitled to recognition in determining the definitive boundary, by authorizing railroad construction upon lands over which Guatemala had previously asserted authority by her grants which in no way infringed any right which Honduras had then established. Nor can Honduras base such an equity upon an extension of the railroad line which was secured only by reason of the special circumstances above recited in connection with the Great War and with the understanding that the extension should be without prejudice to Guatemala's position.

The tribunal established the definitive boundary in its entire extent and held that, in view of the location of the definitive boundary, as established by it, "no award of compensation to either Party is found to be necessary".

Guatemala-Honduras Special Boundary Tribunal, Opinion and Award (1933) 2, 5, 7, 10, 13, 20, 32, 37, 43, 53, 68, 69, 79, 84, 94. For pertinent excerpts from the treaty of 1845, see I *Mediation of the Honduran-Guatemalan Boundary Question, Held Under the Good Offices of the Department of State, 1918–1919* (1919) 16–17. For the convention of 1895, see *ibid.* 17; 87 Br. & For. St. Paps. 530. For the convention of 1914, see 107 *idem* 902. For the arbitration agreement and supplementary convention of July 16, 1930, see 137 League of Nations Treaty Series (1933) 232, 245, 253. For the preliminary decision of the tribunal, see *Guatemala-Honduras Boundary Arbitration, Opinion and Judgment of the Special Tribunal on the Preliminary Question* (1932). See also Fisher, "The Arbitration of the Guatemalan-Honduran Boundary Dispute", in 27 A.J.I.L. (1933) 403. For diplomatic correspondence relating to the boundary dispute, see MS. Department of State, file 714.1515.

The Tacna-Arica dispute involved two former Peruvian provinces, Tacna and Arica. Under article II of the treaty of peace—the so-called Treaty of Ancón—between Chile and Peru, signed at Lima on October 20, 1883, at the end of the War of the Pacific in which Chile was successful, the Peruvian province of Tarapacá was ceded to Chile in perpetuity. Article III provided that "The territory of the provinces of Tacna and Arica . . . shall remain in the possession of Chile, and subject to Chilean laws and authorities, during a period of ten years, to be reckoned from the date of the ratification of the present treaty of peace." Article III further provided that at the expiration of the 10-year period it should be decided by plebiscite which country should have the territory and that the country to which it should be annexed should pay to the other 10 million pesos of Chilean silver or of Peruvian soles of equal weight and fineness.

Shortly before 1894 Peru demanded that Chile temporarily turn over the provinces to her or to a third power upon the expiration of the 10-year period. Chile refused, claiming that she was entitled to

Tacna-Arica; Peru and Chile

Treaty of Ancón

retain the provinces until the plebiscite had been held and resulted favorably to Peru. The Treaty of Ancón having been ratified on March 28, 1884, the 10-year period expired on March 28, 1894. However, the plebiscite was not held on that date.

In response to the invitation of President Harding, representatives of Chile and Peru met in Washington in May-July, 1922, and, as a result of the Conference, the dispute in regard to article III of the Treaty of Ancón was submitted under the terms of a protocol and a complementary act dated July 20, 1922 to the decision of the President of the United States who, on March 4, 1925, delivered his opinion and award. The arbitrator (President Coolidge) defined his duty to be:

> 1. To decide whether in the present circumstances a plebiscite shall or shall not be held . . .
> 2. If the Arbitrator decides in favor of a plebiscite to determine the conditions of that plebiscite . . .
> 3. If the Arbitrator decides against the plebiscite to take no further action as Arbitrator, except that—
> 4. Whether the decision be for or against a plebiscite, the Arbitrator is to decide the pending questions with respect to Tarata and Chilcaya arising respectively on the northern and southern boundaries of the territory.

With respect to the Peruvian contention that Chile had refused to hold the plebiscite for a long period of time for the purpose of Chilenizing the provinces and that such conduct invalidated the provisions of article III, the arbitrator held, after reviewing the negotiations leading up to the arbitration, that he was unable to find any proper basis for the conclusion that Chile had acted in bad faith. The record failed to show, he stated, that Chile "ever arbitrarily refused to negotiate with Peru the terms of the plebiscitary protocol" (as was provided for in article III of the Treaty of Ancón). He held that article III of the Treaty of Ancón was still in effect, that a plebiscite should be had, and that the plebiscite should be held under the supervision of a Plebiscitary Commission composed of three members, one to be appointed by each Government, and a third—the president of the Commission—to be appointed by the President of the United States; and he reserved the right on his own motion to entertain an appeal from the Plebiscitary Commission on any question decided by it. The Commission was given the right to determine the date of holding the plebiscite.

The arbitrator made definite holdings as to the territory, the status of which was to be determined by the plebiscite. Article III of the Treaty of Ancón recited that the territory of the provinces of "Tacna and Arica, bounded on the north by the River Sama from its source in the Cordilleras on the frontier of Bolivia to its mouth at the sea, on the south by the ravine and River Camarones, on the east by the Republic of Bolivia, and on the west by the Pacific Ocean", should continue in the possession of Chile during a period of 10 years. Chile contended that the northern boundary line was the River Sama from its source to its mouth irrespective of any Peruvian provincial lines and that the territory in question included not only the Peruvian provinces of Tacna and Arica but also a portion of the Peruvian province of Tarata. Peru insisted that article III dealt solely with the provinces of Tacna and Arica. The arbitrator found that there was no River Sama having "its source in the Cordilleras on the frontier of Bolivia"; that the treaty contained an inaccurate description of the territory; that the question of including the territory of the province of Tarata was not in the minds of the negotiators of the treaty; and that, if it was thought by Chile that the mention of the river boundary would effect this purpose, "the fact remains that the description of the territory as that 'of the provinces of Tacna and Arica' was put in the treaty and the river line was deprived of a controlling significance by its inaccuracy". He decided—with reference to the northern boundary—that no part of the Peruvian province of Tarata was included in the territory covered by the provisions of article III of the Treaty of Ancón; that the territory to which article III related was exclusively that of the Peruvian provinces of Tacna and Arica as they stood on October 20, 1883; and that the northern boundary of that part of the territory covered by article III which was within the Peruvian province of Tacna "is the River Sama".

The southern boundary of the territory covered by article III is stated in the treaty, as above indicated, to be "the ravine and River Camarones". Article II of the treaty provided for the cession by Peru to Chile in perpetuity of "the territory of the littoral province of Tarapacá, the boundaries of which are, on the north the ravine and River Camarones". The descriptions were identical. There was no dispute as to the boundary thus described between the mouth of the River Camarones at the Pacific Ocean and Arapunta, the junction of two principal tributaries, the Ajatama coming in from the northeast—which Chile claimed was the legal or traditional boundary line between the Peruvian provinces of Arica and Tarapacá— and the Caritaya coming in from the southeast—which Peru claimed was the true boundary from Arapunta to its source. Between the two lines were the valuable borax deposits of Chilcaya. Both parties apparently agreed that the treaty line and the old Peruvian provincial line were the same. The arbitrator decided that the boundary between the provinces of Arica and Tarapacá described in the treaty (art. III) was the boundary as it was on October 20, 1883.

The membership of the Plebiscitary Commission, subsequently appointed, was as follows: Augustin Edwards, of Chile; Manuel de Freyre y Santander, of Peru; and General John J. Pershing, of the United States, president (Major General Lassiter was appointed to succeed him in January 1926). On September 1, 1925 the province of Tarata was delivered by Chile to Peru, in conformity with the arbitral decision. A question having arisen as to the possibility of holding a free and fair plebiscite, a resolution for the termination of the proceedings of the Commission was adopted by it on June 14, 1926, the Chilean Commissioner not voting. On June 21 following the Commission declared itself adjourned.

Meanwhile between April 6 and June 21, 1926 Secretary Kellogg had tendered good offices. However, the negotiations which took place in Washington proved unsuccessful.

The arbitral award of 1925 also contained provision for the appointment of a Special Commission on boundaries, consisting of three members—one to be appointed by Peru, one by Chile, and one by the arbitrator—"to draw the boundary lines of the territory covered by Article 3 of the Treaty of Ancón in accordance with the determination of the Arbitrator in this Opinion and Award". Such a Commission was appointed and proceeded with its work until October 17, 1928, when it was agreed to suspend the work (at first for a period of months and later indefinitely). On August 2, 1929 the President of the United States ordered the labors of the Commission terminated.

Treaty of 1929

On October 3, 1928, pursuant to a suggestion of the Secretary of State of the United States, the two parties resumed direct negotiations on the subject after they had renewed diplomatic relations—broken off since 1910. As a result of these negotiations, the President of the United States (Herbert Hoover), not as arbitrator but in the exercise of good offices, at the request of both countries submitted a proposal for the final settlement of the Tacna-Arica dispute. The proposal was accepted by the two countries and a treaty for the settlement of the dispute was signed by them at Lima on June 3,

Settlement

1929. Article 1 of the treaty states that the dispute arising out of article III of the Treaty of Ancón "is hereby finally settled". Article 2 provides that "The territory of Tacna and Arica shall be divided into two portions of which Tacna shall be allotted to Peru and Arica to Chile" and that—

> . . . The dividing line between the two portions, and consequently the frontier between the territories of Chile and Peru, shall start from a point on the coast to be named "Concordia",

ten kilometres to the north of the bridge over the river Lluta. It shall continue eastwards parallel to the line of the Chilean section of the Arica La Paz railway and at a distance of ten kilometres therefrom, with such sinuosities as may be necessary to allow the local topography to be used, in the demarcation, in such a way that the sulphur mines of the Tacora and their dependencies shall remain within Chilean territory. The line shall then pass through the centre of the Laguna Blanca, so that one portion thereof shall be in Chile and the other in Peru. Chile cedes to Peru in perpetuity all her rights over the irrigation-channels Uchusuma and the Mauri (also known as Azucarero), without prejudice to the sovereignty she will be entitled to exercise over such part of the above-mentioned aqueducts as may come within Chilean territory after the tracing of the dividing line mentioned in the present Article. In respect of both channels, Chile grants to Peru a perpetual and absolute easement over the sections which pass through Chilean territory. Such easement shall include the right to widen the present channels, to change their course and to utilize all the water that may be collected in their passage through Chilean territory, except the waters that at present flow into the river Lluta and those which are used in the Tacora sulphur mines.

Provision was made in the treaty for the marking of this boundary by a mixed commission. It was provided that within 30 days Chile should transfer to the Government of Peru all territories which under the treaty were to come into the possession of the latter (art. 4). Peru was also granted certain rights in the bay and port of Arica (art. 5). It was further agreed that Chile, at the time of the exchange of ratifications, should deliver $6,000,000 and all public works and immovable state property situated in the territories which would come under Peruvian sovereignty, to the Government of Peru. A supplementary protocol signed the same day contains provision, *inter alia*, that the two Governments shall not, without previous agreement between them, cede to any third power the whole or part of the territories which in conformity with the treaty "come under their respective sovereignty" and elaborates upon the meaning of the port facilities granted to Peru under article 5 of the treaty.

In accordance with article 4 of the treaty of 1929, the final act of demarcation of the boundary between Peru and Chile was signed at Lima on August 5, 1930.

Demarcation of boundary

Thomas C. Dawson, Minister in Chile, memorandum, July 16, 1909, MS. Department of State, file 944/77; Presiding Commissioner Lassiter to Secretary Kellogg, June 16, 1926, *ibid.* 723.2515/2464 (plebiscitary proceedings terminated); William C. Dennis to Stokeley Morgan, Oct. 19, 1928, *ibid.* 723.2515/3213½; Department of State, Mimeographed Press Release, May 17, 1929, *ibid.* 723.2515/3394; Chargé Mayer to Secretary Stimson, Aug. 9, 1930, *ibid.* 723.2515/3521; Ambassador Dearing to Secretary Stimson, Oct. 29, 1930, *ibid.* 723.2515/3534; 74 Br. & For. St. Paps. 349 (treaty of 1883); 21 League of Nations Treaty Series (1923–24)

142–145 (protocol and supplementary act of 1922); Ambassador Pezet to Secretary Hughes, July 22, 1922, MS. Department of State, file 723.2515/991 (protocol and supplementary act of 1922); *ibid.* 723.2515/1324 (opinion and award); 94 League of Nations Treaty Series (1929) 406, 410, and 100 *idem* (1930) 467 (treaty of June 3, 1929); MS. Department of State, file 723.2515/3477 (final ruling of arbitrator); *ibid.* file 723.-2515/3534 (final act of demarcation signed Aug. 5, 1930); "Opinion and Award of the Arbitrator" of Mar. 4, 1925 (Washington, 1925) 4, 36–37, 60–64. See also Ireland, *Boundaries, Possessions, and Conflicts in South America* (1938) 160–175.

Ecuador and Peru: Oriente

The so-called "Oriente" controversy between Ecuador and Peru involves the claim of the two countries to a comparatively large area of territory in the headwaters of the Amazon.

Ecuador bases her claim upon exploration; upon her need for the inland territory; upon a Spanish Royal decree of 1740 defining the boundaries of the presidency of Quito, including the "Oriente"; upon a treaty of peace of September 22, 1829 and a protocol of August 11, 1830 between Colombia and Peru, by which Ecuador (as a successor to rights of Colombia) claims that Peru conceded Colombia's claim to territory north of the Amazon, but which Peru denies. Peru bases her claim on "constitution of nationalities", on freedom from obligations under treaties between Colombia and Ecuador, and on the principle that, as between states successors to Spain, sovereignty depends upon permanent control by the state claiming a particular area.

The dispute in its entirety was submitted for arbitration to the King of Spain under the terms of a convention of August 1, 1887, but in 1910, when it was rumored that a decision was about to be given which would not be fully satisfactory, war became imminent but was averted by the joint mediation of Brazil, Argentina, and the United States, and on May 24 of that year the King of Spain withdrew as arbitrator. Thereafter, when the mediating powers suggested that the question should be submitted to a tribunal at The Hague, Ecuador declined, favoring direct negotiations under the convention of 1887. By a protocol of June 21, 1924 the two countries agreed to seek the determination of zones pertaining to each other by direct negotiation (sending delegates to Washington for this purpose and for the purpose of fixing a definite line, if possible) and to submit the determination of boundary in any zone on which it was impossible to agree to the arbitration of the President of the United States, after ratification of the agreement by the Congresses of the two Governments. On July 6, 1936 a further protocol was signed in Lima by the two Governments, implementing the protocol of 1924. By the terms of the protocol the Governments agreed each to name three delegates to meet in Washington on September 30, 1936; to maintain the *status quo* of "their present territorial positions" until the termination of the negotiations at Washington and the arbitral proceedings; and to regard any possible arbitration as purely juridical (*de jure*) in character. Accordingly on that date conferences between the delegates began in Washington. In August 1938 the delegation of Ecuador proposed the submission of the entire dispute to the *de jure* arbitration of the President of the United States. However, on September 29 of that year, the Peruvian Government instructed its delegation to suspend these negotiations. The Peruvian Government claimed that the Ecuadoran insistence upon submission of the entire question to arbitration exceeded the provisions of the protocol of 1924; moreover, the Peruvian Government asserted that it was influenced by the invitation of Ecuador to discuss the boundary controversy directly in Lima in the event that juridical or other reasons delayed or prevented a friendly understanding in negotiations in Washington.

> 1910 For. Rel. 438–507 (mediation) ; 27 League of Nations Treaty Series (1924) 347 (protocol of June 21, 1924) ; Department of State, XV *Press Releases*, weekly issue 354, pp. 17–18 (July 9 and 10, 1936), and *ibid.* weekly issue 366, pp. 283–288 (Sept. 30, 1936), initial sessions of conference in 1936; MS. Department of State, file 722.2315/967 (protocol of July 6, 1936) ; *ibid.* 722.2315/1097, /1199, /1207, /1210 (suspension of conference in 1938) ; League of Nations, *Official Journal* (1938) 1130–1132; Ireland, *Boundaries, Possessions, and Conflicts in South America* (1938) 219–230 (historical summary).

On July 15, 1916 Colombia and Ecuador entered into a boundary treaty for the settlement of their common boundary, including that in dispute on the north side of the "Oriente". On March 24, 1922 Colombia and Peru entered into a treaty with respect to the boundary along the north side of the "Oriente", wherein (art. 1) Colombia ceded to Peru a narrow strip of territory which Ecuador in the 1916 settlement had recognized as belonging to Colombia. To this Ecuador objected, and Brazil, as a neighboring country, also objected to the 1922 agreement on the ground that it dealt with territory to which she had a claim.

As a result of the good offices of Secretary Hughes, an agreement was reached at a meeting at the Department of State in Washington, on March 4, 1925, between the Secretary of State of the United States, the Ambassador of Peru, the Minister of Colombia, and the Chargé d'Affaires ad interim of Brazil. The agreement, in the form of a procès-verbal, provided for (1) the withdrawal by the Brazilian Government of its observations regarding the boundary treaty between Colombia and Peru of March 24, 1922; (2) the ratification by Colombia and Peru of the above-mentioned treaty; and (3) the signing of a convention between Brazil and Colombia by which the boundary between those countries would be agreed to on the

Apaporis –Tabatinga line, Brazil granting in perpetuity in favor of Colombia freedom of navigation on the Amazon and other rivers common to both countries.

> 110 Br. & For. St. Paps. 826 (treaty of July 15, 1916) ; 74 League of Nations Treaty Series (1928) 13 (treaty of Mar. 24, 1922) ; XXV Martens' *Nouveau recueil général* (3d ser., Triepel, 1932) 672 (procès-verbal signed in 1925) ; Ireland, *Boundaries, Possessions*, etc. (1938) 175–185 (controversy between Colombia and Ecuador) ; *ibid.* 188–191 (controversy between Colombia and Peru).

Colombia and Peru

Ratifications of the treaty of March 24, 1922 between Colombia and Peru were exchanged on March 19, 1928. The Mixed Commission of Delimitation created pursuant to the terms thereof completed its work on March 14, 1930, and the transfer of territory from the Putumayo River to the Amazon River, formerly claimed by Peru as part of the Department of Loreto, was delivered to Colombia on August 17, 1930.

Leticia

Leticia, a town with a population of some 300 inhabitants, lies on the Amazon at the southeast corner of the trapezium so transferred. On September 1, 1932 an armed band of Peruvians took possession of the town, incensed, it was claimed, by the treaty of 1922 which had been approved, it was alleged, by the Peruvian Congress under a dictatorial regime in an atmosphere "of silence and terror". The Peruvian Government at once informed the Colombian Government that it had nothing to do with the planning or execution of these acts.

When it was suggested by Peru that the matter be submitted to the Permanent Commission on Inter-American Conciliation under the Gondra treaty of May 3, 1923, or the convention on conciliation signed at Washington in 1929, Colombia took the position that the question of her sovereignty over Leticia was "strictly and exclusively of an internal nature" and that therefore she could not agree to the suggested procedure and meanwhile sent an expeditionary force up the Amazon to restore law and order. On January 14, 1933 the Council of the League transmitted to Peru a copy of a communication from Colombia, dated January 4, 1933, setting forth the views just recited, requested the views of Peru, and expressed confidence that Peru would refrain from acting contrary to the Covenant of the League of Nations, to which Peru replied on January 20 that she desired to "supplement the Salomón-Lozano Treaty [of 1922], to make it more elastic and to infuse new life into it . . . that is to say, a re-examination of the question in dispute for the purpose of dealing with a *de facto* situation which reveals the imperfections of a treaty".

On January 23, 1933 Colombia requested signatories of the Kellogg-Briand pact of August 27, 1928 to remind Peru of her obligations. Brazil offered her mediation, suggesting that the disputed territory be provisionally turned over to her for subsequent transfer to the deposed Colombian officers in the area and that a conference be held in Rio de Janeiro by the riparian states of the Amazon to examine the treaty of 1922 in a broad spirit of conciliation. To this Colombia gave her consent but Peru accepted the proposal with certain amendments which Colombia rejected, and on February 3, 1933 Brazil declared her efforts toward mediation closed.

Meanwhile, on January 25, 1933, Secretary Stimson addressed a note to Peru reminding her of the resolution on "Aggression", adopted at the Habana Conference on February 20, 1928, and the declaration of the American republics denouncing resort to force, signed at Washington on August 3, 1932, and urging compliance with the Brazilian proposal. Peru replied protesting loyalty to her international agreements and refusing to desist from protecting her citizens who seized Leticia.

On February 17 Colombia appealed to the League Council under article 15 of the Covenant. Peru declared that the dispute was purely American and ought to be settled by American commissions or mediators. The Council of the League proposed, on March 1, that a League Commission should take charge of the territory, using Colombian military forces and police "as international" during the negotiations. Colombia accepted the proposal, but Peru made counter suggestions which were unacceptable to the Council. On March 18 the Council adopted a report recommending "the complete evacuation of the area by Peruvian forces . . . and the withdrawal of all support from the Peruvians who have occupied that area". On May 10, 1933 the Advisory Committee of the League Council, with which the United States and Brazil collaborated (the former with reservations), proposed that Leticia be evacuated by Peru and that a Commission of the League in the name of Colombia and at her expense should take over the area and enforce law and supervise negotiations for a settlement of the territorial question. Colombia and Peru accepted the proposals, and on June 23, 1933 the Commission took over Leticia. In September 1933 Peru and Colombia appointed delegates for purposes of direct negotiations.

The agreement for the temporary control by the League Commission expired in June 1934, and on May 24, 1934 Colombia and Peru signed a protocol of peace, friendship, and cooperation (and an additional act) at Rio de Janeiro, wherein Peru deplored events subsequent to September 1, 1932; Peru and Colombia agreed to renew diplomatic relations; the two countries agreed that the treaty of 1922 constituted one of the "juridical ties which may not be modified or affected except by common consent of the parties" or by a decision of the Permanent Court of International Justice; it was agreed not to make war or employ force as a method of settlement of their problems; and it was provided that if, in the future, they could not come to agreement by direct diplomatic negotiations either party might have recourse to the procedure established in article 36 of the Statute of the Permanent Court of International Justice, without reservations. The League Commission transferred Leticia to Colombia on June 19, 1934. The exchange of ratifications of the protocol of May 1934 took place on September 27, 1935.

> 100 League of Nations Treaty Series (1930) 235–246 (procès-verbeaux nos. 4 and 6 of the Mixed Commission of Delimitation, Nov. 11, 1929 and Mar. 14, 1930); League of Nations, *Official Journal* (1933) 516–614; Department of State, *Press Releases*, weekly issue 174, pp. 66–70 (Jan. 25, 1933); League of Nations, *Official Journal* (1934) 283–284, 874–949; *ibid.*, Spec. Supp. 125 (1934), p. 48; Department of State, Treaty Information Bulletin 57 (June 1934) 23; Martínez Pereira, *La paz de Rio de Janeiro*, XXV *Revista de derecho internacional* (Habana, 1934) 280; Woolsey, "The Leticia Dispute Between Colombia and Peru", in 29 A.J.I.L. (1935) 94; 68 Bulletin of the Pan American Union (1934) 546, 549; League of Nations, *Official Journal* (Jan.–June 1935) 443–446; *ibid.* (July–Dec. 1935) 1647; Ireland, *Boundaries, Possessions, and Conflicts in South America* (1938) 196–206.

Bolivia and Paraguay: the Chaco Boreal

A treaty was signed by Bolivia and Paraguay on October 15, 1879 for the settlement of a long-standing boundary dispute in which the whole Chaco Boreal was claimed as Bolivian territory on the ground that it was always under the jurisdiction of the *Audiencia* of Charcas. By the treaty the Bolivian claim was satisfied in part, but neither country ratified it. Another treaty between the two countries, that of February 16, 1887, also failed of ratification, and a similar fate befell agreements of November 23, 1894 and January 12, 1907.

On July 9, 1913 the American Minister in Asunción reported to the Department of State that a recent temporary *modus vivendi* between the two countries, known as "the Ayala-Mujía protocol", provided for the maintenance of the *status quo* in the Chaco for two years and for the conclusion in the meantime of a final boundary treaty or a treaty providing for mediation or arbitration. The time was extended by subsequent protocols.

As a result of the boundary dispute, armed clashes occurred between the troops of the two countries in 1928, 1930, and 1931. A state of armed conflict began in June 1932, which Paraguay declared in 1933 to be "a state of war". It lasted about three years. Finally, by the treaty of peace, friendship, and boundaries concluded on July 21, 1938, the two countries reached agreement on their respective sovereignty over the larger part of the disputed area and agreed to submit the determination of the boundary in the two remaining zones to the Presidents of Argentina, Brazil, Chile, Peru, the United States, and Uruguay "in their capacity as arbitrators in equity, who, acting *ex aequo et bono*", should render their award with reference to these zones. Using the right conferred upon them by article III of the treaty, the Presidents delegated their functions to plenipotentiaries who delivered their award on October 10, 1938. After stating that they took account of a report prepared by an advisory military commission which had made an aerial photographic survey and an inspection of the terrain involved, the plenipotentiaries said:

> Moreover the arbitrators have taken into account the antecedents accumulated by the Peace Conference as well as the needs of the parties with regard to their mutual security and geographic and economic necessities.
>
> The examination of these antecedents and the opinions of the military advisers have convinced the arbitrators that within the zones submitted to arbitration the line described below is equitable . . .

Security, geographic and economic necessities

The award contains a detailed description of the boundary line. It was accepted without reservation by Bolivia and Paraguay.

> Telmo Ichaso, *Antecedents del tratado de límites celebrado con la República del Paraguay* (1894) 1, 4, 319; 1907 For. Rel. 87; Minister Grevstad to Secretary Bryan, July 9, 1913, MS. Department of State, file 724.3415/21; Department of State, Treaty Information Bulletin 106 (July 1938) 256 (treaty of 1938); Department of State, XIX *Press Releases*, weekly issue 472, pp. 263, 264 (Oct. 10, 1938), award of 1938; *ibid.*, XX *Press Releases*, weekly issue 488, p. 94 (Jan. 30, 1939), resolution of closure of the Chaco Peace Conference; *ibid.*, Treaty Information Bulletin 112 (Jan. 1939) 7-9; Ireland, *Boundaries, Possessions, and Conflicts in South America* (1938) 66-95. The volume just cited also contains accounts of other Latin American boundary disputes and adjustments since 1906 not submitted to arbitration.

UNITED STATES – CANADA

§106

By the River and Harbor Act, approved on June 13, 1902, Congress requested the President of the United States to invite the Government of Great Britain to join in the formation of an International Commission to be composed of three members each from the United States and Canada—

International Waterways Commission

> to investigate and report upon the conditions and uses of the waters adjacent to the boundary lines between the United States

and Canada, including all of the waters of the lakes and rivers whose natural outlet is by the River Saint Lawrence to the Atlantic Ocean; also upon the maintenance and regulation of suitable levels; and also upon the effect upon the shores of these waters and the structures thereon, and upon the interests of navigation, by reason of the diversion of these waters from or change in their natural flow; and, further, to report upon the necessary measures to regulate such diversion, and to make such recommendations for improvements and regulations as shall best subserve the interests of navigation in said waters.

The Commission was also authorized to report upon the advisability of locating a dam at the outlet of Lake Erie. Such an invitation was extended to the British Government and was accepted on June 2, 1903.

Powers of Commission

At the first full meeting, held in Washington on May 25, 1905, disagreement arose as to the extent of the Commission's jurisdiction. The instructions from the Department of State, dated April 15, 1905, to the American Commissioners contained the statement that the words "including all of the waters of the lakes and rivers whose natural outlet is by the River St. Lawrence to the Atlantic Ocean" contained in the law, were intended "as a limitation on what precedes them" and that the investigation and report should cover "only such waters, omitting the lower St. Lawrence itself, as well as all other waters not discharging naturally through it". The views of the Canadian Government, looking to a broader interpretation of the act, were set forth in an Order in Council of March 25, 1905. The Canadian Government, however, at length acquiesced in the American view.

Joint reports

The Commission made joint reports on the following subjects:

(1) "The Conditions Existing at Niagara Falls, with Recommendations", May 3, 1906;
(2) "The Conditions Existing at Sault Ste. Marie, with Rules for the Control of the Same, Recommended by the International Waterways Commission", May 3, 1906;
(3) "The Application of the International Development Company for Permission to Construct Regulating Works on the Richelieu River", November 15, 1906;
(4) "The Application of the Minnesota Canal and Power Company, of Duluth, Minnesota, for Permission to Divert Certain Waters in the State of Minnesota from the Boundary Waters Between the United States and Canada, 1906", November 15, 1906.

At the request of the British Government approval of the application of the Minnesota Canal and Power Company, which the Commission had recommended "be not granted without the concurrence of the Canadian Government", was withheld pending the completion of the negotiations subsequently inaugurated for the conclusion of a treaty for the establishment of an international joint commission to have jurisdiction over questions relating to the boundary waters between the United States and Canada. The treaty was concluded on January 11, 1909, and, upon its ratification, the Department of State notified the War Department of the withdrawal of opposition to the granting of the application of the power company, stating that the provisions of article II of the treaty furnished a means for indemnifying property owners on the Canadian side if by any possibility any injury to them should result from the diversion of waters proposed in the power company's project.

32 Stat. 331, 373 (act of 1902); Compiled Reports of the International Waterways Commission, 1905–1913, Sessional Paper No. 19A, Canada (1913), pp. 30, 31, 339, 341, 351, 354. Secretary Root to Ambassador Bryce, no. 219, Jan. 13, 1908, MS. Department of State, file 1718/35; Mr. Bryce to Mr. Root, Jan. 17, 1908, ibid. 1718/38; the Assisant Secretary of State (Wilson) to the Secretary of War, May 12, 1910, ibid. 711.4216B/54; Report of the International Waterways Commission upon the International Boundary Between the United States and the Dominion of Canada through the St. Lawrence River and the Great Lakes, Apr. 29, 1915, ibid. 711.42155/268; 3 Treaties, etc. (Redmond, 1923) 2607 (treaty of 1909).

In its report of Nov. 27, 1912, the American section of the Commission stated that the International Waterways Commission had completed the work for which it had been organized, except the final report upon a dam at the outlet of Lake Erie. The report stated that all new questions arising with respect to the water boundary would be considered by the International Joint Commission created by the treaty of 1909 (art. 7), as that Commission took the place of the International Waterways Commission so far as new questions were concerned. The Waterways Commission, the report added, had one other unfinished task assigned to it by article 4 of the boundary treaty of Apr. 11, 1908, i.e. to ascertain and reestablish accurately the location of the international boundary line between the United States and Canada through the St. Lawrence River and the Great Lakes. 1 Treaties, etc. (Malloy, 1910) 821. MS. Department of State, file 711.42155/212. The work of ascertaining and reestablishing the boundary was completed and a final report made on Apr. 29, 1915.

Article VII of the treaty of 1909 provides for the establishment and maintenance of an International Joint Commission, three commissioners to be named by each country. Article III contains provision that, apart from special agreement, "no further or other uses or obstructions or diversions . . . of boundary waters . . . affecting the natural level or flow of boundary waters on the other side of the line" shall be made except by the authority of the respective countries and with the approval of the International Joint Commission. Article IV provides that, apart from special agreement, the high contracting parties will not permit the construction or maintenance on their respective sides of the boundary of "any remedial or protective works or any dams or other obstructions in waters flowing from boundary waters or in waters at a lower level than the boundary

International Joint Commission

in rivers flowing across the boundary, the effect of which is to raise the natural level of the waters on the other side of the boundary", unless the construction or maintenance thereof is approved by the International Joint Commission. Article VIII provides that in passing upon cases described in articles III and IV, the Commission shall be guided by certain rules, namely, that the two countries shall have, each on its own side of the boundary, "equal and similar rights" in the use of the waters; that the order of precedence which shall be observed among the various uses is (1) domestic and sanitary purposes, (2) navigation, and (3) power and irrigation; that this order of precedence shall not apply to or disturb "existing uses"; and that the Commission may make its approval conditional. By the terms of article IX the two countries further agree that "any other questions or matters of difference arising between them involving the rights, obligations, or interests of either in relation to the other or to the inhabitants of the other along the common frontier" should be referred to the Commission for examination and report, while by the terms of article X it is provided that under certain circumstances the Commission may be granted arbitral powers. Much broader power is conferred upon the Commission in articles VIII, IX, and X than had been advocated by the United States, but the powers of the Commission are much less than had been contemplated in the so-called "Clinton-Gibbons draft", submitted by the American and Canadian members of the International Waterways Commission on September 25, 1907, and generally supported by the Canadian Government.

3 Treaties, etc. (Redmond, 1923) 2607.

For correspondence leading to the conclusion of the convention, see Secretary Root to Judge Clinton, May 17, 1907, MS. Department of State, file 5934/1A; Mr. Clinton to Mr. Root, Sept. 25, 1907, *ibid.* 5934/6; Mr. Root to Ambassador Bryce, Jan. 29, 1908, *ibid.* 5934/18A; Mr. Bryce to Mr. Root, no. 63, Mar. 21, 1908, *ibid.* 5934/19; Mr. Root to Mr. Bryce, June 4, 1908, *ibid.* 5934/25; Mr. Bryce to the Governor General of the Dominion of Canada, no. 104, June 8, 1908, *ibid.* 5934/78; Mr. Anderson to Mr. Root, Aug. 26, 1908, *ibid.* 5934/44.

And see H. Rept. 1612, to accompany S. 8354, 61st Cong., 2d sess., serial no. 5593, and S. Doc. 561, 61st Cong., 2d sess., serial no. 5660.

For a summary of the cases and the functions of the Commission in general, see *Papers Relating to the Work of the International Joint Commission* (Ottawa, 1929), containing a list of the documents of the Commission.

Rainy
River

In 1909 the Government of Great Britain applied to the Government of the United States for its consent to the construction by the Canadian Government of a lock and dam at the foot of Long Sault Rapids in Rainy River. This international stream forms the boundary line between the State of Minnesota and the northwestern portion of the Province of Ontario. Near Rainy Lake are the Falls of Fort Frances, and about 42½ miles below those falls are the Long Sault Rapids where the water descends seven or eight feet within a distance of one and a half miles. It was stated that, by the construction of a dam of the character described at the foot of these falls, the Rainy River could be made navigable to the Falls of Fort Frances. In order to construct the dam it was necessary to use a portion of the territory of the United States. On April 8, 1909 the Secretary of State requested an opinion of the Attorney General on the question of the authority to give consent to a foreign government to occupy, in the manner and for the purposes described, territory of the United States which is situated in the State of Minnesota. On May 10, 1909 Attorney General Wickersham informed him that the President and the Senate, by the exercise of the treaty power and without the consent of the State of Minnesota "can grant to the Canadian government the easement desired".

In connection with a suggestion that the Canadian Government might undertake the construction of the portion of the dam on the American side of the river through a corporation organized under the laws of the State of Minnesota, the construction having been first properly authorized by Congress, the Attorney General said:

> I think this plan entirely feasible, provided the laws of Minnesota are not in conflict therewith; and it would probably present some advantages, as the corporation would be a citizen of the United States and of the State of Minnesota, and its control would not necessitate negotiations with a foreign government. However, I make this suggestion, that when authority is obtained from Congress to construct the dam, its consent be also obtained for the Canadian government to hold the stock of the Minnesota corporation.

27 Op. Att. Gen. (1908–9) 327, 329, 333. See also 33 Stat. 814; 35 Stat. 273; 36 Stat. 931.

Lake of the Woods, a boundary water between the United States and Canada, has two principal outlets, in Canada near Kenora and Keewatin, Ontario, at the extreme northerly end of the lake, where they form the headwaters of the Winnipeg River. In the eighteen eighties the Canadian Government authorized the construction of a dam known as "the Rollerway Dam" in one of these outlets, the primary purpose of which, apparently, was to raise the level of the lake in the interest of navigation—then considerable—on the Canadian side. The work built was said to have effected a rise of from one and a half to three feet in the level of the lake. Several years later (1893–95) another dam, known as "the Norman Dam", was built, by certain power interests, in the Winnipeg River at a point a short distance below the Rollerway Dam. The Rollerway Dam was removed in 1899. In 1906 the other outlet of the lake

Lake of the Woods

was closed by a dam used in connection with a power plant constructed by the town of Kenora. Subsequent to the construction of these dams the increase over the levels which would have prevailed with the natural outlets varied from a little less than a foot to more than six feet.

The increased flooding of lowlands along the southern shore of the lake in the State of Minnesota led to considerable complaint of damage caused by flooding and seepage, and the matter was referred to the International Joint Commission for investigation and report under the provisions of article 9 of the boundary waters treaty of 1909. The Commission submitted its final report and recommendations to the two Governments in June 1917. It found that during the previous 24 years the level of Lake of the Woods had been held at an average of three feet higher than that which would have prevailed had the outlets remained in their natural state, and stated that "subject to the proper compensation and protection being provided for property and interests injuriously affected, the most advantageous use of the waters of the Lake of the Woods and of the waters flowing into and from the lake and of the shores and the harbors of the lake can be secured by maintaining the level of the lake at an ordinary maximum stage of 1061.25 sea level datum". This level was found to be 2.33 feet higher than the computed natural level of the lake and slightly lower than the level prevailing during the preceding 24 years. The report showed that to maintain the lake at the recommended levels it would be necessary, among other things, to acquire for flowage rights 23,968 acres of public and privately owned lands in the United States and 40,792 acres in Canada. The value of the land in the United States, much of which was already covered by water, was estimated at $164,000 and that in Canada at $81,000. The report also included recommendations for the construction of certain protective works on each side of the border, at an estimated cost in Minnesota, including indemnity for certain property to be acquired, of $110,000, and in Canada of $5,000. It was stated in the report that the proposed control of the lake could be effected—

(1) By regulating the outflow capacity of the lake;
(2) By taking advantage of existing reservoir capacity of something over one billion cubic feet on Rainy Lake and the lakes immediately above Kettle Falls;
(3) By enlarging these reservoirs as the demands for power might warrant, so as to be able to store an additional 45 billion cubic feet; and
(4) By international control of all dams and regulating works.

The reservoirs referred to were at the time maintained by dams across Rainy River (connecting Rainy Lake and Lake of the Woods) between the town of International Falls, Minnesota, and Fort Frances, Ontario, operated by the Minnesota and Ontario Paper Company; and by two dams constructed at Kettle Falls (where the waters of Lake Namakan are discharged into Rainy Lake) by the Rainy River Improvement Company.

The Department of State in 1919 called to the attention of the Canadian Government the matter of considering the report of the Commission and of formulating recommendations looking to an agreement. In 1920 William J. Stewart, the Dominion's Hydrographer, was appointed by Canada and Colonel Keller, of the Bureau of Engineers for Rivers and Harbors, War Department, was appointed by the United States to consider jointly the project, but they failed to agree upon a concrete proposal for submission to the two Governments.

In September and November 1922 conferences were held at Ottawa between representatives of the Dominion Government and representatives from the affected areas on both sides of the international boundary. At the November session, attended by the author as the representative of the United States, it was agreed that the two Governments should negotiate a treaty providing for the regulation of the level of Lake of the Woods, the acquisition of a flowage easement on the lowlands bordering on the lake, and the construction of certain protective works, and that the International Joint Commission should be requested to make a further investigation with respect to the feasibility and desirability of control by the two Governments of the upper lakes for storage purposes. As a result of subsequent negotiations, a convention and protocol were signed by the two Governments on February 24, 1925 with respect to Lake of the Woods, and at the same time an agreement was signed referring to the International Joint Commission certain questions to be investigated with respect to the upper lakes. The convention provides that the level of Lake of the Woods shall ordinarily be maintained between elevations 1056 and 1061.25 sea-level datum (art. IV); that the Government of Canada shall maintain a Canadian Lake of the Woods Control Board to be charged with the duty of regulating and controlling the outflow of the lake; that the two Governments shall maintain an International Lake of the Woods Control Board composed of two engineers, one appointed by each Government; and that "whenever the level of the lake rises above elevation 1061 sea level datum or falls below elevation 1056 sea level datum the rate of total discharge of water from the lake shall be subject to the approval of" the International Board (art.

III). It was agreed in the convention that the outflow capacity of the outlets of Lake of the Woods should be enlarged so as to permit the discharge of not less than 47,000 cubic feet of water a second when the level of the lake is at elevation 1061 sea-level datum, the necessary works for this purpose, as well as the necessary works and dams for controlling and regulating the outflow of the water, to be provided for "at the instance of the Government of Canada" (art. VII). It was also agreed that a flowage easement should be permitted up to elevation 1064 sea-level datum upon all lands bordering on Lake of the Woods in the United States, the United States assuming "all liability to the owners of such lands for the costs of such easement"; also that the United States should provide for certain named protective works and measures in the United States along the shores of the lake and the banks of Rainy River (art. VIII). It was further agreed that the United States and the Dominion of Canada should each, on its own side of the boundary, assume responsibility for any damage or injury that might have theretofore resulted to it or to its inhabitants from the fluctuations of the level of the lake or of the outflow therefrom; each likewise to assume responsibility for any damage or injury which might thereafter result to it or to its inhabitants from the regulation of the level of the lake in the manner provided for in the convention (art. IX). In consideration of the undertakings of the United States as set forth in article VIII, the Government of Canada agreed to pay to the United States the sum of $275,000 and to pay, in the event that this sum should prove to be insufficient to cover the cost "of such undertakings [by the United States], one-half of the excess of such cost over the said sum", if the expenditure be incurred within five years of the coming into force of the convention (art. X). Finally, it was provided that no diversion should thenceforth be made of any waters from Lake of the Woods watershed to any other watershed except by authority of the United States or the Dominion of Canada within their respective territories and with the approval of the International Joint Commission (art. XI).

> Memoranda written by Assistant Solicitor Hackworth, dated Oct. 26, Oct. 27, Nov. 19, and Dec. 12, 1921, Nov. 4 and Nov. 25, 1922, and two of Mar. 22, 1923, MS. Department of State, file 711.4216L/172, /173, /197, /198, /196, /199, /200, /201; 4 Treaties, etc. (Trenwith, 1938) 3993 (convention), 3996 (protocol), 3997 (agreement); 44 Stat. 2108.

An act of Congress approved by the President on May 22, 1926 (44 Stat. 617), amended April 18, 1928 (45 Stat. 431) and again on February 28, 1931 (46 Stat. 1455), made provision for carrying into effect the convention between the two Governments. It authorized the Secretary of War to acquire, by purchase or condemnation, the flowage easements on lands bordering on Lake of the Woods and to acquire such lands or interests as might be necessary to provide for protective works and measures in the United States along the shores of the lake and the banks of Rainy River.

> With respect to the act of May 22, 1926, see H. Rept. 908, 69th Cong., 1st sess., serial no. 8533, and S. Rept. 750, 69th Cong., 1st sess., serial no. 8526; regarding the act of Apr. 18, 1928, see S. Rept. 670, 70th Cong., 1st sess., serial no. 8830, and S. Rept. 685, 70th Cong., 1st sess., serial no. 8836; with respect to the act of Feb. 28, 1931, see H. Rept. 2003, 71st Cong., 2d sess., serial no. 9193, and S. Rept. 1580, 71st Cong., 3d sess., serial no. 9323.
>
> Hearings before the House Committee on Foreign Affairs on Lake of the Woods, Mar. 2, 4, 11, 12, 13, 1926, H.R. 9872, 69th Cong., 1st sess., and Jan. 13, 1931, H.R. 5051, 71st Cong., 3d sess., damages sustained by the fluctuation of the water levels; and hearings on an estimate for protective works and measures, Lake of the Woods, and Rainy River, Minn., H. Doc. 175, 74th Cong., 1st sess., serial no. 9928.
>
> A convention for the emergency regulation of the level of Rainy Lake and of certain other boundary waters was signed on Sept. 15, 1938 by the United States and Canada. Department of State, Treaty Information Bulletin 108 (Sept. 1938) 289.

Between 1900 and 1908 communications were exchanged between the Governments of the United States and Great Britain with a view to coming to an arrangement looking to the replacement of lost boundary monuments and the placing of such supplementary monuments as might appear to be necessary along the boundary line between the United States and Canada. On April 11, 1908 there was concluded a boundary treaty having for its purpose "the more complete definition and demarcation" of the boundary and dividing the boundary for that purpose into eight described areas. Article 1, with respect to the boundary through Passamaquoddy Bay from the mouth of the St. Croix River to the Bay of Fundy, provided for the defining and marking of the line as laid down by commissioners appointed under article II of the treaty of 1892, and with respect to the remainder of the boundary line in the area it provided for an arbitration in the event of failure on the part of the two Governments to reach an agreement within six months after the exchange of printed statements setting forth the evidence upon which each Government relied to establish its claims. No agreement was reached within the time specified. After the preliminary steps of the arbitration had been carried out, a compromise agreement was concluded and signed at Washington on May 21, 1910.

In a further treaty of February 24, 1925 to provide for the maintenance of an effective boundary between the United States and Canada, in accordance with the treaties of April 11, 1908 and May

Demarcation of boundaries

21, 1910, certain sections of the boundary covered by the treaty of 1908 were definitively defined. In making surveys looking to the marking of the boundary from the mouth of Pigeon River at the western point of Lake Superior to the northwesternmost point of the Lake of the Woods in accordance with article V of the treaty of 1908, and the marking of the boundary from the northwestern-most point of the Lake of the Woods to the summit of the Rocky Mountains in accordance with the terms of article VI of the treaty of 1908, the commissioners under the treaty of 1908 found that the boundary at the intersection of these two lines at the "northwestern-most point of Lake of the Woods" as previously defined by treaties and marked by surveys left "two small areas of United States waters in Lake of the Woods . . . entirely surrounded by Canadian waters". Article I of the treaty of 1925 defined the terminus of the boundary line "from the mouth of Pigeon River . . . to the northwesternmost point of Lake of the Woods" and the initial point of the boundary line from "the northwesternmost point of Lake of the Woods to the summit of the Rocky Mountains".

Article VI of the treaty of 1908 contained provision for the placing of boundary monuments from the northwesternmost point of Lake of the Woods south to the 49th parallel of north latitude and thence westward along said parallel of latitude to the summit of the Rocky Mountains as established under existing treaties and as surveyed, charted, and monumented by the Joint Commission appointed for that purpose in 1872. The commissioners appointed pursuant to the 1908 treaty found, however, that it was "impracticable to determine the course of a line having the curvature of a parallel of 49° north latitude on the ground between the adjacent monuments" which had been established or reestablished and that the demarcation of the boundary would be more effective if the line between adjacent monuments were defined as a "straight or right" line. Such a definition was adopted in article II of the treaty of 1925.

The treaty of 1910 defined the international boundary line between the United States and Canada from a point in Passamaquoddy Bay lying between Treat Island and Friar Head to the middle of Grand Manan Channel. The commissioners appointed under the 1908 treaty found that the terminus of the boundary line so defined "at the middle of Grand Manan Channel is less than three nautical miles distant both from the shore line of Grand Manan Island in the Dominion of Canada and from the shore line of the State of Maine . . ., and that there is a small zone of waters of controvertible jurisdiction in Grand Manan Channel between said terminus and the High Seas".

Article III of the treaty of 1925 provided that "in order completely to define the boundary line between the United States and the Dominion of Canada in the Grand Manan Channel, . . . an additional course shall be extended from the terminus of the boundary line defined by the said Treaty of May 21, 1910, south 34°42′ west, for a distance of two thousand three hundred eighty-three (2,383) meters, through the middle of Grand Manan Channel, to the High Seas".

Article IV of the treaty provided that in order to maintain an effective boundary line between the United States and Canada and between Alaska and Canada, as established or to be established, the commissioners appointed under the treaty of 1908 and their successors should maintain an effective boundary line and should submit at least annually a joint report accompanied by such plats, tables, and other information as might be necessary to keep the boundary maps and records accurately revised.

Permanent boundary commission

1 Treaties, etc. (Malloy, 1910) 770, 815; 3 Treaties, etc. (Redmond, 1923) 2616; 4 Treaties, etc. (Trenwith, 1938) 3988. XIV *Messages and Papers of the Presidents* (N.Y., 1897) 6370; MS. Department of State, file 839/1–259, 711.42151/259A–334; Secretary Root to Ambassador Durand, May 3, 1906, *ibid.* 27 Notes, Great Britain, 564, 573–577; Mr. Root to the Governor of New York, May 26, 1906, and Chief Clerk Denby to Mr. Van Alstyne, State Engineer and Surveyor, Albany, New York, Nov. 30, 1906. *ibid.* file 268/1, /7. For an account of the gaps in the definition and demarcation of the boundary at the time of the signing of the treaty in 1908, see 2 A.J.I.L. (1908) 634–637. See also report prepared by Mr. Chandler P. Anderson entitled "Northern Boundary of the United States" (1906) and Mr. Anderson's supplementary report on the same subject, dated Nov. 7, 1906, MS. Department of State, file 839/1–3.

By proclamations of June 15, 1908 and May 3, 1912, President Roosevelt and President Taft, respectively, declared and proclaimed that all unpatented public lands of the United States lying within 60 feet of the boundary line between the United States and Canada should be set aside as a public reservation and should not be subject to any other claim, use, or occupation except for public highways.

Reservation of strip on boundary

The Canadian Privy Council in a report of April 14, 1908 stated that it was "in full accord with the principle" of a proposal submitted by the United States Government through the British Ambassador at Washington "that joint action be taken for the reservation of a strip of land sixty feet wide on each side of the Canada-Alaska boundary line". The report of the Privy Council further stated that it would "take steps to give effect to the reservation along the frontier of the Yukon territory". With reference to the matter of a similar reservation along the boundary between the United States and Canada, in addition to the Alaskan boundary, the report contained the following statement:

In connection with this subject the Minister of the Interior desires to suggest consideration of the possibility of making a similar reservation along other parts of the common boundary line, which, besides extensive stretches of water boundary, comprises some 1,900 miles on land.

Of the 1,300 miles or thereabouts from the Straits of Georgia to the Lake of the Woods, some 400 miles lie west of the summit of the Rocky Mountains. Along this distance the Minister understands that the Government of British Columbia has already reserved a strip 66 feet wide, wherever the land has not already been disposed of, along the International Boundary Line. East of the Rocky Mountains, under the original surveys made by the Dominion Government, road allowances were left adjoining the boundary. These road allowances are no longer under the control of the Dominion Government, having now passed under the jurisdiction of the provinces of Alberta, Saskatchewan and Manitoba.

The four provinces mentioned would doubtless agree to make the road allowances and the reservation permanent, though to secure that end, concurrent agreement by the United States or by the several states affected, to reserve a similar strip would appear to be desirable.

By an Order in Council of August 7, 1923, the Canadian Government reserved "a strip sixty feet in width through the crown lands of the province of New Brunswick . . . on the eastern side of the international boundary between the province of New Brunswick and the state of Maine". This reservation was limited to "ungranted crown lands".

In its joint report of 1931, the International Boundary Commission of the United States and Canada stated that the Province of Ontario through its Department of Lands and Forests had in 1925 reserved from sale or disposal all granted crown lands lying within 66 feet of the three portions of the international boundary which extended, respectively, from Cyprus Lake to Swamp Lake, from North Lake to South Lake, and from Watap Lake to Mountain Lake.

35 Stat. 2189; 37 Stat. 1741; Chargé Howard to the Acting Secretary of State (Adee), no. 170, Aug. 15, 1908, MS. Department of State, file 839/92; *Joint Report Upon the Survey and Demarcation of the International Boundary Between the United States and Canada along the 141st Meridian from the Arctic Ocean to Mount St. Elias* (1918) 20–22; *Joint Report Upon the Survey and Demarcation of the Boundary Between the United States and Canada from the Source of the St. Croix River to the St. Lawrence River* (1925) 15, 16; *Joint Report upon the Survey and Demarcation of the International Boundary between the United States and Canada from the Northwesternmost Point of Lake of the Woods to Lake Superior* (1931) 22. For reservations of land adjacent to the boundary line between the United States and Canada by the Provinces of British Columbia, Alberta, Saskatchewan, and Manitoba, see *Joint Report Upon the Survey and Demarcation of the Boundary Between the United States and Canada from the Gulf of Georgia to the Northwesternmost Point of Lake of the Woods* (1937) 23.

In reply to a private inquiry as to the existence of any law pro- Building on
boundary line hibiting the construction of a building on a lot consisting of thirty acres on the Canadian side and one acre on the American side of the boundary, the Department of State said:

> There appear to be no provisions in any of the treaties between the United States and Great Britain concerning the boundary or other relations with Canada touching the construction of buildings intersecting the boundary line, and so far as this Department is informed, there appear to be no provisions in the Statutes of the United States applicable to such buildings. The Department is not in a position to advise you regarding the local laws, if any, which may be applicable to the matter under consideration.
>
> There is enclosed a copy of a proclamation, dated June 15, 1908, issued by former President Roosevelt, which would seem to be relevant to a project to construct a building on the American side within sixty feet of the boundary line if the title to the land upon which it is intended to construct the building was in the United States on the date the proclamation was issued, or has been in the United States at any time since that date. By this proclamation all unpatented public lands of the United States lying within sixty feet of the boundary line between the United States and Canada are set apart as a public reservation subject only to previously acquired and existing rights, and rights for use for public highways.

The Acting Secretary of State (Fletcher) to Representative Tinkham, Mar. 3, 1922, MS. Department of State, file 711.4215/27.

The American and British members of the Joint High Commis- Alaskan
boundary sion for the adjustment of questions at issue between the United States and Great Britain in respect to the relations of the former with Canada (created pursuant to a protocol of the conferences held in Washington in May 1898), meeting at Quebec in August 23, 1898, were unable to come to an agreement as to the meaning of articles 3 and 4 of the convention of February 28/16, 1825 between Great Britain and Russia, defining the boundary between Canada and Alaska. An adjournment of the Commission until the boundary should be adjusted by the two Governments resulted from that disagreement. On October 20, 1899 a *modus vivendi* was agreed upon *Modus*
vivendi, 1899 by the United States and Great Britain, fixing a temporary boundary line between Alaska and Canada in the region about the head of the Lynn Canal.

By a convention concluded on January 24, 1903 between the United States and Great Britain, it was agreed that certain questions regarding the true meaning and application of certain clauses of the convention between Great Britain and Russia of February 28/16, 1825, Arbitration,
1903 relating to the eastern section of the boundary between Alaska and

Canada, should be submitted to an arbitral tribunal of six jurists. The award of the tribunal, containing its answers to those questions, was made on October 20, 1903. Article VI of the convention of 1903 provided that upon receipt of the decision of the arbitral tribunal each Government should at once appoint one or more scientific experts who should, with all convenient speed, proceed together to lay down the boundary line, in conformity with such decision. W. F. King, Chief Astronomer to the Canadian Department of Interior, was appointed British Commissioner, while O. H. Tittmann, Superintendent of the United States Coast and Geodetic Survey (succeeded by E. C. Barnard on April 30, 1915), was appointed American Commissioner. The two Governments, by an exchange of notes on March 25, 1905, formally accepted the recommendation of the two commissioners in the delimitation of the international boundary in accordance with the general principles laid down by the arbitral tribunal. On April 21, 1906 an additional convention was concluded between the United States and Great Britain providing for the appointment of one commissioner by each Government to ascertain, by the telegraphic method, a convenient point on the 141st meridian of west longitude and to trace and mark by intervisible objects so much of a north and south line passing through that point as was necessary to determine the boundary line between Alaska and Canada, defined as the 141st degree of longitude west from Greenwich in the convention between Great Britain and Russia of February 28/16, 1825. The convention was proclaimed on August 21, 1906, and the respective commissioners were appointed (Mr. King—succeeded by Mr. J. J. McArthur on November 29, 1916 "for the whole of the Alaska boundary dealt with under the Conventions of 1903 and 1906"—and Mr. Tittmann).

Commissioners for laying boundary

Convention, 1906

The final report of the commissioners under the convention of 1906 in respect to the 141st meridian from the Arctic Ocean to Mount St. Elias was submitted to the Secretary of State on December 15, 1918. It was published under the title "Joint Report Upon the Survey and Demarcation of the International Boundary between the United States and Canada along the 141st Meridian from the Arctic Ocean to Mount St. Elias".

President McKinley's annual message of 1899, 1 Treaties, etc. (Malloy, 1910) 773; MS. Department of State, files 242 and 711.42151; First Joint Report of the Commissioners for the Demarcation of the 141st Degree of West Longitude, Aug. 27, 1907, *ibid.* file 242/17; Tittmann "Progress of the Demarcation of the Alaska Boundary" in XLVII *Proceedings of the American Philosophical Society* (1908) 86; MS. Department of State, file 242/31.

1 Treaties, etc. (Malloy, 1910) 770 (protocol of the conferences at Washington in May 1898); *ibid.* 777 (*modus vivendi* of 1899); *ibid.* 787 (treaty of 1903); *ibid.* 792 (award of 1903); *ibid.* 796 (exchange of notes, Mar. 25, 1905); *ibid.* 803 (convention of 1906).

See "Canadian boundaries", statement of Otto H. Tittmann before sub-committee of the House Foreign Affairs Committee, Jan. 21, 1908, on diplomatic and consular appropriation bill, fiscal year 1909, relating to boundary line between Alaska and Canada (1908).

On February 3, 1904 the Department of State transmitted to the Speaker of the House of Representatives a memorial of the Wales Island Packing Company, a corporation organized under the laws of the State of New York, engaged in the business of fishing and canning salmon and other fish, whose establishments and interests on Wales Island had, by decision of the Alaska boundary tribunal established under the treaty of January 24, 1903 between the United States and Great Britain, been placed on the Canadian side of the boundary. The change of the location of the boundary deprived the company of the fishing grounds upon which it had relied for its supply of fish and cut it off effectually from United States markets for its supplies and products. The company alleged that in establishing its plant on Wales Island it had relied on the assurance given by the Government of the United States that its jurisdiction extended thereover, and the Court of Claims later so found. (In 1896 the War Department, under the authority of Congress, had built a storehouse on the island on the wallstones of which in a conspicuous place were carved the words "U.S. property. Do not injure", and on February 28, 1902 Secretary Hay had informed the British Ambassador that the United States had been in possession of Wales Island ever since its acquisition from Russia.) It appeared that there were no available fisheries on the Canadian side of the line upon which the company could rely for an adequate supply for its business. The company stated that it looked to the United States Government for relief from the difficulties forced upon it through no fault of its own. In transmitting the memorial to the House of Representatives, the Department of State earnestly invited the attention of Congress to the grounds upon which relief was sought by the company, stating that it submitted the memorial for such action as, in the judgment of Congress, the equities of the case might warrant. A similar letter was addressed to the President of the Senate.

On March 2, 1923 the Senate adopted a resolution referring a bill for the relief of the Wales Island Packing Company to the Court of Claims for findings of fact in accordance with section 151 of the Judicial Code. Special findings of fact and an opinion by that court were filed on February 9, 1931. These, together with a supplemental opinion of the court on a motion for a new trial filed January 18, 1932, were transmitted to the Senate on February 11, 1932. In its opinion of February 9, 1931 the court found the claim of the Wales Island Packing Company to be an equitable one, stating, however, that whether the equity shown by the findings of fact in the court's opinion was of such a nature as to justify Congress in granting the relief was, of course, a question wholly to be determined by that body. In its supplemental opinion of January 18, 1932 the court in considering the proposition that its jurisdiction did not extend to claims growing out of or dependent upon any treaty stipulation said:

> . . . The claim is not founded on the treaty stipulation. It is true that the petition referred to a treaty and that the findings of fact and opinion of the court, in setting forth the history of the case, also refer to the treaty between the United States and Great Britain for the purpose of establishing the boundary line between this country and Canada, but it was entirely unnecessary that this matter should have been mentioned either in the petition, the findings of fact, or the opinion. The foundation of the case was not upon the treaty or any stipulation contained therein. If the treaty had not been entered into it is quite likely the case never would have arisen, but the basis of the case was a matter not mentioned or even referred to indirectly in the treaty.

The court held that the plaintiff had no legal claim of any nature against the Government and that "Its only claim, if it had any, was a moral one which was not enforceable" in that court or any other and which that court had no jurisdiction to adjudicate.

On May 5, 1936 an act of Congress was approved authorizing and directing the Secretary of the Treasury to pay $100,000 to the company "in full settlement of all claims against the Government of the United States for the injury to the business and property of said company on Wales Island on account of the decision of the Alaska boundary tribunal".

> 49 Stat. 2269. *Wales Island Packing Co.* v. *The United States,* 73 Ct. Cls. (1931–32) 615, 624, 625. S. Rept. 116, 61st Cong., 2d sess.; MS. Department of State, file 4491; S. Doc. 61, 72nd Cong., 1st sess., serial no. 9521.

Payment of duties by Alaskans entering Canada

In a letter of March 25, 1929 Dan Sutherland, Delegate to Congress from Alaska, requested an opinion regarding the legality of the collection by Canadian police of license fees and customs duties on guns and camp equipment from Alaskan Indians going across the Canadian boundary line to trap muskrats. The Department of State replied:

> In the case of Paul Diabo (25 F (2d) 71) . . . the Circuit Court of Appeals held on March 9, 1928, that the provisions of Article III of the Jay Treaty were in effect and that the Indians had the right freely to pass and repass the boundary between the United States and Canada.

.   .   .   .

The Department is advised that an appeal from the decision of the Circuit Court of Appeals in the Diabo Case, to the Supreme Court of the United States was not taken for the reason that before the expiration of the time within which the appeal was required to be filed, the President approved, on April 2, 1928, the Act of Congress providing that the Immigration Act of 1924 should not be construed to apply to the right of American Indians born in Canada to pass the borders of the United States (Public Act No. 234, 70th Congress). This Act, however, did not undertake to exempt the Indians from the payment of customs duties.

On April 8, 1929, the Supreme Court of the United States in the case of *Karnuth* v. *United States* . . . held that Article III of the Jay Treaty was terminated by the War of 1812. . . .

While provision is made in Article IX of the Treaty of Ghent concluded between the United States and Great Britain on December 24, 1814, for restoration to the Indians in the United States and Canada on certain conditions of rights which they had in 1811, and which may have included rights granted by the Jay Treaty, it will be noted that that treaty accorded only the right to pass and repass and to take goods and effects across the boundary as it was fixed by the Treaty of Peace concluded between the United States and Great Britain on September 3, 1783. This, of course, did not include the boundary between Alaska and Canada.

Without expressing an opinion as to whether Indians passing and repassing the boundary between the United States and Canada as defined by the Treaty of 1783, are now entitled to exemption from the payment of duties under the provisions of Article IX of the Treaty of Ghent of 1814, I consider that this Government would not be warranted in contending that the Indians in Alaska are entitled to exemption from Canadian customs duties. It is understood that Canadian Indians desiring to bring into Alaska equipment similar to that referred to . . . are required to pay duties to the United States.

I regret, therefore, that the Department does not appear to be in a position to take any action in the matter.

Delegate Sutherland to Secretary Stimson, Mar. 25, 1929, and Mr. Stimson to Mr. Sutherland, May 3, 1928, MS. Department of State, file 711.412/47.

For further discussions of the international boundary between the United States and Canada, see *ante*, "Diversion", §86, "American Rivers", §88, and "The Great Lakes" under "Lakes", §91.

UNITED STATES–MEXICO

§107

The boundary convention of March 1, 1889 between the United States and Mexico provided for the establishment of an International Boundary Commission to be composed of two commissioners, one appointed by each Government; two consulting engineers, appointed in the same manner; and such secretaries and interpreters as either

International Boundary Commission

Government might see fit to add to its section of the Commission. It was provided (art. I) that there should be submitted to this commission for examination and decision:

> All differences or questions that may arise on that portion of the frontier between the United States of America and the United States of Mexico where the Rio Grande and the Colorado rivers form the boundary line, whether such differences or questions grow out of alterations or changes in the bed of the aforesaid Rio Grande and that of the aforesaid Colorado River, or of works that may be constructed in said rivers, or of any other cause affecting the boundary line . . .

The convention was to remain in force for a period of five years (art. IX). Beginning in 1894, the life of the Commission—which is still in existence—was extended annually until 1900 when, by a convention signed November 21 of that year, it was extended indefinitely, subject to the right of either contracting party to dissolve it by giving six months' notice to the other.

Article I of the boundary convention of November 12, 1884 between the two countries provided that the dividing line along the Rio Grande and the Colorado River should follow the center of the normal channel of the rivers, notwithstanding any alterations in the banks or in the course of those rivers, "provided that such alterations be effected by natural causes through the slow and gradual erosion and deposit of alluvium and not by the abandonment of an existing river bed and the opening of a new one", while article II of the same convention stipulated that any other change "wrought by the force of the current . . . shall produce no change in the dividing line as fixed by the surveys of the International Boundary Commissions in 1852, but the line then fixed shall continue to follow the middle of the original channel bed, even though this should become wholly dry or be obstructed by deposits".

Elimination of *bancos*   By article I of the convention signed by the two countries on March 20, 1905 fifty-eight *bancos* cut from one side or the other by changes in the Rio Grande were "eliminated from the effects of Article II" of the convention of 1884, and it was provided that "the dominion and jurisdiction of so many of the aforesaid fifty-eight (58) bancos as may remain on the right bank of the river shall pass to Mexico, and the dominion and jurisdiction of those of the said fifty-eight (58) bancos which may remain on the left bank shall pass to the United States of America". Article II of the convention provides that "The International Commission shall, in the future, be guided by the principle of elimination of the bancos established in the foregoing article, with regard to the labors concerning the boundary line throughout that part of the Rio Grande and the Colo-

rado River which serves as a boundary between the two nations."
It excepted, however, from this provision the portions of land "segregated by the change in the bed of the said rivers" having an area
of over 250 hectares or a population of over 200 persons, which
should not be considered as *bancos* for the purposes of the convention
and should not be eliminated—"the old bed of the river remaining,
therefore, the boundary in such cases".

Article IV stipulates:

> Property of all kinds situated on the said bancos shall be
> inviolably respected, and its present owners, their heirs, and
> those who may subsequently acquire the property legally, shall
> enjoy as complete security with respect thereto as if it belonged
> to citizens of the country where it is situated.

Having become aware of a threatened *banco* cut-off in the Rio *Horcon*
Grande on Mexican soil which would take the channel of the river *Ranch* case
away from the site selected by it for a pumping-station, the Rio
Grande Land and Irrigation Company opened another cut-off by
artificial means in the spring of 1906, changing the natural channel
of the river. The Mexican Government brought the case before the
International Boundary Commission, charging that the company
had violated the convention of 1884. In its session of October 24,
1906 the Commission found that the company "did wrongfully and
knowingly cause a change in the current channel of the Rio Grande
where it constituted the boundary line . . . by artificial means,
and in direct violation of Article III of the Convention of November
12, 1884". It was of the opinion that indemnity should be made for
this wrong, but it had some doubt whether the conventions under
which it was organized conferred jurisdiction—

> (*a*) to restrain a contemplated violation of the treaty by pri-
> vate individuals or corporations;
> (*b*) to punish for a violation already committed;
> (*c*) to award damages to persons injured by the violation, and
> (*d*) to regulate the use of water for irrigating purposes, and
> if so, to what extent.

The questions thus raised were referred by the Department of State
to the Attorney General who advised, on May 16, 1907, that the
authority of the Commission was restricted to the determination of
questions respecting the boundary alone.

Subsequently the United States filed a bill in equity against the
Rio Grande Land and Irrigation Company in the Circuit Court of
the United States for the Southern District of Texas, requesting a
decree compelling the defendant to restore the river to its original
channel or, in the alternative, that the defendant be compelled to
convey certain land to the Mexican citizens affected and to pay dam-

ages, both civil and penal. Mexican citizens affected were brought
into the case, and a decree was issued by Judge Burns, on December
5, 1911 (unreported), to the effect: (1) that the defendant convey
to the Mexican citizens the land contained in the banco created by
the cut-off; (2) that the company pay in damages for the benefit of
the Mexican citizens $5,000; (3) that the company pay $2,000 to cover
the costs and expenses incident to surveying and marking the international boundary line now represented by the former bed or channel
of the Rio Grande before the unlawful diversion of the stream; and
(4) that the company pay in penal damages to the United States
$10,000.

> Commissioner Mills to Secretary Root, Oct. 24, 1906, MS. Department of
> State, file 16893/8; Mr. Mills to Mr. Root, Nov. 8, 1906, and the Acting
> Secretary of State (Bacon) to the Attorney General, Apr. 20, 1907, *ibid.*
> 17119/8; the Acting Secretary of State (Adee) to the Attorney General,
> June 22, 1907, *ibid.* 16893/23; Mr. Adee to Chargé Godoy, no. 332, Aug. 21,
> 1908, *ibid.* 16893/48; Secretary Knox to Chargé Davalos, no. 134, Nov. 15,
> 1909, *ibid.* 16893/65A. Department of Justice to Secretary Knox, Jan. 11,
> 1912, *ibid.* 711.1216D/83; 26 Op. Att. Gen. (1906–8) 250. 1 Treaties, etc.
> (Malloy, 1910) 1159, 1167, 1192, 1199 (conventions of 1884, 1889, 1900, and
> 1905).
>
> See, in this connection, Proceedings of the International (Water) Bound-
> ary Commission, United States and Mexico, Treaties of 1884 and 1889,
> *Equitable Distribution of the Waters of the Rio Grande* (1903), 2 vols.;
> Mexican Boundary, Statement of Wilbur Keblinger, Jan. 21, 1908, Secre-
> tary of the International (Water) Boundary Commission, United States
> and Mexico, regarding elimination of *bancos* in Rio Grande (1908) 16 pp.;
> Hearings before the House Committee on Foreign Affairs regarding United
> States – Mexico Water Boundary, especially regarding *bancos*, origin of
> the International Boundary Commission and El Chamizal, Feb. 5 and 11,
> 1914, 63d Cong., 2d sess.

Testimony
and records

In a telegram of April 2, 1931 the American Commissioner of the
International Boundary Commission, United States and Mexico, informed the Department that subpenas had been issued at the instance
of plaintiffs in a suit pending in a Texas court involving lands in
the San Lorenzo Banco area, summoning the secretary and the consulting engineer of the Commission to bring certain records of the
Commission and to testify. In a telegraphic instruction the Department stated:

> As a general proposition, Department does not look with favor
> upon the summoning of officials Boundary Commission as wit-
> nesses in these private litigations. If, nevertheless, appearance
> is compulsory under the laws of Texas, Secretary and Engineer
> should appear and take such non-confidential records as may
> be requested. They should not testify as to confidential mat-
> ters between the two Governments nor permit records to
> leave their possession. If records are regarded by court as

essential to administration of justice, photostat copies of those not confidential might be furnished at expense of parties making request. Should there be any objection to the procedure just outlined on the part of your Mexican colleague, report such objection to Department for consideration.

Commissioner Lawson to Secretary Stimson, Apr. 2, 1931, and the Acting Secretary of State (Carr) to Mr. Lawson, Apr. 3, 1931, MS. Department of State, file 711.12151A/284.

An act of Congress approved by the President on June 30, 1932, effective July 1, 1932, abolished the American section of the International Water Commission, United States and Mexico (*ante*, §86), and transferred the powers, duties, and functions of that section to the American section of the International Boundary Commission, United States and Mexico. 47 Stat. 382, 417. See also H. Rept. 1025, 72d Cong., 1st sess., serial no. 9492.

An act of Congress approved by the President on Aug. 27, 1935 authorized the Secretary of State to lease to citizens of the United States any land acquired or to be acquired in connection with projects constructed or administered by the Secretary through the American section of the International Boundary Commission, United States and Mexico. 49 Stat. 906. See also S. Rept. 1417, 74th Cong., 1st sess., serial no. 9880.

In September 1907 Commissioner Mills of the International (Water) Boundary Commission, United States and Mexico, established under the convention of March 1, 1889, requested an opinion of the Department of State as to whether the jurisdiction of the State of Texas was to be regarded as extending over the old abandoned bed of the Rio Grande in places where the river had cut for itself a new channel, and the boundary remained in the old channel. The question had its origin in a proposal to establish "an international highway in the bed of the old river around what is known as the 'Cordova Cutoff' within the limits of El Paso, Texas". The Solicitor for the Department was of the view that the title to the land in such old abandoned bed was vested in the State of Texas and that it would be within the power of the Federal Government to take the land by virtue of its power of eminent domain. He recommended, however, that it would be preferable to request Texas "either (*a*) to cede the strip in question to the United States for the purpose of having the central government make of it an international highway . . . or, (*b*) herself to dedicate it for use as a public highway; or, (c) to place the territory at the disposal of the United States for the establishment by the latter of a highway".

Title to abandoned river bed

Opinion of the Solicitor, Sept 23, 1907, MS. Department of State, file 1351/26.

On July 16, 1909 the Treasury Department informed the Department of State that the Rio Grande had cut off "about two hundred acres in one body from Mexico" and requested its views as to the

Avulsion

effect on "all kinds of property" in the area affected. In reply, on July 22, 1909, it was said that—

> it would seem that the recent change in the course of the river has probably been avulsive, and that the land which has been cut off remains Mexican territory in accordance with the provisions of the boundary convention of 1884 [1 Treaties, etc. (Malloy, 1910) 1159]; and the Department suggests that pending an examination of the facts by the International Boundary Commission the land in question be treated by your Department as Mexican territory.

> The Acting Secretary of the Treasury (Reynolds) to the Secretary of State (Knox), July 16, 1909, and the Acting Secretary of State (Adee) to the Secretary of the Treasury, July 22, 1909, MS. Department of State, file 20601.

In the case of *Shapleigh et al.* v. *Mier* the Supreme Court of the United States decided a question of title to certain property in Texas known as "*El Guayuco Banco* No. 319", the *banco* having been cut off from Mexico as a result of an avulsive change in the course of the Rio Grande. Sovereignty over the *banco* was transferred from Mexico to the United States under the provisions of the convention of 1905, proclaimed June 5, 1907, between the United States and Mexico (35 Stat. 1863). The Court, in affirming the judgment of the lower court for the defendant, stated that it granted certiorari to pass upon the contentions of the plaintiffs "that their rights had been illegally divested" through the action of the Mexican Government in expropriating the property prior to the transfer to the United States. Mr. Justice Cardozo, who delivered the opinion of the Court affirming the decision of the district court recognizing the validity of the decree of expropriation under Mexican law, stated:

Effect of avulsive changes on boundaries

The land in controversy was once part of the Mexican state of Chihuahua. In 1926 it was cut by avulsion from the south or right bank of the Rio Grande to the north or left bank, and became part of the United States. By the ordinary rule a change of location resulting from avulsion would have left Mexico still sovereign over the territory thus moved, the centre of the old channel remaining as the boundary. *Missouri* v. *Nebraska*, 196 U.S. 23, 35; *Nebraska* v. *Iowa*, 143 U.S. 359, 361, 367, 370. Here a different rule applied by force of a convention, proclaimed June 5, 1907 (35 Stat. 1863), whereby the boundaries were to shift in the event of future changes, with exceptions not now material as to population and area. A Boundary Commission, previously established but confirmed by the Convention, marked the change upon the ground. Sovereignty was thus transferred, but private ownership remained the same. *United States* v. *Chaves*, 159 U.S. 452, 457; *United States* v. *Percheman*, 7 Pet. 51, 86. To find the title to the land today we must know where title stood while the land was yet in Mexico.

299 U.S. (1937) 468, 469.

During the course of the negotiations looking to a settlement of the dispute concerning the title to the Chamizal tract, the American Commissioner on the International Boundary Commission brought to the attention of the Department certain proceedings before the Commission concerning the Bermudez *banco*. The American claimant to the *banco* having obtained a favorable judgment in the district court of El Paso relative to his claim to the land, the Department requested the Attorney General to take such measures as might be deemed necessary to have the judgment vacated "in order that the Commission may not be embarrassed in any future considerations of the case". The Department declared that the legal situation of the *banco* "as regards matters of jurisdiction, is in all respects similar to that of the larger and more important banco known as El Chamizal". Subsequently, the American claimant having erected a brush dam in the bed of the Rio Grande was compelled, upon the insistence of the Commission, to remove it. In a session of the Commission on Oct. 21, 1908, the Mexican Commissioner declared that he was of the opinion that the entire work was an infringement on the exclusive jurisdiction of the Commission and asked that some action be taken to prevent the occurrence of such infringements and violations in the future. The American Commissioner agreed, stating that he had personally supervised the removal of the obstruction and adding that "should any attempt be made to re-establish the works or to make similar works elsewhere he would join the Mexican Commissioner in rendering a decision declaring them in violation of the treaty; that he had been assured by his government that any decision of the Commission declaring works in violation of existing treaties would be taken up and vigorously prosecuted through the proper channels to the end that . . . treaty obligations be fully enforced and protected".

The Acting Secretary of State (Bacon) to the Attorney General, July 23, 1908, MS. Department of State, file 15844/16; Commissioner Mills to Secretary Root, Oct. 23, 1908, *ibid.* 15844/25.

As regards the Chamizal question, see *ante* §60.

With respect to a statement by the Supreme Court of the United States recognizing that the United States had *de facto* jurisdiction over the tract of land known as "El Chamizal" and that the matter was still pending between the United States and Mexico, see *Cordova* v. *Grant, Executor of Cotton*, 248 U.S. (1919) 413.

On March 21, 1930 the International Boundary Commission, United States and Mexico, eliminated from the effects of article II of the convention of 1884 (described *ante*, this section), a tract of land known as "San Lorenzo *Banco*". Another tract of land, known as "Weber *Banco*", had been eliminated by a decision of the Commission rendered on March 18 of that year. The resolutions eliminating the two *bancos* to the United States were adopted in accordance with the provisions of the convention of 1905 (also described *ante*, this section). Article VIII of the boundary convention concluded on March 1, 1889 (1 Treaties, etc. [Malloy, 1910] 1167) between the two countries, provides that the judgment of the commissioners shall be considered binding upon both Governments unless one of them shall

San Lorenzo and Weber *Bancos*

disapprove it within one month. Attorneys representing certain American citizens claiming property on the San Lorenzo *Banco* objected to the decision of the Commission respecting that *banco* and endeavored to persuade the Government of the United States to disapprove it. On April 18, 1930 the Department of State issued the following statement to the press:

> This Department has given careful consideration to the decisions of the Commissioners and has concluded that it is not called upon to take any action thereon. It is the opinion of this Department that the demarcation of bancos by the International Boundary Commission does not have the legal effect of determining claims of title to the specific properties situated within the bancos.

Mexican protest

On January 12, 1931 the Mexican Embassy at Washington requested the Department of State to take measures to prevent the issuance of documents conveying titles to land situated on the *bancos* eliminated by the International Boundary Commission between the time when the *bancos* were cut from Mexico and the decision of the Commission eliminating them to the United States. In accordance with this request, identic letters were addressed to the Governors of Arizona and Texas reading in part as follows:

> The result of the issuance of American titles to land on bancos in the manner indicated has been to set up controversies between such grantees and Mexican title holders to land on the bancos and to involve the two Governments in much correspondence concerning the matter. In response to a request from the Mexican Government for action by the Government of the United States in assistance of Mexican title holders confronted by the difficulty referred to, the Department advised the Mexican Embassy, September 12, 1930, that it was not aware of any method which might be employed except the usual orderly procedure of application to the courts for relief.
>
> The Embassy has now replied, under date of January 12, 1931, that it has been instructed by its Government to advise the Department that so far as concerns past cases in which the local authorities have given possession of lands to individuals who do not rightly own such lands, the procedure suggested by the Department will be followed, but in order to avoid the occurrence of future cases of the character indicated, the Embassy has requested that the matter be brought to the attention of the appropriate authorities.
>
> Considering that the Embassy's request is entirely reasonable and designed to obviate considerable difficulty which might otherwise arise, I have the honor to request that you will take such action with the appropriate authorities of your State as will tend strongly to prevent the giving of possession or the issuance of titles to lands on bancos which have been cut from Mexican territory, but not yet effectively eliminated to the United States

through decision of the Boundary Commission, acquiesced in by the two Governments.

Commissioner Lawson to Secretary Stimson, Mar. 22, 1930, MS. Department of State, file 711.12151A/199; Mr. Burges to Mr. Stimson, Mar. 26, 1930, and the Acting Secretary of State (Cotton) to Mr. Lawson, Mar. 27, 1930, *ibid.* 711.12151A/208; Mr. Cotton to Mr. Lawson, Apr. 18, 1930, *ibid.* 711.12151A/229A; the Mexican Ambassador (Téllez) to Mr. Stimson, Jan. 12, 1931, and Mr. Stimson to the Governors of Arizona and Texas and to Señor Téllez, Jan. 27, 1931, *ibid.* 711.12151A/271.

Litigation ensued regarding ownership of property situated on the San Lorenzo *Banco*. In the case of *San Lorenzo Title & Improvement Co.* v. *City Mortgage Co.*, 48 S.W. (2d) 310 (1932), the company claimed title under a Mexican grant against the City Mortgage Company claiming title under a grant from Texas. As indicated above, the International Boundary Commission had found on March 21, 1930 that the *banco* had been cut off from Mexico by avulsion in 1898. In the meantime, however, one Alfredo Urias, a Mexican citizen, had obtained a judgment from a Mexican court on February 1, 1927, pursuant to which the land was sold to him on July 19, 1927, and the sale was approved by the Mexican court on August 31, 1927. The defendant, City Mortgage Company, demurred generally, the court sustained the demurrer, and the plaintiff appealed. The Court of Civil Appeals of Texas in examining the judgment of the lower court sustained the demurrer and—referring to the convention of 1905—held that treaties and conventions become binding as to the contracting nations from the day they are signed, citing with approval *Davis* v. *The Police Jury of Concordia*, 9 How. (1850) 280, 289. It was pointed out that, while a different rule prevails as to the effect of treaties on private rights, the plaintiff's assertion as to his rights was made subsequent to the ratification of the convention of 1905. The court also held that since the San Lorenzo *Banco* No. 302 was formed prior to March 20, 1905, the date when the convention was signed, the convention went into effect on that date so far as the *banco* was concerned and that on such date, as between Mexico and the United States, "sovereignty, dominion, and jurisdiction of said banco passed out of the republic of Mexico and into the republic of the United States". The court further held that Mexico's possession of the *banco*, if any, after the signing of the convention of 1905, was a *de facto* possession and that such possession could not confer the power of disposing of title; also that the Mexican court which attempted to dispose of the property was without jurisdiction of the subject-matter and its decision under which the title of Urias was derived was of no effect.

Litigation:
San Lorenzo
Banco

Under circumstances similar to those in the preceding case, the same court held, in the case of *San Lorenzo Title & Improvement Co.* v. *Clardy et al.*, 48 S.W. (2d) 315 (1932), that the purpose of the convention of 1905 between the United States and Mexico was to adjust the boundary line; that the provision of that convention respecting rights of private owners did not protect persons claiming title to lands of *bancos* based on grants from Mexico made subsequent to the conclusion of the convention; that the interpretation of the convention by the International Boundary Commission did not change the purpose and the intention of the representatives who negotiated it; that the convention conveyed equitable title to all *bancos* on the north side of the river coming within its provisions to the United States and that Mexico could not grant land thereon after the convention was signed; that the Commission had no power to decide whether *bancos* should or should not be eliminated, a question which had been decided by the convention; that the only thing the Commission had to decide was "the presence of the facts which would call for the elimination as provided in the treaty"; and that the decision of the Commission placing the *banco* which had been cut off from Mexico by avulsion in 1898 within the provisions of the convention of 1905 related back to the date when the convention was executed.

In the case of *San Lorenzo Title & Improvement Co.* v. *Caples et al.*, 48 S.W. (2d) 329 (1932), in which the facts were similar to those of the two preceding cases (an avulsive change in 1898), the same court held that under the convention of 1905 Mexico could not, after the date of the convention, grant title to lands in a *banco* on the north side of the Rio Grande which was to pass to the jurisdiction of the United States under the convention.

A series of test cases was brought by persons claiming under Mexican titles against persons claiming possession under Texas titles. In one of these, *Willis* v. *First Real Estate and Inv. Co. et al.*, 68 F. (2d) 671 (C.C.A. 5th, 1934), involving land forming part of the San Lorenzo *Banco*, the Mexican title was based on a decision of a Mexican court as a result of which a sale to Urias culminated on August 31, 1927; the Texas title rested on a patent received from the State of Texas in 1861. The plaintiff claimed that the *banco*, although it had been attached to the soil of Texas prior to 1930, had become part of Texas only since the decision of the International Boundary Commission in 1930 found it to be a *banco* within the terms of the convention of 1905. The plaintiff also contended that since the attachment of the land to Texas was made by an avulsive change in 1898, it was, under articles I, II, and V of the convention of 1884 and under principles of international law, in 1927 and until 1930, Mexican territory and subject to Mexican law. The defendants contended that the land had never been a part of Mexican soil, that long before 1848 it had been a part of the Texas republic, and that in that year, by the Treaty of Guadalupe Hidalgo (1 Treaties, etc. (Malloy, 1910) 1107), fixing the Rio Grande as a boundary, it had been recognized to be a part of Texas. The defendants also maintained that the San Lorenzo *Banco* was cut off for a short time between 1897 and 1898 and that during all of the time Texas maintained an uninterrupted assertion of jurisdiction over it. The court found void the proceedings of the Mexican court under which Mexican title was held and said (Circuit Judge Hutcheson speaking) :

> We have examined the Treaties of 1884 and 1905, and the correspondence preceding and following the Treaty of 1905 in the light of the erratic action of the river in so making its changes as to make it difficult, if not impossible, for the boundary commission proceeding under article 4 of the Treaty of 1884 to say whether a true avulsion under article 2 or a mere erosion under article 1 had occurred, and in the light of the great difficulties inherent in the attempt of one country to exert sovereignty over land attached to the other across the boundary. We are left no doubt as to the paramount purpose, intent and effect of the Treaty of 1905. It was to change the international boundary from the shifting and troublesome one provided for in articles 1 and 2 of the old Treaty to the fixed one established by the 1905 Treaty. It was to fix the territory of and sovereignty over all bank lands in accordance with their actual situation on the left or the right bank as thus fixed. It is clear, also, we think, that the function of the boundary commission was to set at rest, not by way of cession, but by way of a definitive boundary decision as to all banco lands, that is, lands which had been affected by avulsive changes, all questions of jurisdiction and sovereignty over them. To declare that they have been, since the Treaty of 1905, settled in favor of the country to which they are attached, this to be determined entirely by their position with reference to the fixed boundary line is unwarranted. We think it clear, then, that the Treaty of 1905 settled by the force of its terms, and from the date of its ratification, all questions of territorial jurisdiction and sovereignty with respect to the lands lying on either side of the fixed boundary.

68 F. (2d) 674.

An act of Congress approved by the President on January 27, 1932 (42 Stat. 359) provided that all lands or *bancos* acquired by the United States by virtue of the convention with Mexico of 1905, and subsequent thereto, which lie adjacent to Texas should, upon the acceptance of the act by Texas, become a part of that State and subject to its jurisdiction.

1 Treaties, etc. (Malloy, 1910) 1199; S. Rept. 230, 67th Cong., 1st sess., serial no. 7918.

Treaty of 1933, U. S. and Mex.

The United States and Mexico concluded a treaty at Mexico City on February 1, 1933 with a view to rectifying the course of the Rio Grande in the El Paso – Juarez Valley so as to prevent flood dangers and with a further view to stabilizing the international boundary line. The rectification on the Mexican side of the Rio Grande is carried on under the supervision of the Mexican Commissioner of the International Boundary Commission, United States and Mexico, while the work on the American side is being supervised by the American member of the Commission.

Treaty Series 864; 4 Treaties, etc. (Trenwith, 1938) 4462; 48 Stat. 1621. Secretary Hull to the President, Aug. 24, 1935, MS. Department of State, file 711.1216A/702A.

For further discussions of the international boundary between the United States and Mexico, see the discussion of the Rio Grande and Colorado River under "Diversion", *ante* §86, and the discussion of the Rio Grande under "American Rivers", *ante* §88.

Land boundary

In 1906 the International (Water) Boundary Commission, United States and Mexico, recommended "that a space sixty feet wide on each side of the international boundary be reserved and set aside by the two Governments, wherever their respective laws permit, as an international highway, upon which no buildings, railroad tracks or other improvements shall be allowed to be placed, except where the main tracks of international railroads cross the boundary line, and then as near as practicable at right angles". In transmitting this recommendation to the Department, on November 6, 1906, the American Commissioner stated that it was his understanding, in which the Mexican Commissioner had indicated his concurrence, that this recommendation would necessarily be restricted to the public lands directly under the control of the Federal Government.

In an opinion of April 24, 1907 the solicitor for the Department of State expressed the view that, pending an agreement with Mexico concerning this matter, such a strip might be reserved from entry by proclamation by the President. President Roosevelt issued such a proclamation on May 27, 1907, the operative portions of which provided that—

> there are hereby reserved from entry, settlement or other form of appropriation under the public land laws and set apart as a public reservation, all public lands within sixty feet of the international boundary between the United States and the Republic of Mexico, within the State of California and the Territories of Arizona and New Mexico; and where any river

or stream forms any part of said international boundary line, this reservation shall be construed and taken as extending to and including all public lands belonging to the United States which lie within sixty feet of the margin of such river or stream.

Brigadier General Mills to Secretary Root, Nov. 6, 1906, Acting Secretary of State (Bacon) to the Secretary of the Interior, May 24, 1907, MS. Department of State, file 2263/11 and /22. 35 Stat. 2136. The proclamation exempted certain vested rights.

In Mar. 1909 the Department of Agriculture solicited the views of the Department of State as to a proposed fence to be constructed along sections of the United States – Mexican boundary for the purpose of preventing diseased Mexican cattle from straying into the United States. The Department of State referred the matter to the American Commissioner on the International Boundary Commission, United States and Mexico, who replied:

"I can see no objection to the construction and maintenance of this fence for the purpose indicated. On the public lands it should be placed sixty feet from the international line, so that when the necessity for it no longer exists it will not be an obstruction within the zone reserved free from entry by the Proclamation of May 27, 1907 (35 Stats., Part 2 [p. 2136], Proclamation 22). Where private property abuts the international line the consent of the owners would have to be obtained to carry the fence sixty feet from same, and if this consent cannot be had it would have to be placed directly on the international line, in which event the consent of Mexico would have to be obtained."

These views were transmitted to the Department of Agriculture, which in Apr. 1910 requested the Department of State to procure the assent of the Mexican Government to the construction and maintenance of such a fence along the boundary line. The desired permission was granted by the Mexican Government on July 16, 1910.

The Secretary of Agriculture (Wilson) to the Secretary of State (Knox), Mar. 26, 1909, MS. Department of State, file 18781; Commissioner Mills to Mr. Knox, Nov. 10, 1909, and Secretary Knox to Secretary Wilson, Nov. 19, 1909, *ibid.* 18781/1; Secretary Wilson to Secretary Knox, Apr. 21, 1910, *ibid.* 611.1257/3; Secretary Knox to Ambassador Wilson, no. 45, June 1, 1910, *ibid.* 812.6217/4; Ambassador Wilson to Secretary Knox, no. 94, June 17, 1910, *ibid.* 611.1257/6; Secretary Knox to Secretary Wilson, July 6, 1910, *ibid.* 812.6217/6.

FISHERIES

NORTHEASTERN FISHERIES

§108

Under the convention of October 20, 1818 (art. I) between the United States and Great Britain it was agreed that the inhabitants of the United States "shall have forever, in common with the subjects of His Britannic Majesty, the liberty to take fish of every kind" on certain parts of the coasts of Newfoundland and of the coasts, bays, harbors, and creeks of Labrador and that American fishermen should also have liberty forever, to dry and cure fish in any of the "unsettled

North Atlantic Coast Fisheries arbitration

bays, harbours, and creeks of the southern part of the coast of Newfoundland" described therein, and of the "coast of Labrador". By the same convention the United States renounced forever "any liberty heretofore enjoyed or claimed by the inhabitants thereof, to take, dry, or cure fish on, or within three marine miles of any of the coasts, bays, creeks or harbours of His Britannic Majesty's dominions in America not included within the abovementioned limits; Provided however, that the American fishermen shall be admitted to enter such bays or harbours for the purpose of shelter and of repairing damages therein, of purchasing wood, and of obtaining water, and for no other purpose". 1 Treaties, etc. (Malloy, 1910) 631. From time to time, beginning as early as 1821 and culminating in 1905–6, because of restrictive legislation by Newfoundland, differences arose as to the meaning of these provisions.

In 1905, after failure of ratification of the Hay-Bond convention signed November 8, 1902 providing that "United States' fishing-vessels" entering the waters of Newfoundland should have the privilege of purchasing bait, of trading, buying, and selling fish and oil, and of procuring supplies in Newfoundland on the same terms and conditions as Newfoundland vessels, Newfoundland enacted "An Act respecting Foreign Fishing Vessels" (5 Edw. VII, c. 4) containing provision that the possession by foreign vessels of certain named articles used in fishery was *prima facie* evidence of unlawful purchase and subjected the vessel to forfeiture. The act of 1905 repealed an earlier Newfoundland act of May 24, 1893 (56 Vict., c. 6), which had contained provision permitting the Governor in Council to authorize the issuance of licenses to foreign fishing vessels enabling them to enter any port on the coast of Newfoundland in order to purchase bait, ice, seines, lines, and all other supplies and outfits for fishery and in order to ship crews. (For the Newfoundland Foreign Fishing Vessels Act of May 10, 1906, repealing the act of 1905, see 6 Edw. VII, c. 1.)

On October 12, and again on October 19, 1905, Secretary Root protested against the enforcement of the 1905 act on the ground that under the convention of 1818 American vessels were entitled to go into the waters of the "treaty coast" and take fish of any kind, that they were entitled to fish without licenses, that unless they purposed to trade as well as fish they were not bound to enter at any Newfoundland customhouse, and that "American vessels are of right entitled to have on them in the waters of the treaty coast both fish of every kind and the gear for the taking of fish, and that a law undertaking to make that possession *prima facie* proof of crime deprives them of that presumption of innocence to which all citizens of Great Britain and America are entitled".

Sir Edward Grey, British Secretary of State for Foreign Affairs, replied on February 2, 1906, by a memorandum addressed to the American Ambassador, that the privilege of fishing contained in article I of the 1818 convention was conceded only when the fishery was "carried on by inhabitants of the United States" and that the convention did not confer rights on American vessels as such; that His Majesty's Government did not share the view that the Newfoundland law was inconsistent with the convention of 1818 "if applied to American vessels which do not purpose to trade, but only to fish"; that it was admitted that the possession by inhabitants of the United States of any fish and gear which they might lawfully take or use in the exercise of their rights under the convention of 1818 could not properly be made *prima facie* evidence of the commission of an offense and that it was not believed that "a Court of Law would take a different view".

On June 30, 1906 Secretary Root replied to the memorandum just discussed, stating that the United States could not admit that an American vessel was bound to furnish evidence that all the members of the crew were inhabitants of the United States and that it could not agree with the British contention that the only ground on which the application of any provisions of the Colonial law to American vessels engaged in the fishery was that of unreasonable interference with the American right of fishery, because the convention did not contain "any grant of right to the makers of Colonial law to interfere at all, whether reasonably or unreasonably".

Secretary Root to Ambassador Durand, Oct. 12 and 19, 1905, MS. Department of State, 27 Notes, Great Britain, 392, 398; Ambassador Reid to Mr. Root, Feb. 6, 1906, *ibid.* 214 Despatches, Great Britain; Mr. Root to Mr. Reid, June 30, 1906, *ibid.* 35 Instructions, Great Britain, 319.

For the text of the unratified Hay-Bond convention, see IV *North Atlantic Coast Fisheries Arbitration*, Appendix to the British Case (S. Doc. 870, 61st Cong., 3d sess.), p. 79.

In 1906 a *modus vivendi* for the fishing season of 1906-7 was concluded; this was renewed for three successive seasons. 1 Treaties, etc. (Malloy, 1910) 805, 811, 832, 844.

On June 20, 1907 Sir Edward Grey addressed a further communication to the American Ambassador in which he stated:

. . . His Majesty's Government do not contend that every person on board an American vessel fishing in the Treaty waters must be an inhabitant of the United States, but merely that no such person is entitled to take fish unless he is an inhabitant of the United States. . . .

Whatever may be the correct interpretation of the Treaty as to the employment of foreigners generally on board American vessels, His Majesty's Government do not suppose that the United States Government lay claim to withdraw Newfoundlanders from the jurisdiction of their own Government so as to entitle them to fish in the employment of Americans in violation of Newfoundland laws.

Proposal of arbitration

In reply, Ambassador Reid proposed that "the pending questions under the treaty of 1818" should be submitted for decision to the Permanent Court of Arbitration at The Hague. He stated at the same time that—

the surrender of the right to hire local fishermen, who eagerly seek to have us employ them, and the surrender at the same time of the use of purse seines and of fishing on Sunday would, under existing circumstances, render the Treaty stipulation worthless to us.

My Government holds this opinion so strongly that the task of reconciling it with the positions maintained in your letter of June 20th seems hopeless.

Sir Edward Grey to Ambassador Reid, June 20, 1907, MS. Department of State, file 17931/1–2; Mr. Reid to Sir Edward Grey, July 12, 1907, *ibid.* 17931/6–9.

On Sept. 24, 1907 an Order in Council of Sept. 9, 1907 was published in the *Royal Gazette* of St. John's, Newfoundland, stipulating that provisions relating to boarding of vessels found in Newfoundland waters should not apply to vessels in which American inhabitants resort to those waters for the purpose of exercising the liberty assured to them by article I of the convention of 1818. It also prohibited the service of process on board any American vessel or arrest of any vessel or its gear, the purpose thereof being to prevent the application of such provisions of the laws of Newfoundland as interfered with the *modus vivendi*. As recited in the text, the order was issued in pursuance of the act of Parliament of June 19, 1819 (59 Geo. III, c. 38), passed to carry into effect the provisions of the convention of 1818 between Great Britain and the United States. The instructions to the Governor of Newfoundland from the British Colonial Office to publish the Order in Council stated that the refusal of the former's Ministers to cooperate in carrying out the *modus vivendi* for 1907 (cited *ante*) left the British Government no alternative but to issue instructions for the publication of the Order in Council. The Order in Council was revoked the following year by another Order in Council dated Sept. 26, 1908.

For the text of the Order in Council of Sept. 9, 1907, see 100 Br. & For. St. Paps. 114; MS. Department of State, file 573/201–202; the Colonial Secretary, Lord Elgin, to Governor MacGregor, Sept. 14 and 16, 1907, III *North Atlantic Coast Fisheries Arbitration* (S. Doc. 870, 61st Cong., 3d sess.), p. 1022. For the text of the Order in Council of Sept. 26, 1908, see VII *idem* 340; 101 Br. & For. St. Paps. 106.

On January 27, 1909 a special agreement was signed by the two countries containing provision for the submission of seven questions, arising out of the dispute, to the arbitration of a tribunal to be selected from the panel of the Permanent Court of Arbitration. The tribunal as organized was composed of Mr. Heinrich Lammasch, of Austria-Hungary; His Excellency A. F. de Savornin Lohman, of the Netherlands; Dr. Luis M. Drago, of Argentina; Judge George Gray, of the United States; and Sir Charles Fitzpatrick, of Great Britain. The arbitration was conducted at The Hague in the summer of 1910, and on September 7 of that year the decision was announced.

Briefly the tribunal decided, with reference to the seven questions submitted to it, (1) that Great Britain had the inherent sovereign right, without the consent of the United States, to make reasonable regulations, not in violation of the convention, as to the exercise of the liberty to take fish referred to in article I of the convention, the question of reasonableness to be determined by an impartial authority; (2) that inhabitants of the United States have the right to employ as members of fishing crews of their vessels persons not inhabitants of the United States; (3) that the inhabitants of the United States "should not be subjected to the purely commercial formalities of report, entry and clearance at a custom-house, nor to light, harbor or other dues not imposed upon Newfoundland fishermen", although American fishing vessels might be required to report if reasonable conveniences for doing so are at hand; (4) that the right granted under the convention to American fishermen to enter bays or harbors on the non-treaty coast "for the purpose of shelter and of repairing damages therein, of purchasing wood and of obtaining water" was not dependent upon the payment of dues, or of entering and reporting at customhouses at these places, as such requirements would be "inconsistent with the grounds upon which such privileges rest"; (5) that, in interpreting the right renounced by the United States to take, dry, or cure fish on or within three marine miles of any of the coasts, bays, creeks, or harbors of His Britannic Majesty's Dominions in America, the word "bays" must be construed as applying to geographical bays, the three marine miles being measured "from a straight line drawn across the body of water at the place where it ceases to have the configuration and characteristics of a bay", but that at all other places "the three marine miles are to be measured following the sinuosities of the coast", and that as to certain bays, the procedure for the limitation of which was not particularly specified, "the limits of exclusion shall be drawn three miles seaward from a straight line across the bay in the part nearest the entrance at the first point where the width does not exceed ten miles" (see *ante* §100); (6) that inhabitants of the United States have the liberty of fishing "in the bays, creeks and harbours of the Treaty coasts of Newfoundland and the Magdalen Islands"; and (7) that inhabitants of the United States whose vessels resort to the fishing grounds for the purpose of exercising the liberties granted in article I of the convention of 1818, are entitled to the commercial privileges on those coasts accorded by agreement or otherwise to United States trading vessels generally, "provided the Treaty liberty of fishing and the commercial privileges are not exercised concurrently".

Per Ct. Arb., *North Atlantic Coast Fisheries Arbitration* (The Hague, 1910) 104, 133, 134, 139, 140, 143, 144; MS. Department of State, file 711.438A/363; Scott, *Hague Court Reports* (1916) 146, 180, 181, 187, 188, 192, 193.

In the so-called case of the *Fishing Claims—Group I* (United States *v.* Great Britain), decided by the Anglo-American tribunal established under the special agreement of August 18, 1910, claims were made for the refund of customs duties, light dues, and other charges imposed on American fishing vessels by Newfoundland authorities between the years 1897–1910, alleged to have been exacted in contravention of the convention of October 20, 1818 between the United States and Great Britain. The tribunal was of the opinion:

There can be no doubt that purchase of herring from independent fishermen in Newfoundland waters could not be regarded as an exercise of the fishing privilege belonging to the United States under the Treaty of 1818.

.   .   .   .

Under the answer of the Permanent Court of Arbitration at The Hague to the seventh question in the North Atlantic Coast Fisheries Arbitration, an American vessel could not exercise fishing privileges and commercial privileges on the same voyage. As to any voyage there must be wholly and purely fishing activities or the vessel must be regarded as trading. Concession of the fishing privilege in the Treaty of 1818 carried with it tacitly (or by implication) the privilege of doing such things as are reasonably necessary to its exercise in view of the nature of the fishery to be carried on. It is contended, on behalf of the United States, that the privilege extends to all customary means and methods of carrying on the fishery. But in our opinion this is true only provided and to the extent that the customary means and methods are reasonably necessary to the exercise of the fishing privilege. We consider that the disposing of fishing outfit and gear to Newfoundland fishermen in Newfoundland waters as a part of their compensation, such outfit and gear remaining their property after use in the employment and entering into the general stock of the country, was not a reasonably necessary mode of or incident of exercising the fishing privilege and must be held to have been trading.
    . . . we must hold that all of the claimant vessels, at all the times in question, were to that extent engaged in trading and hence were not exclusively exercising fishing privileges.

Nielsen's Report (1926) 554, 565; 1 Treaties, etc. (Malloy, 1910) 631.
In the case of *The David J. Adams* (United States *v.* Great Britain) the same tribunal disallowed a claim submitted on account of the seizure

on May 7, 1886 of the schooner *David J. Adams* by Canadian authorities in Digby Basin, Nova Scotia—an area wherein the United States under the convention of 1818 had renounced the liberty to take fish within three marine miles of the coast and had been granted the right to enter "such bays or harbours" for certain specified purposes only, not including the purchase of bait—and the subsequent condemnation of the vessel by a Canadian court on the charge of having, in violation of Canadian legislation and of the convention of 1818, entered Canadian waters for the purpose of procuring bait.

Nielsen's Report (1926) 524, 530. In disallowing the claim the tribunal suggested the payment of compensation as an act of grace.

In the case of *The Thomas F. Bayard* (United States *v.* Great Britain), decided by the same tribunal, damages were awarded the United States on account of the refusal of Newfoundland authorities to permit an American vessel, enrolled and licensed for the fisheries, to exercise the right of purchasing bait in Bonne Bay on the treaty coast of Newfoundland wherein the inhabitants of the United States were entitled to fish under the convention of 1818, as construed by the tribunal of arbitration in 1910 in the case of the *North Atlantic Coast Fisheries* (sixth holding). *Ibid.* 573.

In the case of *The Frederick Gerring, Jr.* (United States *v.* Great Britain), submitted to the tribunal established under the agreement of 1910, the question at issue was whether the act of bailing fish out of a seine in Canadian territorial waters where the fish were caught outside of the three-mile limit constituted "fishing" within the marine league, such fishing being prohibited by article I of the convention of 1818. The tribunal approved an amicable settlement previously reached between the two Governments under the terms of which it was agreed that the Canadian Government should pay $9,000 "to be employed in blotting out the recollection" of the incident. *Ibid.* 575, 577.

In the case of *The Horace B. Parker* (United States *v.* Great Britain), also decided by the Anglo-American tribunal established under the special agreement of 1910, liability in the amount of $1,600 was predicated upon the refusal of Newfoundland authorities to permit an American fishing vessel to make repairs, a right secured to American fishermen by the 1818 convention. The tribunal said that—

"it is enough to say that replacing a sail needed for fishing purposes ['and . . . not necessary for the sailing of a vessel'] where such a sail has been blown away, seems to us clearly within the phrase 'repairing damages,' and we so hold." *Ibid.* 570.

A claim submitted to the same tribunal for indemnity based on the seizure by Canadian authorities of the American fishing schooner *Tattler* in 1905 for not having a fishing license, resulted in an award for $630 in favor of the United States. The master of the vessel, after entering the Canadian port of North Sydney, had repeatedly applied to the authorities for a license so as to enable the ship to obtain additional members for the crew, and the license had been erroneously refused. *The Tattler* (United States *v.* Great Britain), *ibid.* 489.

In the case of the *S.S. May* v. *The King* the Supreme Court of Canada affirmed the judgment of a lower court condemning the vessel under the Customs and Fisheries Protection Act (R.S.C., 1927, c. 43) on the ground that she was within three miles of the Canadian coast in Murray Bay on the Pacific Coast for a purpose not permitted by treaty or convention or by any law of Great Britain or Canada and in violation of the act. The Court stated:

"It is common ground that this section, although primarily enacted as a customs provision for the protection of the revenue, does, by the exception contained in the words 'unless from stress of weather or other unavoidable cause' give effect to a principle of international law recognized by both countries, namely, that vessels of one nation will be excused for entering the territory of another if there is an actual necessity for their so doing. It is a well recognized principle, both in this country and in the United States, that the jurisdiction of a nation is exclusive and absolute within its own territory, of which its territorial waters within three marine miles from shore are as clearly a part, as the land. All exceptions, therefore, to the full and complete power of a nation within its own territory must be traced to the consent of the nation itself given as a general rule by treaty, convention or statute. From this it follows that each nation has the absolute right to prescribe the conditions upon which the vessels of another nation will be permitted to enter its territorial waters. . . .

". . . In 1846 the two nations entered into a treaty defining the boundary line between them from the Rocky Mountains, where it had been fixed by the Convention of 1818, to the Pacific Ocean, at the 49th parallel of north latitude. All north of that line to parallel 54°40' was awarded to Great Britain, and all south of it to the United States. It was not until the ratification of this treaty that the Sovereignty of Great Britain to any part of the Pacific Slope, north of the 49th parallel of latitude, was recognized by the United States. . . .

"In view of the fact that at the date of the Convention of 1818 the United States had not recognized the Sovereignty of Great Britain to the Pacific Slope, it is, in my opinion, impossible to hold that the reference to the 'coasts, bays, creeks and harbours of His Britannic Majesty's dominions in America' contained in art. 1 of the Convention [of 1818], was intended by either party to apply to the Pacific coast. I, therefore, agree with the conclusion reached by Martin, L.J., Adm., in *The King* v. *'Valiant'*, 16 D.L.R. 824, that the Convention of 1818 did not apply to the Pacific waters so far as fisheries were concerned."

[1931] 3 D.L.R. 15, 20, 26; 1 Treaties, etc. (Malloy, 1910) 631.

WHALE FISHERIES

§109

Whaling, etc., by aliens in Alaskan waters

In response to an inquiry from the Norwegian Minister in Washington, on May 13, 1907, whether there would be any objection to the carrying on of whale fishery in Alaskan waters by a Norwegian company, to the landing of the whales in Alaska, to the acquiring of land there for building factories, and whether the vessels to be used for the purpose should be of American build and registry, the Department of State replied July 1, 1907 that—

the Secretary of Commerce and Labor advises me, under date of June 25th, that while he is aware of no provision of the laws relating to the fisheries which would interfere with the enterprise and while he is unable to point to any specific provision of the navigation laws, or of any other laws administered by his Department, expressly providing for such a contingency, he is, nevertheless, of the opinion that the navigation laws are so framed as to indicate by their general scope and spirit a purpose quite inconsistent with the authorization of a project of the sort in question.

Secretary Straus adds that, generally speaking, it would appear that the navigation laws contemplate that the American fisheries are open only to vessels built and owned, and registered or enrolled, in the United States; and that inasmuch as the laws in question impose numerous and exacting duties and obligations to which all vesesls of the United States must conform, it would give foreign vessels an obvious advantage over domestic vessels to permit the former to engage in a domestic pursuit free from all the burdens imposed by the navigation laws.

In further reference to the subject, the Department transmitted to the Norwegian Minister a copy of a letter from the Department of Justice, dated August 29, 1907, reading in part as follows:

> . . . I have the honor to refer you to the act of Congress, dated March 2, 1897, (29 Stat. 618), amending the act of March 3, 1887 (1 Supp. Rev. Stat. 556) which provides "that no alien or person not a citizen of the United States or who has not declared his intention to become a citizen of the United States in the manner provided by law, shall acquire title to or own any land in the Territories of the United States", unless such right is secured by treaty. There is no treaty giving such right to Norwegian citizens. There does not appear to be any law prohibiting whaling by a foreign corporation or company in the waters of Alaska. The act of June 14, 1906 (34 Stat. 263), does not seem to apply.

> The Acting Secretary of State (Bacon) to Minister Hauge, no. 57, July 1, 1907, MS. Department of State, file 6480/1; the Acting Attorney General (Russell) to the Secretary of State, Aug. 29, 1907, *ibid.* 6480/3.

An international agreement for the regulation of whaling was concluded at Geneva on September 24, 1931. Under article 1 the signatory powers agree to take appropriate measures to insure the application of its provisions. The killing of certain kinds of whales is prohibited by articles 4 and 5, while article 6 provides for the fullest possible use of whales taken. The compensation of crews of whaling vessels is made, by article 7, to depend on certain factors including the size, specie, value and yield of oil of whales taken and not upon the number of whales taken. Article 9 provides that the convention is to be applied on the high seas as well as in territorial and national waters. Whaling convention, 1931

Under an act of Congress approved by the President on May 1, 1936 (49 Stat. 1246) to give effect to the convention, the Secretary Act of 1936 of the Treasury and the Secretary of Commence [Interior: 53 Stat. 1433] are authorized to make regulations for the enforcement of the act, such regulations to become effective upon approval by the President.

Agreement of 1937

On June 8, 1937 an agreement for the regulation of whaling was signed at London by the United States and several other countries. This agreement supplements and extends but does not supplant the convention of 1931. It is applicable to factory ships and whale-catchers and to land stations under the jurisdiction of the contracting parties. It prohibits the taking of baleen whales, *inter alia*, in waters south of 40° south latitude except during certain specified seasons. It also limits the period during which whales may be taken or treated in any area to not more than six months in any period of twelve months. The agreement provides for the furnishing to the International Bureau for Whaling Statistics at Sandefjord, in Norway, of statistics regarding whaling operations. The agreement which came into force on May 7, 1938 was amended by a protocol concluded at London on June 24, 1938.

> 49 Stat. 3079, and 4 Treaties, etc. (Trenwith, 1938) 5372 (convention of 1931) ; I Fed. Reg. (1936) 1616 (regulations) ; Treaty Series 933 (convention of 1937) ; Department of State, Treaty Information Bulletin 108 (Sept. 1938) 310 (protocol of 1938) ; *ibid.* 110 (Nov. 1938) 359.

SEAL FISHERIES

§110

On January 21, 1909 the Government of the United States addressed a note to the Japanese Ambassador in the United States proposing an international conference or joint commission on the protection and preservation of the fur seals and reading in part as follows:

> I desire to bring to your attention the question of the protection and preservation of the fur seal herds frequenting the waters of the North Pacific Ocean, including the Seas of Behring, Okhotsk and Kamchatka.

Conference proposed

> It appears from the official reports of observations made under the authority of this Government, that as recently as the year 1891 the seal herd, having its breeding ground on the Pribilof Islands in Behring Sea, numbered upwards of one million seals, and that since then it has steadily decreased in size until at the present time its total number is estimated to be less than one hundred and fifty thousand. A proportionate decrease is understood to have taken place in the size of the Japanese and Russian seal herds frequenting Robben Island and the Commander Islands.
> The ineffectiveness of the protective regulations and conditions imposed under the award of the Fur Seal Arbitration Tribunal at Paris in 1893 upon pelagic sealing by American and

British sealers is no doubt due in part to their lack of application to pelagic sealing carried on under the flags of other nations; but it is also true that in their practical application they have proved to be not well devised for securing for the seals the protection which was intended. It is also evident from the rapidly diminishing size of the Japanese and Russian herds that the protection afforded to those herds by existing regulations is inadequate to prevent their destruction so far as their value for commercial purposes is concerned.

As a result of scientific investigation and study of the subject for a number of years, this Government is strongly of the opinion that any permanent solution of this difficult question should include an international agreement absolutely prohibiting pelagic sealing; but whatever may be the degree and kind of protection essential for the preservation of the seals, it would seem to be no longer open to question that if the present methods of seal hunting are persisted in for a few years longer, the fur seals will be practically exterminated.

Similar notes were addressed on the same day to the Russian and British Ambassadors.

Secretary Root to Baron Takahira, Baron Rosen, and Ambassador Bryce, Jan. 21, 1909, MS. Department of State, file 99/21a.

On February 27, 1911 the British Ambassador notified the Secretary of State that the British Government was prepared to accept the proposal. The Governments of Russia and Japan having previously expressed a willingness to join the United States in a conference, such a conference was convened in Washington on May 11, 1911.

Ambassador Bryce to Secretary Knox, no. 36, Feb. 27, 1911, *ibid.* 711.417/95; memorandum from the Department of State to the Russian Embassy, Dec. 2, 1909, *ibid.* 99/54.

For material with reference to the calling of the conference, see Secretary Knox to Baron Uchida, Prince Koudacheff, and Ambassador Bryce, Mar. 3, 1911, *ibid.* 711.417/95. The Third Assistant Secretary of State (Hale) to Mr. Forster, May 11, 1911, *ibid.* 711.417/123a.

The international aspect of the problem of fur-seal fishing in the Pacific Ocean dates from the issuance of a ukase by Emperor Alexander of Russia on Sept. 7, 1821 granting exclusive whaling and fishing privileges to Russian subjects north of the 51st degree of latitude in the Pacific Ocean and forbidding all foreign vessels, except in case of distress, not only to land on the coasts and islands belonging to Russia but also to approach them within less than 100 Italian miles.

As the result of the diplomatic protests of both the United States and Great Britain against that ukase, conventions were concluded between Russia and those governments on April 17, 1824 and February 28/16, 1825, respectively. By the terms of the convention between the United States and Russia, it was provided, briefly, that citizens or subjects of the two countries should not be disturbed either in navigation or fishing "in any part of the Great Ocean, commonly called the Pacific Ocean, or South Sea" and that citizens of the United States should not resort to any point where there was a Russian establishment without permission, nor Russian subjects to any point where there was any establishment of the United States on the northwest coast. The provisions of the convention between Great Britain and Russia were substantially the same.

By a convention signed on Mar. 30, 1867 the Emperor of Russia, in consideration of the sum of $7,200,000 in gold, ceded to the United States "all the territory and dominion" which he possessed "on the continent of America and in the adjacent islands". The cession included the Pribilof Islands, the principal breeding ground of the fur seals in the Pacific Ocean.

As the result of the seizure of certain British sealing schooners in Bering Sea by United States revenue cutters during the years 1886–89, against which the British Government protested, a treaty of arbitration was signed in Washington on Feb. 29, 1892 between the United States and Great Britain. Specific questions in regard to the extent of the jurisdiction of the United States in Bering Sea were submitted to arbitrators, and it was agreed that the latter should draw up regulations for the protection and preservation of fur seals in or habitually resorting to Bering Sea, which should be binding on both Governments. The tribunal made its award on Aug. 15, 1893, deciding, *inter alia*, that the United States had no right of protection or property in the fur seals frequenting the islands belonging to it in the Bering Sea, when such seals were found outside of the ordinary three-mile limit. The regulations drawn up by the arbitrators contained a stipulation (art. 2) prohibiting the killing, capture, or pursuit of fur seals on the high seas north of the 35th degree of north latitude and east of the 180th degree of longitude and the water boundary line between the United States and Russia from the first of May through the thirty-first of July of each year.

For instances of seizure of vessels for violation of laws and regulations adopted conformably to the Bering Sea award of Aug. 15, 1893 (1 Treaties, etc. [Malloy, 1910] 746, 751), see *The King* v. *The Carlotta G. Cox*, 13 B.C.R. (1908) 460 (irregularity in seizure cured where vessel properly before court); *The Kate* (Great Britain v. United States), Anglo-American tribunal established in accordance with the special agreement of Aug. 18, 1910, Neilsen's Report (1926) 472, 476 (although a *bona-fide* seizure, the superior officer did not consider that there was reasonable ground for seizure; indemnity awarded); *The Jessie, The Thomas F. Bayard*, and *The Pescawha* (Great Britain v. United States), same tribunal, *ibid.* 479, 480 (firearms placed under seal while the vessel was on the high seas; indemnity allowed); *The Wanderer* (Great Britain v. United States), same tribunal, *ibid.* 459, 462–465 (vessel seized on high seas for possession of and not for use of firearms, prohibited by the Bering Sea award and regulations; indemnity allowed); *The Favourite* (Great Britain v. United States), same tribunal, *ibid.* 515 (indemnity allowed for reasons stated in the award in the case of *The Wanderer*).

The United States also concluded an agreement with Russia on Aug. 26/Sept. 8, 1900 submitting to arbitration certain claims of the United States on account of the seizure of American sealing vessels by Russian cruisers beyond the territorial waters of Russia. Awards were made by the arbitrator on account of such seizures. 2 Treaties, etc. (Malloy, 1910) 1532 (agreement, 1900); 1902 For. Rel., App. I, pp. 451 *et seq.* (awards).

It became increasingly apparent after 1900 that the regulations drawn up by the arbitrators under the British-American arbitration agreement of 1892—binding only on the United States and Great Britain—were inadequate to prevent the growing decimation of the seal herds through pelagic sealing. Immediately after the rendition of that award the United States proposed to Great Britain that the two Governments enter into an agreement for the complete suppression of pelagic sealing for a certain time. The proposal was renewed from time to time thereafter without success.

1894 For. Rel., app. I, p. 228; 1895 For. Rel., pt. I, pp. 610, 615, 665–666; 1896 For. Rel., lxxii; 1897 For. Rel., 258 *et seq.;* S. Doc. 40, 55th Cong., 2d sess., serial no. 3592. For a complete history of the controversy regarding fur-seal fishing in the Pacific Ocean prior to 1906, see I Moore's Dig. 890–929, and 1 Moore's Arb. 755 *et seq.* For a detailed diplomatic history of the Alaskan fur-seals question up to 1906, see *Alaskan Fur Seals,* Report Prepared for the Department of State by Chandler P. Anderson, (Government Printing Office, 1906).

For the purpose of avoiding difficulties and disputes in regard to the taking of fur seal in the waters of Bering Sea and the North Pacific Ocean, and to aid in the preservation of seal life, the United States and Russia entered into a temporary agreement on May 4, 1894 with the understanding that it was not to create a precedent for the future, by the terms of which the United States agreed to prohibit its citizens from hunting fur seal within a zone of 10 nautical miles along the Russian coasts of Bering Sea and of the North Pacific Ocean, as well as within a zone of 30 nautical miles around the Commander Islands and Robben Island. 2 Treaties, etc. (Malloy, 1910) 1531.

With reference to the Washington Conference of 1897 and the convention signed on Oct. 6, 1897 by Japan, Russia, and the United States, see 5 A.J.I.L. (1911) 1027–1028. The convention would have prohibited the killing of fur seals in all the waters of the North Pacific Ocean outside of territorial limits for the period of one year. It was made conditional upon the adherence of Great Britain, which was not obtained.

By an act of Congress approved on Apr. 21, 1910 (amending an earlier act of Dec. 29, 1897, 30 Stat. 226), it was provided that no citizen of the United States, nor person owing duty of obedience to the laws thereof, nor any person belonging to or on board a vessel of the United States, "shall kill, capture, or hunt, . . . any fur seal in the waters of the Pacific Ocean, including Bering Sea and the sea of Okhotsk, whether in the territorial waters of the United States or in the open sea". 36 Stat. 326, 328. But see section 1 of the act approved Aug. 24, 1912, cited *post,* p. 797.

An act of Congress approved June 7, 1924 conferred jurisdiction on the District Court of the United States for the Northern District of California to adjudicate claims of American citizens, their heirs and legal representatives, for damages from the seizure, etc., of vessels charged with unlawful sealing in the Bering Sea and water contiguous thereto and outside of the three-mile limit during the years 1886 to 1896. The act barred claims not presented within two years. 43 Stat. 595; H. Rept. 253, 68th Cong., 1st sess., serial no. 8227. See also H. Rept. 784, 67th Cong., 2d sess., serial no. 7956.

Convention, 1911

By article I of the convention concluded on July 7, 1911 between the United States, Great Britain, Russia, and Japan, it was agreed that citizens and subjects of the contracting powers, and all persons subject to their laws and treaties, and their vessels should be prohibited "from engaging in pelagic sealing in the waters of the North

Pacific Ocean, north of the thirtieth parallel of north latitude and including the Seas of Bering, Kamchatka, Okhotsk and Japan". Provision was made in the same article for the seizure and detention (except within territorial waters) by the naval or other duly commissioned officers of any of the parties to the convention, of any person or vessel offending against such prohibition, to be delivered as soon as practicable to an authorized official of the nation to which such person or vessel belonged. The contracting parties agreed in article II not to permit the use of any of their ports or harbors or any part of their territory for any purposes connected with the operations of pelagic sealing within the protected area. By article III it was provided that no sealskins taken within that area and no sealskins identified as the species known as "*Callorhinus alascanus, Callorhinus ursinus* and *Callorhinus kurilensis*" and belonging to the American, Russian, or Japanese herds, except those taken under the authority of the respective powers to which the breeding grounds belonged and officially marked and certified as so taken, should be permitted to be imported or brought into the territory of any of the parties to the convention. Article IV exempted from the provisions of the convention natives of coasts of the waters in the protected area, provided they were not in the employ of other persons or under a contract to deliver the skin to any person. Article V forbade the killing, capture, or pursuit of sea-otters beyond the three-mile limit of the territories in the protected area. Under article VI the contracting parties agreed to enact appropriate legislation to make effective the foregoing provisions. Japan, Russia, and the United States agreed under article VII that each would maintain a guard or patrol in the waters frequented by the seal herd in the protection of which it was especially interested, so far as might be necessary for the enforcement of the foregoing provisions. All of the contracting parties agreed in article VIII to cooperate in taking such measures as might be appropriate and available in order to prevent pelagic sealing in the prohibited area.

"Pelagic sealing" is defined under article IX, for the purposes of the convention, as "the killing, capturing or pursuing in any manner whatsoever of fur seals at sea".

Under articles X and XI detailed provision was made for the delivery, at the end of each season by the United States to the Governments of Japan and Canada, respectively, of 15 percent gross in number and value of the sealskins taken annually under the authority of the United States in the Pribilof Islands, and for the advance payment to Great Britain and Japan of $200,000 each on the coming into force of the convention "in lieu of such number of fur-seal skins to which Great Britain and Japan respectively would be entitled under the provisions of this Convention". Further provision was made for a minimum number of sealskins as the annual share of Japan and Great Britain in those taken from the American herd and for minimum annual payments to those Governments should the United States absolutely prohibit the killing of seals on the Pribilof Islands. Similar detailed provisions were made in article XII for the annual delivery by Russia of 15 percent of the total number of sealskins taken annually on the Commander Islands or any other island or shores within the protected area, to the Canadian and Japanese Governments, respectively. In article XIII, likewise, it was agreed that Japan should deliver annually 10 percent of the total number of sealskins taken annually on Robben Island or any other island or shores within the protected area to the Governments of the United States, Canada, and Russia, respectively. Great Britain agreed in article XIV that, if any seal herd thereafter resorted to any islands or shores in the prohibited area within the jurisdiction of Great Britain, it would deliver at the end of each season 10 percent of the gross number of sealskins taken from such herd to the Governments of the United States, Japan, and Russia respectively.

It was agreed in article XV that the provisions of that convention should supersede those of the treaty entered into February 7, 1911 by the United States and Great Britain, so far as they were inconsistent therewith or in duplication thereof.

Article XVI provided that the convention should go into effect on December 15, 1911 and should continue in force for 15 years from that date, and thereafter "until terminated by twelve (12) months' written notice given by one or more of the parties to all of the others", which notice might be given at the expiration of 14 years or at any time afterward. And it was further agreed that at any time prior to the termination of the convention, upon the request of anyone of the contracting parties, a conference should be held forthwith between representatives of all the parties thereto to consider and if possible agree upon a further extension of the convention with such additions and modifications, if any, as might be found desirable.

3 Treaties, etc. (Redmond, 1923) 2966.

By the act of Congress approved Aug. 24, 1912, to give effect to the convention of July 7, 1911, the killing, etc., of fur seal in "the north Pacific Ocean north of the thirtieth parallel of north latitude and including the seas of Bering, Kamchatka, Okhotsk, and Japan" was forbidden. 37 Stat. 499, 500.

Meanwhile, on Feb. 7, 1911 the United States and Great Britain concluded a treaty looking to the preservation and protection of fur seals. By the terms thereof, pelagic sealing in Bering Sea and the North Pacific Ocean north of the 35th degree of north latitude and east of the 180th meridian was forbidden to the citizens and subjects of the two Governments (art. 1). The United States undertook to surrender to Canada annually one-fifth of the sealskins taken on the Pribilof Islands and to make a certain advance payment to Great Britain in lieu of the number of skins to which the latter would be entitled under the treaty (arts. II and III). The two Governments agreed to maintain a guard or patrol in the waters of the North Pacific and Bering Sea (art. V). Article VI provided that the treaty—

"shall go into effect as soon as, but not before, an international agreement is concluded and ratified by the Governments of the United States, Great Britain, Japan, and Russia".

3 Treaties, etc. (Redmond, 1923) 2629; 1911 For. Rel. 256.

The last paragraph above quoted was inserted in order to meet the objection of the Canadian Government, which did not desire to enter into an agreement contemplating an indefinite cessation of pelagic sealing and not its suspension for a term of years. Ambassador Bryce to Secretary Knox, May 16, 1910, and Mr. Knox to Mr. Bryce, May 17, 1910, MS. Department of State, file 711.417/69.

MISCELLANEOUS FISHERIES

§111

Convention, 1908; International Fisheries Commission

On April 11, 1908 a convention concerning fisheries in United States and Canadian waters was concluded by the United States and Great Britain. Articles I and II contained provision for the creation of an International Fisheries Commission, consisting of one representative of each Government, to prepare a system of uniform and common international regulations as to the times, seasons, and methods of fishing in the waters contiguous to the United States and Canada for the protection and preservation of food fishes. The two Governments were required to put into operation and to enforce by legislation and executive action the regulations, restrictions, and provisions with appropriate penalties. Each Government was to exercise jurisdiction over its own citizens or subjects found within its jurisdiction who had violated the regulations within the waters of the other party, as well as over citizens or subjects of either party apprehended for violation of the regulations in any of its own waters. Article IV specified the waters within which the regulations were to be applied.

1 Treaties, etc. (Malloy, 1910) 827.

With respect to United States – Canada fisheries, see H. Doc. 638, 61st Cong., 2d sess., serial no. 5834 (regulations prepared on May 29, 1909 by the International Fisheries Commission under the convention of 1908)˙; S. Rept. 290, 63d Cong., 2d sess., serial no. 6552, on S. 4437, to give effect to the provisions of the treaty of 1908; H. Rept. 312, 63d Cong., 2d sess., serial no. 6558, on H.R. 13005, to give effect to the provisions of the treaty of 1908.

The regulations of May 29, 1909 were adopted in their entirety and without modification by the Canadian Parliament in 1910. *Ibid.*, p. 2.

They were submitted to Congress by President Taft on Feb. 2, 1910. See H. Doc. 638, *ante*. On May 22, 1911 a bill, S. 12, approving all the regulations except ten, was passed in the Senate of the United States (47 Cong. Rec. 1433) and was referred to the House Committee on Foreign Affairs. *Ibid.* 1530. No further action was taken. Secretary Knox to Representative D. S. Alexander, Apr. 1, 1911, MS. Department of State, file 711.428/260. The regulations were, therefore, never proclaimed by the President. As a result of the non-approval of the regulations, the British Ambassador notified the Department on Oct. 19, 1914 that the "Government of Canada now purpose to resume their liberty of action in the matter of the administration of the fisheries in Canadian waters contiguous to the international boundary". Ambassador Spring Rice to Secretary Bryan, Oct. 19, 1914, *ibid.* 711.428/395. The Commission established under the convention of Apr. 11, 1908 became inactive. Another International Fisheries Commission between Great Britain and the United States was established under a convention of Mar. 2, 1923. 3 Treaties, etc. (Redmond, 1923) 2659. As to the latter commission, see *post*, this section.

Six commissioners appointed by the United States and Canada—constituting the American-Canadian Fisheries Conference—met in Washington on January 16, 1918 to consider pending questions concerning the fisheries on both the Atlantic and Pacific coasts. Hearings were held at various cities and, on September 6, 1918, a final report was signed, recommending: (*a*) the amendment of article 1 of the convention of October 20, 1818 between the United States and Great Britain so as to make liberal port privileges available in either country to the fishing vessels of the other; (*b*) a treaty and regulations for the protection of sockeye salmon of the Fraser River system; (*c*) reciprocal legislation on the subject of a "close time" on halibut fishing in the Pacific off the coasts of the two countries; and (*d*) the prohibition of lobster well-smack fishing just outside of the territorial waters off the coast of Nova Scotia. An Order in Council of February 18, 1918 was considered as settling the question of net fishing in Missisquoi Bay, the Canadian portion of Lake Champlain; and contemporaneous instructions from the Department of Commerce abolishing requirements with respect to entry and clearance imposed on Canadian fishing vessels passing through territorial waters of Alaska bound for the fishing grounds of the high seas beyond, were considered as settling that question. State legislation by New York, Pennsylvania, and Ohio, similar to a Canadian regulation with respect to a four-year prohibition of sturgeon fishing in Lake Erie, was recommended. Finally, a world-wide international conference to consider the protection of whales was suggested.

American-Canadian Fisheries Conference, 1918

Recommendations

The Secretary of Commerce (Redfield) to the Secretary of State (Lansing), June 21, 1917, MS. Department of State, file 711.428/438; Mr. Lansing to Mr. Redfield, Oct. 8, 1917, *ibid.* 711.428/453; Mr. Lansing to Ambassador Spring Rice, Dec. 10, 1917, *ibid.* 711.428/459; Mr. Spring Rice to Mr. Lansing, Dec. 19, 1917, *ibid.* 711.428/460. For the report of the Conference, see Commissioners for the United States to Mr. Lansing, Sept. 6, 1918, *ibid.* files 711.428/488, 711.428/640; 1918 For. Rel. 432–480. For the convention of 1818, see 1 Treaties, etc. (Malloy, 1910) 631.

Port
privileges

As a result of the hearings held by the American-Canadian Fisheries Conference of 1918 and of the urgent need of removing all obstacles to the greatest possible production and movement of food during the World War, the United States section of the Conference recommended the removal of restrictions imposed on Canadian fishing vessels in United States ports. This recommendation was approved by the President, and on February 21, 1918 the Secretary of Commerce issued an order to the collectors of customs directing them to permit Canadian vessels "to enter from and clear for the high seas and the fisheries, disposing of their catch and taking on supplies, stores, etc., under supervision as in the case of merchant vessels entering and clearing for foreign ports", except as to tonnage tax and other charges imposed on this latter class of vessels. At the suggestion of the Canadian section of the Conference of 1918, an Order in Council was approved on March 8, 1918 providing that during the war American fishing vessels could enter any Canadian port for certain purposes specified in the order without the requirement of a license or the payment of fees not charged to Canadian fishing vessels.

The Commissioner of Navigation called the attention of the Secretary of Commerce to the fact that under section 4311 of the Revised Statutes of the United States only American vessels were entitled to engage in the coasting trade and fisheries and to the fact that the order of the Secretary of Commerce of February 21, 1918, which had been issued as a war measure, contravened the provisions of that section, and on July 6, 1921 the Secretary of Commerce issued an order notifying collectors of customs that the port privileges accorded to Canadian vessels were terminated. On October 3, 1921 the British Ambassador informed Secretary Hughes that unless the temporary privileges accorded to Canadian vessels were restored the Canadian Government would have to consider the withdrawal of all privileges to United States fishing vessels, "thus bringing again into operation the provisions of article 1 of the treaty of 1818".

Report of the American-Canadian Fisheries Conference, 1918, MS. Department of State, file 711.428/640; the Secretary of Commerce (Hoover) to the Secretary of State (Hughes), Mar. 9, 1921, and Commissioner Chamberlain to Mr. Hoover, Mar. 9, 1921, *ibid.* 711.428/631; Mr. Hoover to Mr. Hughes, July 11, 1921, *ibid.* 711.428/644; Ambassador Geddes to Mr. Hughes, Oct. 3, 1921, *ibid.* 711.428/655; Mr. Hughes to Mr. Geddes, Nov. 15, 1921, *ibid.* 711.428/672. For the origin of the dispute regarding port privileges, see pages 5 *et seq.* of the Report of the American-Canadian Fisheries Conference, 1918, *ibid.* 711.428/640. For the order of the Secretary of Commerce of Feb. 21, 1918, see *ibid.* 30. For the text of the Canadian order in council of Mar. 8, 1918, see *ibid.* 31.

In March 1923 a convention for the preservation of the halibut fishery of the northern Pacific Ocean was concluded between the United States and Great Britain. Article III established an International Fisheries Commission, to continue in existence so long as the convention should remain in force. The convention was supplanted by a convention for the preservation of halibut fishery of the northern Pacific Ocean and Bering Sea signed at Ottawa on May 9, 1930 between the United States and Great Britain in respect of the Dominion of Canada. It provided for the continuance of the International Fisheries Commission established under the convention of 1923. It also provided for closed seasons and prohibited waters for halibut fishing and authorized the commission to modify the closed season as to part or all of the convention waters. The Northern Pacific Halibut Act of May 2, 1932 (47 Stat. 142) was passed by Congress for the purpose of enforcing the provisions of this convention. *Convention, 1923*

Halibut fishery convention, 1930

On January 29, 1937 there was signed at Ottawa a convention between the United States and Great Britain in respect of the Dominion of Canada, supplanting the convention of 1930. The convention is designed to provide more effectively for the preservation of the halibut fishery of the northern Pacific Ocean and the Bering Sea and continues, with certain specified duties, the International Fisheries Commission established by the convention of 1923. An act of June 28, 1938 (50 Stat. 325, 328) was passed by Congress to give effect to it, by providing for the issuance of joint rules and regulations by the Secretary of the Treasury and the Secretary of Commerce. *Convention, 1937*

Treaty Series 701; 4 Treaties, etc. (Trenwith, 1938) 3982; 43 Stat. 1841 (convention of 1923). Treaty Series 837; 4 Treaties, etc. (Trenwith, 1938) 3999; 47 Stat. 1872 (convention of 1930). Treaty Series 917; 4 Treaties, etc. (Trenwith, 1938) 4014; 50 Stat. 1351 (convention of 1937).

On June 6, 1924 an act of Congress was approved for the purpose of protecting and conserving the fisheries of the United States in all waters of Alaska. The Secretary of Commerce was granted authority to set apart and reserve fishing areas in any of the waters of Alaska over which the United States has jurisdiction, and within such areas to establish closed seasons during which fishing may be limited or prohibited. He was further authorized to issue regulations with respect to the time, means, methods, and extent of fishing within any such area. The act contains provisions dealing particu- *Alaskan fishing* larly with the preservation of salmon fisheries. A further act of Congress was approved on June 18, 1926, amending the 1924 act, also having for its purpose the protection of the fisheries of Alaska. Section 1 of the act of 1924, as amended, has been twice amended, first by an act approved August 14, 1937 and later by an act approved April 7, 1938, with special reference to Bristol Bay. It is provided by the act of 1938 that in the area embracing Bristol Bay and the arms and tributaries thereof, no person shall at any time fish for or take salmon with a stake-net or set-net for commercial purposes, unless such person shall be a citizen of the United States and shall have theretofore continuously resided for the period of at least two years "within said area".

On June 25, 1938 an act of Congress was approved, amending the earlier act approved June 14, 1906, an act to prevent aliens from fishing in the waters of Alaska. It makes it unlawful "for any person not a citizen of the United States, or who has declared his intention to become a citizen of the United States, and is not a bona fide resident therein, or for any company, corporation, or association not organized or authorized to transact business under the laws of any State, Territory, or district thereof, or for any person not a native of Alaska, to catch or kill, or attempt to catch or kill, except with rod, spear, or gaff, any fish of any kind or species whatsoever in any of the waters of Alaska under the jurisdiction of the United States". It is provided that it is permissible to sell fish to aliens or to employ aliens, under certain conditions, and that *bona-fide* residents of Alaska for three consecutive years prior to the date of the approval of the act, who theretofore engaged in fishing in the waters of Alaska for commercial purposes, may continue to engage in fishing therein for commercial purposes for three years after the date of the approval of the act, although not citizens of the United States.

> 34 Stat. 263 (act of 1906) ; 43 Stat. 464 (act of 1924) ; 44 Stat. 752 (act of 1926) ; 50 Stat. 639 (act of 1937) ; 52 Stat. 208 (act of Apr. 7, 1938) ; *ibid.* 1174 (act of June 25, 1938).

Convention of 1930, sockeye-salmon fisheries

On May 26, 1930 a convention was concluded between the United States and Great Britain in respect of the Dominion of Canada for the protection, preservation, and extension of the sockeye-salmon fisheries of the Fraser River system. Ratifications thereof were exchanged at Washington on July 28, 1937.

> Treaty Series 918; 4 Treaties, etc. (Trenwith, 1938) 4002, 4007 (reservations of the Senate of the United States) ; 50 Stat. 1355.

Salmon-fishing activities of Japanese nationals in the offshore waters of Alaska, especially in the Bristol Bay area during the season of 1937. led to apprehension on the part of American fishing interests. As a result of discussions between the American Government and the Japanese Government the latter gave, without prejudice to the question of rights under international law, assurances that the three-year scientific salmon-fishery survey in the waters in question, undertaken by it in 1936, would be suspended; that it would continue to suspend the issuance of licenses for salmon fishing in the Bristol Bay area; and that it would take measures to prevent further salmon fishing by any Japanese vessel shown to be engaged in such operations.

Secretary Hull to Ambassador Grew, Nov. 20, 1937, MS. Department of State, file 711.008 North Pacific/211a; Mr. Grew to Mr. Hull, Mar. 25, 1938, *ibid.* 711.008 North Pacific/315.

On Dec. 17, 1929 Denmark, Danzig, Germany, Poland, and Sweden concluded an agreement concerning the regulation of plaice and flounder fishing in the Baltic Sea, 115 League of Nations Treaty Series (1931) 93. Another agreement concerning the regulation of plaice fishing was signed at Stockholm on Dec. 31, 1932 by Denmark, Norway, and Sweden, 139 *idem* (1933) 198. For other international agreements respecting fisheries, see the following: July 15/28, 1907, Japan and Russia, 101 Br. & For. St. Paps. 453; Jan. 18, 1908, France and Italy, *ibid.* 1059; Feb. 9, 1920, Denmark, France, Great Britain, Italy, Japan, Netherlands, Norway, Sweden, and United States, 2 League of Nations Treaty Series (1920) 8; Sept. 14, 1921, Italy and the Kingdom of the Serbs, Croats, and Slovenes, 19 *idem* (1923) 39, 41; Oct. 24, 1921 (art. 232), Danzig and Poland, 116 *idem* (1931) 137, 293; Apr. 10, 1922, Denmark and Germany, 10 *idem* (1922) 73; Sept. 20, 1922, Finland and Russian Soviet Republic, 19 *idem* (1923) 143; Oct. 21, 1922, Finland and U.S.S.R., 29 *idem* (1924) 197; Sept. 29, 1923, France and Great Britain, 21 *idem* (1923–24) 137; Jan. 20, 1924, Albania and Italy, 44 *idem* (1926) 359; July 9, 1924, Denmark and Norway, 120 Br. & For. St. Paps. 238; Jan. 20, 1925, Japan and U.S.S.R., XV Martens' *Nouveau recueil général* (3d ser., Triepel, 1926) 323; Apr. 23/June 4, 1925, Denmark and Great Britain, 121 Br. & For. St. Paps. 767; July 20, 1925, Italy and Kingdom of Serbs, Croats, and Slovenes, 83 League of Nations Treaty Series (1928–29) 87; Oct. 28, 1925, Estonia and Latvia, 54 *idem* (1926–27) 231; Oct. 12/19, 1925, Denmark and France, 122 Br. & For. St. Paps. 385; Nov. 24, 1926, Greece and Italy, 63 League of Nations Treaty Series (1927) 91; Jan. 23, 1928, Japan and U.S.S.R., 80 *idem* (1928) 341; Jan. 29, 1928, Germany and Lithuania, 89 *idem* (1929) 309; Dec. 20, 1928, France and Great Britain, 86 *idem* (1929) 429; May 22, 1930, Great Britain and U.S.S.R., Gr. Br. Treaty Ser. no. 22 (1930) Cmd. 3583; Aug. 8/Nov. 5, 1930, Great Britain (Canada) and Norway, 24 Martens' *Nouveau recueil général* (3d ser., Triepel, 1931) 345.

While it will be seen from the preceding pages that steps have been taken to preserve fur-seals, whales, and certain other fisheries, these steps are by no means adequate, particularly with respect to food fish. If supplies of these fish are to be assured for future generations the nations should forthwith come to a more definite understanding on measures to be adopted by them to prevent the promiscuous depletion of these fish.

O